BAEDEKER'S EGYPT 1929

Also published by David & Charles (in conjunction with George Allen & Unwin)

BAEDEKER'S RUSSIA 1914

BAEDEKER'S EGYPT 1929

DAVID & CHARLES : NEWTON ABBOT

ISBN 0 7153 6392 1

George Allen & Unwin, London, are the publishers of the current Baedeker series in the United Kingdom

Printed in Great Britain by
Page Bros (Norwich) Limited, Norwich
for David & Charles (Holdings) Limited
South Devon House Newton Abbot Devon

INTRODUCTION

The first English edition of Baedeker's handbook for travellers to Egypt was published in 1878. Its publication, like that of the handbook for travellers to Palestine and Syria which came out in 1876, must be seen as a response to a growing interest on the part of educated people in Western Europe and North America in the ancient civilisations of the Middle East and the opportunities for travel in this area that were created by the opening of the Suez Canal in 1869.

At the time of the handbook's publication, little information on the historical and geographical background required by travellers to Egypt was available in book form. Because of this a series of specially written articles on these topics was included in the handbook which consequently differs from other handbooks in the same series in the amount of space that is devoted to general background information.

The first edition of *Baedeker's Egypt* was prepared under the direction of Professor Ebers. It dealt only with Lower Egypt, that is the area stretching from Cairo to the coast, apart from an excursion to the Sinai peninsula. Subsequent editions indicate the widening of the geographical horizons of travellers in Egypt during the next half century. A second volume dealing with Upper Egypt, including Nubia, was published in 1892. The two Egyptian volumes were combined for the fourth English edition of 1898. This incorporated a series of major textual revisions directed by Professor Steindorf, during which the original text of the itineraries was drastically pruned and some of the original articles were replaced by freshly commissioned material. Later editions extended the coverage of the handbook to include the Sudan. The eighth edition that is reprinted here, incorporates further textual revisions which take account of archaeological discoveries after the First World war, including the finding of the tomb of Tutankhamen in 1922.

I. Masser

PUBLISHING HISTORY OF ENGLISH EDITIONS

Lower Egypt with the Fayum and the Peninsula of Sinai
with 16 maps and 29 plans, 7 views and 76 vignettes
1st ed 1878

Lower Egypt with the Fayum and the Peninsula of Sinai
with 16 maps, 30 plans, 7 views and 76 vignettes 2nd Ed 1885

Egypt Part First Lower Egypt and the Peninsula of Sinai
with 14 maps, 33 plans, 7 views and 76 vignettes 3rd Ed 1895

Egypt Part Second Upper Egypt with Nubia as far as the second cataract and the western oases
with 11 maps and 26 plans 1892

Egypt and Nubia as far as the second cataract
with 22 maps, 55 plans and 66 views and vignettes
4th Ed 1898

Egypt
with 23 maps, 66 plans and 59 vignettes 5th Ed 1902

Egypt
with 24 maps, 76 plans and 57 vignettes 6th Ed 1908

Egypt and the Sudan
with 21 maps, 84 plans and 55 vignettes 7th Ed 1914

Egypt and the Sudan
with 106 maps and plans and 56 woodcuts 8th Ed 1929

EGYPT

MONEY TABLE

(Comp. p. xv).

Approximate Equivalents

Arabic Name	Egyptian: Piastres	Egyptian: Millièmes	British: Shillings	British: Pence	French: Francs (gold)	French: Centimes	American: Dollars	American: Cents
Gold Coins.								
Gineih Maṣri (Egypt. pound, £E)	100 =	1000	20	6	25	92	5	—
Nuṣṣe Gineih (half £E)	50 =	500	10	3	12	96	2	50
Silver Coins.								
Riyâl (Maṣri), also *ʿIshrînîya* .	20 =	200	4	1	5	18	1	—
Nuṣṣe Riyâl	10 =	100	2	0 1/2	2	59	—	50
Rubʿ Riyâl	5 =	50	1	0 1/4	1	30	—	25
Qirshein (double piastre), also *Nuṣṣe Frank*	2 =	20	—	5	—	52	—	10
Qirsh *(Qirsh Ṣâgh)* †	1 =	10	—	2 1/2	—	26	—	5
Nickel Coins.								
Qirsh (big piastre; ***Qirsh Ṣâgh***) †	1 =	10	—	2 1/2	—	26	—	5
Nuṣṣe Qirsh (small or half piastre; *Qirsh ʿtaʿrîfa*, popularly *Qirsh Abyad*) †	1/2 =	5	—	1 1/4	—	13	—	2
2 Millièmes (Millimein)	1/5 =	2	—	1/2	—	5	—	1
1 Millième (Millîm, Nickel) . . .	1/10 =	1	—	1/4	—	2 1/2	—	1/2
Bronze Coins.								
1 Millième (Millîm)	1/10 =	1	—	1/4	—	2 1/2	—	1/2
1/2 Millième (Nuṣṣe Millîm) . . .	1/20 =	1/2	—	1/8	—	1 1/4	—	1/4

† The big piastre (rarely met in silver) is generally indicated by P. T. ('piastre tariff', 'piastre tarifée'), sometimes also by P. E. ('piastre égyptienne').

Weights and Measures.

In all official transactions the metrical system of weights and measures is employed.

1 ***Dirhem*** = 3.12 grammes = 48.15 grains troy.

1 ***Wuqîya*** (*Oqîya;* 12 dirhem) = 37.44 grammes = 1.32 oz. avoirdupois.

1 ***Roṭl*** (*Raṭl;* 12 wuqîya) = 449.28 grammes = 15.85 oz. (just under 1 lb.).

1 ***Wuqqa*** (*Oqqa, Oke;* 400 dirhem) = 1.248 kilogrammes = 2.7513 lb. (about 2 lb. 12 oz.).

1 ***Qanṭâr*** = 100 roṭl = 36 wuqqa = 44.928 kilogrammes = 99.0498 lb. (about 99 lb. 4/5 oz.).

1 ***Rubʿ*** = 8.25 litres = 1 gal. 3 qts. 1/2 pint.

1 ***Weiba*** = 4 rubʿ = 33 litres = 7 gals. 1 qt.

1 ***Ardabb*** (*Ardeb*) = 6 weiba = 198 litres = 43 gals. 2 qts.

1 ***Dirâʿ Baladi*** (ell) = 0.58 metre = 22.835 inches.

1 ***Qaṣaba*** = 3.55 metres = 11 ft. 7.763 inches = 3.882 yds.

1 ***Square Qaṣaba*** = 12.60 square metres = 15.072 sq. yds.

1 ***Feddân*** = 4200.83 sq. metres (1 sq. m. = 616,54 feddân) = 5024.17 sq. yds. = 1.038 acre.

EGYPT

AND

THE SÛDÂN

HANDBOOK FOR TRAVELLERS

BY

KARL BAEDEKER

WITH 106 MAPS AND PLANS, AND 56 WOODCUTS

EIGHTH REVISED EDITION

LEIPZIG: KARL BAEDEKER, PUBLISHER

LONDON: GEORGE ALLEN & UNWIN LTD., 40 MUSEUM ST., W. C. 1
NEW YORK: CHAS. SCRIBNER'S SONS, FIFTH AVE., AT 48TH ST.

1929

"Go lytel boke god sende the good passage . . .
And specyally let this be thy prayere
Unto hem al that the wyl rede or here
Where thou art wronge after her helpe to cal
The to correcte in any parte or al."

Sir Richard Ros.

PREFACE

Ever since the attention of the civilized world was redirected to Egypt at the beginning of the 19th century, the ancient civilization of the Nile valley has exercised a potent and ever-increasing attraction to visitors from all parts of the globe. At the same time Egypt possesses peculiar natural charms in its warm winter climate, its clear atmosphere, its wonderful colouring, the fertility of its cultivated districts with their great modern irrigation works, the romance of its deserts, and the manners, customs, and appearance of a most diversified population.

The HANDBOOK TO EGYPT †, which is now in its eighth edition, is founded on the combined work of several Egyptologists and other Oriental scholars. The first edition, which appeared in 1878, was founded on the manuscript of *Professor Georg Ebers* (1837-98). Since 1897 the supervision of the handbook has been in the hands of *Professor Georg Steindorff*, of Leipzig University, who, for the purposes of its revision, has made repeated visits to Egypt (lastly in the winter of 1928-29). The authors of the special articles are named on pp. vii and viii; in this edition two new chapters on Christian and Islamic Architecture in Egypt have been added, from the pens of leading authorities on these subjects, *Professor Ugo Monneret de Villard* and *Captain K. A. C. Creswell*, R. A. F. Special thanks are due also to *Col. Sir Henry Lyons*, F. R. S., who kindly revised the special articles formerly contributed by him, and to several other expert collaborators. The Editor gratefully acknowledges also the information received from numerous correspondents and official sources, which has often proved most useful.

The Editor hopes that, by confining himself to essential points and by careful arrangement of his material, he has succeeded, within small compass, in supplying the traveller, whether savant or simple tourist, with the necessary information regarding the country and the people he is about to visit and in enabling him to dispense with the useless services of uneducated dragomans (p. xxvi). An attempt has been made to indicate clearly the most important among the bewildering multiplicity of the monuments of antiquity, and the descriptions of these have been so arranged that he will find adequate guid-

† The volume is divided into FOUR SECTIONS (Introductory Matter, Approaches to Egypt, pp. i-ccviii and 1-6; Lower Egypt, pp. 7-210; Upper Egypt, Lower Nubia, Upper Nubia and the Sûdân, pp. 211-468; Index, pp. 469-495), each of which may be separately removed by cutting the gauze backing visible on opening the book at the requisite pages.

ance on the spot in that portion of our description that is printed in larger type, while those who have time and inclination for a more thorough examination will find additional particulars in small type. — For the transliteration of ancient Egyptian and of Arabic names, see pp. cxxxix, xxviii.

The MAPS and PLANS have been the object of the Editor's special care, and all have been carefully revised by Prof. Steindorff. Among the plans redrawn for this edition are those of Cairo, the Tombs of the Caliphs, Luxor, Port Said, and Suez, the Necropolis at Thebes, the Ramesseum, and the Temples of Dendera and Abu Simbel. Several smaller plans (Osireion, Temple of Es-Sebû'a, etc.) appear for the first time in the present edition. The spelling of the names on the maps of the Delta, of the Nile from Cairo to Aswân (3 sheets), and of the Faiyûm still follows the official French transliteration of 1897, for the reason that it was not possible at the time to discover the correct Arabic spelling of the names of most of the villages. It is hoped to redraw these maps in a subsequent edition.

HOTELS. To hotel-proprietors, tradesmen, and others the Editor begs to intimate that a character for fair dealing towards travellers is the sole passport to his commendation, and that no advertisements of any kind are admitted to his handbooks.

Perfect accuracy in a guide-book is impossible of attainment, especially in these days when changes are so frequent. For the improvement of this work, therefore, the Editor looks forward confidently to a continuance of the highly valued CORRECTIONS and SUGGESTIONS with which travellers have long been in the habit of favouring him.

Abbreviations.

B. = breakfast.
c. = circa (about) or French centime.
d. = pence.
D. = dinner.
Dyn. = dynasty.
fr. = French franc (gold).
gr. = gramme.
kg. = kilogramme.
km. = kilometre.
l. = left.
l. = pound sterling.
L. = luncheon.
L. = Italian lira.
£E = Egyptian pound (p. xv).
m. = metre.
M. = mile.
mill. = millième (p. xv).
pens. = pension (board and lodging).
pl. = plural.
Pl. = plan.
P.T. = piastre (p. xv).
r. = right.
R. = route or room.
s. = shilling.
$ = dollar.

The number of feet given after the name of a place shows its height above sea-level. The number of miles placed before the principal places on railway-routes, steamer-routes, and high-roads indicates their distance from the starting-point of the route.

Asterisks denote objects of special interest or imply commendation.

CONTENTS

I. Lower Egypt.

II. Upper Egypt.

III. Lower Nubia.

IV. Upper Nubia and the Sûdân.

Maps.

Plans.

Woodcuts.

I. Preliminary Information.

(1) Plan of Tour. Season. Expenses. Equipment. Tourist Parties.

Plan of Tour. The intending visitor to Egypt may make an outline of his tour at home with as great ease as for any of the countries of Europe. A glimpse of the country may be obtained in four or five weeks (exclusive of the journey out) as follows: two days may be devoted to Alexandria and the journey thence to Cairo — travellers landing at Port Said should take the first train to Cairo, as the town is uninteresting — eight to ten days may be spent in Cairo and its neighbourhood (pp. 37 seqq.), twelve days suffice for the railway journey to Aswân and back (or twenty days by a tourist-steamer), and three days may be given to Aswân (p. 378), while a few days must be set aside for resting. An excursion to the Faiyûm (R. 14) or to the oasis of Khârga (p. 405) takes two or three days. — An expedition to Upper Nubia (from Aswân to Wâdi Ḥalfa and back, p. 410) requires seven days by tourist-steamer; if the quicker government steamer is used and the railway from Wâdi Ḥalfa, the extension of the excursion to Kharṭûm (p. 445) takes another week. A month should be allowed for the steamer-trip from Kharṭûm to Juba and back (p. 463), and four days for the return from Kharṭûm to Suez viâ Port Sudan (R. 36).

An excursion to *Jerusalem* and *Palestine* should be undertaken if possible; for a brief visit, there and back by railway from Cairo, 10-14 days may be allowed (4 days for Jerusalem alone).

Season. The best time for a tour in Egypt is between November 1st and May 1st, Jan. to the end of March being the favourite period. In Alexandria stormy and rainy weather very often prevails from December to March, but in the interior of Egypt, to the S. of a line joining Damanhûr, Ṭanṭa, and Manṣûra, the climate is quite different. Even in the Delta, however, marked falls in temperature (sometimes to 43° Fahr.) occur between the end of November and the end of March, and rain-storms are not infrequent. In Cairo December, January, and sometimes February are distinctly chilly, which is the more inconvenient as there are no adequate heating arrangements in the houses; but November and March are very fine, as also usually are October, April, and May, especially for travellers who do not object to a little heat. In Upper Egypt, from the beginning of November till the middle or end of March, the prevalent weather is that of a delicious spring or moderate summer. Those who intend to winter in Egypt should spend November in Cairo, move on thence in December, on the approach of cold weather, to Upper Egypt (Luxor, Aswân), and return to Cairo at

the end of February. — In summer prices are naturally much lower, but many of the larger hotels are closed.

Expenses. The cost of a tour in Egypt is greater than that of a visit to most parts of Europe, and the traveller should estimate his average daily expenditure at not less than 40-50*s.*, apart from steamer and railway fares. The traveller whose time is very limited, or who is accompanied by ladies, may require also the services of a guide or 'dragoman' (comp. pp. xxvi, 42). With modest requirements, however, it is possible to live more cheaply. — A small sum of money for the early part of the journey may be taken in English or American notes, but large sums should always be in the form of Letters of Credit (in English pounds or American dollars) issued by a bank dealing direct with the East or by one of the principal tourist agencies (p. xv) or steamship companies (pp. 1 seqq.). Travellers proceeding to Upper Egypt may deposit their letters of credit in Cairo and have supplies sent after them, as required, by money order (see p. xx). For European bankers in Alexandria and Cairo, see pp. 11, 39. The National Bank of Egypt (London agency at 6 & 7 King William St., E.C. 4) and Barclay's (Anglo-Egyptian Bank; head office in London, 54 Lombard St., E.C. 3) have branches or agents in most Egyptian and Sudanese towns. The Travellers' Cheques issued by the American Bankers Association and the American Express Co., or the circular notes of Messrs. Thos. Cook & Son, are convenient also.

Equipment. For a journey lasting several months and subject to varying climates and seasons, it is not advisable to limit one's luggage in too niggardly a fashion. Wardrobe trunks are very convenient but they are expensive for railway travelling. For the sea voyage a cabin trunk and a small suit-case for night requirements are useful. It is advisable to have one's name and coloured distinguishing stripes painted on each trunk, so as to be able to collect them easily. — Clothing. For the cool season (Dec. and Jan.) light tweed suits, a cardigan, and a moderately warm overcoat; for the warmer weather, light summer clothes. For men: light washable flannel suits, a light knickerbocker suit for excursions, and linen or silk suits (to be bought cheaply in Cairo); a comfortable felt or straw hat with a wide brim and a pith helmet for excursions; leggings. For ladies: one light and one warmer costume (of tweed or other woollen material), several jumpers or blouses (including one or two warm ones), and white or fadeless washing frocks. Evening dress (for men, dinner jackets) is worn at dinner at the principal hotels. The following articles should not be forgotten: writing and sewing materials, small medicine chest (p. xxv), thermometer, pocket-compass, binoculars, electric torch, drinking cup, large flask or thermos, and body belt. — Cameras should not be too large. Photographic materials are obtainable everywhere. Films can be developed and printed at any of the larger towns.

Tourist Parties. The facilities for travel in Egypt are now such that even inexperienced travellers will have little difficulty in managing an independent tour, without recourse to the assistance of tourist agents or dragomans (p. xxvi), which add considerably to the cost. — In spring and autumn tourist parties are organized by *Messrs. Thos. Cook & Son* (Berkeley St., London; p. 214), the *American Express Co.* (6 Haymarket, London; p. 214), the *Anglo-American Nile & Tourist Co.* (p. 214), *D. E. Munari* (Cairo, p. 40), and the chief steamship companies, programmes of which may be obtained free on application. Travellers who join such parties are enabled to inspect the principal points of interest with the minimum expenditure of time and trouble, but must naturally surrender, to a great extent, both their freedom of choice of companions and the disposal of their time. The expenses are not below those of an independent tour.

The *Tourist Development Association of Egypt* (Cairo, Main Station) maintains inquiry offices in London (41 Tothill St., S.W. 1) and Paris (9 Rue La Pérouse, XVIe). The *Egyptian State Railways* (p. xvii) also have an inquiry office in London (63 Regent St., S.W. 1). — The London office of the *Sudan Government Railways and Steamers* is at Wellington House, Buckingham Gate, S.W. 1.

(2) Coinage. Passports. Custom House. Antiquities. Time.

Coinage (comp. the table before the title-page). The *Egyptian Pound* ('livre égyptienne'; £E) is worth about 20*s.* 6*d.* or $ 5 and is divided into 1000 *Millièmes* (M. or mill.) or 100 *Piastres* (P.T.; worth nearly 2½*d.* or 5 cents). The Arabic name for the piastre is *Qirsh* (pl. *Qurûsh;* pronounced in Cairo *'irsh*, *'urûsh*), but the European name is everywhere current. Travellers should note the distinction that is still frequently made by Europeans in Cairo and Alexandria between the 'big piastre' *(qirsh ṣâgh)* or *Tariff Piastre* (usually abbreviated to 'P.T.'), worth 10 millièmes, and the 'small (or half) piastre' *(petite piastre; qirsh ta'rîfa)*, worth 5 millièmes. — Egyptian gold coins (£E 5, 1, and ½, and P.T. 20) are no longer in circulation, but there are silver coins of P.T. 20 *(riyâl)*, 10 *(nuṣṣe riyâl)*, 5 *(rub' riyâl)*, and 2 *(qirshein)*, nickel coins of 10 millièmes (P.T. 1), 5 mill. (P.T. ½), 2 mill., and 1 millième, and bronze coins of 1 and ½ millième. The older coins bear on the reverse the name of the former Turkish sultan in ornamental flourishes; most of the new ones have the portrait of King Fu'âd I. — The notes of the National Bank of Egypt (£ E 100, 50, 10, 5, and 1) are legal currency. English and American bank-notes (pound = P.T. 97½, dollar = P.T. 20) are readily changed. In some places, especially at Alexandria and on the Suez Canal, reckoning also in *francs* (20 gold francs = P.T. $77._{15}$) is still common. Where British influence is strong, notably in Cairo, the word *Shilling* is used for the rub' riyâl (see above).

When obtaining change, travellers should be on their guard against counterfeit or damaged (i.e. worn or perforated) pieces, which are common enough.

Passports with the Egyptian visa are essential. The passport examination takes place before landing and before crossing the Egypt-Palestine frontier. For Palestine British subjects require an endorsement on their passports, while Americans require a British visa. A French visa is necessary for Syria.

The Egyptian consulates in Great Britain are at London (26 South St., Mayfair, W. 1; office-hours 11-1), Liverpool (Dominion Buildings, 28 Brunswick St.; 9.30-12.30 & 2.30-4.30), and Manchester (Ship Canal House, King St.; 10-1 & 2-4), to which application may be made personally or by post. The Egyptian consulates in the United States of America are at New York (103 Park Avenue) and New Orleans (406-407 Hibernia Bank Building; office-hours at both 9.30-12.30 & 1.30-3.30). The application for the visa (available for one year; fee 8*s.* in 1929, for Americans 10 $) must be accompanied by a small unmounted photograph and a banker's guarantee that the applicant has at least £ 50 at his disposal in Egypt. A transit visa (valid for three days) costs 1*s.*, for Americans 20 cents. — At arrival in and departure from Egypt a sanitary officer's fee of P.T. 25 is exacted. — Tourists touching at Egyptian ports and wishing to visit the country while their boats are at anchor, may obtain from the Passport Office a permit for a temporary sojourn (not exceeding 48 hrs.; fee P.T. 20).

Custom House. Tourists' luggage is subjected to a custom-house examination at the port of entry. The objects chiefly sought for are tobacco and cigars, on which a high tax is levied (tobacco and cigarettes P.T. 80-120 per kg. or $2^1/_5$ lb., cigars £E 1 per kg.). The importation of dangerous drugs (hashish, cocaine, opium; comp. p. lxxvi) is strictly forbidden. Unused articles are subject to an ad valorem duty of 8%; at Alexandria an additional $^1/_2$% (at Port Said ·7-·8%) is charged for quay dues. A similar duty is levied on motor-cars, cycles, typewriting machines, field-glasses, and firearms (special permit necessary; comp. p. 444), but the amount (less 10-20%) is refunded if the article is re-exported within six months, on production of the customs receipt (certificat du payement de droits en dépôt). The duty is paid at the port of entry, at the Egypt-Palestine frontier (custom-houses at El-Qanṭara and El-ʿArîsh), or in the Bonded Warehouse at Cairo. In case of difficulty or dispute one of the higher officials should be appealed to.

Good, though somewhat expensive, cigars (*sigâra afrangi*) may be obtained in Cairo and Alexandria. The importation of one's own cigars is attended with so much trouble as hardly to be worth while. Cigarettes (*sigâra*, pl. *sagâyir*) and tobacco (*dukhkhân*; comp. p. lxxvi) should be purchased in small quantities only, as they get dry very soon.

Antiquities. The inexpert traveller should confine his purchases to reliable dealers or to the sale room of the Cairo Museum (p. 88); expensive objects should not be bought without previous consultation with a connoisseur. For the export of antiquities a permit from the Department of Antiquities is necessary. Applications for leave to export should contain a complete description of the objects, with a statement of their value and the name of the port through which they are to be sent. The objects should be sent to the Cairo Museum for examination in the cases in which they are to be exported, but the lids should not be fastened down. A sealing fee of 60 mill. per box and an export duty of $2^1/_2$% on the value are charged.

Time. *East European Time* (i.e. that of 30° E. long.) has been officially adopted for Egypt and the Sûdân. Egyptian time (comp. p. 75) is thus 1 hr. in advance of Mid-European time (Italy, Switzerland, Germany) and 2 hrs. in advance of Greenwich time. There is no daylight-saving 'summer time' in Egypt.

(3) Conveyances.

Steamers. The necessary information about the steamer-lines between Europe (and America) and Egypt is given on pp. 1-6. For the Nile steamers to Upper Egypt, see p. 213; to Lower Nubia, see p. 409; in the Sûdân, see p. 463.

Railways. Most of the lines (1942 M. in all) belong to the *Egyptian State Railways*, but many branch-lines and light railways (861 M.) belong to private companies. The official time-tables for both state and private lines are published in the *Indicateur des Chemins de Fer de l'Etat Egyptien* (20 mill., pocket edition 10 mill.; sold at the railway stations, the Cairo central telegraph office, and at bookshops). Time-tables are exhibited also in the larger hotels. There are inquiry offices (bureaux de renseignements) at Cairo, Alexandria, Port Said, and Suez stations. — The railway carriages resemble those of France or Italy. The second-class carriages are comfortable enough for day journeys on the main routes (Alexandria to Cairo, Cairo to Manṣûra, Cairo to Port Said or Suez, Cairo to Aswân), and their use makes a saving of nearly 50% in fares. But on branch-lines all travellers should take first-class tickets, especially at night. The third-class carriages are quite unsuited for Europeans.

The trains are somewhat slower than in Europe but are usually punctual. The traveller should be at the station in good time, especially as heavy luggage must be booked $^1/_4$ hr. before the departure of the train. The luggage-tariff is complicated. Hand-luggage up to 55 lb. is free if taken in the carriage. The cloak-room charge is $12^1/_2$ millièmes each package per day. Passenger-fares are calculated on a zone-system, applicable to both express and slow trains: for 100km. (62 M.) 1st cl. P.T. $66^1/_2$, 2nd cl. P.T. 36, 3rd cl. P.T. 16; for 500km. £E 2 P.T. $27^1/_2$, £E 1 P.T. $22^1/_2$, P.T. $54^1/_2$. The journey may be broken once if the station-master's permission be obtained. Passenger-tickets and luggage-tickets are printed in English and Arabic. Return Tickets at reduced prices are issued between certain stations (reduction of 5%) and on suburban lines (lignes de banlieue). They are usually available for four days only, but the availability increases with the distance, e.g. between Cairo and Luxor 8 days, between Cairo and Aswân 15 days, between Alexandria or Port Said and Aswân 20 days. — In hot weather the dust, which penetrates the carriages even when the windows are closed, renders railway travelling in Egypt exceedingly unpleasant. At the chief stations on the express routes there are *Railway Buffets* (usually drinks only; no hot viands). Luncheon and tea baskets also may

be ordered by telegram which is despatched free of charge by any station-master. At other stations refreshments are brought to the carriage windows (comp. p. 216; bargaining necessary; 3 oranges P.T. 1). The water offered for sale should be abstained from. On most of the express trains there are dining and sleeping cars. Train de luxe, see p. 216; Pullman cars (1st class), see pp. 33, 187, 216; seats may be booked in advance through the Sleeping Car Co. at Cairo (p. 40) and at Alexandria, Port Said, Qanṭara, and Luxor stations. Combined railway tickets and sleeping car and hotel coupons for journeys to Upper Egypt, see p. 213.

Light Railways. A network of light or narrow-gauge lines, run by the state or by private companies (Egyptian Delta Light Railways; Société Anonyme des Chemins de Fer de la Basse-Egypte; Fayûm Light Railways Co.), cover the Delta and the Faiyûm (p. 204). These, though of little importance to the tourist, convey the business man and the explorer to various remote points with comparative ease.

The numerous **Motorbus** services are very popular with the lower-class Egyptians and as a rule are not recommended to tourists (cars often overcrowded and very dirty).

An **Air Service** (Imperial Airways Ltd., Airways House, Charles St., S.W. 1) from London to India viâ *Alexandria*, with passengers and mails (comp. p. xx), was inaugurated on March 30th, 1929. The journey occupies 7 days (the actual flying time being 57 hrs.), passengers leaving London every Sat. morning and arriving at Alexandria on Wed. morning. In addition there is a service (in conjunction with the Società Anonima Navigazione Aerea) to Alexandria only, leaving London on Wed. morning and arriving on Sat. morning. Fare to Alexandria 52*l*., to Karachi 124*l*.

1st Day. From *London* (Croydon aerodrome) viâ *Paris* to (485 M.) *Bâle*, by Armstrong Siddeley Argosy aircraft with three engines. Then by night express to (150 M.) *Genoa*.

2nd Day. From Genoa viâ *Rome* to (374 M.) *Naples*, by Short Calcutta flying boats with three Bristol Jupiter engines.

3rd Day. From Naples viâ *Corfu* to (518 M.) *Athens*.

4th Day. From Athens viâ *Suda Bay* (Crete) to (388 M.) *Tobruk* (Italian Lybia).

5th Day. From Tobruk to (310 M.) **Alexandria**, where we land at the harbour (combined marine and land airport at Dikheila, 6 M. to the S.W. of Alexandria, under construction). Thence by motor-car to Abuqîr (p. 32); here we catch the Cairo (Heliopolis)-India machine (comp. p. 128) and proceed to (212 M.) *Gaza* (Palestine) by three-engined De Havilland Hercules aircraft.

6th Day. From Gaza viâ *Rutba* (Syrian Desert) and *Baghdâd* to (906 M.) *Baṣra*.

7th Day. From Baṣra viâ *Bushire* (Persia) and *Lingeh* to (738 M.) *Jask*.

8th Day. From Jask viâ *Gwadar* (Baluchistan) to (605 M.) *Karachi*, which is reached about noon on Saturday.

Heliopolis (p. 128) is the starting-point of the service run by the Imperial Airways from Cairo to India viâ Abuqîr (London-India route, see above) every Tuesday. Fare to Gaza 7*l*., to Baghdâd 32*l*., to Baṣra 39*l*., to Karachi 72*l*.

The **Cabs** (sing. *ʿarabîya*) in the large towns are generally very good. The official tariffs must be shown on demand and are advertised in the 'Indicateur des Chemins de Fer' (p. xvii). At Alexandria and Cairo there are also *Taxicabs.* The cab-drivers (comp. pp. xxv, 41) are seldom able to read the names of the streets, while many of them know the various points only by names of their own. The hotel-porter should therefore be employed as interpreter. The traveller should keep his eye on the direction taken by the cab, as sometimes the cabman drives straight ahead in complete ignorance of the way and requires to be guided, e.g. by being touched with a stick on the right or left arm according to the turning, or with the words *yamînak* (to the right), *shimâlak* (to the left), *dughri* (straight on), *ʿandak* (stop). The cabs usually drive rapidly, and their use saves time and strength. — *Garages* with motor-cars for hire are to be found at Alexandria, Cairo, Port Said, Suez, and other towns.

Donkeys (*ḥomâr*, pl. *ḥamîr*) are found everywhere. The better ones belong to a finer race than the European breed. In Alexandria and Cairo they are, however, no longer used by Europeans for riding within the town. In the towns the donkeys are generally well bridled and saddled; side-saddles are not always obtainable, and when they are an extra charge is sometimes made for them. The proclivities of the donkey-boys for prodding the animals with pointed sticks and urging them to gallop should be sternly repressed. When a slower pace is desired the rider shouts *ʿala mahlak* or *ʿala mahlakum;* if a quicker pace is wanted, *yalla, yalla*, or *mashshi*, or *sûq el-ḥomâr;* if a halt is to be made, *ʿandak*, *ḥûsh*, or 'stop'.

(4) Hotels.

In *Cairo* and its environs and at *Luxor* and *Aswân* (comp. pp. xxii, xxiii) there are hotels of the first class. There are good hotels also at *Alexandria*, *Port Said*, and a few other places. These are managed according to international methods; the waiters and chamber-maids are chiefly Italians, Greeks, or Swiss, while the 'boots' are generally Nubians (Barâbra, p. lxii; often wrongly termed Arabs) who in most cases understand one or more European languages. As on the American system a fixed sum daily is paid for board and lodging, the former consisting of breakfast, luncheon, and dinner. Wine, beer, mineral water, and other liquors are dear. 'Tips' should be calculated at about 10% of the bill. At Pensions the average charge is P.T. 50-100 per day, or £E 10-18 per month. The hotel laundries are expensive but usually good (tariff at the hotels); the Arab 'washermen' are very good and much cheaper.

In other towns the hotels are much inferior. They are mostly kept by Greeks, some (in the Delta) by Italians; the charge for a night's lodging is P.T. 15-30. A café or bar (*bursa*) is frequently connected with the 'hotel' but no restaurant, so that meals have to be taken in a neighbouring eating-house.

(5) Postal Information.

Full details will be found in the *Egyptian Postal Guide*, the *Telegraph Guide* (each P.T. 5, at any post or telegraph office), in the official time-tables (p. xvii), and in the *Egyptian Government Almanac* (P.T. 7).

The **Postal System** is well organized, not only in the principal towns but also in the smaller towns of the Delta and Upper Egypt. The General Post Office is at Alexandria (p. 10). The addresses of letters destined for Egypt should be written very distinctly, particularly the initial letters. They had better be directed to a bank or tourist agency, or to the hotel at which the traveller intends to stay; or they may be sent to the Central Post Office (Poste Restante) in Cairo, in which case the traveller should inform the officials at the Inquiry Office (Bureau de Renseignements) by letter of his local address, and his letters will be forwarded thither. On leaving for Upper Egypt travellers should notify the postal authorities at Cairo, so that letters may be punctually forwarded; passengers by the Nile steamers may have their correspondence looked after by the steamer company.

	Egypt and the Sûdân	Other Countries
Letters	5 mill. for 30 gr. ($1^1/_{14}$ oz.)	15 mill. for 20 gr. ($^5/_7$ oz.); British Empire 10 mill. for 20 gr.
Post Cards	3 mill.	10 mill.; British Empire 8 mill.
Printed Papers	2 mill. for 50 gr. ($1^{11}/_{14}$ oz.); maximum weight 2 kg. ($4^2/_5$ lb.)	2 mill. for 50 gr. ($1^{11}/_{14}$ oz.); maximum weight 2 kg. ($4^2/_5$ lb.)
Registration	10 mill.	15 mill.
Money Orders	5 mill. for each £E 1 (Sûdân 6 mill.); minimum fee (for Egypt and the Sûdân) 15 mill.	
Parcels	30 mill. for 1 kg. ($2^1/_5$ lb.) 40 mill. for 3 kg. ($7^1/_5$ lb.) 50 mill. for 5 kg (12 lb.) (Sûdân 65, 95, and 125 mill.)	To England: for 1 kg. ($2^1/_5$ lb.) P.T. $10^1/_2$ for 3 kg. ($7^1/_5$ lb.) P.T. 15 for 5 kg. (12 lb.) P.T. $18^1/_2$
Telegrams (comp. below)	20 mill. for 6 words, then 5 mill. per word (Sûdân and Palestine 60 and 10 mill.)	See below.
Urgent Telegrams	Triple tariff	Triple tariff.

Air Mail. Correspondence of all categories (bearing a special label obtainable from all post offices) will be accepted for transmission by the London-India route (p. xviii). The special charge from Egypt to London, in addition to the ordinary postage, is 17 mill. for 20 gr. or fraction thereof.

Telegrams. There are two telegraph systems in Egypt, the Egyptian and the British. Messages within Egypt may be sent only

by the *Egyptian State Telegraph* (tariff, see p. xx). Telegrams may be sent in any European language, except from the smaller offices, where Arabic messages only are accepted. The larger state telegraph offices accept telegrams for abroad. — Telegrams to Europe and America should be sent by the *Eastern Telegraph Co.*, viâ Malta and Vigo. To Great Britain 'viâ Eastern' each word costs 48 mill. from Lower Egypt, 53 mill. from Upper Egypt, 63 mill. from the Sûdân; to the United States 87-179 mill. Wireless telegrams to Great Britain and the Continent of Europe are transmitted by the *Marconi Radio Telegraph Co. of Egypt* ('viâ Marconi', Abu Zaʿbal wireless station, p. 129) or 'viâ Radio Syria'. To Great Britain 'viâ Marconi' or 'Radio Syria' each word costs 37 mill. from Lower Egypt, 41 mill. from Upper Egypt. At places where there are no offices of the Eastern Telegraph Co. and of the Marconi Co. (comp. pp. 10, 40) the telegrams should be handed in at the state telegraph office (wireless telegrams are accepted at the larger offices only).

Deferred Telegrams ('télégrammes différés') are forwarded for certain countries by the State Telegraph, by the Eastern Telegraph Co., and by wireless at half rates; they are not dispatched until all the telegrams at full rates have been got rid of (in any case within twenty-four hours).

Telephones. There are state telephone offices (the principal ones open day and night) in most towns and large villages, besides about 200 public call-offices. The tariff is posted up, or it may be consulted in the *State Telephone Directories* (for Cairo, Alexandria and the Provinces; three parts, each at P.T. 5). The operators speak English.

(6) Public Safety. Legations and Consulates. Courts of Justice.

Public Safety. In ordinary times travellers in any part of Egypt are as safe as in Europe. Weapons for self-defence are an unnecessary encumbrance. The police officers at Alexandria, Cairo, Port Said, etc., include many Europeans. — Firearms and ammunition may be imported by special permit only (see p. 444).

Legations and **Consulates.** Most of the European powers and the U. S. A. are represented in Egypt by legations (see p. 39). The diplomatic representative of Great Britain bears the title of 'High Commissioner'. — There are consulates of many European and other nations at Cairo, Alexandria, Port Said, and a few other towns. Consuls in the East enjoy the same privilege of exterritoriality as ambassadors in other countries. A distinction is made between professional ('consules missi') and commercial consuls; and there are consuls general, consuls, vice-consuls, and consular agents, possessing various degrees of authority. In all cases of emergency the traveller should apply for advice to the nearest consul of his country.

There are no consuls within the Anglo-Egyptian Sûdân (p. 441).

Courts of Justice. The consular jurisdiction to which foreigners were formerly liable now applies only to criminal cases and to civil and commercial cases between foreigners of the same nationality. Civil and commercial cases between foreigners of different nationalities (also between foreigners of the same nationality concerning real estate in Egypt), and cases between foreigners and Egyptians (including the King and the Government) are tried by the *Mixed Courts (Tribunaux Mixtes)* established in 1876. The judges are appointed by the King of Egypt, in the case of foreigners after nomination by the Great Powers. The cases are tried in accordance with the 'Mixed Codes', based on those of France and Italy. The courts of first instance are at Cairo, Alexandria, and Manṣûra; the appeal court is at Alexandria. Further information is obtainable at the consulates. — All native cases, civil and criminal, are tried by the *Native Courts*, established in 1883, in which Arabic is the official language. — The law of Islam (Sharʿ or Sharîʿa, p. lxxxix) is used by the *Moslem Courts* (supreme court at Cairo, p. 81), known as *Maḥkama Sharʿîya*, in cases of family or succession disputes, in legal questions concerning pious foundations (p. lxxxix), and in questions of religious rites.

(7) Egypt as a Winter Resort. Medical Hints.

By *Leigh Canney*, M. D. (Lond.), F. R. Met. Soc.

The beneficial influence of the climate of Egypt (comp. p. lxxix) has been known since the Roman period at least, and of late years an increasing number of visitors have flocked to the Nile to enjoy the benefits of its remarkably dry winter climate. Phthisis (if not too far advanced and if the patient has a sound heart and little or no fever), asthma, chronic bronchitis, rheumatoid arthritis, gout, Bright's disease, and other diseases of the kidneys are some of the most important ailments that are at least alleviated by a visit to Egypt. Invalids should remember that a stay of a few weeks only is not sufficient, and should remain from the beginning of November to the middle of April. In deciding which of the health resorts in Egypt a given case should be sent to, the physician must of course consider whether or not warmth must be secured along with dryness of air, whether purity of air alone or also a bright stimulating climate is to be specially sought, and whether cold winds and blowing sand are harmful or not. It is advisable in all cases to secure the advice of the physician resident at the spot selected.

Cairo itself cannot properly be considered a health resort. The presence of a large city with its noise and bustle, the higher relative humidity, owing to the N. wind and the neighbourhood of the Delta, the dust, and other causes, all combine to compel those who seek health from the climate of Egypt to look to other stations. There are, however, excellent health resorts in the immediate vicinity of the capital, such as the Mena House Hotel and Ḥelwân. Luxor and

(still better) Aswân, in Upper Egypt, offer still more favourable climatic conditions.

Mena House Hotel (p. 38), 8 M. to the W. of Cairo, stands near the Great Pyramid of Gîza, on the verge of the Libyan Desert. The mean maximum temperature is 69° Fahr. in Dec., 66° in Jan., 72° in Feb., 74° in March, and 80° in April. The mean minimum for the four months Dec. to March is 50°. The relative humidity (i.e. the amount of moisture, in relation to the temperature at the time, that the air holds out of a possible 100 %) from Dec. to March is 58 % by day (8 a.m. to 6 p.m.) and 80 % at night (8 p.m. to 6 a.m.). The purity of the air is marked; the medical and sanitary arrangements are excellent.

Ḥelwân (p. 178), $15\frac{1}{2}$ M. to the S. of Cairo and 3 M. from the cultivated land, is 115 ft. above the river. The mean maximum temperature is 70° in Dec., 67° in Jan., 73° in Feb., and 76° in March. The mean minimum for these four months is 50°. The daily range of temperature is here also 21°. The relative humidity from Dec. to March is 47 % by day, 66 % at night. Ḥelwân has the advantage of being in the pure atmosphere of the desert. It also has warm sulphurated and saline springs, richer in natural constituents than the corresponding springs at Aix-les-Bains, Harrogate, Buxton, etc. The cases suitable for the baths here are such as would derive benefit from hydro-therapeutic treatment as carried on at Harrogate, Bath, Aix, etc.; of late years Helwân has been especially recommended to sufferers from kidney diseases, and suitable diet is provided at all the hotels and pensions.

Luxor (p. 267) is situated about 400 M. to the S. of Cairo, in the Theban plain on the right bank of the river. The prevailing winds are N.W. and N., as in the whole country. The mean maximum temperature is 76° in Dec., 74° in Jan., 78° in Feb., and 85° in March. The mean minimum for these four months is 50°. The relative humidity is 41 % by day, 64 % at night. In addition to the advantage of its warm and dry climate Luxor has an almost inexhaustible interest in its numerous antiquities, temples, and tombs. The temperature is 7-9° warmer than at Mena House and Ḥelwân; but the sudden drop of temperature at sunset (comp. p. xxiv) must be guarded against. The importance of the extra warmth of Upper Egypt must not be lost sight of, in cases where it is imperative that the action of the skin should be at its highest level, especially as with this warmth a bracing effect is obtained from the dryness of the air.

Aswân (p. 378), situated at the First Cataract, also on the right bank of the river, is the driest of the Egyptian health resorts and may be specially recommended in winter, when N. Egypt is often decidedly chilly. The prevailing winds are, as at Luxor, N.W. and N. in winter. The mean maximum temperature is 78° in Dec., $74\frac{1}{2}$° in Jan., 82° in Feb., and 91° in March. The mean minimum for

these four months is 55°; and the relative humidity is 35% by day, 49% at night. Aswân is more under the immediate influence of the desert; the air is bracing, although about 5° warmer than at Luxor, and the drop of temperature at sunset (see below) is not so marked. The beauty of the surroundings lends a peculiar charm to Aswân. The accommodation for invalids is very good.

Patients should not leave Upper Egypt until the middle of March, on account of the cold N. wind. They will find at Athens, Corfu, Sicily, Capri and other points near Naples, the Riviera, and the Italian Lakes admirable transition stations in spring.

Medical Hints. Revaccination is a safeguard to travellers in Egypt, if not already performed within six years. Special care should be taken to avoid ophthalmia (comp. p. lvi), and it is inadvisable to allow one's field-glasses to be used by strangers, especially natives, for fear of infection. It is unwise to shake hands with lower-class natives without washing as soon as possible. Those, too, who come into contact with natives should above all avoid rubbing their eyes with their hands. A useful precaution is to bathe the eyes regularly with boracic solution (3%), especially on dusty days or after excursions. Visitors to Upper Egypt should have spectacles with smoked glasses. — Against sunstroke, which, however, is rare in the winter months, the best protection is afforded by broad-brimmed hats, sunshades, or cloths tied round the hat so as to fall down over the neck. A pith helmet with a large flap to protect the neck may be recommended also. The remedies for headache resulting from sunstroke are rest and shade; the clothing should at once be loosened and cold applications made to the head and neck.

Colds are frequently followed by fever or by diarrhœa, which is apt to develop into dysentery. Iced drinks should be avoided, also unpeeled fruit (especially strawberries) and green salads. Water and milk should never be drunk unboiled, for fear of typhoid. In cases of diarrhœa meat should be avoided and a simple farinaceous diet adopted (boiled rice, gruel, etc.); the beverages should be milk and soda, tea, or French red wine. There are European doctors at Cairo, Alexandria, Ḥelwân, Luxor, Aswân, etc., also on board most of the tourist steamers.

Sprains are most effectually treated with cold compresses of lead lotion, while the injured limb should be tightly bandaged. — The sting of a scorpion (as of mosquitoes, flies, etc.) is relieved by immediately applying ammonia; strong doses of alcohol may be administered internally.

Travellers should be careful to pay attention to the daily changes of temperature (p. lxxx), particularly at sunset in cultivated districts, when the air cools very quickly and colds are easily caught. Warmer clothing or a cloak is useful in the early morning, then lighter clothing till nearly sunset, when the cloak should be resumed. The hour for returning to the hotel varies with the place and the month,

being earliest in Jan. and latest in March and April. If the traveller be guided by the relative humidity, it would be earliest at Mena House, say about sunset; a little later at Ḥelwân; at Luxor still later, 6 p.m. (except in Jan.), and 8 p.m. in March; and latest of all at Aswân — it being always understood that precautions as to extra clothing have been taken.

Those who wish to take a small **Medicine Chest** with them, a proceeding strongly recommended to anyone making long independent excursions, should consult their physician at home as to the best drugs with which to stock it. The following suggestions may, however, be useful: for colds and fever, *aspirin;* for headaches, *veramon* and *pyramidon;* for insomnia, *adalin* and *bromural;* for constipation, *castor oil*, *cascara*, etc.; for diarrhœa, first castor oil, then *charcoal tablets*, the use of a *body belt*, rest, and a strict diet (comp. p. xxiv; opium is to be avoided); for insect bites, *ammonia*, which should always be carried, and *Insectol;* for inflammation of the eyes (comp. p. xxiv), *boracic solution;* for external injuries, *cotton wool*, *bandages*, *court plaster*, *boracic powder*, *iodine*, and *corrosive sublimate tablets;* for snake-bites, *permanganate of potash;* finally a *clinical thermometer*.

(8) Intercourse with Orientals. Dragomans.

The average Oriental regards the European traveller as a Crœsus, therefore as fair game, and feels justified in pressing upon him with a perpetual demand for bakshish *(baqshîsh, bakhshîsh)*, which simply means 'a gift'. The number of beggars is enormous, but bakshish should never be given either to adults or children, except for services rendered or to the aged and crippled (comp. p. 50); and the government appeals to the tourist by public placards not to encourage the habit of begging. A beggar may be generally silenced with the words *'al Allâh* or *Allâh yiḥannin 'aleik* (God have mercy on thee) or *Allâh ya'ṭîk* (may God give thee). The best reply for more importunate cases is *mâ fîsh, mâ fîsh* (I have nothing for you) or *mâfîsh baqshîsh* (there is no present), which will generally have the effect of dispersing the assailants for a time.

It is, of course, inevitable that cabmen, guides, donkey-boys, and the like should expect a gratuity in addition to the stipulated fee for their services, and the traveller should therefore take care to be amply supplied with Small Change at all times, and especially with pieces of half a piastre (comp. p. ii). Payment should never be made until the service stipulated for has been rendered, after which an absolutely deaf ear should be turned to the protestations and entreaties which almost invariably follow. Even when an express bargain has been made, and more than the stipulated sum paid, they are almost sure to pester the traveller in the way indicated. When there is no fixed tariff, the fees and prices mentioned in the handbook, all of which are ample, should be paid without remark; and if the attacks which ensue are not silenced by an air of calm indifference the traveller may use the word *rûḥ* or *imshi* (be off) or *uskut* (be quiet) in a quiet but decided and imperative tone. At the same time it must be admitted that the increasing number of

visitors to Egypt tends to raise prices during the height of the season, so that a larger bakshish than is mentioned in the handbook may sometimes be necessary.

While much caution and firmness are desirable in dealing with the people, it need hardly be added that the traveller should avoid being too exacting or suspicious. He should bear in mind that many of the natives with whom he comes in contact are mere children, whose demands should excite amusement rather than anger, and who often display a touching simplicity and kindliness of disposition. The native communities hold together with remarkable faithfulness, and the bond of a common religion, which takes the place of 'party' in other countries, and requires its adherents to address each other as '*yâ akhûya*' (my brother), is far more than a mere name. On the other hand, intimate acquaintance with Orientals of the lower classes is to be avoided, especially with the dragomans, who sometimes presume on their opportunities of social intercourse (comp. below). In Lower Egypt travellers can usually make themselves understood in French or Italian; in Upper Egypt English is more useful. A good deal can usually be done by signs.

Notwithstanding all the suggestions we have ventured to offer, the traveller will to some extent have to buy his experience. In most cases the overcharges to which he will be exposed will be comparatively trifling; but if extortion is attempted on a larger scale he had better refer the matter to the police.

For the tours described in this book the services of a **Dragoman** (accent on 1st syllable; Arabic *turgumân*) may easily be dispensed with, even by those less accustomed to travelling. They are sometimes useful, however, for visiting mosques. Only well-recommended dragomans should be engaged, preferably those for whom the hotels assume some responsibility. They must be treated from the first as servants and all familiarity should be discouraged. The dragomans are with few exceptions quite uneducated, without the least knowledge of the historic or æsthetic significance of the monuments; and their 'explanations' of them are only too often merely garbled versions of what they have picked up from guide-books or from the remarks of previous travellers. Special schools for dragomans, however, are to be established by the government at Gîza and Luxor.

Those who wish to make long tours in the desert or hunting excursions are advised to consult residents learned in these matters. The tourist agents also can give good advice, and the necessary outfit (tents, kitchen utensils, etc.) may be bought or hired through them. — For sporting and other expeditions in the Anglo-Egyptian Sûdân, see pp. 443, 444.

On the successful termination of the journey travellers are too apt from motives of good nature to write a more favourable testimonial for their dragoman than he really deserves; but this is truly an act of injustice to his subsequent employers. The testimonial therefore should not omit to mention any serious cause for dissatisfaction.

(9) Arab Cafés. Story Tellers. Musicians. Baths.

Arab Cafés (sing. *qahwa*) are frequented by the lower classes almost exclusively. The front consists of woodwork with a few open arches. Outside the door generally runs a *masṭaba*, or raised seat of stone or brick, covered with mats, and there are similar seats in the interior. Coffee is served by the *qahwâgi* at P.T. ½-1 per cup *(fingân)*, and several *nârgîla* or *shîsha* (water-pipes with a long tube) and *gôza* (water-pipes with a coconut) are kept in readiness for the use of customers. The *tumbâk* (Persian tobacco) smoked in the gôza is sometimes mixed with the intoxicating *ḥashîsh* (hemp, Cannabis indica), which has an unmistakable smell and which is not allowed to be either imported or sold (comp. p. lxxvi).

Story Tellers (who in private domestic circles are generally women) are still a characteristic oriental institution, but in Cairo they are now very scarce. Wherever they make their appearance, whether in the public streets or the coffee-house, in the densely peopled alleys of the large towns or in the smallest country villages, they are sure to attract an attentive, easily pleased, and exceedingly grateful crowd. The more sensational the tale, the better, and the oftener is the narrator applauded with protracted cries of 'Aah', or 'Allâh', or 'Allâhu akbar' (God is the greatest). Most of the story-tellers belong to the so-called *Shû'arâ* (sing. *Shâ'ir*), literally 'poets' or 'singers'. They are known also as *'Anâtira* (sing. *'Antari*) or *Abu Zeidîya*, according as their theme consists of tales and romances from the history of 'Antar, a Beduin hero, or from that of Abu Zeid. Others again are called *Miḥadditâti*, i.e. narrators of history, their province being the recital in prose of passages from the history of Sultan Beibars (p. cxxii) and other historical heroes. The entertainments of the *'alf leila u leila'* (thousand and one nights) are, however, no longer heard, as popular superstition has branded this collection of tales as unlucky. The themes of the whole fraternity are often of an obscene character.

Musicians by profession, called *Âlâtîya* (sing. *Âlâti*), are indispensable on every festive occasion. The usual instruments are the *riqq* or tambourine with little bells, the *naqqâra* or hemispherical tambourine, the *zemr* or oboe, the *ṭabl baladi* or drum, the *ṭabl shâmi* or kettledrum, and the *darâbukka*, a kind of funnel-shaped drum (generally made of earthenware, but sometimes of wood inlaid with mother-of-pearl and tortoise-shell, with a fish-skin stretched over the broad end), which last is accompanied by the *zummâra*, a kind of double flute. A better class of instruments, used for chamber music, includes the *nâi*, a kind of flute, the *kamanga* or two-stringed violin, the body of which consists of a coconut shell, the *rebâba*, or one-stringed violin with a square wooden body, the *qânûn*, a kind of zither with strings of sheep-gut, and lastly the *'ûd*, the lute or mandoline, the oldest of all the instruments.

The Egyptians consider themselves a highly musical people. The Egyptian sings when indulging in his keif (i.e. dolce far niente), when driving his donkey, when carrying stones and mortar up a scaffolding, when working in the fields, when at the sâqiya (p. lxxiv), and when rowing. He regards his vocal music as a means of lightening his labour and of sweetening his repose. The Egyptian songs, however, have no melody, though they have a certain rhythm, which is always dependent on the text. They are sung through the nose on seven or eight different notes, on which the performer wanders up and down. The songs (*mauwâl* or *shughl*) are generally of a lyrical, religious, or erotic description, though some of them extol the pleasures of friendship and rational enjoyment, or express derision of an enemy and contempt for the rustic fellah. — Comp. 'The Songs of an Egyptian Peasant', by *Heinrich Schäfer* (English edition, Leipzig, 1904).

Female Singers (*'Awâlim*, sing. *'Alma*; i.e. 'learned women') perform only in the harems of wealthy natives. — Good Female Dancers, or *Ghawâzi* (sing. *Ghâzîya*), were formerly one of the chief curiosities of Egypt, but are now almost extinct; the performances in the cafés chantants in Cairo are as a rule very inferior. — The Snake Charmers (*Rifâ'îya*, sing. *Rifâ'i*; p. xcv) exhibit performances of a very marvellous character, as credible European residents in Cairo have testified; but the traveller will rarely come in contact with them except by lucky accident. The men and boys who exhibit small snakes in the streets or at the hotels must not be confounded with the Rifâ'îya. — The Jugglers or *Ḥuwâ* (sing. *Ḥâwi*) of Egypt are often exceedingly skilful. — The performances of the Buffoons (*Qurûdâtîya* or *Muḥabbazîn*, sing. *Qurûdâti* or *Muḥabbaz*) are indelicate.

Arab Baths (*Ḥammâm*, pl. *Ḥammâmât*). The baths of Egypt, with their hot-air chambers, are those commonly known as Turkish, but they are neither so clean nor so well fitted up as those in the larger cities of Europe. They are therefore seldom visited by Europeans. Those who wish to try them once should do so early in the morning, and should avoid Fridays, as numerous Moslems bathe on that day, which is their Sabbath. When a cloth is hung up at the entrance to the baths, it indicates that women only are admitted.

(10) The Egyptian Dialect of Arabic.

By *Dr. Curt Prüfer.*

The Transliteration of Arabic vocal sounds, some of them so intensely different from our own, into the ordinary Latin alphabet is rendered additionally difficult by the varied international relations of Egypt. In maps and plans, in railway time-tables, and in other publications we find the transliteration differing widely according as the French or the English view has been adopted. In this handbook we have transliterated the consonantal sounds so far as possible according to English scientific and official usage (e.g. *sh* instead of the French *ch*). The pronunciation of the vowels and diphthongs is as follows: *â* as *a* in father, *e* as *e* in belong or as *a* in final; *a* usually as *a* in final, especially at the end of a word; *î* as *ee* in been, *i* as *i* in did, final *i* as *ee* in been; *ô* as *o* in bone, *o* as *o* in on; *û* as *oo* in fool, *u* as *u* in full; *ai* as *i* in ice; *au* as *ow* in owl; *ei* as *a* in lane; *oi* as *oy* in boy. Thus *amîr* (or *emîr*) is pronounced 'ameer', *fulûs* 'fulloos', *sheikh* 'shake' (*kh* = *ch* in 'loch'), etc. — The *l* of the article is frequently unassimilated; e.g. *el-râs* instead of *er-râs* (comp. p. xxxi).

Arabic belongs to the Semitic group of languages and has no relationship with the tongues of Europe. The classic language of the Koran (comp. p. xcii) is still regarded as the unrivalled model of literary Arabic, but side by side with it there have developed various colloquial dialects, differing widely among themselves, of which that spoken in Egypt is one. In the following brief sketch references to the classic literary language are avoided as far as possible; for that, recourse must be had to the accepted grammars. Even in Egyptian Arabic there are local variations, but the following remarks apply especially to the language as spoken in Cairo, which is generally understood throughout the country.

On p. xxx we give the Arabic **Alphabet,** with the transliteration used in the handbook and the sounds corresponding to the different letters so far as it is possible to represent or describe them to the English reader. — Arab writing runs from right to left. Long vowels are indicated by the letters Elif, Wau, and Yei (comp. p. **xxx**), while short vowels are often left out altogether or represented by special signs placed above or below the consonants.

Quantity and Accentuation of Vowels. Vowels with a circumflex accent (^) are long; other vowels are short. The accent falls on the last syllable when that contains a long vowel or a short vowel followed by two consonants. It falls on the penultimate (1) when that is long, (2) when it ends in a single consonant, and (3) when the preceding syllable is long or ends in a single consonant. In all other cases the accent falls on the antepenultimate. Diphthongs *(ai, ei, au)* must be reckoned as equivalent to long vowels.

Grammatical Hints.

Pronouns.	*ana*, I	*hîya*, she
	inta, thou (masc.)	*iḥna*, we
	inti, thou (fem.)	*intum*, *intu*, ye or you
	hûwa, he	*hum*, *humma*, they

The possessive pronouns, and the personal pronouns used as the object of a verb or connected with prepositions, are indicated by suffixes.

my, mine = *-i* (after a final vowel *-ya*, after verbs *-ni*)
thine (masc.) = *-ak* (after a final vowel *-k*); thine (fem.) = *-ik* (after a final vowel *-ki*)
his = *-uh* (after a final vowel *-h*); her = *-ha*
our = *-na*
your = *-kum*
their = *-hum*

In the case of most feminine nouns a *t* is inserted before the suffix. When otherwise three consonants would come together a short vowel is inserted between the stem and the suffix. Examples:

ARABIC ALPHABET.

1	Elif, Alif	ا	[ʾ]	like the Greek soft breathing, accompanies an initial vowel, and is not pronounced except as a hiatus in the middle of a word. It is also the sign for *â*.
2.	Bâ, Bei	ب	b	as in English.
3.	Tâ, Tei	ت	t	
4.	Thâ, Thei	ث	t, s	originally as *th* in 'thing', but now pronounced *t*, *s*, or *th*.
5.	Gîm	ج	g	generally pronounced hard in Egypt, but soft in the desert and in parts of Upper Egypt.
6.	Ḥâ	ح	ḥ	a peculiar guttural *h*, pronounced with emphasis at the back of the palate.
7.	Khâ	خ	kh	like *ch* in the Scotch word 'loch', or the harsh Swiss-German *ch*.
8.	Dâl	د	d	as in English.
9.	Dhâl	ذ	d, z	originally as *th* in 'the', but now pronounced *d* or *z*.
10.	Rei	ر	r	like the French or Italian *r*.
11.	Zei	ز	z	as in English.
12.	Sîn	س	s	
13.	Shîn	ش	sh	
14.	Ṣâd	ص	ṣ	emphasized *s*, like *ss* in 'hiss'.
15.	Ḍâd	ض	ḍ	both emphasized by pressing the tongue firmly against the palate.
16.	Ṭâ	ط	ṭ	
17.	Ẓâ	ظ	ẓ	an emphatic *z*, now usually pronounced like No. 11 or No. 15.
18.	ʿEin, ʿAin	ع	ʿ	a harsh and very peculiar guttural.
19.	Ghein	غ	gh	a guttural resembling the Parisian *r*.
20.	Fei	ف	f	as in English.
21.	Qâf	ق	q	a very guttural *k*, pronounced in Lower Egypt (particularly in Cairo) in the same way as Elif (see above, No. 1), but in the desert and parts of Upper Egypt as *g* (No. 5) in 'get'.
22.	Kâf	ك ک	k	as in English.
23.	Lâm	ل	l	
24.	Mîm	م	m	
25.	Nûn	ن	n	
26.	Hei	ه	h	
27.	Wau	و	w	as in English. Also the sign for *û*, *ô*, and *au*.
28.	Yei	ى	y	as in English. Also the sign for *î*, *ai*, and *ei*.

kalbi, my dog; *kursîya*, my chair; *kalbîna*, our dog; *shagarâtkum*, your tree; *ḍarabni*, he struck me; *misiktúhum*, thou tookest them; *ʿandi*, beside me, i.e. I have; *ʿandak*, beside thee, i.e. thou hast; *ʿaleikum*, over you.

mîn, who?	*lei*, why?	
ei, what?	*izaiy*, how?	
enhû, which? (masc.)	*illi*, which (relative)	
enhî, which? (fem.)	*di* or *da*, this (masc.)	placed after the noun and its article
enhúm, which? (pl.)	*dî*, *di*, this (fem.)	placed after the noun and its article
kâm, how much?	*dôl*, these	placed after the noun and its article
fein, where? whither?	*duk-ha*, that	placed after the noun and its article
min ein, whence?	*duk-hamma*, those	placed after the noun and its article
imta, when?	*kull*, each, all	

ARTICLE. *El* is the definite article for all genders and numbers. Before words beginning with *t*, *d*, *r*, *z*, *s*, *sh*, *ṣ*, *ḍ*, *ṭ*, or *n* (frequently also *g* and *k*) the *l* of the article is, in educated speech, assimilated with such initial consonants, e.g. *er-râgil*, the man. There is no indefinite article (*el-muʿallim*, the teacher, *muʿallim*, a teacher), but it is sometimes expressed by uneducated people through the numeral *wâḥid*, fem. *waḥda*, e.g. *wâḥid beit*, a house.

NOUNS. Most feminine nouns end in *a*: *el-muʿallíma*, the female teacher. The regular plural is formed by adding *în* to the masculine nouns, *ât* to the stem of feminine nouns; *el-muʿallimîn*, the teachers, *el-muʿallimât*, the female teachers. But there are numerous irregular plurals that must be learned individually, e.g. *beit*, house, *buyût* or *biyût*, houses. The dual ends in *ein* for the masculine, *tein* for the feminine; *kalbein*, two dogs, *kalbatein*, two bitches.

There is no regular declension of nouns. The genitive case is expressed by the juxtaposition of the two nouns, the former always without the article, or by the use of the auxiliary word *bitâʿ*, *bitâʿet*, pl. *bitûʿ*; e.g. *beit el-khawâga*, or *el-beit bitâʿ el-khawâga*, the house of the European. The dative case is formed by the use of the preposition *li* (to); *li 'l-khawâga*, to the European. The accusative (objective) is the same as the nominative. The vocative case is *yâ khawâga*, Sir!

ADJECTIVES are always placed after their nouns, with which they generally agree in gender; e.g. *gineina kwaiyisa*, a beautiful garden, *el-gineina el-kwaiyisa*, the beautiful garden. The verb 'to be' is omitted in the present tense; *el-gineina kwaiyisa*, the garden is beautiful.

VERBS. The typical Arabic verb has three root-consonants; comp. *ksr* 'break', *ktb* 'write' on p. xxxii. The pure stem of regular verbs is seen in the 3rd person singular (masculine) of the perfect tense; *kasar*, he has broken.

Perfect	Present and Future
I broke or have broken, *kasârt*	I break or shall break, *áksar*
Thou hast broken, *kasârt* (masc.), *kasârti* (fem.)	Thou breakest or wilt break, *tíksar* (masc.), *tiksâri* (fem.)
He has broken, *kâsar*	He breaks or will break, *yíksar*
She „ „ *kâsaret*	She „ „ „ „ *tíksar*
We have „ *kasárna*	We break or shall „ *níksar*
You „ „ *kasártu*	You „ „ will „ *tiksáru*
They „ „ *kásaru*	They „ „ „ „ *yiksáru*

Imperatives: Break (sing.), *íksar* (masc.), *iksári* (fem.). Break (plur.), *iksáru.*

Participles. Pres. Breaking, *kâsir;* Perf. Broken, *maksûr.*

So also: I have written, *katábt*	I write, *áktub*
katábt, katábti	*tíktub, tiktúbi*
kátab, etc.	*yíktub*, etc.

In the case of most verbs other tenses and moods are indicated by prefixing or interpolating letters; e.g. *kasar*, he has broken, *inkâsar*, he has been broken. For irregular verbs the grammar (comp. p. ccvi) must be consulted.

To express a negative with verbs the separable form *mâ . . . sh(i)* is used, the verb being inserted in the middle (comp. the French ne . . . pas); e.g. *mâḍarábsh*, he did not strike.

Numerals.

1 (١) *wâḥid*, fem. *waḥda*	the first	*el-auwil (auwal)*, fem. *el-auwilânîya (el-ûla)*		
2 (٢) *itnein*	the second	*tâni*,	fem.	*tâniya*
3 (٣) *talâta*	the third	*tâlit*,	„	*talta*
4 (٤) *arbá'a*	the fourth	*râbiʿ*,	„	*rabʿa*
5 (٥) *khamsa*	the fifth	*khâmis*,	„	*khamsa*
6 (٦) *sitta*	the sixth	*sâtit*,	„	*satta*
7 (٧) *sabʿa*	the seventh	*sâbiʿ*,	„	*sabʿa*
8 (٨) *tamânya*	the eighth	*tâmin*,	„	*tamna*
9 (٩) *tisʿa*	the ninth	*tâsiʿ*,	„	*tasʿa*
10 (١٠) *ʿâshara*	the tenth	*ʿâshir*,	„	*ʿashra*

11 *ḥidâshar*	30 *talâtîn*	500 *khumsemîya*
12 *itnâshar*	40 *arbaʿîn*	600 *suttemîya*
13 *talatâshar*	50 *khamsîn*	700 *subʿamîya*
14 *arbaḥtâshar*	60 *sittîn*	800 *tumnemîya*
15 *khamastâshar*	70 *sabʿîn*	900 *tusʿamîya*
16 *sittâshar*	80 *tamânîn*	1000 *alf*
17 *sabaḥtâshar*	90 *tisʿîn*	2000 *alfein*
18 *tamantâshar*	100 *mîya;* before nouns, [*mît.*	3000 *tálat âlâf*
19 *tisʿatâshar*	200 *mîtein*	4000 *árbaḥt âlâf*
20 *ʿishrîn*	300 *tultemîya*	5000 *khâmast âlâf*
21 *wâḥid u ʿishrîn*	400 *rubʿamîya*	100,000 *mît alf*

1,000,000 *malyûn*

once	*marra waḥda, marra,*	a half	*nuṣṣ*
twice	*marratein* [or *nôba*	a third	*tult, tilt*
thrice	*talat marrât*	a fourth	*rub'*
four times	*arba' marrât*	three-fourths	*talat irbâ'*
five times	*khamas marrât*	a fifth	*khums*
six times	*sitta marrât*	a sixth	*suds*
seven times	*saba' marrât*	a seventh	*sub'*
eight times	*taman marrât*	an eighth	*tumn*
nine times	*tisa' marrât*	a ninth	*tus'*
ten times	*'ashar marrât*	a tenth	*'oshr*

Substantives following the numerals 2-10 are used in the plural, those following numerals above 10 in the singular; thus *talâta kilâb*, 3 dogs, but *talâtîn kalb*, 30 dogs. Educated people generally employ the dual form of the noun instead of the numeral two: *kalbein*, 2 dogs.

Arabic Vocabulary.

Above, *fôq.*

Add, to, *zâd.* Add a little more (i.e. bid a little higher), *zîd shwaiya.*

Address, *'unwân.*

Aeroplane, *ṭaiyâra.*

Africa, *Ifrîqîya.* African, *ifrîqi.*

After, *ba'd;* afterwards, *ba'dein.*

Afternoon, *ba'd ed-ḍuhr, 'aṣr.*

Against, *ḍidd.*

Air, *hawâ.*

All, *el-kull,* all people, *kull en-nâs* (lit. the total of the people).

Almonds, *lôz,* sing. *lôza.*

Always, *dâiman* or *tamalli.*

America, *Amerîka.* American, *marakâni, malakâni,* pl. *marakân, imrikân.*

Anchorage, roads, *mirsâ.*

Angry, *za'lân.* To get angry, *zi'il.* Do not be angry, *mâ tiz'âlsh.*

Apricots, *mishmish.*

Arabia, *Bilâd el-'Arab.* Arab, *râgil 'árabi,* pl. *úlâd el-'arab.*

Arabic, *'árabi.* What is that called in Arabic? *ismuh ei bil-'árabi?*

Arable land, *ṭîn.*

Arm, *dirâ'.*

Arrive, *wiṣil.* When does the steamer arrive, *el-wâbûr yûṣal imta?* Arrival, *wuṣûl.*

Ask, to, *sa'al.*

At, *'and* (*'andi* = with me; see Have).

Aunt, *'amma* (paternal aunt), *khâla* (maternal aunt).

Austria, *Bilâd en-Nimsa.* Austrian, *nimsâwi.*

Autumn, *kharîf.*

Awaken, to, *ṣaḥḥâ.* Awake me, *ṣaḥḥîni.*

Back, *ḍahr.*

Bad, *baṭṭâl.*

Baker, *farrân.*

Bananas, *môz,* sing. *môza.*

Barber, *daqn,* *ḥallâq, mizaiyin.*

Barley, *sha'îr, shi'îr.*

Basket, *quffa,* pl. *qufaf.*

Bath, bath establishment, *ḥammâm.* [*mâm.*

Bazaar, see Market.

Be, to. The copula 'is' (are) is not translated; comp. p. xxxi.

Beans, *faṣûlya.* Broad beans, *fûl.* Haricot beans, *lûbiya.*

Beard, *daqn.* Full beard, *liḥya.* Moustache, *shanab.*

Beat, to, *ḍarab.* Beat him, *iḍrabuh!*

Beautiful, *kwaiyis, gamîl.*

Bed, *serîr,* pl. *sarâyir.*

Beduin, *badawi,* pl. *bidu, 'arab, 'orban.* Beduin sheikh, *sheikh el-'arab.*

Bee, *nahla*, pl. *nahl*.
Beer, *bîra*.
Before, *qabl* (time), *quddâm* (place).
Behind, *wara*.
Below, *taht*.
Bench (of stone or mud), *mastaba*, pl. *masâtib* (also used for certain kinds of tombs, p. clxxvi).
Beside, *'and*, *gamb*.
Better, *ahsan*, *kheir*.
Between, *bein*.
Bicycle, *'agala; bisiklett* or *biskelitt*.
Bill, account, *hisâb*.
Bird, *teir*, pl. *tiyûr*. Singing-bird, *'asfûr*, pl. *'asâfîr*.
Bite, to, *'add*. It (she) has bitten me, *'addétni;* it (she) will bite, *te'udd*.
Bitter, *murr*.
Black, *iswid*, fem. *sôda*.
Blacksmith, *haddâd*.
Blind, *a'ma*, fem. *'amya*.
Blood, *damm*.
Blue, *azraq*, fem. *zarqa*.
Board, *lôha*, pl. *ilwâh*.
Boat, *filûka*.
Boil, to. The water is boiling, *el-maiya tighli*. Boiled, *maslûq*.
Book, *kitâb*, pl. *kutub*. Bookseller, *kutbi*, pl. *kutbîya*.
Boot, *gazma*, pl. *gizam*.
Bottle, *qizâza*, pl. *qazâyiz*. Water-bottle, *qulla*, pl. *qulal*.
Box, *sandûq*, pl. *sanâdîq*.
Boy, *walad*, pl. *ûlâd*.
Brandy, *'áraqi*.
Bread, *'eish*. See also Loaf.
Break, to, *kasar* (trans.); *inkásar* (intrans.). Broken, *maksûr*.
Breakfast, *futûr*. Breakfast, to, *fitir*.
Bride, *'arûsa*. Bridegroom, *'arîs*.
Bridge, *kubri*, *qantara* (comp. p. 197).
Bridle, *ligâm*.
Bring, to, *gâb*. Bring the eggs, *gîb el-beid!*
Broad, *'arîd*.
Brother, *akh* (before suffixes and genitives *akhû*, as *akhûna*, our brother), pl. *ikhwân*.
Brown, *asmar* or *ahmar*, fem. *samra* or *hamra*.
Bucket, *gardal* or *satl*, pl. *garâdil*, *sutûl*.
Burn, to. The fire burns, *en-nâr beyûla'*. The sun burns me, *esh-shams* (or *es-sams*) *tihraqni*.
Bury, to, *dafan*. They have buried him, *dafanûh*.—Burial, *dafna*.
Butcher, *gazzâr*.
Butter, *zibda*.
Button, *zirr*, pl. *zirâr*.
Buy, to. What dost thou wish to buy, *'âuz tishtíri ei?* Hast thou bought the eggs, *inta ishtareit el-beid?* See also p. 53.
Cab, *'arabîya*. Cabman, *'arbági*. He is hailed with the expression *usta*.
Café, see Coffee.
Cairo, *Masr*.
Calf, *'igl*, pl. *'igûl*.
Call, to, *nadah*. Call the cook, *indáh-li't-tabbâkh*.
Call, to, see Name.
Camel, *gamal* (masc.), pl. *gimâl*. Riding camel, *hagîn*. Camel-driver, *gammâl*.
Candle, *sham'a*, pl. *shama'(ât)*. Candlestick, *sham'adân*.
Cape (promontory), *râs*.
Care. Take care, *khalli bâlak* (of the luggage, *min el-'afsh*), *û'â*.
Carpet, *siggâda; busât*.
Carriage, *'arabîya* (also a railway carriage).
Castle, *qasr*, pl. *qusûr; sarâya*, pl. *sarâyât*.
Cattle, *baqar*.
Cause, *sabab*.
Cave, *maghâra*.

The staple of his food consists of a peculiar kind of bread made of sorghum flour (comp. p. lxxvi) in Upper Egypt, or of maize in the Delta, wheaten bread being eaten by the wealthier only. This poor kind of bread often has a greenish colour, owing to an admixture of flour made from the kernels of fenugreek (see below). Next in importance in the bill of fare are broad beans *(fûl)*. For supper, however, even the poorest cause a hot repast to be prepared. This usually consists of a highly salted sauce made of onions and butter, or in the poorer houses of onions and linseed or sesame oil. Into this sauce, which in summer acquires a gelatinous consistency by the addition of the universal bâmiya (the capsular fruit of the hibiscus esculentus, p. lxxvii) and various herbs, each member of the family dips pieces of bread held in the fingers. Both in town and country, goat's, sheep's, or buffalo's milk also forms a daily article of food, but always in a sour condition or half converted into cheese, and in moderate quantities only. In the height of summer the consumption of cucumbers, pumpkins, etc., which the land yields in abundance, is enormous. In spring large quantities of lettuce, radish-leaves, and similar green vegetables are eaten; and the lower classes consume, for medical purposes during January and February, considerable amounts of ḥilba or fenugreek (p. lxxvi), a clover-like plant with a disagreeable odour. In the month of Ramaḍân alone (p. xcix), when a rigorous fast is observed during the day, and on the three days of the great Bairam festival (Qurbân Bairâm, p. c), even the poorest indulge in meat, and it is customary to distribute that rare luxury to beggars at these seasons.

The peasant works in the fields divested of everything except a scanty apron. The chief articles of his wardrobe at other times are an indigo-dyed cotton shirt *(qamîṣ)*, a pair of short and wide cotton breeches, a kind of cloak *('abâya)* of brown, home-spun goats' wool or simply a blanket of sheep's wool *(ḥirâm)*, and lastly a close-fitting felt skull-cap *(libda)*. He is generally barefooted, but occasionally wears pointed red *(markûb)* or broad yellow shoes *(balgha)*. The headmen and wealthier peasants wear wide, black woollen cloaks and the thick red 'Tunisian' *ṭarbûsh* with a blue silk tassel, round which they coil a turban (*'imma;* usually white). They often carry a long and thick stick *(nabbût)*, made of ash imported from Caramania in S. Asia Minor. All watchmen carry similar sticks as a badge of office.

The sole wealth of Egypt is derived from its agriculture, and to the fellahin alone is committed the important task of tilling the soil. They are, indeed, neither fitted nor inclined for other work, a circumstance which proves how completely the settled character of the ancient Egyptians has predominated over the restless Arab blood, which has been largely infused into the native population ever since the valley of the Nile was conquered by the armies of Islâm. The ancient Egyptian racial type has been preserved in extraordinary

purity in many fellah families, especially in Upper Egypt. This is particularly evident in the case of the children and women, whose features are not concealed and distorted by veils (which the ancient Egyptians despised). Even among the Nubians (p. lxii), between the First and Second Cataracts, faces occur that might almost lead us to think that some of the pictures of the period of the Pharaohs had come to life and stood before us in flesh and blood. In Lower Egypt, especially in the Delta, the Semitic type has sometimes prevailed over the African in consequence of the stream of Arab immigration that has now been flowing for more than a thousand years. The modern Egyptians, moreover, resemble the ancient in character and in the lot to which they are condemned. In ancient times the fellah, pressed into the service of priests and princes, was compelled to yield to them the fruits of his toil, and his position is nearly the same at the present day, save that the names of his masters (now mostly merchants) are changed. Among the benefits of the British occupation are the abolition of compulsory labour and the 'five feddân law' introduced by Kitchener in 1912, whereby a mortgage on a property of 5 feddân ($5^1/_5$ acres) or less can no longer be foreclosed. This has improved the lot of the fellahin by putting a check on usury, which has been rampant in Egypt during the last fifty years.

In early life the Egyptian peasant is remarkably docile, active, and intelligent, but at a later period this freshness and buoyancy are crushed out of him by care and poverty and the never-ceasing struggle for his daily bread. In his own fields the fellah is an industrious labourer, and his work is more continuous than that of the peasant of northern countries. He enjoys no period of repose during the winter, and the whole of his spare time is occupied in drawing water for the irrigation of the land (comp. p. lxxiv). The fellah is peaceful in disposition, kindly and helpful to his neighbour. Foreigners see his best side by observing his dealings with his fellows.

Among the common diseases of the fellahin and the lower classes on the whole are ophthalmia (trachoma), ankylostomiasis, and bilharziosis. Ankylostomiasis or hookworm disease is due to a small nematode (Ankylostomum duodenale or Necator americanus) in the duodenum and small intestine, which causes pernicious anæmia. Bilharziosis is due to the bilharzia (Schistosomum hæmatobium), a trematode parasite discovered in 1851 by the German physician Bilharz (professor at the medical school of Qaṣr el-ʿAini, p. 56), which, by its presence in the portal system and renal veins, causes hæmaturia, stone, etc.

(2) Copts *(qibṭ, 'ibṭ)*. While we regard the fellahin as genuine Egyptians in consequence of their uninterrupted occupation of the soil, the religion of the Copts affords us an additional guarantee for the purity of their descent. The Copts are undoubtedly the most direct descendants of the ancient Egyptians, there being no ground for the assumption that their ancestors were immigrants who embraced Christianity after the conquest of the country by the Mohammedans, while on the other hand the obstinacy with which they defended their monophysite Christianity (p. lviii) for several cen-

turies against the inroads of the creed of Byzantium affords another indication of their Egyptian character. At the census of 1917 the number of Copts in Egypt was 834,474. They are most numerous in the towns of Upper Egypt (627,848), around the ancient Koptos (p. 232), at Naqâda, Luxor, Esna, Dendera, Girga, Ṭahṭa, and particularly at Asyûṭ and Akhmîm, where they form the bulk of the population. The proportion of Copts to Moslems (11,656,408) was as 1 to 14. Adherents of other religions and confessions in Egypt numbered 260,036.

At the head of the Orthodox Coptic church is the Patriarch (Yoannes XIX., consecrated in 1928), who has his headquarters in Cairo (p. 85) and has the title of 'Patriarch of the Orthodox Copts of Alexandria, Abyssinia, Nubia, the five Western Cities, Africa, and Syria'. He is elected by the metropolitans, bishops, and heads of monasteries, by members and representatives of the Court of Personal Statute (Maglis Milli, i.e. National Council) of the Coptic Church, and by specially nominated Coptic notables. Below the Patriarch are the bishops *(muṭrân)*, who reside in the chief towns of their dioceses *(muṭrânîya)*, the seat of the bishop of the E. Delta province being at Jerusalem. Outside Egypt the Coptic church includes also the dioceses of Nûba-Kharṭûm (with its seat at Kharṭûm) and of Abyssinia (with its seat at Addîs Ábaba). The priests *(qassîs)* are educated at seminaries (one in Alexandria, another in Cairo), while a special school trains blind youths *('arîf)* to fill humbler positions in the church (as precentors, etc.). Since the first centuries of the Christian era (comp. p. cxvi) monasteries *(deir)* have been scattered throughout the country. Most of them have an arch-priest *(qummuṣ)* at their head. The most important, which have the right of electing the Patriarch (see above), are the monastery of El-Maḥarraq near Manfalûṭ (p. 225; ruled by a bishop), those of St. Anthony (Deir Amba Intaniôs; also under a bishop) and St. Paul (Deir Amba Bôlos) near the Red Sea (p. 218), and the four monasteries in the Wâdi en-Naṭrûn (Deir el-Barâmûs, Deir Suryâni, Deir Amba Bishôi, Deir Abu Maqâr; p. 35). The Deir Amba Samû'îl (Gebel el-Gharbi, near Minya, p. 220) is another large monastery. There are also five nunneries in Cairo.

Most of the Copts that dwell in towns are engaged in the more refined handicrafts (as watchmakers, goldsmiths, embroiderers, tailors, weavers, cabinet-makers, etc.), or in trade, or as clerks and notaries. Their physique is accordingly materially different from that of the fellahin and even from that of Coptic peasants. They are of more delicate frame, with small hands and feet; their necks are longer and their skulls are higher and narrower than those of the peasantry; and, lastly, their complexion is fairer. These differences are sufficiently accounted for by their mode of life; for, when we compare those Copts who are engaged in rustic pursuits, or the Coptic camel-drivers of Upper Egypt, with the fellahin, we find that the two races are not distinguishable from each other. This dualism of type in bodily structure, the robust peasant and the more delicate town-dweller, has been recognized even in the skeletons of the ancient mummies.

Few nations in the East embraced the Gospel more zealously than the dwellers on the Nile. Accustomed as they had long been to regard life as a school of preparation for another world, and weary of their motley Pantheon of divinities, whose self-seeking priesthood designedly disguised the truth, they welcomed the simple

doctrines of Christianity, which appeared so well adapted to their condition and promised them succour and redemption. They took a darker view of Christianity than any other nation; they were the first in whom repentance for sin led to asceticism and the desire of abandoning things of the world to the adoption of a hermit's life (comp. p. cxvi). Like Eutyches, the archimandrite at Constantinople, they revered the divine nature of the Saviour only, in which they held that every human element was absorbed; and when the Council of Chalcedon (p. cxvii) in 451 sanctioned the doctrine that Christ combined a human with a divine nature, the Egyptians with their characteristic tenacity adhered to their old views, and formed a sect termed *Eutychians*, or *Monophysites*, to which the Copts of the present day, and also the Abyssinians, still belong.

The name of the Copts is an ethnical one, being simply an Arabic corruption of the Greek name of Egyptians. The theory is now exploded that they derive their name from a certain itinerant preacher named Jacobus, who according to El-Maqrîzi (p. 78) was termed El-Barâdi'i, or 'blanket-bearer', from the old saddle-cloth worn by him when preaching. [The monk Ya'qôb Burde'anâ (Jacobus Baradæus, d. 578) was consecrated bishop of Edessa (Urfa) c. 542-543 and founded the Monophysite Church in Syria.] This Jacobus promulgated the monophysite doctrine of Eutyches, which had found its most zealous supporter in Dioscurus, a bishop of Alexandria (p. cxvii), declared a heretic and banished after the Council of Chalcedon; and his disciples were sometimes called Jacobites. If this name had ever been abbreviated to Cobit or Cobt, it would probably have occurred frequently in the writings of Monophysites; but there we find no trace of it. It is, on the other hand, quite intelligible that the word Copt, though originally synonymous with Egyptian, should gradually have come to denote a particular religious sect; for, at the period when the Nile valley was conquered by 'Amr (pp. cxvii, cxviii), the native Egyptians, who almost exclusively held the monophysite creed, were chiefly distinguished by their religion from their invaders, who brought a new religious system from the East.

These Egyptian Christians strenuously opposed the resolutions of the Council of Chalcedon, and thousands sacrificed their lives or their welfare in the fierce conflicts of the 6th cent., the causes of which were imperfectly understood by the majority of the belligerents. The subtle dogmatic differences which gave rise to these wars aroused such hatred among these professors of the religion of love, that the defeated Monophysites readily welcomed the armies of Islâm, or perhaps even invited them to their country.

After the conquest of Egypt by the Arabs (p. 46) the Copts were at first treated with lenity, and were even appointed to the highest government offices; but they were soon doomed to suffer persecutions and privations of every description. These persecutions were mainly due to their unbounded arrogance and their perpetual conspiracies against their new masters, and their Mohammedan contemporaries even attributed to them the disastrous conflagrations from which the new capital of the country so frequently suffered. Their hopes were doomed to bitter disappointment, and their national pride to utter humiliation. The conquerors succeeded in maintaining their position, and though apparently at first inclined to moderation, were

at length driven by the conduct and the previous example of the Copts themselves to persecute and oppress them to the uttermost.

In spite, however, of all these disasters a numerous community of Copts has always existed in Egypt, a fact which is mainly to be accounted for by the remarkable tenacity and constancy of the Egyptian character. Owing, however, to the continual oppression and contempt to which they were formerly subjected, they have degenerated in every respect, while their character has been correspondingly altered. Their divine worship will strike the traveller as strange, and anything but edifying or elevating (comp. p. 116). It is true that the Copt is a regular attendant at church ('kinîsa'), but his conduct while there and the amount of benefit he receives are somewhat questionable. In the service the Coptic language, i.e. the language of the Egyptians of the 3rd cent. of the Christian era (comp. p. cxxxiii), is used for praying and chanting. But as the majority even of the priests themselves, though able to read this ancient speech, do not understand it, the Arabic translation of the prayers is given at the same time, and the sermon is delivered in Arabic. Since the 6th cent. the doctrine of the Jacobites has been in a state of deathlike lethargy which has made even the slightest attempt at further development impossible. In no other religious community is fasting so common as among the Christians of Egypt and Abyssinia. They still found their creed upon Old Testament institutions, and so show pretty clearly that had Christianity been confined to the East it would never have become the chief religion of the world.

The Copts are no longer distinguished from the Arabs by their dress. Only the priests (p. lvii) now wear the black or dark blue turban and the dark-coloured clothes originally prescribed by their oppressors. Many Copts have been converted to Protestantism by American missionaries (comp. p. 226), particularly in Upper Egypt, chiefly through the foundation of good schools and the distribution of cheap Bibles. Even the orthodox Copts have a great reverence for the sacred volume, and it is not uncommon to meet with members of their sect who know the Gospels by heart. Roman propaganda, which was begun by Franciscans at the end of the 17th and beginning of the 18th cent., has been less successful among the Copts. There are, however, a few small Roman Catholic communities in Upper Egypt (at Girga, Akhmîm, and Naqâda) and in Cairo (p. 44), forming the 'Church of the Catholic Copts', whose patriarch, Kyrillos II., consecrated in 1899, is a native Copt.

(3) Beduin. *Bidu* (sing. *badawi*) is the name applied to the nomadic Arabs, and *'Arab* (sing. *'Arabi*) to those who immigrated at a later period and settled in the Nile valley. They both differ materially from the town-dwellers and from the fellahin. The subdivisions of the Beduin tribes are called *Qabîla* (whence the name of 'Kabyles' for the Berber inhabitants of Algeria), with a sheikh at

the head of each. Though differing greatly in origin and language, the wandering tribes of Egypt all profess Islâm. Again, while some have immigrated from Arabia or Syria, partly in very ancient and partly in modern times, and while others are supposed to be the aboriginal inhabitants of the territories claimed by them (as the Berbers of N. Africa and the Ethiopians and Blemmyes of Nubia), or former dwellers on the Nile expelled from their homes by foreign invaders, they all differ greatly from the settled Egyptian population; and this contrast is accounted for by the radical difference between the influences of the desert and those of the Nile valley. According to the census of 1927 there were 35,504 Beduin in Egypt.

The Beduin may be divided into two leading groups: (1) *Beduin* in the narrower sense, i.e. Arabic-speaking tribes, most of whom have probably immigrated from Arabia or Syria, and who occupy the deserts adjoining Middle and Northern Egypt, besides to a considerable extent settling in the Nile valley; (2) *Bega (Beja)*, who range over the regions of Upper Egypt and Nubia situated between the Nile and the Red Sea, and extending to the frontiers of the Abyssinian mountains. These are the descendants of the ancient Blemmyes (p. 413; their territory being known as 'Edbai'). The two principal races of the second group, with whom alone we have to deal as inhabitants of Egypt, are the *Bishârîn* and the *ʿAbâbda.* They are widely scattered in the valleys of the desert (pp. 397 seqq.), between the tropics and the latitude of Qena and Qoṣeir, and lead a poverty-stricken life with their very scanty stock of camels, goats, and sheep. Though closely resembling the other Bega tribes in appearance, the ʿAbâbda (sing. ʿAbbâdi) possess an original language of their own ('to-bedjawîya'), which, however, they have long since exchanged for bad Arabic. They have adopted also the costume of the fellahin, while the Bishârîn (sing. Bishâri) tend their large flocks of sheep and herds of camels in a half-naked condition, girded with a leathern apron and wrapped in a cotton shawl ('milâya'; comp. p. 363). All these groups are remarkable for their fine and almost Caucasian cast of features, their bronze-coloured complexion, and their luxuriant hair, which they wear loose or hanging down in numberless plaits. Their figures are beautifully symmetrical, and more or less slender in accordance with their means of subsistence, and their limbs are gracefully formed. In other respects they resemble all the other children of the desert, as in the purity of their complexion, the peculiar thinness of their necks, and the premature wrinkling of their faces. Compared with their quarrelsome neighbours the Bishârîn, the ʿAbâbda are generally gentle and inoffensive.

Besides the two above-mentioned Bega races there are numerous Beduin, including other Bega tribes (Hadendoa, Beni ʿÂmir, Ḥabâb, etc.; comp. p. 453), who inhabit the steppes and deserts belonging to the region of the Nile, but beyond the limits of Egypt, and range as far as the confines of the heathen negro races on the

left bank of the Nile, nearly to 9° N. latitude; but with these we have not at present to deal. As regards the Beduin proper of the N., their common home, the desert, seems to have exerted a unifying effect upon races that were originally different, and the peculiar characteristics of each have gradually disappeared before the uniform environment of all.

There are three important Beduin tribes in the peninsula of Mount Sinai: the *Terâbîyîn;* the *Tîyâha*, who occupy the heart of the peninsula, between Suez and ʿAqaba; and the *Sawârqa* or *El-ʿArayîsh*, to the north of the latter. In Upper Egypt, besides the ʿAbâbda, the most important tribes who occupy the E. bank of the Nile are the *Beni Waṣel* and the *Atwâni*, who, however, have now settled on both banks of the Theban Nile valley and are gradually blending with the fellahin, and the *Maʿâza*, who dwell in groups among the limestone mountains between Suez and Qena, where there are good pastures at places. Most of the Arabian Beduin, on the other hand, who belong to Egypt, confine themselves to the W. bank of the Nile. They occupy the whole of this side of the river from the Faiyûm as far as Abydos near Balyana (p. 231), and by their aid communication is maintained with the western oases, peopled by a totally different race, who till the ground and possess no camels, being probably allied to the Berbers of N. Africa (one of the Libyan tribes mentioned in ancient inscriptions; comp. p. 404).

The Beduin of the North, and especially the tribe of the *Ûlâd ʿAli*, have inherited with comparative purity the fiery blood of the desert tribes, who achieved such marvellous exploits under the banner of the Prophet, but the traveller will rarely come in contact with them unless he undertakes a journey across the desert. The sophisticated Beduin who assist travellers in the ascent of the Pyramids (comp. p. 137) belong to the Nagâma tribe. Genuine Beduin are to be found nowhere except in their desert home, where to a great extent they still retain the spirit of independence, the courage, and the restlessness of their ancestors. As in the time of Herodotus, the tent of the Badawi is still his home. Where it is pitched is a matter of indifference to him, if only the pegs which secure it be firmly driven into the earth, if it shelter his wife and child from the burning sunshine and the chilly night air, and if pasturage ground and a spring be within reach. At Ramleh (p. 27) the traveller may see numerous Beduin families of the poorest class encamped in their tents, where they live in the most frugal possible manner, with a few miserable goats and the fowls which subsist on the rubbish in their neighbourhood. Though professing Islâm, the Beduin of Egypt are considerably less strict in their observances than the fellahin of the Nile valley, who are themselves sufficiently lax, and above all they pay little attention to the religious distinction between clean and unclean (comp. p. xci). They do not observe the practice of praying five times a day (p. xc), and they are as a rule but slightly

acquainted with the Koran. Relics of the old star-worship, which with its lunar calendar is a part of desert life, can still be traced among their customs. To the tillers of the soil, on the other hand, it is the sun and the solar year, by which agricultural seasons are regulated, that are sacred.

The traveller will occasionally observe Beduin in the streets and in the bazaars of armourers and leather-merchants, and will be struck with the proud bearing of these bronzed desert-folk, whose sharp, bearded features and steady gaze betoken virility and resolution. In Egypt the traveller need not fear their predatory propensities.

(4) Arab Town-Dwellers. Those Arabs with whom the traveller usually comes in contact in towns are shopkeepers, officials, servants, cabmen, and donkey-attendants. These are generally of a much more mixed origin than the fellahin. It thus happens that the citizens of the Egyptian towns consist of persons of every complexion from dark-brown to white, with the features of the worshippers of Osiris or the sharp profile of the Beduin, and with the slender figure of the fellah or the corpulence of the Turk. Among the lower classes intermarriage with negro-women has sometimes darkened the complexion and thickened the features of their offspring; while the higher ranks, including many descendants of white slaves or Turkish mothers, more nearly resemble the European type. As the inhabitants of the towns could not be so much oppressed by their rulers as the peasantry, we find that they exhibit a more independent spirit, greater enterprise, and a more cheerful disposition than the fellahin. At the same time they are not free from the dreamy character peculiar to Orientals, nor from a tinge of the apathy of fatalism. Of late years, however, they have begun to occupy themselves with scientific studies and to produce a considerable number of higher officials, barristers, doctors, architects, engineers, etc. The townspeople profess Islâm, but, in their youth particularly, they are becoming more and more lax in their obedience to the Koran. Thus the custom of praying in public, outside the house-doors and shops, is gradually falling into disuse. Likewise the European dress is superseding the oriental (comp. p. 49), though the latter is far more picturesque and better suited to the climate. On the whole they are bigoted Mohammedans, and share the contempt with which the fellahin regard all other religions. Their daily intercourse with unbelievers tends, however, to keep their fanaticism in check, and has even induced them sometimes to admit strangers to witness the sacred ceremonies in their mosques.

(5) Nubians. The name *Barâbra* (sing. *Barbari*, *Berberi*) is applied to the Nubian inhabitants of the Nile valley between the neighbourhood of Aswân and the Fourth Cataract (comp. p. 410). The Egyptians and Nubians are radically different, and the dislike between the two races is carried to such an extent that Nubians, even in Egypt, very rarely marry Egyptian wives. The Nubians are

of the small steam-mills that abound in the villages, and of the numerous small banks which lend money on good security, both to the peasantry and to the government officials, at a rate of interest sometimes amounting to 6% monthly, the maximum permitted by law. Of recent years many Greeks have been active as physicians, lawyers, engineers, architects, and especially landowners. The commercial superiority of the Greeks to the Orientals is nowhere so strikingly manifested as in Egypt, where it affords a modern reflex of their ancient success in colonization.

The *Italian* residents (45,106 in 1927) include many merchants, barristers, and scholars, but consist chiefly of traders of a humble class. — *Maltese* are frequently met with as shoemakers, carpenters, etc. — The *French* (12,000 in 1927) are mostly shopkeepers or artisans of the higher class. The chief European officials of the government, including several architects and engineers, were until recently French. — *British* residents numbered 6118 in 1882 and 26,000 in 1927. The special British interests in Egypt (Suez Canal) are emphasized by the presence of a High Commissioner (p. cxxxii) and of British troops (10,022 of all ranks and arms in 1928). The British are now the only Europeans to hold important government posts; e.g. the control of the Egyptian army and the customs service is in their hands. Many British engineers also are employed in the manufacture of machinery and the construction of Nile barrages and irrigation works, railways, and harbours. The posts and telegraphs, the railways, and the ordnance survey (p. 87) have been remodelled after the British pattern, but are now under Egyptian management. — Before 1914 the *Austrian* and *German* community included a number of merchants of the best class, many physicians and teachers, hotel-keepers, musicians, and clever craftsmen. During the war their number was greatly decreased, but since 1923 it has been slowly on the rise again.

With regard to the capability of Europeans of becoming acclimatized in Egypt there are a number of widely divergent opinions. It has been asserted that European families settled in Egypt die out in the second or third generation, but of this there is no sufficient proof, and many examples to the contrary might be cited. Moreover as the Europeans in Egypt dwell exclusively in the large cities, they do not afford very conclusive evidence on the general question; for city life, as opposed to country life, is even less propitious to health and vigour in warm countries than it is in northern climes. Thus the Mamelukes (pp. cxxi, cxxiii) have left no descendants in Egypt. The climate of Egypt (comp. p. lxxix) is less enervating than that of most other hot countries, an advantage attributed to the dryness of the air.

C. The Nile.

By *Colonel Sir Henry Lyons*, F.R.S.

From the sources of the river *Kagera* (to the S.W. of Lake Victoria) to the sea the Nile is the second longest continuous waterway in the world (about 4000 M.), being surpassed only by the Mississippi-Missouri, which is probably two or three hundred miles longer. From the Ripon Falls at Lake Victoria to the sea the distance is about 3400 M., so that the Nile proper is (with the possible exception of the Amazon) the longest single river in the world.

The Kagera flows into the great *Lake Victoria* or *Victoria Nyanza* (27,600 sq. M. in area; 3724 ft. above sea-level; comp. p. 467), on the N. shore of which, at the Ripon Falls, begins the true Nile. After a course of 242 M. this enters *Lake Albert* or *Albert Nyanza* (2037 ft.; 2240 sq. M.; p. 467). From this point, under the name of *Baḥr el-Gebel*, it traverses a rocky channel as far as Gondókoro, and it then flows for 470 M. through the swamps of the 'sudd' (p. 465). In latitude 9° 30′ N. the main stream receives two tributaries, the *Baḥr el-Ghazâl* and the *Baḥr ez-Zerâf* (*Baḥr ez-Zarâfa;* p. 465), and a little farther on it is joined by the important river *Sobat*, to which the annual flood of the White Nile is due. From this point to Kharṭûm the *Baḥr el-Abyaḍ* or 'White Nile', as it is here called, flows through a shallow valley of considerable width, until it is joined by the *Baḥr el-Azraq* (comp. p. lxviii), i.e. the 'blue', 'dark', or 'turbid' Nile, so called in contradistinction to the White Nile, the 'clear' water of which has been filtered in its passage through the marshes of the Baḥr el-Gebel or has deposited its silt in the upper reaches of the Sobat (comp. p. 457). Between Kharṭûm and the Mediterranean, a distance of 1900 M., the Nile receives no further addition to its supply except from the river *Atbara*, while it is being continually diminished by evaporation, by percolation into the sandstone of the desert through which it flows, and especially by the irrigation of its flood-plains in Egypt. — Between Wâdi Ḥalfa and Aswân the average breadth of the Nile is about 550 yds., to the N. of Aswân it varies from 550 to 980 yds.

As practically no rain falls within its limits (comp. p. lxxx), Egypt would cease to exist as a habitable country and would become a desert valley, similar to those of the Sahara, were it not for its constant supply of water from the Nile. Thus the all-important annual Inundation of that river merits special notice as the great event of the Egyptian year.

The heavy rains which fall from June to September on the Abyssinian tableland cause the Blue Nile and the Atbara to rise rapidly, and their waters carry down in suspension vast quantities of the mud which has during many centuries formed the fertile valley and Delta of Egypt, and of which a fresh layer is still deposited annually in those portions of Upper Egypt where flood-irrigation has not yet been replaced by perennial irrigation (comp. p. lxxiii).

The volume of the Blue Nile flood, which may reach and even exceed 350,000 cubic feet per second, holds back the waters of the White Nile above the junction of the two streams, so that in August and September the waters of the Baḥr el-Gebel and the Sobat are penned up in the White Nile valley and contribute only a very small share to the inundation of the Nile proper. The rains of Abyssinia may therefore be regarded as practically regulating the height of the inundation of the Nile, and it is their variations which occasion the fluctuation from year to year. The region of the equatorial lakes has no effect whatever on the flood.

The Nile begins to rise at Kharṭûm about the middle of May, and at Aswân by the beginning of June, reaching its maximum height at both places about the end of the first week in September. The mean difference between the highest and lowest levels of the river is 21 ft. at Kharṭûm, 20 ft. at Wâdi Ḥalfa, 23 ft. at Aswân, 22 ft. at Asyûṭ, 22 ft. at Minya, and 16 ft. at Cairo. After the flood has reached its maximum height the Blue Nile falls rapidly, but the water of the White Nile, which is now liberated, prevents too rapid a fall of the river below Kharṭûm. By January the Blue Nile supply has diminished to a small amount, while that of the White Nile is several times as great, and this state of affairs continues until June, when the Blue Nile again rises. Thus, for these five months the mainstay of the Nile supply is the constant quantity furnished by the White Nile, amounting to some 14,000 cubic ft. per second.

From time immemorial the Nile flooded its valley annually. Crops were sown on the fertile mud flats left by the water as it subsided and were harvested in April and May, after which time only land in the neighbourhood of the river or where there were wells could be cultivated until the July following the next flood.

A great change took place when the cultivation of cotton was introduced into the Delta by Muḥammed ʿAli in 1821 (comp. p. lxxvi) and afterwards spread to Upper Egypt. It then became necessary to replace basin-irrigation, which was confined to a certain time of the year (comp. p. lxxiii), by perennial irrigation throughout the year. It was decided to construct large dams in order to save the surplus of water in November, December, and January, and to release it gradually during the following months, until the beginning of the new flood. Muḥammed ʿAli deepened the old canals and began in 1835 the Delta Barrage (p. 131), which was not completed till 1890. This raised the water-level sufficiently to feed the three main canals of the Delta, the Raiyâḥ et-Taufîqi, the Raiyâḥ el-Minûfîya, and the Raiyâḥ el-Beḥeira. From the middle of February till the beginning of August the water supply is dependent on these canals alone, as the rivers during that period are completely dried up. The dams of Aswân and Asyûṭ were completed in 1902. The former, which was subsequently heightened and is to be still further raised (p. 396), collects the surplus water (comp. p. lxxiv) in a large storage

reservoir and augments the whole water supply of Egypt when the Nile is low, especially from April to July. The Asyûṭ Barrage (p. 237) regulates, viâ the great Ibrâhîmîya Canal, an extensive system of canals, which supply the provinces of Asyûṭ, Minya, Beni Suef, and Gîza, besides the Faiyûm (viâ the Baḥr Yûsuf, p. 202). The Esna Barrage (completed in 1909; p. 363) is used for the flood-irrigation of the province of Qena, while the Nag' Ḥammâdi Dam (begun in 1927; p. 239) will provide perennial irrigation for the province of Girga also. The great Sennâr Dam (p. 461) in the Sûdân irrigates a large part of the Gezîra, or the stĕppe between the Blue and White Niles, which is being opened up for the cultivation of cotton. — All these works serve to hold up the flow of the Nile and to augment the water supply during the period (April-July) when the river-level is low and when plenty of water is needed for the cultivation of cotton (comp. p. lxxvi). Owing to the increase in perennial irrigation far more water has to be released during the flood season than can be utilized for the summer crops, as those districts which now bear crops throughout the year no longer need the water formerly contained in the basins. A danger thus arose of the low-lying districts in the Delta becoming water-logged. Special pumping works and an efficient system of drainage had to be constructed and the capacity of the Rosetta branch of the Nile (p. 32) increased. — Another dam is to be constructed on the White Nile at Gebel Aulia (p. 463), to increase the water supply of Egypt when the level of the Nile is low, while the course of the Baḥr el-Gebel through the Sudd region (p. 465) and the effluxes of Lake Albert (p. 467) and of *Lake Tana* or *Tsana* in Abyssinia (5758 ft. above sea-level; 1400 sq. M.), through which flows the Abbai (afterwards the Blue Nile), are to be regulated for the same purpose (comp. p. cxxxii).

The breadth of the Nile valley is nowhere great, and only a portion of it is occupied by the cultivated alluvial plain, the rest consisting of desert-sands at too high a level to be reached by the inundation. In Nubia the cultivable land is restricted to isolated patches, while the valley is rarely as much as 2-3 M. wide; in Egypt it is wider, varying from 15 M. at Beni Suef to 5 M. at Edfu, of which 13 M. and 4 M. respectively are cultivated.

The alluvial deposit which is annually brought down by the Nile in flood has accumulated in the course of centuries to an average depth of 35-40 ft., occasionally even more. In composition it varies slightly from place to place. As a rule it forms a good light soil, being rather above the average in potash but deficient in nitrates. The view formerly held that it had a high manurial value was an exaggerated one, and it should be considered rather as a virgin soil which, so long as it is added annually to the surface of the land, enables it to bear luxuriant crops year after year.

Every year during the flood a considerable deposit of silt takes place in the river-bed, part of which is carried away as the river

falls, but the general result is that for thousands of years the bed of the Nile has been slowly rising by deposit at an average rate of about 4 inches per century. One consequence of this is that temples, which were built on the banks of the river, well above the annual inundation, are now below it, and foundations which were originally dry are now below the infiltration-level and in consequence have deteriorated.

This remarkable river has exercised a unique influence on the history of civilization. The necessity of controlling its course and utilizing its water taught the ancient Egyptians the art of river engineering and the kindred science of land-surveying, while in the starry heavens they beheld the eternal calendar which regulated the approach and the departure of the inundation, so that the river may perhaps have given the first impulse to the study of astronomy. As the annual overflow of the water obliterated all landmarks, it was necessary annually to measure the land anew, and to keep a register of the area belonging to each proprietor; and above all it became an important duty of the rulers of the people to impress them with a strong sense of the sacredness of property. Similar causes produced a like result in Babylonia. Every succeeding year, however, there arose new disputes, and these showed the necessity of establishing settled laws and enforcing judicial decisions. The Nile thus led to the foundation of social, legal, and political order.

Subsequently, when the engineers and architects, in the service of the state or of the priestly communities, erected those colossal structures with which we are about to become acquainted, it was the Nile that facilitated the transport of their materials, and enabled the builders of the pyramids and the other ancient Egyptians to employ the granite of Aswân for the structures of Memphis (p. 153), and even for those of Tanis (p. 182), near the coast of the Mediterranean. As the river, moreover, was also an admirable commercial highway, we find that the Egyptians had acquired considerable skill at a very early period in constructing vessels with oars, masts, sails, and even cabins and other conveniences.

From the earliest historical period down to the present time the course of the Nile, from the cataracts down to its bifurcation to the N. of Cairo, has undergone very little change. This, however, is not the case with its **Embouchures**; for, while ancient writers mention seven (the Pelusiac, the Tanitic, the Mendesian, the Bucolic or Phatnitic, the Sebennytic, the Bolbitinic, and the Canopic), there are now practically two channels only through which the river is discharged into the sea. These are the mouths at Rosetta (Rashîd; p. 32) and Damietta (Dumyâṭ; pp. 186, 187), situated near the middle of the Delta. The Pelusiac and Canopic mouths, the most important in ancient times, lay at the extreme E. and W. ends of the coast respectively.

D. The Geology of Egypt.

1. The Nile Valley and the Isthmus of Suez. The building stone generally used at *Alexandria* is obtained from the quarries of Mex (p. 28) and on the coast to the E. of Alexandria. This is a calcareous light-coloured stone of the quaternary period, formed of fragments of shells and foraminifera, intermixed with oolitic granules and grains of quartz sand, or even with fine gravel. This rock forms low hills to the W. of Alexandria and the coast-strip from Alexandria to Abuqîr. In many places it is covered by sand dunes and other recent formations.

The cultivated plains of the *Delta* and the *Nile Valley* consist of recent alluvial deposits, ranging from fine sand to the finest silt, laid down by the water of the annual inundation. Under these lie coarser yellowish sands and gravels of pleistocene age, which here and there reach the surface in the Delta as islands of sandy waste among the rich cultivation of the surrounding country. These are related to the later sand and gravel deposits on the neighbouring deserts, and to the traces of marine cliffs and beaches of the same period which may be seen on both sides of the valley at Cairo and at other places. At Abu Zaʿbal (p. 129) occurs a low hill of basalt which supplies excellent road-metal for Cairo and Alexandria.

The N. portion of the *Isthmus of Suez* consists of the recent marine deposits of the Mediterranean, while in the central portion, near the low hill of El-Gisr and round Lake Timsâḥ (p. 198), are deposits of Nile mud with fresh-water shells. To the S. of the Bitter Lakes (p. 198) are found marine quaternary deposits of the Red Sea. Reefs of fossil coral of quaternary age occur over a large part of the coasts of the Gulf of Suez, and the highest of these are now 1000 ft. above sea-level. The land here, or at least the coast line, must therefore have risen considerably in comparatively recent times, and the salines which are now forming appear to show that the movement has not yet ceased. The shores and islands of the Red Sea (see p. 451) are to-day fringed with live coral reefs which are dangerous to shipping.

Sands and loams occur to the S. of the pyramids of Gîza, and at numerous places on the E. side of the Nile valley between Cairo and Fashn (p. 219), belonging, as is shown by the numerous fossils which they contain, to the pliocene age. The small valley immediately to the S. of the pyramid of Zâwiyet el-ʿAryân (p. 150) has been cut out in these beds, and a rich collection of pliocene fossils may be made here. These deposits are intimately connected with the formation of the Nile valley in pliocene times, when it was at first a funnel-shaped bay of the Mediterranean.

In the time of the older miocene sea the Nile valley did not exist, but instead a large river flowed from a S.W. direction towards the region that is now Lower Egypt. The fluvio-marine deposits of Moghara in the Libyan Desert (p. 404) and the silicified wood of the same district also belong to these miocene times, as do the marine

limestones of the plateau of Cyrenaica, to the N. of the Sîwa Oasis and on the E. edge of the Arabian Desert (at the foot of Gebel Gineifa and Gebel ʿAtâqa, p. 193), and on the shore of the Gulf of Suez near Gebel Zeit.

The 'Petrified Forest' near Cairo (pp. 127, 128) consists of scattered fragments of the silicified stems of trees; and these, together with the red sandstone of Gebel el-Aḥmar (p. 123) and conical hills of the same material in the N. parts of the Arabian and Libyan deserts, are connected with the silicious thermal springs which bubbled forth amid the network of lagoons which existed in these parts in oligocene times. To the N.W. of the Birket Qârûn (p. 208) these fossil trees are even more numerous, while in the sands of oligocene age innumerable bones of extinct terrestrial and marine mammals and reptiles have been found, which were carried down by the river and buried in its estuarine deposits. A fine collection of these fossil animals may be seen in the Geological Museum at Cairo (p. 55).

The cliffs of the Nile valley above Cairo consist of middle and lower eocene limestone, containing numerous nummulites (p. 125) and other fossils. The strata are gently inclined to the N.N.W., so that the strata increase in age as we go towards the S.

In the vicinity of Edfu begins the upper cretaceous formation, here represented by the sandstone which at Gebel es-Silsila (p. 364) forms steep walls of rock and confines the river in a narrow channel. This 'Nubian Sandstone' covers an area of many thousand square miles, extending from the oases (comp. p. 403) to the Sûdân. At certain points, such as Aswân (pp. 379, 381), Kalâbsha (p. 415), Wâdi Ḥalfa (p. 438), and the Third and Fourth Cataracts (pp. 447, 445), ridges of crystalline rocks (granite, gneiss, diorite, etc.) rise through it, and form black or reddish hills in sharp contrast to the low tabular masses of the sandstone.

2. In the Arabian or Eastern Desert (pp. 388, 397 seqq.) a line of hills, some peaks of which are 7000 ft. in height, runs parallel to the Red Sea and at short distance from it. This is wholly formed of crystalline rocks (granite, gneiss, diorite, hornblende-schist, mica-schist, talc-schist, and the andesites and allied rocks), which form a great series of very ancient volcanic rocks, the imperial porphyry of Gebel ed-Dukhkhân (quarried by the Romans; p. 398) being a well-known representative. The E. and W. slopes of this range are overlaid by sedimentary rocks, usually the Nubian sandstone, but also (in the N. part) by limestones and marls (see pp. 399, 400). These stretch away toward the W., forming a great plateau of limestone in the N. and of sandstone in the S., in which the Nile valley forms a narrow trough. Numerous deeply eroded valleys give a characteristic appearance to the Eastern Desert. The open plains are almost bare of vegetation, but numerous plants may be seen in the valleys, especially after rain, while in the sheltered ravines among the hills where springs occur they grow luxuriantly.

3. The Libyan or Western Desert (pp. 403 seqq.) is totally different. The level limestone plateau, about 1000 ft. above the sea, extends to the W., its S. escarpment overlooking the lower plain of the Nubian sandstone to the S. In deep bays in this escarpment lie the oases of El-Khârga (p. 405), Ed-Dâkhla (p. 408), and El-Farâfra (p. 405), while that of El-Baḥarîya (p. 405) is situated in a depression surrounded by the higher plateau. The plateau is waterless and practically devoid of vegetation, while isolated knolls show how rapidly the erosion of the desert surface by wind is proceeding. In certain parts lines of sand dunes 100-200 ft. high stretch across the desert plateau in a N.N.W. and S.S.E. direction, sometimes for several hundred miles with hardly a break. They are most developed to the W. of the oasis of Ed-Dâkhla. The floor of the oases of El-Khârga and Ed-Dâkhla consists mostly of dark-coloured sands and clays of the upper cretaceous formation. Some beds contain alum and others are phosphatic. Springs well up at many points from a depth of about 400 ft. and furnish an abundant water supply to the cultivated lands. Some of these rise through natural fissures and others through artificial bore-holes.

To the S. of the oases lies the lower plain of the Nubian sandstone. This plain presents a low rolling surface covered with blackened flint pebbles and concretions of iron and manganese oxide, while the silicified trunks of fossil trees are frequently met with. Yellow drift-sand is seen everywhere, but it is only occasionally that it forms dunes of any size.

The oasis of El-Farâfra lies farther W., and to the N. and W. of it extends the plateau of eocene limestone as far as the oasis of *Sîwa* (p. 403). The strata here are mostly of miocene age, and they contain numerous fossils, a fact recorded by Herodotus (p. cx) and Eratosthenes (p. 380).

E. Agriculture and Vegetation.

1. Capabilities of the Soil. The land is extremely fertile, but by no means incapable of exhaustion. The common belief that all the fields of Egypt yield three harvests in the year is entirely erroneous. Many of the crops, as elsewhere, must occasionally be followed by a fallow period; others thrive only when a certain rotation is observed; and some fields require to be manured. Occasionally two crops are yielded by the same field in the same season (wheat and saffron, wheat and clover, etc.). So long as the inundation deposited a thick layer of fresh mud on the basin-lands (p. lxxiii) every year, and a single crop was raised off the greater part of the area, while the soil lay fallow during the hot months before the flood, the land could go on producing crops indefinitely. The great extension within the last fifty years of the cultivation of the sugar-cane and the cotton-plant (comp. p. lxxvi) has necessitated considerable modifications in the modes of irrigation (comp. p. lxxiii) and cultivation

hitherto in use. Now that most of the land is irrigated throughout the year a very small amount of mud is deposited, while two or more crops are raised annually. As both sugar and cotton are very exhausting crops, the land must either be more frequently left fallow or must be artificially manured. As the dung of the domestic animals is used as fuel throughout Egypt, where wood is very scarce while that of the numerous pigeons (comp. p. 237) is mainly used for horticultural purposes, resource must be had to other manures. One of these is afforded by the ruins of ancient towns, which were once built of unbaked clay, but now consist of mounds of earth, recognizable only as masses of ruins by the fragments of pottery they contain. Out of these mounds, which conceal the rubbish of thousands of years, is dug a kind of earth, known as *Sabakh*, sometimes containing as much as 12 % of salts (mainly potassium nitrate, but also sodium carbonate and sal ammoniac). This source of supply, however, will be exhausted at no very distant date. The only alternative is artificial manuring, and large quantities of fertilizers are imported. The bulk of the phosphates produced in Egypt (at El-Qoṣeir and Safâga on the Red Sea, p. 400, and at Es-Sibâʿîya in Upper Egypt, p. 358) are exported (175,123 metric tons in 1926) for use in the manufacture of superphosphates, as the soil of Egypt is already rich enough in those salts.

2. Irrigation. As the annual flooding of the Nile was the source of Egypt's prosperity, efforts were made even at the earliest times to derive as much benefit from it as possible. The land was divided up by earthen walls into basins, into which the flood-water was conducted by means of canals. Thus the too rapid ebbing of the floods was prevented and the soil was properly moistened. This system, when the dam at Nagʿ Ḥammâdi (p. 239) has been completed, will only survive to the S. of that point, in the province of Girga, on the edge of the W. desert, and on the right bank of the Nile above Cairo. The rest of Egypt, from Asyûṭ to the Mediterranean, now enjoys perennial irrigation through innumerable canals and watercourses. The annual procedure is as follows. At the time of the Nile flood, which begins in July, the sluices of the Aswân dam are opened (comp. p. 396) to allow the reddish-brown water to find its way into the plain. When the basins to the S. of Asyûṭ (see above) are full enough, the water therein is kept at a certain level for about forty days, until the ground is thoroughly saturated and all the silt has settled. The clear water is then drained back to the river, or, in years of extraordinarily low flood, conducted into lower basins. Seeds are sown in the silt that is left behind, and the crops grow without further watering. When the flood is weak, the inundation does not reach the higher districts, which are known as 'Sharâqi' and are freed from taxation in the years when they receive no flood-water (comp. p. 113).

The perennially irrigated provinces of Middle Egypt and the Delta take from their canals only the amount of water required by

standing crops. In the present conditions of intensive cultivation, therefore, they receive a much smaller share of flood-silt than the districts with basin irrigation and their lack of silt must be compensated for by extensive manuring (comp. p. lxxiii).

In November, when the Nile is falling and the whole country is amply supplied, the sluice-gates of the Aswân Dam (p. 396) are gradually closed, so as to fill the reservoir slowly. This is usually accomplished about the end of January. The gates of the Asyûṭ Barrage (p. 237) are similarly manipulated so as to maintain the necessary depth of water in the supply-canals. In the middle of February the gates of the Delta Barrage (p. 131) are completely closed. In April the supply falls below the requirements of the country, and, besides drawing upon the Aswân reservoir, it then often becomes necessary to restrict landowners on different parts of a canal to drawing water from it in rotation. The supply steadily diminishes until the flood rises about the beginning of July.

The irrigation is effected by means of: (1) The *Sâqiya*, a large wheel (rarely exceeding 30 ft. in diameter) turned by cattle or buffaloes, and sometimes by camels, and fitted with scoops or buckets *(qâdûs)* of wood or clay, resembling a dredging machine. (2) The *Shâdûf*, an apparatus resembling an ordinary 'well-sweep' (with bucket and counter-weight), set in motion by one person only, and drawing the water in buckets resembling baskets in appearance. As a substitute for the sâqiya several shâdûfs are sometimes arranged one above the other. (3) The Archimedean screw or *Ṭunbûr* (a tube in the form of a screw wound round a cylinder), chiefly seen in the Delta. (4) When it is possible to store the water in reservoirs above the level of the land to be watered, it is allowed to overflow the fields whenever required. This is the only method available in the oases, where fortunately the springs rise with such force as to admit of their being easily dammed up at a sufficiently high level. (5) Pumps driven by steam are used also, particularly when a large supply of water is required, as in the case of the sugar-plantations on the banks ('gefs') of the Nile in the N. part of Upper Egypt (e.g. near Kôm Ombo, p. 362). (6) The *Tâbût*, a peculiar, very light, and easily moved wooden wheel, which raises the water by means of numerous compartments in the hollow felloes, used mainly in the Lower Delta in places where the level of the water in the canals remains nearly the same. — Undershot water-wheels also are found in the Faiyûm. Occasionally irrigation is effected by means of a basket *(naṭṭâl)* slung on a rope between two labourers. — In order to distribute the water equally over flat fields, these are sometimes divided into a number of small squares by means of embankments of earth, a few inches in height, which are easily opened or closed so as to regulate the height of the water within them.

3. Agricultural Seasons. In the time of the Pharaohs the Egyptian agricultural year, which originally began on July 19th,

was divided into three equal parts, each consisting of four months of thirty days: the period of the inundation, winter, and summer. At the present day there are, strictly speaking, but two seasons: the hot season lasting from May to September and a cooler one from November to March, while October and April are transition months; but the effect which the annual Nile flood has upon the agriculture of the country rather than upon the climate has caused the months of September and October to be considered as a third season, comparable to our late-summer or autumn.

(a) The *Winter Cultivation (Esh-Shitwi)* lasts on the flooded lands of Upper Egypt from November till April; on perennially irrigated land the winter sowing takes place from October onwards, while the grain harvest is reaped in April in Middle Egypt and in May in the Delta. In this season the principal crops are wheat, barley, beans, and barsîm (Egyptian clover).

(b) The *Summer Crops (Eṣ-Ṣeifi)* may be considered as growing from May to August in the basin-lands and to October wherever there is perennial irrigation. The principal crops are rice (p. lxxvi), which is sown in May and harvested in October, and cotton, sown in March and picked in September and October. Most of the latter is grown from seed, but a limited amount is grown from two-year-old plants which have been cut back. On basin-lands of Upper Egypt where sufficient water from wells is available a crop of durra (sorghum vulgare, p. lxxvi) is grown and harvested before the flood-water arrives.

(c) The *Autumn Season (En-Nîl,* or flood) is the shortest, lasting barely seventy days. On the rich land of the Delta maize (p. lxxvi) is grown. A large crop of durra is raised on the perennially irrigated lands of Upper Egypt, and a considerable amount also grown on those which are not reached by the inundation. This crop is cut about November.

The Agricultural Implements of the Egyptians are exceedingly primitive and defective. The chief of these is the plough *(miḥrât)*, the form of which is the same as it was five thousand years ago (comp. p. 166); and the traveller will recognize it on many of the monuments and in the system of hieroglyphics (p. cxxxiii). It consists of a pole about 6 ft. long, drawn by an ox, buffalo, or other draught-animal, attached to it by means of a yoke, while to the other end is fastened a piece of wood bent inwards at an acute angle and shod with a three-pronged piece of iron *(lisân)*. Connected with the pole is the handle which is held by the fellah. These rude and light ploughs penetrate but slightly into the ground. The harrow is replaced in Egypt by a roller provided with iron spikes *(qunfud*, literally 'hedgehog'). The only tool used by the fellahin on their fields, or in making embankments of earth, is a kind of hoe *(fâs, ṭûrîya, qaddûm)* or shovel *(migrafa)*. The process of reaping consists in cutting the grain with a sickle *(mingal)*, or simply uprooting it by hand. The *nôrag*, or 'threshing sledge', consists of a kind of sledge resting on a roller provided with sharp semicircular pieces of iron, and drawn by oxen or buffaloes. This primitive machine, being driven over the corn to be threshed, crushes the stalks and ears; the grain or seeds is then separated by means of winnowing fans and a large sieve *(ghurbâl)*. The chopped straw *(tibn)* is used as fodder for stable animals.

4. Farm Produce of Egypt. The following is an enumeration of all the most important industrial crops cultivated in Egypt.

a. Cereals. 1. Wheat *(qamh)*. — 2. Maize (*dura shâmi*, i.e. Syrian durra, also known as *dura frangi*, i.e. European durra, or simply as *dura*, as it is called in Syria). — 3. Barley *(sha'îr, shi'îr)*. — 4. Rice *(ruzz)*, cultivated in the lower part of the Delta, from Alexandria and Rahmânîya as far as Manṣûra, Zagazig, and Ṣâliḥîya, and in the Wâdi et-Ṭumîlât, the Faiyûm, and the oases of the Libyan desert. In 1926 17,995,459 kg. (39,679,987 lb.), with a value of £E 319,892 were exported; in 1927 the exports reached £E 518,000. — 5. Sorghum (Sorghum vulgare, Andropōgon sorghum, see p. 455; *dura baladi*, i.e. durra of the country, or *dura 'aweiga*, simply called *dura* in the Sûdân; Ital. sorgho, Engl. Indian millet, Guinea corn, or Kaffir corn, the Tyrolese sirch). — 6. Pennisetum typhoideum, Penicillaria spicata, reed-mace or pearl millet *(dukhn)*.

b. Leguminous Plants. 1. Broad beans, Vicia faba *(fûl)*. — 2. Lentils *('ads)*. — 3. Chick-peas, Cicer arietinum *(ḥummuṣ)*. — 4. Lupins *(tirmis)*. — 5. Peas *(bisilla)*. — 6. Vigna sinensis, vigna beans or 'chowlee' *(lûbiya)*. — 7. Dolichos lablab, Egyptian kidney-bean *(liblâb)*, which are very frequently seen festooning walls and hedges, but are grown also as shrubs in fields *(lûbiya 'âfin)*.

c. Green Crops. 1. White Egyptian clover, Trifolium Alexandrinum *(barsîm)*. — 2. Fenugreek, Fænum græcum *(ḥilba)*, frequently ground into flour and used in making bread; also eaten raw by the lower classes in spring (comp. p. lv); not to be confounded with clover. — 3. Medicago sativa, or lucerne *(barsîm ḥigâzi)*. — 4. Lathyrus sativus, or flat pea *(gilbân)*. — 5. Sorghum halepense *(gerau)*.

d. Narcotics. The growing of tobacco *(dukhkhân)* has been forbidden since 1890, although the government has recently been making experimental plantings. Egyptian cigarettes (in 1928 exported to the value of £E 341,140) are mostly made of tobacco from Asia Minor. The cultivation of the opium poppy, Papaver somniferum *(abu 'n-nôm*, 'father of the sleep'), has been recently forbidden by Act of Parliament in order to stop the manufacture of opium *(afyûn)*. The growing of hemp (Cannabis indica), owing to its use as an intoxicant (*ḥashîsh*, p. xxvii), is also prohibited.

e. Textiles. 1. Cotton (*quṭn*; see below). — 2. Flax *(kittân)*. — 3. Indian hemp, Hibiscus cannabinus *(tîl)*. — 4. Sisal-hemp, Agave rigida *(ṣabbâr)*. — Cotton, which seems to have been known to the ancients, was reintroduced from India in 1821, but has been extensively cultivated since 1863 only. It is now the principal crop of Egypt, occupying in normal years nearly one-third of the arable land (= 1,573,815 acres in 1927) and yielding an average harvest of over 7,500,000 qanṭâr (742,875,000 lb.). In 1927 7,383,201 qanṭâr (about 731,300,000 lb.), with a value of £E 38,999,192 were exported, besides cotton seed, cotton-seed cakes and oil to the value of £E 4,247,000. During 1928 the cotton exports reached £E 45,137,823. The advantage of Egyptian cotton lies not in the quantity but in the quality of the produce; it is especially suited to the mercerizing process, which gives the cotton a silky gloss. A Cotton Research Board, attached to the Ministry of Agriculture (p. 56), was founded at Gîza (p. 87) in 1919. Cotton-growing in the Sûdân, see pp. 442, 462.

f. Dyes. 1. Indigofera argentea, a peculiar kind of indigo *(nîla)*. — 2. Lawsonia inermis *(ḥinna)*, used for dyeing the nails, the palms of the hands, and the soles of the feet yellowish red (a very ancient custom); properly a tree, but, like the tea-plant, cultivated in fields in the form of a dwarfed bush. — 3. Safflower, bastard saffron, or bulrush millet, Carthamus tinctorius (*qurṭum*, seeds *'uṣfur*). Real saffron (Crocus sativus; *za'farân*) comes from Europe. -- 4. Dyer's weed, Reseda luteola *(bliya)*, used as a yellow dye.

g. Oil Plants. 1. Castor-oil plant (Ricinus communis; *kharwa'*). — 2. Sesame *(simsim)*. — 3. Rape (Brassica napus; *salgam*). — 4. Mustard (Brassica lanceolata or nigra; *khardal*, *kabar*). — 5. Arachis hypogæa, ground-nut, pea-nut, or monkey-nut (*fûl sinnâri*, *fûl sûdâni*). — 6. Saff-

lower (comp. p. lxxvi under f). — 7. Poppy (comp. p. lxxvi under d). — 8. Garden cress, Lepidium sativum *(rashâd)*.

h. Spices. 1. Capsicum annuum, 'chillies', the Italian peperone *(filfil aḥmar, filfil rûmi)*. — 2. Capsicum frutescens, Cayenne pepper *(shaṭṭa)*. — 3. Aniseed (Pimpinella Anisum; *yansûn*). — 4. Coriander *(kuzbara)*. — 5. Cummin *(kammûn, kammûn abyaḍ)*. — 6. Black cummin or fennel-flowers, Nigella sativa *(kammûn aswad)*. — 7. Dill *(shabat)*. — 8. White mustard, Sinapis alba *(khardal)*. — 9. Fennel (Fœniculum capillaceum; *shamar*).

i. The Sugar Cane *(qaṣab)* is largely cultivated in the N. part of Upper Egypt, where it was first grown by Ismâ'îl (p. cxxvii) on his estates in 1867. An inferior variety, which is now only eaten raw, was introduced from India in the time of the Caliphs.

j. Vegetables. 1. Bâmiyas, Hibiscus esculentus (*bâmiya*; comp. p. lv). — 2. Pumpkins *(qar', sing. qar'a)*. — 3. Cucumbers *(khiyâr)*. — 4. Egyptian cucumbers (frequently trumpet-shaped and ribbed; different varieties called *'abdallâwi, 'aggûr, faqqûs*, etc.). — 5. Melons *(qâwûn*; the best kind is the sugar or musk melon, *shammâm)*. — 6. Water-melons (Citrullus vulgaris; *baṭṭîkh*). — 7. Aubergines or the egg-plant, Solanum melongena, Solanum esculentum *(bâdingân)*. — 8. Tomatoes *(ṭamâṭim)*. — 9. Jew's mallow, a kind of jute, Corchorus olitorius *(mulûkhiya)*. — 10. Mallows *(khûbbeiza)*. — 11. Cabbage *(kurumb)*. — 12. Celery *(karafs)*. — 13. Lettuces *(khass)*. — 14. Sorrel *(ḥummeiḍ)*. — 15. Spinach *(isbânikh)*. — 16. Parsley *(baqdûnis)*. — 17. Purslane (Portulaca oleracea; *rigla*). — 18. Garden rocket (Eruca sativa; *gargîr*). — A variety of other vegetables are cultivated in small quantities in gardens, exclusively for the use of European residents, e.g. the artichoke *(kharshûf)*, cauliflower *(qarnabîṭ)*, asparagus *(halyûn; kishk almâs)*, etc.

Root Vegetables. 1. Onions *(baṣal)*, one of the chief exports of Egypt (in 1926, 135,243 metric tons with a value of £E 710,289; in 1927, to the value of £E 863,000). — 2. Garlic *(tûm)*. — 3. Leeks (Allium porrum; *kurrât*). — 4. Batatas, sweet potatoes (Ipomœa batatas; *baṭâṭa ḥilu*). — 5. Potatoes *(baṭâṭa)*. — 6. Colocasia *(qulqâs)*. — 7. Jerusalem artichokes *(truff)*. — 8. Radishes, a peculiar kind, with a white skin and fleshy, edible leaves *(figl)*. — 9. Carrots *(gazar baladi*, a peculiar kind, with blood-red juice; *gazar frangi*, European carrots). — 10. Turnips (Brasscia rapa; *lift*). — 11. Beetroot (Beta rapa; *bangar*).

5. Trees. The extensive planting of trees since the middle of the 19th cent. has introduced a new feature into the Egyptian landscape. In ancient times most of the timber required for shipbuilding and other purposes seems to have been imported from abroad. Muḥammed 'Ali (p. cxxv), a great patron of horticulture, at one time offered prizes for the planting of trees, but his efforts were unattended with success, as he lacked expert advice. Ibrahîm followed the example of his predecessor, but 'Abbâs I. and Sâ'îd were sworn enemies to trees of every kind, and they were content that their palaces should be exposed to the full glare of the sun. A new epoch, however, began in 1869, when the Khedive Ismâ'îl (p. cxxvii) summoned to Egypt M. Barillet, one of the most skilful landscape-gardeners of the day (comp. p. 53). The finest of the shade-trees, both on account of its umbrageousness and the excellence of its wood, and one which thrives admirably, is the lebbakh (Albizzia lebbek). Within forty years the lebbakh attains a height of 80 ft., while the branches project to a long distance over the roads, covering them with a dense leafy canopy. Of late years, however, especially in the Cairo district, most of the lebbakhs have been destroyed by insects; they have been replaced by other species, chiefly

the beautiful poinciana ('Flamboyer des Indes', 'Barbados pride') and the violet-flowered bauhinia (known from the shape of its leaves as 'Khuff el-Gamal' or 'camel hoof'). Among other kinds of trees the most important are the rapidly growing jacaranda (rosewood; with blue flowers), the casuarina and eucalyptus, tropical fig-trees, and several rare varieties of palms.

The commonest trees of an earlier period which the traveller will encounter in every town in Egypt are the following: — The Nile acacia (Acacia nilotica or arabica; *sanṭ*, *ṣunṭ*), the thorn-tree of antiquity, the pods *(qaraḍ)* of which, resembling the beads of a rosary, yield an excellent material for tanning purposes. Next to the date-palm, this is the tree most frequently seen by the wayside and in the villages. Then, the Acacia farnesiana *(futna)*, with blossoms of delicious perfume; sycamore (Ficus sycomorus, *gimmeiz;* comp. pp. lii, cxlvi), anciently considered sacred; Zizyphus spina Christi, thorn jujube or Christ's thorn *(nabq)*; tamarisk *(atl);* parkinsonia *(seisabân);* mulberry *(tût);* and carob or St. John's bread (Ceratonia siliqua; *kharrûb*).

Among fruit-trees the most important is the date-palm (Phœnix dactylifera, *nakhla;* dates, *balaḥ;* ribs of the leaf, *garîd;* points of the leaf, *sa'af;* terminal bud, *gummâr;* bast, *lîf*). The date-palm blossoms in March and April, and the fruit ripens in August and September. Fresh dates are rough in appearance, blood-red or pale yellow in colour, and harsh and astringent in taste. Like the medlar they become more palatable (and digestible for Europeans) after fermentation has set in. There are at least twenty-seven kinds of dates commonly offered for sale. The largest attain a length of three inches, and are called *ibrîmi*, or *sukkôti*, coming from N. Nubia. The most delicately flavoured are the soft, dark-brown, late-season dates from Alexandria, known as *amhât* and *bint 'eish,* which are eaten fresh. Few dates are exported, as they realize a high price in the country itself. — The dûm palm (Hyphæne thebaica) occurs principally in Upper Egypt and Nubia (comp. p. 239). It is a broad-leafed palm of medium height, and its timber and bast are of considerable value. Buttons and other objects are made out of the hard kernels of the fruits, which are largely exported, while the soft and fibrous rind is edible and tastes like ginger-bread.

The vine thrives admirably in Egypt, especially in the Faiyûm, and grapes *('inab)* abound from July to September. Wine was extensively made from them in ancient times (e.g. in the Mareotis, p. 29, and the Faiyûm, p. 202), and this might still easily be done, were it not that Egypt is already amply supplied with cheap and excellent wines from every part of the Mediterranean. The vine blossoms in March and April, like the palm, and the grapes ripen in June and July. Oranges *(burtuqân)* are abundant and cheap (the harvest beginning in September), and so also are mandarins (Citrus nobilis; *Yûsuf afandi*, 'Lord Joseph') and lemons (*lamûn* or *lîmûn;*

a small and juicy variety of the Citrus limonum); citrons are of less frequent occurrence. Among other fruit-trees we may mention also the pomegranate (Punica granatum; *rummân*) and the apricot *(mishmish)*, which yield a handsome return. The common European fruits, e.g. peaches *(khôkh)*, likewise abound, but their flavour is generally very inferior. Figs *(tîn)* are very common in summer. The mango-tree (Mangifera indica; *manga*) and the American guava (Psidium guayava; *gawâfa*), the latter introduced since the beginning of the century, are frequently grown for the sake of their fruit.

The principal decorative plants are roses (*ward;* of which the musk-rose, Rosa damascena moschata, and the evergreen rose, Rosa sempervirens, used to be specially cultivated for the manufacture of attar of roses), oleanders *(difla)* of astonishing height, carnations, and geraniums, all of which have been grown in Egypt from a very early period. A bushy shrub, which in its half-leafless condition attracts the attention of every traveller in winter, is the poinsettia (Euphorbia pulcherrima; *bint el-qunṣul*, 'the consul's daughter'). The insignificant blossom is surrounded by leaves of the most brilliant red, presenting a very picturesque and striking appearance. — Natural forests, or even solitary wild trees, are never met with in the valley of the Nile or in the valleys of the northern deserts.

The papyrus plant (Cyperus papyrus), which had been grown in Egypt since the earliest times, was almost extinct when its cultivation was recently revived in the Cairo district. Formerly common in the lower Nile district, it became the emblem of Lower Egypt and found its way into art, especially (like the lotus) as a basic form of the Egyptian columns (comp. pp. clxvi, clxvii). The ancients manufactured the pith of its stout stems into a material for writing upon. — The lotus or water-lily is represented in Egypt by two species, the Nymphæa lotus, with perfumed white flowers that open at night, and the Nymphæa cærulea, blue and flowering by day.

F. The Climate of Egypt.

By *Colonel Sir Henry Lyons*, F.R.S.

The blue cloudless sky, the powerful sunlight, and the dry warm air are among the first facts that strike the traveller on his arrival in Egypt; and his surprise increases when he observes that the conditions remain uniform day after day, and are, in short, so generally the rule that 'the weather' ceases to be a topic of conversation. If from the top of the hills or cliffs bordering the Nile valley to the S. of Cairo he looks out on the boundless deserts on either side, the visitor will realize at once that Egypt is practically a part of the Sahara, a verdant strip of fertile soil, 8-12 M. wide, dependent for its existence upon the Nile; and that the refreshing purity of the atmosphere is essentially due to the proximity of the desert.

During the summer months (May-Sept.; comp. p. lxxv) there prevails throughout the whole of Egypt dry and hot weather, temp-

ered by steady N. winds, but in the other half of the year, and especially in December, January, and February, the storms of the Mediterranean exercise so much effect on the Delta that comparatively cold weather, with cloudy days, is sometimes experienced as far as Cairo and even up to Beni Suef (p. 218). The temperature is sometimes high even in winter, but the dryness of the air prevents it from being trying, while as soon as the sun gets low the temperature falls so rapidly as to necessitate precautions against a chill (comp. p. xxiv).

The mean maximum and minimum temperatures at some of the more important points are given in the following table.

	January		April		July		October	
	Max. °F.	Min. °F.	Max. °F.	Min. °F.	Max. °F.	Min. °F.	Max. °F.	Min. °F.
Alexandria. . . .	65.1	50.4	74.8	58.1	89.8	72.3	82.4	68.0
Cairo (ʿAbbâsîya)	65.1	44.8	82.9	56.3	95.7	69.8	84.7	62.8
Asyûṭ	68.2	42.4	89.1	58.1	98.8	72.7	86.5	64.4
Aswân	74.7	49.2	94.4	64.8	107.2	78.1	98.6	69.4
Wâdi Ḥalfa . . .	75.4	46.2	97.3	62.6	105.4	73.8	97.3	66.7

In spite of the essential dryness of the climate, the rapid fall of temperature at night causes morning fog to be common in the Nile valley in winter. It is, however, rapidly dissipated when the sun rises. The following table shows the percentage of relative humidity (comp. p. xxiii).

	January	February	March	April	May
Alexandria . . .	70	70	70	71	72
Cairo (ʿAbbâsîya)	75	70	65	58	52
Asyûṭ	70	64	55	44	38
Aswân	46	42	36	31	33
Wâdi Ḥalfa . . .	49	39	31	25	23

Rain is rare in Upper Egypt, a slight shower in winter being the most that is usually recorded. Heavier rain-bursts take place not infrequently in the desert, and on rare occasions extend to the Nile valley.

At Cairo rain usually falls on 4-6 days in the year, the average amount being about one inch. In some years, however, as much as two inches are recorded, while in others hardly any rain falls. At Alexandria and on the coast the regular winter rains of the Mediterranean occur, and the average annual rainfall is 8 inches, most of which falls from November to February. The rainfall at Asyûṭ, Aswân, and Wâdi Ḥalfa is practically nil.

From Asyûṭ southwards the prevalent winds blow from the N. throughout the year, being slightly to the E. of N. in the spring months and more to the W. in the late summer. In winter and spring

dry S. winds occur occasionally. In the N. portion of the country the winds are more variable, for although N. winds prevail, S. and S.W. winds may continue for several days in the winter and are a great hindrance to the sailing craft on the Nile at this season. These S. winds are due to the Mediterranean winter storms, which sweep by from W. to E., and if they follow a track between Crete and Egypt produce S. winds blowing from the Egyptian deserts towards the storm centre. The winds blowing from the open desert are cold and by their dryness seem to be even colder than they really are, so that visitors to Cairo in the winter months may experience the sensation of a somewhat greater degree of cold than would be expected from the temperatures quoted above.

Similar conditions in the Mediterranean are also primarily the cause of the *Khamsîn* or hot S. wind, which occasionally blows for two or three days at a time in March, April, and May. This wind comes from the now heated deserts and often attains considerable strength, carrying with it sand and dust until a thick yellow fog may prevail, sufficiently dense to hide the sun. The shade temperature under these conditions frequently exceeds 100° Fahr.

On the desert plateau the range of temperature is at all times of the year considerably greater than in the valley, where the temperature sinks to freezing point only for very brief periods. In the desert, however, the thermometer often stands at freezing point and may even fall several degrees below it.

The opinion frequently expressed of recent years that the climate of Egypt has deteriorated, i.e. become more rainy, owing to the numerous irrigation works, is devoid of foundation.

III. El-Islâm.

By *Professor C. H. Becker.*

The term *Islâm* is used to connote the peculiar civilization of the Nearer East, which owes its characteristic features to the spread of the Arabs and to the religion of Mohammed. However strange and novel it may appear to us at first sight, it is nevertheless based upon the same general principles as the civilization of mediæval Europe, from which it differs mainly in being represented by other peoples and other races, to whom the brilliant intellectual development of Europe has been denied.

The rise of Islâm has become historically intelligible only within recent years. Formerly it was tacitly assumed on all hands that the Arabs had imposed upon the East not only a new language, but also a new, specifically Arab, civilization. This view agreed with Christian conceptions, which recognized in Islâm only a new religion and founded its opposition to Arab dominion on religious and ecclesiastical motives only. In Christian eyes Mohammed was identified with Antichrist; he instigated his barbarian hordes to hurl themselves upon the Christian countries of the East in order to convert them to Islâm by the sword; the course of development since antiquity was abruptly broken off; and the Islamic Arab civilization superseded its early-Christian predecessor. When, with such preconceptions as these, the Arabian historical sources were consulted, they seemed at first to yield confirmation. The Arab tradition was as ecclesiastically coloured as the European; there, too, the starting-point was Mohammed and the Arab migrations; Mohammed and the early Caliphs were supposed to have reorganized everything and to have created, in all essentials, the new Islamic civilization. As a matter of fact, the erroneousness of all these current conceptions cannot be too emphatically insisted on.

In the first place it must be clearly understood that the triumphant campaigns of the Mohammedans were nothing else than an *Arab Migration*, the latest and, for us, the most obvious of the great Semitic migrations, absolutely analogous with the great migrations of the Germanic peoples in Europe. The main difference between the Arab and the Germanic migrations is this, that the Arabs, owing to their religious organization, were directed by a central authority, so that the establishment of a homogeneous Islamic empire became a possibility. It was not only religious zeal, it was not only the fiery words of an inspired prophet that urged the Arabs on their warlike mission to the outer world; simple necessity, the long continued economic decline of Arabia, in a word sheer hunger, drove them into the rich lands of the settled countries. The movement had begun centuries before Mohammed. The tribes of Inner Arabia were already on the move, a peaceful immigration of Arabs into Mesopotamia and Syria had already begun, and the standing

hostility between Byzantium and Persia had many times led to incursions into the settled districts by the savage border-tribes of both empires. The tide had thus begun to flow long before Islâm gave the movement a unifying watchword and an organization. Universal dominion for the Arabs was the watchword; that was the interpretation put upon Islâm by the conquerors, in contrast with the initial position of their prophet. They had no thought of converting the defeated nations by force; so long as tribute was paid and Arab supremacy recognized, every religious and civil right was confirmed to the conquered. At first conversion to Islâm was possible only by connecting the convert with the Arab tribal system as a client; then, as a Moslem, he became, in theory at least, a burgess of the Islamic theocracy and no longer required to pay tribute. Thus the flood of converts to Islâm became larger than was pleasing to the Arabs; but the impelling force was not terror of the sword but the economic advantages that attended the transition of a subject into even the lowest rank among the rulers.

The key to an appreciation of Islamic civilization lies in an understanding of the relations between the thin Arab upper layer and the huge mass of their subjects. In the case of kindred peoples at least, it was easy for the Arabs to impose their language as the language of common intercourse; and for the reasons given above their religion also was bound to spread. But for the rest the Arabs, comparatively few in number and on a lower stage of culture, could hardly hope to stamp a new civilization upon the inhabitants of the ancient empire. In each new-won province, therefore, they simply took over the arrangements for governing as they found them, and with them the problems of economic and intellectual life. Even their religion, to be effective, was forced to come to an understanding with the ecclesiastical conceptions of expiring antiquity. Islâm, born of the religious spirit of W. Asia, did not of its own strength impose upon a population of a widely different nature that religious temper which is to this day characteristic of the Islamic world, permeating state and society, family and individual. On the contrary, it was by the conquered peoples that Islâm was converted to that view of existence, as we now see it, which infuses religion into everything; for these new converts, in contrast with the religiously indifferent Arabs, could neither do anything nor leave anything undone without bringing it into direct relation with God and the future life. We must therefore think of early Islamic civilization, not as something quite new, introduced from elsewhere by the Arabs, but as the self-assertion of the mixed civilization of the Near East that had developed in the first six Christian centuries. In other words, Islâm is the heir of the late-Hellenistic Christian civilization, which we must regard as the hybrid product of Greek and Asiatic feelings and philosophy.

When that point is established, Islamic civilization falls into its

natural position in the general scheme of the world's history. From the days of Alexander down to the Roman empire the East had been forced to bow to European ideas and to submit to European domination. But just as in the days of the early emperors the Hellenic spirit was suffocated in the embrace of the Orient and the classical world hungrily assimilated the cults of the East, so an ethnical renaissance of the East began in the 2nd cent. and the Semitic element steadily asserted itself beneath the Hellenistic surface. With the spread of the Arabs the Orient once more achieved an independence in the political sphere, corresponding with that which had slowly been growing in the intellectual sphere. The first result of the political union of the whole of the Near East was that the Greek intellectual impulses there, cut off from their original sources of inspiration and operating only through Semites, were submerged by orientalism. On the other hand the seeds of Asiatic civilization found fresh nourishment in the new whole formed by the permanent political connection between the Near East and Central Asia; and the Asiatic reaction against the expansion of the Greek spirit operated until far on in the Islamic period. Thus Islamic civilization finds its organic connection with and place in the general course of history. Further, we recognize another important bond; for, if Islâm simply carried Christian civilization a step farther, we are no longer surprised by the profound inner relationship between the mental outlook of mediæval Christianity and that of Islâm; both systems are based upon the common foundation of the Greek-Oriental civilization of Christian antiquity. The Arabs consistently stressed the oriental elements in this civilization; while on the other hand, on European soil, the Germanic spirit turned away from these and elaborated from its inner consciousness the typical western forms of the middle ages.

From these principles it becomes clear why Arabia could not permanently remain the seat of the caliphate. Damascus superseded Medîna. It was only in the agitated period of the Arab empire, the period of expansion, that the artificial condition of the political supremacy of the *Arabs* over subjects superior to them in culture could be maintained. In the long run the economic and intellectual influence of the subjugated races was bound to tell and the deposition of the Arab ruling class was inevitable. The levelling influence of Islâm, as it was understood by the majority of its converts, destroyed the economic basis of the Arab dominion and with it the prerogatives of the Arabs as such. The results of the Arab period of Islamic civilization were a continuance of previously existing elements of civilization, an advance to a kind of syncretism among the varied civilizations of the Near East, and the spread of the Arab tongue and the religion of Islâm.

By-and-by the people that was nationally the strongest and the most advanced in culture within the empire of the caliphs began to

assert itself. That people was the *Persians*, whose civilization even in pre-Islamic days had permeated the Near East and was the chief factor in orientalizing it. It is almost impossible to exaggerate the importance of the Persian element in Islamic civilization, which is so often erroneously spoken of as Arab. If we are to connect that civilization with any one people, it must be with the Persians; for all the notable achievements of the period of the caliphs, the sumptuous buildings, the works of literature, even the higher developments of the religion of Islâm, are utterly un-Arab and, so far as they are not inspired by Greek influences, are due to the Persian spirit. Only the domain of law, so intimately connected with the beginnings of a religion, betrays the stamp of the Prophet's native land. The decisive ascendancy of the Persians is apparent in the facts that the Arabic language never established itself on Persian soil and that under the Abbasid caliphs it was a matter of course that court and government, architecture and literature, should be modelled after Persian patterns. Moreover, when the separate provinces developed into independent kingdoms, it was the Persian rulers alone that followed local traditions, while, e.g., the Tulunid sultans of Egypt could only imitate the Persianized Baghdâd and the residence of the caliphs at Sâmarrâ (comp. pp. cxciii, cxciv). Even the civilization of the Fatimid empire was thoroughly Persian (see p. cxciv seqq.).

The transference of the imperial residence from Damascus to Baghdâd (comp. p. cxciii) heralded a new era, and the Arab military aristocracy was changed into a despotism on the ancient oriental pattern. This was the consequence of the deposition of the Arabs as a ruling caste (p. lxxxiv). The Arab aristocracy of birth was superseded by a bureaucratic aristocracy of mostly Persian officials, the free warriors became paid troops, and were finally replaced by an army of slaves.

With these slaves, who were a constantly growing factor in the Islamic world from the 9th cent. onwards, the third national element powerfully affecting Islâm enters upon the scene. The *Turks*, appearing at first in groups of slaves but afterwards as strong tribes from Central Asia, introduced new traditions and forms into the empire of the caliphs. This third phase in the development of Islâm begins with the appearance of the *Seljuks* (p. cxx), the most powerful of these Turkish tribes. The union of the empire had long before begun to crumble, but the Seljuks postponed its disintegration. Egypt at first stood out against them, but even Egypt in the long run was unable to repel Seljuk influence; and Turkish civilization penetrated to the Nile under Saladin, who himself stood upon the ruins of the Seljuk power. The religious reaction was accompanied by a change in ecclesiastical architecture (p. cxcvi), and the establishment of a feudal system (very different indeed from the European system) coincided with a total alteration of all titles of honour. The

traditions of Saladin's epoch were carried on in all departments by the Mamelukes (comp. p. cxxi), whose influence is most conspicuous in Egypt; while the reinforcements from Central Asia conduced at the same time to the accentuation of Asiatic elements. The Mongol invasion, which overthrew the Seljuk civilization in Asia, came to a halt before the gates of Egypt. Egypt's brilliant period ended when she lost her political independence and became subject to a foreign people from Central Asia, viz. the Osman Turks (1517; p. cxxiv).

A glance over the historical development thus briefly sketched shows why Islamic civilization cannot be named after any particular nation; from the very first it was a hybrid civilization resting upon the international basis of religion. Yet amid all the mingling of the various elements, amid all the shiftings of peoples, one unifying principle is clear: the steady growth of *Asiatic Ideas.* Antedating Islâm, the process had begun in a reaction against Greek intellectual supremacy and Roman political dominion; European fetters were shaken off; and in the course of subsequent development both the Near East and Egypt passed under the direct influence of Asiatic conceptions, first in the intellectual and finally also in the political sphere. But that accomplished, the vital ethnic force and the intellectual energy of Asia were exhausted. This is the true reason of the decline of Islâm under Osman rule. Its civilization has culminated; strength fails it for a renaissance. At the present day, just as in the Hellenistic period, the European spirit and European domination are pressing forward in the East. This western movement in the historical process will certainly be followed by an eastern reaction. In any case only the form and not the essence will be common to the East and West in the intellectual sphere so long as racial differences exist among nations.

Doctrines of El-Islâm. El-Islâm, the state religion of Egypt, professed by the bulk of the population (comp. p. lvii), counts to-day about 235 million adherents, mostly in Asia and Africa, but to be found in Europe and America also, and even in Australia. It is rapidly extending, especially in Africa.

Mohammed (Muḥammad, Mahomet), the founder of the religion, son of *ʿAbdallâh*, was born at Mecca (p. 452) about A.D. 570 and at the age of forty announced himself as a prophet. As he found no acceptance in his native Mecca, he emigrated in 622 to Medîna. This was the famous *Hegîra*, *Hejira*, or *Hijra* ('departure', not 'flight'), the date of which, on the introduction of the Mohammedan calendar (p. xcviii), was fixed as July 16th, 622. At Medîna he met with more success, and from the position of a kind of magistrate he rose to be the head of a new state. After years of fighting he captured Mecca in 630, but two years later he died at Medîna in the prime of life. Mohammed never represented himself as anything beyond a mortal

man, but in legend, which in the East has the authority of history, he is invested with the halo of the miraculous. God, it is said, created the Light of the Prophet even before the creation of the divine throne; and this Light wandered through all the generations of men until it manifested itself at the centre of the world in the best of created beings, a noble scion of the noblest family of Mecca. Angels, opening the breast of the boy, expunged the last drop of sin from his heart. A little later the Archangel Gabriel brought him the Revelations, the Korans, which were then formed into a book (p. xcii). Mohammed wrought many miracles and even raised the dead to life, as in the case of his parents, who turned their brief resurrection to account by embracing Islâm. Among his feats was the splitting of the moon and his nocturnal journey *(mi'râg)* on a miraculous steed from Jerusalem to heaven, where he treated with the Deity as to the number of prayers to be offered by the faithful.

The starting-point of Mohammed's teaching was the conception of the Last Judgment. Borrowing the idea of a future life and of future rewards and punishments from the Jews and Christians, who were found all over Arabia, Mohammed exhorted his fellow-countrymen, who lived merely from day to day, to adopt a serious conception of life. Paradise and hell were drawn in striking colours (p. xciii). The idea of the Judgment involves the idea of a just and single deity; from the beginning Mohammed had to preach the strictest monotheism in opposition to the fetishism of the Arabs. This he named *Islâm*, resignation to the will of God. He believed at first that Christianity and Judaism were identical, and he desired to bring the same gospel to the Arabs. When he learned the real historical relation of these faiths, he postulated an ascending series of revelations, culminating in Islâm (p. xcii). At Medîna he endeavoured to accommodate himself to the doctrines of the Jewish community there, but finding this impossible he shook himself free of both Christian and Jewish fetters, although he still adhered to Abraham (Ibrâhîm), who was venerated by Jews and Christians alike and was, moreover, according to the Bible the ancestor, through Ishmael (Ismâ'îl), of the Arabs. The ancient temple of stone at Mecca, the *Kaaba* (p. c), became to him an analogue of the temple of Jerusalem. The entire native creed of the Meccans was re-interpreted on an Abrahamistic basis, so that its incorporation with Islâm was rendered possible. On the other hand the reception of Islâm by the Meccans was facilitated. In addition to this assertion of religious independence the Hegira had another consequence of moment for the future of Islâm: the position of the Prophet as also the head of a state entailed a mingling of political and religious life, and the present markedly political character of Islâm is a result of this short-lived theocracy. Mohammed further had definite conceptions of a revealed religion, for which he deemed necessary a sacred book, a prophet, and a fixed ritual with recitations and liturgies. But at the date of his death neither Islamic law nor

dogma, not even the number of daily prayers (p. lxxxix), was fixed. The comprehensive system now known as the religion of Islâm grew up in the course of time.

The foundation is the *Koran* (p. xcii), the very word of God, which was collected and written down as early as A.D. 650. This contains few rescripts or laws. Next to it as a rule of conduct ranks the *Sunna*, the practice of the Prophet and his earliest associates. To follow this example in all its details became, under the influence of the Jewish spirit, the aim of every believer. The Sunna was glossed by the sayings of the Prophet and by reports as to his practice and as to the things that he suffered to happen without comment. These formed the traditions or *Ḥadîth*. Originally the traditions were substantially genuine, but in the course of the general effort to live as the Prophet did they finally became the literary vehicles of religious controversy. To sift them and to harmonize their contradictory sayings has given rise to a science of itself. In this process the consensus of the learned *(Igmâʿ)* was the deciding authority, which became authoritative over the Sunna, and indeed over the Koran itself, for only the Igmâʿ was able rightly to interpret the Koran. The early scholars of Islâm too received the Igmâʿ as the most important principle of development next to the Sunna and the Koran.

Founded on the Koran, the Sunna, and the Igmâʿ, **Mohammedan Law** has been developed into a canonical system, embracing every department of life, in the manner of the Jewish and Christian systems. When the Arabs became masters of the ancient civilized countries of the Near East, there arose a crop of legal problems, which had to be solved according to the Sunna, or at least in their spirit. The impulse to independent legal activity in the newly conquered lands was given (as in *ʿIrâq* by *Abu Ḥanîfa*, d. 767) by the pre-Justinian Roman law that had been accepted by the Christian church. Against this intellectual independence, which allowed room for differences of opinion, arose the orthodox party at Medîna (*Mâlik ibn Anas*, d. 795), who admitted only the letter of the ancient tradition. Afterwards a compromise was attained by the admission of analogous decisions *(Qiyâs)*, as a legal-theological principle (*Esh-Shâfiʿi*, d. 820; comp. p. 124). A number of schools of jurisprudence *(madhhab*, pl. *madhâhib)* arose, named after their founders; but of these only four survived: the *Malikites*, *Hanafites*, *Shafiites*, and *Hanbalites* (pronounced ḥambalites). In Egypt the Shafiites and Malikites are most influential to-day, though the Moslem law courts (p. xxii) base their decisions on the Hanafite madhhab, as a result of the former connection with Turkey, which is Hanafite. West Africa is Malikite. The Hanbalites, restricted to Arabia, are of less importance. Every believer must belong to one or other of these rites or schools (which are not sects). They recognize each other as orthodox and differ only in their distribution of actions among the five recognized classes of 'commanded', 'recommended', 'indifferent', 'blameworthy', and

'forbidden'. The science of law is known as *Fiqh* (recognition). It forms practically the entire sphere of Islamic mental activity. Its results, varying slightly according to the rites and adapting themselves to the interpretation of each, constitute the *Sharî'a*, or *Shar'*, the holy law. It contains the collection of those precepts from the Koran and the Sunna that have been approved by the Igmâ' and are therefore authoritative. Certain later text-books also have attained canonical authority. The theologian who is officially entrusted with the exposition of the law is called *Muftî*, his decision *Fetwâ*. The chief mufti bears the title *Sheikh u'l-Islâm*, which acquired its greatest prestige as it became more and more exclusively attached to the Mufti of Constantinople. His office attained to considerable religious and political importance under the Turkish Empire but gradually lost its power during the 19th cent. and was finally abolished by the Turkish Government in Nov. 1922. The highest Islamic authorities in Egypt are the Rector of the Azhar University (*Sheikh el-Gâmi' el-Azhar*, p. 61) and the Grand Mufti of Egypt (*Muftî ed-Diyâr el-Maṣrîya*). These experts are necessary, for only the learned can grasp the complicated system. These learned men (*'Ulamâ*, sing. *'Âlim*) and jurists (*Fúqahâ*, sing. *Faqîh*) resemble Jewish scribes rather than Christian priests. A sinner may reckon upon divine pardon even if he transgress the precepts of the Sharî'a daily or hourly, but if he doubt their theoretical authority he is an infidel. This is why Mohammedans are always ready to fly to arms when the Sharî'a is threatened. In practice they trouble themselves little about its precepts.

The five pillars (i.e. chief duties) of Islâm are the profession of the true faith, the repetition of the daily prayers, the payment of the charitable tax, the fast during Ramaḍân, and the pilgrimage to Mecca (p. xc). Other matters dealt with by the Sharî'a are the laws relating to family duties, inheritance, and marriage; the management of religious endowments (*Waqf*, pl. *Auqâf*), which occupies a special ministry (p. 55) in Egypt; and the regulation of ceremonies and custom. The precepts of the law as regards these, being regarded as religious in the narrower sense, are carried out in practice as far as possible. In other matters, regarded as more theoretical (such as constitutional law, criminal law, the law of real property, and the law of obligations), local customary law (*'Ada*) has from the first outweighed the Sharî'a. The distinction between the 'Âda, commands of custom, and the Sharî'a, commands of religion, is recognized in every sphere of life. The extent to which the Sharî'a prevails in any country is a measure of the real strength of Islâm in that country. At times of fanatical excitement its prescriptions are fulfilled with unusual zeal. Among uneducated people the 'Âda and the Sharî'a are often identified.

The hours of PRAYER (*ṣalât*) are proclaimed by the muezzins (*mu'addin*) from the minarets of the mosques five times a day: (1) *Maghrib*, a little after sunset; (2) *'Isha*, nightfall, about $1^1/_2$ hour after sunset; (3) *Subḥ*, daybreak; (4) *Ḍuhr*, midday; (5) *'Aṣr*, afternoon, about 3 hours after midday.

On Fridays the midday prayer takes place three-quarters of an hour earlier than usual and is followed by a sermon. Friday, however, is not regarded as a day of rest in the Christian sense. The sonorous call of the muezzin is as follows: *Allâhu akbar* (four times); *ashhadu anna lâ ilâha illa'llâh; ashhadu anna Muhammadan rasûlu'llâh* (twice); *ḥeiya 'ala 's-ṣalâh* (twice); (*heiya 'ala 'l-falâḥ* (twice); *Allâhu akbar* (twice); *lâ ilâha illa'llâh* ["Allah God) is greatest; I testify that there is no God but Allah, I testify that Mohammed is the Prophet of Allah; come to prayer; come to salvation; Allah is greatest; there is no God but Allah"]. — The duty of washing before prayer is enforced by the ritual. In the desert the faithful are permitted to use sand for this religious ablution. The person praying must remove his shoes or sandals and turn his face towards Mecca, as the Jews used to turn towards Jerusalem (comp. p. cxcii). He begins his orisons by holding his hands to the lobes of his ears, then a little below his girdle, the left within the right, and he interrupts his recitations from the Koran with certain prostrations in a given order. The most usual prayer is the first Sûra of the Koran (p. xcii), one of the shortest, which is used as we

employ the Lord's prayer. It is called *el-fâtḥa* ('the opening [sûra]') and is to the following effect: "In the name of Allah, the merciful and compassionate. Praise be to Allah, the Lord of the worlds, the merciful and compassionate, the Prince of the day of judgment; Thee we serve, and to Thee we pray for help; lead us in the right way, the way of those to whom thou hast shown mercy, upon whom no wrath resteth, and who go not astray." After praying the Moslem looks over his right, then over his left shoulder, in greeting to the two recording angels who write down his good and evil actions (comp. p. xciii).

The Charitable Tax *(zakât)* is a very high religious tax upon property, graduated according to the kind of property, and earmarked for certain purposes, chiefly charity and the 'holy war' (Jihâd, Gihâd). Now, however, it is paid only by the very pious. But in religious risings the zakât is an inexhaustible source of supply. A special kind of charitable tax, called the *zakât el-fiṭr*, or tax for breaking the fast, is almost universal.

For the Fast *(ṣôm)* of the month of *Ramaḍân*, the third of the chief duties of Islâm, comp. p. xcix.

For the Pilgrimage to Mecca *(ḥagg)* the pilgrims from the different countries assemble at particular points. Those from Egypt (14,545 in 1929)

usually proceed by sea to Jidda on the Red Sea (p. 452), from which Mecca is about 59 M. distant. On approaching Mecca the pilgrims undress, laying aside even their headgear, and put on aprons and a piece of cloth over the left shoulder. They then perform the circuit of the Kaaba (p. c), kiss the black stone at its E. corner, hear the sermon on Mt. ʿArafât near Mecca, perform stone-throwing ceremonies (popularly considered the stoning of Satan) in the valley of Muna, and conclude their pilgrimage with a great sacrificial feast (*ʿîd el-aḍhâ*). On the day when this takes place at Mecca, sheep are slaughtered and a festival called the Great Bairam (p. c) is observed throughout all Mohammedan countries. The Mahmal (p. xcviii), the Kiswa (p. xcix), and the gifts to the city of Mecca, which the Egyptian government used to send along with the Egyptian caravan, were not despatched in 1927-29 (comp. p. c).

Other Religious Precepts forbid the use of intoxicating liquors or of the flesh of swine and the eating of the flesh of any animal not slaughtered in the prescribed fashion or of blood. The position of women is clearly defined. Every Moslem is permitted to have four wives at a time, though monogamy is the rule, owing to economic conditions. A woman has full rights under the law of property, but under the law of succession and as a witness she is regarded as equivalent only to half a man. The veiling of women, usual in the higher circles and the middle classes in the towns (comp. p. 49, 50; the women of the fellahin do not veil as a rule), is a matter coming under the ʿâda not the sharîʿa (p. lxxxix). This practice, however, is no longer observed with its former rigour, owing to the influence of European ideas and the prohibition of the veil in Turkey. The ease with which Islâm permits a husband to divorce his wife by the mere threefold pronunciation of the formula "Thou art divorced", or "I divorce thee", is a grave moral danger. When a man divorces his wife, he pays her a portion, generally one-third, of the mahr or dowry (p. xcvi) which had been settled upon her at the time of the marriage, to be paid in the case of divorce or of his death. The Egyptian government proposes to reform the marriage laws by making polygamy more difficult and by strengthening the protection of the wife against arbitrary repudiation. Further details as to Islamic law may be found in the 'Handbuch des islamischen Gesetzes', by Th. W. Juynboll of Leyden (Leipzig, 1908-10), a work adapted for the layman as well as for the legal expert.

Dogma by no means plays such an important part in Islâm as in Christianity; for the simple Moslem creed is embodied in the words: "There is no God but Allah and Mohammed is the Prophet of Allah". But lively controversies over dogma have not been absent in the development of Islâm, mainly owing to the influence of Græco-Christian thought. Just as in the sphere of law, we find here a literal and a speculative interpretation; and in the sphere of dogma also orthodoxy triumphed by adopting the speculative method in a modified form. The process of amalgamation is associated with the name of *El-Ashʿarî* (d. 935). The questions most eagerly canvassed were those relating to the freedom of the will, the attributes of God, and the nature of the Koran (i.e. whether it is 'eternal' or 'created'). The orthodox solutions of these problems are as follows. There is but one God, in whom certain universal attributes inhere (knowledge, seeing, hearing, etc.), but who must not be conceived of under a human form. He is all-mighty and has therefore created also evil, which serves his purposes of salvation in a manner inconceivable by our limited human intelligence. Above all, God is the Creator, who at every moment re-creates all things. Causality is the creative operation of the divine will. In this connection man is not free, for

everything is immutably foreordained by God's will. God operates everything in man, but man is responsible, according as he assents to or dissents from the operations of God. The Koran (see below), like the Logos of the Christians, is conceived of as uncreated and coexistent with God from all eternity. The cardinal points which every Moslem is bound to hold are the beliefs in God and the angels, in written revelation and the prophets, and in the last judgment and predestination.

God and the Angels. Ninety-nine of the different attributes of God were gathered from the Koran, each of which is represented by a bead of the Moslem rosary (comp. p. 52). Great importance is attached to the fact that the creation of the world was effected by a simple effort of the divine will. (God said 'Let there be', and there was.) The story of the creation in the Koran is taken from the Bible, with variations from Rabbinical, Persian, and other sources. God first created his throne; beneath the throne was water; then the earth was formed. In order to keep the earth steady God created an angel and placed him on a huge rock, which in its turn rests on the back and horns of the bull of the world. In connection with the creation of the firmament was that of the *Jinn* (demons; sing. *jinni*), beings occupying a middle rank between men and angels, some of them believing, others unbelieving. When the jinn became arrogant an angel was ordered to banish them, and he drove them to the mountains of Qâf by which the earth is surrounded, whence they occasionally make incursions. Adam was then created, on the evening of the sixth day, and the Moslems on that account observe Friday as their Sabbath. As the angel who conquered the jinn refused to bow down before Adam, he was exiled and thenceforward called *Iblîs*, or the devil. After this Adam himself fell and became a solitary wanderer, but was afterwards reunited to Eve at Mecca (comp. p. xcviii), where the sacred stone in the Kaaba derives its black colour from Adam's tears. Adam is regarded as the first Moslem.

The *Angels* are the bearers of God's throne and execute his commands. They act as mediators between God and men. While there are legions of good angels, there are also satellites of Satan who seduce men to error.

Written Revelation and the Prophets. The earliest men were all believers, but they fell away from the true faith. A revelation became necessary. The prophets are very numerous, amounting in all, it is said, to 124,000; but they differ in rank. They are free from all gross sins and are endowed by God with power to work miracles, which power forms their credentials; nevertheless they are generally derided and disbelieved. The greater prophets are *Adam*, *Noah* (Nûḥ), *Abraham* (Ibrâhîm; comp. p. lxxxvii), *Moses* (Mûsa), *Jesus* (ʿIsa), and *Mohammed* (Muḥammad), Jesus being the next greatest after Mohammed. Moses and Christ prophesied the advent of Mohammed, who is the promised Paraclete, the Comforter (John xiv. 16, 26, and xv. 26), the last and greatest of the prophets.

The Koran (*Qurân*), the name of which signifies 'rehearsal' or 'reading', is divided into 114 chapters or parts called *Sûras*. It was committed piecemeal to the Prophet by the angel Gabriel. The first revelation vouchsafed to the Prophet took place in the 'blessed night' in the year 609. With many interruptions the 'sending down' of the Koran extended over twenty-three years, until the whole book was in the prophet's possession. The earlier or Meccan sûras, placed at the end of the book on account of their brevity, are characterized by great freshness and vigour of style. In the longer sûras of a later period the style is more studied and the narrative often tedious. The Koran is nevertheless regarded as the masterpiece of Arabic literature (p. xxix). The English translations of the Koran are those of *George Sale* (1734), the best version in any language, obtainable in a cheap form (latest edition, London 1927) or with a preliminary discourse and copious notes, edited by E. M. Wherry (1882-86, 4 vols.); *John Medows Rodwell* (arranged chronologically: London, 1861; 2nd edit., 1876; obtainable also in Everyman's Library, 1909); *Edward Henry Palmer*

(London, 1880; published in the World's Classics, 1928); *Mîrzâ Abu 'l-Faḍl* (Arabic text and English translation, arranged chronologically, with abstract; Allahabad, 1911, etc.; in progress), and *Maulvi Muḥammed ʿAli* (Arabic text with English translation and commentary; Islamic Review, Woking 1917). — See also *Sir William Muir*, 'The Côran, its Composition and Teaching' (1878; new ed. 1896); *W. St. Clair Tisdall*, The Original Sources of the Qur'an' (London, 1905); and *H. U. W. Stanton*, 'The Teaching of the Qúr'an' (London, 1919).

Last Judgment. The doctrine of the resurrection has been highly elaborated in the Koran and subsequent tradition; but its main features have doubtless been borrowed from the Christians, as has also the appearance of Antichrist, and the part to be played by Christ at the Last Day. On that day Christ will establish Islâm as the religion of the world. Before him will reappear the *Mahdi*, the 'well-directed one', the twelfth Imâm (comp. p. xcv), who will establish the Islamic ideal empire and will render Islamic law supreme. The Last Judgment will begin on the appearance of Christ. The first trumpet-blast of the angel *Asrâfîl* will kill every living being; a second will awaken the dead. Then follows the Judgment; the righteous cross to Paradise by a bridge of a hair's breadth, while the wicked fall from the bridge into the abyss of hell. At the Judgment every man is judged according to the books of the recording angels (p. cx). The book is placed in the right hand of the good, but is bound in the left hand of the wicked behind their backs. The scales in which good and evil deeds are weighed play an important part in deciding the soul's fate, and the doctrine of the efficacy of works is carried so far that it is believed works of supererogation may be placed to the credit of other believers. Hell, as well as heaven, has different grades; and Islâm assumes the existence also of a purgatory, from which release is possible. Paradise is depicted by Mohammed as a place of material delights.

Mysticism, the third great branch of religious thought under Islâm, aims at an immediate union with the divine on the basis of emotion, in contradistinction to the hair-splitting of the dogmatists and to the doctrine of the efficacy of works taught by the moralists. The mystics seek their end in two ways. They bridge over the vast gulf between God and humanity by the conception of mediators with God, viz. *Saints*, who with reference to an expression in the Koran are known as 'those who stand near God' (*Auliyâ*, sing. *Walî*); and on the other hand, by emotional exercises in company, they aim at producing an ecstatic exaltation of mind, i.e. the immediate blending of their own individuality with that of the Deity. The latter is the explanation of the practices of the dervishes (p. xcv). In the worship of saints, which centres principally at tombs and ancient holy sites, we trace the same popular polytheistic tendencies as appear in Christianity, connected with the traditions of the heroic age. An attempt has been made to deduce the fundamental forms of early Semitic religious conceptions from the practices current to-day in Islamic saint-worship. The recognition of saints became possible in Islâm when Mohammed himself was exalted above the infirmities of humanity. The tomb of Mohammed at Medîna and that of his grandson Ḥusein at Kerbelâ (comp. p. 58) became particularly famous, and every little town soon boasted of the tomb of its particular saint. In many villages the traveller will observe small dome-buildings with grated windows. These are saints' tombs and are called *Sheikhs*. 'Sheikh' also means a chief or old man.

Shreds of cloth are seen suspended from the gratings of these tombs, or on certain trees which are considered sacred, having been placed there by devout persons or by those who have made vows. About the end of the 18th cent. a reaction against the abuses of Islâm sprang up in Central Arabia. The *Wahhabis* or *Wahabis*, named after their founder *Muḥammed (Ibn) ʿAbd el-Wahhâb* (1703-91) but calling themselves *Ikhwân*, i.e. brothers, endeavoured to restore the religion to its original purity; they destroyed all tombs of saints, including Ḥusein's (1801) and even Mohammed's (1804), as objects of superstitious reverence, and sought to restore the primitive simplicity of the prophet's code of morals. As a political power they were suppressed for the time being, by Muḥammed ʿAli (p. cxxvi). *ʿAbd el-Azîz Ibn Saʿûd*, however, ruler of the Central Arabian plateau (Nejd), succeeded, even before the Great War, in reviving the importance of the Wahhabite state of his forebears, and in the last ten years he has brought nearly the whole of Arabia within the Wahhabite sphere of influence. He captured Mecca (Oct. 1924) and Medîna after a successful war with Ḥusein Ibn ʿAli, the former Grand Sherîf (comp. p. 49) of Mecca, who assumed the title of 'King of the Ḥijâz' in Nov. 1916 and claimed recognition (after March 1924) as 'Caliph' (comp. p. cxxiv). After Ḥusein's abdication Ibn Saʿûd put an end to his son ʿAli's reign (Oct. 1924 to Dec. 1925) by the capture of Jidda (p. 452). In Jan. 1926 Ibn Saʿûd was proclaimed in Mecca as 'King of the Ḥijâz and Sultan of Nejd'.

Another development quite foreign to the original spirit of Islâm is that of the Religious Orders (*Ṭuruq*, sing. *Ṭarîqa)*, or orders of Dervishes, who owed their rise to the influence of other religions. Starting with the Christian doctrine of asceticism (hence *Darwîsh*, *Faqîr*, poor man, *Ṣûfi*, man in a woollen shirt), the mystics borrowed Neo-Platonic ideas (Dionysos Areopagita, the alleged author of mystical writings dating from about A.D. 500) and subsequently also Buddhist ideas. Even the Buddhist nirvana was adopted under the form of *fanâ*, the extinction of individuality. As a consequence pantheistic and other heresies found their way into Islâm. The orthodox party long opposed the recognition of the mystics, and mysticism did not effect its footing until the time of the philosopher *El-Ghazâli* (d. 1111). To-day all those orders that accept the formulæ of the faith and the received doctrine of religious duties are recognized as orthodox. Each order has its own fixed system, with an ascending series of degrees. A man may reach the lower degrees in several different orders, the higher degrees in one only. The *zikrs*, or religious exercises, are directed towards producing a state of mental excitement by means of invocations or dancing (hence howling or dancing dervishes; comp. p. 76); the souls of those who reach a condition of ecstasy are considered to be absorbed in the Deity. These orders represent in the East the religious and other associations of Europe. They are more important economically

than politically, though great political movements, even in modern times, have been brought about by organizations resembling these orders, e.g. the insurrection of the Mahdi in the Sûdân (p. cxxix). The original orders were few, but numerous subdivisions have in course of time established themselves on an independent footing. In Egypt all the orders are under the control of the *Sheikh el-Bekri*, who is the political representative of their interests and presides at public functions.

The following are the principal orders of dervishes (*ṭarîqat ed-darâwîsh*) in Egypt. (1) The *Rifâ'îya* (sing. *rifâ'i*), an order founded by Saiyid Aḥmad er-Rifâ'i el-Kebîr (d. 1180), are recognizable by their black flags and black or dark blue turbans. The best-known branches of this order are the *Ûlâd 'Ilwân*, or *'Ilwânîya Dervishes*, and the *Sa'dîya Dervishes*. The former are noted for their extraordinary performances at festivals, such as thrusting iron nails into their eyes and arms, breaking large stones against their chests, as they lie on their backs on the ground, and swallowing burning charcoal and fragments of glass. The Sa'dîya, who usually carry green flags, are snake-charmers (p. xxviii). Belonging to this group but actually independent and peculiar to Egypt, are (2) the *Aḥmadîya* (sing. *Aḥmadi*), the order of the Egyptian national saint Saiyid Aḥmad el-Badawi (d. 1276), who is buried at Ṭanṭa (p. 36). They are recognized by their red banners and turbans. This order is divided into many branches, but of these the two most important are the much-respected *Baiyûmîya* or *Shinnâwîya*, who play an important part in the ceremonies at Ṭanṭa (p. 36), and the *Ûlâd Nûḥ*, who are generally young men, wearing high pointed caps and carrying wooden swords and a kind of whip. Connected with this group by a mystic genealogy are (3) the *Mîrghanîya* or *Khatmîya*, an order conspicuous for the energy of its zikrs on dervish festivals (e.g. the Mûlid of the Prophet, p. xcviii). The Nubians (p. lxii) have joined this order in large numbers, and it is widespread in the Sûdân. The *Senussi (Sanûsi)*, too, that come to Cairo usually join it. Their order, the *Sanûsîya*, founded at Mecca in 1837 by the Algerian Sîdi Muhammed Ibn 'Ali es-Sanûsi (d. 1859), has spread throughout the E. Sahara as far as the Sûdân. To the same group belong (4) the *Burhâmîya*, the order of Ibrâhîm ed-Disûqi (p. 34), an exceedingly popular saint in Egypt. Their colour is green. (5) The *Qâdirîya* (sing. *Qâdiri*), one of the most widely distributed orders, founded by Saiyid 'Abd el-Qâdir el-Gîlâni (d. 1166), are quite independent. Their banners and turbans are white (monastery, see p. 76). In addition to these there are thirty or forty less important orders and groups of orders. The religious functions connected with the royal court are discharged by the *Mawlawîya*, the Turkish *Mewlewi* order (p. 76), founded at Konia by Jelâl ed-Din Rûmi (surnamed Mewlânâ, 'our master'; 1207-73), the greatest mystic poet of the Persians. Another Turkish order is that of the *Baktâshîya* or *Bektashi* dervishes (p. 126), which has existed since the 16th cent. at least and is named after its alleged founder Ḥadji Bektash.

Sects are much less important in Islâm than in other religions. They separate on a point of constitutional law, the question being which of the early caliphs (*khalîfa*, 'deputy') were the legitimate successors of Mohammed. The *Orthodox Party*, which alone prevails in Egypt, recognizes all the 'rightly directed' caliphs — Abu Bekr, 'Omar, Othmân, and 'Ali (p. cxviii). The *Shiites* (from *shî'a*, party, i.e. the party of 'Ali) regard 'Ali and his sons Ḥasan and Ḥusein (p. 58) as the only legitimate caliphs and imâms (i.e. leaders in prayer), the twelfth (or seventh) of whom is believed to be awaiting in concealment the day of restoration. The *Kharigites* (*Khawârig*, sing. *Khârigi*, i.e. seceder) recognize only Abu Bekr and 'Omar. All the

sects have their traditions, and when the Shiites are said to reject the Sunna (p. lxxxviii), the remark applies only to the orthodox Sunna. Their Sunna has developed in the same manner as that of the Orthodox, but along different lines. The same is true of all the Moslem sects. Egypt has been under a Shiite régime only in the time of the Fatimids (p. cxix), who recognized the seventh Imâm. They professed a secret doctrine which resulted in scepticism (comp. p. cxix).

Mohammedan Manners and Customs.

The rite of Circumcision is performed on boys of five, six, or more years, the ceremony being attended with great pomp. The child is previously conducted through the streets on horseback or in a carriage; in order to save expense, the procession is frequently united with some bridal party (see below), or two or more boys are driven together in a carriage. The boy generally wears a turban of red cashmere, girls' clothes, and conspicuous female ornaments, which are designed to avert the evil eye from his person. He half covers his face with an embroidered handkerchief; and the barber who performs the operation and a troop of musicians head the procession. The first personage in the procession is usually the barber's boy, carrying the *ḥeml*, or barber's sign, a small cupboard made of wood, in the form of a half-cylinder, with four short legs.

Marriage. Girls were formerly married in their twelfth or thirteenth, and sometimes as early as their tenth year. In 1927, however, the marriage age was raised by law to sixteen. The youth has his bride found for him by relatives or professional female matchmakers, and he has no opportunity of seeing his bride until the wedding day, unless she belongs to the lowest classes. When everything is arranged, the bridegroom has to pay a dowry or bridal-portion *(mahr)* amounting to about 25*l.*, less being paid when the bride is a widow. Generally about two-thirds of the sum, the amount of which forms a subject of lively discussion, is paid down, while one-third is settled upon the wife, being payable on the death of the husband or on his divorcing her against her will (comp. p. xci). Before the wedding the bride is conducted in gala attire to the bath. This procession is called *Zaffet el-Ḥammâm*. It is headed by musicians with one or two oboes and drums; these are followed by married female friends and relatives of the bride in pairs, and after these come a number of young girls. The bride follows, under a silken canopy open in front. In Cairo, however, this canopy is now generally replaced by a carriage or motor-car. Musicians bring up the rear. The cries of joy which women of the lower classes utter on such occasions are called *zaghârîṭ* (sing. *zaghrûṭa*). The bride is conducted with the same pomp to the house of her husband.

The ceremonies observed at Funerals are not less remarkable than those that attend weddings. If the death occurs in the morn-

ing, the funeral takes place the same day; but if in the evening, it is postponed till next day. The body is washed and mourned over by the family and the professional mourning women (*naddâbât*, sing. *naddâba*); the schoolmasters (*fúqahâ*, sing. *fiqî*; p. 52) read several sûras of the Koran by its side; after this, it is wrapped in its white or green winding sheet, placed on the bier, and carried forth in procession. The foremost persons in the cortège are usually six or more poor, and generally blind, men, who walk in twos or threes, chanting the creed: "There is no God but Allah; Mohammed is the Prophet of Allah; God be gracious to him and preserve him!" These are followed by male relatives of the deceased, and sometimes by dervishes with the flags of their order, and then by a few boys, one of whom carries a copy of the Koran adorned with palm-branches. The boys usually chant in a loud and shrill voice several passages from the *Ḥashrîya*, a poem describing the last judgment. The bier, with the head of the deceased foremost, comes next, borne by three or four of his friends, who are relieved from time to time. After the bier come the female relatives, with dishevelled hair, sobbing aloud, and frequently accompanied by professional mourning women, whose business it is to extol the merits of the deceased. If he was a husband or father of a family one of the cries is: "O thou camel of my house", the camel being the emblem of the bread-winner of the household. The body is first carried into that mosque for whose patron saints the relatives entertain the greatest veneration, and prayers are offered on its behalf. It is then borne to the cemetery, where it is laid in the tomb in such a position that the face is turned towards Mecca.

The female relatives and friends of the deceased are distinguished by a strip (usually blue) of linen or cotton bound round the head, with the end hanging down behind. Men wear no mourning. The women, especially in the country, frequently put dust on their brows and breasts, a practice that is a survival from antiquity, as may be seen on comparing the representations of funerals at Thebes and elsewhere. Rich men or pious sheikhs and ʿulamâ (p. lxxxix) are buried with greater pomp, to which religious fraternities and dervishes with their flags contribute; water is distributed; and the riding horse and a buffalo are led in the procession. The buffalo is slaughtered at the tomb and its flesh distributed among the poor.

A custom peculiar to the Moslems is the separation of the sexes after death. In family vaults one side is set apart for the men, the other for the women. Between these vaults is the entrance to the tomb, covered with a large slab. The vaults are high enough to admit of the deceased sitting upright when he is examined by the angels Munkar and Nakîr (vulgarly called Nâkir and Nikîr) on the first night after his interment.

Mohammedan Calendar. Festivals.

The Mohammedan era begins with July 16th of the year 622 of our era, which corresponds with the 1st of Muḥarram (p. xl) in the year of the Hegira (p. lxxxvi), the actual date of which, however, is now generally agreed to have been the 8th of Rabîʿ el-Auwal (Sept. 20th, 622). The Moslem year is purely lunar and has no reference to the sun; it contains 354 days, or 355 in leap-years, eleven of which occur in each cycle of 30 years. There are 12 months (see p. xl), the first, third, etc., of which have 29 days each, the second, fourth, etc., 30 days. The Mohammedan day begins at sunset. The Moslem year 1348 began on the evening of June 8th, 1929.

The Gregorian calendar was introduced into Egypt in 1875, but is observed by government in the finance department only. For all other purposes the Mohammedan calendar is used, and the dates even of fixed festivals cannot easily be stated according to the European computation of time, as they occur at constantly shifting periods, according to the solar year. Calendars (e.g. the Government Almanac, p. xx) reducing the Mohammedan and Coptic reckoning of time to the European system may, however, be obtained at any bookseller's. The so-called 'Era of the Martyrs', by which the Copts reckon their chronology, begins with the day of Diocletian's (p. cxvi) accession to the throne, i.e. August 29th, A.D. 284. The Coptic year 1645 began on Sept. 11th, 1928 (comp. p. xl).

Religious Festivals. The first month of the year is Muḥarram, the first ten days of which (*ʿashar*), and particularly the 10th (*yôm el-ʿâshûrâ*, see below), are considered holy. On these days alms are distributed and amulets purchased. Mothers, even of the upper classes, carry their children on their shoulders, or cause them to be carried, through the streets, and sew into the children's caps the copper coins presented to them by passers-by. On the 10th Muḥarram, the highly revered *ʿÂshûrâ* day, on which Adam and Eve are said first to have met again after their expulsion from Paradise (comp. p. xcii), on which Noah is said to have left the ark, and on which Ḥusein, the grandson of the Prophet, fell as a martyr to his religion at the battle of Kerbelâ, the Ḥusein Mosque (p. 58) is visited about 8 p.m. by a vast concourse of noisy religious devotees. Troops of Persians in long white robes parade the streets, striking their bare backs with iron chains and cutting themselves with swords on their shaved heads until the blood streams down and stains their snowy garments. Two boys, representing the brothers Ḥasan and Ḥusein, are led through the streets on horseback, with blood-stained clothes.

At the end of Ṣafar, the second month, or at the beginning of Rabîʿ el-Auwal, the third, the ***Mecca Caravan*** (comp. p. xc) returns home. A pyramidal wooden erection, called the *Maḥmal*, hung with beautifully embroidered stuffs, and carried by a camel, accompanies the procession as a symbol of royalty. The interior of the Maḥmal is empty, and to the outside of it are attached two copies of the Koran. The procession usually enters the city by the Bâb en-Naṣr (p. 84). In 1½-2 hrs. it reaches Saladin Square (p. 73), in front of the citadel, from which twelve cannon-shots are fired as a salute. The cortège finally enters the citadel (p. 73) through the Bâb el-Wazîr.

The great festival of the ***Mûlid en-Nabi***, the birthday of the prophet, is celebrated in the first half of Rabîʿ el-Auwal. The preparations for it begin on the second day of the month, and the most important ceremonies take place on the evening of the eleventh. The city, particularly the scene of the festival, near ʿAbbâsîya (p. 85), is then illuminated. Processions of dervishes parade the streets with flags by day and with lamps by night. The ***Dôsa***, or ceremony in which the sheikh of the Saʿdîya (p. xcv) rode over the prostrate bodies of dervishes, which took place on the twelfth of this month, was suppressed in 1881 by the Khedive Taufîq, and the ceremonies are now confined to the sheikh's walking over some dervishes, his procession, and the reading of the Koran in the royal tent. At night a great zikr (p. xciv) is performed by the dervishes.

In the fourth month, that of Rabîʿ el-Âkhir (***Rabîʿ et-Tâni***), occurs he peculiarly solemn festival of the birthday or ***Mûlid of Ḥusein***, the pro-

phet's grandson, the principal scene of which is the mosque of Ḥusein (p. 58). This festival lasts fifteen days and fourteen nights, the most important day being always a Tuesday *(yôm et-talât)*. On the chief days, and on their eves, the Koran is read aloud to the people, the streets adjoining the mosque are illuminated, the shops are kept open, and story-tellers, jugglers, and others of the same class attract numerous patrons.

In the middle of RAGAB, the seventh month, is the *Mûlid of Es-Saiyida Zeinab* ('Our Lady Zeinab'), the grand-daughter of the prophet. The festival, which lasts fourteen days, the most important being a Tuesday, is celebrated at the mosque of the Saiyida Zeinab (p. 79). — On the 27th of this month is the *Leilet el-Miʿrâg*, or night of the ascension of the prophet (p. lxxxvii), the celebration of which takes place outside the former Bâb el-ʿAdawi (near the Shâriʿ el-ʿAdawi, Pl. F 3), in the N. suburb of Cairo. The minarets of all the mosques are illuminated on this night.

On the first, or sometimes on the second, Wednesday of SHAʿBÂN, the eighth month, the *Mûlid of Imâm esh-Shâfiʿi* is commemorated, the centre of attraction being the mosque mentioned on p. 124. This festival is numerously attended, as most of the Cairenes are Shafiites (p. lxxxviii). Minarets are illuminated on the night of the 14-15th of this month (*Leilet en-Nuṣf min Shaʿbân*, 'the night of the middle of Shaʿbân').

The month of RAMAḌÂN, the ninth, is the month of fasting, which begins as soon as a Moslem declares that he has seen the new moon. This watching for the new moon *(Er-Ru'ya, Leilet er-Ru'ya)* is celebrated in large towns by a ceremony at the government buildings, in which delegates from the workmen's corporations take part. At Cairo there is a procession, accompanied by a band, to the Beit el-Qâḍi (p. 81), where three witnesses affirm that they have seen the new moon. During Ramaḍân the fast is strictly observed during the day, but the faithful indemnify themselves by eating, drinking, and smoking throughout the greater part of the night. At dusk the streets begin to be thronged, the story-tellers in the cafés attract numbers of visitors, and many devotees assemble at the mosques. The *Leilet el-Qadr*, or 'night of the divine decree', one of the last ten nights of the month, generally supposed to be the eve of the 27th of Ramaḍân, is considered peculiarly holy. On this night the Koran is said to have been sent down to Mohammed. On the last Friday of Ramaḍân the king takes part in solemn prayer at the old mosque of ʿAmr (p. 119).

The month of Ramaḍân is succeeded by that of SHAUWÂL, on the first three days of which is celebrated the festival of rejoicing, called by the Arabs *El-ʿÎd eṣ-Ṣughaiyar* (*El-ʿÎd eṣ-Ṣaghîr;* the lesser feast) or *ʿÎd el-Fiṭr* (the festival of the breaking of the fast) but better known by its Turkish name of *Bairâm (Ramaḍân Bairâm)*. The object of the festival is to give expression to the general rejoicing at the termination of the fast; and as at our Christmas, parents give presents to their children, and masters to their servants at this festive season. Friends embrace each other on meeting, and visits of ceremony are exchanged. At this season the traveller may also pay a visit to the cemetery by the Bâb en-Naṣr, or to one of the others (p. 120). The richer classes possess tiny houses by the graves of their relatives and spend a day or two there; the former custom, however, of spending the night is now rarely observed.

A few days after the Bairâm, the pieces of the *Kiswa*, or the so-called *Holy Carpet*, a covering of black brocade manufactured in Cairo at the cost of the Egyptian state for the Kaaba (see below), used every year to be conveyed in procession to the Citadel, where they were sewn together and lined and subsequently carried to Mecca by the great caravan of pilgrims. In 1928, however, it was made at Delhi to the order of King Ibn Saʿûd (p. xciv). [The *Kaaba* (Kaʿba, i.e. 'cube'; $39^1/_2$ ft. in length, 33 ft. in breadth, and $49^1/_4$ ft. in height), the most venerated shrine of Islâm, is situated in the courtyard of the Great Mosque at Mecca, and in its E. corner is immured the famous black stone known as *El-Ḥagar el-Aswad*.] The ceremonies that take place in Cairo on this occasion are repeated on a grander scale in the second half of DHÛ 'L-QAʿDA, the eleventh month,

on the departure of the great pilgrimage caravan for Mecca, accompanied by the Maḥmal (see p. xcviii and below). On this occasion every true believer in the prophet, if he possibly can, spends the whole day in the streets. The women don their smartest attire. Many of the harem windows are opened and the veiled inmates gaze into the streets. The chief scene of the ceremonies is Saladin Square (p. 73), where a sumptuous tent of red velvet and gold is pitched for the reception of the King and the high officials. The King himself leads the camel carrying the Maḥmal by the bridle and hands it over formally to the Amîr el-Ḥagg (the leader of the pilgrimage). The procession is headed by soldiers, who are followed by camels adorned with gaily coloured rugs and bearing on their humps bunches of palm-branches with oranges attached. Each section of the cavalcade is preceded by a band of Arab musicians, the largest section being that which accompanies the *Takhtarawân*, or litter of the Amîr el-Ḥagg, which is covered with red material and is borne by two camels; the next in order is that of the *Dalîl el-Ḥagg*, or guide of the pilgrimage, with his attendants. Next follow various detachments of pilgrims and dervishes with banners, and lastly the Maḥmal. As the customary despatch of a detachment of Egyptian troops to accompany the Maḥmal and the pilgrimage caravan to Mecca led to differences of opinion with King Ibn Sa'ûd (p. xciv), the Egyptian government has abstained from sending the Maḥmal to the Ḥijâz since 1927.

On the 10th of Dhû'l-Ḥigga, the twelfth month, begins the great festival of *El-'Îd el-Kebîr* (also called *'Îd el-Qurbân* or *'Îd el-Aḍḥâ*, the Turkish *Qurbân Bairâm*, 'sacrificial feast', see p. xci), which resembles the lesser feast already mentioned on p. xcix.

The great **Nile Festivals**, closely resembling those of the ancient period of the Pharaohs, take place in summer. As they have reference to a regularly recurring phenomenon of nature, their dates are necessarily fixed in accordance with the Coptic solar reckoning of time (p. xl), instead of the variable Arabian lunar year. The night of the 11th of the Coptic month Baûna (June 18th) is called *Leilet en-Nuqṭa*, 'night of the drop', as it is believed that a drop from heaven (or a tear of Isis, according to the ancient Egyptian myth) falls into the Nile on this night and causes its rise. The astrologers professed to calculate precisely the hour of the fall of the sacred drop. The Copts and others formerly spent this night on the banks of the Nile, and practised all kinds of superstitious customs. One of these consisted in the placing of a piece of dough by each member of a family on the roof of the house; if the dough rose, happiness was in store for the person who placed it there. On June 21st the river begins slowly to rise. On the 27th of the Coptic month Baûna (July 4th) the *Munâdi en-Nîl*, or Nile-criers, are frequently heard in the morning, announcing to the citizens the number of inches that the river has risen. Each munâdi is accompanied by a boy, with whom he enters on a long religious dialogue by way of preface to his statements, which, however, are generally inaccurate. The next important day is that of the *Cutting of the Dam (yôm gabr el-baḥr*, or *yôm wafâ el-bahr)*, about the middle of the Coptic month of Misra (i.e. the middle of August), when the principal ceremonies are performed in the open space to the N. of the Fumm el-Khalîg (p. 112). The Nile-crier, attended by boys carrying flags, announces the *Wafâ en-Nîl* (superfluity of the Nile), or period when the water has reached its normal height of about sixteen ells (p. 113). The actual cutting through of the dam can no longer take place, but the festivities, which culminate in a firework display attended by the Governor, go on as before.

The only general holiday celebrated by adherents of all religions is the ancient **Spring Festival** of the *Shamm en-Nesîm* ('the smell of the West wind'), on the Coptic-Orthodox Easter Monday. All the shops are closed, and many families spend the day in the country. — The **Official Holidays**, to which, however, the people pay little attention, are *Independence Day* (March 15th; see p. cxxxi), the *King's Birthday* (March 26th), and the *Anniversary of the King's Accession* (Oct. 9th).

IV. Outline of the History of Egypt.

By *Professor Georg Steindorff.*

I. Ancient History.

A. From the Earliest Times to the Macedonian Conquest
(from before 3200 B.C. to 332 B.C.).

Exact systems of chronology were as little known to the ancient Egyptians as to the other peoples of antiquity. The events they desired to record were usually dated according to the years of the king reigning at the time. The priests drew up long lists of monarchs, fragments of which have survived to the present day (comp. pp. 94, 257, 291). The chronological epitomes, moreover, which are all that has been transmitted to us of the historical works written in Greek by Manetho, were founded on these native registers. Manetho of Sebennytos (p. 185), who flourished c. 300 B.C., in the reigns of Ptolemy I. Soter I. and Ptolemy II. Philadelphus, was probably a priest at Heliopolis and wrote his three books of Αἰγυπτιακὰ Ὑπομνήματα ('Egyptian Memoirs') in the reign of Ptolemy II. He arranged all the rulers of Egypt, from Menes, the first king, to Alexander the Great, in thirty dynasties, which correspond, generally speaking, to the various royal houses that held sway in Egypt successively or (at certain periods) simultaneously. This arrangement has been generally adopted by writers on the subject; but at the same time, for the sake of convenience, several dynasties are frequently grouped together under the name of a 'period', 'empire', or 'kingdom'. It is impossible to assign anything like exact dates for the kings before Psammetichos I. (p. cix). The dates, therefore, in the following outline are given as approximate merely, and in the earliest period may sometimes be even a century or more out.

(1) Primæval (Pre-Dynastic) Period (before 3200 B.C.).

The dark primæval period, which later traditions fill up with dynasties of gods and demigods, is illumined by a few scattered rays of light only (comp. p. 229). It may be taken as certain that the country did not originally form one single kingdom, but was divided into two states: the Lower Egyptian kingdom of the Delta, and the Upper Egyptian kingdom, stretching from the neighbourhood of Memphis (Cairo) to the First Cataract. Each of these states was subdivided into a number of 'nomes' (νομός, a province), which probably originated as small independent principalities. The capital of Lower Egypt was Behdet (Damanhûr, p. 34), its chief deity the falcon-god Horus (p. clvii), while the capital of Upper Egypt was Ombos (near Naqâda, p. 233) and its chief deity Seth (p. clviii). The religious centre of the land was at Heliopolis (On, pp. 129, 130). At a later period Buto (p. 34) became the capital of Lower Egypt, and Hierakonpolis (Nekhen, p. 369), in conjunction with Nekhab (Elkâb, p. 365), that of Upper Egypt. The snake-goddess Buto (p. clvi) and

the vulture-goddess Nekhbeyet (p. clvii) were the patron deities of both kingdoms and of their rulers. The two Egyptian kingdoms were for a time hostile to each other. Their final union seems to have been operated from Upper Egypt by King Menes (see below), just how is unknown. The memory of the ancient division subsisted beyond the dawn of the historic period; thus the arms of the united empire were formed by the union of the sedge (Carex or perhaps Juncus globulosus; pp. cxxxiii, cxxxiv) and the papyrus, the symbolical plants of Upper and Lower Egypt (comp. p. clxxxvi); the king styled himself 'King of Upper and Lower Egypt' or 'Lord of both Lands', and wore the double tiara  consisting of the white crown 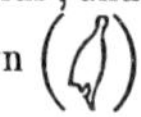 of Upper Egypt and the red crown  of Lower Egypt; and at the base of the temple walls were represented on one side the provinces of the S., and on the other the provinces of the N. Even in matters of administration respect was paid to this distinction, which was further emphasized by the physical differences of the two regions. The introduction of the Egyptian calendar perhaps belongs also to the primæval period and begins with July 19th, 4241.

(2) Ancient Empire (c. 3200-2270 B.C.). †

a. *Archaic Period. The Earliest Kings* (c. 3200-2780 B.C.).

1st & 2nd DYNASTIES, residing at This (p. 231).

Menes united Egypt c. 3200 B.C. and founded the 'White Walls', a fortified city on the site afterwards occupied by Memphis (p. 153). The tombs of his successors (Athothis, Wenephês, Usaphaïs, Khasekhem, etc.) are at Abydos (p. 260; comp. p. 98).

b. *Pyramid Period* (c. 2780-2270 B.C.).

3rd DYNASTY (2780-2720 B.C.).

Djoser *(Zoser)* removes his capital to Memphis, where he builds his tomb, the Step Pyramid at Ṣaqqâra (p. 156). The most ancient maṣṭabas (p. clxxvi) date from this period.

4th DYNASTY (2720-2560 B.C.).

An epoch of a great expansion of the royal power.

Snofru *(Soris)*, builder of the pyramid of Meidûm (p. 217) and of the great stone pyramid at Dahshûr (p. 177).

Kheops or **Cheops** (*Khufu;* c. 2690 B.C.), builder of the great pyramid of Gîza (p. 136).

Dedf-rē (reigned eight years), builder of the pyramid of Abu Roâsh (p. 149).

---

† Only the most important kings of each dynasty are mentioned. Dynasties given in full are prefixed by an asterisk. — The names of the kings are here given in the Greek form, with the Egyptian form in brackets (or vice versa).

Khephren (*Khefrē;* c. 2650 B.C.), builder of the second pyramid of Gîza (p. 142).

Mencheres or **Mykerinos** (*Menkewrē;* c. 2600 B.C.), builder of the third pyramid of Gîza (p. 143).

Shepseskaf (c. 2560 B.C.), the last king of the 4th Dyn.; his tomb is the Maṣṭabat Fara'ûn (p. 176).

5TH DYNASTY (2560-2420 B.C.).

Egypt now reached the zenith of her civilization; art, in particular, attained a perfection never again reached. The pyramids of the kings are at Abuṣîr (p. 151), where special sanctuaries were built also for the sun-god Rē (p. 152).

Userkaf built his pyramid at Ṣaqqâra (p. 157).

Sehurē (c. 2550 B.C.) carried on wars against the Libyans and Asiatics.

Niuserrē (c. 2500 B.C.) built the sanctuary of Abu Gurâb (p. 150).

Onnos (*Unis*), the last king of the 5th Dyn., built his pyramid at Ṣaqqâra (p. 175). After his death internal dissensions seem to have broken out, resulting in the accession of a new dynasty.

6TH DYNASTY (c. 2420-2270 B.C.).

The power of the kings was more limited, and the small principalities recovered some of their independence. Far-reaching commercial relations were entered into with the Upper Nile (comp. p. 411), Punt (p. 233), Syria, etc.

Othoes (*Teti*) **Phiops I.** (*Pyopi*, c. 2375 B.C.) **Methusuphis** (*Merenrē Ment-em-sof*) **Phiops II.** (*Nefer-ke-rē Pyopi*)	Builders of pyramids at Ṣaqqâra (pp. 175, 176).

(3) **Intermediate Period** (c. 2270-2100 B.C.).

7-10TH DYNASTIES.

Towards the end of the 6th Dyn. a great disaster befell the monarchy. While the successors of the 6th Dyn. (*8th Dynasty*) may have maintained themselves at Memphis, a new race of independent kings (*9th & 10th Dynasties;* c. 2240-2100 B.C.) established themselves at Heracleopolis (p. 218) and for a time ruled perhaps the whole of Egypt. Literature flourished at the court of Heracleopolis (*King Akhthoës*).

(4) **Middle Empire** (2100-1700 B.C.).

11TH DYNASTY (2100-2000 B.C.).

In Upper Egypt the Theban princes succeeded in extending their power beyond their own nomes and in gradually gaining the sovereignty over all Egypt. Most of them were named **Mentuhotep.** The mortuary temple of two of these has been found at Deir el-Baḥari (p. 322). The Mentuhoteps finally overthrew the kings of Heracleopolis and reunited the whole country.

*12th DYNASTY (2000-1790 B.C.).

This was Egypt's most prosperous period, and an epoch of great buildings. There is hardly a considerable town in Egypt without some traces of the building activity of the kings of this dynasty. Literature and art flourished.

Amenemmēs I. (*Amenemḥēt*, c. 1980 B.C.; comp. p. clii) restored peace and ruled over the whole of Egypt. His tomb is the N. pyramid at Lisht (p. 217).

Sesostris I. (*Senwosret*, c. 1950 B.C.) conquered Nubia (comp. p. 411); his tomb is the S. pyramid at Lisht (p. 217).

Amenemmēs II.; his tomb is at Dahshûr (p. 177).

Sesostris II., builder of the pyramid of El-Lâhûn (p. 207).

Sesostris III. (the famous *Sesostris* of the Greeks, c. 1860 B.C.) consolidates the sovereignty over Nubia (comp. p. 412). Pyramid at Dahshûr (p. 177).

Amenemmēs III. (c. 1820 B.C.), builder of the pyramid and great temple (so-called Labyrinth) at Hauwâra (p. 206).

Amenemmēs IV.

Sebek-nofru, a queen.

13th DYNASTY (1790-c. 1700 B.C.).

The monarchs of the *13th Dynasty*, mostly named **Sebek-hotep,** maintained the power of Egypt for some time.

(5) Hyksos Period (c. 1700-1555 B.C.).

14-16th DYNASTIES (c. 1700-1600 B.C.).

Another period of decline sets in. There is no age of Egyptian history at which kings were more numerous, most of them reigning but a short time. The South was probably ruled by the descendants of the ancient Theban kings, while in the town of Xoïs, in the W. Delta, another family raised themselves to power *(14th Dynasty).*

About this time Egypt was conquered by a Semitic people, known as *Hyksos*, i.e. 'Shepherd Kings' *(15th & 16th Dynasties).* Few of their monuments have been preserved, but it is evident that they conformed to the ancient culture of Egypt. While the Hyksos were established in the N. part of the land, the S. was ruled by Theban princes, who were at first vassals of the foreign intruders. The tombs of these princes lay near Dirâʿ Abu'n-Naga (p. 300). They form the —

17th DYNASTY (1600-1555 B.C.).

Sekenyenrē, whose mummy was found at Deir el-Baḥari (comp. p. 105). His queen was *Ahhotep* (comp. p. 104).

Kemose, son of the last, waged successful war against the Hyksos.

Amosis (*Ahmose*, 1580-1555 B.C.), brother of Kemose, conquered Auaris, the chief fortress of the Hyksos, and expelled the intruders from Egypt, which was reunited under one sceptre. The Biblical story of the Exodus may possibly be connected with the expulsion of the Hyksos.

(6) New Empire (1555-712 B.C.).

*18TH DYNASTY (1555-1350 B.C.).

Egypt became a great power during this period. At first the culture of the New Empire differed little from that of the Middle Empire, but under Thutmosis III. political and social life as well as the art of Egypt underwent a radical change, owing to the new relations with W. Asia. The tribute paid by foreign states caused an enormous flood of wealth to pour into Egypt, and especially into Thebes, the capital (p. 270). The earlier buildings, that had fallen into disrepair, were replaced by imposing monuments.

Amenophis I. (*Amenhotep*, 1555-c. 1540 B.C.). This king and his mother *Ahmes-Nofreteroy* were afterwards regarded as the patron saints of the Necropolis of Thebes (for the mortuary temple of Amenophis I., see p. 328).

Thutmosis I. (*Tuthmosis*, *Dhutmose*, *Thothmes;* 1540-1501 B.C.) conquered Upper Nubia (p. 447). His tomb at Bîbân el-Mulûk (p. 314) was the first royal rock-tomb of the Pharaohs. During his lifetime his children fought for the succession.

Kemarē-Hatshepsut (1495-1475 B.C.), queen and builder of the temple of Deir el-Baḥari (p. 317). Her tomb is at Bîbân el-Mulûk (p. 312). **Thutmosis II.** (c. 1480 B.C.; mortuary temple, see p. 347). **Thutmosis III.** (1501-1448 B.C.).	reigned alternately.

After the death of his sister and brother Thutmosis III. reigned alone. He was one of the most notable Egyptian kings, conquered Syria (comp. p. 289), and established the influence of Egypt in W. Asia. Builder of temples at Thebes (pp. 281, 317, 354), El-ʿAmada (p. 426), Buhen (p. 438), etc. His tomb is at Bîbân el-Mulûk (p. 313; mortuary temple, see p. 327).

Amenophis II. (*Amenhotep;* 1448-1420 B.C.), builder of a temple at Karnak (p. 296); tomb at Bîbân el-Mulûk (p. 313; mortuary temple, see p. 328).

Thutmosis IV. (1420-1411 B.C.) excavated the Sphinx at Gîza (comp. p. 145). Tomb at Bîbân el-Mulûk (p. 314; mortuary temple, see p. 328); mummy at Cairo (comp. p. 105).

Amenophis III. (1411-1375 B.C.; called *Memnon* by the Greeks), whose wife was named *Teye*, maintained intercourse with the kings of Babylon, Assyria, Mitanni (on the upper Euphrates), etc. (see cuneiform tablets from Tell el-ʿAmârna, p. 246), and built temples in Nubia, Luxor (p. 272), Karnak (p. 281), Medînet Habu (Colossi of Memnon, p. 345), and elsewhere. His tomb and that of his wife are both at Bîbân el-Mulûk (pp. 316, 315).

Amenophis IV. (1375-1358 B.C.), whose wife was *Nofretête*, replaced the old religion by the worship of a single deity, viz. the sun (*Aton;* p. clii). The movement was soon directed against

Amun and his fellow-deities, who, during the New Empire, had thrown all others into the shade. Many of the ancient deities also were fanatically 'persecuted', their images and names being removed from all monuments. For his own original name, in which the name of Amun occurs, the king substituted that of *Akhenaten* (*Ekh-n-Aton*, *Akhnaton*, i.e. 'the disk of the sun is content'). Tell el-ʿAmârna (p. 245) was made the capital instead of Thebes and became the centre of a special art style ('Amârna art). After his death internal commotions broke out and the new religion was abolished (temple of Sesebi, see p. 447).

Among his successors (1358-1350 B.C.) were **Tutankhamûn** *(Tut-ankhamen)*, who died at the age of 18 after a reign of 6-7 years (tomb at Bîbân el-Mulûk, p. 315; tomb treasure at Cairo, pp. 105 seqq.), and **Eye** (tombs at Tell el-ʿAmârna, p. 250, and at Bîbân el-Mulûk, p. 316), who transferred the royal residence back to Thebes.

*19th Dynasty (1350-1200 B.C.).

Egypt recovered her strength and under Sethos I. and Ramses II. regained her position as a great power.

Haremhab (*Harmaïs;* 1350-1315 B.C.), commander-in-chief and viceroy under Amenophis IV. and his successors, restored peace (expedition against Nubia, p. 360). Tomb at Bîbân el-Mulûk (p. 315).

Ramses I. *(Ramesse)* had a short reign. His tomb is at Bîbân el-Mulûk (p. 308).

Sethos I. (*Seti*, 1313-1292 B.C.) fought against the Libyans, the Syrians, and the Hittites (Khatti), a powerful people that under the 18th Dyn. had penetrated from Asia Minor into N. Syria and threatened the Egyptian possessions in Syria and Palestine. Sethos built temples at Karnak, Qurna, and Abydos. His tomb is at Bîbân el-Mulûk (p. 308), his mummy at Cairo (comp. p. 102).

Ramses II. (*Ramesse*, c. 1292-1225 B.C.), the most celebrated of all Egyptian kings. He waged tedious wars against the Hittites (battle of Kadesh, p. 326), finally making a peace with them in the 21st year of his reign (p. 288), which left Palestine proper in the possession of the Egyptians, while N. Syria was acknowledged to be tributary to the Hittites. Ramses developed an extraordinary building activity in the course of his reign of sixty-seven years. About one-half of all the extant temples date from this reign; and the name of Ramses is found in nearly every group of ruins in Egypt. His largest temples were those of Abu Simbel (p. 431), Karnak (p. 281), Luxor (p. 273), the Ramesseum (p. 324), Abydos (p. 259), Memphis (p. 154), and Bubastis (p. 181). His tomb is at Bîbân el-Mulûk (p. 304), his mummy at Cairo (comp. p. 102). Ramses II. is frequently identified, but groundlessly, with the 'Pharaoh of the Oppression' (Exodus i. 11). Of his numerous sons only Menephthes (p. cvii) survived him,

Menephthes (*Merneptah*, 1225-1215 B.C.) carried on campaigns against the Libyans and their allies (p. 93), the peoples of the Mediterranean, and against the Ethiopians (p. 427). His mortuary temple is at Thebes (p. 328), his tomb at Bîbân el-Mulûk (p. 304), and his mummy at Cairo.

Amen-meses **Siptah** (c. 1210 B.C.) **Sethos II.** (c. 1205 B.C.)	are all buried at Bîbân el-Mulûk (pp. 305, 315, 308). Their short reigns were followed by a period of anarchy. **Decline of the kingdom.**

*20TH DYNASTY (1200-1090 B.C.).

Seth-nakht succeeded in restoring peace. Tomb at Bîbân el-Mulûk (p. 308).

Ramses III. (*Ramesse*, 1198-1167 B.C.) conquered the Libyans and in two great battles repelled an invasion of barbarians (Philistines, etc.) who approached from Asia Minor by land and by water, threatening Egypt. His reign of twenty-one years was thereafter an epoch of peace and quiet, in which several large buildings (e.g. the temple and palaces at Medînet Habu, p. 347) were erected. The king presented great gifts to the gods, especially to the Theban Amun, who had been richly endowed by former kings also. The high-priest of Amun gradually became the greatest power in the state (comp. p. 271). The king's tomb is at Bîbân el-Mulûk (p. 305), his mummy at Cairo.

Ramses IV.-Ramses XII. gradually fell more and more under the control of the priests of Amun. Their tombs are at Bîbân el-Mulûk (pp. 303 seqq.).

Herihor, high-priest of Amun, occupied the throne for a short time after the death of Ramses XII.

21ST DYNASTY (TANITES; 1090-945 B.C.).

The empire now fell to pieces. At Tanis (p. 182) a new dynasty arose (*Psusennes*, *Amenemōpet*), which contested the rule of the high-priests of Thebes (p. 271). *Pinutem I.*, a Theban priest-king, became king of all Egypt through marriage alliances with the Tanite dynasty, while his sons obtained the influential and lucrative dignity of high-priests of Thebes. The decay of the empire was accelerated. Nubia recovered its independence (p. 412); and the Egyptian dominion in Palestine terminated.

22ND DYNASTY (945-745 B.C.).

The kings of this dynasty were of Libyan origin. Their ancestors, members of the Mashwesh (Maxyes) and other tribes, had come to Egypt as the leaders of mercenary troops. Settling in the E. Delta, they grew in power as that of the monarchy declined. The royal residence was Bubastis (p. 181); Thebes steadily declined in importance. Royal princes assumed the office of high-priests of Amun.

Sheshonk I. (*Sesonchis*, c. 940 B.C.; the *Shishak* of the Bible) overthrew the Tanites. In the fifth year of Rehoboam of Judah he

captured Jerusalem and plundered the Temple of Solomon (c. 930 B.C.). For his monument of victory, see p. 288. He built the temple of El-Ḥîba (p. 219).

Under his successors (*Osorkon*, *Takelothis*, *Sheshonk*, etc.) the throne once more lost power, and the country was subdivided into small independent principalities. Among these are reckoned the members of the —

23RD DYNASTY (745-718 B.C.),

who reigned in Tanis, but of whom we know little. The kings of Ethiopia (Kush, p. 411), whose capital was Napata (p. 445), made themselves masters of Upper Egypt.

Tefnakhte (c. 730 B.C.), prince of Saïs and Memphis, attempted to seize the sovereignty of Lower Egypt, but was defeated by **Piankhi,** king of Ethiopia, who captured Memphis. (For Piankhi's monument of victory, see p. 96.)

*24TH DYNASTY (718-712 B.C.).

Bocchoris *(Bekenranf)*, son and successor of Tefnakhte, secured the sovereignty of Lower Egypt, while Upper Egypt remained subject to the Ethiopians. *Sabakon* of Ethiopia (Kush), son of *Kashta*, overthrew Bocchoris and burned him to death. All Egypt fell for a time into the hands of the Ethiopians.

(7) **Late-Egyptian Period** (712-332 B.C.).

*25TH DYNASTY (Ethiopians; 712-663 B.C.).

712-700 **Shabako** *(Sabakon)* assisted the smaller Syrian states (Hezekiah of Judah) against the Assyrians.

700-688 **Sebichos** *(Shabataka)*.

688-663 **Taharka** (the *Tirhakah* of the Bible) also assisted the princes of Syria and Palestine against the Assyrians, but was defeated in 670 by Esarhaddon, king of Assyria, and after the capture of Memphis compelled to take refuge in Ethiopia. Both Upper and Lower Egypt became subject to the Assyrians, the various local princes (such as Necho of Saïs, etc.) becoming vassals of the invaders. Various attempts to expel the latter failed.

663 **Tanutamun,** son of *Shabako*, succeeded in recovering Egypt for a brief period, but was finally defeated by the Assyrians and driven back into Upper Egypt and Ethiopia (comp. pp. 412, 446). The absence of the main Assyrian forces, which were engaged in wars in Babylon and Elam, afforded an opportunity of shaking off the yoke, which was seized by *Psammetichos* of Saïs (p. 36), son of Necho (see above), with the help of Gyges, king of Lydia. The foreign garrisons were expelled; the authority of the small native princes was gradually curbed; and Egypt was again united. Since then Ethiopia has been definitively separate from Egypt.

*26th DYNASTY (663-525 B.C.).

Egypt now enjoyed another period of prosperity. Trade began to flourish owing to the new relations with Greece. Art also received a fresh impetus; even before the Ethiopian kings artists had begun to imitate the models of the classic periods of Egyptian art under the Ancient and Middle Empires, and even those of the 18th Dynasty. This reversion to an earlier era appeared also in other departments, such as literature, the spelling of inscriptions, and even the titles of officials.

663-609 **Psammetichos I.** *(Psametik)*, see p. cviii.

609-593 **Necho** *(Nekaw)*. While the Assyrians were engrossed in a deadly contest with the Babylonians and Medes Necho invaded Syria, defeating and slaying Josiah, king of Judah, at the battle of Megiddo. The Egyptians were, however, defeated at Carchemish (on the Euphrates) by Nebuchadnezzar, king of Babylon, and thus lost their possessions in Syria and Palestine. — Necho began to construct a canal from the Nile to the Red Sea, but was stopped by an oracle (p. 193).

593-588 **Psammetichos II.** warred against Ethiopia (p. 412).

588-569 **Apries** or **Uaphris** (*Weh-eb-rē*; the *Hophrah* of the Bible) made another attempt to recover Syria, but was unable to prevent the capture of Jerusalem by Nebuchadnezzar in 587. A military rebellion in Libya dethroned Apries, and his general Amasis was proclaimed king.

569-526 **Amasis** *(Ahmose)* secured his supremacy by marriage with a daughter of Psammetichos II. A campaign undertaken by Nebuchadnezzar against Egypt led to the final abandonment of the Egyptian claims upon Syria. Amasis assigned the city of Naucratis (p. 34) to Greek colonists, who speedily made it the most important commercial town in the empire. A friendly alliance was made with Polycrates, tyrant of Samos.

525 **Psammetichos III.** was defeated at Pelusium (pp. 197, 198) by the Persian king Cambyses, and Egypt became a Persian province.

PERSIAN DOMINATION (525-332 B.C.).

The Persian monarchs appeared as successors to the native rulers. The old religion was unmolested.

*27th DYNASTY.

525-521 **Cambyses** led an unsuccessful expedition against the oases of the Libyan Desert and a campaign against Ethiopia (p. 412).

521-486 **Darius I.** endeavoured to promote the prosperity of Egypt in every possible way. The canal from the Nile to the

Red Sea was completed (p. 194). A strong garrison was sent to the oasis of Khârga and a temple was built there to Amun (p. 406). After the battle of Marathon (490 B.C.)
487 the Egyptians expelled the Persians. The insurrection, however, was quelled by —
486-465 **Xerxes I.**, who appointed his brother Achæmenes satrap.
465-425 **Artaxerxes I.** During his reign the Egyptians again revolted.
463 *Inaros (Ert-Har-erow)*, prince of Mareia (on Lake Mareotis, p. 29), aided by the Athenians, defeated Achæmenes but was himself defeated and crucified by the Persian general Megabyzos near Prosopitis in the Delta.
After 449 *Herodotus* visited Egypt.
424-404 **Darius II.** The Persian power declined. Under —
404-362 **Artaxerxes II.** and his successor —
362-338 **Artaxerxes III.** the Egyptians once more revolted and succeeded in regaining their independence for a brief period (404-341) under native rulers, whom Manetho assigns to the 28-30th Dynasties.

*28th DYNASTY.

404-399 **Amyrtæos** of Saïs (p. 36) maintained his authority for a short time only. In Lower Egypt several dynasties contended for sovereignty.

*29th DYNASTY (398-379 B.C.).

This dynasty came from Mendes (p. 183) and relied for support chiefly upon Greek mercenaries.
398-393 **Nepherites I.** *(Nefarēt).*
392-380 **Achoris** *(Hagor)* repelled a Persian invasion after a three years' struggle.
379 **Psamuthis** *(Pshe-Mut).*
Nepherites III. reigned a few months only.

*30th DYNASTY (378-341 B.C.).

378-361 **Nektanebis I.** *(Nekhte-nebof)*, of Sebennytos (p. 185), a strong ruler and a great builder, built temples at Philæ (pp. 390, 391) and at Medînet Habu (pp. 348, 354) and a gate at Karnak (p. 292).
360-359 **Tachos** *(Djehor)* was dethroned, and died at the Persian court.
358-341 **Nektanebis II.** *(Nekht-Har-ehbēt)* built the temple of Isis at Bahbît el-Ḥigâra (p. 185) and a gate at Karnak (p. 294).
341 Egypt, however, was reconquered by the Persians; Nektanebis fled to Ethiopia and the temples were plundered. — *Khababash* (p. 159), perhaps a member of an Ethiopian dynasty, became king of all Egypt for a short while.
323 *Alexander the Great* took possession of Egypt.

B. Græco-Roman Period

(332 B.C.-A.D. 638).

(1) Alexander the Great and the Ptolemies.

"Under the Ptolemies the lower valley of the Nile became once more for three centuries the seat of a brilliant kingdom, at first under gifted rulers of the most prosperous, richest, and most powerful state in the world, but afterwards condemned to shameful impotence under their vicious and degenerate posterity, torn by fratricidal wars, and existing only by the favour of Rome, until it was involved in the domestic struggles of Rome and finally perished" (Eduard Meyer). The customs and religious views of the Egyptians were respected by the Ptolemies, who represented themselves to the native population as the descendants of the ancient Pharaohs. Large temples were built.

332-323 **Alexander the Great** tolerated the native religion and visited the oasis of Zeus Ammon (Sîwa Oasis, p. 403) in 331, where he was hailed by the priests as a son of Ammon. He founded *Alexandria* (p. 12), which soon became the centre of Greek culture and of the commerce of the whole world. After his death in 323 the Macedonian empire fell to pieces. Egypt became the satrapy of —

323-285 **Ptolemy I. Soter I.,** son of Lagus (whence the Ptolemaic dynasty is often known as the *Lagid* dynasty), who carried on the government at first as satrap for *Philippus Arrhidaeus*, the imbecile half-brother of Alexander the Great, and for *Alexander II.*, son of Alexander the Great, and then for the latter alone. Alexander II. died in 311, and Ptolemy assumed the title of king in 305. The Museum at Alexandria (p. 14) and Ptolemaïs Hermiou (p. 230), in Upper Egypt, were founded.

285-246 **Ptolemy II. Philadelphus** married first *Arsinoë I.*, daughter of Lysimachus, then his sister *Arsinoë II.* The power of Egypt abroad was now at its zenith; friendship with Rome. Arsinoë II. (d. 270) was named patron-goddess of the Faiyûm, which was entitled the 'Arsinoite nome' (p. 204) in her honour. Under Philadelphus and his successors great elephant-hunts took place on the Somali coast. The elephants were brought to Egypt and trained for military purposes.

246-222 **Ptolemy III. Euergetes I.** married *Berenice* of Cyrene. He
246 temporarily conquered the empire of the Seleucidæ in Asia Minor and advanced victoriously on Babylonia. When
245 he was recalled to Egypt by a rising, Seleucus regained most of his lost territory. In spite of this, however, Euergetes succeeded in restoring the ancient frontiers of the
238 kingdom. An unsuccessful attempt was made by the Egyptian priests to reform the calendar by intercalating a day in every fourth year (comp. p. 96, No. 983).

222-203 **Ptolemy IV. Philopator.** Under the misgovernment of this king and his successors the empire of the Ptolemies began
217 to totter. Ptolemy IV. defeated Antiochus the Great (III.) of Syria, who had threatened the Egyptian frontier, at the battle of Raphia (Tell Rifaḥ, S. Palestine), but concluded a dishonourable peace with him. The king married his sister *Arsinoë III.* For nineteen years a series of native Pharaohs ruled at Thebes (p. 271).

203-181 **Ptolemy V. Epiphanes** (comp. p. cxxxiii) ascended the throne, when five years of age, under the guardianship of Agathocles and Œnanthe, the mother of the latter. In consequence of a revolt at Alexandria his guardians were obliged to resign their office. Advantage of these dissensions was taken by Antiochus the Great of Syria and Philip V. of Macedonia to invade the foreign possessions of Egypt. Egypt offered the guardianship of Epiphanes to the *Roman Senate*, which ceded Cœlesyria and Palestine to Antiochus, while Egypt continued to be independent, although it lost all its foreign possessions except Cyprus and Cyrene. Epiphanes married
193 *Cleopatra I.*, daughter of Antiochus. The internal affairs of the country fell into deplorable confusion; rebellion succeeded rebellion, and anarchy prevailed everywhere.

181 Ptolemy V. was poisoned.

181-146 **Ptolemy VI. Philometor,** his son, ascended the throne under the guardianship of his mother Cleopatra. Onias was permitted by the king to build a Jewish temple at Leontopolis (p. 181).

169 Antiochus IV. Epiphanes of Syria invaded Egypt and captured Memphis, but in the course of a subsequent campaign was induced to withdraw from Egypt by the Roman ambassador C. Popilius Lænas. Philometor's younger brother —

Ptolemy IX. (*Physcon*, i.e. Big Belly), at first also surnamed Philometor, was summoned to the throne by the Alexandrians. The Lagid kingdom grew constantly weaker and in its foreign policy became completely dependent upon Rome.

170-163 Philometor and Physcon reigned jointly, having become reconciled, and with them also their sister *Cleopatra*, wife of Philometor.

163 The brothers again quarrelled. Philometor fled to Rome, was
163-146 reinstated by the Roman Senate, and thenceforth reigned alone, while the younger brother became king of Cyrene.

146 After the death of Philometor he was succeeded by his son, **Ptolemy VII. Eupator,** who, after a very short reign, gave place to —

146-117 **Ptolemy IX.,** sole ruler, who now assumed the title of **Euergetes (II.).** He married his brother's widow and afterwards also his niece Cleopatra.

130 Expelled by a revolution, Ptolemy IX. sought refuge in Cyprus, while Cleopatra reigned in Egypt as Philometor Soteira. Memphites, a son of Euergetes, became, under the name **Ptolemy VIII. Neos Philopator**, a rival to his father, who succeeded in murdering him.

127 Euergetes II. regained possession of the throne. After his
117 death the government was shared by his widow —

Cleopatra Cocce and her son **Ptolemy X. Soter II.** *(Lathyrus).*

106 Soter II. was banished, and his brother **Ptolemy XI. Alexander I.** became co-regent in his stead.

96 Cyrenaica was bequeathed to the Romans and later became a Roman province.

88 Alexander, expelled by a rebellion, perished in a naval battle. Soter II. was recalled.

Thebes rebelled but was recaptured after a lengthy siege and destroyed (p. 271).

81 After the death of Soter II. **Ptolemy XII. Alexander II.** married *Cleopatra Berenice*, with whom he reigned jointly.

80 He assassinated his wife and was himself slain.

80-51 **Ptolemy XIII. Neos Dionysos** (popularly called *Auletes*, i.e. 'the flute-player') next ascended the throne and was form-
59 ally recognized by Rome. Cyprus was annexed by the Romans in 58, wherefore Ptolemy XIII. was expelled by the Alexandrians; after living in exile in Rome he was restored in 55. The temple at Edfu (p. 370) was completed and that at Dendera was begun (p. 261). — Ptolemy XIII. was succeeded by his children —

51-47 **Cleopatra** and **Ptolemy XIV.**, under the guardianship of the Roman Senate. *Pompey* was appointed guardian.

48 Ptolemy banished his sister Cleopatra. Pompey, having been defeated at the battle of Pharsalia (47 B. C.), sought refuge in Egypt, but on landing at Pelusium (pp. 197, 198) was slain at the instigation of Ptolemy, his ward.

Julius Cæsar landed at Alexandria (p. 13), took the part of the banished Cleopatra, and defeated the rebellious Ptolemy, who was drowned in the Nile. — Cæsar, having meanwhile become dictator of Rome, appointed —

47 **Ptolemy XV.**, the brother of Cleopatra, a boy of eleven, coregent.

45 Ptolemy XV. was assassinated at the instigation of Cleopatra, and —

Ptolemy XVI. Cæsar (also called **Cæsarion**), her son by Cæsar, was appointed co-regent.

44 Cæsar was murdered.

41 **Antony,** having summoned Cleopatra to answer for the conduct of her general Allienus, who contrary to her wishes had aided the army of Brutus and Cassius at Philippi, was capt-

ivated by her beauty and talent. After having spent years
of debauchery with the Egyptian queen, he was at length
31 declared by the Roman Senate to be an enemy of his country.
Octavianus took up arms against him, defeated him at the
naval battle of Actium, and captured Alexandria. Antony
30 committed suicide, and Cleopatra also took her own life
(it is said by the bite of an asp).

Egypt now became a Roman province subject only to the emperor and was governed by prefects nominated by the emperor.

(2) Roman Period
(30 B.C.-A.D. 395).

The Roman emperors followed the example of the Ptolemies in representing themselves to the Egyptian people as successors of the Pharaohs and in maintaining the appearance of a national Egyptian state. — Christianity was early introduced into Egypt, where it spread rapidly.

B.C. 30-29 *Cornelius Gallus*, whom Ovid ranked first among Roman elegiac poets, was appointed first prefect. He repressed an insurrection in Upper Egypt (p. 272) and fought against the Ethiopians. Having afterwards fallen into disgrace with the emperor, he was recalled (27-26) and committed suicide (26). — The reformed calendar was finally introduced by Augustus.

27 *Caesar Octavianus*, under the title of **Augustus**, became sole ruler of the vast Roman empire (p. 13).

24 The Ethiopians, under their queen *Candace* (p. 413), invaded Egypt.

Strabo travelled in Egypt (pp. 13, 272).

A.D. 14-37 **Tiberius** erected the Sebasteum at Alexandria.

19 *Germanicus*, heir to the imperial throne, visited Egypt.

30 (?) Death of Jesus Christ on the Cross.

37-41 **Caligula.** In Alexandria civic disturbances took place between the Hellenes and the Jews.

41-54 **Claudius.** The building of the pronaos of the temple at Esna (p. 357) was begun; a temple at Philæ (p. 395) begun.

54-68 **Nero.** Egypt acquired a new source of wealth as a commercial station between India and Rome.

64 St. Paul beheaded at Rome.

68-69 *Galba. Otho. Vitellius.*

69-79 **Vespasian** (p. 14) was first proclaimed emperor at Alexandria. From this city his son **Titus** (79-81) started on his expedition against Palestine, which terminated with the destruction of Jerusalem in the year 70. The temple of Onias (p. cxii) was closed.

81-96 **Domitian** favoured the worship of Isis and Sarapis at Rome.

96-98 **Nerva.**

98-117 **Trajan** (p. 14). The canal connecting the Nile with the Red Sea was reopened (Amnis Trajanus; p. 194).
117-138 **Hadrian** (pp. 14, 346, 394) visited Egypt in 130. His favourite Antinous was drowned in the Nile, and was commemorated by the founding of the town of Antinoupolis (p. 221).
138-161 **Antoninus Pius.**
c. 150 Ptolemy, the astronomer and mathematician, working at Alexandria.
161-180 **Marcus Aurelius** (p. 14); his throne shared by *Lucius Verus* (pp. 238, 394) till 169.
172-173 Rebellion of the *Bucolians*, or cowherds, who had long been settled among the marshes to the E. of Alexandria, quelled by *Avidius Cassius*.
175 Avidius Cassius was proclaimed emperor by the Egyptian legions, but was assassinated in Syria.
176 Marcus Aurelius visited Alexandria (p. 14).
180-192 **Commodus.**
c. 190 School of the Catechists (p. 15) flourished at Alexandria under Pantænus, Clement (c. 200), and Origen (after 203).
193-211 **Septimius Severus** (p. 14).
204 Edict prohibiting Roman subjects from embracing Christianity. The Delta at this period was thickly studded with Christian communities.
211-217 **Caracalla** (p. 14) visited Egypt. Massacre at Alexandria.
212 The Constitutio Antonina admitted provincials to the Roman citizenship.
Caracalla was assassinated by the prefect of his guards —
217-218 **Macrinus,** who was recognized as emperor by the Egyptians. After his death a series of contests for the possession of the throne took place at Alexandria.
249-251 **Decius** (p. 15). Persecution of the Christians under Bishop Dionysius of Alexandria in A.D. 250.
253-260 **Valerian.** Persecution of the Christians (p. 15).
260-268 **Gallienus** accorded a certain measure of religious toleration to the Christians. Plague in Egypt.
260 Rebellion of *Macrianus*, who was recognized as emperor by the Egyptians. He was defeated in Illyria by *Domitian*, the general of Gallienus, and put to death.
265 *Æmilianus (Alexander)* was proclaimed emperor by the army at Alexandria and recognized by the people, but was defeated and put to death by the Roman legions.
268 Lower Egypt occupied by an army of *Queen Zenobia* of Palmyra (comp. p. 15), and part of Upper Egypt by the Blemmyes (p. 413).
268-270 **Claudius II.**
270-275 **Aurelian.**
270 Probus (p. cxvi) reconquered Egypt for the empire.

c. 271 | Anthony of Coma in Middle Egypt (c. 251-356), a Copt, became the first hermit (comp. pp. 217, 218).
276-282 | **Probus** (p. cxv) obtained the purple at Alexandria.
278 | His successful campaign against the Blemmyes.
284-305 | **Diocletian** (comp. p. xcviii).
292 | Rebellion in Upper Egypt (comp. p. 232).
294 | Insurrection of the Alexandrians.
295 | Diocletian took Alexandria.
303 | Persecution of the Christians.
305-313 | **Maximinus.** Beginning of the Arian controversies.
c. 320 | Pachomius founded the first convent in Tabennēse (p. 232).
324-337 | **Constantine the Great,** the first emperor (son of St. Helena, d. about 330), who was really a friend of the Christians. The government of Egypt was reorganized; the country was made into a diocese and subdivided into six provinces, viz. Egypt, Augustamnica, Heptanomis (afterwards called Arcadia), Thebaïs, Upper Egypt, and Lower Egypt.
325 | Council of Nicæa. The doctrine of the presbyter *Arius* of Alexandria that Christ was begotten by God before all time, for the purpose of creating the world, and was godlike, but not very God, was condemned; while the doctrine that Father and Son are homoousioi, or of the same nature, was sanctioned.
328 | *Athanasius*, Archbishop of Alexandria (comp. p. 15).
330 | Byzantium became the capital (Nova Roma, Constantinopolis) and the new metropolis of Greek art and science.
c. 330 | Beginning of the communities of anchorites in the Sketian and Nitrian deserts (comp. p. 35; Macarius, Amûn).
337-361 | **Constantius** favoured Arianism. Athanasius was banished from Alexandria more than once (comp. p. 407).
346 | Death of St. Pachomius (see above).
c. 350 | The earliest Coptic translations of the Bible.
361-363 | **Julian,** surnamed the *Apostate* from his renunciation of Christianity (p. 15).
373 | Athanasius died, after witnessing the success of his cause in the last years of his life.
379-395 | **Theodosius (I.) the Great.** He formally declared Christianity to be the religion of the empire. Persecution of the Arians and heathens (p. 15). Destruction of the Serapeum (p. 15).
395 | Partition of the Roman empire, *Arcadius* being emperor of the East, and *Honorius* of the West.

(3) Byzantine Period (395-638).

395-408 | **Arcadius** (p. 30). *Theophilus*, the bigoted Patriarch of Alexandria (p. 15), carried fire and sword against the opponents of anthropomorphism, the doctrine that God must be considered to have a human form.
Shenute (d. 466), founder of the national Egyptian or Coptic church (comp. p. lvi seqq.) and head of the White Convent (p. 229) from c. 383 onwards.

395 *St. Augustine* (354-430), doctor of the Church, became Bishop of Hippo (N. Africa).

408-450 **Theodosius II.**

412 Theophilus died and was succeeded by *Cyril* (p. 15).

415 Hypatia, the female pagan philosopher (p. 15), stoned to death at Alexandria.

431 The Patriarch Cyril defended his view, that Mary was Theotokos ('Mother of God') against Nestorius, Patriarch of Constantinople after 428 (comp. p. 230), at the Third Œcumenical Council, held at Ephesus.

444 Cyril died and was succeeded by *Dioscurus* (till 451).

449 In the 'Robber Council' at Ephesus the Patriarch Dioscurus of Alexandria obtained a victory as representative of the monophysite view (see below).

450-457 **Marcian.** Wars with the Nubians and the Blemmyes (p. 390).

451 At the Fourth Œcumenical Council, that of Chalcedon, the monophysite doctrine, to the effect that Christ possessed a double nature before His incarnation, but that His human nature was afterwards absorbed by His divine, was condemned, chiefly through the influence of Pope Leo the Great. The doctrine that Christ possesses two natures, ἀσυγχύτως and ἀτρέπτως, but at the same time ἀδιαιρέτως and ἀχωρίστως, i.e. unmixed and unchangeable, but also indistinguishable and inseparable, was formally adopted by the Church. The Egyptian Christians, to this day, adhere to the monophysite doctrine.

474-491 **Zeno.**

491-518 **Anastasius.**

502 Famine in Egypt.

527-565 **Justinian** (p. 15). New administrative measures.

610-641 **Heraclius** (p. 15).

619 The **Persians** under **Chosroes II.** invaded Egypt (p. 15). Alexandria was taken. Chosroes ruled with moderation.

622 The **Hegira** (Mohammed's 'flight' from Mecca to Medina, p. lxxxvi), beginning of the Mohammedan calendar.

626 The Persians expelled by Heraclius.

632 Death of Mohammed. **Abu Bekr**, his successor, becomes the first caliph (comp. pp. cxxiv, cxxv).

634 Beginning of the conquest of Syria by the Arabs. Death of Abu Bekr. **'Omar** becomes the second caliph.

636 Decisive victory of the Arabs over the Byzantines on the Yarmûk. Fall of Damascus.

637 Victory of the Arabs over the Persians at El-Qâdisîya; fall of Ctesiphon. End of the Sassanian empire.

638 Fall of Jerusalem. 'Omar in Syria.

II. The Middle Ages.

Egypt as a Province of the Empire of the Caliphs.

640 *'Amr ibn el-'Aṣ* (pp. 15, 46, 119), general of Caliph 'Omar, conquered Pelusium (p. 197) and defeated the Byzantines at Heliopolis (p. 129).

641 The fortified city of Babylon (p. 46) was handed over through the intervention of the Patriarch Cyrus (Muqauqis, comp. p. 154).

642 *Fusṭâṭ* was founded as military headquarters and seat of government (p. 46). Capture of Alexandria (p. 15).

644-656 **ʿOthmân** was overthrown in a revolt which had its origin in Egypt.

645 Alexandria was relieved by the Byzantine fleet.

646 ʿAmr recaptured Alexandria. Egypt now became an undisputed possession of the Arabs and the base for their naval campaigns against Byzantium and for their conquest of N. Africa.

656-661 Civil war between **Caliph ʿAli**, son-in-law of Mohammed, and **Muʿâwiya**, founder of the dynasty of the Umaiyads. Egypt belonged at first to ʿAli (comp. p. 58), but after 658 to the Umaiyads.

UMAIYADS (658-750).

This illustrious Arab dynasty had its residence in Damascus (comp. p. lxxxiv). Arab tribes were settled in the Nile valley and the system of government was based on Arab models. Many Copts embraced Islâm. Egypt was ruled by governors, who were often princes of the house of the caliphs.

744-750 **Marwân II.**, the last of this dynasty, fled to Egypt, and was put to death there. His tomb is at Abuṣîr el-Meleq (p. 218). The Umaiyads were then exterminated, with the exception of ʿAbd er-Raḥmân, who fled to Spain and founded an independent caliphate at Cordova (756).

ABBASIDS (750-868).

The new dynasty, which had risen to power on Iranian soil and with Persian assistance, transferred the royal residence and seat of government from Syria to ʿIrâq. Baghdâd was founded (p. cxciii) and the caliphate reached its zenith. Egypt was ruled by frequently changing governors. The Copts were oppressed and frequent revolts occurred (p. lviii).

813-833 **Ma'mûn,** son of Hârûn er-Rashîd, visited Egypt and quelled the resistance of the Copts and the Beduin tribes. The fusion between Arabs and Copts began and Arabic became the language of the fellahin.

Under Ma'mûn's successors the power of the caliphs began to decline; the government became dependent upon Turkish slaves (p. lxxxv), and the provinces regained their independence.

TULUNIDS (868-905).

Egypt became again for a short time independent.

868-883 **Aḥmad ibn Ṭûlûn,** governor of Egypt, declared himself an independent sultan, and extended the boundaries of Egypt beyond Syria and as far as Mesopotamia. Numerous buildings were erected during his reign (pp. 46, 76 seqq.) and that of his son —

883-895 **Khumâraweih** (p. 46). The latter and his successors were unable to preserve their independence.

ABBASIDS (905-935).

Egypt again came under the dominion of the Abbasid caliphs at Baghdâd.

925 The Shiite *Fatimid Caliphs* (see below) of Qairawân (Kairwan, p. cxcv) attacked Egypt, but were defeated.

IKHSHIDIDS (935-969).

935-946 **Muḥammed el-Ikhshîd,** a Turk and governor of Egypt, took possession of the throne and founded a short-lived dynasty. His successors ruled under the direction of —

966-968 **Kâfûr,** an Abyssinian eunuch, who afterwards usurped the throne and recognized the suzerainty of the Abbasids. Syria and Palestine were subordinate to Egypt, and the court at Old Cairo was very brilliant. On his death Kâfûr was succeeded by Muḥammed el-Ikhshîd's grandson Aḥmad, who was not yet of age, and the Fatimids took advantage of this moment of weakness to conquer Egypt.

Egypt under Independent Rulers.

FATIMIDS (969-1171).

The Fatimids, rulers of a kingdom which had arisen in the W. part of N. Africa in 909, as the result of a religious Shiite movement (p. xcv), attributed their origin to Fâṭima, daughter of Mohammed.

969 *Gôhar (Gawhar)* conquered Egypt for the Fatimid **El-Muʿizz,** and founded the new capital Cairo (pp. cxciv, 47).

970 Founding of the Azhar Mosque (p. 58).

973 El-Muʿizz came himself to Cairo and resided there until his death (975). He conquered Syria also.

975-996 **El-ʿAzîz,** son of Muʿizz, distinguished himself by his tolerance and his love of science (p. 58); Egypt prospered under his rule.

996-1021 **El-Ḥâkim** (p. 83), his son by a Christian mother, was a fanatic, capable of extraordinary cruelty. Subsequently, at the instigation of Ed-Darazi, a Persian sectary, he declared himself to be an incarnation of ʿAli (p. cxviii), and exacted the veneration due to a god. Ed-Darazi became the founder of the sect of the Druzes. Ḥâkim disap-

peared on one of his nightly rides on the Moqaṭṭam hills (p. 125), where he was probably assassinated (at the instigation of his sister Sitt el-Mulk?). The Druzes believe that he voluntarily withdrew from the world in consequence of its sinfulness and that he will one day reappear as a divine prophet.

1021-1036 **Eẓ-Ẓâhir,** Ḥâkim's effeminate and cruel son, succeeded at the age of sixteen. Until 1024 Egypt was under the regency of his aunt *Sitt el-Mulk.*

1036-1094 **El-Mustanṣir,** a weak and incapable prince.

1047-1077 Under Christodulos, the Coptic Patriarch, the seat of the Patriarchate was removed from Alexandria to Cairo.

1065 The country was ravaged for seven years by pestilence and famine, owing to the failure of the Nile inundation. Palestine and Syria were overrun by the Seljuks (p. lxxxv), who attacked them from the E. There were revolts among the Turkish and Berber mercenaries. The palace and the library were plundered.

1074-1094 *Badr el-Gamâli,* Mustanṣir's Armenian vizier, restored order in the capital and governed with almost unlimited power, to the great advantage of Egypt. Building of the stone walls and great gates of Cairo (pp. cxcv, 84), and of the Giyûshi Mosque (p. 125). Badr el-Gamâli's son —

1094 *El-Afḍal* became vizier to the young caliph —

1094-1101 **El-Musta'li,** son of Mustanṣir, who conquered —

1096-1098 Jerusalem and the towns on the Syrian coast, but was deprived of his conquests by the army of the First Crusade.

1099 *King Baldwin* of Jerusalem attacked Egypt unsuccessfully.

1101-1159 Owing to a succession of incapable caliphs the empire of the Fatimids gradually fell to pieces. The viziers, *El-Afḍal* (assassinated in 1121) and his successors, were the actual rulers of the country.

1160-1171 **El-'Âḍid,** the last Fatimid caliph.

Contests for the office of vizier took place during this reign between *Shâwar* and *Ḍirghâm.* The former, being exiled, obtained an asylum with *Nûr ed-Dîn,* ruler of N. Syria (resident at Damascus after 1154), who assisted him to regain his office with Kurd mercenary troops, under the brave generals *Shîrkûh* and *Saladin.* Shâwar, quarrelling
1164 with the Kurds, invoked the aid of *Amalrich I.,* King of Jerusalem, who came to Egypt and expelled the Kurds. A second army of Kurds, which was about to invade Egypt in 1167, was driven back in the same way, whereupon Amalrich himself endeavoured to obtain possession of
1168 Egypt. Shâwar next invoked the aid of Nûr ed-Dîn and set fire to Fusṭâṭ (p. 118, Nov. 1168). In a third invasion
1169 of Egypt Shîrkûh and Saladin forced Amalrich to retire and

obtained possession of the country. Shâwar was executed on account of his uncertain attitude. Shîrkûh became chief vizier, and on his death (in March 1169) —

1169-1193 **Saladin** (*Salâḥ ed-Dîn Yûsuf ibn Aiyûb*, p. 47) ruled in the name of the incapable caliph. On the death of the latter

1171 Saladin became sole ruler of Egypt, and founded the dynasty of the —

AIYUBIDS (1171-1250).

Saladin's reign was the most brilliant in the mediæval history of Cairo, though he resided only eight years in the city and spent the rest of the time in campaigns in Palestine, Syria, and Mesopotamia. He began the citadel (p. 73) and the city walls (p. 118). The Shiite doctrines, introduced into Egypt by the Fatimids were abolished. Syria was conquered.

1200-1218 **Malik el-ʿÂdil,** his brother, for a short time preserved the dominions intact, which had been temporarily divided on Saladin's death. In 1211 his wife, the sultana Esh-Shamsa, built the mausoleum of the Imâm esh-Shâfiʿi at Cairo (p. 124). After Malik el-ʿÂdil's death the empire was again dismembered, Egypt falling to the share of his son —

1218-1238 **Malik el-Kâmil** (p. 183), a prudent and vigorous ruler.

1218 Damietta (Dumyâṭ) was captured by the army of the Fifth Crusade, but was surrendered again in 1221 (p. 186).

1229 Kâmil concluded a treaty with the Emperor Frederick II., who led an army into Palestine. By this compact Jerusalem and the coast towns were surrendered to the emperor for ten years. — Kâmil was succeeded by his sons —

1238-1240 **El-ʿÂdil II.** and —

1240-1250 **Es-Ṣâliḥ Aiyûb.** The latter built the castle on the island of Rôḍa in the Nile (p. 112). For his mausoleum, see p. 81.

1249 *Louis IX.* of France (St. Louis) undertook the Sixth Crusade against Egypt and took Damietta, but was captured with

1250 his army at Manṣûra (p. 183) by **Tûrânshâh,** who had succeeded his father Eṣ-Ṣâliḥ. During the negotiations for the release of Louis Tûrânshâh was murdered by his bodyguards, the Mamelukes. After the short interregnum of *Shagaret ed-Durr*, widow of the sultan Eṣ-Ṣâliḥ Aiyûb, one of the Mameluke leaders, named *Aibak*, was raised to the throne and married Shagaret ed-Durr; both were put to death in 1257 (for the mausoleum of Shagaret ed-Durr, see p. 80). Aibak was the first ruler in the dynasty of the —

BAHRITE MAMELUKES (1250-1382).

In the space of 132 years there were twenty-five sultans, some of whom reigned several times. Comp. pp. lxxxvi, cxcvi, 47.

The MAMELUKES were slaves (the word *mamlûk* means a 'white slave'), purchased by the sultans and trained as soldiers for the

purpose of forming their bodyguard and the nucleus of their army. They became known as the *Bahrite* Mamelukes from the fact that their barracks lay on the island of Rôḍa (p. 112) in the river *(Baḥr)*.

1260-1277 **Beibars I.** *(Bîbars)*, one of the ablest of this dynasty, annihilated the last remnants of the kingdom of Jerusalem in the course of four campaigns. He brought to Cairo a representative of the Abbasid caliphs (p. cxviii), who had
1258 been expelled from Baghdâd after its capture by the Mongols under Hûlâgû, grandson of Chingiz Khân, and the execution of the last caliph El-Musta'ṣim, and permitted him and his successors nominally to occupy the throne (1261-1517). Building of the Eẓ-Ẓâhir Mosque (1269; p. 85).

1279-1290 **Qalâûn,** *El-Manṣûr Qalâûn*, succeeded to the sultanate, to the exclusion of a youthful son of Beibars, opposed the Mongols with success, and entered into treaties with the Emperor Rudolph of Habsburg and other princes. Great building activity in Cairo (p. 81), Egypt developing its own style of Islamic architecture.

1290-1293 **El-Ashraf Khalîl** captured Acre, the last place in the Holy Land still held by the Christians (1291).

1293-1340 **Muḥammed en-Nâṣir,** *Muḥammed ibn Qalâûn* (p. 47), succeeded his brother Khalîl at the age of nine years, but owing to internal dissensions was compelled to retire to Syria, while *El-Manṣûr Lâgîn* ruled in Egypt from 1296 (comp. p. 76). With the aid of the Syrian emirs, however, he regained his throne in 1298. In order to escape the influence of the Emirs Beibars and Salâr, who held the reins of power, En-Nâṣir fled in 1309 to the castle of El-Kerak (to the E. of the Dead Sea). *Beibars (II.)* was chosen sultan but was compelled to abdicate on En-Nâṣir's return in 1310 and was put to death (for his convent-mosque, see p. 84). En-Nâṣir retained possession of the throne till his death in 1340. Distrustful, vindictive, and avaricious, he treated his emirs with the utmost capriciousness, loading them with rich gifts or ordering them to execution as the humour seized him. The Aiyubid emir *Ismâ'îl Abulfidâ*, known also as a historian, succeeded, however, in retaining his master's favour and died as prince of Ḥamâ (Syria) in 1331. Towards the mass of the population En-Nâṣir was liberal and condescending, and towards the clergy indulgent. In order to provide the enormous sums required for the expenses of his court and for his love of building (mosque and tomb, see p. 82; mosque in the Citadel, see p. 75; aqueduct, see p. 124) he appointed Christian officials in the administration of taxes and the finance department, as they were considered especially clever and cunning.

1303 An earthquake destroyed a large part of Cairo.

1347-1361 **Ḥasan**, the sixth son of En-Nâṣir, was still a minor when he ascended the throne. The lawless independence of the Mamelukes and emirs was aggravated by a plague in 1348-1349 which exterminated whole families, whose property was seized by the government. Ḥasan was dethroned in 1351, regained his sceptre three years later, after the reign of the sultan *Ṣâliḥ* (p. 47), and was assassinated in 1361. His mosque (madrasa; p. 71) marks the climax of Islamic architecture in Egypt. — The following sultans (comp. p. 47) became more and more dependent on the emirs.

CIRCASSIAN MAMELUKES (1382-1517).

1382-1399 **Barqûq**, a Circassian slave, succeeded in usurping the throne by treacherously setting aside *Ḥâggi*, a boy of six years and great-grandson of En-Nâṣir. The exasperated emirs dethroned him in 1389 (comp. p. 47); but he triumphantly re-entered Cairo in 1390. He fought successfully against the Mongols under Tamerlane, whose proper name was Tîmûr or Tîmûr-i Lang (i.e. Lame Timur; d. 1405), and against the Osmans under Bâyazîd I. For his mosque (madrasa), see p. 82; tomb, see p. 121.

1399-1412 **Farag** (pp. 47, 121), his son, had scarcely ascended the throne, as a boy of thirteen years of age, before the Osmans, and a little later the Mongols, again began to threaten the Egyptian dominions. Farag proceeded victoriously as far as Damascus; but owing to dissensions among his emirs he was obliged to return to Cairo. After the defeat of the Turks by the Mongols under Tamerlane at the battle of Angora (1402), Farag had to enter into negotiations with Tamerlane. The latter years of Farag's reign were constantly disturbed by the rebellions of his emirs, particularly *Sheikh el-Maḥmûdi*, who afterwards became *Sultan El-Mu'aiyad*. Farag was at length compelled by the insurgents to capitulate at Damascus, and his execution was followed by the accession of —

1412-1421 **Sheikh el-Mu'aiyad.** His reign was chiefly occupied with victorious campaigns against his unruly Syrian vassals, in which he was greatly aided by the military talents of his son *Ibrâhîm*. For his mosque, see p. 63; muristan, see p. 73.

Mu'aiyad exacted heavy contributions from Christians and Jews, and he re-enacted and rigorously enforced the sumptuary laws of ʿOmar (p. cxvii), El-Mutawakkil (847-861), El-Ḥâkim (p. cxix), and En-Nâṣir (p. cxxii). Not only were the colours to be worn by the Christians and Jews prescribed (the costume of the former being dark-blue, with black turbans, and a wooden cross weighing 5lb. hung round their necks; that of the latter, yellow, with black turbans, and a black ball hung from their necks); but the fashion of their dress and length of their turbans, and even the costume of their women, were so regulated as entirely to distinguish them from the followers of the Prophet.

1422-1438 **El-Ashraf Bars Bey,** who had for a time been regent on behalf of an infant sultan, ascended the throne in 1422. He waged successful campaigns against Cyprus and the Mongols. For his mosque, see p. 57; tomb, see p. 122.

1468-1496 **Qâït Bey** was one of the last independent Mameluke sultans of Egypt. Both as a general and a diplomatist he successfully maintained his position against the Turks (Sultans Muḥammed II. and Bâyazîd II.), and even inflicted serious losses on them (Emir Ezbek, p. 53); but the refractory Mamelukes obstructed his undertakings and in 1496 compelled him to abdicate in favour of his son Muḥammed, a boy of fourteen.

1501-1516 **El-Ghûri,** *Qânṣûh el-Ghûri*, once a slave of Qâït Bey, was upwards of sixty years of age when he ascended the throne, but he still possessed sufficient vigour to keep the unruly emirs in check. Already seriously injured by the discovery of the Cape route to India by the Portuguese, the trade of Egypt was terribly depressed by high taxes and by the accompanying debasement of the coinage. At the instigation of the Venetians, El-Ghûri equipped a fleet against the Portuguese in India, and in 1508 he gained a naval victory over Lorenzo, son of the viceroy Francisco d'Almeida, at Chaul, S. of Bombay; but in 1509 his fleet was compelled to retreat to Arabia. El-Ghûri fell while fighting against the army of the Osman sultan Selîm I. on the plain of Merj Dâbiq (N. of Aleppo). For his mosque (madrasa and mausoleum), see p. 62.

1517 *Ṭûmân Bey* was dethroned by the **Osman Sultan Selîm I.** of Constantinople (pp. 48, 129). Cairo was taken by storm. Egypt thenceforth became a *Turkish Pashalic.* Selîm brought Mutawakkil III., the last scion of the family of the Abbasid caliphs (comp. p. cxviii), to Constantinople, whence he returned to Cairo after the sultan's death (1520) and died in 1543. According to the tradition, the historical truth of which is not absolutely certain, Selîm compelled Mutawakkil to convey to him his nominal supremacy, and thus became *Caliph* (Khalif, Khalîfa), the chief of all the professors of Islâm.

The Osman sultans' claim to the caliphate was based upon this act. The caliph (p. xcv) was not in any sense the 'pope' of the Mohammedans, as he claims no spiritual power. He was the temporal head of the true believers and their champion in the holy war (p. xc). The caliphate of the Osmans was divested of its temporal power by the Turkish National Assembly at Angora, when the sultanate was abolished (Nov. 1922), and was finally done away with at the beginning of March 1924. It was only a de facto caliphate, as according to the Sharîʿa (p. lxxxix) the caliph must be a descendant of the Quraish, the Arab tribe to which Mohammed and the earlier caliphs belonged. On this account many of the Sunnites did not recognize the cali-

phate of the Osmans. The Turkish court theologians declared that this was not a necessary condition, but that God made the final decision in the success with which he endowed the caliph. The Shiites (p. xcv) had never recognized the Osman caliphs as they were not descended from ʿAli. — Attempts to restore the caliphate, made since 1924 (com. pp. xciv), have been unsuccessful.

III. Modern History.

Turkish Domination after 1517.

The authority of the Osman sultans soon declined, and with it that of their governors. The Egyptian pashas were now obliged, before passing any new measure, to obtain the consent of the twenty-four Mameluke *Beys*, or princes, who governed the different provinces. These beys collected the taxes, commanded the militia, and merely paid tribute to the pasha.

1768 *ʿAli Bey*, originally a slave, raised himself to the dignity of sultan of Egypt. He conquered Syria, but was treacherously slain on the point of returning to Egypt, where his son-in-law *Muḥammed Bey Abu Dahab* (p. 62) had seized

1773 the throne. After Muḥammed's death the beys *Murâd* and *Ibrâhîm* shared the supremacy.

French Occupation.

1798, July 1st **Napoleon Bonaparte** arrived at Alexandria, hoping to destroy the British trade in the Mediterranean and, by occupying Egypt, to neutralize the power of England in India.

July 2nd Storming of Alexandria.

July 13th The Mameluke Bey Murâd defeated.

July 21st Battle of the Pyramids (p. 87).

Aug. 1st Destruction of the French fleet at Abuqîr by the British fleet commanded by Nelson (p. 32).

Sept. 13-25th Insurrection at Cairo quelled.

1799, Jan.-May Middle and Upper Egypt conquered (comp. p. 392).

July 25th Defeat of the Turks at Abuqîr (p. 32).

Aug. 24th Napoleon returned from Alexandria to France.

1800, March 20th Kléber defeated the Turks at Maṭarîya (p. 129).

June 14th Kléber assassinated at Cairo (p. 48).

1801, Sept. The French were compelled by a British army (comp. p. 32) to capitulate in Cairo (p. 48) and Alexandria, and to evacuate Egypt.

Muḥammed ʿAli and his Successors.

The retirement of the French was contemporary with the rise of the star of **Muḥammed ʿAli,** the ablest ruler that the East has produced for a long time. Born of Albanian parentage at Kavalla in Macedonia in 1769 (the year of Napoleon's

birth), he became a coffee-dealer in his native town. He was sent to Egypt in 1798 in the contingent from Kavalla and so distinguished himself in action against the French that *Khusraw Pasha*, the new governor, appointed him to the command of a corps of Albanians in the contests between the Turks and the Mamelukes. In this position Muḥammed adopted the policy of apparent impartiality, while he worked in secret for the destruction of both parties. When the Turkish governor was expelled Muḥammed ʿAli
1805 became pasha, with the approval of the Porte, and in 1805 he took possession of the citadel of Cairo (p. 48). The British meanwhile had occupied Alexandria and Rosetta, but Muḥammed, allying himself with the Mamelukes, inflicted two defeats upon them, in consequence of which the British fleet
1807 withdrew in the autumn of 1807. The pasha next disembarrassed himself of his allies by inviting the Mameluke beys to Cairo, where they, with their followers (480 in all), were treacherously massacred in the citadel by Muḥammed's Albanians, on March 1st, 1811 (p. 73; comp. p. 429).

1811 A campaign, begun in 1811 by Muḥammed on behalf of the Porte against the Wahhabis (p. xciv), who had taken possession of Arabia, was carried on successfully till 1816 by Muḥammed's son *Ṭûsûn*. Muḥammed's son (or adopted son) *Ibrâhîm Pasha* (b. 1789), a first-class general, then took over the command and after severe fighting completely crushed the resistance of the Wahhabis in 1819.

Muḥammed now turned his attention to military reforms. He employed his lawless Albanians in Nubia (p. 413) and the Sûdân (where his son Ismâʿîl perished, p. 449) and created a home army of fellahin, which showed its prowess in 1824-1827, under Ibrâhîm, in helping the sultan in the Greek war of independence, until the Turkish-Egyptian fleet was annihilated at the battle of Navarino by the united squad-
1827 rons of Russia, Britain, and France (1827).

To increase the strength and resources of Egypt Muḥammed energetically encouraged agricultural improvements and introduced various manufacturing industries (comp. p. lxvii). After the Russian victories over Turkey in 1828-29 he decided that the moment had come to free himself from the suzerainty of the Porte. At the beginning of 1832 Ibrâhîm invaded Syria and within a year he was master of Asia Minor, but the intervention of the European powers compelled Mu-
1833 ḥammed to conclude the peace of Kutâhiya or Konia in 1833, which was favourable to the Porte. Sultan Maḥmûd II.
1839 renewed hostilites in 1839 against Muḥammed ʿAli, who had extended his power over S.W. Arabia, but the Turkish army was decisively defeated on June 24th by Ibrâhîm at

Nisib, near Bîrejik, to the W. of the Euphrates, and on the death of the sultan (July 1st, 1839) Aḥmed Pasha, the Turkish high admiral, and the entire Turkish fleet declared for Muḥammed. The armed intervention of England and Austria, however, obliged Muḥammed to yield to the Porte a
1841 second time. By the so-called firman of investiture of 1841 the sultan assured the hereditary governorship (pashalic) of Egypt to the family of Muḥammed ʿAli, according to the Turkish law of succession (seniorate), and granted to the governor (wâli) the right of concluding non-political treaties and of appointing all Egyptian officials and officers up to the rank of colonel. In return the governor was required to pay to the Porte an annual tribute of 80,000 purses (318,930*l.*). During the last years of his life Muḥammed fell into a state of imbecility. He died on Aug. 2nd, 1849 (comp. p. 74).

1848 **Ibrâhîm** had already taken the reins of government, in consequence of Muḥammed's incapacity, in June 1848, but he died in November of the same year, before his father.

1849 **ʿAbbâs I.**, a son of Ṭûsûn (p. cxxvi), had a dislike for European innovations. He maintained, however, the strictest discipline among his officials.

1854 **Saʿîd** (b. 1823), his successor, was Muḥammed ʿAli's fourth son. He equalized the incidence of taxation, abolished monopolies, completed the railways from Cairo to Alexandria and to Suez, and supported the scheme for the Suez Canal (p. 195). During the Crimean war (1853-56) he was obliged to send troops and money to the aid of the Porte. He died in 1863 and was succeeded by —

1863 **Ismâʿîl** (b. 1830), second son of Ibrâhîm Pasha. Ismâʿîl had been educated in France and had acquired a preference for European institutions. Most of his innovations, however, such as factories, canals, railways, bridges, and telegraphs, were planned in his own interest, though the country shared in the advantage, while even in the setting up of schools, the reorganization of the system of justice (p. xxii), and the like, he acted rather with an eye to produce an impression in Europe than from concern for the needs of his subjects. He succeeded in appropriating for his own
1866 use about one-fifth of the cultivable land of Egypt. In 1866, in consideration of a sum of money, he obtained the sanction of the Porte to a new order of succession based on
1867 the law of primogeniture, and in 1867 he was raised to the rank of *Khedive*, or viceroy, having previously borne
1869 only the title of *Wâli*, or governor of a province. In 1869
1873 the Suez Canal was opened (p. 195). In 1873 the Khedive obtained a firman extending his privileges (indepen-

dence of administration and judiciaries; right of concluding treaties with foreign countries; right of coining and borrowing money; permission to increase his army to 30,000 men). The annual tribute payable to the Porte was fixed at 700,000*l.* The military successes of Ismâʿîl resulted in the extension of his dominions to the borders of Abyssinia and, on the S., to the 2nd parallel of N. latitude. — The burden of the public debt increased to 100,000,000*l.* The Powers brought such pressure to bear on the Khedive that in 1878 he was compelled to resign his private and family estates to the state and to accept a ministry under the presidency of Nûbâr Pasha (p. 17), with the portfolio of public works entrusted to E. de Blignières and that of finance to Sir Rivers Wilson. This coalition,
1879 however, proved unworkable; and early in 1879 the cabinet was replaced by a native ministry under Sherîf Pasha. The patience of the Great Powers was now at an end; and on the initiative of Germany they demanded from the Porte the deposition of Ismâʿîl, which took place on June 26th. He died at Constantinople in 1895.

1879 Ismâʿîl was succeeded by his son **Taufîq** (or in Turkish **Tewfîq,** b. 1852), under whom the government was carried on in a more rational spirit. The debts were regulated, an international commission of liquidation was appointed, and a scheme of reform was undertaken. On Sept. 8th,
1881 1881, however, a military revolution broke out in Cairo, which had for its object the emancipation of Egypt from European influences. The Khedive was besieged in his palace and had to yield; he appointed Sherîf prime minister and arranged for an election of notables, or representatives. As the latter espoused the nationalist cause ('Egypt for the
1882 Egyptians') Sherîf resigned in Feb. 1882, and Maḥmûd Pasha formed a new ministry, the soul of which was *ʿArâbi (ʿAurâbi) Bey*, the energetic minister of war. This cabinet proceeded, without the Khedive's consent, to pass measures intended to diminish European influence in the administration of the country. At the end of May the British and French fleets made their appearance before Alexandria. In the middle of June disturbances broke out in that town, in the course of which Europeans were killed. On July 11-12th Alexandria was bombarded by the British fleet, and on Sept. 13th the fortified camp of ʿArâbi at Tell el-Kebîr (p. 192) was stormed by a British force under Sir Garnet Wolseley. ʿArâbi and his associates were captured and sent to Ceylon. Since then British influence has been paramount in Egypt. ʿArâbi, who had been released and pensioned in 1901, died at Cairo in 1911.

1883 In 1883 Sir Evelyn Baring (afterwards *Earl of Cromer*) became British diplomatic agent and consul-general in Egypt. In his hands lay the control of British policy and he won distinction as one of the makers of modern Egypt. In the autumn a rebellion broke out among the Nubian tribes of the Sûdân under the leadership of Muḥammed Aḥmad, the so-called 'Mahdi' (p. xciii), which proved fatal to Egyptian supremacy in the Sûdân. An Egyptian force of 10,000 men under Hicks Pasha (William Hicks, 1830-83) was annihilated in Nov. 1883 by the Mahdi's forces (comp. p. 463), and a second expedition of less than 4000 gendarmes and conscripts, led by Baker Pasha (Valentine Baker, 1827-87), was likewise vanquished at Tokar (90 M. to the S.E. of
1884 Port Sudan) in Feb. 1884. On Feb. 18th, General Gordon, who had been Governor-General of the Sûdân in 1877-79, entered Kharṭûm, which he had undertaken to save from the Mahdi; while on Jan. 29th and March 13th the rebels under the Mahdi's lieutenant ʿOsmân Digna (d. 1926) were defeated at *Et-Teb* (78 M. to the S.E. of Port Sudan) and *Tamâï* (47 M. to the S. of Port Sudan) by the British under Sir Gerald Graham. The Mahdi himself, however, still maintained his position near Kharṭûm, and towards the close of the year a second British expedition (of 7000 men) was sent out under Wolseley to rescue Gordon (p. 446).

Wolseley selected the laborious Nile route in preference to the shorter but more dangerous desert route from Suâkin to Berber. An advanced brigade under Sir Herbert Stewart was, however, sent on from Kôrti (p. 446) at the beginning
1885 of 1885, which accomplished its march across the *Bayûḍa Desert* with complete success, gaining victories over the Mahdi's followers at *Abu Klea* (Jan. 17th) and at *Abu Khrûg*, near El-Metemma (Jan. 19th; p. 449). Stewart, however, was mortally wounded in the latter engagement. The British reached the Nile at *Gubat*, just above Metemma, on Jan. 19th, and on Jan. 24th a small body of men under Sir Charles Wilson set out for Kharṭûm in two steamers which Gordon had sent to meet them. Sir Charles reached Kharṭûm on the 28th, but found that it had already fallen on the 26th and that Gordon had perished (comp. p. 455).

The project of reconquering the Egyptian Sûdân from the Mahdists was temporarily abandoned, and Wâdi Ḥalfa remained the S. limit of the Khedive's dominions (p. xlviii). In 1885 the Mahdi died and was succeeded by the *Khalîfa ʿAbdullâhi* (pp. 458, 460). Suâkin (p. 453) became the base of desultory operations against ʿOsmân Digna (see above). — The British devoted their chief attention to improving the administration of Egypt. Negotiations on the

part of the Porte, instigated by France and Russia, to bring the British occupation of Egypt to a close, proved fruitless. A loan of 9,000,000*l.* was raised by the British for the pur-

1887 pose of regulating Egyptian finances. In 1887 a convention with France established the neutrality of the Suez Canal.

1892 The Khedive Taufîq died on Jan. 7th, 1892, and was succeeded by his eldest son **ʿAbbâs II. Ḥilmi** (b. 1874). His independence of action was controlled by the British diplomatic agent (see below).

1896 In the spring of 1896 an Anglo-Egyptian military force under Sir Herbert Kitchener (see below) commenced operations against the Mahdists to the S. of Wâdi Ḥalfa. On Sept. 2nd,

1898 1898, the army of the Khalîfa ʿAbdullâhi was defeated in a decisive engagement at Kerreri (p. 460), and Omdurmân, the Mahdist capital, on the left bank of the Nile, opposite Kharṭûm, was taken.

A small French expedition under Major Marchand which had occupied Fâshôda (Kodok, p. 464) on July 10th, aroused hostile feeling in Britain and, on Kitchener's appearance, was compelled to withdraw on Dec. 11th.

1899 By the Sûdân Convention of Jan. 19th the Anglo-Egyptian Sûdân was reunited to Egypt and placed under a British Governor-General (see p. 441).

In Egypt itself numerous reforms were accomplished by the British administration, and, in especial, much was done to further agriculture by light railways and irrigation.

1902 The Nile Dam at Aswân was opened (p. 396).

1904 Anglo-French understanding (April 8th) by which England promised not to alter conditions in Egypt, while France gave up all claim to set any period for evacuation. Growth of the nationalist and anti-British movement.

1907 Lord Cromer (d. 1917) succeeded as British diplomatic agent by *Sir Eldon Gorst*, who was succeeded in 1911 by —

1911 *Field-Marshal Viscount Kitchener of Khartoum*, who was given extended powers. [An earldom was conferred on Kitchener in June 1914. On Aug. 6th, 1914, he became British secretary-of-state for war; sailing for Russia on June 5th, 1916, he went down with H. M. S. Hampshire off the Orkneys.]

1914 Aug. 12th Egypt declared war on Germany and her allies. Alexandria became a British naval base. *General Sir John Maxwell* (1859-1929), commander-in-chief of the forces in Egypt,

Nov. 1st proclaimed martial law.

Nov. 12th Turkish declaration of war against the Allies.

Dec. 18th Great Britain declared Egypt to be a *British Protectorate*.

Dec. 19th Khedive ʿAbbâs II. Ḥilmi (see above) was deposed, his uncle **Ḥusein Kâmil** being proclaimed Sultan of Egypt. *Sir Henry MacMahon* was appointed *High Commissioner* for Egypt.

1915, Feb.	Repulse of the Turkish attacks on the *Suez Canal* (p. 197).
Nov.	Attacks of the *Senussi* (p. xcv) under Sheikh Sîdi Aḥmad Sherîf on the W. frontier of Egypt, Sollûm (p. 31) and the oases of Baḥarîya, Farâfra, and Dâkhla (p. 405 seqq.) being temporarily occupied by them. Hostilities in this quarter last till Feb. 1917.
1916 March 19th	Retirement of Sir John Maxwell, *General Sir Archibald Murray* becoming commander-in-chief of the Egyptian Expeditionary Force.
July, Aug., Dec.	Repulse of the second Turkish advance (p. 197). *General Sir Reginald Wingate* appointed High Commissioner.
1917, March	The British advance into Palestine began, supported by the Palestine Railway (p. 190), a pipe-line, and a wire road.
June 28th	*General Sir Edmund Allenby* (created a viscount in 1919) appointed commander-in-chief.
Oct. 9th	Death of the Sultan Ḥusein Kâmil, and accession of his brother **Aḥmad Fu'âd** (born March 26th, 1868) as sultan.
1918 Oct. 30th	Armistice with Turkey.
Nov. 11th	Armistice between the Allies and Germany.
Nov. 13th	The Nationalists, led by *Sa'd Zaghlûl Pasha* (a peasant's son from Muṭûbis in the Delta, p. 32, but by training a lawyer), requested the High Commissioner to afford facilities for the despatch of an Egyptian delegation (wafd) to London in order to negotiate concerning the Egyptian question.
1919 March End of May	The Nationalists demanded complete independence. Rioting broke out when Zaghlûl was deported to Malta. Allenby became 'Special High Commissioner' and restored order. Zaghlûl Pasha (see below) allowed to return to Egypt.
1922 Feb. 28th	On Allenby's advice the British government proclaimed the abolition of the protectorate and recognized independence of Egypt as a sovereign state.
March 15th	This step ratified by the British Parliament. Great Britain reserved four cardinal points for subsequent settlement: 1. Security of communications (i.e. Suez Canal) between the various parts of the British Empire; 2. Defence of Egypt against foreign attacks; 3. Protection of European interests; 4. The Sûdân question. — Sultan Aḥmad Fu'âd assumed the royal dignity as **King Fu'âd I.**
1923 April 19th	Proclamation of the constitution (dustûr) of the kingdom of Egypt as an hereditary constitutional monarchy.
Nov.	General election, resulting in a large majority of the 'Wafd' (comp. above), the Nationalist party of Zaghlûl Pasha.
Dec.	Zaghlûl prime minister. The parliamentary majority demanded the complete independence of Egypt, the withdrawal of British troops, and the return of the Sûdân. A new *National Flag* chosen (green with a white crescent and three stars).

1924 March 15th	Opening of the first Egyptian parliament (p. 55).
Nov. 19th	Assassination of Gen. Sir Lee Stack, Governor-General of the Sûdân, by Egyptian Nationalists at Cairo. The Egyptian detachments withdrawn from the Sûdân on British demand.
1925, Oct.	*Lord Lloyd* appointed High Commissioner.
1926, May	New victory of the Nationalists (Wafdists) at the elections.
1927, July	Visit of King Fu'âd I. to England. Conversations between *ʿAbd el-Khâliq Sarwat Pasha* (d. Sept. 1928), the prime minister, and Sir Austen Chamberlain regarding the draft of a treaty to regulate Anglo-Egyptian relations.
Aug. 23th	Death of Zaghlûl Pasha. *Muṣṭafa en-Naḥḥâs Pasha* chosen as his successor as leader of the Wafd.
1928, Feb.	The treaty offered by the British government as a result of the negotiations with Sarwat Pasha included the following terms: Egypt to join the League of Nations; the British troops to remain in Egypt for another ten years, after which a fresh agreement was to be made; Great Britain to be represented in Egypt by an ambassador, who was to take precedence in the diplomatic corps; the organization of the Egyptian army and the present administration of the Sûdân to remain unaltered, etc. The Wafdists, however, refused to accept the treaty; the Sarwat ministry
March	resigned (March 4th), and Muṣṭafa en-Naḥḥâs Pasha (see above) became prime minister (March 16th).
June 24th	Dismissal of Muṣṭafa en-Naḥḥâs Pasha's ministry. Muḥammed Maḥmûd Pasha appointed prime minister (June 27th).
July 19th	Parliament dissolved by royal decree and the Parliamentary régime suspended for three years.
1929 May 7th	Agreement between Great Britain and Egypt regarding the rights of Egypt and the Sûdân in the waters of the Nile and the regulation of irrigation works.

V. Hieroglyphics.

By *Professor Georg Steindorff.*

Repeated attempts were made in the 17th and 18th centuries to decipher the peculiar picture-writing of the ancient Egyptians, the Jesuit priest Athanasius Kircher (1601-80) being among the earliest to take up the subject. It was not, however, until the beginning of the 19th century that the key was found, though Silvestre de Sacy, a Frenchman, Åkerblad, a Swede, and Thomas Young, the English physicist (1773-1829), had previously attained a certain amount of success in their efforts. Jean François Champollion, a Frenchman, succeeded in 1822 in discovering the long-sought alphabet from a comparison of royal cartouches, and so found the clue to the principles of the Egyptian style of writing. Champollion afterwards followed up his initial discovery with such success that he may fairly rank as the real interpreter of the Egyptian hieroglyphics.

The first clue was afforded by the famous 'Rosetta Stone' (now in the British Museum), discovered in 1799 in the Fort St. Julien at Rosetta (p. 33). This tablet of basalt bears three inscriptions: one in the ancient Egyptian language, written in hieroglyphics, one in the popular language of a later period, inscribed in demotic characters, and a third in Greek, the two last being translations of the first. The subject of the triple inscription is a decree of the Egyptian priests issued in 196 B.C. in honour of Ptolemy V. Epiphanes. The first step towards deciphering the hieroglyphics was made when it was ascertained that the frequently occurring groups of signs each enclosed in an oval (so-called cartouche, p. cxxxvii) were the names of kings and that the name of Ptolemy must be found among them. — Comp. *Sir E. A. Wallis Budge's* 'The Rosetta Stone' (London, 1927).

Champollion and his successors established the phonetic signification of a large number of hieroglyphic characters, and it then became possible, from a knowledge of Coptic, the latest form of the ancient Egyptian language (comp. p. cxxxviii), not only to read but also to interpret the inscriptions. Heinrich Brugsch (1827-94), who led the way to the complete interpretation of demotic texts, was also the first to point out that in hieroglyphic writing, as in the Semitic systems of writing, only the consonants were inscribed, while the vowels were omitted as not essential.

The Egyptian hieroglyphics form a system of picture-writing, in which concrete objects were originally expressed by pictures representing them (i.e. by so-called *ideograms*); e.g.

'Face' *ḥr* 	'Eye' *yr-t* 
'Moon' *yʿḥ* 	'Sun' *rʿ* ⊙
'Swallow' *wr* 	'Plough' *hb'* 

Abstract ideas and verbs were represented on the same principle by the use of pictures of objects suggesting in some sort the idea to be expressed. Thus the idea 'to rule' *ḥq'* was expressed by the picture of a crook or sceptre , 'Upper Egypt' *šmʿ* by a plant ,

perhaps the sedge (comp. p. cii), regarded as the emblem of Upper Egypt, 'to write' *sẖ*, by a writing apparatus , etc.

A great advance was made when words, for which there was no special sign, began to be expressed by the pictures of other and different objects, the phonetic significance of which, however, happened to be the same. Thus *pry* 'to go out' was expressed by the picture of a house , because a 'house' also was called *pry*; *s'* 'son' by a 'goose' *s'*; *tp* 'first' by the sign *tp* 'dagger'. This phonetic transference was facilitated by the fact that it was only the consonantal skeleton to which the meaning of the word is attached.

Many of these characters gradually came to be used for so many different words that their original word-signification was lost, and they thenceforth were used merely as PHONETIC SIGNS for groups of consonants. Thus, the sign *p'*, originally 'to fly', was afterwards used for the combination *p'* in any signification; *wr*, originally 'swallow' and afterwards also *wr* 'great', was used for any combination of the two consonants *wr*. In this way word-signs also came to be used as letters; e.g. *r'* 'mouth' was used for *r*; *š* 'lake' for *š*; *dj-t* 'serpent' (*t* is the feminine termination) for *dj* (or *d*); etc. The letters of the alphabet, like the phonetic symbols for groups of consonants, were exclusively consonant-signs (comp. p. cxxxiii), although at a later period certain consonants were occasionally used to express vowels.

These phonetic signs were joined together to form whole words and were also used for grammatical purposes (as suffixes), but afterwards, owing to frequent ambiguities in the significance of the word-signs, they were used to indicate the pronunciation in each particular case and thus to render the reading easier. Thus to the sign *wr* 'great' a *r* was frequently added, written thus *wr*, in order to indicate the pronunciation; or *ʿnḫ* 'to live' was followed by the two explanatory consonants *n* and *ḫ*, thus *ʿnḫ*; or *nb* 'lord' was preceded by *n*, thus *nb*. Frequently all the consonants in a word were written instead of merely the word-sign, thus *śḫ-t* 'field' instead of *śḫ-t*.

In addition to these there was another class of hieroglyphics, known as DETERMINATIVES (p. cxxxvii), which were placed after the word in order to give some hint as to its meaning. Thus, *śwr*

with the sun-god under the name of *Amon-Rē* and was rescued from obscurity (comp. p. 280) as early as the period of the 12th Dyn. (p. civ), some of the kings of which named themselves after him (e.g. Amenemhēt, 'Amun is at the head', Greek Amenemmēs). At the beginning of the New Empire (p. cv), when Thebes (p. 270) became the capital instead of Memphis, Amun became the head of the Egyptian pantheon. The great campaigns against Nubia and Asia were waged in his name by the Theban kings, temples were erected to him in the conquered lands (comp. p. 412), and the lion's share of the spoil fell to his shrines in Egypt, especially to the temples at Thebes (pp. 270, 271). Under the 18th Dyn. Amun, in short, became the national god, the successful rival of his predecessor Horus (Rē-Harakhte). It was not to be expected that the priests of Heliopolis should tamely submit to this weakening of their influence. They therefore eagerly seized the first opportunity of overthrowing Amun and of restoring the sun-god to his former official dignity. When Amenophis IV. (p. cv) succeeded to the throne a special form of the sun-god of Heliopolis (Rē-Harakhte) regained the position of supreme deity, and shortly afterwards, in the sixth year of the king's reign, the sun itself (Egyptian *Aton*) was announced as the one and only god. This revolution was doubtless to some extent prompted by the king's desire to put a stop to the prevailing religious confusion at a blow, and to make practice square with theory, for theoretically all the numerous deities had long been explained as in reality one with the great sun-god (comp. p. 245). The representations and names of Amun and his fellow-gods were everywhere obliterated. But after the death of Amenophis and under the rule of Tutankhamûn (p. cvi) the partisans of Amun speedily regained the upper hand; the new religion was abolished and the earlier creed restored. The Egyptian religion remained in its former confusion; the process of amalgamating different gods became more and more common; and religious belief gradually lost all living reality. Men clung anxiously to the ancient traditions, and the superstitious belief in amulets and magic as the only protection against harmful influences gained universal sway. But no fresh religious conceptions are to be found in the innumerable texts inscribed upon the temples, tombs, and sarcophagi of the later period. After the decline of Thebes Amun began to lose his prestige, and his place was taken by the deities of the Delta, such as *Osiris* and his group (*Isis*, *Harpocrates*, and *Anubis*). Under the Ptolemies *Osorapis* (Sarapis, Serapis), i.e. the deceased Apis-bull identified with Osiris (comp. p. 158), became the national deity of Greek Egypt, and the worship of this god (an infernal deity, like the Pluto of the Greeks) gradually spread beyond Egypt to the East and subsequently also to the Roman empire. The old religion of Egypt was gradually vanquished only by the power of Christianity.

The Future Life. A considerable diversity of doctrine as to the

of particular gods. In the primitive period two independent kingdoms were formed in Upper and Lower Egypt (p. ci), and *Seth*, of Ombos (p. 233), and *Horus*, of Behdet (p. 34), the local deities of the two capitals, were recognized as guardians of the two states. After the temporary union of the two kingdoms had been operated from Lower Egypt and Heliopolis had become of pre-eminent importance (perhaps politically also; see below), Horus became recognized as the sole Royal God, and henceforth remained the patron of the Pharaohs and god of the empire. In the latest period of the primæval epoch Egypt was again divided into two kingdoms, the capitals being Nekhab-Nekhen (pp. 365, 369) and Buto (p. 34); the patron deity of the former was the vulture-goddess *Nekhbeyet*, of the latter the serpent-goddess *Buto*. These thus became the royal goddesses of Upper and Lower Egypt. In a similar way after the end of the Ancient Empire *Ptah*, the deity of the capital Memphis (p. 153), became one of the chief deities of Egypt. An important rôle in the religious history of Egypt has been played by the city of **On-Heliopolis** (p. 129), which was probably the religious centre of Egypt in the earliest period. The coronation ceremonies of the sovereign seem to have taken place in the temple of this city, and here, too, according to legend, the goddess *Seshet* inscribed the years of the reign on the leaves of the sacred tree. At On stood also the obelisk-like stone column of *Benben*, the chosen seat of the Sun-God. The local deity, strictly speaking, was, however, *Atum;* and the priests of On put this god on a par with the god of the sun and asserted that he was only another form, another name of Rē-Harakhte (p. cxlviii). This doctrine obtained a wide currency throughout the country and other local gods were promptly identified with Rē and invested with the symbol of Rē, viz. the sun-disk with the poisonous royal serpent (uræus, p. clxxxvi) coiled round it. Thus even the crocodile-god *Suchos* and *Amun*, the god of Karnak (see below), became sun-gods. This amalgamation of local deities with Rē, which began under the Middle Empire and was carried to great lengths under the New Empire, was a fertile source of confusion in the Egyptian religion. Attempts indeed were made to draw a distinction among the various forms of Rē, Harakhte for example being regarded as the morning sun and Atum as the evening sun, but nothing like a systematic scheme was ever achieved.

In the same way a number of Female Local Deities, especially when they were of a similar character, were welded into one. Thus *Hathor*, the goddess of the sky, was identified with *Isis;* the cat-goddess *Bastet* with the lion-goddesses *Sakhmet* and *Pekhet*, while Sakhmet was identified also with the vulture-goddess *Mut*.

When the centre of the empire was carried farther S. after the beginning of the New Empire, a new phase began in the development of the Egyptian religion. Amun, the god of Karnak, who was hardly known at all under the Ancient Empire, became identified

The Sun and the Moon, the principal heavenly bodies, were in particular the subject of many theories, probably representing the teachings of the different colleges of priests throughout the country (comp. p. 130). A very early idea represented the sun and moon as the eyes of the great god who created the world. At the same time this great god is no other than the sun-god Rē himself, so that we have the contradictory idea that the incorporation of the sun (Rē) had the sun as an eye. When Horus became a sun-god the sun and moon were considered to be his eyes. In one way or another the eye of the sun played a very important part in Egyptian mythology. It was thought of as a sun and was transformed into an independent goddess proceeding from the sun-god. With this eye of the sun are identified the serpent-goddess Buto, of Lower Egypt, and afterwards other goddesses also, such as the lion-headed Tefnut and the cow-goddess Hathor. The eye of the sun was sometimes thought of as a poisonous serpent (uræus serpent) rearing itself on the forehead of the sun-god and breathing fire against his enemies. This idea gave rise to the custom adopted by the kings of Egypt of wearing the uræus serpent as a diadem or as an ornament in their crowns (p. clxxxvi). — Another conception was that the sun-god Rē, in the guise of an Egyptian fisherman, sailed in a boat on the waters of the sky by day, and in the evening stepped into another boat and continued his voyage through the underworld. As the sun-god Rē-Harakhte was a falcon the sun was sometimes regarded as a brilliantly plumaged falcon soaring in the firmament; or like Horus the sun was a powerful young hero, waging a ceaseless combat with the hostile powers of darkness. It was conceived of also under the form of a *Scarabaeus* or beetle (p. clxxxvi); the sun-god was represented in the form of a scarabæus rolling the round disk of the sun in front of him, in the same way as a scarabæus rolls the small ball in which it has laid its egg. The scarabæus was more particularly held to be the morning or day sun, while the night sun, which journeys through the underworld, was represented as a ram-headed deity.

The Egyptians of course did not believe that the world, the gods, and human beings had always existed, but that they were created. The most widespread belief was that *Geb*, the god of the earth, and *Nut*, the goddess of the sky, lay in close union in *Nun*, the primæval ocean, until *Show*, the god of the air, separated them by raising Nut aloft in his arms. The sun-god *Rē* also was supposed to have arisen from Nun; another view, however, made him the child of Geb and Nut, new-born every morning. These ideas of course conflict with the other conception that Rē himself created the world.

In the course of its history the religion of Egypt underwent many transformations. The dominant position in the Egyptian pantheon shifted from one god to another, either through theological speculation and the growth of legends, or through the coming into prominence of royal houses and cities that were devoted to the cult

Osiris, which in antiquity also was one of the most widely spread. Osiris ruled as king over Egypt and the country enjoyed the blessings of prosperity. But *Seth*, his wicked brother, conspired against him, and at a banquet persuaded him to enter a cunningly wrought chest, which he and his seventy-two accomplices then closed and threw into the Nile. The river carried the chest down to the sea, and the waves at length washed it ashore near the Phœnician Byblos. Meanwhile *Isis* roamed in distress throughout the world, seeking her lost husband; and she at length succeeded in discovering his coffin, which she carried to Egypt and there mourned over her husband in solitude. She then buried the coffin before going to visit her son *Horus*, who was being brought up at Buto (p. 34). During her absence Seth, while engaged in a boar-hunt, found the body of his brother, cut it into fourteen pieces, and scattered them in every direction. As soon as Isis learned what had happened she sought for the fragments, and wherever one was found she buried it and erected a monument on the spot to its memory; and this accounts for the numerous tombs of Osiris mentioned as existing in Egypt and elsewhere (comp. pp. 258, 260, 395). When Horus grew up he set out to avenge his father's murder. and after terrible contests was at last victorious (comp. pp. 46, 369, 238). According to other accounts the combatants were separated by Thoth. They then divided the country, the S. of Egypt falling to Horus and the N. to Seth. Osiris was afterwards magically restored to life by Horus and continued to rule the W. land as king of the dead.

Among the Egyptians as with other peoples the SPECULATIONS ABOUT THE ORIGIN OF THE WORLD, the movements of the heavenly bodies, and the alternation of day and night took the form of myths. Their conception of the world reveals the limited geographical horizon of the ancient Egyptians. They regarded the earth as a huge oval plain, floating upon the ocean. From one end to the other it was traversed by a broad stream, the Nile, which flows out of the ocean on the S. or rises from two springs near the cataracts of Aswân (comp. pp. 364, 395). All around rose high mountains, and the sky was pictured as a flat slab resting upon four mountains, with the stars hanging from it like lamps. Another view was that the sky had the same form as the earth, and was traversed by a river and intersected by numerous canals; and under the earth there was believed to be an underworld, called *Dēt (Duat)*, which was exactly like heaven and, according to a later conception, was peopled by the dead. After the cow-goddess Hathor had become a goddess of the heavens (see p. cxlviii) the sky was sometimes conceived of as a cow, with the sun seated between its horns illuminating the world. Another view was that the sun sailed in a boat by day on the cow, as on the ocean of the sky, while the stars were represented on the body of the cow; Show, the god of the air, stood below the cow of the heavens and supported it.

of Memphis (p. 154) was the patron of artists, metal-workers, and smiths, and was thus the Egyptian Hephæstos; the powerful *Sakhmet* (p. clviii) of Memphis became a terrible war-goddess, who annihilated the enemy, while on the other hand stress was laid on the more attractive attributes of *Hathor* of Dendera (p. 261), who was worshipped as the goddess of love and joy (resembling Aphrodite). Many local deities were connected with the moon and the sun and other cosmic powers (comp. p. cxlvii). Thus *Thoth* of Hermupolis (p. 221) was regarded as a moon-god, who had created the times of day and the cosmic universe; he was the inventor of hieroglyphic writing and therefore the patron deity of scribes and scholars. Above all *Horus* was transformed into a god of the heavens in connection with the sun and received the name of *Rē-Harakhte*, i.e. 'the sun, the Horus who dwells on the horizon'. The cow-goddess *Hathor* (whose name means 'House of Horus') became a goddess of the heavens. Many local deities came to be worshipped all over the country under these particular characteristics.

Finally there was also a considerable number of LESSER DEITIES, dæmons, and spirits, who could help or harm human beings at particular junctures, and who therefore must be propitiated. Among these rank, for example, the different *Goddesses of Childbirth*, who assisted women and could either cut short or protract their pangs; the grotesque god *Bes*, the protector of the marriage chamber and of women in childbirth; *Heket*, the frog-goddess of childbirth; various *Goddesses of the Harvest*, etc. At a later period unusually distinguished mortals, revered after death as saints, gradually came to be included among the gods, as *Imhotep* of Memphis, physician and architect to King Djoser (p. cii), *Amenhotep*, the learned son of Hapu (18th Dyn.), etc.

Like human beings the god frequently had a wife and a son, and in that case this so-called *Triad* dwelt and was worshipped in one temple. Divine families of this kind are exemplified in *Ptah*, with his wife *Sakhmet* and his son *Nefertēm*, and by *Osiris*, *Isis*, and *Horus*. The theologians of the holy city of On (Heliopolis, p. 130) even created a ninefold group *(Ennead)* of gods, at the head of which stood *Atum*, the local deity of the city (comp. p. cli). Atum was attended by the four cosmogonic deities *Show*, his wife *Tefnut*, *Geb*, and *Nut* (p. cxlvii). The number nine was made up by *Osiris*, his wife *Isis*, *Seth* (the ancient god of Upper Egypt and the legendary antagonist of Osiris; see p. cxlix), and his wife *Nephthys*. The worship of the nine gods became so popular that it was adopted in many different localities, the place of Atum being taken by the chief local god in each.

Human passions and virtues were attributed to the gods; and numerous tales were told by the faithful of the divine exploits and adventures. Unfortunately most of these myths have perished; of the few that have come down to us the best known is the story of

selves certain animals were regarded as sacred to the gods, e.g. the lion of Cybele, the owl of Athena, and the eagle of Zeus.

Anthropomorphism. A stage beyond fetishism was reached when the Egyptians, in the beginning of the historical period, began to form an anthropomorphic conception of their deities. The gods had human faces and forms and wore clothing such as the Egyptians themselves wore. Like princes, they wore on their heads helmets or crowns, and, like the primæval rulers, they had tails fastened to the back of their aprons. They bore the sceptre or the commander's baton as the symbol of their might. The deities that were conceived of as animals now received human figures, but the gods, although figured as men, retained the heads of the animals in which they revealed themselves. Thus *Suchos* appears as a man with a crocodile's head, *Khnum* with a ram's head, *Thoth* with an ibis's head, *Horus* with a falcon's head. The various *Cow Goddesses* have a human head with cow's horns, while over the vulture-goddess *Mut* (worshipped in Thebes, p. 272) a vulture spreads its wings, and the head of *Neith* of Saïs was adorned with a bundle of arrows, which was the form in which she was worshipped (comp. p. cxlvi). Though such a device cannot but appear strange to us as it did to the Greeks, it must be confessed that the Egyptian artists in their reliefs and statues of those animal-headed deities managed the transition from the animal's head to the human body with remarkable skill.

Besides the local deities, whose spheres of influence were limited to particular districts, there were even in the earliest times a certain number of universal deities, who were revered by the whole nation. Among these were the god *Geb* (earth), the goddess *Nut* (sky), the god *Show* (air), the goddess *Tefnut* (dew), the sun-god *Rē*, a masculine deity with the Egyptians as with the Greeks (Helios), *Osiris* (vegetation), *Hapi* (the Nile), and *Nun* (ocean). Among the stars *Orion* and *Sothis* (Sirius or the Dog Star, a female deity) played the leading rôles. These revealed themselves only in natural phenomena; they were therefore not confined to any particular place of worship, but were everywhere revered. Even in early times, however, these forces of nature were frequently assimilated to local deities. The great gods of heaven received human forms and special places of worship. Thus the sun-god *Rē*, through his relations with Atum, came to be specially worshipped at Heliopolis (p. 130), and the divine couple *Show* and *Tefnut* as lion-headed deities at Leontopolis (p. 181).

Already at an early period the religious conceptions regarding many of the gods were deepened or expanded, as certain characteristics became especially emphasized. Thus the falcon-headed *Mont*, the local god of Hermonthis (p. 356), was a war-god; the god *Min* of Koptos (p. 232), where the desert road across the mountains from the Red Sea joins the valley of the Nile, became the patron deity of travellers in the desert, then also a god of fertility and the harvest (comp. p. 230), whence the Greeks identified him with Pan; *Ptah*

Sethy (Seti. Sethos) II. 19.

Ramses III. 20.

Sheshonk (Sesonchis) I. 22.

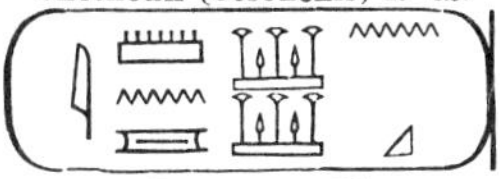

Osorkon I. 22.

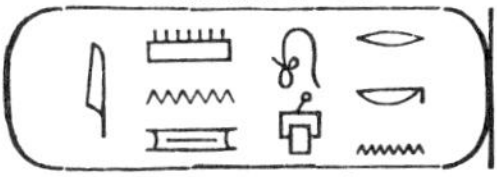

Takelothis I. 22.

Bekenranf (Bocchoris). 24.

Shabako (Sabakon). 25.

Taharka (Tirhakah). 25.

Princess Amenerdaïs.

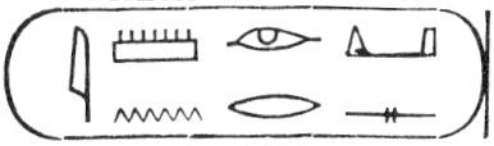

Piankhi.

Psametik (Psammetichos) I. 26.

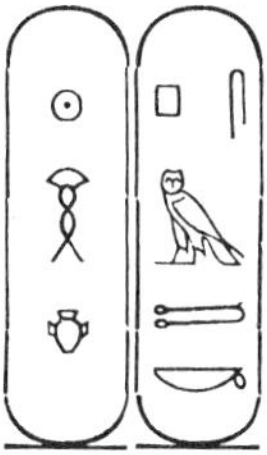

Nekaw (Necho). 26.

Psametik (Psammetichos) II. 26.

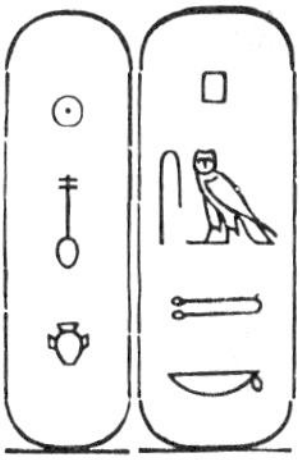

Weh-eb-rē (Apries. Uaphris. Hophrah). 26.

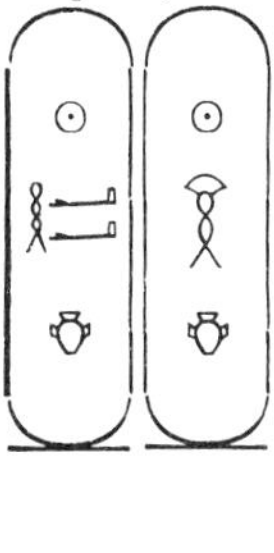

Ahmose II. (Amasis). 26.

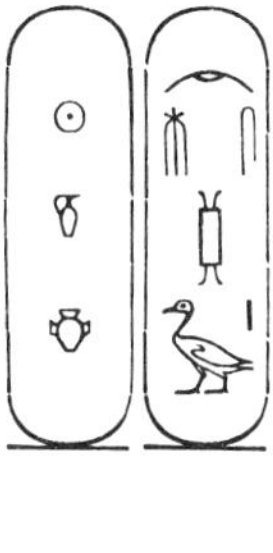

Kambitjet (Cambyses). 27.

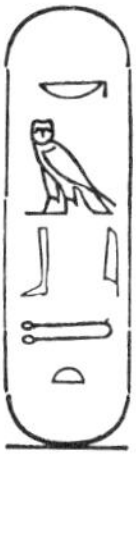

Entaryush (Darius). 27.

Kheshyeresh (Xerxes). 27.

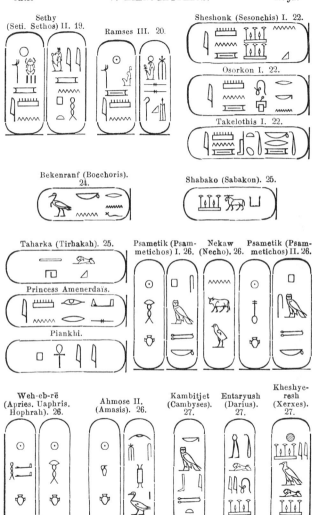

Ahmose (Amosis). 17.

Amenhotep (Amenophis) I. 17.

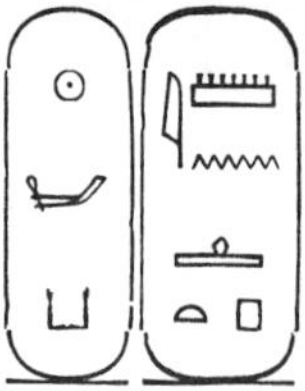

Dhutmose (Thutmosis) I. 18.

Kemarē-Hatshepsut. 18.

Thutmosis II. 18.

Thutmosis III. 18.

Amenophis II. 18.

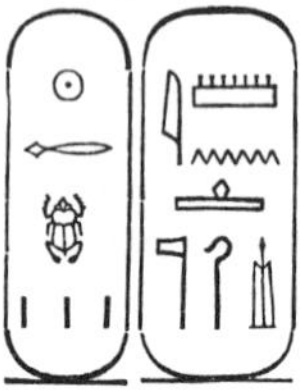

Thutmosis IV. 18.

Amenophis III. 18.

Amenophis IV. (Akhenaten. Ekh-n-Aton). 18.

Tutankhamûn. 18.

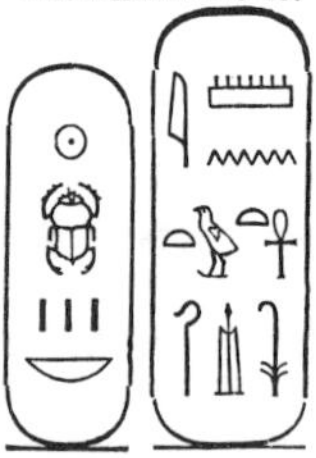

Haremhab (Harmaïs). 19.

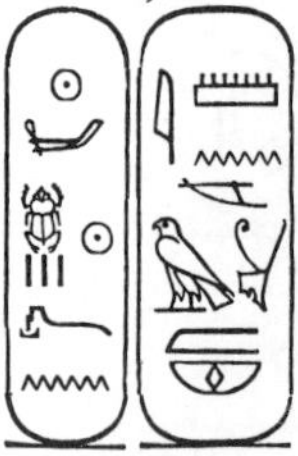

Ramses I. 19.

Sethy (Seti. Sethos) I. 19.

Ramses II. 19.

Merneptah (Menephthes). 19.

4. Frequently Recurring Cartouches of Egyptian Kings.

The Arabic numbers placed after the names are those of the different dynasties. Where two cartouches are given the first contains the official cognomen assumed by the king on his accession, while the second is his individual or birth name.

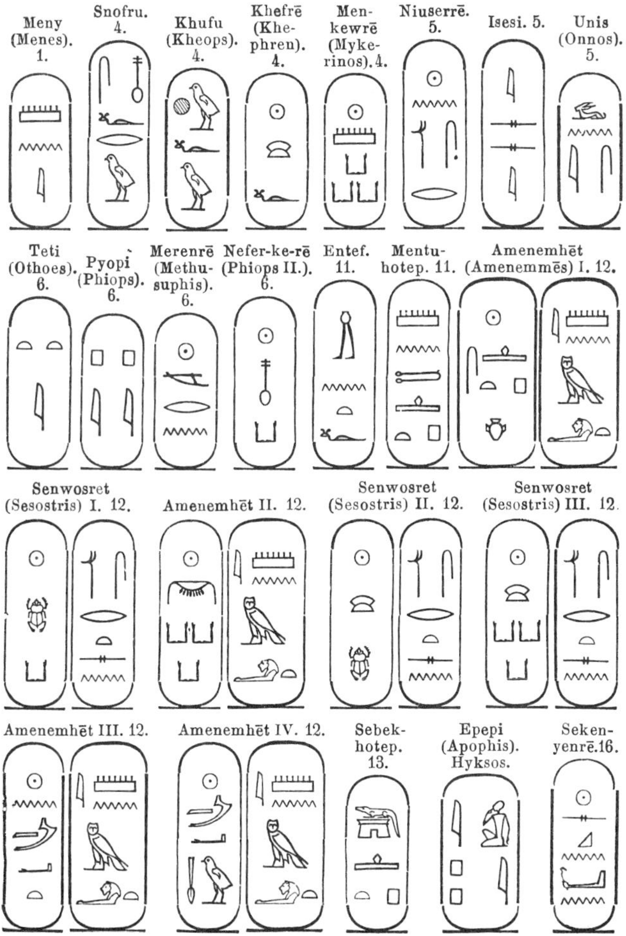

in the post-Christian era (comp. p. 413), now also successfully deciphered by Prof. F. L. Griffith of Oxford University, but with its meaning still lost to us.

The following hints will be of service to those who may try to decipher any of the kings' names with the aid of the foregoing lists, consulting first the list of phonetic signs, then that of the word-signs. The Egyptian kings frequently had several names, the two most important of which, viz. the official name and the individual name, are enclosed within the cartouche (p. cxxxvii). The official name is preceded by the title  *n-św bit*, 'King of Upper and Lower Egypt', and frequently also by  *neb te'wy*, 'lord of both lands' (p. cii), or  *neb ḫe'w*, 'lord of the diadems'. The title  *s' Rʿ (se' Rēʿ)*, 'son of the sun', is a regular addition to the individual or birth name after the Middle Empire (p. ciii). Thutmosis III., for example, a king of the 18th Dyn., was named —

The former is his official name, assumed at his accession to the throne, the latter his individual name. ⊙ is the original word-sign (a 1 on p. cxxxvi) *rʿ*, 'sun, sun-god Rē';  is the biliteral sign (b 1 on p. cxxxv) *mn*, here, however, standing for 'to remain';  is the transferred word-sign (b 22) *ḫpr*, 'to become, to be'. The first name therefore is *Rʿ-mn-ḫpr*, or, rather, as the words signifying god or king are written first out of reverence, *mn-ḫpr-Rʿ*, 'remaining in being (existence) is Rē' (vocalized *Men-ḫeper-Rēʿ*, Greek *Mesphrēs*). In the second cartouche  is the original word-sign (a 10) *Dḥwty*, 'the god Thoth';  is the biliteral sign (b 5) *mś*; and  the letter *s* (a 16 on p. cxxxv), added to show the sound of *mś*. The whole is thus *Dḥwty-mś* (i.e. 'the god Thoth has created'), corresponding to the Greek *Thutmosis*, and probably to be vocalized *Dhut-mose*.

It may here be remarked that the Egyptian names occurring in this handbook are usually written in the traditional Greek form and not in the native Egyptian; e.g. *Sethos* instead of *Sṯhy*, *Kheops* instead of *Khwfw*. For names, however, of which the Egyptian forms are more familiar, or of which there are no known Greek transliterations, the Egyptian forms have been retained, with vowels inserted on the principles explained above. In these cases, however, the diacritical signs are omitted, so that no difference is made between *k* and *q (ḳ)*, *h* and *ḥ*; *w* is sometimes represented by *u* and *y* by *i* (especially at the end of a word); *ẖ* and *ḫ* by *kh*; *ś* by *s*. The apostrophes ' and ʿ are uniformly omitted. In short, the general rules already adopted by the Greeks for the transliteration of Egyptian words are followed.

of Deir el-Baḥari, p. 317) and from the small crowded hieroglyphics of the Ptolemaic period.

When the picture characters instead of being carved by the chisel were written with a reed-pen upon papyrus, fragments of limestone, potsherds, or wooden tablets, they generally assumed a simpler and more rounded form. In this way arose a system of *Cursive Hieroglyphics*, which we meet with mainly in carefully executed religious manuscripts.

For the purposes of ordinary writings this system was still further simplified and abbreviated and for the sake of speed the separate characters were often united, thus forming a still more *Cursive Style*, which is usually termed *Hieratic Writing*. In this style the owl 𓅓 *m*, which in cursive hieroglyphics (written from right to left) had the form , degenerates into , an outline scarcely recognizable as that of an owl. In hieratic writing we possess literary works of almost every kind. — Further abbreviations and amalgamations of letters developed another cursive style from the hieratic, viz. the *Enchorial* or *Demotic*, which was the ordinary character employed in the chanceries of the Græco-Roman period. The sign of the owl, for example, was curtailed to . This writing was chiefly used for contracts, accounts, letters, and similar documents, and it was sometimes termed the *Epistolographic*, or 'epistolary character', by the Greeks.

During the second century after Christ Egyptian magical formulæ were frequently written in Greek characters; and after the introduction of Christianity it became the universal custom to write the Egyptian translations of the Scriptures in the simpler Greek letters instead of in the inconvenient hieroglyphics, which were at the same time more difficult to learn. But as the Greek alphabet was not adequate to represent all the Egyptian sounds (e.g. *sh*, *f*, *kh*, etc.) seven supplementary characters (ϣ *sh*, ϥ *f*, ϧ *kh*, ϩ *h*, ϭ *č*, *tsh*, ϫ *ž*, *dj*, and the syllabic ϯ *ti*) were borrowed from the demotic. Thus arose the *Coptic Writing* of the Egyptian Christians (pp. lvi, lix).

The use of hieroglyphics extended beyond the borders of Egypt, especially into Nubia, where they were employed in the temples built by the Pharaohs (comp. p. 412). And even after the Nubian-Ethiopian kingdom became independent of Egypt, hieroglyphics still continued to be used there. At first, however, only inscriptions in the Egyptian language were thus written; some time elapsed before hieroglyphics were adapted to the native language. In the course of this adaptation various formal modifications took place, resulting in a *Meroïtic Hieroglyphic System*, the bulk of which it is now possible to read although still an unknown language. A *Meroïtic Cursive Style* also, probably based on the demotic, was developed

9. *śtp* (orig. 'axe'), to choose.

10. *b'* (orig. 'ram'), soul.

11. *ḥtp* (orig. 'mat and loaf'), to be content.

12. *mr* (orig. 'lake'), to love.

13. *ywn* (originally 'column'), On (Heliopolis, pp. 129, 130).

14. *nṯr*, *ntr* (orig. 'cloth wound on a pole'), god.

15. *ś-t* (orig. 'seat'), Isis.

16. *'ḫ* (orig. 'bird'), spirit, brilliant.

17. *Nr-t* (orig. 'two bows tied in a package'), the goddess Neith.

18. *w'ḥ* (orig. 'a swab'), to add to.

19. *'nḫ* (orig. 'sandal-strap'), to live.

20. *rwḏ* (orig. 'bow-string'), to grow.

21. *nb* (orig. 'chain'), gold.

22. *ḫpr* (orig. 'beetle', p. clxxxvi), to become, be, exist.

3. Determinatives (p. cxxxiv).

E.g. man; woman; tree; house; town; abstract idea. To this class belong also the sign of the plural ||| (|) and the oval ring (the so-called 'cartouche') placed round the names of kings.

These various classes of signs, which were used in accordance with certain fixed rules of orthography, were employed in writing Egyptian words; e.g. *mn*, 'to remain' (phonetic biliteral sign *mn*, alphabetic sign *n* as phonetic complement, determinative for an abstract idea); *sp*, 'occasion, time' (*s*, *p*, word-sign *sp*). We cannot, of course, pronounce these words that are written without vowels; but in many instances, by the aid of Coptic (p. cxxxviii) or of cuneiform or Greek transliterations (especially in the case of proper names), we learn what was the pronunciation at later periods, and are thus able to supply vowels to the consonantal skeletons. We know, e.g., that the Coptic *mun* means 'to remain' and we therefore read the Egyptian *mn* as *mun;* in the same way we read *sp* as *sop*, the Coptic word for 'time' being *sop*. When, however, no such guide is obtainable it is the custom of Egyptologists to render the words articulate by inserting an *e*; thus *k'*, 'bull', is read *ke'*.

Hieroglyphics are usually written from right to left, sometimes in perpendicular rows, sometimes in horizontal rows; occasionally, but quite exceptionally, they are written from left to right. Modern reproductions of hieroglyphics, however, are written or printed from left to right. It was almost a matter of course that both the shapes of the hieroglyphics and the orthography of the words should vary very greatly in the course of the thousands of years during which the system was used; and with a little trouble the traveller will soon learn to distinguish the simple and bold characters of the Ancient Empire from the ornate symbols of the 18th Dyn. (e.g. in the temple

6. ʿʾ.
7. *mr*.
8. *św*.
9. *wp*.
10. *tʾ*.
11. *śʾ*.
12. *bʾ*.
13. *śn*.
14. *mʾ*.
15. *ḥm*.
16. *rw*.
17. *wʾ*.
18. *śʾ*.
19. *my*.
20. *św*.
21. *nw*.
22. *wn*.
23. *yr*.
24. *tm*.

2. Word Signs.

a. In their original signification.

1. *rʿ*, Sun, the sun-god Rē.
2. *ḥʾ-t*, fore-part; front.
3. *yʿḥ*, moon.
4. *Mʾʿt*, the goddess **Mʾʿ-t** ***(Maat)***.
5. *Śtẖ*, the god Seth.
6. *Rʿ*, the sun-god Rē.
7. *Ymn* (*ʾmn*), the god Amun.
8. *Ptḥ*, the god Ptah.
9. *Ḥr*, the god Horus.
10. *Dḥwty*, the god Thoth
11. *Śbk*, the crocodile-god Sobk (Suchos).
12. *ḥqʾ*, to rule; prince.
13. *yb*, heart.
14. *kʾ*, bull.
15. *nḫt*, to be strong.
16. *ḫw*, to reign.
17. *śbʾ*, star.

b. In their derived signification.

1. *wʾś* (originally 'sceptre'), welfare.
2. *ḏd* (*dd*) (orig. 'sacred pillar of Osiris), to be enduring.
3. *ḥm* (orig. 'hammer'), majesty.
4. *pḥ-ty* (orig. 'chessman'), strength.
5. *ḥb* (orig. 'basket'), festival.
6. *ḏśr* (*djśr*; orig. 'arm with hand holding a wand'), splendid.
7. *sʾ* (orig. 'goose'), son.
8. *whm* (orig. 'leg of an animal'), to repeat.

(sowr) 'to drink' is written, with the determinative (a man with his finger in his mouth) in order to indicate that the idea expressed by *śwr (sowr)* has something to do with the mouth. These determinatives, which greatly facilitate the reading of inscriptions, were freely used, especially in later hieroglyphic periods.

The hieroglyphic system, as we find it in the earlier Egyptian inscriptions, is already complete; its development, briefly sketched above, had already come to a close. The following different classes of hieroglyphic characters were used simultaneously.

1. Phonetic Signs.

a. *Alphabetic Signs* or *Letters*.

1. (corresponds to the Arabic *Elif*, p. xxx).
2. consonantal *y* (in many cases in later inscriptions this sound disappears and is replaced by a simple breathing like ').
3. ʿ (a guttural breathing, unknown in English, corresponding to the Arabic *ʿAin*, p. xxx).
4. *w* (as in 'well'), *u*.
5. *b*.
6. *p*.
7. *f*.
8. *m*.
9. *n*.
10. *r*.
11. *h*.
12. *ḥ* (an emphasized h-sound, like the Arabic *Ḥâ*, p. xxx).
13. *ḫ* (*kh*, as 'ch' in the Scottish 'loch').
14. *ẖ* (*kh*, perhaps like the German 'ch' in 'ich'.
15. *s* (more correctly *z*, a soft *s*).
16. *ś* (emphatic s).
17. , better , , *š (sh)*
18. *q* (*ḳ*, a sharp k-sound, pronounced at the back of the throat, corresponding to the Arabic *Qâf*, p. xxx).
19. *k*.
20. hard *g*.
21. *t*.
22. *ṯ* (*tj*, a rather indefinite t-sound) and sometimes *t* (in consequence of an ancient change of pronunciation).
23. *d* (also *ṭ*, a clear, sharp t-sound, like the Arabic *Ṭâ*).
24. *ḏ* (*dj*), sometimes *d* (in consequence of an ancient change in pronunciation).

Several other alphabetic signs were afterwards added; *e.g.* *y*, *y*, *w*, *m*, *n*, etc. For the vowels, comp. p. cxxxiii.

b. *Biliteral Signs*, of which (as of the word-signs, p. cxxxvi) we mention only the most important, especially those which occur in the list of kings (p. cxl seqq.).

1. *mn*.
2. *ḫʿ*.
3. *kʾ*.
4. *nb*.
5. *mb*.

fate of man after death prevailed amongst the Egyptians, and the various views were never reduced to a single authoritative creed. The only point that was common to the whole people was the firm conviction that the life of man did not end at death, but that on the contrary men continued to live just as they had lived upon earth, provided that the necessaries of existence were assured to them. It thus seemed specially necessary that the body should be carefully interred and protected from decay. The next step was to build a house for the deceased, after the pattern of his earthly abode, in which he might dwell, and which, according to the popular belief, he could quit at pleasure during the day. Statues, erected in a special room for the purpose, represented the owner of the house, his family, and his domestics (p. clxxvi). Sacrificial offerings provided the deceased with food, and pious endowments ensured him against hunger and thirst even in the distant future. Nor was this all; representations of food, utensils, etc., were painted or carved upon the walls of the tomb or the sides of the sarcophagus, and it was believed that through magic these representations could serve the deceased in place of the real things. Ornaments, clothing, etc., were likewise placed in the tomb or depicted on the walls for the same purpose. The occupations that engrossed the deceased while on earth, the pleasures that he delighted in, the dignities that he enjoyed, awaited him beyond the tomb, and these too were represented on the walls in order that he might really possess them. To this belief we owe those sepulchral paintings that give us so exact a picture of the life of the ancient Egyptians. In the earliest times the grandees alone were allowed to build themselves tombs. Those who were not attached to the court had to content themselves with simple graves. But at a later period even the ordinary citizens built 'everlasting houses' for themselves, at least so far as they possessed the means to do so.

The dead were under the protection of the local deities, whose duty it was to superintend the funeral ceremonies and afford security in the tomb. There was also in many towns a special God of the Dead, named *Khenti-Amentiu*, 'the first of the inhabitants of the Western Kingdom' (i.e. of the dead; p. 252), who was represented in the form of a dog. At a later date these local gods retired in favour of *Osiris*. Owing to the well-known myth attaching to his name (see p. cxlix) this ancient god of vegetation was gradually recognized as the ruler of the dead by all Egypt, and dominion over the departed was assigned to him almost exclusively. Abydos became the chief religious centre of his cult (pp. 252, 260). The death which, according to the legend, Osiris suffered was the common lot of mortals; but just as Osiris rose again, so a man also could begin a new life, provided that the same formulæ were pronounced for him by some faithful son; he went to Osiris, became united with the slain god, in fact was himself Osiris. Admission to the realm of

Osiris depended upon the recitation of magical formulæ and incantations, a knowledge of which must be communicated to the deceased. A virtuous earthly life was required to assure the deceased eternal happiness, and he had therefore to undergo a trial before Osiris and to prove before forty-two judges that he was free from mortal sin. Before this, and before his heart had been weighed by Thoth in the scales of righteousness and found perfect, he might not enter the future land.

Opinions differed as to the Abode of the Blessed Dead. Their dwelling was usually located in the West, among the mountains, and in the desert where the sun set. The conception expressed in the Pyramid Texts (p. 136) placed the land of the dead near the circumpolar stars, in the N. part of the heavens; there, too, the king's journeyings through the heavens usually came to an end. Some believed that they inhabited the heavenly fields of *Earu*, a fruitful country where ploughing and reaping were carried on as upon earth, and where the corn grew seven ells high, forming a veritable paradise for the Egyptian peasant. As the labour in this future land might often be too great for the strength of the deceased, it became the custom at the period of the Middle Empire to place funerary statuettes, the so-called *Ushebtis* (*Ushabtis*, *Shabtis*) in the tomb along with him. These little figures of men were imbued with life by a magic spell written upon them and assisted the deceased when he was called to work beyond the tomb. Another doctrine sought to unite the different conceptions of the future life and placed the abodes of the blessed in *Dēt*, the underworld (see p. cxlix). This was divided into twelve parts, corresponding to the twelve hours of night, and, according to a certain view, separated from each other by massive gates (comp. pp. 301 seqq.).

In flat contradiction to these doctrines was the popular belief that man possessed not only a body but also a soul (*baï*), which lived after death. This was originally conceived of as a bird; at a later period as a bird with a human head. It was believed that the soul left the body at death and flew freely about, but could return to the body at pleasure, provided, of course, that the latter did not decay. Thus from ancient times everything was done in Egypt to prevent the destruction of the body, and so to enable the soul to recognize its mortal tenement. A certain place in the belief of the ancient Egyptians was taken also by the *Ka*, personification of vitality, provider of nourishment, and thus a kind of guardian spirit or genius, which was born with the individual and accompanied him through life. The Ka did not expire with its protégé but continued to live in order to preserve the vitality of the deceased in the future world.

In the earliest period the dead were buried in a crouching posture with their knees drawn up and lying on their left side. In the Ancient Empire, under the influence of the Osiris doctrine, the custom

of leaving the corpse at full length began to be followed, probably at first in the case of the kings. At the same time EMBALMING was attempted. The bodies were treated with saline solutions and bitumen and rolled in linen bandages and wrappings. The process of preparing the mummy was more elaborate at later times. The brains were first removed through the nostrils by means of an iron hook; the stomach was then opened with a flint knife and the viscera removed (Herodotus ii. 86) and placed in four jars, known as *Canopi*. In later times these were closed with lids, bearing the heads of the four sons of Osiris (comp. Emset, p. cli), to whose protection the intestines were committed. The heart also was removed from the body, and was replaced by a stone scarabæus (p. clxxxvi), laid upon the breast of the deceased, beneath the wrappings. Herodotus states that at a later period there were three methods of embalming, differing according to the expense involved. So much care was given to the preservation of the corpses that to this day the features of many of the mummies may be clearly made out (comp. pp. 99 seqq.).

Comp. 'The Mummy: A Handbook of Egyptian Funerary Archæology', by *Sir E. A. Wallis Budge* (Cambridge 1893, 2nd ed. 1925); 'Egyptian Mummies', by *G. Elliot Smith* and *Warren R. Dawson* (London, 1924).

List of the Chief Egyptian Deities and Sacred Animals.

AMUN, AMON, or AMMON (Fig. 1), specially worshipped at Thebes, was made a sun-god under the name ***Amon-Rē*** and became the national god under the New Empire. For his persecution by Amenophis IV., see p. clii. His sacred animal was the ram. Amun was related to the oasis-god (Zeus or Jupiter) Ammon, whose special shrine was at the Ammon Oasis of Sîwa (p. 403), named after him.

AMSET, see Emset.

ANTÆUS or ANTAIOS, the Greek name for a strange Egyptian god, worshipped at Antæopolis (p. 238).

ANUBIS (Fig. 2), local god of Kaïs (p. 219) and the special god of the 12th, 17th, and 18th Nomes of Upper Egypt; a primæval god of the dead, whose function later on was connected with the interment. A still later myth makes him a brother of Osiris. The dog (or jackal?) was sacred to him.

ANUKET (Greek *Anukis*), goddess of the district of the Cataracts (island of Siheil, p. 389).

APIS, the sacred bull of Memphis. For his distinctive markings, see p. cxlvi. The apis was buried in the Serapeum (p. 158).

ATUM (Fig. 3), the local deity of Heliopolis (p. 130), Pithom (p. 192), etc., was afterwards regarded as a sun-god (specifically the evening sun; p. cli). His sacred animals were the lion, serpent, and ichneumon.

BASTET, the goddess of Bubastis (p. 181), a goddess of joy. Sacred animal, the cat.

Bes, a popular deity, represented as a dwarf, introduced from the land of Punt (p. 233). He was the god of matrimony and also had influence over births.

Buchis, the sacred bull of Hermonthis and Medamût (pp. 356, 297).

Buto, see *Utō*.

Dedun, guardian deity of Nubia (pp. 412, 440).

Dwe-metf, one of the four guardian deities of the dead; see *Emset*.

Eme-wet, a god of the dead, represented, like Anubis, with a dog's head. His symbol was a post with a skin hanging on it .

Emset, one of the four sons of Osiris and guardian deities of the dead, who protected them from hunger and thirst, and to whom therefore the viscera of the deceased were dedicated. He was represented with a human head. The other three guardians were *Hapi*, *Dwe-metf*, and *Kebeh-senuf*.

Enhuret (Greek *Onuris*; p. cxlv), the god of This (p. 231) and Sebennytos (p. 185).

Epet, a popular goddess of childbirth. In Thebes, where she was revered as the mother of Osiris (p. 279), she was represented as a pregnant hippopotamus. See also *Toëris*.

Eri-hems-nufer ('the good companion'; Greek *Harensnuphis*), another name for Show, under which he was worshipped on the islands of Bigga and Philæ (pp. 395, 390).

Ews-os, goddess of Heliopolis, the consort of Harakhte (see below).

Geb or Keb, the earth-god, husband of Nut (pp. cxlvii, cl).

Hapi, a name given to the Nile and the Nile-god (p. 364).

Hapi, one of the guardian deities of the dead. See *Emset*.

Harakhte ('Horus of the horizon'; Fig. 4), a special form of Horus (p. cxlviii). He was the god of Heliopolis (p. 130). The falcon was sacred to him.

Harendotes (Fig. 5; Egyptian *Har-nedj-yotf*), 'Horus who protects his father' (Osiris), a form of Horus.

Har-khentekhtaï, god of Athribis (p. 37). Sacred animal, the serpent.

Harmachis, a name given to the Sphinx at Gîza (p. 145).

Harpocrates, Horus the child, represented with a side-lock and a finger on his lips. The Greeks regarded him as god of silence. He was much revered, especially at a late date (p. clii).

Har-sem-tewe *(Harsomtus)*, 'Horus the uniter of the two lands', a form of Horus (pp. 261, 370).

Harsiēsis, 'Horus, son of Isis', a form of Horus.

Hathor (Fig. 6), a deity of the sky (p. cxlviii) and a goddess of joy and love, identified by the Greeks with Aphrodite (pp. 217, 356). She was the goddess of Dendera (p. 261) and Aphroditopolis (p. 217), and was worshipped also in Thebes as guardian of the necropolis (pp. 320, 339). The cow was sacred to her, and she was frequently represented with cow's horns or a cow's head (Fig. 7).

HEKET, the frog-goddess of childbirth.

HERISHEF, the ram-headed god of Heracleopolis (p. 218).

HORUS received universal homage as the sun-god (see Harakhte). He was the local deity of Behdet (p. 34) and the patron of the Pharaohs (p. cli); at Edfu (p. 369) he is represented as a winged sun (Fig. 20). He is usually described as the son of Osiris and Isis (p. cxlix), sometimes as the son of Rē and brother of Seth. The falcon was sacred to him.

IMHOTEP *(Imuthes)*, a deified saint of Memphis, the famous architect of King Djoser (p. 156), revered as a priest and physician, was identified by the Greeks with *Asklepios (Æsculapius)*. He had a temple at Philæ also (p. 391; comp. also p. 322).

ISIS (Figs. 8 & 9), the sister and wife of Osiris and mother of Horus (Harsiēsis), was a goddess of Philæ (p. 390) and was highly revered at a late period (p. clii).

KA, the guardian spirit of men (p. cliv).

KEB, see Geb.

KEBEH-SENUF, one of the four guardian deities of the dead. See *Emset*.

KHEPRE, the scarabæus (dung-beetle), regarded as a form of the sun-god (p. cl).

KHNUM (Fig. 10) was the god of Herwēr (near Beniḥasan, p. 240), Shes-hotep (p. 229), Esna (p. 357), Elephantine (comp. p. 384) and the Cataract districts (comp. p. 390), etc. His sacred animal was the ram.

KHONS, the moon-god of Thebes, was the son of Amun and Mut, with whom he forms the Theban triad. Sacred animal, the falcon.

MAAT (Fig. 11), goddess of truth. Her symbol is an ostrich-feather (p. clxxxvi).

MIN (Fig. 12), the local deity of Akhmîm and Koptos (pp. 230, 232), was also the god of travellers in the desert. Later he was revered as a god of the harvest (pp. 326, 350) and was frequently amalgamated with Amun (pp. 322, 377); the Greeks identified him with Pan (p. cxlvii). He is ithyphallically represented.

MNEVIS, the sacred bull of Heliopolis (p. 130).

MONT *(Montu)*, the god of Thebes, Medamût, and Hermonthis (pp. 270, 297, 356); was regarded from an early period as the god of war. He was represented with a falcon's head.

MUT, the wife of Amun of Thebes and mother of Khons (pp. 272, 297). Her sacred animal was the vulture.

NEFERTĒM, son of Ptah of Memphis (p. cxlviii).

NEITH, goddess of Saïs, Esna (pp. 36, 357), etc. Comp. p. cxlvii.

NEKHBEYET (p. cxlv; Greek *Smithis*), goddess of Elkâb (Nekhab, p. 365) and guardian deity of Upper Egypt. As she presided over childbirth the Greeks identified her with Eileithyia. Sacred animal, the vulture.

NEPHTHYS (Fig. 13), originally a goddess of the dead. Sister of Osiris, Isis, and Seth (also wife of the last, p. cxlviii).

NUN, the primæval waters beneath the earth, which was represented as a floating disk (p. cl).

NUT, the goddess of the sky and wife of Geb (pp. cxlvii, cl).

ONNOPHRIS, see *Wen-nofre.*

OSIRIS (Fig. 14), originally the god of vegetation; at Busiris (in the Delta) identified with Anedjti, the god of that place; already from an early period amalgamated with the death-god of Abydos, the 'Lord of the Western Folk', and universally worshipped as god of the dead (p. cliii). His tomb was at Abydos (p. 253). For his legend, see p. cxlix. His fetish was a post or column 𓊽 *(Djed).*

PEKHET, the goddess of Speos Artemidos (p. 241), to whom the cat was sacred.

PTAH (Fig. 15), the god of Memphis (p. 154) and patron deity of Egypt (p. cli), was regarded as the guardian of artists (p. cxlviii) and identified by the Greeks with Hephæstos.

PTAH-TENEN, a special form of Ptah (p. 421).

RĒ, the sun-god (p. cl). He was identified at an early period with Harakhte of Heliopolis (p. clvi) and named Rē-Harakhte (p. cxlviii). During the night he traverses the underworld and is then named *Yfu-Rē* and represented with a ram's head.

SAKHMET (*Sekhmet*; Fig. 16), lion-goddess of war (pp. cxlv, cxlviii). Sacred animal, the lioness.

SARAPIS *(Serapis)*, a foreign god introduced into Egypt under the Ptolemies (p. clii), and identified with the ancient Egyptian Osiris-Apis (Osorapis), the deceased Apis bull (p. 158).

SATET (Greek *Satis*), guardian deity of the Cataract district, was worshipped at Esna (p. 357), Elephantine (p. 382), Siheil (p. 389), and Philæ (p. 390).

SELKET, a goddess to whom the scorpion was sacred

SESHET (Fig. 17), goddess of writing (p. cli).

SETH *(Setekh)*, god of Ombos (near Naqâda, p. 233), was the patron deity of Upper Egypt in prehistoric times (p. cli), and was worshipped also at Tanis (p. 182) and Auaris (p. civ). He was the brother of Osiris, whom he is said to have slain (p. cxlix). Another myth makes him brother and enemy of Horus (p. cxlix). Later he became a god of war and god of the Semites, who identified him with Baʿal. After the 22nd Dyn. he was expelled from the Egyptian pantheon and was thenceforth regarded as god of the impure (Typhon; p. 240). His sacred animal, with a peculiar muzzle and grotesque ears and tail, is, according to Schweinfurth, the aard-vark or ant-bear (Orycteropus æthiopicus).

SHOW *(Shu)*, god of the air (p. cxlvii), the local deity of Leontopolis (p. 181). The Egyptians believed that he supported the sky (p. cl). The lion was sacred to him. See also Eri-hems-nufer.

Soker, a falcon-headed god of the dead worshipped in the neighbourhood of Memphis (comp. pp. 258, 351).

Suchos or Sobk (Fig. 18), worshipped in the Faiyûm (p. 204), at Ombos (Kôm Ombo, p. 374), etc. The crocodile was sacred to him.

Tefnut *(Tefênet)*, the goddess of the dew (p. cxlvii), sister and consort of Show, along with whom she was worshipped (in the form of a lioness).

Thoth (*Thout*, *Dḥuti;* Fig. 19), the moon-deity and god of the sciences (p. cxlviii), therefore identified by the Greeks with Hermes (Hermes Trismegistus). He was the local deity of Hermupolis (p. 221). The ibis and baboon (cynocephalus) were sacred to him.

Toëris, 'the great (sc. Epet)', another name of Epet (see p. clvi).

Utō (Greek *Buto*), goddess of the town of Buto (p. 34) in the Delta; also the guardian deity of Lower Egypt. The serpent, ichneumon, and shrew-mouse were sacred to her. This goddess was represented also with a lion's head.

Wen-nofre (Greek *Onnophris*), another form of Osiris (p. 394).

Wep-wawet (p. cxlv), local deity of Asyûṭ (p. 226), also worshipped as a god of the dead. The wolf was sacred to him.

Wert-hekew ('the great in magic'), a lion-headed goddess, wife of Rē-Harakhte.

Representations of the most important Deities.

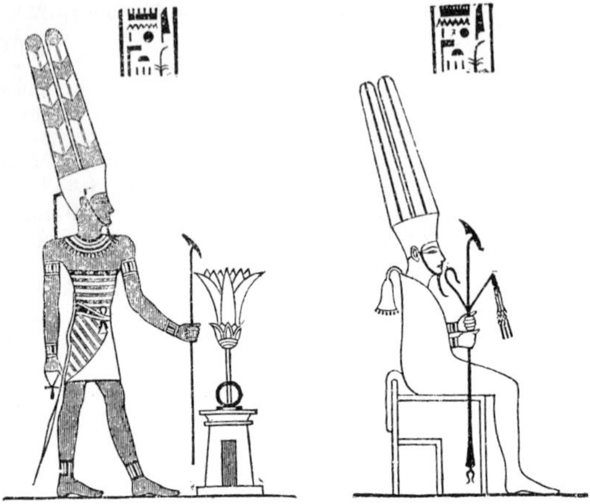

1. Amon-Rē.

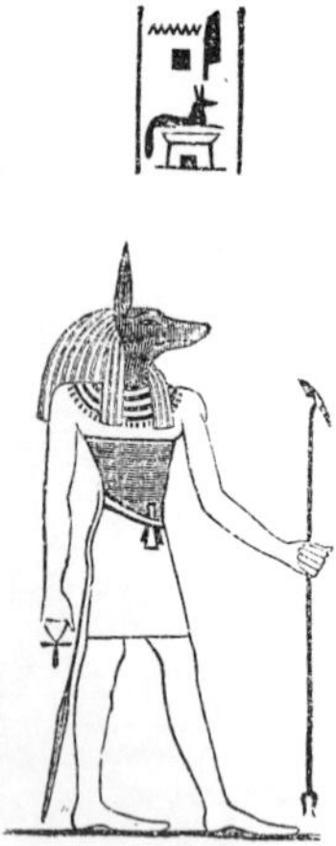

2. Anubis.

3. Atum.

4. Harakhte.

5. Harendotes.

6. Hathor.

7. Cow-headed Hathor.

8. Isis.

9. Isis, suckling the infant Horus.

10. Khnum.

11. Maat, goddess of truth.

12. Min; behind is the curious shrine of the god.

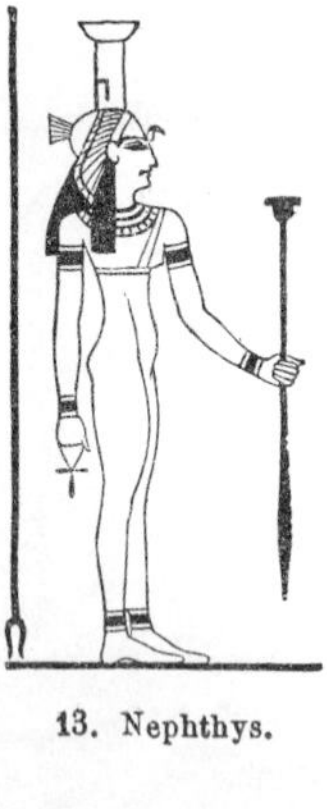

13. Nephthys.

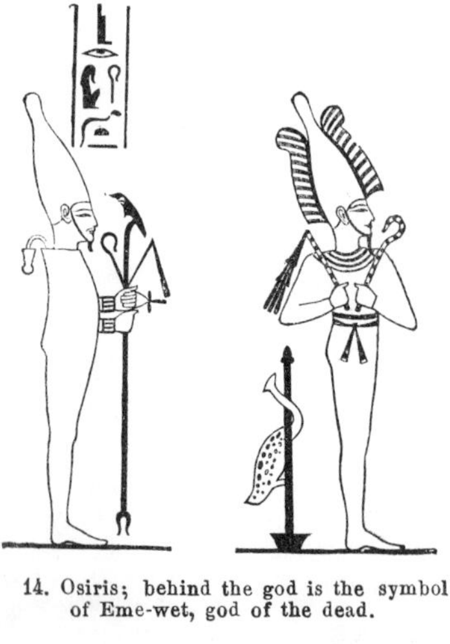

14. Osiris; behind the god is the symbol of Eme-wet, god of the dead.

15. Ptah.

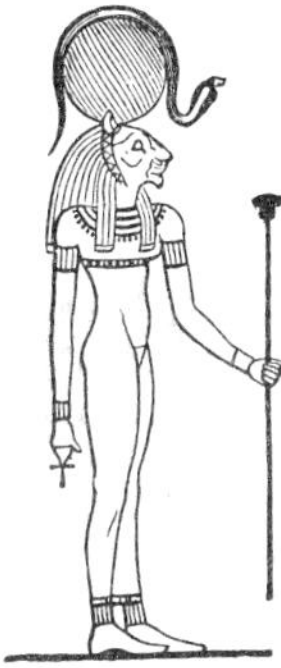

16. Sakhmet.

17. Seshet writing the king's name on the sacred tree of Heliopolis.

18 Suchos.

19. Thoth.

20. The winged Sun.

VII. Historical Notice of Egyptian Art.

By *Professor Georg Steindorff.*

1. Architecture.

Of Egyptian buildings dating from the prehistoric period or from the earliest dynasties little has been preserved — very little compared with what remains of the buildings of the period extending from the Ancient Empire to the Græco-Roman epoch. The remains that do exist are chiefly tombs, of clay or of sun-dried bricks of Nile mud, materials which were used also for houses and temples of the period. For the roof-supports, and frequently for the roofs also, round trunks of palms were used. In many other cases the chambers were covered with barrel-vaulting. — Stone began to be used for tombs and temples at the beginning of the Ancient Empire, but brick never ceased to be the characteristic building material of Egypt. The characteristic Egyptian architectural members, such as the cavetto (concave) cornice and the round moulding (torus or roll), had their origin in the primitive structures of wattle-and-daub and survived in the later buildings of stone; the form of the circular *Column*, too, was borrowed from the wooden supports used in brick buildings. The square *Pillar* or *Pier*, on the other hand, came into existence with stone architecture. Of stone also were the fluted half-pillar, the half-column with a papyrus-capital, and the three-quarter column imitating a bundle of reeds, which are found at the beginning of the 3rd Dyn. in the temples belonging to the Step Pyramid of Ṣaqqâra (pp. 156, 157), but these forms very soon disappeared again as decorative members.

Square **Pillars** are first met with in tombs of the Ancient Empire. They have neither abacus nor stylobate. Their lateral surfaces are frequently occupied by reliefs or inscriptions and their fronts by other ornamental designs. Thus tall papyrus-plants and lilies occur on pillars of the time of Thutmosis III. at Karnak (p. 290), and a sistrum (a rattle used by women) with a head of Hathor at Abu Simbel (p. 436). The four-sided pier was converted into an octagonal or sixteen-sided pillar by bevelling off the corners, part of the pier, however, being left square at the top so as to blend with the roof; at the foot was a round, cushion-like base. By grooving or fluting the flat surfaces of the pillar a play of light and shade was obtained. Sixteen-sided fluted pillars, which have received the name of *Proto-Doric Columns* (Fig. I), occur at first in tombs of the Middle Empire (at Beniḥasan, p. 244, and Aswân, p. 384) and afterwards in temples of the time of Thutmosis III. (Karnak, p. 293; Deir el-Baḥari, p. 320). The name was suggested by certain points of resemblance to the Doric columns of the Greeks, the chief of which are the marked fluting and the tapering (entasis); but the Proto-Doric differs from the Greek Doric in being destitute of the

echinus, a member resembling an overhanging wreath of leaves, forming an important part of the capital of the true Doric column. The chief difference, however, is that the shaft of the Egyptian column rests upon a base, while the Doric column springs immediately from the ground. Another difference is that some of the sides of the Proto-Doric column are frequently unfluted and left flat for the reception of inscriptions. The fluted half-pillars of the structures

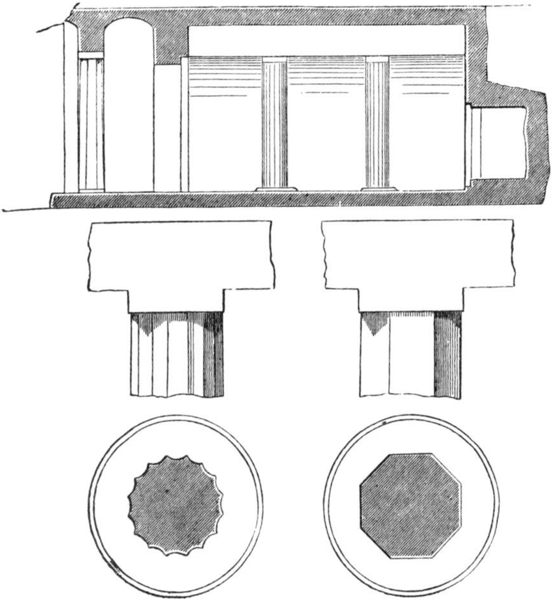

I. Tomb Chamber and Columns of Beniḥasan.

near the Step Pyramid of Ṣaqqâra, mentioned on pp. 156, 157, are unparalleled elsewhere and their origin is still obscure.

Along with the pillar and the allied Proto-Doric column the round **Column** began to be used in Egyptian stone architecture after the beginning of the 5th Dynasty. Its simplest form was the *Tree-Trunk Column* of two members, which was an imitation of the ancient palm-tree supports and is first found in the mortuary temple of Sehurē at Abuṣîr (p. 151). This consists of a low circular base and a cylindrical shaft, which was adorned in front with a band of

inscriptions. Usually, however, the column had three parts, i.e. it was crowned by a capital, ending in a square slab known as the abacus, upon which rest the beams of the architrave, supporting the slabs of the roof. The Egyptian love of plants is well known from various sources, and consistently with this the favourite forms for columns as early as the Ancient Empire were borrowed from plant-life. Two plants (comp. p. lxxix) especially were most frequently copied, viz. a variety of lotus (Nymphæa lotus) and the papyrus (Cyperus papyrus). Sometimes the column represents a single plant-stalk, sometimes a cluster of stalks held together by bands; while the capital imitates in turn the closed bud (closed umbel) or the open calyx (open umbel; Fig. II). Thus there arise four varieties of plant-columns: the simple plant-column with bud-capitals and the same with calyx-capitals; and the clustered plant-column with bud or calyx capitals.

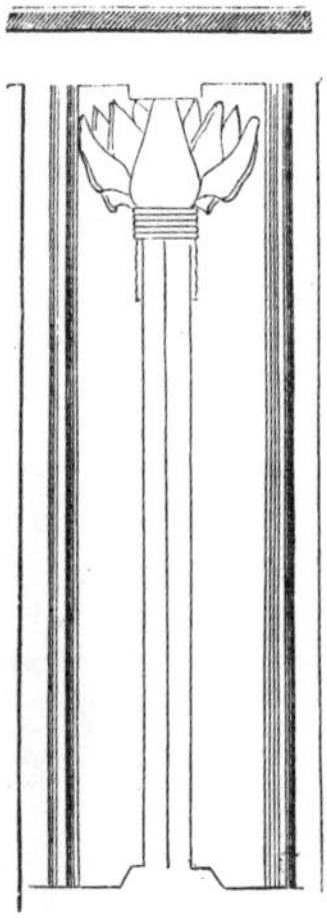

II.

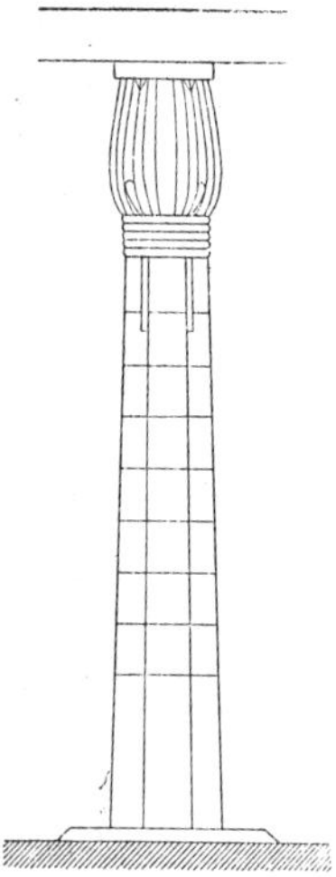

III.

Of the various *Lotus Columns* (which seem to have been freely used if we may judge from the numerous pictures of them) comparatively few have been preserved. Clustered columns of this kind with bud-capitals occur during the Ancient (maṣṭaba of Ptahshepses, p. 152) and Middle Empires (in a tomb at Benihasan, p. 242), but appear to have died out under the New Empire. The above-mentioned shaft at Beniḥasan is formed of four round stalks, rising from a round base, and fastened together at the top by bands (Fig. III). The capital is formed of closed buds, the green sepals of which extend quite to the top of the white petals of the corolla. Between the bands which hold the main stalks together are inserted smaller stalks. Examples of clustered lotus-columns with open (calyx) capitals (Fig. II) are frequently seen in reliefs on tombs of the Ancient and Middle Empires; but they occur most often in buildings of the later period.

The *Papyrus Columns* are much more numerous. They differ widely from the lotus-columns. The stalks in the latter are circular

in section, while in the papyrus-columns they are triangular, and moreover taper rapidly at the base, where they are encircled with pointed leaves — characteristics that are wanting in the lotus-columns. There is a difference also in the capitals, the sepals of the lotus reaching to the upper edge of the flower, while the leaves surrounding the umbel of the papyrus are considerably shorter. The simple papyrus-column with a bud-capital is seen only in paintings and reliefs, whereas the clustered column is common enough (Fig. IV a). The latter usually consists of eight stalks held together by bands at the top, while between these stalks smaller clusters of three fastened together by bands, were inserted. These inserted stalks, however, lost their independent treatment at an early period. — Towards the close of the 18th Dyn. the clustered papyrus-column underwent an essential change. In order to adapt the shaft for the reception of inscriptions and pictures, all its irregularities were abandoned and it was made perfectly smooth. For the same reason the capital also was rounded off and transformed into a blunt cone, the original clustering being recalled by painting alone (Fig. IV b). — Papyrus-columns with calyx-capitals (Fig. V a; representing the opened umbel of the plant), in which it is difficult to distinguish between simple and clustered columns, occur in most temples of the New Empire, where they generally appear supporting the lofty roof of the central passage in such hypostyle halls as consist of nave and aisles (see p. 285). They invariably consist of a single rounded shaft, no longer articulated into separate stalks (and generally covered with inscriptions and reliefs).

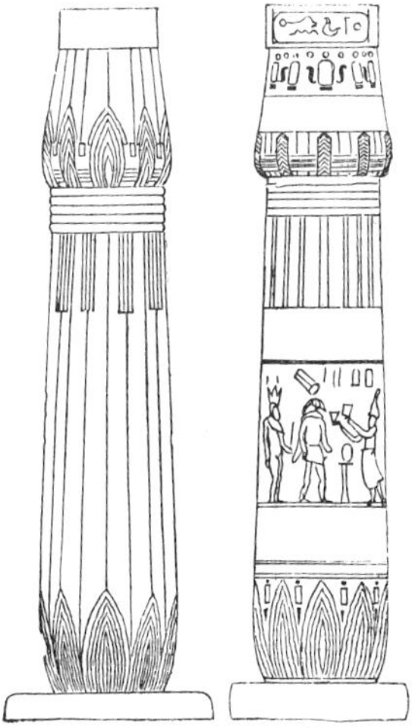

a b

IV.

Amongst the other and rarer varieties the *Palm Column* deserves mention. Its shaft is round (without the tapering foot of the papyrus column) and supports a capital formed of a bundle of palm-leaves, bending slightly outwards, and held together by bands (Fig. V c). The earliest and finest palm-columns were found in the mortuary temple of Sehurē at Abuṣîr (p. 151). At a later period the base of the column was often omitted. — The comparatively simple plant-capitals of the earlier periods were elaborately developed during the Ptolemaic epoch, until they almost assumed the form of bouquets

of different plants (papyrus, cyperus, sedges), resplendent with brilliant colours (Fig. V b).

Besides these plant-columns other varieties occur. The so-called *Hathor* or *Sistrum Columns*, symbols of the goddess Hathor, have round shafts crowned on four sides with the head of the goddess Hathor (with cow's ears), above which was a temple-like addition. These are doubtless reproductions of the sistrum (p. clxiv), with its handle; they are exclusively confined to temples of female deities and are most numerous in the Ptolemaic period (e.g. at Dendera, p. 261, 262). Another curious column is the ***Tent-Pole Column***, an imitation of the primitive  form of tent-poles. This occurs in the festal temple of Thutmosis III. at Karnak (p. 291), where the capitals are altered to the form of inverted calices.

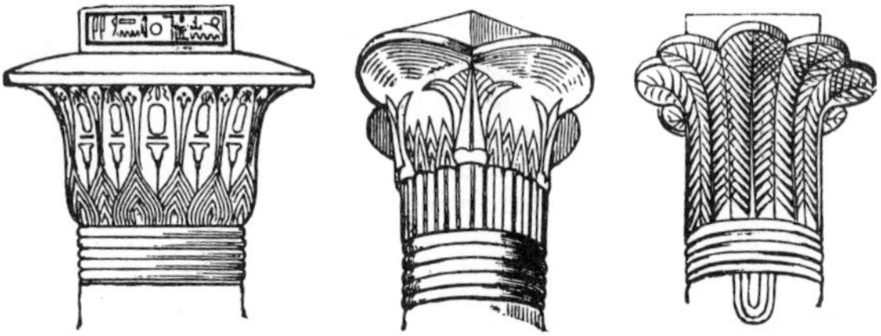

a — Calyx (Open Umbel) Capital of a Papyrus Column. b — Composite Plant Capital. c — Palm Capital.

V.

Comparatively few of the ancient Egyptian **Secular Buildings**, even of the later historical periods, have been preserved (comp. p. 153). The number of ruined towns is not, indeed, insignificant; but the remains of the earlier houses are almost invariably concealed by those of later date and are thus very difficult to examine. The remains of earlier houses have come down to us directly in only a few exceptional instances, e.g. beside the valley temple of the Mykerinos Pyramid (p. 143), at El-Lâhûn (pp. 206, 207), and especially at Tell el-ʿAmârna (pp. 245, 246). These, in connection with representations preserved on the monuments and models of houses found in tombs, afford us some knowledge of the structure and interior arrangements of Egyptian Private Houses, which in many respects resembled the Arab houses of modern Egypt (p. cci). The house of the humble peasant or workman was as simple then as it is to-day. An open court, in which the family spent the day (and in summer the night also), was adjoined by a few dimly lighted sleeping rooms and stables for the cattle, while a staircase led from

the court to the flat roof, upon which a few smaller apartments were often found. The houses of the more prosperous Egyptians of the Middle Empire also had a court as their central point, at the back of which, on a terrace, was a colonnade or vestibule of light columns, generally open towards the N. and affording protection from

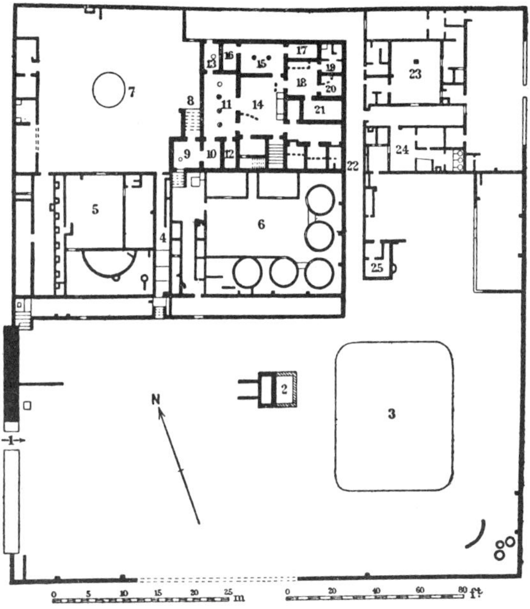

Ancient Egyptian Private House at Tell el-ʿAmârna.

1. Entrance. 2. Kiosk. 3. Pond. 4. Passage. 5. Cattle Sheds. 6. Store Rooms & Granaries. 7. Courtyard and Well. 8. Main Entrance of the House. 9. Porter's Lodge. 10. Vestibule. 11. West Loggia. 12, 13. Guest Rooms (?). 14. Central Hall (lighted by clerestory windows from above). 15. North Loggia. 16, 17. Bedrooms (?). 18. Private Sitting Room (?). 19. Bathroom and Wardrobe. 20. Small Bedroom. 21. Master's Bedroom (?). 22. Passage. 23. Servants' Quarters & Offices. 24. Kitchen. 25. Overseer's Cottage.

the sun. Thence a door led to a wide hall, the roof of which rested on columns, and beyond that was a deep hall, also with columns, probably used as the dining room. Beyond that again were other apartments (bedrooms) for the master of the house and his grown-up sons. On one side of the four principal divisions of the house (court, vestibule, broad hall, deep hall) were the women's apart-

ments, or harem (ḥarîm, p. cci), the middle point of which was another open court; and on the other side were the slaves' apartments, the store-rooms, the kitchens, and the stables. This arrangement of the Egyptian dwelling-house was probably the same in essential details at all periods, and even in the Royal Palaces (e.g. at Tell el-ʿAmârna, p. 246, and Medînet Habu, pp. 352, 355) the four principal divisions occur in the same order. The houses of the 18th Dyn. which have been excavated at Tell el-ʿAmârna are built upon a slightly different plan. The ground-plan on p. clxix is that of the house Q 44 I (comp. p. 246), a typical specimen of its class.

The walls of the houses and palaces were built of unburnt bricks of Nile mud; the roofs were made of wooden beams, covered with straw or reeds and daubed within and without with Nile mud; the columns were either of stone or of wood, and in palaces were inlaid with coloured stones or glass-paste. Colour was extensively used also in the interiors; the walls were whitewashed and adorned with bright-coloured rugs or with paintings, and even the pavements were often covered with colouring matter (comp. pp. 246, 94, 98).

Numerous Fortified Structures have been preserved. Amongst these may be mentioned the Nubian forts at Kuri (p. 421), at Kûbân (p. 423), and to the S. of Wâdi Ḥalfa (p. 440), where a chain of fortifications closed the roads beside the Cataract, and the Egyptian forts at Elkâb (p. 365) and El-Aḥâïwa (p. 238), and the fortified town of El-Lâhûn (Kahun, p. 207), all of which probably date from the Middle Empire. Mention must be made also of the Sham Fortresses, i.e. royal palaces constructed in the style of fortresses, such as those extant at Abydos (p. 260), Kôm el-Aḥmar (p. 369), and Medînet Habu (p. 347).

As taxes and salaries were paid in kind, large Magazines were required for the reception of tribute, not only by the state but also by temples. The remains of such storehouses have been found beside the Ramesseum (p. 327) and elsewhere.

Probably in no other country have so many **Temples** within such narrow limits survived from antiquity as in Egypt. Most of these, it is true, date from the New Empire and the Ptolemaic epoch, so that we have a clear conception of the temples of these periods only. Few or no complete temples have survived from the Ancient or Middle Empires or from the late-Egyptian period.

Of the Temples of the Ancient Empire, apart from the mortuary temples beside the pyramids (pp. 140, 142, 143), only one example of a particular kind has been preserved. This is the *Sanctuary of the Sun* at Abu Gurâb, erected by King Niuserrē (p. 150). This temple consisted of a large court bounded by covered passages and containing only a few buildings; at the back of the court rose a huge obelisk. The walls of the passages and of some of the rooms were covered with reliefs representing festivities, hunting scenes, and country life.

The remains of the TEMPLES OF THE MIDDLE EMPIRE are even scantier than those of the Ancient Empire. Large sanctuaries, sometimes even superior in size to those of later times, were built during this period at *Luxor* (p. 272), *Karnak* (p. 278), *Koptos* (p. 232), *Abydos* (p. 252), *Madînet el-Faiyûm* (pp. 203, 204), *Heliopolis* (p. 130), *Bubastis* (p. 181), and *Tanis* (p. 182); but none has left any considerable traces. All probably fell into decay during the troublous times of the Hyksos supremacy (p. civ) and were replaced under the 18th Dyn. by new buildings, in which the materials of the earlier edifices were utilized as far as possible. In plan they seem to have corresponded exactly with the later sanctuaries, and probably many temples of the later period were erected on the plans of the earlier buildings. In decoration also they exactly resembled the later temples. The inner walls were adorned with reliefs showing the king in communion with the gods; the ceilings of their halls were supported by columns of various patterns; and in front of their entrances rose tall obelisks (p. 130) and colossal statues of the Pharaohs.

However different from each other the TEMPLES OF THE NEW EMPIRE appear at first sight, there is but little difficulty in referring them all to two general fundamental forms. One of these, recalling, probably quite accidentally, the Greek *Peripteros* or temple surrounded by a colonnade, was especially popular during the 18th Dyn., the age of Thutmosis III. and his successors. The rectangular cella (or sanctuary), containing the sacred boat with the image of the god and provided with doors at each end, rose upon a basement of masonry, crowned with a cavetto cornice and approached by a flight of steps. On all four sides it was surrounded by a colonnade, the roof of which rested upon square pillars or on Proto-Doric columns (p. clxiv), connected by low screens. Occasionally this main structure was adjoined at the back by several smaller apartments, also used for religious rites. Among the peripteral structures of this kind are the small temples of Thutmosis III. at Karnak and Medînet Habu (pp. 295, 354), the S. temple of Buhen near Wâdi Ḥalfa (pp. 438, 439), and a sanctuary of Amenophis III. upon the island of Elephantine, which has now vanished (see p. 384). Curiously enough this form of peripteros was revived in the Ptolemaic period, though with various modifications, being used in the so-called *Birth Houses (Mammisi)*, which stood beside the principal temples (e.g. at Dendera, p. 266, Edfu, p. 374, and Philæ, p. 392) and were dedicated to the worship of the maternal deity (Isis or Hathor) and her child. The inner rooms in these birth-houses also were surrounded with colonnades, the roofs of which, however, were borne by the curious sistrum-columns (p. clxviii) crowned with heads of Hathor or with figures of Bes (p. clvi).

The second fundamental form of the Egyptian temple is most simply and clearly illustrated in the small temples built by Ram-

ses III. at Karnak in honour of Khons and of Amun (pp. 278, 282; see special plan of the great temple of Amun at Karnak, p. 279). The approach to the temple is formed by the *Pylon*, two large towers of masonry flanking the entrance-door. The slightly inclining walls, framed with round mouldings and crowned by a cavetto cornice, offer the greatest available space for reliefs. The towers were imposing from their sheer size, and this impression was heightened (from the Middle Empire onwards) by the obelisks and colossal statues placed in front of them, and by the lofty flagstaffs which

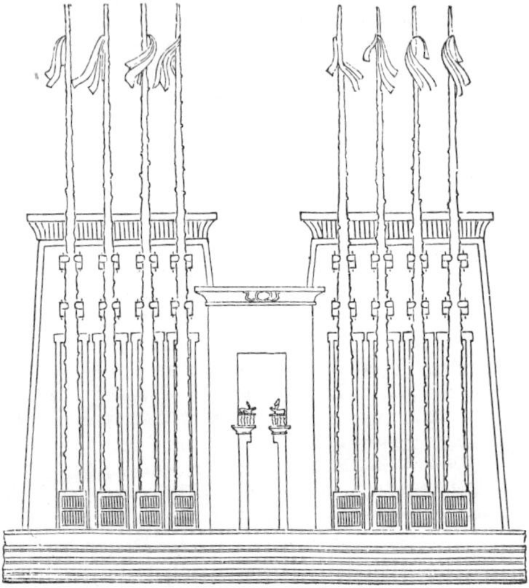

VI. The Second Pylon at Karnak decorated for a festival (from an ancient Egyptian representation).

were placed in shallow niches in the masonry and fastened by huge clamps (Fig. VI). Beyond the pylon we enter a broad open *Court*, flanked on the right and left by covered colonnades. In the centre stood the great altar, round which the people assembled on festivals. This court was adjoined by the *Temple* proper, which stood on a terrace of moderate height adorned with a cavetto cornice and reached from the court by one or more ramps. At the top we first reach a *Pronaos* or *Vestibule*, borne by columns. The columns in the front row are connected by stone screens, shutting off the temple from the court. Behind this lies a *Hypostyle Hall*, occupying the whole breadth of the building. In the larger temples of the 19th Dyn. and later

(e.g. the Ramesseum, p. 327, and the temple of Khons at Karnak, p. 279) this hall consisted of a tripartite nave and two or more aisles, the latter considerably lower than the former. In these cases the roof above the nave is supported by four rows of columns, of which the two central rows are tall papyrus-columns with calyx-capitals, that above the aisles by lower columns with bud-capitals. To overcome the difference in height the lower columns support a row of square pillars, the spaces between which are occupied by windows (comp. the illustration on p. 285). Beyond the hypostyle hall lies the innermost *Sanctuary*, a comparatively narrow and deep chamber. This contained the image of the god, usually in a sacred boat, which was borne by the priests in processions. Only the king or his representative, the high-priest, might enter this chamber and 'look upon the god'. When the temple, e.g. the sanctuary of Ramses III. at Karnak (p. 282), was dedicated to a triad of gods, the sanctuary of the chief god (Amun) was flanked by the chapels of the other two (Mut and Khons). Chambers of various sizes used for religious rites or for the storage of temple property surrounded the sanctuary; staircases led to the roof and to various rooms, which were used in the celebration of special ceremonies, etc.

This form of Egyptian temple, which recurs in most of the larger sacred buildings of the New Empire and lingered until after the beginning of the Ptolemaic period, closely corresponds with the ground-plan of the early Egyptian house or palace previously described. The open court of the house, accessible to every visitor, is represented by the great temple-court; the pronaos of the temple corresponds to the vestibule, the colonnaded (hypostyle) hall to the broad hall of the dwelling; and the deep hall in which the master of the house spent his time finds its analogue in the sanctuary, the dwelling-place of the god. And just as these apartments in the dwelling-house were adjoined by chambers and rooms for various purposes, so the sanctuary in the temple was adjoined by a series of small apartments, store-rooms, etc. Thus the temple was literally what the Egyptians called it, the *House of the God*.

In many temples the hypostyle hall is further separated from the sanctuary by one or more *Smaller Halls* (with or without columns) of narrower proportions and diminishing in height. Frequently also the sanctuary is followed by several other halls and chambers; and not unfrequently the temple proper is preceded by two colonnaded courts instead of by one. The particular purposes of all these various rooms are in most cases hard to determine.

Though many temples, such as the temple at Luxor (p. 272) and the great temple of Amun at Karnak (p. 280), exhibit a much more complicated form than that just described, the explanation is that they were not built on one uniform plan but owe their construction to various builders. In the descriptions of the particular temples concerned this matter is treated with due attention to detail.

Occasionally the nature of the site compelled further deviations from the above-described form. In Lower Nubia the sandstone cliffs approach so close to the bank of the Nile that the temple had to be partly or wholly constructed in the rock, the necessary rooms being hewn out. At Garf Ḥusein (p. 420) the court is built as usual, while the hypostyle hall and the sanctuary are hewn out of the rock. The larger temple of Abu Simbel (p. 431) is entirely a rock building, the pylon and the colossi included. At Abydos the difficulty of excavating the rock was avoided by placing the part of the temple containing the slaughter-court and other offices at right angles to the main edifice, so that the whole now presents the form of a ┐ (comp. the Plan, p. 253).

Although many small temple-buildings of the Libyan Epoch (p. cvii) and the Late Period are still in existence, almost nothing has come down to our day of the large temples, with the exception of the temple of Hibis, in the oasis of Khârga (p. 406), which was erected in the time of the Persians. Nearly all the kings of that period resided in the Delta (Bubastis, p. 181; Saïs, p. 36), and therefore markedly favoured the North in erecting their monuments. There the sanctuaries were built of limestone, and in mediæval and modern times the blocks have either found their way into lime-kilns, or, since the Delta itself yields but scanty building materials, have been utilized for new buildings, usually leaving only the more refractory blocks of granite behind. It was not until the days of the Ptolemies (p. cxi) that attention was once more directed to the South. Under these kings the priesthood again acquired great wealth and was able to erect large temples, usually on the site of earlier ruined buildings. All these temples are built on one uniform plan, differing but slightly from the older forms (comp. the plan of the temple at Edfu, p. 370, with that of the Ramesseum, p. 325). There is a difference in only two essential points. The hypostyle hall is no longer basilican (with raised nave), but forms a large uniform hall; moreover, the sanctuary for the boat is surrounded on three sides by corridors, on which open smaller chambers. This innovation, which is seen for the first time in the temple of Khons at Karnak (20th Dyn.; p. 278), provided the temple proper with a chapel closed all round. The earlier temples were often altered to conform to this new plan, and a separate boat-chamber was inserted among the older rooms (e.g. in the temple at Luxor, pp. 276, 277, and in the great temple at Karnak, p. 290). The side-rooms also are numerous at this period and among these special mention must be made of a small *Sacrificial Court* situated on the right side (see the plan of Edfu, p. 370) and an elegant *Kiosk* adjoining it (ib.).

From an early period all flat surfaces on pylons, interior walls, column-shafts, and ceilings were covered with representations and inscriptions. The external walls, the pylons, and the walls of the

courts, i.e. those parts of the temple that were exposed to the vulgar eye, commemorated above all the exploits of the king, campaigns, great festivals, or other important events of his reign; the representations were intended to keep the power and nobility of the Pharaoh constantly before his people. On the other hand the representations in the interior of the temple were exclusively devoted to the religious proceedings that took place there. The king, who theoretically was the only mortal who might have intercourse with the gods, appears again and again, offering gifts and homage to the deities and receiving from them earthly blessings. In the late period and especially under the Ptolemies the secular representations on the external walls and the walls of the court gave place to religious scenes; the battle-scenes and triumphs of the ruler are superseded by sacrificial and other sacred scenes depicted at tedious length. On the pylons, however, the primitive typical figure of the Pharaoh smiting his enemies in presence of the god still appears. — The temple, moreover, was in the eyes of the Egyptian a type in small of the world. The roof corresponded to the sky, and was, therefore, appropriately adorned with stars upon a blue ground, while above the middle passage hovered vultures, protecting the king as he passed along below. Not unfrequently, and especially in the temples of the Ptolemaic period, the ceiling is adorned with astronomical representations — the gods and goddesses of the months and days, the planets, various constellations, and the goddess of the sky herself, on whose body rested the boat of the sun. Similarly the pavement represented the earth. Here (i.e. on the bottom of the walls) we see flowers blooming or long processions of the representatives of the nomes and other divisions of the country, and of the river and canals, bringing their characteristic products as offerings to the deities of the temple. Egypt was traditionally regarded as divided into two portions — a northern and a southern (pp. ci, cii) — and similarly the entire world as represented in the temple was also regarded as consisting of a N. half and a S. half. The representatives of the N. appear on one side, those of the S. on the other; and even in the ceremonial religious scenes on the walls this distinction may frequently be traced. The entire temple precincts were enclosed by a massive brick wall, the monumental portal of which was approached by a dromos or avenue of sphinxes or of animals sacred to the god (e.g. in Thebes recumbent rams). Within this wall stood also the dwellings of the priests, besides storehouses and stables, so that the temple proper, like an Arab mosque of to-day, stood in the midst of a complex of domestic buildings.

Owing to the great value of arable land in Egypt **Tombs** were not placed in the lower portions of the Nile valley, but in the more elevated desert regions, which, moreover, being beyond the reach of the inundation, were in any case better adapted for the preservation of the dead. The Egyptian tomb always had a double

function to fulfil; it not only served as a safe resting-place for the dead, but it was also a place where the survivors could meet on certain days and offer gifts to the deceased. Thus the tomb was in two parts, the actual *Tomb* in the ground, and the *Place of Worship* above ground. — The most ancient graves were simple pits, in which the corpses were laid; these were frequently walled with bricks and covered over with beams. Larger pits were divided into chambers by partition walls. Over the grave heaps of stones were piled or a mound was formed of bricks made of Nile mud, on the E. side of which a shallow niche (in the form of a door) or a stele was set up; in front of this a small court was made, which served as a place of worship, where the gifts for the deceased were deposited. From this early form of Egyptian tomb were developed the Maṣṭabas, as the tombs of the aristocrats of the Ancient Empire are called; these were erections of limestone blocks or of bricks, with a rectangular ground-plan and sloping walls. A perpendicular shaft (10-100 ft. in depth) or a staircase led down to the sepulchral chamber, containing the corpse, which frequently lay in a coffin of wood or stone. On the E. side of the upper structure lay the place of worship, a courtyard that is now seldom discernible. Here a narrow niche, usually a door-shaped stone or a stele resembling a false door, marked the spot that was regarded as the entrance to the grave and to the realm of the dead. In front of this the surviving relatives laid the food, drink, and other offerings to the dead upon the flat *Table of Offerings*, or recited their prayers for the welfare of the departed. After the close of the 3rd Dyn. a chapel was frequently built in front of the recess or a regular chamber of worship formed in the masonry of the maṣṭaba, and the stele was then removed to its W. side. In the time of the 5th Dyn. the inner chamber was enlarged and a number of additional rooms added. The extent to which these 'everlasting abodes' might be enlarged and developed is best illustrated by the maṣṭaba of Mereruka at Ṣaqqâra (p. 171), which, like any ordinary well-to-do house (see p. clxviii), contains a suite of rooms for the master, another (the harem) for his wife, a third, behind, for the son, besides various store-rooms. The inner walls were embellished with inscriptions and representations (usually in relief), depicting the deceased at his favourite occupations, hunting and fishing, the various activities on his estates, his workmen at work, etc. (pp. 160 seqq.). The object of these representations was to enable the deceased to continue his occupations in the land beyond the grave (comp. p. cliii). The deceased and the members of his family were represented by statues, which were placed in one or more special rooms (the so-called *Serdâbs*, i.e. cellars), generally built in the thickness of the walls but sometimes separate structures. These received light and air by means of small apertures only. Most of the fine statues of the Ancient Empire now in the Cairo Museum (pp. 90 seqq.) were found in such serdâbs.

Just as the streets of a town were arranged round the palace of the king, so the rows of maṣṭabas were grouped around the tomb of the king (comp. p. 140). Originally the royal tombs were large brick maṣṭabas like the others, in or beneath which were chambers for the body of the king, for those of his suite, and for the various funeral gifts. At the beginning of the 3rd Dyn. King Djoser and his clever architect Imhotep invented a new type of royal tomb. The maṣṭaba, composed entirely of hewn stone, was enlarged by heightening it and surrounding it with several outer casings, each of which was lower than the one inside it. A Step Maṣṭaba (step-pyramid) was thus developed, such as may still be seen in the step-pyramid at Ṣaqqâra (comp. p. 156), where the original simple rectangular maṣṭaba appears as it were to rest upon a five-stepped base. The normal form of the true pyramid, with a square ground-plan and smooth facing, was evolved from the step-pyramid at the beginning of the 4th Dyn., and thenceforward it remained the usual form for royal tombs until the 18th Dynasty. The oldest of such pyramids are those of Snofru at Meidûm and Dahshûr (pp. 217, 177). In the rock beneath the massive stone erection of the pyramid a sloping shaft (Pl. *a*) led to a subterranean passage, closed by means of a stone trap-door, and to the chamber (Pl. *b*) in which the sarcophagus stood. The great pyramids at Gîza, the step-pyramid at Ṣaqqâra, and various others contain several passages and several chambers, but the existence of these is due to modifications of the original plan or to later alterations (pp. 135, 156). The inner rooms of the pyramids, and particularly the sarcophagus-chambers, which were made inaccessible after the interment, were almost entirely destitute of ornament in the ancient period. It was not until the end of the 5th Dyn. that it began to be customary to adorn the walls with religious texts (the so-called 'Pyramid Texts', p. 136). The open court with niche or the chapel in which sacrifices were offered to the dead in the maṣṭabas was represented in the case of the pyramids by a detached temple on the E. side. These temples were divided into two portions, one public, the other private. The centre of the public portion was occupied by a large open court, surrounded with arcades, off which opened five chambers for the statues of the deceased monarch; the principal apartment in the private temple was the sanctuary containing the stele. On the edge of the cultivated land, moreover,

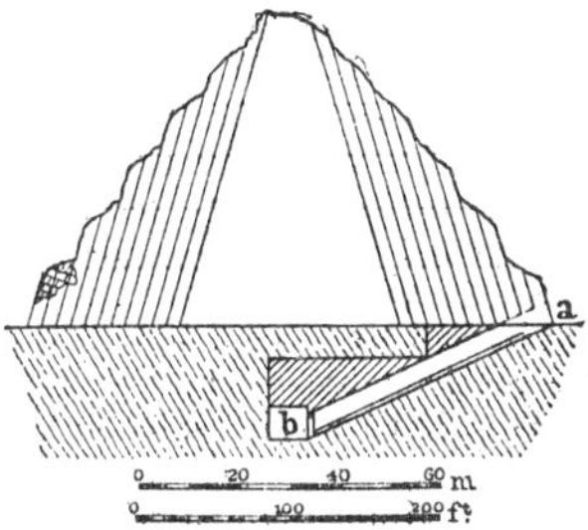

VII. Elevation of the Step Pyramid of Ṣaqqâra.

stood a temple, forming a monumental gateway, rising on a terrace and connected by a long covered approach with the mortuary temple, which lay on the desert plateau. The walls of the pyramid-temples of the 3rd and 4th Dyn. were left bare, but those of the temples at Abuṣîr (p. 151) are partly covered with reliefs, which to some extent display the same types as are seen in the temples of the gods (the king as a griffin triumphing over foreign foes, military campaigns, booty captured from the enemy, etc.). The best-preserved mortuary temples of the Ancient Empire are the temple of *Djoser* beside the step-pyramid of Ṣaqqâra (p. 156), the temple beside the pyramid of *Meidûm* (p. 217; apparently unfinished), the temples of Khephren and Mykerinos beside the pyramids of *Gîza* (pp. 142, 143), and those of Sehurē, Nefer-er-ke-rē, and Niuserrē at *Abuṣîr* (pp. 151, 152). The mortuary temples beside the pyramids of Lisht (p. 217), Dahshûr (p. 177), El-Lâhûn (p. 207), and Hauwâra (p. 206) belong to the Middle Empire. Most of these are in a very ruinous condition, like the temple of Amenemmēs III., the so-called Labyrinth (p. 206), while others have not been fully excavated. The best-preserved is the mortuary temple of Mentuhotep II. and Mentuhotep III. (11th Dyn.) at *Deir el-Baḥari* (p. 322), but that is built on a peculiar plan with terraces and cannot be considered typical. For the way in which the pyramids were built, comp. p. 134. At a later period the kings of Napata and Meroë (pp. 445, 448) re-adopted the pyramidal form for the royal tombs. — The enormous extent to which a royal burial-place could be developed ist best shown by the tomb of Djoser, which has been almost completely excavated in recent years (comp. pp. 156, 157). Its girdle-wall, an elaborate piece of architecture, encloses — besides the tomb proper, or step-maṣṭaba, and its annexed mortuary temple — two princesses' maṣṭabas, a large festal temple probably intended for the celebration of the king's jubilee, a magnificent festal hall, a small temple of unknown purport, and other buildings.

The custom of placing their tombs at the foot of a royal pyramid was gradually abandoned by the nobles and officials after the end of the 4th Dyn.; they preferred to be buried near their own homes. As in the royal cemeteries, so in the provincial deserts, they built for themselves small maṣṭabas or small brick pyramids upon rectangular or square bases. The tomb-chamber was formed in the thickness of the wall or dug out of the ground beneath; and a tombstone was erected on the outside in the shape of a false door or of a tablet rounded at the top, before which the survivors recited their prayers or presented their offerings. Mostly the tombs were sited on the slope of a desert mountain. The simpler *Rock Tombs* consisted merely of a chamber with a false-door recess, and often an attempt was made, even inside the rock, to imitate the interior of a maṣṭaba. As a rule, however, in accordance with the fundamental conception of the tomb as the *House of the Dead*, each tomb had to contain the four principal divisions of the ancient Egyptian dwelling-house

(p. clxviii). Thus a *Forecourt*, usually surrounded with a brick wall, was provided in the open air in front of the tomb, generally ending in a small *Porch* with two pillars or columns hewn in the solid rock. Beyond this was a wide *Hall* with columns or pillars, followed by a *Chamber* or deep *Recess*, which contained the rock-hewn statue of the deceased (frequently accompanied by that of his wife) and thus replaced the serdâb (p. clxxvi) of the old maṣṭabas.

This dwelling-house arrangement is most distinctly seen in the rock-tombs of Beniḥasan and Aswân (comp. pp. 241, 384). The inner walls are covered with inscriptions and representations intended to provide for the enjoyment of the deceased and to inform posterity of his exploits. The unembellished sarcophagus-chamber was reached from the first hall by a perpendicular shaft hewn in the rock.

The Tombs of the New Empire coincide in their general features with those of the Middle Empire. At this date also both free-standing tombs (maṣṭabas and pyramidal tombs) and rock-tombs occur. The former variety of tomb is now, however, represented by very few examples. In the rock-tombs a narrow corridor is frequently found between the first hall and the small inner chamber with the statues; for their general arrangement and decoration, see the remarks on p. 301. After the beginning of the 18th Dyn. the Pharaohs also ceased to build pyramids as their last resting-places, and prepared their tombs in the slopes of a sequestered mountain valley on the W. bank of the Nile near Thebes (comp. pp. 302, 314). These Royal Tombs of the New Empire comprised long corridors and halls, the walls of which were occupied by religious inscriptions and scenes (comp. p. 301). Like the passages within the pyramids, these were exclusively destined for the reception of the sarcophagus, while the rock itself represented the pyramid built over the grave. Since there was no room among the mountains for mortuary temples, the latter were built on the plain, where their ruins remain to this day (comp. pp. 327, 328).

The grandees of the late period followed the example of their predecessors under the Middle Empire by imitating the tombs of the Pharaohs in preparing their own private graves. This was the case in Thebes at least, where the tombs of important individuals are constructed after the model of the royal tombs at Bîbân el-Mulûk. Thus at ʿAsâsîf (p. 323) the burial-places of high officials of the 25th and 26th Dyn. consist of a series of corridors and halls, the walls of which are decorated with religious texts and representations. Unfortunately none of the royal tombs of the last native dynasties have as yet been discovered; these must have lain near the large capitals in the Delta. Even of the larger private tombs of this epoch few have been found, with the exception of those at Thebes and a few others at Gîza (p. 148) and Ṣaqqâra (pp. 175, 176).

The Tombs of the Humbler Classes must, of course, have largely outnumbered those of the grandees; but beyond the pits

which contained the bodies, and some gravestones, they have left no traces. From pictures we know that under the New Empire they were frequently in the form of small brick pyramids; but nearly all have fallen victims to time. The poorer classes were frequently buried in Common Tombs, constructed by speculators in ruined temples or in long corridors underground. In these the corpses were laid in plain coffins (sometimes merely on planks or mats made of the fibres of palm-leaves), accompanied by simple gifts for their use in the future world.

2. Sculpture and Painting.

Egyptian art is the only national art of which we can follow the undisturbed development from its primitive beginnings, through a long history, to the full expression of its guiding principles. But no fair estimate of Egyptian art can be formed unless it be remembered that it is based on principles quite different from those to which Greek classical art has accustomed us. The art of the Egyptians, Babylonians and Assyrians, Hittites and Cretans, is far anterior to the classical age of Greece, and they share with savage races and children the peculiarity that they reproduce the outside world not simply as the eye sees it, but as it appears in the Imagination of man. In a manner surprising to us they avoid visual impressions; neither in sculpture nor in painting do they deal with oblique views and consequent foreshortening and shifting of angles. It was the Greeks of c. 500 B.C. who accomplished the momentous transition from 'imaginative' art to a 'perspective' art founded on visual impressions.

Reliefs and **Paintings**. As the pre-Hellenic artist was quite unconscious of perspective foreshortening, he represents the body and its limbs on the flat, as viewed not obliquely but from a point straight in front. Nothing is depicted as one sees it from a single point, but the picture is built up of its separate, undiminished parts. Simple objects of three dimensions generally appear in their most characteristic view; complex objects are shown in a mentally reconstructed aspect as though in one plane, but the various parts may be separately treated and the picture built up, item by item, into an artificial composition. It is impossible, without other sources of knowledge, accurately to retranspose these drawings (e.g. houses) into the realities they represent. Objects, persons, and animals which to the view of the bystander are placed one behind the other are arranged in the picture in rows, next to or above one another. Objects lying on a table are drawn as if they were standing on it. Bodies usually are shown separately, without hiding or intersecting one another, but even at an early period it has apparently been observed that things that lie behind one another hide one another. The chief personage in a scene, e.g. in battle scenes the king charging in his chariot, is represented as taller than the other figures.

The central element in the Egyptian art of drawing is the human figure, which is represented as a composition of the various parts of the body drawn from different points of view. The head is seen from the side, while the eyes are drawn from the front. The shoulders are shown facing us, without foreshortening, and the rest of the body and the feet and legs in profile. Alongside of this basic type, an excellent example of which are the reliefs of Hesirē (p. 91, No. 88), there gradually developed the use of a correct profile representation. This is sometimes met as early as the 5th Dyn. but was not handled with perfect certainty until the second half of the 18th Dynasty. At this time the Egyptian art of drawing had attained its zenith. Nothing of equal excellence is found of a later date. The traveller will find the best opportunity to study the works of this period at Sheikh ʿAbd el-Qurna and Tell el-ʿAmârna (pp. 328, 245).

The art of drawing in Egypt was hampered from time immemorial by a number of *Types* that were copied again and again, though some alterations were gradually introduced. In the course of centuries the ancient treasury of types was increased by the addition of new and valuable motives. Thus the Ancient Empire furnishes numerous scenes from the life of the people on the large landed estates, which are often marked by a charming naïveté and a delicate observation of nature. In the 5th Dyn. pictures of military import join the circle of representations used in the mortuary temples, while under the Middle Empire we find scenes of the life at the courts of the provincial princes, and various new burial scenes. The supply of material, however, dates its greatest increase from the period of the 18th Dyn. (p. cv), when Egypt became a world power through its political relations with Asia Minor, and when the horizon of the artists had consequently become much more extensive. Under Amenophis IV. (p. cv) even the intimate life of the royal family and the court, which no one had previously ventured to represent, was, for a time, drawn into the field of art. Under the 19th Dyn. (p. cvi) and under Ramses III. (p. cvii) new tasks were imposed upon the artists, who were called upon to represent the warlike deeds of the king, and to execute huge pictures of battles. The beginning of this new tendency may indeed be recognized in the 18th Dyn., as in the reliefs on the chariot of Thutmosis IV. in the Cairo Museum (No. 3000, p. 98). With the end of the New Empire the supply of types again shrinks and becomes inferior even to that of the Ancient Empire. In scenes of the kind here referred to the artist found a free field for his powers of invention. When, however, he had to reproduce ceremonial scenes, he had naturally to adhere more or less rigidly to the ancient models. Among the subjects thus stereotyped were scenes relating to the intercourse of the king with the gods (in prayer or sacrifice), the celebration of certain festivals, and the slaughtering of animals for sacrifice.

Egyptian reliefs are either *Bas-Reliefs*, the earliest and at all periods the commonest form, which, always of comparatively shallow dimensions, were developed to an especial degree of refinement, or *Incised Reliefs* ('reliefs en creux'), in which the design is sunk below the surface. This form, which is peculiar to Egypt, first appears under the 4th Dyn. (p. cii) and always serves as a cheap substitute for bas-reliefs. The sculptors of the New Empire, however, often succeeded in producing very attractive effects by the skilful use of its peculiarities. Egyptian relief attained its highest point under the 5th Dyn. (p. ciii). The high level of technical and artistic skill at that period is best illustrated in the maṣṭabas of Ti and Ptahhotep at Ṣaqqâra (pp. 159, 169), and in the reliefs from the mortuary temples of the kings of the 5th Dyn. (p. 90). Under the 6th Dyn. and during the Middle Empire the execution of the reliefs had distinctly begun to decline, and it is not till we reach the works of the 18th Dyn. (e.g. in the temples of Luxor, p. 272, and Deir el-Baḥari, p. 317, and in some of the graves of Sheikh 'Abd el-Qurna, p. 328) that we find some approach to the old excellence. From this period on the decline is steady, though a few graceful and attractive reliefs were produced in the time of Sethos I. (e.g. in the temples of Qurna, p. 299, and at Abydos, p. 252). The too lavish demands made upon artistic resource for the decoration of the numerous new temples led, under Ramses II. (p. CVI), to a rough and ready style of work, the defects of which were multiplied under Menephthes. — In the SAÏTE PERIOD (pp. CVIII, CIX) the works of the Ancient Empire were again selected as models for sculptures in this branch of the plastic art, though the standard of the ancient masters was rarely attained. But all the same the reliefs of this period please by their delicate and exact execution, and by a certain elegance and charming softness of form. — Art under the PTOLEMIES (p. cxi) was at first content to follow in the track of the Saïte artists; but it gradually grew more and more crude, and the temple walls were overladen with rows of tasteless reliefs, contrasting with the good taste shown by the earlier artists in interspersing decorated with undecorated surfaces. The figures of men and gods in these became heavy and shapeless, so that their features and limbs have a swollen appearance. Unfortunately the reliefs of this late period of Egyptian art are the most numerous and most conspicuous in Upper Egypt, and thus it is that a much lower rank was assigned to Egyptian relief-sculpture than even its mediocre productions deserve. — All reliefs were painted, but many of them have now lost every trace of colour. When *Painting* was used instead of sculpture (as in the tombs of the 18th Dyn. at Sheikh 'Abd el-Qurna, p. 328), to save expense or because the available stone was not suitable for carvings, it need scarcely be stated that the same rules of style applied to paintings as to reliefs.

Statues. The pre-Hellenic attitude to the representation of nature, which differs so much from ours, applies also to sculpture in the round, especially to statues and figures of men and animals, and involves important divergences from visual impressions. The Egyptian statues show the body square to the spectator, with neither shoulder advanced, and the only permissible lateral movement of the head is at right angles. The limbs are added in a plane at right angles to the trunk. Exceptionally, however, freer figures occur among statues, just as foreshortening is sometimes found among reliefs. — Personages meant to be invested with a certain dignity are shown standing or sitting in a quiet posture, or even seated on the ground with their legs folded beneath them. They are often combined in family groups. The attendants, on the other hand, whose statues were placed in the grave of the deceased, are represented as indulging freely in their usual occupations (comp. p. cliv).

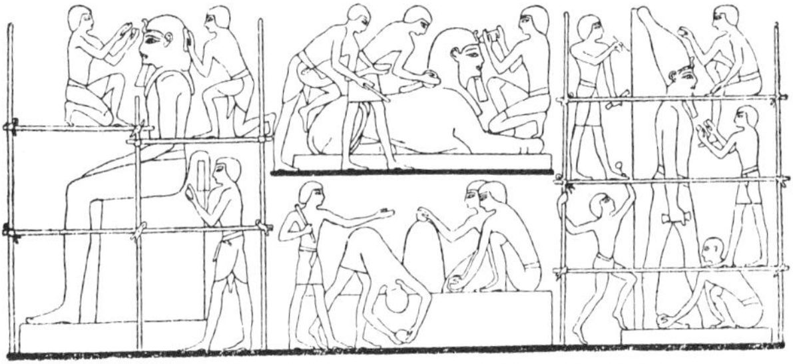

Sculptors at work (from an ancient Egyptian relief).

We possess specimens of the art of even the Earliest Period of Egyptian history in the shape of primitive figures of men and animals, mostly carved in bone or ivory, some of which (especially among the animal figures) display a high degree of finish. The statues dating from the end of the 2nd Dyn. and the beginning of the Ancient Empire already possess all the merits of Egyptian sculpture, though they still show traces of archaic stiffness, often due to the difficulty of working the material (granite, metamorphic slate, and occasionally limestone). They are mostly seated figures of moderate size, with a constrained arrangement of the limbs; the right hand usually rests on the breast, the left hand upon the thigh. When an inscription occurs it is usually given in relief. But even these primitive works (among the best of which are the royal statues of Khasekhem, No. 3056, p. 98, and Djoser, No. 6008, p. 90) show an effort on the part of the artist to render the features in as portrait-like a manner as possible.

The art of the statuary reached one of its highest points in the

4th and 5th Dynasties. Among the works of this period preserved in the Cairo Museum, most of which are of limestone or wood, the best are indicated on pp. 89-91. In all these statues the chief stress is laid upon a faithful reproduction of the face; the rest of the body, especially the hands and feet, are conventionally treated. The artist frequently imparted a curiously striking effect to his statue by inserting eyes of black and white quartz, with a wooden or copper stud to represent the pupil.

After a period of decay the art of sculpture entered upon a new period of prosperity under the Middle Empire. Among its masterpieces were the fine statue of Amenemmēs III. at Cairo (No. 284, p. 91), and the statues and sphinxes which were formerly attributed to the Hyksos (p. civ), but which probably also represent Amenemmēs III. or other kings of the close of the 12th Dyn. (p. 92). These are marked by an emphatic rendering of the spiritual expression, and are permeated by an appealing seriousness. The period, however, furnishes us also with creations of much less intrinsic value, such as the conventional statues of Sesostris I. from Lisht (pp. 91, 92), with their vacant faces.

The comparatively numerous Statues of the New Empire which have come down to us present a striking contrast to those of the Middle Empire. In place of the melancholy earnestness shown by the latter we find a certain placid and attractive cheerfulness. Examples of incomparable verisimilitude, worthy to rank with the best productions of the earlier period, are not wanting. Among these may be mentioned the statue of Thutmosis III. (No. 400, p. 92), the portraits-heads of Queen Nofretête (No. 3611, p. 101), the busts of a married couple (Nos. 745, 746, p. 94), the head of King Haremhạb (?), the statue of the god Khons, and the head of the goddess Mut in the Cairo Museum (Nos. 451, 462, 456, p. 93), besides a few other specimens in European museums. In many cases the artists have abandoned an attempt to produce a faithful portrait in favour of ideal beauty, devoting much of their energy to the representation of the coiffure, the ornaments, and the flowing garments then fashionable. Many new types were invented in this period, such as the figure of a man crouching on the ground and enveloped in a voluminous mantle.

After the 20th Dyn. (p. cvii) art steadily declined until the time of the Ethiopian monarchs (p. cviii), when it again revived under the inspiration of the models of the Ancient, the Middle, and (occasionally) the New Empires. At last began a later period of bloom, which has been styled the Egyptian Renaissance (comp. p. cix). Many of these late works are so like their ancient type-models that it is hard even for an expert to tell the difference. Simultaneously a new school arose in the Ethiopian period (c. 675 B.C.), which emancipated itself from slavish imitations and, by diligent study of the art of portrait-making and by a valiant effort to pour new

wine into old bottles, succeeded in producing masterpieces such as the head of the negroid old man (No. 1184, p. 95) and the statue of Mentemhēt (No. 935, p. 96), who was governor of Upper Egypt under Taharka of Ethiopia (No. 1185, p. 95). The same school, but perhaps several hundred years later, produced the portraits of bald-headed priests, in which the characteristic points (such as the shape of the skull) are indicated in a masterly manner, while the less significant details are ignored. — Though these productions of an art that strove after fidelity to nature, but was yet highly conventional, show no trace of Greek influence, the development of sculpture from the time of the Ptolemies on (p. cxi) betrays the influence of Greek art in an ever-increasing degree. Side by side with purely Greek works (chiefly in Alexandria) and purely Egyptian works, the sculptors of which clung anxiously and mechanically to the ancient style, we meet with specimens of a peculiar hybrid Græco-Egyptian style, in which the figures are Greek in attitude and Egyptian in drapery, coiffure, and adornment, or (e.g. in the tomb of Petosiris, p. 222) vice versa. However valuable these may be for an appreciation of Egyptian civilization at a late period, they certainly carry no satisfaction to the eye intent upon artistic effects.

In the practice of the **Artistic Handicrafts**, such as ivory and wood working, glass-blowing, and the production of coloured faience, Egypt was perfect. The goldsmiths and workers in metal in particular had attained the most complete mastery of their craft; they thoroughly understood all its ancillary arts, such as enamelling and damascene work, and they were thus able to produce, especially with the aid of coloured gems and faience inlays, works of a degree of finish and brilliancy such as a highly civilized nation alone could execute and appreciate. Egyptian jewellery attained its zenith under the Middle Empire and 18th Dynasty.

Owing to the strangeness of the Egyptian methods of representing nature it is not at all easy for the present-day visitor to form a real appreciation of their plastic arts and to distinguish the creations of true artists. For such an estimate an acquaintance must be obtained with the portrait-statues and reliefs now preserved in the Cairo Museum, and the reliefs on the walls of maṣṭabas, of rock tombs, and of a few special temples (notably the temples of Deir el-Baḥari and Luxor, at Thebes, pp. 317, 272, and the temple of Sethos at Abydos, p. 253). Genuine art-works, it is true, are but thinly sown in Egypt, and the more conspicuous colossal statues, sphinxes, and temple reliefs, with few exceptions, served only a decorative purpose.

The art of the Egyptians is far more closely connected with nature than is the case with any other race. It is but rarely that they give play to their imagination. On the other hand a truly charming sympathy with nature is apparent even in details. Combined with this, however, is an astonishing and at first somewhat repellent ten-

dency to a geometrical rendering of art forms, while a decided prepossession in favour of the monumental shows itself not only in gigantic dimensions, but even in their smallest productions.

Even those who cannot appreciate the genuine beauty of Egyptian art will not fail to be charmed by their extraordinary technical skill, which even to-day commands our unbounded admiration.

The following are some of the SYMBOLS and SIGNS most commonly used in sculpture and as architectural ornamentations. Thus, is the crook or shepherd's staff, the emblem of the prince or monarch (No. a12 on p. cxxxvi);  a flail or ceremonial whip, the symbol of kingly power;  the sign of life (No. b19 on p. cxxxvii);  the symbol of Osiris and the sign of steadfastness (No. b2 on p. cxxxvi);  the symbol of Isis;  the red crown of Lower Egypt;  the white crown of Upper Egypt;  the united crown of Upper Egypt and Lower Egypt (p. cii);  the blue head-dress of the king;  and  the uræus or royal serpent, represented on diadems and suns by . Its function was to avert hostile influences, just as the uræus serpent had once destroyed with its poison the enemies of the sun-god. The winged sun-disk,  (p. clxiii), the emblem of Horus of Edfu, was frequently placed over the doors of temples to avert everything evil. The sceptre,  *wes (w'ś)*, denoted welfare (No. b1 on p. cxxxvi);  *maat*, an ostrich-feather, truth and justice (comp. p. clvii);  *khepre*, the scarabæus or dung-beetle, is a form of the sun-god (p. cl) and was frequently worn as an amulet. The symbol  (originally meaning a lung and windpipe) signifies union. It is frequently entwined with sedge and papyrus, the typical plants of Upper and Lower Egypt, when it is symbolical of the union of the 'two lands' and is equivalent to the national arms of Egypt (p. cii). The lock  on the temple of a figure marks it as a child, at a later period generally the offspring of the gods or of the kings.

VIII. Christian Art in Egypt.

By *Professor Ugo Monneret de Villard.*

The history of Christian Art in Egypt may be divided into two periods, presenting entirely different characteristics. The first extends from the beginning of the 4th cent. to the Arab conquest (640-642), the second from that date to the present day. During the first period Egypt was a province of the Byzantine empire in the domain of art also, and its art exhibits the close relations between the Nile valley and the capital and other provinces, especially Syria. Alexandria was then one of the most important cities of the East, wealthy, learned, and highly cultured; and its position in the history of commerce is no less remarkable than its eminence in the history of civilization. All the products of the East came to its port, and it was frequented by merchants from the remotest countries. Thus the artistic influences of Asia found easy access to spread throughout Egypt. Superficially the interior of the country was hellenized, and, although the mass of the people maintained their national traditions, artistic productions reflect the domination of the cultured classes. Through the reactions between these two elements a local art of great importance came into being.

The oldest monuments of Christian art known to us are Tombs: the catacombs of Alexandria situated near the so-called Pompey's Pillar (p. 17), the mausolea of the necropolis in the oasis of Khârga (p. 407), and the tombs in the cemetery of Oxyrhynchus (El-Bahnasa, p. 219), the last-named showing a perfect type of small sepulchral Basilicas. Over the tomb of St. Menas in the Mareotis district the Emperor Arcadius (345-408) built a large basilica with transept (p. 30), which is the first monument of certain date in the Christian architecture of Egypt. Later, c. 430, the Byzantine count Cæsarius erected the great basilica of Deir el-Abyaḍ (p. 229), the church of the convent to which Shenute, one of the greatest Egyptian monks, belonged. This basilica is characterized by the form of its sanctuary, which is composed of three apses disposed in the form of a cross, a form which was copied in the Deir el-Aḥmar (p. 230) and in the basilica near the temple of Dendera (p. 266). These large columnar basilicas, with their numerous richly decorated niches and their frescoes that originally covered the whole of the wall-surfaces, are without doubt the most important monuments in the first period of Christian architecture in Egypt. Of somewhat later date, of smaller size, but also very interesting on account of their wealth of decorative sculptures, are the churches of the monastery of St. Jeremiah at Ṣaqqâra (p. 156) and of that of St. Apollo at Bâwîṭ (pp. 224, 225). Their best fragments are now in the Cairo Museum (p. 97). The type of these churches approaches more to that of the Syrian basilicas. The church of the Deir Abu Ḥinnis (p. 222) is a monument of great importance, unhappily spoilt by later mediæval

restorations and alterations. In Upper Egypt the savants of Napoleon's expedition (p. cxxv) discovered near Armant (p. 355) a large basilica with an apse at either end; this has since vanished, but a building of the same type is to be seen in the 'basilica of the baths' in the City of St. Menas (p. 30) and in a ruin at Mirsa Maṭrûḥ (p. 31).

In the earliest times the numerous hermits that peopled the Egyptian desert chose as their place of retreat ancient tombs of the Pharaonic period, which were converted into churches by the addition of a large niche serving as an apse. The most interesting examples of this adaptation are to be seen chiefly in some of the tombs at Beniḥasan (p. 241) and Mîr (p. 225), a tomb at Esh-Sheikh Saʿîd (p. 236), that of Penehse at Tell el-ʿAmârna (p. 248), that of Ramses IV. at Bîbân el-Mulûk (p. 303), and those of Sheikh ʿAbd el-Qurna at Thebes (pp. 328 seqq.) bearing the Nos. 84 (p. 330), 95, and 97. Several of these tombs contain Christian inscriptions and frescoes of the highest interest. Around these HERMITAGES gradually arose small MONASTERIES, the grotto serving as the church of the community. On the open space in front of the entrance were the cells, the storehouses, and a tower (jausaq, gausaq) that served as a place of refuge. One of the best examples of the type is the monastery of Epiphanius at Sheikh ʿAbd el-Qurna (p. 328).

Not content with utilizing the tombs of the Pharaonic period, the Christians took possession of the ancient temples. As a rule the vestibule was fitted up as a church (as at Dendera, Edfu, Esna, and Philæ), but the recent clearing of the temples from débris has in nearly every case caused the disappearance of every vestige of the Christian church. Elsewhere it was installed in an inner chamber, as may still be seen at Luxor (p. 276, Pl. E) or at Karnak, where it occupied the whole of the Great Festal Hall of Thutmosis III. (p. 291), the columns of which retain traces of frescoes representing saints of the Coptic church. Or the church was placed in one of the temple courts; a splendid example of this type, demolished a few years ago, was the church in the second court of the temple of Medînet Habu (p. 350). In Upper Egypt the Christians rarely destroyed the ancient temples; sometimes they obliterated the bas-reliefs, but more often they simply covered them with a thick coat of whitewash, a process to which we owe their preservation.

The buildings of this period were generally executed with great care; the columns were fine monoliths of Aswân granite and bear reliefs of crosses or other religious symbols and sometimes the donors' inscriptions; walls were of skilfully cut stone (usually limestone); roofs were of timber, except in the case of the apses, which had conches. There is a wealth of DECORATIVE SCULPTURE, with foliage, flowers, and interlacing patterns as motives, sometimes too with geometrical designs. One particular school of sculpture of Middle Egypt, which seems to have had its centre at Ahnâs (Ihnâsya

el-Madîna), the ancient Heracleopolis (p. 218), produced large compositions grouped around human figures, treated in a high-relief of great depth and effectiveness, with a skilful handling of masses and a play of light and shade that obtains results comparable with those of baroque sculpture. Although the general form of the elements (capitals, architraves, pilasters) is derived from Syria or Byzantium, their decoration has an altogether individual character and a repertoire of forms and motives that has never been attained by any other architecture in the Christian Orient.

Christian art in Egypt was profoundly, and almost essentially, a decorative art: walls, columns, capitals were covered with Paintings and Frescoes. Unfortunately very few examples of such paintings have survived to our day, but the little that remains enables us to trace its history. Like the Alexandrian art from which it derives, it is extremely fond of realism; the so-called Faiyûm portraits (comp. the Cairo Museum, Room O, Cases H-M, p. 110) exemplify a tradition that passed into Christian art and which we find again in the frescoes of Ṣaqqâra and Bâwîṭ (Cairo Museum, Gallery X and Room V, p. 97). With these Alexandrian traditions were mingled more definitely Oriental influences. The Hellenistic style shows itself persistently in the decoration; plinths have paintings in imitation of marble incrustation and friezes with circles and lozenges framing flowers, fruit, baskets, birds, and even portraits or symbolical figures and genre-figures. Above the plinths are large friezes with figures of prophets and saints, or monks, archangels, and the Virgin Mary. In the conch of the apses Christ frequently appears on a chariot with the beasts of the Apocalypse. The same style of art is found in the celebrated miniatures of the 'Christian Topography' composed c. 547-549 by Cosmas Indicopleustes of Alexandria, in which the picturesque, beloved by the Alexandrians, is mingled with the monumental style more appropriate to Asiatic æsthetics.

The conquest of Egypt by the Arabs had a great effect on the development of Christian art. Above all, the impoverishment of the church prevented the construction of expensive buildings, and the fact that Christianity was no longer the state religion, even though persecution was never rife in Egypt, brought about a failure of resources. Another consequence of the Arab domination was the victory of the Monophysite party (p. lviii) over the Catholics; the latter were imbued with classical traditions and Greek culture, the former with a nationalist spirit and local traditions. Nor must we forget the great influence which Asiatic monophysitism, which prevailed in the interior of Syria and in Mesopotamia, exercised upon the development of Christianity in Egypt. A deep Hellenistic tinge was succeeded by a still more remarkable Asiatic influence. Methods of construction at once alter: buildings are no longer constructed of hewn stone but of bricks and very often of unbaked bricks; granite columns are replaced by brick pillars; wood for roofing being exhausted, every

building is vaulted or domed. All this involved a change in the ground-plan of the churches, and one may say that the basilican type is completely abandoned (save at Old Cairo, pp. 113 seqq.).

In the extreme North of Egypt the Convents of the Wâdi en-Naṭrûn (p. 35) present monuments of the highest importance. The most interesting is the Deir Suryâni, rebuilt at the beginning of the 9th cent.; here the great church of the Virgin is an aisled and pillared basilica with barrel-vaults, a choir sited like a transverse nave, and a sanctuary formed of three square chambers. The central chamber is decorated with superb stuccoes in the Mesopotamian style, akin to those of the 3rd style of Sâmarrâ (pp. cxciii, cxciv) and probably executed in the time of Abbot Moses of Nisibis (Neṣîbîn; 10th cent.). Of great interest too are two doors of wood inlaid with ivory, dated 913-914 and 926-927. The small church of the Virgin at the same convent reproduces the form of the churches of the Ṭûr ʿAbdîn (a mountainous district about 25 M. to the N.E. of Neṣîbîn). The buildings of Deir Amba Bishôi and Deir Abu Maqâr are of later date than the Deir Suryâni, while the Deir el-Barâmûs was almost completely rebuilt in the 14th century. In Upper Egypt another group of buildings displays Mesopotamian influences still more perspicuously. The monastic church of St. Simeon near Aswân (p. 386) had a nave covered with two cupolas resting on squinches and aisles roofed with barrel-vaulting flanked by 'voûtains', two peculiarities clearly of Asiatic origin; the plan of the church too recalls a similar building at Amida (Diarbekr). The monastery of St. Simeon is the best-preserved specimen of a great Egyptian monastic foundation. The church of the Deir esh-Shuhadâ, or convent of the Martyrs, near Esna (p. 358) is an analogous structure. — Another important group of monastic buildings is found between Naqâda and Qamûla (p. 233); these are not all of the same age, and even in a single convent the various churches belong to quite different periods. The most interesting are the churches of El-ʿAdra and Mâri Girgis in the Deir el-Magmaʿ, the latter showing a system of parallel vaults on transverse arches after a model of Sassanian Persia.

During the 12th cent. a new type of church was developed in Egypt, which rapidly spread throughout the country and was employed down to the latest period. The church is rectangular in form, and within the rectangle columns or pillars form square bays each covered with a cupola. These cupolas may be very numerous, e.g. the church of Amba Pakhôm near El-Madamûd (p. 297) boasts twenty-nine. The most interesting of this series is the church of the Deir el-Maḥarraq (p. 225), where, according to Coptic legend, Christ sojourned during the Flight into Egypt.

The churches of Old Cairo (pp. 112-117) belong to another tradition, being mediæval reconstructions of churches antedating the Arab conquest. From early times they retain the general form

and 24*l.*, 3rd class 16*l.* — Nippon Yusen Kaisha (4 Lloyds Avenue, E.C. 3 and 25 Cockspur St., S.W. 1) fortnightly in 13 days, viâ Gibraltar, Marseilles, and Naples; fares 34*l.*, 22*l.*

From Liverpool to Port Said. Bibby Line (26 Chapel St., Liverpool; 22 Pall Mall, London, S.W. 1) every other Fri. in 13 days, viâ Marseilles; 1st class only, 32*l.* — Ellerman's City & Hall Lines (22 Water St., Liverpool, and 104-106 Leadenhall St., London, E.C. 3) every 7-12 days, sometimes calling at Marseilles or Naples; fares 33*l.*, 25*l.* — Anchor Line (Cunard Building, Liverpool, and 48 Fenchurch St., E.C. 3) fortnightly; fare 30*l.*, in summer 18*l.*, return 28*l.* — Henderson Line (153 St. Vincent St., Glasgow; London agents, 7 Billiter Square, E. C. 3) fortnightly viâ Marseilles; fare 30*l.*, in summer 20*l.* — Blue Funnel Line (India Buildings, Liverpool; London agents, 8 Billiter Square, E.C.3) every fourth Sat. in 9 days; 1st class only, 32*l.* (in summer 22*l.*). Also cargo steamer every Sat., carrying 1st class passengers (20*l.*, in summer 16*l.*).

From Liverpool to Alexandria. Ellerman and Papayanni Lines (22 Water St., Liverpool; London agents, 104-106 Leadenhall St.) in 14 days; fare 25-28*l.*, return 45*l.*-50*l.* 8*s.*

From London or Manchester to Alexandria. Prince Line (56 Leadenhall St., E.C. 3) every three weeks from London and every 10 days from Manchester, calling at Malta; fare 15-25*l.*

From Southampton to Port Said. Rotterdam Lloyd (London agents, 13 Fenchurch Avenue, E.C. 3) every other Fri. in 11 days, viâ Tangier and Marseilles; fares 35*l.* 10*s.*, 21*l.*, 12*l.* 10*s.* — Nederland Line (London agents, 60 Haymarket, S.W. 1) every other Thurs. in 12 days, viâ Algiers and Genoa; fares 30*l.* 15*s.*, 22*l.* — German African Services (German East Africa, Woermann, and Hamburg-America Lines; London agents, 66-68 Haymarket, S.W. 1) every three weeks viâ Lisbon, Tangier, Malaga, and Genoa; fares 33*l.*, 24*l.* 15*s.*, 16*l.* 10*s.*

From New York to Port Said or Alexandria. White Star Line (1 Broadway) monthly in about three weeks to *Alexandria* viâ Madeira, Gibraltar, Algiers, Monaco, Naples, Athens, Constantinople, and Haifa; 1st class $ 325, tourist 3rd cabin $ 145. — Ellerman & Bucknall Steamship Co. (agency, 26 Beaver St.) monthly to *Port Said* viâ Marseilles in 20 days; fares $ 250, $ 190. — Fabre Line (p. 5; agency, 17 State St.) from New York (and Providence or Boston) monthly in 3-5 weeks to *Alexandria* viâ the Piræus, Constantinople, Jaffa, etc.

B. Steamship Lines from Mediterranean Ports.

Overland Routes from London to Mediterranean Ports. *Brindisi* is 49 hrs. from London by ordinary express (1st class 10*l.* 12*s.* 7*d.*, 2nd class 7*l.* 6*s.* 1*d.*; sleeping car supplement from Paris 4*l.* 0*s.* 11*d.*) and 51 hrs. by the Rome Express (sleeper 7*l.* 16*s.* 3*d.*). — *Genoa* is 29¼ hrs. from London by ordinary express (7*l.* 10*s.* 9*d*, 5*l.* 4*s.* 8*d.*) and 25¾ hrs. by the Rome Express (sleeper 4*l.* 14*s.* 9*d.*). — *Venice* is 28½ hrs. from London (8*l.* 12*s.* 7*d.*, 5*l.* 19*s.* 11*d.*). — *Naples* is 45 hrs. from London by ordinary express (9*l.* 18*s.* 9*d.*, 6*l.* 16*s.* 11*d.*) and 38½ hrs. by the Rome Express (sleeper 6*l.* 8*s.* 3*d.*). — The 'P. & O. Express'

IX. Islamic Architecture in Egypt.

By *Captain K. A. C. Creswell.*

Although the Moslem architecture of Egypt begins in the 8th-9th cent. with the Nilometer (p. 112) and the mosque of Ibn Ṭûlûn (p. 76), it is quite impossible to understand these without a few words on the beginnings of Islâm.

In the days of Mohammed the Arabs had nothing worthy of the name of architecture. The house which he built at Medîna after his migration from Mecca (see p. lxxxvi) consisted of an open courtyard, about 60 yds. square, surrounded by walls 10-11 ft. high, built of dry rubble below and mud bricks above. This courtyard, which afterwards served as a place of prayer, was at first quite open, but, as the Companions complained of being exposed to the burning heat of the sun, a shelter was erected, consisting of palm-trunks used as columns supporting a roof of palm-leaves and mud. At the S.E. corner of the courtyard, against the outer wall, were the huts occupied by Saudâ and ʿÂisha, the wives of Mohammed, also built of mud bricks and thatched with palm-leaves. As Mohammed took other wives additional huts were constructed. All these huts opened into the courtyard. There were no lamps, and the evening devotions were accomplished by the light of a fire of palm-leaves.

At first the congregation turned towards Jerusalem when praying, a practice due to contact with the Jews, who occupied an important position in Medîna at this time, and from whom Mohammed had drawn a great part of his religious and political conceptions. Failing to bring about an entente with them after eighteen months of effort, he ultimately decided to break with them, and the first outward and visible sign of this decision was the change in the *qibla* or direction of prayer (Jan. 10th, 624), which henceforth became Mecca.

After Mohammed's death in 632 a period of great campaigns opens. The advance of the Arabs from their peninsula as champions of Islâm was, as it were, fan-wise; N.W. they spread into Syria and made contact with its Syro-Byzantine civilization, N.E. they spread into Mesopotamia (ʿIrâq) and Persia and made contact with the civilization of the Sassanian empire. This fact is of paramount importance for the development of Islamic architecture, as became manifest by the second half of the 7th century. — The armies of Islâm, composed chiefly of coarse Beduin from the heart of E. Arabia, knowing Mohammed and the Koran merely by name, and taking part, not in a religious war for the propagation of the faith, but in the hope of gratifying their insatiable lust for loot, had no soul for art or architecture, and, like all true nomads, no wish to dwell in towns. After about two generations, when the Arabs began to settle down and to require permanent habitations, it was to Sassanian architects that they turned on the Mesopotamian front, and to Byzantine architects on the Syrian.

The concave *miḥrâb* (or niche indicating the direction of prayer), the *maqṣûra* (or enclosure for the Caliph, p. cxvii, or the provincial governor), and the *minbar* (pulpit, p. cc), all of which are of non-Moslem origin, appear at the end of the 7th or beginning of the 8th century.

In Syria most of the early **Mosques** were converted churches, conversion being effected by closing the W. entrances, by making openings in the N. side, and by praying towards the S. wall (i.e. towards Mecca). Hence the distinct predilection in Syria for a sanctuary with two rows of arcades (the ancient three-aisled basilica). In Mesopotamia, where the chief centres of Arab settlement were new foundations such as Kûfa and Baṣra, a different type of mosque was evolved. At Baṣra the first mosque was simply marked out on the ground, and the people prayed there without any buildings. At Kûfa the boundaries of the mosque were marked out by a man who stood on the chosen site and threw an arrow in the direction of the qibla, then another towards the N., another to the W., and a fourth to the E. A square, with each side two arrow-casts long, was thus obtained. The area was enclosed by a ditch, and the only structural part was a covered colonnade *(ẓulla)*, open on all sides, which ran the whole length of the S. side. The columns were taken from the ruins of Ḥîra. Against the S. side was built the dwelling of the Commander-in-Chief. It is important to observe that we have here, as early as the year 638, a group — a square mosque, with the Governor's residence built against the S. side — that was destined to persist for several centuries.

In A.D. 750 occurred an event which had a profound influence on Islâm — the fall of the only real Arab dynasty, the Umaiyad (comp. p. cxviii), and the rise of the Abbasids (p. cxviii), who transferred the seat of government to Baghdâd, which was founded by El-Manṣûr in 762. This change was as fundamental as the transfer of the capital of the Roman Empire from Rome to Constantinople, the centre of gravity of the empire in each case being displaced towards the E. The influence of Syria and Byzance on Moslem art thereby decreased, and the influence of the traditions of Sassanian Persia and Central Asia enormously increased. The first great mosque of Baghdâd appears to have been about 125 yds. square, with a courtyard *(ṣaḥn)* in the centre, a sanctuary five arcades deep on the qibla side, and arcades two aisles deep on the other three sides, all covered with flat roofs. From 836 to 892 the seat of the caliphate was at Sâmarrâ, about 60 M. higher up the Tigris. Here considerable remains have been preserved above ground, and an enormous quantity of stucco ornament has been recovered by the excavations of Sarre and Herzfeld. The pointed arch is found here in the ruins of the Caliph's palace.

We must now turn to Egypt, which had remained extremely backward architecturally, having been a conquered province for over

two centuries, bled white for tribute under a series of extortioners, scarcely any of whom remained in office for more than three years. The Umaiyad period is consequently quite unrepresented there. At last, however, Egypt became the seat of an independent ruler, *Aḥmad Ibn Ṭûlûn* (p. cxix), who came from Sâmarrâ bringing with him the architectural traditions of that great city. His mosque (p. 76), in plan related to that of Baghdâd, in ornament to the monuments of Sâmarrâ, is thus an absolutely foreign (Mesopotamian) product, planted down on the soil of Egypt. The legend of the Christian architect, invented solely to explain the use of piers (a novelty in Egypt) instead of columns, may be unhesitatingly rejected. The three types, under which Herzfeld has classified the ornament found at Sâmarrâ, are all found in the mosque of Ibn Ṭûlûn, together with the simplest and earliest examples of geometrical ornament in Islâm (soffits of arches on the S.W. side of the court). The whole structure is built of brick, and the slightly stilted pointed arch is employed throughout.

The Fatimid Period (969-1171; p. cxix) commenced with the conquest of Egypt by Gôhar, the general of the Fatimid caliph El-Muʿizz, in 969. From this year dates the foundation of Cairo (El-Qâhira, p. 47) on unoccupied ground to the N. of Fusṭâṭ and El-Qaṭâ'iʿ (the town of Ibn Ṭûlûn; p. 46). The city was a fortified enclosure about 1200 yds. square, containing two palaces for the caliph (a larger one on the E. and a smaller one on the W., p. 81), government offices, quarters for the garrison, treasury, mint, library, imperial mausoleum, arsenal, etc. Until the fall of the Fatimid dynasty in 1171, no person was allowed to enter the walls of the city except the soldiers of the garrison and the highest officers of state. In this respect it recalls the arrangement at Peking of the Chinese City, the Tartar City, and the Forbidden City, as laid out by Qubilai Khân three centuries later.

No fragment of the enclosure remains to-day, but some carved wooden friezes from the smaller Fatimid palace (see above) are fortunately to be seen in the Museum of Arab Art (p. 67). Gôhar also built a mosque, the *Gâmiʿ el-Azhar* (p. 58), which was commenced in 970 and completed in the following year. Columns are used instead of piers. Though it has been much altered, it is easy to see that the original sanctuary was five aisles deep and the side ones three, but the number on the N. side remains doubtful. Its most striking feature is the transept, which runs from the ṣaḥn to the miḥrâb (prayer-niche; p. 61), and against which the arcades on either side stop short. This is the first example of a transept in the mosques of Egypt, but it is found earlier in Syria, since the Great Mosque at Damascus, built by El-Walîd in 705-715, has one. It would appear that this feature was taken to the W. (comp. the mosque of Cordova) by ʿAbd er-Raḥmân (p. cxviii), the last of the Umaiyads, and came back to Egypt viâ N. Africa, where it is found

in the mosque of Sîdi ʿOqba at Qairawân (Kairouan in Tunis), the capital of the Fatimids. In the Azhar Mosque there was probably a dome at each of the back corners, exactly as may be seen in the *Mosque of El-Ḥâkim* at Cairo (p. 83), built 990-1012. A detailed examination of the latter enables us to analyse its sources of inspiration. Its nearly square plan, its numerous doors, the five sanctuary aisles of seventeen arches each, the piers, and the little arches over them, which lighten the masonry, are all Mesopotamian features; the transept is ultimately derived from Syria, as also are the entrances (now walled up) in the middle of the N.E. and S.E. sides. The semi-fortified appearance, given by the two great salients containing the minarets, is another Mesopotamian feature, which characterized the mosques of Baghdâd and Sâmarrâ, and also the Great Mosque of Bosṭâm in N. Persia, which El-Muqaddasi, the Arab geographer (985), says stood like a fortress in the centre of the market-place.

Cairo was refortified by Badr el-Gamâli (p. cxx) in 1087-92, the town having outgrown the original enclosure. Of this new work three well-preserved *Gateways* remain, the Bâb en-Naṣr (p. 84), the Bâb el-Futûḥ (p. 84), and the Bâb Zuweila (p. 64), and over 300 yds. of the city wall, set with square towers. Each of these gates has a distinct individuality and is the work of different architects, three Armenian refugees from Edessa (Urfa), which had fallen into the hands of the Seljuk Turks (p. cxx) the previous year (1086). These gates, curtain-wall, and towers are of exceptional interest as being among the few examples remaining of Moslem military architecture prior to the Crusades. The Bâb en-Naṣr is defended by a pair of mâchicoulis, a device in fortification not found in Europe until the end of the 12th century. The passage-ways of the Bâb el-Futûḥ and the Bâb Zuweila are covered by a shallow dome of cut stone resting on spherical-triangle pendentives of the same curvature ('calotte sur pendentifs'), the earliest example of this feature in Egypt. Practically every architectural feature of these fortifications can be traced to N. Syria, and their inspiration, as fortifications, is Byzantine.

The chief glory of Fatimid architecture lay in its ornamentation, which compels universal admiration by the boldness and variety of its designs. This ornament consists of decorative writing and of arabesqe patterns of a very high order, sometimes worked into a geometrical framework, sometimes not. Geometrical ornament at this time played quite a subordinate part, and the famous interlacing star pattern, which in later times had ten, twelve, or even more points, is only found in its simplest form, the eight-pointed star. Unlike the Tulunid period, in which Mesopotamian influences predominate, the Fatimid period is noteworthy for the beginning of Syrian influences, which later on became such a dominating feature under the Aiyubids and early Mamelukes. In decorative script,

Persian and N. Mesopotamian influences appear to be the dominant factor, and the development of many distinctive features, such as the plaiting of the shafts of the letters, etc., is often a century in advance of Egypt in those countries. An adequate analysis of the question, however, cannot yet be made, owing to the scarcity of contemporary monuments outside Egypt, and this fact alone adds immensely to the importance of the wonderful series of Fatimid monuments preserved in Cairo.

The Aiyubid Period (1171-1250; p. cxxi) opens with the military works of Saladin, who built a great part of the present walls of Cairo, besides the mighty Citadel (p. 73) which is so conspicuous an object as one approaches the city. Unfortunately none of the religious buildings erected by him in Egypt have survived. Unlike the Fatimids, who used square towers, Saladin always employed half-round towers about 20 ft. wide, with two arrow-slits giving one a flanking and the other forward fire. His curtain-walls at the Citadel have a continuous internal gallery 3 ft. wide running through them, but his city walls are without this feature, except in the case of the E. wall, where there is a short length of gallery attached to each tower.

The most noteworthy device in fortification introduced by Saladin was the bent entrance. Something of the sort seems to have been known in ancient Egypt, but Babylon, Rome, Byzance, and early Islâm apparently knew it not. The Bâb el-Mudarrag at the Citadel (hidden away behind Muḥammed ʿAli's Bâb el-Gedîd; p. 73), is the earliest dated example in the Middle East (1184). The object of such an entrance is of course to break the rush of a storming party. The Bâb el-Qarâfa, on the opposite side of the Citadel, excavated by the writer in 1923, is another example of the same date.

Saladin's brother El-ʿÂdil reinforced the Citadel, in some places with great square towers, in others by building round the half-round towers and trebling their diameter, e.g. the two great towers facing ʿAbbâsîya. — Saladin introduced the madrasa or theological school (p. cxcviii) into Egypt, but the cruciform type did not appear until nearly a century later.

The Aiyubid period was therefore marked by the military architecture of Saladin, the introduction of the madrasa, the increasing use of hewn stone, the introduction of marble panelling for miḥrâbs (e.g. in the mosque of the Sultan Eṣ-Ṣâliḥ Aiyûb, p. 81), by the development of stucco ornament in the direction of almost excessive fineness, by the first use of glass in connection with pierced stucco grilles (mausoleum of the Abbasid caliphs, p. 80), and by the first steps in the evolution of the stalactite pendentive (see p. cc, under Mausolea).

Bahrite Mamelukes (1250-1382; p. cxxi). This period witnessed an important development in the early mosque plan, whereby the little dome which, in the Ḥâkim Mosque (p. 83) for example,

covers the space in front of the miḥrâb, is replaced by a really large dome of wood which covers nine bays (3 by 3) and dominates the sanctuary, e.g. in the mosques of Beibars I. (at ʿAbbâsîya, p. 85; 1269), Muḥammed en-Nâṣir (in the Citadel; 1318-35), El-Mârdâni (p. 65; 1340), etc. The Syrian number (three) and arrangement of the doors were also adopted. It was Beibars I. also who introduced the stalactite portal from Syria, henceforth such a distinctive feature in the architecture of Egypt. The greatest achievement of the period was the Madrasa of Sultan Ḥasan (1356-63; p. 71). Its dimensions are truly colossal: in length it measures about 490 ft. and its greatest breadth is about 220 ft.; it covers an area of nearly 8000 sq. yds. When one stands at the entrance to the great ṣaḥn (p. 72), and observes its vast proportions, its rich yet restrained decoration, the grandeur and simplicity of its lines, the height and breadth of its great vaults, and the rich stalactite balconies of the minaret rising over the S.W. corner (p. 71), one feels bound to admit that this madrasa is one of the great things of the world. Richer and more delicate monuments were built in Egypt under the following dynasty, but as an expression of power and majesty we shall never find its equal.

The period of the Bahrite Mamelukes is marked also by the invention of the cruciform madrasa (comp. p. cxcviii); by the introduction of striped *(ablaq)* masonry for the decoration of façades; by the final development and gradual extinction of stucco ornament; and by the introduction of splendid dados of many-coloured marble.

Circassian Mamelukes (1382-1517; p. cxxiii, comp. also p. 78). The architecture of this period follows that of the previous one without any break in development. The rich stucco decoration which had become extinct towards the end of the previous period is not immediately replaced; at first the stone surfaces were left smooth and marble panelling was the chief enrichment, but when plastic skill in the new material was once acquired (c. 1440), elaborate carved surface decoration once more became a regular feature. The period is noteworthy for the last stages in the development of the stalactite pendentive; niches are set out Syrian fashion in a triangular frame, but, unlike Syrian pendentives, each tier is curved in plan instead of cutting across the corner in a straight line; there is a great increase in the number of tiers, seven, eight, or nine being common and even as many as thirteen being known. Domical construction culminated; the domes of this period, which are always of stone, are without rivals for lightness, beauty of outline, and richness of decoration, a notable example being the Barqûq Mosque (pp. 121, 122), among the Tombs of the Caliphs. The ancient type of mosque is replaced towards the end of this period by a type of structure hitherto used for madrasas only (see p. cxcviii).

Turkish Period (pp. cxxiv, cxxv). The Turkish conquest in 1517 caused at first a serious diminution in every branch of industry:

a large number of craftsmen were sent to Constantinople, and it is even stated that many crafts became extinct in Cairo. It has been the custom to belittle the Turkish period, nevertheless it would appear that the enormous reduction in the amount of money hitherto spent on grandiose monuments by the rich Mameluke court was a more serious factor than an actual falling off in the quality of work. The small mosques of Sîdi Sâriya in the Citadel (p. 75), Sinân Pasha at Bûlâq (p. 86), and El-Malika Ṣafîya (p. 71) suffice to justify this opinion. The withering effect of European influence was destined to deal the final blow at all spontaneous self-expression in architecture, but fortunately not so soon in Egypt as elsewhere. This fatal influence, whose arrival is signalled at Constantinople by the Nuri Osmaniye Mosque, finished about 1753, and at Damascus by a baroque fountain, built in 1798, does not appear to have reached Egypt until after 1820.

Mosques, the most important monuments of Islamic art, may be divided into two categories, the *Gâmiʿ* or mosque for the congregational prayer on Friday, and the *Masgid* or praying place. Besides these there is the *Zâwiya* or small chapel. The oldest type of congregational mosque found in Egypt is of Mesopotamian origin (e.g. Ibn Ṭûlûn, p. cxciv). Around a nearly square court *(ṣaḥn)* are four flat-roofed porticos *(riwâq)*. The chief riwâq, or sanctuary, placed on the side towards Mecca, has usually five aisles (Ibn Ṭûlûn, p. 77; El-Azhar, p. 59; El-Ḥâkim, pp. 83, 84) or six aisles (Beibars I., p. 85), while the other sides have only two (Ibn Ṭûlûn) or three (El-Azhar, El-Ḥâkim, and Beibars I.).

The religious, dogmatic, ceremonial, social, and moral precepts of Islâm have taken form under four principal rites, founded by the Imâms Abu Ḥanîfa, Mâlik ibn Anas, Esh-Shâfiʿi, and Aḥmad ibn Ḥanbal (p. lxxxviii). The **Madrasa** was a kind of theological college introduced by the Seljuk Sultans (p. cxx) in the 11th cent. for the teaching of these rites, and for the training of the large body of officials needed by the Seljuk administration. As there was no hostility between the various rites, they sometimes made provision for more than one rite in the same building. Nûr ed-Dîn introduced the institution into Syria, and Saladin (p. cxxi), after the fall of the Fatimid dynasty, carried it into Egypt, in order to combat the Shiite heresy of the Fatimids and insure the triumph of the Sunnite reaction.

The architectural form usually taken by the madrasa in Egypt after the middle of the 13th cent. was as follows: a square central court flanked by four open halls or *lîwâns*, forming the branches of a cross. This figure is inscribed in a rectangle, the angles of which are occupied by the dependencies: the great entrance-bay, a staircase to the roof, halls, cells for the professors, etc. In early examples the lîwâns are covered by tunnel-vaults, in later examples there is merely a frontal arch with a flat timber roof behind it. The prevalence

of this type gave rise to the idea that Egyptian madrasas were always built for all four rites, and the fact that the institution was introduced from Syria gave rise to the theory that the cruciform type was introduced from Syria also. Both these ideas are erroneous. We now know that although no less that eight madrasas built before 1270 exist in Syria, none of them has either a cruciform plan or four great lîwâns, but that a cruciform madrasa was built in Egypt as early as 1263 by Sultan Beibars I., and we are therefore justified in saying that the cruciform plan was first employed for a madrasa in Egypt.

To return to the evolution of the mosque proper. The disadvantages of the arcaded type of mosque for preaching in may be realized by mounting the pulpit (say in the mosque of Ibn Ṭûlûn) and observing how little of the congregation would be visible from it, owing to the obstruction caused by the piers of the arcades (comp. the plan, p. 77). In the madrasa, on the contrary, one's vision of the congregation is not obstructed, and it is therefore not surprising to find that the madrasa plan gradually ousts the older plan, and that it is sometimes adopted for mosques as early as the 14th cent. (mosques of the Emir Yl-Malak, 1319, and Aṣlam el-Bahâ'i, 1345, p. 65) and frequently in the 15th cent. (mosques of Gamâl ed-Dîn el-Ustâdâr, 1408; Gânî Bek, 1427; Gôhar el-Lâlâ, 1430, p. 73; Qigmâs el-Isḥâqi, 1481, p. 65; etc.). In the last century of the Mameluke period the size of the ṣaḥn was much reduced and a skylight placed over it.

After the conquest of Egypt by the Turks in 1517, the influence of the Byzantine-Ottoman style caused the introduction of a sanctuary covered by a large dome and preceded by a court surrounded by arcades roofed with little domes (e.g. El-Malika Ṣafîya, 1610, p. 71).

The Exteriors of the earliest mosques were very plain. The enclosing wall was pierced by many doorways without architecture and capped by stepped crenellations. Later on the influence of Syria (e.g. the Great Mosque at Damascus) caused the doors to be reduced to three in number (e.g. Beibars I., 1269, p. 85; En-Nâṣir Muḥammed, 1318-35, p. 75; and El-Mârdâni, 1340, p. 65). The walls were now broken up into narrow panels, in which the windows, usually quite small, were placed. The entrances were treated in an imposing manner, usually consisting of a slight salient with a deep entrance-bay vaulted with stalactites; at the back of this bay was the actual doorway, usually covered by a joggled lintel with a joggled relieving arch above. The door was often covered with bronze plaques arranged in an elaborate geometrical pattern. The sill was frequently a block of granite taken from an old Egyptian monument, with hieroglyphics still visible.

Internal Equipment. The centre of the court *(ṣaḥn)* was usually occupied by a fountain *(fasqîya)* under a little wooden dome resting on columns. This, however, was not for ablution (p. xc), which, until

after the Turkish conquest, was performed in an adjoining court. It then became usual to have a structure with taps all round (*ḥanafîya)* in the centre of the ṣaḥn, a practice which, in an earlier age, would have been regarded as polluting the mosque.

At the back of the sanctuary is to be found (1) the prayer-niche (*miḥrâb*; not *qibla*, which merely means the direction of Mecca): (2) the pulpit (*minbar*, pron. 'mimbar'), frequently a fine piece of cabinet-maker's work; (3) the *dikka*, or platform supported on columns, on which the *muballighîn* (assistants of the imâm or leader in prayer) repeat the genuflections, etc. (pp. lxxxix, xc), at the same time being visible to the whole congregation, who are therefore enabled to keep time; (4) the lamps and lanterns (*tannûr*, a large chandelier), hanging from the ceiling. All the great bronze chandeliers and enamelled glass lamps have been removed to the Museum of Arab Art (p. 69) for safety.

The first mosques had no *Minarets*, the call to prayer being given from the roof. The first minaret of Ibn Ṭûlûn's mosque (pp. 76, 78), was apparently a spiral copied from the minaret of the Great Mosque at Sâmarrâ. In the 11th cent. we find a tall square shaft surmounted by a little domed kiosk (El-Giyûshi, 1085; p. 125). This little kiosk becomes more and more elaborate, its cap becoming fluted and its lower part drawn out to such an extent that eventually the minaret becomes three-storied, successively square, octagonal, and circular (e.g. the mosque of Sangar el-Gâwli, 1303; p. 79). This evolution is so clear and so gradual that the Pharos theory of the origin of the minaret must be given up (comp. p. 13). After c. 1340 the prevailing type consisted of an octagonal shaft, with a little domed kiosk at the summit (El-Mârdâni Mosque, 1340, p. 65; Sheikhûn Mosque, 1355, p. 76).

The **Mausolea** of sultans and emirs are generally, though not invariably, built as annexes to mosques or madrasas founded by them. The actual subterranean chamber containing the body or bodies are destitute of decoration. The corpse, wrapped in white cotton cloth, is placed with the face towards Mecca. In the chamber above the vault stands a cenotaph (*tarkîba*, when of stone or brick; *tâbût*, when of wood). This chamber is almost invariably square and covered by a dome, the transition to which from the square ground-plan provides a most interesting study for architects. The earliest Moslem domes in Egypt (mosques of El-Ḥâkim, p. 83, and El-Giyûshi, p. 125) rest on semi-domed niches (known as squinches), which are placed in the corners of the square below the dome. The square is thereby converted into an octagon, on which it is easy to set a dome. In the first departure from this scheme the octagon is formed, not by a squinch, but by three niches surmounted by one (mausoleum of El-Ga'fari and Saiyida 'Âtika, c. 1125; p. 80). The next step was to fill the blank space on either side of the upper niche with another one, thus producing a pendentive of two tiers of

three niches (mausoleum of the Abbasid Caliphs, 1242-43; p. 80). The next step occurs in the mausoleum of Sultan Eṣ-Ṣâliḥ Aiyûb (1250; p. 81), which has a comparatively large dome. Here, apparently, it was felt that a more gradual transition was necessary. The earlier procedure was repeated; just as the squinch was shrunk into the corner, so we now find a pendentive, modelled on that of the Abbasid caliphs, shrunk into the corner, and the final transition effected by a row of four niches placed above it. The next step was to make the pendentive of four tiers of stalactites (mausoleum of Beibars II. el-Gâshankîr, 1306-9; p. 84). Five tiers first appear in the mausoleum of the Emir Ṣarghatmish (1356; p. 79). This type must have been evolved in Egypt, as the Syrian type is constructed quite differently, the tiers of niches, instead of being curved in plan, run straight across the corners, and are really nothing more than blind niches carved on tiers of oversailing lintels. Moreover the number of niches in each tier is generally more or less equal in Egypt, whereas in Syria there is only one niche in the lowest tier, two in the second, three in the third, and so on.

Among Secular Buildings the **Fortifications** have already been discussed (pp. cxcv, cxcvi), and the special importance of the Fatimid walls and gates emphasized.

Of the ancient **Palaces** several fortunately remain, but none earlier than the middle of the 14th century. The ground-floors are of good solid masonry entirely vaulted, but the ceilings of the first floor are almost invariably of timber painted and gilded, and sometimes beautifully coffered, as in the palace of the Emir Bishtâk (d. 1341; p. 83). Projecting balconies were also a feature.

Dwelling Houses (comp. the plans at pp. ccii, cciii) rarely had more than two stories. On the ground-floor is the *Salâmlik*, or men's apartments, and on the first floor the *Ḥarîm* or women's apartments and rooms for the family.

The chief decoration of the façade is provided by exquisite *Mashrabîya* balconies. During the last thirty years it can scarcely be an exaggeration to say that 90% of these have disappeared, and the streets of Cairo have thereby lost their most distinctive cachet. Perhaps the best vista to be seen to-day is in the street which runs W. from the madrasa of Gamâl ed-Dîn, skirting the Bishtâk Palace (p. 83), and comes out into the Shâriʿ Bein es-Sûrein (Pl. G F 4).

The following rules are generally observed in the construction of a house. (1) The principal rooms face N. (direction of the prevailing wind; comp. p. 75) and look into the court. (2) The windows looking on to the street are few and placed high. (3) The passage leading from the street to the court is built with a right-angled turn to prevent passers-by from seeing into the court. (4) The entrance to the harem is placed in a second court, or on the far side of the first court. (5) The reception rooms of the master of the house, servants' quarters, kitchen, etc., are arranged round the first court.

The principal rooms, which are usually the only rooms with any decoration are the *Mandara* (No. 7 on the first plan), or reception room for male visitors, with its *Khazna* or cabinet; the *Takhtabôsh* or *Maqʿad* (No. 1 on the second plan), a veranda placed in a kind of entresol and raised one or two steps above the level of the court. To these may be added a *Court* paved with marble. All these belong to the salâmlik. On the upper floor is the *Qâʿa*, the chief living room of the family, resembling the mandara. In some exceptional

Plan I.

Ground Floor.

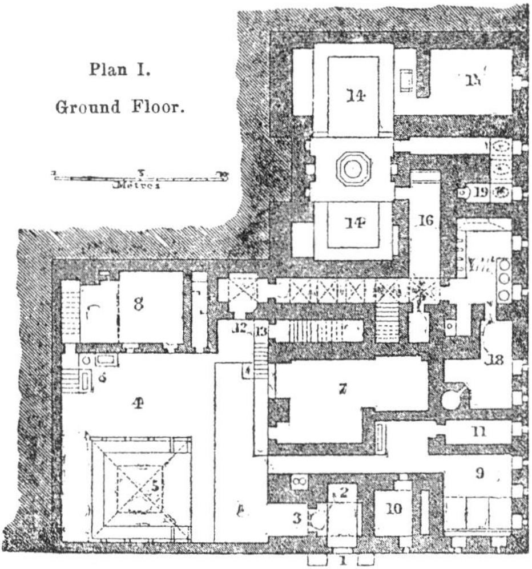

1. Entrance. 2. Seat (maṣṭaba) for the doorkeeper (bauwâb). 3. Corridor (dirka). 4. Court (hôsh). 5. An arbour in which visitors are received in summer. 6. Fountain. 7. Mandara. 8. Servants' rooms. 9. Donkey-stable. 10. Harness-room. 11. Room for fodder. 12. Door leading to the women's apartments (bâb el-harîm). 13. Staircase leading to the takhtabôsh. 14. Principal sitting room (el-qâʿa). 15. Cabinet (khazna). 16. Small court. 17. Kitchen. 18. Bakehouse. 19. Privy.

cases the qâʿa is on the ground-floor (comp. No. 14 on the first plan, also in the palace of Muḥammed Muḥibb ed-Dîn, known as the Hall of ʿOsmân Katkhudâ and situated near the Shâriʿ Beit el-Qâḍi, p. 81). The qâʿa is a long narrow room and, strictly speaking, consists of three sections, differentiated in shape and height of ceiling. The floor of the square central portion, known as the *Durqâʿa*, is one step lower than the *Liwâns* on each side. The latter are not always of the same width, in which case the broader one is regarded as the place of honour. The ceiling of the durqâʿa generally takes

the form of a wooden dome or lantern with coloured glass windows of the kind known as *Qamarîya (qamrîya, qimrîya).* The latter consist of plaster slabs perforated with patterns representing vases of flowers, geometrical patterns, etc., the openings being covered with coloured glass fixed on the outside. The durqâʿa is generally paved with marble, and there is usually a basin with a fountain in the centre. On one side there is a marble shelf resting on an attractive little open arcade; this shelf is known as the *Ṣuffa*, and on it

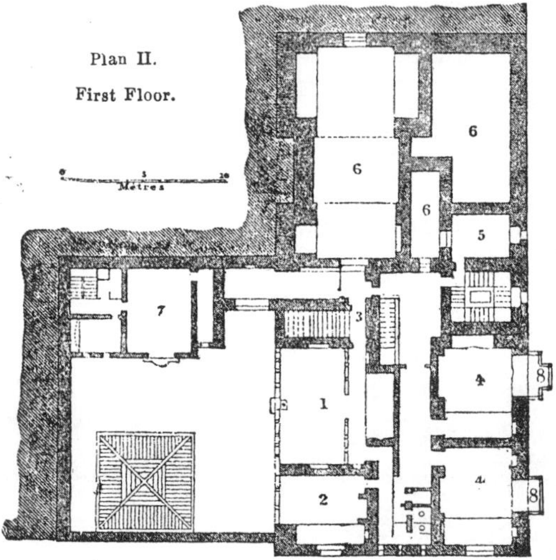

1. Open hall (takhtabôsh or maqʿad). 2. Cabinet. 3. Door of the harem. 4. Rooms of the harem with mashrabîyas. 5. Store-room. 6. Open courts. 7. Guest-chambers with khazna and privy. 8. Balcony with mashrabîyas.

are placed the coffee cups, etc. The walls of the lîwâns are panelled with marble to a height of 6-10 ft. Above this there is sometimes a shelf for metal vessels, porcelain vases, etc., and above that the wall is generally covered with plain white plaster. The lîwâns are roofed with a ceiling of painted and gilded woodwork resting on a deep cavetto cornice in the same style. Light and air are admitted to the room from one of the ends, where mashrabîyas are inserted in the lower part of the wall and qamarîyas in the upper part.

The **Public Baths** are usually of quite plain exterior, though one of them, the Bath of the Emir Bishtâk (p. 83) in the Sûq es-Silâḥ (Pl. F 5, 6), has an exquisite little portal.

A **Wakâla** (or *Wikâla*, storehouse, caravanserai), commonly called *Okala* (*Okella*, *Occaleh;* p. 53) is frequently a very large building, several stories high, with a courtyard in the centre. The ground-floor on the exterior consists of a number of rooms open to the street, which are let out as shops. Above are living quarters, let out to passing merchants or permanent residents. A monumental gateway in the centre of the façade leads to the courtyard, round which are store-rooms for merchandise, with living quarters above, frequently served by outer galleries or balconies, running all round. These buildings, warehouses and tenements in one, were a form of investment before the days of limited liability companies, and benefactors, wishing to endow a mosque or madrasa, frequently built okalas, the rents derived from them being administered by trustees. Such an arrangement is called a *Waqf* (comp. p. 55).

The neglect from which the study of the Moslem architecture of Egypt has hitherto suffered is chiefly due to the rival glamour of the immensely old monuments of ancient Egypt. There are few visitors, however, who can fail to be thrilled by the charm of Islamic art, the splendid façades of the 14th and 15th cent., the beautiful forms of its innumerable domes and minarets, and the extraordinary refinement of its ornament.

X. Books about Egypt.

We mention only some of the more important and more modern works. Several books on special subjects and individual sites are mentioned in the text of the handbook.

Books about Alexandria, see p. 11; Aswân Dam, p. 397; Cairo, p. 48; Cairo Museum, p. 88; Eastern Desert, p. 397; Faiyûm, p. 203; Islamic Law and the Koran, pp. xci, xcii; Oasis of Kurkur, p. 388; Luxor, p. 269; Meroë, p. 448; Mummies, p. clv; Western Oases, pp. 403-5, 408; City of St. Menas, p. 30; Ṣaqqâra, p. 153; Egyptian Songs, p. xxviii; Sûdân, p. 444; Thebes, p. 269.

Scientific Societies in Egypt, see p. 44. The *Egypt Exploration Society* (formerly Egypt Exploration Fund), founded in 1883 by Miss Amelia Edwards (p. 435), has its seat in London, 13 Tavistock Square, W.C. 1.

History of Ancient Egypt.

Bevan, Edwyn Robert, A History of Egypt under the Ptolemaic Dynasty; London, 1927; 15*s*.

Breasted, James Henry, History of Egypt; 2nd ed., New York, 1909 (London 1906; new ed. 1923). A detailed and clearly written account.

—, Ancient Records of Egypt (a collection of translations of Egyptian historical documents); 5 vols., Chicago, 1906-7.

Cambridge Ancient History. Vols. I-III; Cambridge, 1924-25.

Hall, Harry Reginald Holland, The Ancient History of the Near East from the Earliest Times to the Battle of Salamis; 7th ed., London, 1927.

King, L. W., and *Hall, H. R. H.*, History of Egypt, Chaldea, Syria, Babylonia, and Assyria in the Light of Recent Discovery; London, 1906 (reissued in 1907: Egypt and Western Asia in the Light of Recent Discoveries).

Meyer, Eduard, Geschichte des Altertums. Vol. I, 3rd ed., Stuttgart & Berlin, 1911, 4th and 5th ed. (phototype) 1925; Vol. II, Part I, 2nd ed., 1928.

Milne, *J. Grafton*, A History of Egypt under Roman Rule; 3rd ed., London, 1924; 12*s*.
Peet, *T. Eric*, Egypt and the Old Testament; London, 1922; 5*s*.
Quibell, *Annie A.*, Egyptian History and Art; 2nd ed., London, 1926; 6*s*.
Rawlinson, *George*, Ancient Egypt; 10th ed., London, 1923 (Story of the Nations series); 7*s*. 6*d*.
Scharff, *Alexander*, Grundzüge der ägyptischen Vorgeschichte; Leipzig, 1927; 4 marks 20 pf.
Smith, *G. Elliot*, The Ancient Egyptians and their Influence upon the Civilization of Europe; London & New York, 1911 (revised ed. 1923: The Ancient Egyptians and the Origin of Civilization).
Steindorff, *Georg*, Die Blütezeit des Pharaonenreichs; 2nd ed., Bielefeld, 1926; 10 marks.

Mediæval and Modern History of Egypt. Mohammedanism.

Arnold, *Sir Thomas*, The Preaching of Islam; 2nd ed., London, 1913; 12*s*. 6*d*.
—, The Islamic Faith; London, 1928 (Benn's Sixpenny Library).
Becker, *C. H.*, Islamstudien. Vom Werden und Wesen der Islamischen Welt; Vol. I, Leipzig, 1924; 14 marks.
Butler, *A. J.*, The Arab Conquest of Egypt; London, 1902.
Devonshire. *Mrs. R. L.*, L'Egypte Musulmane et les Fondateurs de ses Monuments; Paris, 1926.
Elgood, *Lt.-Col. P. G.*, The Transit of Egypt; London, 1928; 18*s*. The best book on the British occupation.
Ghorbal, *Shafik*, The Beginning of the Egyptian Question and the Rise of Mehemet Ali; London, 1928; 12*s*. 6*d*.
Hasenclever, *Adolf*, Geschichte Ägyptens im 19. Jahrhundert; Halle, 1917; 15 marks.
Lammens, *Henri*, S. J., Islâm; translated from the French by Sir E. Denison Ross; London, 1929; 8*s*. 6*d*.
Lane-Poole, *Stanley*, History of Egypt in the Middle Ages; 2nd ed., London, 1914.
Margoliouth, *D. S.*, The Early Development of Mohammedanism; London, 1914.
Muir, *Sir William*, The Mameluke or Slave Dynasty of Egypt (1260-1517 A.D.); London, 1896.
Newman, *Major E. W. Polson*, Great Britain in Egypt; London, 1928; 15*s*.
Ross, *Sir E. Denison*, Islâm; London, 1927 (Benn's Sixpenny Library).
Weigall, *Arthur E. P. B.*, A History of Events in Egypt from 1798 to 1914; London & New York, 1915; 10*s*. 6*d*.
The Campaign in Egypt and Palestine (vol. 1), an official history of the War (London, 1928; 12*s*. 6*d*., maps 5*s*. 6*d*.).

Civilization of Ancient Egypt.

Breasted, *James Henry*, Development of Religion and Thought in Ancient Egypt; London, 1923; 15*s*.
Budge, *Sir E. A. Wallis*, The Gods of the Egyptians; 2 vols., London, 1904.
—, The Dwellers on the Nile; new ed., London, 1926; 10*s*. 6*d*.
Carter, *Howard*, and *Mace*, *A. C.*, The Tomb of Tut-Ankh-Amen (see p. 315); London, 2 vols., 1923 and 1927; 31*s*. 6*d*. each.
Erman, *Adolf*, A Handbook of Egyptian Religion, translated by A. S. Griffith; London, 1907.
—, Ägypten und ägyptisches Leben im Altertum, new ed. by *Hermann Ranke*; Tübingen, 1923; 36 marks.
Moret, *Alexandre*, Kings and Gods of Egypt, translated by Mme. Moret; London, 1912; 7*s*. 6*d*.
—, The Nile and Egyptian Civilization, translated by M. R. Dobie; London, 1927; 25*s*.
Petrie, *Sir Flinders*, The Religion of Ancient Egypt; London, 1906.
—, Religious Life in Ancient Egypt; London, 1924; 6*s*.
—, Social Life in Ancient Egypt; London, 1923; 6*s*.

Sayce, A. H., The Religion of Ancient Egypt; 2nd ed., Edinburgh, 1913.
Scott-Moncrieff, P. D., Paganism and Christianity in Egypt; Cambridge, 1913; 6*s*.
Steindorff, Georg, The Religion of the Ancient Egyptians; New York and London, 1905.
Wilkinson, Sir John Gardner, The Manners and Customs of the Ancient Egyptians, 4th ed. by S. Birch; 3 vols., London, 1878.

Classical scholars should provide themselves with the 2nd book of *Herodotus* (which may be suitably supplemented by the commentary by *W. W. How* and *J. Wells*, published at Oxford in 1912), the 17th book of *Strabo*, and the 1st book of *Diodorus Siculus*.

Language and Literature of the Ancient Egyptians.

Erman, Adolf, Ägyptische Grammatik; 4th ed., Berlin, 1928; Schrifttafel und Ergänzungsband, 1929; 23 marks.
—, The Literature of the Ancient Egyptians, translated by A. M. Blackman; London, 1927; 21*s*.
Gardiner, Alan Henderson, Egyptian Grammar, being an Introduction to the Study of Hieroglyphs; Oxford, 1927.
Maspero, Sir Gaston, Popular Stories of Ancient Egypt, translated by Mrs. C. H. W. Johns from the 4th French ed.; London & New York, 1915.
Murray, M. A., Elementary Coptic (Sahidic) Grammar; 2nd ed., London, 1927.
Petrie, Sir Flinders, Egyptian Tales, illustrated by Tristram Ellis; 2 vols., 4th ed., London, 1926.
Steindorff, Georg, Kurzer Abriss der Koptischen Grammatik; Berlin, 1920; 3 marks.

Language of the Modern Egyptians.

Dirr, A., Colloquial Egyptian Arabic Grammar, translated by W. H. Lyall; London, 1904; 4*s*.
Elias, A. Elias, Modern Dictionary, English-Arabic; 2nd ed., Cairo, 1923; 17*s*.
—, Pocket Dictionary, Arabic-English; Cairo, 1924; 5*s*.
—, The School Dictionary, English-Arabic and Arabic-English; 2nd ed., Cairo, 1928; 11*s*.
Gairdner, Canon W. H. Temple, Egyptian Colloquial Arabic, a Conversation Grammar; 2nd ed., London, 1926; 10*s*. 6*d*. With phonetic transcription.
Marriott, Major R. A., Egyptian Self-Taught (Arabic); Thimm's System; 5th ed., London, 1921; 3*s*. (Marlborough's Self-Taught series).
Phillott, Lt.-Col. D. C., and *Powell, A.*, Manual of Egyptian Arabic; Cairo, 1928; 15*s*.
Spiro, S., Arabic-English Dictionary of the Modern Arabic of Egypt; 2nd ed., Cairo, 1923; P.T. 70.
Vollers, K., The Modern Egyptian Dialect of Arabic, translated by F. C. Burkitt; Cambridge, 1895.
Willmore, J. Selden, The Spoken Arabic of Egypt; London 1901, 3rd ed. 1919; 15*s*.
—, Handbook of Spoken Egyptian Arabic; 4th ed., London, 1927; 3*s*. 6*d*.

Modern Egypt and Modern Egyptians.

Blackman, Miss Winifred S., The Fellâḥîn of Upper Egypt; London, 1927; 15*s*.
Colvin, Sir Auckland, The Making of Modern Egypt; London, 1906, 18*s*.; cheap ed., 1909. 1*s*.
Cromer, Earl of, Modern Egypt; 2 vols., London, 1908; one-vol. edition, 1911. The standard work dealing with modern developments in Egypt.
Kennett, A., Bedouin Justice. Laws and Customs among the Egyptian Bedouin; Cambridge, 1925.
Lane, Edward William, An Account of the Manners and Customs of the Modern Egyptians, written in Egypt during the years 1833-35; London, 1836; several new editions (published in Everyman's Library, 1908; reprinted 1923).
Lorin, Henry, L'Egypte d'Aujourd'hui. Le Pays et les Hommes; Cairo, 1926.

Milner, *Viscount*, England in Egypt; 11th ed., London, 1904.
Royle, *Chas.*, The Egyptian Campaigns, 1882-85; new ed., revised to 1899, London, 1900.
L'Egypte, Aperçu Historique et Géographique. Gouvernement et Institutions, Vie Economique et Sociale; Cairo 1926, Imprimerie de l'Institut Français d'Archéologie Orientale. A comprehensive work including expert monographs on archæology by Pierre Lacau (p. 88) and E. Breccia (p. 22), geography by H. Lorin (see p. ccvi), and geology by W. F. Hume (see below), and J. Ball (see pp. 403, 405).

Scientific and Medical Works.

Brooksbank, *F. H.*, Egyptian Birds; London, 1925.
Canney, *Leigh*, The Winter Meteorology of Egypt and its influence on disease; London, 1897.
Hume, *W. F.*, Geology of Egypt; Vol. I, Cairo, 1925.
Lyons, *Sir Henry*, The Physiography of the River Nile and its Basin; Cairo, 1906.
Muschler, *R.*, A Manual Flora of Egypt; 2 vols., Berlin, 1912; 40 marks.
Nicoll, *M. J.*, Handlist of the Birds of Egypt (Ministry of Public Works, Egypt Zoological Service, Publication No. 29); Cairo, 1919; P.T. 15.
Tottenham, *Percy Marmaduke*, The Irrigation Service, its Organisation and Administration; Cairo, 1927; P.T. 20.
Willcocks, *Sir William*, Egyptian Irrigation; 2 vols.; 3rd ed., London, 1913; 42*s*.

History of Egyptian Art.

Boreux, *Charles*, L'Art Egyptien; Paris & Brussels, 1926.
Briggs, *Martin S.*, Muhammadan Architecture in Egypt and Palestine; London, 1924; 84*s*.
Capart, *Jean*, Primitive Art in Egypt, translated by A. S. Griffith; Philadelphia, 1905.
—, L'Art Egyptien. I. L'Architecture. Choix de Documents accompagnés d'Indications Bibliographiques; Brussels & Paris, 1922.
—, Egyptian Art: Introductory Studies, translated by Warren R. Dawson; London, 1923; 16*s*.
—, Lectures on Egyptian Art; Chapel Hill (University of North Carolina) & Brussels, 1928; 23*s*.
Clarke, *Somers*, Christian Antiquities in the Nile Valley; Oxford, 1912; 38*s*.
Creswell, *K. A. C.*, Early Muslim architecture: Umayyads, early ʿAbbâsids and Tûlûnids. Oxford, 1928.
Maspero, *Sir Gaston*, Art in Egypt; 1st ed., London, 1912 (reissued in the Ars Una, Species Mille series).
—, Manual of Egyptian Archæology, translated and enlarged by Agnes S. Johns; 6th ed., London, 1914; 6*s*.
—, New Light on Ancient Egypt; London, 1908, 12*s*. 6*d*.; cheap ed., 1910, 6*s*.
Migeon, *Gaston*, Manuel d'Art Musulman. Arts Plastiques et Industriels; 2 vols., 2nd ed., Paris, 1927.
Mileham, *G. S.*, Churches in Lower Nubia; London, 1910.
Petrie, *Sir Flinders*, Ten Years' Digging in Egypt, 1881-1891; London, 1892, 3rd ed. 1923; 2*s*. 6*d*.
—, Egyptian Decorative Art; London, 1895.
—, The Arts and Crafts of Ancient Egypt; London, 1909; new ed. 1923, 7*s*. 6*d*.
—, Methods and Aims in Archæology; London, 1904.
Steindorff, *Georg*, Die Kunst der Ägypter: Bauten, Plastik, Kunstgewerbe (with 200 plates); Leipzig, 1928; 14 marks.

Books of Travel.

Gordon, *Lady Duff*, Letters from Egypt; London, 1865-67; new ed., 1902.
Lepsius, *K. Richard*, Letters from Egypt, Ethiopia, etc.; London, 1853.
Martin, *Percy Falcke*, Egypt, Old and New; London, 1923, reprinted 1924; 21*s*.
Quibell, *Annie A.*, A Wayfarer in Egypt; London, 1925; 7*s*. 6*d*.
Weigall, *Arthur E. P. B.*, A Guide to the Antiquities of Upper Egypt; London, 1910; 7*s*. 6*d*.

Works of Fiction.

The Arabian Nights' Entertainments, translated by Edward William Lane (London, 1830-40; various new editions). The learned editor is of opinion that these popular tales were written in 1474-1525, being based mainly on earlier traditions, that they were probably compiled by an Egyptian, and that they afford an admirable picture of Arabian, and particularly of Egyptian, life at that period.
David M. Beddoe, The Lost Mameluke (1913).
Georg Ebers, An Egyptian Princess (1864), etc.
Robert Hichens, Bella Donna (1909), etc.
Charles Kingsley, Hypatia (1863; comp. p. 15).
Marmaduke Pickthall, The Children of the Nile (1908), etc.
Mark Twain, The Innocents Abroad, or The New Pilgrims' Progress (1869).
Arthur E. P. B. Weigall, Madeline of the Desert (1920), etc.

Maps.

The best special map of Egypt is the topographical map issued by the *Survey of Egypt* on a scale of 1:100,000 (P.T. 10 per sheet, on linen P.T. 15), with names in English. Orders are received at the Consultation Map Room of the Survey Department at Gîza (p. 87; surveyor-general, Maḥmûd Fahmi Bey), where also other maps of the Survey of Egypt (land-register sheets, etc.) may be examined free of charge (adm. daily, except Fri. and official holidays, 8-1.30). At Alexandria a sale-room of the Survey of Egypt has been installed at the Bureau des Hypothèques (20 Rue de Stamboul, Pl. G 4; open 8-12 & 3-5 or 6, Sun. and Fri. 9-12). The Survey of Egypt also published in 1928 a very interesting *Atlas of Egypt:* a series of maps and diagrams with a descriptive text illustrating the orography, geology, meteorology, and economic conditions (31 plates, £E 3½). — The excellent maps by Prof. Schweinfurth are mentioned on pp. 178, 269, 397, and the tourist-maps (Luxor & Karnak; El-Qurna) of the Survey of Egypt on p. 269.

For the Sûdân the best maps are those issued by the *Sudan Survey Department* at Kharṭûm (p. 454) on a scale of 1:250,000 (2*s.* per sheet, on linen 3*s.*) and of 1:1,000,000 (3*s.* per sheet).

1. Approaches to Egypt.

The best steamers calling at Egyptian ports are those of the *Peninsular & Oriental Co.* ('P. & O.') and *Orient Line*, of London, the *Norddeutscher Lloyd* of Bremen, the *Messageries Maritimes* of Marseilles, the *Rotterdam Lloyd*, the *Nederland Line* of Amsterdam, the *Lloyd Triestino* of Trieste (the quickest route), and the *Società Italiana di Servizi Marittimi* ('Sitmar') of Rome.

The time-tables and handbooks of the various steamship companies give full information both as to the direct sea routes from England and as to the steamers from Mediterranean ports. Overland routes from England to the Mediterranean, see p. 2. The principal steamship companies issue return-tickets at a reduction of 20-33⅓ % on the return-journey if made within 6 or 12 months. Heavy baggage should in all cases, if possible, be sent round by steamer. — Travellers from America may sail direct from New York to Alexandria or Port Said (comp. p. 2). From Boston, Philadelphia, or Montreal they may take a steamer bound for any Mediterranean port and proceed thence by one of the steamers mentioned on pp. 3-6. — For occasional steamers and pleasure-cruises from England or America, including a visit to Egypt, see advertisements or apply to the tourist agencies.

Travellers who desire to return from Egypt by one of the larger mail lines should secure a berth as soon as possible by applying to the shipping offices in Cairo (p. 40), as these steamers are apt to be crowded from February to April inclusive. Information as to available accommodation is telegraphed from Aden to Cairo. The days and hours given below for the arrival and sailing of the steamers are approximate only, except in the case of the terminal ports. At intermediate ports the steamers are sometimes behind itinerary time, and not unfrequently several hours or even a day in advance. In either case they proceed at once on their voyage.

Alexandria, the chief seaport of Egypt, is regularly visited by British, German, French, Italian, Rumanian, and Egyptian steamers. *Port Said* and *Ismailia*, on the Suez Canal, are touched at by liners on their way to and from India, China, Australia, and E. Africa. — For the return-journey from Port Said to Europe, comp. p. 193. — *Cairo* is reached by rail from Alexandria in 3-3½ hrs., from Ismailia in 2½-3 hrs., from Port Said in 4 hrs., and through-tickets are issued by some of the steamship companies.

Passengers should be ready to embark at least one hour before the advertised time of departure. As a rule the ships berth at the quay or passengers are embarked by tender, but in Italy, at Port Said, etc., it may be necessary to hire a rowing boat (best through Cook's).

EGYPTIAN TIME, see p. xvii.

A. Steamship Lines from England and America direct.

From London to Port Said. P. & O. (comp. above; 122 Leadenhall St., E.C. 3, and 14 Cockspur St.). Mail-steamer every Fri. from Tilbury, Royal Albert, or King George V. Dock in 12 days, viâ Gibraltar and Marseilles; 1st class fare 38*l.*, 2nd class 26*l.* (reduced fares from April to Aug.). — BRITISH INDIA STEAM NAVIGATION Co. (same addresses) from Royal Albert Dock three or four times monthly in 12 days (34*l.*, 24*l.*; reduced fares from April to Aug.). — ORIENT LINE (5 Fenchurch Avenue, E.C. 3, 14 Cockspur St., S.W. 1, and 1 Australia House, Strand, W.C. 2). From Tilbury Dock every other Sat. in 12 days, viâ Gibraltar, Toulon, and Naples; 1st class 38*l.*, 3rd class 16*l.* — UNION-CASTLE LINE (3 Fenchurch St., E.C. 3) about once monthly from London viâ Marseilles and Genoa; 1st class 34*l.*

of the ground-plan, many elements such as columns, bases, and capitals, and the practice of covering the nave with wooden roofs. The type of timber-work clearly shows a Western influence, a consequence of the Crusades and the commercial relations between Egypt and the maritime republics of Italy.

Decoration is in a state of complete decadence during this second period of Christian art. Stone sculpture disappeared almost entirely after the 8th cent.; a few slabs crudely adorned with interlacing patterns and capitals of a very simple type are found, but one may fairly say that by the 11th cent. work in stone was abandoned. — Of the painting of the period we have some examples at the Deir Suryâni and the Deir Abu Maqâr (p. 35), at the White Convent near Sohâg (p. 229), and at the monastery of St. Simeon near Aswân (p. 386); but all these frescoes, interesting enough from the iconographical point of view, show strong foreign influences, mainly Armenian. Decorative effort may be said to concentrate on the carving and inlay of wood. The ikonostasis of the church of Abu Sarga (p. 114) at Old Cairo incorporates six carved panels (p. 116) of the 11th cent. that are, with others formerly in the church of El-Muʿallaqa (p. 117) and now in the British Museum, the best examples of their kind. But it is chiefly in geometric polygonal decoration that Coptic craftsmen excelled, and all such work betrays Arab influence By the 14th cent. Coptic art may be said to be extinct; neither its buildings nor its decorations show sufficient character to distinguish them from the productions of Arab art, henceforth the sole true art throughout Egypt.

to *Marseilles* is despatched from Boulogne on Thurs. on the arrival of the connecting service leaving London at 1.50 p.m. The express calls at Paris and runs alongside the steamer at Marseilles, which awaits its arrival. Fare, including sleeping-car, 12*l.* (tickets obtainable only from the P. & O.). By ordinary express Marseilles is reached in 20$^1/_2$-23 hrs. (6*l.* 15*s.* 8*d.*, 4*l.* 14*s.* 6*d.*; sleeper on the Blue Train 4*l.* 4*s.* 7*d.*). — *Trieste* is 32$^3/_4$ hrs. from London (9*l.* 4*s.* 1*d.*, 6*l.* 7*s.* 8*d.*; sleeper on the Simplon-Orient Express 3*l.* 2*s.* 5*d.*). — *Constantinople* is 76$^1/_2$ hrs. from London by the Simplon-Orient Express (18*l.* 0*s.* 1*d.*; sleeper 6*l.* 9*s.* 2*d.*).

Sleeping-car tickets are obtained from the *International Sleeping Car Co.*, 20 St. James's St., London, S.W. 1.

1. **From Brindisi.** Lloyd Triestino (agency at the Grand-Hôtel International) to *Alexandria* or *Port Said*, see p. 5, under Trieste.

Brindisi (Grand-Hôtel International, at the harbour; Albergo Europa Nuova, in the Corso Garibaldi, 5 min. from the station and the harbour, Alb. Ferrovia, in the same street, near the harbour, both plain), with 30,000 inhab., is the *Brentesion* or *Brundisium* of antiquity; it has regained its ancient importance as a place of embarkation for the East. Comp. Baedeker's 'Southern Italy'.

2. **From Naples.** Sitmar (agency, Piazza Giovanni Bovio) to *Alexandria* or *Port Said*, see p. 4, under Genoa.

Orient Line (p. 1; agency, Via Guglielmo Sanfelice 24) to *Port Said*, see p. 6, under Toulon.

Marittima Italiana (agency, Via Agostino Depretis 88) and Citra (office, Traversa Municipio 17) to *Port Said*, see p. 4, under Genoa.

Nippon Yusen Kaisha (p. 2; agency, Via Guglielmo Sanfelice 59) fortnightly to *Port Said* in 4 days; fares 23*l.*, 13*l.*

Hugo Stinnes Lines (agency, Viâ Agostino Depretis 65) once monthly to *Port Said;* fare 16-20*l.*

Naples (Bertolini's Palace Hotel, 150 beds from 60, P. from 95*L.*, Parker's, 175 beds from 20, P. from 65*L.*, Britannique, 100 beds from 20 *L.*, all three in the Corso Vittorio Emanuele, high up; Grand, by the sea, 250 beds from 40*L.*; Excelsior, 150 beds from 50*L.*; Hôtel Royal des Etrangers; Grand-Hôtel du Vésuve; Santa Lucia Hotel; Continental, 120 beds from 24*L.*; Hôtel de Londres; Terminus, at the station; etc.), Ital. *Napoli*, with 771,900 inhab., is the largest town in Italy after Milan, and its environs are famous for their beauty. Hurried travellers should drive along the *Via Tasso* and the *Via di Posillipo*, visit the *Museo Nazionale*, and take a walk in the gardens of the *Villa Comunale*. The finest view-point is *San Martino*, near the *Castel Sant' Elmo* (tram and cable railway). — Comp. Baedeker's 'Italy' or 'Southern Italy'.

3. **From Venice.** Lloyd Triestino (agency in the Piazza of St. Mark) to *Alexandria* or *Port Said*, see p. 5, under Trieste.

Venice (Hôtel Royal Daniele, 400 beds from 35*L.*, Hôtel de l'Europe, 125 beds from 50*L.*, Grand, 200 beds from 60*L.*, all three fashionable; Italie-Bauer-Grünwald; Bristol-Britannia, 300 beds from 30*L.*; Grand Canal & Monaco, Regina & de Rome, both on the Canal Grande; Vittoria, R. from 18*L.*; Luna, near the Piazza of St. Mark; Londres, Beau-Rivage, Métropole, these three on the Riva degli Schiavoni; and many others), Ital. *Venezia*, with 183,700 inhab., was till 1797 the capital of a powerful republic. The station (restaurant) lies at the N.W. end of the Canal Grande. A visit to the piazza and church of *St. Mark* and the *Palace of the Doges*, and a trip on the *Canal Grande*, will give the hurried traveller an idea of this incomparable city. Comp. Baedeker's 'Italy' or 'Northern Italy'.

4. **From Genoa.** Sitmar (comp. p. 1; agency, Piazza Nunziata 64 R; agency in London, C. I. T., 16 Waterloo Place, S.W. 1), express

steamer (S. S. 'Esperia' or 'Ausonia') every Thurs., calling at *Naples* on Fri. and *Syracuse* on Sat., and arriving at *Alexandria* on Monday. Fares: cabin de luxe 42*l.*, 1st class 38*l.*, 2nd class 24*l.*, from Naples 39*l.*, 36*l.*, 22*l.*; from Syracuse 35*l.*, 33*l.*, 20*l.* Also by the Circular Tour A (Genoa, Naples, Sicily, Alexandria, Port Said, Palestine, Syria, Cyprus, Smyrna, Constantinople, Genoa) every other Sun., calling at *Naples* on Tues. and arriving at *Alexandria* on Sat.; 1st class 29*l.*, 2nd class 19*l.*, from Naples 27*l.*, 17*l.* The steamer goes on from Alexandria every other Mon. and arrives at *Port Said* on Tues.; fare from Genoa 31*l.*, 20*l.* 8*s.*, from Naples 29*l.*, 18*l.* 8*s.*

NORDDEUTSCHER LLOYD (agency, Piazza Santa Sabina 2; agency in London, 25 Cockspur St., S.W.1) monthly to *Port Said* in 5 days; cabin class 20*l.*, intermediate class 14*l.*

GERMAN AFRICAN SERVICES (p. 2; agency, Via Sottoripa 5) every three weeks to *Port Said;* 1st class 24*l.*, 2nd class 18*l.* — HAMBURG-AMERICA LINE (E. Asian service; agency, Via Cairoli 15) fortnightly to *Port Said;* by passenger steamer 20*l.*, by cargo steamer 16*l.*

MARITTIMA ITALIANA (office, Piazza Meridiana; agency in London, 110 Fenchurch St., E.C. 3) every 4th Fri., calling at *Naples* on Sat. and arriving at *Port Said* on Wed.; 1st class 30*l.*, 2nd class 18*l.*, from Naples 25*l.*, 15*l.*

COMPAGNIA ITALIANA TRANSATLANTICA or 'CITRA' (office, Via Balbi 6; agency in London, C.I.T., 16 Waterloo Place, S.W. 1) to *Port Said* on the 5th of each month, calling at *Naples* on the 7th; 1st class 26*l.*, 2nd class 17*l.*

NEDERLAND LINE (p. 2; agency, Via Roma 30 R) every other Fri.; 1st class 19*l.* 10*s.*, 2nd class 14*l.* 5*s.*

UNION-CASTLE LINE (p. 1; agency, Piazza Nunziata 41) about once monthly to *Port Said;* 1st class 25*l.* and 15*l.*, 3rd class 11*l.*

Genoa (Grand-Hôtel Miramare, 250 beds from 65*L.*, Grand-Hôtel Columbia, both near the central station and fashionable; Grand-Hôtel Bristol, Via Venti Settembre 35, R. from 65*L.*; Grand-Hôtel Savoy-Majestic, close to the central station, R. from 40*L.*; Grand-Hôtel de Gênes, Piazza De Ferrari, R. from 30*L.*; Grand-Hôtel & des Princes, Via Balbi 36, 150 beds from 25*L.*; Grand-Hôtel Isotta, Via Roma 7, R. from 20*L.*; Hôtel de Londres & Continental, Britannia, both in the Via Balbi; etc.), Ital. *Genova*, is the chief seaport of Italy (316,200 inhab.) A walk should be taken through the *Via Balbi*, *Via Cairoli* and *Via Garibaldi*, with their numerous palazzi, and there is a splendid view from the *Castellaccio* (cable railway). Comp. Baedeker's 'Italy' or 'Northern Italy'.

5. **From Marseilles.** P. & O. (p. 1; agency, 18 Rue Colbert) every Fri., arriving at *Port Said* on Wed.; 1st class 30*l.*, 2nd class 18*l.*

BRITISH INDIA STEAM NAVIGATION CO. (p. 1; agency, 8 Rue Beauvau) every 4th Sat.. arriving at *Port Said* on Fri.; fares 26*l.*, 16*l.*

BIBBY LINE (p. 2; agency, 8 Rue Beauvau) every alternate Sat. to *Port Said;* 1st class only; 25*l.*

MESSAGERIES MARITIMES (agency, 3 Place Sadi-Carnot; London offices, 72-75 Fenchurch St., E.C. 3, and 62 Pall Mall, S.W. 1) to *Port Said* 5 or 6 times monthly; 1st class 20-28*l.* (according to

steamer), 2nd class 13-19*l.* To *Alexandria* 3-5 times monthly in 4-5 days; 1st class 29-38*l.*. 2nd class 19-24*l.*

Nippon Yusen Kaisha (p. 2; agency, 8 Rue Cannebière) fortnightly in 6 days to *Port Said* viâ *Naples;* 1st class 26*l.*, 2nd class 14*l.*

Rotterdam Lloyd (p. 2; agency, 5 Boulevard Dugommier) fortnightly to *Port Said;* 1st class 30*l.* 10*s.*, 2nd class 18*l.* 10*s.*

Henderson Line (p. 2; agency, 28 Rue Grignan) fortnightly to *Port Said;* fare 23*l.*, in summer 17*l.*

Ellerman's City & Hall Lines (p. 2; agency, 8 Rue Beauvau) to *Port Said;* fares 25*l.*. 16*l.*

Fabre Line (p. 2; 15 Rue Beauvau; agency in London, 166 Piccadilly, W. 1) 1-4 times monthly in 5 days to *Alexandria;* fares 24-33*l.*, 18-21*l.*

Union-Castle Line (agency, 14 Rue Beauvau) about once monthly to *Port Said;* 1st class 26*l.* and 16*l.*, 3rd class 12*l.*

Marseilles (Hôtel de Noailles & Métropole, 64 Canebière, Splendid, 61 Boulevard Dugommier, Louvre & de la Paix, Le Grand, 53 and 66-68 Canebière, Regina, Place Sadi-Carnot, all first-class; Terminus, Bordeaux & d'Orient, both near the Gare St-Charles; Beauvau, near the Vieux Port, Astoria, 10 Boul. Garibaldi, both hôtels garnis; La Réserve, restaurant of the highest class, Promenade de la Corniche), French *Marseille*, is the second largest town (652,200 inhab.) and the chief seaport in France. The pride of the Marseillais is the *Canebière*, a street starting from the *Vieux Port*, or inner harbour. The best view of the city and its environs is obtained from the church of *Notre-Dame de la Garde*, to the S. of the Vieux Port (cable railway). — Comp. Baedeker's 'Southern France'.

6. **From Trieste.** Lloyd Triestino (comp. p. 1; offices at the harbour; agency in London, 110 Fenchurch St., E. C. 3), by the express line (S.S. 'Helouan' and 'Vienna') every Sat., calling at *Venice* (from the end of Aug. to the middle of Feb. only) on Sat. and *Brindisi* on Sun. and arriving at *Alexandria* on Tuesday. Fares: from Trieste or Venice 1st class 35*l.*, 2nd class 24*l.*; from Brindisi 31*l.*, 21*l.* — By the Indian express line every 4th Fri., calling at Venice on Sat. and Brindisi on Mon., and arriving at *Port Said* on Thursday. Fares: from Trieste or Venice 1st class 30*l.*, 2nd class 18*l.*; from Brindisi 25*l.*, 15*l.* — By the Far East line every 4th Mon., calling at Venice on Tues. and Brindisi on Thurs. and arriving at *Port Said* on Monday. Fares ('cabin class') from Trieste or Venice 24*l.*, from Brindisi 19*l.* 10*s.* — By the Syrian line A every other Thurs., calling at *Venice* (Fri.), *Brindisi* (Tues.), the *Piraeus* (for Athens; Thurs.), etc., and arriving at *Alexandria* (Sun.) in 10 days (from Venice 9, from Brindisi 5 days) and *Port Said* (Wed.) in 13 days (from Venice 12, from Brindisi 8 days). Fares: from Trieste or Venice 1st class 26*l.*, 2nd class 16*l.* (to Port Said 28*l.* and 17*l.* 8*s.*), from Brindisi 23*l.* and 14*l.* (to Port Said 25*l.* and 15*l.* 8*s.*).

Trieste (Savoia Excelsior Palace, with café-restaurant, 350 beds from 35*L.*; Hôtel de la Ville, with restaurant, 160 beds from 25*L.*; Regina; Milano, 120 beds at 16-22*L.*; etc.), formerly the chief seaport of Austria, is now the capital of an Italian province (238,700 inhab.). The Stazione Centrale (restaurant) lies to the N. of the city, to the E. of the Porto Nuovo, where

the Lloyd steamers berth. The Stazione Campomarzio is to the S. For further details, see Baedeker's 'Italy' or 'Northern Italy'.

7. **From Toulon.** ORIENT LINE (p. 1; agency, Quai de Cronstadt) to *Port Said* every 2nd Fri., calling at *Naples* on Sun.; 1st class 30*l*., 3rd class 12*l*., from Naples 26*l*., 10*l*.

8. **From Constantinople.** KHEDIVIAL MAIL LINE (London office, 122 Leadenhall St., E.C.3; brokers, Gilchrist, Walker & Co., Galata) every Sun., calling at the *Piraeus* (Athens) on Tues. and arriving at *Alexandria* on Thurs.; 1st class £E 16, 2nd class £E 11.

SITMAR (p. 4; agency, Galata Quay) every 2nd Thurs., arriving at *Alexandria* on Sat. (a 9 days' trip); 1st class 19*l*. 4*s*., 2nd class 13*l*. 8*s*.

ROYAL RUMANIAN STATE LINE (with connection from Constantza; agency, Galata Quay), every Tues., calling at the *Piraeus* (Athens) on Thurs. and arriving at *Alexandria* on Sat.; 1st class 19*l*., 2nd class 12*l*. 10*s*., from the Piræus 12*l*. 10*s*., 8*l*. 10*s*.

Constantinople (hotels in the Pera quarter, 1/2 hr. from the station and 20 min. from the quay: Tokatlian, opposite the Galata Serai; Pera Palace, Bristol, Londres, Continental & Français, all facing the Petits-Champs gardens; Novotny, Kohout, both in Kabristan Street, a little below the Petits-Champs; Khedivial Palace, in Great Pera St.; etc.) was the capital of Turkey till 1923 and is now the second capital, with 807,000 inhab., including the suburbs, in 1927. It consists of the port of *Galata* and the European quarter of *Pera*, to the E. of the Golden Horn, and of *Stambul* to the W. *Scutari*, on the Asiatic coast, is also reckoned a part of Constantinople. Visitors should ascend the *Galata Tower*, drive over the *New Bridge* to inspect the *Mosque of St. Sophia* and the *Museums* of the old Serai in Stambul, walk through the *Great Bazaar* in the company of a dragoman, and take a steamer-trip on the *Bosporus*. Comp. Baedeker's 'Konstantinopel und Kleinasien'.

C. The Land Route to Egypt.

The 'Simplon-Orient Express' (Calais-Paris-Lausanne-Simplon-Milan-Venice-Trieste-Belgrade-Sofia-Constantinople) goes on twice weekly (Mon. & Fri.) through Asia Minor, Syria, and Palestine to Egypt. From the main station at Constantinople (Sirkedji) by ferry-boat over the Bosporus to Haidar Pasha, and by railway viâ *Eskishehir* (junction for Angora), *Konia*, the *Taurus Tunnel*, *Adana*, and *Aleppo* to *Tripolis* in Syria. Thence by motor-car of the International Sleeping Car Co. in 8 1/2 hrs. to *Haifa* or *Jaffa* in Palestine. Finally by railway to *Qanṭara East* (p. 190), where we cross the Suez Canal by ferry and proceed to *Cairo* by train (see pp. 190-192). The journey from Calais to Cairo takes about a week.

Fares from London to Cairo: first-class 32*l*. 12*s*. 6*d*., sleeping and Pullman car supplement 11*l*. 3*s*. 1*d*. (from Calais 30*l*. 2*s*. 11*d*. and 10*l*. 19*s*. 7*d*.); mixed class (i. e. first-class from London to Paris, on the Bosporus ferry, and from Tripolis to Qanṭara, second-class for the rest of the journey) 26*l*. 18*s*. 8*d*., sleeping car supplement 8*l*. 7*s*. 1*d*. (from Calais 24*l*. 9*s*. 1*d*. and 8*l*. 7*s*. 1*d*.). Those travelling second-class in Palestine and Egypt deduct 1*l*. 15*s*. 8*d*. from the railway fare or 21*l*. 8*s*. 1*d*. from the inclusive fare, as there are no second-class sleeping cars on that section.

I. LOWER EGYPT.

2. Alexandria and its Environs.

Arrival by Sea. Most of the steamers berth at the wharf of the Inner Harbour. As soon as the passport examination and health inspection is over the traveller should have his luggage conveyed to the hotel or station by the hotel-servants, or by one of the representatives of Cook's or the Cairo hotels, who swarm out in small boats to meet the incoming steamer (about P.T. 5 per trunk). These are recognizable by their official caps. Those who employ unauthorized persons will certainly be cheated. On most of the steamers railway-tickets to Cairo are issued by the purser before landing; through-carriages are run from the harbour during the season in connection with the principal steamship lines. The custom-house examination is usually made easy for tourists.

The **Aerodrome** for the London-India air service (p. xviii) is at *Dikheila*, 6 M. to the S.W. of Alexandria (under construction in 1929).

Railway Station. *Gare du Caire* (Pl. H 5), the main station, with restaurant.

Hotels (comp. p. xix). **Claridge's* (Pl. g; H 4), 35 Rue Fouad Premier, with roof-garden, 150 R. (100 with bath) at 60-150, B. 15, L. 35, D. 40, pens. 120-180 P.T., hotel motor (including lugagge) from the station 15, from the harbour 40 P.T.; **Majestic* (Pl. f; F 4), 4 Place Saad Zaghloul, 200 R. (80 with bath) from 50, B. 12, L. 30, D. 35, pens. (for more than three days) from 100 P.T., service 10%. — *Regina Palace* (Pl. k, F G 3; new building under construction close by), Avenue-Promenade de la Reine Nazli, 110 R. (40 with bath) at 40-60, B. 10, L. 30, D. 35, pens. 90-120, omnibus 6 P.T.; *Windsor* (Pl. d; G 3), 12 Rue Avéroff, 82 R. (8 with bath) at 40-80, B. 10, L. 25, D. 30, pens. 80-90 P.T.; *Bonnard* (Pl. e; F 3), 7 Place Saad Zaghloul, 50 R. from 30, B. 10, L. 20, D. 25, pens. from 70 P.T., with garden. — *Excelsior & du Nil* (Pl. h; F 3), 11 Rue de l'Ancienne Bourse, 50 R. (10 with bath) from 7*s.* (English money), B. 2*s.* 6*d.*, L. 5*s.*, D. 6*s.*, pens. from 18*s.*, omnibus from the station 5, from the harbour 10 P.T., Jewish; *Grand Palace*, Rue de la Poste (Pl. F 3, 4); *Canal de Suez* (Inset Plan i; F 3, 4), 9 Rue de l'Ancienne Bourse, 60 R. at 20-25, B. 6-8, D. 16-18, pens. 50-60 P.T.; *Hôtel de France*, Place Saad Zaghloul (W. side; Pl. F 3, 4), 50 R. at 20-25, B. 7-10, omnibus 5-10 P.T., Jewish.

Pensions. *Iorio*, 35 Boulevard Saad Zaghloul (Pl. F G 3, 4), 50 R., pens. P.T. 50-70; *New Savoy* (E. Iorio), 148 Promenade de la Reine Nazli, near the Post Office (Pl. F 3), 24 R., pens. P.T. 60; *Syracuse*, 5 Place Ismaïl (at the Ramleh station, Pl. G 3), 100 R., pens. P.T. 60-100; *York*, 26 beds, pens. P.T. 40-50, *Khedivial*, both in the Central Buildings, near the Exchange (Pl. F 4); *Astoria*, 15a Rue Fouad Premier, pens. P.T. 80, English; *Allenby House* (Y.M.C.A.), 8 Place Saad Zaghloul.

Cafés (Arabian coffee P.T. 1 per cup), in the Place Mohammed Ali (Pl. F 4), frequented mostly by Egyptians. — **Confectioners.** *Baudrot-Groppi*, 33 Rue Chérif Pacha; *Athenaios*, 11 Rue Fouad Premier and Place Ismaïl (see below); *Grand Trianon*, 35 Boulevard Saad Zaghloul.

Restaurants. *Giovannidis*, 33 Boulevard Saad Zaghloul, near the Ramleh station; *Union*, 2 Rue de l'Ancienne Bourse (Inset Plan F 3, 4); *Athenaios*, Place Ismaïl, near the Ramleh station. — Beer Restaurants (lager beer). *Brasserie Germania*, *Gambrinus*, *Centrale*, and *St. James's*, all in the Rue de l'Ancienne Bourse; *Brasserie Viennoise*, 11 Rue Saïd Premier, near the Ramleh station (Pl. G 3); *Brasserie Serreli*, 6 Rue Saïd Premier. — Bars near the Exchange (Pl. F 4) and at the above-mentioned confectioners.

Baths at the hotels. — Sea Bathing in the Bay of Anfûshi (p. 20), and at various spots on the Ramleh beach, e.g. at Bulkeley (p. 27; Stanley Bay), Glymenopoulo (p. 27), and San Stefano (p. 28).

Clubs. *Sultan Hussein Club* (formerly Cercle Khédivial), on the first floor of the Exchange (Pl. F 4), 2 Rue Chérif Pacha, frequented by Europeans of all nations; introduction by a member necessary; after a week visitors must purchase a subscription ticket. — *Cercle Mohammed Ali*,

2 Rue Fouad Premier, similar. — *Royal Yacht Club of Egypt*, at Râs et-Tîn (p. 20). — *Union Club*, *Deutscher Club*, 6 and 8 Rue de l'Ancienne Bourse. — *Circolo Italiano*, 4 Rue Fouad Premier. — *Cercle Suisse*, Rue Ambroise Ralli (Pl. K L 1), Chatby-les-Bains (p. 26). Numerous newspapers at these, and also in the reading room of the Exchange. — *Sporting Club* (comp. Pl. L 1), Ibrâhîmîya (p. 26). — *Royal Automobile Club of Egypt*, Rue de la Gare du Caire.

Tramways, focussing in the Place Mohammed Ali (Pl. F 4). Fares: 1st class 10, 2nd class 5 mill. — **1** (white star). From the *Rond-Point* (Pl. K 3) viâ Rue Sultan Hussein, Ramleh Station (Pl. G 3), Rue Saïd Premier, Place Mohammed Ali, Rue des Sœurs, and Gabbari (Pl. C D 8; p. 27) to *Mex* (p. 28). — **2** (red disk). From the *Rue Moharrem Bey* (Champs Elysées, Pl. L 5) viâ the Main Station, Place Mohammed Ali, and Rue Bâb el-Karasta to the *Custom House* (Douane; Pl. D 5). — **3** (green triangle; circular route). From *Ramleh Station* (Pl. G 3) viâ Rue Saïd Premier, Anfûshi Bay (Pl. C 1, 2; p. 20), Râs et-Tîn (Pl. A B 3), Rue de la Marine, Minet el-Bassal (Pl. D E 6), Rue du Premier Khédive (Pl. E-G 5, 6), Rue Nébi Daniel, and Rue Missalla back to *Ramleh Station*. — **4** (green lozenge). From the *Place Mohammed Ali* (Place Saad Zaghloul) viâ Rue Sidi Abil Dardar (Pl. F 4, 5; p. 17) and Rue de la Colonne Pompée (Pompey's Pillar, p. 17) to *Karmous* (Kôm esh-Shuqâfa, p. 18). — **5** (red crescent). From the *Place Mohammed Ali* (Place Saad Zaghloul) viâ Rue Tewfik Premier, Rue Masguid el-Attarine, and Rue Ragheb Pacha to *Gheit el-Enab* (Pl. H 7, 8). — **6** (green clover leaf). From the *Boulevard Saad Zaghloul* (corner of Rue Adib, Inset Plan F 4) viâ Rue Missalla, Rue Sultan Hussein, and Rond-Point (Pl. K 3) to *Nuzha Garden* (p. 22). — **7** (green triangle above a red semicircle). *Rue Moharrem Bey* (Champs Elysées, Pl. L 5) viâ the Main Station, Rue Nébi Daniel (Pl. G 5, 4), Rue Missalla, Ramleh Station (Pl. G 3), and Rue Saïd Premier to *Anfûshi Bay* (Pl. C 1, 2; p. 20). — To *Ramleh*, see p. 26.

Cabs (comp. p. xix). Within the town: one-horse cab for drive not exceeding 10 min. P.T. 3, two-horse P.T. 4. For a long drive or to the suburbs, comp. the tariff inside each cab. — Motor Cabs: fare P.T. 3 for 1200 metres (1312 yds.), each 500 m. (547 yds.) more P.T. 1; the large cabs marked 'Taxe Spéciale' are allowed to charge 25% extra.

Post Office (Pl. F 3; p. xx), open from 7.30 a.m. to 9.30 p.m. (on Sun. and holidays from 8 to 11 a.m.). Branch-offices at the Main Station and at Bulkeley, Bacós, and San Stefano stations on the Ramleh tram route (pp. 27, 28). France has a post office of its own, at 4 Boulevard Saad Zaghloul. — **Telegraph Offices** (comp. p. xx), *Egyptian* and *British* (Inset Plan F 4), both in the Boulevard Saad Zaghloul; *Marconi Radio Telegraph Co.*, Rue St-Marc (Inset Plan F 4).

Consulates. *British*, 53 Rue Fouad Premier (Pl. G-I 4, 3; new building under construction in the Avenue Alexandre le Grand, to the N. of the Cricket Club, Pl. H 3); *American*, 29 Rue Fouad Premier. There are also Danish, Dutch, French, German, Italian, Norwegian, Spanish, Swedish, and other consular representatives.

Chambers of Commerce. *British*, 6 Rue de l'Ancienne Bourse (Inset Plan F 3, 4); *American*, 5 Rue Fouad Premier.

Tourist Agents. *Thos. Cook & Son*, 2 Rue Fouad Premier; *Cox & King's Shipping Agency*, 13 Rue Chérif Pacha (Pl. F G 4); *The Libyan Oases Association* (G. N. Hillier & Co.), 26 Rue de l'Eglise Copte (Pl. G 4), for excursions in the Mareotis (p. 28) and the Libyan Desert (Sîwa Oasis, p. 403); *Sudan Government Railways & Steamers*, 6 Rue de l'Ancienne Bourse (Inset Plan F 3, 4).

Steamship Offices (comp. pp. 1-6). *P. & O.*, *British India*, and *Khedivial Mail Line*, Curwen & Co., 7 Rue Adib (Inset Plan F 4); *Orient*, R. J. Moss & Co., 6 Boulevard Saad Zaghloul (Pl. F G 4, 3); *White Star* and *Red Star*, John Ross & Co., 8 Rue de la Marine (Pl. D E 4, 5); *Cunard*, Cox & King's (see above); *Lloyd Triestino*, 3 Rue de l'Ancienne Bourse; *Sitmar Line*, 30 Rue Chérif Pacha; *Messageries Maritimes*, 1 Rue Fouad Premier; *Royal Rumanian State Line* and *Norddeutscher Lloyd*, Müller & Co., 14 Rue de Stamboul (Pl. G 4); *Fabre Line*, 'Abdallah Zehil & Co., 4 Rue Chérif Pacha; *Dollar Steamship Line*, 3 Rue de la Gare du Caire, Kelada Building; *Prince*

Line, Furness (Egypt) Ltd., 21 Rue Nébi Daniel (Pl. G 3-5); *Ellerman & Papayanni Lines,* N. E. Tamvaco & Co., 16 Rue Sésostris (Inset Plan G 4).

Banks (usually open 9-12 & 3-4.30; in summer 8.30-1.30). *National Bank of Egypt,* 4 Rue Toussoun Pacha (Pl. G 4); *Barclay's* (formerly Anglo-Egyptian Bank), 7 Rue Chérif Pacha; *Banque Misr,* 6 Rue Toussoun Pacha; *Ottoman Bank,* 5 Place Mohammed Ali; *Crédit Lyonnais,* 4 Rue Chérif Pacha; *Banque Belge & Internationale,* 10 Rue de Stamboul; *Deutsche Orient-bank,* 4 Rue Adib (Pl. F 4); *Banco Italo-Egiziano,* 2 Rue Toussoun Pacha.

Physicians (addresses may be obtained from the chemists). *Dr. Russell, Dr. Curtis* (both English); *Dr. Preiswerk* (Swiss). — SPECIALISTS. Surgeons: *Dr. Harlow, Dr. Cooke* (both English), *Dr. Escher* (Swiss), *Dr. Calzolari,* and *Prof. Crescenzi* (Italian). — Oculists: *Dr. Weakley* (English; see below), *Dr. Osborne.* — Skin specialist: *Dr. Strassberg* (Austrian). — **Dentists.** Dr. *Leuty* and *Dr. Campion* (both American); *Dr. Wittich* (German); *Dr. Maurer* (Swiss). — **Chemists.** *Moraïtis & Co.,* 18 Rue Chérif Pacha; *Rosette* (Moine & Fissekis), 23 Rue Fouad Premier; *Fletcher & Co.,* 29 Boulevard Saad Zaghloul; *Pangalos,* 1 Rue de l'Ancienne Bourse. — **Hospitals.** *Anglo-Swiss* (Pl. L 3, 4; formerly German Deaconesses' Hospital; director, Dr. Weakley, see above), at Ḥadra (p. 21); *European* (Pl. F 4, 5; French), Rue Sidi el-Mitwalli; *Italian* (Pl. L 3), Rue du Palais No. 3; *Government Hospital* (Pl. H 3), Rue de l'Hôpital Egyptien; *Jewish* (Pl. I 5), 40 Rue Moharrem Bey; *Greek* (Pl. G 4), Rue de l'Hôpital Grec.

Booksellers. *L. Schuler,* 6 Rue Chérif Pacha; *Spiros N. Grivas* ('The Central Library'), 11 Rue Boulevard Saad Zaghloul; etc. — STATIONERS: *Standard Stationery Co.,* 6 Rue de l'Ancienne Bourse; *Victoria Stationery & Book Stores,* 25 Boulevard Saad Zaghloul. — MUSIC. *Papasian & Co.,* 6 Rue Fouad Premier. — CIRCULATING LIBRARY: *British Book Club,* 5 Rue Adib (Inset Plan F 4; daily 9-1 and, except Sat., 3-6.30). — ENGLISH NEWSPAPER: *Egyptian Gazette* (P.T. 1; daily), the leading English paper in Egypt. — PHOTOGRAPHIC MATERIALS. *Egypt Kodak,* Rue Chérif Pacha; *Société des Drogueries d'Egypte,* 29 Rue Chérif Pasha and 2 Rue Tewfik Premier.

Shops for all kinds of European goods are to be found in the Rue Chérif Pacha (Davies Bryan & Co.), the Rue Sidi el-Mitwalli (S. Sednaoui & Co.), and the Place Mohammed Ali (Rothenberg). — ORIENTAL GOODS in the Rue Chérif Pacha (Tawa) and in the Rue Fouad Premier.

Theatres. *Théâtre Mohammed Ali* (Pl. G 4; built in 1921), 13 Rue Fouad Premier; *Nuovo Teatro Alhambra* (Pl. G 3), corner of Rue Missalla and Rue de l'Hôpital Egyptien, varieties (also comedies and operettas), with garden.

Churches. ANGLICAN: *St. Mark's* (Pl. F 4), Place Mohammed Ali, services on Sun. at 8, 11 (summer 10), and 6.30. — ROMAN CATHOLIC: *St. Catherine's Cathedral* (Pl. F 4), *Lazarist Church* (Pl. F 4), *St-Antoine* (Pl. I 4, 5), *St. François,* Rue de la Marine (Pl. D E 4). — SCOTTISH PRESBYTERIAN: *St. Andrew's* (p. 16; with a boys' school). Sun. at 10.30 & 6.15. — *American Mission Church* ('Egl. améric.' on Pl. G 4), with a mission school. — *Protestant Church* (Pl. F 3), Rue de la Poste. Sun. at 10.15; German and French services alternately.— *Coptic Orthodox* (Pl. G 4), Rue de l'Eglise Copte. — *Greek Orthodox* (2), *Greek Catholic* (4), and *Armenian Churches,* several *Synagogues,* etc. — *British Boys' School,* 16 Rue des Pharaons (Pl. H I 3), opened in 1928.

Chief Attractions. 1st Day. In the morning walk through the inner town, by the *Rue Fouad Premier, Rue Chérif Pacha,* and *Place Mohammed Ali;* go by tram or cab to *Pompey's Pillar* (p. 17) and the Catacombs of *Ḳôm esh-Shuqâfa* (p. 18). Return viâ the *Maḥmûdîya Canal* and the *Nuzha* and *Antoniadis Gardens* (p. 22). — 2nd Day. Visit the *Museum* (p. 22) in the morning. In the afternoon go to *Ramleh* (*San Stefano,* p. 28) or by motor-car to *Abuqîr* (p. 32). — Those who stay only one day should visit *Pompey's Pillar, Ḳôm esh-Shuqâfa,* and the *Museum* (combination-tickets, see p. 22).

Comp. *Evaristo Breccia's* 'Alexandrea ad Aegyptum', a guide to the ancient and modern town, and to its Græco-Roman Museum (Bergamo, 1922).

Alexandria, Arabic *El-Iskandarîya,* the second town of Egypt and one of the most important commercial cities on the Mediterranean,

is situated at the W. extremity of the Nile delta, on the narrow sandy strip separating Lake Mareotis from the sea, in E. long. 29° 58′ and N. lat. 31° 13′. In 1927 the population numbered 573,063, of whom 473,548 were Egyptians. The European element consists chiefly of Greeks (37,106) and Italians (24,280), but includes also British (14,394), French (9429) and Austrians, and a few Russians, Germans, etc. The Mohammedans (421,930) live chiefly in the N. and W. quarters of the city, the Europeans in the E. quarter and at Ramleh. The town has a governor of its own (p. xlix). In the summer the Egyptian government moves from Cairo to Alexandria (Bulkeley, p. 27), and also the Court (palaces of Râs et-Tîn and El-Muntazah, pp. 20, 32) and the diplomatic corps (p. 39).

Alexandria has two Harbours. The *Port Est*, or E. harbour, known in antiquity as the 'Great Harbour' and then sheltered by a massive mole, is now accessible only for fishing-boats. It is surrounded by wide esplanades (p. 16). The *Port Ouest*, or W. harbour, originally named *Eunostos* or 'Harbour of the Safe Return', was not freely used until the time of the later Roman emperors. Since 1871 it has been enlarged by the addition of an *Outer Harbour*, over 1700 acres in area. This is protected by a breakwater nearly 2 M. in length, constructed of solid masses of masonry. A second pier, or mole, nearly 1000 yds. in length, protects the *Inner Harbour*, which is about 470 acres in area and on an average 28 ft. deep. From the beginning of the pier a series of quays, backed by warehouses, extends along the whole E. side of the harbour to the Arsenal. The *Maḥmûdîya Canal* (p. 16) enters the inner harbour by several locks (Pl. D 6). The port was entered in 1927 by 2125 vessels of a registered tonnage of 4,865,845, of which 605, with a tonnage of 1,446,599, flew the British flag. After cotton the chief exports are grain, cotton-seed, beans, rice, sugar, onions, tomatoes, etc.

I. History and Topography of Ancient Alexandria.

Alexandria was founded in 331 B.C. by *Alexander the Great* and forms a magnificent and lasting memorial of his Egyptian campaign. He conceived the plan of founding a new and splendid seaport in Egypt, both to facilitate the flow of Egypt's wealth towards Greece and the Archipelago, and to connect the venerable kingdom of the Pharaohs with that widely extended Greek empire which it was his great ambition to found. The site chosen was opposite the island of Pharos, near the ancient Egyptian village of *Rhakotis*, between the Mediterranean and the Mareotic Lake (p. 29), which was connected with the Nile by several navigable channels. The choice was judicious and far-seeing. For the older and apparently more favourably situated harbours at the E. end of the Delta were exposed to the danger of being choked by Nile mud, owing to a current in the Mediterranean, beginning at the Straits of Gibraltar and washing the whole of the N. African coast. *Deinocrates*, the

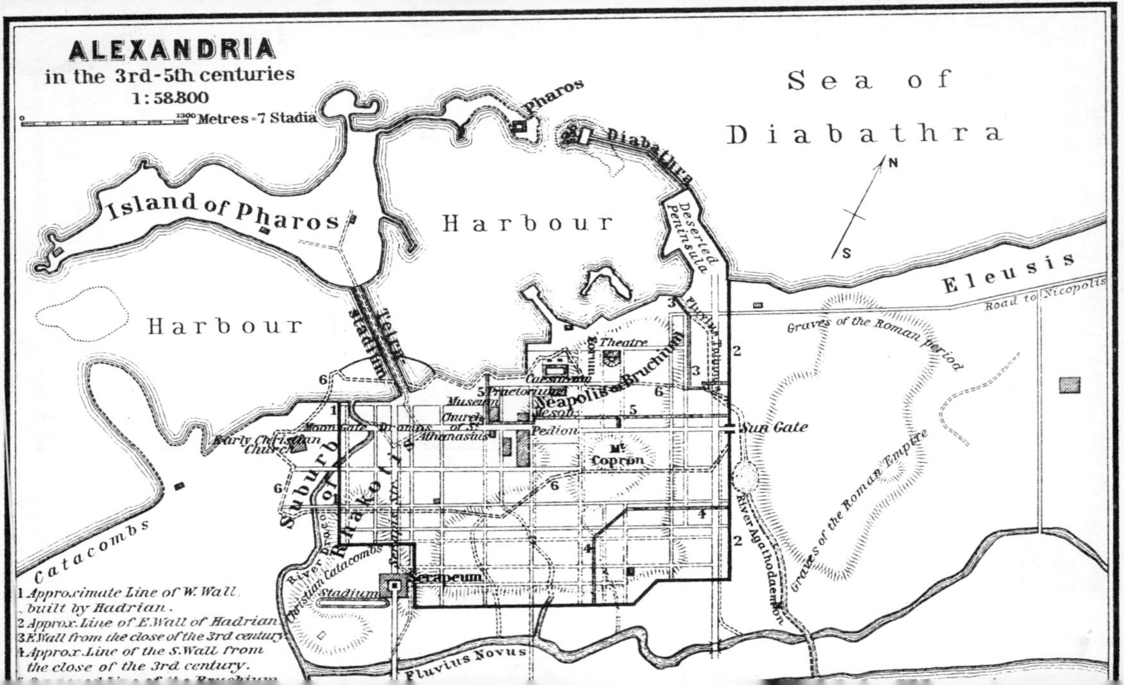
ALEXANDRIA
in the 3rd-5th centuries
1:58800
0 1300 Metres = 7 Stadia
Sea of Diabathra
Pharos
Diabathra
Island of Pharos
Harbour
Harbour
Deserted Peninsula
Eleusis
Road to Nicopolis
Graves of the Roman period
Graves of the Roman Empire
Tetrastadium
Theatre
Forum
Caesareum
Praetorium
Museum
Church of St. Athanasius
Neapolis or Bruchium
Pedion
Mt. Copron
Sun Gate
Moon Gate
Dromos
Early Christian Church
Suburb of Rhakotis
Serapeum
Stadium
Christian Catacombs
River Draco
River Agathodaemon
Fluvius Novus
Catacombs
1 Approximate Line of W. Wall, built by Hadrian.
2 Approx. Line of E. Wall of Hadrian
3 E. Wall from the close of the 3rd century
4 Approx. Line of the S. Wall from the close of the 3rd century.

architect, was entrusted with the planning and building of the new city. Its organization was that of a Greek city, the only previously existing example of which in Egypt was Naucratis (p. 34). After Alexander's death his general *Ptolemy I. Soter* (322-285 B.C.) came into possession of Egypt. During the wise and upright reigns of him and his immediate successors Alexandria became a resort of artists and scholars, including Demetrius Phalereus, the orator, who suggested the foundation of the famous Museum and library (p. 14), Apelles and Antiphilus, the painters, Euclid, the mathematician, and Erasistratus and Herophilus, the physicians.

Notwithstanding the continual dissensions among the Ptolemies with regard to the succession to the throne (pp. cxi seqq.), which seriously disturbed the peace of the city, the fame of Alexandria, as the greatest centre of commerce in the world and the chief seat of Greek learning, steadily increased, and it had reached its zenith by 48 B.C., when the Romans interfered in the quarrels of *Cleopatra* and her husband and brother *Ptolemy XIV.* (p. cxii). After the murder of Pompey at Pelusium (p. 197) *Cæsar* entered Alexandria in triumph, but was attacked by the citizens and the army of Ptolemy XIV. and had considerable difficulty in maintaining himself in the Regia (p. 14). Cæsar was afterwards conquered by the charms of the Egyptian queen, but *Antony* fell more fatally into her toils and spent years of dissipation with her at Alexandria (42-30). *Augustus* enlarged the city by the addition of the suburb of *Nicopolis* (see pp. 14, 27). At this period Alexandria is said to have numbered more than half-a-million inhabitants. The Greek element predominated, next in importance to which was the Egyptian, while a Jewish community was settled here as early as the 4th cent. B.C.

The Greek scholar and traveller *Strabo* describes Alexandria, as it was in the decades immediately before the beginning of our era, in the 17th Book of his Geography. The former island of **Pharos** had been united to the mainland by an embankment known as the Heptastadium (see below), and on the E. extremity of the island rose the famous lighthouse built of white limestone by Sostratus, the Cnidian, in the reign of Ptolemy II. Philadelphus (completed in 280-279 B.C.), which was regarded by the ancients as one of the wonders of the world, and gave its name of 'Pharos' to all lighthouses afterwards erected (comp. p. cc). Its original height is said to have been 400 ells (590 ft.) or, according to recent researches, 360-390 feet. Though even in antiquity it threatened more than once to collapse, part of the ancient tower still stood erect after the great earthquakes of 1303 and 1326. This was overwhelmed by the sea a little later, and the present fortifications ('Fort du Phare' or 'Fort Qâït Bey') were erected on its ruins in the 15th century. The *Heptastadium*, a vast embankment seven stadia (1400 yds.) in length, as its name imports, was constructed by Ptolemy Soter or by his son Philadelphus. It was pierced by two passages, both bridged over, and before Cæsar's time served also as an aqueduct. Having since that period been artificially enlarged by débris from the ancient city, thrown into the sea, as well as by natural deposits, it has attained a width of more than 1600 yds. and now forms the site of a great part of the modern city.

Among the Principal Quarters of the ancient city Strabo particularly mentions the *Necropolis* or city of the dead, at the extreme W. end, "where there are many gardens, tombs, and establishments for em-

balming bodies"; *Rhakotis*, "the quarter of Alexandria situated above the ships' magazines", chiefly inhabited by Egyptians (comp. above); the *Royal City (Regia;* afterwards called *Bruchium)*, which was subsequently walled in and contained the palaces and public buildings, on the mainland between the promontory of Lochias and the Heptastadium; and the *Jews' Quarter*, situated to the E. of the Lochias. Outside the Canopic gate (p. 21), on the E., lay the hippodrome, and farther E., 30 stadia from Alexandria, was the suburb of *Nicopolis*, with an amphitheatre and a racecourse.

The town was regularly built, with streets intersecting each other at right angles. The main artery of traffic seems to have been the long street beginning at the Canopic Gate (comp. p. 21).

Of the Principal Buildings of ancient Alexandria the scanty relics of a few only can be identified. The **Cæsareum**, a great temple begun by Cleopatra in honour of Antony and completed by Augustus for the divine worship of the Cæsars, lay in the Rue Missalla ('Obelisk Street'), N. of the Rue Fouad Premier; the 'Cleopatra's Needles' (now in London and New York; comp. p. 130) formerly stood at the entrance of this temple. The **Paneum** is doubtless identical with the modern Kôm ed-Dikka (p. 21). The **Gymnasium** may have lain to the E. of this point. The theatre, the Sema, and the Museum were all three situated in the 'Royal City' (see p. 13). The Alexandrian **Theatre** lay on the site now occupied by the Government Hospital (p. 21), opposite the island of Antirrhodus, so that the spectators had a view of the sea in the background. The **Sema**, which lay near the royal palaces, close to the mosque of Nébi Daniel (p. 21), was an enclosed space containing the tombs of Alexander the Great and the Ptolemies.

The **Museum**, the site of which is believed to have lain in the area bounded by the Rue Missalla, Rue de l'Hôpital Grec, Rue Nébi Daniel, Rue Fouad Premier, and Rue Chérif Pacha, was a sort of academy or research institute (in the modern sense), the members of which, appointed by the king and freed from all material cares by the receipt of ample salaries, were able to devote themselves to scientific labours. It contained "a hall for walking, another for sitting, and a large building with the refectory of the scholars residing at the Museum". Connected with it were an observatory, a zoological garden, an anatomical institute, and especially the famous *Alexandrian Library*, which contained 400,000 scrolls as early as the reign of Ptolemy II. Philadelphus, while in Cæsar's time, when it was burned, the number had risen to about 900,000. The library, which numbered some excellent philologists among its staff and which edited standard texts of Homer and other classical authors, lay to the N. of the Museum, near the harbour.

The **Serapeum** (Greek *Sarapeion*), or great temple of Sarapis (p. clviii), whose worship was introduced by the Ptolemies, was situated on the hill on which stands Pompey's Pillar (p. 17).

In A.D. 69 *Vespasian* was proclaimed emperor by the Alexandrians, his recognition having been to a great extent due to the influence of the philosophers then resident at the Museum. In *Trajan's* reign (98-117) the Jews, who constituted one-third of the whole population, caused sanguinary riots. *Hadrian* (117-138), who visited the city in 130, held disputations with the professors at the Museum. *Marcus Aurelius* (161-180) attended the lectures of the grammarians Athenæus, Harpocration, Hephæstion, Julius Pollux, and others. Lucian, the Greek satirist, also lived at Alexandria at this period, in the capacity of secretary to the prefect of Egypt. In 199 *Septimius Severus* (193-211) visited Alexandria and established a municipal constitution. A disastrous visit was that of *Caracalla* (211-217), who revenged himself for the derision of the citizens by a bloody massacre and also caused the academy to be closed

Still more disastrous were the contests between the Palmyrenes and the imperialists (p. cxv), in which a large part of the population was swept away by the sword, pestilence, and famine.

Christianity early found its way to Alexandria. According to tradition the Gospel was first preached to the Alexandrians by St. Mark (whose bones were removed to Venice in 829). The first great persecution of the Christians, which took place in the reign of *Decius* (250), was a terrible blow to the Alexandrians. The city had for a considerable time been the seat of a bishop, and had since 190 possessed a theological school, presided over by Pantænus and Clement of Alexandria (beginning of the 3rd cent.), who endeavoured to combine Christianity with the Neo-Platonism which sprang up about this period at Alexandria and was taught by Ammonius Saccas, Herennius, Plotinus (p. 227), Porphyrius, Iamblichus, and others. A second persecution took place in 257, during the reign of *Valerian;* and shortly afterwards, in the reign of *Gallienus*, the plague carried off a large portion of the population. Alexandria, however, still continued to be regarded as the chief seat of Christian erudition and of the orthodox faith (Athanasian Creed), until it was eventually obliged to yield to Constantinople its proud position as the centre of Greek thought and science. Sanguinary quarrels took place between the Athanasian party (p. cxvi) and the Arians under their unworthy bishop Georgius. On the accession of *Julian the Apostate* (361-363) the pagans of Alexandria again instituted a persecution of the Christians. In the reign of *Theodosius* (379-395), however, paganism received its death-blow, and Theophilus, the patriarch of Alexandria, displayed the utmost zeal in destroying the heathen temples and monuments. It was at this time that the famous statue of Sarapis was burned. The material prosperity of the city also declined so greatly that the municipality was no longer able to defray the cost of cleansing the Nile and keeping the canals open. The revenues of Alexandria were still further diminished by the proceedings of the patriarch Cyril (p. cxvii), who expelled the Jews from the city; and in 415 the learned and beautiful pagan Hypatia, daughter of the mathematician Theon, was stoned to death by an infuriated crowd. Under *Justinian* (527-565) all the still existing pagan schools were finally closed.

In 619 Alexandria was captured by *Chosroes II.*, king of Persia, but the Christians were left unmolested and the Persians were expelled by Heraclius in 626. The troops of the *Caliph ʿOmar* then invaded the country and took Alexandria after a prolonged siege. In October 642 ʿAmr ibn el-ʿÂṣ, ʿOmar's general, entered the city; but he treated the inhabitants with moderation. The decline of Alexandria now became rapid in the same proportion as the growing prosperity of the newly founded capital on the Nile, the modern Cairo, and its commerce received a death-blow by the discovery of America and of the sea-route to India round the Cape of Good Hope.

The decay of the once powerful seaport, which contained only 5000 inhab. in 1800, was at length effectually arrested by the vigorous hand of *Muḥammed ʿAli* (p. cxxv), who improved the harbours and constructed several canals. The chief benefit he conferred on Alexandria was the construction of the *Maḥmûdîya Canal* (p. 12); begun in 1819 and finished in six months by compulsory labour (over 20,000 of the workmen died from fatigue and famine), it was named after the reigning Sultan Maḥmûd II. Through this channel the adjoining fields were irrigated anew and Alexandria was again connected with the Nile and the rest of Egypt, the products of which had long found their only outlets through the Rosetta and Damietta mouths of the river. Subsequent viceroys also made great efforts to improve the position of the town. It suffered severely, however, during ʿArâbi's rising in 1882 (bombardment by the British fleet on July 11th and 12th; p. cxxviii), and a great part of the European quarter was laid in ashes; but all traces of this misfortune have disappeared and the town is again quite prosperous.

II. Modern Alexandria.

1. The Central and Western Quarters.

The centre of European life is the long **Place Mohammed Ali** (Pl. F 4; formerly *Place des Consuls*), known to the Arabs as *El-Manshîya* and embellished with trees. In the centre is the equestrian statue of *Muḥammed ʿAli* (Pl. 3; see above), designed by A. Jacquemart and cast in Paris. The pedestal is of Tuscan marble. On the N.E. side stands the *English Church* (St. Mark's; 'Eglise anglicane', Pl. F 4; p. 11), adjoined by *St. Mark's Building*, belonging to the British community, with a school; on the E. side is the *Exchange* (Bourse); on the S.W. are the *Law Courts* (Tribunal Mixte, p. xxii). These are the only buildings in the square which escaped the fury of the natives in 1882 (see above). In the garden beside St. Mark's Building is a bust of *Major-General William Earle* (1833-85), who fell at the battle of Kirbekân (p. 435).

To the N. of the Place Mohammed Ali lies the Place Saʿad Zaghloul (Pl. F 3, 4); on its E. side is the *Scottish Presbyterian Church* (St. Andrew's, Pl. 1). If we continue N. we reach the *Quai Port Est* (Avenue-Promenade de la Reine Nazli, Pl. D-H 1-3), i.e. the new quays of the E. harbour, with the *French Consulate* and the *Ramleh Station* (Pl. G 3; for the electric railway mentioned on p. 26).

From the E. side of the Place Mohammed Ali runs the busy *Rue Chérif Pacha*, the chief seat of the retail trade, with attractive shops (in the side-streets also); from the S. side the *Rue des Sœurs* (tram No. 1, p. 10), with its continuation, the long *Rue Ibrahim Premier*, constructed through an old and crowded Arab quarter, leads to the quarter of *Mînet el-Bassal* (Pl. D E 6), the focus of the cotton trade, with the *Cotton Exchange* (shown in the forenoon to visitors introduced by a cotton merchant). The Rue Ibrahim ends at the *Pont*

Neuf or *Pont Ibrahim* (Pl. E 7), over the Maḥmûdîya Canal (p. 12); thence to Gabbari and Mex, see p. 28. On the S. bank of the canal lies the quarter of *Mînet esh-Sharqâwîya* (Minet el-Charkaouiyeh, Pl. D E 7), occupied by wholesale dealers in grain, sugar, onions, etc.

To the S.E. of the Place Mohammed Ali is the triangular *Square Ste-Catherine* (Pl. F 4), with the Roman Catholic church of *St. Catherine*. The Rue Sidi Abil Dardar (Shâri' Sîdi Abi'd-Dirdâ or Dardaa; tram No. 4, p. 10) leads hence to the S. On the left is the *European Hospital* (Pl. F 4 5). Nûbâr Pasha (p. 21; monument by Denys Puech) is buried in the graveyard of the *Armenian Church* (Pl. F 5), in the Armenian quarter. Farther on we pass the *Old Protestant Cemetery* (corner of Rue du Prince Abd el-Moneim), the *Governorate* (Pl. F G 5), the *Municipal Library* (Bibliothèque Municipale; open 9-12 & 4-7, closed on Sun. and Fri.), and the *Picture Gallery*, founded by the German Eduard Friedheim, with modern paintings of minor importance. The *Sîdi 'Amr Mosque* (Pl. G 6) lies at the S. end of the Rue Sidi Abil Dardar.

We now turn to the right into the *Rue du Premier Khédive* and then, by the *Italian School* (Pl. F 6), to the left into the *Rue de la Colonne Pompée*, which leads S., past a large Arab cemetery (Pl. F 6 7), to a bare eminence covered with rubbish and fragments of ruins, the site of the *Serapeum* (p. 14). Here rises ***Pompey's Pillar** (Arabic *El-'Amûd*; Pl. F G 7; open 9-5.30, in summer till 6; adm. P.T. 3, comp. p. 22; guide quite unnecessary), the largest well-preserved relic of antiquity in the city. We reach the top of the plateau by a flight of steps. All around lie fragments of Roman and other buildings revealed by the excavations begun by Botti (p. 22) and continued by the Von Sieglin Expedition (1898-1902) and by E. Breccia (p. 22; 1905-7). The pillar is composed of red granite from Aswân. Its height, including the pedestal and the Corinthian capital, is 88 ft.; the shaft, 68 ft. high, is about 9 ft. in diameter at the bottom and not quite 8 ft. at the top. The foundations, composed of several blocks (one with the name and figure of Sethos I., another with the name of Arsinoë Philadelphos) which once belonged to other buldings, are much damaged. On the W. side is a much-defaced inscription in honour of the Emperor Diocletian (p. cxvi), placed here in A.D. 292 by a Roman prefect named Posidius. The column, which may once have belonged to the temple of Sarapis, was perhaps erected here by the Emperor Theodosius to commemorate the victory of Christianity and the destruction of the Serapeum (A.D. 391; see p. 15). The present name of the pillar is due to the mediæval belief that it marked the tomb of Pompey the Great. — To the N. of the pillar is an ancient water-basin; to the S. are two sphinxes of red granite, a headless sphinx of Haremhab (p. cvi), a scarabæus in red granite, a headless seated figure of Ramses II., etc., all of which probably came from the temple at Heliopolis (p. 129).

About 55 yds. W. of Pompey's Pillar are several granite columns marking the remains of the *Serapeum* (p. 14). Its subterranean passages (of little interest) are reached by a flight of wooden steps descending into an open court, from the N. and S. corners of which long passages are cut into the rock, with small niches of unknown purport.

Continuing to follow the Rue de la Colonne Pompée and its prolongation, the *Rue Karmous*, a little farther, and then diverging to the right by the Rue Bab el-Melouk, we pass the small El-Mîri Mosque and reach the entrance (Pl. 'E.'; F 8) to the ***Catacombs of Kôm esh-Shuqâfa** (Kôm el-Chogafa, Pl. F 8; 'hill of potsherds'), on the S. slope of a hill crowned by an abandoned fort and now used as a quarry (open 9-5.30, in summer till 6; adm. P.T. 5, comp. p. 22). This burial-ground, discovered in 1900, is the most important in Alexandria and probably dates from the 2nd cent. of our

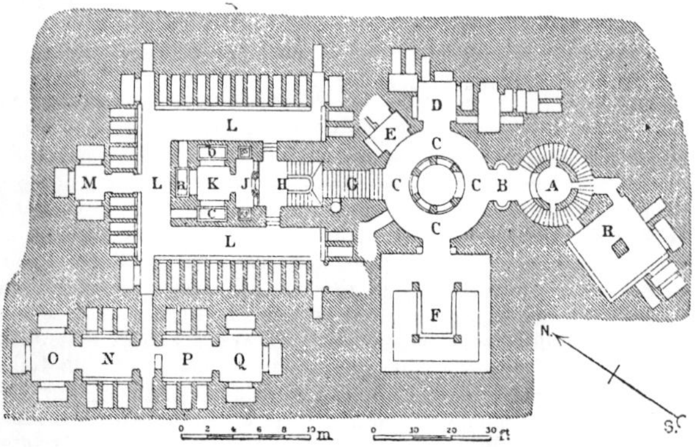

era; it is an admirable example of the characteristic Alexandrian fusion of Egyptian and Græco-Roman styles. Modern flights of steps on the side of the hill lead to the old entrance, which has been restored. The chambers lie in several stories one above another. They were perhaps excavated as the burying place of a religious society, the main chambers being reserved for the founder and his family. The exploration of the interior is facilitated by wooden bridges and electric light.

A Winding Staircase (Pl. A), with a large circular light-shaft, descends into two stories of the catacomb, the lower of which is generally under water; near the top of the staircase is a Sarcophagus Chamber (R) of later construction. From the entrance to the upper floor (B), on each side of which is a semicircular recess with benches, we enter a Rotunda (C). In the middle of this, covered by a kind of cupola, is a shaft leading to the lower stories.

To the right lie two Smaller Rooms (D, E), with niches and sarcophagi. Above the latter are 'loculi' or shelf-tombs. To the left is the Triclinium Funebre (F), a large room with a ceiling borne by four pillars. Three wide platforms or divans have been hewn out of the rock for the banquets held in honour of the deceased. — The Staircase (G), which commands a good view of the chief sepulchral chambers, divides farther down into two flights, flanking the entrance to the lower story (H) and leading to the Vestibule (J) of the grave-chamber proper.

The façade of the Vestibule is articulated by two Egyptian columns, with elaborate flower-capitals, which bear a cornice adorned with the winged solar disk and with falcons; above this is the flat arch of the pediment. Inside, in deep niches to the right and left, are Statues of the deceased and his wife in Egyptian dress, carved in white limestone. The door in the rear wall of the vestibule is surmounted by the winged sun's disk and a frieze of serpents. To the right and left, on pedestals, are two large serpents with the Egyptian double crown, the caduceus of Hermes, and the thyrsus of Dionysos. Above are shields with heads of Medusa.

We now enter the Sepulchral Chamber (K). The sarcophagi containing the remains stand in niches (a-c) and are hewn, like their lids, out of the solid rock. The fronts are adorned, after the Greek fashion, with festoons, masks, heads of Medusa, bucrania, and bunches of grapes. On the middle one is a reclining figure of the deceased. The walls of the niches are decorated with representations of religious import.

Central Niche (a). *Rear Wall:* On a bier in the shape of a lion rests the mummy, surrounded by Horus, Thoth, and Anubis, the three gods of the lower world; below the bier are three canopic jars (p. clv). *Left Wall:* On the right a priest, wearing a panther-skin, reads from the book of ritual; on the left the deceased is seen before an altar. *Right Wall:* A priest of Isis sacrifices to the goddess. — Right Niche (b). *Rear Wall:* King or emperor offering a collar to an Apis bull, protected by the wings of Isis. *Left Wall:* King sacrificing to the deceased as Osiris. *Right Wall:* Figures of two gods of the dead, one with the head of a cynocephalus. — The representations in the Left Niche (c) are similar. — To the right and left of the door are the dog-headed Anubis, as a warrior, and a dog-headed dæmon with a serpent's body.

Round the sepulchral chamber runs a Gallery (L), entered from the passage in front of the vestibule, with two rows of shelf-tombs (ninety-one in all). Each of these contained at least three mummies. The names and ages of the deceased, in red paint, are still visible on some of the slabs. — At the back of the gallery is a Sarcophagus Chamber (M), with three tomb-niches and plain pillars. Adjoining the W. part of the gallery are four Later Rooms (N-Q), with shelf-tombs and sarcophagus-niches.

Close by is a *Graeco-Roman Catacomb* of the 3rd or 4th cent. after Christ, in three stories (excavated in 1910). — Farther W. lie some other tombs, of less interest and not worth visiting.

The main portion of the Arab Quarter lies on the ancient

Heptastadium (p. 13), between the E. and W. harbours. It contains several bazaars. The chief thoroughfare is the *Rue de France* (Pl. E 3 4), which leads W. from the Place Mohammed Ali (p. 16) and is prolonged by the Rue Masguid Terbana and the *Rue Râs et-Tîn*. The *Terbâna Mosque* (Pl. F 3) in the Rue Masguid Terbâna was built in 1684 but incorporates antique columns. The Rue Râs et-Tîn (Pl. C D 3) turns W. farther on and intersects the TURKISH QUARTER, on what was formerly the island of *Pharos* (p. 13), with less narrow streets and picturesque houses and gardens. The Rue Sidi Abou el-Abbas leads N. past the Institute for Ulemas (see below) to the square of the same name, the centre of the quarter, with the *Tomb Mosque of Abu'l-ʿAbbâs el-Mursi* (Pl. D 2; d. 1288), built by Algerians in 1767. Both these quarters present interesting scenes of oriental life.

The *Institute for Ulemas* (Mashyakhet el-ʿUlamâ el-Iskandarîya; comp. p. lxxxix), on the W. side of the Rue Sidi Abou el-Abbas (see above), is a Mohammedan religious institution (founded in 1903) on the same footing as El-Azhar University (pp. 58-61), with (1926) 82 professors and 808 students and a library of 13,391 volumes.

Farther on, to the N. of the Rue Râs et-Tîn, near the shore of the *Bay of Anfûshi*, lie two **Greek Rock Tombs** (Tombeaux d'Anfouchi; Pl. B C 3), dating from c. 200 B.C. Permission to visit them must be obtained through the museum officials (p. 22).

SOUTHERN BURIAL PLACE. By means of a flight of steps and a terraced slope we reach a rectangular court or atrium (now uncovered) off which open two tombs, each comprising a large vestibule and the tomb proper. The ceilings consist of barrel-vaulting. The walls of the vestibule of the *South Tomb* (right) bear numerous Greek inscriptions and drawings, including a cleverly sketched ship with a tower. In the rear wall of the sepulchral chamber is a niche in the Egyptian style. The *East Tomb* (left) is the finest of all. The walls of the vestibule terminate in a concave cornice and are painted to imitate alabaster and black and white marble. The painting of the ceiling is intended to make it look as if divided into coffers. The ceiling of the sepulchral chamber seems to have been painted with great taste; in front of the niche in the rear wall is an altar of limestone. — Close by is the NORTHERN BURIAL PLACE, which is very similar to that just described. The vestibule of the *East Tomb* (right) served as a triclinium in which the banquet for the dead was held. The tomb still contains its granite sarcophagus, in which a whole family was interred. In the vestibule of the *North Tomb* (left) are three tombs of later date, constructed of bricks. The wall-paintings here also imitate alabaster and limestone. — Close by are other, recently discovered tombs of a similar character.

The Rue Râs et-Tîn ends at the **Royal Palace of Râs et-Tîn** (Pl. A B 3), which was renovated by Italian artists in 1925 and is not accessible at present. — The street skirts the N. side of the palace to reach the *Yacht Club* and the *Military Hospital* (Pl. A 4), finely situated at the extremity of the RÂS ET-TÎN ('promontory of figs'); in its courtyard is the *Lighthouse* marking the entrance of the West Harbour.

The best return-route to the Place Mohammed Ali leads past the *Naval Arsenal* (Pl. C D 3), along the West Harbour (p. 12), and through the Rues Moutouch Pacha, de la Marine, Bab el-Karasta, and Anastasi. *Fort Cafarelli* (Pl. E 5) or *Kôm en-Nâḍûra*, one of Napoleon's chief defences, is now a signal-station. In the *Rue Bâb el-Akhḍar* (Pl. E 4, 5) is the gold and silver bazaar.

2. The Eastern Quarters.

The chief thoroughfare of the E. quarters is the Rue Fouad Premier (Pl. G-I 4, 3; formerly Rue de la Porte de Rosette), the continuation of the Rue Sidi el-Mitwalli, leading to the E. from the Rue Chérif Pacha. It corresponds with the E. half of the ancient main street (p. 14) and leads past the town hall (p. 22) to the *Porte Fouad Premier* (Pl. K 3), the former Porte de Rosette, on the site of the ancient *Canopic Gate.* To the S. is the *Stadium* (Pl. I K 4; completed in 1929). — On the top of the *Kôm ed-Dikka* (Kôm ed-Dîk, Pl. H I 4; 115 ft.; comp. p. 14), to the S. of the Rue Fouad Premier, is the reservoir of the waterworks. The water is obtained from the Maḥmûdîya Canal and pumped into the *Farkha Canal* (Pl. K L 4, 5), the main pumping station being at the Rond-Point (Pl. K L 3).

In the Rue Nébi Daniel, to the S. of the Rue Fouad Premier, is a *Mosque* (Pl. H 4), with the tombs of Sa'îd Pasha (p. cxxvii), Prince Hassan, and other members of the royal family. Farther on is the new *Railway Station* (Pl. H 5; p. 9), opened in 1927. — In the prolongation of the street towards the N. are the *Coptic-Orthodox Church of St. Mark* (Pl. G 4; l.) and the handsome *Synagogue* (r.).

In the Rue Sultan Hussein (Pl. H I 3; trams 1 & 6, p. 10), the former Rue d'Allemagne, are the *Jewish School* (right) and the *Asylum for Old Men* (left formerly the Kaiser-Wilhelm-Heim), managed by the Borromean sisters. Farther on, on a height adjoining the Jewish cemetery, stands the *Government Hospital* (p. 11). In the gardens of the *Place Saïd* is the *Omdurmân Column*, an ancient granite column found in the vicinity and erected to commemorate the taking of Omdurmân (p. cxxx). On the base are inscriptions in English and Arabic and two figures of Sakhmet, the Egyptian lion-headed goddess of war. The gardens of the hospital contain antiquities excavated on the spot and the tomb (a Roman sarcophagus flanked with Coptic columns) of Dr. Schiess Pasha, a former director. On a hill affording a view of the new harbour is the *Victoria Column*, also found in this neighbourhood and named after Queen Victoria.

The Rue Sultan Hussein goes on to the beautiful *City Park*, laid out on the site of the Arab fortifications and containing a bronze monument to Nûbâr Pasha, the Egyptian statesman (1825-99). On the left is an old three-storied cistern (El-Nabih). We continue to follow the tram-lines to the Porte Fouad Premier (see above), near which is a monument to French soldiers who died in Alexandria during the Great War. On the left, farther on, are the large *Roman Catholic Cemeteries*, the further of which contains an antique tomb.

The tram-lines go on to the Rond-Point (Pl. K 3), whence three streets radiate. To the S.W. the Rue Menascé, with its continuation the Rue el-Rassafah, runs to the *Maḥmûdîya Canal* (p. 12). On the S.E. the Rue Sign el-Hadra leads to the Anglo-Swiss Hospital (p. 11) and the *Prisons* (Pl. L 4). The Rue du Palais No. 3 (tram No. 6, p. 10), to the E. of the Rond-Point, runs past the Italian Hospital

(p. 11) and through the suburb of Ḥaḍra, with its ancient necropolis and a British military cemetery, to the **Nuzha Garden* (café; band), a most attractive public resort on the Maḥmûdîya Canal, with a small zoological collection. Adjacent is the **Antoniadis Garden* (adm. P.T. 2), presented to the city by Anthony J. Antoniadis (d. 1922); to the N. of the villa is a rock-tomb of the Roman period. We may return to the city either along the highly picturesque canal and viâ the Rue Karmous (p. 18), or across the *Champs Elysées* (Pl. L 5; trams 2 & 7, see p. 10) and viâ the Rue Moharrem Bey (Pl. L-H 5).

In the Rue du Musée, which diverges N. from the Rue Fouad Premier (p. 21), are the *Town Hall* (Municipalité) and, adjoining it, an edifice in the Greek style, accommodating the —

***Museum of Græco-Roman Antiquities** (Pl. H 3), founded by *G. Botti* (d. 1903), an Italian, with the co-operation of the Athenæum Society and the municipal authorities. The museum soon attained considerable importance. Most of the contents are of Alexandrian origin and were generally brought to light either in digging for old stones for building houses (a common practice here) or by the excavations of the Société Royale d'Archéologie d'Alexandrie. Most of them come from the extensive catacombs constructed on the outskirts of the ancient city. The importance of the museum lies in the comprehensive collections of objects of significance in the history of the city.

The museum is open daily, 9-12.30 and 3-5.30 (in summer 4-6); adm. P.T. 2; ticket-office at Pl. 29, p. 23); it is closed on Mon. and Thurs. afternoons in summer. Combination-tickets (billets cumulatifs; P.T. 8) are issued for the museum, Pompey's Pillar (p. 17), and the catacombs of Kôm esh-Shuqâfa (p. 18). Hand-cameras are allowed. Director, *Prof. E. Breccia.* Catalogue, see p. 11.

From the **Vestibule** (Pl. X) we have a view of the statue of Hercules in the transverse gallery (p. 25) connecting the two main wings of the museum. The vestibule contains a collection of palæolithic and neolithic stone implements and flint knives, mostly found in the Western Desert (Kôm el-Qanâṭir, 19 M. to the S.W. of Mex) and in the Faiyûm. — On the right are Rooms 1-5, but it is better to begin with Room 6, on the left, and leave Rooms 1-5 to the end.

Room 1. Christian Antiquities. Two fine capitals of columns from Alexandria. Nos. 1-17 (right and left of the entrance). Tombstones of monks of a convent at Alexandria (Ed-Dikheila), dating from the 6th century. Græco-Christian and Coptic tombstones, chiefly from Upper Egypt, with ansated crosses ('the sign of life'; p. 100), peacocks, palms, and other decorations; the inscriptions often close with the words "Be not sad; no one on earth is immortal". Columns and architectural fragments of the Christian period. — In the *Cases:* Terracotta lamps; vessels. In glass-case I, cushion from Antinoë (p. 221). Bone and ivory carvings (in several show-cases). *Glass Cases La* and *M:* Flasks (ampullae) for holding miracle-working oil from the tomb of St. Menas the martyr (p. 30). Between the two cases: 240. Marble relief of St. Menas, standing between two kneeling camels, from Ed-Dikheila. — In the centre: Magnificent sarcophagus-lid of porphyry; Christian mummies.

Rooms 2-5 contain the collection of Coins. Room 2: in the centre, a capital from Alexandria; coins of the Roman emperors. — Room 3: Coins of the Ptolemaic period (table-cases A-D); on the walls, Coptic textiles; niche (with representation of a saint in Paradise) and other wall-paintings

from a Christian building at Abu Girga (Maryûṭ). — Room 4: in the entrance, a large Coptic terracotta vessel with the figure of a saint praying, birds, plants, etc.; in the desk-cases, coins of the imperial era; colossal seated figure of a woman with a girl at her side (tomb-monument); on the walls, Coptic embroideries. — Room 5: in the desk-cases, Roman and other coins; on the walls, Coptic tombstones from Upper Egypt; Menas flasks (see p. 22); vessels of the Christian period from the city of St. Menas (p. 30) and Kôm esh-Shuqâfa (p. 18).

Room 6. Greek and Latin Inscriptions, Papyri, Tombstones. To the right: 18-146. Votive and memorial inscriptions of the Ptolemaic period; Ptolemaic tombstones with inscriptions and representations resembling Attic tombs of the 4th cent., with small pediments, the enclosed space being occupied sometimes by reliefs, sometimes merely with names in red paint; 83. Tombstone with a dying woman attended by her two daughters; 87. Tombstone with relief of a seated woman; 88. Tombstone with two women from Pisidia; 97. Tombstone with seated figure of an old man; 150. Relief from the tombstone of a boy, represented as carrying a goose and playing with his little dog; 96. Tombstone of a soldier named Lycomedes. — To the left: 1-18, 146-303. Votive and memorial inscriptions, military diplomas (176, 177), and tombstones of the Roman period (note especially 252, 253. Tombstones of a Roman and a Syrian soldier). — In the middle: 351. Lifesize figure of Apis in granite, found in the Serapeum, with dedication to Sarapis by Hadrian (on small pillar below); 350. Sphinx. — The *Glass Cases* contain papyri of the Ptolemaic and Roman periods.

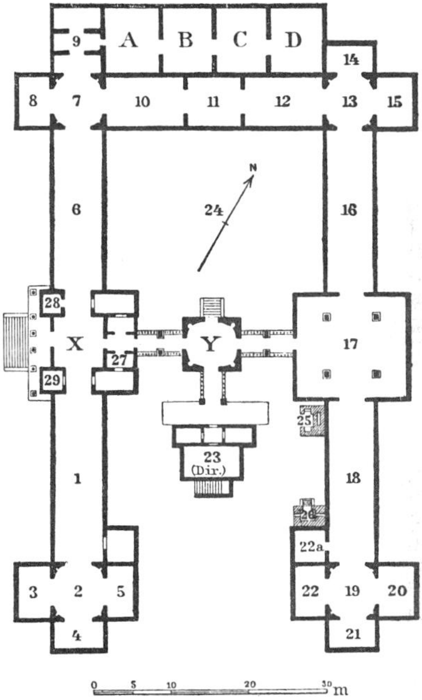

Room 7. Egyptian Antiquities. In the centre: 359. Colossal statue in pink granite of one of the Pharaohs, afterwards usurped by Ramses II., with an incised relief of his consort at the side, from Abuqîr. 361, 363. Two sphinxes of Amenemmēs III. from Abuqîr, afterwards usurped by Ramses II. 18. Bust of Ramses II., from Abuqîr. In the *Glass Cases:* Fragments of two statues of Pshereptah; heads of kings, late period.

Room 8 (continuation of the Egyptian collection). Capital of a sistrum-column (p. clxviii), with fine heads of Hathor. 385, 386-389. Wooden coffins from the common tomb of the Theban priests of Amun in Deir el-Bahari (p. 323); 388. Mummy of a late-Egyptian period. — *380. Fine bas-relief of the Saïte period, with a man (l.) in a flowing robe, a harper, and singing

women. 378, 379, 381-383. Limestone coffins in the shape of mummies, from Upper Egypt.

Room 9. In the centre, a wooden bier with the mummy of a sacred crocodile, from the temple of the crocodile-god Pnepherōs at Baṭn Harît (Theadelphia, p. 210), with a representation of priests carrying the bier in a procession. — Wooden door with Greek votive inscription and other objects from Baṭn Harît; 21. Fragment of an obelisk of Sethos I. — Farther on we turn to the right to visit Rooms A-D.

Room A. Topographical Collection. Plans of old and new Alexandria, photographs and drawings of Alexandrian monuments. — **Room B.** Mosaic of the Hellenistic period, representing two winged genii killing a stag and, on the border, a lion, a stag, a bull, a boar, and fabulous animals (found at Shâṭbi in 1921). The wall-cases contain painted tombstones of the Ptolemaic period. — **Room C.** Architectural fragments; busts; portions of statues; colossal head of a Queen Berenice. — **Room D.** Interesting mosaics of the Hellenistic period (one from Thmuis, p. 183, with a personified seaport and the name of the maker, Sophilos); plaster casts. — We return to Room 9.

Room 10 (Salle Antoniadis). Smaller Egyptian Sculptures. In the entrance (*B*): Basin for sacrificial offerings, with the votive inscription of Amenemmēs I., from Samannûd (p. 185). — *Wall Cases C, AA, E:* Figures of gods and sacred animals in bronze and faience. — *Case H:* Alabaster vases; canopic jars. — *Case BB:* Bronze figures of deities (Isis, Neith, Amun, Harpocrates, etc.); folding chair with heads of geese. — *Case L:* Funerary statuettes (p. cliv) in faience. — *Glass Case O:* Scarabæi, amulets, and rings in faience. — *Glass Case P:* Small vases from Rhodes and Cyprus; gold ornaments of the Ptolemaic, Roman, and Byzantine periods (armlets, necklaces, rings, and ear-rings). — In the centre, a plaster cast of the statue of Princess Amenerdaïs (Cairo Museum, p. 96).

Room 11. Egyptian Sculptures of the Græco-Roman Period. 78. Upper portion of the granite statue of a goddess in Greek costume; 33, 34. Osiris and Isis in the form of serpents. 43-53. Statues of priests and officials of the Roman era, from Dimai (p. 208). — 61. Fragments of a temple-relief with deities, from Benha (Athribis, p. 37). — 62. Chapel with the badly preserved figure of the nursing Isis; above, memorial stone with the falcon-shaped Horus in a chapel borne by floral pillars. — 75. Tombstone in the form of a chapel, with a man in Greek costume. — *Case A:* 69. Fine fragment of a female statue, by an Egyptian sculptor working under Greek influence.

Room 12. Portrait Busts and Smaller Sculptures. 1. Charming head of a youth, from Kôm esh-Shuqâfa; 2. Head of a boy; 3. Roman woman; 16. Head of a youth, of the Attic school of the 4th cent. B.C.; 17. Alexander the Great (?) in red granite; 18. Young warrior; 19. Cleopatra (?); *20. Head of a youthful goddess. — *Case A:* Small sculptures, heads of women; 10-12. Busts of Ptolemaic queens; 20. Pan; 21, 22. Fauns. — 32, 32a (3337, 3339). Male busts, from Alexandria (W. necropolis); 33 (3357). Colossal head of one of the Ptolemies, with the royal Egyptian headgear; 60. Colossal head of Ptolemy IV. Philopator (p. cxii), with the double crown (p. cii). — In *Case C:* 30. Portrait of a young Libyan. — 55. Portrait of Septimius Severus. — In *Case B:* *20-24. Small busts of Alexander the Great; charming marble heads of children and others; below, statuettes of Venus. — In the centre, 30. Colossal marble statue of Marcus Aurelius (the eagle on the armour replaced in the Christian period by the monogram of Christ). — 27. Torso of a statuette of Venus.

Room 13. Sculptures and Architectural Fragments. 1. Statue of an emperor (the head of Septimius Severus does not belong to it); 3. Egyptian naos from Ḥadra. — In the recesses, 4-7. Draped female statues. — *Case F:* 2. Young faun; 5. Bronze head of a negress.

Room 14 (left of the preceding). 1. Torso of a marble statue of a philosopher; 6. Tombstone in the shape of a small temple; sphinxes; 2-4. Pillars with half-columns and rich foliage-capitals, found in the Rue Sultan Hussein (p. 21).

Room 15 (adjoining R. 13 on the E.). 29, 50. Frescoes from a tomb at Gabbari (p. 28). — Round the room are architectural fragments and small

altars from tombs at Gabbari, made of Mex limestone and executed in the mixed Greek and Egyptian style, some of very fine workmanship. The same style is shown in Nos. 2 and 3, brightly painted capitals (in which the Egyptian papyrus motive is used) from the quarter of the palace of the Ptolemies.

Room 16. SCULPTURES. 39. Arm bearing a globe, probably part of a colossal statue of an emperor, from Benha (p. 37). — On the left wall: 41-43, 45. Four fragments of statues, probably parts of a group; 47. Colossal seated marble figure of Zeus-Sarapis; 49, 52, 52a. Colossal heads of Zeus-Sarapis; 53. Roman head; 54. Apollo on the omphalos; on two syenite columns are fine Ionic capitals of the 3rd cent. B.C.; 61. Recumbent tomb-figure of a Roman, from Abuqîr. — In the centre: 31. Bath; 34. Colossal eagle; 35. Hip-bath; 37. Sarcophagus in the form of a bath. — By the right wall: 5. Mænad; 13. Draped female figure; 17. Venus. — By the door-posts at the entrance to the following room: 62. Sleeping genii.

Room 17. MUMMIES AND SMALL OBJECTS OF ART. *U*, *X*, *Y*. Mummies with the portraits of the deceased painted on wood; coffins with mummies. — *MM.* Plaster masks of the Roman period (2nd cent. of our era) from Antinoë (p. 221). — *Cases A*, *A*[1], *O*, *P:* Glass bottles. — *Table Case RR:* Ornaments and amulets in gold, silver, etc., found on the mummies at Wardiân (p. 28); engraved stones and cameos. — *Table Case ZZ:* Glass-pastes used as inlay for coffins. — Colossal statue of porphyry. — Sarcophagus of white marble, with scenes from the Dionysos myth. — Case with Greek vases and terracotta figures. — *Table Case VV:* Two golden bracelets from Abuqîr, lamps, ivory carvings. — *Case F:* Faience figures of the Hellenistic and Roman period. — *Case G:* Funerary furniture from the necropolis at Shâṭbi (p. 26); 7. Garland of flowers in painted terracotta: 8, 9. Laurel and ivy garlands in gilded bronze and terracotta. — *Cases EE*, *NN:* Plaster masks. — *Case H:* Cinerary urns of the so-called Ḥadra type. — In the centre, a *Mosaic Pavement (family in a tent on the Nile), from Thmuis (p. 183). — *Case K:* Cinerary urns. — *Case L:* Urns, garlands, terracotta figurines. — *Case M:* Terracotta figure of a man lighting a lantern, etc. — On either side of the garden door, two marble sarcophagi adorned with garlands; fragments of a mosaic (the river-god Alpheus pursuing the nymph Arethusa). — *Case LL:* Black cinerary urn with reliefs and white painting, from Ḥadra.

Room 18. CERAMICS AND OBJECTS FROM TOMBS. *Glass Case HH:* Large cinerary urn in black-varnished terracotta, with reliefs and a figure of the deceased on the lid. — Left side of the room. *Glass Cases B-E:* Greek vases; lamps of the Roman period. — *Case F:* Terracottas of the beginning of the Ptolemaic period. The *Figures of girls are distinguished by delicacy of execution and colouring, and some of them (e.g. one with a lute, No. 4) rival the best Tanagra figurines. — *Cases G-I:* Greek terracotta figurines. — *Case K:* Lamps and lanterns. — *Case L:* Moulds for terracotta figurines. — Right side of the room: in *Case A* cinerary urns, in other cases Græco-Egyptian terracottas, notably figures of deities, which seem to have served as images of saints in the houses of the common people. — In the centre: *Mosaics from a temple at Abuqîr (p. 32).

Room 19. *Mosaic and cinerary urns from Shâṭbi (p. 26). *Case I:* Fine faience vase, adorned with three heads and the figure of the god Bes.

Room 20. OBJECTS FROM TOMBS. In the middle: Torsos of a fine group of Dionysos and the Faun, executed under the influence of the school of Praxiteles. — *Cases A* and *B:* Greek vases and terracotta figures.

Room 21. In a covered *Glass Case:* Objects from tombs; sepulchral wreaths in terracotta and gilded bronze; 5. Double flute in ivory. — *Case B:* Cinerary urns and clay figures from Shâṭbi. — *Cases D* and *F:* Similar objects from the necropolis of Ibrâhîmîya (p. 26).

Room 22 (Room of Prince ʿOmar Ṭûsûn). FRAGMENTS FROM CANOPUS (p. 32). Mosaic of a warrior surrounded by griffins (found in Alexandria); on the walls, architectural fragments. — We return to R. 17 and there turn to the left.

TRANSVERSE GALLERY (Pl. Y). *3. Colossal seated marble figure of Hercules. A side-room (Pl. 27; adm. by special permission only) contains copies and articles not adapted for public exhibition.

In the Garden (Pl. 24): Two sphinxes of Apries (p. cix), originally erected at Heliopolis. — Reconstitution of the gates and the chapel of the crocodile-god Pnepherōs at Theadelphia (Baṭn Harît, p. 210); flanking the first gate (with a Greek votive inscription, 137 B.C.) are two recumbent lions; the chapel contains the bier for the sacred crocodile (original in R. 9, p. 24). — 24. Colossal head of Antony (p. cxiii) as Osiris, from Ḥadra; large limestone, granite, and marble sarcophagi from Abuqîr, Ḥadra, Kôm esh-Shuqâfa, and other places; architectural fragments. — Beyond the transverse gallery is a reconstitution of two rock-tombs of the 3rd and 1st cent. B.C., from the W. necropolis near Wardiân (p. 28); the one (Pl. 25) is a cella with a large funeral couch and remains of colouring, the other (Pl. 26) plain, with three niches and sarcophagi.

III. Environs of Alexandria (Ramleh, Mex).

From Alexandria to Ramleh the best route is by the electric railway starting from the Ramleh Station (Pl. G 3; from 5.30 a.m. till 1 a.m.; 1st cl. fare P.T. 2, book containing 50 tickets P.T. 75). The 'Service Victoria' runs on the N. line, the 'Service Bacos' on the S. line (diverging from each other at Bulkeley, see p. 27). The journey takes about 1/2 hr. — The Rue de Ramleh et d'Aboukir, with much motor and carriage traffic, starts from the Porte Fouad (Pl. K 3; p. 20) and leads viâ Sîdi Gâbir (see below) to Ramleh and Abuqîr (p. 32). — The railway (Abuqîr-Rosetta line, p. 32) is of practically no use to tourists.

From the starting-point we have a fine view of the E. harbour; projecting into the sea, to the left, is the small *Fort Silsila* (Pl. H 1). The line runs along the Avenue Alexandre le Grand, parallel with the quay; on the right lies the Government Hospital (p. 11). — *Mazarita* station. The road on the right leads to the *City Park* (p. 21), that on the left to *Fort Silsila* (see above). — *Chatby* station (Pl. I 2; Arabic *Esh-Shâṭbi*) derives its name from a Moslem saint. On the right are the large buildings of the Greek orphanage and the Greek school, and the institutions (industrial school, hospital, almshouse) of the ʿOrwa el-Woska, a Moslem benevolent society, on the left, the *Royal Institute of Hydro-Biology* (Pl. I 1, 2). Then, to the right, the Jewish and Christian cemeteries (Pl. K 2; British war cemetery). — To the left of *Chatby-les-Bains* station (Pl. K 1) are sea-baths and a necropolis of the first Ptolemaic era, the tombs of which (tombs with superstructures and rock-tombs) are the oldest in the vicinity of Alexandria (adm. by permit from the museum authorities, p. 22). On the hill to the right is the handsome *Lycée Français* (Pl. K L 1); to the left is the imposing *Collège St-Marc* of the Frères des Ecoles Chrétiennes (1928). We pass stations for the suburbs of *Camp de César* (Pl. L 1) and *Ibrâhîmîya* (*Ibrahimieh;* Daly's House, pens. from £E 9 per month), with a Franciscan church (Sacré-Cœur), a Greek Orthodox church, and numerous villas. Near Ibrâhîmîya is a Græco-Jewish necropolis of the 3rd cent. B.C.

The next stations are *Sporting Club* (a British club with a race-course) and *Cleopatra;* on the right the Rue du Prince Hussein leads to the Nuzha Garden (p. 22). Beside the station of *Sîdi Gâbir* (*Sidi Gaber;* a station on the railway to Cairo, p. 33, and on the Abuqîr-Rosetta line, p. 32) is (l.) a mosque containing the tomb of the Mohammedan saint Sîdi Gâbir. Close by a marble monument com-

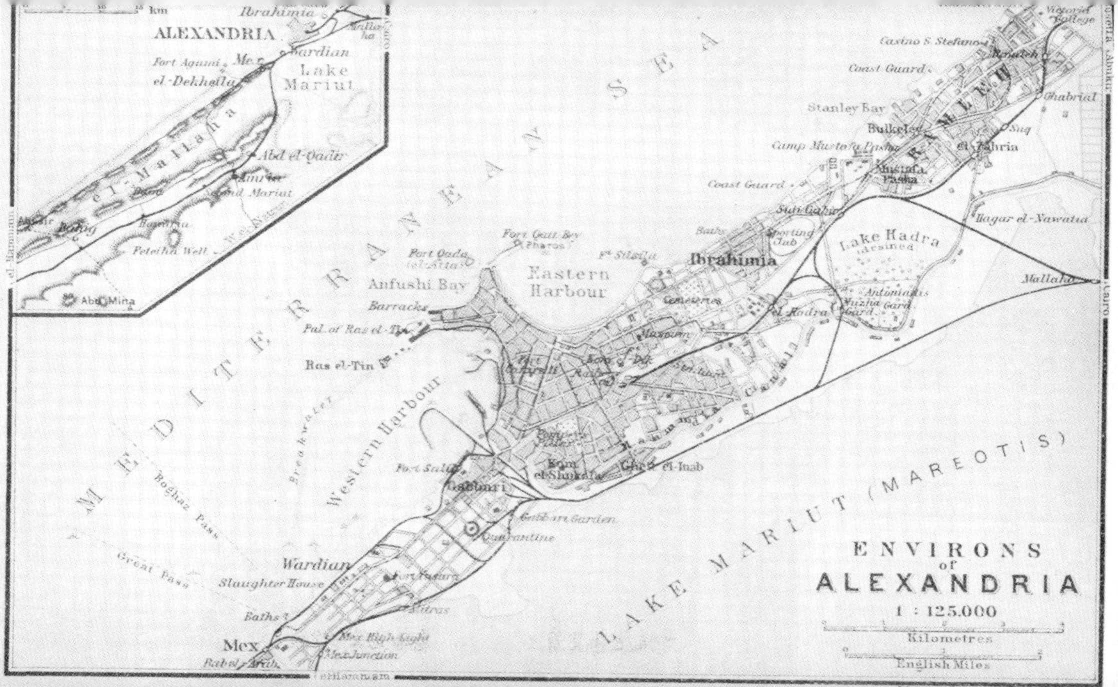
ENVIRONS
of
ALEXANDRIA
1 : 125.000
Kilometres
English Miles
MEDITERRANEAN SEA
LAKE MARIUT (MAREOTIS)
Eastern Harbour
Western Harbour
Breakwater
Boghaz Pass
Great Pass
Anfushi Bay
Barracks
Pal. of Ras el-Tin
Ras el-Tin
Fort Qada (el-Atta)
Fort Qait Bey (Pharos)
Ft. Silsila
Ibrahimia
Cemeteries
Museum
el-Hadra
Lake Hadra (drained)
Antoniadis
Nuzha Gard.
Sporting Club
Baths
Sidi Gabir
Coast Guard
Camp Mustafa Pasha
Mustafa Pasha
Bulkeley
Stanley Bay
el-Bahria
Suq
Ghabrial
Ramleh
Casino S. Stefano
Victoria College
Hagar el-Nawatia
Mallaha
Cairo
Rosetta
Abukir
Kom el-Shukafa
Gheit el-Inab
Gabbari
Fort Salib
Gabbari Garden
Quarantine
Wardian
Slaughter House
Baths
Mex
Mex High Light
Mex Junction
Rabat Arab
el-Hammam
ALEXANDRIA
Ibrahimia
Mallaha
Wardian
Lake Mariut
Fort Agami
Mex
el-Dekheila
el-Mallaha
Abd el-Qadir
Amria
Sand Mariut
Hamra
Feteiha Well
Abu Mina
el-Hammam
km
Wagner & Debes' Geogr. Estab. Leipzig

memorates *General Sir Ralph Abercromby*, who fell in battle against the French in 1801 (comp. p. 32).

The track now runs parallel with the road from Alexandria. Station *Moustapha Pacha*. The hill of *Abu Nawâtîr*, on the right, commands a fine view of Lake Mareotis. On an eminence to the left are the remains of a château built by Ismâ'îl Pasha, now used by the British military authorities, and barracks for British troops (parade service in the garrison church of St. George at 9.30 a.m.). The building material for the château was taken from the ruins of the *Qaṣr el-Qayâṣira* ('Castle of the Cæsars'), an old fortified Roman

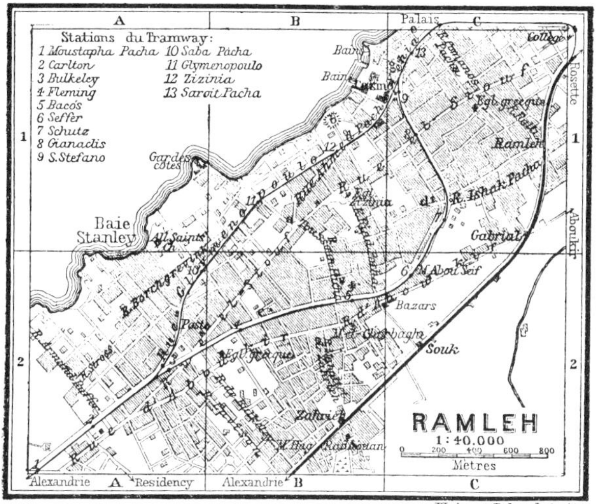

Wagner & Debes, Leipzig

camp in the vicinity. — The attractive villas of Ramleh begin at *Carlton* and *Bulkeley*, and cover the site of the ancient *Nicopolis* (p. 14), a suburb of Alexandria founded by Augustus to commemorate his victory over Antony. The favourite bathing place is Stanley Bay (Pl. A 1). Bulkeley, which contains the English church of All Saints (Pl. A 1) and the *British Residency* (beyond Pl. A 2; used in summer, comp. p. 12) is named, like most of the following stations, after one of the promoters of the railway.

Ramleh (Arabic Er-Raml, i.e. 'sand'), with 51,500 inhab., is the favourite summer resort of well-to-do Alexandrians and Cairenes; in winter it is not so attractive to tourists. The N. line (p. 26) runs viâ *Saba Pacha*, *Glymenopoulo* (Summer Palace, Pl. a, B 1, 42 R., pens.

P.T. 75), and *Zizinia* to *San Stefano.* Thence past the stations of *Saroit Pacha* (Sarwat Pasha), *Laurens*, *Palais* (with the palace of the King's aunt; no adm.), *Sidi Bichr* (Sîdi Bishr; mosque), and *Siouf* (Es-Siyûf) to *Victoria* (railway to Abuqîr and Rosetta, see p. 32), near which is the handsome *Victoria College*. The latter, opened in 1909, was founded by public subscription in 1901 in memory of Queen Victoria, to provide a liberal education on the lines of the English public schools.

To the S. of Victoria station, in Victoria Road (connecting the Abuqîr and Cairo roads), is the new 'garden city' of *Taftîsh Siyûf* (Domaine de Siouf).

The S. line runs to the right viâ *Fleming*, *Bacós*, *Seffer*, *Schutz*, and *Gianaclis*, and reaches its terminus at *San Stefano*. Bacos, the central part of Ramleh, has a bazaar, a mosque, and a Roman Catholic church and school. Near San Stefano, on the shore, are the **Hôtel-Casino San Stefano* (Pl. B C 1; 150 beds, pens. 100-160 P.T., closed in winter), with garden, terrace, sea-baths, etc., the *Hôtel Beau-Rivage* (Pl. e, C 1), with fine garden, the *New Victoria Hotel* (Pl. b, B 1; 54 R., pens. 13-20 gold fr.), and the *Villa Margherita* (Pl. g; C 1).

From Alexandria to Mex (Meks): Tramway (line 1, see p. 10) viâ Gabbari, every 7 min. in 3/4 hr. (fare 15 or 6 mill.).

From the suburb of *Gabbari* (Pl. C D 8; Arabic *El-Qabbâri*), with a large goods station of the Egyptian Railways, the tram runs S.W. by the Route du Meks, traversing the hilly *Necropolis* of the Roman imperial age (p. 13). On the left are the gardens, the picturesque mosque, and the palace of Gabbari, the last now a *Quarantine Station*. Farther on we pass through the Arab village of *Wardiân* (El-Wardyân); to the right is the slaughter-house. — A number of interesting Ptolemaic tomb-chambers, called *Baths of Cleopatra*, are cut out of the limestone of the coast-hills (comp. p. 32).

Mex or *Meks* (El-Maks), the terminus of the tramway, is visited for sea-bathing. On the beach are several hotels, the *Nuovo Casino Restaurant*, and the *Bâb el-ʿArab* ('Beduin Gate'), part of the old fortifications. Farther S.W. are the quarries mentioned on p. lxx.

IV. Mareotis District (City of St. Menas, Abuṣîr).

An excursion to the Mareotis district, interesting both for its scenery and history, is recommended, especially in Feb.-April, when the superb desert *Flora (anemone and narcissus in Jan. and Feb., ranunculus in March, asphodel and yellow daisy in April) is seen at its best. A visit to the ruins of *Abuṣîr* and the *City of St. Menas* is best made by Motor Car and takes a whole day; full information is obtainable at the Museum (p. 22) and the tourist agencies (p. 10). By Railway two days are required; the point of departure for both places is *Bahîg*, a station on the Maryût Railway, a line constructed by the ex-Khedive ʿAbbâs II. (48 1/2 M. in 1 3/4 hr.; 1st class P.T. 39, 2nd class P.T. 21; comp. p. 31). As riding-animals cannot be procured at Bahîg, the traveller must bring a donkey with him from Alexandria (from Bahîg to the City of St. Menas 2 hrs., to Abuṣîr c. 1 1/2 hr.).

— The drive by motor-car from Alexandria to ***Mirsa Maṭrûḥ*** (p. 31) takes 10-12 hrs. (for information apply to the Libyan Oases Association, p. 10).

History. To the S. of the narrow strip of sand on which Alexandria stands there has lain from time immemorial a large inland sheet of water, named by the ancients **Lake Mareotis** or *Mareia* (Arabic *Beḥeiret Maryûṭ*). The lake lies below the level of the sea and was connected with the Nile by channels through which the products of Egypt were brought to Alexandria. In the lake lay eight islands, covered with luxurious country-houses; its banks were exuberantly fertile, and its white wines are celebrated by Horace and Virgil. In the middle ages the lake dried up. During the siege of Alexandria in 1801 the British cut through the dunes at Abuqîr. The sea at once rushed in, destroying 150 villages, and it still covers over 77 sq. M., although Muḥammed ʿAli (p. 16) spared no cost to win back the land for cultivation. The Egyptian government has recently resumed the task of reclamation. Pumping works at Mex (p. 28) keep the water-level at $8^1/_4$ ft. below the level of the sea. The ex-Khedive ʿAbbâs II. succeeded by a carefully planned system of agriculture in improving the arable coast-plain, which extends on the W. into the Libyan Desert. The district is mainly inhabited by Beduin (Ûlâd ʿAli, p. lxi), who live partly in small villages and partly in tents, trade in camels, and raise sheep. Barley flourishes with especial success; vineyards and orchards have been replanted.

The Maryûṭ railway (Main station, see p. 9) diverges from the main line near *Ḥadra* station (p. 33), crosses the Maḥmûdîya Canal beyond *Nuzha* station (3 M.; p. 22), and runs W. between the canal and Lake Mareotis to the station of ($7^1/_2$ M.) *Gabbari Garden* (*Jardin Gabbary;* comp. p. 28). The line then runs along the N. bank of Lake Mareotis, with the houses of *Mex* (p. 28) to the right, to ($9^3/_4$ M.) *El-Mitrâs (Metras)* and ($10^1/_2$ M.) *Mex Junction*, with the large factory of the Egyptian Salt & Soda Co. (comp. p. 35). — The train now runs S. along an embankment ($2^3/_4$ M. long) through the lake, then turns W. and traverses cultivated land to ($18^2/_3$ M.) *ʿAbd el-Qâdir.* Above the village stands the small mosque dedicated to the saint of that name. — 21 M. *El-ʿAmirîya (Amria)*, with pretty gardens and a villa of King Fu'âd I. The Beduin market held here on Wednesdays presents an animated scene, when camels, horses, grain, etc., are offered for sale; it is especially interesting in Dec., Jan., and Feb., when the date caravans arrive from the oasis of Sîwa (p. 403). — $23^2/_3$ M. *Ikingi Maryûṭ (Second Mariût)*, with vineyards. Farther on we pass through cultivated land and desert. — $29^1/_4$ M. *El-Hauwârîya (Hawaria).*

$34^3/_4$ M. **Bahîg.** Thence to El-Ḥammâm, see p. 31.

The Motor Road from Alexandria (31 M.) runs through the suburb of *Mex* (p. 28), crosses the above-mentioned embankment, and then follows the railway-line to Bahîg.

From Bahîg to the City of St. Menas, $7^1/_2$ M. — From the station we proceed S.E. across the railway embankment to ($^2/_3$ M.) *Zâwyet el-Iseila*, a few houses and a small school. Close by is a deep cistern with good drinking-water, at which the Beduin water their herds of camels. Continuing S.E. we ascend an eminence from which we have a pretty view of Bahîg, of Gebel el-Bâṭin (concealing the sea), and of Abuṣîr. Farther on our route passes between fields of grain till the plateau on the edge of the desert is reached and the hills of the City of St. Menas appear.

The **City of St. Menas**, called by the Beduin *Karm Abûm* (i.e. *Karm Abu Mîna*, 'vineyard of Menas') or *Bu Mna*, lies in the Mareotic Desert, about halfway between Alexandria and the Wâdi Naṭrûn. The extensive site was rediscovered and successfully excavated in 1905-7 by Mgr. Carl Maria Kaufmann of Frankfurt. The objects found among the ruins are in the museums of Alexandria and Frankfurt. St. Menas (d. A.D. 296), who was looked upon as a kind of patron saint of the Libyan Desert, was buried here, and, in the 5-6th cent. especially, his tomb was a favourite place of pilgrimage, whence the pilgrims carried away clay flasks filled with its wonder-working water and oil (so-called Menas flasks). In the 7-8th cent. a town of some size grew up here, which was destroyed c. 900. Comp. 'Three Years in the Libyan Desert', by *J. C. Ewald Falls* (English translation, London 1913; illus.).

The great Basilica of Arcadius, the building of which was begun by that emperor (395-408) and completed by the Patriarch Timothy, forms the central point of the ancient city, the streets and houses of which are clearly distinguishable. The church, which is orientated with great exactitude, is built on the early-Christian cruciform plan (p. clxxxvii). It consists of nave, aisles, and transept supported by fifty-six columns and adjoined on the E. by an apse or chancel, 35 ft. in width. The transept, 164 ft. long and 66 ft. wide, has a small apsidal recess at each end; in the centre stand four columns, formerly bearing a canopy and marking the site of the altar. Access is obtained from the apse into some vaulted tomb-chambers. The chief entrance (atrium), consisting of three portals, is in the S. aisle, and there are other entrances at the beginning of the N. aisle and in the N. transept. A number of other rooms, subterranean tomb-chambers, corridors, and cellars adjoin the aisles. — At the W. end of the basilica stands a tower-like building, the main apse of the original *Burial Church of St. Menas*, of earlier date. This consists of a basilica, 125 ft. long and 74 ft. broad, with nave and aisles each terminating in an apse. The whole is built over an extensive crypt lying 26 ft. below and reached by a broad flight of marble steps (now closed by iron railings). — Close by the burial church on the W., is an octagonal *Baptistery*, with a large baptismal basin in the middle.

On the outer circumference of the town, in the midst of a cemetery on the N., stands another *Basilica* (the so-called 'basilica of the baths', p. clxxxviii), with apse, prothesis (room used for preparing the Eucharist), diakonikon (sacristy), and numerous other chambers, including an elegant baptistery adjoining the right aisle. — In various quarters of the town are potteries and kilns, in which the clay flasks for pilgrims (comp. above) were made. Among the other secular buildings are some cisterns and an early-Christian hospice (with baths).

To visit the Wâdi en-Naṭrûn (p. 35) from the City of St. Menas 2-3 days are required; the ride to the edge of the valley takes 1/2 day. Besides the riding-camels a camel to carry water is necessary. The camp should

be pitched near Bîr Hooker, the terminus of the light railway from Khaṭâṭba (p. 35). — For the salt-lakes and convents, comp. p. 35.

From Bahîg to Abuṣîr, 5 M. — From the station we proceed N. to the prettily situated village of *Bahîg* and thence N.W. across deserts and fields to (c. $1^1/_2$ hr.) ***Abuṣîr** *(Abu Ṣîr)*, the ruins of the ancient *Taposiris Magna.* The remains of this town, which lay on the plain, are very scanty. The Egyptian Temple, however, situated on a limestone ridge rising from the seashore, is in good preservation as far as its enclosing walls are concerned. To judge from the Greek name of the place, it was probably dedicated to Osiris. The sanctuary lay from E. to W. and was entered by a handsome pylon, which, like the rest of the walls, is built of blocks of limestone. In the interior of each of the two towers is an ancient stairway; from the top we enjoy a magnificent *View of the blue sea, the desert, and the fertile land in the distance. The pylon is adjoined by the temple, which was surrounded by lofty walls and had a length of 295 ft. The rooms in the interior (partly converted into a Christian church) are now destroyed. — A few minutes N. of the temple lie the ruins of a *Lighthouse* of the Roman period. The rocks in the neighbourhood contain many quarries and Roman tombs, and near the temple a bath has been excavated which deserves a visit.

The Railway runs on from Bahîg to ($38^1/_2$ M.) *Burg el-ʿArab*, founded in 1917 as the administrative centre of the E. district of the Western Desert province (see p. 403), with a large carpet factory. — $41^2/_3$ M. *El-Gharbânîyât*, with extensive gypsum deposits. — $48^1/_2$ M. *El-Ḥammâm* (i.e. 'bath'; Beduin market on Sat.) is the present terminus of the railway (extension to Mirsa Maṭrûḥ is planned). Thence a motor-road runs alongside the railway (now abandoned) viâ ($91^1/_3$ M.) *ʿAbd er-Raḥmân*, with the mosque of the saint of that name, and (111 M.) *Eḍ-Ḍabʿa*, the ancient *Zephyrium* and former terminus of the Maryûṭ railway, to (205 M.) *Mirsa Maṭrûḥ* (rest-house of the Libyan Oases Association, p. 10, on the shore, good), a little seaport (sponge-fishing) with a small fort, a mosque, and the headquarters of a camel corps. It has a Greek church and the ruin of a 6th cent. Christian basilica, with two apses opposite each other (p. clxxxviii). Mirsa Maṭrûḥ is the capital of the Western Desert Province (p. xlix); it was the ancient *Paraetonium*, whence Alexander the Great marched to the oasis of Jupiter Ammon (p. 403). Motor-road S. to the oasis of *Sîwa* (p. 403). On the W. the motor-road goes on to the harbour of **Es-Sollûm** *(Es-Sallûm)*, on the gulf of that name. The little town (new mosque, 1928), which adjoins the E. frontier of the Italian colony of Cyrenaica, was occupied by Egypt in 1911, but was not acknowledged as an Egyptian possession until the treaty with Italy of Dec. 1925.

Sollûm is the starting-point for the oasis of *Jarabûb* (Arabic *Jaghbûb*, *Gaghbûb*), situated in N. Lat. 29° 44′ and E. Long. 24° 31′, about 130 M. to the S.W. (75 M. to the N.W. of Sîwa, p. 403). Jarabûb, recognized as Italian territory in Dec. 1925, was formerly (1855-95) the chief stronghold of the Senussi order (with the tomb-mosque of its founder, p. xcv).

V. Excursion to Abuqir and Rosetta.

Railway to (44 M.) *Rosetta* in $2^1/_4$-$2^1/_2$ hrs. (two trains daily; fare 1st class P.T. $48^1/_2$, 2nd class P.T. $26^1/_2$); to ($14^1/_3$ M.) *Abuqîr* in 1 hr. (10-12 trains daily; fare P.T. 7 or $4^1/_2$, return P.T. 9 or 6). — Those who wish to combine a visit to the temple of Sarapis at Abuqîr with the excursion to Rosetta should take the first train in the morning from Alexandria to Maʿmûra (see below) and go on thence by the next train to Rosetta (see below). — Good Motor Road to *Abuqîr* and *Rosetta* (c. 2 hrs.).

As far as (4 M.) *Sîdi Gâbir* (p. 26) the train follows the line to Cairo (p. 33), from which it then diverges E. past *Ramleh* (p. 27), afterwards crossing the desert. — 10 M. *El-Mandara;* $^3/_4$ M. to the S. rises the hill of *Kôm et-Terbân*, commanding an extensive view. — $10^3/_4$ M. *El-Muntazah (Montaza)*, with a royal château. The train now skirts the edge of the fertile region. — $12^1/_2$ M. *El-Maʿmûra*, junction for Abuqîr and Rosetta. On either side lies the aerodrome of the British Royal Air Force (see below).

$14^1/_3$ M. **Abuqîr,** *Abu Qîr*, or *Aboukir* (Hotel Canopos, 25 R. at 20-25, pens. 50-60 P.T.; Nelson Hotel), a village with a shallow harbour, has become a favourite summer resort and contains the villas of many rich Alexandrians and a club-house of the Royal Egyptian Automobile Club (p. 10). It is the seaplane base for the Royal Air Force in Egypt (London-India air service, see p. xviii). At Abuqîr, in the 'Battle of the Nile' (Aug. 1st, 1798), the British fleet under Nelson signally defeated the French, destroying thirteen of their seventeen vessels, which were intended to cover Bonaparte's army of invasion. On July 25th, 1799, Bonaparte here repulsed the Turkish army, which had landed near Abuqîr; and on March 8th, 1801, Sir Ralph Abercromby (p. 27) defeated the remnants of the French army and compelled the evacuation of Egypt in Sept. 1801.

From the station, where donkeys are in waiting (bargaining necessary), we turn left (W.) for (c. 20 min.) *Et-Taufîqîya Fort.* Close to this are the insignificant ruins of the ancient **Canopus,** where Greek legend placed the burial of Canopus, the helmsman of Menelaus. To the S. of the fort are the remains of the famous *Temple of Sarapis*, visited by many pilgrims in search of health. Orgiastic feasts were celebrated at Canopus. The antiquities found here are in the Alexandria Museum (p. 25). For the 'Decree of Canopus' see p. 96, No. 983. To the N., in the direction of the coast, is a large tomb of the Hellenistic period; on the shore are remains of ancient baths, and not far off are fragments of a colossal granite statue. If time permit, a very attractive walk may be taken hence past the old Es-Sabʿ Fort to *Fort Qâït Bey* (Ṭâbiyat el-Burg), on the point of the ancient promontory of *Zephyrium* (superb view). Thence we follow Abuqîr Bay S. to the former Ramleh Fort (Ṭâbiyat er-Raml), the ancient *Menuthis*, now waterworks. The ruins of the ancient '*Baths of Cleopatra*' lie $^1/_3$ M. to the S.W. We return to Abuqîr village and the railway station.

18 M. *Eṭ-Ṭarḥ.* The train traverses the narrow neck of land between *Lake Idku* (area c. 104 sq. M.) and the Mediterranean. — 21 M. *El-Maʿaddîya (El-Maʿdîya, Maadia)*, near the former Canopic mouth of the Nile. — 29 M. *Idku (Edkou)*; the village lies to the left on a hill. — 36 M. *El-Buṣeili (El-Buṣîli).*

44 M. **Rosetta** (Hôtel Royal), Arabic *Rashîd* (a Coptic name), with 23,048 inhab. in 1927, almost exclusively Arabs, lies at the

mouth of the Rosetta arm of the Nile *(Far' el-Gharbi)*, probably on the site of the town of *Bolbitine*, whence in ancient times this arm of the Nile received the name of Bolbitinic (p. lxix). During the middle ages and in more recent times its commercial prosperity was considerable, until the construction of the Maḥmûdîya Canal (p. 16) diverted its trade to Alexandria. In the main street, which runs S. from the station, is the *Mosque of 'Ali el-Mehalli* (on the left; built in 1721); the picturesque covered bazaars are farther on, to the left. Numerous antique marble columns are built into the four and five storied houses; the house of 'Ali el-Faṭâïri in the Ḥâret el-Ghazl (dating from 1620) should not be missed. The large *Sakhlûn Mosque* lies at the end of the main street, and to the E., close to the river, is the *Mosque of Muḥammed el-'Abbâsi* (1809), with a tasteful minaret. An attractive excursion may be made to the *Mosque of Abu Mandûr*, to the S. of the town, beside the river; visitors should go by boat if the wind is favourable, otherwise by donkey ($^1/_2$ hr.). The hill of the same name commands a fine view. — The fortifications to the N. of the town are shown by permission of the commandant. The famous *Rosetta Stone* (p. cxxxiii) was discovered in Fort St. Julien.

From Rosetta to *Damietta* viâ *Lake Burullus*, see p. 187.

From Rosetta the train returns to El-Buṣeili (p. 32) and thence runs S.E. to ($43^1/_2$ M.) *Idfîna (Edfina)*, on the Rosetta arm of the Nile. Hence a light railway runs viâ 'Aṭf to Damanhûr (see p. 34). — Opposite Idfîna lies the village of *Muṭûbis (Metoubès)*, $1^1/_4$ M. to the N. of which, on the Rosetta arm, is *Ibyâna*, with the house (now state property) in which Zaghlûl Pasha (p. cxxxi) was born in 1850.

3. From Alexandria to Cairo.

130 M. Railway (comp. p. xvii). Express train in $3\text{-}3^1/_2$, ordinary train in $6\text{-}7^1/_4$ hrs. (fares 1st class £E 1 P.T. 23, 2nd class P.T. 66). Seats in the Pullman cars (1st class, P.T. 25 supplement) are obtained through the Sleeping Car Co. (p. 40) at the station (p. 9). Restaurant-cars on the midday and evening expresses, sleeping cars on the night train. — Travellers should engage the commissionnaire of the hotel or one of the tourist agents (comp. p. 10) to assist in booking their luggage. — The Alexandria and Cairo line, the first railway of the East, was constructed by Robert Stephenson (p. 195) under Sa'îd Pasha in 1855.

The railway crosses the Farkha Canal (p. 21) and soon comes into sight of *Lake Mareotis* (p. 29), the water of which washes the railway-embankment at places during the period of the inundation. Beyond *Ḥaḍra* ($2^1/_2$ M.; p. 22) the Maryût line (p. 29) diverges to the right, and beyond *Sîdi Gâbir* ($4^1/_3$ M.; p. 26) the Rosetta line (p. 32) diverges to the left. We cross the *Maḥmûdîya Canal* (p. 16) by a drawbridge, and the triangular sails of the boats which appear above its banks enable its course to be traced for quite a distance. — 8 M. *El-Mallâḥa*. Cotton-fields now appear to the left. — 17 M. *Kafr ed-Dauwâr*. In the vicinity are the ruins of *Kôm el-Gîza*, marking the site of *Schedia*, the Nile-harbour of ancient Alexandria.

A Light Railway diverging at Kafr ed-Dauwâr (two trains daily in each direction) serves a number of villages on the W. margin of the Delta and rejoins the main line at Damanhûr (see below).

We pass several unimportant villages, with the clay-built grey houses, crowned by cupolas, which are so characteristic a feature of the whole Delta landscape. — 28 M. *Abu Ḥummuṣ.*

38 M. **Damanhûr** (buffet and restaurant, with bedrooms), with 51,720 inhab. in 1927, is an important cotton emporium and the capital of the province of *Beḥeira* (p. xlix), which extends from the Rosetta arm of the Nile to the Libyan desert. Damanhûr was the ancient Egyptian *Behdet* (p. ci), afterwards *Time-en-Hōr* (city of Horus, p. clvii) and the Roman *Hermopolis Parva.* The town lies on an eminence, with the towers of a church rising from among its houses. In the vicinity are several ginning mills, for the separation of the cotton from the seeds. The Arab cemetery lies close to the railway.

From Damanhûr to Maḥallet Rôḥ, 46 M., railway in $2^1/_4$-$3^1/_4$ hrs. (fare P.T. 50). — Beyond *Sanhûr* and *Er-Raḥmânîya* the train crosses the Rosetta arm of the Nile by an iron bridge completed in 1927 by Messrs. Dorman, Long & Co. to replace the original bridge of 1895. It consists of ten spans (one a swing span of 195 ft.) and has a total length of 2010 ft. — 13 M. **Disûq** (*Desûq, Dessuk*), a town with 7000 inhab., to the right, on the Rosetta arm, is also a station on the Ṭanṭa-Fuwa light railway (p. 36). A large fair is held here to celebrate the birthday (mûlid) of the local saint Ibrâhîm ed-Disûqi (p. xcv), the founder of an order of dervishes. The mosque established by him and equipped with a madrasa (p. cxcviii) by Sultan Qâït Bey (p. cxxiv) was rebuilt in 1885 and converted by Khedive ʿAbbâs II. into a college (Disûq Institute) after the model of the Azhar University (p. 58), with 19 professors and 290 students in 1925. Between the villages of Ibṭu and Shâba, $7^1/_2$ M. to the N.E. of Disûq, are the débris-heaps of *Tell el-Faráʿîn*, on the site of *Buto* (p. ci), the ancient capital of Lower Egypt. — The railway runs S.E. from Disûq, crossing numerous canals and passing *Shabâs (Chabas)* and ($27^1/_3$ M.) *Qallîn* (*Kalline;* buffet), where the branch to *Shirbîn* (p. 185) diverges. — Then come *Esh-Shîn* (p. 36), *Quṭûr* (*Kutur;* p. 36), and *El-Kunaiyisa* (*Konaiesa*). — 46 M. *Maḥallet Rôḥ* lies on the railway from Ṭanṭa to Manṣûra (p. 184).

Damanhûr is also the starting-point of several Light Railways: (1) S. to *Teh el-Bârûd* (p. 35) viâ *Ed-Dilingât (Delingat)* and *Ṭôd* (junction for *Kherbeta*). Near Ṭôd the rubbish-mounds of *Kôm el-Hiṣn* mark the site of the 'House of the Lady of the Trees', the capital of the 3rd nome of Lower Egypt. — (2) E. to *Teh el-Bârûd* viâ Shubra Khit (*Choubra Khît, Shibrikhît;* Hôtel du Nil; 2746 inhab.), on the Rosetta arm of the Nile, and *Shandîd* (p. 35). — (3) N. to *Idfîna* (p. 33) viâ *Zarqûn* and *El-ʿAṭf.* At ʿAṭf the *Maḥmûdîya Canal* (p. 16) diverges from the Nile; and on it barges and small steamers maintain communication with Alexandria. The machines which here impel the waters of the Nile towards Alexandria are very striking. — (4) To *Kafr ed-Dauwâr*, see above.

From Shubra Khît (see above) we may visit the ruins of *Ṣâ el-Ḥagar* (Saïs, p. 36) by boat or on donkey-back in 1-$1^1/_2$ hr. In the latter case we cross the Rosetta arm and follow the E. bank.

The line skirts an irrigation-canal of considerable size, *El-Khandaq Canal*, an offshoot of the Raiyâḥ el-Beḥeira (p. 35).

48 M. *Ṣafṭ el-Melûk.* About 1 hr. S.E., near *Nibîra (En-Nebeira)*, on the Canopic arm of the Nile (p. 32), lie the ruins of *Naucratis*, a Greek commercial city founded by Amasis (p. cix). The ruins do not repay a visit.

53¹/₂ M. *Teḥ* (or *Ityâi*) *el-Bârûd* (buffet) is a village with a large mound of ruins.

FROM TEH EL-BÂRÛD TO CAIRO, 76 M., branch-railway along the W. margin of the Nile delta in 3¹/₄ hrs. (two trains daily). — 9¹/₂ M. *Kôm Hamâda*; 14¹/₂M. *Wâqid* (*Waked*). To the right extends the Libyan Desert. — Beyond (19¹/₂ M.) *Et-Teiriya* (*Et-Teirieh*) the train skirts the *Raiyâh el-Beḥeira* (called in part the *Khaṭâtba Canal*), which diverges from the Rosetta arm (p. 131). — 31 M. *Kafr Dâwûd*, a village with 3000 inhabitants. — 38¹/₂ M. *El-Khaṭâtba* (to Bîr Hooker, see below). — 45¹/₂M. *Wardân*, with 5000 inhabitants. — 47¹/₄ M. *Abu Ghâlib*. — 54³/₄ M. *El-Qaṭṭâ* (*Katta*) has the remains of an early settlement (near the station), and in the desert is a large burial-ground of the Middle Empire. — 62 M. *El-Manâshi* (p. 131). — 67 M. *Ausim* (*Oussim*), a large village with three mosques. This was the ancient *Letopolis*; the temple of Horus erected here by Nectanebis I. (p. cx) is now represented by a few blocks of stone. — Beyond (71¹/₂ M.) *Imbâba* (Embaba, p. 87) we cross the Nile to (76 M.) *Cairo* (see p. 153).

LIGHT RAILWAYS run from Teh el-Bârûd to *Damanhûr* viâ *Dilingât* or *Shubra Khit* (p. 34) and to *Kafr 'Awâna* viâ *Shandîd* (p. 34).

From *Khaṭâtba* (see above) a private railway of the Egyptian Salt & Soda Co. (p. 29) leads to (34 M.; 3 hrs.) *Bîr Hooker*, on the E. edge of the Wâdi en-Naṭrûn ('natron valley'). This valley (c. 20 M. long) in the Libyan desert contains ten salt lakes, which are supposed to be connected with the Nile and which dry up almost entirely in summer. These lakes and the surrounding soil yield salt and soda, which are used in Egypt for bleaching and in the manufacture of soap and glass. The Wâdi Naṭrûn is celebrated for its hermitages and convents, which were established here as early as the 4th cent. (comp. p. cxvi) and had great influence in the development of Christianity. Only four of them are still inhabited (by Coptic monks; p. lvii); they are old, fortress-like buildings, with peculiar domed churches (p. cxc), and are most conveniently visited from Bîr Hooker. Close to Bîr Hooker are the *Deir Suryâni* ('Syrian Monastery') and, 10 min. from it, the *Deir Amba Bishôi* ('Monastery of St. Pshoi'; good water at both); farther N. is the *Deir el-Barâmûs*, while the *Deir Abu Maqâr* ('Monastery of St. Macarius'), the oldest of all, lies at the S. end of the valley. — From Bîr Hooker to the *City of St. Menas*, see pp. 30, 31. — The motor drive from Alexandria or Cairo to the Wadi Naṭrûn is recommended, but care should be taken to employ a driver that knows the way. On application to the Salt & Soda Co. at Alexandria (5 Rue Adib) visitors to the Wâdi Nâṭrûn may obtain board and lodging at the manager's house.

The line continues skirting the Khandaq Canal (p. 34), from which numerous small branches radiate. The fellahin may be observed raising water from the canals by means of Archimedean screws or by large wheels (sâqiya) hung with buckets or scoops (comp. p. lxxiv). The cultivated land becomes richer. Beyond *Taufiqîya* (*Tewfikieh*) the train crosses the Sâḥil Marqaṣ Canal (the N. continuation of the Raiyâḥ el-Beḥeira, see above) and an iron bridge over the Rosetta arm of the Nile (fine view to the left).

64¹/₂ M. **Kafr ez-Zaiyât** (buffet), on the right bank of the Nile. The town carries on a busy trade in grain, cotton, and other products of the Delta, and contains large cotton warehouses and ginning factories.

A BRANCH LINE leads S., parallel with the Rosetta arm of the Nile, to *Dinshawai* (*Denshawai*) and *Minûf* (p. 36), a station on the Ṭanṭa-Barrage-Cairo line (p. 36). — A LIGHT RAILWAY, to the N. of the main line, runs from Kafr ez-Zaiyât to Ṭanṭa viâ *Birma* (*Berma*; p. 36), a large village of 9000 inhabitants.

We cross several canals, enlivened by numerous ships.

76 M. **Tanta.** — *Buffet* and *Restaurant.* — Hotels. *Claridge, Orient,* R. 20-25 P.T., meals taken at a restaurant. It is best, if possible, to spend the night in Cairo or Manṣûra.

Banks. *Barclay's, National, Commercial Bank of Egypt, Banque Misr, Banco Italo-Egiziano.* — Hospital of the American Mission (p. 226), with 100 beds and four American doctors. — British Consular Agency. — Clubs. *British Club; International Sporting Club.*

Ṭanṭa, on the Qâṣid Canal, the thriving capital of the province of *Gharbîya* (p. xlix), which lies between the Rosetta and Damietta arms of the Nile, has a population of (1927) 89,712 and possesses large public buildings, churches, bazaars, and an extensive palace of the King of Egypt. It is an important cotton-market.

The *Mosque of Saiyid Aḥmad el-Badawi*, the most popular saint in Egypt (p. xcv), who was born in the 12th cent. at Fez and settled at Ṭanṭa after a pilgrimage to Mecca, is a handsome domed building, erected by ʿAbbâs I. and Ismâʿîl Pasha on the site of the original building, which dated from 1276. The large forecourt contains the basin for ablutions. Europeans are often denied access to the interior. The catafalque of the saint is covered with red velvet adorned with gold embroidery and is enclosed by a handsome bronze railing. Connected with the mosque are the Tanta Institute, the largest but one of the Mohammedan religious institutions in Egypt (comp. p. 58; 2536 students and 79 professors; library of 8873 vols., including 1985 MSS.), and two small schools (madrasas, p. cxcviii). The sibîl, or public fountain, with the small school above it, in the space adjoining the mosque, is older. A large market is held on Mondays.

From Ṭanṭa to *Maḥallet Rôḥ*, *Manṣûra*, and *Damietta*, see R. 10.

From Ṭanṭa to Cairo, 66½ M., branch-railway viâ the Barrage in 2¾-3½ hrs. — The line runs S. to (17½ M.) *Shibîn el-Kôm* (27,335 inhab.), the capital of the province of *Minûfîya*, one of the most fertile regions in the Delta. — 25½ M. *Minûf* (*Menûf;* buffet) is the central point of the province. Branch-lines to Kafr ez-Zaiyât (p. 35) and to Benha (p. 37). — 38½ M. *Ashmûn*. — At (52 M.) *Delta Barrage*, or *Barrage du Nil*, we join the route to Cairo mentioned on p. 131.

Ṭanṭa is also the starting-point of a branch-line, under construction in 1928, to (8¾ M.) *Es-Sanṭa* (p. 184), and of several Light Railways: 1. Viâ *Birma* (p. 35) and *Tanẓîm* (or *Qanṭaret*) *Basyûn* (*Bassioun Régulateur*), and then along the right bank of the Rosetta arm viâ *Ṣâ el-Hagar* (*Salhagar;* see below), *Maḥallet Diyâi* (*Mehallet Diai*), and *Disûq* (p. 34) to *Fuwa* (*Fua*). — 2. Viâ *Tanẓîm Basyûn* (see above), *Esh-Shîn* (p. 34), *Sakha* (p. 184), and *Kafr esh-Sheikh* (p. 185) to *Sîdi Sâlim*. — 3. Viâ *Quṭûr* (p. 34) to *Maḥalla el-Kubra*, and thence viâ *Tîra* and *Biyala* to *Balṭîm* (see p. 184). — 4. To *Kafr ez-Zaiyât*, see p. 35.

About ½ hr. N. of *Ṣâ el-Hagar* (see above; accommodation at the ʿomda's, or village headman's) lie the inconsiderable ruins of *Saïs*, the residence of Psammetichos I. and the kings of the 26th Dynasty (p. cix) and the centre of the cult of Neith (p. clvii).

At (80 M.) *Difra (Defra)* the train crosses the Qâṣid Canal and, beyond the station of (87 M.) *Birket es-Sabʿ* (light railway to Maḥalla el-Kubra, see p. 184), the *Baḥr Shibîn* (p. 185), the ancient Sebennytic arm of the Nile. A number of cotton-ginning mills testify to the wealth of the country. — 93 M. *Quweisna (Kuesna).* Near Benha, on the Damietta arm of the Nile, is a large royal palace, where ʿAbbâs I.

(p. cxxvii) died in 1854, probably by violence. — The train crosses the Damietta branch of the Nile by a large iron bridge.

100½ M. **Benha** (buffet), with 28,412 inhab. in 1927, is the capital of the province of *Qalyûbîya* (p. xlix) and the junction for the railway to Zagazig and Port Said (p. 192); a branch to Minûf (15 M.; p. 36) was opened in 1929. It is noted for its oranges, mandarins, and grapes (comp. p. lxxviii) and has branches of the National Bank and the Banque Misr. A considerable market is held here on Mondays.

To the N.E. of Benha, about 1 M. from the station and to the left of the railway, are the insignificant ruins of the ancient *Athribis*, now named *Tell Atrîb*. — A branch-line (five trains daily) leads to (8 M.) *Mît Bira* (p. 184), on the left bank of the Damietta arm, and light railways run to *Manṣûra* and the *Delta Barrage* (see p. 184).

Beyond Benha the train crosses the large *Taufîqîya Canal* (Raiyâḥ eṭ-Taufîqi; p. 131). Near (108½ M.) *Ṭûkh* (light railway to Biltân and Shibîn el-Qanâṭir, see p. 181) the mountains enclosing the Nile valley become visible in the distance. — 113½ M. *Qaha (Kaha).*

120½ M. **Qalyûb** (*Kalioub;* buffet), a district capital with 16,798 inhab., is the junction of lines to Zagazig (p. 181) and to Ṭanṭa (p. 36) viâ the Delta Barrage (p. 131). The outlines of the Pyramids then begin to loom in the distance on the right. The track crosses the *Sharqâwîya Canal.*

The Libyan chain becomes more distinctly visible, and we observe also the Moqaṭṭam range with the citadel, and the mosque of Muḥammed ʿAli with its slender minarets. Gardens and villas come in sight. To the left lie the site of the ruins of Heliopolis (the obelisk of which is not seen from the railway), Maṭarîya with its sycamores, Qubba, the residence of the King, and the suburb of ʿAbbâsîya.

130 M. **Cairo** (Main Station), see below.

4. Cairo.

Plan. The commonest word for a street is *Shâriʿ* (or *Sharia;* French *Chareh*), meaning a main street, avenue, or boulevard; other words used are *Sikka* (street), *Darb* (road, also caravan-track), *Ḥâra* (lane, also quarter of a town), and *ʿAṭfa* (blind alley). *Mîdân* is a square. — Since the British occupation the names of the streets have been written up at the corners in Arabic, accompanied by English or French transliterations (p. xxviii). Our plan follows the modern English system; the ending often written up as *e* or *eh* appears in our plan and text as *a* (e.g. Gîza, not Gîzeh).

A. Railway Stations. Air Service. Hotels and Pensions. Restaurants and Cafés.

Railway Stations. 1. The Main Station (Pl. E 2; buffet), on the N. side of the city, 12 min. from the Ezbekîya Garden, for *Alexandria, Port Said, Suez,* the whole of the *Delta,* and *Upper Egypt.* — 2. Pont Limoun Station, adjoining the main station, for *Shibîn el-Qanâṭir* (comp. p. 181) viâ *Demirdâsh* (for *ʿAbbâsîya*), and for *Qubba, Zeitûn, Maṭarîya (Old Heliopolis),* and *El-Marg.* — 3. Bâb el-Lûq Station (Pl. D 5), for *Ḥelwân* viâ

El-Ma'âdi and for *'Ain eṣ-Ṣîra* (p. 124). — The hotel commissionaires, with omnibuses, and representatives of the tourist agents (p. 40) await the arrival of the fast trains. Luggage may be entrusted also to the Arab porters with numbered metal badges on their arms (trunk P.T. $1^1/_2$, several articles P.T. 1 each), who will conduct the traveller to the hotel omnibus or procure a cab for him (tariff, see p. 41). Heavy luggage is sent on to the hotel in special vehicles.

Air Service, see p. xviii. For details apply to Imperial Airways Ltd. (at *Heliopolis Aerodrome*, p. 128) or to a tourist agency (p. 40).

Hotels (comp. p. xix). The leading hotels at Cairo are excellent; at most of them evening dress is 'de rigueur' at dinner. Even the second-class hotels are well fitted up, nearly all having electric light, baths, etc. As all the hotels are frequently full, especially in Jan., Feb., and March, it is advisable to wire for rooms from Alexandria or Port Said, if they have not been engaged even sooner. In summer many of the hotels are closed, and the others lower their prices. Children and servants pay half-price.

In the Interior of the City. **Shepheard's* (Pl. sh, E 3; owned by the Egyptian Hotels Ltd.), 8 Shâri' Kâmil, with 350 rooms (150 with bath), suites of apartments, a large terrace (concerts), garden, restaurant and grill room, bar, post and telegraph office, etc., pens. from P.T. 160, open from Nov. 1st to May 15th; **Semiramis* (Pl. s, C 5; same ownership as Shepheard's), Qaṣr ed-Dûbâra, on the Nile, a fashionable house with 200 R. (120 with bath), central heating, bar, post office, garden, restaurant, and roof-terrace (view), open from Dec. 1st to April 15th, pens. from P.T. 190; **Continental-Savoy* (Pl. cs, E 4; same ownership as Shepheard's), 2 Shâri' Kâmil, in Opera Square, with 400 R. (140 with bath), suites of apartments, terrace, garden, grill room, bar, and post office, pens. from P.T. 140 (cheaper from May to Nov.), motorbus P.T. 8. — **Victoria & New Khedivial* (Pl. vk, E 3; proprietor J. Vocles), 2 Shâri' Nûbâr Pasha, 120 R. (35 with bath), pens. from P.T. 100. — **National* (Pl. n; D 4), 30 Shâri' Sulîmân Pasha, corner of Shâri' Deir el-Banât, with 150 R. (50 with bath), garden, and restaurant, pens. P.T. 100-120, omnibus P.T. 6; *The Metropolitan* (formerly Grosvenor; owned by the Egyptian Hotels Ltd.), 1 Shâri' el-Borṣa el-Gedîda (Pl. D 4), 100 R. (all with bath), pens. P.T. 100-120 (P.T. 90 from April to Oct.), new. — *Windsor & des Voyageurs* (Pl. v; E 3), 5 Shâri' Nûbâr Pasha, 60 R. (8 with bath) at 30-40, B. 10, L. or D. 35, pens. 60-100 P.T.; *Bristol & du Nil* (Pl. bn; E 3), Mîdân el-Khâzindâr, N.E. of the Ezbekîya, 75 R. at 30-35, B. 10, L. 20, D. 25, pens. 65-80 P.T., evening dress optional; *New York*, 11 Shâri' Nûbâr Pasha. — Hôtels Garnis (bed and breakfast only). *Moderne* (Pl. m; E 3), Shâri' 'Imâd ed-Dîn, corner of Shâri' el-Malika Nâzli, 55 R. (6 with bath) from 30, B. 7 or 10 P.T.; *Hôtel du Nord*, Shâri' 'Imâd ed-Dîn (Pl. E 3), near the main station, 76 R. (16 with bath); *Hôtel de Paris*, 10 Shâri' el-Maghrabi (Pl. D E 4; Passage Groppi), 30 R. at 38-54, B. 8-12 P.T.

At Heliopolis Oasis (p. 128): **Heliopolis Palace*, on the electric railway mentioned on p. 41, a first-class house with restaurant, garden, etc., open Dec.-April, with 500 R. (300 with bath), pens. from P.T. 140. — *Heliopolis House*, a first-class family hotel, with a large terrace (concerts), restaurant, and bar, 80 R. (10 with bath) at 40-80, L. 25, D. 30, pens. 80-100 P.T.

Near the Pyramids of Gîza (p. 133). **Mena House* (same ownership as Shepheard's), at the terminus of the tramway to the Pyramids (p. 40; No. 14), with 200 beds, post office, gardens, baths and swimming pool (open to non-residents), grass golf-course, tennis courts, etc., open all the year round, L. (at 1 p.m.) 40, D. (at 7.30 p.m.) 50, pens. from 130 P.T., motorbus from the station P.T. 15.

Pensions (generally well spoken of). *Gresham House*, 20 Shâri' Sulîmân Pasha (Pl. D 4); *Drummond* (Mme. Frizell), 6 Mîdân Sulîmân Pasha (Pl. D 4), 12 R., pens. P.T. 60-100; *Britannia* (Mme. E. Rosenfeld), 13 Shâri' el-Maghrabi (Pl. D E 4), 14 R., pens. £E 12-15 per month; *Morandi* (Tivoli), 12 Shâri' Fu'âd el-Auwal (Pl. A-E 2-4); *Morisson*, 9 Shâri' Fu'âd el-Auwal (Pl. A-E 2-4), pens. P.T. 50-60; *Ex-Tadey*, 9 Shâri' Fu'âd el-Auwal (3rd floor), 70 R., pens. P.T. 50; *Albion House*, 18 Shâri' el-Maghrabi (Pl. D E 4); *Osborne House*, 22 Shâri' esh-Sheikh Abu 's-Sibâ' (Pl. D 4); *Killiney House*, 15 Shâri' el-

Madâbigh (Pl. D 4); *Warwick House*, 44 Shâri' Sulîmân Pasha. — *Pension Viennoise* (Austrian), 14 Shâri' el-Antîkkhâna (Pl. C D 4), 16 R., pens. P.T. 50; *Imperia House* (Swiss), 3 Mîdân Sulîmân Pasha, pens. P.T. 50; *Renner* (German), Shâri' 'Imâd ed-Dîn (Pl. E 3-5), Immeuble (block) T, 18 R., pens. P.T. 60-80; *Cecil House* (Danish), 2 Shâri' Nâṣir ed-Dîn, next to the Muḥammed 'Ali Club (Pl. D 4), 80 R., pens. P.T. 60-80; *Pension Maffet* (formerly Hanrion), Shâri' 'Imâd ed-Dîn (Pl. E 3-5), Immeuble (block) B, 25 R., pens. P.T. 40-60; *Anglo-Swiss Home*, 27 Shâri' Sulîmân Pasha, opposite the National Hotel (Pl. n; D 4), 22 R.; *Minerva House*, Shâri' Sulîmân Pasha, corner of Shâri' el-Madâbigh (Pl. D 4), Immeuble (block) Rofe B; *Pension Riche*, 45 Shâri' Qaṣr en-Nîl. — Good and cheap lodgings are provided by the *Catholic Sisters* of St. Charles Borromeo, 8 Shâri' el-Qâṣid (Pl. D 5).

Restaurants. Besides the grill rooms at the best hotels: **Celestino*, 4 Shâri' Alfi Bey (Pl. D E 3), **Flasch*, at the same address; **Ritz*, 14 Shâri' Taufîq (Pl. D 3); **Groppi*, Mîdân Sulîmân Pasha (Pl. D 4); *Café Bauer*, 6 Shâri' Fu'âd el-Auwal; *Waqf*, 18 Shâri' Gâmi' Sharkas, opposite the Ministry of Waqfs (Pl. D 4), with rooms; *Finisch*, *Bologna*, both in the Shâri' el-Mahdi (Pl. E 3); *Luna Park*, *Parisiana*, *Brasserie du Nil & Suisse*, all in the Shâri' Alfi Bey (Pl. D E 3); *St. James's*, 14 Shâri' Fu'âd el-Auwal.

Bars and Cafés. *New Bar*, *Mahroussa Bar*, *Café Khédivial*, all in Opera Square (Mîdân et-Tiyâtro, Pl. E 4); *Café Bauer*, see above; *Splendid Bar*, Shâri' Kâmil (Pl. E 3, 4); *Opera Bar*, in Opera Square (drinks only). — Cafés in the European style, at which beer and other beverages are obtainable, abound in and near the Ezbekîya (none of them suitable for ladies). — The numerous Arab Cafés are small and often dirty; coffee in the Arab style is easily obtained elsewhere. — Confectioners. *Sault*, 5 Shâri' Fu'âd el-Auwal (also restaurant) and 33 Shâri' Qaṣr en-Nîl (tea-room for ladies). *Groppi*, 11 Shâri' el-Manâkh (Pl. D E 4), for afternoon tea, with garden, and in the Mîdân Sulîmân Pasha (comp. above); *Lemonia Bros.*, 44 Shâri' Qaṣr en-Nîl (Pl. D 4) — Bakers. *Simonds & Co.*, 26 Shâri' el-Maghrabi (Pl. D E 4).

B. Legations and Consulates. Banks. Post & Telegraph Offices. Tourist Agents. Steamship Offices.

Legations and Consulates (comp. p. 12). *Great Britain* is represented by the High Commissioner at the British Residency (Pl. C 5; p. 55), Shâri' el-Wâlda, Qaṣr ed-Dûbâra. Consulate, 19 Shâri' Gâmi' Sharkas (Pl. D 4). — *United States:* 8 Shâri' Lazoghli (Pl. C 5), Qaṣr ed-Dûbâra. — There are also Belgian, Danish, Dutch, French, German, Italian, Norwegian, Spanish, Swedish, Turkish, and other diplomatic and consular representatives. — Sûdân Agency, 6 Mîdân Taufîq (Pl. D 3).

Banks (comp. p. xiv; usually open 9-12 and, except Sat., 3-5, in summer 9-1 only; most of them with branch-offices in the larger Egyptian towns). *National Bank of Egypt* (Pl. D 4), 31 Shâri' Qaṣr en-Nîl; *Barclay's* (Pl. E 4; formerly Anglo-Egyptian Bank), 51 Shâri' Qaṣr en-Nîl; *Ottoman Bank* (Pl. E 4), 10 Shâri' el-Manâkh; *Crédit Lyonnais* (Pl. E 4), Shâri' el-Busta; *Banque Belge & Internationale*, 45 Shâri' Qaṣr en-Nîl; *Thos. Cook & Son* and *American Express Co.*, see p. 40; *Banque d'Athènes* (Pl. D E 4), 37 Shâri' Qaṣr en-Nîl; *Banca Commerciale Italiana*, 23 Shâri' el-Manâkh (Pl. D E 4); *Banque Misr*, 18 Shâri' 'Imâd ed-Dîn (Pl. E 3-5); *Crédit Foncier Egyptien* (Pl. E 4), 14 Shâri' el-Manâkh. — Small change can always be obtained from the money-changers in the streets, from the hotel-porter, or in making purchases in the shops or at the post office.

Post Office (Pl. E 4; p. xx), at the corner of Shâri' Ṭâhir and Shâri' el-Beidaq (parcels office in the Shâri' el-Beidaq). The office on the street, open from 7.30 a.m. to 9.30 p.m. (on Sun. and public holidays 8-7), sells postage-stamps only. The office in the courtyard is open from 8 a.m. till 8 p.m. (with a short interruption from about 12.30 p.m.), the inquiry office 8.30-12.30 & 3-6. Information regarding the mails to Europe, etc., is exhibited in the vestibule. The arrival of *Registered Letters*, etc., is intimated to the addressee by a notice, which must be produced, bearing the stamp of the hotel or the endorsement of a well-known resident, when the letters are applied for. There are

several branch-offices in the town; also at some of the hotels. Letter-boxes at all the hotels. — **Telegraph Offices** (comp. p. xx). *Eastern Telegraph Co.* (Pl. E 4), 8 Shâriʿ ʿImâd ed-Dîn; *Egyptian Telegraph*, Shâriʿ el-Malika Nâzli, off Shâriʿ Zaki (Pl. D 3); *Marconi Radio Telegraph Co.*, Shâriʿ Sherîf, near the National Bank (Pl. D 4).

Tourist Agents. *Thos. Cook & Son*, 6 Shâriʿ Kâmil (Pl. E 3, 4); *American Express Co.*, at the Continental-Savoy Hotel (Pl. c3; E 4); *Cox & King's Shipping Agency*, Opera Square; *D. E. Munari*, 4 Shâriʿ Kâmil; *M. S. Farajallah & Co.*, 9 Shâriʿ Kâmil; *H. A. Zarb & Co.* (formerly A. Liggeri & Co.), 8 Shâriʿ el-Maghrabi. — *International Sleeping Car Co.*, 8 Shâriʿ el-Manâkh (Pl. D E 4). — *Tourist Development Association of Egypt*, at the main station.

Steamship Offices. *Thos. Cook & Son* (see above); *Anglo-American Nile & Tourist Co.*, 8 Shâriʿ el-Manâkh; *P. & O.*, *British India*, and *Khedivial Mail Line*, Curwen & Co., 15 Shâriʿ Kâmil; *Orient*, *Bibby*, at Cook's (see above); *White Star*, *Red Star*, and *Royal Mail Steam Packet Co.*, 9 Shâriʿ Kâmil; *Norddeutscher Lloyd*, *German African Services* (p. 2), and *Royal Rumanian State Line*, William H. Müller & Co., 48 Opera Square; *Lloyd Triestino*, D. E. Munari (see above); *Nederland Line* (G. Vogel), 7 Shâriʿ Gâmiʿ el-Banât (Pl. F 4), near Mîdân Bâb el-Khalq; *Messageries Maritimes*, 7 Shâriʿ Kâmil; *Sitmar* (p. 1), 4 Shâriʿ Kâmil, also for the Italian State Railways.

C. Tramways. Steamers. Cabs. Donkeys. Dragomans.

The **Tramways** are numbered and have special compartments for women (fare 1st class 12 mill., 2nd class 6 mill., unless otherwise stated). The chief points of intersection are the ʿATABA EL-KHAḌRA square (Pl. E 4; p. 54), S.E. of the Ezbekîya, and the MAIN STATION (Pl. E 2; Mîdân Bâb el-Ḥadîd). — **1** (white disk; every 6 min.). From the *Mîdân el-Khâzindâr* (Pl. E 3) viâ ʿAtaba el-Khaḍra (see above), Mîdân Bâb el-Lûq, Mîdân Ismâʿilîya (Pl. D 5; Qaṣr en-Nil Bridge, Egyptian Museum), Shâriʿ Qaṣr el-ʿAini, and Fumm el-Khalîg (Pl. C 8) to *Atar en-Nabi* (p. 113), in 40 min. — **2** (green; every 12 min.). From the *Sporting Club* at Gezîra (Pl. B 3; p. 86) viâ Bûlâq Bridge and Shâriʿ Fu'âd el-Auwal to *ʿAtaba el-Khaḍra*. — **3** (red; every 3 min.). From *ʿAtaba el-Khaḍra* viâ Shâriʿ el-Amîr Fârûq (Pl. F G 4-2) direct, or viâ Shâriʿ Fu'âd el-Auwal, the Main Station (Mîdân Bâb el-Ḥadîd, Pl. E 2), and Mîdân eẓ-Ẓâhir (Pl. G 2), to *ʿAbbâsîya* (beyond Pl. G 2; p. 85). — **4** (white and red; every 4 min.). From *Sabtîya* (or *Saptia*; Pl. C D 2) viâ the Main Station (Pl. E 2), Shâriʿ Clot Bey, ʿAtaba el-Khaḍra, and Mîdân Bâb el-Khalq (Pl. F 5; or Mîdân Bâb el-Lûq and Mîdân en-Nâṣrîya, Pl. D 6) to *Saiyida Zeinab* (Pl. D 6). — **5** (orange; every 4 min.). From *Mîdân el-Ghamra* (Pl. G 1, 2) viâ Mîdân eẓ-Ẓâhir (Pl. G 2), Bâb esh-Shaʿrîya, Mûski, Bâb el-Khalq (Pl. F 5; Arab Museum), Shâriʿ Khalîg el-Maṣri, and Saiyida Zeinab (Pl. D 6) to the *Cemeteries* (Pl. C D 7). — **6** (green and orange; every 6 min.). From *Imbâba* (beyond Pl. A 2; p. 87) viâ Gezîra (Pl. B 3; p. 86) and Bûlâq Bridge (Pl. B C 3) to *ʿAtaba el-Khaḍra*. — **8** (blue; every 5 min.). From *ʿAtaba el-Khaḍra* viâ Shâriʿ Fu'âd el-Auwal (Pl. D E 3, 4; p. 54), Shâriʿ el-Malika Nâzli (Pl. D E 3), and the Main Station to *Shubra Village* (beyond Pl. E 1; p. 85). — **9** (white and blue; every 5 min.). From *ʿAtaba el-Khaḍra* viâ Shâriʿ Clot Bey and the Main Station to *Rôḍ el-Farag* (beyond Pl. E 1; p. 85). — **10** (red and white; every 5 min.). From *ʿAtaba el-Khaḍra* viâ Shâriʿ Fu'âd el-Auwal, Shâriʿ el-Malika Nâzli, the Main Station (Mîdân Bâb el-Ḥadîd), and Shâriʿ el-Faggâla to *Sakâkîni* (beyond Pl. G 2). — **11** (white and green; every 6 min.). From *Mîdân el-Khâzindâr* viâ ʿAtaba el-Khaḍra and the Citadel (Pl. F G 6, 7) to *Imâm esh-Shâfiʿi* (beyond Pl. F 8; p. 124). — **12** (white and orange; every 3 min.). From the *Main Station* viâ Shâriʿ el-Malika Nâzli (or Shâriʿ Clot Bey), Shâriʿ Mariette Pasha (Egyptian Museum; Pl. C 4), Qaṣr en-Nîl, Mîdân el-Azhâr (Pl. D 4, 5), and Mîdân en-Nâṣrîya to *Saiyida Zeinab* (Pl. D 6). — **13** (green and white; every 7 min.). From the *Citadel* (Pl. F G 6, 7) viâ Mîdân Bâb el-Khalq (Pl. F 5), ʿAtaba el-Khaḍra, and Shâriʿ Fu'âd el-Auwal to the E. end of Bûlâq Bridge, then N. to the *Technical School* (Pl. C 1) at Bûlâq (p. 86). — **14** (green and red; Pyramids Line). From *ʿAtaba el-Khaḍra* (Pl. E 4) viâ Shâriʿ Fu'âd el-Auwal, Bûlâq Bridge (Pl. B C 3), Gezîra (p. 86), Zamâlik Bridge (Pl. A 2),

6 Mîdân Taufîq (Pl. D 3), open on week-days 10-12 and 4.30-7 p.m. — MUSIC: *Papasian & Co.*, 9 Shâri' el-Maghrabi.

Photographs (films developed). *Kodak*, 20 Shâri' el-Maghrabi (opposite the Turf Club, Pl. D 4), Opera Square, and Shâri' Kâmil; *Lehnert & Landrock*, 21 Shâri' el-Maghrabi and 4 Shâri' Kâmil; *Cairo Studio* (Kofler), Shâri' el-Manâkh (opposite Davies Bryan); *Anglo-Swiss Studio* (Hanselmann), Shâri' Qaṣr en-Nîl. — PHOTOGRAPHIC MATERIALS. *Kodak* (see above); *Société des Drogueries d'Egypte*, Mîdân Suarès (Pl. E 4) and Shâri' Fu'âd I.

European Goods. Clothing, shoes, travelling and shooting requisites, etc.: *Davies Bryan & Co.*, Shâri' 'Imâd ed-Dîn, corner of Shâri' el-Manâkh; *Salamandre*, *Cicurel*, *Chemla Frères*, all in the Shâri' Fu'âd I.; *Au Bon Marché*, *Carnaval de Venise*, both in Shâri' 'Imâd ed-Dîn; *Orosdi-Back & Co.*, Shâri' 'Abd el-'Azîz (Pl. E 4); *Tiring*, Shâri' 'Imâd ed-Dîn, corner of Shâri' el-Maghrabi; *Karmann*, in the Mûski. — Drapers, etc.: *Au Printemps*, 23 Shâri' Qaṣr en-Nîl; *Mlles. Cécile*, 7 Shâri' Shawârbi Pasha (Pl. D 4). — Tailors: *Phillips & Co.*, 23 Shâri' Qaṣr en-Nîl; *Collacott*, 2 Shâri' el-Maghrabi. — Sports outfitters: *Roberts, Hughes & Co.*, Mîdân Suarès (Pl. E 4). — Household requisites: *Lappas Frères*, Shâri' Qaṣr en-Nîl; *J. & H. Fleurent*, 6 Shâri' Alfi Bey. — Watchmakers and goldsmiths: *Lattès*, 30 Shâri' el-Manâkh; *Kramer*, 4 Shâri' el-Manâkh and 38 Mûski; *Süssmann*, 37 Mûski. — Opticians: *Lawrence & Mayo*, at Shepheard's; *Thompson Optical Co.*, 2 Shâri' Fu'âd I.; *Beinisch*, Shâri' Fu'âd I. and 46 Mûski; *Davidson & Regenstreif*, at the Continental-Savoy Hotel (p. 38); *Süssmann*, *Kramer*, see above.

Arab Bazaars, see p. 52 and pp. 56 seqq. The most important for visitors is the *Khân el-Khalîli* (p. 57). Many so-called oriental articles are, however, manufactured in Europe and are to be obtained at home equally genuine and as cheap. — The prices demanded by the dealers for ANTIQUES are absurd, though many travellers are foolish enough to pay them, in spite of the notorious fact that most of the articles are forgeries (comp. p. 268). Genuine antiques are sold by *M. Nahman*, 27 Shâri' el-Madâbigh, and *E. A. Abemayor*, *N. Tano*, and *R. H. Blanchard*, all in the Shâri' Kâmil. Those sold in the sale-room (Salle de Vente) of the Museum are reasonably priced (p. 88). For the export of antiques, see p. xvi.

Arab Woodwork, etc., is sold by *E. Hatoun*, Shâri' es-Sikka el-Gedîda (Pl. F G 4), by *Furino*, Shâri' Sulîmân Pasha (Pl. D 4), and by the *Helmieh School of Arabic and Egyptian Arts and Crafts*, Shâri' Sulîmân Pasha.

Oriental Embroidery, Carpets, etc. *Vitali Madjar*, at Shepheard's; *Chellaram*, at the Continental-Savoy (p. 38); *The Oriental Galleries*, 13 Shâri' el-Manâkh; *Kerestezoglou*, Mîdân Sulîmân Pasha; *Ispenian*, Shâri' Qaṣr en-Nîl; *Pohoomull Bros.*, opposite Shepheard's; *Hatoun* (see above); also at various shops in the Khân el-Khalîli (p. 57).

Goods Agents. *Thos. Cook & Son* (p. 40); *American Express Co.* (p. 40); *William H. Müller & Co.* (p. 40); *F. Bancel & Co.*, Shâri' el-Maghrabi, and opposite Shepheard's; *John Ross & Co.*, 31 Shâri' el-Maghrabi; *Egyptian Bonded Warehouse Co.*, Shâri' Sabtîya (Pl. D 2), near the main station; *H. A. Zarb & Co.* (p. 40). Those who make purchases in Egypt to any extent are recommended to send them home through a goods agent, in order to avoid the worries of the custom house examinations, porterage, etc. The consigner should satisfy himself that the packing is properly done, as subsequent complaints are generally futile. — *Parcel Post*, see p. xx.

F. Theatres. Clubs. Churches. Schools.

Theatres. At the *Royal Opera House* (Pl. E 4; p. 54) a French or Italian opera company performs during the latter half of the winter season (chiefly grand opera; arrangement of seats and their prices in the Italian style). Box-office open 8-12 and 2-5; boxes dear (evening dress compulsory; closed boxes for Moslem ladies). — *Kursaal* (Pl. D E 3), a variety theatre in the Shâri' 'Imâd ed-Dîn (French and Italian companies). — Arabic performances in the *Ezbekîya Garden Theatre* (p. 54) and the *Ramses Theatre*, Shâri' 'Imâd ed-Dîn. — ARAB MUSIC HALL. *Théâtre Mille et Une Nuits*, rebuilding in the Shâri' 'Imâd ed-Dîn. — Numerous CINEMAS in the Shâri' 'Imâd ed-Dîn

and elsewhere. — British Military Band several times weekly in the evening at the Ezbekîya Garden (p. 53).

Scientific Societies. The *Société Royale de Géographie d'Egypte* (Pl. D 5; p. 55), Shâri' Qaṣr el-'Aini, founded in 1875 on the initiative of the African explorer Georg Schweinfurth (d. 1925), possesses a library and a reading room (for members only), a collection of plants from the Sûdân, and a small ethnographical museum (open daily, except on official holidays and during the summer vacation, 9-12; catalogue, 1924, P.T. 25); president, Dr. W. F. Hume (p. 55); secretary, H. Munier. — *Institut d'Egypte* (Pl. C D 5; p. 55), 1 Shâri' esh-Sheikh Rîḥân, founded at Alexandria in 1859 (comp. p. 79), with library (27,000 vols.); president M. Mosseri. — *Institut Français d'Archéologie Orientale* (Pl. C D 6; p. 56), with an oriental library (19,000 vols.; open also to foreign students; librarian, St. Paul Girard) and a printing press; director Pierre Jouguet. — *Deutsches Institut für Ägyptische Altertumskunde* (*German Institute for Egyptian Archaeology;* Pl. B 2; p. 87), at Gezîra, 11 Shâri' el-Amîr Sa'îd, with an Egyptologic library; director, Prof. Hermann Junker. — *Société Royale de Médecine* (at the Institut d'Egypte, see above); president, Shâhîn Pasha. — *Société Royale d'Economie Politique, de Statistique et de Législation*, 16 Shâri' el-Malika Nâzli. — *Cairo Scientific Society* (School of Medicine; Qaṣr el-'Aini, Pl. C 7). — *Zoological Society of Egypt*, at the Zoological Institute of the Egyptian University, 'Abbâsîya (pp. 85, 86). President, Rashwân Pasha Mahfûẓ; vice-president, Prof. Jollos. — *Société Royale Entomologique d'Egypte*, 14 Shâri' el-Malika Nâzli. — *Royal Agricultural Society*, at Gezîra (p. 87). — *Société des Amis de l'Art*, 4 Shâri' Nûbâr Pasha. — Colleges. *Azhar University* (Pl. G 4; p. 58); *Egyptian University* (p. 85); *School of Engineering* (Pl. A 7), at Gîza; *Agricultural College* (p. 87); *Higher School of Commerce; Higher Training Colleges* for teachers (one for men, one for women); *American University* (p. 55), a free university in the American style.

Clubs. *Muḥammed 'Ali Club* (Pl. D 4), Shâri' Sulîmân Pasha, fitted up in the English style (introduction by a member necessary). — *Turf Club* (Pl. D 4), 12 Shâri' el-Maghrabi. — *Gezîra Sporting Club* (Pl. B 4), at Gezîra, with golf-course (18 holes) and cricket ground. — *Heliopolis Sporting Club*, *Heliopolis Racing Club*, and *Heliopolis Polo Club*, at Heliopolis Oasis (p. 128). — *Ma'âdi Sporting Club*, at Ma'âdi (p. 177). — *Royal Automobile Club of Egypt*, 25 Shâri' el-Madâbigh. — *British Recreation Club* (Pl. D 3), Shâri' el-Malika Nâzli.

Churches. Anglican: *St. Mary's* (Pl. C 5), Shâri' Qaṣr el-'Aini. — Scottish Presbyterian: *St. Andrew's* (Pl. D 3), Shâri' Fu'âd I., at the Abu'l-'Ela level crossing. — *American Services* at the American Mission (Pl. E 3), at 6 p.m. — *French Protestant Church* ('Egl. Franç. Prot.', Pl. D 3), Shâri' Fu'âd I., by the Abu'l-'Ela level crossing. — *German Protestant Church*, Shâri' et-Tir'a el-Bûlâqîya, next to the English School (Pl. D 3). — Roman Catholic: *Holy Assumption* (Pl. F 4), in the Mûski, with dependent churches in the Shâri' 'Imâd ed-Dîn (*St. Joseph's;* Pl. E 4) and at Bûlâq (*Mount Carmel Church*, Pl. C 2); *Jesuit Church* (Pl. E 2), Shâri' el-Malika Nâzli; *Eglise du Sacré-Cœur* (Church of the Central African Mission), Shâri' Deir el-Banât (Pl. D 4). — *Greek Catholic Church of St. Nicholas* (Pl. F 4), in the Ḥamzâwi (p. 62). — *Coptic Orthodox Church* (*St. Mark's;* Pl. E 3), services on Sun. at 10 a.m., on the Eastern Christmas Eve, the eve of the 'Îd el-Ghiṭâs (p. 116), and the Sat. of Holy Week at 10 p.m.; *Coptic Catholic Church* (Pl. F 4; comp. p. lix). — *New Synagogue* (Pl. D E 4), Shâri' el-Maghrabi. The Jews are of two sects, the Talmudists and the Karaïtes, the former being by far the more numerous. Most of the synagogues are in the Jewish quarter (Ḥâret el-Yahûd; Pl. F 4).

Schools. *St. Mary's English School*, Shâri' Qaṣr el-'Aini, near the English church mentioned above. — *English School* (Pl. D 3), for boys and girls (headmaster, C. V. W. Grose), at Bûlâq (p. 86). — *Church Missionary Society's Schools*, for native girls at Bûlâq (p. 86), for native boys on Rôḍa Island (p. 112). — *English Mission College*, Shâri' Seif ed-Dîn el-Mahrâni (Pl. E 2, 3). — There are several *American Mission Schools* (comp. p. 226), most of which are for girls. — *American Mission College for Girls*, 4 Shâri' el-Malika Nâzli (p. 85), with 360 pupils (about half of whom are non-Christian) from well-

to-do families. — *German Catholic School*, kept by the Sisters of St. Charles Borromeo, 8 Shâriʿ el-Qâṣid (Pl. D 5). — Besides these there are a *Lycée Français* (Pl. D 4), several *Collèges des Frères* (Rom. Cath.), a *Pensionnat des Dames du Sacré-Cœur* (Pl. G 1; for girls), an *Institution des Dames du Bon-Pasteur* (p. 85), a *Collège de la Ste-Famille* (a Jesuit school, connected with their church mentioned on p. 44), a British *Institute for the Blind* at ʿEzbet ez-Zeitûn (p. 129); etc. — *Government School of Arts and Crafts*, in the Ḥamzâwi (Pl. F 4; p. 62). — The Ministry of Education maintains at Cairo twenty-six primary schools in the European style (eighteen for boys, eight for girls) and seven secondary schools (six for boys, one for girls), a special school for girls, seven training colleges for elementary teachers (three for men, four for women); etc. For the numerous native elementary schools, see p. 52. — Instruction in Arabic is given at the *Berlitz School*, 8 Shâriʿ ʿImâd ed-Dîn, and the *School of Oriental Studies of the American University* (p. 55).

G. Plan of Visit.

Unbelievers are admitted to most of the *Mosques*, the restoration of which has been taken in hand by the *Monuments Office* (Committee for the Preservation of Monuments of Arab Art) of the Ministry of Waqfs (p. 55). No adm. on Fri., festivals (p. xcviii), and at the time of the midday prayer (about noon). Entrance tickets (P.T. 4 for each building) may be obtained at the Ministry of Waqfs (Pl. D 4; Mosque Section), 7 Shâriʿ esh-Sheikh Ḥamza (1st floor, Room 4), open 9-11 & 3-4.30 (in summer 4-6; on Fri. in the morning only) or through the hotel-porters or dragomans. On leaving the mosques bakshish (P.T. 1) should be given for the use of slippers (worn over the shoes). The taking of photographs in mosques used for educational purposes (El-Azhar, El-Mu'aiyad, El-Mârdâni) is forbidden.

1st Day. Morning: Tour of inspection in the neighbourhood of the *Ezbekîya* (p. 53); then by cab to the *Bazaars* (most animated on Mon. and Thurs., pp. 56-62). — Afternoon (by cab): **Tombs of the Caliphs* (p. 120) and **Citadel*, with the mosque of *Muḥammed ʿAli* (*View of Cairo; p. 74), returning (by tram if preferred) viâ the Shâriʿ Muḥammed ʿAli (p. 66).

2nd Day. Morning: **Egyptian Museum* (p. 88; closed on Mon.). — Afternoon: Mosques of **Sultan Ḥasan* (p. 71), **Ibn Ṭûlûn* (view of Cairo, p. 76), and *Qâït Bey* (p. 78).

3rd Day. **Pyramids of Gîza* (p. 132), which may be seen in half-a-day if necessary.

4th Day. Morning: Mosques of **El-Azhar* (p. 58), *El-Ghûri* (p. 62), and **El-Mu'aiyad* (p. 63), the *Bâb Zuweila* (p. 64), and the house of *Gamâl ed-Dîn* (p. 63); spare time may be spent in the bazaars (pp. 56-62). — Afternoon: by railway (or by carriage along the ʿAbbâsîya road, viâ Qubba) to *Maṭarîya* (Old Heliopolis, p. 129), or by electric railway to *Heliopolis Oasis* (p. 128).

5th Day. Morning: Second visit to the *Egyptian Museum* or the bazaars. — Afternoon: Ascent of the **Moqaṭṭam* (p. 124; view at sunset) and visit to the monastery of the *Bektashi Dervishes* (p. 126).

6th Day. Morning: **Arab Museum* (p. 66; closed on Mon.) and *Egyptian Library* (p. 69). — Afternoon: *Zoological Gardens* (p. 87).

7th Day. By railway (lunch should be brought) to Badrashein and thence on donkey-back to *Memphis* and **Saqqâra* (pp. 152 seqq.), or by motor-car direct to Ṣaqqâra. It is well worth while to return viâ Abusîr (p. 151) to the Mena House Hotel, and thence to Cairo by tram (comp. p. 152).

8th Day. Morning: Mosques of **Qalâûn* (p. 81), **Muḥammed en-Nâṣir* and *Barqûq* (p. 82); **Bâb el-Futûḥ* (old city wall) and **Bâb en-Naṣr* (p. 84). — Afternoon (cab, tram, or train): *Rôḍa* (p. 112) and *Old Cairo* (p. 113), with the Coptic churches of Abu Sarga (p. 114) and El-Muʿallaqa (Coptic Museum, p. 117); also, if time permit, the *Mosque of ʿAmr* (p. 119) and the excavations at *Fusṭâṭ* (p. 118).

9th Day. *Delta Barrage* (p. 131), either by railway (from the Main Station; luncheon should be taken) or (preferably) by steamer.

10th Day. To *Abu Roâsh* (p. 149) or *Abuṣîr* (p. 151).

The *Egyptian Museum* (p. 88), the *Arab Museum* (p. 66), the *El-Azhar Mosque* (p. 58), and the *Bazaars* deserve repeated visits.

Cairo, *El-Qâhira*, *Maṣr (Miṣr) el-Qâhira*, or simply *Maṣr*, is situated in 30° 4′ N. latitude and 31° 17′ E. longitude, on the right bank of the *Nile*, 12 M. to the S. of the 'Cow's Belly', the point where the stream divides into the Rosetta and Damietta arms. It has been styled "the diamond stud on the handle of the fan of the Delta". On the E. rise the barren, reddish Moqaṭṭam Hills (p. 124), forming the commencement of the Eastern Desert. On the S. the city extends as far as Old Cairo (p. 113), on the W. it reaches the bank of the river and the island of Gezîra, having absorbed the suburb of Bûlâq (p. 86).

Cairo is by far the largest city in Africa, as well as in the Arab world. It is the residence of the King of Egypt and of the principal authorities and has a governor of its own (comp. p. xlix). In 1927 the population was returned as 1,064,567, including the suburb of Helwân (p. 177). Among the Europeans the majority are Greeks (20,115), Italians (18,575), and British (11,221). The non-European population includes, besides 988,394 Egyptians, Turks (3877) and Syrians (3111); there are also many Sudanese, negroes of various tribes, Persians, Hindus, etc. The great majority of the inhabitants are Mohammedans (851,700); the Christians (177,806) include Orthodox and Catholic Copts, Orthodox Greeks, Roman Catholics, oriental Christians of various sects, and Protestants. The Jews number 34 103.

History. At a very remote period a city lay on the E. bank of the Nile, opposite the great pyramids, and was called by the Egyptians *Khere-ohe*, or 'place of combat', because Horus and Seth were said to have contended here (p. cxlix). This formed a kind of suburb of Heliopolis. The Greeks named it *Babylon* (comp. p. 114), probably in imitation of the Egyptian name of the island of Rôḍa, viz. *Per-hapi-n-On* or the 'House of the Nile of On' (Heliopolis). The citadel of this town (p. 114) was fortified by the Romans and under Augustus became the headquarters of one of the three legions stationed in Egypt. In A.D. 641 Babylon was captured by *ʿAmr ibn el-ʿÂṣ*, the general of Caliph ʿOmar, who established a new capital of the country to the N. of the fortress, extending as far as the Gebel Yashkur (p. 76). This, named *El-Fusṭâṭ* (Lat. fossatum, surrounded by trenches; p. 118), was, like Egypt itself, also called *Miṣr* or *Maṣr el-Fusṭâṭ* by the Arabs; its present name of *Old Cairo (Maṣr el-ʿAtîqa* or *Maṣr el-Qadîma)* was introduced later. A mosque is said to have been built by ʿAmr on the site of his tent. When, after the fall of the Umaiyads in A.D. 750, Fusṭâṭ, with the exception of the great mosque, was burned to the ground, a new residence was built still farther N. by the Abbasid governors, and around this sprang up the new quarter of *El-ʿAskar*. The town was extended N.E. as far as the base of the citadel by *Aḥmad ibn Ṭûlûn* (868-883), who transferred his residence to the Yashkur hill and erected the quarter of *El-Qaṭâʾiʿ*. Aḥmad's splendour-loving son *Khumâraweih* embellished the town

with lavish magnificence. The modern city of Cairo was founded by *Gôhar (Gawhar)*, general of the Fatimid caliph *El-Muʿizz*, after the conquest of Egypt in 969. He erected a residence for the caliph and barracks for his soldiers to the N. of El-Qaṭâʾiʿ (comp. p. cxciv). At the hour when the foundation of the walls was laid the planet Mars, which the Arabs call El-Qâhir, or 'the victorious', crossed the meridian of the new city, and El-Muʿizz accordingly named the place *El-Qâhira* (Cairo). Its N. and its S. limits are to-day marked by the Bâb el-Futûḥ (p. 84) and the Bâb Zuweila (p. 64) respectively. A street 82 ft. wide divided it into two approximately equal halves, and two magnificent palaces were built for the caliph in the centre of the city, on either side of the main street. In 973 El-Muʿizz took up his permanent residence in Cairo, two years after the foundation of the mosque of El-Azhar (p. 58). — A new period of prosperity began under the Aiyubids. *Saladin* endeavoured to unite the still separated cities of Cairo and Fusṭâṭ by means of a common wall (pp. 118, 120), which, however, was never finished, and in 1176 he founded the citadel. Under his luxurious and extravagant successors Cairo was greatly extended and magnificently embellished, and in the 14th cent. it reached its zenith. At that period, however, it was fearfully devastated by the plague, as it had been on former occasions (e.g. in 1065 and in 1295) and was also several times subsequently (especially in 1492, when about 12,000 people are said to have been carried off by it in one day). The town suffered severely in other ways also, and indeed its whole history, like that of the sultans and the Mamelukes themselves, seems to have presented an almost continuous succession of revolutions, rapine, and bloodshed. As most of the Mameluke sultans who resided in the citadel died a violent death, so the reign of almost every new potentate began with sanguinary contests among the emirs for the office of vizier, while but few reigns were undisturbed by insurrections in the capital. During the third régime of *En-Nâṣir* (1293-1340), who had been twice deposed and as often recovered his throne, a persecution of the Christians took place at Cairo. The churches which had been built in the capital and elsewhere were closed or demolished, while the Christians themselves were so ill-treated and oppressed, especially in the reign of the sultan *Eṣ-Ṣâliḥ* (1351-54), that many of them are said to have embraced Islamism. In 1366 and 1367, in the reign of the sultan *Shaʿbân* (p. 66), bloody conflicts took place in the streets of Cairo between hostile parties of Mamelukes, and in 1377 Shaʿbân himself was tortured and strangled in the citadel. The wildest anarchy attended the dethronement of the sultan *Barqûq* (1389), when the convicts escaped from their prisons and plundered the houses of the emirs and the public magazines. The following year another rebellion among the Mamelukes restored Barqûq to the throne. Scarcely, however, had he closed his eyes and been succeeded by *Farag* (1399), when the Mamelukes again revolted and renewed conflicts took

place for possession of the citadel, during which the city was partly plundered. Similar scenes were repeated on almost every change of government. The turbulence of the Mamelukes, who were treated with too much consideration by the sultans, became more and more unbearable; they robbed the people in the markets and assaulted citizens in the public streets.

On Jan. 26th, 1517, the Osman sultan *Selîm I.*, after having gained a victory in the neighbourhood of Heliopolis (p. 129), entered the city. *Ṭûmân Bey*, the last Mameluke sultan, was taken prisoner and executed (p. 64). Selîm caused the finest marble columns which adorned the palace in the citadel to be removed to Constantinople. Under the Turks few new buildings were erected in Cairo and the city was freely exposed to the exactions of the soldiery, but it still remained a busy and brilliant provincial capital. — After the Battle of the Pyramids (p. 87) in 1798 Cairo was occupied by *Bonaparte*, who established his headquarters for several months on a site now occupied by Shepheard's Hotel. On his return to France Kléber was left as commander-in-chief of the French troops at Cairo, where he was assassinated on June 14th, 1800. In 1801 the French garrison under Belliard, being hard pressed by the grand vizier, was compelled to capitulate. On August 3rd, 1805, *Muḥammed ʿAli*, as the recognized pasha of Egypt, took possession of the citadel, which for the last time witnessed a bloody scene on March 1st, 1811 (comp. p. 73). Since that time Cairo has entered upon a new period of prosperity, and a great influx of European ideas has begun. A new E. to W. artery, the present-day Mûski (p. 56), was pierced through the old quarters. The rule of *Ismâʿîl* witnessed great modern improvements. The neighbourhood of the *Ezbekîya* (p. 53) was remodelled, the great thoroughfare known as the Shâriʿ Clot Bey and Shâriʿ Muḥammed ʿAli was formed, and the new suburb of *Ismâʿîlîya* was begun to the S.W. of the Ezbekîya. To the N. of the last the *Taufîqîya* was added under *Taufîq*. The insurrection of ʿArâbi in 1882 (p. cxxviii) scarcely affected Cairo. — The 20th cent. has brought important accretions to the city. A new thoroughfare has been constructed in place of the city canal (El-Khalîg), which was filled up in 1897-1900; the island of *El-Gezîra* has been built over, and the villa quarters of *Qaṣr ed-Dûbâra* and *Garden City* have sprung up on the S., while to the N. of ʿAbbâsîya is the suburb of *New Heliopolis* (p. 128). Cairo, 345 acres in area under the Fatimids, now covers an area of 64 sq. M.; with its mixture of mediæval Arab streets and European quarters of the most modern type, it is one of the most attractive cities in the world.

Comp. 'The Story of Cairo', by *Stanley Lane-Poole*, in the Mediæval Towns Series (London 1900, reprinted 1924); 'Oriental Cairo', by *Douglas Sladen* (illus.; London 1911, 2nd ed. 1913); 'Cairo and its Environs', by *A. O. Lamplough* and *R. Francis* (illus.; London, 1909); 'The City of the Caliphs', by *E. A. Reynolds-Ball* (Boston, 1897); 'Cairo Fifty Years Ago', by *Edward William Lane*, edited by Stanley Lane-Poole (London, 1896); 'Some Cairo Mosques and their Founders' (London, 1921; 17*s.* 6*d.*), 'Quatre-Vingts

Mosquées et Autres Monuments Musulmans du Caire' (Cairo, 1925), 'Rambles in Cairo' (Cairo, 1917), all of them by *Mrs. R. L. Devonshire;* 'Le Caire, le Nil et Memphis', by *G. Migeon*, in the 'Villes d'art célèbres' series (illus.; Paris, 1928).

The ***Street Scenes** presented by the city of the Caliphs admirably illustrate the whole world of oriental fiction and produce an indelible impression on the uninitiated denizen of the West. The busy traffic in the principal streets of the old Arab quarters presents an "interminable, ravelled, and twisted string" of men, women, and animals, of walkers, riders, motor-cars, omnibuses, and carts of every description. It is not, however, until the traveller has learned to distinguish the various individuals who throng the streets, and to know their different pursuits, that he can thoroughly appreciate his walks or drives.

From a very early period it has been customary for the Arabs to distinguish their different sects, families, and dynasties by the colour of their *Turbans*. And the custom still prevails to a certain extent. The 'Sherîf' (plural 'Shúrafâ'), a descendant of the prophet, now frequently wears a white turban, though originally he wore green, the colour of the prophet. Green turbans are now worn by last year's Mecca pilgrims. The various orders of dervishes (p. xcv) are similarly distinguished; the Rifâ'îya wear black or dark-blue turbans, the Aḥmadîya red, the Qâdirîya white. The 'Ulamâ, or clergy and scholars, usually wear a very wide, evenly folded turban of light colour. The orthodox length of a believer's turban is seven times that of his head, being equivalent to the whole length of his body, in order that the turban may afterwards be used as the wearer's winding-sheet, and that this circumstance may familiarize him with the thought of death. Many Mohammedans now, however, wear European dress or adopt a semi-European, semi-oriental costume; a common headgear is the red *ṭarbûsh* (erroneously known as a *fez* by most Europeans). Little difference is now observable between the costume of the Copts, Jews, and other oriental 'unbelievers' and that of the Moslem Egyptians, except that the Coptic priests and Jewish rabbis usually wear a black turban.

The *Women* of the poorer and rustic classes wear nothing but a blue gown and a veil. Their ornaments consist of silver, copper, glass, or bead bracelets, ear-rings, and anklets, while their chins, arms, and chests are often tattooed with blue marks. Similar tattooing is common also among the men. In Upper Egypt nose-rings also are frequently seen. The women of the upper classes are never so handsomely dressed in the streets as at home. When equipped for riding or walking they wear a silk cloak, with very wide sleeves *(tôb* or *sabla)*, over their home attire. They don also the *burqu'*, or veil, which consists of a long strip of muslin, covering the whole of the face except the eyes and reaching nearly to the feet. Lastly they put on the *ḥabara*, a kind of mantle, which in the case of married women consists of two breadths of glossy black silk. The

Coptic, Jewish, and Syrian women wear the same costume, but are generally unveiled. The wealthier ladies, who drive in their carriages or motor-cars attended by eunuchs, usually veil their faces up to their eyes with thin white gauze or black silk. European dress, however, is becoming more and more common, and the rigour of the veiling is gradually diminishing. Egyptian women colour their eyelashes and eyelids with kohl (p. liv), and their finger and toe nails with henna (p. lxxvi) which gives them a brownish-yellow tint. (Circumcision, weddings, and funerals, see pp. xcvi seqq.)

Amid this busy throng of men and animals resound the warning shouts of coachmen, donkey-attendants, and camel-drivers. The words most commonly heard are — *'riglak, riglak'*, *'shimâlak'*, *'yamînak'*, *'û'â, û'â'*. As a rule, these warnings are accompanied

by some particularizing title. Thus, *'riglak yâ músyu'* (monsieur), or *'riglak yâ khawâga'* ('thy foot, sir', i.e. 'take care of your foot'; *khawâga* is the usual title given to Europeans by the Arabs and is said to have originally meant 'merchant' only); *'wishshak yâ gada''* ('thy face, young man'); *'shimâlak yâ sheikh'* ('to thy left, O sheikh'); *'yamînik yâ bint'* ('to thy right, girl'); *'ḍahrik yâ sitt'* ('thy back, lady'); *'yâ 'arûsa'* (bride); *'yâ sharîf'* (descendant of the prophet); *'yâ afandi'* (the title for a native gentleman). — Beggars are very numerous at Cairo, most of them being blind. They endeavour to excite compassion by invoking the aid of Allah: *'yâ Muḥannin yâ Rabb'* ('O awakener of pity, O Master'); *'ṭâlib min Allâh ḥaqq luqmet 'eish'* ('I seek from my Lord the price of a morsel of bread'); *'ana ḍeif Allâh wa'n-nabi'* ('I am the guest of God and of the Prophet'). The usual answer of the passer-by is *'Allâh yiḥannin 'aleik'* ('God will have mercy on thee'; comp. p. xxv).

The *Saqqa*, or water-carrier, with his goatskin of water, carried either by himself or by a donkey, still plies his trade in Cairo although the waterworks supply every house in the city, as well as the public fountains *(sabîl* or *sibîl)*, and though on many of the houses there are brass tubes through which passers-by may take a draught from the main pipes. The *Ḥemali* also, who belong to one of the orders of dervishes (p. xciv), are engaged in selling water, which they flavour with orange-blossom *(zahr)*, while others use liquorice *(ʿerqsûs* or *ʿirqisûs)* or raisins *(zebîb* or *zibîb)*. There are also numerous itinerant vendors of fruit, vegetables, and sweetmeats, which to Europeans usually look very uninviting. The *Rammâl* or soothsayer, squatting by the side of the road, offers to tell the fortune of the passer-by by consulting the sand. Lastly, there are itinerant *Cooks (ṭabbâkhîn*, sing. *ṭabbâkh)*, with portable kitchens, who sell small meat puddings, fish, and other comestibles.

Most of the Arab *Barbers (muzaiyin)* have their shops open to the street. Besides cutting the hair of their customers they may be seen shaving their heads, an art in which they are very expert.

Several times during the day and also at night the solemn and sonorous cry of the *Muezzin (mu'addin)* summoning the faithful to prayer (see p. lxxxix), reverberates from the tops of the minarets *(mâdna)*.

When the shops are shut the watchmen *(bauwâb)* place their beds *(serîr)* of palm-twigs in the streets outside the entrances and prepare to spend the night there; sometimes they have only mats or rugs to sleep on. The street traffic ceases in the Arab quarters comparatively early, while in the European districts it goes on till nearly midnight. But during the month of Ramaḍân (p. xcix) it continues throughout the whole night even in the Arab quarters.

The traveller will observe the *Elementary Schools (maktab)*, of which there are 79 in Cairo, and one of which is attached to almost every public fountain (sibîl; p. 51). He will find it very amusing to watch the schoolmaster (*fiqî*, a corruption of faqîh, p. lxxxix), teaching his pupils with the aid of admonitions and blows, while the boys themselves recite verses of the Koran with a swaying motion of their bodies (a practice supposed to 'strengthen the memory') or bend over their wooden or metal writing tablets. They do not fail, however, to find time for the same tricks as European schoolboys. It is not advisable to watch the fiqî too closely, as he is easily disconcerted.

These schools, mostly belonging to pious foundations controlled by the Ministry of Waqfs (p. lxxxix), are now supervised by the Ministry of Education. The mere reading and recitation of verses from the Koran being in itself considered a meritorious act, the great object of these schools is to teach the pupils to recite the Koran by heart. Although the language is often antiquated and obscure, no explanations are given, so that the boy who knows the whole book by heart usually understands but little of it. After learning the alphabet the pupil is taught to write a few simple words, such as the names of his friends, and then learns the ninety-nine 'beautiful' names of Allah, a knowledge of which is necessary to enable him to repeat the ninety-nine prayers of the Mohammedan rosary (sibḥa or subḥa). The boy is next made to learn the *Fâtḥa* (p. xc), or first chapter (sûra) of the Koran, after which he proceeds to learn the last, the last but one, and the others in the same inverted order, until he reaches the second, the reason being that the chapters gradually diminish in length from the second to the last. The course of study frequently takes 4-6 years and its completion is commemorated by the celebration of the *Khatma*, a family festival, to which the schoolmaster is invited.

The **Bazaars** of Cairo present many interesting traits of oriental character. As is the universal custom in the East, shops of the same kind, with their workshops, are congregated together in the same quarter, named sometimes after a mosque but more usually after the wares there sold, e.g. *Sûq en-Naḥḥâsîn*, bazaar of the coppersmiths, *Sûq el-Khurdagîya*, bazaar of the ironmongers. Most of the bazaars consist of narrow, and often dirty, lanes, generally covered over with an awning to shade them from the sun, and flanked with shops about 6 ft. wide. These shops *(dukkân)* are open towards the street, and in front of each is a *maṣṭaba* or seat on which the customer takes his place and on which the shopkeeper offers his prayers at the appointed hours. These lanes usually enclose a massive storehouse of considerable size *(khân)*, consisting of two stories. Several such khâns together form a quarter of the city *(ḥâra)*. These were formerly closed at night by massive, iron-mounted gates, still in some cases preserved, though no longer used.

Bâzâr is a Persian word, the Arabic equivalent for which is *sûq*. The magazines of the wholesale merchants, with their large courts, are called *wakâla*, which the Franks have corrupted to *occaleh* or *okella* (comp. p. cciv).

The principal market-days are Monday and Thursday, when the traffic in the narrow streets is so great that it becomes difficult to traverse them. Pedlars force their way through the crowd, shouting at the top of their voices. So, too, we observe coffee-sellers, water-carriers, sweetmeat-vendors, and others, elbowing their way.

In walking through bazaars and other streets the traveller will be interested in observing how industriously and skilfully the ARTISANS work, with tools of the most primitive description. The turners *(kharrâṭ)*, for example, are equally adroit with hand and foot.

European travellers who purpose making large purchases in the bazaars should make previous inquiries as to the prevailing prices and should then arm themselves with the most inexhaustible patience. Time has no value for an Oriental. Everything must be haggled for, sometimes in the most obstinate fashion. When the customer offers the proper price, the dealer will remark '*shwaiya*' (it is little), but will eventually close the bargain. Sometimes the shopkeeper sends for coffee or tea from a neighbouring coffee-house in the course of the bargaining. If no satisfactory agreement can be reached, the customer should calmly proceed on his way. Every step he takes will lower the demands of the obdurate dealer. It is advisable to offer at first rather a lower sum than the purchaser is willing to pay, in order that the offer may be raised. A common phrase in the ceremonious East is '*khuduh balâsh*' (take it for nothing), which, of course, is never seriously meant. Foreigners, however, must be prepared to pay more than natives. Dragomans and commissionnaires usually have a private understanding with the dealer, so that to make purchases in their company is to add 10-20% to the price. The street-hawkers often ask as much as ten or even twenty times the value of their wares.

I. The Ezbekîya and the New Quarters.

On the square in front of the Main Station, the MÎDÂN EL-MAḤAṬṬA and MÎDÂN BÂB EL-ḤADÎD (Pl. E 2), stands the *National Monument* ('The Awakening of Egypt'), in pink granite, by Mukhtâr Bey (1928). To the S. of the square, at the N. end of the Shâri' Nûbâr Pasha, is the *Sibîl of the Mother of Muḥammed 'Ali* (Pl. E 3), a handsome fountain, opposite the pretty modern *Mosque of Aulâd 'Inân*. Thence the Shari' Nûbâr Pasha, continued by the Shâri' Kâmil, leads to the Ezbekîya Garden.

The *Ezbekîya Garden (Pl. E 3, 4), or simply the *Ezbekîya*, is the centre of the foreign quarter, between the old Arab Cairo and the new town built in the European style since the middle of the 19th century. It occupies the site of a lake and is named after the heroic Emir Ezbek, the general of Sultan Qâït Bey (1468-96; p. cxxiv). A mosque, pulled down in 1869, was erected here in 1495 in honour of his victory over the Turks. The gardens, which have several entrances (adm. 5 mill.), were laid out in 1870 by M. Barillet, formerly chief gardener to the city of Paris. They cover an area of $20^1/_2$ acres and contain a variety of rare trees and shrubs. In the N.

part of the gardens are a café and a British soldiers' club, and in the S.E. part is the Arab theatre (p. 43). Military bands, see p. 44.

To the S. of the Ezbekîya lies the *Opera House* (Pl. E 4; p. 43), hastily constructed in five months to be ready for the opening of the Suez Canal (p. 193) and inaugurated on Nov. 1, 1869, with Verdi's 'Rigoletto' ('Aida', composed specially for the opening of the opera house, was not finished in time). In front of the building, to the W., stretches the Opera Square (Mîdân et-Tiyâtro; Pl. E 4), with an equestrian statue of *Ibrâhîm Pasha* (p. cxxvii; by Charles Cordier, 1872). Thence the Shâri' 'Abdîn leads S. to the *Mîdân 'Abdîn*, on the left side of which lies the *Royal Palace* ('Abdîn Palace; Pl. E 5).

No. 2 in the Ḥâret el-Mabdûli, opposite the S.W. corner of the 'Abdîn Palace, is *King Fuâd's Museum of Hygiene*, established in 1927 with the collaboration of the officials of the Dresden Museum of Hygiene. It contains numerous models dealing with human anatomy, physiology, and pathology, infant welfare, etc. (open daily, except Mon., 9-12 & 3-6; reserved for women on Tues.; adm. free, Sun. and Fri. P.T. 1).

Between the Ezbekîya and the Opera House the Shâri' et-Tiyâtro leads to the small Mîdân Ezbek, with the *Mixed Tribunal* (Pl. E 4; comp. p. xxii) and the *Crédit Lyonnais* (p. 39). Parallel with this street and its continuation, the Shâri' Ezbek, runs the Shâri' Ṭâhir, on the right of which are the *Caisse de la Dette Publique*, the *General Post Office* (Pl. E 4; p. 39), and the headquarters of the *Fire Brigade*. Both these streets end at the Mîdân el-'Ataba el-Khaḍra, an important tramway centre, whence radiate the Mûski (p. 56), the Shâri' Muḥammed 'Ali (p. 66), the Shâri' el-Azhar (p. 58) and Shâri' el-Amîr Fârûq (Pl. FG 4-2; both constructed in 1927), etc.

Adjoining the Ezbekîya on the N.E. is the small *Mîdân el-Khâzindâr* (Pl. E 3; Shâri' Clot Bey, see p. 85).

Westwards from the Ezbekîya and the Opera Square, and to the W. of the Shâri' Kâmil and the Shâri' 'Abdîn, as far as the Nile and the Shâri' el-Malika Nâzli, extend the quarters of **Ismâ'îlîya** and **Taufîqîya** *(Tewfikiyeh)*. The Ismâ'îlîya was begun by the Khedive Ismâ'îl (p. cxxvii), who desired to rival the modern quarters of Paris and presented sites gratuitously to anyone who would undertake to erect on each a house worth at least 30,000 fr. within eighteen months. This is no longer the most fashionable residential quarter, but it is the seat of European commerce. Several of the principal hotels and banks are situated here, also the offices of the great business firms, several department stores, most of the consulates, and many palaces of European, Levantine, and Egyptian grandees. The Ismâ'îlîya and Taufîqîya quarters are separated from each other by the wide and busy Shâri' Fu'âd el-Auwal (Avenue Fouad Premier, formerly Shâri' Bûlâq), which, beginning on the W. side of the Ezbekîya, leads through the quarter of Bûlâq (p. 86), crosses the Nile, intersects Gezîra (p. 86), and ends at the *Zamâlik Bridge*

(Pl. A 2). — To the S. of and parallel with the E. half of the Shâriʿ Fu'âd I. run the Shâriʿ el-Maghrabi and the fashionable Shâri el-Manâkh. Farther S. is the Shâriʿ Qaṣr en-Nîl, leading from the Shâriʿ ʿAbdîn (p. 54) to the *Mîdân Sulîmân Pasha* (Pl. D 4), with the monument of *Sulîmân Pasha*, a former French officer (Octave de Sèves; 1788-1860), the reorganizer of the army of Muḥammed ʿAli. Beyond this point the street leads to the barracks of *Qaṣr en-Nîl* (Pl. C 4) and the *Egyptian Museum* (p. 83), in the Shâriʿ Mariette Pasha. The Shâriʿ el-Bustân likewise ends at the barracks, leading W. from the Mîdân ʿAbdîn.

The Shâriʿ Sulîmân Pasha (Pl. D 4), at No. 2 in which is the *American Legation*, leads from the Shâriʿ Fu'âd I. to the Mîdân Sulîmân Pasha, and thence to the *Mîdân el-Ismâʿîlîya* (Pl. D 5). This square is crossed by the Shâriʿ Kubri Qaṣr en-Nîl, which leads from the Shâriʿ ʿAbdîn to the great bridge over the Nile and in which, at the corner of the Shâriʿ el-Madâbigh, is the ***Ministry of Waqfs*** (Pl. D 4; in charge of pious foundations, mosques, etc.), a building in the Arab style. — In the Shâriʿ Qaṣr el-ʿAini, leading S. from the Mîdân el-Ismâʿîlîya (see above), is, to the right, a fashionable quarter recently erected on the site of the palace of *Qaṣr ed-Dûbâra*, including the *Residency* of the British High Commissioner (Pl. C 5; comp. p. 39) and adjoined on the S. by the new *Garden City*. On the E. side of the Shâriʿ Qaṣr el-ʿAini are the College of Arts and Sciences (No. 113; founded in 1920), belonging to the *American University* (p. 44) and including a school of oriental studies for foreigners; the *Institut d'Egypte* (p. 44) with its gardens, the *Chemical Department* of the Ministry of Finance, the *Société Royale de Géographie* (p. 44), and the *Ministry of Public Works* (Wizâret el-Ashghâl el-ʿUmûmîya).

The **Geological Museum** (Pl. D 5), in the Shâriʿ esh-Sheikh Rîḥân, is open daily, except Fri. and government holidays, from 8.30 to 1. Guide to the exhibits (1923), P.T. 1. Director, *Dr. W. F. Hume.*

Ground Floor. The entrance hall contains specimens of the valuable minerals of Egypt (gold, petroleum, phosphates, etc.), flint implements, etc. The East Hall is devoted to building stones, clays, and wells. — On the First Floor is an extensive collection of Egyptian fossils (eocene and oligocene), found by H. J. L. Beadnell in the Libyan desert. In the central room are three skulls of the Arsinoïtherium Zittelii (an extinct monster resembling a rhinoceros; from the Faiyûm); bones of the Palæomastodon and Mœritherium, the earliest known representatives of the elephants; and two complete specimens of a monster tortoise (Testudo Ammonis). The East Room contains a complete collection of fossils characteristic of the various geological formations of Egypt and Sinai; in the West room is a representative collection of the rocks and minerals of Egypt and Sinai.

On the E. side of the ministerial buildings, in the Shâriʿ el-Falaki, are the offices of the *Public Health Administration.* — In the Shâriʿ Dâr en-Niyâba (i.e. 'Parliament Street'; Pl. D 5), which diverges E. from the Shâriʿ Qaṣr el-ʿAini, are (on the N. side) the ***Ministry of Communications***, the Cooperative Section of the Ministry of Agriculture, and the new *Parliament Buildings* (by B. R. Hebblethwaite,

1923); on the S. side is the *Ministry of Agriculture* (Wizâret ez-Zirâʿa). At the E. end of the street (Mîdân Lazoghli) lie the Ministry of Justice (N.) and the Ministries of Finance and the Interior (S.).

Farther on in the Shâriʿ Qaṣr el-ʿAini are (r.) the English church of *St. Mary* (p. 44) and (l.) the *Ministry of Education* (Wizâret el-Maʿârif el-ʿUmûmîya; entrance in the Shâriʿ eṭ-Ṭurqa el-Gharbi). The *Ministry of Foreign Affairs*, in the Shâriʿ el Insha, diverging to the left, occupies a former palace of Muḥammed ʿIzzet Pasha. Then follow, in the Shâriʿ el-Munîra, (l.) the *Higher Training College* for teachers (entrance in the Shâriʿ el-Madrasa) and the *Institut Français d'Archéologie Orientale* (p. 44). Next comes, on the right, beyond the street leading to the Muḥammed ʿAli Bridge and the island of Rôḍa (pp. 112, 113), the large hospital of *Qaṣr el-ʿAini* (Pl. C 6; p. 42). Originally a palace built in 1446 by Aḥmad Ibn el-ʿAini, Master of the Horse to Sultan Khushqadam, it was turned into a hospital in 1837, when the adjoining *School of Medicine and Pharmacy* (Faculty of Medicine of the Egyptian University, p. 85), created by the French doctor Antoine Clot (Clot Bey, 1793-1868) at Abu Zaʿbal (p. 129) in 1827, was transferred to Cairo. [New buildings for the hospital and medical school are under construction at Manyal er-Rôḍa (comp. p. 112).] Thence to the *Mîdân Fumm el-Khalîg* and to *Old Cairo*, see pp. 112 seqq. — The Shâriʿ Ḥelwân, parallel with the Shâriʿ Qaṣr el-ʿAini, contains the station of *Es-Saiyida Zeinab* (Pl. D 6), on the line to Ḥelwân (p. 177).

II. The Mûski and its Side Streets.

A visit to the chief *Bazaars* (comp. p. 52), to which this section is devoted, is so full of novelty and interest that the traveller will scarcely have time to combine with the first visit the inspection of the *Mosques* (tickets of admission, see p. 45) passed on the way. Both ladies and gentlemen, aided by the following description and the plan of the city (p. 37), may plunge fearlessly into the thickest of the crowd, especially if they do not mind taking an occasional wrong turning.

The chief thoroughfare of the Arab part of Cairo is the ***Mûski** (Pl. F 4), dating from the first half of the 19th cent., which leads from the square of ʿAtaba el-Khaḍra (p. 54) to the circular *Mîdân Sûq el-Kantu;* its continuations, the Shâriʿ es-Sikka el-Gedîda (p. 57), Shâriʿ esh-Shanawâni (Pl. G 4), and Shâriʿ ed-Darrâsa, traverse the entire breadth of the old town (nearly 1 M.). This street has now almost entirely lost its external oriental characteristics. The tobacco and clothing stores, etc., present quite a European exterior. But the oriental features of the traffic (p. 49) that surges up and down the street from morning till night are still unchanged. To the left, in the Shâriʿ esh-Shawâzlîya, is the recently restored *Mosque of ʿAbd er-Raḥmân Katkhudâ* or *Kikhya* (pp. 60, 61), dating from the middle of the 18th century. At the end of the Mûski, where we cross the Shâriʿ el-Khalîg el-Maṣri (Pl. F4; p. 57), we enter the old city of

the Fatimids (p. 47), the second wall of which, erected after 1074, is still represented by the Bâb el-Futûḥ and the Bâb en-Naṣr (p. 84), its N. gates, and the Bâb Zuweila (p. 64), its S. gate. Its W. boundary was the old canal of El-Khalîg (p. 112), now the Shâri' el-Khalîg el-Maṣri (Pl. D-G 6-2; tram No. 5, p. 40).

On the right in the Shâri' Bein es-Sûrein, which runs parallel with and close to the Shâri' el-Khalîg el-Maṣri, are the *Armenian Gregorian Church of the Holy Virgin* (Pl. F 4) and the Armenian *Patriarchate*. Farther on, in the Shari' Zuweila, which diverges right, are three Coptic Orthodox Churches (Pl. F 4), adjoining one another: *El-'Adra (Blessed Virgin)*, the oldest in the city, said to date from the Fatimid era, but in its present state a 12th cent. reconstruction (in front of the sanctuary, a screen decorated with beautiful ivory inlay); *St. Mercurios (Abu's-Seifein*, 'the two-sworded'), a small church altered in 1780; and, in the upper story, the church of *Mâri Girgis (St. George)*. Adjacent are two nunneries.

We follow the Shâri' es-Sikka el-Gedîda (Pl. F G 4; p. 56), the continuation of the Mûski. The *Ghetto* (Ḥâret el-Yahûd) to the left contains numerous synagogues and the old 'school' (i.e. synagogue) of the philosopher Maimonides (d. at Fusṭâṭ 1204). The *Bars Bey Mosque* (*El-Madrasa el-Ashrafîya;* Pl. F 4), farther on to the right, was built by Sultan el-Ashraf Bars Bey in 1424 and has a noteworthy portal. Here we turn to the left (on the right is the Shâri' el-Ashrafîya, p. 62) into the long line of thoroughfare beginning with the Shâri' el-Khurdagîya (p. 80), and at the first cross-street on the right (Shâri' el-Qumṣânwîya) we enter a large covered bazaar, known as the Khân el-Khalîli.

The **Khân el-Khalîli** (Pl. G 4), still the centre of the market traffic of Cairo, was founded in 1400 by Garkas el-Khalîli, master of the horse to Sultan Barqûq, on the site of a palace of the Fatimids. It forms a distinct quarter of the city, and is intersected by a main street and numerous cross-lanes, formed by long rows of stalls of tradesmen and artisans, all covered over. Here are the headquarters of the silk and carpet merchants and the vendors of trinkets. We follow the main avenue, the Shari' el-Khân el-Khalîli. In the first lane on the left is a *Bazaar of the Shoemakers*, in which the red shoes (*markûb*, plural *marâkîb*) of the Arabs may be purchased. On the right are large *Carpet Bazaars*.

The purchase of expensive carpets without expert knowledge is dangerous, as many of the examples are modern. As soon as a purchaser appears the dealers spread their wares over the whole court for his inspection. Patience and time are essential for a satisfactory bargain (comp. p. 53). Many of the so-called Damascene silks, and particularly those in the most pleasing colours, are manufactured at Lyons and Krefeld.

The Shâri' el-Khân el-Khalîli turns right and leads through the **Brass Bazaar** to the Sikka el-Gedîda, while the Sikket el-Bâdistân leads straight on to the Ḥasanein Mosque (p. 58). Passing through a fine gateway on the right, the *Sikket el-Qabwa*, which dates from the beginning of the 16th cent. (note the decoration of stalactites and inscription-friezes) and is occupied by brass-workers, we reach the Sikket and the parallel Ḥâret Khân el-Khalîli, both of which lead also to the Ḥasanein Mosque.

The **Mosque of Saiyidna'l-Ḥusein** (Pl. E 3) or **El-Ḥasanein** ('the two Ḥasans', i.e. the brothers Ḥasan and Ḥusein) is the mosque of the youthful Ḥusein, who fell at Kerbelâ in Mesopotamia in A.D. 680 fighting against the enemies of his father ʿAli, son-in-law of the prophet (p. cxviii), who was slain in 661. Ḥusein is still highly venerated by Shiite Mohammedans (p. xcv), particularly in Persia. The mosque (inaccessible to non-Moslems), of no architectural importance, has been almost completely modernized. The chief attraction is the modern mausoleum, which contains the head of Ḥusein, said to have been brought to Cairo in a green silk bag. This mosque is chiefly visited by men on Thurs. and by women on Saturdays.

Opposite the Ḥasanein Mosque on the S. is the Azhar Mosque (see below), from which the SHÂRIʿ EL-AZHAR (Pl. F G 4) runs to the square of ʿAtaba el-Khaḍra (p. 54), parallel with the Mûski.

Between the E. end of the Shâriʿ el-Azhar and the Sikka el-Gedîda lies the **Bazaar of the Booksellers.** Most of them are scholars, and their shops are the resort of the learned Mohammedan world of Cairo.

As the prices of books vary greatly in accordance with the demand and other circumstances, and as there is no such thing as a fixed publishing price, purchasers should always endeavour to ascertain beforehand the true value of any work they wish to buy. As in the case of many other wares, the line between new and second-hand books is not so strictly drawn in the East as in Europe. The booksellers generally keep catalogues, several feet in length, to refresh their memories regarding the state of their stock. The Koran, which is shown very reluctantly to non-Moslems, is kept separate from the other books. The books are piled up in a very inconvenient fashion. Many of them are sold in loose sheets, in which case the purchaser should see that the work is complete, as gaps are of frequent occurrence. The bindings usually consist of leather or cardboard. Valuable books are often kept in cases of red sheepskin. — The workmanship of the bookbinders, who, like other oriental artisans, work in the open street, is very cheap and far inferior to that of European productions. Red is their favourite colour.

We now follow the Shâriʿ el-Azhar, which leads to the left to the main entrance of the Azhar Mosque.

The ***Mosque of El-Azhar** (*El-Gâmiʿ el-Azhar;* Pl. G 4), the 'most blooming', the most important monument of the Fatimid period, was completed in A.D. 971 by *Gôhar*, general of the Fatimid caliph El-Muʿizz, and here, two years later, El-Muʿizz offered his first prayer after his entry into Cairo. Admission, see p. 45; cameras are forbidden and the visitor should carefully abstain from any manifestation of amusement or contempt. The mosque was created a **University** in 988 by *Caliph El-ʿAzîz* (p. cxix). The rectangular ground-plan of the original building, almost entirely rebuilt by the Emirs Salâr (after the earthquake of 1303) and Ṣarghatmish, and by the sultans Ḥasan and Qâït Bey, is easily recognizable, but it has been so frequently restored that no part of it can be said to date actually from the Fatimid period except the central part of the sanctuary, with its cupolas. Everything outside this rectangle is known positively to be of later date. The characteristic old ornamentation of the arcades and cupolas in the sanctuary deserves special

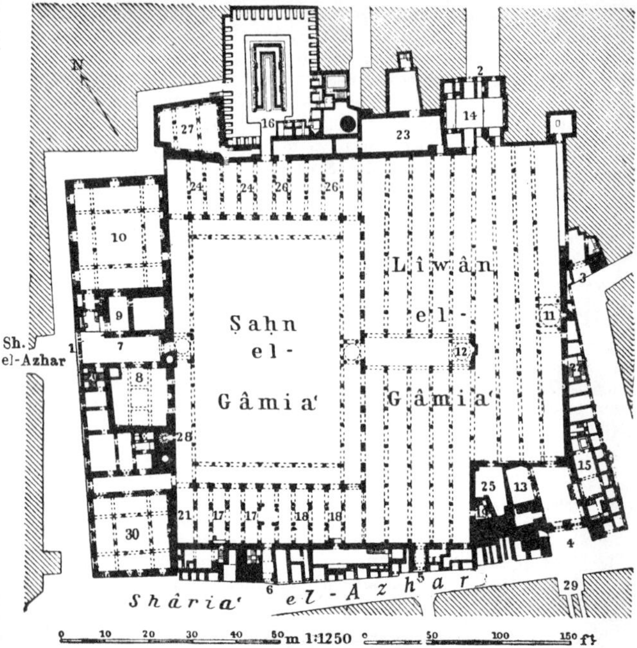

After Herz Pasha.

Gates: 1. *Bâb el-Muzaiyinîn* ('Gate of the Barbers'), on the W.; 2. *Bâb el-Gôharîya*, on the N.; 3. *Bâb esh-Shorba* ('Soup Gate'), on the E.; 4. *Bâb es-Sa'âida* ('Gate of the Upper Egyptians'); 5. *Bâb esh-Shauwâm* ('Gate of the Syrians'); 6. *Bâb el-Maghârba* ('Gate of the North West Africans'), these three on the S. and closed 2-6 p.m.

7. Forecourt. 8. *El-Madrasa* (school-mosque) *et-Ṭaibarsîya*. 9. Steward's office. 10. *El-Madrasa el-Aqbughâwîya* (library). — Lîwân el-Gâmi', the principal hall for instruction. — 11. Prayer-niche of 'Abd er-Raḥmân Kikhya. 12. Dome in front of the old prayer-niche. 13. Tomb of 'Abd er-Raḥmân Kikhya. 14. *El-Madrasa el-Gôharîya*. 15. Sabîl (fountain). 16. Court of Ablutions, with a tank in the centre and latrines all round. — 17-27. Riwâqs (bedrooms and studies). 17. *Riwâq el-Atrâk* (Turks); 18. *Riwâq el-Maghârba* (N.W. Africans); 19. Staircase to the *Riwâq esh-Shauwâm* (Syrians); 20. Staircase to the *Riwâq el-Baghdâdîyîn* (natives of Bagdad) and to the *Riwâq el-Hunûd* (natives of India); 21. *Riwâq el-Gabart* (E. Africans from Somaliland, Zeila', Berbera, and Tajurra); 22. Staircase to the *Riwâq el-Makkîyîn* (natives of Mecca); 23. *Riwâq esh-Sharâkwa* (natives of the province of Sharqîya, p. xlix); 24. *Riwâq el-Fashnîyîn* (Upper Egyptians from Fashn); 25. *Riwâq es-Sûdânîyîn* (natives of the Sûdân); 26. *Riwâq el-Balâbisa* (natives of Lower Egypt); 27. *Riwâq el-Ḥanafîya* (Hanafites, see p. lxxxviii). — 28. Steps to the terrace and to the Minaret of Ghûri. — 29. Gate of the *Okella Qâït Bey* (ruinous but interesting façade). — 30. *Riwâq el-'Abbâsi*.

attention; that of the walls has been for the most part renewed after vanished patterns. The arcades of the court *(ṣaḥn)* were rebuilt under the Khedive Taufîq with scrupulous reproduction of the old style and the retention of the old columns. — The successive rulers of Egypt have emulated each other in maintaining and enlarging this venerable building. In the 18th cent. the wealthy ʿAbd er-Raḥmân Kikhya (or Kiaḥya, p. 61) added four aisles to the sanctuary, and in more recent days Saʿîd Pasha and the Khedives Taufîq and ʿAbbâs II. have been notable benefactors. ʿAbbâs II. erected a new building in place of the dilapidated N.W. side of the mosque, and his neo-Arab façade is practically the only one the mosque boasts, the other sides being all devoid of decoration.

The university is considered the most important in the territory of Islâm. Before the British occupation the average number of students was some 7600, taught by 230 professors. After that the numbers sensibly diminished, as no students came from the former equatorial provinces of Egypt during the domination of the Mahdi. By 1912 the numbers had risen to 14,959 students and 587 teachers, but since then they have fallen again, as the instruction in Islamic studies is now shared with six other institutions (at Ṭanṭa, Zagazig, Asyûṭ, Alexandria, Damietta, and Disûq). In 1926-27 there were 246 teachers and 4838 students, of whom only 700 were non-Egyptians, so that the Egyptian riwâqs (p. 59; Upper Egypt, Lower Egypt, Eastern Egypt) are the largest. The rest are Syrians, Turks, or N. Africans, while a few come from Afghanistan, Bagdad, India, Java, Persia, Sennâr, Somaliland, and other Moslem countries.

No lectures are delivered on Thurs. or during the fasting month of Ramaḍân (p. xcix). When teaching, the professor *(sheikh)* sits cross-legged on a straw-mat or chair and reads from a book placed on a desk *(raḥla)* before him, explaining each sentence as he proceeds; or he directs one of the more advanced students to read aloud, adding his own explanations from time to time. The students sit in a circle around the teacher, listening or attentively taking notes. As soon as a student knows by heart and can explain the whole of the book that is being studied by the class, the sheikh makes an entry (*Igâza*, i.e. permission) in the student's copy of the work, whereby authority to lecture on the subject concerned is conferred. But the student cannot avail himself of this permission until he has passed the final examination, to which he may submit himself after receiving an igâza in each of the subjects of examination.

The complete CURRICULUM at the Azhar now lasts for fifteen years. If the student *(mugâwir)* successfully passes the examination at the end of the twelfth he receives the *Shahâdet el-ʿâlimîya*, or 'diploma of learning', which qualifies him to teach at the Azhar or other institutions of similar standing (see above); after another three years' course in the 'specialization section' (qism et-takhaṣṣuṣ) he may obtain the *Shahâdet et-takhaṣṣuṣ* ('diploma of specialization'). At the end of the eighth year a preliminary examination is held, success in which secures the *Shahâdet el-ahlîya* ('certificate of proficiency'), a diploma qualifying for the minor offices in the mosques and for the post of elementary teacher. The aim of the curriculum is to impart a thorough knowledge of not only the religious and civil teaching of Islam but also of classical Arabic (p. xxix). The subjects taught at the university fall into two classes: preparatory studies and professional studies. The former embrace grammatical inflexion *(ṣarf)* and syntax *(naḥw)*, rhetoric *(balâgha)*, logic *(manṭiq)*, versification *(ʿarûḍ* and *qâfiya)*,

algebra *(gabr)*, arithmetic *(hisâb)*, and the terminology of traditional science *(muṣṭalah el-ḥadîth)*. The professional subjects are theology *(kalâm)*, jurisprudence *(fiqh;* p. lxxxix), the explanation of the Koran *(tafsîr)*, and the teaching of the traditions *(ḥadîth;* p. lxxxviii). History, geography, mathematics, and style are optional subjects. — This list of subjects will serve to convey an idea of the intellectual condition of orthodox Mohammedans at the present day. Of recent years reformatory efforts have been directed, not only towards the compilation and systematic arrangement of traditional knowledge, but also towards its reorganization in accordance with modern ideas and its adaptation to present-day needs. This scheme of reform is to be initiated in 1929.

At the head of the university is the Rector *(Sheikh el-Gâmiʿ)*, one of the chief Mohammedan authorities in Egypt (comp. p. lxxxix), with an administrative committee of five. Control, especially in matters of finance, is exercised by a Conseil Supérieur. Instruction is free; the university is supported by pious endowments, from which also bread (replaced in 1929 by money) and pocket money are provided for the students. Within the last few years numerous 'strikes' have taken place among the students in consequence of the alleged misappropriation of the endowments by government. The budget for 1929-30 is estimated at £E 320,000.

The principal entrance (Pl. 1), where strangers receive a guide, is on the N.W. side, and is called *Bâb el-Muzaiyinîn*, or 'Gate of the Barbers', because the students used to have their heads shaved here. It leads to a small forecourt (Pl. 7), on the right of which is the *Madrasa et-Ṭaibarsîya* (Pl. 8), with a magnificent miḥrâb, or prayer-niche, of 1309, and to the left are the office of the steward (Pl. 9), in a restored mausoleum, and the *Madrasa el-Aqbughâwîya* (Pl. 10), now used as the El-Azhar Central Library (52,000 vols., of which 15,000 are MSS.). The branch-libraries of the different riwâqs (see p. 59) contain mostly ancient MSS.

The forecourt (Pl. 7), ending in a portal added by Qâït Bey (by whom the adjacent minaret also was built), leads directly into the large *Ṣaḥn el-Gâmiʿ*, or mosque court, enclosed by an arcade, with Persian keel-arches, shallow niches, medallions, and pinnacles.

The *Sanctuary* (Lîwân el-Gâmiʿ; p. cc), with its nine aisles, now forming the principal lecture-hall, has 140 marble columns (100 antique) and covers an area of about 3600 sq. yds. The front and older part, with the transept (p. cxciv) leading to the miḥrâb, is low in the ceiling. The part at the back, to which we ascend by a few steps, has considerably higher arcades (restored). The hall is imperfectly lighted. To the right of ʿAbd er-Raḥmân's prayer-niche (Pl. 11) is the pulpit *(minbar);* a staircase on the right ascends to the upper story. On the S. side is the tomb of ʿAbd er-Raḥmân Kikhya (Pl. 13; p. 56). The N. side is bounded by the elegant *Madrasa el-Gôharîya* (Pl. 14), which dates from the 15th cent. and has a roofed central court.

The ceilings of the *Northern* and *Southern Lîwâns* are supported by double colonnades. The N. lîwân is adjoined by the Court of Ablutions (Pl. 16), with a basin (meiḍa'a) in the centre.

The *Lateral Lîwâns* and many of the subsidiary buildings of the mosque are set apart as sleeping or working apartments (riwâqs, literally 'galleries') for the use of students of particular countries or

provinces (comp. the plan and its reference numbers 17-27, p. 59, most of the names of which still hold good). At the W. angle of the Great Court is the *Riwâq el-ʿAbbâsi* (Pl. 30), built by ʿAbbâs II. (p. cxxx) and used for lectures. One of its doors leads to the Shâriʿ el-Azhar.

Leaving the insignificant *Mosque of Muḥammed Bey Abu Dahab* (1773; p. cxxv) on the left (N.), we follow the Shâriʿ eṣ-Ṣanâdqîya (Pl. F G 4), called also *Sûq es-Sûdân*, formerly reserved for the dealers in Sudanese wares but now housing also other branches of trade (many druggists). It leads direct to the junction of the Shâriʿ el-Ashrafîya, opposite the mosque of Bars Bey (p. 57).

From the Shâriʿ el-Ashrafîya, on the left side of the mosque of Bars Bey, the Shâriʿ el-Ḥamzâwi eṣ-Ṣaghîr, with the bazaar of the same name, leads to the W. The **Sûq el-Ḥamzâwi** (comp. Pl. F 4) is the bazaar of the 'Christian merchants' (Syrians and Copts), who vie with their Mohammedan fellow-tradesmen in the exorbitance of their demands, and whose chief wares are European calico, porcelain, and drugs (which last are sold in nearly all the bazaars). This narrow winding street debouches in the Shâriʿ el-Azhar (p. 58), a little to the N. of the chief *Greek Catholic Church of St. Nicholas* (Pl. F 4). — Just at the beginning of the Shâriʿ el-Ḥamzâwi eṣ-Ṣaghîr we observe on the left the covered *Shâriʿ et-Tarbîʿa* (Pl. E 3), with the **Sûq el-ʿAṭṭârîn**, or spice-market. The perfumes of Arabia, genuine and adulterated, wax candles, and drugs are the chief commodities here. Attar of roses is sold by weight at high prices. The small bottles into which it is usually put contain only one drop. Then follow the weavers and the tailors. The Shâriʿ et-Tarbîʿa ends at the Shâriʿ el-Azhar, opposite the Ghûri Mosque (see below).

The Shâriʿ el-Faḥḥâmîn runs S. from the S.W. corner of the Ghûri Mosque and contains the bazaar for wares from Tunis and Algiers. We first observe drug-stalls and then magazines for light-coloured woollen and other stuffs, Beduin rugs, etc. — We now proceed to the left direct to the Shâriʿ el-Ghûri (see below), or turn sharp to the right, then sharp to the left, and pursue the same direction, parallel with the Shâriʿ el-ʿAqqâdîn (see below) and passing a number of slipper-makers' stalls *(bawâbîgi)*, till we come to the *Shâriʿ el-Minaggidîn*, a passage which turns first right, then left, and is inhabited chiefly by tailors, cloth-merchants, and dealers in undressed wool. A short abrupt curve of this lane, to the left, then brings us to the Shâriʿ el-ʿAqqâdîn.

The Shâriʿ el-Ashrafîya, which skirts the E. side of the Ashraf Mosque (Pl. F 4; p. 57), forms the first part of a long line of streets leading S. and farther on taking successively the names of Shâriʿ el-Ghûri, Shâriʿ el-ʿAqqâdîn, Shâriʿ el-Manâkhlîya, and Shâriʿ es-Sukkarîya (p. 63).

In the Shâriʿ el-Ghûri the first things to catch our eye are the beautiful façades of the **Madrasa and Mausoleum of Sulṭân El-Ghûri** (Pl. F 4), one of the last monuments of the time before the Turkish conquest and often depicted by the brushes of famous artists. The Madrasa, to the W. (r.), was finished in 1503 and has a minaret (213 ft. high) inappropriately crowned with five modern dwarf cupolas. Like the mosque of Qâït Bey (p. 122) it is cruciform, with a flat-vaulted central court. The most notable features of the interior are the beautiful pulpit and the tasteful marble panelling of

the lower part of the walls. Opposite the madrasa, on the E. side of the street, is the MAUSOLEUM, dating from 1504. The sultan, who fell in Syria (p. cxxiv), is not, however, buried here. It was restored under ʿAbbâs II., the last Khedive, and now houses the library of Aḥmad Pasha Zaki. From the rectangular vestibule we pass to the right into the oratory, covered by a dome. From this a door leads into the maqʿad, or hall in which the sultan was wont to await the hour of prayer. To the left of the vestibule lies a second chapel, now used as a school office. Adjacent is a charming *Sibîl* (fountain) with a school (p. 52).

To the E. of the Shâriʿ el-ʿAqqâdîn lies the quarter of *Khushqadam.* In its main street stands the *House of Gamâl ed-Din ez-Zahabi (No. 6; Pl. FG 5), president of the merchants, one of the best preserved of the earlier Arab private houses in Cairo (comp. p. cci). The building dates from 1637 (visitors knock; adm. P.T. 2). Through a crooked passage *(dirka)* we reach the court of the salâmlik, or living rooms of the owner, with two well-preserved façades. In the S.W. corner is a flight of steps leading to the maqʿad, an open colonnade with two arches. The inscription on the cornice in the interior gives information about the building. Adjoining the maqʿad is an oriel window with mashrabîyas (p. cci), whence the ladies of the harem could overlook the court. Adjacent is the bath. Proceeding straight on we enter the beautiful qâʿa, or drawing-room, adorned with fine mosaics. The middle and lower-lying part of the room is covered with a wooden dome, and the flat wooden ceiling of the other parts of the chamber is also very beautiful.

The SHÂRIʿ ES-SUKKARÎYA, which continues the Shâriʿ el-ʿAqqâdîn farther on, is the bazaar for sugar, dried fruits *(nuql)*, and fish, candles, etc. On the left is the *Sibîl of Muḥammed ʿAli*, a modern marble fountain, and on the right the ***Mosque of El-Mu'aiyad** (Pl. F 5), called also *El-Aḥmar* (i. e. 'the red') after the adjoining Darb el-Aḥmar (p. 65). It was erected by *Sheikh el-Maḥmûdi Mu'aiyad* (p. cxxiii), the Mameluke sultan, who had been captured in a street fight against Sultan Farag and vowed that he would build a mosque on this site if he were released from prison. The mosque was not finished till 1422, a year after the sultan's death. The massive enclosure walls of the courtyard were erected during a thorough restoration in the second half of the 19th cent. (modern portions shaded grey on the ground-plan). The bronze gate at the entrance (Pl. 1), considered the handsomest in Cairo, originally belonged to the Sultan Ḥasan Mosque (p. 71). — To the left of the vestibule is a bronze-mounted wooden door, leading to the mausoleum of the sultan (Pl. 2), which is covered with a beautiful dome. To the right is a corridor (Pl. 3) leading to the old sanctuary (Pl. 4; restored in 1890), a magnificent apartment with lofty stilted arches. The decoration is rich and effective. The lower part of the wall with its niches is adorned with panels of coloured marble and other stones, surmounted by charming dwarf arcades with colonnettes of blue glass-paste and a rich mosaic of coloured marbles. Above the niches are stucco windows and inscriptions in finely carved and gilded letters, interspersed with gilded arabesques and rosettes. The coloured wooden ceiling and the inlaid ornamentation of the pulpit

(Pl. 5) and doors also deserve notice. This hall is now used as a lecture-room when the Azhar Mosque (p. 58) is overcrowded. In the S.E. angle is the mausoleum of the sultan's family (Pl. 6). The

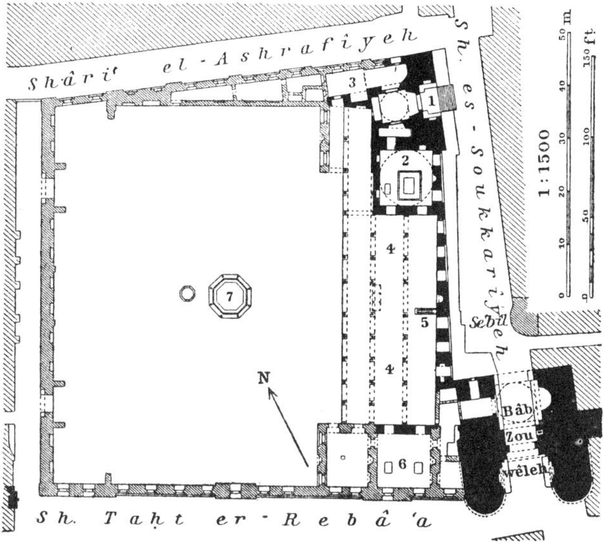

sanctuary is separated by a modern iron railing from the court, which was once surrounded by colonnades and is now planted with trees and furnished with a modern ḥanafîya, or fountain for ablution (Pl. 7).

Adjoining the mosque is the town-gate **Bâb Zuweila** (Pl. F 5; p. cxcv), at the end of the street. This is built of massive ashlar masonry and in plan resembles the two other gates of the Fatimid period, the Bâb el-Futûḥ and the Bâb en-Naṣr (p. 84). It was erected at the end of the 11th cent. by three builders from Edessa (Urfa). The S. side consists of two huge towers, surmounted by the elegant minarets of the Mu'aiyad Mosque. On the W. tower are a number of stone and wooden balls, probably dating from the Mameluke period. Ṭûmân Bey, the last of the Circassian sultans of Egypt, was hanged on this tower by Sultan Selîm I., on April 15th, 1517 (p. 48). This gate is commonly called *Bauwâbet* (or *Bâb*) *el-Mitwalli*, from the popular opinion that the mysterious Quṭb el-Mitwalli (Mutawalli), the most holy of the saints (p. xciii), has his abode behind the W. half of the gate, where he sometimes makes his presence known by a gleam of light. On both wings of the gate hang shreds of cloth-

ing, teeth, and other votive offerings, placed here by sufferers in hope of cure.

In the recently cleared space outside the gate, to the right, is the *Sibîl* (fountain) *of Sultan Farag*, by the bronze railings of which executions by strangulation took place down to the middle of the 19th century. To the left is the *Mosque of Ṣâliḥ Ṭalâ'i'*, built under the last Fatimid sultan in 1160 and recently restored. The sanctuary arches rest on Corinthian columns and are adorned with delicate plaster sculptures, inscriptions, and decorations.

Immediately to the S. of the Zuweila Gate is a *Bazaar of the Shoemakers*, and farther on, in the *Shâri' el-Khiyâmîya*, is the bazaar of the tentmakers, where gaily coloured tent-covers (the designs of which, however, are now very degenerate) are offered for sale. The streets continuing the Shâri' el-Khiyâmîya are less interesting and lead to the Shâri' Muḥammed 'Ali.

From the Zuweila Gate the Shâri' ed-Darb el-Aḥmar (Pl. F 5) leads S.E. Not far from the gate is (No. 36) the small ***Mosque of the Emir Qigmâs el-Is-ḥâqi,** erected in 1481 in the style of Qâït Bey (comp. p. 78) and admirably restored at the end of the 19th century. The fine portal is approached by steps, and on the left of it is the projecting sibîl (fountain). The mausoleum, which is large in proportion to the mosque, long remained empty, as the emir Qigmâs (Qijmâs) el-Isḥâqi, master of the horse to Qâït Bey, died and was buried in Syria, of which he was governor. In 1851, however, the pious Sheikh Abu Hurîba was interred here. The interior, dimly lighted by beautiful plaster windows (partly renewed), makes a deep impression with its subtly harmonious colouring. While the lateral lîwâns are contracted almost into niches, the W. lîwân and the E. sanctuary are deeper and roofed with flat and richly decorated ceilings. The lower part of the walls is faced to a height of 6 ft. with marble panelling, finished off with an ornamental frieze in flat relief. The cornice of the W. lîwân is adorned with stalactite ornament, that of the sanctuary with an inscription-frieze. The valuable old pulpit is decorated with ivory and ebony inlay. The enamelled glass lamps are modern, made in Bohemia after ancient models (see p. 69). A door in the S. wall of the sanctuary leads to the mausoleum of Abu Hurîba.

From the Qigmâs Mosque a narrow street leads to the Ḥâret Abu Kalba, opposite the end of which, some distance off, lies the small *Mosque of Aṣlam el-Bahâ'i* (Pl. G 5; p. cxcix), or *Aslân Mosque*, built in 1345, with a noteworthy façade, recently exposed to view, and interior decoration of Persian faience.

To the S. of the Qigmâs Mosque, in the Shâri' et-Tabbâna (Pl. F 5), lies the ***Mârdâni Mosque** *(Gâmi' el-Mârdâni)*, one of the largest in Cairo, built in 1338-40 by the emir Altunbogha el-Mârdâni, cup-bearer of Sultan Muḥammed en-Nâṣir. The building was in a ruinous condition in the 19th cent., but was restored by Herz Pasha (p. 66). It is now a branch of the Azhar University (p. 58) and is used

for educational purposes. The nearly square court is surrounded by colonnades. The prayer-niche and the walls on each side of it are covered with costly mosaics. The new concrete dome (comp. p. cxcvii) in front of the prayer-niche is borne by superb ancient Egyptian granite columns. The side-colonnades also contain ancient columns, probably from a temple of the Ptolemaic period. The sanctuary, or main hall, is separated from the court by an ancient wooden railing *(maqṣûra)*, much of which has had to be renewed. The ḥanafîya (p. cc) in the court formerly stood in the mosque of Sultan Ḥasan and here occupies the site of the original fountain. — The Shâri' Bâb el-Wazîr goes on to the gate of that name and to the *Citadel* (p. 73). About halfway it passes on the right the *Madrasa and Mausoleum of Sultan Sha'bân* (Pl. F G 5, 6), known also as *Madraset Umm es-Sulṭân* and built in 1369. It has a deeply recessed portal; strangers are not admitted. The porch is used as an infants' school. — A few paces farther on, to the left, is the picturesque ***Aqsunqur Mosque** or *Gâmi' Ibrâhîm Agha* (Pl. F G 6), known also as *El-Azraq*, or 'the blue', from the rich blue tiles on the walls. Built in 1346 by the emir Aqsunqur, this mosque was restored and decorated with blue tiles by Ibrâhîm Agha, the Turkish governor, in 1653.

III. The South-Eastern Quarters.

The route described in this section leads viâ the Shâri' Muḥammed Ali to the *Citadel*, and thence by a wide curve to the S. back to the same street. *Trams*, see pp. 40, 41 (Nos. 5, 11, 13, 23).

Starting from Mîdân el-'Ataba el-Khaḍra (see p. 54), the Shâri' Muḥammed 'Ali (Pl. E F 4-6), 1 M. in length, leads S.E. straight to the foot of the citadel (tram 11, p. 40). On the left, about one-third of the way down the street, lies the square of Bâb el-Khalq, with the *Governorate* (Pl. F 5), containing the *Police Headquarters*, and the building of the Arab Museum and Egyptian Library.

The ***Arab Museum** (Pl. E F 5; entrance on the E. side), or *Dâr el-Athâr el-'Arabîya* (Museum of Arab Antiquities), consisting of objects of artistic or antiquarian interest from ruined mosques and other Egyptian buildings, especially those of Cairo, is due to the zeal of *Franz Pasha* (d. 1915), the Austrian technical director of the Waqfs Ministry (p. lxxxix). The collections were formerly exhibited in the El-Ḥâkim Mosque but, constantly increased by the efforts of Max Herz Pasha (d. 1919), were transferred in the year 1903 to the ground-floor of the present handsome new building in the Arab style. The museum is open daily from Nov. to April, except on Mon. and official holidays, 9-4.30, on Thurs. 9-2, Fri. 9-11 and 1-4.30 (adm. P.T. 10); from May to Oct., 8-1, Fri. 9-11 (adm. P.T. 1). Director, Prof. G. Wiet, the French Arabist; curator, Ḥusein Râshid; assistant curator, Ḥasan Muḥammed el-Hawâri.

The walls of the Vestibule are occupied by a chronological survey of the Islamic dynasties of Egypt.

Room I contains models of two houses discovered during the excavations at Fusṭâṭ (p. 118). — Room II (to the right). Model of a group of houses at Fusṭâṭ; mosaics, mashrabîyas, benches.

Room III. *Tombstones.* On the N. wall and in the centre, tombstones in marble (from a cemetery to the S. of Cairo) and sandstone (from Aswân), of the first centuries of the Hegira (p. lxxxvi), with good illustrations of the development of Arabic scripts, the ornamental Kûfi (Cufic, p. 70) and the cursive Nas'khi. By the window are marble cenotaphs. — In the passage to Room II, fragments of cenotaphs, head-dresses from the tombstones of Mohammedan men and women.

Room IV. *Marble and Other Stone Carvings.* Architectural fragments; jars and their stands, with ornamentation; tombstones; fragments of stone panelling with arabesques and other decoration; jars and their stands, some with fabulous animals; marble stand with lions' feet and a woman clutching her breast (thought to date from the 12th cent.); capitals and shafts of columns, mostly from ancient buildings and utilized by the Arabs.

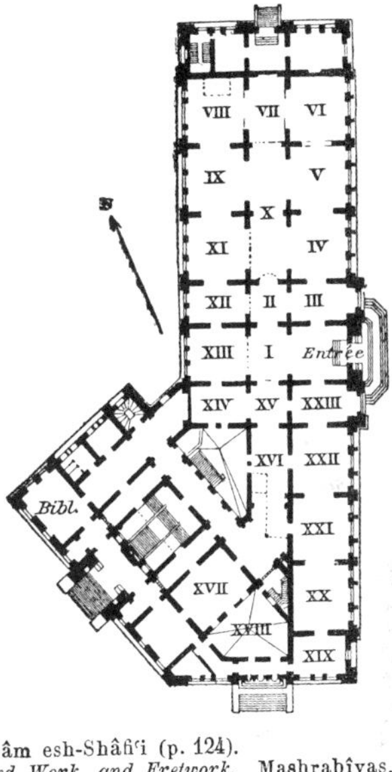

Room V. *Plaster and Tile Ornaments, mostly from Fusṭâṭ* (p. 118). Coloured marble mosaic; old capitals, used as well-heads. Stained-glass windows from various mosques in Cairo. *Fountain from a house of the 14th (?) century. Small oil-seed mill from Fusṭâṭ. The show-cases contain finds from the ruins at Fusṭâṭ: moulds for ornaments, etc.; incense-burners of plaster, decorated with animals and genii, plaster ornaments, weights. Hanging bronze lamp from the mosque of Sultan Ḥasan. Wooden door from the tomb-mosque of Sultan Eṣ-Ṣâliḥ Aiyûb (p. 81; 1249).

Room VI. *Wood Carvings.* Pulpits, reading desks for the Koran; prayer-niches (p. cc) of carved wood, one of which (No. 107), according to the two lines of Cufic script, was made by order of the wife of the Caliph El-ʿÂmir for the mausoleum of Saiyida Ruqîya (1132; p. 80). Cenotaphs, including one (No. 119) from a tomb near the tomb-mosque of Imâm esh-Shâfiʿi (p. 124).

Room VII. *Wood Carvings, Turned Work, and Fretwork.* Mashrabîyas, balconies, window-frames, lattice-work; in the entrance, door from a house at Damietta (p. 186); pulpits; bronze lamp from the mosque of Emir ʿAbd el-Bâsiṭ, keeper of the wardrobe to Sultan el-Mu'aiyad (15th cent.).

Room VIII. *Wood Carvings.* Carved woodwork showing the development of Islamic ornament. On the E. wall, fragments of cenotaphs from the cemetery of Fusṭâṭ, of the first centuries of the Hegira. Wooden doors with fine ivory inlay, from various Cairo buildings. On the N. wall (No. 69), two fragments of a cenotaph from the tomb-mosque of Imam esh-Shafiʿi (12th cent.), of the finest workmanship in various woods; panel with an inscription in Hebrew (Fatimid period). Carved frieze with hunting scenes, dancers, musicians, and women riding on camels, from a palace of the Fatimids (comp. p. cxciv), found in the Muristân of Qalâûn (p. 81).

Room IX. *Wood and Ivory Carvings.* On the ceiling, old wooden ceilings. 250-253. Four caskets inlaid with ivory, ebony, or tortoise-shell. Mosque-fittings; carved doors with ivory inlay; wooden tables (*kursi*), one especially

fine example in mosaic, from the mosque of Sultan Shaʿbân (p. 66); Koran chests (No. 156, with mosaic and hinges, from the same mosque); jewel-boxes. Small wooden ceiling, richly painted and gilded, from the sibîl (fountain) of Sulîmân Sâri; another with painted and gilded stucco ornament from a house in Cairo, the inscription being an invocation of the Prophet (17th cent.). In Cases A and D: dice of ivory and bone, dolls of bone, shoulder-blades of animals with inscriptions, bathing sandals inlaid with ivory, from Fusṭâṭ; carved wooden panels.

Room X (to the E. of R. IX and XI). *Mosaic pavement and fountain from an Arab house in the Ḥilmîya quarter of Cairo. Finely carved wooden ceiling from a 17th cent. house. Stucco ceiling of geometrical pattern, formed of two rows of thin strips of wood nailed together, with stucco ornaments in the panels.

Room XI. *Metal Work.* Bronze-mounted doors: 1. From the mosque of Ṣâliḥ Ṭalâʾiʿ (1160; Fatimid period); 3. From the mosque of Bars Bey at El-Khânqâh (N. of Cairo; p. 130). The show-cases contain candelabra, Koran boxes, and chests from mosques; *105, 106. Small perfume tables, richly inlaid with silver (No. 105 has the name of Sultan En-Nâṣir, 14th cent.); 12. Bronze drum from the mosque of Saiyid Aḥmad el-Badawi at Ṭanṭa (p. 36). Domestic utensils, brass dishes, bronze vessels, plates, mortars; magic bowls, writing materials, perfume-boxes, small vessels inlaid with gold and silver. Below the window are finds from Fusṭâṭ (p. 118); objects in copper and bronze, lamps, handles, spoons, needles, surgical instruments, birds and animals in bronze, weights and measures, armlets, ear-rings, etc. Between the windows, astronomical instruments (astrolabes, globes, etc.); gold and silver coins; locks and keys, likewise from Fusṭâṭ. From the ceiling hang beautiful metal lamps from various mosques.

Room XII. *Metal Work.* Weapons of all kinds inlaid with gold, muskets, pistols, dress-swords (including one with the names of the sultans El-Ghûri and Ṭûmân Bey, beginning of 16th cent.); candelabra; bronze-mounted doors; silver-mounted door. 129. Bronze cauldron. Door-bolt from the mosque of Sultan Barqûq (p. 82). Arab steelyards. Fine hanging lamp with arabesques and the name of Sultan El-Ghûri.

Room XIII. *Faience* from the recent excavations at Fusṭâṭ. The cases by the N. wall contain fragments with coats-of-arms. E. wall: Lamps of various periods, lids, grenades for Greek fire. S. wall: Chinese porcelain and imitations thereof in faience; potter's samples, glass pastes, firing failures, tools for grinding colours, etc. W. wall: Fragments of earthenware water-bottles (qullas, p. 119), Fatimid potsherds. In the centre of the room, faience of the Fatimid and Mameluke periods, fragments with names of sultans or potters, with representations of animals, plants, etc.

Room XIV. *Faience.* N. wall: Tiles from Egyptian potteries, removed from buildings in Cairo. W. wall: Syrian tiles, one with a picture of the Kaaba at Mecca (Damascus, 1726); above, stucco decorations of an Arab room in Old Cairo. S. wall: Tiles from Rhodes. E. wall: Tiles from Italy and Tunis. The desk-cases contain finds from Fusṭâṭ: filters from water-bottles (qullas) with charming patterns; lamps, earthenware toys.

Room XV. On the walls, Italian and Hispano-Moresque faience. The show-cases contain terracottas from Fusṭâṭ.

Room XVI (corridor). *Faience*, mostly of foreign origin. E. wall: show-cases with vases, plates, pots, and flasks from Persia, Mesopotamia, Syria, and China; fragments of faience vessels of various origin (from the ruins of Fusṭâṭ). In the centre, hanging lamps and dishes, mostly from Cairo mosques. Suspended from the ceiling, balls and faience lamps. A show-case contains a superb *Dish of cornelian, 17$^{3}/_{4}$ in. in diameter and 4 in. in height, with nineteen cut marginal facets, from the mosque of Sultan Qalâûn. W. wall: Stucco decorations from buildings in Cairo. At the end of the corridor: Wood panelling from a house in Rosetta (p. 32).

Room XVII. Collection of objects of the time of Muḥammed ʿAli (p. cxxv); ornaments, silver dinner service, coffee cups. Portrait of Muḥammed ʿAli. Sword worn by Ibrâhîm Pasha at the battle of Nisib (p. cxxvii).

Courtyard (XVIII). Tombstones and inscriptions of the Turkish period (16-19th cent.). Sundials. On the right of the door leading to Room XIX is a marble door with rich ornamentation (end of 18th cent.), presented in 1928 by King Amânullâh of Afghanistan.

Room XIX (Room of Prince Yûsuf Kâmil). In the centre is a Persian *Carpet of silk interwoven with silver thread (Iṣfahân, 16th cent.). The show-cases contain faience, four fine glass mosque-lamps (see below), Coptic textiles, carpets, ornate weapons (sword bearing the name of the Turkish sultan Suleimân I., 'the Magnificent', 1520-66; another with the name of the sultan Muḥammed II. 'the Conqueror', 1451-81).

Room XX. *Textiles and Carpets.* The textiles are partly of native manufacture, found in old Mohammedan graves, and partly of foreign origin, of comparatively late date. E. wall (window side): Pieces of Arab embroidered or printed stuffs. In Case I: Blocks for printing textiles, weaving tools, combs for carding wool, spools, spindles, etc., mostly from Fusṭâṭ. Case II: Embroidered caps; textiles with inscriptions. S. wall: Admirable Persian and Turkish carpets. W. wall: Textile patterns; in the centre, dated pieces in chronological order.

Room XXI. **Enamelled Hanging Lamps from Mosques*, most of them made of pale-green glass, with enamelled flowers, foliage, inscriptions, medallions, and coats-of-arms. The places of manufacture were probably Aleppo and Damascus. Only about two hundred of these lamps are now extant; most of those in this museum (over 70) date from the end of the 13th cent. to the middle of the 15th. The oldest specimens bear the titles of the Sultan El-Ashraf Khalîl, of his brother En-Nâṣir, and of several of En-Nâṣir's emirs. Numerous lamps, with the name of the Sultan Ḥasan, are from his mosque; the six finest specimens are to be seen in the two glass-cases at the entrance to the following room. **Enamelled Glass Lamps* (see above) from the tomb-mosques of Sultans Barqûq and Sha'bân.

Room XXII. Glass lamps of foreign manufacture. Glass bracelets, beads, flasks, weights, etc., mostly from Fusṭâṭ. On the N. wall are two pictures of the holy cities of Mecca and Medina.

Room XXIII. In the centre, a Koran box, with 'cuir bouilli' ornamentation and the name of the sultan El-Ghûri (1501-16), the donor. The show-cases contain oriental book-bindings. In the case of new acquisitions is a bronze statuette of a man with a tamburine, a unique example of the representation of a human figure preserved from the Arab period. The case to the left of the window contains weapons presented by King Amânullâh of Afghanistan in 1928.

The **Egyptian Library** (*Dâr el-Kutub el-Maṣrîya;* special entrance from the Shâri' Muḥammed 'Ali), on the first floor of the Arab Museum, was founded in 1869 by Khedive Ismâ'îl. The chief credit of arranging this fine collection of books belongs to five Germans, Dr. Stern, Dr. Spitta Bey (d. 1883), Dr. Vollers (d. 1909), Dr. Moritz, and Dr. Schaade, followed, since 1914, by Egyptian directors. Present director, Muḥammed A'sad Barrâda Bey. At the end of 1926 the whole library consisted of about 126,000 vols. (58,000 printed in Arabic and other oriental languages, 68,000 in European languages) and 24,000 MSS. (Arabic, Persian, Turkish, Amharic, and Syrian) and photographic facsimiles. The Koran alone accounts for no fewer than 2677 volumes. The illuminated Persian MSS. from the library of Muṣṭafa Fâḍil Pasha (d. 1875), brother of Khedive Ismâ'îl, are extremely valuable. The library contains also a collection of *Coins* (about 5000) of the Mohammedan rulers of Egypt. — The reading room is open daily (except on Mon., official holidays, and during the hour of midday prayer on Fri.) 9-1 and 4-8 (June-Sept. 8-12

and 5-8). Visitors to the other rooms require a special permit from the director, while those who wish to borrow books must obtain a guarantee from some high official (e.g. a consul) or other personage in Cairo known to the director.

The **Show Room** (open free, 9-4) contains coins and specimens of oriental MSS. and printed works. We begin with the table-cases to the right. — *Shelves 1, 2.* Arabic papyri (8-9th cent.); *3-5.* Arabic documents on papyrus, paper, parchment, potsherds, and flakes of limestone (9-13th cent.); *6.* Early Arabic books (9-13th cent.); *7.* Autographs of famous oriental authors; *8.* Arabic MSS. from North Africa and Spain (11-17th cent.). — *9-20.* Fine examples of the Koran. These are remarkable for their large size, superb execution, and great age. The Mohammedans have always exercised the greatest care in preparing the MSS. of the Koran, and have always regarded the sacred book (comp. p. xcii) with the most profound reverence. The oldest specimens of the Koran (Shelves 9 seqq.), dating from the 8-10th cent., are in the *Cufic* character, an early form of Arabic script, and are written on parchment. Note on Shelf 9 a Koran written c. 725, on Shelf 11 a copy dating from 719-912, both from the ʿAmr Mosque. Among the fine large copies of the Koran on paper which were executed for the sultans of the Bahrite Mamelukes (1250-1382) and their emirs, the most notable are those (Shelves 14 seqq.) made for the sultans Ḥasan and Shaʿbân and their emirs Sheikhûn and Ṣarghatmish (14th cent.). — *21-36:* Korans of the 14-15th cent. made for the emirs Qigmâs and Arghûn and the Mameluke Sultans Barqûq, Farag, En-Nâṣir, El-Mu'aiyad, and Bars Bey; Korans and other books of the 15th cent., prepared for the sultans Khushqadam, Qâït Bey, and El-Ghûri. The largest Koran in the collection, measuring 44¾ by 35 inches, belonged to Qâït Bey. — Table-case with Arab coins, the oldest piece being a dînâr of the caliph ʿAbd el-Malik ibn Marwân (77 of the Hegira, i.e. A.D. 696). — *37.* Korans of the 14-15th cent. (Mameluke period). — *Shelf 38.* Korans written in India.

Shelves 39-44. *Persian MSS. with miniatures. The origin and development of this branch of art have not yet been adequately investigated. The specimens here exhibited are all the work of Islamic artists, though the influence of E. Asiatic taste is noticeable in those of later date. These book-illustrations are distinguished from the purely ornamental art of the Korans by a greater freedom of conception and variety of motive, particularly by the frequent employment of living forms. Nearly all are illustrations of poetical or historical works. The chronological arrangement shows that this art was at its best in the 14-16th cent., and that thereafter a rapid decline set in. *39.* *Dîwân (collection of poems) of Farîd ud-Dîn ʿAṭṭâr, written in 1454; poems of Jâmi (1414-92), written in the N.E. Provinces of India, perhaps in the 17th century. *40.* Anthology of Persian poetry, written for the library of Bâyazîd, Sultan of Turkey (15th cent.); Persian MSS. of the 16th cent., one of which is the *Bûstân or 'fruit-garden' of the poet Saʿdi (d. 1291). *41.* Korans written in Persia. *42.* Korans and other books written in India; two albums with Indian miniatures and autographs of celebrated Persian and Turkish calligraphers (1670-1703); the poem of Yûsuf and Zuleikha, by Jâmi (see above), written in 1604, with full-page illustrations. *43.* Persian miniatures of the 15-16th cent.; a second specimen of Jâmi's poem of Yûsuf and Zuleikha, written in 1533; the Arabic Cosmography ('Wonders of the Creation') of Qazwîni (d. 1283), translated into Persian, with diagrams in the E. Asiatic style (1567); two MSS. of Mihr u Mushtari or 'Sun and Jupiter', a poem by ʿAṣṣâr (1493); several MSS. of the Shâhnâmeh or Book of Kings of Firdausi (d. 1020). *44.* Persian miniatures of the 16-17th cent.; three copies of the Dîwân of Ḥâfiẓ (d. 1389) of Shîrâz (1556, 1565, and 1680); Gulistân or 'rose-garden' of Saʿdi (see above), written by Sultan Muḥammed Nûr (16th cent.). — *45.* Korans written by Turks. *46.* Turkish MSS. with miniatures; a copy of the Qudatku Bilik, the first work of Turkish literature in Arabic characters, composed about 1070 and written in Cairo about 1350; Cosmography of Qazwîni (comp. above; 1685). — *47.* Turkish albums (16-17th cent.);

48. Autographs of Turkish sultans; *49.* Arabic books, printed in Africa (Zanzibar, Sûdân, Egypt, Tunis, Algiers, Morocco); *50.* Arabic books printed in Asia (China, East Indies, Persia, etc.), and also the earliest European specimens; *51-54.* Arab, Persian, and Turkish book-bindings (14-19th cent.). On the walls: Koran written for the Sultan Uljaitu of Persia (1314) and later (1326) acquired by the Mameluke Sultan En-Nâṣir.

From the Bâb el-Khalq Square we continue to follow the Shâriʿ Muḥammed ʿAli. A side-street soon leads to the left to the *Mosque of El-Malika Ṣafîya* (Pl. F 5), a centralized building in the Byzantine-Ottoman style (1610; p. cxcix), the dome borne by six monolithic antique columns. Behind it, in the Shâriʿ ed-Dâwûdîya, lies the small ***Mosque of El-Burdeini** (Pl. F 5), built perhaps in 1690 and restored in 1885, lavishly adorned with mosaics and adjoined by an elegant minaret. The beautiful wooden ceilings and the elaborate pulpit are especially notable.

Farther on the Shâriʿ Muḥammed ʿAli passes the *Mosque of Qûṣûn es-Sâqi* (Pl. F 5), built in 1330 but much altered, and leads to the Mîdân Muḥammed ʿAli (Pl. F 6), which has two large mosques on its S. side. That on the left is the **Mosque of Er-Rifâʿi,** a handsome columned edifice completed in 1912. It stands over the tomb of Sheikh ʿAli er-Rifâʿi (comp. p. xcv) and contains the family vault of the Khedive Ismâʿîl (p. cxxvii; interesting memorials).

On the right rises the ****Sultan Ḥasan Mosque** (Pl. F 6; *Madraset es-Sulṭân Ḥasan*), the school-mosque (madrasa) of Sultan Ḥasan, perhaps the finest existing monument of Egyptian-Arab architecture. It was built in 1356-63 for Sultan Ḥasan (p. cxxiii), perhaps by a Syrian architect, and has been well restored by Herz Pasha. The huge proportions of the building, which occupies a shelving rock below the citadel, taken in conjunction with the masterly execution of its details, produce an effect of great majesty (comp. p. cxcvii). Admission, see p. 45.

The exterior recalls the broad surfaces of the early-Egyptian temples. All the *Façades* are crowned by a unique and boldly projecting cornice of 'stalactite' formation and are furnished with pinnacles (restored). The broad wall-surfaces are relieved by blind recesses and round-arched windows in couples. The mausoleum, which projects boldly from the S.E. façade, is covered by a dome (180 ft. high), renewed in the 18th cent. in the Turkish-Arab style, after the Constantinople pattern. The N.W. façade is unfinished. — The massive ***Gateway* (Pl. 1), 85 ft. high, though its ornamentation was never fully carried out, has been more or less imitated in many other Egyptian mosques. The original magnificent bronze gate now adorns the mosque of El-Mu'aiyad (p. 63). — The *South Minaret* (Pl. 11a; 285 ft. high) is the highest minaret in Cairo (that of El-Ghûri 213 ft., Qalâûn 193 ft., El-Mu'aiyad 167 ft., El-Azhar 167 ft., Qâït Bey and Barqûq 164 ft., Ibn Ṭûlûn 131 ft., ʿAmr 105 ft.). Its fellow minaret (Pl. 11b) collapsed, but was afterwards rebuilt on a smaller scale.

The building is in the form of an irregular pentagon, 85,000 sq. ft. in area, in which the cruciform shape of the *Madrasa* (school-mosque, p. cxcviii) has been skilfully incorporated. — From the main entrance (Pl. 1) we enter first a domed vestibule (Pl. 2) and then a smaller anteroom, whence steps ascend to the corridor (Pl. 3) adjoining the large Ṣaḥn el-Gâmiʿ or mosque court (115 ft. long and 105 ft. broad). In the centre of the court is the ḥanafîya (Pl. 4), or fountain for ablutions. The four arms of the cross are occupied by four large halls (lîwân), with lofty barrel-vaulting. These serve as praying rooms. The lecture-rooms for the four orthodox rites of Islâm (p. lxxxviii) were fitted up in the four small madrasas (Pl. 12).

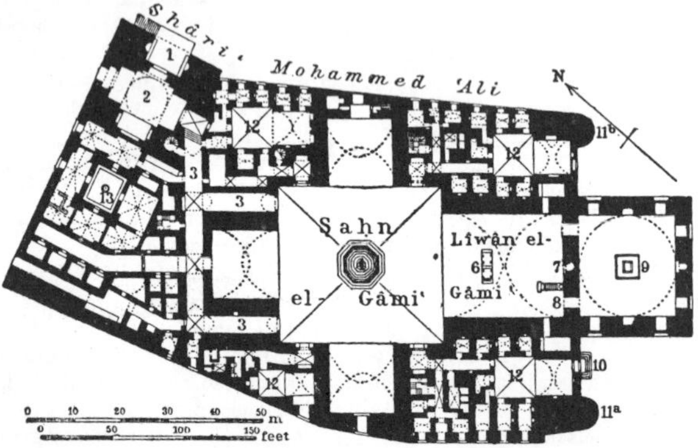

1. Chief Entrance (from the Shâriʿ Muḥammed ʿAli). 2. Vestibule. 3. Corridor. 4. Ḥanafîya. 6. Dikka. 7. Prayer-niche (miḥrâb). 8. Pulpit (minbar). 9. Mausoleum of Sultan Ḥasan. 10. South Entrance. 11 a and b. Minarets. 12. Madrasas (lecture-rooms) for the four rites of Islâm. 13. Old court of ablutions in the sunk floor (ruinous).

The Lîwân el-Gâmiʿ or sanctuary has as its chief embellishment an elaborate inscribed *Frieze, cut in the stucco and much restored, with fine Cufic letters on a tasteful background of arabesques. The rear wall, with the prayer-niche, is adorned with marble. The only remains of the once sumptuous fittings of this hall are the dikka (p. cc; Pl. 6), the pulpit (Pl. 8), with a wooden door, inlaid with gold and silver and mounted with bronze, and the chains of the innumerable lamps (p. 69). To the right of the pulpit is a bronze door (now closed), damascened with gold and silver, leading to the mausoleum. The present entrance to the *Mausoleum* (Pl. 9) is an iron door to the left of the pulpit. The square domed apartment, with the simple sarcophagus of the sultan, has a beautiful inscribed frieze of carved wooden letters. The stalactitic pendentives of the original dome still exist. The ceiling and the painted friezes have been partly restored.

To the E. of the Er-Rifâ'i Mosque (p. 71) the Shâri' Dâyir er-Rifâ'i leads to the small *Mosque of Gôhar El-Lâlâ* (Pl. F 6; built in 1430). Thence we follow narrow lanes E. to the ruins of the *Muristân of Sultan El-Mu'aiyad* (1418); a great part of the hospital (comp. p. 82) is still standing and is being gradually freed from encumbrances; it has a fine doorway (also approachable from the Shâri' el-Maḥgar, see below).

To the S. of the Sultan Ḥasan Mosque extends **Saladin Square** (*Mîdân Salâḥ ed-Dîn;* Pl. F 6, 7), the finest in the city, formed at Lord Kitchener's instigation in 1913 out of the *Rumeila Square* and by the demolition of several small streets and buildings. A busy market *(Sûq el-Qaṣr)* is held in the afternoon, and the festivities attending the departure and return of the Mecca caravan (p. xcviii) take place here. At the N. end of the square, on elevated ground, stand the *Amîr Akhôr Mosque* (Pl. F 6; built in 1503) and the unimportant *El-Maḥmûdîya Mosque* (1567). On the E. side rises the citadel (see below), with its former main entrance, the *Bâb el-'Azab* (Pl. F 6; now closed to civilians), flanked with huge towers. The crooked lane behind the gate, enclosed by lofty walls, was the scene of the massacre of the Mamelukes on March 1st, 1811, by order of Muḥammed 'Ali (p. cxxvi); only one is said to have escaped, Amîn Bey, who made his horse leap through a gap in the wall into the moat. The *Prison* lies at the S. end of the square, and from its N.E. corner the Shâri' Maṣṭabat el-Maḥmal, and farther on the Shâri' Bauwâbet el-Gebel, lead along the N. edge of the Tombs of the Mamelukes (p. 123) to the Monastery of the Bektashi Dervishes (p. 126).

From the N.E. corner of Saladin Square, the Shâri' el-Maḥgar, a carriage-road, and then the winding Shâri' Bâb el-Gedîd (view of the Tombs of the Caliphs on the left) lead to the citadel. Pedestrians follow the Shâri' ed-Daftarkhâna, on the left side of which are the *Archives* (*Daftarkhâna;* Pl. F G 6), in a building erected by Muḥammed 'Ali in 1828.

The **Citadel** (*El-Qal'a;* Pl. F G 5, 6) was begun in 1176 by Saladin (p. 47) and was built of stones taken, according to the very credible statements of Arab historians, from the smaller pyramids at Gîza. Of the original structure three-quarters of the N. half now remains. Although the fortress commands the city, it is itself commanded by the Moqaṭṭam heights, rising above it immediately to the S.; thus in 1805 Muḥammed 'Ali was enabled, by means of a battery planted on the Gebel Giyûshi (p. 125), to compel the Turkish governor, Khurshîd Pasha, to surrender the citadel. — We enter the outer court of the citadel by the main entrance or *Bâb el-Gedîd* ('New Gate'), and then pass through the *Bâb el-Waṣṭâni* ('Middle Gate') into the main court, where the Alabaster Mosque rises in front of us, with the En-Nâṣir Mosque to the left.

The ***Muḥammed 'Ali Mosque** (Pl. F 7; *Gâmi' Muḥammed 'Ali*), or 'Alabaster Mosque', the lofty and over-slender minarets of which

form one of the landmarks of Cairo, was begun by Muḥammed ʿAli on the site of a palace which was blown up in 1824; and by 1857 it was completed in its present form by Saʿîd (p. cxxvii). The architect was the Greek *Yûsuf Boshna* of Constantinople, who, aided by Greek foremen, built it on the model of the Nuri Osmaniye mosque at Constantinople. The columns are built, and the walls incrusted, with poor yellow alabaster. Wood painted to resemble alabaster is used also.

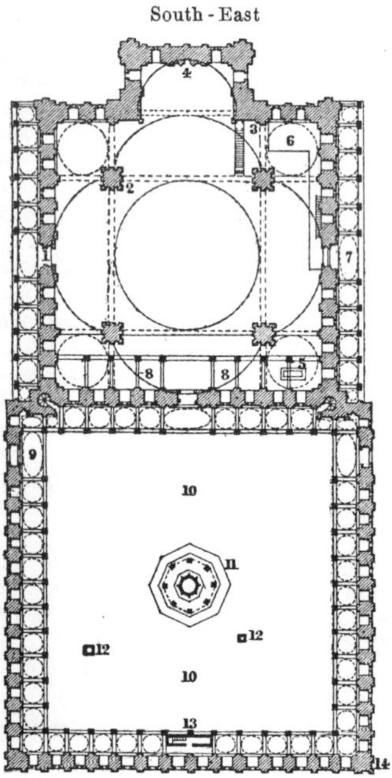

1. Sultan's Entrance. 2. Kursi (reading-desk). 3. Pulpit. 4. Prayer-niche. 5. Tomb of Muhammed ʿAli 7. Entrance. 8. Great Gallery. 9. Usual Entrance. 10. Ṣaḥn el-Gâmiʿ. 11. Ḥanafîya. 12. Openings to the great cistern under the court. 13. Ascent to the clock-tower. 14. View Point.

The entrance (Pl. 9), in the centre of the N. side, leads into the *Ṣaḥn el-Gâmiʿ* (Pl. 10), or *Fore-court*, enclosed by vaulted galleries, in the upper parts of which limestone has been used instead of alabaster. In the centre is the *Ḥanafîya* (Pl. 11), or basin for ablution, in the debased Turkish style. On the W. side is the approach to a tower (Pl. 13), which terminates in a pavilion with Moorish arabesques and contains a clock presented to Muḥammed ʿAli by Louis Philippe.

The Interior is entered through the centre of the E. gallery. It consists of a large quadrangle, with Byzantine domes resting on four huge square pillars. The size and lighting of the place produce a very striking impression. The Turkish decoration is unimportant, and the reading-desk, pulpit, and prayer-niche (Pl. 2, 3, 4) possess no particular attraction. To the right of the entrance is the *Tomb of Muḥammed ʿAli* (d. 1849), enclosed by a handsome railing (Pl. 5).

A magnificent *View is obtained from the parapet at the W. angle of the mosque (Pl. 14), which is reached by walking round outside the building, within the railing. From this point we survey

attractive public gardens and the *Gezîra Palace* (formerly an hotel, now private property). In the Gezîra Grotto is an *Aquarium* (open 8 till sunset; adm. 5 mill.), containing a good collection of Nile fish A shorter route from the City to Gezîra is offered by the Bûlâq Bridge (p. 86). In the Shâriʿ el-Amîr Saʿîd, which diverges N. (r.) from the W. or Gezîra end of the bridge, is the *German Institute for Egyptian Archaeology* (Pl. B 2; p. 44).

Near the aquarium (p. 86) the Shâriʿ el-Gezîra turns S. and is continued along the El-Aʿma branch of the Nile (see below) by the Shâriʿ el-Gabalâya, leading to the English Bridge and the Shâriʿ el-Gîza (see below).

Below Gezîra the Nile is spanned by the *Imbâba* or *Embâba Bridge* (Pl. B C 1), used by foot-passengers and carriages as well as by the railway. On the left bank is the station of *Imbâba* (pp. 35, 153), to the N.W. of which was fought the 'Battle of the Pyramids', in which Bonaparte defeated the Mamelukes on his march from Alexandria to Cairo (July 21st, 1798).

The Shâriʿ Kubri el-Aʿma runs to the left from the Mîdân el-Gezîra (p. 86) through the S. part of Gezîra, which is occupied by **Gardens*, much frequented in the afternoon. To the r. is the exhibition hall (Pl. B 5) of the *Royal Agricultural Society* (p. 44). This road crosses the *English* or *El-Aʿma Bridge* (Pl. B 5; built in 1914; opened to river traffic 12.15-1 p.m.), spanning the W. arm of the Nile (the *Baḥr el-Aʿma*, i.e. 'blind river'), and, under the name of *Shâriʿ el-Gîza*, skirts the river through *Gîza Suburb*, a new villa-quarter. [The Shâriʿ Maḥaṭṭet Bûlâq ed-Dakrûr, which diverges to the right, leads to Bûlâq ed-Dakrûr station (p. 153).] On the right, at the corner of the *Shâriʿ el-Birinsât*, are the offices of the *Survey of Egypt* (Pl. A 6; comp. p. ccviii) and the *Mudîrîya* (government building) of the province of Gîza. The *School of Law*, on the left, belongs to the University of Egypt (p. 85). New buildings for the faculties of arts and science are being erected here. Farther on (right) are the public *El-Urmân Gardens*, botanic gardens managed by the Ministry of Agriculture, beyond which lie the *School of Engineering* (Pl. A 7) and the ***Zoological Gardens** (Arabic *Ḥadîqat el-Ḥaiwânât;* open daily, 8 till sunset; adm. 5 mill.; plan 5 mill.), which are maintained by the government and are rich in rare African and Sudanese animals. The beautiful park itself, 52 acres in extent, is worth visiting for the magnificent royal palms (Oreodoxa regia) and water-lily pond. There is also a grotto with a view-terrace (adm. P.T. 1). — The road next reaches the N. end of the little town of Gîza, where, at the station known as *Gîza Village*, the tramway (Lines 14 & 15; comp. pp. 40, 41) joins the branch crossing the ʿAbbâs Bridge (comp. p. 132). To the right are the *Agricultural College* (Pl. A 8) and the adjoining *School of Veterinary Medicine*.

Gîza, an uninteresting town of 26,773 inhab., is the capital of a province comprising the districts of El-ʿAiyâṭ, Imbâba, Gîza (left bank of the Nile), and Eṣ-Ṣaff (right bank). Tuesday is market-day. — For the Pyramids of Gîza, see p. 132.

VI. The Egyptian Museum.

Tramways (Nos. 11, 12, & 14), see pp. 40, 41.

The ***Egyptian Museum* (Pl. C 4; *Musée Egyptien du Caire*, Arabic *El-Antîkkhâna el-Maṣrîya*), containing Egyptian and Greek antiquities found in the valley of the Nile, lies in the Shâriʿ Mariette Pasha, not far from the Qaṣr en-Nîl Bridge. Founded by the French Egyptologist *Auguste Mariette* (1821-81) in 1857 and originally housed at Bûlâq, the museum was greatly enlarged by later directors (Grébaut, De Morgan, Loret, and especially Maspero, d. 1916) and is the largest and most important collection of its kind. Its growth is steady and rapid, owing to the regular archæological enterprises of the Egyptian Department of Antiquities, to purchases, and to the proceeds of foreign excavations, which (except for such pieces as may be presented to the excavator as an act of grace) have to be surrendered to the museum. — The present Director (and also Director-General of the Egyptian Department of Antiquities) is the French archæologist *Pierre Lacau*; the Secretary-General is *Henri Gauthier*; and the Conservators are *Reginald Engelbach*, *Battiscombe Gunn*, *Sâmi Effendi Gabra*, and *Maḥmûd Effendi Ḥamza*. — 'Guide to the Cairo Museum' (French edition 1915, English 1910), by Maspero, P.T. 20; brief guide by G. Daressy (in English and French, 1925; P.T. 5).

The museum is open in winter daily, except on Mon. and public holidays, from 9 till 4 or 4.30, on Fri. 9-11.15 and 1.30-4; in summer (May-Oct.) from 8.30 to 1, on Fri. 8.30-11.15. Admission P.T. 10 (in summer P.T. 1).

The museum buildings, covering an area of 14,330 sq. yds., were erected in the Græco-Roman style in 1897-1902 by *M. Dourgnon*, a French architect. In the front garden rises a bronze *Statue of Mariette* (see above), by Denys Puech (1904), behind the marble sarcophagus of the great Egyptologist.

The centre of the main façade is occupied by a porch flanked with two massive pillars. Above these are two high-reliefs by Ferdinand Faivre (1867), representing Upper and Lower Egypt. On both sides of the porch are colonnades for the exhibition of large monuments. At the corners are two pavilions, that to the left accommodating the *Library*, that to the right the *Sale Room* (Salle de Vente) for antiquities (the genuineness of which is guaranteed by the museum authorities), photographs, picture post-cards, and scientific publications. The general admission tickets (p. 212) for Upper Egypt are obtainable here.

The brown lettering on our PLAN refers to the rooms on the ground-floor, the black lettering to the corresponding rooms of the upper floor. The letters designating the different rooms are marked on the walls. — At the entrance to each room of the ground-floor hangs a diagram showing the positions of the larger and more important objects. This should in each case be consulted as the frequent rearrangement of the exhibits prevents absolute accuracy in our description.

STUDENTS of special subjects should apply to the director or to one of the conservators. — COPYING, SKETCHING, or PHOTOGRAPHING the exhibits

(the goddess of writing making an inventory of booty from Libya). — *Case B:* Statues of the Ancient Empire. — *88. Wooden reliefs of Hesirē, represented standing and then seated at a meal. — 91-94. Rock reliefs from the Wâdi Maghâra (Sinai; 91A. King Snofru slaying a Semitic Beduin). — 502, 505, 6050. Groups of heads of foreign captives, perhaps parts of the bases of statues, from Damanhûr, Tanis, and Ṣaqqâra (3rd Dyn.).

Room D. **223. Limestone statues of Prince Ra-hotep and his wife Nofret, from his maṣṭaba at Meidûm (p. 217), the colouring still remarkably fresh and the facial expression excellent (end of 3rd Dyn.).

*225. Limestone statue of the priest Ra-nufer, from Ṣaqqâra; 233. Fragments of the wall of a tomb: flute and harp players, singers, dancing girls, and two persons beating time; *136. Six geese, painted on stucco, from a tomb at Meidûm; *224. Limestone statue of the priest Ra-nufer (see No. 225); 239. False door of Atoti (with the deceased, in the half-round, emerging from it); *229. Statue of Ti, from Ṣaqqâra (p. 164); 232. Fragments of tomb-reliefs (potters, bakers, brewers); 6010. False door from the tomb of a noble dwarf, from Gîza; in the glass-case in front, 6055. Group of the dwarf Seneb and his family, with the limestone box it was found in. *230. Copper statue of King Phiops I., 231. His son Methusuphis (p. ciii), both from Hierakonpolis (p. 369), partly of cast, partly of beaten metal; 235. Ape biting a man in the leg, 236. Boatmen fighting, two fragments of tomb-reliefs with well-preserved colouring.

Monuments of the Middle Empire and Hyksos Period
(11-17th Dynasties; 2100-1555 B.C.).

Room F. In the centre, *280. Wooden statue of the tutelary genius *(Ka)* of King Hor, represented as a nude man, bearing the hieroglyph *Ka* (two raised arms) on his head; the statue was found in the king's tomb by the South Brick Pyramid at Dahshûr (p. 177) and stands in a wooden shrine (No. 195). — *284. Limestone statue of Amenemmēs III., from his mortuary temple (p. 206); 287. Rude painted sandstone statue of King Mentuhotep III., from his rock-tomb at Deir el-Baḥari (p. 322); 286. Granite statue of Queen Nofret, wife of Sesostris I., from Tanis (p. 182); 283. Granite statue of Nakht, steward of the palace, from Lisht (p. 217).

Gallery J. 517. Seated figure of an official of the Middle Empire, quite similar in style to that of the Amenhotep of the 18th Dyn. (No. 3, p. 89); squatting figure of Hotep. — Two show-cases with painted tombstones and small statues of the Middle Empire.

*Room G. In the centre, *300. Tomb-chamber of Harhotep, containing his limestone coffin and adorned with pictures of household utensils required by the deceased; *Ten over-lifesize limestone statues of Sesostris I., from his mortuary temple in the S. pyramid at Lisht (p. 217; note the fine reliefs on the throne). By the pillars, 301-306. Six statues of Sesostris I., from Lisht (three with the

Upper Egyptian and three with the Lower Egyptian crown, p. cii; the king represented as Osiris, with crossed arms). 311. Lower part of a tomb-wall with relief of King Entef and his hounds (11th Dyn.); *6049. Portrait-head of Sesostris III., from Medamût; 307-310, 361. Stone chests for canopic jars (p. clv). On either side of No. 361, two granite statues of viziers, of the end of the Middle Empire.

The show-cases contain excellent sculptures of the Middle Empire. Portrait-figures of kings and private persons, notably a wooden figure of *Sesostris I. with the white crown, from Lisht.

319, 320. Relief of a vizier, seated in front of a table of offerings. Above is a painted relief of a girl, from El-Barsha (p. 224).

We return to Gallery J. Monuments of the Middle and New Empires. 507a-507d. Sphinxes of Amenemmēs III. in black granite, from Tanis (p. 182); 508. Group in grey granite, from Tanis (two water-gods offer fishes on lotus-stalks and carry strings of fishes and birds; in front is the cartouche of King Psusennes, p. cvii); 506. Bust of an unknown king with a curious head-dress, in black granite; 503. Thutmosis IV. and his mother Tio, from Karnak; 500. Sennufer, a prince of the 'Southern Residence', and his wife (18th Dyn.).

Monuments of the New Empire
(18-24th Dyn.; 1555-712 B.C.).

Room I. Statues, tombstones, and stelæ of the 18th Dynasty. — *400. Thutmosis III. as a youth wearing the Upper Egyptian crown, in grey schist, from Karnak. — *Case A:* Tombstones of the beginning of the 18th Dynasty. — 404. Thutmosis III.; 407. Stele of Amenophis III., referring to his victories; 408. Thutmosis III. erect, in pink granite; 410. The god Ptah-Tenen, dedicated by Amenophis II.; 418. Senmut with Princess Nefrurē; over-lifesize granite statue of Hatshepsut as king, from Deir el-Baḥari (p. 317); *420. Triumphant monument of Thutmosis III., from Karnak.

In the upper part is the king sacrificing to Amon-Rē, with the patron goddess of Thebes behind him. In the poetic inscription the king is hailed as victor by Amun, and the conquered lands are enumerated.

Case B: *424. Statue of Êset, mother of Thutmosis III., with a gilded diadem, from Karnak; Thutmosis III. as a sphinx; *428. Thutmosis III. kneeling and offering wine. — 444. Painted sandstone statue of Mut-nofret, mother of Thutmosis II.; two kneeling figures of Hatshepsut, from Deir el-Baḥari; **445, 446. The chapel and sacred cow of the goddess Hathor, dedicated by Thutmosis III., discovered in the rocks near the temple of Deir el-Baḥari (p. 323). The walls of the chapel, the ceiling of which is painted so as to imitate the vault of heaven, are decorated with coloured reliefs representing Thutmosis III. and women of his family before the sacred cow and the goddess Hathor herself. The cow is a masterpiece of Egyptian sculpture, the head especially showing close observation of nature; in front of it stands the dead king, painted in black, while the living king is represented as drawing milk from the udder. —

Case C: 455. Head of Amenophis III.; *451. Head in black granite, with a mild expression, perhaps King Haremhab (p. cvi). — *457. Statue of Tutankhamûn; 456. Head of the goddess Mut (thought also to be Teye, wife of Amenophis III.), from Karnak; *459, 461, 465, 467. Statues of the sage Amenhotep at different ages (comp. p. 89); *462. Statue of the god Khons, with the features of Tutankhamûn; *452, 453. Queen of Punt, accompanied by slaves and donkeys laden with gifts, a relief from the temple of Deir el-Baḥari (p. 319); 470. Amenophis II., protected by the snake-goddess; 496. The snake-god Har-khentekhtaï, dedicated by Amenophis III.

We return to Gallery J, at the N. end of which are exhibited monuments of the time of Amenophis IV. (p. cv). By the pillars, two over-lifesize portrait-figures of Amenophis IV. from Karnak. — 3875. Coffin-lid of Amenophis IV., gilded and inlaid with glass-paste. — In a case: Statuettes of Amenophis IV., heads of princesses, etc., from El-ʿAmârna; 482. Folding altar; 478. Death-mask (?) of Amenophis IV. — In another case: 6056. Model pylon with sculptures of Amenophis and his family.

By the *Staircase to the Upper Floor:* (l.) 550. Colossal seated lion, in pink granite, from Tell Muqdâm (p. 184); (r.) 551. Praying baboon, in pink granite, from the base of the great obelisk at Luxor (p. 273; now in Paris).

Gallery K. Tombstones and fragments of walls of tombs, of the New Empire. — Left, 560. Stele of King Tutankhamûn, referring to his buildings at Karnak (see p. 272); 562. Relief of women dancing and making music, scenes from a funeral procession; right, 559. Funeral obsequies, from the tomb of Harmin.

Room L. 578, 579. Statues of the vizier Pramessu (time of Haremhab, p. cvi), who is supposed to have afterwards become Ramses I., as a scribe with crossed legs; 6017. Stone with inscription of Merneptah commemorating his victory over the Libyans. *590. Sacred boat in red granite, from the temple of Ptah at Memphis; 592. Statue of Senmut holding an image of Hathor.

North Portico *(Portique du Nord).* 595. Ramses II., seated between Isis and Hathor; 597. Ramses II. and the god Ptah-Tenen. — *599. Stone with memorial inscriptions of Amenophis III., referring to his buildings for Amun, and of Menephthes (Merneptah), referring to his victories over the Libyans ('Israel Stele').

This stood originally in a temple of Amenophis III. at Thebes and was afterwards used by King Menephthes, who inscribed upon the back (turned towards the room) a hymn, concluding with the words: "Israel is wasted and his seed is brought to nought". This is the earliest mention of Israel in any Egyptian inscription. The stele was discovered by Sir Flinders Petrie in 1896.

460, 463. Fine reliefs (scenes with gods) from a chapel of King Mentuhotep at Dendera (p. 261).

Central Atrium. This court contains the largest monuments, including colossal statues from the Temple of Tanis (p. 182). On

the N. staircase: *610. Colossal group of Amenophis III. and his consort Teye, with their three daughters; 612. Two chapels dedicated by Ramses II. — 613, 616, 617, 630, 633. Colossal statues of kings of the Middle Empire, with the name of Ramses II. added at a later date (from Tanis); 611. Altar from the mortuary temple of Sesostris I. at Lisht; *3848. Funerary tent of Queen Est-em-khebet; *627. Stucco pavement from the palace at El-ʿAmârna (p. 246); 632. Statue of a king, usurped by Haremhab, from Medînet Habu (p. 347); 619, 620. Sarcophagi of Thutmosis I. and Hatshepsut (as king; comp. p. 318), with the stone chests for the canopic jars; 6024. Sarcophagus of Queen Hatshepsut, executed before her accession to the throne; *621. Bed of Osiris, found at Umm el-Gaʿâb (p. 260), with a falcon perched on it and two falcons at either end; 626. Apex of the pyramid of Amenemmēs III. at Dahshûr, in black granite. — On the S. staircase: 624. Sarcophagus of King Eye (p. cvi). — We return to the North Portico.

Gallery M (continuation of Gallery K). 654. Black granite sarcophagus of Khay; *660. The celebrated 'Tablet of Ṣaqqâra', found in a tomb at Ṣaqqâra, on one side of which is inscribed a hymn to Osiris, while on the other appears the scribe Thunri praying to fifty-eight Egyptian kings, beginning with Miebis (1st Dyn.) and ending with Ramses II.; 6018, 6019. Two groups from Abydos, representing King Haremhab with Osiris, Isis, and Horus; 655. Fragmentary relief of men leading horses; 666. Memorial stone of Ramses II., referring to the working of a sandstone quarry near Heliopolis. By the stairs: 664. Granite statue of Ramses II.; 665. Statue of Thutmosis IV.; good reliefs of the New Empire.

Gallery N. Monuments of the New Empire and the later period. Sarcophagi in the form of mummies; statues of officials. — 674. Ramses III. holding a pole with the ram's head of Amun; 673. Statue of Amun; 675. Superb granite head from a colossal statue of Ramses II.; 682. Two arms from a colossal statue of Ramses II. at Luxor. — *Case A* (in the centre): 741. Bust of a princess, with well-preserved colouring, of the time of Ramses II.; *745, 746. Busts of a man and woman from Thebes; 42146. King as sphinx, holding a vessel with a ram's head. — *Case B.* Statuettes of the 19-20th Dyn.: 42142. Ramses II. kneeling to dedicate a table of offerings; 42163. Ramses-nakht, high-priest of Amun, dedicating three images of gods (Amun, Mut, Khons; comp. p. 95, No. 768). — *Case C.* Statuettes of the 22nd-25th Dyn.: 42197. King Osorkon kneeling to dedicate a (missing) boat; 848. Harmakhis, the first prophet of Amun; 846. A fat man; 42194. Sheshonk, high-priest of Amun and generalissimo, with an image of Isis. — *Case D.* Statuettes of the 26-30th Dyn. (Saïte): 890. Statuette of the priest Ahmose, probably of the early Ptolemaic period; 847. Statuette of Djedkhons-efonekh. — *Case E:* 822. Statuette of an abbess of Amun; statuette of Hor, prophet of Mont, in a squatting posture. — We now retrace our steps.

Room O. Chiefly monuments of the 19-20th Dynasties. 767. Group of Kay and Naya (19th Dyn.); 765. The gods Horus and Seth crowning Ramses III. (figure of Seth lacking), from Medînet Habu; 768. The high-priest Ramses-nakht, with Thoth sitting on his shoulder in the form of a cynocephalus; 743. Ramses VI. seizing a Libyan. — *Case A:* 744. Head of a king; 42153. Ramses III. holding an image of Amun; 42141. Ramses II. on his knees, under the protection of Amun. — 729. Upper part of the statue of a king (from Tanis, p. 182); 728. Two obelisks of Ramses II., praying cynocephali, and small chapel with a scarabæus and the god Thoth in the form of a cynocephalus, from Abu Simbel (p. 435); 725. Bust of King Menephthes (Merneptah); 724. Alabaster statue of Sethos I.

Monuments of the Later Period (712-332 B.C.).

Room Q ('Naos Room'). On the pillars of the entrance-wall are eight delicate reliefs in the style of the Ancient Empire, from tombs (870. The deceased watching the delivery of jewellery intended for him). By the walls, shrines of the gods (naoi) in granite. In the centre: 854-857. Table of offerings, statues of Osiris, Isis, Hathor in the form of a cow, and, in front of her, a man named Psamtik, all found in his tomb at Ṣaqqâra, good sculptures of the later period; right, *1185. Head of the Ethiopian king Taharka (the Tirhakah of 2 Kings xix. 9 and Isaiah xxxvii. 9), of a negro type; left, *1184. Head of a high official, with curious, probably negroid features; behind, 790. Parts of a chapel dedicated by Nektanebis I. (p. cx) in the temple of Ṣafṭ el-Ḥina (p. 192) near Bubastis (Zagazig), covered with texts and religious representations. — *791. Statue in green schist of Toëris, a goddess in the form of a hippopotamus, of marvellous workmanship, found at Karnak (26th Dyn.). — 795. Stele of Ptolemy I. Soter, found among the foundations of the mosque of Sheikhûn at Cairo (p. 76); it relates to a gift of lands to the gods of Buto (p. 34) and is dated in the 7th year of the nominal reign of Alexander II. (son of Alexander the Great), whose satrap Ptolemy calls himself; in front, 872. Fine statue of Neskenshuti, a high official.

By the pillars near Room R, which is used as a store: 850. Memorial stone of Nektanebis I., with a decree relating to the taxation of the Greek factories and to the imports of Naucratis, found in the ruins of that town (p. 34); *851. 'Pithom Stele', or memorial stone of King Ptolemy II. Philadelphus, from Tell el-Maskhûṭa (p. 192), recording his exploits and his benefactions to Egyptian temples.

Among the points mentioned are the facts that the king went to Persia and brought back to Egypt the images of gods which the Persians had carried off, and that he sent a fleet of four ships under a general to the S. parts of the Red Sea.

829. Fine vase of black granite, dedicated to the god Thoth by King Apries (26th Dyn.). Wall Cases A-D contain statuettes of the Saïte and Ptolemaic periods. — We retrace our steps.

Room S. Ethiopian monuments (comp. p. clxxxv). In the middle, *930. Alabaster statue of Princess Amenerdaïs (25th Dyn.; comp. p. 294). — 935. Statue of Mentemhēt (25th Dyn.). — 937. Stele of Piankhi (p. cviii), referring to his victories over the minor Egyptian princes; 938. Memorial stone of Tanutamun (p. cviii), referring to his campaign against the Assyrians and their vassals in Lower Egypt; 941. Stele of Harsiotef, referring to his victories over the Nubians; 939. Stele of King Espelut, referring to his accession. — By the pillar: 932. Statue of Osiris, dedicated by Nitocris, daughter of Psammetichos I.

Monuments of the Græco-Roman and Coptic Periods
(4th cent. B.C.-7th cent. of our era).

Gallery X, divided into three sections, contains monuments of the later period and of Ethiopian and Coptic art.

1st Section. 1180. Hathor column, dedicated by Apries to Neith; 1202. Water-spout in the form of a lion, in red sandstone. — *Cases A and B:* Clay tablets from El-'Amârna. – Two show-cases with funerary statuettes (ushabtis; p. cliv) and foundation deposits from the pyramids of the Ethiopian kings near Gebel Barkal, Nûri, Kurru, and Meroë (pp. 445-49). — *Case C:* Statuettes of the late period. — *Case D:* Foreign antiquities found in Egypt. — Under the window, 6054. Stelæ and statue with inscriptions in a peculiar hieroglyphic character, found in the Sinai peninsula. 1210. Roman emperor in the guise of Pharaoh. — Relief of Isis under the sycamore, from the temple of El-Maḥarraqa (p. 423).

Room T. Monuments of the Græco-Roman period (300 B.C.-A.D. 200). In the entrance: left, 997. High-relief of Emperor Antoninus Pius and his family (2nd cent.); right, 6021. Sarapis, Mithras, and Isis. — In the centre, 6022. Statue of a Roman orator, from Ihnâsya (p. 218).

In the show-case: *993. Marble head of a Galatian, an original Greek work of the beginning of the Ptolemaic period, from Rhodes; marble heads of Aphrodite. — 972. Black granite statue of an Egyptian official named Hor, in the Græco-Egyptian style; 973. Statue of a man bearing a naos with an image of the god Horus, from Mît Rahîna (p. 154).

By the rear wall: *Case A*, with Greek sculptures and tomb-stelæ. — 996. Black granite stele, surmounted by a head (2nd cent. of our era); 990. Mithraic reliefs from Mît Rahîna; 964. Lid of a money-box in the form of a snake, from the temple of Æsculapius at Ptolemaïs (p. 230).

N. wall. *983. The famous Decree of Canopus (p. 32), in three languages, found at Kôm el-Ḥiṣn (p. 34) in 1881.

The decree appears above in the ancient Egyptian language written in hieroglyphics, in the middle in the popular dialect written in the demotic character, and below in the Greek language and lettering. The decree was pronounced by an assembly of the priests in the temple of Canopus on March 7th (17th Tybi), 238 B.C., in the reign of Ptolemy III. Euergetes I.

It praises the king for having brought back the images of the gods from Asia, gained many victories, preserved peace in the land, and saved it from imminent famine by remitting taxes and importing corn. In token of gratitude a resolution is passed to institute new festivals in honour of the king and queen and their ancestors, to call all priests also 'priests of the divine Euergetæ', to found a new sacerdotal class to be named after Euergetes, and to introduce an improvement in the popular calendar (comp. p cxi) so that the festival of Euergetes may always be celebrated on the first day of the year as in the year of the decree. It is resolved also to pay permanent honour to the Princess Berenice, who died young, and to celebrate an annual festival to her memory. The inscriptions lastly declare that the decree is to be inscribed in the holy (hieroglyphic), the Egyptian (demotic), and the Greek languages.

Adjacent, a cast of the Rosetta Stone (p. 33); 980. Another copy of the Decree of Canopus, found at Tanis (p. 182) in 1866.

W. wall. *Case B.* *1010. Aphrodite wringing the water from her hair (from Alexandria, 2nd cent. B.C.). — 1016. Statue of a priest of Suchos, carrying a crocodile, the animal sacred to that god.

We return to Gallery X. 2nd Section. 1200. Relief from Luxor of Isis and Sarapis, the latter cutting the throat of a gazelle. — *Cases G and H:* Nubian antiquities of the Roman period, from Karanóg (p. 429), painted clay vessels, statuettes, etc. — 1220. Large niche from the monastery of Apa Apollo at Bâwîṭ (p. 224), with figures of the Virgin and Child, apostles, and saints.

3rd Section. Architectural fragments, capitals from Coptic monasteries; 1232. Niche with tombstone of a man.

Room V. Coptic monuments, tombstones, portions of buildings, fine capitals, and decorative friezes from the monastery of St. Jeremiah at Ṣaqqâra (p. 156) and the monastery at Bâwîṭ (p. clxxxvi), illustrating the transition from Byzantine to Arab ornament (comp. p. clxxxix). — 1130. Reader's seat (ambo) with six steps and a column on either side, from the monastery of St. Jeremiah. — 1116. Tombstone with the Virgin and Child between two angels.

Great Gallery *(Grande Galerie d'Honneur)*, East Wing. Four columns and an architrave from the temple of Augustus on the island of Philæ (p. 395); 982. Siren; 1241. Marble statue of a Roman woman; 1280. Statue of a governor of the colony of Naucratis (p. 34); 1281. Colossal statue of a Ptolemaic king, perhaps Alexander II. (p. cxi). — Large stone sarcophagi of the Saïte and Ptolemaic periods; 1294. Coffin of a dwarf, with his portrait on the adjacent lid; 1295, 1296. Statues of the god Ptah dedicated by Ramses II. in the temple of Memphis (p. 153). — For the W. wing, see p. 89.

We now ascend by the S.E. staircase to the upper floor.

B. Upper Floor.

Great Gallery *(Grande Galerie d'Honneur)*. On the landing of the S.E. staircase are coffins of the priests and priestesses of Amun. — By the pillars, 4940. Water-clock with astronomical figures; model of an ancient Egyptian villa; in front, a reproduction

of a chariot (original in the Archæological Museum at Florence). — The N. and S. wall-cabinets contain furniture, jewellery, vases, etc.

We turn to the right from the E. wing of the Great Gallery to enter the SOUTH BALCONY *(Salon Méridional).* *623. Two fine limestone sarcophagi of princesses, from Deir el-Baḥari, reliefs outside and paintings inside, in the clumsy style of the 11th Dyn.; wooden coffins of the Middle Empire, on some of which stand (in their original arrangement) models of ships, granaries, etc., and statuettes of attendants; 3108. Wooden coffin of the priest Iti. — *Cases A and E.* Two groups of soldiers from the tomb of a provincial prince at Asyûṭ: *3345. Forty Egyptians with shields and spears; *3346. Forty Nubians with bows and flint-pointed arrows. — *Case C:* 3347. Small boat and alabaster figure of the deceased. — *Case I:* 3000. Body of the battle chariot of Thutmosis IV. — *Case H.* Small figures of delicate workmanship in wood, faience, or bronze, of various periods: 4244. Ivory figurine of King Kheops; 4249, 4232. Heads of women; 4220. Gilded censer; 4221. Hippopotamus in blue faience (Middle Empire); seated figure of a king in red stone (Ancient Empire). — 4920. Part of a carved-wood shrine with figures of Thutmosis II.

The room to the S. of the principal gallery is occupied by the *Panthéon de l'Egyptologie*, with busts of famous Egyptologists and glass-cases with stone implements. — The adjoining room on the right contains the **Natural History Collections** *(Objets d'Histoire Naturelle):* mummies and skeletons of animals, remains of plants found in tombs, loaves. Note, in Case R, the skeleton of a horse, found in a large wooden coffin at Ṣaqqâra (20th Dyn.). On the walls, portions of a beautiful stucco pavement from a palace of Amenophis IV. at El-ʿAmârna (p. 246).

GALLERY A, entered from the W. wing of the principal gallery, contains wooden coffins of various periods (but mostly of the Middle Empire and the early part of the New Empire).

ROOM B. Earliest period. 3055. Large slate palette belonging to King Narmer-Menes, with reliefs of his victories, from Hierakonpolis (p. 369). — Between the cases, tombstones of kings of the earliest dynasties, from Abydos (p. 253).

Case A: Finds from the brick masṭaba near Naqâda (p. 233), including a lion in rock-crystal, a lion and hounds in ivory, and a small ivory tablet engraved with representations ('Menes Tablet'). — *Case B:* Objects from tombs of the earliest dynasties, stone vessels, lions and hounds in ivory, stone vessels with golden lids. — *Case C.* Objects from the royal tombs of Abydos, etc.; stone vessels; flint implements; copper utensils; slate palette, with bull's head and stars (from Gerza); 3054. Elegant alabaster vase, with ornamentation imitating the cord by which the vessel was carried; 3056. Seated figure of King Khasekhem (2nd Dyn.); 3072. Kneeling figure in granite. — *Cases D and E:* Vases of various stones; vases of black and red earthenware, flint knives, combs and toilet articles, from burial-places in Upper Egypt; 3059. Vessel of diorite (the ears of the vase, to which copper handles are attached, are plated with gold); 3062. Flint dagger with an engraved hilt of gold plate; 3063. Dagger with a gold handle; combs. — *Case F.* Vessels of painted clay. Desk-case with small vessels of stone and alabaster. Club-heads; bracelets. — *Case G:* Black-and-red

and painted clay vessels; palettes. — *Case H:* Tombstones of various persons, of dwarfs, and of favourite hounds, from the royal tombs at Abydos. — Between Cases H and I: 3052. Vase of red granite, with the figure of King Khasekhmui (3rd Dyn.). — *Cases I and J:* Clay stoppers for beer-jugs. — *Cases K and L:* Alabaster and stone vessels of fine workmanship, rock-crystal bowls, of the early Ancient Empire, from Ṣaqqâra. — Between Cases K and L: 3073. Large kneeling figure in limestone, from Hierakonpolis (p. 369).

Room C. Coffins and mummies of the Middle Empire. *Case H.* 3105. Mummy of Ament, a lady of the royal harem, with necklaces and tattooing (11th Dyn.). — In the centre: 38. Wooden coffins and wooden chest for the canopic jars of Prince Amenemmēs.

Room D. Funerary furniture, dating from the Ancient and Middle Empires.

Case A: Wooden models of boats which were used for pleasure-trips or for conveying the dead. — *Case B:* Wooden statuettes of female servants with offerings; 3123. Model of a kitchen yard (brewing); 3124. Potter's workshop; 3125. Joiner's workshop; 3126. Master and mistress of a house listening to a concert of singers and harpers. — *Case C:* 3137. Wooden box with bronze models of sacrificial vessels. Between Cases C and D: 3136. Model of a kitchen in which a butcher, a cook, and a brewer are at work. The two flat cases by the balustrade contain models of sacrificial objects (joints of meat and poultry). — *Case D:* *3155. Limestone statue of a harp-player (Middle Empire; see above, No. 3126); 3156, 3157. Small copper tables of offerings; head-rests; models of sacrificial geese. — *Case E.* Models of boats and granaries; kitchen yard; servants with sacrificial offerings; wooden and gilded models of sandals; head-rests. — *Cases F and G:* Wooden models of boats. — *Case H:* Boats; wooden figures; statuettes of servants; 3195, 3196. Two female servants, each with a basket on her head and a goose in her hand; 3194 Kitchen yard. — *Case I:* Boats, in one of which are soldiers with shields; models of granaries. — *Case J:* Brewery; figures of servants; woman grinding corn; oxen at pasture and at the plough; laden donkeys. — *Case K:* Figures of attendants; woman milling; brewer; baker; 3224. Man carrying baggage. In the middle: 3220. Wooden figure of a man in whose tomb at Mîr (p. 225) most of these figures were found (6th Dyn.). — *Case L.* Models of boats; models of the sacred boat of the sun (p. cxlix).

Pillar Room E. Coffins of the 22nd-26th Dyn., with fine painting (No. 3040 with jewellery painted on the breast).

Room F. *Funeral equipment, from tombs of the Middle Empire. *Case A:* 'Soul-houses', destined for the use of the dead, and models of granaries. — *Case B:* Alabaster canopic jars with men's heads, from Dahshûr. — *Case C:* Head-rests, funerary statuettes, small figures of apes, miniature tools. — *Case D:* Weapons and sticks. — *Case E:* Mummy-masks and wooden shields. — *Case F:* Wooden couch for a mummy; plates and dishes with imitation food; tables of offerings, in clay. — *Case G:* Tables of offerings and wooden boxes with pots of ointments. — *Case H:* Wooden swan; vessels and canopic jars in alabaster.

Objects from the tomb of a noble of the 11th Dyn., found near Deir el-Baḥari. — *Case I:* Three sailing boats, one of which is the cook's boat. — **Case J:* The deceased with his scribes and officials in an arbour, his herds driven in front of him. — *Case K:* Servant carrying a basket on her head. — **Case L:* Spinning and weaving women; joiner's workshop; porch of a house, with garden and pond. — *Case M:* Two ships with a drag-net; rowing boat and pilots, the deceased seated beneath a shelter, with an official discoursing to him; a similar boat with the crew hoisting the sail.

Room G. Funeral equipment, from tombs of the New Empire; ornaments and amulets of mummies.

Case B. Above, wooden sepulchral tablets, or stelæ, of the later period; head-rests; in the desk-case, scarabæi, which were laid on the breast of the mummy in place of the heart ('heart-scarabs'; p. clv). — *Case C.* Above, wooden sepulchral tablets; models of women, some lying on beds, the harem of the deceased. In the desk-case, heart-scarabs. — *Case E.* Above, wooden boxes for funerary statuettes; in the desk-case, heart-amulets; wax tablets with sacred eyes, which were laid on the dead at the spot where the incision was made for the embalming. — *Case G.* Above, wooden boxes for funerary statuettes. In the desk-case, tablets with sacred eyes (see above); falcons with outspread wings, placed on the breast of the mummy; small wax figures of the four deities protecting the entrails (p. clv). — *Cases I and J.* Funerary figures with agricultural implements, including one (No. 3381) in white and blue faience made for the vizier Ptahmose; 3380 A, 3380 B. Funerary figures in bronze, bearing the names of Amenmose and Herey; 3383. Bier with a mummy beside which is seated the soul; small coffins with funerary statuettes. — *Cases F and S.* 3376, 3505. Nephthys and Isis, laying their protecting hands on the (missing) mummy. — *Cases O, P, R, T, V, W:* Mummy-masks; objects inlaid in the cartonnage of mummies; nets and mummy-coverings in bead-work; small wooden coffins with falcons' heads, for the entrails of the deceased. In the desk-cases: Amulets; pectorals (breast tablets) in the form of little chapels; sacred eyes; amulets of the 'two fingers'; magic wands with curious representations.

Room H. *Finds from the tomb of the fan-bearer Mey-her-peri (p. 314; 18th Dyn.). *Case E:* Large rectangular wooden coffin, within it, a mummy-shaped wooden coffin, black, with gilding. — *Case F:* Gilded coffin. — *Case B:* Coffin with mummy. — *Case C:* 3806. Chest to hold canopic jars, shaped like a temple and standing on runners. — *Case I:* 3801 A, 3808. Two quivers of stamped red leather with lids; arrows; two dog-collars of reddish leather, with the animal's name; bracelets and necklaces; blue faience bowl; coloured glass vase; draughts board and men. — *Case A:* Wooden boxes with legs of veal, etc., for the sustenance of the deceased. — *Case H:* Alabaster canopic jars, earthenware jugs, etc. — *Case G:* 3820. Wooden bier, on the linen of which a figure of Osiris, god of the dead, has been covered with a layer of earth sown with barley. — By the walls: The *'Book of the Dead' (comp. p. 111) of Mey-her-peri, with coloured vignettes, one of the finest examples of its kind.

Finds from the tomb of Sennutem (p. 340). *Cases O and P:* Coffins of Sennutem and his relative Khonsu, on runners. — *Case J:* Coffin and mummy of Sennutem, with lid in the shape of the deceased's body. — *Case N:* Coffin and mummy of Êset, a female relative of Sennutem. — *Case K:* Chairs and stools; measures. — *Case M:* Funerary statuettes, chests, etc. — *Case L:* 4912. Painted leaf of the door of the tomb-chamber of Sennutem.

*Room I. Objects found in the royal tombs at Thebes (comp. p. 102). — *Case A:* Objects from the tomb of King Haremhab (p. 315), including 3840 A, B. Figure of Osiris with perforated base; alabaster lid of a canopic box with portrait of Haremhab; funerary figures of Haremhab. — *Case B:* Models of barks of the sun (p. cl). — *Case C.* Objects from the tomb of Thutmosis IV. (p. 314). Above: Cow's head,

vases, and ansated ('handled') crosses (☥; 'crux ansata'), in blue faience; 3738. Fragment of embroidery in the so-called Kelim technique, with lilies and the name of Thutmosis IV.; magic wands in blue faience. In the desk: blue glazed funerary statuettes and coffins for them. — Between Cases C and D is a stone box for the canopic jars of Thutmosis I. — *Cases D, E, F.* Objects from the tomb of Amenophis II. (p. 313). In Case D, above: Large cow's head and calf's head, carved in wood; vases in faience and glass. In the desk: Fragments of coloured glass vessels. Case E: Black wooden figures of the king; two wooden panthers; wooden vulture. In the desk: Magic wands and ansated crosses (see above) of blue faience. Case F, above: Wooden swan; wooden figures of kings and gods. In the desk: Blue faience vases in the shape of the ansated cross. In a show-case: *3610-3612. Three alabaster canopic jars, the lids of which bear portraits of Queen Nofretête (p. cv). — *Case G:* Objects from the tomb of Thutmosis III. Above: Wooden swan; papyrus. Below: Models of magic wands, tools, etc.

Case H. Above: Large wig; mummy of a child; canopic jars; in the desk, funerary statuettes in blue faience. — *Case I.* Above: Gazelle-shaped mummy box with an embalmed gazelle; wigs; in the desk, blue funerary statuettes. — *Case J.* Above: 3782. Wooden box for the funerary statuettes of King Pinutem (p. cvii); goblets in glass and faience; 3733. Wooden tablet with a decree in favour of Queen Nes-khons; 3785. Small coffer of wood and ivory with the name of Ramses IX. In the desk: Small coffin, in which a human liver was found; embalmed portions of sacrificial animals; fruit. — *Case K.* Above: 3794. Box in white basketwork with the wig of Queen Est-em-khebet (see below); 3792. Coffer of Queen Kemarē-Hatshepsut (18th Dyn.) with the entrails of another queen of the same name belonging to the 21st Dyn. (comp. p. 102, No. 3853); 3793. Marvellously fine piece of stuff from the mummy of Thutmosis III.; in the desk, faience goblet of Nes-khons; 3794 Mirror-case inlaid with the ivory figure of a nude girl. — *Case L.* Box of palm-leaves, for the offerings to Queen Est-em-khebet; wigs; pieces of fine linen from mummies.

Gallery J. Coffins of the later and Greek periods: 4275. Leaden coffin; *6036. Mummy-shaped wooden coffin of Petosiris, with hieroglyphics inlaid in coloured glass, from the tomb of Petosiris near Dirwa (p. 222); 4276. Gilded mummy-mask.

At the junction of Galleries J and K are desk-cases with scarabæi and three cases (A, B, and C) with collars and strings of beads, of various periods.

Royal Mummies.

Towards the close of the New Empire the power of the Egyptian state was no longer in a position to protect even the last resting-places of the dead. Not only the necropolis at Dirâ' Abu'n-Naga (p. 300), but even the secluded tombs in the Valley of Kings (p. 301) were plundered. The authorities contented themselves with rescuing the mummies of the ancient Pharaohs. Thus the bodies of nine kings were walled up in a side-chamber of the tomb of Amenophis II. For the same reason the mummy of Ramses II. was transferred from its tomb at Bîbân el-Mulûk (p. 304) to that of Sethos I., and later to the tomb of Amenophis I. Finally, towards the beginning of the 22nd Dyn., it was resolved to protect the royal mummies from further profanation by interring them all together, mixed pell-mell with the coffins of the priest-kings of the 21st Dyn., in an old tomb of the 11th Dyn. near

Deir el-Baḥari (p. 323). Thus at last the remains of the great monarchs of the New Empire — Amosis I., Thutmosis III., Sethos I., and Ramses II. — were left in peace until in 1875 the fellahin discovered their secret resting-place and the plundering of the mummies began again. In 1881 the modern thieves were traced, and their finds secured for the museum. It was not till 1898 that Victor Loret discovered the group of mummies in the tomb of Amenophis II.; and these were transferred to the museum in 1901. Comparatively few mummies of kings or their relatives have been discovered in their original tombs. — The royal mummies were withdrawn from the public gaze in 1928 and are now placed in a special room, admission to which is obtainable only by a permit from the Minister of Education (p. 56).

**Gallery K (comp. p. 89). Coffins of kings and members of the royal family of the 21st Dynasty. Note especially: *Case D*, 3858. Coffin of Queen Notmet, mother of the priest-king Herihor, with faience inlay; *Case B*, 3853. Coffin with the mummies of Kemarē, wife of Pinutem I., and her still-born daughter; in the centre, 6026. Coffin of a royal prince, perhaps a son of Ramses III.

North Portico *(Salon Septentrional). Case O:* 3877. Lid from the coffin of Ramses II.; 3872. Coffin of Queen Ahhotep, wife of Amenophis I. (18th Dyn.); 3892. Coffin of Queen Ahmes-Nofreteroy, mother of Amenophis I.; 3881. Coffin-lid of Sethos I (see p. 105).

Finds from the Tomb of Queen Hetep-heres, mother of Kheops (p. 141). *Case I:* 6041. Carrying-chair of the queen (only the gold is original, the wooden framework being a reconstruction). — *Case II:* 6042. Alabaster jars. — *Case III:* 6043. Three golden vases, two golden razors, and various other objects of gold; 6044. Copper washing utensils; 6045. Copper tools; 6046. Wooden box (modern) with eight small alabaster jars for fine oils and eye-cosmetics, and a copper spoon.

*Coffins and funerary furniture from the tomb (p. 315) of Yu'e, father-in-law of Amenophis III., and his wife Tu'e. *Case A:* 3680. Bed with representations of the deities Bes and Toëris; 3613, 3679. Two beds with well-preserved stringing. — *Cases C-F:* 3666-3669. Four wooden coffins of Yu'e, which were placed one within the other, the outermost resting on a sledge, the three mummiform inner ones gilded and inlaid with glass paste. — *Case G:* 3614, 3615. Two biers, on the linen of which the figures of Osiris were outlined in sown barley (comp. p. 100 No. 3820). — ***Case H:* 3676. Chariot of Tu'e; 3672. Wooden arm-chair with decoration of women's heads, well-preserved string-plaiting, and, on the back, Princess Sitamun receiving the 'gold of the southern countries'; 3673, 3674. Child's chairs belonging to Princess Sitamun; 3677, 3678. Two jewel-coffers richly adorned with enamel and bearing the name of Amenophis III. — *Case I:* Funerary furniture. 3651. Wig-box made of rushes, in the form of a house; dummy vases, in wood, painted to simulate various stones; painted wooden chest; sandals; death-masks; funerary statuettes; 3647. Mummy on a bier; decorated staff. — *Case J.* Above, wooden boxes with mummified articles of food; sandals. Below, boxes for canopic jars; canopic jars of alabaster, with

men's heads; 3662. Alabaster jar; funerary statuettes. — *Cases N-P:* 3705, 3704, 3671. Three coffins of Tu'e, the innermost richly gilded, with inscriptions and ornamentation inlaid in coloured glass and stones, the outermost with an arched lid and standing on a sledge.

Jewellery.

**Room L (Jewel Room) contains the Egyptian jewellery, illustrating the art of working in gold and other metals from the earliest times down to the Græco-Roman and Byzantine eras.

Case 1 (at the N.W. corner): Jewellery of the 1st Dyn. (4005. Ox, 4006. Antelope), already of excellent workmanship, from Nagʿ ed-Deir (p. 231). — *Case 2.* Ancient Empire: 4000-4003. Four bracelets from the tomb of King Djer at Umm el-Gaʿâb (p. 260; 1st Dyn.). — *Case 3:* *4010. Golden hawk's head with inserted eyes, from a copper figure of a hawk (6th Dyn.), from Hierakonpolis (p. 369).

In Cases 4-6 is the ****Treasure of Dahshûr**, which was discovered by Jacques de Morgan in 1894-95 in the tombs of various princesses of the 12th Dyn. near the pyramids of Dahshûr (p. 177), and shows the work of the Egyptian goldsmiths at its very best.

Case 4. Jewels of King Hor and Princess Nebhetepti-khrod: 3986, 3987. Two golden hawks' heads, necklace-clasp; 3990. Portions of a flail in semi-precious stones. — Jewels of Princess Sit-Hathor-Yunut: 3983. Gold pectoral or breast-tablet inlaid with stones (with the name of Sesostris II. between two hawks); 3965. Gold shell inlaid with a lotus-flower; 3982. Gold pendant inlaid with stones, in the form of two water-lilies tied together, from which a sistrum (rattle) depends; scarabæi; 3976-3981. Six gold lions; gold shells from chains. — Jewels of Princess Mereret: Silver mirrors; gold necklace with pendent shells, larger gold shells and double lion-heads, from chains; 3970. Golden pectoral inlaid with stones (above, the goddess Nekhbeyet in the form of a vulture; below, the cartouche of Sesostris III.; on either side, a griffin representing the king trampling on his Asiatic enemies); 3971. A similar pectoral (above, the vulture; below, right and left, Amenemmēs III. smiting a kneeling Asiatic with his mace); 3968, 3969. Two gold bracelet-clasps with the name of Amenemmēs III.; gold necklaces and portions of necklaces, including numerous admirably worked examples; scarabæi in semi-precious stones; rings with scarabæi.

Case 5. Jewels of Princesses Khnumet and Ite: Dagger with inlaid hilt and pommel of lapis lazuli; *3925, 3926. Two golden crowns inlaid with stones, one consisting of a net of gold threads held by six flower-ornaments and adorned with forget-me-nots, the other of rosettes and lyre-shaped ornaments. To the latter belong two other ornaments, a hovering vulture and a golden branch. 3901-3904. Four gold necklaces of the finest workmanship, one (No. 3902) adorned with a butterfly, another (3901) with stars;

3904. Chain with pendants (blue plaquette with a cow, stars in the granular technique); 3905-3909. Pendants of gold with hieroglyphics inlaid in stone. Bracelets of gold beads, chains, etc.

Case 6. Jewels of Princess Ite-weret: 3945. Large pectoral; necklaces; bracelets; small golden razors.

Case 7: Chains. — *Case 8.* *Jewels from a princess's tomb near the pyramid of El-Lâhûn (p. 207): 3999. Gold diadem with bands; 3998. Pectoral with the cartouche of Amenemmēs III.; 3997. Mirror with Hathor's head in gold. — *Case 9.* Metalwork of the Middle Empire; chains; 4012. Inscribed dagger of the Hyksos period (p. civ).

Case 10. ****Jewels and Funerary Furniture of Queen Ahhotep** (p. civ), mother of Kemose and Amosis, which were found in 1859 with the mummy of the queen at Dirâʿ Abu'n-Naga (p. 300). 4031. Necklace with three large flies; 4039. Double-hinged bracelet, with delicately engraved figures on blue enamel, representing (twice) King Amosis kneeling with the earth-god Geb behind him, and two falcon-headed and two dog-headed genii; 4052-4054. Gold bracelets and anklets. 4055. Dagger and sheath, both of gold; the hilt is adorned with gold and semi-precious stones, while the pommel is formed of four female heads; the junction of blade and hilt is artistically covered with the head of a bull; the centre of the blade is inlaid with fine damascening. 4056, 4057. Two daggers of simpler style; 4043. The queen's mirror. — 4049. Golden boat, on a small wooden carriage with bronze wheels, the crew in silver; 4040. Diadem with the cartouche of Amosis and two sphinxes. — 4035. Ceremonial axe, with handle of cedar-wood covered with gold-leaf and inscribed with the cartouche of Amosis, the blade being of gold inlaid with blue paste; 4038. Pectoral inlaid with stones (the gods Amon-Rē and Rē-Horus, in a bark, pour over Amosis the water for his purification; on either side are hawks); 4036. Gold chain with two golden goose-heads as clasp and a gold scarabæus inlaid with blue paste as pendant; 4041, 4044, 4045. Three bead bracelets belonging to Amosis; 4046. Gold bracelet with a hovering vulture. — 4030. Silver boat with crew; 4037. Elaborate breast-ornament formed of rows of knots, flowers, lions, antelopes, etc., with two hawk's heads at the ends; 4042. Fan-handle of wood covered with sheet gold.

Case 11. ***Gold Treasure of the 19th Dynasty**, found in 1906 at Zagazig (Bubastis, p. 181). 4214, 4215. Two gold vases; *4216. Silver vase with a gold handle in the form of a goat; 4217. Silver bowl with beautiful ornamentation; 4218. Lotus-shaped gold cup with the name of Queen Tewosret; 4212, 4213. Two gold bracelets with the name of Ramses II.; necklaces, ear-rings, etc.

Case 12: Silver objects (19th Dyn.). — *Cases 13* and *14* contain the ***Gold Ornaments of Queen Teye** (18th Dyn.) **and Queen Tewosret** (19th Dyn.), found by Theodore M. Davis (comp. p. 315) in 1907 and 1908 at Bîbân el-Mulûk (pp. 315, 308). *Case 13:* 4190, 4191. Collars of Queen Teye, one in the form of a vulture, the other with

rows of gold beads. — *Case 14:* 4192. Crown of Tewosret, consisting of fifteen blossoms; 4193. Two large ear-rings with the name of King Siptah; 4199. Necklace of pierced gold beads.

Case 15: Pectorals of the 20th-21st Dyn.; small golden images, of deities; 4060. Ear-rings with the cartouche of Ramses XII.; 4064, 4065. Bracelets from the mummy of Pinutem I. — *Case 16:* Diadem with the uræus (p. cli); large scarabæi (22nd Dyn.). — *Case 17:* Golden images of deities, amulets, and jewellery, found with a mummy of the 26th Dyn. at Hauwâra (p. 205). — *Case 18:* Gold and silver finger-rings, some with scarabæi. — *Case 19:* Ear-rings.

Case 20: Portions of mummy-wrappings, amulets, and images, of the later period; 4115. Golden mummy-mask of the royal admiral Tjenhebu, from Saqqâra (p. 176).

Case 21: Mummy-ornaments and amulets of Tjenhebu. — *Case 22:* Silver vessels found in the ruins of Mendes (p. 183), probably used in a temple. — *Case 23:* Ptolemaic jewellery.

Case 24. ****Treasure of Tûkh el-Qarâmûs**, found in 1905 and 1906 about $2^1/_2$ M. to the S.W. of Abu Kebîr (p. 182), dating from c. 300 B.C.: 4172. Large bracelet in the form of a snake, with a large shaped ruby on the head; 4177. Bracelet, the clasp of which imitates a tied knot, exuberantly adorned with gold wire; 4173, 4175. Two small bracelets, at the ends of which are winged sphinxes in the Hellenistic style; 4174, 4176. Two gold armlets or anklets, ending in the heads of fabulous animals resembling deer; 4170. Necklace with two griffins' heads. — 4178. Figures of gods; 4171. Necklace, with falcons' heads. Silver dishes, bowls, and cups.

Case 25: Græco-Roman jewellery.

Gallery M. Royal coffins, mostly from Deir-el-Bahari (continuation of Gallery K). 3874. Coffin of Amenophis I. (comp. below, No. 3868); 3886. Coffin of Kemose (found at Dirâʿ Abu'n-Naga in 1860). — *Case T:* 3888. Gilded lid of the coffin of Queen Ahhotep (p. 104). — *Case V:* 3895. Coffin of Siamûn, son of Amosis I.; 3894. Coffin of Amosis I.; 3893. Coffin of King Sekenyenrē (with shattered skull; p. civ). — *Case U:* 3891, 3890, 3889. Coffins of Thutmosis II., Thutmosis III., and Thutmosis I. — *Case I:* 3868. Coffin-lid of Amenophis I. (comp. above, No. 3874). — *Case R:* 3884. Coffin of a daughter of King Amosis I.; 3883. Coffin-lid of Sethos I. (see p. 102); 3882. Coffin of Thutmosis IV.

The ****Finds from the Tomb of Tutankhamûn** (pp. cvi, 315) are shown in Galleries M, N, R, and T (Cases 1-28, 43-62, and A-I) and in the room to the N. of Gallery M (Cases 29-42).

The tomb was discovered by Howard Carter in the Valley of the Kings in Nov. 1922. Its contents are among the finest productions of Egyptian craftsmanship, the artistic value of the gold and precious objects far surpassing all other hoards while the collection of furniture is the finest ever discovered. — Only about a half of the treasure is exhibited in the museum, many objects being still in the laboratory at Thebes. Its arrangement therefore is provisional and subject to alterations.

Case 1: 16. Wooden bust of the king. — *Case 2:* 20. Ebony bedstead (on the foot-panel, the god Bes and lion-goddesses). — *Case 2a:* 530. Gold-plated bedstead. — *Case 3:* 221. Large couch of gilded wood, the sides carved in the form of two fabulous animals with the heads of hippopotami, the bodies of serpents, and the feet of lions. — *Case 3a:* 521. A second couch, similar to No. 221, supported by cows. — *Case 4:* 95. Bed. — *Cases 5 and 6:* 96, 181. Two lifesize wooden statues of the king, which stood like sentinels in front of the tomb-chamber. — *Case 7:* *98. Chariot-body of gilded wood, with representations of prisoners and of the king in the form of a sphinx trampling on his enemies. — *Case 8:* 97. Chariot-body, similar to No. 98, made of gilded wood with coloured glass inlay, representations of prisoners, and, on the front, the names of the king and his consort. — *Cases 9 and 10:* 99, 100. Chariot-wheels; 113-116. Disks armed with spikes, pieces of harness. — *Case 11:* 101-110. Axles, yokes, and other chariot-parts; 111, 112. Two gilded hawks with the sun's disk on their heads, probably from the outer ends of the poles of a royal chariot. — *Case 12:* 13. Wooden casket with blue faience inlay and gilded ornaments; 15. Folding stool of ebony with ivory inlay, gold mountings, seat imitating an animal's skin, and legs terminating in ducks' heads. — *Case 13:* Gilded walking-sticks with curved ends, No. 175 with two enemies (Asiatic and negro) bound together at the knees, Nos. 176 and 179, similar. — *Case 14:* 6-9. Two-handled alabaster vases with the heraldic plants of Upper and Lower Egypt (p. cii); 185. Alabaster vase with handles in the form of Nile-gods carrying the heraldic plants of Lower and Upper Egypt. — *Case 15:* 189-191, 197. Sticks of the finest workmanship, with gold and ivory inlay; *187. Fan-handle covered with sheet gold, decorated with representations of the king hunting ostriches; 125, 186. Bronze and silver trumpets. — *Case 16.* Alabaster vases and box: *184. Alabaster lamp (the design, which shows through, depicts the queen standing in front of the king; the handles are in the form of papyrus plants with the god of eternity); 11. Alabaster lotus-shaped wishing cup; 12. Box with inlaid wreath designs (on the lid, the king's titles between two bunches of flowers); 182. Alabaster lamp, formed of lotus flowers and foliage; *183. Cylindrical alabaster box with prisoners' heads on the feet (on the sides, two columns surmounted by heads of Bes; on the lid, a recumbent lion; around the casket runs an extremely lifelike representation of a hound and a lion chasing desert animals). — *Case 17:* 188. Gilded fan-handle with coloured inlay; *195. Golden staff with the figure of the young king; 196. Similar staff in silver; 216. Golden ceremonial stick. — *Case 18:* *14. Wooden shrine overlaid with sheet gold (scenes from the intimate life of the royal pair, in the ʿAmârna style). — *Case 19:* 22. Child's chair, with figures of antelopes on the arms; 23. Footstool belonging to No. 22; 24. Child's chair. — *Case 20:* *324. Wooden casket, adorned with the finest miniature paintings, artistic-

ally one of the most valuable finds. On the vaulted lid: right, the king hunting desert animals; left, hunting lions; on the right side of the chest, a battle with Asiatics; left, a battle with negroes; at the ends, the king as sphinx, trampling on his enemies. — *Case 21:* *1. Throne with figures of the king and queen inlaid in coloured stones on the back, and arms formed of crowned and winged serpents; 2. Footstool with representations of prisoners. — *Case 22:* *3. Chair of cedar-wood with gold mounts and a representation of the god of eternity on the back; 4. Footstool resembling No. 2 (see above). — *Case 23:* 21. Linen-chest with the names of the king and queen; 25. Wooden stool with openwork pattern symbolizing the union of Upper and Lower Egypt; 26. Stool. — *Case 24:* 5. Cedar-wood chest with ebony and ivory inlay. — *Case 25:* 94. White-washed chest; 337-340. The king's gloves, of linen fabric. — *Case 25bis:* Alabaster jars. — *Case 26:* 18, 19. Small shrine with the figure of a serpent-shaped deity; 332, 333. Shrine and serpent, resembling Nos. 18, 19. — *Case 27:* 117-135. Staves, bows, etc., some of them marvellously decorated with patterns in filigree work; 123. Curved stick with the name of the king and hunting scenes, partly in the granular technique; 127. Bow with the heads of captives at each end; 132. Whip-stock of ivory with inlaid inscription. — In the show-case in front: 441. Bow-case of wood, overlaid with bark, gilded and adorned with hunting scenes; 514. Gold mounted reed, cut (according to the inscription) by the king's own hand; 520. Double bow, of composite construction. — *Case 27bis:* 522-524. Bows; 525-528. Sticks; four gold-plated whips. — *Cases 28 and 28bis:* 168-171. Pieces of gilded wood imitating rolls of linen.

Cases 29-42, placed in a separate room (comp. p. 105), contain the king's coffins and jewellery. — *Case 29.* 219. The innermost or third **Coffin of the King** (comp. pp. 108, 316), made of solid gold and shaped like a mummy, a work of unparalleled splendour and sumptuousness. Upon the forehead, the vulture and serpent (Nekhbeyet and Buto, Upper and Lower Egypt), symbols of royalty, in gold and lapis lazuli inlaid with faience; the arms, worked in the round, are crossed over the breast, while the hands hold a flail and a crook; encircling the abdomen are the protective vulture and serpent goddesses Nekhbeyet and Buto with outspread wings. The coffin is most delicately chased with inscriptions, figures of Isis and Nephthys with wings outspread over the legs, and designs imitating a feather covering. The weight of the coffin is about $4^1/_2$ cwt., and the value of the gold 31,500*l.* — *Case 30:* 312-316. Collars from the king's mummy, with the symbols of Upper and Lower Egypt (vulture and falcon, winged serpent), Nos. 312 and 313 being of chased gold; 314. Flexible ornament composed of thirty-eight gold plaquettes with polychrome glass inlay; 315, 316. Similar ornaments, but even finer and more elaborate. — *Case 31:* 318-323. Six pectoral-collars in chased sheet gold, resembling Nos. 312 and 313 (see above). — *Case 32:*

220. The *Golden Mask of massive burnished gold, inlaid with precious stones and polychrome glass. It was placed on the head and shoulders of the mummy inside the golden coffin (p. 107) and reproduces the king's features exactly; the eyes are inlaid with lapis lazuli, white and black stone. The head-dress is adorned with the vulture and serpent; on the breast is a wide collar ending in two hawks' heads, inlaid with lapis lazuli. The hieroglyphic text on the back of the mask contains a chapter of the 'Book of the Dead' (p. 111) relating to mummy-masks. — 265. Beard belonging to the mask; 266. Necklace with a scarabæus of resin; 267. Necklace made of three rows of thin disks, from the mask. — *Case 33:* Finger-rings of gold and stone, some with scarabæi, others with religious representations or the king's names; golden bracelets with fine ornaments. — *Case 33bis:* *225. Golden dagger, the sheath adorned with representations of wild animals in the Mycenæan style; 226. Iron dagger with rock-crystal pommel and sheath decorated with a flower design; 227-232. Gold necklets with beautiful pendants in the shape of a vulture, a falcon, the king's name, and the mystic eye. — *Case 34.* Scarabs, necklaces, amulets; 86. Sceptre of gold and blue glass; 65. Superb scarabæus with a representation of the king being guided by the gods Atum and Harakhte; 84. Gold pendant, the king's first name formed of three characters (scarabæus, sun, basket); 85. Necklace, to which is attached a pendant representing the king supported by a serpent-goddess (Wert-hekew); *224. Golden pectoral in the form of the soul-bird (p. cliv) with the king's portrait, taken from the mummy; 233. Uræus serpent in gold and polychrome glass; 66, 83. Plaques of perforated sheet gold. — *Case 34bis:* Gold rings, bracelets, and amulets. — *Case 35:* 317. The king's gold diadem, adorned with the vulture and serpent (comp. p. 107); 258, 259. The strips of gold by which the hair-bag was attached to the skull of the mummy; 223. Small gold perfume-box in the form of two royal cartouches, with coloured inlay and silver base; 445. Chain with a golden figure of the king seated on the ground, a charming piece. — *Case 36:* *222. Inner or second coffin of wood covered with sheet gold, which contained the golden coffin (p. 107) and is decorated with a feather pattern in polychrome glass, the arms and abdomen being protected by the patron-goddesses of Upper and Lower Egypt in the form of vultures. — *Case 37:* 327. Golden sandals from the mummy's feet; 328-331. Gold sheaths from the fingers and toes of the mummy. — *Case 38:* *17. Wooden funerary figure, a portrait of the king. — *Case 39:* 336. Strips of gold placed over the mummy-wrappings. — The jewels exhibited in Cases 40 and 41 were found in caskets placed in the treasury of the tomb (comp. p. 316). *Case 40.* *Bracelets; rings; chains with breast-ornaments of the finest workmanship and in the best taste: 342. Falcon with outspread wings; 344. Sun-god in the form of a scarabæus, seated in the boat of the sun between two baboons representing the moon-god; 345. The

king between Ptah and Sakhmet; 347. The goddess Nekhbeyet in the form of a vulture with outspread wings; 350. Sun-god in the form of a scarabæus in his boat. — Case 41: *363-367. Ear-rings; 368. Pendant consisting of a scarab of lapis lazuli between two uræi; 369-376. Pectorals in the form of ships, which are occupied by divine figures; 379. Papyrus-polisher of ivory and gold; 380-383. Scribe's palettes; 383. Case for writing reeds in the form of a palm-column. — *Case 42:* 403, 406. Sceptres; 404, 405. Flails; *452. Miniature gold coffin, one of the four from the canopic chest containing the viscera of the king.

Case 43: 407-411. Statuettes in gilded wood of the king standing upon a flat boat and throwing a harpoon (No. 407), carried on the head of a goddess (No. 408), and standing on the back of a leopard (No. 410). — *Case 44:* 412-419. Images of deities in gilded wood. — *Case 45:* 395. Head of a cow. — *Cases 46 and 47:* Statuettes of deities. — *Case 48:* *396. Box in the form of a cartouche, with the king's name on the lid (hieroglyphics in ebony and coloured ivory); *397. Wooden box with ebony and ivory inlay, of the finest workmanship. — *Case 49:* Casket of ivory and gilt wood, with the king's titles in full detail. — *Case 50:* 459. Painted wooden model of the royal boat, with rigging. — *Case 51:* 462-469, 472-475. Funerary statuettes (shabti) of the king with various crowns and head-dresses, inscribed with the 6th chapter of the Book of the Dead. — *Case 52:* *454-457. Four statuettes of the tutelary goddesses Isis, Nephthys, Selket, and Neith, in gilt wood, which stood at the four sides of the shrine enclosing the canopic chest (exhibited here provisionally). — *Case 53:* 460. Model boat of painted wood. — *Case 54:* Bier with the image of Anubis, in the form of a jackal, lying on a shrine of gilt and painted wood; it contained jewellery, the faience amulets shown in Case F (p. 110), etc. — *Case 55:* *448. Ostrich-feather fan with ivory handle and the inlaid name of the king. — *Case 56:* Nest of three small wooden coffins, the innermost of which contained a lock of Queen Teye's hair. — *Case 57:* *Alabaster lids from the four canopic jars with portrait-heads of the king; the jars are not separate but form part of the canopic chest which is not yet exhibited. — *Case 58:* 533. Ivory head-rest in the form of a deity supporting the heavens, with two recumbent lions; 534. Head-rest in the form of a folding chair, decorated with grotesque heads of Bes and with legs ending in goose feet; 531. Head-rest of pale-blue glass; 532. Head-rest of dark-blue faience; 577, 580, 581, 586. Scribes' palettes. *535. Alabaster table-decoration in the form of a boat floating on a lake, on a stand inlaid with red and blue paste; it is decorated with ibex heads and contains the figures of a seated girl and a female dwarf. — *Case 59:* Alabaster jars. — *Case 60:* 543-548. Alabaster ointment pots with inlaid designs (No. 544 in the shape of a lion-headed demon). — *Case 61:* 537, 538. Curved swords; 560. Fire-drill; 565. State sandals; 568. Tool (a sort of chisel) with the king's

name in gold inlay; 575. Cushion with bead embroidery; Bread, with a net used to shape it. — *Case 62:* Coronation robe of the king, with embroidery. — *Case A:* Vases of alabaster, rings and armlets, amulets, models of tools; 87, 88. Head-rests; cosmetic boxes, vases of glass and faience, etc.; 143. Wine-strainer; 192. Wooden symbol of Osiris (p. clviii). — *Case B:* Fine vases and cups of dark-blue faience; 174. Basket filled with fruit of the dûm-palm (p. lxxviii); 173. Box made of papyrus rushes; 54-59. Cubit-rods, each measuring 20 in.; 193. Two small shrines covered with black resin containing vessels and an amulet, 194. Wooden swan, covered with black resin; 172. Peculiar emblem in the form of a vase between two pylons. — *Cases C & D:* Models of boats. — *Case E:* 89. Ivory casket of the best workmanship; 31, 32. Sistra (rattles); 217, 218. Maces of gilded wood; 27-30. Bronze torch-holders in the form of the 'life' character (p. cxxxviii); 90. Ointment-box in the shape of a goose; 92. Lid of a casket with the crouching figure of a princess; 64, 74, 80. Small crouching figures of the king with his finger in his mouth; 93. Toilet-casket in cedar-wood. — *Case F:* 435, 436. Emblems of Anubis (rods with animals' skins, on alabaster stands); 401. Small basket with a representation of the king among the gods; amulets and images of deities in blue faience. — *Case G:* 446. Hand-mill; 449. The king lying on a bier supported by lions, with his falcon-headed and human-headed souls at his side (a 'cenotaph' presented by the official Meye); *453. Casket with the finest ebony and ivory inlay; 476-478. Funerary statuettes. — *Case H:* 612-640. Boomerangs of wood, faience, and ivory, some meant for use (apparently of the Australian type), others merely funerary gifts; 573. Sickle; castanets with the names of Queen Teye and Princess Merit-Aton; 558 seqq. Sham vases of blue faience; *540. Gaming board with a stand in the form of a bed with lions' feet; 541, 542. Small ivory gaming boards; 566. Finely ornamented gaming board of ivory. — *Case I:* 502-504. Wine-jars with the vintage year marked in the hieratic script; 499-501. Decorated vases.

Room O. North Wall: Coffins, mummies, portraits and masks from mummies of the Roman period; 4312. Small shrine with the portrait of a girl. — South Wall, *Cases H-M* (comp. p. clxxxix): Mummy-masks; *Mummy-portraits (in Case J, portrait of a man and wife). *Case C:* 4270. Large wooden shield.

Room P. Figures of gods and sacred animals. Note, 4752. Squatting figure of Djed-Hor in black granite, with inscriptions; in front, a protective stele with Horus upon the crocodiles. — In the doorway leading to the outer gallery: 4750. Large protective stele, Horus upon the crocodiles; votive inscription to Shedu, god of hunting, and Isis, from El-ʿAmârna.

Room Q. Funerary papyri; drawings on splinters of limestone; sculptors' models and statues at various stages of execution.

In the entrance, right, 4371. Plan of a royal tomb (probably that of Ramses IX.). — In the desks by the N. wall: 4785. Wrestlers; 4784. King in a battle; 4783. A fight with arrows between a king and a queen in chariots.

Room S. Papyri, mostly 'Books of the Dead' (i.e. texts and spells referring to the life after death; pp. 301, 302), which were placed in the tomb with the mummy; some of them have beautiful coloured drawings. *Case A:* Writing implements.

Gallery T. Finds from the tomb of Tutankhamûn (see p. 105 seqq.).

Room U *(Salle Civile).* Tools, weapons, games and toys, architectural fragments, objects used in daily life, etc. By the entrance, ceiling and wall paintings. — **Show Case:* Ointment-boxes in the shape of animals; anointing spoons, with handles in the form of bunches of flowers, figures of girls, etc.

Case A (desk): Faience inlay from temple and palace walls. — *Case B.* Tools: wall-clamps, mallets, levels, chisels, etc. — *Case C:* Tools; bronze door-hinges (one with the name of Piankhi), etc. — *Case D:* Bronze bolts in the form of lions, twibills (5205), chisels. — *Case E:* Musical instruments, mirrors. — *Case F:* Wooden boxes, mirrors, kohl vases, combs. — *Case G:* Cosmetic boxes, anointing spoons and ointment vases, often in human or animal shapes; *5323. Cosmetic pot in the form of a kneeling man with a jar on his shoulder. — *Show Case:* Castanets. — In the doorway, lion-bolts from temple doors. — *Case H:* Ointment vases, mirror and fan handles. — *Case I:* Games, toys, draughts, dolls, and balls. — *Cases J and K:* Weapons. — Between Cases K and L: 5460. Sledge for transporting a coffin, from the tomb of Ramses V. at Thebes. — *Case L:* Agricultural and weaving implements. — *Case M:* Weights and measures; 5510. Alabaster vessel with the name of Thutmosis III. (according to the inscription its capacity is 21 'hin', a hin being 4/5 pint); 5512. Weight in the form of a calf's head with the name of Sethos I.; 5511. Hemispherical weight with the name of Taharka. In the desk, ointment vases in the form of animals. — *Case N:* Architectural models. In the desk, faience tiles with representations of fettered enemies.

Room V. Small Græco-Roman works of art.

Case A: Stamps, etc. — *Case B:* Bronze figures. — *Case C:* Terracotta figures from Alexandria. — *Case P:* Portions of furniture in bronze. — *Case D:* Greek vases; terracotta figures of the Roman period; ivory carvings (parts of boxes). — *Case E:* Græco-Egyptian terracotta statuettes, important as illustrations of popular religion in the Roman period. — *Case F:* Lamps and lanterns. — *Case H:* Glass vessels. — *Case I:* Græco-Egyptian terracotta figures. — *Case J:* Faience of the Græco-Roman period; 5653, 5654. Two triangular pediments of wood with figures of Sirens in painted and gilded stucco (belonging to coffin No. 4278, of the Ptolemaic period). — *Case K:* Bronze lamps and candelabra; vase-handles. — *Case L:* Mummy-labels with the names of the deceased. — In the centre are *Cases M* (bronze figures), *N* (glass), and *Q* (faience).

Room X contains Christian, i.e. Coptic antiquities (5-7th cent.).

By the walls between the cases are coloured textiles and painted clay vessels. *Case B:* Lamps. — *Cases C and D:* Bronze vessels. — *Case E:* Wooden or metal utensils, writing implements. — *Case G:* Consecration crosses, armlets, etc. — *Case H:* Wooden castanets; ivory carvings; ivory comb with reliefs. — *Case I:* Architectural fragments in carved wood. — *Case J:* Wood-carvings; iron helmet. — *Case K:* Fragments of mural paintings; stamps for consecrated bread. — *Case L:* Textiles with figures of dancing girls. In the desk, musical instruments, swords, writing implements, shoes, and aprons. — *Case M:* Painted vases; plaques with consecration crosses (No. 5773 in silver, with the name of a Bishop Abraham).

5. The Environs of Cairo.

I. Old Cairo, the Island of Rôḍa, and Fusṭâṭ.

Tramways (Nos. 1 and 15), see pp. 40, 41. — Those who wish to visit only the *Qaṣr esh-Shamʿ* (p. 114) may take the Ḥelwân railway as far as the station of St-Georges (p. 177).

Through the quarter of Ismâʿîlîya to the *Qaṣr el-ʿAini* (Pl. C, 6), see pp. 54-56. — Thence the *Shâriʿ Qaṣr el-ʿAini* goes on to the *Mîdân Fumm el-Khalîg*, where the city canal *El-Khalîg* (filled in at the end of the 19th cent.) formerly diverged from the *Saiyâlet er-Rôḍa*, or small arm of the Nile separating the island of Rôḍa from the E. bank. On the right is the scene of the annual festival of the 'Cutting of the Dam' (p. c).

To the S.E. of the Shâriʿ es-Sadd el-Barrâni, which begins at the Mîdân Fumm el-Khalîg, are the *Christian Cemeteries* (Pl. C D 7, 8; Armenian, Coptic, Roman Catholic, Protestant). The first is the Old British Protestant Cemetery. — At the junction of the Shâriʿ es-Sadd el-Barrâni and the Shâriʿ ed-Diyûra stands the *Mosque of Sîdi Muḥammed eṭ-Ṭîbi*, about 100 yds. to the S. of which lies the entrance (between the Armenian and Coptic cemeteries) of the **Deir Mâri Mina**, or monastery of St. Menas (p. 30), a brick-walled enclosure containing the *Church of St. Menas* (Pl. D 7), founded in the 4th cent. and restored in the 15th (comp. p. cxc).

Beyond the Mîdân Fumm el-Khalîg rises the *Head of the Old Aqueduct* (Pl. C 7, 8; p. 124), constructed of masonry in an hexagonal form, 151 ft. in diameter. — The main road, here called *Shâriʿ Maṣr el-Qadîma* (Pl. C 8), skirts the Nile. A road, diverging to the right viâ the *El-Malik eṣ-Ṣâliḥ Bridge* (Pl. C 8), traverses the island of Rôḍa, passing the new building of the hospital of Qaṣr el-ʿAini and the School of Medicine (p. 56), which were begun in 1928 from the plans of Charles Nicholas and J. E. Dixon-Spain; it then crosses the Nile to Gîza by the *ʿAbbâs II. Bridge* (comp. p. 132). — To the left diverges the Shâriʿ Gâmiʿ ʿAmr, leading across the Ḥelwân railway to the new *English Cemetery* (including graves of British soldiers who fell in the Great War and a cenotaph in their memory), the Deir Abu' s-Seifein, and the Mosque of ʿAmr (p. 119).

The Coptic convent of **Deir Abu's-Seifein** is named after the largest, though not the oldest, church within its precincts (comp. p. 57). The convent includes three partly restored churches (*El-ʿAdra; Amba Shenûda*, 8th and 14th cent.; *Abu' s-Seifein*, 11th cent.) and a nunnery (*Deir el-Banât*). The entrance is by the small gate at the S.W. angle, near the level crossing.

The Shâriʿ Maṣr el-Qadîma continues to follow the direction of the arm of the Nile and leads to Old Cairo, passing the *Church Missionary Society's Hospital* (p. 42) and the mosque of Sulîmân Pasha el-Fransâwi (p. 55). Opposite the Shâriʿ el-Qabwa (A 1 on plan, p. 114) is the ferry crossing to the **Island of Rôḍa** (*Gezîret er-Rôḍa*; payment made on returning). A guide is easily found to conduct travellers through the intricate lanes to the garden at the S. extremity of the island, belonging to the heirs of *Ḥasan Pasha*.

At the S. end of the garden is a Nilometer *(Miqyâs)*, constructed in A.D. 716 by order of the Umaiyad caliph Sulîmân.

It consists of a well, with an octagonal column in the centre, on which are inscribed the ancient Arab measures. The *dirâʿ*, or old Arabian ell, is 54 centimetres, or about 21¼ inches long, and is divided into 24 qîrâṭ. The Cufic inscriptions (p. 70) on the central column and on marble slabs built into the walls refer to restorations of the nilometer in the 9th cent., under the Abbasid caliph El-Mutawakkil (861). Numerous later restorations have taken place, the last in 1893. The office of measuring the water is entrusted to a sheikh.

The zero point of the nilometer (according to Maḥmûd Bey) is 28 ft. above the average level of the Mediterranean, so that the top of the column is nearly 59 ft. above sea-level. The water of the Nile, when at its lowest, covers 7 ells of the nilometer, and when it reaches a height of 15 ells and 16 qîrâṭ, the sheikh of the Nile measurement proclaims the *Wafâ* (comp. p. c), i.e. the height of the water necessary for irrigating every part of the Nile valley. The announcement of the wafâ was formerly the signal for cutting the embankments of the irrigation canals, and noisy popular merry-makings still take place (about the middle of August) at the Mîdân Fumm el-Khalîg (p. 112). The rate of taxation (see p. lxxiii) was determined in ancient times in accordance with the height of the inundation, and even to this day part of the land tax is remitted by parliamentary vote in bad seasons.

Adjoining the nilometer is a large *Kiosk* in the Turkish style (no adm.). — To the N. of a smaller round kiosk on the E. quay-wall is a modern nilometer. — The S. end of the island commands a fine view of the Nile, with Gîza to the right, the Pyramids in the background, and Old Cairo on the left, with its imposing quay.

In a garden farther N. (c. 5 min. S. of the bridge of El-Malik eṣ-Ṣâliḥ, p. 112) stands the wonder-working tree of *Saiyida Mandûra*, a huge nabq-tree (p. lxxviii), hung with innumerable little flags and rags. According to a popular superstition the patient must thus offer to the saint the cloth which enveloped the affected limb (especially in the case of the eyes), pluck off two leaves, and tie them on the affected part with another cloth. — From the N. end of the island the *Muḥammed ʿAli Bridge* (Pl. C 6) leads to the hospital of Qaṣr el-ʿAini (p. 56).

To the left of the Shâriʿ Maṣr el-Qadîma lie the bazaars and alleys of the suburb of **Old Cairo** (*Maṣr el-Qadîma;* comp. p. 46). The Shâriʿ el-Qabwa (p. 112) and its continuation lead to the Qaṣr esh-Shamʿ (p. 114). — The No. 1 trams follow the road along the river to *Sâḥil Atar en-Nabi*, the chief harbour of Cairo for goods from Upper Egypt (especially corn). From the quay, which is about ½ M. long, a flight of forty steps descends to the river. The granaries and warehouses, which cover an area of 28,800 sq. yds., are divided from one another by wide streets with the dealers' booths. From Sâḥil Atar en-Nabi a fine high-road, between the Helwân railway and the river, leads S. to Maʿâdi and Ḥelwân (p. 177). — Among the mounds of débris beyond the railway are several Coptic churches (comp. p. cxc): *El-ʿAdra bi Bâblûn*, the 'Blessed Virgin of Babylon'; *Aba Kîr and Yûḥanna; El-Amîr Tâdros*, and farther S. is *St. Michael's*, formerly the frequent headquarters of the Coptic Patriarch (p. 85). — Turning left from the Shâriʿ Maṣr el-Qadîma by the police station (Pl. A 2) and the adjoining small English church,

we reach the Shâri' eṣ-Ṣaghîr (Pl. B 1, 2) and follow it to the left for a little while. Farther on a road leads right, past some gardens (l.), to the railway station of *St. George* (Pl. B 2; p. 177). Beyond the railway lies the Coptic quarter of *Qaṣr esh-Sham'* (Pl. C 1, 2). It is built within the still partly preserved walls of the ancient Roman citadel of *Babylon* (*Bâblûn*, p. 46).

We cross the railway by a wooden staircase. To the left lie the church of El-Mu'allaqa (p. 117) and *St. George's Monastery* (Pl.

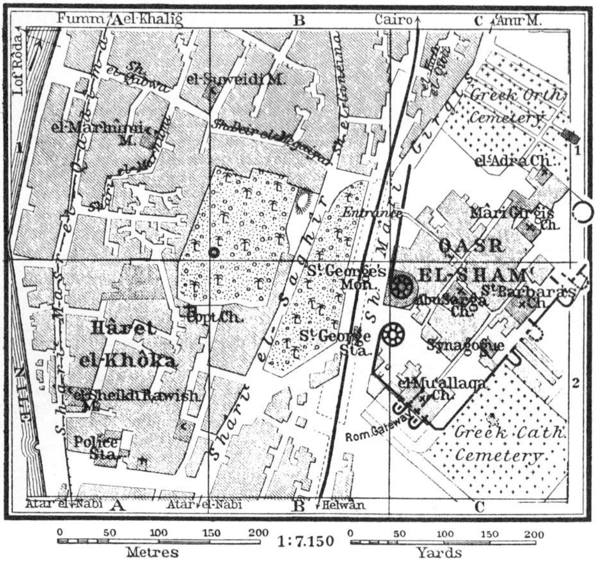

Old Cairo.

B C 2) of the Orthodox Greeks, the circular domed church of which (the burial-place of the Greek Patriarchs) rests on the foundations of a late-Roman or Byzantine tower.

A winding street leads thence to the citadel and the Coptic church of ***Abu Sarga** (*St. Sergius;* Pl. C 2), enclosed by a dense mass of houses. This church is a reconstruction of the Fatimid era. The crypt, however, where according to tradition the Virgin and Child spent a month after their flight into Egypt, is probably of earlier date.

This church may be regarded as the original model of the older Egyptian-Byzantine churches in which the Coptic Christians now

worship (comp. pp. cxc, cxci). The basilica consists of a nave and aisles, the latter with flat roofs and provided with galleries. The nave and the choir, which is raised, have open ceilings. The lofty side-walls of the nave consist of two rows of columns, one above the other, the columns of the lower row being separated by keel-arches, while the upper series, supporting the gallery, comprises alternate groups of two marble columns and one pillar of masonry. The columns of marble originally belonged to ancient edifices, and have been placed here without the least regard to their suitability in

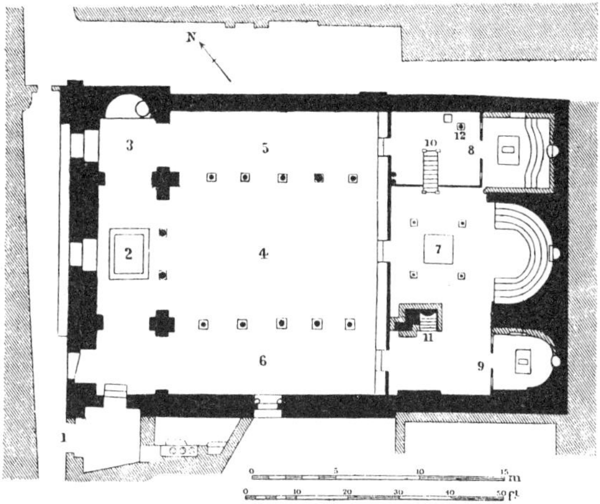

1. Entrance. 2. Vestibule or narthex, with water-basin. 3. Baptistery. 4. Nave. 5, 6. Aisles. 7. Sanctuary (heikal), with the high altar. 8. 9. Side-chapels. 10, 11. Entrances to the crypt. 12. Well. — The original walls are shown in black, the later ones are shaded.

point of size or architectural features. — The entrance (Pl. 1) is at the S.W. corner (P.T. 1 to the guide and P.T. 1 per person to be placed in the collection plate). The three original entrances on the W. side are now built up; they all led into the narthex, or old vestibule, whence the catechumens used to watch the divine services. This narthex is divided by wooden screens into three sections, the central one of which (Pl. 2) contains an ancient water-basin, in which the priest still washes the feet of the men at the feast of Epiphany (comp. p. 116). The N. section (with a niche; Pl. 3) serves as the baptistery. A wooden screen divides the narthex from the body of the church.

The nave (Pl. 4), which has a pointed wooden ceiling, is reserved for the men, the aisles (Pl. 5, 6) being generally used by the women, who only sit in the galleries when the church is crowded. The separation of men and women, however, is no longer so strictly observed as in former times. A few steps ascend to the sanctuary (Pl. 7) and two side-chapels (Pl. 8, 9), which are shut off by wooden screens, panelled and richly adorned with carvings in wood and ivory (p. cxci). The finest and oldest of these are on the screen to the left; besides ornamental designs they include representations of the Nativity, St. Demetrius, St. George, St. Theodore (?), and the Last Supper. The sanctuary or *Heikal* contains the high altar, surmounted by a canopy, and a stepped niche, formerly seats for the priests. The S. side-chapel (r.; Pl. 9) is dedicated to St. George, that on the N. (l.; Pl. 8) to St. Michael.

Steps (Pl. 10, 11) descend from the side-chapels to the *Crypt*, the oldest part of the church (6th cent.), a small vaulted and aisled chapel with antique marble columns. In its nave is an altar in the form of an early-Christian tomb-niche, which tradition indicates as the spot where the Virgin and Child reposed. The right aisle contains the font, into which, according to the Coptic ritual, the child to be baptized is dipped three times. The crypt is often flooded and is used for service on five occasions only during the year (Feast of the Flight into Egypt, Christmas Eve, the Sun. before Palm Sunday, the Feast of the Death of the Virgin, and the Assumption).

Coptic Worship resembles that of the Greek Orthodox Church in many particulars. On entering the church the members of the congregation first pay their homage to a number of pictures of saints hanging on the walls and then kneel before the altar and kiss the hand of the priest. The service, which often lasts for three hours or more, begins with the reading or chanting of prayers and passages from the Gospels, partly in the Coptic language and partly in Arabic, in which the priest is assisted by a schoolmaster and a choir of boys. During this performance the worshippers engage freely in conversation. After a time the burning of incense begins. The priest, swinging his censer, leaves the heikal and joins the congregation, each member of which he blesses, placing his hand on their heads. The celebration of the Eucharist is very frequent in the Coptic churches, immediately following the ordinary service. — On January 19th, the anniversary of the Baptism of Christ (*'îd el-ghiṭâs*), men and boys plunge into the large font or bath, the water having been first blessed by the priest. In former times they performed the same ceremony in the Nile, into which they first poured some holy water. On the eve of this festival, as well as at Epiphany, on Maundy Thursday, and on the festival of the Apostles, the priest washes the feet of the whole of his congregation. On Palm Sunday plaits of palm are blessed by the priest, which are then worn by the Copts under their headgear during the whole of the following year as amulets against every misfortune that can befall body or soul. — The Copts attach great weight to the observance of fasts, during which all kinds of animal food, not excepting eggs, butter, cheese, etc., are prohibited. — Comp. *Alfred J. Butler*'s 'The Ancient Coptic Churches of Egypt' (1884) and 'Babylon of Egypt' (Oxford, 1914).

The citadel contains several other Coptic churches, interesting only to those who are making a special study of this kind of architecture (comp. p. cxc). Among them we may mention those of

St. Barbara (*Es-Sitt Burbâra;* Pl. C 2; restored), which contains good carvings and paintings; *St. George* (*Mâri Girgis;* Pl. C 1), partly destroyed by fire, a fine chamber retaining some of its old decorations and now used for wedding receptions; and the *Blessed Virgin* (*El-ʿAdra;* Pl. C 1). The Jews say that Elijah once appeared in the modern *Synagogue* (*Esh-Shamyân* or *Kenîset Eliâhu*), and show a place in it where Moses once prayed.

About 20 yds. to the right of Abu Sarga we enter a picturesque lane on the left, which leads to a low iron-bound door (marked 'Entrance' on the plan, B C 1). Thence a road leads to the left, past St. George's Monastery (p. 114) and the railway station, to the church of **El-Muʿallaqa** (Pl. C 2; 'resting upon columns'; p. cxci) and the adjoining Coptic Museum, situated at the S.E. corner of the citadel. We pass through a vestibule into a garden and thence to a courtyard whence a broad flight of steps leads up to the church. The latter is built on the E. tower of the S. gate of the citadel and was originally much larger, probably occupying the space above both towers. Beyond a narthex is the main body of the church, consisting of four (originally five or more) aisles and containing the pulpit. Of the three chapels shut off by old carved screens, the central one or sanctuary (heikal) is dedicated to Christ, that on the S. (r.) to John the Baptist, and that on the N. (l.) to St. George.

The **Coptic Museum** (adm. P.T. 5; closed on Fri. & Sun. during divine service), to the left of the entrance to the church, was founded in 1910 by Morkos Pasha Simaika, the present director.

Room I. In the show-cases and on the walls are embroidered priestly vestments, processional banners, curtains hung in front of sanctuaries, one of them from the monastery of El-Maharraq, to the N.W. of Manfalût (p. 225; 13th cent.). *Mashrabîya from the patriarchal palace in Cairo. — All the rooms have carved wooden ceilings and window-screens removed from old Coptic houses.

Room II. By the wall and in the show-case, fragments of glazed pottery with Christian emblems, from the ruins of Fusṭâṭ (p. 118).

Room III. Carved door from the church of St. Barbara (see above): on the front, Christ, the Apostles, and angels supporting the head of Christ (4th cent.). The show-case contains glazed pottery and glass.

Room IV. Wood-carvings: on the wall, scenes from the life of Christ (Entry into Jerusalem, Resurrection, etc.; 5th cent.) and door of the Fatimid period, from the church of El-Muʿallaqa (see above).

Room V. Wood-carvings; carved screen from an altar with hunting scenes (Fatimid period), from St. Barbara's (see above).

Room VI. In the show-case, wood-carvings with ivory inlay; four ivories with verses from the Psalms (from the church of Amba Shenûda in Old Cairo, p. 112). On the walls, wood-carvings of camels, elephants, etc. Carved chest for altar vessels, inlaid with ivory.

Room VII. Carved cupboard; lecterns; cabinets inlaid with ivory. On the walls, ikons. In the bay-window is a mashrabîya with an Arabic inscription. We descend the staircase to —

Room VIII. Two carved episcopal chairs; carved altar from the church of Abu Sarga (6th cent.), beneath a wooden dome from El-Muʿallaqa (10th cent.). The walls are hung with pictures of saints. In the show-case, stamps for eucharistic bread; carved panels of doors. — We ascend the steps and pass through Room IX, which contains a bench, a chest, and pictures of saints, and R. X to Room XI.

Room XI. In the three cases, copper church-vessels, dishes, two of them with Coptic inscriptions, from the Faiyûm (p. 202). On the walls, pictures of saints. On either side of the stairs to R. XII are bronze-mounted wooden doors from the Faiyûm, one of them with an inscription in corrupt Greek.

Room XII. The first show-case contains bronze lamps and candelabra; oil-ladles; incense-burners and candlesticks, from the monastery of St. Menas in Old Cairo (p. 112). In the second show-case are beautiful church-vessels and three silver *Gospel Chests, adorned with gold and coloured stones. In the centre is a copper baldacchino for an altar, adorned at the four corners with crosses (the Coptic inscriptions mention the 'Year of the Martyrs' 650 [= A.D. 934]); above the hemispherical dome is a crucifix. By the wall is a patriarchal throne of bronze (10th cent.). The semicircular cabinet and the cases in front of it contain valuable church-utensils, consecration crosses, and candelabra. Fine carved wooden dome from a Coptic house. We descend the steps to —

Rooms XIII and XIV, which are devoted to a large collection of Coptic textiles and embroideries (4-12th cent.). Note the piece of embroidery with four female heads (the Virtues).

We now return to R. VIII and descend to the Courtyard, with four colonnades (A-D) containing Coptic tombstones (A), fragments of lattice-windows and wood-carvings (B, D), and architectural fragments (C; finely carved bow windows), whence we descend steps to the *South Gate* of old Babylon (p. 114), which lies $29^1/_2$ ft. below the street-level and has two projecting towers. — We return through the courtyard and colonnade to visit the Library, which is adorned with old fountains and wall-facing with a mantel-shelf *(suffa)* of mosaic. The library consists of about 1050 Coptic and 950 Arabic MSS., collected from various Coptic churches and monasteries. The exit leads to a courtyard with a recently excavated tower of the Roman wall.

From the Qaṣr esh-Shamʻ the Shâriʻ Mâri Girgis leads N. to the ʻAmr Mosque (p. 119). We diverge to the right beyond the Greek Orthodox cemetery (Pl. C 1) to reach the new excavations at **Fusṭâṭ**, the oldest Arab settlement in the Cairo district (p. 46). In 1168, rather than surrender it to Amalrich, King of Jerusalem, it was burnt and destroyed by the vizier Shâwar (p. cxx). A side-street leads to the office, where the custodian issues tickets of admission (P.T. 5 per person). The ground-plans and foundations of numerous houses (some of which were very large), built of burnt bricks and hewn stone, are easily recognizable. In the centre of the house, which was several stories in height, is an open court, in which was a bath and fountain *(fasqîya)* surrounded by flower-beds. The four chief rooms were arranged round this in the form of a cross. The houses contained also smaller rooms, baths, and sanitary arrangements. Numerous cisterns (care necessary), water-pipes, drains, cess-pits, mills, an oil-press, and a church have also been excavated. The streets are mostly only $3^1/_4$-10 ft. wide, never more than 33 ft. On the E. side is a long excavated section of the *City Wall* with its gate-towers, erected c. 1176 by Qaraqush, one of Sultan Saladin's emirs; for its continuation (recently excavated) to the N., near the Tombs of the Caliphs, see p. 120.

To the S. of Fusṭâṭ the road goes on E. to the baths of ʻAin eṣ-Ṣîra and the Tombs of the Mamelukes (Imâm esh-Shâfiʻi); see p. 124. — If we return from Fusṭâṭ by the same route and turn to the right (N.) near the above-mentioned Greek cemetery, we reach

in a few minutes the white and red striped W. façade of the externally insignificant mosque of 'Amr (comp. Pl. C 1).

The **Mosque of 'Amr** *(Gâmi' 'Amr ibn el-'Âs)*, with a minaret 105 ft. high, owes its name to the general of the caliph 'Omar (p. 46), though not a trace now remains of the original mosque of c. 642, which was only 50 ells long and 30 ells broad. Indeed there is scarcely a building in Egypt that has so frequently been destroyed by water, fire, and earthquake, and that has been so regularly rebuilt. Tickets of admission, see p. 45.

The interior exhibits the usual plan of a court surrounded by colonnades. The columns are represented on the N. and S. sides by their bases only. Their heterogeneous nature is accounted for by the fact that they were brought from Roman and Byzantine buildings.

The façades of the *Court (ṣaḥn)* have no pretensions to antiquity; the arches are of an unusually clumsy shape. In the centre, which is now planted with trees, is a ḥanafîya (p. cc); the deep well is popularly believed to have a connection with the Zemzem well in Mecca. The *South-Eastern Lîwân* is the sanctuary. In front of the pulpit, within an iron railing, is a column of grey marble, on which, by a freak of nature, the names of Allah, Muḥammed, and Sultan Sulimân in Arabic characters, and the outline of the prophet's 'kurbâg' (whip) appear in veins of a lighter colour. This column is believed by the Moslems to have been transported miraculously from Mecca to Cairo by the caliph 'Omar. In the N.E. corner is the tomb of Sheikh 'Abdallâh, son of 'Amr. In the N.W. corner is a recess with two low columns; the blood-stains on the top are caused by patients in search of health, who here rub their tongues until they bleed. In the W. colonnade, which consists of a single row of columns only, is a pair of columns, placed very close together, and it is said that none but honest men could squeeze themselves between them.

The mosque of 'Amr is almost entirely disused. On the last Friday in Pamaḍân (p. xcix), the month of fasting, however, a solemn service is annually held here, in which the King takes part. — In 1808 this mosque witnessed a very remarkable scene. The whole of the Mohammedan priesthood, the Christian clergy of every sect, and the Jewish rabbis, with one accord, assembled to pray for the rise of the Nile, which had delayed beyond the usual period.

Near the mosque of 'Amr are several *Qulla Factories*, in which the process of making the porous water-jars (Arabic *qulla*, pl. *qûlal*) used throughout Egypt may be seen. The chief seat of manufacture is, however, Qena (p. 232). The material is a light-grey clay; the remarkably delicate porosity of the vessels is produced by mixing the clay with ashes. The rapid evaporation caused by the porosity of the qulla cools the liquid within to a temperature of 12–14° Fahr. lower than that of the surrounding air. — To the convent of Deir Abu 's-Seifein, see p. 112.

The Shâri' Sîdi Ḥasan el-Anwar (Pl. C D 8) leads from the mosque of 'Amr to the *Mîdân es-Salakhâna* (Pl. D 7), adjoining the

abattoir, and to the Christian cemeteries (p. 112). Some distance to the E. of this street lie the Jewish cemetery and, on an eminence, the ruined *Mosque of Sîdi Abu 's-Su'ûd* (Pl. D 8).

II. The Tombs of the Caliphs and Mamelukes.

Tickets of Admission, see p. 45; *Motor Cars* and *Carriages*, see p. 41. The general effect is most striking towards sunset. The enjoyment of the scenery is, however, greatly impaired by the dustiness of the roads.

The mediæval Arab mausolea of Egyptian rulers, which, under the names *Tombs of the Caliphs* and *Tombs of the Mamelukes*, stretch along the E. side of the city, were erected mainly by the later Circassian Mameluke sultans (p. cxxiii). The name 'Tombs of the Caliphs', however, is historically a misnomer, for the tombs have no connection with the Abbasid caliphs then resident in Egypt and treated as mere titled puppets. These mosque-tombs were once each provided with a numerous staff of sheikhs and attendants. The revenues of the mosques having been confiscated at the beginning of the 19th century, the tombs gradually fell to ruin. Now, however, the Waqfs Ministry (comp. p. 45) has taken them into its keeping.

The usual route to the ***Tombs of the Caliphs** (Arabic *Turab el-Khulafâ* or *Turab Qâït Bey*) leaves the city viâ the Mûski (p. 56) and its prolongations. It then traverses the mounds of potsherds known as the Windmill Hills or Tell Qaṭ' el-Mar'a, and reaches the still-used Mohammedan cemeteries of *El-Qarâfa esh-Sharqîya* ('East Cemetery') and *Qarâfet el-'Afîfi*. By the main street, the *Shâri' es-Sulṭân Aḥmad* (A-C 5-3 on the plan opposite), and its side-turnings lie large mausolea (Arabic *ḥôsh*), with courts and rooms occupied during certain festivals by the relatives of the deceased (comp. p. xcix). Proceeding E., we first reach the tomb-mosque of Qâït Bey, to the N.E. of which is that of Barqûq. Hence we return to the city by one of the routes described below.

Those who wish to combine a visit to the *Citadel* (p. 73) with that to the Tombs of the Caliphs should select the route from the *Bâb el-Atâbki* (Pl. G 6), which divides the necropolis from the citadel on its S. The *Shâri' Qarâfet Bâb el-Wazîr* leads from the gate to the Shâri' es-Sulṭân Aḥmad (see above). To the E., adjoining the gate, is the *Sibîl Sheikhûn* (comp. p. 76), a rock-hewn well dating from 1349.

It is, however, more convenient to begin with the N. group of tombs. In this case we quit Cairo by the *Bâb en-Naṣr* (Pl. G 3; p. 84) and pass the Mohammedan cemetery. To the right, among the rubbish-heaps, is a recently excavated section of the *City Wall* (p. 47) constructed by Saladin in 1176-93, with a large defence work known as the *Burg eẓ-Ẓafar* ('victory fort'; B 1 on the plan opposite) at its N.E. corner. On the E. side is a walled-up city gate. Beyond the unimportant tomb of *Sheikh Sîdi Galâl* (Pl. B 1) we have one of the finest *Views of the city of the dead.

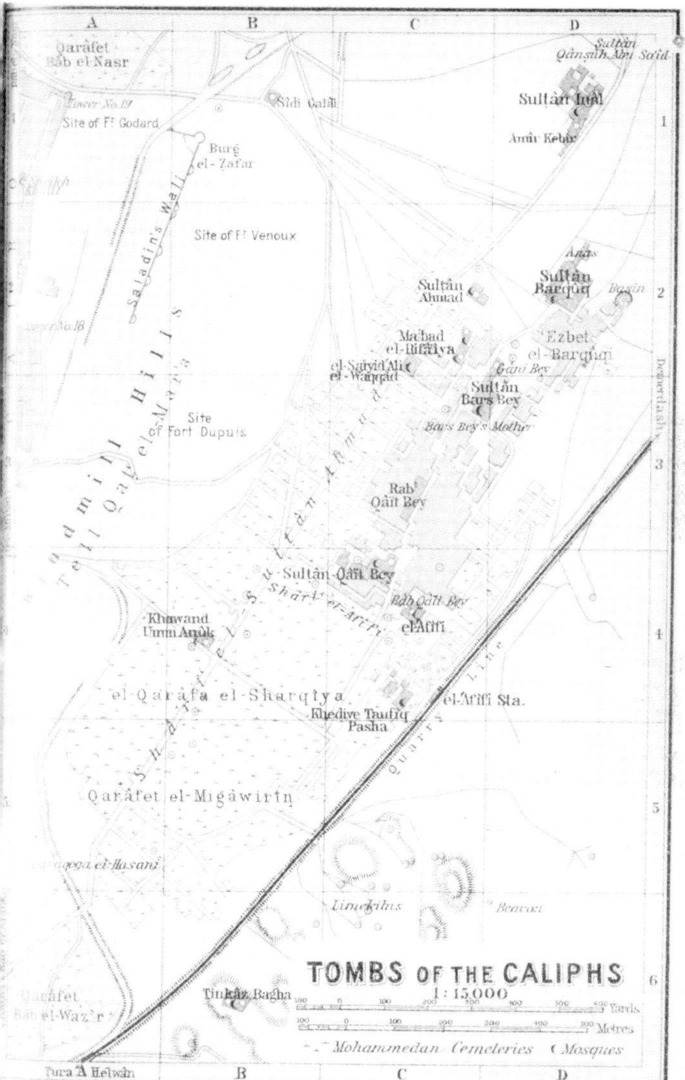
TOMBS OF THE CALIPHS
1:15000
Yards
Metres
Mohammedan Cemeteries
Mosques
Qarâfet Bâb el-Nasr
Site of Ft Godard
Burg el-Zafar
Saladin's Wall
Site of Ft Venoux
Site of Fort Dupuis
Tell el-Qaf el-Mâma
Sîdi Galâl
Sultân Qânsûh Abu Sa'îd
Sultân Inâl
Amîr Kebîr
Sultân Ahmad
Sultân Barqûq
Basin
Ma'bad el-Rifâ'iya
el-Saiyid Ali el-Waqqâd
'Ezbet el-Barqûqi
Sultân Bars Bey
Bars Bey's Mother
Rab' Qâit Bey
Sultân Qâit Bey
Bâb Qâit Bey
Shâri' el-Afîfi
el-Afîfi
Khawand Umm Anûk
el-Qarâfa el-Sharqîya
el-Afîfi Sta.
Khedive Taufîq Pasha
Quarry Line
Qarâfet el-Migâwirîn
Limekilns
Beacon
Tinkiz Bagha
Qarâfet Bâb el-Wazîr
Tura & Helwân
Demerdash
Wagner & Debes, Leipzig

The N.E. group of mausolea consists of the buildings (Pl. D 1; tomb-mosque and convent, with a fine minaret; 1450-56) connected with ***Sultan Inâl***, and of the adjoining madrasa and mausoleum of ***Qurqumâs***, known as ***Amîr Kebîr***, one of the emirs of Sultan El-Ghûri (1506).

Straight on are the partly ruined ***Tomb-Mosque and Convent of Sultan Barqûq** (Pl. D 2). The N. dome was completed in 1400-5 by Barqûq's sons, *Farag* (p. cxxiii) and *ʿAbd el-ʿAzîz*, the S. dome and the convent *(khânqâh)* in 1410 by Farag. — The ground-plan is square (each side 240 ft.) and resembles that of the madrasas (p. cxcviii), The lîwans, however, are not covered with barrel-vaulting but are protected against sun and shower by colonnades with spherical domes. The present entrance (Pl. 1) is in an outbuilding at the S.W. angle. It leads to a domed vestibule, whence a corridor (Pl. 2) runs to the fine Ṣaḥn el-Gâmiʿ or large inner quadrangle, in the middle of which, beneath two tamarisk-trees, is the old ḥanafîya (Pl. 3), or fountain for ablutions. To the right (E.) is the exquisitely proportioned main lîwân or sanctuary (Pl. 6), with three aisles, simple prayer-niches (Pl. 4), and a beautiful stone *Minbar or pulpit (Pl. 5) presented by Qâït Bey. To the left (N.) of the sanctuary is the mausoleum (Pl. 7), with the cenotaphs of Barqûq and of his sons ʿAbd el-ʿAzîz and Farag. The column at the head of Barqûq's cenotaph is said to indicate the stature of the deceased. The S. (r.) mausoleum (Pl. 8) contains women's graves. The two *Domes of the mausolea, considered to be the earliest built of stone, are

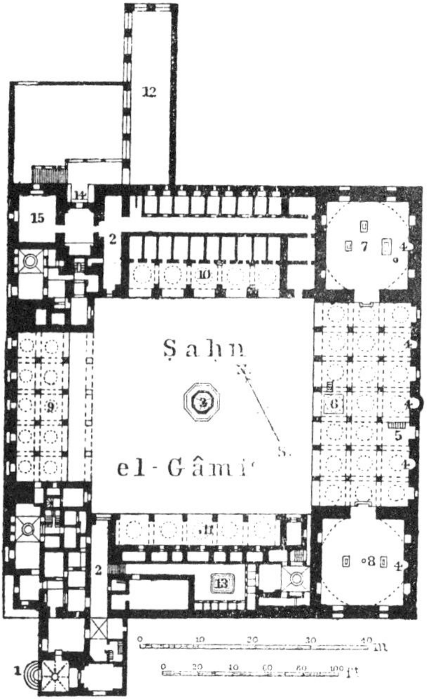

masterpieces of Arab architecture, marvels of proportion (p. cxcvii). The W. lîwân (Pl. 9) had three aisles also, but the arcade next the court has collapsed. The two side-lîwâns (Pl. 10 & 11) have one aisle only, the S. one being partly destroyed. Behind that to the N. are four-storied monks' cells and a hall (Pl. 12; now very dilapidated), which forms an outbuilding to the mosque and connects the khânqâh with the small mausoleum of Barqûq's father, *Sharaf ed-Dîn Anas*, who died in 1382. Behind the S. lîwân is a ruined court of ablution (Pl. 13), with a water-basin and other accessories; adjoining the former main entrance (Pl. 14) is a sibîl (fountain) with a school (Pl. 15). — One of the two *Minarets* was restored in 1900. Both had originally three stories.

To the W. of the Barqûq Mosque, within a walled court, is the mausoleum of Barsbâi en-Nakhkhâsi (c. 1456), usually known as the tomb of *Es-Sultân Aḥmad* (Pl. C 2). It contains interesting sculpture in the dome and inscriptions in blue faience, now partly destroyed. On the right of the road leading from the mosque of Barqûq S.W. to the tomb of Qâït Bey (see below) is the *Ma'bad er-Rifâ'îya*, a large depressed dome of the Turkish period.

Opposite, to the left, is the *Tomb of Bars Bey* (Pl. C D 3; p. cxxiv), completed in 1432. It includes a mosque, a mausoleum, and the ruins of a convent and of a sibîl. Within the enclosing walls are the tombs of relatives of Bars Bey. The lîwân contains good mosaics. The dome of the mausoleum is interesting. — Farther on, to the right, is the *Tomb of the Mother of Bars Bey* (Pl. C 3), a small dome with pentagonal and hexagonal openings (c. 1440).

In the same street, farther S., we observe on the right the *Rab' Qâït Bey* (Pl. C 3), a dwelling-house 260 ft. long, completed in 1473, but now in ruins. The façade is plain but the gateway is very tasteful. A little farther S., in an angle, is a *Water Trough* (Pl. 15, p. 123), now in ruins, with its once beautiful rear wall protected by a roof. The rab', the trough (ḥôḍ), and the tomb-mosque (see below) all belonged to the burial-place (ḥôsh) of Qâït Bey, which covered an area 330 yds. long. Its exact limits cannot now be determined, and a number of modern buildings have been erected within them.

The ***Tomb-Mosque of Qâït Bey** (Pl. C 4; p. 78), completed in 1474 and restored in 1898, is the finest edifice among the Tombs of the Caliphs. It has a beautiful dome, a slender minaret (130 ft. high), harmonious proportions, and handsome ornamentation, in which stalactites are profusely used. In the interior we notice the beautiful marble mosaic, the tasteful ceilings, the pulpit, and the lattice windows of stucco (qamarîyas, p. cciii; partly modern). Within the mausoleum (Pl. 8, p. 123) are shown a finely carved desk and two stones, which are said to have been brought from Mecca by Qâït Bey and to bear impressions of the feet of the Prophet.

To the S.E. of the mosque of Qâït Bey the Shâri' el-'Afîfi leads to the *Tomb-Mosque of the Khedive Taufîq* (Pl. C 4, 5; p. cxxviii).

Short Walks in the Desert. Those who enjoy the silence and pure air of the desert may proceed from the Tombs of the Caliphs (or from ʿAbbâsîya, p. 85) into one of the small lateral valleys to the S. of the Gebel el-Aḥmar (see below). A small round hill of red sandstone in this vicinity commands a superb panorama of the Arabian desert, the Suez road, ʿAbbâsîya, Heliopolis Oasis, and the extremity of the Delta. — We may return S. viâ the *Gebel Giyûshi* (p. 125) or N. viâ the **Gebel el-Aḥmar**, or *Red Mountain* (394 ft.), rising to the E. of ʿAbbâsîya. The mountain consists of a very hard conglomerate of sand, pebbles, and fragments of fossil wood (p. lxxi), coloured red or yellowish brown by oxide of iron. Centuries ago the quarries here yielded material for statues as they now do for excellent and durable mill-stones and road material.

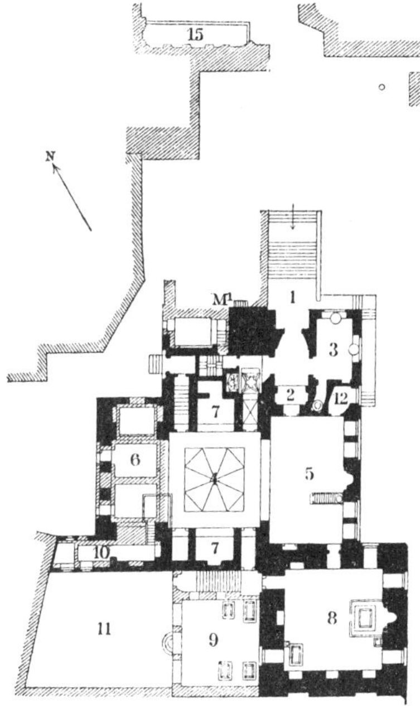

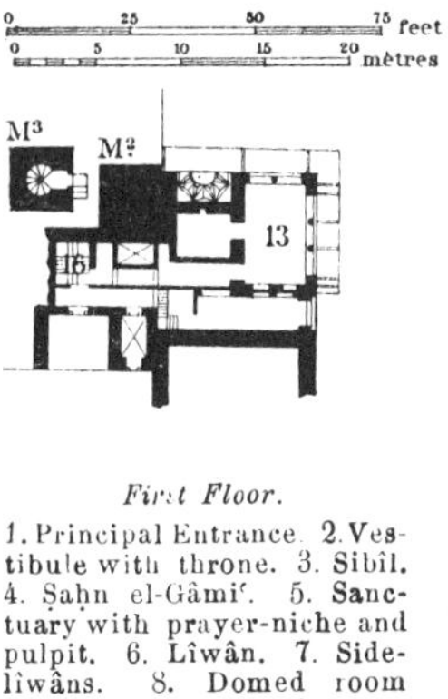

First Floor.

1. Principal Entrance. 2. Vestibule with throne. 3. Sibîl. 4. Ṣaḥn el-Gâmiʿ. 5. Sanctuary with prayer-niche and pulpit. 6. Lîwân. 7. Side-lîwâns. 8. Domed room with cenotaph of Qâït Bey. 9. Hall with tombs of Qâït Bey's four wives. 10. Library. 11. Uncovered court. 12. Khilwa (chamber) for the Imâm. 13 (first floor). Kuttâb (elementary school). 15. Water-trough. 16. Staircase to the minaret. M1, M2, M3. Minaret in the three stories.

The **Tombs of the Mamelukes**, to the S. of the citadel, are most conveniently visited from *Saladin Square* (*Mîdân Ṣalâḥ ed-Dîn*, Pl. F 6, 7; p. 73; tram No. 11, see p. 40). The tombs, both old and new, approach close to the city and extend E. as far as the slopes of the Moqaṭṭam. The older tombs are in much poorer preservation

than the Tombs of the Caliphs, owing to their conversion into modern burial-places. Some are now represented only by their minarets. A few are of architectural interest. The extant inscriptions upon them are almost exclusively verses of the Koran. To the left, half-way up the Moqaṭṭam, is the Bektashi monastery.

The busy SHÂRIʿ ES-SAIYIDA ʿAISHA (Âïsha, p. cxcii, the favourite wife of Mohammed), runs S. from Saladin Square and is continued by the SHÂRIʿ EL-FATḤ, at the end of which is a portion of the old city wall with the *Bâb Qâït Bey* (*Bâb el-Qarâfa*, Pl. F 7), also called *Bâb es-Saiyida ʿAisha*, a gate built in 1475-84. Next follow the SHÂRIʿ EL-QÂDRÎYA and SHÂRIʿ EL-IMÂM ESH-SHÂFIʿI (family tombs on both sides), leading to the *Mîdân el-Imâm esh-Shâfiʿi*. Here to the right, with a conspicuous blue-grey dome, lie the **Mosque and *Mausoleum of Imâm esh-Shâfiʿi**, the founder of one of the four orthodox rites of Islâm (p. lxxxviii). The *Mosque*, dominated by a modern minaret over-decorated in the Mameluke style, was erected by Khedive Taufîq about forty years ago and is of no artistic importance. A passage adjoined by tomb-chambers leads thence to the superb domed **Mausoleum*, built in 1211 by the sultana *Esh-Shamsa*, mother of the Aiyubid sultan El-Kâmil. The frieze of carved wood is noteworthy. The tomb of the imâm, enclosed by a modern screen, is a great place of pilgrimage for both men and women and is inaccessible to unbelievers. The adjacent tomb of the sultana Shamsa has beautiful wood-carving.

Near the mosque of Imâm esh-Shâfiʿi is the **Ḥôsh el-Bâshâ** ('Mausoleum of the Pasha'), the family tomb of Muḥammed ʿAli. The monuments (including those of Ibrâhîm and ʿAbbâs I., p. cxxvii) are in white marble and were executed by Greek and Armenian sculptors. The inscriptions and ornamentation are richly gilded and painted. — About 1/2 M. to the S.W. of the mosque of Imâm esh-Shâfiʿi, beyond the quarry railway, lie the sulphur-baths of *ʿAin eṣ-Ṣîra*, frequented by the Egyptians. They are reached by a side-turning out of the Shâriʿ el-Imâm esh-Shâfiʿi. Thence to the mosque of ʿAmr and Old Cairo, see p. 118.

From the Bâb Qâït Bey the AQUEDUCT (Arabic *El-Qanâṭir*), built in 1311 by Sultan Muḥammed en-Nâṣir (p. cxxii; formerly ascribed to Saladin) and restored by El-Ghûri (p. cxxiv), runs in a wide sweep towards the Nile (see p. 112). It supplied the citadel with water before the construction of the new waterworks.

III. The Moqaṭṭam Hills.

An excursion to the Moqaṭṭam Hills is best made from the citadel (trams Nos. 11, 13, and 23 to Saladin Square, see pp. 40, 41). The route from the Tombs of the Caliphs is to be avoided on account of the intolerable dust. The excursion may be combined with the visit to the smaller Petrified Forest in the manner indicated on p. 127. The VIEW is best between 8 and 9 a.m., towards sunset, or at the time of the full moon.

From the *Citadel* (p. 73) the route ascends in an almost straight direction, passing through the *Bâb el-Moqaṭṭam* (Pl. G 7; p. 75) and over the railway-bridge. About 1/2 hr. brings us to the top.

The **Moqaṭṭam Hills** (*Gebel el-Muqaṭṭam;* maximum height above sea-level 700 ft.), to the E. of Cairo, also called *Gebel el-Giyûshi* after the conspicuous mosque situated on the summit, belong to the great range of nummulitic limestone mountains which extend from N.W. Africa, across Egypt and India, to China. This formation is one of the eocene, or oldest deposits of the tertiary period. It yields a favourite building stone, and there are numerous quarries on the slopes of the hills.

Nummulitic limestone is remarkably rich in fossils, the chief mass of which consists of millions of nummulites (so called from their resemblance to coins) or rhizopods of the polythalamia group. The larger kinds are about an inch and a half in diameter and the smaller about 1/8 inch. They are frequently seen also in the stones of the Pyramids, part of the material for which was taken from the quarries of the Moqaṭṭam. The quarries yield also a profusion of sea-urchins (clypeaster, cidaris, echinolampas, etc.), various kinds of bivalves (including many oysters), cerithium, ovula, strombus, nerita, turritella, nautilus, sharks' teeth, and bones of the halicore. Beautiful crystals of selenite and of strontianite also occur.

The **VIEW from the top is magnificent and in a good light is finer than any other in the neighbourhood of Cairo (e.g. that from the citadel, p. 74). The citadel, the mosque of Muḥammed ʿAli, and the grand burial-grounds of the desert form a noble foreground; the Nile dotted with sailing boats flows below us; to the W., on the borders of the desert, tower the huge Pyramids. At sunset the thousand minarets of the city and the citadel are tinted with a delicate rosy hue. The view from a steep projection S. of the mosque is still more varied, the foreground being especially picturesque.

The **Giyûshi Mosque**, one of the oldest in Cairo (comp. p. cc), was built in 1085 by the Emir Badr el-Gamâli (p. cxx), the grand vizier of the Fatimid caliph El-Mustanṣir. According to tradition he chose this high-lying situation (525 ft.) that he might still, even after death, be able to see the mausolea of his seven favourite wives in the valley below.

The entrance to the mosque lies on the N.W. side, in the lower part of the minaret, which is built in the earlier style of architecture (p. cc). The open court is adjoined by a vaulted prayer-room decorated in the Byzantine-Persian taste. To the left of it is the tomb of the founder.

Below the mosque are the *Rock Caves* of Coptic monks, with Coptic and Arabic inscriptions. Some of them may be reached by a steep path.

At the N. end of the plateau is an old Turkish *Fort* (El-Gebel Fort, Pl. G 7), whence a causeway descends to the citadel. On the N.E. and higher part of the Moqaṭṭam, separated from the citadel by a large quarry, is a memorial stone, to the right, adjoining the summit, erected in 1874 by the British party of scientific men who observed the transit of Venus from this point (673 ft.). The projecting rock in front of this commands the most extensive panorama in the neighbourhood of Cairo, and should certainly be visited if time permit. The S. end of these hills is skirted by the road to

the smaller Petrified Forest, which may be reached from this point in about 1 hr. (see p. 127).

On the steep slope of the Moqaṭṭam, to the S. of the Giyûshi Mosque, lies the so-called *Castle of the Mamelukes* or *Mosque of Shâhîn el-Khalwati,* built in 1533. The ruinous interior may be entered from below. A steep path, practicable for expert climbers only, ascends hence to the plateau through the Coptic caves mentioned on p. 125.

The ***Bektashi Monastery** (*Baktâshîya Dervishes*, Pl. G 7), with its palms and gardens, lies on the bare W. slopes of the Moqaṭṭam. It belongs to a Turkish order of dervishes (p. xcv) and was founded by ʿAbdallâh el-Maghâwri; it is best visited by the road starting from Saladin Square (see p. 73) or, in connection with a visit to the citadel, from the Bâb el-Muqaṭṭam (p. 75). Visitors are admitted. An easy flight of steps ascends to the court adjoined by the dervishes' residences. The terraced gardens in front command a superb view of the city, the Nile valley, and the desert. From the court a deep cave (once a stone-quarry) enters the mountain side and contains tombs of the dervishes. At the end is a chamber with the tomb of a sheikh, where worshippers are frequently observed. There is another large quarry beneath the N. terrace.

IV. The Spring of Moses and the Petrified Forest.

The geologist will certainly find it profitable to visit the Petrified Forest (comp. p. lxxi), but for other travellers its chief interest lies in the fact that they here obtain their first glimpse of the E. desert. The latter may therefore content themselves with an excursion to the *Little Petrified Forest*, the outskirts of which may be reached in $1^1/_2$-2 hrs. The expedition may be made in half-a-day on donkey-back (p. 41). Carriages require extra horses and even then sometimes stick in the sand. — The deviation to the *Spring of Moses* adds rather less than an hour to the expedition, and if the donkey-boy knows the route a guide may be dispensed with. A visit to the *Great Petrified Forest* can hardly be accomplished without the aid of a well-informed guide. — The desert excursions made from Ḥelwân (p. 180), however, are more attractive.

Starting at the Bâb en-Naṣr (p. 84), or from the point where the route to the Tombs of the Caliphs leaves the Mûski (p. 120), we ride by the Tombs of the Caliphs, pass between the Moqaṭṭam (p. 124) and the Red Mountain (p. 123), and ascend a desert valley, into which the E. spurs of the Moqaṭṭam descend. Farther on an isolated hill of red and black sandstone resembling the Red Mountain is visible in the desert on our left. We cross a watercourse (usually dry), where the paths separate. That to the right (S.E.) leads to the Spring of Moses and the Little Petrified Forest (p. 127), while that to the left (E.) is the route to the Great Petrified Forest and the Bîr el-Faḥm (p. 128).

About 100 paces to the right, at the foot of the mountain-slope behind the Tombs of the Caliphs, which we ascend on this side past some large lime-kilns, we may trace the high-water level of the sea in the pliocene age, 235 ft. above the present sea-level, on a rocky face of the nummulite plateau, thickly dotted over with holes made by boring molluscs (piddocks, pholades).

Following the path to the right, we observe a yellowish hill at the foot of the spurs of the Moqaṭṭam and reach it in $^1/_4$ hr. more. This hill stands at the mouth of the narrow, winding valley, $^3/_4$ M.

VI. Old Heliopolis.

This expedition is best made by MOTOR CAR or by tariffed CARRIAGE (p. 41; drive to the obelisk $1\frac{1}{2}$ hr.), though it may be accomplished also by RAILWAY to Maṭarîya starting from the Pont Limoun Station (Pl. E 2; p. 41). Trains run every $\frac{1}{4}$ or $\frac{1}{2}$ hr. and take 17-23 min. for the journey (return-tickets P.T. 6 or 4). — To *New Heliopolis*, see p. 128.

The road to Old Heliopolis diverges to the left from the Shâri' el-Malika Nâzli (p. 85) at the Girls' College of the American Mission and, passing under the railway to Marg, leads past the gardens of the *Royal Palace of Qubba* (no adm.). The plain between Qubba and Maṭarîya has been the scene of two important battles. On Jan. 22nd, 1517, the Battle of Heliopolis made Selîm I. and the Turks masters of Egypt; and on March 20th, 1800, General Kléber with 10,000 French troops succeeded in defeating 60,000 Orientals, and in consequence of this victory regained possession of Cairo (p. 48), although for a short time only. We then reach the Shâri' el-Maṭarîya and the village of *Maṭarîya*, in which, to the right of the street, is the garden with the Virgin's Tree (see below).

The RAILWAY passes the following stations: $1\frac{3}{4}$ M. *Demirdâsh (Demerdash)*, station for 'Abbâsîya (p. 85); $2\frac{1}{2}$ M. *Manshîyet eṣ-Ṣadr*. — 3 M. *Pont de Qubba (Kûbri el-Qubba)*; $3\frac{1}{2}$ M. *Qubba-les-Bains (Ḥammâmât el-Qubba)*; $4\frac{1}{4}$ M. *Palais de Qubba* (*Sarâi el-Qubba*; royal palace, see above; tram to Helipolis Oasis, p. 128). — 5 M. *'Ezbet ez-Zeitûn* (Hotel Zeitûn, at the station), with numerous villas, and a British Institute for the Blind. — $5\frac{1}{2}$ M. *Ḥilmîya (Helmia)*, with a British military camp. — $6\frac{1}{4}$ M. *El-Maṭarîya (Mataria)*, station for Old Heliopolis (see below). Beyond the station (W.) is a road leading direct to the ($\frac{1}{2}$ M.) Virgin's Tree.

The railway goes on, viâ *'Aîn Shams (Ein Shems)* and *'Ezbet en-Nakhl* to ($8\frac{3}{4}$ M.) *El-Marg* (p. 130), junction of a line to *El-Khânqâh (Khanka*; p. 130), *Abu Za'bal* (wireless station, p. xxi, and basalt quarries, p. lxx; workshops of the Egyptian State Railways in course of construction, comp. p. 86), and *Shibîn el-Qanâṭir* (p. 181).

El-Maṭarîya (New Khedivial Hotel) is a village of 12,000 inhab., but noteworthy only for its possession of the *Virgin's Tree*, an ancient sycamore, under which, according to the legend, the Virgin and Child once rested during the Flight into Egypt. The sycamore, planted after 1672, was seriously injured in 1906, but a shoot still flourishes. The garden in which it grows, in the Shâri' el-Maṭarîya (adm. P.T. 5), is watered by means of a double sâqiya (p. lxxiv), supplied from a shallow reservoir fed by springs. This water is drinkable, while that of the other springs, which percolates from the Nile, is usually brackish; and it is supposed to possess this peculiar quality because the spring was called into being by the Child Jesus. Adjoining the garden is the *Chapelle de la Sainte-Famille*, belonging to the Jesuits.

From the garden the *Shâri' el-Misalla* leads in 12-15 minutes to the obelisk and ruins of ancient **Heliopolis** (p. cli), the famous

'city of the sun', called *On* by the Egyptians. The latter name frequently occurs in the Bible. Thus, in Genesis (xli. 45), Pharaoh gives Joseph "to wife Asenath the daughter of Poti-pherah [Egyptian *Pede-prē*, 'he whom the sun-god Rē has given'] priest of On".

Heliopolis-On was one of the most ancient Egyptian cities and in prehistoric times was for a while the capital of Egypt. Even in the historical period, when it was the chief town of a separate province included in Lower Egypt, it remained the religious and intellectual centre of the country. The deities of the place were the falcon-headed Rē-Harakhte (the sun-god, whence the Greek name Heliopolis) and the human-headed Atum, to whom the sacred Mnevis Bull (p. clvii) was consecrated. To these was dedicated the famous temple, 'the House of Rē', built on the site of an earlier edifice by *Amenemmēs I.*, first king of the 12th Dyn., in front of which his son and successor *Sesostris I.* erected two great obelisks (see below) in celebration of an important anniversary. A large section of the Egyptian religious literature was due to the priests of Heliopolis, and their doctrines were widely disseminated throughout the country at a very early period, so that Rē-Harakhte was one of the most highly venerated deities in Egypt. — Even during the Greek period these priests enjoyed a high reputation for wisdom; Herodotus conversed with them and Plato is fabulously said to have spent thirteen years with them. — Under the New Empire the temple of Heliopolis was the largest and most richly endowed in all Egypt, next to the temple of Amun at Thebes. — When Strabo visited Egypt in 24-20 B.C. the city had been destroyed, but the temple was still intact, except for some minor injuries attributed to Cambyses; even the houses of the priests and the apartments of Plato and his friend Eudoxus were shown to the traveller. The priestly school, however, had ceased to exist, and only a few officiating priests and guides for foreigners resided there.

The outer walls, rising in all directions from the fields, are now the only vestiges of the city; of the temple nothing is left but scanty ruins and a solitary *Obelisk* (Arabic *El-Misalla*). The latter (66 ft. high) is of red granite of Syene (Aswân, p. 379). Each of the four sides bears the same inscription in bold hieroglyphics, recording that Sesostris I. (Senwosret), King of Upper and Lower Egypt, lord of the diadems and son of the sun, whom the (divine) spirits of On love, etc., founded the obelisk on the first festival of Sed (a kind of jubilee celebration). The pyramidium at the top and the falcons which begin the inscriptions on each side were once covered with metal. The companion obelisk (for these monuments were always erected in pairs) stood down to the 12th century.

The two obelisks erected by Thutmosis III. (p. cv) in front of the temple of the sun-god were taken to Alexandria in 23 B.C. by order of the prefect Barbarus and set up in front of the Cæsareum (p. 14). One of them, which had lain prostrate for centuries, was presented by Muḥammed ʿAli to the British government in 1819, but was not removed for many years. It was erected in 1878 on the Thames Embankment in London. The other, given by Khedive Ismâʿîl to the City of New York, stands since 1880 in the Central Park. Both obelisks are known as 'Cleopatra's Needles', but have no connection with Cleopatra.

To the W. of the obelisk (see above) the remains of the temple may be recognized in a few blocks of granite, bearing inscriptions by Ramses II. On one Ramses II. appears offering a libation to Atum. — The *Necropolis of Heliopolis* lies about 3 M. to the E. of the obelisk.

The excursion may be extended to the villages of *El-Marg* (2½ M.), with some ruins of the 18th Dyn., and *El-Khânqâh*, on the outskirts of the desert (7½ M. from Maṭarîya), both stations on the railway from Cairo to Shibîn el-Qanâṭir (see p. 129). The palm-groves at El-Marg afford pleasant walks.

VII. The Delta Barrage.

The Railway to the Barrage is traversed by ten trains daily from Cairo (16½ M., in 40 min.; fare P.T. 9 or 6, return-tickets P.T. 13 or 8½, on Sun. and Fri. P.T. 8 and 6). Five of the trains run to the old station, and five to the new (¼ M. away, on the Cairo-Minûf-Tanta line, p. 36; buffet). The intermediate stations are *Shubra*, *Qalyûb* (p. 37), and *Qalyûb Town (Calioub-Ville)*. The best plan is to walk from either the old or the new station and to return by the small 'trolley', pushed by Arabs, which unites Barrage with the station of *El-Manâshi*, on the West Nile Railway (p. 35; 1 pers. P.T. 8, 2 pers. 11, 3-4 pers. 15 per hour); from the station to the gardens 1 pers. P.T. 2-4 (3 or 4 pers P.T. 5-10) per hour; from the station to the village of El-Manâshi across the river, or vice versa, P.T. 3 (3-4 pers. P.T. 8). Opposite the old Barrage station is the Restaurant Tewfikieh. — Messrs. Cook & Son arrange special excursions twice weekly by Steam Launch to the Barrage (see notices at the hotels and in the trams). Also steamers daily of the Compagnie des Bateaux-Omnibus (p. 41) from Rôd el-Farag. — Motor Road viâ Shubra and Qalyûb.

The object of the ***Delta Barrage** (*Barrage du Nil*, Arabic *El-Qanâṭir el-Khairîya*), one of the largest structures of the kind in the world, is to keep the water-level in the Delta uniform in all seasons, so as to obviate the necessity for the old irrigation machinery, with its great expenditure of labour, and to remove the difficulties of navigation during the three months when the Nile is at its lowest. The work was begun under Muḥammed ʿAli, about 1835. *Linant Bey* (1800-83; p. 195), the viceroy's French engineer of waterworks, proposed to alter the course of the river and to build a weir farther N., where the configuration of the ground appeared more favourable; but his plan was judged too costly and was rejected in favour of one proposed by another French engineer named *Mougel Bey*. The cost of establishing foundations in the shifting soil of the Delta, however, far exceeded the estimates; and, after all, the erection was found to be too insecure for its intended purpose. For nearly twenty years after 1867 the Barrage lay useless, as a costly failure; but in 1885-90 *Sir Colin Scott-Moncrieff* successfully completed it at a cost of 460,000*l.*, so that now a depth of water of about 12 ft. can be maintained in the W. branch of the Nile. In consequence of a burst in the winter of 1909-10 considerable strengthening works became necessary.

Nearest the station are the *Weirs* on the *Taufîqîya Canal* (p. 37) and on the *Eastern* or *Damietta Branch of the Nile.* The latter weir is over 500 yds. in length and has 68 vertical iron sluices. From the farther end a pretty avenue of lebbakh-trees (p. lxxvii) leads across the isthmus (about ½ M. wide) between the arms, in the middle of which is the *Minûfîya Canal*, constructed both for irrigation and for communication with the province of Minûfîya (p. 36). The *Weir* on the *Western* or *Rosetta Branch of the Nile* is 480 yds. across and has 58 vertical iron sluices. Farther W. is a fourth *Weir*, on the *Beḥeira Canal* (p. 35). The navigation of the river is carried on by means of spacious basins and locks, fitted with swing-bridges, at either end of the two weirs and also on the Minûfîya Canal. The

superstructures of the works are built in a Norman castellated style. A junction-canal above the weirs connects the two branches of the Nile, and is used to regulate the depth of water in each. When the river is low the W. branch receives all its water through this canal.

The island, formerly occupied by fortifications, is now covered with attractive and extensive **Gardens*, laid out by Walter Draper with flower-beds, lawns, artificial rocks, etc. Tea and rfmts. are obtainable at the little 'Casino'. — In the garden is a *Museum*, with models of the various waterworks of Egypt. — If not pressed for time the traveller should visit the little Arab village of *Shalaqân*, which stretches along the river near the railway stations. A charming and picturesque impression of Egyptian country-life is obtained here on market-days.

6. The Pyramids of Gîza.

This excursion requires at least half-a-day. TRAMWAY No. 14 from the ʿAtaba el-Khaḍra to the (1 hr.) *Mena House Hotel;* also No. 15 as far as Gîza Village only, see pp. 40, 41. — MOTORISTS will find the road excellent. — *RESTAURANT at the Mena House Hotel (p. 133). There is also a mall restaurant at the tram terminus. Or tourists may bring provisions with them from their hotel (included in the pension charge).

WHEN TIME IS LIMITED travellers should devote their attention to the ***Great Pyramid* (p. 136; ascend to the summit and visit the interior), the ***Sphinx* (p. 145), and the **Valley Temple of Khephren* (p. 146). The inspection of these chief objects of interest occupies about 2 hrs. The **Circuit* described on pp. 147-149 will occupy $1^1/_2$-2 hrs. more. — A fine and calm day should be selected for a visit to the Pyramids, the driving sand in windy weather being very unpleasant. *Sun Umbrellas* and *Smoked Spectacles* are advisable precautions against the glare of the sun. Ladies who intend to ascend the pyramids should dress as they would for mountain-climbing. A repetition of the excursion by moonlight produces an ineffaceable impression.

The tramway to the Pyramids (No. 14) follows the Shâriʿ Fu'âd I. and crosses the *Bûlâq Bridge* to *Gezîra* (comp. pp. 86, 87). Continuing along the Shâriʿ Fu'âd I., we cross the *Zamâlik Bridge* and then skirt the W. arm of the Nile S. to the *English Bridge* (p. 87). Here we join the *Shâriʿ el-Gîza* and follow it past the Zoological Gardens (p. 87) to the N. end of Gîza (station *Gîza Village*, p. 87), terminus of tram 15 (p. 41). [The route viâ Rôḍa, which tram 14 sometimes follows, diverges to the right at *Old Cairo*, about 750 yds. S. of the water-tower (p. 112), crosses the narrow branch of the Nile by the *El-Malik eṣ-Ṣâliḥ Bridge*, traverses the island of Rôḍa (p. 112), and crosses the main arm of the Nile by the *ʿAbbâs II. Bridge* (Pl. A B 8; open 10-10.45 a.m. and 3.15-4 p.m. to river traffic), which was completed in 1907 and is 489 yds. in length. It then runs W. to Gîza Village (see above).] On the left is the *Government Ophthalmic Hospital*, the laboratory of which (designed by N. Dawson, bronze panels by L. F. Rosslyn) was presented by the Imperial War Graves Commission in 1924-25 to commemorate the services of the Egyptian Labour and Camel Transport Corps in the Great War.

Thence the road to the Pyramids *(Shâri' el-Haram)*, constructed by Khedive Ismâʿîl for the visit of the Empress Eugénie (1869; comp. p. 195), which the tram follows, crosses a canal and intersects the Upper Egypt Railway (tram station; Gîza station lies 5 min. S., p. 153). After crossing a second canal it leads straight towards the Pyramids, which are still nearly 5 M. distant. On the left lie two villages, *Eṭ-Ṭâlibîya* and *El-Kôm el-Akhḍar* (tram stations). The fields on each side are intersected by canals and are flooded at the rising of the Nile. The huge angular forms of the Pyramids gradually become more distinct, and soon stand out in clear outlines.

At the tram terminus, on the edge of the desert, are the extensive buildings of the **Mena House Hotel** (p. 38); opposite are a police station, a post office, various shops, etc. The road goes on in a curve up the steep N. slope of the plateau on which the Pyramids stand.

At the tram terminus is a stand for donkeys and camels (P.T. 5 and 8 per hour). The porter of the Mena House Hotel also will procure riding animals at a fixed tariff. Sand-cart P.T. 15 per hr., 100 for the whole day; guide P.T. 6 per hr., 25 per day.

Tickets for the inspection of the Pyramids and other monuments are sold in a small office at the upper end of the street: for the ascent of the Great Pyramid P.T. 10; for a visit to the interior of the Pyramid P.T. 10; for a visit to the monuments (i.e. the Valley Temple) P.T. 5. For the entire expedition, including the ascent of the Great Pyramid and the visit to its interior, the charge is P.T. 20. Guides (Beduin; comp. pp. lix, lxi) are procured here through application to their sheikh. Bakshish is entirely optional (comp. the notice posted up). The inspection of the minor points of interest is free; our plan and description render the assistance of a guide entirely superfluous. The public is not admitted to the areas now being excavated by the Harvard-Boston Expedition and the Vienna Academy of Sciences (comp. p. 136). — No attention should be paid to the begging of the Beduin, and visitors are advised to have nothing to do with the vendors of 'antiquities' (almost invariably spurious). Other guides who press their services on the traveller should be repelled, if necessary with the help of the police.

The ****Pyramids of Gîza** or *Gizeh* form the second and most imposing of the six groups of pyramids which stand on the margin of the Libyan Desert and extend in a line measuring about 25 M. from N. to S. To the N. lies the group of *Abu Roâsh* (p. 149); southwards follow the groups of *Abuṣîr* (p. 151), *Ṣaqqâra* (p. 155), *Dahshûr* (p. 177), and *Lisht* (p. 217). The Arab word for pyramid is *hâram* (pl. *ahrâm*).

The Pyramids of Gîza rank among the oldest monuments of mankind, and their colossal proportions extort from us to-day the same astonishment as was felt in antiquity by Greek and Roman travellers. We marvel not only at the technical knowledge and ability of the Egyptians, but also at the might of their kings, who must have had absolute control over thousands of their subjects to be able to rear such monuments. Some conception of the enormous amount of labour involved may be obtained when we learn that, according to Sir Flinders Petrie's calculation, about 2,300,000 separate blocks of stone, averaging about $2^1/_2$ tons, were required for the Pyramid of Kheops, and that some of them were quarried on

the E. bank of the Nile and had to be ferried across the river and conveyed to the plateau.

The Construction of the Pyramids has been admirably described by Herodotus, the earliest writer on the subject, who visited Egypt about 450 B.C.

Herodotus states (ii. 124. 125) that there were some 100,000 men employed annually for three months in constructing the *Great Pyramid* of Kheops †. "They first made the road for the transport of the stones from the Nile to the Libyan Mts.; the length of the road amounts to five stadia (1017 yds.), its breadth is ten fathoms (60 ft.), and its height, at the highest places, is eight fathoms (48 ft.), and it is constructed entirely of smoothed stone with pictures engraved on it ††. Ten years were thus consumed in making this road and the subterranean chambers (for the coffins). The construction of the Pyramid itself occupied twenty years. Each of the four sides measures eight plethra (820 ft.), and the height is the same. It is covered with smoothed stones, well jointed, none of which is less than thirty feet long. This pyramid was first built in the form of a flight of steps. After the workmen had completed the pyramid in this form, they raised the other stones (used for the casing) by means of machines, made of short beams, from the ground to the first tier of steps; and after the stone was placed there it was raised to the second tier by another machine; for there were as many machines as there were tiers of steps; or perhaps there was but one machine, easily moved, that was raised from one tier to the other, as it was required for lifting the stones. The highest part of the pyramid was thus finished first (by smoothing), the parts adjoining it were taken next, and the lowest part, next to the ground, was completed last. It was recorded on the pyramid, in Egyptian writing, how much was spent on radishes, onions, and roots of garlic for distribution among the workmen and, if I rightly remember what the interpreter who read the writing told me †††, the money they cost amounted to sixteen hundred talents of silver [upwards of 350,000*l*.]. If this was really the case, how much more must then have been spent on the iron with which they worked, and on the food and clothing of the workmen."

In modern times many eager discussions have been held as to the mode in which the Pyramids were erected and the meaning of the account given by Herodotus. The most important questions seem to be: (1) How could Kheops, when he ascended the throne and chose an area of 82,000 sq. yds. for his monument, know that his reign would be so unusually long as to enable him to complete it? (2) If one of the builders of the great pyramids had died in the second or third year of his reign, how could their sons or successors, however willing to carry out the plan, have succeeded in

† According to Sir Flinders Petrie, these three months fell during the inundation, when field-work was at a standstill and the services of 100,000 men for transporting the stones could be easily enough obtained. The stonecutters and masons were probably engaged all the year round in the quarries and on the pyramid itself.

†† This causeway is still traceable. It terminated on the E. side of the Pyramid of Kheops (see the plan and p. 148). The 'pictures' said to have been engraved on the causeway wall probably included the hieroglyphic inscriptions by which subsequent visitors sought to immortalize their names.

††† It is unlikely that the interpreters, who attended travellers like the dragomans of the present day, were able to read hieroglyphics. They probably repeated mere popular traditions regarding the pyramids and other monuments, with embellishments and exaggerations of their own.

completing so gigantic a task and in erecting monuments for themselves at the same time? (3) And how comes it that many other kings did not, like Kheops, boldly anticipate a reign of twenty-five years and begin a work of the same kind, the design for which might so easily have been drawn, and might so readily have been carried out by his subjects? — To these questions Lepsius (p. 136), Erbkam, and Ebers (p. v) answer. "Each king", says Lepsius in his letters from Egypt (p. ccvii), "began to build his pyramid when he ascended the throne. He began it on a small scale, in order that, if a short reign should be in store for him, his tomb might be a complete one. As years rolled on, however, he continued enlarging it by the addition of outer coatings of stone, until he felt that his career was drawing to a close. If he died before the work was completed the last coating was then finished, and the size of the monument was accordingly proportioned to the length of the builder's reign." — This 'layer theory' of the construction of the Pyramids has been opposed by Sir Flinders Petrie, who has sought to show that the initial plan of each pyramid practically contemplated the full extent reached by the completed work. But more recently Borchardt (p. 151) has demonstrated conclusively that Lepsius's theory is not altogether incorrect, though it requires modification in some essential points. According to Borchardt, each pyramid-builder began by planning a monument of moderate size. In many instances this original small conception was permanently adhered to; but it not unfrequently happened that kings who enjoyed long reigns or found themselves in control of more extensive powers expanded their original designs and enlarged their buildings, either by mere additions without altering the passages or chambers (as in the Step Pyramid at Ṣaqqâra) or by revising the whole original design, including the chambers, etc., on a new and more extensive scale (as in the second and third pyramids of Gîza). Occasionally a second enlargement took place, as in the case of the Great Pyramid.

The Pyramids were opened by sacrilegious robbers at a very early period, certainly under the 12th Dyn. and perhaps even earlier. Attempts were made to force an entrance into the inner chambers, and passages were laboriously cut through the solid masonry in order to reach the expected treasures. In the course of this mining and tunnelling the passages and chambers sustained much damage. Somewhere about the period of the 25th or 26th Dyn. these injuries were repaired and the Pyramids restored. But they seem to have been again invaded by the Persians; and also at later periods, under the Romans and under the Arabs, renewed attempts were made to penetrate to the treasures supposed to lie in the interior.

The first modern traveller who carefully and successfully examined the Pyramids was *Nicholas Shaw* in 1721; but he still entertained the notion that the Sphinx had a subterranean connection with the Great Pyramid. He was followed by *Norden* in 1737; *Richard Pococke*, who visited Egypt in 1737-38 and gave a plan and dimensions; *Claude-Louis*

Fourmont in 1755; *Carsten Niebuhr* in 1761; *Davison* in 1763; *James Bruce* in 1768; *Volney* in 1783; *W. G. Browne* in 1792-98; and *D. V. Denon*, *Coutelle*, *Jomard* (p. 79), and other savants of the French expedition under Bonaparte in 1799-1801. Jomard in particular has the merit of having taken comparatively accurate measurements. *William Richard Hamilton*, in 1801, was a dispassionate and critical observer. In 1817 *Caviglia*, a bold but illiterate and fanciful seaman, was fortunate in eliciting new facts regarding the interior of the Great Pyramid, and excavated the Sphinx (p. 145). *Giovanni Battista Belzoni* (1775-1823), an intelligent explorer and accurate draughtsman, was originally a novice at Rome, but when the French occupied that city he retired to London, where he devoted himself to study in spite of many hardships. In 1815 he reached Egypt, where, besides opening the Second Pyramid of Gîza in 1818, he discovered the tomb of Sethos I. at Thebes, etc. The next eminent explorer was *Sir Gardner Wilkinson* in 1831. In 1837 and 1838 *Gen. R. W. Howard Vyse* and *John Shae Perring* made very thorough investigations and took careful measurements which will always be considered authoritative. In 1842-45 *Richard Lepsius*, the German Egyptologist, made several very important discoveries and furnished us with much valuable information. He found no fewer than thirty pyramids which had been quite unknown to previous travellers. *Sir Gaston Maspero* (p. 88) opened the small pyramids of Ṣaqqâra in 1880-81 and inside the pyramids of Onnos and the 6th Dyn. kings discovered the 'Pyramid Texts' (p. clxxvii), which are of great importance in the history of religion. *Sir W. M. Flinders Petrie* subjected the Pyramids of Gîza to new measurements in 1881-82. The Pyramids of Dahshûr were examined in 1894-95 by *De Morgan;* those of Lisht by *Gautier* and *Jéquier* in 1895, and by the expedition of the *Metropolitan Museum of New York* since 1906; and those of Abu Roâsh by the *Institut Français* (p. 44) in 1900-2. Excavations were carried on by German explorers at Abu Gurâb in 1898-1901. A renewed examination of the pyramids and tombs of Ṣaqqâra was undertaken by the Egyptian *Department of Antiquities* in 1900 and continued since 1923 by Cecil M. Firth, with particularly successful results in the case of the Step Pyramid (p. 156). The *German Oriental Society* carried on excavations at Abuṣîr in 1902-8, while Germans and Americans have been exploring the Necropolis of Gîza since 1903, and Austrians (Vienna Academy of Sciences) since 1912. The excavation of the Valley Temple of Khephren was accomplished by the German *Von Sieglin* expedition in 1909-10. The *Harvard-Boston Expedition* discovered the tomb-shaft of Queen Hetep-heres in 1925.

The Pyramids of Gîza stand upon a plateau, which extends 1600 yds. from E. to W. and 1300 yds. from N. to S., the E. and N. margins being precipitous at places. The Pyramids are built exactly facing the four cardinal points. The diagonal of the largest pyramid from N.E. to S.W. is precisely in a line with the diagonal of the second pyramid. The various numerical or metrical theories concerning the building of the Pyramids, and the belief that the ancient Egyptians might have concealed certain esoteric secrets within the Great Pyramid, are devoid of any scientific foundation.

The ****Great Pyramid**, or *Pyramid of Kheops*, which we reach first, was called by the Egyptians *Ekhet Khufu* ('horizon of Khufu'), and was built by *Kheops*, the *Khufu* of the Egyptians (p. cii). The outermost covering has mostly disappeared, except at several places on the N. side. The length of each side (Pl. *A A*) is now 746 ft., but was formerly (Pl. *B B*) about 756 ft. (i.e. 440 Egyptian ells); the present perpendicular height (Pl. *C D*) is 450 ft., while originally

(Pl. *C E*), including the nucleus of rock (Pl. *F F*) at the bottom and the apex (Pl. *D E*), which has now disappeared, it is said to have been 481 ft. The length of each sloping side (Pl. *A D*) is now 568 ft. and was formerly (Pl. *B E*) 610 ft. The angle at which the sides rise is 51° 50′. The cubic content of the masonry, deducting the foundation of rock in the interior, as well as the hollow chambers, was formerly no less than 3,277,000 cubic yards and it still amounts to 3,057,000 cubic yards. The stupendous structure covers an area of nearly thirteen acres. The material of which it is constructed is yellowish limestone quarried in the vicinity and containing numerous fossils, chiefly nummulites (p. 125). The outer covering was formed of blocks of a finer white limestone, which was obtained from the quarries at Ṭura (p. 180) and other parts of the Moqaṭṭam.

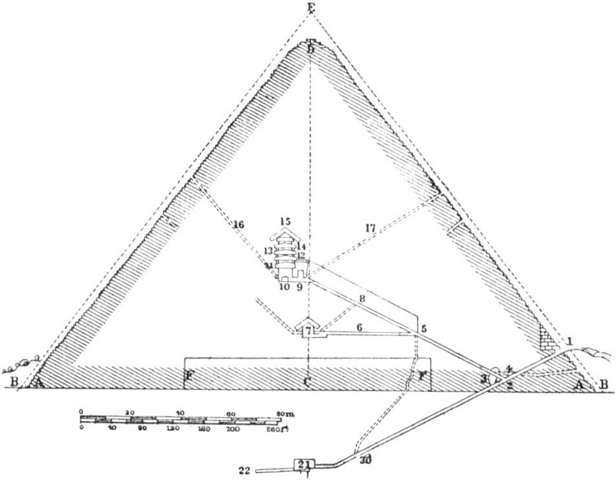

Construction of the Great Pyramid. According to Borchardt's theory this pyramid was not built on a single homogeneous plan (p. 135). It was originally designed to contain only one sloping corridor hewn in the rocky ground *(2-20)* and leading through an antechamber *(21)* to Passage *22*. But before this design was completely carried out it was exchanged for a more comprehensive plan, involving the construction of another chamber, now called the Queen's Chamber *(7)*, reached by the corridor marked *2*, *5*, *6*. But even this was not final, for Kheops undertook another and greater extension, resulting in the construction of the Great Hall *(8)* and the King's Chamber *(10)*.

The Ascent of the Pyramid, though fatiguing, is perfectly safe. The traveller selects two or three of the Beduin (p. 133). With one

holding each hand, and the third pushing behind, he begins the ascent of the steps (usually at the N.E. corner), which are each about 3 ft. high. The strong and active attendants assist the traveller to mount by pushing, pulling, and supporting him, and will scarcely allow him a moment's rest until the top is reached. As, however, the unwonted exertion is fatiguing, the traveller should insist on resting as often as he feels inclined. All requests for bakshish should be refused, and it is as well to keep an eye upon one's pockets. — The ascent may be made in 10-15 min. but, in hot weather especially, the traveller is recommended to take nearly double that time, in order to avoid the discomfort of arriving breathless and heated at the summit.

The space at the top at present is about 12 yds. square, so that there is abundant room for a large party of visitors. The **View is remarkably interesting and striking. There is perhaps no other prospect in the world in which life and death, fertility and desolation, are seen in so close juxtaposition and in such marked contrast. To the W., S., and N.W. extend yellowish-brown tracts of sand, interspersed with barren cliffs. The huge and colourless monuments erected here by the hand of man remind the spectator, like the desert itself, of death and eternity. On a bare plateau of rock stand the other pyramids, while the Sphinx reposes majestically in its pit. The arrangement of the extensive burial-ground to the E. and W., with its various streets of tombs, is plainly seen. To the S., in the distance, rise the pyramids of Abuṣîr, Ṣaqqâra, and Dahshûr. To the N. are the palm-groves of Kirdâsa and the fields of the valley of the Nile. Towards the E., on the other hand, glitters the river, on each bank of which stretches a tract of rich arable land, luxuriantly clothed with blue-green vegetation and varying in breadth. The fields are intersected in every direction by canals, on the banks of which stately palms wave their flexible fan-like leaves. In the direction of Cairo runs the long straight carriage-road. Immediately before us rises the Citadel with its striking minarets, while the Moqaṭṭam hills, which form the chief mass of colour in the landscape, gleam in the morning with a pale golden tint and in the evening with a violet hue.

The descent of the Great Pyramid is hardly less fatiguing than the ascent. Persons liable to giddiness may find it a little trying, but the help of the Beduin removes all danger.

A visit to the Interior of the Great Pyramid is facilitated by modern staircases, but should be omitted by nervous or delicate persons, especially those predisposed to apoplectic or fainting fits.

The original entrance (Pl. *1*) is on the N. side (as in all pyramids), on the thirteenth tier of stones, at a perpendicular height of 49 ft. from the ground. The long passage *1-20*, which is only 3 ft. 11 in. in height and 3 ft. 4 in. in width, descends in a straight direction at an angle of 26° 41′, and is altogether 106½ yds. in length.

The present entrance, made by treasure-hunting Arabs, is a few tiers lower (comp. the plan). We follow this passage as far as the point 2 only, 20 yds. from the original entrance. Here diverges the ascending passage 2-5, the lower end of which is filled with massive blocks of granite, placed in position after the interment of the mummy to protect the grave from robbers. The hardness of the material of which this barrier consists compelled the treasure-hunters (see above) to avoid it and to force a new passage (Pl. *4*) through the softer limestone. Beyond the granite blocks we enter the passage (Pl. *3-5*), 41 yds. in length, beyond which lies the Great Hall (Pl. *8*).

In front of the entrance to the latter a formerly concealed opening gives access to the horizontal passage *6* which terminates in the so-called *Queen's Chamber* (Pl. *7*). This passage is at first 3 ft. 9 in. only in height, but at a distance of $6^1/_2$ yds. from the chamber the paving has been removed so that the height increases to 5 ft. 8 inches. The N. and S. sides of the chamber are each 17 ft. in length, and the E. and W. sides 18 ft. 10 inches. The height is 20 ft. 4 in., including the pointed roof, which rises $5^1/_2$ ft. above the top of the walls and consists of enormous blocks with their ends sunk into the surrounding masonry.

The jointing and polish of the fine-grained Moqaṭṭam limestone in the *Great Hall* (Pl. *8*) form an unsurpassable marvel of skilful masonry, of which the Arab historian ʿAbd el-Laṭîf (1162-1231) accurately remarks, that neither a needle nor even a hair can be inserted into the joints of the stones. The Great Hall is 28 ft. high and 155 ft. long. The lower part is 3 ft. 4 in. in width; and the upper part, above the stone ramps on each side, which are 1 ft. 8 in. thick and 2 ft. high, is $6^3/_4$ ft. in width. The roof is formed of seven courses of stone projecting one above the other and crowned by horizontal slabs. At the end of the Great Hall is a small horizontal passage, 22 ft. long and 3 ft. 8 in. high, expanding about the middle into an antechamber (Pl. *9*), which was once closed by four trap-doors of granite. The remains of one of these slabs, in its pendent position, should be noticed. We next enter the tomb-chamber proper, commonly called the *King's Chamber* (Pl. *10*). The N. and S. sides are each 17 ft. in length, the E. and W. sides $34^1/_2$ ft., and the height is 19 ft.; the floor of the chamber is $139^1/_2$ ft. above the plateau on which the pyramid stands. The chamber is entirely lined with granite and is roofed with nine enormous slabs of granite, each $18^1/_2$ ft. in length, above which five chambers *(11-15)* have been formed, which may be reached from the Hall *8* by means of ladders.

In constructing these hollow chambers the over-cautious builders made an error in their calculations, for as a matter of fact the uppermost chamber by it'elf would have been sufficient to prevent the roof of the King's Chamber being crushed by the superincumbent weight. The name of Kheops was found in the two highest chambers (Pl. *14*, *15*).

The King's Chamber now contains nothing but an empty and mutilated *Sarcophagus* of granite, bearing no trace of an inscription, the lid of which had disappeared before the time of the French

expedition (p. 136). The sarcophagus, which once contained the mummy of Kheops is, 7½ ft. long, 3 ft. 3 in. wide, and 3 ft. 4 in. high. The very massive sides ring with a clear tone when struck. Curiously enough, the King's Chamber does not lie exactly in a line with the diagonal of the pyramid but is 16 ft. 4 in. to the S. of it.

The *Air Shafts* (Pl. *16, 17*), the ends of which are seen about 3 ft. above the floor of the chamber, were perhaps constructed from religious motives. They are about 6 in. in height and 8 in. in width only, expanding by a few inches at the outer extremities.

The other chambers discovered in the interior of the Great Pyramid are inaccessible to visitors. The first passage *1-20*, which is blocked at *2*, leads downwards in a straight line, 319 ft. in length, and terminates in a horizontal corridor, 27 ft. in length, 3 ft. in height, and 2 ft. in width, which leads to the unfinished subterranean chamber *21*, hewn in the rock. The E. and W. sides of this chamber are each 46 ft. in length, the N. and S. sides 27 ft., and the height 10½ ft. Its floor is 101½ ft. below the level on which the pyramid is built. The subterranean horizontal passage *22*, 60 ft. long, ends in a cul-de-sac. The statement of Herodotus, that the subterranean chamber planned by Kheops for the reception of his body was surrounded by a canal conducted hither from the Nile, is erroneous, as the chamber lies above the highest level of the overflow of the river, and it has, moreover, been ascertained that no channel from the river ever led in this direction. — From the lower end of the Great Hall a shaft *(5-20)*, discovered by Davison in 1763, descends to the lower passage. The enterprising Caviglia (p. 136) found that it terminated in the passage *(20)* leading to the subterranean chamber *(21)*. To all appearance it was bored through the masonry after the latter had been finished.

The vast **Cemetery of the Kings** (no adm.), extending to the W. of the Great Pyramid, was laid out on a uniform plan under the 4th Dyn. for members of the royal household and high officials. Its roads run from N. to S. and from E. to W. and are bordered by stone maṣṭabas, each preceded, at the S. end of its E. side, by a sacrificial chamber constructed of brick or stone. The necropolis was bounded by a wall on the S. side, towards the middle of which lay a hollow originally unoccupied by tombs. After the fall of the 4th Dyn. the royal cemetery lost its privileged position; under the 5th and 6th Dyn. smaller tombs filled the gaps between the large maṣṭabas; the open spaces were likewise utilized and the cemetery was extended to the W. A labyrinth of roads and paths came into being, through which it was difficult to find one's way. The necropolis has been excavated by Germans, Austrians, and Americans (comp. p. 136). The best general view of it is from the summit of the Great Pyramid.

To the E. of the pyramid is the wired-off enclosure of the Harvard-Boston Expedition, the area of which includes some of the monuments described below. — To the E. of the pyramid stood the *Temple* for the worship of the deceased Kheops such as was erected in the case of every pyramid (comp. p. clxxvii). Nothing of this now exists, however, except some remnants of the basaltic pavement. The neighbouring 'mortar-pits' (marked *m* on the plan at p. 132)

hewn out of the rock, once contained three boat-shaped structures of brick or wood, intended to represent 'boats of the sun' (which played a part in the Egyptian ritual; comp. p. cl). Part of the long covered *Causeway* ascending from the valley to the temple is still preserved; the tunnel constructed below it to connect the two sections of the necropolis is the oldest known road-tunnel. — On the E. side lie also *Three Small Pyramids* intended for wives of the king. The middle one of these (Pl. *l*) is said by Herodotus to have been the tomb of a daughter of Kheops. That to the S., according to an inscription in the Cairo Museum, belonged to the queen of Kheops, named Henwetsen. — At the E. base of the small pyramid to the S. lies a small *Sanctuary of Isis* (Pl. *o*), the 'mistress of the Pyramids', which was erected by a King Psusennes (21st Dyn.) and rebuilt in the 26th Dyn., when it was used as a mortuary temple. — Between the N. and middle pyramids is a pit (about 66 ft. long) for a fourth 'boat of the sun' (see above), belonging to the queen and walled across later on to form storehouses.

Between the enclosure of the small N. pyramid and the causeway of the Pyramid of Kheops is a *Shaft*, 99 ft. deep, descending to a *Tomb Chamber*. This belonged to *Queen Hetep-heres*, wife of Snofru (p. cii) and mother of Kheops, and when discovered in 1925 was completely undisturbed. Some of its contents are now in the Cairo Museum (pp. 89, 102). — Close by are *Two Tombs* (6th Dyn.) with underground sacrificial chambers, the larger on the W. being that of *Kar*, a private secretary of Phiops II. and priest of the Pyramid of Kheops, that on the E. belonging to *Iduw*, son of Kar, who bore the same titles as his father. A winding staircase leads to an open court adjoined by the sacrificial chamber on the S., next to which is a chamber with a false door. On the right of Iduw's tomb-chamber is a curious representation of the deceased; from a deep recess in the rock, which is painted to resemble a granite slab, emerges his half-length figure with the hands stretched towards the table of offerings. — To the E. of the small pyramids are five rows of large *Maṣṭabas*, extending from W. to E. behind one another. These are tombs of sons and daughters of Kheops, and their cult-chapels, adjoining them on the E., still survive in part.

About 100 yds. to the E. of the tomb-shaft of Queen Hetep-heres (see above) lies the maṣṭaba of Queen Hetep-heres (II.), a granddaughter of Hetep-heres I. and probably the wife of Dedfrē (p. cii). In the rock below its N. part is the *Tomb of Queen Meryes-onkh*, a daughter of Hetep-heres II. and probably the wife of Khephren (p. 142). Two staircases descend from the street-level to the entrance of the tomb, which consists of a main chamber and two side-chambers. In the N. wall of the N. side-chamber are ten statues hewn out of the rock and representing Hetep-heres (II.), Meryes-onkh, and the latter's daughters. There are four similar statues (of Hetep-heres II. and Meryes-onkh) in the W. side-chamber. In the S. wall of the main chamber are the six squatting figures of the funeral priests. The walls are decorated in part with fine inscriptions and paintings with well-preserved colouring; note the portrait of the fair-haired Hetep-heres II. From the W. side-chamber the tomb-shaft descends to the tomb-chamber (the granite sarcophagus in the chamber itself has been rifled).

The **Second Pyramid,** called by the Egyptians *Wer-Khefrē* ('Great is Khefrē'), was erected by ***Khefrē***, who was called ***Khephren*** by Herodotus (p. ciii). Owing to the greater height of the rocky plateau on which it stands, it appears taller than its larger neighbour. The perpendicular height of this pyramid is now 447½ ft. (originally 471 ft.), each side of the base measures 690½ ft. (originally 707¾ ft.), and the height of each sloping side is 563½ ft. (originally 572½ ft.), while the sides rise at an angle of 52°20′. The solid content of the masonry is now 2,156,960 cubic yds., equivalent to 4,883,000 tons in weight (originally 2,426,710 cubic yds., equivalent to 5,309,000 tons). As the rocky site rises towards the

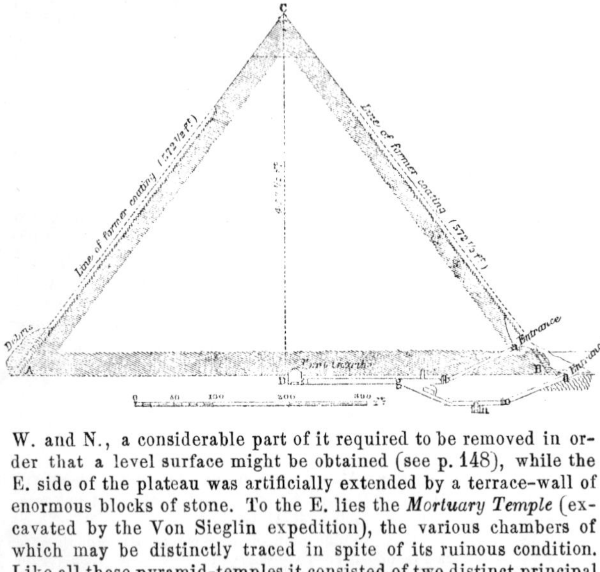

W. and N., a considerable part of it required to be removed in order that a level surface might be obtained (see p. 148), while the E. side of the plateau was artificially extended by a terrace-wall of enormous blocks of stone. To the E. lies the ***Mortuary Temple*** (excavated by the Von Sieglin expedition), the various chambers of which may be distinctly traced in spite of its ruinous condition. Like all these pyramid-temples it consisted of two distinct principal portions, the public temple and the reserved sanctuary. The main part of the public temple was a large open court, surrounded by a passage like the cloisters of a mediæval monastery and embellished with colossal statues of the king. This was the scene of the great funeral festivals. The causeway ascending to it from the valley, the monumental entrance to which was formed by the so-called 'Granite Temple' (p. 146), is still traceable. To the S., within the wall that surrounded this pyramid, stood another small pyramid, now almost level with the ground, in which the queen was probably buried. —

The casing of the Second Pyramid, of which a considerable part still remains at the top, consisted of limestone slabs in the upper courses and of partially unpolished granite slabs in the two lower (well preserved on the W. side). The merit of having opened this pyramid belongs to *Belzoni* (p. 136). An inscription over the entrance records that the opening took place on March 2nd, 1818.

The plan of the Second Pyramid also appears to have been altered in the course of building. The original intention seems to have been to erect a small pyramid over the subterranean chamber. Afterwards a larger pyramid was decided upon and the chamber moved towards the S., to its present position.

The INTERIOR is thus entered by two passages, both on the N. side. The mouth of one of these, blocked up on the abandonment of the first plan, is in the level surface in front of the pyramid and was concealed by the pavement (Pl. *d*); that of the other, which still forms the entrance to the pyramid, is on the N. side of the pyramid itself, and is now 38 ft., but formerly 49 ft., above the level of the ground (Pl. *a*). This *Upper Passage*, which was lined with granite at the beginning, descends at an angle of 25° 55′ for 105 ft. (Pl. *a b*) and then leads as a horizontal corridor (Pl. *b g c*) to 'Belzoni's Chamber', which once contained the tomb of the deceased, situated 3 ft. 10 in. E. of the diagonal of the pyramid. This chamber is hewn in the rock and roofed with painted slabs of limestone, placed obliquely at the same angle as the sides of the pyramid. It is 22½ ft. in height, 46½ ft. in length from E. to W., and 16⅓ ft. in width from N. to S. Belzoni here found a granite sarcophagus let into the ground and filled with rubbish, 3 ft. in height, 6 ft. 7 in. in length, and 3½ ft. in width, and destitute of inscription. The lid was broken. — The *Lower Passage* (Pl. *d*) descends at first at an angle of 21° 40′, reaches a trap-door (Pl. *e*), runs in a horizontal direction for 59 ft. (Pl. *e f*), and then ascends, terminating, after a distance of 97 ft. in all (Pl. *g*), in the horizontal corridor leading to Belzoni's Chamber. This ascending passage was perhaps made to permit the introduction of a broad trap-door of granite and to permit of the transportation of the coffin from the old to the new tomb-chamber. On the E. (left) side of the middle of the horizontal portion of this lower passage was introduced a small recess, and on the W. side is a steep passage, 22 ft. in length, descending to a chamber (Pl. *h*) hewn in the rock, 8 ft. 5 in. in height, 34 ft. 3 in. in length, and 10 ft. 4 in. in width. This chamber was originally designed to receive the sarcophagus, but was never used.

The **Third Pyramid**, named by the Egyptians *Neter-Menkewrē* ('Divine is Menkewrē'), was erected by *Menkewrē*, the *Mykerinos* of Herodotus and the *Mencheres* of Manetho (p. ciii). Its present perpendicular height (Pl. *B B*, p. 144) is 204 ft., its former height *(B C)* was 218 ft.; the side of the base *(A A)* is 356½ ft.; the present height *(A B)* of the sloping sides is 263¾ ft., being originally *(A C)* 279¾ ft.; these rise at an angle of 51°. The upper part of the casing of the pyramid was formed of limestone blocks, the lower part of granite, left partly unsmoothed. The granite covering is in good preservation, especially on the N. and W. sides. On the E. side lie the ruins of the customary mortuary temple, laid bare during the American excavations of 1907 under Dr. Reisner and, as usual, approached from the valley by a still recognizable causeway, beginning near the modern Arab cemetery with a so-called valley-temple, a smaller sanctuary built of brick but no longer recognizable.

The *Interior* is reached only with difficulty. The entrance is on the N. side. A passage *a c* descends at an angle of 26° 2′ for a distance of 104½ ft.,

being lined with red granite where it passes through the masonry from *a* to *b* and then penetrating the solid rock from *b* to *c*. From *c* a horizontal passage *c d* leads to an antechamber *f*, 7 ft. in height, 12 ft. in length, 10 ft. in width, and decorated with door-shaped ornaments. Beyond this chamber it passes three trap-doors *g*, descends slightly from *h* to *d* (gradient 4°), a distance of 41½ ft., and finally descends to the chamber *e*, in a cavity in which the sarcophagus of the king seems to have originally stood (comp. below). This chamber is 44½ ft. long, 12½ ft. broad, and, owing to the unevenness of the rock, from which the pavement has been removed, varies from 13 ft. to 13 ft. 5 in. in height.

In the pavement of the chamber *e* is the mouth (formerly covered) of a shaft 30 ft. in length, which has a fine granite lining at its upper end and could be closed by a trap-door at its lower end. It is continued by a horizontal shaft, 10 ft. in length, to the granite *Tomb Chamber* (Pl. *i*). Immediately before the latter is reached a flight of seven steps leads to

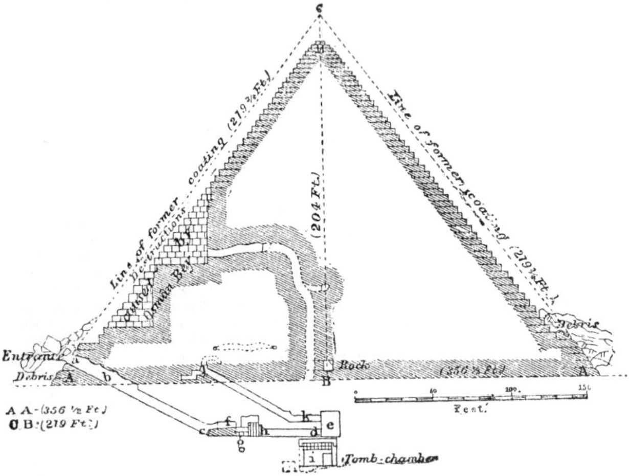

the right to a chamber with recesses on the right and back walls. The tomb-chamber is paved with blocks of granite, 2½ ft. in thickness, and its ceiling has been formed by placing the stones against each other at an angle so as to resemble a roof and then hollowing them out on the inside in the form of a Gothic arch. The richly decorated sarcophagus of Menkewrē was found here by Gen. Vyse (p. 136) in a good state of preservation. It was made of basalt and measured externally 2 ft. 7 in. in height. The lid was gone. Fragments of the inner wooden coffin and of a mummy (now in the British Museum) were found in the chamber *e*. The vessel in which the sarcophagus was being conveyed to England was unfortunately lost off the coast of Spain.

The original intention of the builder was to construct a pyramid on a small scale, containing only the sloping corridor *l k*, leading to a chamber at *e*, smaller than that now existing. But when a larger pyramid was projected the corridor *a b c d* was formed, leading first to an antechamber and then to a tomb-chamber at *e*, enlarged by deepening the earlier chamber at that point. Under the New Empire the interior of the pyramid

was ruined by the forcible entry of treasure-seekers; but probably during the Saïte period a restoration took place. To this restoration are due the sloping shaft and the granite chamber *(i)* in which the stone sarcophagus of Menkewrē was concealed, as well as the lower-lying room with the recesses.

The Second and Third Pyramids are most conveniently visited in the course of the circuit of the pyramid plateau mentioned on p. 147. After inspecting the Great Pyramid visitors may follow the wide road, lined with stones, which skirts the E. side of the pyramid, passes the maṣṭabas on its S. side (excavated by the Vienna Academy in 1928 and 1929) and Campbell's Tomb (p. 148), and leads to the Sphinx, which lies about 350 yds. from the S.E. corner of the pyramid.

The ****Sphinx**, the guardian of the sacred enclosure of the Second Pyramid and next to the Pyramids themselves the most famous monument in this vast burial-ground, is a colossal recumbent lion with the head of a king wearing the royal head-dress, which is adorned with the royal serpent (p. clxxxvi). It lies in the middle of a large quarry, which supplied Kheops with the stone for the building of his pyramid and the large maṣṭabas in the Cemetery of the Kings, which immediately adjoins it on the N. In the course of the quarrying operations a knoll of hard grey and soft yellowish limestone was left behind as being useless for building material. When Khephren, the successor of Kheops, was erecting his own pyramid and the temple buildings in connection with it, this mass of rock attracted the attention of the king and his builders, and the happy idea was conceived of shaping it into a sphinx. Such was the origin of this gigantic figure, which from the earliest times till the present day has aroused universal admiration and must always be reckoned among the greatest wonders of the world. Afterwards it was taken for the sun-god and named *Harmachis* (i.e. 'Horus on the horizon'). In front of the breast was once an image of a god, the weathered remains of which are still to be seen. The head is now deplorably mutilated; the neck has become too thin, the nose and beard have been broken off, and the reddish tint which enlivened the body has almost disappeared. But in spite of all injuries it preserves even now an impressive expression of strength and majesty. The entire height of the monument, from the pavement to the crown of the head, is about 66 ft., while its total length is 240 ft. The ear, according to Mariette, is $4^1/_2$ ft., the nose 5 ft. 7 in., and the mouth 7 ft. 7 in. in length; and the extreme breadth of the face is 13 ft. 8 inches. There is a hollow in the head which originally held a thead-ornament and is now closed with an iron plate. — In Egyptian art the sphinxes are nearly always male figures, and it is only rarely that they have the female head ascribed to them by Greek legend.

The first Excavation and Restoration of the Sphinx, so far as is now known, was undertaken by Thutmosis IV. (see p. 146). During the Ptolemaic or Roman period the colossus was several times freed from the encroaching sand and restored. At the same time a sacrificial platform, with a still surviving altar, was constructed in front of it, walls of brick

and stone being erected, without permanent success, to prevent the encroachment of the sand. The great staircases on the E. also date from this period. Curiously enough, the Sphinx was mentioned neither by Herodotus nor by any later Greek traveller. The mutilations which now disfigure it date from the Arab domination. In 1380 it fell a victim to the iconoclastic zeal of a fanatic sheikh, and it was afterwards used as a target by the Mamelukes. — In 1818 the Sphinx was first completely excavated by *Caviglia* (p. 136), at the cost (450*l.*) of an English society. He discovered the flight of steps which ascended to the monument, and also found between the paws of the lion a carefully laid pavement, at the end of which, between the paws, rose a kind of open temple. The latter was enclosed by two partitions, through which ran a passage; in the middle of the latter was a small figure of a lion, facing the Sphinx. In the background and at each side were memorial stones erected by Thutmosis IV. and Ramses II. The Sphinx was again excavated by ***Maspero*** in 1886. A new and complete excavation and restoration was undertaken by ***E. Baraize*** in **1925-26** on behalf of the Egyptian Department of Antiquities. Several pieces of the colossus that had fallen off were refixed by cement in their original positions; the head-dress, which was in a dangerous condition, was supported by means of stays; and loose places at the back of the head were made firm with cement. No reconstitution of missing parts has been attempted.

The large ***Valley Temple of Khephren**, long known as the 'Granite Temple', 50 yds. S.E. of the Sphinx, was discovered by Mariette in 1853 and almost completely excavated by the Von Sieglin expedition in 1909-10. This was the sanctuary erected as

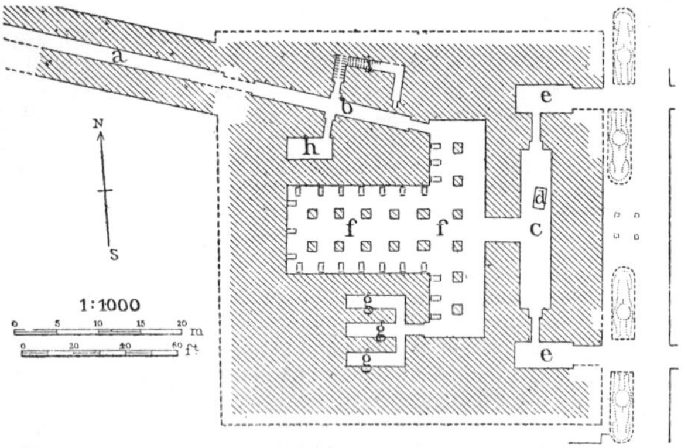

an entrance to the causeway which ascended from the valley to the mortuary temple and pyramid of Khephren. It is an example of the simple and majestic architecture of a period when the art of working the hardest kinds of stone had already attained perfection.

The total structure is 147 ft. square and 43 ft. in height; externally the walls batter. The façade, on the E. side, was pierced by two huge portals (now closed), surrounded by monumental royal inscriptions. The present entrance is from the ancient *Causeway*

leading to the pyramid-temple (p. 142), the first part of which has been laid bare (Pl. a). We descend the corridor (Pl. b) to the *Antechamber* (Pl. c), constructed of red granite, in which the passages leading from the two portals unite. Here is also the shaft (Pl. d), at present full of water, in which Mariette found the famous statue of Khephren now in the Cairo Museum (p. 90), etc. We return through the large doorway in the central axis of the building into the main *Hypostyle Hall* (Pl. f), which is shaped like an inverted T, the main arm being 57 ft. long and 29½ ft. broad, and the cross arm 82 ft. long and 23 ft. broad. Sixteen monolithic granite pillars divide the main arm into three aisles, the cross arm into two. The stone beams of the architrave still preserve their sharp edges. These rooms were lighted by means of small oblique openings, still seen in the upper part of the side-walls. Against the walls originally stood twenty-three colossal royal statues, the bases of which have left rectangular marks on the pavement. Several of these statues are now in Cairo. — From the S.W. angle of the hypostyle hall a dark passage leads to a group of *Storerooms* (Pl. g), arranged in two stories with three rooms in each. Thence we return to the entrance corridor (Pl. b), quit it by a door on the left, and follow a short oblique passage to the *Porter's Room* (Pl. h), which is constructed of slabs of alabaster. To the right in the corridor is the entrance to an *Inclined Plane* (Pl. i), which turns twice at a right angle and leads to the *Roof* of the temple. The pavement and walls of this plane are likewise constructed of alabaster.

To the S. of the Sphinx lies a recently excavated group of three Maṣtabas of the 5th Dyn. (opened by the custodian). The largest, that of *Khafrē-onkh*, comprises a large hall supported by eight pillars, with wall-niches containing figures of the deceased and his relatives; on either side is a serdâb (p. clxxvi) with niches and statues. The cult-chamber, to the W. of this hall, has two false doors; the deceased and persons bringing offerings are represented in the doorway. — On the N. is the maṣṭaba of *Sankhku*, 'custodian of gold in the palace'; that of *Pu*, on the S., has a pillared hall adorned with wall-decorations (hunting in the swamps, sacrifice of animals, field-work, etc.).

Travellers who are not pressed for time and who desire to obtain a closer view of the Second and Third Pyramids are recommended to make the following ***Circuit of the Pyramid Plateau** (comp. p. 132; donkeys and camels, see p. 133).

After having inspected the Great Pyramid (p. 136), we turn W. from the entrance and descend as far as the N.W. angle of the pyramid, where the levelled space on the ground (Pl. *b*), intended for the reception of the corner-stone, has been exposed to view. Towards the W. lies the large cemetery belonging to the 4-6th Dynasties (p. 140).

Leaving this portion of the necropolis, which is inaccessible, to the right, we turn towards the N. side of the court of the *Second Pyramid* (p. 142). On the floor of the levelled plateau prepared for this pyramid (p. 142) are a number of regularly arranged square incisions, separated from each other by furrows about 2 ft. wide. These date from the quarrying operations (comp. p. 382) carried on here during the building of the pyramid.

On the rock above is an inscription in honour of *Mey*, chief architect in the temple called 'Ramses shines in the Great House of the Prince' (i.e. Heliopolis) and son of Bek-en-Amun, chief architect of Thebes. In the reign of Ramses II. Mey systematically demolished the temple of Khephren or part of the facing of the pyramid to obtain materials for building a temple at Heliopolis.

We follow the W. side of the pyramid. On the rock to the right is another hieroglyphic inscription (Pl. *f*) by the above-mentioned *Mey*, near which are several rock-tombs. One of these (Pl. *g*), that of *Neb-em-ekhet*, nearly opposite the S.W. angle of the pyramid, has a fine ceiling hewn in the rock in imitation of palm-stems. On the E. side of the pyramid are remains of the mortuary temple connected with it (p. 142).

Our route now leads S.W. to the *Third Pyramid* (p. 143). To the S. of it stand three small pyramids, belonging to near relatives of King Mykerinos; on the E. side of each is a small brick cult-chapel.

We now turn to the remains of the mortuary temple to the E. of the Third Pyramid and descend E. by the ancient causeway (p. 134). Here, on the left, is another series of rock-tombs dating from the 4-5th Dynasties. Among these is that of *Debehne* (Pl. *h*), with several chambers and recesses. This is now closed by a wooden door and is regarded as the sacred tomb of Sîdi Ḥamed Samʿân. Numerous villagers assemble here on Friday for religious exercises.

In the valley before us, to the right, rises a projecting ridge of rock containing tombs of no interest. Adjoining this rock, on the left, is a picturesque Arab cemetery. Still farther E. we observe the remains of a wall (perhaps the ancient town wall), with a gateway. — After passing a high mound of débris, consisting of a pyramidal mass of masonry on a projecting rock and supposed to be the remains of an uncompleted pyramid, we come to other tombs on the left, covered with sand. Among these is the tomb of *Wer-khewew* (Pl. *k*), a judge under the 5th Dynasty.

We now proceed to the left (N.) to **Campbell's Tomb**, a family tomb of the 26th Dyn., discovered by Gen. Vyse (p. 136) in 1837 and named by him after Col. Campbell, the British consul-general in Egypt at that period. The upper part, the maṣṭaba proper, has vanished. The shaft (53 ft. deep), now uncovered, led to a tomb-chamber (now destroyed) which was vaulted with an arch having a span of 11 ft. The sides of the shaft are separated from the surrounding rock by a trench, which is spanned by bridges of stone at only a few points. Similar tombs of the Persian period are described on p. 175.

The sarcophagus which stands in the tomb-chamber contained the remains of the royal scribe *Pe-kop Wah-eb-rē-em-ekhet*, a contemporary of King Apries. Beside the sarcophagus lies a stone lid shaped like a mummy. In niches in the S. and W. sides of the shaft are two other sarcophagi; a fourth found here is now in the British Museum. All these sarcophagi had been opened and plundered.

We return past the *Sphinx* (p. 145) and the *Valley Temple of Khephren* (p. 146) to the Great Pyramid and the three small pyramids lying in front of it to the E.

To the E., on the verge of the desert plateau, near the Arab village of *Kafr es-Sammân*, are several Rock Tombs of the Ancient Empire. The largest of these (locked) is that of *Ankhmerē*, keeper of the granaries, and contains numerous figures of the deceased in the half-round and badly preserved mural representations. — A little to the S. is the partly ruined *Tomb of Numbers* (Pl. *n*), which belonged to a certain *Khafrē-onkh*, a courtier of Khephren. On the E. wall appear the deceased and his brother, accompanied by a dog, inspecting the cattle (the numbers of which are given) that are driven towards them by peasants. Other scenes represent field-work and the snaring of birds with the clap-net. On the left (S.) wall are the deceased and his wife at table. On the rear (W.) wall are decorative false doors and a niche with a statue of the deceased.

An expedition across the desert to the Western Petrified Forest (*Kôm el-Khashab*) is attractive (guide necessary). To the N. of the Mena House Hotel we strike off to the W. and after a ride of 3 hrs. across a sandy valley reach the beginning of the petrified forest, which extends as far as the Wâdi en-Naṭrûn (p. 35). The specimens of petrified trees here are much finer than those in the petrified forest in the Eastern Desert (pp. 127, 128).

The Excursion to the Pyramids of Abu Roâsh, which lie 5 M. to the N. of the Pyramids of Gîza, takes half-a-day and is most conveniently made from the Mena House Hotel, where donkeys, camels, or sand-carts may be obtained (see p. 133). — The route leads through the desert, skirting the edge of the cultivated land. It then bends E. through fields and reaches (3/4 hr.) the village of *Kirdâsa*, which is prettily situated amid palm-groves and is itself a sufficient attraction for an excursion, especially on Monday, the weekly market-day. We then proceed through palm-groves to (1 hr.) the village of *Abu Roâsh (Abu Rauwâsh)*, with the tomb of the saint of that name. Here we again turn W. across the desert, enter the Wâdi el-Qarn, and ascend by the ancient approach from the N.E., of which about 1 M. is still preserved, to the (1/2 hr.) abrupt rocky plateau. On this stands the great **Pyramid of Abu Roâsh,** known by the natives as *El-Qâ'a*, the tomb of the king Dedfrē (4th Dyn.; p. cii). The pyramid itself has almost entirely disappeared, but we can look down into the hollow hewn in the rock which contains the sepulchral chamber, and on the passage descending to it. The

remains of brick buildings to the E. of the pyramid belong to the mortuary temple; the neighbouring cleft in the rock was probably shaped to receive a boat of the sun (comp. p. 141). Adjacent is the house of the Institut Français d'Archéologie Orientale. — A smaller stone pyramid to the S.W. is now represented by a few fragments only. The plateau commands a fine view of the Nile valley and of the gorges of the Libyan desert. — There is a third pyramid, built of brick, in the plain to the N. of the village of Abu Roâsh. The brick superstructure, which was 55 ft. in height when Lepsius saw it in 1842, has since been entirely demolished, and nothing now remains but the rock core with the tomb-chamber.

On a spur of the plateau above the village, 1 M. to the E. of the pyramid of Abu Roâsh (p. 149), lies a *Necropolis of the Ancient Empire*, with large mastabas, excavated by the Institut Français in 1922-24; and a little to the S. of this, on another spur, are tombs of the 2nd-4th Dynasties.

The Excursion to the Pyramids of Abuṣîr, to the S. of Gîza, is interesting. We take the tram to the Mena House Hotel and proceed thence in $1^1/_2$-2 hrs. by donkey, camel, or sand-cart (see p. 133). Or, best of all, the excursion may be combined with that to Ṣaqqâra (p. 152; comp. the plan, p. 156).

Quitting the Mena House Hotel we ride along the verge of the desert, leaving the Pyramids of Gîza on the right. To the left is the cultivated country, with several villages. After about 1 hr. we have the large cemetery of the village of *Zâwiyet Abu Musallam* on our right. A low mound of rubbish on the summit of the desert plateau marks the site of the stone pyramid of *Zâwiyet el-ʿAryân* (comp. p. lxx). In the desert, $^1/_4$ hr. N.W., lies a second and *Unfinished Pyramid*, known to the natives as *Shughl Iskandar* ('Alexander's excavation'), which seems to have been begun by King Nebka (3rd Dyn.). This has been excavated by Alessandro Barsanti, and plainly shows the sloping passage cut in the rock and leading to a large square shaft, in which the tomb-chamber was to have been made. The foundation and pavement of the last were completed (both of red granite), and in it stands the finely worked red granite sarcophagus of the king, which was to have been half-embedded in the pavement. — In $1^1/_2$ hr. we reach the rubbish heaps of Abu Gurâb. [Another, somewhat longer route leads viâ the village of *Zâwiyet Abu Musallam*, which has a picturesque sheikh's tomb.]

Abu Gurâb *(Abu Girab)*, formerly called also the Pyramid of Righa, was explored in 1898-1901, on behalf of the Berlin Museum and at the expense of Baron von Bissing (comp. p. clxx). The building was a *Sanctuary of the Sun God*, erected by King Niuserrē (5th Dyn.) on the occasion of the 'Thirty Year Feast' (a royal jubilee).

The sanctuary stands upon a low, artificially altered hill and consists of an uncovered court, 330 ft. long by 250 ft. broad, with its entrance on the E. side, while in the posterior (W.) and main part of it rose the large *Obelisk of the Sun*. In front of it stands the *Altar*, 19 ft. long, 18 ft. broad, and 4 ft. high, built of five massive blocks of alabaster. From the entrance-

gate a (once) covered passage, ornamented with fine reliefs, led to the left along the E. and S. sides of the court, and then turned right (N.) to reach the obelisk. The obelisk itself has totally vanished, but part of the platform of masonry on which it stood is still extant; and the top of this, reached by an internal staircase, commands a fine view. In the front half of the court was the place for slaughtering the sacrificial bulls; the gutters in the pavement empty themselves into nine alabaster basins (originally ten). On the S. side of the obelisk is a ruined chapel (probably the king's robing room), which was embellished with admirable reliefs (now in the museums of Cairo and Berlin); its entrance (on the E.) was flanked with two plain granite stelæ and two ablution-basins let into the ground. — On the N. side of the obelisk was another sacrificial court. The N. side of the court was flanked by treasure-houses, reached from the entrance-gate by a passage (to the right) similar to that described above. To the S. of the temple lie the brick foundations of a boat of the sun (comp. p. 141). The temple was connected by a covered causeway with a gateway situated in the valley near the N.E. slope of the hill.

The three largest **Pyramids of Abuṣîr** *(Abu Sîr)*, erected by kings of the 5th Dyn., stand close together, about 20 min. S.E. of the sanctuary of Abu Gurâb (comp. the inset plan II at p. 156). They were explored in 1902-8 by the German Oriental Society under Prof. Borchardt. The masonry of these monuments, having originally been constructed with no great care, is now much damaged. The entrances are on the N. sides, and the interior chambers are almost completely in ruins. The northernmost is the **Pyramid of King Sehurē**. Its perpendicular height was 162¾ ft. (now 118 ft.), its sides were 257 ft. (now 216 ft.) in length, and they were inclined at the angle of 51° 42′ 35″. On the E. side of the pyramid lie the extensive remains of the *Mortuary Temple*, to which a slightly sloping causeway ascended from a small temple in the valley. The vestibule on the E. side of the temple opens into the large *Colonnaded Court*, the centre of the building, with a well-preserved pavement of basalt. Fragments of the sixteen granite palm-columns (p. clxvii), which once supported the roof of the colonnade around the walls of the court, are scattered about (reliefs, see p. 90). The court is adjoined by a *Transverse Room* and by a *Room with Five Recesses*, in which stood statues of the king. A side-door on the left admits to the narrow passages leading to the *Sanctuary*, in which, at the foot of the pyramid, stood the large door-shaped stele. Among the other apartments we may note the *Storerooms for the Sacrificial Offerings*, a series of two-storied chambers on the S. side, and the two-storied *Treasuries* on the N. side. At the S.E. angle of the pyramid, in a separate court with a side-entrance flanked by two tree-trunk columns (p. clxv), stands the small *Queen's Pyramid*.

Next, to the S., is the **Pyramid of Niuserrē**, to which an easy winding path ascends (fine panorama). It too had a *Mortuary Temple* on the E. side. From the plain a sloping causeway ascends to the main entrance and the forecourt, on each side of which lie storerooms. This is adjoined by an open court, with columns and a basalt pavement. Fragments of the granite papyrus-columns (p. clxvi) lie scattered about. The following chambers, extending to the N. at the

base of the pyramid, are in a very ruinous state. To the N. of the temple are some large *Maṣṭabas* of the 5th Dynasty. At the S.E. corner of the pyramid is a smaller pyramid, perhaps that of the queen. — The builder of the largest pyramid (sides 325, formerly 360 ft.; perpendicular height 164, formerly 228 ft.), situated a little to the S.W., was *King Nefer-er-ke-rē* (5th Dyn.). On the E. side are the remains of the mortuary temple, built of freestone and brick. — The other buildings, some of which were pyramids and others sanctuaries of the sun, are mere heaps of ruins.

A few paces S.E. of the Pyramid of Sehurē is the *Maṣṭaba of Ptahshepses* (5th Dyn.), excavated by De Morgan in 1893. It is mostly covered up again; the locked chambers are opened by the keeper of Abuṣîr. We first enter a large hall (only partly excavated), with twenty square pillars. Thence a door opens into another hall, with three recesses containing statues; on the walls are reliefs of goldsmiths and workmen carving statues of the deceased in wood and stone. A third hall contains the lower parts of two interesting lotus-columns with bud-capitals (p. clxvi) and remains of fine wall-reliefs (boats, etc.).

Continuing our ROUTE TO ṢAQQÂRA we leave to the left a pond and the village of *Abuṣîr*, situated beyond a group of palms to the S.E., and soon reach the sandy eminences of the Necropolis of Memphis and Mariette's House (p. 157), 3/4 hr. from the first pyramid of Abuṣîr. In the village pond of Abuṣîr are the remains of a temple of the New Empire.

7. The Site of Ancient Memphis and the Necropolis of Ṣaqqâra.

A visit to Memphis and Ṣaqqâra may easily be accomplished by railway in one day and by motor-car in half-a-day (see p. 153). Provisions should not be forgotten. — TICKETS admitting to the monuments of Ṣaqqâra may be obtained for P.T. 10 each at Mariette's House (p. 157), at the Tomb of Mereruka (p. 171), and the Pyramid of Onnos (p. 175). Travellers, however, who possess a general admission-ticket (p. 212) do not require these special tickets. The custodians are forbidden to ask for gratuities, but, when candles are supplied, a single traveller generally gives P.T. 1, parties P.T. 3-5.

The following TOUR will be found convenient. Take an early train to (1 hr.) *Badrashein* (1st cl. 23, 2nd cl. 13 P.T.), where donkeys and drivers (P.T. 14 there and back, gratuity 5, lady's side-saddle 5; refuse further demands) and motor-cars are in waiting. Ride viâ the site of *Memphis*, where the **Colossi of Ramses* (p. 154) are inspected, and thence, passing the **Step Pyramid* (p. 156), to (about 1 1/2 hr. in all) *Mariette's House* (p. 157), in the middle of the *Necropolis of Ṣaqqâra*. For luncheon and a visit to the **Serapeum* (p. 158) and the ***Tombs of Ti* and *Ptahhotep* (pp. 159, 169), the three chief sights, about 2-3 hrs. should be allowed; we then preceed to inspect the **Step Pyramid* (p. 156), the *Onnos Pyramid* (p. 175), and the *Persian Tombs* (p. 175), or, if time permit, the **Tomb of Mereruka* (p. 171), the *Tomb of Ka-gem-ni* (p. 173), the *Street of Tombs* (p. 174), and the *Teti Pyramid* (p. 175). Hurried travellers may content themselves with an inspection of the Tomb of Ti, Serapeum, Tomb of Ptahhotep, and Step Pyramid (about 3 hrs. in all). — A highly attractive return-route is as described above viâ Abuṣîr to the Mena House Hotel (2 1/2 hrs.; bargain beforehand with the donkey-driver at Badrashein; donkey from Badrashein

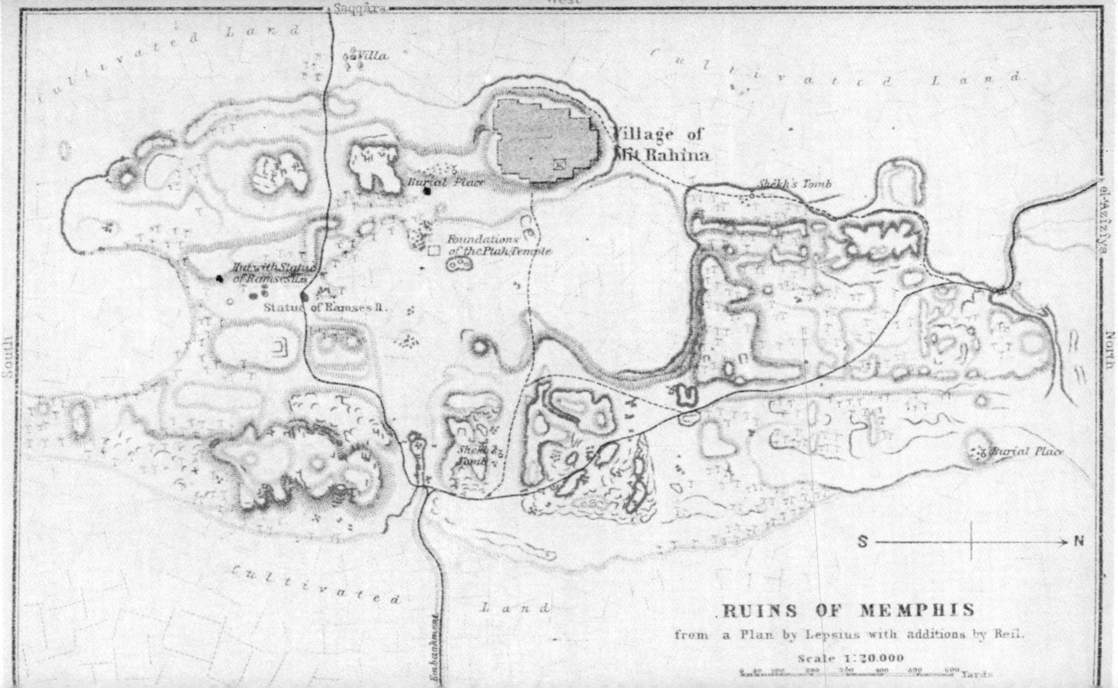

RUINS OF MEMPHIS

from a Plan by Lepsius with additions by Reil.

to the hotel about P.T. 40), whence we take the tramway to Cairo. The excursion is more comfortably and speedily accomplished by motor-car from Cairo (half-a-day): the route (well signposted) diverges S. from the road to the Pyramids, short of the level crossing (comp. p. 133), and runs between the Nile and a canal (on the left is the sugar factory of Ḥawâmdîya) to Badrashein station (see below). The return journey should be made by the W. motor-road (which leads to El-Wâsṭa, p. 217) alongside a canal to Shabramant and the Mena House. Memphis and Ṣaqqâra may be visited also by motor-boat daily from Cairo (apply to M.S. Farajallah's tourist agency, p. 40): fare, including donkey, guide, and tickets of admission, P.T. 90. — Comp. 'The Tombs of Sakkara', by *A. A. Quibell* (Cairo, 1911; P.T. 5).

The trains start from the *Main Station* at Cairo (p. 37). The railway crosses the Nile beyond *Bûlâq* (p. 86), passes (1³/₄ M.) *Imbâba* (p. 87), and makes a wide curve to (6 M.) *Bûlâq ed-Dakrûr*, on a canal. To the right appear the Pyramids of Gîza. We cross the road to the Pyramids. — At (8¹/₂ M.) *Gîza* (p. 87) we see Old Cairo (p. 113) on the left, above which extends the long ridge of the Moqaṭṭam and to the S.E. the Gebel Ṭura (p. 180). — To the right, beyond (11¹/₂ M.) *Abu'n-Numrus*, rise the hills of the Libyan desert with the sun-temple of Abu Gurâb (p. 150), the Pyramids of Abuṣîr, and the Step Pyramid (p. 156). Fine groves of palms. — 14 M. *Ṭammûh;* 17¹/₂ M. *El-Ḥawâmdîya (Hawamdia)*, with a large sugar factory.

At (20¹/₂ M.) **Badrashein** (*El-Badrshein;* buffet, on the opposite or Cairo platform) visitors bound for Memphis and Ṣaqqâra leave the train, which goes on to Upper Egypt (see p. 217). The station is on the left side of the line. Opposite Badrashein, on the E. bank of the Nile, lie the baths of *Ḥelwân* (p. 177).

From Badrashein to *Dahshûr*, see p. 177; to *Ṣaqqâra* viâ *Ḥelwân*, see p. 180.

Viâ Memphis (Colossi of Ramses) and Mît Rahîna to the Necropolis of Ṣaqqâra. We cross the railway, go through the market street of Badrashein, and follow the embankment towards the palm-grove, within which lies the village of Mît Rahîna. At the end of the embankment, where the path divides, we keep straight on. The mounds of rubbish before us, the ruins of brick buildings, between which the lines of ancient streets may often be traced, scattered blocks of granite, and broken pottery mark the site of Memphis.

Site of Memphis.

Were it not for the vast necropolis to the W. of the ancient city, no one would imagine that one of the most famous and populous capitals of antiquity had once stood here. The Egyptians, from the earliest period down to the Roman imperial epoch, built their private houses of large sun-dried bricks of Nile mud, reserving better material, such as limestone and granite, for palaces and temples. But even the public buildings of Memphis have almost disappeared, as the stones were early carried off to build other edifices elsewhere.

History. The story of Memphis stretches back to the beginning of Egyptian history. According to a very probable tradition, Menes, the

first historical ruler in Egypt, is said to have founded the 'white walls' of a fortress in a reclaimed district on the borders between the two ancient kingdoms of Upper and Lower Egypt (p. cii), in order to keep the conquered inhabitants of Lower Egypt in subjection. To the S. of this he is said to have built also the temple of Ptah (Hephæstos, p. clviii), the patron-god of the city. The new settlement rapidly became of importance; it was made the capital of a separate district, and the kings of the early dynasties sometimes planted their court here. Under the 6th Dyn. a new quarter was founded, in which King Phiops I. fixed the residence of his court and near which the sepulchral pyramid of the ruler was situated. This quarter, as well as the pyramid, was called *Men-nefru-Mirē*, i.e. 'The beauty of King Mirē (Phiops) remains', and this name (in the later abbreviated form *Menfe*, in Greek *Memphis*) was afterwards applied to the whole city. Memphis attained its greatest prosperity under the monarchs of the Ancient Empire, who resided here or in the vicinity (near Gîza and Abuṣîr). Even under the Middle and New Empires, when Thebes became the centre of Egypt and the Theban Amun the most revered among the gods, Memphis appears to have retrograded but little. In the time of the 20th Dyn. the temple of Ptah was still the largest in the country but two. In the course of the contests for the possession of Egypt, which raged after the 22nd Dyn. (comp. p. cviii), the city was captured by the Ethiopian Piankhi and by the Assyrians.

Cambyses, the first monarch of the Persian dynasty (p. cix), took Memphis by storm after his victory at Pelusium (525 B.C.) over Psammetichos III.; and even after the foundation of Alexandria (331 B.C.) it appears to have retained some importance. Under Augustus it was a large and populous city, though its palaces, elevated on an eminence, lay ruined and deserted. Among the temples that still existed were those of Ptah, of Apis (p. 158), and of a female deity who was identified with the Aphrodite of the Greeks. In consequence of the edict of Theodosius (A.D. 379-395; comp. p. cxvi) the temples and statues were destroyed, and under the later Byzantine monarchs the heretical Monophysites (p. cxvii) seem to have been very numerous here. Muqauqis (p. cxviii), the leader of the Copts, was established at Memphis while negotiating with ʿAmr ibn el-ʿÂṣ, the general of ʿOmar (p. 46). The Mohammedan conquerors transferred their residence to the right bank of the Nile, opposite the northernmost part of Memphis, using the well-hewn blocks, which had once composed the venerable palaces and temples of the ancient city of Menes, for the construction of their palaces, castles, and mosques at Cairo. But down to a late period the ruins of Memphis excited the admiration of all visitors. Thus ʿAbd el-Laṭîf (p. 139) assures us that even in his time the ruins contained a profusion of wonders which bewildered the mind and baffled description. After his time the rapidly dwindling ruins of Memphis are rarely mentioned.

The path continuing in the original direction (W.) from the fork (p. 153), and leading through the palm-grove of the village of *Mît Rahîna (Mît Riheina)*, brings us to the ***Colossal Statues of Ramses II.**, which once marked the entrance to the temple. The first of these, discovered in 1888, is made of granite and lies on its back on a slight eminence. Its length is 26 ft., not including the crown, which is 6$^1/_2$ ft. long. The square hole in the head of the colossus was for the insertion of the crown, which lies on the ground beside it. On both shoulders, breast, girdle, and bracelet occurs the name of the king; and on the pillar at the back is an inscription. On the left of the statue is an incised relief of Princess Bent-Anat. — Beside the statue stands a memorial inscription with a decree of Apries (p. cix), in the rounded pediment of which appear Ptah and the falcon-headed Soker (p. clix). A little farther on lies a

gigantic alabaster *Sphinx* of the 18th or 19th Dynasty, excavated in 1912. It is 26 ft. long and 14 ft. high, and weighs about 80 tons.

We next reach the mud-hut that conceals the *Second Colossus* (admission by ticket, p. 152), discovered by Caviglia and Sloane in 1820. A wooden flight of steps ascends to a platform from which the statue is inspected. It consists of remarkably hard and fine-grained alabaster, and before it lost its legs was about 42 ft. in height (ear more than $1^1/_2$ ft. long), corresponding to the measurement given by Herodotus (30 cubits of $1^1/_2$ ft. each). The workmanship is excellent. The handsome and gentle features of the king are admirably reproduced. A conventional beard is attached to the chin. In the girdle is a dagger with two falcons' heads. On the right shoulder, the breast, and the girdle appear the prænomina of Ramses II. — In front of the hut are several fragments of monuments, showing the name of Ramses II. — The ruins of the great *Temple of Ptah* at Memphis lie to the N.W. of the colossi, at the foot of the white sheikh's tomb of Mît Rahîna and near the house of the Philadelphia Museum Expedition, close to which are, to the E. of the colossi, the débris of a large *Palace of Menephthes* (Merneptah, p. cvii; excavated by the Philadelphia Expedition).

Our route continues W. from the colossi. On quitting the palm-grove we obtain an attractive view; immediately to the left is a small well. Beyond the cultivated fields is another long palm-grove surrounding the village of Ṣaqqâra and bordering the desert; beyond this, on the yellow sand of the desert, rise eleven pyramids. The first of these, to the left, is the S. brick pyramid, beyond which are the blunted pyramid, the N. brick pyramid, and the great pyramid, all belonging to the group of Dahshûr (p. 177). Not far from these we next perceive the Maṣṭabat Fara'ûn, with the pyramid of Phiops II.; then, exactly above the houses of Ṣaqqâra, two pyramids, the lesser of which is that of Phiops I.; and, lastly, to the right, the pyramid of Onnos, the great Step Pyramid, and two smaller ones (left, that of Userkaf; right, that of Teti). — We follow the embankment, cross a bridge over a canal, and turn to the right (N.). At a signpost we turn left (W.), crossing a sluice-bridge over the Baḥr el-Libeini. Thence we make straight across the fields to the Râs el-Gisr (see below). — An alternative route leads from the first bridge (see above) due W. to Ṣaqqâra village. Here we turn N., passing a sheikh's tomb picturesquely sited by a sycamore, and arrive at the *Râs el-Gisr* ('head of the embankment'), on the edge of the desert. Monastery of St. Jeremiah, see p. 156.

We now ascend the sandy plateau and come in sight of the vast ****Necropolis of Ṣaqqâra** *(Sakkara)*, which extends about $4^1/_3$ M. from N. to S., and $^1/_4$-1 M. from E. to W. It contains sepulchral monuments of almost every period of Egyptian history. The whole necropolis has been repeatedly ransacked by the Byzantines and the Caliphs, as well as by modern explorers. Loose heaps of light-

coloured sand indicate recent excavations. Important finds have been made even in recent years (comp. p. 157).

On a hill close to the Râs el-Gisr (p. 155) lie the ruins of the large **Monastery of St. Jeremiah,** excavated in 1907-9 by J. E. Quibell for the Egyptian Department of Antiquities (comp. p. clxxxvii). The monastery, founded in the second half of the 5th cent. of our era and destroyed by the Arabs about 960, includes two churches, a refectory, a bake-house, oil-press, wine-press, etc. The cell of St. Jeremiah also is preserved. Many of the monks' cells have remained intact, each with a recess in the E. wall, which served as an oratory and was sometimes adorned with paintings of the Madonna, the archangels, and the founder of the convent. These paintings, like the fine capitals and reliefs from the churches, are now in the Cairo Museum (p. 97).

From the monastery we ride N.W., straight to the Step Pyramid.

The ***Step Pyramid** or *Step Maṣṭaba* of Ṣaqqâra (Arabic *El-Haram el-Mudarrag*, i.e. 'the pyramid provided with steps'; comp. the illustration on p. clxxvii), a very conspicuous feature in the landscape, may be regarded as the cognizance of Ṣaqqâra. It was the tomb of the ancient king *Djoser* or *Zoser* (3rd Dyn.; p. cii) and is probably the earliest stone building of importance erected in Egypt. It lies within a rectangular court (temenos) about 490 yds. long and 295 yds. wide, which contains several other buildings of the greatest architectural interest; part of the enclosure-wall (originally 23 ft. in height) still survives (p. 157). The pyramid or step-maṣṭaba is rectangular in ground-plan (413 ft. by 344 ft.) and rises in six stages, the lowest of which is 37$^1/_2$ ft. in height, the next 36 ft., the third 34$^1/_4$ ft., the fourth 32$^1/_2$ ft., the fifth 30$^3/_4$ ft., and the sixth 29 ft., while each stage recedes about 6$^1/_2$ ft. as compared with the one below it. The perpendicular height is 200 ft. For the graduated construction, comp. p. clxxvii. The pyramid is built of an inferior clayey limestone quarried in the neighbourhood. The entrance is on the N. side, at the foot of the lowest step; in front are the remains of the mortuary temple (Pl. 1), with a chamber for the king's statue (p. 90). The interior (opened in 1821; now closed to the public) contains a complicated series of passages and chambers, which, however, are due in part to treasure-hunters and to later attempts at restoration. Two of the original chambers had their walls decorated with plaques of blue-green faience in imitation of woven reed-mats. In 1928 Mr. Cecil Firth found another gallery decorated with blue tiles and with three false doors or niches containing reliefs of King Djoser. The pyramid is seldom climbed, as the stone of which it is composed is very friable, but the top commands an interesting view. — Two large maṣṭabas (Pl. 2 & 3), with chapels, lie to the N.E. of the pyramid; these were probably the tombs of the royal daughters Int-kas and Hetep-hernebti. In front of each maṣṭaba is a courtyard about 27 yds. square. Its N. side, formed by the façade of the maṣṭaba, is decorated with four engaged fluted columns and with two panels of ribbed

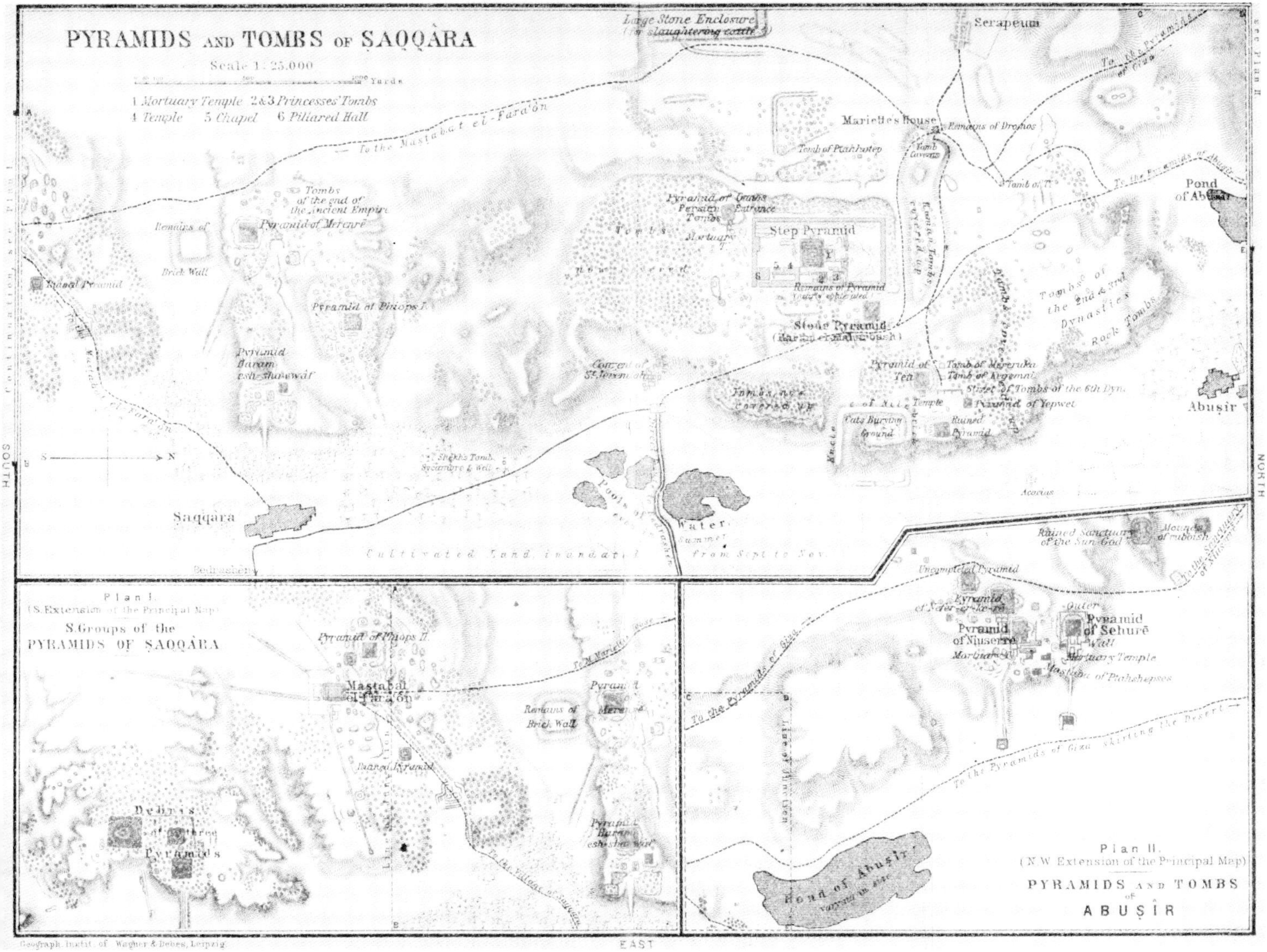
PYRAMIDS AND TOMBS OF ṢAQQÂRA
Scale 1:25,000
Yards
1 Mortuary Temple 2&3 Princesses' Tombs
4 Temple 5 Chapel 6 Pillared Hall
Large Stone Enclosure (for slaughtering cattle)
Serapeum
To the Mastabat el-Fara'ôn
To the Pyramids of Giza
Mariette's House
Remains of Dromos
Tomb of Ptahhotep
Tomb of Ti
To the Pyramids of Abuṣîr
Pond of Abuṣîr
Tombs of the end of the Ancient Empire
Pyramid of Merenrē
Remains of
Brick Wall
Ruined Pyramid
Pyramid of Piiops I
Pyramid Baram esh-Shawwâf
Tombs
Step Pyramid
Remains of Pyramid
Stone Pyramid
Convent of St. Jeremiah
Pyramid of Teti
Tomb of Mereruka
Tomb of Kegemni
Street of Tombs of the 6th Dyn.
Pyramid of Yepwet
Temple
Cats Burying Ground
Ruined Pyramid
Tombs of the 2nd & 3rd Dynasties
Rock Tombs
Abuṣîr
S N
Sheikh's Tomb, Sycamore & Well
Pools of Water
Saqqâra
Acacias
Cultivated Land, inundated from Sept. to Nov.
Bedrashên
SOUTH
NORTH
Plan I.
(S. Extension of the Principal Map)
S. Groups of the
PYRAMIDS OF ṢAQQÂRA
Pyramid of Piiops II.
Mastabat el-Fara'ôn
To M. Mariette's House
Pyramid Merenrē
Remains of Brick Wall
Ruined Pyramid
Debris of three Pyramids
Pyramid Baram esh-Shawwâf
To the Village of Saqqâra
Ruined Sanctuary of the Sun God
Mounds of rubbish
Uncompleted Pyramid
Pyramid of Nefer-er-ke-re
Pyramid of Niuserrē
Pyramid of Sehurē
Mortuary Temple
Mastaba of Ptahshepses
To the Pyramids of Giza
To the Pyramids of Giza skirting the Desert
Line of Junction
Pond of Abuṣîr
Plan II.
(N.W. Extension of the Principal Map)
PYRAMIDS AND TOMBS of ABUṢÎR
Geograph. Instit. of Wagner & Debes, Leipzig
EAST

pattern representing the wood or reed protection of the angle of the building. The side-walls of the court were in part decorated with small engaged columns in exact imitation of a single papyrus stalk and flower (p. lxxix). — To the S.E. is a *Temple* (Pl. 4), perhaps erected on the occasion of the king's 'Thirty Year Feast' (comp. p. 150) and containing a series of chapels with fences reproduced in stone. Inside, staircases ascend to an upper story. In the court is a substructure with steps, on which the king's throne was probably placed. — To the S.E. of this temple part of the enclosure-wall (p. 156), faced with limestone and adorned with towers and recesses, has been preserved to a considerable height; lower portions (on the N., E., etc.) have also been laid bare. Between two prominent towers is the main entrance of the whole enclosure. Thence we enter the great *Pillared* or *Festal Hall* (Pl. 6). It contains forty pairs of piers with a three-quarter-column carved at each end (originally over 18 ft. in height) imitating bundles of reeds; the false doors at the E. end imitate wooden doors swung open. The pillared hall is adjoined on the W. by a small *Transverse Chamber* with four pairs of piers, whence a doorway adorned also with false doors leads to the pyramid court.

In the middle S. enclosure-wall is an earlier *Tomb of Djoser* (discovered by Cecil Firth in 1927), a large maṣṭaba constructed by the king before the building of the Step Maṣṭaba and never actually used. Subterranean staircases and passages lead to antechambers that contained large alabaster jars and to four rooms with wall-decoration of blue-green faience plaques in imitation of reed mats (comp. the chamber inside the Step Pyramid, p. 156). The second chamber contains three false doors with wonderful reliefs representing Djoser (comp. p. 156). — To the S., outside the enclosure-wall (comp. above), is a *Maṣṭaba of the 6th Dynasty*, belonging originally to Ikh, an official, and later to the lady Idut; it contains several rooms with good reliefs of well-preserved colouring (cat and ichneumon robbing birds' nests among the papyrus swamps). — Inside the N. wall of the temenos are underground galleries, in which were found quantities of grain and fruit sealed with the clay seals of Kings Khasekhmui and Djoser and stored here since the time of the 3rd Dynasty. Somewhat to the E. of these store-rooms is a large structure about 16½ yds. square, perhaps a gigantic altar or the base of a solar obelisk.

To the N.E. of the Step Pyramid lie the ruined *Pyramid of Userkaf* (5th Dyn.; Arabic Haram el-Maharbash) and, on its S. side, the very dilapidated *Mortuary Temple* (excavated by Firth in 1928), chiefly consisting of a courtyard surrounded on three sides by colonnades with square granite columns. On its W. side is a small pyramid, perhaps used for ritual purposes, and to the S.E. is the small pyramid of the queen, with a mortuary chapel (on the E. side). These early buildings were subsequently incorporated in large 26th Dyn. maṣṭabas.

The path turns to the left and soon reaches **Mariette's House.** Auguste Mariette, the famous French Egyptologist (p. 88), first rose into notice by his discovery of the Apis tombs in 1851, and from 1858 till his death in 1881 was director of the official excavations in Egypt. Visitors generally eat their luncheon (brought from Cairo) on the terrace. A fee of P.T. 2½ or more, according to the number of the party, is given to the keepers in charge of the house, who supply coffee prepared in the Arab style. From this point paths lead to the various points of interest.

A few hundred yards W. of Mariette's House lies the Egyptian ***Serapeum,** or subterranean *Tombs of Apis*, hewn in the rock.

Apis (p. clv), the sacred bull of the god Ptah (p. 154), which was worshipped in a special temple at Memphis, was after death embalmed like a human being and interred with great pomp in the necropolis. As early as the reign of Amenophis III., and probably still earlier, the Apis tombs consisted of a subterranean tomb-chamber, reached by a sloping shaft, over which a chapel was erected in honour of the bull. Under Ramses II. a large common grave was prepared for the Apis bulls by Prince Khaem-weset; a subterranean gallery, over 100 yds. in length, was hewn in the rock and flanked with chambers, which were walled up after receiving the wooden coffin containing the sacred remains. Psammetichos I. caused a similar gallery with side-vaults to be constructed at right angles to the first one. These vaults, which were added to at intervals down to the Ptolemaic period, were much larger and more carefully constructed than the previous series. They have an aggregate length of about 380 yds. and are about 10 ft. in width and 17½ ft. in height. Above them rose a large temple for the cult of the dead god. — The ancient Egyptians believed that like man (p. cliii) the deceased bull was united with Osiris, and became the 'Osiris-Apis' (Egyptian *Oser-hape;* Greek *Osorapis*). He thus became a kind of god of the dead and was called, like Osiris, 'Lord of the Western Land'; pilgrims crowded to the tomb to pay their devotions

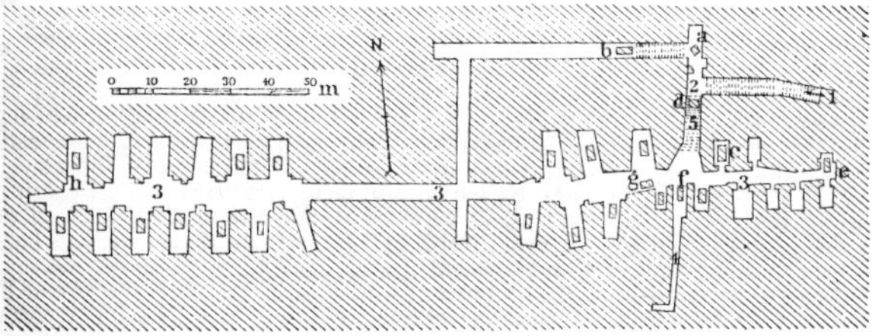

and to present votive offerings. The last were usually small memorial tablets, which were inserted in the walls of the subterranean galleries. The worship of the foreign god *Sarapis* or *Serapis*, introduced under Ptolemy I., rapidly spread in Egypt, and it is easy to understand how the new *Sarapis* was confounded with *Osorapis* and worshipped along with the latter in the ancient temple in the necropolis of Memphis. The temple itself came to be commonly known as the *Sarapeion* or *Serapeum.*

A second temple of Osorapis, built by Nektanebis II. (p. cx), once stood opposite the temple covering the Apis tombs (W. of Mariette's House). These temples were connected by a path enclosed by walls, on which stood Greek statues; a few of these are still on their original site (but now covered with sand). The great *Sphinx Avenue*, which led to the W. through the necropolis to the *Serapeum*, terminated in front of the temple of Nektanebis in a semicircular space adorned with statues of Greek philosophers. But the remains of all these monuments are now covered with sand, and only the later gallery of *Apis Tombs* constructed by Psammetichos is accessible to visitors.

From the Entrance (Pl. 1) we enter a chamber (Pl. 2) of considerable dimensions, with niches in the bare limestone walls, where many tombstones of deceased bulls and votive tablets (see above) were found. The guide now proceeds to the right. After a few paces we observe at our feet a huge block of black granite (Pl. *a*),

which once formed the lid of a sarcophagus. Beyond it we turn to the left and after twenty paces we reach an enormous granite sarcophagus (Pl. *b*), which nearly fills the passage. The lid and the sarcophagus, which belong to each other, were probably stopped here on their way to the vault for which they were destined, in consequence of the abolition of the worship of Apis. Near the end of this passage we turn to the left (S.) into another.

This leads to the PRINCIPAL PASSAGE (Pl. 3), running parallel with the first, from E. to W., and penetrating the solid rock. The passage is flanked with side-chambers, about 26 ft. high, the pavements and vaulted ceilings of which are constructed of excellent Moqaṭṭam stone. Twenty of the chambers still contain sarcophagi for the Apis mummies. These monster coffins each consist of a single block of black or red polished granite or of limestone, and average 13 ft. in length, 7 ft. in width, and 11 ft. in height, and no less than 65 tons in weight. The covers have in many instances been pushed on one side. All the sarcophagi, when discovered by Mariette, had been emptied of their contents, with the exception of two, which still contained a number of trinkets. Only three of the sarcophagi have inscriptions; one bears the name of *Amasis* (Pl. *c*; the lid at Pl. *d*), another that of *Cambyses* (Pl. *e*), and a third that of *Khababash* (Pl. *f*; the lid at Pl. *g*), the last ruler of Egypt before its conquest by Alexander the Great (p. cx). The finest is the last sarcophagus on the right side (Pl. *h*), to which a flight of steps descends. It consists of black and finely polished granite and is covered with inscriptions and door-shaped ornaments.

Near the E. end of the principal passage we reach a side-passage (Pl. 4) diverging to the right, some 22 yds. in length, from which another leads to the right, in a direction parallel with the main corridor, but now built up. Opposite the side-passage we pass over the lid (Pl. *d*) of the Amasis sarcophagus (see above) by means of modern steps (Pl. 5) and thus regain the door by which we entered the vaults. The temperature in these subterranean chambers is always nearly 80° Fahr., so visitors should beware of taking cold on leaving.

Far more interesting then the Apis tombs are the private tombs (*maṣṭabas*, p. clxxvi), though only a few are accessible to tourists. The most celebrated of these, to the N.E. of Mariette's House, is the ****Maṣṭaba of Ti** *(Tjï)*, a high court official and wealthy landowner of the beginning of the 5th Dynasty. The building originally stood above ground, but it is now entirely sunk in the sand. It was discovered by Mariette and has been restored by the Department of Antiquities, as is recorded on a tablet at the entrance. The mural reliefs, besides being interesting on account of their subjects, are among the finest and best-preserved examples of the art of the Ancient Empire (comp. p. clxxxii).

From the street we first enter the SMALL VESTIBULE (Pl. 1), which contains two pillars (upper parts restored), on each of which

Ti is represented, in a long wig and a short, broad apron, holding a staff in one hand and a kind of club in the other. On the E. wall are women (representing the villages belonging to Ti) bringing food to the tomb; on the S. wall are poultry and doves being fattened in a pen. The other reliefs are obliterated.

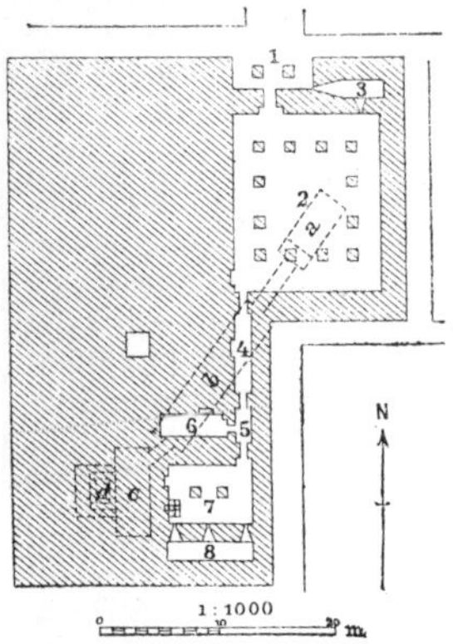

We next pass through a doorway, the sides of which show figures of Ti and inscriptions, and enter the Great Colonnaded Court (Pl. 2), with a modern wooden roof borne by twelve ancient square pillars (restored). This court was the scene of the offerings to the deceased. In the centre is a flight of steps (Pl. *a*), by which we may descend to a low subterranean passage (Pl. *b*) extending the whole length of the building and leading first to a kind of vestibule (Pl. *c*) and then to the tomb-chamber (Pl. *d*). The now empty sarcophagus completely fills the niche in which it stands.

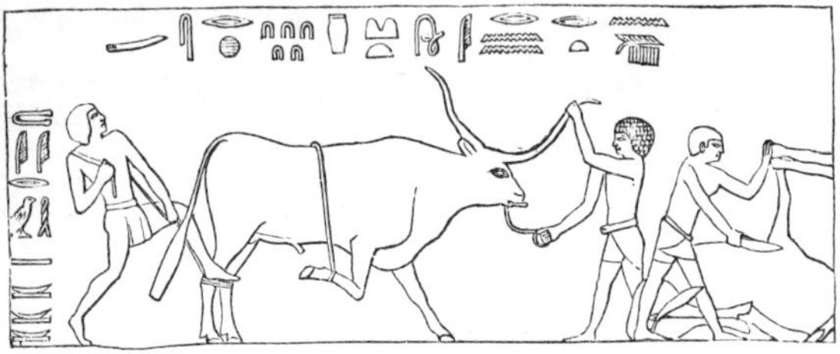

Throwing the victim.

Cooking poultry.

The *Mural Reliefs* in the great court deserve no long examination; they are much injured by exposure and some have become

altogether unrecognizable. On the *North Wall* Ti is represented superintending the sacrifice and cutting up of cattle, shown in the woodcut on p. 160, and servants with gifts. Behind the wall here was another chamber (*serdâb;* Pl. 3; p. clxxvi), containing statues. On the *East Wall* there are reliefs only to the left: Ti borne in a litter, preceded by attendants carrying fans,

Fattening geese.

Fattening cranes; the two men above are preparing the food.

boxes, and chairs. On the *West Wall* (right to left): Ti and his wife inspect the fattening of geese and the feeding of cranes (see the woodcuts); a poultry yard; Ti receiving the accounts of his officials, who stand in a house supported by columns; Ti (upper part

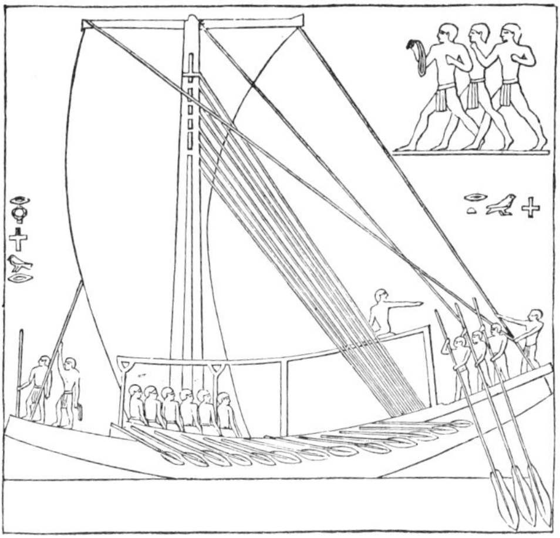

Sailing ship.

injured) superintending the arrival of his Nile boats, while herds of various kinds are driven towards him; false door dedicated to Ti's son.

We pass through the door in the corner, noticing on each side three figures of Ti, represented as walking from within, each time in a different costume. The door admits to a Corridor (Pl. 4). On each side-wall are servants bearing offerings into the tomb. On the right is also a false door dedicated to *Neferhotpes*, the wife of Ti. Another door admits us to a Second Corridor (Pl. 5). In the lower row on the *Left Wall* the slaughter of cattle for sacrifice is represented; in the upper row statues of the deceased are being drawn to the tomb on sledges, in front of which a man pours water to prevent the heavily laden sledges from taking fire by friction. On the *Right Wall* appear ships in which Ti has inspected his estates in the Delta. The curious steering gear should be noticed. Over the door by which we entered are Ti and his wife in a boat in a thicket of papyrus. Over the door leading to the tomb-chapel (Pl. 7) are dancers and singers. A door on the right leads into a Side Chamber (Pl. 6), or pantry, in which the original colours of the reliefs are admirably preserved. On the upper part of the left door-post a piece of the sycamore wood to which the door was attached is still in its place. *Right Wall:* Ti, who stands to the right, receives from his servants sacrificial gifts (flowers, cakes, poultry, etc.); in the top row, tables with sacrificial gifts. *Back Wall:* at the top, potters, bakers, and brewers; below, a man measures corn, while scribes note down the quantity. *Left Wall:* Ti; to the right, servants with gifts; above, tables and vessels of various kinds. *Entrance Wall:* Tables and vessels. — Leaving the corridor we pass through a door (with a figure of Ti on each side) and enter the Tomb Chapel (Pl. 7) itself, which is 16 ft. wide, 23 ft. long, and 15 ft. high. The ceiling rests on two square pillars, coloured to imitate red granite. The names and titles of Ti are inscribed on the pillars. The reliefs here, the colouring of which is also for the most part well preserved, repay careful examination.

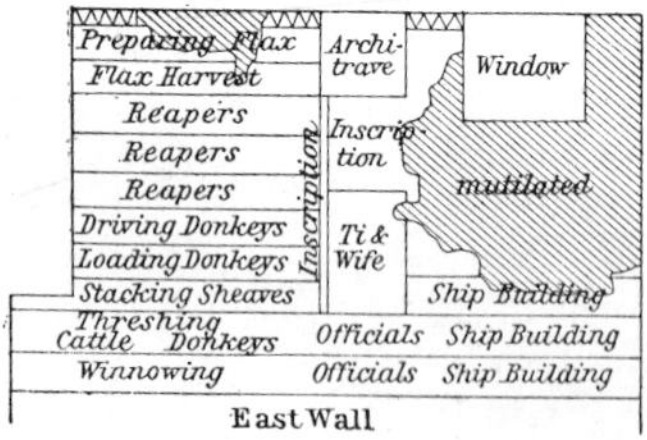

On the *East Side* (left of the entrance; comp. the key-plan) Ti, to the right, with his wife kneeling at his side, inspects the harvest operations, which are represented in ten rows of scenes (beginning at the top; comp. the woodcuts on p. 163): flax is harvested and prepared; corn is reaped, placed in sacks, and loaded upon asses, which bear it to the threshing floor; the ears are taken from the sacks and piled in heaps; then follows the treading out of the corn by [illegible] asses; the threshed

Winnowing corn.

Reaping.

Ass with a sack of corn.

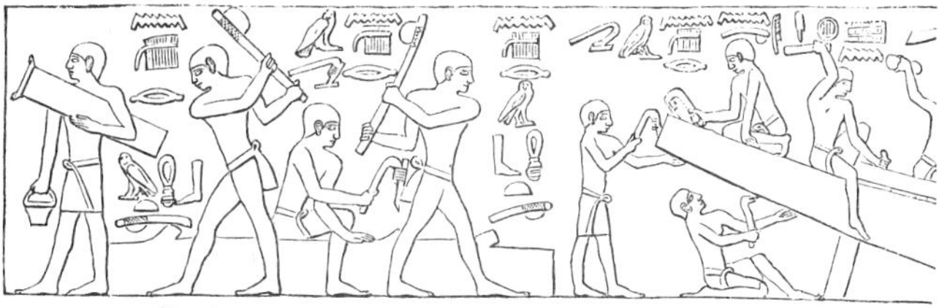

Shaping a tree-trunk. Ship-building.

Ship-building. Sawing. Shaping a beam.

grain along with the chaff is piled in a great heap by means of three-pronged forks, then sifted, and winnowed with two small boards; finally it is placed in a sack by a woman.

Farther to the right on this wall are two well-preserved and several damaged ship-building scenes, representing the various operations: shaping the tree-trunks, sawing boards, and the actual construction of the ship, on which some workmen are using hammer, adze, and chisel, while others are placing the planks. In one of the ships stands Ti, inspecting the work. The primitive saws, axes, hammers, drills, and other tools used by the workmen are particularly interesting (comp. the woodcuts on p. 163).

The *South Side* of the tomb-chapel (comp. the key-plan below) is richly covered with representations, but the upper parts are damaged. From left to right: at the top (left), Ti. A small cleft below this figure to the left leads to a second serdâb (Pl. 8), in which a complete statue of Ti (p. 91) and several broken ones were found.

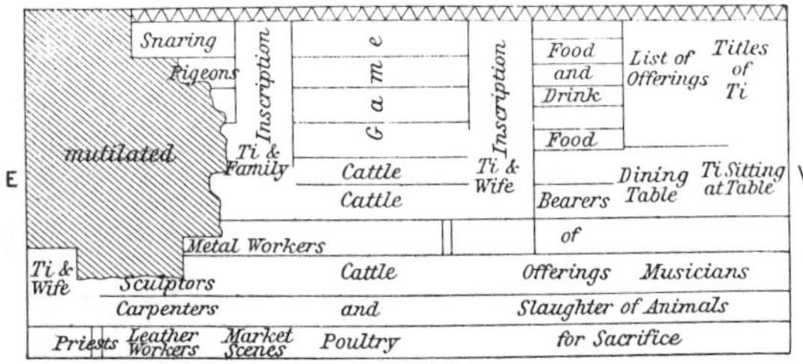

South Wall

To the right and left of the cleft are two men offering incense to Ti. Ti and his wife inspect their workmen, who are represented in four rows: from above downwards, 1. Men blowing a furnace (for gold-smelting); 2. Sculptors and makers of stone vessels; 3. Carpenters; to the left are men polishing a door and a chest; then, men sawing planks; two men polishing a bedstead, below which lies a head-rest; a man using a drill; 4. Leather-workers and market-scenes; one dealer has a skin and two pots of oil for sale; another has a wallet for which a man offers him a pair of sandals; a stamp-cutter makes a stone seal; to the right a man is selling sticks. — At the top (in the middle), Ti, with his wife seated at his feet, inspects the different kinds of animals (antelopes, gazelles, goats, stags, cattle; each with the name above) which are being brought for sacrifice by the peasantry of his estates. Below, three rows of cattle; three village elders are forcibly brought to the estate office to give evidence as to taxes; at the bottom, poultry of all kinds (cranes, geese, pigeons). — At the top (to the right), Ti is sitting at table, while attendants bring sacrificial gifts. Below are attendants with gifts for sacrifice,

and flute-players and harpers, who perform music during the meal; slaughter and cutting up of cattle for sacrifice.

On the *West Side* of the tomb-chapel are two large false doors, representing the entrance to the realm of the dead. In front of the

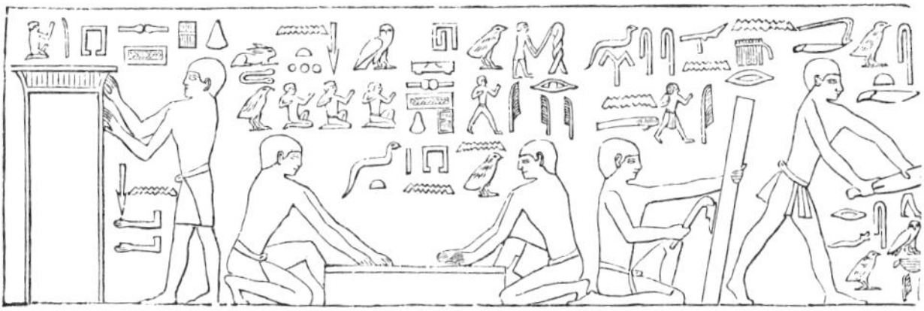

Carpenters.

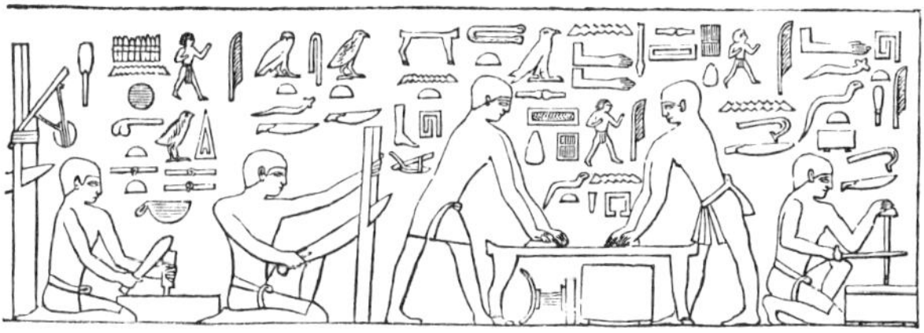

left door is a slab for the reception of offerings. In the centre of the wall are slaughterers and the presentation of gifts (damaged); above are tables.

Village elders brought to give evidence.

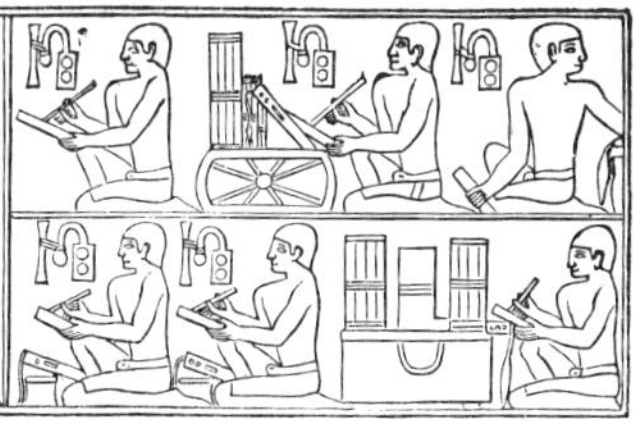

Estate office.

The ***North Side* of the tomb-chapel (key-plan, p. 166) is adorned with scenes representing life in the marshes of the Delta. To the left (beginning at the top): Ti superintending bird-snaring and fishing; a hut with a catch of birds and fishes; two men seated at

a small table cutting up fish; below, cattle pasturing; a cow is represented calving, another is being milked, while an overseer leans on his staff close by and a herdsman grasping a calf by the legs prevents it running to its mother; to the left, calves tethered to

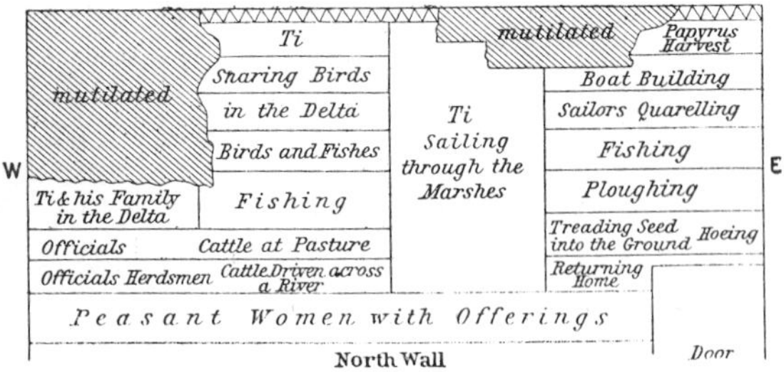

pegs in the ground try to tear themselves free, others are browsing; to the right, herdsmen in small papyrus boats drive a herd of cattle across a river in which lurk two crocodiles; to the left are two dwarfs with their master's pet ape and a leash of greyhounds. — In the

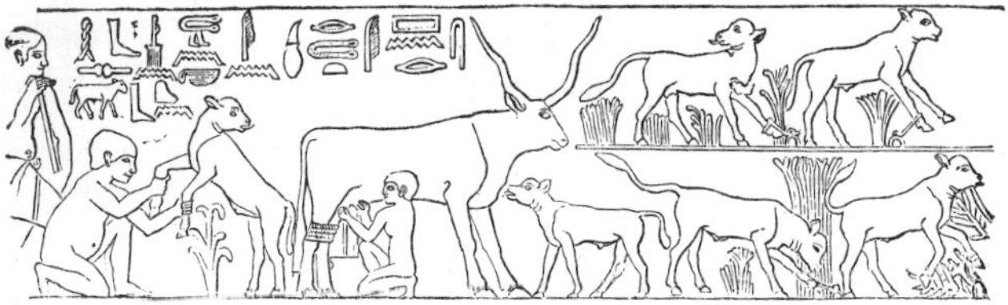

Cattle at pasture.

Ploughing. Tilling. Sowing.

centre: Ti sailing through the marshes in a boat of papyrus. In front of him is a second boat, whose crew is engaged in hunting hippopotami with harpoons, near which a hippopotamus bites a crocodile. In a smaller boat behind is a man catching a sheat-fish,

In the surrounding papyrus thicket various birds are sitting on their nests or fluttering about. — To the right: papyrus harvest and the construction of papyrus boats; boatmen quarrelling and fighting;

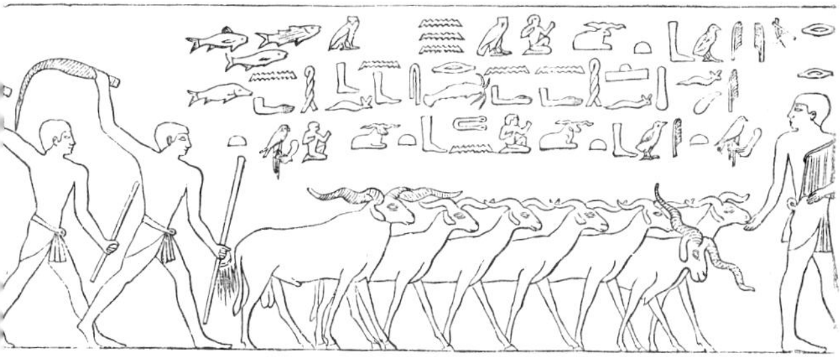
Rams treading in the seed.

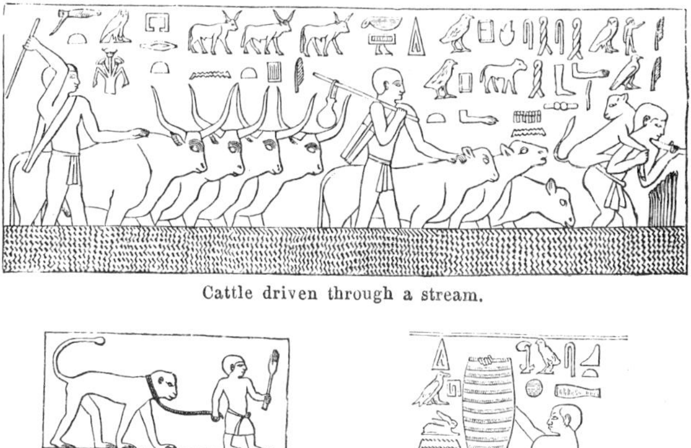
Cattle driven through a stream.

Dwarfs with ape and hounds.

Catch of fish.

fishing, a fisherman shakes fish from a bow-net into a basket; tilling the ground, a man ploughs with two oxen, which another man drives (note the shape of the plough), a third man breaks the clods,

Ti sailing through the marshes.

Peasant women with offerings.

while a fourth is sowing; close by is a scribe. Rams are driven over the newly sown ground to tread in the seed, while men hoe the ground, to the right. Cattle, returning from pasturage in the Delta, are driven through the water; one of the herdsmen, in front, carries a young calf on his shoulders.

The narrow strip running along the entire N. wall at the bottom consists of a procession of thirty-six peasant women bearing sacrificial offerings of meat, poultry, vegetables, fruits, and drink. The different figures represent the various estates of the deceased Ti, the name of each being inscribed beside its representative.

The mastaba of Ti is rivalled in beauty by the reliefs in the ****Mastaba of Ptahhotep,** which lies a few minutes to the S. of Mariette's House. It dates from the 5th Dyn., under which the deceased held one of the highest offices of state. Only Rooms A-F, described below, are accessible.

From the entrance (A on the plan, p. 170), on the N. side, we enter a CORRIDOR (Pl. B), the walls of wich are adorned with interesting preliminary sketches and half-finished reliefs (r.) and with royal cartouches, partly empty (l.). On the right is the PILLARED HALL (Pl. C), a large square apartment with its roof supported by four pillars. A door in the S.E. angle admits us to a vestibule (Pl. E), beyond which is the tomb-chamber.

The SACRIFICIAL CHAMBER OF PTAHHOTEP (Pl. F) is adorned with mural reliefs that are among the highest achievements of ancient Egyptian art at its zenith (p. clxxxii), some of them even surpassing those in the mastaba of Ti. The colours are still well preserved. The ceiling imitates the trunks of palm-trees.

In the Doorway: Servants with sacrificial gifts. *North Wall:* over the door, Ptahhotep at his morning toilet, with his greyhounds under his chair and a pet ape held by an attendant; in front of him are harpers and singers; dwarfs stringing beads (upper row); officials seated on the ground (next two rows); harpers and flute-players and a singer beating time with his hands (lowest row). To the left of the door are servants with gifts; slaughter of the sacrificial oxen. — *West Wall:* In the right and left angles are false doors; that on the right, very elaborate, perhaps representing the façade of a palace. On the left door (at the foot) the deceased is represented seated in a chapel (right) and borne in a litter (left); in front is the table of offerings. The wall-reliefs represent Ptahhotep seated at a richly furnished banquet (left); before him are priests making offerings (upper row) and servants bearing various gifts (three lower rows); above is the list of offerings. — On the *South Wall* is a similar representation of the deceased at table; before him are peasant women with gifts (top row; injured); in the second row the sacrificial animals are being cut up; in the lowest two rows are servants with all kinds of offerings. — The representations on the *East Wall* are the finest and most interesting. On the right Ptahhotep

inspects the "gifts and tribute that are brought by the estates of the N. and S."; in the upper row are boys wrestling and seven boys running (the first having his arms tied). In the next two rows are shown the spoils of the chase: four men drag two cages containing lions, a man carries a frame loaded with young gazelles, bound together in groups, another has cages with hares and hedgehogs.

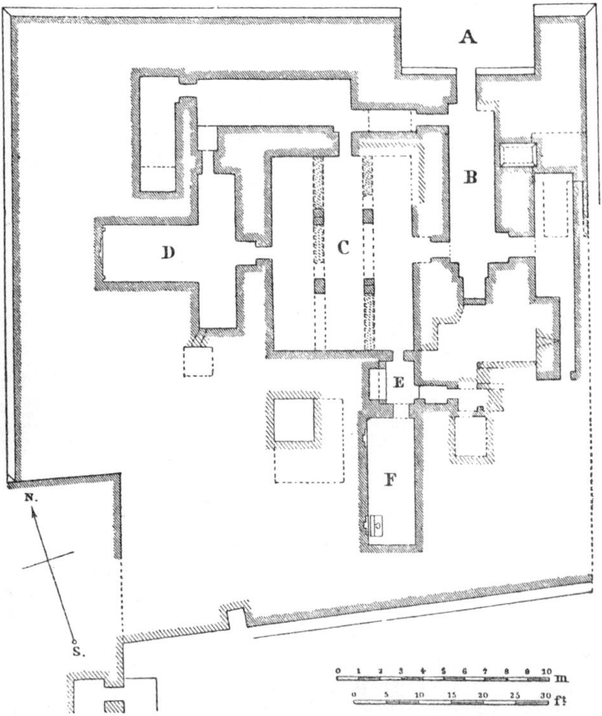

In the fourth row are herdsmen and cattle in the fields, the calves being tethered to pegs; in the two following rows cattle are brought for inspection (note the lame herdsman leading a bull with a neck-ornament); in the lowest row, poultry. On the left Ptahhotep is shown "contemplating all the pleasant diversions that take place throughout the country"; in the top row a herd of cattle is being driven through a marsh, and men are engaged in plucking papyrus

plants, tying them in bundles, and carrying them away; in the second row are boys playing; the vintage is represented in the third, with vines upon trellises, watered by a servant, while others gather the grapes and tread them in the wine-press or crush them in sacks; the fourth and fifth rows are devoted to animal life and hunting in the desert; in the sixth are men labouring in the marsh, cleaning fish, and making ropes and papyrus boats; in the seventh row are fowlers with nets and other men placing the captured birds in boxes and bearing them away; in the lowest row are peasants in boats upon the Nile, with plants and fishes; some of the peasants are fighting. In the boat to the left appears Ni-ankh-Ptah, sculptor-in-chief, receiving a drink from a boy; this is doubtless the artist who designed the reliefs and has here immortalized himself.

We now return to the Pillared Hall and pass through a door in the W. wall into the Chapel of Ekhet-hotep (Pl. D), a son of Ptahhotep. To the right and left are representations of the deceased at a banquet, with servants bringing him sacrificial gifts. On the W. wall is a false door, with a large table of offerings.

The ***Tomb of Mereruka** is another grave well worthy of a visit. It is situated at the N.W. angle of the Pyramid of Teti (p. 175), which lies to the E. of Mariette's house, beyond the ruined pyramid of User-kaf (p. 157). The tomb dates from the beginning of the 6th Dyn. and contains thirty-one rooms and passages, divided into three sections, of which that marked A on the plan (p. 172) belonged to *Mereruka*, that marked B to *Hert-watet-khet*, his wife, and that marked C to their son *Meri-Teti*. The tablet at the entrance records the discovery in 1893.

Rooms marked A. To the right and left of the *Entrance:* Mereruka and his wife (the latter on a small scale). To the right in the entrance: the artist who designed the reliefs (perhaps Mereruka himself), seated before an easel, painting the three seasons of the Egyptian year (p. lxxv), represented by deities; in one hand he holds a shell containing colour, and in the other a pen, while a writing apparatus hangs from his shoulder; in front of him stands his son Khenu. To the left: Mereruka, before whom is his little son Meri-Teti, holding a lotus-stalk and a bird; behind Mereruka appear his wife and several rows of attendants. — A 1. *North Wall.* Mereruka, in a papyrus boat with his wife, spearing fish; in two smaller boats are men harpooning three hippopotami; in the reeds are birds and in the river fish. *South Wall.* Mereruka hunting in the marshes, in a boat, accompanied by his wife. The details are beautifully rendered (birds, fish, etc., hippopotamus with a crocodile in its mouth). Below, to the left, cattle crossing a stream; above, cattle thrown on the ground in order to be slaughtered; gardens being watered. The positions of the cattle are accurately observed and reproduced. — A 2 contains the mummy-shaft. — A 3. *East Wall.* Mereruka and his wife (to the left) inspecting various operations, which are represented in six rows. In the two lowest rows are goldsmiths and makers of necklaces and vessels; in the 3rd row, three statues are being drawn to the tomb, while a priest swings a censer; in the 4th row are carpenters making bedsteads; and in the 5th row are men making stone vessels. *West Wall.* Mereruka and his wife, accompanied by attendants, at a hunt in the desert; desert animals; hound seizing an antelope; lion devouring a bull; hedgehogs; hares. — A 4. *East Wall.* To the right, Mereruka and his wife, with attendants, watching the capture of fish; the fat brother of the deceased is shown sailing in a boat and

drinking from a cup; to the left, Mereruka and his wife; before them are servants, one leading a monkey and two hounds in a leash. *West Wall.* To the left is the estate office, a hall with columns, in which the clerks sit, while the village elders are being dragged, not without cudgelling, to give evidence as to taxes (comp. p. 165); one has been stripped and is being beaten at a whipping-post. To the right, Mereruka and his wife inspect the offering of sacrifices to the statues of the deceased. — A 5 contains no reliefs. — Leaving A 6-A 9 unvisited for the present (see p. 173), we turn to the right.

A 10 (Bedroom). The roof is supported by four pillars, bearing incised reliefs of the deceased. *West Wall* (beginning to the left). Bedroom scenes. The bed, standing beneath a canopy, is prepared in presence of Mereruka and his wife; the deceased, along with his wife, who plays upon a harp, sits upon a large couch with lions' feet, beneath which are two rows of vases; Mereruka, seated in an easy chair, receives gifts of various kinds in vases and boxes from his retainers. *North Wall.* Priests of the dead bring stands loaded with meat and drink to the deceased. *East Wall.* Mereruka and his wife, with attendants; servants bringing sacrificial gifts; male and female dancers (two lowest rows). *South Wall.* The deceased receiving sacrificial gifts.— A11. Only a few reliefs are preserved here, together with the false door on the *West Wall*, behind which is a serdâb (p. clxxvi). In the floor is the opening of the *Shaft* descending to the *Tomb Chamber*; it was blocked by a vertically grooved stone slab. The walls of the chamber are decorated with reliefs of sacrificial gifts, lists of offerings, and false doors. The huge sarcophagus stands against the back wall. — A 12. *North Wall.* The deceased receiving gifts; in the second row from the bottom are ten granaries; in the lowest row, treading grapes and pressing the trodden grapes in a sack. On the other walls are the deceased receiving food and drink, and cattle being slaughtered.

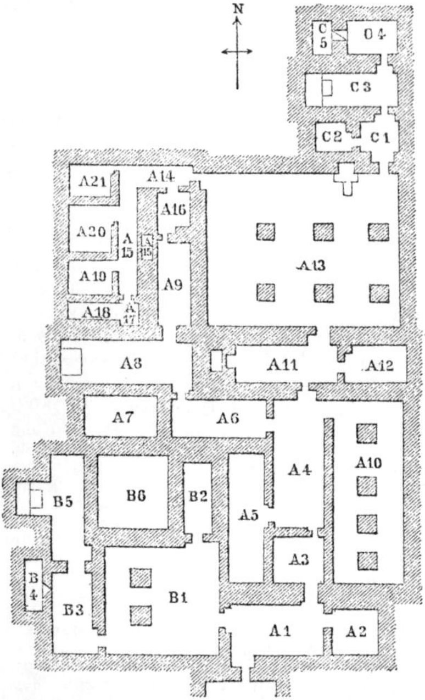

*A 13, the sacrificial chapel, has six square pillars, on which Mereruka is represented standing. In the middle is a stone ring for tethering the sacrificial ox. *North Wall.* In a recess is a statue of Mereruka (front view), with a table of offerings in front. Mural reliefs (right to left): Mereruka inspecting domestic animals, etc. (in the top row, boat-building; in the four lower rows, gazelles, antelopes, and cattle; in the lowest row, feeding tame hyænas); the aged Mereruka conducted by his two sons; Mereruka

in a sedan chair, with a large retinue, including two dwarfs leading dogs. *West Wall* (much damaged). Ships. *South Wall* (bottom row only preserved). Funeral: entrance to the tomb, with a priest and dancers in front of it; left, men carrying a large chest; sacrificial gifts; four ships, with several men in the water; the funeral procession with professional mourners (very graphic). To the left of the door, the deceased, accompanied by two women, sails in a boat through the marshes; crocodiles and fish in the water. *East Wall.* To the right, harvest operations in presence of the deceased and his wife and mother. To the left, Mereruka and his wife playing draughts. Over and beside the door to C1: Mereruka, his wife, and mother, with female dancers and musicians; various games. We now pass through a doorway of modern construction.

Rooms marked C. — C 1. *East Wall.* To the right, poultry yard, fattening geese; left, cattle and antelopes. *North Wall*, Meri-Teti, son of Mereruka, receiving sacrificial gifts from servants. *West Wall.* The deceased witnessing a hunt in the desert; gazelles and antelopes. *South Wall.* Servants with poultry and fish as sacrificial gifts. — C 2 has no reliefs. — C 3. *East Wall.* In the two lowest rows, cattle being slaughtered for sacrifice; upper rows, servants bringing gifts, cattle, gazelles, etc. *North* and *South Walls.* Meri-Teti at table; servants bringing sacrificial gifts. *West Wall.* False door, with the deceased's name inserted in place of an earlier one; in front is a table of offerings. — C 4. *East Wall.* Men bearing large chests full of clothing and vessels to Meri-Teti, who stands on the left. *North Wall.* In the centre, the deceased; at the sides, servants bringing jars and boxes; right, large jars brought on sledges. *West Wall.* Attendants with gifts (unfinished); square hole leading to C 5, the serdâb. *South Wall*, unfinished (reliefs similar to those on the N. wall). — We now regain A 13 and turn to the right (W.).

Rooms marked A (continued). A 14 leads to several store-chambers (A 15 - A 21), only about 3 ft. high; the names are inscribed above the doors. — From A 16 we enter A 9. *West Wall.* In the centre are Mereruka and his wife, right and left are servants bearing pieces of cloth, vessels of sacred oil, boxes of clothing, and stands of ornaments; sledge with three large jars. *East Wall.* Similar scenes. — A 8. Beyond the false door on the *West Wall*, in front of which stood the table of offerings, nothing of interest. — A 6. *West Wall.* Feeding of poultry (pigeons, geese, cranes). A narrow cleft in this wall leads to the serdâb (A 7), in which a painted statue of Mereruka was found. *South Wall.* To the left, cattle, antelopes, etc., are being driven before the deceased, while scribes note down the numbers; right, peasant women, representing villages the names of which are inscribed, bringing gifts. *North Wall.* Left, the slaughtering of cattle; right, Mereruka inspecting his fishermen.

Rooms marked B. — B 1. *North and South Walls.* The wife of Mereruka, a princess, receiving various gifts from her attendants. *West Wall.* Right, Mereruka's wife, son, and daughter; four servants bearing a litter adorned with lions; left, fishing scene; above, capture of wild bulls. — B 2. Staircase. — B 3. *North Wall* (left of the door leading to B 5). Dancers. On the other walls are servants bringing food for the deceased, and cattle. — B 4. Serdâb (inaccessible). — B 5. *West Wall.* In the centre is an elaborate false door, in front of which is a square block once supporting a table of offerings; to the right and left is the deceased at table, with servants bringing food, flowers, etc. *North Wall.* Mereruka's wife and son Meri-Teti carried by women in a litter adorned with a lion, near which are three dogs and a pet ape. On the other walls, attendants bringing gifts to the deceased; cattle being slaughtered. — B 6. Empty.

To the right (E.) of Mereruka's tomb, and likewise excavated in 1893, lies the large **Maṣṭaba of Ka-gem-ni,** vizier and judge under three kings of the 6th Dynasty.

The Entrance is at the S. end of the East Front, which has a frieze inscribed with the names and titles of the deceased. We first enter an

ANTEROOM (Pl. 1), with representations of fishermen and persons carrying sacrificial gifts. Thence we reach a HALL supported by three pillars (Pl. 2), with attractive reliefs of dancers, hunting in the marches, farmyard, boats, cattle crossing a ford, boys feeding a puppy, and a court of justice. On the W. is a CORRIDOR (Pl. 3) serving five storehouses that were once probably two-storied. From the pillared hall we enter, to the N., ROOM I (Pl. 4). On the left wall, Ka-gem-ni inspects his cattle and poultry; hyænas being fed; feeding poultry; bird-snaring. On the right wall the deceased inspects the fisheries; the captured fish are recorded and carried away. Above the door to the next room is the deceased in his litter. The SERDÂB (Pl. 5), to the W. of this, is inaccessible. — ROOM II (Pl. 6). Ka-gem-ni receiving gifts from his attendants. To the left is a chamber (Pl. 7) in which figures of the deceased are chiselled out at two places. — ROOM III (Pl. 8). On the side-walls, Ka-gem-ni, seated in a chair, receives sacrificial gifts. On the end-wall is the false door, in front of which was the table of offerings, reached by a flight of steps. — ROOM IV (Pl. 9). Two representations of Ka-gem-ni, standing, and receiving gifts from his attendants; tables with vessels; large ointment-jars dragged on sledges. — We return to the anteroom, whence a door leads N. to a HALL (Pl. 10). Farther on is a staircase ascending to the roof of the mastaba, where there were originally two chambers 36 ft. long, which probably contained boats of the sun.

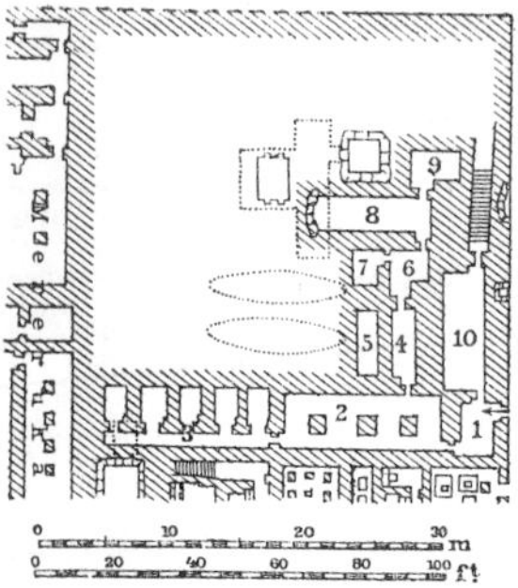

A few paces E. of the tomb of Ka-gem-ni, and N. of the Teti pyramid (p. 175), is a **Street of Tombs,** exhumed by Victor Loret in 1899 but partly covered up again. Several interesting structures of the 6th Dyn. were discovered here (left). The first is the somewhat ruinous tomb of *Nefer-seshem-Rē*, surnamed *Sheshi*, a vizier and judge, the chief remains of which are a hall with six square pillars, bearing the figure of the deceased, and a fine false door.

The first tomb on the left in the Street of Tombs proper is that of **Ankh-me-Hor*, surnamed *Sesi*, also called the 'Tomb of the Physician' on account of the surgical operations represented. The upper part of the walls has been destroyed.

ROOM I. To the left of the entrance: Farming scenes, including a representation of cattle fording a river. — In ROOM II, lying behind R. I, the deceased is represented on the left wall inspecting the catching of birds. On the rear wall are interesting representations of statues being prepared for the tomb. In the doorway to the next room is represented the slaughter of sacrificial animals; right, the attendants are seen throwing an ox to the ground. — The THREE FOLLOWING ROOMS contain the customary representations, such as the bringing of offerings to the dead and the slaughtering of cattle. — We return to the first room and enter the room lying to one side of it, which was formerly supported by five pillars. In the doorway are representations of surgical operations; on the right, circumcision, on the left, an operation on a man's toe. On the entrance-wall of the PILLARED ROOM, to the right, are representations of attendants and women bewailing the dead, while to the left are dancers.

The next tomb belongs to *Udje-he-Teti*, or *Nefer-seshem-Ptah*, surnamed *Sheshi*, 'the first next to the king'.

From the Entrance Room we proceed through a door, with representations of attendants and sacrificial animals, into a Second Chamber, with some fine reliefs. On the right wall: catching of wild ducks with a net; above, a poultry yard, catching of fowls, feeding of geese; on the other walls are attendants with sacrificial gifts, several of them in boats. — On the W. wall of the Last Room is the false door, through which the deceased is twice represented as emerging; above is a window, out of which he is looking; in front is the table of offerings; on the other walls are the deceased at a banquet, attendants with gifts, and the slaughtering of cattle for an offering to the dead.

If not pressed for time the traveller may now ascend to the *Pyramid of Teti*, to the E. of which lie the scanty ruins of the mortuary temple, with remains of the alabaster altar and a number of table-shaped pedestals for statues (displaced). Farther E. lies a chaos of buildings, brought to light during the excavations carried on by J. E. Quibell of the Department of Antiquities, and dating from various times from the Ancient Empire down to the Greek period. The oldest monuments are two large stone maṣṭabas, belonging to the Ancient Empire, surmounted by brick tombs added in the Middle Empire. The brick wall by which these are surrounded is 30-33 ft. thick and dates from the Greek period. — Close by is the *House of the Egyptian Department of Antiquities*. In front of this, to the N.W., stretches a cemetery excavated by Quibell, with *Brick Maṣṭabas* of the 2nd and 3rd Dynasties.

The ***Pyramid of King Onnos** or **Unis** (p. ciii), which lies to the S.W. of the Step Pyramid, may easily be climbed without assistance. The view from the top includes, to the N., the Pyramids of Abuṣîr and Gîza; S., those of Ṣaqqâra and Dahshûr; and E., the Step Pyramid and the palm-groves and fields of Ṣaqqâra and Mît Rahîna.

Interior. The pyramid was opened by Sir Gaston Maspero (p. 136) in 1881 and is accessible to visitors (apply to the keeper; tickets, see p. 152). A sloping *Passage*, the mouth of which was formerly covered by the pavement, runs from the middle of the N. side to an *Antechamber*, beyond which a straight *Corridor*, originally blocked at the farther end by three trap-doors, leads to a *Central Chamber*, with the *Tomb Chamber* on the right (W.) and another *Small Room* on the left (E.). The last, which was originally closed by a slab of stone, has a flat roof and three recesses, while the central chamber and the tomb-chamber have pointed roofs and walls covered with inscriptions, the so-called pyramid-texts (p. clxxvii). These hieroglyphics are cut into the stone and filled with blue pigment. They relate to the life beyond the tomb and are the oldest religious Egyptian texts known. The granite sarcophagus of the king stands in the tomb-chamber, close to the W. wall. To the right and left are false doors of alabaster.

The small *Mortuary Temple*, E. of the pyramid, is much dilapidated. It contained a court with palm-columns (p. clxvii), fragments of which lie scattered about. At the foot of the pyramid, probably on the site of the sanctuary, are vestiges of a false door of granite.

On the S. side of the Pyramid of Onnos are three **Shaft Tombs of the Persian Epoch**, all of similar arrangement. A vertical square shaft descends to a chamber constructed of blocks of stone, at the

bottom of a larger shaft sunk for the purposes of construction and then again filled in. These tombs are now accessible by a spiral staircase and are connected with each other by tunnels.

The descent is somewhat toilsome. The shaft, 72 ft. deep, leads viâ a corridor 16 ft. long to the vaulted tomb-chamber of the physician *Psamtik*, a contemporary of Darius I. (p. cvii). The walls are decorated with religious inscriptions. The lid of the large limestone coffin is raised and the arrangement for lowering it is plainly visible. This coffin contained a smaller one of basalt and, like those in the two other tombs, is let into the floor. — To the W. is a modern tunnel, leading to the tomb-shaft and sarcophagus-chamber of the royal admiral *Tjenhebu* (p. 105), which contains beautifully carved inscriptions. — Towards the E. we descend by steps to the shaft (88 ft. deep) and the chamber of *Pede-ēse*. The walls are decorated with inscriptions in fine low relief, the colouring of which is well preserved, and with representations of sacrificial gifts. The vaulted ceiling is covered with coloured stars upon a white ground.

If time permit the traveller may now proceed to the SOUTHERN PYRAMIDS OF ṢAQQÂRA, a ride of $1^1/_4$ hr. to the S. from Mariette's House. We pass near a piece of ground about 440 yds. square, enclosed by broad and massive, but now very dilapidated walls on the E., N., and W. sides, while the S. side is bounded by the natural hills of the desert. The route leads thence straight to the Maṣṭabat Fara'ûn (see below). To the left are the dilapidated *Pyramids of Phiops I.* and *Merenrē* (p. ciii) and a pyramid called by the Arabs *El-Haram esh-Shauwâf*.

On the N.W. (r.) side of the Maṣṭabat Fara'ûn is the *Pyramid of Phiops II.*, constructed and adorned, like the rest of these pyramids, in the same manner as that of King Onnos (p. 175). To the E. lie the remains of the *Mortuary Temple*, excavated by G. L. Jéquier of Neuchâtel in 1926-27 on behalf of the Egyptian Department of Antiquities. Like the mortuary temples of the 5th Dyn. at Abuṣîr (p. 151) it has a central courtyard with a colonnade; beyond is a chamber with five chapels for statues, while the sanctuary is approached by two anterooms. The relief-decoration of the walls and pillars is well preserved in parts.

The *Maṣṭabat Fara'ûn*, the most important monument in the S. group, takes the form of an immense coffin with barrel-vaulting. It was a king's grave, as its name ('grave of Pharaoh') implies, being the burial-place of *Shepseskaf*, the last ruler of the 4th Dynasty.

The lay-out of the INTERIOR, which may be inspected, shows the transition from the pyramid of Mykerinos (p. 143) to the 5th Dyn. pyramids at Abuṣîr (pp. 151, 152). The entrance (unlocked by the custodian) is on the N. side. A passage descends to a small anteroom; next come three granite trap-doors and then a horizontal passage leading to a vestibule, which has the tomb-chamber (with a ridged roof) on its right. Another passage, with niches (one on the right, four on the left), runs from the S.E. corner of the vestibule. All the walls of these inner chambers are faced with rough granite slabs.

The remains of the *Mortuary Temple* are on the E. side of the maṣṭaba, within a temenos enclosed by a well-preserved brick wall. — About 100 yds. W. of the N.W. corner of the Maṣṭabat Fara'ûn lies the *Tomb of Queen Udjebten*, wife of Phiops II.

An interesting but somewhat tiring day's ride (6-7 hrs.) is from Badrashein (p. 153) across the desert and viâ the Maṣṭabat Fara'ûn (p. 176) to the Pyramids of Dahshûr (see below), and back to Badrashein (donkey P.T. 30 there and back). — The necropolis and pyramids of **Dahshûr** lie 1/2 hr. S. of the Maṣṭabat Fara'ûn. Here rise two large pyramids and a smaller one of limestone, and two of Nile-mud bricks (*El-Ahrâm es-Sûd*, 'Black Pyramids'), together with remains of others, all of which are at a considerable distance from each other. The *North Brick Pyramid*, once covered with slabs of stone, is probably the tomb of Sesostris (Senwosret) III. (12th Dyn.). The length of the side at the base is 344 ft., while the height is now only about 90 ft. To the N. of this pyramid, but within the wall that formerly enclosed it, are two subterranean galleries with tomb-chambers in which female members of the royal family were interred (jewels now in the Cairo Museum, p. 103).

To the S.W. of the North Brick Pyramid lies a larger *Stone Pyramid*. This is still 325 ft. in height and 709 ft. in width, being nearly as large as the Great Pyramid of Gîza (p. 136), and in its solitude presents a very imposing appearance. Like the Pyramid of Meidûm (p. 217) it was built by Snofru, and is thus the most ancient royal tomb in the form of a pure pyramid.

To the E. is the ruinous pyramid of *Amenemmēs II.* (12th Dyn.), while to the E. and S. are remains of several other pyramids. Still farther S. rises a pyramid of peculiar form, called the *Blunted Pyramid* or *Pyramid of the Two Angles*, known to the Arabs as *El-Haram el-Kaddâb*, or the *False Pyramid*, the lower part rising at an angle of 54° 41′, while the sides of the apex form an angle of 42° 59′. This pyramid is 618 1/2 ft. square and 319 ft. in height, and presents the appearance of a pointed pyramid resting on a truncated one or on a huge maṣṭaba. The exterior coating is in good preservation and gives a very good notion of the original appearance of the pyramids. The interior was explored as early as the year 1660 by an English traveller named Edward Melton. In 1860 Le Brun found a small chamber in the interior. No clue to the name of the builder has been discovered, but it is believed to be the burial-place of Hu, the last king of the 3rd Dynasty. To the S. is the pyramid of the queen.

To the E. of the Blunted Pyramid and about 2 M. to the S. of the North Brick Pyramid, near the village of Minshât Dahshûr, which lies on the edge of the desert to the N. of Dahshûr, rises the *South Brick Pyramid*. This, which was originally covered with limestone slabs, was perhaps built by Amenemmēs III. (12th Dyn.). To the N. of it, but enclosed by the former girdle-wall, are the graves of *King Hor* (pp. 91, 103) and *Princess Nebhetepti-khrod* (p. 103).

8. Ḥelwân.

Railway (to be electrified) from Cairo to (15 1/2 M.) Ḥelwân in 30-40 min.; 30 trains daily. Return-tickets, 1st cl. P.T. 12, 2nd cl. 7 1/2 (on Sun. and Fri. P.T. 8 and 6). — There is also an excellent Road from Cairo to Ḥelwân viâ Old Cairo (comp. p. 113), much used by motorists.

The trains start from the *Bâb el-Lûq* station (p. 37). — Beyond the stations of (1 1/4 M.) *Es-Saiyida Zeinab* (*Saida Zenab;* Pl. D 6) and (3 M.) *St. George* (p. 114) the railway traverses the narrow plain on the E. bank of the Nile, generally on the boundary between the cultivated land and the desert. — At (7 M.) *El-Ma'âdi (Meadi)* is a villa-colony with pretty gardens (Pensions Cecil House and Windermere House; Café Diamanti, on the Nile). Near the village are the grounds of the Ma'âdi Sporting Club (p. 44; golf, tennis, swimming) and a machine for utilizing the sun's rays (1912), which provides steam for the 50 h.p. engine of an irrigation system. — 8 M. *Ṭura*. To the right are the 'Egyptian Army Bakery & Supply Stores' and

a penitentiary; about ¹/₂ hr. to the left are the quarries (p. 180). On the hill stand the ruins of an old Mameluke fort. — 11 M. *El-Maʻṣara (Massara)*, a village on the Nile, with a cement factory. — The line leaves the Nile and ascends along the slopes of the *Gebel Tura* and *Gebel Ḥôf;* on the left are old stone-quarries.

15¹/₂ M. **Ḥelwân**. — *Buffet.* — HOTELS and PENSIONS. *ᵉGrand-Hôtel Hélouan* (Pl. a, A B 2; Egyptian Hotels Ltd., comp. p. 88), opposite the Casino, with gardens and terrace, closed in summer, 130 R. (50 with bath), pens. from 120, motorbus 5 P.T.; *Hôtel des Bains* (Pl. b; B 3), same ownership as Grand-Hôtel, opposite the Bath House, with garden and veranda, 52 R., closed in 1929; *English Winter Hotel* (Mrs. M. Dodd; Pl. e, B 2), with garden, 31 R., pens. P.T. 60-80; *Hôtel-Pension Claremont* (Pl. f; B 3), 35 R., pens. 14 gold fr.; *Hôtel-Pension Antonio* (Pl. g; B 3), with garden, closed from June to Sept., 42 R., pens. from P.T. 60, well spoken of; *Hôtel-Pension Kouchnir* (Pl. q; B 3), 40 beds, pens. P.T. 50-70; *Villa Wanda* (Pl. i, B 3; 'Datsha Wanda', Russian), closed from June to Aug., 42 R., pens. P.T. 50-60, quite good; *Pension Savoy*, Rue Mansour Pacha and Rue Hussein Kamel Pacha (Pl. B 2); *Hôtel-Pension Sphinx* (Pl. h; B 3), Rue ʻAbd er-Rahman Pacha, with garden, closed from May to Sept., 24 R., pens. P.T. 50; *Pension Villa Kitty*, 12 Rue Riad Pacha, beside the Bath House, open all the year round, 12 R., pens. P.T. 40-60, with garden. Invalid cooking and diet on request at any of the hotels or pensions. — FURNISHED APARTMENTS, £E 10-20 per month.

SANATORIA. *Dr. Glanz* (Pl. l; C 2), 60 beds, pens. 20-30 gold fr.; *Dr. Preminger's Medical Institute* (Pl. m; C 2); *Dr. Roger*, for nerve cases; *Sanatorium Fuad* (Pl. c, C 2; formerly Al-Hayat), a state institution for tubercular patients (Dr. René Burnand), pens. P.T. 100-120.

PHYSICIANS. *Dr. Moore* (medical superintendent of the Bath House), *Dr. Roger* (see above), both English; *Dr. Glanz* (Russian, see above); *Dr. Preminger* (German-Bohemian; see above); *Dr. Papas* (Greek). — LADY OCULIST. *Dr. Hélène Glanz.* — LADY DENTIST. Mme. R. Niemtshenko (Russian). — CHEMIST. *Anglo-Egyptian Pharmacy.* — POST AND TELEGRAPH OFFICE (Pl. P.O.; B 2). — PHOTOGRAPHER. *Mohammed Helmy* (films developed), Rue Zaki Pacha 33, near the Roman Catholic church.

CHURCHES. *St. Paul's* (English Ch., Pl. A 2), Rue Sabet Pacha, Anglican services at 8.15, 11, and 6.30. — *Roman Catholic* (Pl. B 2), Rue Nubar Pacha, belonging to the Central African Mission. — *Greek Orthodox* (Pl. A 2), *Greek Catholic*, and *Coptic Churches.*

CABS at the station (fares according to tariff): P.T. 4 per km., 10 per hour; to the Nile P.T. 19, there and back 30; to the Wâdi Ḥôf (p. 180) P.T. 20 and 45; to the Wâdi Gerraui (Wâdi Girâwi, p. 180) P.T. 35 and 53. — DONKEYS (difficult to obtain): P.T. 5 per hour, 25 per day. For excursions without a guide the visitor should provide himself with Schweinfurth's map of the environs of Ḥelwân (scale 1 : 30,000; 'Aufnahmen in der Östlichen Wüste von Ägypten, Blatt l', comp. p. 397; Berlin 1897; 6s. 6d., on linen 9s.).

Ḥelwân, French *Hélouan-les-Bains*, Arabic *Hammâmât Hilwân*, an artificial oasis in the desert, 3 M. to the E. of the Nile and 115 ft. above the average water-level, is situated on a plateau enclosed from N.W. to S.E. by steep limestone hills. Before the war it had about 8000 inhab., but its population, together with the number of patients, has since decreased. It owes its repute partly to its thermal springs, partly to its climate. The sulphur and saline springs, which were made available for medicinal purposes in 1871-72, have a temperature of 91° Fahr. and resemble those of Harrogate and Aix-les-Bains in their ingredients. They are efficacious in cases of rheumatism, lumbago, sciatica, neuritis, and gout. The dry and warm climate is specially adapted for rheumatic and kidney

diseases, and for all cases in which cold and damp should be avoided (comp. p. xxiii). Between Nov. and Feb. rain falls for a few hours only at Ḥelwân, and the atmosphere is free from all perceptible moisture. The mean temperature in winter is 61° 5′ Fahr., with a daily range of 21° (51-72°). The amount of daily sunshine averages 8 hrs. and the fall of temperature after sunset is very slight.

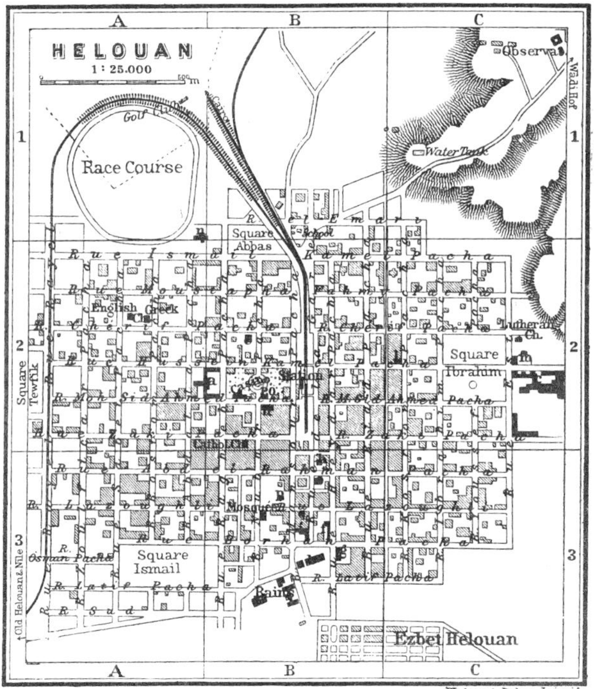

Wagner & Debes, Leipzig

In consequence of the rocky soil and the powerful rays of the sun, the air is extraordinarily pure, dustless, and bracing.

The *Bath Establishment* (Bains; Pl. B 3), in the Moorish style, built by the Egyptian government in 1899, rebuilt in 1911, and now leased by the Egyptian Hotels Co. (p. 178), is equipped with immersion-baths for fresh and sulphur water, electric, hot-air, vapour, swimming baths, etc. There are arrangements also for inhalation and massage and for sun and air baths.

To the N.E. of Ḥelwân, on the plateau, stands the *Astronomical & Meteorological Observatory* (Pl. C 1; 374½ ft.; lat. 29°51′31″ N., long. 31°20′27″ E.; adm. 3.30-5 from Nov. 1st to April 30th, also occasionally on winter evenings). Adjacent are the *Waterworks.*

Ḥelwân is within easy motoring distance of Cairo, and it has the good golf-course (Pl. A 1; 18 holes) of the Helouan Golf Club, a tennis club, the International Club ('Casino', Pl. B 2), etc. Excursions may be made to the gorge-like valleys of the desert and to Ṣaqqâra, while the banks of the Nile afford good wild-fowl shooting. — Pleasant drives (carriages, see p. 178) may be taken, past the aerodrome (Royal Air Force), to the village of *Old Ḥelwân* (beyond Pl. A 3), picturesquely situated on the Nile, and to the *Princesses' Garden* near the palace of the mother of ʿAbbâs II. Ḥilmi (p. cxxx).

The quarries of **Maʿṣara** and **Ṭura**, to the N. of Ḥelwân, are 1½ hr.'s donkey-ride; a guide and candles are necessary. These quarries, which are still worked, yielded the fine white limestone used for the outer coating of pyramids and masṭabas and other ancient buildings down to the Ptolemaic period. The stone is transported to the bank of the Nile by means of tramways, carts, camels, and mules. The Arabs of the present day quarry the stone on the outside of the rocky slopes only, while the quarrymen of the Pharaohs penetrated into the interior of the mountain and excavated large chambers when they came to serviceable stone. The roofs are supported by pillars of rock. A few inscriptions, recording the opening of new halls in the quarries, some demotic inscriptions, and reliefs (Kings Amenemmēs, Amosis, Amenophis III., Nektanebis II.) are still preserved. The Egyptians named these the quarries of *Royu* (or *T-royu*), which the Greeks corrupted into *Troja*, while Strabo relates that the village beside the quarries was "an ancient residence of captive Trojans who had followed Menelaus to Egypt and remained there".

From Ḥelwân an excursion to the *Wâdi Ḥôf (beyond Pl. C 1), with its picturesque scenery, curious fossils, and remarkable desert vegetation, which is finest after rain, may be made in ½ day either by carriage (p. 178) or by donkey (P.T. 15). The road, which is possible for vehicles nearly to the wâdi, leads N. past the Observatory (see above) to 'Sarcophagus Corner' (shown on Schweinfurth's map), opposite the Reil ravine. Thence we follow the picturesque windings of the valley for about ¾ hr. to its head, where visitors should give orders for their carriages to rejoin them (the valley bottom is quite practicable for riders). A footpath ascends 'Bastion Hill', which commands a fine view. The Reil ravine (see above), with its magnificent termination, should also be visited.

Another pleasant excursion may be made to the **Wâdi Risheid**, S.E. of Ḥelwân (to the end of the valley 6-8 hrs.; guide, water, and provisions necessary). The valley contracts until it becomes a very picturesque gorge, at the end of which pools known to the Beduins rise in stages one above the other.

About 7 M. to the S.E. of Ḥelwân (2 hrs. by donkey; carriages, see p. 178) is the **Wâdi Gerraui** (*Wâdi Garâwi* or *Girâwi*), a desert ravine running E. and W. between abrupt limestone cliffs. Schweinfurth discovered here the remains of a large *Dam* of masonry (*Sadd el-Kafara*), probably erected under the Ancient Empire to arrest the water flowing down the ravine in rainy winters and so to provide drinking water for the workmen employed in the alabaster quarries, 2½ M. to the E. It consists of an embankment, 33 ft. high, 200-260 ft. long, and 150 ft. thick, stretching across the ravine, and constructed of solid masonry faced with limestone slabs on the E. side. Remains of stone huts were found on the top of the hill N.W. of the dam.

The Excursion from Ḥelwân to Ṣaqqâra takes a whole day. We ride to Old Ḥelwân and thence ferry across the Nile to *Badrashein.* Travellers are carried ashore on the backs of the Arabs. Thence, see p. 153. Donkeys and carriages can be hired at Badrashein.

9. From Cairo to Mansûra viâ Bilbeis and Zagazig.

92 M. RAILWAY viâ Bilbeis in 3-4¾ hrs.; six trains daily (fares 1st cl. P.T. 93½, 2nd cl. 50½). — The route viâ Ṭanṭa (comp. pp. 37, 36, 184, 185) is shorter and pleasanter.

From Cairo to (9½ M.) *Qalyûb*, see p. 37. — The main line to Alexandria and to Ismailia and Port Said diverges to the left. Our train turns N.E. and traverses a fertile district. — 13½ M. *Nawa*. — 20 M. *Shibîn el-Qanâṭir*.

About 2 M. to the S.E. of Shibîn el-Qanâṭir is the ruined site of **Tell el-Yahûdiya** (Hill of the Jews), the ancient *Leontopolis*. Ramses III. erected a temple here, partly ornamented with glazed mosaic tiles, most of which are now in the **Cairo Museum**. Their colouring is produced partly by variations in the glazing and partly by the use of separate inlaid pieces of glass. At a later date (170 B.C.) a Jewish high-priest named Onias, aided by Ptolemy VI. Philometor, erected a temple after the model of the Temple of Solomon for his countrymen who had been expelled from Jerusalem by the Syrian party. A visit to the ruins scarcely repays the trouble, as most of them are again buried in rubbish.

A branch-line runs S. from Shibîn to *Marg* (13½ M.; p. 129), and a light railway N.W. to *Ṭûkh* (p. 37) and *Biltân* (p. 184).

29 M. *Inshâṣ*. — 36 M. *Bilbeis (Belbeis)*, with an old mosque, lies on the old caravan road from Cairo to the East.

A light railway runs from Bilbeis to *Mînyet el-Qamḥ* (p. 192), *Mît Abu Khâlid* (see below), and *Ṣahragt* (p. 184).

We now approach the Fresh Water Canal (p. 191). — Beyond (41½ M.) *Burdein* we cross the Fâqûs Canal. To the right short of Zagazig, appear the ruins of Bubastis (see below).

48 M. **Zagazig**. — *Buffet*. — The other station, on the line from Benha to Ismailia, is reached by a subway. — HOTELS. *Royal*, 20 beds, R. 20 P.T., clean; *Egyptien*, R. 20 P.T. — RESTAURANT. *Central*, well spoken of.

BRITISH CONSULAR AGENCY. — BANKS. *National Bank of Egypt; Barclay's* (Anglo-Egyptian Bank).

SERVICES at the chapel of the *American Mission* (see below); also Anglican services once monthly.

Zagazig (Zaqâzîq), the capital of the province of *Sharqîya* (p. xlix) and the seat of a mudîr, is a thriving town, with 52,351 inhabitants in 1927. Its favourable situation on the *Muʿizz* (or *Moez*) *Canal* (*Baḥr Muweis*, the ancient Tanitic arm of the Nile), from which the *Mashtûl Canal* here diverges N., has largely contributed to the prosperity of the town, which is the chief centre of the Egyptian cotton and grain trade. Many European merchants have offices here, and the large cotton-ginning factories give parts of the town an almost European appearance. The *Zagazig Institute*, opened in 1925, is a Mohammedan religious institution (comp. p. 58) with 102 teachers and 1336 students in 1926-27. The American Mission maintains schools for boys and girls here. A market is held every Tuesday.

LIGHT RAILWAYS: 1. To *Mît Ghamr* (p. 184) viâ *Mît Abu Khâlid* (see above) and *Ṣahragt* (p. 184). — 2. To *Simbillâwein* (p. 182) and *Âga* (p. 184).

About ½ hr. S.E. of Zagazig, on the *Tell Basta*, lie the extensive ruins of the ancient **Bubastis** (Egyptian *Per-Baste;* the *Pi-beseth* of Ezekiel xxx. 17), the capital of the Bubastite nome. Some of the remains of the brick walls of the houses are of considerable height. The temple of Bastet, the

patron-goddess of the town, at the S.W. foot of the hill, was excavated in 1887-89 at the expense of the Egypt Exploration Fund; but the remains (granite blocks, columns, architraves, etc., some with inscriptions, and a few statues) are in too ruinous a state to repay a visit. The temple, begun by the pyramid-builders Kheops and Khephren, underwent frequent alterations at the hands of Ramses II. and other later kings, but owed its final form to the monarchs of the 22nd Dyn., who resided at Bubastis, and to Nektanebis II. (Nekht-Har-ehbēt; p. cx). At this period it consisted of four large halls, of an aggregate length of 600 ft.; and in these were celebrated the joyous and licentious festivals in honour of Bastet. "When the Egyptians travel to Bubastis", says Herodotus, "they do so in this manner. Men and women sail together, and in each boat there are many persons of both sexes. Some of the women make a noise with rattles, and some of the men blow pipes during the whole journey, while the other men and women sing and clap their hands. If they pass a town on the way, they lay to, and some of the women land and shout and mock at the women of the place, while others dance and make a disturbance. They do this at every town that lies on the Nile; and when they arrive at Bubastis they begin the festival with great sacrifices, and on this occasion more wine is consumed than during the whole of the rest of the year. The natives assert that men and women to the number of 700,000, besides children, make the annual pilgrimage hither."

Beyond Zagazig we cross the line to Ismailia and Port Said and follow the E. bank of the Muʿizz Canal. The country is fertile. 56 M. *Hihya* (*Hehia;* light railway to Ibrâhîmîya, see below).

62 M. *Abu Kebîr* (buffet) is a village with 8600 inhabitants.

From Abu Kebîr a branch-line runs E. viâ ($8^1/_2$ M.) *Fâqûs* (*Fakus;* branch to Ṣân el-Ḥagar, see below, projected) to ($20^1/_2$ M.) *Eṣ-Ṣâliḥîya* (*Salhia;* p. 197). — About 4 M. to the N. of Fâqûs, the ancient *Phakussa*, near the hamlet of *El-Khatâʿna*, are the ruins of a large town; buildings dating from the time of the 12th Dyn. and of the Ramessids were discovered here by Naville. About $2^3/_4$ M. to the N. of Khatâʿna, near the village of *Qantîr*, stood a temple built by Ramses II.

About 20 M. to the N.E. of Fâqûs (see above) are the ruins of the ancient **Tanis** (Egyptian *Djanet;* the *Zoan* of Numbers xiii. 22 and Psalms lxxviii. 12), situated near the fishing village of *Ṣân el-Ḥagar* on the Muʿizz Canal (comp. below and p. 181). The temple of the patron-god Seth, built by Ramses II., partly with the material of earlier structures, is now a confused heap of ruins (statues, carvings, obelisks in wild disorder). Most of the larger monuments have been transferred to the Cairo Museum (pp. 92, 93).

About 8 M. to the S.E. of Tanis, and 9 M. to the N.W. of Eṣ-Ṣâliḥîya (see above), lie the mounds of débris known as *Nebesha*, the ancient Egyptian *Yemet*. These were excavated in 1886, at the instance of the Egypt Exploration Fund, by Sir Flinders Petrie, who discovered the remains of a temple, built by Ramses II. with the aid of older monuments, and a sanctuary of the town-goddess Buto, founded by Amasis (p. cix). In the cemetery, among the Egyptian tombs of the 19th Dyn. and later, were found the graves of Cyprian mercenaries stationed here under Amasis.

LIGHT RAILWAYS FROM ABU KEBÎR. (1) W. viâ *Hurbeit* (*Khorbetta*, the ancient *Pharbaethus*, chief seat of the worship of Har-merti), on the Muʿizz Canal, and *Ibrâhîmîya* (branch to Hihya, see above) to *Diyarb* (or *Diarb*) *Nigm* (p. 183). — (2) S. to *Abu Ḥammâd* (p. 192).

Beyond Abu Kebîr the line turns N.W. and crosses the Muʿizz Canal and a number of smaller canals. — $66^1/_2$ M. *El-Bûha*. — 68 M. *Kafr Ṣaqr* (light railway to Manṣûra, see p. 184). — $70^1/_2$ M. *Abu'sh Shuqûq (Abu el-Shekuk)*.

$79^1/_2$ M. *Es-Simbillâwein (Simbellawin)*.

About 6 M. to the N.E. of the station, on either side of the village of *Timai* (or *Tmai*) *el-Amdîd* (*Tumay;* on the light railway from Manṣûra to

Kafr Ṣaqr, p. 184; road to Manṣûra, see p. 184) and a canal, rise two mounds of ruins. That to the S., the *Tell Timai el-Amdîd* or *Tell ibn es-Salâm*, is Roman and perhaps marks the site of the ancient *Thmuis*. That to the N., the *Tell er-Rubʿ* or *Tell el-Qaṣr*, was known in the middle ages as *El-Mondîd* and contains the ruins of the ancient *Mendes* (pp. cx, cxlv). A shrine dedicated in the temple by Amasis (p. cix) and coffins of sacred rams, which were revered in Mendes, still exist.

Light Railways from Simbillâwein. 1. Viâ *Diyarb Nigm* (p. 182) and *El-Qanâyât* (*Kanayat*) to *Zagazig* (p. 181). — 2. Viâ *Âga* (p. 181) to *Minyet* (or *Mît*) *Samannûd*, on the E. bank of the Damietta arm of the Nile (on the W. bank lies *Samannûd*, p. 185). — 3. To *Fumm el-Bûhîya (Foum el-Bouhia)*, where the *Bûhîya Canal* diverges from the Damietta arm. Thence to *Mît Ghamr*, see p. 184.

85 M. *Baqlîya (Baklia)*, with the unimportant remains of the ancient *Hermupolis* (Egyptian *Bah;* comp. p. 221). — 88 M. *Shâwa*.

92 M. **El-Manṣûra**. — *Buffet*. — Hotels. *Claridge's*, Place de la Gare, 40 R. at P.T. 40-50, new and good; *Hôtel de la Bourse*, facing the Nile, R. 20-25 P.T.; *de Paris*, Rue Fouad Ier, *Royal*, Rue Ismaïl, at both 30 R. at P.T. 15-20; *Savoy*, Rue Ismaïl.

Post and Telegraph Office, near the police station. — Banks. *National Bank of Egypt*, *Barclay's* (Anglo-Egyptian Bank), *Ottoman*, *Crédit Lyonnais*.

British Consular Agency.

Church Services in English are held during winter by the chaplain of the *Delta Chaplaincy* and by the *American Mission*.

El-Manṣûra (Mansourah), a thriving town with 62,815 inhabitants in 1927 and numerous new houses in the European style, is the capital of the province of *Daqahlîya* (p. xlix) and lies on the right bank of the ancient Phatnitic arm of the Nile, now the Damietta branch, from which diverges the *Baḥr eṣ-Ṣaghîr*, a canal emptying into Lake Manzala. On the opposite bank of the river lies *Ṭalkha* (p. 185). Manṣûra is an emporium for the cotton and other products of the Nile Delta.

El-Manṣûra (i.e. 'the victorious') was founded by Sultan Malik el-Kâmil (p. cxxi) in 1221, as an advantageous substitute for Damietta (comp. p. 186). The first serious attack made on Manṣûra was by the Crusaders under Louis IX. of France (St. Louis; comp. p. 186) in 1249. After encountering great difficulties they succeeded in crossing the Ushmûm Canal (Baḥr eṣ-Ṣaghîr), but in the neighbourhood of Manṣûra they were defeated by the young Sultan El-Muʿaẓẓam Tûrânshâh (p. cxxi). Their fleet was destroyed and 'famine-fever' broke out. When the ill-fated Crusaders attempted to escape they were intercepted by the Saracens, who thinned their ranks terribly and captured the king (April, 1250). On May 6th, 1250, St. Louis was released on payment of a heavy ransom and on surrendering Damietta.

The town is regularly laid out and the crowded Arab quarter is gradually disappearing before modern streets. The main street runs W. from the railway station to the Nile. In a square near the police station is the unassuming mosque of El-Muwâfiq. An unfounded tradition points out an old house of Saladin's time, close by, as the prison of St. Louis (see above). Farther on is the bazaar. — In the quarter between the main street and the Nile are the former *Khedivial Palace*, a large and unattractive building now used as a mixed tribunal (p. xxii), and the small mosque of *Sanga*. The latter contains columns brought from older edifices, with Byzantine capitals of Corinthian tendency, bearing Saracenic arches. The

minbar (pulpit) and ceiling are still embellished with remains of fine wood-carving, which was originally painted.

Railway to *Damietta* or *Tanta*, see R. 10.

LIGHT RAILWAYS FROM MANSÛRA. 1. To *Âga* (p. 183), *Fumm el-Bûhîya* (to Simbillâwein, see p. 183), **Mit Ghamr** (a district-capital of 12,000 inhab. on the right bank of the Damietta arm of the Nile), *Fumm es-Sâfûrîya (Foum el-Safouria)*, *Sahragt* (7000 inhab.; branch-line to Zagazig, p. 181), and *Benha* (p. 37), and thence viâ *Biltân* (*Beltân*; p. 181) to the *Delta Barrage* (p. 131). — 2. On the right bank of the Damietta arm to *El-Barâmûn*, *Mahallet Inshâq* (p. 185), *Mît el-Khôli ʿAbdallâh (Ez-Zarqa)*, *Fâriskûr* (p. 185), and *Damietta* (p. 186). — 3. To *Matarîya*. This line runs along the right bank of the Bahr es-Saghîr (p. 183). The intervening stations are *Mahallet Damana*, *Mît Dâfir (Mit Dafer)*, *Dikirnis* (*Dekernès*; a district-capital; comp. below), *Ashmûn er-Rummân* (2500 inhab.), *Mît Salsîl* (3500 inhab.), and *El-Manzala* (*Menzaleh*; a village with fully 10,000 inhab.). **Matariya** *(Matarieh)* is a village with over 15,000 inhab., the centre of the inland fisheries, situated on a peninsula in Lake Manzala (p. 197). Steamer across the lake to Port Said and Damietta, see p. 190. — 4. To *Godeida* (*Gedaiyidet el-Hâla*; see below), *Tannâh (Tanah)*, and *Dikirnis* (see above), and thence to *Mahallet Inshâq* (see above). — 5. To *Kafr Saqr* (p. 182) viâ *Godeida* (see above) and *Timai el-Amdîd* (p. 182), 2-3 hrs.

ROAD (carriage P.T. 60-70) from Mansûra to *Timai el-Amdîd* (p. 182). — Excursion to *Bahbît el-Higâra* viâ *Mît ʿAssâs*, see p. 185.

10. From Tanta to Damietta viâ Mansûra.

74 M. RAILWAY in 3-3¾ hrs. (1st cl. P.T. 76½, 2nd cl. 41½; six or seven trains daily to Mansûra, three to Damietta).

Tanta, see p. 36. — 5 M. *Er-Ragdîya (Ragdia)*. — 8½ M. *Mahallet Rôh* or *Rûh (Mehallet Roh)* is the junction for Zifta (see below) and for Disûq and Damanhûr (see p. 34).

FROM MAHALLET RÔH TO ZIFTA, 19¼ M., branch-line in 1 hr. (1st cl. P.T. 21½, 2nd cl. 12). Stations: *El-Qurashîya (Korashia)*, *El-Gimmeiza (Gemaiza, Guemmézah)*, *Es-Santa* (see p. 36). — **Zifta**, a district-capital with 15,850 inhab., lies on the left bank of the Damietta arm. Branch-line to Mît Bira (19¼ M.; p. 37; under construction in 1929); light railway to Birket es-Sabʿ (see below). About 2 M. lower down, reached in 5 min. by the light railway to Mahalla el-Kubra (see below), lies the *Zifta Barrage*, constructed in 1903 and containing fifty sluices, each 16 ft. in width. This construction resembles the Asyût Barrage (p. 237) and is intended to collect water for the canals of the E. provinces (Gharbîya, Daqahlîya, and Sharqîya), which were formerly supplied from the Delta Barrage (p. 131). — Opposite Zifta, on the right bank, lies *Mît Ghamr* (see above). About 6 M. to the S.E., in one of the most beautiful parts of the Delta, is the *Kôm* (or *Tell*) *el-Muqdâm*, with a ruined temple of Osorkon II. (22nd Dyn.), probably on the site of the *Leontopolis* of Strabo.

17½ M. **El-Mahalla el-Kubra** *(Mehalla Kebîr)*, a district-capital with 45,642 inhab. (1927), has numerous European houses, entrepôts (halaqa) for cotton, cotton ginning and weaving mills, and an interesting old synagogue.

LIGHT RAILWAYS. (1.) First N. to *Kafr es-Sârim (Kafr Sarem)*, then in a curve S. to *Samannûd* (p. 185), *Sumbât* (*Sombat*; a village of 5645 inhab., on the Damietta arm), *Zifta Barrage*, *Zifta* (see above), and *Birket es-Sabʿ* (p. 36). — (2.) To *Sakha* (p. 36) and *Kafr esh-Sheikh* (p. 185). — (3.) To *Qutûr* and *Tanta*, see p. 36. — 4. Viâ *Tîra* E. to *Talkha* (p. 185) and N. to *Biyala* and *Baltîm* (see p. 36).

20 M. *Er-Râhbein.* — 22 M. *Samannûd*, a village with 14,408 inhabitants. To the N. of the station are the scanty ruins of the ancient *Sebennytos* (Egyptian *Tjeb-nuter*, Coptic *Jemnuti*), the birthplace of Manetho (p. ci). Samannûd is situated on the Damietta arm of the Nile and has a station on the light railway from Maḥalla el-Kubra to Zifta and Birket es-Sabʿ (see p. 184). On the opposite (right) bank is *Minyet* (or *Mît*) *Samannûd* (p. 183). — 26 M. *Mît ʿAssâs.*

Proceeding N. from the station of Mît ʿAssâs for 10 min. along the canal, then turning to the left, we reach in $^3/_4$ hr. the ($2^1/_2$ M.) ruins of **Bahbît el-Ḥigâra** (*Behbît el-Hagar*), the ancient **Iseum** or *Isidis Oppidum* of the Romans. The Egyptian name of the place was *Hebet* or *Per-ehbēt*, 'House of the god of Hebet' (i.e. Horus), of which the modern name is a corruption. Horus and Osiris, as well as Isis, were worshipped here. Within a still partly extant girdle-wall of unburnt brick, used by the Arabs as a place of burial, rises a large heap of ruins, which form the remains of the once magnificent Temple of Isis, built by Nektanebis II. (30th Dyn.) and Ptolemy II. Philadelphus (p. cxi). The ruins form a most picturesque mass of fragments, altogether about 400 paces in circumference. The structure consisted entirely of granite, chiefly grey but partly red in colour, brought hither from a great distance.

The Reliefs all date from the time of Ptolemy II. The position of one of them enables us to identify the ancient sanctuary. In this relief the king appears offering incense before the sacred bark of Isis, which is here shown in a form hitherto found only in bronzes: the cabin resembles a house of two stories; above, the goddess, with cow's horns and the sun's disk, is enthroned on a lotus-flower, guarded on each side by a winged goddess. On the W. side of the ruins, near the ancient entrance, is an interesting large slab of grey granite, veined with red, on which is represented the king offering a gift of land to Osiris and Isis. On the N. side lies an unusually large Hathor capital, in granite. Numerous remains of pillars, architraves, friezes with heads of Hathor, and waterspouts in the shape of recumbent lions also still exist. A little farther on the remains of a staircase built in the walls may be observed.

The sacred lake of the temple still exists near the village of Bahbît, to the N.W. of the ruins.

32 M. *Ṭalkha* is the junction for Maḥalla el-Kubra (p. 184). — The train crosses the Damietta arm to (34 M.) **Manṣûra** (p. 183).

On leaving Manṣûra the train recrosses the river to the left bank, which it follows to Damietta. The land is carefully cultivated, and we observe a number of steam-engines used for the irrigation of the soil. — 42 M. *Baṭra.*

$48^1/_2$ M. *Shirbîn* (*Sherbin*, *Cherbine*), a district-capital with 8500 inhabitants. Opposite, on the right bank of the Damietta arm, is *Maḥallet Inshâq* (*Meḥallet Ingâq* or *Ingag*; p. 184).

From Shirbîn to Qallîn, 51 M., railway in about $2^1/_2$ hrs. — Beyond ($5^1/_2$ M.) *Basandîla* (*Bessandila*) the line crosses the *Baḥr Shibîn* (p. 36; here called also *Baḥr Basandîla*) and beyond the stations of *Bilqâs* (*Belkas*; 25,473 inhab.) and *Biyala* (*Biela*; p. 184) we cross the *Baḥr Tîra*. Stations: 38 M. *Kafr esh-Sheikh* (6702 inhab.), connected by light railways with Ṭanṭa (p. 36) and Sîdi Sâlim (p. 36) and with Maḥalla el-Kubra (p. 184); *Nashart.* — 51 M. *Qallîn* (p. 34).

55 M. *Râs el-Khalîg.* The rubbish-mounds of *Tell el-Balamûn*, near the station, mark the site of *Diospolis Inferior* (Egyptian *Per-Amun*). — 64 M. *Fâriskûr* (*Faraskur*; see p. 184); the town lies on

the right bank of the Damietta arm. Lake Manzala (p. 197) is seen to the E. — 70 M. *Kafr el-Baṭṭîkh* lies in a sandy plain, extending as far as Lake Burullus and covered in summer with crops of water-melons (baṭṭîkh; large melon-market in July). — The station of (74 M.) *Damietta* lies on the left bank of the arm of the Nile (ferry to the upper landing-place in 1/4 hr.).

Damietta. — HOTEL. *Egyptien*, on the river, R. 20-25 P.T. Manṣûra (p. 183) offers better accommodation.

Damietta, French *Damiette*, Coptic *Tamiati*, Greek *Tamiathis*, Arabic *Dumyâṭ*, situated between the Damietta branch of the Nile and Lake Manzala (p. 197), 7 1/2 M. from the sea, is a town of 34,812 inhab. (few Europeans) in 1927 and is the seat of a separate governorate (p. xlix). Trade is inconsiderable and is chiefly in the hands of native merchants (Arabs and Levantines). The industries to which the town owed its former prosperity still exist to some extent (e.g. silk and cotton weaving).

Little or nothing is known of the early history of Damietta. During the Arab era it attained a great reputation on account of the resistance it offered to the Crusaders; but the town of that period stood farther N. than its modern successor (see below). In 1218 it was besieged by King John of Jerusalem. With the aid of an ingenious double boat, constructed and fortified in accordance with a design by Oliverius, an engineer of Cologne, the Frisians, Germans, and others of the besiegers succeeded after a fight of twenty-five hours in capturing the tower to which the chain stretched across the river was attached. The success of the Christians was, however, considerably marred by the interference of the ambitious though energetic Pelagius Galvani, the papal legate, and by the vigilance of the Egyptian Sultan Malik el-Kâmil. At length, after various vicissitudes, the Christians captured the place. They obtained valuable spoil, sold the surviving townspeople as slaves, and converted the mosques into churches, but in 1221 they were compelled to evacuate the town. In 1249, when St. Louis landed near Damietta, it was abandoned by its inhabitants. Without striking a blow the Crusaders marched into the deserted streets of the fortress, but in the course of the following year they were obliged to restore it to the Moslems as part of the ransom of St. Louis, who had been taken prisoner at Manṣûra (p. 183). During the same year, by a resolution of the Emirs, the town was destroyed, and was re-erected on the E. bank of the river, farther S. The new town soon became an important manufacturing and commercial place. Its staple products were leather goods, cloth, and oil of sesame, for which it was famous, and its harbour was visited by ships of many different nations. Owing to the construction of the Maḥmûdîya Canal (p. 16) Damietta lost most of its trade, and its decay was hastened by the rise of the Suez Canal ports.

Seen from the railway station Damietta still presents an imposing appearance, with its lofty houses flanking the river; but this by no means corresponds with the interior of the town, where the buildings are mostly humble brick erections. The European quarter lies upstream, with the spacious *Government Hospital* and the *Coastguards' Barracks*. Here is also the principal *Mosque* (Gâmiʿ el-Baḥr; with two lofty minarets and a spacious dome); the date of its foundation is not known, but, according to an inscription on the roof, the building was renewed in 1600. In the vicinity are a Roman Catholic and a Greek church. Close to the river stands the *Madrasa*

el-Matbûlîya (comp. p. cxcviii), a college *(Ashrafîya Institute)* and mosque erected by Sultan El-Ashraf Qâït Bey (p. cxxiv) in 1475 and now amalgamated with the Gâmi ʿel-Baḥr to form the *Damietta Institute.* The latter is one of the six Mohammedan religious institutions in Egypt (apart from the Azhar University; pp. 58-61) and has 22 professors and 320 students. — The principal street, upwards of **1 M.** long, forms the busy bazaar of the town. Many of the houses are provided with handsomely carved wooden bay windows and lattice-work, which are in most cases very ancient and differ materially in style from the mashrabîyas of Cairo (comp. p. cci).

To the N. of the town, in the suburb of *El-Gabbâna* (i.e. 'the cemetery'), is the dilapidated mosque of *Abu'l Maʿâta.* The building appears to date from the period of the old town of Damietta and has Cufic (p. 70) inscriptions in front. The interior contains numerous antique columns, two of which, standing on the same base, offer a test of honesty, while another in the same row is licked by sufferers in the hope of cure (comp. p. 119). The minaret is embellished with early-Arab ornamentation.

Steamers ply three or four times daily from June to Sept. down to the *Mouth of the Nile (Boghâz)* and (1 hr.) the *Râs el-Barr*, a peninsula jutting out into the sea to the W. of the Nile and visited for sea-bathing by both Europeans and Egyptians (primitive accommodation). The trip by boat takes 3-3½ hrs. there and back (1½ hr. only with a favourable wind). Dolphins are often seen in the river near its mouth.

From Damietta to Port Said viâ Lake Manzala (8 hrs.), see p. 190. The boats start thrice weekly from the fishing village of *Gheiṭ en-Naṣâra*, 2 M. to the E. of Damietta (carriage in 20 min., P.T. 6-8). — From Damietta to Rosetta (p. 32) viâ *Lake Burullus (Burlus)*, a route which is not recommended, takes 2-3 days at least and sometimes much longer.

11. From Port Said to Cairo or Suez viâ Ismailia.

Railway to *Ismailia*, 50 M., in 1½-1¾ hr. (1st cl. P.T. 54½, 2nd. cl. 29½); to *Cairo*, 148½ M., express in 4-4¼, ordinary train in 4¾ hrs. (fares P.T. 135½ and 73); to *Suez* (Town Station), 107 M., in 3¾-4¾ hrs. (fares P.T. 105½ and 57). — Pullman cars (P.T. 25 supplement; comp. p. 33) or dining cars are attached to the expresses on the Port Said and Cairo line.

Port Said.

Arrival by Sea. The coast consists of low sandhills, and the sea inshore is clouded by the muddy waters of the Nile (comp. p. 12). The entrance of the harbour, marked by buoys, is ½ M. wide. To the right is the Lesseps Monument (p. 189). — The custom house examination takes place on shore. As the steamer does not berth at the pier (though a floating bridge was constructed in 1927), passengers have to disembark at the custom house (Pl. C 2, 3) by small boats (P.T. 2 each pers., at night 4; trunk P.T. 1½, hand-luggage ½). The agents of Cook, Cox & King, the steamship lines, and the hotels will, for a small fee, relieve travellers of all trouble connected with the landing and examination of their luggage.

Railway Station (Pl. B 2; buffet), 10 min. W. of the custom house.

Hotels. **Eastern Exchange* (Pl. a; C 2), Shâriᶜ Fu'âd el-Auwal, with lifts and garden, 80 R., pens. P.T. 80-100; **Casino Palace* (Pl. c; D 1), on the N. shore, with bathing-place, garden, and a large veranda (sea view), 85 beds at P.T. 60-70, pens. 120-130; *Marina Palace* (Pl. b; C 2), near the custom house, with restaurant and bar, 110 beds at P.T. 40-60, pens. 80-100; *Continental* (Pl. d; C 2), Shâriᶜ Fu'âd el-Auwal, 40 R.; *Hôtel de la Poste* (Pl. e; C 2), 27 Shâriᶜ Fu'âd el-Auwal, 60 R., pens. P.T. 70-90, well spoken of.

Cabs. For a drive in the town with two horses P.T. 4, to the station 5, per hour 12. — Motor Taxicabs. Within the town: for the first kilometre P.T. 4, each 333 m. more P.T. 1; waiting P.T. 3 per 1/4 hr.

Tramways. 1. From the Mîdân de Lesseps (Pl. C 2) through Shâriᶜ de Lesseps and the native quarter (p. 189) to the cemeteries; 2. From the Commercial Basin viâ the station (Pl. B 2) to *El-Qâbûṭi* (beyond Pl. A 2), on Lake Manzala (p. 197).

Banks. *National Bank of Egypt* (Pl. 4; D 2), *Barclay's Bank* (Pl. 1, D 2; formerly Anglo-Egyptian Bank), *Crédit Lyonnais* (Pl. 3; C 2), *Comptoir d'Escompte de Paris* (Pl. 2; C 2), all four in the Shâriᶜ Fu'âd el-Auwal; *Ottoman Bank* (Pl. 5; C 2), Shâriᶜ de Lesseps.

Post Office. *Egyptian* (Pl. C 2), Shâriᶜ Fu'âd el-Auwal; *French* (Pl. C 2) Shâriᶜ Eugénie. — **Telegraph Offices.** *Egyptian* (Pl. C D 2), Shâriᶜ el-Amîr Fârûq; *Eastern Telegraph Co.* (Pl. D 2), Shâriᶜ es-Sulṭân Ḥusein, for foreign cables only.

Consulates. *British*, Shâriᶜ el-Gabarti (Pl. CD 1, 2). — *American*, Shâriᶜ es-Sulṭân Ḥusein (Pl. C D 2, 1). Also French, German, Belgian, Danish, Italian, Dutch, Norwegian, Swedish, Spanish, and other consulates.

Shops of all kinds abound, but the 'oriental goods' are usually manufactured in Europe and are sold at high prices. Genuine articles can be obtained at *Simon Arzt's;* also good Chinese and Japanese articles, etc., from *Fioravanti & Chimenz* (Au Nippon) and *G. C. Sarolides* (Au Mikado). — Booksellers. *Colonial Book & News Stores* (Victoria), *Librairie Hachette*, both in the Shâriᶜ el-Amîr Fârûq (Pl. BC 2).

Tourist Agents. *Thos. Cook & Son* (Pl. 6; D 2), *Cox & King's Shipping Agency*, 15 and 27 Shâriᶜ es Sulṭân Ḥusein; *Wm. Stapledon & Sons*, Shâriᶜ Waghorn, at the station; *Walter Hilpern*, Shâriᶜ Saᶜîd, corner of Shâriᶜ Memphis (Pl. C D 2, 1).

Steamship Offices. *P. & O.* (comp. p. 1); *British India Steam Navigation Co.* and *Khedivial Mail Line* (Pl. D 2), English Coaling Co., Shâriᶜ Fu'âd el-Auwal (Pl. C D 3-1); *Orient*, *Union Castle*, and *Bibby*, Stapledon & Sons (see above); *Ellerman's City & Hall Lines*, *Anchor Line*, Cory Bros., 25 Shâriᶜ es-Sulṭân Ḥusein (Pl. C D 3-1); *Henderson Line*, *Dollar Line*, *Nederland Line*, and *Nippon Yusen Kaisha*, Worms & Co., 3 Shâri' Fu'âd el-Auwal; *Norddeutscher Lloyd*, Wm. H. Müller & Co., Shâriᶜ el-Muqaṭṭam (Pl. C D 2); *Hamburg-America Line* and *German African Services* (comp. p. 2), German Coaling Depot, 27 Shâriᶜ es-Sulṭân Ḥusein; *Lloyd Triestino*, 23 Shâriᶜ es-Sulṭân Ḥusein (Pl. D 2, 1); *Sitmar* (comp. p. 1), L. Savon & Co., 1 Shâriᶜ el-Furât, corner of Shâriᶜ es-Sulṭân Ḥusein (Pl. D 1, 2); *Marittima Italiana* and *Citra* (comp. p. 4), G. de Castro, Shâriᶜ Fu'âd el-Auwal; *Rotterdam Lloyd*, Port Said & Suez Coal Co., Shâriᶜ es-Sulṭân Ḥusein; *Messageries Maritimes* (Pl. 7; C D 2), 8-9 Shâriᶜ es-Sulṭân Ḥusein.

Physicians. *Dr. D. G. Kennard* (British Hospital, Pl. A 1); *Dr. H. E. Stiven* (Government Hospital, Pl. B 2); *Dr. P. Sander* (for affections of the eyes, ears, nose, and throat), Shâriᶜ eẓ-Ẓâhir (Pl. C 1); *Dr. Scarpalezo*, Shâriᶜ Eugénie (Pl. A-D 1, 2); *Dr. Stipanovich*, Shâriᶜ Ibrâhîm (Pl. A-D 1).

Churches. *Anglican* (Holy Epiphany, Pl. B 2); *Roman Catholic* (Ste-Eugénie, Pl. BC 2); *Greek Orthodox* (St. John's, Pl. B 2); *Coptic* (St. Mary's, Pl. A B 2).

Clubs. *Golf Club* (Pl. A 3); *Sporting Club.*

Port Said (Bôr Saᶜîd), the chief town of the Egyptian governorate of the Suez Canal (El-Qanâl; p. xlix), lies in a dismal and infertile district at the E. extremity of an island which belongs to

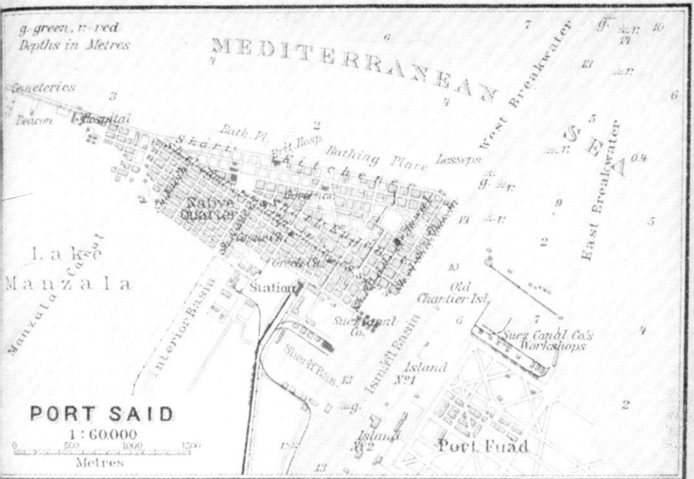

g. green, r. red
Depths in Metres
MEDITERRANEAN SEA
Cemeteries
Beacon
Hospital
Bath. Pl.
Brit. Hosp.
Bathing Place
Lesseps
West Breakwater
East Breakwater
Native Quarter
Lake Manzala
Manzala Canal
Interior Basin
Station
Greek Ch.
Old Chantier Isl.
Suez Canal Co.
Suez Canal Co.'s Workshops
Ismailia Basin
Sherif Bas.
Island No. 1
Island No. 2
Port Fuad
PORT SAID
1 : 60.000
Metres

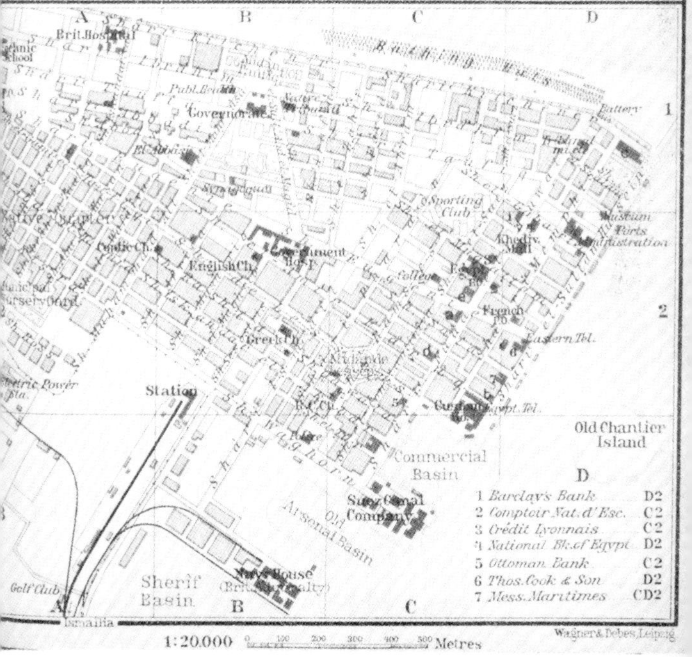

A B C D
1 2
Brit. Hospital
Bathing Huts
Publ. Garden
Governorate
Native Tribunal
El Abbasi
Sporting Club
Battery
Custom
Ports Administration
Native Quarter
Coptic Ch.
English Ch.
Government Hosp.
College
Khediv. Mail
French P.O.
Eastern Tel.
Greek Ch.
Electric Power Sta.
Station
R.C. Ch.
Egypt. Tel.
Old Chantier Island
Commercial Basin
Suez Canal Company
Old Arsenal Basin
Navy House (Brit. Admiralty)
Sherif Basin
Golf Club
Ismailia
1 Barclay's Bank D2
2 Comptoir Nat. d'Esc. C2
3 Crédit Lyonnais C2
4 National Bk. of Egypt D2
5 Ottoman Bank C2
6 Thos. Cook & Son D2
7 Mess. Maritimes CD2
1 : 20.000
Metres
Wagner & Debes, Leipzig

the narrow strip of land separating Lake Manzala (p. 197) from the Mediterranean. It owes its origin to the Suez Canal and its name to Khedive Saʿîd (p. cxxvii), and its prosperity since the beginning of the century has been marked. The population, which in 1883 was only 17,000, had risen to 75,192 by 1917 and was returned at the census of 1927 as 104,603.

The town is laid out on a regular plan, with streets crossing each other at right angles. On the quay, the *Shâriʿ es-Sulṭân Ḥusein* (Pl. D 1, 2), are the offices of the chief steamship companies; a small museum of Egyptian antiquities (Pl. D 2; adm. P.T. 2½); the offices of the Ports Administration, with a **Lighthouse* (184 ft. in height), the light of which is visible for twenty nautical miles; and, at the S.W. end, the Custom House. The parallel street on the W., or *Shâri Fu'âd el-Auwal* (Pl. CD 1-3; Boulevard Fouad Premier), is crossed by the wide *Shâriʿ Eugénie* (Pl. A-D 1, 2; with the Government Hospital) and *Shâriʿ de Lesseps* (Pl. BC 2). The latter is continued W. by the *Shâriʿ el-Gâmi et-Taufîqi* (Pl. A 1) to the NATIVE QUARTER (Pl. A 2). Farther W., between the sea and the Birket esh-Shagara, or N. end of Lake Manzala, are the European and Mohammedan *Cemeteries* (including a British war cemetery; tram, see p. 188). — From the N.E. end of the Shâriʿ es-Sulṭân Ḥusein (see above), which is prolonged by the *Quai de Lesseps*, the *Shâriʿ Kitchener* (Pl. A-D 1; formerly Shâriʿ el-Gharbîya), with its avenue of trees, leads past the bathing place.

The *Harbour* occupies an area of 575 acres and has been excavated to a depth of 42 ft. by means of laborious dredging. It is protected by two massive piers: the *West Breakwater*, recently extended to a length of about 6000 yds., and the *East Breakwater*, now about 2200 yds. long. The former protects the harbour from the mud-deposits of the Nile (comp. p. 12); the waves dashing over it provide a fine spectacle when a storm from the W. is raging. Near its landward end is a statue of *Ferdinand de Lesseps* (p. 195), by E. Frémiet, unveiled by the Suez Canal Co. in 1899. The statue, 22½ ft. high, stands on a pedestal 34½ ft. in height. The inner harbour pier, opposite the lighthouse (see above), is 550 yds. long and shelters the anchorage from the E. wind.

The inner harbour (222 acres) includes the *Ismâʿîl Basin* and three adjoining docks: the *Commercial Basin* (Pl. C 3), the *Old Arsenal Basin* (Pl. BC 3), and the *Sherîf Basin* (Pl. AB 3). Between the first two are the handsome buildings of the Canal Co. (Pl. C 3), and between the second and third is a magnificent group of buildings erected by Prince Henry of the Netherlands as a factory for the Dutch trade, but now used as the Navy House (Pl. B 3) or headquarters of the British naval authorities. The Ismâʿîl Basin is adjoined on the S. by the *ʿAbbâs Ḥilmi* or *Africa Basin*, with a quarantine station for cattle and the waterworks. On the E. bank of the canal lie (from N. to S.) the *Suez Maritime Canal Co.'s Basin*, with docks and work-

shops, the *Coaling Basin*, the *Sulṭân Ḥusein Basin*, and the *Petroleum Basin*.

Opposite Port Said on the E. (steam ferry) and to the S. of the Canal Co.'s Basin (p. 189) lies the town of **Port Fuâd,** inaugurated in 1926 by the Canal Co. as a residential quarter for its employees and workmen. It has been designed on a uniform plan, with wide streets and gardens, and is administered by a board of four (the governor of Port Said, a representative of the Egyptian government, and two members appointed by the Canal Co.). Farther S. are the works of the Port Said Salt Association.

From Port Said to Maṭarîya and Damietta by steamer across Lake Manzala (p. 197) in 9 hrs., not recommended. Flat-bottomed stern-wheel steamers of the *Menzaleh Canal & Navigation Co.* (pier on the W. side of the native quarter, p. 189) sail on Mon., Wed., and Sat. (water-level permitting). Provisions should be taken. — *Maṭarîya* (for the railway to Manṣûra) and *Damietta*, see pp. 184, 186.

The Railway to Cairo at first skirts the Suez Canal (comp. R. 12); to the right lies Lake Manzala (p. 197). — $8^1/_2$ M. *Râs el-ʿIsh* (*Ras el-Esh;* p. 197); 15 M. *Et-Tîna (Ṭîna);* 22 M. *El-Kâb (Le Cap).*

29 M. **Qanṭara** (*Kantara West*; buffet). The village (p. 197) lies on the opposite bank of the canal (ferry), near the station of *Qanṭara East*, which is the starting-point of the *Palestine Railway* constructed during the war (to Jerusalem viâ Gaza and Ludd in $9^1/_2$ hrs., to Ḥaifa in 10 hrs.). Comp. the plan, p. 196.

The train runs along an embankment through *Lakes Ballâḥ* (p. 198). — $35^1/_2$ M. *El-Ballâḥ*. — Beyond ($41^1/_2$ M.) *El-Firdân* (*Ferdan;* p. 198) we leave the Suez Canal and turn S.W.

50 M. **Ismailia.** — *Buffet.* — Hotels. *Hôtel-Restaurant des Voyageurs*, near the station; *Splendid*, Avenue Guichard, 12 R. at P.T. 20.

Post Office, Place Champollion, near the station. — Egyptian Telegraph Office, beside the station. — Bank. *Ottoman Bank.*

Physicians. *Dr. Alio; Dr. Jardry*, at the hospital of the Suez Canal Co. — Chemists. *London Pharmacy*, 59 Rue Negrelli; *Pharmacie Française*, Place Champollion. — English Church at Moascar (see below). Also *Roman Catholic*, *Protestant*, *Greek Orthodox*, and *Coptic Orthodox Churches.*

Motor Cars: P.T. 4 for 1 km. ($^2/_3$ M.), then P.T. 1 per 333 m. (364 yds.); to Moascar (p. 191) or the hospital (p. 191) P.T. 13 there and back; to Nifîsha P.T. 23; to Abu Ṣuweir P.T. 83.

Ismailia (Ismâʿîlîya), a pleasant town of 15,507 inhab., with numerous and luxuriant gardens and parks, lies on the N. bank of *Lake Timsâḥ* (p. 198; comp. the map, p. 196). It owes its name to the Khedive Ismâʿîl (p. cxxvii) and was the main centre of operations during the construction of the Suez Canal. For a time it lost its importance, which, however, it has since regained as the seat of a large British garrison (barracks in the suburb of *Moascar*, p. 191; British war cemetery, adjoining the town cemetery, to the W. of Ismailia station). The town has a governor of its own. — The wide *Avenue de l'Impératrice* and (farther on, beyond the suspension bridge over the Fresh Water Canal) the *Avenue Guichard* lead from the railway

station to the shore of Lake Timsâḥ (station of the steam-launches). Thence we follow the Rue de Chancel and the Rue d'Italie to the left to the *Place Champollion*, beyond which the *Rue Negrelli*, the main street of the town, with shops and cafés, runs E. to the extensive gardens belonging to the Suez Canal Co., which contain several large monuments found at Tell el-Maskhûṭa (p. 192).

2245. Large memorial inscription of Ramses II., in granite, with a representation of the king offering to the falcon-headed Rē-Harakhte an image of the goddess of truth; group of Ramses II. between the gods Khepre and Atum; 2241. Recumbent sphinx, dedicated by Ramses II. to Atum and Harmakhis; 2242. Similar sphinx, headless; 2246. Fragment of a naos dedicated by Ramses II. in the temple at Tell el-Maskhûṭa; 2247. Coffin-lid of a high palace-official, in black granite, from Tell el-Maskhûṭa; 2248. Granite naos from El-ʿArîsh (Sinai Province) with inscriptions referring to the rule of the gods upon earth, etc.

The *Quai Mohammed Ali* runs E. along the Fresh Water Canal, passing the house of the Comte de Serionne, which encloses the actual chalet in which De Lesseps lived and worked (furniture, books, etc., left exactly as in 1865). Farther on are the offices of the Suez Canal Co., the police station (markaz), and the Canal Co.'s gardens (see above). The shaded *Rue Lamasson*, diverging to the right, leads to ($1^3/_4$ M.) the Canal Co.'s hospital (motor cars, see p. 190) and the former khedivial chalet (now a convalescent home). Superb view of Lake Timsâḥ, the Suez Canal, and the desert.

At the corner of Rue Lisbonne and Rue de Paris is a small *Museum* of antiquities mostly found near the canal (apply at the offices of the Suez Canal Co., see above, as the custodian is frequently absent): on the walls, several mosaic pavements, one with Phædra and Hippolytus, the mysteries of Dionysus, and Greek verses in a border of birds; Græco-Egyptian terracottas, bronze figures (some from Tell el-Maskhûṭa), etc. The garden contains fragments of the monuments erected by Darius (p. 194).

On quitting Ismailia we obtain another glimpse of the azure waters of Lake Timsâḥ (p. 198). — Near (51 M.) *Moascar Ismailia* (p. 190) the ʿAbbâsîya Fresh Water Canal diverges on the right. — 52 M. *Nifîsha (Nefisha, Neficheh)*, junction for Suez (see p. 193). An arm of the Fresh Water Canal (see below) diverges to the left. — The Cairo line traverses the Arabian Desert, which is intersected from E. to W. by the *Wâdi eṭ-Ṭumîlât*, with its narrow strips of arable land, and we skirt the Fresh Water or Ismâʿîlîya Canal (see below). The fertile tract which we now traverse is part of the *Goshen* of the Bible (p. 192) and has been reclaimed for cultivation by means of the canal.Behind the fertile strip rise the desert hills.

The **Fresh** or **Sweet Water Canal**, called also **Ismâʿîliya Canal**, constructed in 1858-63 to supply the villages on the Suez Canal with drinking water and enlarged in 1876, is in great part a restoration of an earlier canal dating from the Middle Empire. This ancient canal, which began at the Nile, watered the land of Goshen with its branches, and entering the Bitter Lakes (p. 198), changed their character, according to Strabo, and connected them with the Red Sea. The channel of the old canal, which was rediscovered by the French expedition of 1798, is still traceable at places, and its direction was frequently followed by the engineers of De Lesseps. The remains of scarps of masonry show it to have been about 50 yds. in width and 16-$17^1/_2$ ft. in depth. The canal is now chiefly used

for irrigation purposes. It diverges from the Nile near Cairo and marks the boundary between the Arabian plateau (N.) and the land of Goshen (S.). To the E. of Abu Ḥammâd (see below) it intersects the ancient fresh-water canal coming from Zagazig, and then runs E., parallel with this, through the *Wâdi eṭ-Ṭumîlât*, which is over 30 M. in length. From *Nifîsha* (p. 191) a S. arm of the canal leads to Suez, while near *Moascar Ismailia* (p. 191) the ʿAbbâsîya Fresh Water Canal leads to Port Said.

The **Goshen** of the Bible (Egyptian *Gosem*) is first mentioned in Genesis, xlv. 10, where Joseph sends word to Jacob, his father: "And thou shalt dwell in the land of Goshen, and thou shalt be near unto me, thou, and thy children, and thy children's children, and thy flocks, and thy herds, and all that thou hast". Mention is made of Goshen also in Genesis xlvi. 28, 29, 34, and xlvii. 1, 4, 6, 27, and Exodus viii. 22, and ix. 26. Exodus i. 11 mentions the cities in Goshen in which the Israelites were compelled to work at the tasks imposed on them by Pharaoh: "Therefore they did set over them taskmasters to afflict them with their burdens. And they built for Pharaoh treasure cities [or storehouses], Pithom and Raamses" (see below). Goshen lay in the triangle between Zagazig, Bilbeis, and Abu Ḥammâd and formed part of the Egyptian nome of Arabia, the capital of which was *Per-Sopd* (the *Phakusa* of the Greeks), rediscovered by Edouard Naville (p. 318) near the modern *Ṣafṭ el-Hina*, not far from Ṣuwa station (see below). The ruins have disappeared (comp. p. 95, No. 790), but a few ancient stones have been built into the houses of the village and two stelæ are preserved in the garden of the ʿomda' or village headman.

60 M. *Abu Ṣuweir (Abou-Soueir).* To the N. of the station is a large British military camp, with an aerodrome (training school of the Royal Air Force). — 66 M. *El-Maḥsama.*

The neighbouring ruins of *Tell el-Maskhûṭa* mark the site of the ancient Egyptian 'Fortress of Tjeku' (the *Succoth* of Exodus xii. 37). The spot was explored for the Egypt Exploration Fund in 1883, when among the temple buildings were discovered several grain-stores, in the form of deep, rectangular chambers without doors, into which the corn was poured from above. These perhaps date from the time of Ramses II., and may possibly be the actual 'storehouses' of the Bible. Later excavators, however, recognize in these buildings parts of the platform of a fort. The débris-heap of *Tell er-Reṭâba*, to the W. of the Tell el-Maskhûṭa, is the probable site of the Biblical *Pithom* (Egyptian *Per-Atum*, i.e. 'house of the god Atum').

71 M. *El-Qaṣṣâṣîn (Kassassin).* — 80 M. *Tell el-Kebîr*, noted as the scene of ʿArâbi's defeat by the British troops in 1882 (p. cxxviii). On approaching the station the train passes (left) the cemetery of the British soldiers who fell in the battle, with a tasteful monument, and the British war cemetery (1914-18).

At (84½ M.) *Abu Ḥammâd* (p. 182) the train enters the fertile district of the E. Delta, which is richer both in watercourses and in trees than the W. Delta. — 89½ M. *Ṣuwa (Sowa*; see above). — 93 M. *Abu el-Akhḍar.* — 98 M. **Zagazig**, see p. 181. — 102 M. *Ez-Zankalûn;* 106¼ M. *El-Gudaiyida (Godaieda);* 109 M. *Minyet el-Qamḥ (Minet el-Gamh, Mîna el-Qamḥ;* p. 181); 110 M. *Mît Yazîd;* 114½ M. *Shiblanga (Sheblanga).* The train crosses the Taufîqîya Canal and reaches (120½ M.) *Benha* (p. 37), where our line is joined by that from Alexandria.

148½ M. *Cairo* (Main Station), see p. 37.

B. The Voyage through the Suez Canal.

Port Said, see p. 187. Opposite, on the left, is *Port Fuâd* (p. 190). The forest of masts in the harbour remains in sight long after we quit the town. The canal, on the W. bank of which runs the railway to Ismailia (p. 190), is constructed in a perfectly straight line through **Lake Manzala** (*Menzaleh*), but the part of the lake adjoining the canal on the E. (and to a less extent on the W.) has been drained. The brackish waters of this lake extend over an area of about 660 sq. M., covering what was once one of the most fertile districts in Egypt, formerly intersected by the three most important arms of the Nile (p. lxix) in ancient times, the Pelusiac, the Tanitic, and the Mendesian. Among the numerous towns and villages situated here were the important cities of Tanis (p. 182) and Tennis. The chief village is now Maṭarîya (p. 184). Immense flocks of pelicans and silver herons and some flamingoes are to be seen on the lake, and its waters are fished by about 7000 boats, each of which pays a monthly tax of £E 2. For the steamers of the Menzaleh Canal & Navigation Co., see p. 190. — The first station is (10 M.) *Râs el-ʿIsh* (p. 190).

Lake Manzala ends at ($27^1/_2$ M.) **El-Qanṭara** (*Kantara*, 'the bridge'), an isthmus separating it from Lake Ballâḥ. Over this isthmus led the ancient military road from Egypt to Syria. The railway from Port Said to Cairo (p. 190) passes through Qanṭara, which is also the starting-point of the Palestine railway (see p. 190). The village, with a post office and custom house, lies on the Asiatic bank of the canal (ferry). To the N.E. is an aerodrome.

The British military cemetery near Qanṭara, where the Egypt Expeditionary Force (p. cxxxi) had its base in 1915-18, the remains of trenches and barbed-wire entanglements visible from the steamers on the E. bank of the canal, and a war memorial (S. of Ismailia, p. 198; Indian war memorial, see p. 201) are reminders of the British defence of the Suez Canal during the war. The Turkish advance on the canal through the Sinai desert in February 1915 was a complete failure, and the Turkish and German attack in July 1916 was likewise repulsed on Aug. 4-5th at *Rumâni* (25 M. to the N.E. of Qanṭara, on the Palestine railway).

The mounds of débris named *Tell Dafana* (*Kôm Dafana*, *Tell ed-Daffâna*, or *Tell Defenneh*; 'hill of the grave-diggers'), situated to the N. of the caravan route between Eṣ-Ṣâliḥîya (p. 182) and Qanṭara, at the ancient Pelusiac mouth of the Nile, are reached from Qanṭara by donkey in $2^1/_2$-3 hrs. They contain the remains of a camp of the Greek mercenaries of Psammetichos I. and were excavated in 1886 by Sir Flinders Petrie, who found numerous fragments of Greek pottery, arrow-heads, and weapons. Sir Flinders identifies the spot with the Greek *Daphnae* and with the *Tahapanes*, *Tahpanhes*, or *Tehaphnehes* of the Bible (Jeremiah ii. 16 and xliii. 7; Ezekiel. xxx. 18, etc.). — About $^1/_2$ hr. from Qanṭara, to the S. of the old caravan road, lies the hill of *Tell el-Aḥmar* ('red hill') or *Tell Abu Seifa*, with the ruins of a temple of Ramses II. and remains of the Ptolemaic and Roman periods.

About $2^1/_2$ M. to the N. of (18 M.) Pelusium station on the Palestine railway, and 6 M. to the W. of Rumâni station (see above), are situated the ruin-strewn *Tell el-Farama* and *Tell el-Faḍḍa*, occupying the site of **Pelusium**, the celebrated eastern seaport and key to Egypt (pp. ix, cxvii),

which now contains no objects of interest. Here too lay the Delta residence of the Ramessids, the Biblical town of Rameses (Raamses; Gen. xlvii. 11).

The canal traverses **Lakes Ballâḥ,** now drained. At *El-Firdân* (p. 190), at the S. end of the lakes, the canal passes through the first cutting. At the next passing-place we obtain a glimpse of the desert.

The hills of **El-Gisr** ('the embankment'), which cross the course of the canal at an average height of 52 ft. above sea-level (comp. p. lxx), presented the most serious obstacle to its construction. In order to form a cutting through it about 18,800,000 cubic yds. of earth had to be removed. At the top of the hill is the deserted village of *El-Gisr*, with a chapel to the Virgin of the Desert and a ruined mosque. A flight of steps ascends to this point from the canal. The view hence embraces a great part of the Isthmus, the frowning Gebel ʿAtâqa (p. 193) above Suez, the mountains of the Sinai peninsula, the course of the canal, and the green expanse of the Bitter Lakes.

At the end of the cutting the canal enters **Lake Timsâḥ** ('crocodile lake'), the dredged channel through which is indicated by stakes. As we enter the lake we see the khedivial chalet (see p. 191) above us to the right, and to the S. the mountains of Gebel Abu Ballâḥ. The lake, which is now about $5^1/_2$ sq. M. in area and of a beautiful pale-blue colour, was, before the construction of the canal, a mere pond of brackish water, full of reeds. On its N. bank lies the town of **Ismailia** (p. 190).

After quitting Lake Timsâḥ we pass (r.) the foot of the *Gebel Maryam*, which an Arab legend points out as the place where Miriam, when smitten with leprosy for her disapproval of the marriage of Moses with an Ethiopian woman, spent seven days, beyond the precincts of the camp of the Israelites (Numbers xii). — On the W. side of the canal, about 5 M. to the S. of Ismailia and $1^1/_2$ M. to the N. of Ṭûsûm (see below), the spot where the Turks tried to cross the canal in 1915 (comp. p. 197) is marked by a *War Memorial*, two obelisks, each 164 ft. high, erected by the Suez Canal Co. — At the 87th kilometre is situated (r.) the small village of *Ṭûsûm*, which is easily recognized by the whitewashed dome of the tomb of a sheikh. Excavations near here have led to the discovery of many interesting fossil remains of large animals belonging to the miocene tertiary formation, and pieces of fossil wood also have been found here (comp. p. 127). — A little farther on (near the 92nd kilometre) is the cutting which conducts the canal through the rocky barrier of the *Serapeum* (station, see p. 193).

The canal now passes the signal station of *Le Déversoir* ('weir'), with its lighthouse, and enters the blue-green **Bitter Lakes**, which have been identified with the *Marah* of the Bible (Exodus xv. 23; "they could not drink of the waters of Marah, for they were bitter"; comp. p. 201). The banks are flat and sandy, but to the S.W. (r.)

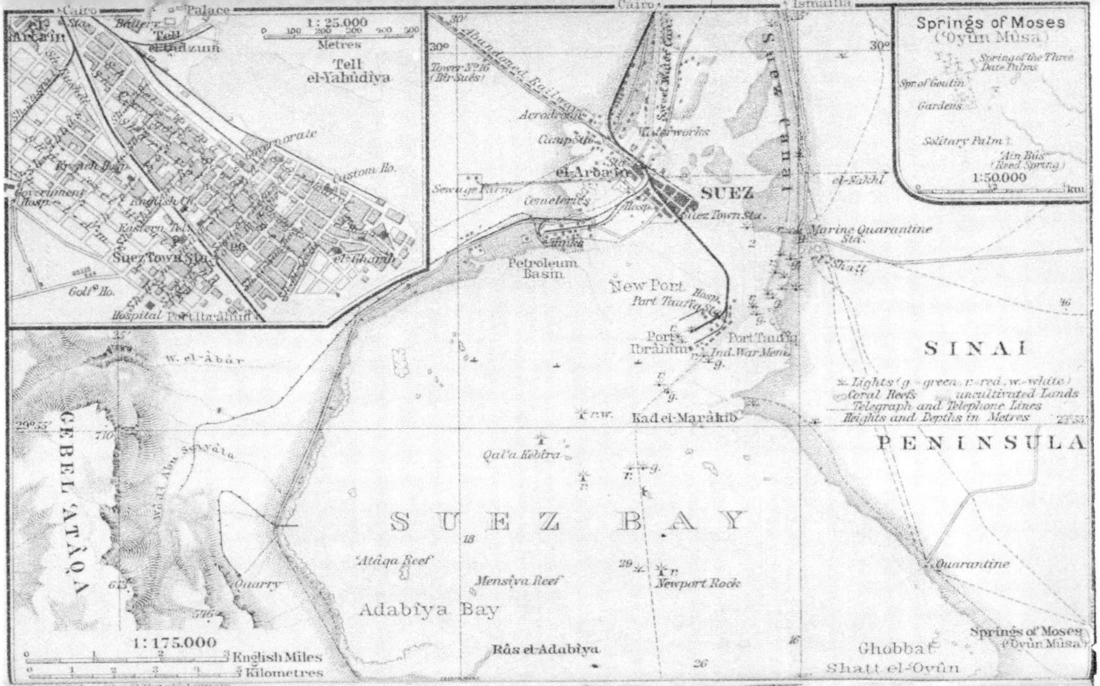

Cairo
Palace
Cairo
Ismailia
1: 25.000
0 100 200 300 400 500
Metres
Tell el-Yahûdiya
Governorate
Custom Ho.
English Ch.
Eastern Tel.
Suez Town Sta.
el-Gharîb
Golf Ho.
Hospital
Port Ibrahim
30°
Tower No. 16 (Bir Sues)
Abandoned Railway
Sweet Water Canal
Aerodrome
Camp Site
Waterworks
el-Arba'în
Sewage Farm
Cemeteries
Hosp.
SUEZ
Suez Town Sta.
Suez Canal
el-Nakhl
Marine Quarantine Sta.
el-Shatt
Petroleum Basin
New Port
Hosp.
Port Taufiq Sta.
Port Ibrâhîm
Port Taufiq
Ind. War Mem.
Springs of Moses
('Oyûn Mûsa)
Spring of the Three Date Palms
Spr. of Goutin
Gardens
Solitary Palm
'Ain Bûs (Reed Spring)
1:50.000
km
SINAI
PENINSULA
Lights (g = green, r = red, w = white)
Coral Reefs
uncultivated Lands
Telegraph and Telephone Lines
Heights and Depths in Metres
W. el-'Âbûr
GEBEL 'ATÂQA
Kad el-Marâkib
Qal'a Kebîra
SUEZ BAY
'Atâqa Reef
Mensîya Reef
Newport Rock
Adabîya Bay
Râs el-Adabîya
Quarry
Quarantine
Springs of Moses ('Oyûn Mûsa)
Ghobbat Shatt el-'Oyûn
1: 175.000
English Miles
Kilometres

rises the range of the *Gebel Gineifa* (p. 193). At the S.E. end of the Large Basin is (121 km.) the signal station of *El-Kabrît*. The bed of the Little Basin, which we next traverse, consists entirely of shell-formations. The signal station of *Gineifa* lies at its end (134 km.).

Near *Esh-Shallûfa* (139 km.) no less than 45,000 cubic yds. of limestone, coloured red and brown with iron, had to be removed in the course of the excavation of the canal. This stone contained teeth and vertebræ of sharks (Carcharodon megalodon Ag.), bivalve shells, and remains of Bryozoa. In the layer of sand above the limestone were found crocodiles' teeth and the remains of hippopotami and other large quadrupeds. The monument of Darius near Shallûfa is mentioned on p. 194.

We finally reach the Gulf of Suez, which is here so shallow that, but for the canal, it might be crossed on foot at low tide. It contains several islands. On the W. bank are the docks, workshops, and warehouses of the Canal Co. Passengers are landed at Suez in steam-launches.

Suez (*Port Taufîq*; 160 km.), see below.

13. Suez and its Environs.

Railway Stations. *Arba'în*, for local trains; *Suez Town; Port Taufîq (Port Taufik)*, for the docks. — **Arrival** by steamer, see above.

Hotels. *Bel-Air* (Pl. a), opposite the Eastern Telegraph Office, 40 R. at 25-30, B. 10, L. or D. 25, pens. 70-80 P.T., plain but good. At Port Taufîq: *Hôtel du Sinai*, to the E. of the station.

Post Office, Rue Colmar. — **Telegraph Offices** (comp. p. xx). *Egyptian*, at the Governorate; *Eastern Telegraph Co.*, Shâri' Hammâm Shiuûda. — Custom House near the harbour. — At Port Taufîq there are branch-offices of the Egyptian post office and the two telegraph offices, and a sub-office of customs.

Physicians. *Dr. J. Mitchell; Dr. Rogier; Dr. Gauthier* (physician to the Suez Canal Co.), at Port Taufîq. — **Chemists.** *Hippocrate*, *Eliades*, *Pharmacie Suez*, all three in the Rue Colmar.

Consulates. *British*, at Port Taufîq (vice-consulate). There are also French, German, Italian, Danish, Dutch, Norwegian, Swedish, Spanish, and other consulates.

Steamship Offices (most of them at Port Taufîq). *P. & O.* (comp. p. 1), *British India*, English Coaling Co.; *Union Castle*, *Bibby*, *Orient*, *Blue Funnel Line*, Wm. Stapledon & Sons; *Lloyd Triestino*, *Sitmar Line* (comp. p. 1), G. Lazzerini & Co., Rue des Messageries; *Hamburg-America Line* and *German African Services* (comp. p. 2), at the German Coaling Depot; *Rotterdam Lloyd*, Port Said & Suez Coal Co.; *Henderson Line*, *Nederland Line*, *Nippon Yusen Kaisha*, Worms & Co.; *Anchor Line*, G. Beyts & Co.; *Messageries Maritimes*, M. Lecouflet; *Khedivial Mail Line*, Curwen & Co.

Junction Railway between the town (Arba'în station, see above) and Port Taufîq; trains every half-hour, in 9 min.; 1st class fare P.T. $1^1/_2$.

Boats by the hour according to previous arrangement. The boatmen are apt to be extortionate in their demands, as they have been spoiled by passengers on the large liners making a short stay only. Comp. p. 201.

Chief Attractions. The afternoon of the day of arrival may be devoted to a visit to the *Harbour*. The next morning (early start necessary; comp. p. 201) may be spent in a visit to the *Springs of Moses*.

Suez (Arabic *Es-Suweis*), a town of 40,523 inhabitants in 1927, lies at the head of the gulf of that name, one of the N. extremities of the Red Sea, and to the N.W. of the mouth of the Suez Canal. Before the construction of the canal it was a miserable Arab village. Neither the Arab quarter, with its seven mosques and unimportant bazaar, nor the European quarter, which has grown considerably of recent years and in which the principal street is the Rue Colmar (Shâri' Sûq en-Nemsa), presents any attraction. The town has a governor of its own (p. xlix).

A mound of débris to the N. of the town, the *Kôm* or *Tell el-Qulzum*, commands a fine view of the mountains of the Sinai peninsula, the sea, the harbour, and the town. This hill, which is shown by the road-cutting to be a heap of ruins of the Græco-Roman period, was probably the site of the Ptolemaic fortress of *Klysma* as well as of an earlier settlement of the period of the Pharaohs. Near it are the remains of a large temple of that date. Beyond the railway, to the W., is the Arab quarter of *El-Arba'în*. — Farther N. is the mouth of the *Fresh* or *Sweet Water Canal* (p. 191), the flow of which into the conduits, as well as its discharge into the sea, is regulated by means of a large lock. The level of the canal is here $6^1/_2$ ft. above that of the Red Sea. On its banks, and also near the *British Cemetery* (including a war cemetery), are luxuriant gardens. The large buildings to the N. of it are the former *British Naval Hospital* and the engine-house of the *Waterworks*. — To the E. of the canal are the quarantine station and a large camping-ground for caravans.

To the S.W. of El-Arba'în (see above) are *Petroleum Refineries* of the Anglo-Egyptian Oilfields Ltd. and of the Egyptian government; here the crude petroleum from El-Hurghâda (p. 400) and other wells on the Red Sea is treated.

As the N. extremity of the Gulf of Suez ends in a shoal, which is dry at low water, the entrance of the Suez Canal and the necessary harbour-works were constructed 2 M. to the S., at the beginning of the deep water. A stone *Causeway*, 50 ft. wide, on which run a road and railway, connects the town with these works and affords beautiful views of the 'Atâqa Mts. on the W. and the range of the Sinai peninsula on the E.

At the end of the pier is *Port Taufîq* or *Tewfik*, on an artificial island 50 acres in area, constructed of the large quantities of earth dredged from the canal. The main street of Port Taufîq is the *Avenue Hélène*, over 1000 yds. in length, at the N. end of which is a bronze bust erected by De Lesseps to *Lieutenant Thomas Waghorn* (1800-50; p. 195), an enterprising British naval officer, who, after having spent the best years of his life in the endeavour to establish regular communication between England and India viâ Egypt, died in poverty in London. The large docks of *Port Ibrâhîm* lie to the S.W., and on the extreme W. is the *Petroleum Basin*. The outer anchorage of the harbour is spacious and well-protected, and war-ships moor

here. A new quay, 186 yds. long, is under construction. The situation of the sand-banks and of the navigable channel is of course best seen at low tide. — The *Indian War Memorial* (1926), a granite obelisk 65 ft. high, designed by Sir John Burnet and placed at the S. extremity of Port Taufîq, commemorates the Indian soldiers who fell in Egypt and Palestine during the war.

Excursion to the Springs of Moses (7-8 hrs.). — *Boats* (p. 199) and *Donkeys* (there and back about P.T. 20) should be ordered a day in advance, and an early morning start should be made (about 6 a.m.). A motor-boat, for which application should be made to the consul or to a steamship agent, is preferable to a rowing boat. Calm weather is very desirable for this excursion, not only for the passage in the boat (by which the donkeys also must be conveyed) but also because the driving sand in the desert is very disagreeable in a high wind. About 2 hrs. should be allowed for the stay at the springs, including time for luncheon (brought by the traveller) and for a walk on the beach.

The distance from the usual landing-place of the boats, in the entrance to the Suez Canal (comp. the map, p. 199), to the springs is about $6^1/_2$ M. (2 hrs.' ride). The whole of the route thence by land traverses the sand of the desert, skirting the sea, which lies to the right. On the W. towers the imposing Gebel ʿAtâqa (p. 193), which presents a most picturesque appearance on the return-route. To the left rise the yellowish ranges of the *Gebel er-Râḥa*, belonging to the long chain of the *Gebel et-Tîh*, and facing the S.E. We are now traversing Asiatic soil, while at the same time the eye ranges over part of the African continent.

In favourable weather the expedition is usually made by sea to the pier at the quarantine station (Esh-Shaṭṭ), about 2 M. to the N.W. of the springs, which are thence reached on foot. This part of the Red Sea was long regarded as that across which the Israelites fled from Pharaoh; now, however, this is generally located farther N., in the vicinity of the Bitter Lakes, which at that epoch may have been connected with the Red Sea.

The **Springs of Moses** (*ʿOyûn* or *ʿIyûn Mûsa)* form an oasis of luxuriant vegetation, about five furlongs in circumference. Some of the springs, which vary in temperature from 70° to 84° Fahr., are only slightly brackish, while others are undrinkably bitter. The largest, in the garden farthest S., is said to have been the bitter spring which Moses sweetened by casting into it a particular tree (Exodus xv. 25).

A mound, 10 min. S.E. of the gardens, which is about 15 ft. high and is marked by a solitary palm-tree, commands a fine view. On the top of it is a small spring. — Conchologists will find a number of interesting shells on the beach at low tide, but the best places are much farther S.

Motor-road from Suez across the desert to *Heliopolis* (Cairo), see p. 128.
From Suez to *Port Sudan* and *Kharṭûm*, see R. 36.
From Suez to *Sinai*, see Baedeker's 'Palestine and Syria'.

14. The Faiyûm.

A visit to the Faiyûm, a fertile and attractive district with many historical associations, can be accomplished in two or three days, by making use of motor-cars. Travellers with a slight knowledge of the language and customs may dispense with a dragoman. 1st Day: Railway or motor-car (new motor-road, see below; good road also viâ Ṣaqqâra) from Cairo to *Madînet el-Faiyûm;* inspect that town and its environs (site of Crocodilopolis-Arsinoë); by railway or carriage to *Biyahmu.* 2nd Day: Excursion by motor-car to *Lake Mœris* viâ *Ibshawâi.* 3rd Day: Excursion to *Hauwâra* (Labyrinth) and *El-Lâhûn;* return to Cairo. — Hurried travellers should take the early train from Cairo to Madînet el-Faiyûm and make the excursion to Lake Mœris on the same day; next day they visit the pyramids of Hauwâra and El-Lâhûn. — A favourite plan is to motor to El-Lâhûn and on to *Beni Suef*, where the Cairo-Luxor railway is reached (p. 218); this drive takes $3^1/_2$ hrs. (including 1 hr.'s stay at the pyramid of El-Lâhûn). There is also a branch-railway from El-Lâhûn to Beni Suef (see p. 218). — Messrs. Thos. Cook & Son organize six-day and eight-day desert-excursions on camels from the Pyramids of Gîza viâ Ṣaqqâra and Dahshûr to Ṭâmîya, Lake Mœris, and Madînet el-Faiyûm, details of which may be learned at Cook's office in Cairo (p. 40).

Railway from Cairo viâ Wâsṭa to Madînet el-Faiyûm, $80^3/_4$ M., in $2^1/_2$-$2^3/_4$ hrs., five trains daily in either direction. A new Motor Road leads from the Pyramids of Gîza (p. 132) straight across the desert to Kôm Aushîm (p. 209), and thence on to Madînet el-Faiyûm. — From Madînet el-Faiyûm radiate numerous light railways (besides the main line), which facilitate visits even to remote points. — Carriages, Motor Cars, and Riding Animals may be obtained at the Hôtel Karoun in El-Madîna (p. 203).

Situation and History. In the great plateau of the *Libyan Desert*, which rises 300-400 ft. above sea-level, is situated the province of the Faiyûm (*Fayum*, *Fayoum*; from the ancient Egyptian 'Phiom', i.e. the lake), the first of the oases, which is usually considered to belong to the valley of the Nile, and is justly celebrated for its extraordinary fertility. This tract is in the form of an oval basin and is enclosed by the Libyan hills, which are here of moderate height, and lies about three-fifths of a degree to the S. of Cairo. It enjoys a remarkably fine climate. Even at the period of the Ptolemies and the Romans the Faiyûm was extolled. "The Arsinoïte Nome" [comp. p. 204], says Strabo, "is the most remarkable of all, both on account of its scenery and its fertility and cultivation. For it alone is planted with large and richly productive olive-trees, and the oil is good when the olives are carefully gathered; those who are neglectful may indeed obtain oil in abundance, but it has a bad smell. In the rest of Egypt the olive-tree is never seen, except in the gardens of Alexandria, where under favourable circumstances it yields olives but no oil. Vines, corn, podded plants, and many other products also thrive in this district in no small abundance." The Faiyûm is indebted for its fertility to the *Bahr Yûsuf* or *Youssef* ('Canal of Joseph'), which diverges from the Ibrâhîmîya Canal at Dairûṭ (see p. 224) and flows at El-Lâhûn (p. 206) through a narrow opening in the Libyan chain into the Faiyûm, where it divides into numerous ramifications, abundantly watering the whole district. At the point where the Baḥr Yûsuf enters the Faiyûm the district forms a plateau of moderate height, descending W. in two gradations to the E. bank of the Birket Qârûn (p. 208).

In antiquity the Faiyûm was known as *Te-she* or 'lake-land' (Gr. *Limnē*, lake), from the great inland lake frequently mentioned and described by Greek travellers and geographers under the name of *Lake Mœris* (from Egyptian *me(r)-wēr*, *mwēr*, great lake), of which the last trace must be recognized in the present *Birket Qârûn* (p. 208). At the most remote period the lake occupied almost the entire basin of the Faiyûm, but within the historical period its area became contracted, and it extended from the desert temple discovered by Schweinfurth (p. 203), on the N., to Biyahmu and the district between Ibshawâi and ʿAgamîyîn, on the S. Its circum-

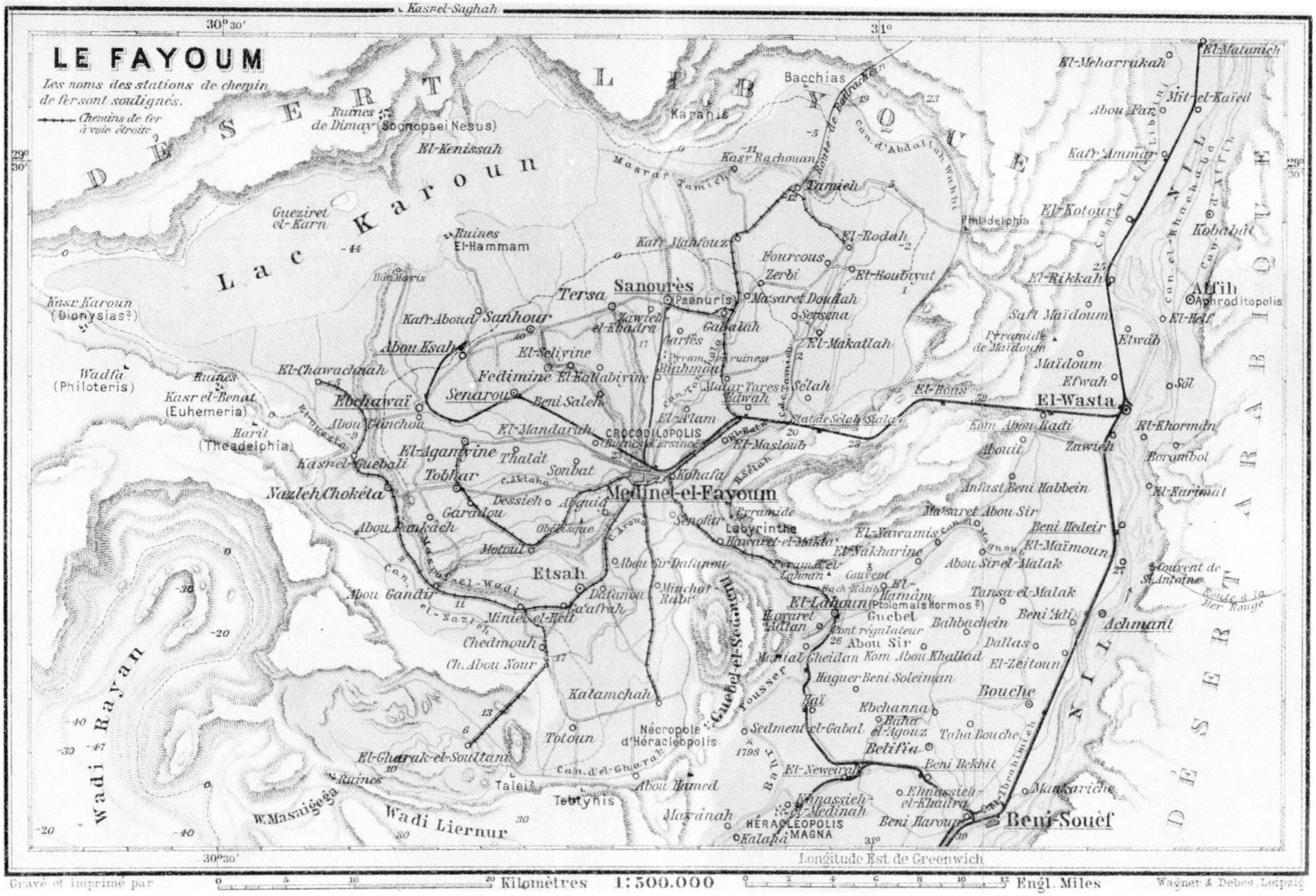
LE FAYOUM
Les noms des stations de chemin de fer sont soulignés.
Chemins de fer à voie étroite
Kasr-el-Saghah
30° 30'
31°
29° 30'
DÉSERT LIBYQUE
DÉSERT ARABIQUE
Lac Karoun
NIL
Ruines de Dimay (Socnopaei Nesus)
El-Kenissah
Gueziret el-Karn
Ruines El-Hammam
Bacchias
Karanis
Kasr Rachouan
Tamieh
Philadelphia
Kasr Karoun (Dionysias?)
Wadfa (Philoteris)
Kasr el-Benat (Euhemeria)
Harit (Theadelphia)
Sanhour
Tersa
Sanourès
Psenuris
Abou Ksah
Fedimine
Senarou
El-Chawachnah
Ebchawaï
CROCODILOPOLIS
Médinet-el-Fayoum
Nazleh Chokéta
Tobhar
Etsah
Pyramide Labyrinthe
El-Lahoun
Pyramide de Maïdoum
Maïdoum
El-Wasta
Alfih
Aphroditopolis
El-Meharrakah
El-Matanieh
Mit-el-Kaïed
El-Rikkah
Achmant
Beni-Souef
Bouche
Belifia
Ehnassieh-el-Medinah
HÉRACLÉOPOLIS MAGNA
Nécropole d'Héracléopolis
Guebel el-Sedmant
Sedment-el-Gabal
El-Gharak-el-Soultani
Kalamchah
Tebtynis
Wadi Rayan
Wadi Liernur
W. Masaïgega
Couvent de St Antoine
Route à la Mer Rouge
Longitude Est de Greenwich
Gravé et imprimé par
Kilomètres 1:500.000 Engl. Miles
Wagner & Debes, Leipzig

ference seems to have been about 140 M. and its area about 770 sq. M. According to recent calculations it lay 73ft. above the level of the Mediterranean; the present lake is 144 ft. below sea-level. The ancient Lake Mœris thus left uncovered only the narrow strip of the fertile 'lake-land' on the S., on which stood the capital *Shedet* (Crocodilopolis, p. 204), protected by embankments against inundation. Several rulers of the 12th Dyn. established their residences on the E. margin of the lake-land, and Amenemmēs III. seems to have shown a special predilection for it. Teye, the wife of Amenophis III. (18th Dyn.), fixed her residence near El-Lâhûn. In the Greek period, chiefly under Ptolemy II. Philadelphus (p. cxi), the lake area was reduced by means of embankments, approximately to the size of the modern Birket Qârûn. Land was reclaimed for agricultural purposes by draining the marshes, and the success of these efforts is attested by the fertile fields and prosperous villages that have occupied for twenty centuries the erstwhile site of Lake Mœris. The extensive irrigation works constructed by Philadelphus were discovered in 1927-28. Strabo describes the lake in the following terms: "Owing to its size and depth Lake Mœris is capable of receiving the superabundance of water during the inundation without overflowing the habitations and crops; but later, when the water subsides, and after the lake has given up its excess through the same canal [i.e. the Baḥr Yûsuf], both it and the canal retain water enough for purposes of irrigation. At both ends of the canal there are lock-gates by means of which the engineers can regulate the influx and efflux of the water." Near the modern El-Lâhûn there is a large lock to this day. — The statement of Herodotus that Lake Mœris was an artificial construction thus rests upon an error and is moreover in direct contradiction to Strabo's account. For the two pyramids and statues mentioned by Herodotus as standing in the lake, see p. 205.

The Faiyûm forms a separate province. The *Inhabitants* are fellahin, or tillers of the soil, and Beduin. To the latter race belong the poor fishermen who inhabit the banks of the Birket Qârûn. — Comp. 'The Topography and Geology of the Fayum Province', by *H. J. L. Beadnell* (Report of the Egyptian Survey Department; Cairo, 1905), and 'Recent Work on the Problem of Lake Mœris', by *Miss G. Caton-Thompson* and *Miss E. W. Gardner* (Geographical Journal, Jan. 1929).

From Cairo to *El-Wâsṭa* ($57^1/_4$ M.; buffet), see p. 217. Travellers change trains.

The branch-railway to the Faiyûm runs W., across cultivated land (with the pyramid of Meidûm on the plateau to the right; p. 217), to the ($4^1/_4$ M.) station of *Kôm Abu Râḍi*, beyond which it traverses a desert tract and crosses the low and bleak Libyan chain of hills, attaining its highest point at 190 ft. above the sea. On reaching the cultivated districts of the Faiyûm the train crosses the *'Abdallâh Wahbi Canal.* The pyramid of Hauwâra (p. 206) is seen to the left. Beyond ($15^1/_2$ M.) *Seila (Siala)* we cross the *Baḥr Seila el-Gedîd* (p. 206) and the *Baḥr el-Wâdi* or *El-Baṭs Canal* (p. 207; now reclaimed for tillage). — Near ($18^1/_2$ M.) *El-'Idwa* (*Edwa;* 69 ft.; p. 204) is a cemetery. In the distance is the pyramid of El-Lâhûn (p. 207), nearer is that of Hauwâra (p. 206). We traverse rich arable land.

$23^1/_2$ M. **Madînet el-Faiyûm.** — Hotels (near the station). *Karoun*, 21 R., pens. P.T. 60-80, with restaurant, *National*, both comparatively good. — Bank. *National Bank of Egypt.*

Madînet el-Faiyûm (Fayoum), usually known as *El-Madîna*, is the chief town of the province of Faiyûm with 52,372 inhab. in 1927

(including many Greeks). There are several mosques, a Roman Catholic, and a large Coptic church, and a station of the American Mission. The long covered bazaars are of no great interest. The mosque of *Qâït Bey*, built on a bridge over the *Baḥr Yûsuf* (p. 202), has an ancient portal with bronze-mounted doors. The interior has been completely restored. At the W. end of the town the Baḥr Yûsuf radiates through sluices into numerous branches.

To the N. of the town, and intersected by the railway to Abuksâh (see below), are the rubbish-mounds known as *Kîmân Fâris*, or 'rider's hills', covering an area of 560 acres. These mark the site of **Crocodilopolis-Arsinoë**, one of the most extensive ruins of any old Egyptian town. The rubbish-heaps have recently been much diminished by brick-burners and diggers for sabakh (p. lxxiii).

The ancient Egyptian name of this town was *Shedet*. It was the centre of the worship of the crocodile-headed water-god *Suchos* or *Sobk*, under whose protection the entire lake-land stood. The crocodile was sacred to him, and the Greeks therefore named the city *Crocodilopolis* or 'crocodile town'. It never attained to any political importance. Ptolemy II. Philadelphus (p. cxi) seems to have converted it into an essentially Hellenic city by adding new quarters, founding Greek temples and educational institutions, and introducing the Greek language. This monarch also raised Queen Arsinoë to the dignity of patron-goddess, and the district became known as the 'Arsinoïte Nome' and the capital as the 'City of the Dwellers in the Arsinoïte Nome', or, more briefly, as *Arsinoë*. At the time of its greatest prosperity it had over 100,000 inhabitants.

On the extreme N. edge of the ruins, near the farm of ʿEzbet Faraḥât Farîd, is the site of the principal ancient temple, which was dedicated to Suchos. This existed as early as the 12th Dyn. and was afterwards rebuilt by Ramses II. Beside the temple lay a sacred pond in which the crocodile of Suchos was kept.

Railways run from Madînet el-Faiyûm to *Abuksâh* (see p. 208), and viâ *Biyahmu* to ($7^1/_2$ M.) *Sinnûris* (*Sennures*, *Sennorès*; light railway, see below), a district capital.

The **Faiyûm Light Railways** also radiate in various directions, their starting-point adjoining the main railway station. 1. Viâ *Quḥâfa*, *Hauwâra*, and *Dimishqîn* to *El-Lâhûn*, see pp. 205, 206. — 2. Viâ *Sheikh Hasan* and *ʿEzbet Matar (Ezbet Mattar)* to *Qalamshâh (Qalamsha)*, whence *Dishâsha* (p. 218), about 12 M. to the S., may be reached on donkey-back viâ *Abu Ḥâmid* in $2^1/_2$-3 hrs. — 3. Viâ *Abgîg* (p. 205), *Itsa* (*Etsa*; a district capital), *Minyet el-Heiṭ* (*Miniet*, *El-Minya*; see below), *Shidmûh (Shidmo)*, and *Sheikh Abu Nûr (Abou Nour)* to *El-Gharaq*. About 6 M. to the S.E. of El-Gharaq, on the Bahr el-Gharaq canal, by the S.W. border of the Faiyûm, and near the Tell Umm el-Breigât, lay the ancient *Tebtynis*, in the necropolis of which a number of mummified crocodiles and numerous papyri were found in 1899-1900. From El-Gharaq an interesting desert expedition may be made in one day on camels to the *Wâdi Raiyân*, a valley on the way to the oasis of Baharîya (p. 405). — 4. To *Itsa* and *Minyet el-Heiṭ* (see above), and viâ *Abu Gandîr (Abou Guandir)*, *En-Nazla (Nezleh-Balad)*, and *Qaṣr el-Gebâli (Kasr-el-Guibali)* to *Esh-Shawâshna* (p. 209). — 5. Viâ *Ṣûfi (Soufi)*, *Mutûl (Moutoul)*, *Garadu (Guaradu)*, and *Ṭubhâr (Tobhar)*, to *El-ʿAgamîyîn (Agamiine)*. — 6. Viâ *El-ʿIdwa* (p. 203), *Maṭir Ṭâris (Mittertaris, Matar Tares)*, *Maʿsaret Dûda (Massaret Douda)* to *Sinnûris* (see above), *Ṭâmîya* (*Tamieh*; p. 209) and *Er-Rôḍa (Rodah)*. To the S. of Er-Rôḍa, in the necropolis near the village of *Er-Rûbîyât*, Theodore Graf found the famous mummy-portraits (2nd-3rd cent. of our era) now distributed over the museums of the world. About 5 M. to the N.E. of Er-Rôḍa, on the desert plateau above the

ʿAbdallâh Wahbi Canal and near the beginning of the desert route to Er-Riqqa (p. 217), is the site of the ancient *Philadelphia*, a colony of Greek soldiers founded c. 250 B.C. under Ptolemy II. Philadelphus.

The village of **Biyahmu** (*Biahmu*, *Biahmo*, *Bîhamu*), which lies on the railway to Sinnûris (p. 204), 4½ M. to the N. of Madînet el-Faiyûm, is usually visited by carriage or motor-car, or on donkey-back. The fine high-road running to Sinnûris leads past the Government School, the Government Hospital, and several country-houses. It then traverses fertile fields and passes palm groves and fig orchards, affording an idea of the fertility of the district. — By the railway embankment, ½ M. to the N. of Biyahmu station, rise two large stone *Piles*, which present the appearance of ruined pyramids and are called by the natives *Kursi Faraʿûn* ('Pharaoh's chair') or *Eṣ-Ṣanam* ('the idol'). These were the pedestals of two colossal sandstone *Statues of King Amenemmēs III.*, remains of which have been found by Lepsius and by Sir Flinders Petrie, who estimates their original height at 40 ft. The learned Father Vansleb of Erfurt saw the lower portion of one of these figures in 1672. The pedestals were once washed by the waters of Lake Mœris, and there is little doubt that they are the two pyramids described by Herodotus as standing in Lake Mœris, each with a colossal seated human figure upon it.

From Madînet el-Faiyûm to Sanhûr, 9½ M. This fine route leads through a remarkably fertile and well-cultivated region, viâ the villages of *Beni Ṣâliḥ* and *Es-Silîyîn*. Picturesquely situated on a cliff to the left appears the village of *Fidîmîn*. **Sanhûr** is a large village occupying the site of a considerable ancient town.

Near **Abgig** (*Begîg;* railway station, see p. 204), 2 M. to the S.W. of Madînet el-Faiyûm, lies a red granite obelisk, erected by Sesostris I., now broken, which was once 46 ft. in height. The natives call it *El-ʿAmûd*, or the column.

Pyramids of Hauwâra (Labyrinth) and El-Lâhûn.

The excursion to the pyramid of Hauwâra may be comfortably accomplished in half-a-day. We take the light railway (p. 204) to (½ hr.) *Hauwâra*, and ride thence by donkey, which we must bring with us (comp. p. 202). From the pyramid we ride all the way back to Madînet el-Faiyûm. Or we may ride all the way to the pyramid and back (c. 3 hrs.). The drive by carriage or motor-car is more convenient and enables the pyramid of El-Lâhûn to be included in the excursion. — A visit to the pyramid of El-Lâhûn by railway and donkey requires an entire day, but Hauwâra may be included on the return-route. We take the light railway to Bâsh Kâtib, ride thence to the pyramid of El-Lâhûn, and thence, in 1½ hr., to the pyramid of Hauwâra. — Carriages and motor-cars, see p. 202.

1. **Railway Journey to Hauwâra and El-Lâhûn.** The railway, following the same course as the high-road, leads at first along the bank of the *Baḥr Yûsuf*, with the pyramid of Hauwâra to the left, to the village of *Quḥâfa*. Farther on it traverses cultivated fields, with the heights of Gebel Sidmant to the right, and reaches the station of *Hauwâra (Hawara)*, beside the village of *Hauwâret el-Maqtaʿ*, with its pretty mosque (route hence to the pyramid, see p. 206). To the left is a large cemetery, with the graves of sheikhs. — The railway now again approaches the Baḥr Yûsuf. The remains of old embankments which we see from the train date from the period of the Caliphs. We then cross the *Baḥr Seila el-Gedîd*, which diverges from the Baḥr Yûsuf. The pyramid of El-Lâhûn becomes visible on the left. The train approaches the margin of the desert. — *Dimishqîn (Dimishkine)* station. — The station of *Bâsh Kâtib*

(Bash-Kateb) is the starting-point for the pyramid of El-Lâhûn (p. 207). — The train then traverses fertile land to the village of **El-Lâhûn** or *Illâhûn* (*Lahoun;* Egyptian *Le-hône*, i.e. 'mouth of the canal', see p. 202), situated on the right bank of the Baḥr Yûsuf. Branch-line to Beni Suef, see p. 218. — Close to the railway station is the sluice-bridge ('pont régulateur') through which the Baḥr Yûsuf enters the Faiyûm. Beyond the bridge is the village of *Hauwâret 'Adlân*, a picturesque place situated on the water. About 2 M. to the S.W. of El-Lâhûn, close to the edge of the desert, is the ruined town of *Madînet Gurôb (Kôm Madînet Ghurâb)*, discovered by Sir Flinders Petrie. It owed its origin to Thutmosis III., who built a temple here.

2. The **Pyramid of Hauwâra** *(Hawâra)*, the tomb of *Amenemmēs III.*, is reached on donkey-back from the village of *Hauwâret el-Maqṭa'* (p. 205) in about $^3/_4$ hr. The route leads N., through fields, to the desert plateau on which the pyramid stands. We then cross a bridge over the *Baḥr Seila el-Gedîd* (p. 203), which intersects the plateau. The pyramid consists of unburnt Nile bricks mixed with straw, and, when its sides were perfect, covered an area about 115 yds. square. The limestone casing, however, had disappeared even in the Roman period. The nucleus of the structure is a natural mass of rock, 39 ft. in height. The dilapidated summit is easily reached in a few minutes by a well-worn path. The entrance to the pyramid, on the S. side (now impassable), was discovered in 1889 by Sir Flinders Petrie. An intricate series of passages in the interior leads to the tomb-chamber in which Amenemmēs III. and his daughter Ptah-nofru were interred.

On the S. the pyramid was adjoined by the large mortuary temple of Amenemmēs. This edifice, however, which served as a quarry for centuries after the Roman period, has completely vanished, with the exception of an extensive space strewn with small splinters of stone and fragments of fine granite and limestone columns. Traces of its walls may be recognized also in the sloping banks of the Baḥr Seila el-Gedîd. There is no doubt that this edifice was the famous **Labyrinth**, of which ancient travellers speak with such unbounded admiration.

For the best description we are indebted to Strabo, who visited the Labyrinth in person. He says: "There is also the Labyrinth here, a work as important as the Pyramids, adjoining which is the tomb of the king who built the Labyrinth. After advancing about 30-40 stadia beyond the first entrance of the canal we reach a table-shaped surface, on which rise a small town and a vast palace, consisting of as many royal dwellings as there were formerly nomes. For there is that precise number of courts, bordered with columns and adjoining each other, all being in the same row, and forming one building, like a long wall having the courts in front of it. The entrances to the courts are on the opposite side from the wall. In front of the entrances are numerous long covered passages, intersecting each other and thus forming such a winding path that a stranger cannot find his way into or out of each court without a guide. It is a marvellous fact that each of the ceilings of the chambers consists of a

single stone, and also that the passages are covered in the same way with single slabs of extraordinary size, neither wood nor other building material having been employed. On ascending to the roof, the height of which is inconsiderable as there is only one story, we have a survey of the flat stone surface consisting of these large slabs. On emerging from the covered passages we have a view of them extending in one line, each borne by twenty-seven monolithic columns. The walls also are constructed of stones of similar size. At the end of this structure, which is more than a stadium in length, is the tomb, consisting of a square pyramid, each side of which is four plethra (400 ft.) in length, and of equal height. The deceased who is buried here is called Imandes. It is asserted that so many palaces were built because it was the custom for all the nomes, represented by their magnates, with their priests and victims, to assemble here to offer sacrifice and gifts to the gods, and to deliberate on the most important concerns. Each nome then took possession of the hall destined for it."

The remains of brick buildings, which still linger on the mounds of rubbish to the E. of the temple and were erroneously regarded by Lepsius as remains of the Labyrinth, date from a village of the Roman period. — To the N. of the pyramid stretches the large *Necropolis* used since the period of the Middle Empire by the richer inhabitants of Shedet-Crocodilopolis (p. 204).

The Return to Madînet el-Faiyûm may be made in $1^1/_2$ hr. without again touching Hauwâret el-Maqṭaʿ, as follows. We cross the Baḥr Seila el-Gedîd (p. 206) and ride along its W. bank for some distance, next continue W. through the fields, and cross the filled-in *Baḥr el-Wâdi* (p. 203), which is partly cultivated and partly covered with reeds. We proceed through desert and fertile land to the village of *Quḥâfa* (p. 205), charmingly situated on the Baḥr Yûsuf, whence we follow the railway embankment to the town.

3. The **Pyramid of El-Lâhûn** *(Illâhûn)*, tomb of *Sesostris II.*, is most easily visited (20 min.) from Bâsh Kâtib (p. 205) or El-Lâhûn station (p. 206). The pyramid is constructed of Nile bricks, piled up upon a rocky nucleus bearing a star-shaped framework of low walls built of massive limestone blocks. To the N. of the pyramid are eight tombs hewn in the rock and the remains of the queen's pyramid. To the S. are four shaft-tombs of near relatives of the king, in one of which, that of the princess *Sit-Hathor-Yunut*, Sir Flinders Petrie discovered in 1914 a large collection of gold ornaments of outstanding artistic merit, now divided between the Cairo Museum (p. 104) and the Metropolitan Museum of New York.

About $1^1/_4$ M. to the N. of the pyramid of El-Lâhûn Sir Flinders Petrie discovered in 1889 the ruins of the town of *Hetep-Senwosret* ('Contented is Sesostris'), which he called *Kahun*. This town was founded by Sesostris II. (12th Dyn.) and had but a brief existence. Numerous domestic articles were found among the ruined houses.

Birket Qârûn (Lake Mœris) and its Environs.

This excursion is easily accomplished by motor-car from Madînet el-Faiyûm in one day; the route leads viâ Ibshawâi (see below) direct to the bank of the lake. A more laborious route, not recommended for those ignorant of Arabic, is to take the train to Abuksâh and to hire there (apply at the police station) a donkey or carriage to take them to the lake. Travellers who wish to make a lengthier stay near the lake and to visit the ruins of *Dimai* and the temple of *Qaṣr Qârûn* must employ a dragoman, who will provide tents and provisions (information at the Hotel Karoun, p. 203).

The railway journey from Madînet el-Faiyûm to (12$^1/_2$ M.) *Abuksâh (Abuxah)* takes c. 1 hr. Beyond (7$^1/_2$ M.) *Sînaru (Senaro)* lie the ruins of an ancient town. — 12 M. *Ibshawâi (Abshawâi).* The carriage route to the lake (comp. above) leads first through cultivated land, then crosses the ancient bed of the lake. — If we start from Abuksâh we reach the lake at the ruins of *El-Ḥammâm.*

The **Birket Qârûn,** i.e. 'Lake of Qârûn' (the Korah of Numbers xvi), is the *Lake Mœris* of the Greeks (comp. p. 202). It lies 144 ft. below the level of the Mediterranean and measures 93 sq. M. in area, 25 M. in length, and, at its broadest part, barely 6 M. in width. The depth of the E. part of the lake is 12 ft., of the W. part 18 ft. The greenish water is slightly brackish and is not fit for drinking. The N. bank is sterile, but on the S. the cultivated land often reaches as far as the lake. The right of fishing is let by government, and the whole of the fishermen on the lake are in the service of the lessee. Waterfowl are sometimes abundant but are far too shy to approach within gunshot.

The lake is crossed with a favourable wind in about 2 hrs. To the E. appears a peninsula, with rubbish-heaps. In the lake lies the large island called *Gezîret el-Qarn*, or 'island of the horn'. On the N. bank of the lake are barren hills of considerable height.

From the landing-place a somewhat steep path ascends to the (1$^3/_4$ M.) ruins and temple of **Dimai** *(Dimê).* The fortified position of this town (230 ft. above the level of the lake), named in antiquity *Soknopaiou Nēsos*, i.e. 'island of Soknopaios' (a form of Suchos, the Faiyûm deity, p. 204), provided a secure point of departure for the caravans trading with the oases in the Libyan Desert. The ruins cover an area of about 125 acres. A street 400 yds. in length, formerly embellished with figures of recumbent lions, leads past well-preserved houses to a platform on which an important temple once stood. This temple, built under the Ptolemies, was dedicated to Soknopaios and the 'beautifully enthroned Isis'. The precinct was surrounded by a brick wall, and the temple itself contained several apartments, those in the rear being lined with well-jointed limestone-blocks and those in front having walls of roughly hewn stone coated with stucco. Very few reliefs have been found here; on one appears a Ptolemy praying before a ram-headed deity (probably Amun).

At the foot of a steep descent in the Libyan desert, about 5 M. to the N. of Dimai, Prof. Schweinfurth (p. 44) discovered in 1885-86 the small

Temple of Qaṣr eṣ-Ṣâgha. It consists of blocks of limestone and contains seven recesses and several other apartments, but no sculptures or inscriptions. In the vicinity are remains of an ancient quay.

In the desert, to the E. of the lake and to the N.W. of Ṭâmîya (p. 204), rises the mound of *Kôm Aushîm*, covering the ruins of *Karanis*, a Greek town frequently mentioned in local history, with a temple of Pnepherōs and Petesuchos. It lies on the motor-road from the Pyramids of Gîza to Madînet el-Faiyûm (p. 202). — The mound called *Tell Umm el-Qatl*, or *Kôm el-Asl*, 7 M. to the E. of Karanis, marks the site of *Bacchias*, with a ruined Greek temple. Both mounds were explored in 1896 by Hogarth and Grenfell, at the expense of the Egypt Exploration Fund, and Kôm Aushîm was excavated in 1924-26 by the University of Michigan (Ann Arbor).

The ruins marking the site of Qaṣr Qârûn lie at the S.W. end of the Birket Qârûn. We land on the promontory of *Khashm Khalîl*, which is overgrown with tamarisks and reeds. Ascending thence across the desert for about an hour, we reach the temple, which is now $2^1/_4$ M. from the lake, though it originally stood on its bank. The fishermen object to passing the night here, being afraid of the Beduin and evil spirits (ʿafârît, sing. ʿafrît).

Qaṣr Qârûn is most conveniently visited from *Esh-Shawâshna*, a station on the light railway (p. 204).

Qaṣr Qârûn is a fairly well preserved temple of the late Ptolemaic period. The numerous traces of an ancient town that surround it are probably those of *Dionysias*, which was situated on the extreme W. verge of the Roman province of Egypt, at the beginning of the caravan-route to the 'Small Oasis' (Baḥarîya, p. 405). A circular foundation-wall indicates the site of an ancient cistern. The walls of the temple consist of carefully hewn blocks of hard limestone. This temple, like almost all the shrines in the oases, was dedicated to the ram-headed Amun-Khnum, as is proved by two figures of this deity standing at the highest part of the posterior wall of the upper story of the open roof. The winged sun-disk occurs over each gateway in the building. There are no ancient inscriptions.

The temple is 21 yds. in width across the façade and $29^1/_2$ yds. in length. The entrance, facing the E., is approached by a lofty and carefully constructed platform, 14 yds. in length, forming a forecourt. On the façade of the temple, to the right (N.) of the entrance-door, is a huge half-column, forming a relic of a pillared hall. On the lower floor are the apartments of the temple which were dedicated to worship. In the first three *Anterooms* the ground slopes down towards the *Sanctuary*, which was divided into three small rooms at the back. The sanctuary is flanked by two narrow passages, each of which is adjoined by three rooms. The anterooms also have adjacent chambers from which we may enter the cellars or ascend by two flights of steps to the upper floor, with its different apartments, and thence to the roof, which affords an extensive view of the remains of the ancient city, the lake, and the desert. Over the doors leading into the second and third anterooms and into the sanctuary, instead of the ordinary cavetto cornice, there is a series of uræus snakes.

To the E. of the large temple are two smaller temples, in a tolerable state of preservation. One of them, which has the same axis as the large temple, is a kiosk, resembling in ground-plan the kiosk of Philæ (p. 395); the second and larger of the two is situated

300 paces from the smaller. Its walls (18 ft. by 19 ft.) consist of good burnt bricks and its substructures of solid stone. The sanctuary terminates in a niche resembling an apse; on each of the side-walls are two half-columns which, as the fragments lying on the ground show, belong to the Ionic order.

About 8½ M. to the S.E. of Qaṣr Qârûn are the ruins of **Qaṣr el-Banât**, the ancient *Euhemeria*, including the remains of a temple of Suchos (p. 204) and Isis. — About 5 M. to the W. of Qaṣr el-Banât are the ruins of the ancient *Philoteris*, now known as *Wâṭfa;* 1¾ M. to the S.E., beside the village of *Harît (Baṭn Ihrît)*, lie the ruins (*Kharâbet Ihrît;* with a temple of the crocodile-god Pnepherōs, p. 24) and the necropolis of the ancient *Theadelphia.*

II. UPPER EGYPT.

Visitors to the temples and tombs of Upper Egypt and Nubia should be provided with a General Admission Ticket of the Egyptian Department of Antiquities, valid for a year (June 1st to May 31st), which may be obtained (price £ E 1 P.T. 80) from the Cairo Museum (p. 88), Thos. Cook & Son (p. 40), the Anglo-American Nile & Tourist Co. (p. 40), and in Upper Egypt from the inspectors of antiquities or at Karnak.

The ordinary traveller, desiring to visit only the principal points of interest, may ascend the valley of the Nile either by railway or by steamer. By Railway not less than a fortnight is required for a visit to the chief points. Those who use the Nile Steamers, spending three or four weeks on the voyage, enjoy a much more thorough and convenient survey; while the voyage on the Nile has so many attractions of its own that even the most hurried traveller should make a point of proceeding by river at least between Luxor and Aswân. At the same time it must not be forgotten that in travelling by tourist steamer one is a member of a party and has to surrender some of the free control of one's time (comp. p. xv). The most attractive, but also the slowest and most expensive method of ascending the Nile is by Dahabîya (p. 216). — Moonlight adds a peculiar charm to a visit of Luxor, Karnak, and Aswân. It is as well for the independent traveller to avoid as far as possible coming into contact with the large parties organized by the tourist agents, for otherwise circumstances are apt to arise in which he is pushed to the wall, without any redress.

Railway. Travellers who desire to see as much as possible in a short time and are impatient of the restrictions of an organized party may visit Upper Egypt by train, making occasional use of motor-cars. Fast trains daily from Cairo to Luxor in $12^1/_2$-$13^1/_2$ hrs., see R. 15; from Cairo to Aswân in 17, from Luxor to Aswân in $4^1/_2$ hrs., see R. 22. The following scheme, which is recommended to somewhat experienced travellers only, takes about $2^1/_2$-3 weeks from Cairo to Aswân and back (according to the time spent at Luxor and Aswân) and includes the chief points of interest.

1st Day. To *Minya* (p. 220).

2nd Day. Visit the rock-tombs of *Beniḥasan* (p. 240).

From Cairo to (20½ M.) *Badrashein*, see p. 153.

Farther on we have a view, to the right, of the pyramids of Dahshûr, including the great Stone Pyramid, the Blunted Pyramid, and the small Brick Pyramids (p. 177). To the left are the Nile and a Beduin village shaded by palm-trees. — 28 M. *Mazghûna;* 32⅓ M. *El-Bileida (Beleida, Balîda)*; 36½ M. *El-ʿAiyâṭ* (*Ayat;* p. 234), with a large ginning factory. — 40½ M. *El-Matânya (Matania).* To the W., on the edge of the desert (40 min. donkey-ride), are the pyramids of *El-Lisht;* that to the N. is the tomb of Amenemmēs I. (12th Dyn.), that to the S. the tomb of his successor Sesostris I. Their mortuary temples and the surrounding tombs have been excavated by the Metropolitan Museum of New York. — 45½ M. *Kafr ʿAmmâr.* Near *Kafr Ṭarkhân*, 1¼ M. to the S.W. of the station, beyond the canal of Baḥr el-Libeini, is a large prehistoric burial-ground, excavated by Sir Flinders Petrie in 1911-12.

51½ M. *Er-Riqqa* (*Rekkah;* p. 234), a large village with brick and cement works, is the starting-point for the excursion to the pyramid of Meidûm; for the visit from El-Wâsṭa, see below.

A visit to Meidûm may be accomplished in about 4-5 hrs. (donkey P.T. 20, and P.T. 2½ for fodder). Crossing the railway, we proceed in about 1¼ hr. to the pyramid, which rises on the soil of the desert close to the cultivated country and ½ hr. N.W. of the village of ***Meidûm.***

The **Pyramid of Meidûm** *(Maidûm)*, the unfinished and never used tomb of ***Snofru*** (p. cii), predecessor of Kheops, is the first true pyramid with a square ground-plan (comp. p. clxxvii). Its three (originally seven) square receding stories rise to a height of about 214 ft. in smooth and steep stages at an angle of 74° 10′. The first section is 81 ft. 6 in., the second 98 ft. 11 in., while the third, now almost entirely destroyed, is 34 ft. 3 in. in height. The outer walls are admirably jointed of blocks of limestone. On the N. side is an isolated section of the outer casing, with the entrance. The examinations by Maspero and Petrie prove that the pyramid was pillaged as early as under the 20th Dynasty. On its E. side is the small ***Mortuary Temple of Snofru***, now again covered up. This temple, built of limestone, consists of two bare chambers and an open court. The masṭabas, or tombs of Snofru's courtiers, to the N. and E. of the pyramid, are now covered with sand; their best reliefs are in the Cairo Museum (pp. 90, 91).

On the E. bank of the Nile, opposite Riqqa station and ½ hr. from the river, lies the village of **Aṭfîḥ**, with scanty remains of the ancient *Aphroditopolis*, named after Hathor-Aphrodite. The Egyptian name of the town was *Tep-yeh* or *Per-Hathor nebt Tep-yeh*, i.e. 'House of Hathor, Mistress of Tep-yeh', whence the shortened Coptic form *Petpeh* and the Arabic *Aṭfîḥ* are derived. Strabo states that a white cow, sacred to Hathor, was worshipped here (comp. p. clvi).

In the Christian period (c. A.D. 310) Aphroditopolis gained some celebrity from *St. Anthony* (p. cxvi), who fixed his hermitage in the mountains to the E. of the town but afterwards fled from his admirers and buried himself deeper in the mountains (comp. p. 218). The portrayal of his contests with demon-tempters was a favourite subject of 16-17th cent. painters.

57 M. **El-Wâsṭa** (p. 234; buffet; 92 ft. above sea-level), a district capital and junction for the Faiyûm railway (p. 203). The expresses wait 4-5 min. here. The town is pleasantly situated in a

grove of palms. The pyramid of Meidûm (p. 217) lies $4^1/_2$ M. to the N.W. and is conveniently visited from here.

Beyond Wâsṭa, on the left, are the storage-reservoirs of *Qusheisha*, $1^1/_2$ M. to the W. of the river. The Ibrâhîmîya Canal (p. 237) continues skirting the railway on the right. — 63 M. *Beni Ḥideir (Beni Ḥodeir)*. — 67 M. *Ishmant (Ashment, Achmant)*. A road leads hence to the Faiyûm (p. 202; motor-cars and motorbuses at the station). To the right appears the small black pyramid of El-Lâhûn (p. 207). The E. hills rise on the left.

About 3 hrs. N.W. of Ishmant is the village of **Abuṣir el-Meleq** *(Abu Ṣîr el-Malaq)*, the 'Lower Egyptian Abydos' of the Egyptians, containing extensive ancient cemeteries excavated in 1905-6 by the German Orient Society. In the vicinity is the tomb of Marwân II. (p. cxviii).

$72^1/_2$ M. *Bûsh* (*Bouche;* p. 234), inhabited by Copts.

77 M. **Beni Suef** (*Beni Suweif;* buffet; Semiramis Hotel, at the station; Continental, very fair) is a town of 39,478 inhab. (1927), pleasantly situated between the railway and the Nile, which is $^1/_4$ hr. from the station. As the capital of a province, it is the seat of a mudîr (the mudîrîya lying to the left of the station) and contains several banks. The linen manufacture for which this place was celebrated in the middle ages has greatly declined, but several ginning factories, numerous cotton plantations, and a small bazaar still lend it a certain importance.

A secondary line viâ *Nazlet Shâwîsh* (8 M.; for Ihnâsya el-Madîna, see below) runs in 1 hr. to (16 M.) *El-Lâhûn*, at the entrance of the Faiyûm (p. 202). Thence a light railway goes on to Madînet el-Faiyûm.

On the right bank of the Baḥr Yûsuf, 10 M. to the W. of Beni Suef, and connected with Nazlet Shâwîsh (see above) by a branch-line (3 M. in 20 min.), lies the village of *Ihnâsya* or *Ahnâsya el-Madîna* (*Ahnasia* or *Ehnassieh el-Medîna*, locally *Ahnâsya Umm el-Kimân*, 'Ahnâsya of the rubbish-heaps'), beside the mounds of débris, covering an area of $^1/_2$ sq. M., which mark the site of the ancient **Heracleopolis**. The Egyptian name of the town was *Hat-nen-nesut*, from which are derived the Coptic *Hnēs* and the Arabic *Ahnâs* and *Henassîya*. It was the capital of a nome (the Græco-Roman Heracleopolites) and the chief seat of the worship of the ram-headed god Herishef, identified by the Greeks with Heracles. The ichneumon also was revered here. Among the chief shrines were a temple erected under the Middle Empire and a new building by Ramses II., but all have practically vanished; four columns of a late period, probably dating from a Byzantine church, are all that projects above the rubbish-heaps (comp. pp. clxxxviii, clxxxix). The ancient necropolis (excavated by Sir Flinders Petrie in 1920-21) lies on the left bank of the Baḥr Yûsuf near *Sidmant* (or *Sedment*) *el-Gebel.*

A road beginning at the village of *Bayâḍ en-Naṣâra* (p. 234), on the E. bank of the Nile, leads through the desert (36 hrs. by camel) to the very ancient *Monasteries of SS. Anthony and Paul* (pp. lvii, 217), situated about 25 M. from the Red Sea.

$90^1/_2$ M. *Biba (Beba)*, a district capital, is the junction of a secondary line running parallel with the main line on the W. bank as far as Maghâgha ($27^1/_2$ M.; two trains daily in either direction). At Biba is a Coptic church with a tall bell-tower.

At Dishâsha *(Dechachah)*, beyond the Baḥr Yûsuf, on the edge of the desert, 14 M. to the N.W. of Biba (accessible by motor-car), are tombs of the rulers of this nome under the 5th Dyn. (first examined by Sir

Flinders Petrie in 1897). Those of *Inti* and *Shedu* contain interesting sculptures of battle scenes, a siege in Syria, etc. The tombs are unlocked by the caretaker. Dishâsha may also be reached viâ Qalamshâh (see p. 204).

99 M. **El-Fashn** *(Fashen, Fachen)* is a district capital.

To the S.E., a little above Fashn, at the village of **El-Ḥiba**, are the ruins of the Greek town of *Ankyronpolis*. The village, hidden by palms, lies on the E. side of an eminence that becomes an island when the floods are out. The town walls, several yards in thickness and still in good preservation, were built under the 21st Dynasty. Within the walls, picturesquely situated among palms, are the ruins of a temple of Amun, built by Sheshonk I. (22nd Dyn.).

104 M. *El-Fant.* — 112 M. **Maghâgha** (p. 235), a district capital with a sugar factory, is the junction for the secondary lines to Biba (p. 218) and Maṭâi (p. 220).

A road leads from Maghâgha to the oasis of *Baḥarîya* (p. 405), which is connected with Bahnasa and Ṣandafa by another desert route (comp. below). — Opposite Maghâgha, near the village of *Qarâra* (the ancient *Phylakē Hippōnos*), are Coptic cemeteries of about the 8th cent., excavated by the Germans in 1913-14; and ½ hr. N., near the village of *Aulâd esh-Sheikh*, is a burial-ground of c. 3000 B.C. About 12-20 M. to the E. of the Nile, near the wide *Wâdi esh-Sheikh*, are some prehistoric *Flint Factories*, discovered by H. W. Seton-Karr in 1896.

The railway approaches the Nile again. To the E. rise the *Gebel esh-Sheikh Embârak* (or *Sîdi Mubârik*) and the *Gebel Qarâra*. — The village of *Shârûna* lies on the E. bank, a little higher up.

To the E. of Shârûna, on the E. edge of the hill of *Kôm el-Aḥmar* ('red mound'), is a partly destroyed rock-tomb of the end of the 6th Dynasty. It belonged to Pepi-onkh and besides a wide vestibule, where the deceased is portrayed catching birds and spearing fish, it contains three small chambers, one of which is adorned with reliefs and inscriptions. — Farther S. are a ruined temple of Ptolemy I. (p. cxi) and rock-tombs of the later period, believed to have belonged to the town of *Hat-nesut*, in the Kynopolitan nome.

122 M. *Beni Mazâr* (p. 235), a district capital. About 1½ M. to the S.W. lies the village of *El-Qeis*, Egyptian *Kaïs*, whose local deity was Anubis, and which probably occupies the site of *Kynopolis*, capital of the province under the Greeks.

From Beni Mazâr a secondary line leads N.W. to (10 M.) *Ṣandafa*, a village on the Baḥr Yûsuf (p. 202). Beyond the canal lies the village of **El-Bahnasa** *(Behnesa)*, on the site of the ancient *Oxyrhynchus* (Egyptian *Per-medjet*, Coptic *Pemdje*, Greek *Pemptē*; comp. p. clxxxvii), once the capital of a nome but now represented only by a few desolate heaps of débris. The fish *Oxyrhynchus*, a species of mormyrus (Arabic mizda), was worshipped here. In the neighbouring town of Kynopolis the dog was held in equal honour, and Plutarch relates how a 'very pretty quarrel', the settlement of which required the intervention of the Romans, arose between the two towns, because the citizens of each had killed and dined on the sacred animals of the other. On the introduction of Christianity Oxyrhynchus became a veritable town of monks. In the town itself were twelve churches, and all round it convent jostled convent. In the 5th cent. the diocese of Oxyrhynchus is said to have contained 10,000 monks and 12,000 nuns. In the Mameluke period it was still of some importance, but it afterwards declined. Excavations begun here in 1897 by B. P. Grenfell and A. S. Hunt have yielded large quantities of Greek, Coptic, and Arabic papyri. Remains of colonnades and of a large theatre of the Roman period were discovered in 1922, and in the cemetery are the ruins of early-Christian tomb-chapels. — From Ṣandafa a desert route (125 M.; practicable for motor-cars) leads to the oasis of *Baḥarîya* (p. 405).

Beyond (129 M.) **Maṭâi** (p. 235) a handsome bridge crosses a canal. Maṭâi is the junction of the secondary line to Maghâgha (p. 219) and Minya (see below). — 134 M. *Qulûṣna (Kolosna)* is situated between the Nile and the Ibrâhîmîya Canal; opposite, on the E. bank of the Nile, is the village of *Es-Sirîrîya* (p. 235). Our line crosses the Abu Baqara Canal, which diverges from the Nile. — 138 M. **Samâlûṭ** is a district capital on the Ibrâhîmîya Canal, 1 M. from the river, with a fine station, a Coptic church, and sugar factories. On the E. bank of the Nile rises the massive *Gebel eṭ-Ṭeir* (p. 235), forming a picturesque background for the numerous sails on the Nile. Extensive cotton-fields and sugar-plantations are passed; the vegetation is rich.

144 M. *Itsa (Etsa).* On the E. bank of the Nile lies the village of *Ṭihna el-Gebel.*

To the S. of the village we follow a river embankment shaded with ṣunṭ-trees (p. lxxviii), cross a small canal, and walk across the fields to a ridge 65-80 ft. in height, with some early-Egyptian *Rock Tombs* which were again used in the Greek period. On the ridge is a sanctuary of the Roman period with limestone columns, built partly in the open and partly as a cave-temple. In a chapel on the river side of the ridge is the representation of a bald-headed man in Roman costume sacrificing to Egyptian deities. To the N., in the direction of the village, are the brick ruins of the ancient town of *Tĕnis*, also called *Akōris*, belonging to the nome of Hermopolis. — About 1/2 hr. farther S., hidden among débris halfway up the hillside, are three *Rock Tombs* of the Ancient Empire with interesting inscriptions (last wills and testaments). A colossal image carved out of the rock represents Ramses III. sacrificing to the gods Suchos and Amun. — In the valley between the rocky ridge just mentioned and the E. mountains, to the N. of the Mohammedan cemetery, lie a Græco-Roman and a Christian necropolis.

153 M. **El-Minya** (*Minia;* buffet and clean waiting rooms at the station; Majestic Hotel, Savoy Hotel, both well spoken of), a town with 43,973 inhab. (1927), is the centre of the Upper Egyptian cotton trade and has a British war cemetery. It lies between the Ibrâhîmîya Canal and the Nile, which is here over 1000 yds. broad. The Shâriʿ el-Maḥaṭṭa leads from the station to the town. On the quay is a small museum. A handsome bridge, with locks, spans the canal. Market-day (Mon.) in Minya presents a gay picture of oriental life. Minya is the junction of secondary lines to Maṭâi (see above) and Dairût (p. 224). — To *Beniḥasan*, see p. 240.

Opposite Minya, on the E. bank, lies *Kôm el-Kafara*, with tombs of the Middle Empire. Farther S., 4 1/2 M. above Minya, is situated *Zâwiyet el-Amwât (Zâwiyet el-Meitîn).* On the E. side of the village lies the Minya cemetery, with its domed tombs and chapels. Faithful to the custom of their ancestors under the Pharaohs, the inhabitants still ferry their dead across the river and bury them near the ancient necropolis.

A few minutes' walk towards the S. brings us to the large mound of rubbish known as *Kôm el-Aḥmar* ('red mound'), and beyond this we reach the rock-tombs (buried in débris) of the princes and grandees of the ancient town of *Hebenu*, which date

mainly from the end of the Ancient Empire. The only one that is accessible is that of Nefer-sekheru, superintendent of storehouses under the New Empire.

At *Aulâd Nuweir (Nueirât* or *En-Neweirât)*, a village farther S., are some small rock-tombs belonging to the Ancient Empire.

To the E. appear the hills of Zâwiyet el-Amwât and Kôm el-Aḥmar (p. 220), with a sheikh's tomb at the farther end. Low rugged hills are seen on the left and a plain on the right. — 160 M. *Mansâfîs.* — 166 M. *Abu Qurqâṣ (Abou Kerkas)*, a district capital with a sugar factory. Opposite are the rock-tombs of Beniḥasan (p. 241). The village of *Balanṣûra*, 8 M. to the W. of Abu Qurqâṣ, on the Baḥr Yûsuf, represents the ancient Egyptian *Nefrus.* — 170 M. *Itlîdim (Etlîdem).* Near *Qaṣr Hôr (Qaṣr el-Hûr)*, 7 M. to the S.W., are the ruins of the 6th cent. monastery of *Abu Jânâ.*

177 M. **Er-Rôḍa.** The town, with its large sugar factory, lies on the Nile, at some distance from the station (Roda Junction), with which it is connected by a light railway (nine trains daily; 2 M. in 7 min.). The nearest night-quarters are at Mallawi (p. 222) or (better) at Minya (p. 220). About 4 M. to the W., between the Ibrâhîmîya Canal and the Baḥr Yûsuf and on a light railway from Roda Town to Idâra (which may be used in one direction at least), is the village of *El-Ashmûnein* (accessible also from Mallawi). Near it (close to Idâra station) lie the ruins of the once famous city of *Khmunu* (Coptic *Shmun*), the ***Hermupolis*** of the Greeks, which from a remote period was the chief seat of the worship of Thoth, god of writing and science. Numerous papyri of the Roman and Byzantine periods have been discovered here. This town was also the capital of the 'hare' nome, in Upper Egypt, whose princes under the Middle Empire were buried at Deir el-Barsha (p. 224).

Several granite columns, probably belonging to the colonnade of the Greek agora, are still standing. To the N., in a palm grove, are the meagre remains of a temple of Philip Arrhidæus, half-brother of Alexander the Great (p. cxi). To the N.W., beyond the palm-grove, are the considerable relics of the pylon and the pillared hall of a 19th Dyn. sanctuary. The remains of a lengthy inscription referring to Menephthes (p. cvii) are to be seen on the E. outer wall of the N. tower of the pylon; the reliefs on the inner walls of the pylon date from Sethos II. — At *Tûna el-Gebel*, on the opposite bank of the Baḥr Yûsuf, are the extensive necropolis of the ancient city and two rock-inscriptions (much dilapidated) of Amenophis IV. (p. 245).

Opposite Rôḍa, on the E. bank, amid palms, lies the village of *Esh-Sheikh ʿIbâda*, to the E. of which are the ruins of **Antinoupolis** or *Antinoë*, the town erected by the Emperor Hadrian in A.D. 130 in honour of his favourite Antinous. The handsome youth, whose features are known to us from numerous antique sculptures, is said to have drowned himself here, to fulfil the oracle which predicted a heavy loss to the emperor and so to prevent a more serious disaster. The remains of a *Temple of Ramses II.*, the relic of an earlier foundation on this site, may be traced to the N. of Sheikh ʿIbâda; of this only the columns of the forecourt and the main hall project from the

rubbish-heaps. The vestiges of public buildings are now exceedingly scanty, though the French expedition (p. 136) saw a triumphal arch, a theatre, and streets flanked with columns. Granite columns and capitals lie scattered about. Near the ruins of a large building on the road running E. from the mosque lies a broken marble basin, which must have had a diameter of about 10 ft. The Roman and Christian cemeteries have recently been much injured.

To the S.W. of Sheikh 'Ibâda we reach **Deir Abu Ḥinnis** (*Deir Abu Hennes*, i.e. 'Monastery of St. John'; p. clxxxvii), called also simply *Ed-Deir*, a village inhabited by about 2000 Copts. Near it is a ruined town of the Christian epoch, known as *El-Madîna*. The oldest portions of its church date from the 5th century. On the N. side of a ravine in the hill behind the village are many ancient cave-like quarries, which were fitted up at an early date as Christian *Chapels* or anchorites' dwellings (p. clxxxviii). The largest chapel, in which divine service is held, is believed to date from the time of the Empress Helena (p. cxvi) and contains wall-paintings of saints and scenes from the New Testament, but those in the neighbouring chapel (Raising of Lazarus, Marriage in Cana, etc.) are better. — Deir el-Barsha (p. 224) is within $1/2$ hr. of Deir Abu Ḥinnis.

Immediately beyond Rôḍa the mountains on the E. bank recede farther from the river. During the sugar-cane harvest, at the beginning of February, this region presents a busy scene.

$181^1/_2$ M. **Mallawi** (*Mellawi;* modest inn at the station; Dr. Nadîm's Sanatorium, German, pens. £E 15 per month), a district capital on the W. bank of the Ibrâhîmîya Canal, with 20,250 inhab., has a market frequented on Sundays. To the left we have a view of the E. range of hills, in which are the tombs of El-Barsha (p. 224) and Sheikh Sa'îd (p. 236). A shady route, skirting the Dairûṭîya Canal, leads hence to Ashmûnein and Hermupolis (p. 221; by motor-car in $3/4$ hr.). To Tell el-'Amârna, see p. 245.

In the desert, to the W. of Mallawi and near the village of Dirwa, lies the ***Tomb of Petosiris**, excavated by Gustave Lefebvre in 1920. A visit to it takes 6 hrs. We reach it by motor-car from Mallawi (P.T. 50 there and back, with a gratuity of P.T. 10, bargaining necessary), following a good road viâ the village of *Umm Qummuṣ* to ($6^1/_4$ M.) the bank of the Baḥr Yûsuf, opposite Dirwa. We leave the car here and cross the canal by ferry to *Dirwa.* The village headman ('omda) provides donkeys for the ride across the desert, if notified from Mallawi through the ma'mûr (p. xlix) or other responsible person. From Dirwa our route lies at first through cultivated fields, then across the level desert and past old mounds of débris (Kôm el-Aḥmar) to (1 hr.) the tomb, which lies not far from the escarpment of the Libyan Desert.

The elegant structure, now surrounded by débris-heaps, was built c. 300 B.C. as a family tomb by *Petosiris*, a prominent citizen of Hermupolis (p. 221) and high priest of the temple of Thoth. It

comprises only two chambers: a vestibule, the later portion of the structure, dedicated to the memory of Petosiris himself, and an almost square chapel supported by pillars, erected by Petosiris for the cult of his father Es-Show and his elder brother Djed-Dhut-efonkh. Both rooms were adorned by Egyptian artists with reliefs (colouring well preserved in part) of high importance in the history of art (p. clxxxv). While the religious representations, especially in the chapel, are in the pure Egyptian style, more or less after models of the 18th Dyn., the secular reliefs, reproducing scenes of daily life, in the vestibule and at the base of the chapel walls are in an Egyptian style adulterated with Greek elements, some indeed being purely Greek in character.

The tomb is approached by a paved way about 65 ft. long and 13 ft. wide, to the left of which is an altar 8 ft. high, with horn-shaped decorations at the four corners. The FAÇADE of the tomb shows four columns with rich plant-capitals; on either side of the portal the columns are connected by tall screens, which, like the lateral pilasters, are adorned with reliefs of Petosiris praying and sacrificing to the gods of his native nome. — In the VESTIBULE the reliefs at the back of the four screens (N. wall) portray secular motives in a mixed Græco-Egyptian style. From left to right: 1, 2. Metal-workers; the making of all kinds of utensils, with a man working at a table decoration; weighing the metal; delivery and packing of the finished pieces. 3, 4. In the two upper rows, the preparation of salves; in the two lower, carpenters; two men at a lathe (the earliest representation known); the manufacture of a state bed. — *East Wall.* Three rows of reliefs (starting at the bottom): ploughing, flax harvest, corn harvest, and the threshing of corn with sticks. — *South Wall:* to the left of the door, the sons of Petosiris with their parents; at the base of the wall, men bringing offerings; right of the door, the daughters with their parents; at the base, mourning women and a sacrificial scene, in a purely Greek style. On the lateral pilasters, above, the deceased is seen playing draughts. — *West Wall:* in the two upper rows, cattle in the fields; in the lower, the vintage, with a wine-press and the delivery of the jars.

The four pillars in the CHAPEL are decorated with long inscriptions and with reliefs (the deceased praying to various gods). *North Wall*, right (E.) section: the goddess Nut produces water out of a tree for the parents of Petosiris; below, Petosiris praying to his father; at the base of the wall, cattle driven through a swamp. — *East Wall:* Funeral procession, with the coffin borne on a hearse, men, gods (the four sons of Osiris, p. clv), and women walking to the tomb, some bearing offerings; on the right, the mummy in front of the tomb and a priest pouring holy water over it. At the base of the wall, men carrying offerings. — *South Wall* (divided into three sections by projecting pilasters). Left Section: The father with nine gods praying to the sun; Djed-Dhut-efonkh and his children praying to his father; below, a marshy landscape with cattle. In the centre, Es-Show (l.) and Djed-Dhut-efonkh praying to Osiris and Isis (or Nephthys), and below, the snake and vulture goddesses protecting with their wings Osiris in the shape of a beetle; right and left, Isis and the soul-bird (p. cliv) perched on a false door; at the base of the wall, the bestowal of water on the soul. Right Section: above, Djed-Dhut-efonkh praying to nine divinities; below, Petosiris and his brother; at the base, a swampy landscape with hippopotami and a crocodile. — *West Wall.* Upper row (left to right): Djed-Dhut-efonkh praying to nine baboons, Djed with twelve snakes, Djed with sacred bulls and deities, Djed conducted to Osiris, Djed praying. Middle row: The deceased praying to various gods (Book of the Dead, chapter xviii). Lower row: Bearers of offerings, partly in the Greek style. — *North Wall*, left (W.) section: the deceased in front of the table of offerings; below, Petosiris with his dead brother. — The TOMB-SHAFT (closed) leads to a chamber in which Petosiris was buried with his wife and one of his sons. His coffin is in the Cairo Museum (p. 101).

Nearly opposite Mallawi, on the E. bank of the Nile, a little way from the river, lies the Coptic village of **Deir el-Barsha** (or *el-Bersha*), with an old church. Beside a Coptic cemetery to the E. begins a desert ravine, running N.W. and S.E. and named *Wâdi en-Nakhla* or *Wâdi Deir el-Barsha*, in the steep sides of which are numerous quarries and ancient tombs. The valley is chiefly noted for the rock-tombs in its N. slope, constructed under the Middle Empire by the princes of the 'hare' nome (p. 221), which included this region. The only one that need be visited is —

Tomb 2, belonging to Dhut-hotep, son of Kay, prince of the nome in the reigns of Amenemmēs II. and Sesostris II. and III. This tomb is constructed in the same way as those at Beniḥasan. The *Vestibule*, originally supported by two palm-columns, has fallen in. A door leads hence to the *Inner Chamber*, the walls of which were embellished with reliefs, now partly destroyed. On the *Left Wall* is a scene representing the transportation of a colossal statue of the deceased from the quarries of Hat-nub (p. 252) to a temple. The inscription informs us that the statue was of alabaster and 13 ells (c. 21 ft.) in height. It is securely fastened with ropes upon a wooden sledge, which is drawn by four rows of workmen with forty-three men in each. A priest precedes the statue scattering incense. On the prow of the sledge stands a man pouring water on the ground to prevent the heavily loaded sledge from taking fire by friction; and on the lap of the figure is another man clapping his hands, probably the leader and fugleman of the song of the workmen, whose task was facilitated by rhythmical movement. Below are other workmen carrying water and a beam; and behind the statue are foremen and other officials. At the top are companies of people with branches in their hands, hastening to meet the procession. To the extreme left stands Dhut-hotep, followed by his bodyguard, observing the spectacle.

Below the rock-tombs are *Tombs of the Ancient Empire*, *Shaft Tombs of the Middle Empire*, and numerous tombs of the Ptolemaic period. Opposite, on the S. side of the valley, is a large *Quarry*, which, according to a now defaced inscription, yielded stone in the first year of Amenophis III. for the temple at Hermupolis (p. 221). Farther up the valley are quarries of the time of Nektanebis I. (p. cx).

Continuation of the Railway. 188 M. *Deir Mawâs (Deir-Moës)*. The village is on the other side of the Ibrâhîmîya Canal; the hamlet beside the station is called *Ḥasabîya (El-Ḥasâïba)*. On the E. bank are the ruins of **Tell el-ʿAmârna** (p. 245), which are visited hence.

194½ M. **Dairûṭ** or *Deirûṭ (Dairûṭ el-Maḥaṭṭa)*, a district capital. Near the station is a great barrage, with sluices through which the *Baḥr Yûsuf* (p. 202) and the *Dairûṭîya Canal* are supplied with water from the *Ibrâhîmîya Canal* (p. 237). About 2 M. to the N. is the considerable village of *Dairûṭ esh-Sherîf*, to the W. of which, on the edge of the desert, lies the village of *Bâwîṭ*, with the rubbish-

mounds of the Coptic monastery of Apa Apollo (p. clxxxvii). Secondary railway to Minya, see p. 220.

203 M. *Nazâli Gânûb*. Beyond the railway and the Ibrâhîmîya Canal lies the town of **El-Qûṣîya,** the ancient *Cusae*, in which, according to Ælian (c. A.D. 200), Aphrodite Urania (i.e. Hathor, the mistress of heaven) and a cow were worshipped. It was the ancient Egyptian *Kis*, capital of the 14th Upper Egyptian nome. — About 2 hrs. W. of Nazâli Gânûb lies *Mîr* (*Meir*; p. clxxxviii), and $1^1/_2$ hr. farther, on the edge of the desert, is the necropolis of Qûṣîya, with **Rock Tombs* of the princes of the nome and their relations, dating from the 6th and 12th Dynasties. Of special interest are the tombs of Senbi, son of Ukh-hotep (time of Amenemmēs I.), and his son Ukh-hotep (time of Sesostris I.), with reliefs partly in the naturalistic style, some of the best produced under the Middle Empire (tombs unlocked by the caretaker).

From Mîr (Nazâli Gânûb) or Manfalûṭ (see below) a desert route leads to the oasis of Farâfra (p. 405).

The village of *El-Quṣeir (Qoṣeir el-ʿAmârna)* is charmingly situated amid palm-groves on the E. bank of the river, opposite Nazâli Gânûb. In the hills near it are several rock-tombs of the 6th Dyn., including that of Khunukh, with slight paintings, and the larger but unfinished tomb of Pepi-onkh. — The E. hills and the railway now approach the Nile.

On the edge of the desert, about 6 M. to the S.W. of Nazâli Gânûb, and conveniently reached thence, is the large Coptic monastery of *Deir el-Maḥarraq* or *Deir el-Muḥarraqa* (pp. lvii, cxc). Its 12th cent. tower is an important example of an Egyptian 'donjon' or keep, containing living-quarters, store-rooms, a church, etc.

$215^1/_2$ M. **Manfalûṭ** (p. 236), a district capital between the Nile and the Ibrâhîmîya Canal, is the seat of a Coptic bishop and has several fine villas and gardens and a Coptic cathedral with two towers. Its market is much frequented on Saturdays, and it possesses a sugar factory. Date-brandy (ʿaraqi) is made here, chiefly for local consumption by the Copts, though it is also exported in large earthenware vessels.

To the S.W. of Manfalûṭ lies *Beni ʿAdi*, where in 1798 an encounter took place between the troops of General Desaix and the Arabs. In the following year General Davout destroyed it. Muḥammed ʿAli concentrated his army here in 1820 for the expedition to Morea (comp. p. cxxvi).

At the foot of the hills on the right bank, opposite Manfalûṭ and some distance inland, lie the villages of *El-Maʿâbda*, *ʿArab el-ʿAṭîyât*, and *Deir el-Gabrâwi*.

The hills to the N.E. of *El-Maʿâbda* contain tombs of the Ancient Empire. About $3^1/_2$ M. to the N.E., on the plateau of the E. hills, is the *Crocodile Grotto*, which, however, is hardly worth visiting, as practically nothing is to be seen except the charred remains of the mummies of crocodiles. — To the S. is the *Gebel Qurna*, with a quarry exhausted in the reign of Sethos II. (inscription). — At *ʿArab el-ʿAṭîyât*, 3 M. to the E. of El-Maʿâbda, are tombs and quarries. About 2 M. farther E. lies the Coptic village of *Deir el-Gabrâwi*, containing a Greek inscription (discovered by Harris) in the form of a dedication of the Lusitanian Cohort, which served under Diocletian and Maximian, to Zeus, Heracles, and Nikē (Victory).

In the *Gebel Marâg*, a ridge $1^1/_2$ hr. distant, commanding a glorious view of the Nile valley, are numerous rock-tombs belonging to princes and grandees of the nome of the '*Serpent Mountain*'. These tombs, mostly dating from the close of the Ancient Empire, are difficult of access and hardly repay a visit. They are divided into a N. and a S. (earlier) group, the former comprising eighty tombs (four with inscriptions and reliefs), the latter about forty (twelve with reliefs). The most interesting are two of the S. group, situated above the village of Deir el-Gabrâwi, belonging to *Djaw* and *Ibi* (6th Dyn.), 'princes of the 12th nome (Serpent Mountain) and of the nome of Abydos'. Like the graves of Beniḥasan (p. 241), these tombs contain interesting representations of craftsmen, harvesters, fishing and hunting scenes, etc.

233 M. **Asyûṭ**. — *Buffet.* — Hotels. *Grand*, by the station, 26 R., *New*, Shâriʿ el-Helâli, beyond the station, 20 R. at P.T. 28, with restaurant, both very fair. — Post Office in the main street (Shâriʿ el-Maḥaṭṭa); Telegraph Office at the station. — Steamer Agencies, on the Nile. — Banks. *National Bank of Egypt; Barclay's* (formerly Anglo-Egyptian Bank).

Carriage to the Barrage (see p. 237) and the Rock Tombs (p. 227), in about 3 hrs., P.T. 30 and a gratuity of P.T. 5; motor-car about P.T. 40.

Hospital of the American Mission (see below), with 130 beds and three American physicians.

Asyûṭ (Asiûṭ, Assiut, Assiout, or *Siûṭ)*, the name of which still preserves the ancient Egyptian *Syowt*, enjoyed considerable importance, even in antiquity, chiefly owing to its favourable situation. It lies in the midst of an extensive and fertile plain, $12^1/_2$ M. in width, between the Libyan and the E. hills, and at the beginning of a great caravan route leading to the oases in the Libyan desert (R. 29) and thence to the Sûdân. Asyûṭ, however, seems to have been of political importance only occasionally (e.g. in the period between the Ancient and the Middle Empire). It was the capital of the 13th nome of Upper Egypt and the chief seat of the worship of the god *Wep-wawet* who was represented as a wolf of the desert. This latter circumstance gave rise to the Greek name *Lycopolis*, or 'wolf town'. The modern Asyûṭ, which extends from E. to W., is the largest town (57,036 inhab. in 1927) in Upper Egypt, the capital of a province, and the residence of the mudîr. The handicrafts for which it was formerly noted (pottery, inlaid wood, ivory carvings, leather and woven goods, and tulle shawls with gold or silver threads) are being rapidly ousted by European factory-made goods. Natron, soda, cotton, and grain are among the principal exports. The streets and bazaars are full of busy life, especially on Tuesdays, when the people of the neighbourhood flock into the market. — The *Asyûṭ Institute*, founded in 1915 by Sultan Ḥusein Kâmil, is directed by a sheikh, like other Mohammedan religious institutions in Egypt (p. 58); it has 64 professors and 931 students. Asyûṭ is also the chief seat of the *American Presbyterian Mission* (director, Dr. C. P. Russell), which has in Egypt 342 stations, including 112 churches, 216 schools, and two large hospitals (at Ṭanṭa and Asyûṭ). *Asyûṭ College*, in the Shâriʿ Sulṭân Ḥusein (near the mouth of the Ibrâhîmîya Canal, p. 227), attended by 750 pupils, and the girls' school of the *Pressly Memorial Institute* (450 pupils), in the Shâriʿ el-Helâli, likewise deserve a visit.

Plotinus, the greatest of the Neo-Platonic philosophers (A.D. 205-270), was born at Asyûṭ, and his system was not uninfluenced by the priestly doctrines of his native town. From the beginning of the 4th cent. onwards Christianity was dominant. Pious believers took up their abode in the caves of the necropolis to live a life of penitence apart from the world. One of these, *John of Lycopolis*, at the end of the 4th cent., bore the reputation of a saint and prophet. The Roman emperor Theodosius sent an embassy to him to inquire the outcome of the civil war. The anchorite foretold a complete but bloody victory, and this prophecy was fulfilled in the victory of Theodosius over Eugenius at Aquileia in A.D. 394.

From the station square (Mîdân el-Maḥaṭṭa) the Shâriʿ el-Helâli leads to the left (E.) to the Nile, along the bank of which the Shâriʿ Fu'âd el-Auwal (to the left, the mudîrîya), with its quays, leads N. to the sluice-bridge of the Ibrâhîmîya Canal and the Shâriʿ Sulṭân Ḥusein. Here are the *Law Courts* (maḥkama), the imposing *Government Ophthalmic Hospital*, and the new buildings of the *Asyûṭ Institute* (see p. 226). Beyond the bridge the road leads past the *Government Secondary School* (left) and a public garden (right) to the Barrage (p. 237). Between the Nile, the Shâriʿ Sulṭân Ḥusein, and the railway is a fashionable new residential quarter *(El-Manshîya)*. — In the Shâriʿ Madraset es-Sanîya, N. of the station square (see above), are the *Asyûṭ Model Workshops*, where instruction is given in various handicrafts (271 pupils in 1926-27).

Close to the post office, in a side-street of the Shâriʿ el-Maḥaṭṭa, which diverges W. from the square, is the **Egyptian Museum** of Saiyid Kháshaba Pasha, a wealthy resident of Asyûṭ, who excavated ancient cemeteries at Asyûṭ and Mîr (p. 225) in 1910-14. Adm. on application at the owner's private house in the Manshîya quarter.

Room to the Right. Wooden coffins from Asyûṭ and Mîr, some with beautifully coloured door-ornamentation. The show-cases contain sepulchral offerings from Mîr (granaries, kitchens, ploughmen, boats). — Central Room. Mummy-shaped granite sarcophagus of Siēse, superintendent of storehouses for Upper and Lower Egypt (New Empire; from Asyûṭ); limestone group of a prince and his consort (Mîr; 6th Dyn.). In the wall-cases, funerary statuettes, scarabæi, vessels, mirrors, etc. To the right, by the pillar, a relief from El-ʿAmârna, showing the interior of a house. — Room to the Left. Wooden coffin from Mîr, mummy-shaped and covered with linen, of Horiaina, a woman who, according to the Greek inscription, died at the age of fifty; wooden and stone coffins; fine reliefs from a tomb of the 19th Dyn. (the deceased at table; the deceased and his relatives in the presence of the gods of the dead); over-lifesize *Statue of the official Yuni, holding a shrine with an image of Osiris.

In the Shâriʿ el-Maḥaṭṭa, which leads to a circular open space, and thence (to the right) to the old town and the bazaar, are the Collège des Frères, the American Mission (p. 226), and a government school.

The street issuing S.W. from the town is continued by a causeway, which crosses the Sohâgîya Canal and leads to the foot of the hill, halfway up which lie the ***Rock Tombs of Ancient Asyûṭ.** From the slaughter-house, near which the keeper of the tombs lives (tickets must be shown, p. 212), we follow a steep zigzag path leading to a **Large Rock Tomb**, which belonged to *Djefay-Hape (Hap-djefaï)*, prince of the nome in the reign of Sesostris I. The Arabs call it *Isṭabl ʿAntar* (comp. p. 241).

From a courtyard in front of the tomb we enter a surprisingly lofty and elongated HALL, the vaulted roof of which was painted with stars; on the right wall is the deceased, with a long and now scarcely legible inscription in front of him. A doorway, on each side of which is a figure of the deceased holding a staff, leads to a TRANSVERSE CHAMBER. On the right half of the *Entrance Wall* is a long inscription in vertical columns containing the text of ten contracts concluded between the deceased and various priesthoods of his native city to secure the proper sacrificial offerings to himself, and to provide for the performance of other ceremonies. The corresponding inscription on the left side of the same wall contains exhortations to visitors to the tomb and an account of the merits of the deceased. The flat roof has coloured ornamentation (snail, meander, and woven patterns). A door between two recesses in the rear wall admits us to a vaulted hall, leading to a SECOND TRANSVERSE ROOM with three recesses. On the rear wall of the central recess appeared the deceased, four women with lotus-flowers standing before him; on the side-walls he is shown at table, while three rows of priests and servants bring gifts to him or perform sacred ceremonies. The left recess leads to the mummy-shaft.

The *View from this tomb is very fine. Below, to the left, is the Arab cemetery (see below). The fertile land forms a pleasant setting for the town of Asyûṭ, with its minarets and its environment of palm-gardens, and for the Ibrâhîmîya Canal, with its boats. The E. mountains provide a fine background. The view is still grander from the higher tombs. Here there is a row of three tombs close to each other, dating from the period before the Middle Empire. The northernmost has been destroyed.

The second or middle tomb is the **Soldiers' Tomb**, or *Kahf el-ʿAsâkir*, so named from the rows of warriors armed with spears and large shields on the S. wall of its pillared hall. On the right side of the vestibule appear *Kheti*, prince of the nome and owner of the tomb, and his wife *Tef-yeb*, with a long and partly effaced inscription, referring to King Meri-ke-rē of the period between the Ancient and the Middle Empire (p. ciii). Only a single column is left standing in the main chamber, in the rear wall of which is a recess for the statues of the deceased. — A passage has been made from this tomb to that adjoining it on the S., which is of imposing dimensions and belonged to *Tef-yeb*, a prince of the nome.

Farther on we scramble over heaps of débris to reach a small *Christian Rock-Chapel (Kenîsa)*, which has Greek and Coptic inscriptions painted in red. By climbing a little further round the spur of the hill, we include in the view the distant range on the E. edge of the Libyan desert.

A large ***Arab Cemetery** stretches across the plain to the N. of the hill of tombs, with hundreds of domed tombs.

At the foot of the hill, behind the slaughter-house, is the tomb of another *Djefay-Hape*, much destroyed. It contains some ceiling ornaments and paintings of harvest scenes, etc., upon stucco.

About 1/2 hr. S. of the rock-tombs, on the slope of the Libyan hills, is the village of *Durunka (Dronka)*, and 2 M. farther S. is the Coptic convent of *Ed-Deir (Deir Rîfa)*; several tombs of princes and grandees of Shes-hotep (see p. 229; Middle and New Empires) near the latter contain nothing of interest save some inscriptions. — About 4 1/2 M. to the S.E. of Asyûṭ, on the railway to Luxor, lies the village of *Shuṭb (Shoṭb)*, the

Egyptian *Shes-hotep* and the Greek *Hypselis*, capital of the Hypselite nome. The chief deity here was the ram-headed Khnum (necropolis, see p. 228).

From Asyûṭ to the *Oasis of El-Farâfra*, see p. 405. — To the Southern Libyan Desert and *El-Fâsher*, see p. 440.

Beyond Asyûṭ the railway approaches the Nile. — 243 M. *El-Muṭî'a (Motia, El-Mati'ah).*

248 M. **Abu Tîg** (*Abutîg, Butîg;* p. 237), a district capital, lies in the ancient Hypselite nome. The name is probably derived from the Greek 'apothēkē', i.e. storehouse. A large weekly market is held on Saturday. — 254 M. *Ṣidfa* (*Sedfa;* p. 237). On the opposite (E.) bank, $1^1/_4$ M. from the Nile, is *El-Badâri*, a district capital, near which burials of the remotest prehistoric age (the so-called Badâri period) were discovered by the British School of Archæology in 1924-25. On the steep edge of the desert to the N. of El-Badâri, between the villages of *El-Khawâlid (Khawaled)* and *Nag' Wîṣa (Naga' Wissa)*, are several settlements and burial-grounds of the same period, examined in 1928 by the British School, under the auspices of the British Museum.

$259^1/_2$ M. *Ṭima* (*Tema;* p. 237), a pretty village in verdant surroundings. Opposite (E. bank) is the fertile plain of *Qâw* (p. 237), the Greek Antæopolis. — $263^1/_2$ M. *Mishṭa (Meshta).* The village of *Kôm Ishqâw*, the ancient *Aphroditopolis*, lies 3 M. to the S.W. — 270 M. *Ṭahṭa* (p. 238), a district capital with a noted cattle-market. The hills of the E. bank now approach close to the river. — 278 M. *El-Marâgha* (p. 238). — 284 M. *Shandawîl* (*Chandawil;* p. 238). A large market is held here every Saturday.

290 M. **Sohâg** or *Souhag* (Hôtel Khédivial, near the station; branch of Barclay's Bank), with 24,991 inhab. (1927), is the capital of the province of Girga. The handsome government buildings (mudîrîya) stand in a neat square. Close by are the hospital and the Protestant church. The Coptic cathedral is modern. The bazaar is small; Monday is market-day.

An excursion to the White and Red Convents (comp. p. clxxxvii) takes about 4 hrs. by carriage (P.T. 60, bargain necessary; gratuity of P.T. 5). An embanked road leads W. from Sohâg, viâ the village of *Mazâlwa*, to (3 M.) the early-Christian settlement of the **White Convent**, or *Deir el-Abyaḍ*, situated on the edge of the Libyan mountains. The convent, named also *Deir Amba Shenûda* after its most important abbot, Shenute (p. cxvi), is occupied by men, women, and children (about 100 souls in all). The present convent was originally the church, built c. 440; it is enclosed by a lofty wall of white limestone blocks and has almost the appearance of a fortress. The wall and the entrance gateway, on the S. side, are adorned with a cavetto cornice like an Egyptian temple. We enter the church by a narthex, which terminates on the W. in a recess. The body of the church was a basilica with nave and aisles, with a trefoil-shaped sanctuary consisting of a square central portion and three apses with half-domes. The central portion originally had a pointed roof but is now covered with a 12th cent. dome. In the church and in the court (formerly the aisles) are some ancient columns, taken from the adjacent ruins of the antique *Atrēpe (Athribis).* The apses are adorned with two superimposed rows of niches (five in each), which alternate with columns. Some of the ceiling-paintings are well preserved (p. cxci). A second narthex to the W. of the basilica has a N. apse adorned with columns. The rich treasures of the

library of the convent have been sold to European collectors. — About 3¾ M. farther N.W. (carriage in ½ hr.) is the **Red Convent**, *Deir el-Ahmar*, also called *Deir Amba Bishôi* and now enclosed on two sides by modern hutments. The church, which is contemporary with the White Convent, was originally a basilica with nave and aisles and elaborate capitals. The sanctuary, trefoil-shaped (comp. p. 229), is decorated with recesses, columns, and badly preserved ceiling-paintings.

From the road on the bank of the Nile a steam-ferry (P.T. 1) crosses the river to the E. bank, and from the landing-place a horse-tram (about ½ hr.) and a motorbus run to **Akhmîm**, a thriving district capital with 23,800 inhab. (6600 Copts), with several Coptic churches and a bazaar. The market on Wed. is much frequented. Akhmîm, which is remarkably free from European influences, stands on the site of *Chemmis* or *Panopolis*, which was the capital of a separate nome. The Egyptians named it *Epu* and also *Khente-Min*, after its god, the ithyphallic harvest-deity *Min* (p. clvii), whence proceed the Coptic *Shmin* and the Arabic Akhmîm. Near an Arab cemetery to the N.E. of the town are limestone blocks forming part of an ancient temple, and not far away is a ruined church with several columns still upright.

Herodotus (ii. 91) distinguishes the citizens of Chemmis as the only Egyptians who favoured Greek customs and relates that they erected a temple to Perseus and worshipped him with Hellenic rites. Strabo mentions the weavers and stone-cutters of Panopolis. — Chemmis still flourished in the Roman period, and its ancient and famous temple was finally completed in the 12th year of Trajan. After Christianity established itself here the vicinity of Panopolis became crowded with monasteries and nunneries. Nestorius, Patriarch of Constantinople, who had been banished to the oasis of Khârga (p. 407) on account of his disbelief in the divine motherhood of the Virgin Mary (p. cxvii), died at Panopolis-Akhmîm (probably in 451). The temples of the 'great town' of Akhmîm were, as Abulfidâ (p. cxxii) and other Arabs relate, among the most important remains of the days of the Pharaohs. But the ruins of these temples are now very scanty.

Extensive ***Necropolises*** have been discovered among the low hills ¾-1 hr. N.E. of Akhmîm. The route thither leads viâ (¾ hr.) *El-Hawâwîsh*, in a hill beyond which are numerous old tombs (now completely destroyed). To the N. and W. is a Christian cemetery, in use from the 5th to the 15th cent., and in the vicinity is a Coptic monastery. The tombs to the N., which are still older, date from the Roman, Ptolemaic, and Egyptian periods. Farther up the mountain are tombs of the 6th Dynasty. — To the S. of Akhmîm is a rock-chapel constructed under King Eye (18th Dyn.).

The railway crosses the *Sohâgîya Canal*, which ends to the N.W. of Manfalûṭ and is intended to convey the water of the rising Nile as far as possible towards the Libyan desert. — 294 M. *Balasfûra*, on the Girgâwîya Canal.

299 M. **El-Manshâh** (p. 238) or *El-Minshâh (Menshah, El-Menshîya)*, a dirty town of fellahin, occupies the site of *Ptolemaïs Hermiou*, which was founded by Ptolemy I. (p. cxi) and described by Strabo as "the largest town in the Thebaïd and not inferior in size to Memphis, with a constitution drawn up in the Hellenic manner." Its Egyptian name was *Psoï*.

About 7½ M. to the W. of El-Manshâh, near the village of *El-Kawâmil*, are large cemeteries of the earliest period.

305½ M. *El-ʿAsîrât (Assirat)*.

312 M. **Girga** *(Guerga)* is a district capital in the province of Girga. A large market is held on Tuesdays. Many of the houses are built of burnt brick and decorated with glazed tiles. There are numerous mosques. Outside the town lies a Roman Catholic monastery (presided over by a Brother of the Holy Sepulchre), which is one of the oldest in Egypt.

The village of *El-Birba*, 3½ M. to the N.W. of Girga, perhaps occupies the site of *This* (Egyptian *Tine*), the capital of the first two dynasties and of a nome of the same name. — About 3½ M. to the W. of Girga, near *Beit Khallâf*, is a large brick maṣṭaba of the time of King Djoser (3rd Dyn.) and often thought to be his tomb (comp. p. 156), excavated by Prof. Garstang. Both here and at the neighbouring village of *Maḥâsna* cemeteries of the beginning of the Ancient Empire have been found. — Upon the E. bank opposite Girga, near *Nagʿed-Deir*, lie several cemeteries, some of them of the prehistoric period, which were excavated by Dr. George A. Reisner in 1901 for the University of California (comp. p. 103). — In the vicinity is the old Coptic monastery of *Deir el-Malâk*, the large cemetery of which is still used by the Christian inhabitants of Girga. The E. mountains, which approach close to the river beyond the village, contain numerous tombs, four of which, at a considerable elevation, belonged to grandees of the ancient This (see above). Their inscriptions and representations are now scarcely visible. — At *Nagʿ el-Mashâyikh (Meshâïkh)*, about 3 M. farther S., are remains of a temple built by Ramses II. and restored by Menephthes (19th Dyn.). Mashâyikh is a village of the Aulâd Yiḥya, on the site of the ancient *Lepidotonpolis*. Above the village are some ancient rock-tombs, the chief of which belonged to Enher-mose, a high-priest of This in the reign of Menephthes.

317½ M. *Bardîs*. — 321½ M. **El-Bályana** *(Baliana)*, a district capital, is the starting-point for the highly interesting excursion to Abydos (see p. 252).

326½ M. *Abu Shûsha (Abou Choucheh)*, the ancient Egyptian *Pe(r)-djōdj*. About 3 M. to the S. lies *Samhûd*, on ancient rubbish-mounds. — 332 M. *Abu Tisht (Abou Tichet)*.

334½ M. *Oasis Junction (Muwâṣlet el-Wâḥât)*, for the oasis railway to El-Khârga (p. 405). A branch to the Nagʿ Ḥammâdi Dam (p. 239) is projected. — Beyond (338½ M.) *Farshûṭ* the railway approaches the Nile.

343½ M. **Nagʿ Ḥammâdi** *(Nag Hamadi)* is a district capital with a large sugar factory. The railway crosses the Nile here (comp. p. 239) by a large iron bridge and remains on the E. bank as far as Luxor and Aswân. For the Nagʿ Ḥammâdi Dam, see p. 239.

347½ M. *Ed-Dâbba*.

A little to the N. of the station, near some large quarries among the E. hills, are the **Tombs of Qaṣr eṣ-Ṣaiyâd** (El-Qaṣr wa'ṣ-Ṣaiyâd, p. 239), belonging to princes of the seventh nome of Upper Egypt, under the 6th Dynasty. The large tomb situated farthest to the left is that of *Tjauti*. It consisted of two chambers, the partition-wall between which has almost wholly disappeared. Its barrel-vaulting was hewn out of the rock. The representations in the interior (ships, figures bearing sacrificial gifts, etc.) have been largely destroyed. — To the S. is the tomb of *Idu*, now comprising only a transverse chamber. In this case also little is left of the inscriptions and reliefs (the deceased catching wildfowl, persons with sacrificial gifts, etc.). — The smaller tombs in the vicinity are uninteresting. Several Coptic inscriptions testify that anchorites found retreats in these tombs during the Christian period (comp. p. clxxxviii).

355 M. **Fâw** *(Fâu, Faou)* is the Coptic *Phbow*, where, at a large monastery founded by Pachomius, the monks of all the convents in Egypt used to assemble twice a year. Pachomius's church is now represented by a number of columns. A little farther S. lay *Tabennēse*, where Pachomius founded the first monastery about A.D. 320.

359 M. **Dishna** *(Deshna, Dechna)*, a district capital, is situated on the ruins of an ancient town. — 363 M. *Es-Samaṭa.* — 367½ M. *Aulâd ʿAmr.* To the right, on the left bank, is seen the ruined temple of Dendera (p. 261).

377½ M. **Qena** (*Kena, Qina:* Hôtel du Nil, in the main street), the ancient *Kainēpolis*, with 27,523 inhab. (1927), is the capital of the province of that name and lies on the E. bank of a canal (sometimes dry), 1 M. from the Nile. The railway station is to the E. of the town, the mudîrîya in a neat square to the S.W. The mosques and Coptic church are not of special interest. Qena has a reputation for its clay vessels, and especially for small porous water-bottles (comp. pp. 119, 239), hundreds of thousands of which are annually exported to Cairo and Alexandria, chiefly by water. Qena is the starting-point of the routes through the Eastern Desert (R. 28; railway to El-Qoṣeir, p. 400, projected).

Railway travellers make the excursion to *Dendera* (p. 261) from Qena in c. 4-5 hrs. (donkey, including ferry, P.T. 15 and gratuity of P.T.5; carriages available only as far as the river). From the station we follow the Shâriʿ Sîdi ʿAbderraḥîm, named after the Muslim local saint ʿAbd er-Raḥîm ibn Ḥajjûn (d. 1196), and pass through the bazaars. We cross the canal near the mudîrîya (see above) and follow the Shâriʿ Gisr el-Ḥimîdât, an avenue of lebbakh-trees (p. lxxvii), passing the prison and the irrigation office on the right, to the Nile (about ½ hr. from the station). The ferry is 5 min. downstream, at the hamlet of *El-Ḥimîdât (El-Ḥamîdât)*, the harbour of Qena. On the W. bank it lands us at the village of *Et-Tarâmsa;* thence the route skirts the river, then strikes off across the fields to the hamlet of *Kafr el-Kahragalla* and the (¾ hr.) temple of Dendera (p. 261). — A shorter route leads W. from Tarâmsa over the fields direct to the N. gate (p. 261) and through the E. side-gate into the temple enclosure.

390 M. **Qifṭ** *(Kift, Quft)*, the ancient *Koptos* (Egyptian *Kebtōyew*), situated beyond the Shanhûrîya Canal. Though now of no importance, this place was in remote antiquity a flourishing commercial town, and down to the Græco-Roman period was one of the chief emporia for the wares of Arabia and India. It stood under the protection of the ithyphallic harvest-god Min (Pan; comp. p. clvii), who was the patron of travellers in the desert. During the great rebellion in Upper Egypt under Diocletian (A.D. 292) Koptos was besieged and destroyed, but it quickly recovered from the blow. Down to the time of the Caliphs it remained a populous trading town. The extant ruins are of no great interest.

At Koptos the great caravan routes to the seaports on the Red Sea quitted the Nile valley. The chief goals of the caravans were the Sinaitic peninsula and the land of *Punt* (probably the modern Somaliland), which yielded incense, ivory, ebony, panther-skins, etc., and was regarded by the Egyptians as a land of fabulous wonders, like India. Other caravans made for the *Wâdi el-Ḥammâmât* in the desert, which produced a hard stone much prized by the Egyptian sculptors (comp. p. 399). At a later period the caravan trade was diverted to the routes viâ Qûṣ and finally to those viâ Qena.

397 M. **Qûṣ** *(Kous)*, a district capital with a busy market (Mon.), occupies the site of the ancient *Apollonopolis Parva*, where the god Haroëris (a form of Horus) was worshipped. According to Abulfidâ (p. cxxii) this town, of which heaps of ruins alone now remain, was second in size only to Fusṭâṭ (Cairo, p. 46) and was the chief centre of the Arabian trade. A few stones with fragmentary inscriptions have been built into the houses of the town. The *El-ʿAmri Mosque*, one of the few interesting Islamic buildings in Upper Egypt, contains a fine pulpit (1155) and a basin formed of a single stone, with the name of Ptolemy Philadelphus upon it.

On the W. bank, nearly opposite Qûṣ, lies *Ṭûkh*, to the N.W. of which, on the edge of the desert, are the ruins of *Ombos* (excavated by Sir Flinders Petrie in 1895), not to be confounded with the town of that name to the S. of Gebel Silsila (p. 374). Seth was the guardian deity of this town, which at a very early period was the capital of Upper Egypt (p. ci). In the neighbourhood are extensive cemeteries dating from the prehistoric age.

Also on the W. bank, to the S. of Ṭûkh, whence it may be reached, is *Naqâda*, a town mainly Coptic in population, picturesquely situated on the river, with post and telegraph offices and a Coptic and a Roman Catholic church.

To the N. of Naqâda a large and much damaged maṣṭaba of brick was discovered by De Morgan in 1897. It dates from the time of Menes, the first historical Egyptian king (p. cii).

On the edge of the desert, between Naqâda and Qamûla (p. 240), lie several Coptic Monasteries, which, except for a few older portions, date from the middle ages (comp. p. cxc). *Deir el-Malâk*, the largest, situated in the Coptic cemetery of Naqâda, is built of crude bricks and contains four connected churches, of which the largest (in the centre) is dedicated to St. Michael. The monastery, which has twenty-eight domes, is now unoccupied, and is used for divine service only on certain festivals by the clergy of Naqâda. To the W. of it is the ruined *Monastery of St. Samuel.* — The other monasteries are those of *Deir Amba Andreas* (or *Deir Abu'l-Lîf*), *Eṣ-Ṣalîb*, and *Amba Shenûda* (in a group to the S.W. of *Danfîq*), *Deir el-Magmaʿ* (with the churches of the Virgin, *El-ʿAdra*, and St. George, *Mâri Girgis;* p. cxc), *Amba Pisentios* (with relics), and *Mâri Buqṭur* (St. Victor), the southernmost and oldest of all, with frescoed domes.

407½ M. *Khuzâm (Khizâm)* has an old necropolis. To the right, on the opposite bank, appear the ruins of Western Thebes, while near the railway are the imposing temples of Karnak.

419 M. **Luxor**, see p. 267.

16. From Cairo to Luxor by the Nile.

460 M. TOURIST STEAMER in seven days (comp. p. 215).

The starting-place of the steamers is above the *Qaṣr en-Nîl Bridge* (p. 86). To the left (E. bank) lie the Semiramis Hotel, the Garden City, and the island of Rôḍa. After passing the ʿAbbâs II. Bridge, we have Old Cairo (p. 113) on the left, beyond which rise the Moqaṭṭam Hills, with the citadel; on the W. bank are Gîza and the Great Pyramids. — To the left (E. bank), farther on, are *El-Maʿâdi*, a pleasant suburb, *Ṭura*, and *El-Maʿṣara* (see pp. 177, 178). Among the hills are the large quarries mentioned on p. 180. Opposite, on the W. bank, rise the pyramids of Abuṣîr, Ṣaqqâra, and Dahshûr. Farther up, to the left, amidst a fine grove of palms, is a Coptic monastery.

The steamer remains for some hours at (14 M.) *Badrashein* (railway station), where donkeys are kept ready for a visit to Ṣaqqâra (see p. 153). Opposite, on the right bank, lies the village of *Ḥelwân* and a little inland is the watering-place of that name (p. 177).

On the W. bank, at (31 M.) *El-ʿAiyâṭ* (railway station, p. 217), are some ancient constructions. On the E. bank lies *Eṣ-Ṣaff* (comp. p. 87), a district capital. Opposite, at *El-Matânya* (p. 217), are the pyramids of *El-Lisht* (p. 217).

Er-Riqqa, on the W. bank, is a starting-point for the excursion to the *Pyramid of Meidûm* (p. 217).

Passing a few islands we reach (56 M.; W. bank) **El-Wâsṭa** (railway station, see p. 217; branch-line to the Faiyûm, p. 203; post and telegraph office at the railway station, $^1/_4$ M. from the Nile).

On the W. bank the mountains recede a little, but on the E. bank their steep and lofty spurs frequently extend down to the river in picturesque forms. None of the Nile villages before Beni Suef need be mentioned. On the E. bank stands the poor Coptic monastery of *Deir Mâr Antonios*, with a dome surmounted by a cross. — On the W. bank lies *Ishmant* (p. 218), and about 2 M. inland is *Bûsh* (railway station, p. 218). On the E. bank, the village of *Bayâḍ en-Naṣâra (Biâḍ)*, hidden by palm-trees, with a white Coptic church of many domes. To the monasteries of St. Anthony and St. Paul, see p. 218.

71$^1/_2$ M. (W. bank) **Beni Suef** (railway station, see p. 218).

The next villages are *Tizmant* and *El-Ḥalâbîya*, picturesquely situated among palms on the W. bank, and *Beni Sulîmân*, on the E. bank. As far as Minya (p. 220) the space between the E. bank and the hills remains narrow, the limestone rocks frequently abutting on the river in unbroken walls or rounded bluffs. The fertile alluvial tract on the W. side, however, 10-12 M. in width, is thickly populated and carefully cultivated, exhibiting in profusion all the cereals that grow on the Nile, date-palms, cotton, and sugar-cane. Cotton-ginning factories abound. Lofty chimneys and steam machinery impart a very modern industrial air to the ancient land of the Pharaohs.

The boat passes several large islands. On the W. bank lie *El-Barânqa* and *Biba*, the latter a railway station (p. 218). The bell-tower of the Coptic church, surmounted by a cross, is visible from afar. On a promontory of the E. bank, opposite Biba, is the tomb of a sheikh; in the river lies the *Gezîret el-Biba*, an island of some size. The channel now contracts and the picturesque hills on the E. approach the river. Numerous islets. — 95 M. *El-Fashn* (railway station, p. 219), on the W. bank, has a white church with two towers and is $1^1/_2$ M. from the river. Above Fashn are the island and village (E. bank) of *El-Ḥîba*, with the great brick walls of the ancient town (p. 219).

On the W. bank lies *El-Fant* (railway station, p. 219), and on the E. bank are the palm-shaded villages of *Aulâd esh-Sheikh* and *Qarâra* (p. 219). The *Gebel esh-Sheikh Embârak* and the *Gebel Qarâra* approach the E. bank.

$108^1/_2$ M. (W. bank) **Maghâgha** (railway station, p. 219).

The Nile channel is very wide here (*Gezîret Shârûna* and other islands); farther on both banks are flat. — Then (E. bank) *Shârûna* (p. 219). — *Beni Mazâr* (W. bank) has a railway station (p. 219).

125 M. *Esh-Sheikh Faḍl*, a village close to the E. bank, with a large sugar factory. Close by is the necropolis of the ancient Kynopolis (p. 219).

Farther on, on the W. bank, $1^3/_4$ M. from the river, is *Maṭâi* (railway station, p. 220). — Short of ($133^1/_2$ M.; W. bank) *Qulûṣna* (railway station, p. 220) the Nile forms the large island of *Es-Sirîrîya*. Opposite (E. bank) lies the village of *Es-Sirîrîya*. To the N. and S. are ancient limestone quarries, among which is (to the S.) a small rock-chapel, built under Menephthes (p. cvii) and dedicated to Hathor, with reliefs of funeral offerings. On one of the rocks is a representation of Ramses III. between Hathor and another deity.

On the W. bank lies the railway station of *Samâlûṭ* (p. 220). A little farther S., at the mouth of a side-valley on the E. bank, rise the steep rocky sides of the **Gebel eṭ-Ṭeir** ('bird mountain'), with a flat top bearing the Coptic convent of *Deir Gebel eṭ-Ṭeir*, known also as *Deir el-Baqara* or *Deir el-ʿAdra* ('Convent of the Virgin'). Visitors reach the top of the hill by a steep stone staircase. The convent, which consists of a group of miserable huts, occupied not only by monks but also by laymen with their wives and children, is surrounded by a wall of hewn stone, erected in the Roman period. The foundation of the church is ascribed to the Empress Helena (p. cxvi); below it is a cave in which the Holy Family is believed to have rested in the Flight into Egypt. The sanctuary is hewn in the solid rock and possesses a gate, now half-buried, adorned with Byzantine ornamentation.

A legend, recorded by El-Maqrîzi (1364-1442), relates that on the saint's day of the convent all the buqîr birds assembled here and thrust their bills, one after the other, into a cleft of the rock until one died. These birds are described as being black and white, with a black neck ringed near the head. The convent is named also *Deir el-Buqîr* after them.

On the E. bank, $^1/_2$ hr. farther on, is the village of *Ṭihna* (p. 220). — 157 M. (W. bank) **El-Minya,** see p. 220.

167 M. **Beniḥasan,** with its rock-tombs, see p. 240.

To the S. of Beniḥasan, on the E. bank, are some rock-tombs dating from the end of the Ancient Empire. On the E. bank the desert extends down to the river; on the W. bank is the picturesque village of *Qalandûl.*

177 M. (W. bank) **Er-Rôḍa** (railway station, p. 221).

On the E. bank, opposite Rôḍa, are the village of *Esh-Sheikh ʿIbâda* (or *ʿAbâda*) and the ruins of *Antinoupolis* (p. 221).

On the W. bank (188 M.), 1 M. from the Nile, is the town of **Mallawi** (railway station, p. 222).

Farther on, on the E. bank, at the foot of the hill crowned with the tomb of Sheikh Saʿîd lies the small settlement of *Esh-Sheikh Saʿîd,* among palms, with tombs of the Ancient Empire, belonging to princes and officials of the Hare Nome (p. 224). The tombs (comp. pp. 224, clxxxviii) are clearly seen from the river.

We next reach the ruins of **Tell el-ʿAmârna,** on the E. bank (p. 245). The steamer stops at *Et-Tell (Tell Beni ʿImrân).* — Farther on, on the E. bank, is (193 M.) *El-Ḥâwaṭa esh-Sharqîya.* In the vicinity are several rock-inscriptions, defining the boundaries of the sacred territory of the sun-city of Amenophis IV. (comp. p. 245).

Beyond *Dairûṭ* (on the W. bank; railway station, p. 224) the Eastern mountains, rising in precipitous rocky walls, approach the river. Swallows, ducks, and other birds inhabit the caves in the porous rock on the banks. The cliffs of this part of the Nile are known as (112 M.) **Gebel Abu Fôda.** Violent winds and numerous sandbanks often render navigation difficult and dangerous. On the E. bank is the Coptic monastery of *Deir el-Quṣeir,* near which are some ancient rock-tombs (p. 225).

On the W. bank, 3 M. from the river, is *El-Qûṣîya* (p. 225). — $223^1/_2$ M. **Manfalûṭ** (railway station, p. 225) lies on the W. bank close to the river, which must have made great encroachments here since the end of the 18th century. Between Manfalûṭ and Asyûṭ (27 M. by river, only 17 M. by land) the Nile makes many curves.

We next observe *Shiqilqîl,* on the E. bank, $1^1/_4$ M. to the S. of *El-Maʿâbda* (p. 225); then *El-Ḥawâtka,* a pretty village among palms, on the W. bank, and *Beni Muḥammed,* on the E. bank. The mountains to the N. (E. bank) recede farther from the river, leaving a broad strip of fertile land at their feet. Close to the mountains lie *ʿArab el-ʿAṭîyât* and *Deir el-Gabrâwi* (p. 225).

Above Beni Muḥammed the Nile makes several great bends and is divided into two arms by the large island of *Gezîret Bahîg.* On the E. arm lies (233 M.) **Abnûb,** a district capital, with a large Coptic population and fine palm-groves.

The foot-hills of the Libyan chain on the W. bank now approach

the river, which is here, near the village of *El-Wilîdîya* (*El-Walîdîya*; W. bank), bridled by the **Asyûṭ Barrage,** an imposing work intended to regulate the amount of water in the Ibrâhîmîya Canal, which irrigates the provinces of Asyûṭ, Minya, and Beni Suef. The dam, which is 910 yds. long and 41 ft. high, was constructed in 1898-1902 by John Aird & Co. (p. 396) from the original design of Sir William Willcocks and plans by Sir Benjamin Baker (d. 1907) and Sir William Garstin (d. 1925). It consists of thirteen sections, the first of which (W.) has three arches and a lock, while the others have nine arches each. Each opening (111 in all) can be shut by an iron door. The dam is crossed by a carriage-road. The steamer passes through the W. lock. — Immediately above the dam, on the W. bank, are the sluice-bridge and the mouth of the *Ibrâhîmîya Canal.* Close by are the neat houses and pretty gardens of the officials.

250 M. **Asyûṭ** (railway station, p. 226). We land at the Shâriʿ Fu'âd el-Auwal (p. 227), the shady avenue on the bank of the Nile, which is lined with handsome houses.

From Asyûṭ the voyage to Sohâg leads through an extremely fertile district. Well-tilled fields, broader on the W. than on the E., adjoin both banks of the river, and are shaded by fine palms and Nile acacias (p. lxxviii), especially near the villages. Here, as in most of Egypt, large quantities of pigeons are kept by the peasants, chiefly for the sake of their droppings, which they use to manure their gardens (p. lxxiii), although the pigeons really consume more than they produce. Most are of the common grey species and attain a considerable size, but many pretty little reddish-grey turtle-doves are seen also. Large pigeon-houses, not unlike forts or pylons, and built of unbaked bricks, clay, and pottery, are visible everywhere in Upper Egypt.

Nearly opposite Asyûṭ lies the village of *El-Wâsṭa.* On the E. bank the next villages are *Biṣra (Boṣra)*, near the Coptic monastery of *Deir Biṣra*, and *El-Ghuraiyib*, to the E. of which, in the *Gebel Rukhâm*, is an alabaster quarry. On the W. bank are *Esh-Shaghaba* and *El-Muṭîʿa* (railway station, p. 229).

264¾ M. (W. bank) **Abu Tig** (railway station, p. 229), with a small harbour filled with Nile boats.

Near the E. bank is *El-Badâri*, a district capital (p. 229); on the W. bank then follow the railway stations of (271 M.) *Ṣidfa* and (277 M.) *Ṭima.*

281 M. *Qâw Gharb* or *Qâw el-Kebîr* (W. bank) is situated opposite the fertile, crescent-shaped plain of **Qâw** *(Qâu, Gau)*, with its girdle of hills. At the village of *El-Hammâmîya*, which lies on the verge of the desert, by the Khizindârîya Canal (p. 238), are three rock-tombs of high officials of the beginning of the 5th Dyn., with reliefs. We may visit (½ hr. S.E.) three large rock-vaults, laid out in terraces, of princes of the 10th or Aphroditopolis nome of the Middle Empire and the extensive necropolises of Antæopolis, with tombs

of later date. Not far off are quarries with demotic inscriptions; in one of them are two pillars bearing remarkable paintings of the god Antæus and the goddess Nephthys. The name *Qâw* recalls the ancient Egyptian name of the town *Tu-Kow* (Coptic *Tkow*); the Greeks named it *Antaeopolis*, after Antæus, whom they identified with the deity worshipped here.

According to the myth, Antæus was a Libyan king of immense strength, who was in the habit of wrestling with all visitors to his dominions and of slaying those whom he vanquished, in order to build a temple to his father Poseidon with their skulls. Heracles came to try conclusions with him and, after overthrowing him in a wrestling match, slew him. — According to Diodorus (p. 324) the final struggle betwixt Horus and Seth took place here (comp. p. 309). In the Roman period Antæopolis was the capital of the Antæopolitan nome. The last remains of a temple, dedicated here by Philometor (p. cxii) to Antæus and restored by Marcus Aurelius and Lucius Verus (A.D. 164), were swept away by the Nile in 1821.

On the W. bank is the railway station of *Mishṭa* (p. 229); on the E. bank, to the S. of the village of *En-Nawâwra*, is the lock-bridge near which the *Khizindârîya Canal* diverges N. The hills of the *Gebel esh-Sheikh el-Harîdi*, with ancient quarries and inscriptions hewn in the rock, approach close to the river.

290 M. *Sâhil Tahṭa*, on the W. bank, is the harbour for the town of *Tahṭa* (p. 229), situated 2 M. inland.

The next railway stations are (293 M.) *Eṣ-Sawâm'a Gharb*, (297½ M.) *El-Marâgha*, and (305 M.) *Shandawîl*, all on the W. bank (comp. p. 229). — On the E. bank of the Nile, which here forms several islands, are some grottoes without inscriptions.

316¼ M. (W. bank) **Sohâg**, a provincial capital and railway station (p. 229). — The Nile makes a wide bend towards the N.E. On the E. bank lies *Akhmîm*, see p. 230.

We next see, close to the E. bank, the conspicuous convent-village of *Deir el-Hadîd*, resembling a fortress. About 100 men, women, and children occupy the convent. The church has aisles and cupolas.

331¼ M. (W. bank) **El-Manshâh**, a railway station (p. 230).

Beside the village of *El-Aḥâiwa*, on the E. bank, are burial places of the prehistoric period and the New Empire. On the hill, close to a sheikh's tomb, are the ruins of an Egyptian brick fortress. — On the W. bank is the village of *El-Aḥâiwa Gharb*.

The *Gebel Ṭûkh* hills, on the E. bank, approach close to the stream. Extensive quarries (with Greek, Latin, and demotic inscriptions) exist here, especially near *Sheikh Mûsa*; these yielded building material for Ptolemaïs (p. 230). — Where the mountains recede a little, opposite Girga, lies the village of *Naġ' ed-Deir* (p. 231). At a lock-bridge on the W. bank diverges the *Girgâwîya Canal*, which joins the *Sohâgîya Canal* at Sohâg.

343 M. (W. bank) **Girga**, a railway station (p. 231).

On the E. bank expands a fertile plain with numerous water-

raising machines. — 354 M. **El-Balyana,** on the W. bank, with a railway station (p. 231), is the starting-point for the interesting visit to Abydos (p. 252).

Above Balyana the course of the Nile lies almost due E. and W. The dûm-palm becomes more and more common and increases in size and beauty as we travel southwards (comp. p. lxxviii). At *Abu Shûsha* (railway station, p. 231) the river makes a wide bend to the N. The hills *(Gebel eṭ-Ṭârif)* approach close to the river.

382 M. **Nagʿ Ḥammâdi,** on the W. bank, is a railway station (p. 231). The large railway-bridge, used also by vehicles and foot-passengers, crossing the river here is opened at certain hours for the passage of ships.

The **Nagʿ Ḥammâdi Dam**, begun in 1928 and to be completed by 1930, is being constructed across the Nile here by Sir John Jackson Ltd., from the designs of A. B. Buckley. The total estimated cost is £E 2,000,000, and the barrage will have a hundred sluices, a navigation lock, and a swing-bridge. Two canals are to be constructed to irrigate an area of 622,800 acres in the province of Girga, to the N. This is the last of the great Egyptian irrigation works on the main stream of the Nile (comp. p. lxviii).

385¼ M. **Hiw** *(Heou)* or **Hû** (W. bank), at one of the sharpest bends in the stream, is a large fellahin village. It was the home of Sheikh Selîm (Sìdi Silîm), who died in 1891, after sitting stark naked for the greater part of his long life on the bank of the Nile at the spot now marked by his tomb a little above the village. He was deemed to possess great powers in helping navigation. In the neighbourhood of Hiw are the scanty ruins of the ancient *Diospolis Parva*, with large prehistoric burial-places.

388¼ M. *El-Qaṣr* (*El-Qaṣr wa's-Ṣaiyâd;* E. bank) is probably the ancient *Chenoboskion.* A little to the N. of the village are the high white walls enclosing the *Monastery of St. George (Deir Mâri Girgis).* — To the N. of the railway station of *Ed-Dâbba*, in the vicinity, are ancient rock-tombs (p. 231).

Farther on we pass a fine mountain mass (N.), especially imposing by afternoon light, and see several thriving villages close to the river: on the E. bank, to the left (N.), *Esh-Shînîya* (*El-Chaʿnieh*) and *El-Yâsînîya;* on the W. bank, to the right (S.), *Er-Raʾîsîya.* The mountains on the N. recede, leaving a wide fertile area at their base.

397½ M. *Fâw* (E. bank), a railway station (p. 232).

401½ M. *Dishna* (E. bank), another railway station (p. 232). — The village of *Dendera* on the left bank gave its name to the great temple of the Ptolemies (p. 261).

417 M. **Qena** (E. bank), also with a railway station (p. 232).

The tourist steamers moor at the W. bank, for the visit to **Dendera** (p. 261 seqq.).

Beyond Qena the river turns S. and we pass several islands. On the W. bank lies the village of *El-Ballâṣ*, with clay deposits from which most of the Qena pottery is made (see p. 232). Balâlîṣ (pl. of ballâṣ, named after the village), qúlal (p. 119), and other kinds

of jars lie on the banks awaiting shipment. This village is situated in the district known to the Greeks as *Typhonia* ('dedicated to Typhon', i.e. Seth).

429¼ M. *Bârûd* (E. bank). — To the E., 1½ M. inland, lies **Qifṭ** (p. 232). On the W. bank is the village of *Ṭûkh* (p. 233). *El-Ḥilla* (E. bank) is the harbour for **Qûṣ** (p. 233). Opposite lies (440 M.) *Naqâda* (p. 233). The Nile forms the island of *Miṭeira*; on the E. bank is the village of *Gezîret Miṭeira*. On the W. bank is *Danfîq* (p. 233). — At *Shanhûr (Chanhour)*, which lies a little inland from the E. bank, 1 hr. S. of Qûṣ, are the ruins of a small temple of Isis, of the Roman period. The Shanhûrîya Canal, which is named after the village, runs N. to Qena.

Khuzâm (E. bank; railway station, p. 233). — 449½ M. (W. bank) *Qamûla*, formerly with plantations of sugar-cane, was, during the rebellion of Sheikh Aḥmad in 1824, the residence of 'Ali Kâshif Abu Ṭarbûsh, who defended it against the insurgents.

On the left bank rise high limestone hills, presenting precipitous sides to the river, from which, however, they are separated by a strip of fertile land. The right bank is flatter, and the E. hills retreat farther into the distance. Before reaching the point where the W. chain projects a long curved mass of rock towards the river, we see to the left first the great obelisk, then the pylons of the temple of Karnak, half-concealed by palm-trees. When we clear the abrupt profile of the W. cliffs and new formations are visible at its foot, we may catch a distant view of Luxor towards the S.E. The columns of the temple of Medamût (p. 297) are seen among the palms to the left of the railway. None of the buildings on the W. bank are visible until the steamer has ascended as high as Karnak; then first the Colossi of Memnon and afterwards the Ramesseum and the Temple of Deir el-Baḥari come into view. As we gradually approach Luxor, we distinguish the flags flying above the consulates. The Winter Palace Hotel and the castellated villa of the widow of Sultan Ḥusein Kâmil (p. cxxx) are conspicuous in the background.

460 M. **Luxor** (p. 267) lies on the E. bank. The steamer berths close to the colonnades of the temple (comp. Pl. A 3, 4).

17. Beniḥasan.

Donkeys (with good saddles) are in waiting at the landing-place of the Steamers (p. 236), for the excursion to the *Speos Artemidos* and the *Rock Tombs* (there and back 3-4 hrs.). — For travellers by Railway the most convenient station is *Minya* (p. 220), whence we reach Beniḥasan by motor-car (there and back £E 1) or by the cheap motorbus to Abu Qurqâṣ (p. 221) and ferry across the Nile.

The rock-tombs of Beniḥasan owe their name to an Arab tribe which settled in several villages (now deserted) in the valley and still occupies the village of Beniḥaṣan esh-Shurûq. — The route from the landing-place to the rock-temple (½ hr.'s ride) descends

the river at first, then strikes off to the right towards the desert along an embankment leading through fields. In the vicinity is the cats' graveyard, in which the cats sacred to Pekhet, patron goddess of this region, were interred. Farther S.E. we reach a wâdi or ravine, from the mouth of which a cemetery of the 22nd-25th Dyn. stretches toward the plain. In the valley are several quarries of ancient date, and on the right (S.) side of the ravine, about 600 paces from its mouth, lies the temple.

The rock-temple of the goddess Pekhet, called **Speos Artémidos** ('Grotto of Artemis') by the Greeks, is known to the Arabs as *Iṣṭabl 'Antar* ('Antar's stable'), after an ancient Beduin hero (comp. p. xxv). It consists of a vestibule and of an inner chamber connected with the vestibule by a short corridor. It was built in the joint reign of Queen Hatshepsut and King Thutmosis III. (p. cv); the latter afterwards erased the names and representations of his sister (comp. p. 317), and Sethos I. (19th Dyn.) inserted his own names in the blanks.

Over the *Entrance* to the temple is a long inscription in praise of the reign of Hatshepsut. Of the eight pillars which supported the VESTIBULE only three now remain; these bear on their sides the names of Thutmosis III. and Sethos I. (comp. above). The fronts seem to have been adorned with sistra (unfinished). *Rear Wall.* To the left of the door, Sethos I. between Amon-Rē (enthroned) and the lion-headed Pekhet; Thoth delivering a speech to the nine great gods of Karnak (comp. p. cxlviii) and to the gods of Upper and Lower Egypt. To the right of the door are three reliefs: Sethos sacrificing to Pekhet; Sethos receiving from Pekhet the hieroglyphics of the word 'life', hanging from two sceptres; Sethos blessed by Thoth. To the left in the CORRIDOR are a long inscription of Sethos I. and a representation of the king offering wine to Pekhet; to the right, he offers her a cynocephalus. In the rear wall of the INNER CHAMBER is a niche intended for a statue of the goddess.

To the W. (right) is a second grotto, on the outside of which, at the entrance, are the cartouches of *Alexander II.*, son of Roxana (p. cxi), and six small scenes representing the king in the company of the gods. The interior, which was supported by pillars, is now in ruins; perhaps it was never completed. In the vicinity are several rock-tombs of the New Empire, in the form of rectangular chambers, with deep shafts.

We now return to the mouth of the desert ravine and proceed N., passing the ruins of *Beniḥasan el-Qadîm* ('Old Beniḥasan'). In $^1/_2$ hr. we reach a ruined tower, whence the path ascends the hill-slope to the tombs.

The ***Rock Tombs of Beniḥasan** or **Beni Ḥasan** ($^1/_2$ hr.'s ride direct from the landing-place) were constructed during the Middle Empire by the princes and grandees of the town of *Monet-Khufu* ('Nurse of Khufu'), and rank among the most interesting monuments in all Egypt, not only on account of their remarkable architectural features, but also for their inscriptions and representations of scenes from the domestic life of the early Egyptians. The latter are painted in bright colours upon stucco, but many of them are so injured or faded that the subjects are difficult to make out.

The tombs of Benihasan, thirty-nine in all, are arranged in a row in the rocks. The best examples are protected by iron doors. Travellers whose time is limited may content themselves with a visit to the four largest and most important tombs (Nos. 17, 15, 3, 2). For remarks on the construction of the tombs, see pp. clxxviii, clxxix.

The path that ascends to the tombs brings us first to No. 32. Here we turn to the N. (left) and proceed to *Tomb 17, which belonged to **Kheti**, nomarch of the 16th or Antelope Nome (11th Dyn.). The façade is simple. We enter the *Rock Chamber*, the roof of which was originally borne by six lotus-columns with bud-capitals, though only two with the original colouring are now standing. The wall-paintings are still in good condition. *Left Wall (N.).* In the top rows is a hunt in the desert, in the lower rows, male and female dancers, the statue of the deceased being borne to its appointed place, carpenters, etc. *Rear Wall (E.).* Above are wrestlers in various attitudes; below, military scenes and an attack on a fortress. *Right Wall (S.).* From left to right: the deceased and his wife; the deceased accompanied by his fan-bearer, sandal-bearer, two dwarfs, etc.; the deceased receiving offerings (notice the barn on the right).

Farther N., at the end of an ancient path ascending from the plain, is *Tomb 15, belonging to **Beket** (or *Baket*), father of Kheti and nomarch of the Antelope Nome (11th Dyn.). The two columns which supported the roof of the rectangular chamber have been destroyed. In the S.E. angle is a small niche (serdâb; p. clxxvi). *Left Wall (N.).* Above, hunting in the desert; barber, washermen, painters, etc. Below, the deceased and his wife, with four rows of women spinning and weaving, female dancers, girls playing at ball; herdsmen bringing animals for sacrifice to the dead; goldsmiths; fishing; various birds, with their names inscribed beside them. *Rear Wall (E.).* Above, wrestlers; below, military scenes (resembling those in Tomb 17). *Right Wall (S.).* The deceased, in front of whom, in several rows, are men drawing a shrine containing a statue of the dead; in front are female dancers and attendants bearing ornaments, etc., for the statue; peasants bringing their flocks and herds; peasants forcibly brought to testify as to taxes, while scribes note down the amounts; potters with wheels; men carrying slaughtered birds; men gambling.

Tomb 3 is that of **Khnemhotep**, the son of Neheri, a scion of a princely family with hereditary jurisdiction over the Antelope Nome and over the E. districts, the capital of which was Monet-Khufu. Khnemhotep was invested by King Amenemmēs II. (p. civ) with the latter districts and married a daughter of the governor of the Dog Nome (Kynopolis, p. 219), which was inherited by a son of this marriage in the reign of Sesostris II.

The Porch, which formerly stood behind an open court, is borne by two sixteen-sided columns (p. clxv) tapering towards the top. The cornice projects considerably above the architrave and is ostensibly supported by fine laths, hewn, like all the rest of the

structure, out of the living rock. The resemblance of these laths to the mutules of the Doric order is worthy of mention.

The MAIN CHAMBER was divided by two pairs of columns into three slightly vaulted sections. The scenes and inscriptions here are much faded and therefore difficult to distinguish. At the foot of the walls is a long inscription cut in the rock, in vertical lines of a greenish colour, $2^1/_2$ ft. high, containing the foregoing interesting excerpt from Egyptian provincial history. In 1890 the royal names were cut out of the rock by some vandal hand.

Entrance Wall (W.). Over the door we see the statue of the deceased being transported to the temple, preceded by female dancers in curious attitudes; below is the deceased, watching carpenters at work. To the *Left (N.)* of the door is the estate office of the deceased, with servants weighing silver, measuring grain, and bringing corn into the barns, while scribes seated in a colonnaded hall register the amounts. The next two rows show the operations of breaking up the ground, ploughing, harvesting, and threshing with cattle. In the fourth row are Nile boats, bearing the mummy of the deceased to Abydos (the grave of Osiris; comp. p. 253). In the fifth row is a representation of the vintage and of the gathering of figs and growing of vegetables. The cattle in the water and the fishing scene (at the foot) depict life by the river. — *North Wall* (to the left on entering). At the top is the deceased hunting in the desert. Below, to the right, he is represented on a large scale inspecting various proceedings in his province. In the third row from the top two of his officials introduce to him a *Caravan of Asiatics*, including men, women, and children, clad in gaily coloured foreign garments and accompanied by their goats and asses. The sharply cut features, hooked noses, and pointed beards of these strangers unmistakably proclaim their Semitic nationality. The inscription describes them as thirty-seven Amu (i.e. Semitic Beduin) bringing eye-paint to the governor of the province. Khnemhotep's secretary hands him a list of the visitors. The lowest rows depict the cattle and poultry of the deceased. — *Rear Wall* (*E;* partly indistinguishable). To the left the deceased appears with his wife in a boat, hunting waterfowl with a throw-stick. All manner of birds fly about and nest in the thicket of reeds; in the water are fish, a crocodile, and a hippopotamus; below is a fishing scene. To the right is a companion picture, showing the deceased in a canoe transfixing two fish with a double-pronged spear. In the centre is a recess, once containing a seated figure of the deceased. Above this door is the deceased catching birds with a net. — *South Wall* (to the right). To the left the deceased is seated at table, with all kinds of sacrificial gifts heaped before him. To the right are processions of servants and priests bringing gifts for the dead. In the lowest rows are cattle, gazelles, antelopes, and poultry, brought to be sacrificed, and the slaughtering and cutting up of the sacrificial animals. — *Entrance*

Wall (to the right, i.e. S. of the door). In the top row are men washing; below, potters, men felling a palm, the deceased in a litter inspecting his ship-carpenters. In the third row are two ships carrying the family of the deceased to the funeral festival at Abydos. In the fourth row are women engaged in spinning and weaving, and bakers. The lowest row contains men constructing a shrine, a sculptor polishing a statue, etc.

In front of Tomb 3 is an ancient path descending to the plain, and another begins opposite *Tomb 2, which belonged to **Ameni-em-hēt**, or *Ameni*, also a nomarch of the Antelope Nome in the reign of Sesostris I. (p. civ). In the Porch are two octagonal columns, bearing a flat vault hewn out of the rock. On the door-posts and lintel are inscribed the prayers for the dead and the titles of Ameni. Inside the door, to the right and left, is a long inscription dated in the 43rd year of Sesostris I., extolling the deeds of Ameni in several military campaigns and the benefits conferred by him upon his province. — Four sixteen-sided columns, with shallow fluting (so-called Proto-Doric columns, p. clxiv), support the roof of the Main Chamber, which has three sections. The wall-paintings closely resemble those in the tomb of Khnemhotep (p. 242). On the *Entrance Wall*, to the left (N.), are shoemakers, carpenters, goldsmiths, potters, and other craftsmen, and agricultural scenes. *Left Wall (N.).* At the top, hunting in the desert; in the second row, the transportation of the statue and ceremonial dances; below, to the right, the deceased receiving tribute from his estates; in the two lowest rows, Ameni's estate office. *Rear Wall.* Wrestlers and military scenes; in the lower row, the mummy being conveyed to the sacred tomb at Abydos (comp. p. 253). In the rear wall opens a recess containing the statues (much dilapidated) of the deceased, his wife Hetpet, and his mother. *Right Wall (S.).* To the left the deceased is seated at table with sacrificial gifts heaped before him; priests and servants bring food and other offerings for the dead; below is seen the slaughtering and cutting up of the sacrificial animals. To the right is Hetpet, wife of Ameni, likewise seated at table and receiving sacrificial gifts.

If time permit, the following tombs also should be visited: Tomb 4, that of *Khnemhotep*, son of the Khnemhotep buried in Tomb 3. In the porch stands a Proto-Doric column (p. clxiv); the tomb-chamber was unfinished. — Tomb 5, with two pillars, unfinished. — Tomb 14, that of *Khnemhotep*, a nomarch under Amenemmēs I. (p. civ). In the tomb-chamber were two plant-columns (unfortunately broken); the wall-paintings are interesting but sadly faded. On the rear wall appear soldiers and a caravan of Libyans, with their wives and children and herds, who visited the province of the deceased; the men are distinguished by the ostrich-feathers in their hair, the women carry their children in baskets on their backs. — Tomb 18, though unfinished, is interesting, as the process of hollowing out the tomb-chamber may be traced. The pavement in the front of the chamber is not fully excavated; and at the back are ten clustered columns with bud-capitals, of which five (still unfinished) remain. — Tomb 21, that of *Nakht*, nomarch of the Antelope Nome under the 12th Dyn., resembles No. 15 (p. 242) in its arrangement. — Tomb 23, that of *Neternakht*, nomarch

of the E. districts, with uninteresting wall-paintings; on the E. wall is a Coptic inscription. — TOMB 27, that of *Remushenti*, nomarch of the Antelope Nome. — TOMB 28, with two lotus-columns, was converted into a church in the Christian period (comp. p. clxxxviii). — TOMB 29, that of *Beket*, nomarch of the Antelope Nome. The doors opening into the adjoining Tombs 28 and 30 were made by the Copts. The wall-paintings are in comparatively good preservation, but offer no novel point of interest: the dwarfs following the deceased, on the W. half of the S. wall, and the wrestling scenes, on the N. wall, may be mentioned. — TOMB 33, that of *Beket*, prince of the Antelope Nome, son of the Beket interred in No. 29; several wall-paintings. — TOMBS 34-39 were left unfinished.

On the slope below the tombs of the grandees are numerous smaller tombs of the Middle Empire in which officials and persons of lower rank were interred.

We descend the path from Tomb 2, and a ride of 1/2 hr., upstream, by the edge of the cultivated ground, brings us back to the landing-place (p. 240).

18. Tell el-ʿAmârna.

The ruins are visited either by motor-car from Mallawi (p. 222) or by RAILWAY, which we leave at the station of *Deir Mawâs* (p. 224). Thence we walk or ride viâ the village of *Beni ʿImrân* to the (20 min.) bank of the Nile, across which we ferry (P.T. 5) to *Et-Tell (Tell Beni ʿImrân)*, where the keeper of the N. tombs lives. The keeper of the S. tombs lives at Ḥâgg Qandîl. Donkey P.T. 15-20.

The name *Tell el-ʿAmârna* (or better *El-ʿAmârna*), derived from a Beduin tribe, is given to the extensive ruins and rock-tombs which lie near the villages of *El-Ḥâgg Qandîl* on the S. and *Et-Tell (Tell Beni ʿImrân)* on the N., and form the last relics of the ancient royal city of *Ekhet-Aton*, 'the horizon of the sun'. The extensive excavations carried on here before the war by the German Orient Society are being continued by the Egypt Exploration Society (formerly Egypt Exploration Fund).

When Amenophis IV. (p. cv) became converted to the exclusive worship of the sun and abjured the ancient gods, he quitted Thebes, the capital until that time, and withdrew with his court to a new sacred spot. This was situated in the Hermopolitan Nome in Upper Egypt, on both banks of the Nile, and its boundaries may be traced to this day by fourteen inscriptions chiselled on the rocks near El-Ḥáwaṭa (p. 236), at the N. and S. groups of tombs, at Sheikh Saʿîd (all on the E. bank), and near Tûna el-Gebel, Dirwa, and Gilda (W. bank). The new royal residence-town was founded on the E. bank and speedily prospered. Temples and palaces sprang up, beside the imposing royal abode arose the dwellings of the nobles, and lordly tombs were prepared for the king and his favourites in the hills to the east. But after the death of Amenophis the ancient religion once more obtained the upper hand, his second successor Tutankhamûn (p. 315) transferred the court again to Thebes, and the new town rapidly decayed. Its life had not lasted for more than thirty years, and the site upon which it stood was never again

occupied. Owing to this circumstance the ancient streets and ground-plans have remained to this day and may be traced with little trouble (comp. below). The religious revolution under Amenophis IV. was accompanied by a revolution in art. The artists who worked in his reign, probably feeling themselves more independent of ancient traditions, attempted to lend their creations a more natural expression. At first, however, they fell into exaggeration, as, for example, in the representations of the lean form of the king. The tombs of El-ʿAmârna contain the best examples of this realistic tendency and are therefore of great importance in the history of art.

About $^1/_4$ hr. from Cook's landing-place are the ruins of the city and *Palace of Amenophis IV.* at Et-Tell. The palace was once situated within the precincts of a great temple. Its fine stucco pavements, discovered by Sir Flinders Petrie in 1891-92, were ruthlessly destroyed in 1912 (fragments in the Cairo Museum, pp. 94, 98). The numerous remains of brick pillars seen to the S. of the palace perhaps belonged to the royal vineyards. — To the E. lay the *Archives*, in which in 1888 the celebrated clay tablets of Tell el-ʿAmârna with cuneiform inscriptions were found (now in the British Museum and the museums of Berlin and Cairo); these are letters written to Kings Amenophis III. and IV. by Babylonian and other kings of W. Asia and by Syrian and Phœnician vassals, and are of the greatest historical value.

To the N. of Et-Tell was a second *Palace* dating from the end of Amenophis IV.'s reign, excavated in 1923-25 by the Egypt Exploration Society. — The *Sikket es-Sultân*, a road leading S. from Et-Tell to Ḥâgg Qandîl, brings us to the excavated portions of the ancient city, which was intersected by three main streets running N. and S. (the westernmost being the Sikket es-Sulṭân) and by several side-streets. The ground-plans of many of the houses can still be made out. Perhaps the most complete so far excavated is that of the house Q 44 I, a typical example of the dwelling of a high official (comp. the ground-plan on p. clxix). It lies about one-third of the way between the palace of Et-Tell and Ḥâgg Qandîl. The house of the *Vizier Nakht* (W. of the society's offices), that of the *General Ramose*, and that of the *Sculptor Dhutmose*, with workshops in which numerous excellent sculptures were found (now in the Berlin and Cairo museums), are also interesting. — There are remains of a *Temple* at the S.W. end of Ḥâgg Qandîl, but they are still partly covered by houses and a sheikh's tomb. — At El-Ḥáwaṭa (p. 236), $1^1/_4$ M. to the S.W. of Ḥâgg Qandîl, are the ruins of a *Summer Palace* (called Maru-Aton) of Amenophis IV.

From the great palace of Amenophis IV. (see above) we proceed N.E., passing the site of the *Great Temple*, and in $^3/_4$ hr. we reach the **North Group of Tombs.**

The rock-tombs of Tell el-ʿAmârna are essentially the same in point of structure as the tombs of the 18th Dyn. at Thebes (p. 328). Each is immediately preceded by a *Forecourt*, which was generally surrounded by a brick wall. Thence a wide door admits to the *Hall*, the roof of which is in many cases supported by columns. The *Chamber* containing the statue of the deceased is next reached, either by another door, or by a corridor which frequently leads first to a narrow anteroom. Many of the tombs are unfinished, in consequence of the death of Amenophis IV. and the subsequent return of the court to Thebes. The tombs are marked with black numbers (1-25), running from N. to S.

Tomb 1 belonged to **Huye**, superintendent of the royal harem and chamberlain to the queen-mother Teye. In the entrance is the deceased praying. The Hall has two clustered columns, of which, however, only that on the left side is standing. *Entrance Wall.* To the right are the king and queen seated at table, below the queen are two princesses facing each other, to the right are guards, etc. Here, as in all similar representations in the tombs at Tell el-ʿAmârna, the sun appears above the royal couple, with rays ending in hands. Below are musicians, a table with offerings, bowing servants, soldiers, etc. *Right Wall.* A temple of the sun is represented with the chief altar in the colonnaded court and statues; to the right the king, escorted by guards behind and below, leads his mother to the temple dedicated to the king's parents, Amenophis III. and Teye; above is the sun. *Rear Wall.* This is occupied, on each side of the door, by two companion-scenes (much injured), showing Amenophis III. and IV., with their consorts. *Left Wall.* The king is being carried to a reception hall (right) in order to receive the tribute of his subject nations; he is accompanied by a large retinue. *Entrance Wall.* To the left, a scene resembling that to the right (see above). — On both sides of the door to the next room the deceased appears in prayer. The following chamber (unfinished) contains the mummy-shaft, surrounded by a parapet hewn in the solid rock. — In the Last Chamber (shrine) is a recess with the colossal seated figure of the deceased, the features of which have been defaced. On the walls are burial scenes, mourners, men with sacrificial gifts, a carriage, chairs, etc.

Tomb 2, belonging to **Meri-rē**, another superintendent of the royal harem, deserves special attention because its construction was still going on under Sake-rē, the son-in-law and successor of Amenophis IV. The Hall has two columns; the rear chambers are unfinished. *Entrance Wall.* To the left is the king seated under a canopy holding a goblet, which the queen is filling with water; adjacent stand three princesses. To the right, the king and queen, on a balcony, are handing down golden ornaments to the deceased; while in the forecourt of the palace (r.) are the royal chariot and fan-bearers and the secretaries and servants of Meri-rē; below are represented the return of Meri-rē and his welcome at his own house. *Right Wall.* The king and queen seated under an elevated canopy receive the tributes of the Asiatics (left) and negroes (right); other captives do homage to the king.

The other tombs lie 1/4 hr. S.E., on another hill-slope.

Tomb 3, belonging to **Ahmose**, 'fan-bearer on the right hand of the king', may be visited by travellers with abundance of time.

Over the entrance-door is the deceased worshipping the names of the sun; to the right and left within the door he appears praying in his official costume (with fan and axe). On the *Left Wall* of the Hall the royal family is shown at a banquet in a hall of the palace; above are four rows of soldiers, armed with shields and spears, etc., marching to the

temple, followed by the royal chariot (merely sketched in red pigment). The Side Chambers, on each side of the corridor, contain mummy-shafts, and on the side-walls are door-shaped steles. In the last room is a statue of the deceased.

Tomb 4, one of the largest and most interesting, belonged to **Meri-rē**, high-priest of the sun. The reliefs are now rather dark and require to be well lighted. — This tomb is preceded by a spacious court. The entrance-door is embellished with a cavetto cornice and, on its inner side, with a representation of the deceased in prayer. It admits us to a Vestibule, on the *Right and Left Walls* of which are door-shaped steles, with the deceased praying in front and large nosegays of flowers behind. The other walls are covered with inscriptions. — The Hall beyond was originally borne by four columns, of which two remain. In the doorway, to the right is the deceased, to the left his wife, praying. *Entrance Wall*, to the left. The king throws down gold to Meri-rē from the window of the palace. *Left Wall.* The scenes here represent the king driving in his chariot from the palace (on the left, above) to the temple of the sun (comp. below), preceded by his guards and followed by the queen, princesses, and retinue in chariots and on foot. The relief is continued on the *Left Half of the Rear Wall,* which exhibits the temple of the sun, at the entrance of which priests and musicians await the king. *Right Wall* (the reliefs continued along the *Right Half of the Rear Wall*). Above is the king visiting the temple; below, Meri-rē is being adorned with golden chains in the presence of the king and queen; to the left are the royal barns and storehouses. *Entrance Wall,* to the right. The king and queen, accompanied by their two daughters, offer sacrifices to the sun; Meri-rē and another priest stand beside the altars. Below are the royal retinue and priests; at the bottom, to the right, is a charming representation of blind singers. — The two following rooms are unfinished.

Tomb 5, that of **Pentu**, a physician, is much damaged. On each side of the entrance is the deceased praying, with an inscription in front of him containing a hymn to the sun. On the *Left Wall* of the first chamber are the king and queen praying to the sun, which rises over the pylon of the temple. The deep mummy-shaft is in the side-passage to the right. The statue of Pentu, which stood in the last room, has been chiselled away.

Tomb 6, that of **Penehse**, is a little to the S.E. In the *Entrance Door*, to the left, are the king and queen followed by their three daughters and the queen's sister, praying to the sun; below is a row of servants, fan-bearers, and other attendants; at the foot, the deceased praying. On the right are similar scenes. The Hall originally contained four papyrus-columns with bud-capitals, of which two still remain. The false door on the rear wall to the left has been converted into a kind of font, probably when the tomb was used as a church (comp. p. clxxxviii). A flight of steps on the right leads to the sarcophagus-chamber. *Entrance Wall* (to the left). The king and queen hand Penehse golden ornaments from the balcony of the palace. On the *Left Wall*, at the top, to the left, appears the temple of the sun, with the king praying at an altar in the forecourt. *Entrance Wall* (to the right). The deceased and his attendants bring offerings to the royal consorts, who are accompanied by four princesses. — A door with a representation of the deceased and his sister leads to a Second Room with four columns, containing the niche which held the statue of the deceased (now chiselled away).

A visit should be paid also to the *Boundary Inscription* (comp. p. 245), which is engraved on a cliff about $1^1/_2$ M. to the E. of Tomb 6.

About halfway between the N. and the S. group of tombs, on a spur of the E. hills some distance from the city proper, lay a *Village* surrounded by a wall. This was the home of the grave-diggers and tomb-attendants of the royal city, a class of men whom for various reasons it was well to keep at a distance and under discipline. Close by is a cemetery with brick chapels.

The **South Group of Tombs** is situated 1 hr. S., amid the low spurs of the *Gebel Abu Ḥaṣâh.* Eighteen of them have been opened (keeper, see p. 245).

Farthest N. is Tomb 8, that of **Tutu.**

On the *Door Jambs* the deceased is represented praying, while his name and titles are inscribed above. In the *Doorway*, to the right, are the king and queen sacrificing to the sun; below, the deceased kneels in prayer. To the left is the deceased praying. The Hall had its ceiling originally supported by twelve columns arranged in two rows (eight still stand), by which it is divided longitudinally into three aisles; the columns in the rear row are united by low stone screens with cornices, and between the central pair gate-jambs are set to mark the entrance. A flight of steps on the left leads to the sarcophagus-chamber. In the two short side-walls are small, partly unfinished recesses with statues. *Entrance Wall.* On the right the king and queen look on from the balcony of the palace (represented on the left), while Tutu is being adorned with golden chains; beneath is the deceased in prayer. To the left the royal pair are seated in the palace, with Tutu and other courtiers in respectful attitudes before them; beneath is the deceased in prayer. — The *Corridor* is unfinished.

Immediately adjoining is Tomb 9, belonging to **Mahu,** an officer of the police. In the *Entrance*, to which a narrow flight of steps descends, are, to the left, the king (holding the hieroglyph for 'truth' towards the sun), the queen, and a princess, with sistra, in presence of the sun; beneath kneels the deceased, with the text of his prayer inscribed in front of him. To the right is the deceased in prayer. — We next enter the Hall. *Entrance Wall* (left half). The king stands on the balcony of the palace (merely sketched in black pigment). *Left Wall.* A tombstone rounded at the top, to which two steps ascend; above are the royal pair; below, the deceased in prayer. To the right is a scene that is continued on the *Left Half of the Rear Wall*, representing men standing before the temple of the sun, among whom, at the head of the lowest row, the deceased is seen kneeling and returning thanks for the king's goodness. On the *Right Half of the Rear Wall*, the representations on which are continued by those on the *Left Half of the Right Wall*, appear the king and queen, driving from the palace, with outrunners in advance, to visit the fortifications of the City of Akhenaten; below, we see them returning. *Right Wall.* In the middle is a door-shaped tombstone. *Entrance Wall* (right half). In the lowest row we see Mahu setting out in his chariot, to the left, and to the right, Mahu bringing prisoners to the vizier, who is accompanied by a retinue. In the second row from the foot is Mahu leaning on a staff and listening to a report from his subordinates; to the right, a chariot and soldiers running. The upper rows are

badly preserved. — The Second Room has no reliefs or paintings. In the rear wall is a false door. To the right a winding staircase of forty-six steps leads to a chamber in which opens the mummy-shaft.

Tomb 10, of **Epy**, is unfinished. To the left, in the entrance, are the king and queen offering two pictures to the sun, the king presenting two princesses who worship the names of the sun, while the queen presents her own portrait, also adoring the names of the sun; behind them are three princesses with sistra; the sun darts his rays upon an altar loaded with food and vessels. — Tomb 11, of **Ramose.** To the left, in the entrance, are the royal pair accompanied by a princess, receiving the symbol of 'Life' from the sun's rays, which are shaped like hands. In the niche are seated figures of the deceased and his wife. — Tombs 12 and 13, though unfinished, are of interest as illustrating the method in which these rock-tombs were hollowed out. — Tomb 14 belonged to *Mey*, a 'military commander and fan-bearer on the king's right hand', whose name has everywhere been carefully obliterated, while the names of the king and queen have been left uninjured. The tomb is unfinished. On the right portion of the entrance-wall are preliminary sketches in black of the quays of the City of Ahkenaten, with ships, gardens, and the palace in the background. — Tomb 17, though a fine specimen, has no representations or inscriptions. — Tomb 19, of *Suti*, had just been begun.

Tomb 23, belonging to **Eny**, a royal house-steward and scribe, differs from the other tombs in its arrangement. A flight of limestone steps ascends to the entrance, which is crowned with a cavetto cornice, and in front of which a colonnade was intended to be erected. On each side of the lintel are the king and queen and three princesses praying to the sun; on the left side in the entrance is the deceased praying, with the text of his prayer in front of him, on the right side he appears with a staff and nosegay (painted on stucco). The walls of the Hall are coated with stucco, but with the exception of the cavetto cornice at the top are unpainted. In the Niche is a colossal statue of the deceased. On the right wall are the deceased and his wife seated before a worshipper; on the left wall, the deceased seated at table and receiving flowers from a priest. These scenes also are painted on stucco but are much faded.

Tomb 25, the farthest S. in this group, belonged to **Eye** *(Aï)*, the successor of Tutankhamûn (p. cvi). This tomb, like so many of the others, was left unfinished, because Amenophis died during its construction and the court was soon afterwards removed back to Thebes, where Eye caused a new tomb to be made for himself (p. 316). On the Door Jambs, to the right and left, are Eye and his wife Teye, kneeling below inscriptions. In the Entrance, to the left, are the king and queen, followed by the princesses and the court, praying to the sun, which directs its arm-shaped rays towards the altar; below are Eye and his wife in prayer. To the right are Eye, in his official costume, and his wife praying, their prayers being inscribed beside them. — The Hall was designed to be supported by twenty-four papyrus-columns with bud-capitals, but only fifteen have been hewn out, and of these only four are finished. The remainder (to the S.) have just been begun in the living rock at the top. On three of the columns appear the deceased and his wife, adoring the names of the sun and of the king and queen. In the centre of the rear wall and in the N.W. angle are unfinished doors; in the N.E. angle is a flight of steps intended to lead to the sarcophagus-chamber, which has not even been begun.

The representation on the left portion of the *Entrance Wall*, the only one finished, deserves notice. To the left are the king and queen at the balcony of the palace throwing down decorations to Eye and his wife (upper parts of their bodies in the Cairo Museum). Beside the queen are the three youthful princesses, one of whom strokes her mother's chin; above shines the sun. In the courtyard of the palace wait the royal retinue (charioteers, scribes, fan-bearers, and soldiers), raising their hands in respectful homage to the royal pair. The curious bent attitudes of the courtiers should be observed. Below are boys frisking for joy. To the right Eye leaves the palace, receiving the congratulations of his retainers, who raise their hands in exultation; servants carry the gifts away. In the top row are the doorkeepers sitting and conversing with their yeomen about the sounds of jubilation that reach their ears.

About 6½ M. from Tell el-ʿAmârna, in a mountain valley stretching towards the E. between the N. and S. groups of tombs, and known by the Arabs as *Darb el-Hamzâwi* or *Darb el-Melek*, are a number of uninscribed rock-tombs and one (No. 26) which, though greatly damaged, contains many interesting decorations.

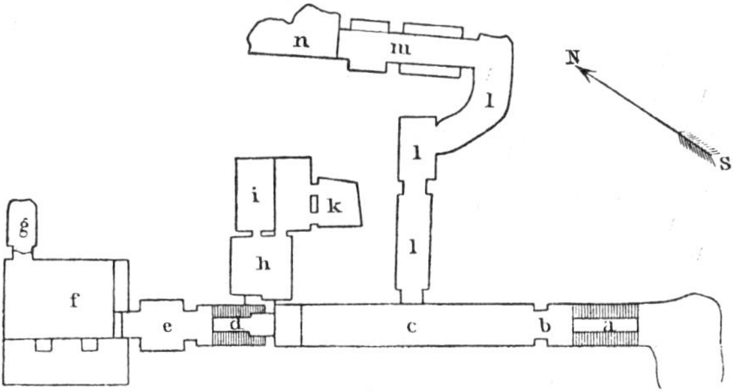

This, the **Family Tomb of Amenophis IV.** (closed; keeper at Ḥâgg Qandîl), is erroneously considered to be that of the king himself (comp. p. 315, No. 55). A flight of twenty *Steps* (Pl. *a*), with a smooth inclined plane in the middle for the transportation of the sarcophagus, leads to the *Entrance* (Pl. *b*), whence a sloping *Corridor* (Pl. *c*) leads to a second flight of sixteen *Steps* (Pl. *d*), beyond which is an *Antechamber* (Pl. *e*), with a shaft, now filled up, and damaged mural reliefs. Beyond this lies the *Tomb Chamber* (Pl. *f*), in which the sarcophagus once stood. All the pillars but one have disappeared. The mural representations were carved in stucco, but all are much damaged with the exception of those on the left portion of the entrance-wall (king, queen, and princesses adoring the sun) and the left wall (king, queen, princess, and professional mourners beside a bier?). In the right wall is a small recess (Pl. *g*). — We now retrace our steps towards the entrance. To the left of the steps at *d* lie three rooms (Pl. *h*, *i*, *k*), embellished with reliefs and inscriptions, forming perhaps the Grave of the Princess Meket-Aton. Both the main walls of the *First Room* (Pl. *h*) show almost exactly the same scene: the king and queen, four princesses, and the royal retinue presenting offerings to the sun, which is seen rising over the mountains behind the pylon of the temple (on the left); at the foot of the mountains are various

animals. To the left (i.e. on the left part of the entrance-wall and between the doors on the rear wall) the king's non-Egyptian subjects, including negroes and Asiatics in their distinctive costume, worship the sun. In the lower row on the right part of the entrance-wall we see the deceased princess on the bier, beside which stand the king and queen and professional mourners; in the upper row the royal pair, the nurse with a little princess, and the mourners vehemently lament the deceased. The *Second Room* (Pl. *i*) contains no representations. On the rear wall of the *Third Room* (Pl. *k*) the mummy of the princess is shown (on the left) standing under a canopy, while in front of it the royal family and court are mourning. This scene is continued on the right wall. On the left wall we see the mummy lying below the same canopy; in front is the mourning royal family, while farther to the right is the nurse with a young princess at her breast. On the entrance-wall are objects with which the tomb was furnished (much injured). — We return to the steps at *d*. Nearer the entrance a *Corridor* (Pl. *l*) leads to the left to a sloping *Passage* (Pl. *m*) ending in an unfinished *Chamber* (Pl. *n*).

In the hills enclosing the plain of Tell el-ʿAmârna are many quarries of limestone and alabaster. The most important are the *Alabaster Quarries of Hat-nub*, or *Het-nub*, about 5 hrs. distant, to which a path running eastwards to the S. of the S. group of tombs leads. These quarries, which were discovered by Prof. Percy Edward Newberry in 1891, are ascertained from inscriptions and graffiti to have been worked under the Ancient Empire and at the beginning of the Middle Empire.

19. Abydos.

The ordinary traveller, with the average amount of time at his disposal, will confine himself to the *Temple of Sethos I.*, the sadly dilapidated *Temple of Ramses II.*, and the ancient fortress of *Shûnet ez-Zebîb*. — CARRIAGES (there and back, with stay of 2 hrs., P.T. 120), MOTOR CARS (P.T. 100), and DONKEYS (P.T. 25), with good saddles, may be obtained at the railway station of Balyana.

Abydos lies about $6^1/_2$ M. from *El-Balyana* (p. 231), a drive of $^1/_2$ hr. by motor-car or about 1 hr. by carriage, or a donkey-ride of $1^1/_4$ hr. The track crosses the railway a little to the N. of the station and follows the telegraph wires along a wide and much-used embankment. Beyond the hamlet of *El-Ḥigz* it crosses a canal, traverses a fertile district dotted with villages, and reaches the village of *El-ʿArâba* or *El-ʿArâba el-Madfûna* (i.e. 'buried ʿArâba'), on the other side of the *Kisra Canal*. The view of the well-cultivated and populous plain, and of the mountains to the E., is very fine. The peasants working in the fields mostly live with their cattle in wattle-huts of durra straw or in flat, brown or striped Beduin tents. On the verge of the arable land lay the ancient Abydos, which extended from El-ʿArâba to El-Khirba (p. 260).

Abydos (Egyptian *Abôdu*) was one of the most ancient cities in Egypt and played an important rôle under the first dynasty as the burial-place of the kings and grandees. The town and its necropolis were both devoted to the worship of the dog-formed death-god Khenti-Amentiu, 'the first of the inhabitants of the Western King-

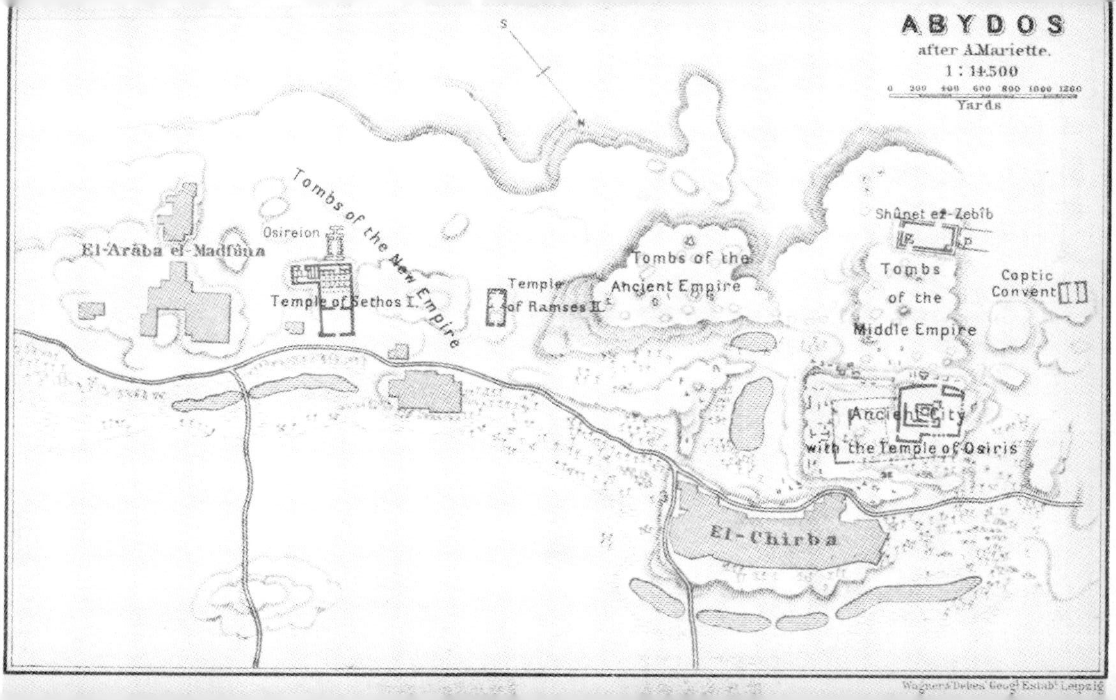
ABYDOS
after A. Mariette.
1 : 14.500
0 200 400 600 800 1000 1200
Yards
S
N
El-Arâba el-Madfûna
Osireion
Tombs of the New Empire
Temple of Sethos I.
Temple of Ramses II.
Tombs of the Ancient Empire
Shûnet ez-Zebîb
Tombs of the Middle Empire
Coptic Convent
Ancient City with the Temple of Osiris
El-Chirba
Wagner & Debes' Geogr. Estabt. Leipzig

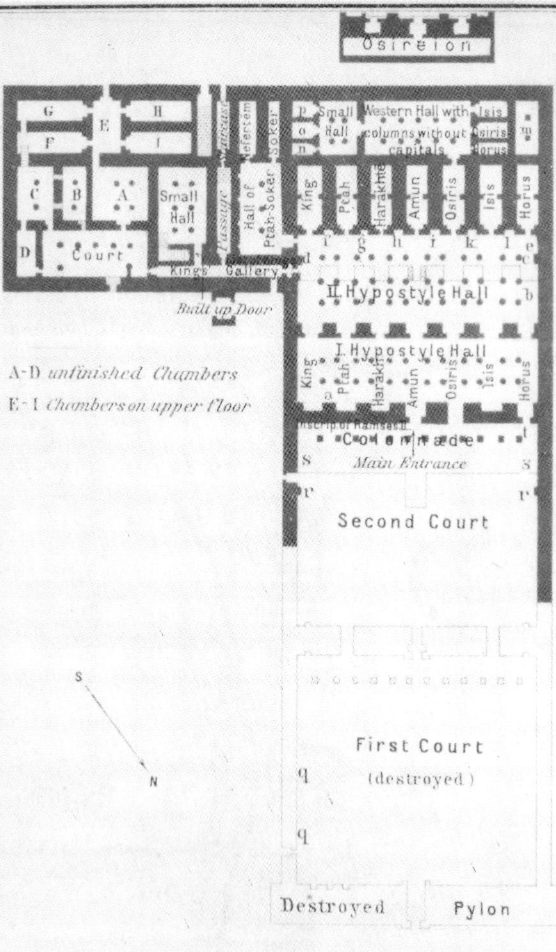

TEMPLE OF SETHOS I, AT ABYDOS

1 : 1500

0 50 100 150 200 250

English Feet

Wagner & Debes' Geogl. Estabt. Leipzig

dom'. Even under the Ancient Empire, however, the cult of Osiris (which originated in the Delta) made good its footing at Abydos. Osiris took possession of the ancient temple and was raised to an equality with Khenti-Amentiu. The tomb of Osiris was transferred to Umm el-Gaʿâb (p. 260), and in the days of the 6th Dynasty it became usual to inter the dead from all parts of Egypt at Abydos. Just as the Shiite Mohammedan cherishes no dearer wish than to be buried near the tomb of Ḥusein (p. 58) at Kerbelâ, so the pious Egyptian desired no better fortune than to have his corpse carried to Abydos, there to find its last abode beside the tomb of Osiris. Those who were unable to do this, or who had built tombs elsewhere, often caused their mummies to be brought temporarily to Abydos, to receive the desired consecration and to spend some time at least with Osiris. Many contented themselves with merely erecting a memorial stone or a cenotaph in the necropolis, thereby assuring to themselves the favour of Osiris, the lord of the underworld. — Isis, the wife of Osiris, his son Horus, and, under the New Empire, Ptah, Harakhte, and Amun were likewise worshipped there.

Strabo gives an interesting account of Abydos: "Above it (Ptolemaïs [p. 230]) lies Abydos, the site of the *Memnonium*, a wonderful palace of stone, built in the manner of the Labyrinth (p. 206), only somewhat less elaborate in its complexity. Below the Memnonium is a spring, reached by passages with low vaults consisting of a single stone and remarkable for their extent and mode of construction. This spring is connected with the Nile by a canal, which flows through a grove of Egyptian thorn-acacias, sacred to Apollo. Abydos seems once to have been a large city, second only to Thebes, but now it is a small place." Ammianus Marcellinus (4th cent. after Christ) speaks of the oracle of the god Bes, which flourished here.

The most important part of ancient Abydos was its extensive *Necropolis*, situated in the desert. Four distinct sections are clearly traceable. In the southernmost, beside El-ʿArâba (p. 252), are tombs of the New Empire and the temples of Sethos I. and Ramses II., and the so-called Osireion. To the N. of this rises a hill, with graves dating from the close of the Ancient Empire. Still farther N., between the sanctuary of Osiris (Kôm es-Sulṭân) and the fortress of Shûnet ez-Zebîb (p. 260), are the tombs of the Middle Empire, many in the form of small brick pyramids. Here are found also graves of the 18-20th Dyn. and of the later period. Finally, in the hill of Umm el-Gaʿâb (p. 260), to the W., are the tombs of the kings of the earliest dynasties and the sacred grave of Osiris.

The chief centre of interest is the ****Temple of Sethos I.**, the *Memnonium* of Strabo. This wonderful structure, built by Sethos I. and completed by Ramses II., was almost completely excavated in 1859 by Mariette (p. 88), at the expense of Khedive Saʿîd. The walls consist of fine-grained limestone, while a harder variety has been selected for the columns, architraves, door-posts, and other burden-bearing portions. The *Reliefs* dating from the reign of Sethos I. are among the finest productions of Egyptian sculpture of any age.

The ground-plan differs materially from that of other great

Egyptian temples. Instead of one sanctuary it has seven, dedicated to Osiris, Isis, Horus, Ptah, Harakhte, Amun, and the deified king; and as each of these had a special cult the entire front portion of the temple is divided into seven parts, each with its separate gateway and portals. The chambers behind the sanctuaries are not arranged behind each other as in other temples, but side by side. Another remarkable peculiarity consists in the wing (p. 257) containing various halls, chambers, etc., which stands at right angles to the main building (comp. p. clxxiv).

We enter the temple from the N.E. In front of the temple, on the left, is the façade of a small building (probably a festal temple), which faces the axis of the whole structure. The first pylon has collapsed; at the back are shallow niches once holding statues of Sethos I. and Ramses II., in the form of Osiris. The **First Court**, recently excavated, is badly ruined. On its S. (or more exactly S.E.) wall are reliefs of the Asiatic wars and victories of Ramses II. (Pl. *q*): Battle with the Hittites; counting the enemies' severed hands; dedication of the booty to Amun. On the W. (S.W.) the court is bounded by a pillared hall to which an incline ascends; on the base of the wall Ramses' children are portrayed. The reliefs are continued on the back of the second pylon. In front of the incline are two wells.

The **Second Court** is in better preservation. On the right and left are memorial inscriptions of Ramses II. (Pl. *r*). Farther on appears Ramses II., sacrificing to different gods and smiting his enemies in the presence of Amun (Pl. *s*). At the back of the court a low incline ascends to the vestibule of the temple proper, which, like the hall of the first court, was supported by twelve pillars composed of blocks of sandstone and limestone and originally had seven doors in its rear wall. On the wall to the left of the main entrance is an inscription in ninety-five vertical lines, in which Ramses II. describes in florid language the completion of the temple. In the adjoining relief Ramses is shown presenting an image of the goddess Maat to a triad consisting of Osiris, Isis, and his father Sethos I., who takes the place of Horus. On the wall are other representations of Ramses in presence of the gods. — The seven original doors corresponded to the seven sanctuaries of the temple. Processions in honour of the king seem to have entered by the door to the extreme left; the next served for processions to Ptah, the third for Harakhte, the fourth for Amun, the fifth for Osiris, the sixth for Isis, and the seventh for Horus. Ramses, however, walled up six of these doors, leaving the central one alone as the main entrance to the temple.

The present approach is by the ancient main door. We enter the **First Hypostyle Hall**, which is about 171 ft. wide by 36 deep. The roof, part of which has fallen in, is supported by twenty-four clustered papyrus-columns, with bud-capitals. The columns are so arranged that two pairs stand on each side of the five central processional aisles, while the two outermost aisles are each flanked

on one side by the walls of the temple. The representations on the shafts of the columns represent the king before the deity to whom the aisle led, sometimes accompanied by the other deities of his triad. Thus in the Amun aisle we see Ramses II. before Amun, Mut, and Khons; in the Ptah aisle, the king before Ptah, Sakhmet (Hathor), and Nefertēm. The sculptures (incised reliefs) are of mediocre workmanship; they date from Ramses II., who chiselled away his father's bas-reliefs to make room for his own (comp., e.g., Pier *a*). The only interesting Mural Representations are those in the lower row on the end-wall to the right. To the right Thoth and Horus pour over Ramses II. the holy water in the form of the hieroglyphics for 'purity' and 'life'; to the left Wep-wawet, with a wolf's head, and Horus, with a falcon's head, 'the avenger of his father', conduct the king to the temple and hold the hieroglyph for 'life' to the king's nose; close by, to the left, is Hathor of Dendera; farther to the left, Ramses hands to Osiris and his companions, Isis and Horus, a case for papyrus-rolls in the shape of a column held by a kneeling king, with a falcon's head on the top as a lid.

Seven doors, which are placed in the axes of the built-up entrance-doors and the sanctuaries, lead from this first hall into the **Second Hypostyle Hall.** The architrave, on which rest the roof-slabs, is supported by thirty-six columns, arranged on either side of the processional aisles in pairs on the same system as in the first hall. The twenty-four columns in the first two rows of columns have papyrus-bud capitals. Beyond the second row the floor of the temple is considerably raised, forming a platform upon which stands the third row of columns. These are tree-trunk columns (p. clxv), with cylindrical shafts and no capitals, on which rest slabs forming an abacus for the support of the architrave. The inscriptions and representations on the walls and columns date from the reign of Sethos and are of admirable workmanship, but their subjects are of little general interest. The wonderful **Reliefs*, however, on the right wall (Pl. *b*) should not be overlooked. Here, to the right, we see Sethos I. standing before Osiris and Horus, holding a censer and pouring water from three vases embellished with flowers. In the next scene the king with the censer appears before a shrine in the midst of which Osiris is enthroned; in front of the god stand Maat and Ronpet (goddess of the year) and behind are Isis, Amentet (goddess of the West), and Nephthys, with nine small gods of the dead in the background. On Pier *c* is a representation of the highly adorned sacred column *Djed*, the symbol of Osiris of Busiris (p. cli), to the right and left of which stands the king, wearing the crown of Lower Egypt (comp. the representation on the pier in the S. wall, Pl. *d*). To the left of Pier *e* the king presents an image of Maat to Osiris, Isis, and Horus. The king's profile is evidently a faithful likeness and is everywhere portrayed with great artistic skill.

Adjoining this hall, in a direct line with the seven entrance

doors, are **Seven Sanctuaries**, of which that in the middle was dedicated to Amun, the chief deity under the New Empire. To the right are the sanctuaries of Osiris, Isis, and Horus; to the left those of Harakhte, Ptah, and the king. Each contained the sacred boat of its god and was shut off by a folding door. The central chapel was approached by a flight of steps, the others by inclined planes. The roofs of these chapels are not vaulted in the strict architectural signification of that word; they are formed of two horizontal courses, each projecting over the one below, and rounded off by the chisel to the form of an arch. The vaults are decorated with stars and the names of Sethos I., while the walls are covered with reliefs, illustrating the ceremonies that took place in the sanctuaries. The colouring is in excellent preservation. In the piers separating the doors are square recesses, which are likewise adorned with reliefs.

Those who desire to examine more particularly the sanctuaries and shrines should begin with the King's Sanctuary, to the left. *Left Wall.* Lower row (from left to right): three dog-headed gods and three falcon-headed gods bear the king into the sanctuary, preceded by a priest, with the lock of youth and a panther-skin, offering incense; the king seated on a throne at a banquet, with his guardian spirit behind him and the ibis-headed god Thoth in front; the gifts offered to the king are recounted in a long list in front of the god. Upper row: the priest in presence of nine gods (in three rows); the king between Thoth and Nekhbeyet, on the right, and Horus and Buto, on the left, who bestow blessings upon him; Thoth and the priest sacrificing to the sacred boat of the king, which is adorned with king's heads on stem and stern and stands in a shrine crowned with serpents; the priest before the king is obliterated. — *Right Wall.* Lower row (from left to right): the king with his guardian spirit and the priest, as on the opposite wall; the king seated beside Nekhbeyet and Buto on a throne supported by the written symbol for 'union', about which Thoth and Horus wind the characteristic plants of Upper and Lower Egypt (p. cii; a scene symbolizing the union of Egypt under the king); to the right Seshet inscribes the king's name for eternity; the priest before nine gods. Upper row: the priest and Thoth before the (defaced) image of the king, while six gods, with the heads of dogs and falcons, bring vases to him; Mont and Atum conduct the ruler to the temple, followed by Isis. — The *Rear Wall* in this and all the other sanctuaries except that of Osiris (see below) was occupied by two false doors (p. clxxvi), surmounted by round pediments and separated by the representation of a flower on which a serpent lies. — Niche *f*. To the left Thoth holds the symbol of 'life' to the king's nose; to the right Thoth and the king sit facing each other; on the rear wall the funeral priest offers incense before the king. — Sanctuary of Ptah (partly destroyed). On the side-walls the king is shown worshipping Ptah. — Niche *g*. Sethos before Ptah (rear), Harakhte (right), and Sakhmet (left). — Sanctuary of Harakhte. The reliefs here represent the king before Harakhte, Atum, the goddess Ews-os of Heliopolis, and Hathor. — Niche *h*. The king before Amon-Rē (rear), Mut (right), and Harakhte (left), to whom he offers an image of Maat. — Sanctuary of Amun. Sethos here sacrifices to the various forms of Amun and offers incense to the sacred boats of Amun (adorned with rams' heads), Khons, and Mut (these two adorned with the heads of the deities), which stand in a shrine. The colouring here is in excellent preservation, and the inscriptions on the false door, dating from the Greek period, should be noticed. — Niche *i*. The king anoints Amun (rear), offers incense to Khons (right), and sacrifices to Mut (left). — Sanctuary of Osiris. The king in the presence of various forms of Osiris, who is frequently accompanied by Isis or other gods; at the top of the right wall he sacrifices to the sacred boat of Osiris, and at the top of the left wall he offers incense to the

reliquary of Osiris at Abydos, which stands beneath a canopy with five images of deities borne on poles in front of it; on each side of the entrance is the king before the wolf-headed Wep-wawet. — NICHE *k*. The king before Osiris, Isis, and Nut. — SANCTUARY OF Isis (now closed). Sethos appears before Isis, who is frequently accompanied by her son, the falcon-headed Horus, and the boat of Isis. — NICHE *l*. The king before Osiris, Horus, and Isis. — SANCTUARY OF HORUS. The king in presence of the falcon-headed Horus, Isis, and the boat of Horus.

A door in the Osiris Chapel leads to a series of chambers dedicated to the special rites in honour of Osiris. We first enter the *Western Hall*, the roof of which was supported by ten columns (without capitals). To the right of this lay three small chambers, adorned with fine coloured sculpture. The chapel on the right is dedicated to Horus, the middle one to the deified king, and that on the left to Osiris and Isis. Behind them lies another room (Pl. *m;* closed). To the left on entering the Western Hall is a door leading to a room with four columns and four recesses with reliefs in the E. wall, which was adjoined by three smaller apartments (Pl. *n*, *o*, *p*). These are much damaged.

South Wing. This building consists of a slaughter-yard, store-rooms, etc. The most important, to which a visit should be paid even if all the others be omitted, is the long, slightly ascending corridor known as the *GALLERY OF THE KINGS, entered from the left side of the second hypostyle hall, between the second and third row of columns. On the right wall is the famous *List of Kings*, which helped to determine the correct order of the Egyptian Pharaohs. Sethos I., with the censer, and the crown-prince Ramses (with the side-lock of youth) reciting hymns from a papyrus-roll, are seen revering their royal ancestors, the names of seventy-six of whom are inscribed in the two upper rows. The list begins with Menes, the first king of Egypt, and extends down to Sethos, the names of unimportant or illegitimate rulers being omitted. Above the list is the inscription: "The performance of the prayer for the dead — 'May Ptah-Soker-Osiris, lord of the tomb, who dwells in the temple of Sethos, increase the gifts for the kings of Upper and Lower Egypt' — by King Sethos; 1000 loaves of bread, 1000 barrels of beer, 1000 cattle, 1000 geese, 1000 incense offerings, etc., by King Sethos for King Menes," etc. (here follows the list). In the lowest row the phrases 'by King Men-ma-rē', 'by the son of Rē, Sethos' are repeated over and over again. — On the left wall we again meet Sethos and the youthful Ramses. The father holds a censer in his left hand, while the son, adorned with the priestly panther-skin, pours a libation on the altar in front of him. The inscription contains a long list of the names and shrines of gods whom Sethos and his son are here honouring with sacrificial gifts.

In the centre of the right wall a door leads into a PASSAGE, beyond which is a vaulted stone staircase, which was built up in ancient times.

The *Reliefs* in the passage date from Ramses II. On the right wall the king and a prince appear lassoing a bull in presence of the wolf-headed god Wep-wawet. Farther to the left this animal is being sacrificed to the god Wep-wawet. On the left wall Ramses conducts four sacred oxen to Khons and King Sethos; farther to the left Ramses paces out the precincts of the temple (comp. p. 325); Ramses and four gods net birds; Ramses

and a prince offer the captured geese to Amun and Mut. — The numerous Phœnician and Aramaic inscriptions on the walls of the staircase are due to Semitic visitors.

Another door in the right wall of the Kings' Gallery led to a hall supported by six columns and adorned partly with representations (painted in preparation for their execution in relief) by Sethos I., partly with reliefs 'en creux' by Ramses II. The benches by the walls were probably intended for the sacrificial gifts.

From the S. end of the Kings' Gallery, where Coptic prayers have been written up in red, we enter the SLAUGHTER COURT, surrounded with seven columns but never completed. The sculptures and hieroglyphics were sketched in colour under Sethos, and only a few of them were afterwards finished as reliefs 'en creux'. They represent Sethos sacrificing. The scenes in the lower row depict the slaughter and cutting up of sacrificial animals. The screen between the first column and the left wall was intended to veil the proceedings in the court from the Kings' Gallery.

Adjoining this court are four unfinished rooms (Pl. A, B, C, D). Room B is inaccessible. In the first three the designs on the walls are merely sketched in; in D they have been completed in colour. — From Room C a staircase ascends to Rooms E-I (H and I inaccessible), which contain unfinished representations dating from the reign of Menephthes. From Room E a door leads into the open air, opposite the Osireion (see below). — Beyond Room D, outside the temple proper, lies a deep circular well.

Returning now to the second hypostyle hall, we may pay a brief visit to the CHAMBER which adjoins it on the left and was dedicated to Ptah-Soker, god of the dead at Memphis. The roof is supported by three tree-trunk columns (p. 255). The fine reliefs show Sethos revering Soker, Nefertēm, and other gods; the E. wall has four recesses adorned with reliefs.

Opening off this chamber are two small sham-vaulted chapels; that to the right dedicated to Soker, that to the left to Nefertēm. On the left wall of the former is a relief of Horus and Isis by the bier of Osiris, on whose mummy sits a falcon (Isis); at the head and feet of the mummy are two other falcons, with drooping wings. On the right wall are Isis and Horus by the bier of Soker-Osiris, whose left hand is raised to his brow, while with his right he holds his phallus.

The large structure to the W. of the Temple of Sethos, with its rear wall separated from it by a distance of only 26 ft., is considered by several authorities to be the *Osireion* or *Tomb of Osiris*, but in reality is a **Cenotaph of Sethos,** closely connected with the main temple. In its simple majesty it is reminiscent of the Valley Temple of Khephren (p. 146). Discovered in 1903 by Margaret A. Murray, it was excavated and examined in 1911-26 by the Egypt Exploration Society under the direction of E. Naville (p. 318) and Dr. Frankfort. The building, which was originally surrounded by trees and lay inside an artificial mound, was erected by Sethos I. but left unfinished. Subsequently some of the chambers were decorated by Menephthes with inscriptions and reliefs. The building material is white limestone and reddish sandstone, red granite being used solely for the pillars, the roof of the main chamber, and some of the doorways. — The *Entrance Gate*, on the N. side, which was

originally approached through the mound by a vertical brick shaft, is roofed with thick brick vaulting. Thence we follow a sloping *Passage* (Pl. 1), 330 ft. long, with walls decorated with funerary texts destined for Sethos I. (and later Menephthes; those on the right wall taken from the 'Book of Portals', those on the left from the 'Book of that which is in the Underworld'; comp. pp. 301, 302). This leads to an *Anteroom* (Pl. 2), likewise furnished with sacred texts and pictures, opening off which is another small chamber (Pl. 3).

From the anteroom a *Second Passage* (Pl. 4) branches off to the E., leading to a large *Transverse Chamber* (Pl. 5), 20 by 65 ft., which was covered with a saddle-roof and adorned by Menephthes with texts from the Books of the Dead. Next follows a large three-aisled *Pillared Hall* (Pl. 6), 100 ft. long and 65 ft. wide, surrounded by sixteen small chambers opening on a passage that is only 2 ft. wide.

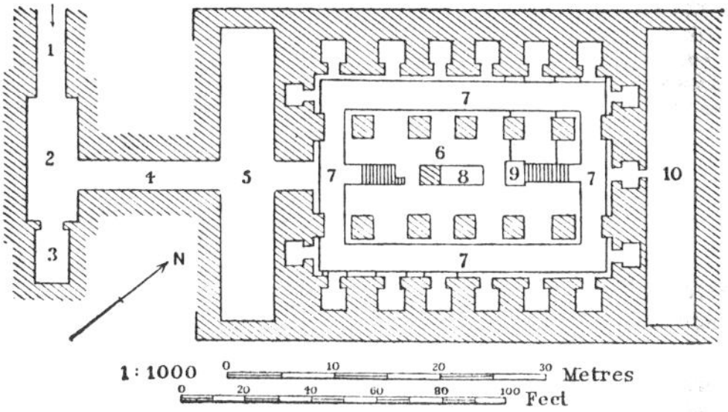

The central space and the chambers are separated by a trench (Pl. 7). At either end of the central space is a staircase descending to the water. In the pavement between the two rows of pillars are two cavities, the oblong one (Pl. 8) in the centre being perhaps intended for the coffin, the square one (Pl. 9) for a canopic chest. In the main axis is the entrance to a second *Transverse Chamber* (Pl. 10), the shape of which is probably meant to represent the royal coffin. Its well-preserved saddle-roof bears admirable reliefs of Sethos I.: Nut, goddess of the sky, raised aloft by Show, god of the air; Nut protecting the dead king with her arms.

A few minutes to the N. of the Temple of Sethos I., partly beneath the modern village, lies a *Temple of Ramses I.*, and close by is the **Temple of Ramses II.**, which also was dedicated to Osiris and the cult of the deceased king. The latter temple is in a very ruinous state. The scanty traces of a spacious court may be made out in front of the present entrance. Within, the ground-plan of a peristyle court (decorated with pillars and figures of Osiris, like the Ramesseum, p. 326), two halls, the sanctuaries beyond them,

and various other rooms can still be traced; but the average height of the remaining walls is only 5-6 ft. To judge by the extant remains, this temple was a much more sumptuous and more carefully built structure than any of the other buildings of Ramses II. known to us. Not only fine-grained limestone, but also red and black granite (for the door-frames), sandstone (for the pillars), and alabaster (for the innermost shrine) were used. The still brilliantly coloured mural decorations in the rear rooms are in delicate low relief recalling the admirable sculptures under Sethos I.; the ruder reliefs 'en creux occur only in the court and the first hall, with the adjoining rooms. The reliefs in the first court depict a grand procession. The outer walls are decorated with warlike scenes, the S. wall with lists of offerings.

On the right (N.) wall peasants are shown bringing oxen, antelopes, geese, and other animals to four priests, of whom the first records the gifts, while the second offers incense; farther to the right, the animals are being slaughtered. On the left (E. and S.) walls are similar scenes. To the left as we enter are persons with sacrificial gifts, who are met by a procession of priests, soldiers, the royal war-chariot, captive negroes and Asiatics, etc. The colouring of the figures is surprisingly well preserved. — In the rooms behind are much-damaged religious representations.

On the outside of the temple (N. and W. sides) are reliefs in fine white limestone, which are among the finest artistic productions of the reign of Ramses II. They represent scenes in the king's war with the Hittites, and adjacent is inscribed a report on the results of the war (comp. pp. 274, 325). The exterior of the S. wall bears a long inscription, recounting the building of the temple and its endowments.

To the N.W. of the temple of Ramses II. lies the ruin of *Shûnet ez-Zebîb*, surrounded by two walls. It is probably an ancient palace in the form of a fortress (see p. clxx).

A few hundred yards N.E. of Shûnet ez-Zebîb, near the village of *El-Khirba*, are the ruins of the ancient city of Abydos and of the *Sanctuary of Osiris*, called by the Arabs *Kôm es-Sulṭân* and dating back to the beginning of Egyptian history. The enclosing walls, built of brick in the Middle Empire, and some scanty traces of the temple are extant.

To the W. of this point lies the Coptic convent of *Deir es-Sitt Dimyâna* or *Damiâna*, called also *Deir Amba Mûsa*, which looks more like a village than a convent. It dates from the year 1306 of the Coptic era (c. A.D. 1590), but scarcely repays a visit.

The rubbish-mounds 20 min. S.W. of the temple of Ramses II., called by the Arabs **Umm el-Ga'âb** ('mother of pots'), contain tombs of kings of the 1st and 2nd Egyptian dynasties, including those of *Djer* (p. 103; regarded even under the Middle Empire as the tomb of Osiris), *Usaphaïs*, and *Miebis* (1st Dyn.). They were explored by E. C. Amélineau and Sir Flinders Petrie, but there is now practically nothing to be seen. — Near *Nag' el-Ghâbât*, to the S. of Abydos, is an ancient quarry.

ceiling admit the light. Four rows of reliefs on the walls exhibit the king before the gods of Dendera. In this and some of the other rooms the cartouches of the king are left empty, probably because the priests were in doubt as to which ruler should be selected for honour in the unsettled times during which the temple was built.

Some of the RELIEFS in the lower row, representing the ceremonies performed by the king at the foundation of the temple, deserve notice. To the right of the entrance (Pl. *g*): the king, wearing the crown of Lower Egypt, quits his palace, preceded by a priest offering incense; to the left the king cleaves the earth with a hoe on the site of the temple, turns the first sod, as we should express it; in front of him is the goddess Hathor. — To the left of the entrance (Pl. *h*): the king, with the crown of Upper Egypt, quits his palace (as above); to the right he presents Hathor with bricks, representing the building material for the new temple.

On each side of this hall are three CHAMBERS (Pl. 1-6), some of which are dark, while others are lighted by apertures in the roof; they were used as laboratory, treasury, and store-rooms for the sacrificial incense, etc. The inscriptions and representations show the Pharaoh in presence of Hathor, the lion-headed Horus of Dendera, and other gods.

We next enter the **First Antechamber** ('Sacrificial Chamber'), which is lighted by apertures in the roof and walls and is decorated with four rows of mural reliefs. The latter, with reference to the purpose of the chamber, represent the king presenting different offerings to Hathor and other deities. To the right and left are passages, leading to the staircases which ascend to the roof of the temple (p. 265). On the left is also a small chamber (Pl. 7) used for sacrificial offerings.

The **Second Antechamber** ('Central Hall'), which we next enter, is lighted by means of apertures in the side-walls and has four rows of bas-reliefs on the walls. A door to the left opens into a small room (Pl. 8) in which perfumes were preserved as well as the sacred garments with which the images of the goddess were embellished at festivals. — The corresponding door on the right side of the hall leads to three connected rooms, which form a special enclosed sanctuary. We see here first a small store-room (Pl. 9), connected by a corridor with the W. staircase (p. 265). Thence we enter an open court (Pl. 10), beyond which is a charming **Kiosk**, approached by modern steps and supported by two sistrum-columns. These are connected with the side-walls by two stone screens rising to half the height of the columns. Here the priests assembled to celebrate the birthday of Hathor and the immediately following New Year festival. The sacrificial gifts were offered in the court, as represented on the walls. The walls of the kiosk are embellished with three rows of representations, showing the king and various deities in presence of the gods of Dendera. Just above the floor is a procession of local deities (l., those of Upper Egypt; r., those of Lower Egypt) bearing gifts. On the ceiling the sky-goddess Nut is depicted with the sun rising from her lap and shining upon a head

of Hathor, which stands on a hill with two trees and typifies the temple of Dendera. Between the three windows high up at the back of the court are pillars with heads of Hathor. A staircase in the pavement descends to a crypt (see below).

We return to the second antechamber in order to visit thence the innermost part of the temple, 'the hidden secret chambers', as they are called in the inscriptions.

The central door leads to the profoundly dark **Sanctuary**, 'the great seat', in which the sacred boats with the images of the gods formerly stood. The king alone, or his sacerdotal representative, might enter this sacred precinct and in solitude commune with the deity. Only once a year was this permitted even to him, at the great festival of the New Year. The reliefs on the walls depict the rites which the king had to perform on entering the sanctuary, and the sacrifices which he had to offer.

There are three rows of Reliefs, but only the lowest can be distinctly seen even with the aid of an electric torch. The reliefs are so arranged that each scene on the *Left Wall* (Pl. *k*), beginning at the entrance, is followed in historical sequence by the corresponding scene on the *Right Wall* (Pl. *l*). 1 (left) The king ascends the steps to the shrine of the gods; 2 (right) removes the band fastening the door; 3 (l.) breaks the seal on the door; 4 (r.) opens the door; 5 (l.) gazes upon the goddess; 6 (r.) prays to her with his arms hanging down; 7 (l.) offers incense before the sacred boats of Hathor and Horus of Edfu; and (8; r.) before the boats of Hathor and Har-sem-tewe. — *Rear Wall* (Pl. *m*). To the left, the king, before whom is the youthful son of Hathor with sistrum and rattle, presents an image of the goddess Maat to Hathor and Horus of Edfu; to the right, the same ceremony before Hathor and Har-sem-tewe.

The sanctuary is surrounded by a Corridor, lighted by apertures in the side-walls and in the ceiling, and entered from the second antechamber by means of two side-doors. Opening off this corridor are eleven Small Chambers (Pl. 11-21), which were used as chapels dedicated to various deities, as store-rooms, and for different religious purposes. Room 11, which is embellished with reliefs like those in the sanctuary, contained a shrine with an image of Hathor. A modern iron staircase in this room leads to a small *Niche* in the S. wall, containing a relief of Hathor.

Before ascending to the roof of the temple, we should visit the subterranean chambers, or **Crypts**, in which were preserved such sacrificial vessels and images of the gods as were no longer in use. They claim attention not only for their remarkable construction but also for the fresh tints of their paintings. The temple contains no fewer than twelve crypts, constructed in the thickness of the temple walls in different stories and entered by narrow flights of steps or by openings concealed by movable stone slabs. Their elaborate mural reliefs date from the reign of Ptolemy XIII. Neos Dionysos (p. cxiii), and are therefore the oldest as well as the best-executed decorations in the temple. The custodian will open, on request, those crypts (entered from Rooms 18 and 19) that are worth a visit.

In the crypt accessible from Room 18, which we enter through a square opening in the pavement, are several narrow chambers, on the walls of which are depicted the objects that used to be preserved here. On the right wall of the second room to the right is an interesting relief of King Phiops (6th Dyn.) kneeling and offering a statuette of the god Ehi to four images of Hathor. In the crypt accessible from Room 19 the king is shown offering sacrifices and slaying hostile gods. — On the walls of the crypt entered through an opening in the pavement of the small sacrificial court (p. 263) Ptolemy XIII. appears presenting gifts (chiefly ornaments) to various gods.

We return to the first antechamber (p. 263) and ascend one of the two **Staircases** (Pl. 22, 23) which lead thence to the roof of the temple. The E. staircase, which ascends straight to the roof with easy steps, is dark. The W. staircase is a kind of spiral staircase, with ten rectangular turns, lighted by several windows, with tasteful symbolical representations of the sun shining through them. The walls of both staircases are embellished with reliefs of the ceremonial procession of the priests with the images of Hathor and her fellow-gods at the great New Year's festival. The left wall presents us with a view of the procession ascending from the lower rooms of the temple to the roof, in order that 'the goddess Hathor might be united with the beams of her father Rē' (the sun-god); the right wall shows the procession descending. The priests are headed by the king; some of them wear masks representing the lesser deities. — The W. staircase passes a small room (situated above the store-room adjoining the second antechamber, Pl. 9) with three windows looking into the court (p. 263). Higher up is a small court (locked) with two rooms opening off it, corresponding to the chambers on the E. side of the terrace (see below) and likewise dedicated to the cult of Osiris. The reliefs in the second room represent the resuscitation of Soker-Osiris.

We now reach the **Temple Roof**, which has various levels, the highest being above the great vestibule (p. 262). At the S.W. angle of the lower terrace, which we reach first, stands a small open *Pavilion*, supported by twelve sistrum-columns with heads of Hathor. Adjoining the terrace on the N. is a small *Shrine of Osiris*, situated above the chambers to the left of the hypostyle hall and used in the worship of the slain and risen Osiris, as curious representations and numerous inscriptions indicate. The second room is separated from the first (an open court) by pillars, and contains a plaster cast of the famous *Zodiac of Dendera* (original in the Bibliothèque Nationale at Paris), the only circular representation of the heavens found in Egypt. The window in the last room, with representations of Osiris dead and returning to life, deserves attention. — A flight of steps ascends from the N.W. end of the terrace to the roof of the first antechamber and thence to the still higher roof of the hypostyle hall. Thence a modern iron staircase leads to the roof of the great vestibule, which commands a beautiful view of the valley of the Nile and the hills of the desert.

Finally a walk round the Outside of the Temple will be found interesting. The exterior walls are covered with inscriptions and representations. The reliefs on the E. and W. walls date from the reign of Nero and other Roman emperors. The large scenes on the S. rear wall show Ptolemy XVI. Cæsar, son of Julius Cæsar, and his mother, Cleopatra, in presence of the gods of Dendera. In the centre is the image of the goddess Hathor. The faces are purely conventional and in no sense portraits. The projecting lions' heads on the sides of the building were intended to carry off the rain-water.

We now turn our attention to the other buildings within the temple precincts. To the right (S.W.) of the N. gateway lies a small temple called the **Birth House.** Similar structures were erected beside all large temples of the Ptolemaic period (e.g. at Edfu and Philæ). They were dedicated to the worship of the sons of the two deities revered in the main temple, in the present case to Har-sem-tewe (p. 261). This birth house was built by Augustus and some of its reliefs were added by Trajan and Hadrian. In the style of a peripteros (p. clxxi) it is surrounded on both sides and at the back by a colonnade of flower-columns, the abaci of which are adorned with figures of Bes, patron deity of women in labour.

An incline leads to a wide Forecourt, in the pavement of which is cut the ground-plan of a late-Roman trefoil-shaped building. — Interior. We first enter a vestibule, from which opens on the right a flight of steps (contrived within the masonry; upper part destroyed) which led to the roof. On the left is a door to the colonnade, while another leads to a chamber. A door in the middle admits to a *Transverse Chamber*, adjoined by the *Sanctuary* or birth-chamber proper, the mural reliefs in which represent the birth and nursing of the divine infant. In the rear wall is a shallow door-recess. The small rooms on either side of the sanctuary are inaccessible.

Immediately to the S. of the Birth House is a large **Coptic Church,** dating from the end of the 5th cent. and interesting as a characteristic example of the arrangements of an early Egyptian church (only the churches near Sohâg are older, see pp. 229, 230). The entrance is at the N.W. corner. Thence we pass through a vestibule (with a shell-niche) to reach the *Narthex*, which occupies the whole width of the church and has a semicircular recess at its N. and S. ends. To the W. are small chambers and a staircase. Three doors lead from the narthex to the *Nave*, the sides of which are adorned with niches. The trefoil-shaped *Sanctuary* is adjoined on either side with other chambers.

To the S. of the church lies a **Second Birth House,** begun by Nektanebis I. and completed under the Ptolemies. On the E. side is a *Colonnade*, which has columns connected by screens and is intersected by the enclosure-wall of the Temple of Hathor. Thence a Ptolemaic doorway leads to a *Transverse Chamber* (on the left, a door leading to the open air), off which open three doors. The middle one leads to the *Sanctuary*, with mural reliefs dating from Nektanebis I. and depicting the birth of the divine child Ehi (p. 261).

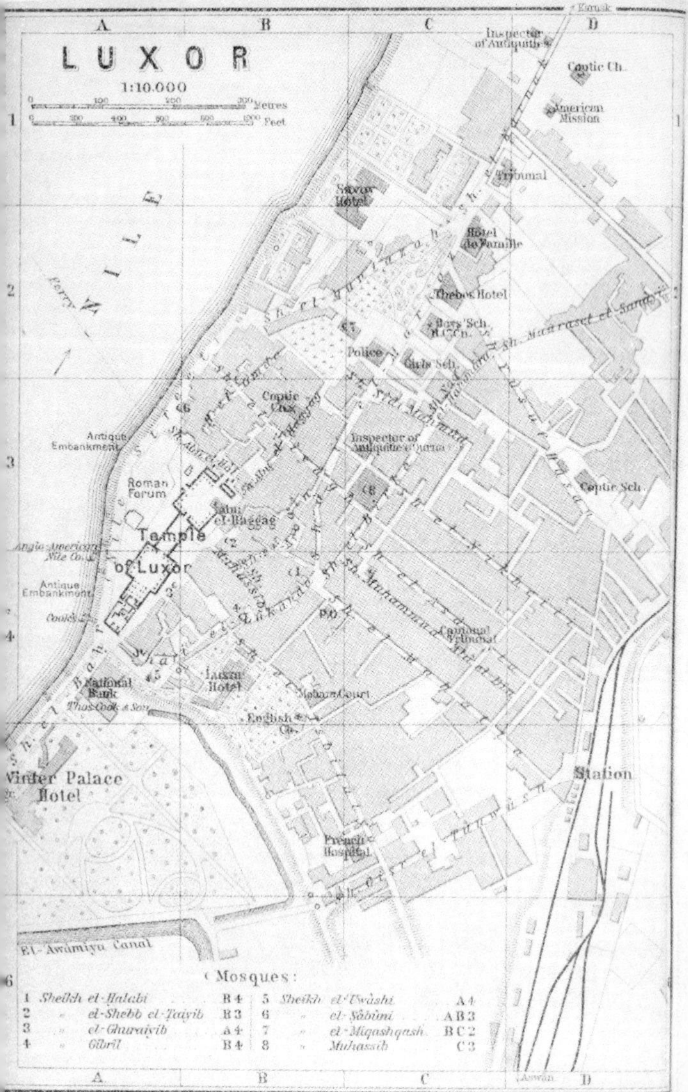
LUXOR
1:10.000
Metres
Feet
NILE
Ferry
Savoy Hotel
Hotel de Famille
Thebes Hotel
Boys' Sch.
Police
Girls' Sch.
Coptic Ch.
American Mission
Tribunal
Inspector of Antiquities
Coptic Chx
Antique Embankment
Roman Forum
Temple of Luxor
Anglo-American Nile Co.
Cook's
National Bank
Thos. Cook & Son
Luxor Hotel
English Ch.
Winter Palace Hotel
French Hospital
Coptic Sch.
Cantonal Tribunal
Station
El-Awamiya Canal
Karnak
Aswan
Mosques:
1 Sheikh el-Halabi B 4
2 " el-Shebb el-Taiyib B 3
3 " el-Ghuraiyib A 4
4 " Gibril B 4
5 Sheikh el-Uwâshi A 4
6 " el-Sabûni A B 3
7 " el-Miqashqash B C 2
8 " Muhassib C 3
Wagner & Debes, Leipzig

The doors at the sides lead to two rooms devoid of ornament; from the left-hand one a spiral staircase ascends to the roof. — The brick buildings to the S. of this birth house are Roman (perhaps baths).

Farther S., to the W. of the Temple of Hathor, is the *Sacred Lake*, a deep basin lined with blocks of stone and entered by a flight of steps at each corner. Doors on the N. and S. sides lead to inner staircases contrived within the masonry and leading to a lower water-level.

The *Temple of Isis*, which stands on a lofty terrace behind the Temple of Hathor to the S.W., owes its origin to the Emperor Augustus. The W. half is destroyed. The entrance is on the N., but the rooms inside are kept locked. — To the E. of this is a large *Temple*, of which only the foundations have survived. It consisted of a forecourt, a wide and a deep hall (each with four columns), and several subsidiary chambers.

21. Luxor and its Environs. The Site of Ancient Thebes.

Arrival. By steamer, see p. 240; by railway, see p. 233. — The *Railway Station* (Pl. D 5; buffet) lies to the S.E. of the town. Cabs (P.T. 2) and hotel-buses (see below) meet the trains.

Hotels. * *Winter Palace* (Pl. A 5), on the quay, to the S. of the landing-places, with restaurant, lift, terrace, and a beautiful view of the Nile, closed from the middle of April to the middle of Nov., 220 R. (150 with bath), at 90-210 (before the season 70-160), B. 15, L. 45, D. 55, pens. 180-300 (140-240), omnibus 16 P.T.; *Luxor* (Pl. B 4), with lift and electric heating, open all the year round, 100 R. (30 with bath) at 60-150 (before the season 40-90), B. 12, L. 35, D. 45, pens. 130-200 (90-150), omnibus 16 P.T., well spoken of. These two, both with large gardens, are owned by the Upper Egypt Hotels Co.; pension rates are granted only for a stay of five days or more. — *Savoy* (Pl. B C 1, 2; German proprietor), with a bar and a pretty garden on the Nile, open from Oct. to April, 72 R., pens. from Jan. to March P.T. 80-120, cheaper from Oct. to Dec. and in April, omnibus P.T. 6, well spoken of. — Plainer: *Hôtel de Famille* (Pl. C 2; M. G. Hedra), Shâriʿ el-Markaz, with garden, 40 R., pens. P.T. 55, *Thebes* (Pl. C 2), in the same street, 24 R., pens. P.T. 60, both clean.

Post Office (Pl. B 4), Shâriʿ el-Maḥaṭṭa; also at the Winter Palace during the season. — **Telegraph Office** near the Winter Palace (Pl. A 5) and at the railway station.

Bank. *National Bank of Egypt* (Pl. A 4), Shâriʿ el-Baḥr.

Tourist Agencies and **Steamship Offices.** *Thos. Cook & Son* (Pl. A 4), *Anglo-American Nile & Tourist Co.*, *American Express Co.*, *Lloyd Triestino* (D. E. Munari), all near the Winter Palace. — *International Sleeping Car Co.*, at the railway station.

Consular Agencies. British, French, German, Italian, and Belgian.

Physicians. English physician, at the Luxor Hotel; *Dr. C. E. Wetter* (Swiss), at the Winter Palace Hotel. — The *French Hospital* (Pl. B C 5), which is supported by the voluntary contributions of travellers, and the *Government Hospital* are in charge of Egyptian physicians.

Chemists. *English Chemist* (P. Hampton), at the Winter Palace; *Rizgallah*, Shâriʿ el-Markaz.

Churches. *Anglican* (Pl. B 4, 5); *American Mission Church* (Arabic services) and *Chapel* (in the girls' school; English services), both in the Shâriʿ el-Karnak; *Roman Catholic* (Pl. C 2), Shâriʿ el-Markaz. The hours of the services are posted up at the hotels.

Guides. On the E. bank, P.T. 20 for the Temple of Luxor, P.T. 30 for Karnak; on the W. bank P.T. 50-70. A guide is of assistance in saving time, but is not indispensable, as the donkey-boys and cabmen usually know the way. The following guides may be recommended, all of whom speak English: *Girgis Mikhâ'îl* (also conducts long expeditions); *Husein Muhammed 'Elwa*, *Khalîl Ibrâhîm*, *'Abdallâh A. 'Abûdi*, *Mustafa Khalîl*, *'Abd el-Galîl 'Awad*, *Tâya Khâlid*, *Salîb Hanna*, *Ahmed Kareim*, *Muhammed Yehya*, *Ahmed Yehya*, *Amîn Muhammed*, and *Ahmed 'Abdallâh*. The hotel-porters will furnish addresses of others.

The **Donkeys** (comp. p. xix) are good and are well saddled (English saddles available at the hotels). To Karnak and back P.T. 10-15 (bakshish included); to all places on the W. bank P. T. 25; side-saddle P.T. 5 extra.

Cabs and **Motor Cars**. From the station to the town, see p. 267; to Karnak and back P.T. 40; for the whole day on the W. bank 150-200, to Qena (Dendera, comp. p. 261) and back £E 5. — **Boats.** Across the river to the W. bank and back, by sailing-boat P.T. 8, by motor-boat 20 (tickets at the hotels); sailing trip on the Nile, 1 hr. P. T. 20, 2 hrs. 30, etc., 3-4 pers. 30 and 45; for longer excursions by motor-boat apply at the Winter Palace.

Books, Photographs, and Photographic Materials. *Luxor Photo Stores* (A. Gaddis & G. Seif), at the Winter Palace Hotel; *English Photo Stores* (Muhammed 'Abûdi), Nile Street (opposite Cook's landing-stage); *H. Leichter*, Nile St.

Gymkhanas are held weekly during the season.

Antiquities may be obtained from *Mohareb Todrus* (attractive museum near the Temple of Luxor, on the quay), and from the dealers *Mahmûd Bey Muhasseb*, *Ahmed 'Abd er-Rahîm*, *Husein 'Abd el-Magîd*, *Mansûr Mahmûd*, and *Girgis Gubriân*, all in the Shâri' el-Lûkanda (Pl. A B 4), and *Kamâl Khâlid*, at the Winter Palace. Prices vary greatly; several pounds must be paid for a good scarabæus with fine colour. Many of the articles offered for sale in the streets are forgeries skilful enough to puzzle even an expert. Travellers should never buy antiquities without the advice of a connoisseur, for which they may apply with confidence to *Mohareb Todrus* (see above).

Plan of Visit. Travellers by the tourist steamers or members of large travelling parties are more or less committed to the prescribed programme (comp. p. 215). Those, however, who are at liberty to arrange their time for themselves will find the following programme convenient. For all-day excursions the hotels provide their guests with luncheon baskets.

Three Days' Visit. 1st Day. Start early and ride to *Karnak* (p. 277). Those who see the *Great Temple of Amun*, the most gigantic of the monuments, on the first day, may then proceed with the satisfactory feeling that Thebes has fulfilled their highest expectations, and will no doubt take a later opportunity to return and refresh their first impressions. The effect by moonlight is enchanting. In the afternoon visit the temple of *Luxor* (p. 272), reached in a few minutes from the hotels. — 2nd Day. Cross the river as early as possible, visit the *Temple of Sethos I.* (p. 299), ride or drive to the Tombs of the Kings at *Bîbân el-Mulûk* (p. 301), then cross the ridge on foot to visit the temple of *Deir el-Bahari* (p. 317; an excursion of 7 hrs.). — 3rd Day. Again cross the river early, visit the *Colossi of Memnon* (p. 345), *Medînet Habu* (p. 347), the *Tombs of the Queens* (p. 342), and *Deir el-Medîna* (p. 338). On the way back (after lunch) visit the *Ramesseum* (p. 324), and finally some of the tombs of *Sheikh 'Abd el-Qurna* (p. 328; another 7 hrs.' day).

On a Longer Stay the traveller will wish to revisit several points, especially the Temple of Amun at Karnak, and will be glad to devote more time to the monuments on the W. bank, particularly the interesting tombs of Qurna. *Medamût* (p. 297) also may be visited, or a half-day trip by railway or motor-boat may be taken to the barrage and temple of *Esna* (p. 357) and the temple of *Edfu* (p. 369). The temples of *Dendera* (p. 261) and *Abydos* (p. 252) also may each be visited in one day from Luxor by railway. To *Qoseir*, see p. 400.

Maps. The best maps of the district are the Luxor & Karnak and El-Qurna sections published by the Survey of Egypt (1:10,000; Tourist Edition, Cairo 1922; each section P.T. 10, on linen 15), and *Georg Schweinfurth's* (p. ccviii) Map of the Western Environs of Luksor and Karnak (Thebes; 1:25,000; Berlin, 1909; 5*s.* 7*d.*).

Comp. *G. Legrain*, 'Louqsor sans les Pharaons, Légendes et Chansons Populaires de la Haute-Egypte' (Brussels and Paris, 1914); *A. M. Blackman*, 'Luxor and its Temples' (London, 1923); *J. Capart* and *M. Werbrouck*, 'Thebes, the Glory of a Great Past' (London, 1926).

On each side of the Nile stretches a wide belt of fertile land, bounded both on the E. and W. by ranges of hills, which are overtopped by finely shaped peaks, especially on the E., where the ridge retires farther from the stream than on the W. The verdant crops and palms which everywhere cheer the traveller as soon as he has quitted the desert, the splendid hues that tinge the valley every morning and evening, the brilliant, unclouded sunshine that bathes every object even in the winter season, lend to the site of ancient Thebes the appearance of a wonderland, richly endowed with the gifts of never-failing fertility. Most of the ruined temples are situated in the level district and are reached by the waters of the Nile when the inundations are at their highest; the tombs, on the other hand, are hewn in the flanks of the hills, where their dark openings are so numerous that the E. slope of the Libyan range might be compared to a piece of cork or to a honeycomb.

On the Right (E.) Bank lies *Luxor* (*Louxor*, *Luqsor*, *Louksor*, etc.), Arabic *El-Uqṣur*, a district capital of 19,000 inhab. and the chief tourist centre in Upper Egypt. The name is derived from the Arabic *El-Quṣûr* (pl. of *El-Qaṣr*) and means 'the castles', having reference to the extensive temple within which part of the place lay till the end of last century. Near the temple traces of antique embankments on the river (Pl. A 3, 4) and of a nilometer may still be seen; and between the river and the temple are ruins of a forum of the Roman age. The most frequented part of the town is *Nile Street* (Shâriʿ el-Baḥr, Pl. A 5-3), extending N. and S. from the temple; here are the Winter Palace Hotel, the National Bank, Cook's offices, and many shops. On the E. the Shâriʿ el-Maḥaṭṭa, with the post office, runs straight to the railway station (p. 267). From the N. end of Nile Street the Shâriʿ el-Muntazah leads to an open space adorned with gardens and skirted by the *Shâriʿ el-Markaz* (Pl. B C 3, 2). Here are the *Markaz* or district offices (with the police station; Pl. C 2), a *Mosque* (Pl. 7), a *Roman Catholic Church*, Italian schools for boys and girls, and the Savoy (Pl. B C 1) and other hotels.

To the N. of Luxor extend the immense ruins of *Karnak* (p. 277), connected with it formerly by the lanes of the city, now by a broad street planted with trees (Pl. C D 2, 1). Even under the Pharaohs the Temple of Amun was considered the most striking creation of an age peculiarly famous for architectural achievements. To this day few other buildings in the world can match its dimensions.

Farther N. is another extensive temple-site at *Medamût* (p. 297), which has replaced *Medu*, the sister-town of Thebes.

On the Left (W.) Bank (p. 298), now often known as 'Thebes', was the *Necropolis*, with vaults in the rock and tombs on the desert soil, adjoined by many temples and dwelling-houses. Even in antiquity the Tombs of the Kings (p. 301) were reckoned among the chief sights of ancient Thebes.

The History of Thebes under the Ancient Empire is veiled in uncertainty. The Egyptian name for the town was *Wēset*, or more shortly *Newt*, 'the city', whence the Scriptural name *No* or *No Amon* ('city', 'city of Amon'; Ezekiel xxx. 14 and Jeremiah xlvi. 25). The W. bank was known as 'the West of Wēset'. No satisfactory explanation has been offered of why the Greeks called it *Thebes* (Thebai), a name they frequently bestowed upon their own cities. Among the Greeks the town was known also as *Diospolis*, 'city of Zeus' (Amun), also called *Diospolis hē megalē* or *Diospolis Magna* to distinguish it from Diospolis Parva or Hiw (p. 239). Wēset was the capital of a nome, and it was ruled by princes of its own, whose tombs (6th Dyn.) were at Dirâ' Abu'n-Naga (p. 300). The local deity was the falcon-headed Mont (p. 293), a god of war, who was worshipped also in the neighbouring towns of Medu (p. 297) and Hermonthis (p. 356).

When Theban princes assumed the royal dignity during the Middle Empire (comp. p. ciii), Thebes rose to a more commanding position and at the same time the worship of the hitherto inconsiderable deity Amun of Karnak came into prominence. But the real greatness of Thebes dates only from the beginning of the New Empire. The liberation of the country from the Hyksos (p. civ) and the reunion of the empire was directed from Thebes, and that city continued for centuries to be the favourite seat of the Pharaohs, and the reservoir into which flowed the untold treasures exacted as tribute or brought as booty from conquered nations. A large share of this wealth was bestowed upon Amun. The magnificent and gigantic temples built at this period to the god are still among the chief sights of Thebes. The already existing sanctuary of *Epet-esowet* at Karnak was enlarged, and the temple of *Apet Resyet* ('the southern house of the women') was erected. The grandees of the kingdom esteemed it an honour to become priests of Amun, the schools beside his temples flourished, and the kings offered their richest gifts to this god. Thebes was now an Oriental world-metropolis, of which the prophet Nahum (iii. 9) could say that "Nubia and Ethiopia were her strength, and it was infinite; Put and Lubim were thy helpers." Even Homer had heard of the great city (Iliad ix. 379-384; possibly a later interpolation): —

"Where, in Egyptian Thebes, the heaps of precious ingots gleam,
The hundred-gated Thebes, where twice ten score in martial state
Of valiant men with steeds and cars march through each massy gate."

The epithet 'hekatompylos' or hundred-gated was applied also by later classical authors to Thebes. Diodorus (1st cent. B.C.), Strabo (p. 272), Pliny (d. 79 of our era), and Stephanus of Byzantium (7th cent.) all make use of it, referring to the gates of the town as symbols of its size and power. The persecution of the god Amun by Amenophis IV. (p. cv) and the temporary transference of the royal residence to Tell el-ʿAmârna (p. 245) affected Thebes but slightly. Its images and inscriptions were restored under Haremhab, Sethos I., and Ramses II., and the wealth of the god became greater than ever. An idea of the endowments of the temple of Amun may be gleaned from the fact that under Ramses III. more than two-thirds of the landed property possessed by the temples of Egypt belonged to it, and that three-quarters of the gifts lavished by Ramses III. upon the gods of Egypt fell to the share of Amun, so that, for example, of 113,433 slaves, no fewer than 86,486 were presented to the Theban deity. Under these circumstances it was natural that the high-priests of Amun should gradually grow to regard themselves as the chief persons in the state; and they finally succeeded in usurping the throne and in uniting for a time the royal title with the priestly office (comp. p. cvii). But the sun of Thebes began to set when the royal residence was transferred to the Delta under the princes of the 21st Dynasty (comp. p. cvii). For a long time, however, Thebes, with a large part of Upper Egypt, formed a distinct political entity, governed by the high-priests of Amun and more or less independent of the kings residing in the N. In the 7th cent. B.C. the armies of the Assyrians penetrated as far as Thebes and plundered it; the Ethiopians planted their rule here and honoured Amun with buildings and inscriptions; the princes of the 26th Dyn. did for Saïs (p. 36) what the princes of the 18th and 19th Dyn. had done for the city of Amun. The invading army of Cambyses (p. cix) ascended as far as Upper Egypt, but seems to have done little or no damage at Thebes. Nektanebis II., one of the native Egyptian princes who maintained themselves against the Persians, added a gate to the temple of Mont. Alexander the Great and the kings of the house of the Ptolemies probably found Thebes still a great though decadent city, and they assisted to embellish it, as many buildings dating from the Ptolemaic period still attest. The town of Ptolemaïs (p. 230), founded and endowed with many privileges by Ptolemy I., became the capital of Upper Egypt, and rapidly proved a dangerous rival to the ancient metropolis. For a brief interval Thebes, though politically and economically weakened, recovered its independence under native princes by putting itself at the head of the revolt in Upper Egypt under Epiphanes (p. cxii) against the Macedonian domination. But the rebellion was speedily crushed and Thebes once more reduced to the rank of a provincial town. Under Ptolemy X. Soter II. it again rebelled, but after a siege of three years was captured and destroyed (comp. p. cxiii). In spite of its evil fate it once

more revolted, taking part in the Upper Egyptian insurrection in 30-29 B.C. against the oppressive taxation of the Romans. The prefect Cornelius Gallus (p. cxiv) overthrew the rebels and utterly destroyed the town. Strabo, who visited Egypt in 24-20 B.C., found only scattered villages on the site of the ancient city. Thenceforward Thebes is mentioned only as a goal of inquisitive travellers, who under the Roman emperors were attracted in particular by the temples and the colossi of Memnon.

The introduction of Christianity and the edicts of Theodosius (p. cxvi) were followed by the destruction of many pagan statues and the obliteration of many of the ancient inscriptions. The Nile, which annually overflowed as far as the temple of Karnak, and the saline exudations of the soil wrought great harm; many tombs were converted into peasants' dwellings; Christian churches and convents were erected in the temple halls (comp. p. clxxxviii), and dwelling-houses were built between the columns of the temple at Luxor. Hewn blocks and slabs were removed from the monuments, which were used as quarries, and many architectural details were thrown into the furnace and reduced to lime.

The Tickets of Admission (p. 212) essential for entering the temples and tombs should not be forgotten.

A. THE EAST BANK AT THEBES.

I. The Temple of Luxor.

The main entrance to the temple by the great pylon (p. 273) is now closed. We therefore proceed from the road on the bank of the river to the court of Amenophis III. (p. 275), whence we visit the great colonnade (B) and the inner parts of the sanctuary (B-X; pp. 275-277). We then return to the court and proceed through the colonnade to the court of Ramses II. (p. 274) and the chapel of Thutmosis III. Thence we pass through the W. gate (p. 275) and inspect the pylon from the exterior.

To the S. of the town and close to the bank of the Nile rises the imposing ***Temple of Luxor** (Pl. A B 3, 4), which still contains, within its N.E. part, the highly venerated little mosque of Abu 'l-Ḥaggâg, the local saint of Luxor. The temple was built by Amenophis III. (p. cv) on the site of an older sanctuary of sandstone, and was called by the Egyptians *Apet Resyet* (p. 270). It was dedicated to *Amun*, his wife *Mut*, and their son, the moon-god *Khons*. Like all Egyptian temples, it included the sanctuaries of the gods with their adjoining rooms and vestibules, a large hypostyle hall, and an open peristyle court approached from the N. by a great double colonnade. The temple was 623 ft. in length, while its greatest breadth was 181 ft. Opposite the temple was a granite chapel, erected by Thutmosis III. During the religious revolution under Amenophis IV. (comp. p. 271) the representations and name of Amun were obliterated, and a sanctuary of Aton was built beside the temple. Tutankhamûn (p. cvi) transferred the royal residence back to Thebes, and caused

the walls of the colonnade to be decorated with reliefs (p. 275), in which Haremhab afterwards substituted his own name for that of his predecessor. The Temple of Aton was destroyed, and in the reign of Sethos I. the figures of Amun were restored. Ramses II., the greatest builder among the Pharaohs, could not refrain from adding to the temple at Luxor. He constructed a large colonnaded court in front of the completed temple; he 'usurped' the ancient chapel of Thutmosis III. and replaced the old reliefs with new ones; and he erected a massive pylon, the entrance of which was formed next the chapel of Thutmosis, so that the longer axis of the main temple was altered. The total length of the temple was now 853 ft. Later centuries brought few alterations to the temple of Luxor. After the introduction of Christianity it was converted into a church. A modern wall on the side next the river protects it against damage from inundation.

In front of the principal **Pylon** (Pl. *P-P*) of the temple were six *Colossal Statues* of Ramses II., two sitting and four standing, of which only the two sitting and the westernmost of the others are now in position. The sitting figures are about 45 ft. in height; that on the E. is buried breast-high in rubbish, while that on the W. is supported at the back by an obelisk. In front of these figures rose two *Obelisks* of pink granite, erected on the occasion of a jubilee of Ramses II., one of which (the W.) has adorned the Place de la Concorde at Paris since 1836. The inscriptions name Ramses the Pharaoh, with many pretentious titles, as the founder of this gorgeous building erected in honour of Amun in Southern Apet.

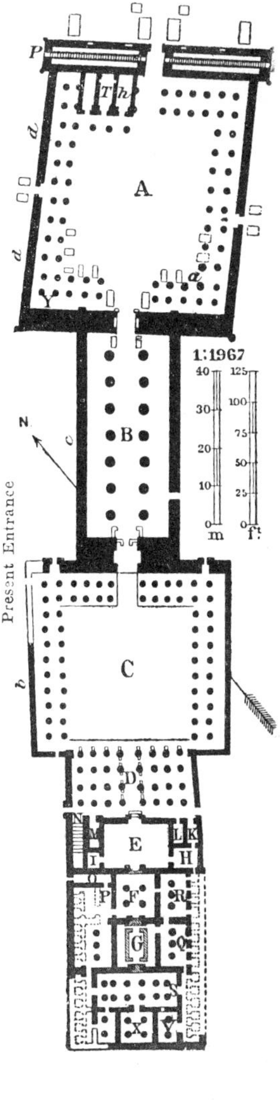

The exterior walls of the pylons are adorned with *Reliefs* 'en creux' referring to the campaign against the Hittites, which Ramses II. carried on in Syria in the 5th year of his reign. They have suffered severely from the hand of time and at several places are almost obliterated. On the *Right (W.) Tower*, to the left, the king on his throne holds a council of war with his princes; in the middle is the camp, fortified by the shields of the soldiers arranged side by side and attacked by the Hittites; to the right, the king in his chariot dashes into the fray. — The scenes on the *Left (E.) Tower* plunge us into the battle; the king in his chariot dashes against the foes who have surrounded him, and launches his arrows against them. The field is strewn with the dead and wounded, while the Hittites flee in wild confusion to the fortress of Kadesh, whence fresh troops issue. Farther to the left Kadesh, girt with water, appears, with the defenders on the battlements. Remote from the battlefield, to the extreme left, the prince of the Hittites stands in his chariot, surrounded by his guards, and 'fears before his majesty'. — Below the reliefs on the W. tower is a long poetical description of the battle of Kadesh, inscribed in vertical lines. It is continued on the E. tower, where, however, the text is still partly concealed by rubbish.

On the front of each tower of the pylon are two large vertical grooves for the reception of flagstaffs, and above these are large square apertures to receive the braces securing the flagstaffs and loopholes to admit light and air to the interior. The portal between the towers is buried in rubbish and in a very ruinous condition. The reliefs represent Ramses II. in presence of the chief deities of the temple. The carvings in the doorway, in somewhat high relief, date from the reign of the Ethiopian king Shabako (p. cviii).

Beyond the principal pylon (though not accessible from this side, comp. p. 272) lies the great **Court of Ramses II.** (Pl. A), which was entirely surrounded by a double row of papyrus-columns (seventy-four in all), with bud-capitals and smooth shafts. It measures 187 ft. in length and 167 ft. in breadth, but, owing to the presence of the mosque of Abu 'l-Ḥaggâg (p. 272) the N.E. portion has not yet been laid bare. On a platform in the N.W. corner lies an ancient *Chapel* (Pl. *Th*), built by Thutmosis III. and restored and adorned with reliefs by Ramses II. It contains three chambers, of which that in the centre was dedicated to Amun, that on the W. to Mut, and that on the E. to Khons, each once containing the sacred bark of the god. On the side facing the court it had a small colonnade of four clustered papyrus-columns in red granite.

The *Walls* of the court are covered with reliefs and inscriptions, including sacrificial scenes, hymns to the gods, representations of conquered nations, etc., most of which date from the reign of Ramses II. The relief on the S.W. wall (Pl. Y) shows the façade of the temple of Luxor, with the pylons and flagstaffs, the colossal statues, and the obelisks, while from the right approaches a procession,

headed by the princes and followed by garlanded animals for sacrifice. (The scene is continued on the W. wall.) — On the W. side is a gate forming an exit from the temple (p. 272); in front are two statues of Ramses II. which have lost their upper portions.

The S. half of the court is further embellished with standing *Colossi of Ramses II.*, placed between the columns in the first row. These, with the exception of one in black granite, are wrought in red granite and average 23 ft. in height. The finest (Pl. *a*) is $17^1/_2$ ft. high; the crown, carved from a separate block, has fallen off; on the pedestal and apron is the name of Ramses II. On each side of the S. doorway is another colossal figure of the king in black granite, seated with the queen by his side.

On the S. side this court is adjoined by a **Colonnade** (Pl. B), which forms the beginning of the processional way leading to the temple. It is in fairly good preservation and contributes essentially to the dignified appearance of the ruins of Luxor when viewed from the river. Seven couples of papyrus-columns, about 52 ft. in height, with calyx-capitals, still support a heavy architrave above a lofty abacus. The whole was built by Amenophis III., but Tutankhamûn (p. 272), Haremhab, Sethos I., Ramses II., and Sethos II. have likewise recorded their names upon it. The walls on each side of the colonnade were embellished by Tutankhamûn (whose name was later replaced by that of his successor, Haremhab) with fine reliefs, representing the voyage of the god Amun and his divine companions to the celebration of the festival of the 'Southern Apet', which took place about the middle of the inundation period and lasted twenty-four days. On that occasion the sacred boats of the gods were brought by the Nile from Karnak to Luxor, borne into the temple at Luxor, and returned to Karnak at the end of the festival. The procession is here depicted in a realistic manner in all its interesting details, though unfortunately a large part of the reliefs has perished with the ruined upper part of the walls. The series begins at the N.W. corner of the colonnade and ends at the N.E. corner.

On the *West Wall* (from N. to S., i.e. beginning on the visitor's right) are represented the following scenes from the festal voyage: 1. The king's sacrifice to the boats in the temple of Karnak; 2. Priests carrying the boats from the temple to the Nile; 3. Voyage on the Nile to Luxor, accompanied by a crowd of pilgrims by land; 4. Procession of the boats from the Nile to the temple of Luxor; 5. The boats of Luxor, with sacrificial offerings. — *East Wall.* Return to Karnak after the conclusion of the festival: 1. The king's sacrifice to the boats in the temple of Luxor; 2. The boats carried back to the Nile; 3. The return journey by water; 4. Procession of the boats from the Nile to the temple of Karnak; 5. Sacrifice of the king to the boats at Karnak.

The (second) **Court of Amenophis III.** (Pl. C), which visitors actually enter first, is 148 ft. deep and 184 ft. broad, and had double rows of columns on three sides. The columns are clustered papyrus-columns with bud-capitals; the E. and W. rows, with the architrave, are in excellent preservation.

The remaining (S.) side of this court is adjoined by the **Pronaos** or *Vestibule* of the temple proper (Pl. D), the roof of which was borne by thirty-two clustered papyrus-columns arranged in four rows of eight. The reliefs on the E. wall show Amenophis III. before the gods of Thebes; at the foot of the wall are personifications of the Egyptian nomes, bearing gifts. On the S. wall (on either side of the apse) is the coronation of Amenophis by the gods. To the left stands an *Altar*, dedicated to the Emperor Constantine, with a Latin inscription. Adjoining the rear wall are two small *Chapels* (Pl. L and M) and a staircase (Pl. N), the latter destroyed. One chapel (L) was dedicated to the goddess Mut, the other (M) to the moon-god Khons. — A door in the centre of the rear wall admits to a smaller hall, which originally had eight columns and was converted into a *Church* (Pl. E) at the end of the 4th century (comp. p. clxxxviii). The ancient entrance to the sanctuary chambers has here been altered into a kind of apsidal recess, bounded on the right and left by two granite Corinthian columns. In the apse and on the walls are remains of important Christian paintings (4th cent.). At a few points the Christian whitewash has peeled off, permitting the beautiful bas-reliefs of Amenophis III. to become visible again. Adjoining the church are several small rooms (Pl. I on the W., Pl. H and K on the E.).

We return to the vestibule and quit the temple by a door on the E. side, then turn to the right and re-enter it almost immediately (three doors) to inspect the **Birth Room** (Pl. R), the roof of which rested upon three clustered columns. The room owes its name to the *Reliefs* on the W. wall, referring to the divine birth of Amenophis III. The reliefs on the S. wall refer to his accession to the throne.

West Wall. *Lowest Row* (from left to right): 1. The god Khnum moulds two infants (Amenophis III. and his guardian spirit) upon the potter's wheel; opposite is seated Isis. 2. Khnum and Amun. 3. Amun and Mut-em-weye, mother of Amenophis III., seated upon the hieroglyphic symbol for 'heaven', and supported by the goddesses Selket and Neith. 4. Amun conversing with Thoth. 5. The king and Amun (much defaced). 6. Isis (defaced) embracing Queen Mut-em-weye; to the right stands Amun. — *Middle Row:* 1. Thoth foretells to Mut-em-weye the birth of her son. 2. The pregnant Mut-em-weye conducted by Isis and Khnum. 3. Confinement of Mut-em-weye; beside and beneath the couch are Bes, Toëris, and other genii. 4. Isis (defaced) presents the new-born prince to Amun. 5. Amun with the child in his arms; beside him are Hathor and Mut. — *Top Row:* 1. To the left is the queen, with the goddess Selket seated behind her; to the right two goddesses suckle the infant prince and his guardian spirit; below, the prince and his guardian spirit suckled by two cows. 2. Nine deities holding the prince. 3. The god Hekew (painted blue) carrying the prince and his guardian spirit; behind is the Nile-god. 4. Horus hands the prince and his guardian spirit to Amun. 5. Khnum and Anubis. 6. The prince and his guardian spirit seated and standing before Amun. 7 (in the corner), Amenophis as king.

From the Birth Room we enter *Room Q*, the roof of which is supported by three columns, and thence, after glancing at the much damaged reliefs, we pass through an arched doorway, of later insertion, into the so-called **Sanctuary of Alexander the Great** (Pl. G).

This chamber was practically rebuilt in the reign of Alexander. The original four supporting columns in the centre were replaced by a chapel (open both front and rear), in which the sacred boat of Amun was preserved. The reliefs covering both the interior and exterior walls of the chapel represent Alexander before Amun and his fellow-gods; those on the walls of the chamber still show Amenophis III. before the Theban deities. — A door in the wall on the N. side of the sanctuary admits us to a small square *Hall* (Pl. F), with four clustered papyrus-columns. The wall-reliefs, which are in three rows, show Amenophis III. before Amun and other Theban deities.

The **Rearmost Rooms** of the temple are of comparatively little interest. From the Sanctuary of Alexander we pass through a gap in the wall into *Room S* (with twelve columns), which is adjoined by three *Chapels*. The central one of these (Pl. X) has a ceiling which was borne by four clustered papyrus-columns. A relief to the left shows Atum and Horus conducting the king into the sanctuary. The other reliefs represent the king in presence of Amun. — *Chapel V*, accessible also from without the temple, was dedicated to the ithyphallic Amun (Kamephis).

We now proceed to inspect the *Pylon* (p. 273). On the way thither the traveller should not omit to cast a glance on the exterior W. walls of the temple (Pl. *b*, *c*, *d*), which were embellished by Ramses II. with reliefs of scenes from his Asiatic campaigns. — The outer S.E. wall of the Court of Ramses II. is inscribed in great vertical lines with the famous poem celebrating the battle against the Hittites.

Between the road on the bank of the Nile (which is blocked up) and the great colonnade are remains of later buildings, including a Christian basilica with a baptistery.

A paved street, flanked on both sides with figures of recumbent rams, each with a small image of Amenophis III. in front of it, led to the N. from this temple to the temples of Karnak. The avenue of sphinxes beside the temple of Khons at Karnak (p. 278) is a remnant of this street.

II. Karnak.

Guides, *Motor Cars*, *Carriages*, and *Donkeys*, see p. 268. — Hurried travellers should see the Temple of Khons and the main portions of the great Temple of Amun (temple of Ramses III., hypostyle hall) and of the Festal Temple of Thutmosis III. They should then walk S. along the great processional way to the 10th pylon and drive thence to the Temple of Mut. The view from the first pylon of the Temple of Amun (p. 282) and the survey of the great Hypostyle Hall (p. 284) are wonderfully effective by moonlight.

The Shâriʿ el-Markaz (p. 269) is prolonged N. by the wide *Shâriʿ el-Karnak* (beyond Pl. C D 1), on the right of which are the law courts, the church and schools of the American Mission, and the Coptic church. Beyond a small bridge over a canal we skirt the Roman Catholic cemetery (left). The motor-road to the right, passing the Temple of Mut (p. 297) and crossing the railway, leads to Qena (comp. p. 268), while the road to the left runs direct to the great Temple of Amun and the house of the director of the excavations at Karnak (p. 280). The main road, straight ahead, brings us to

the village of *Karnak* and the Temple of Khons. On the way we pass the pedestals of numerous recumbent rams (p. 277), while others flank also the old road to the Temple of Mut that diverges here.

a. Temple of Khons and Surrounding Buildings.

A handsome *Portal*, erected by Euergetes I. (p. cxi), with a winged sun-disk in the concave cornice, forms the S.W. entrance to the precincts of Karnak, which are enclosed by a brick wall. The reliefs show Euergetes praying and sacrificing to the Theban deities. Beyond this portal another avenue of sphinxes, erected by Ramses XI., last of the Ramessids, brings us to the beautiful temple of Khons.

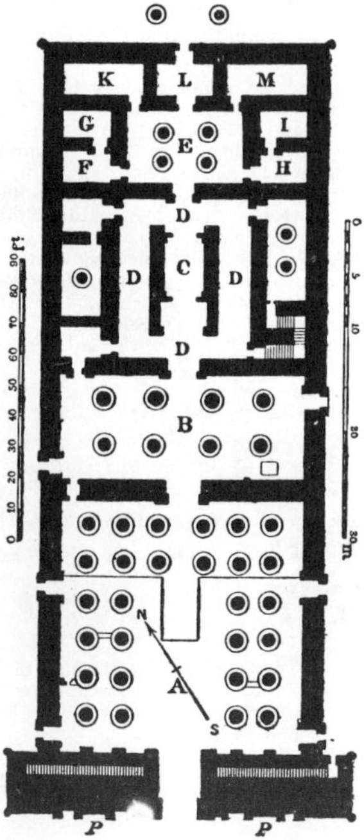

The **Temple of Khons** was dedicated to the Theban moon-god Khons, son of Amun and Mut, and, like Ramses III.'s temple to Amun (p. 282), may be regarded as a typical example of an Egyptian sanctuary under the New Empire. Ramses III. reared the walls of this temple, but placed reliefs only in the innermost chambers; the completion of the decoration was left for his successors Ramses IV., Ramses XI., and the priest-king Herihor (p. cvii), the last of whom built also the court (Pl. **A**).

The entrance is formed by a large **Pylon** (Pl. *P-P*), 105 ft. in length, 33 ft. in breadth, and 59 ft. in height. Upon the front may be seen the four vertical grooves, with the corresponding apertures in the masonry, used in fastening the flagstaffs. The reliefs on the towers of the pylon show the high-priest Pinutem I. (21st Dyn.) and his wife Hent-tewe sacrificing to various Theban deities. In front of each tower lay a porch, borne by columns and surmounted by a wooden ceiling. The bases of the columns are still in situ.

The central portal (reliefs of Alexander II.) admits to the **Court** (Pl. A), which is surrounded on two sides by a colonnade with a double row of papyrus-columns with bud-capitals. On the smooth shafts and on the walls are representations of Herihor offering sacrifices. The court had four side-exits.

On the right (E.) wall is a noteworthy relief: Herihor offering incense before the sacred boats of Amun (ram's head), Mut (goddess's head), and Khons (falcon's head). To the right is a relief of the façade of the temple, showing the pylon with its flagstaffs.

In the rear of the court is an incline leading to the PRONAOS or *Vestibule*, which is borne by twelve columns. Beyond this lies a **Hypostyle Hall** (Pl. B), occupying the entire breadth of the building. The central aisle has four papyrus-columns with calyx-capitals, while the two aisles on each side, which are 5 ft. lower, are separated by two columns with bud-capitals. On the walls and columns appear Ramses XI. and Herihor (p. 278), high-priest of Amun, sacrificing to various deities.

A door in the centre of the rear wall leads to the **Sanctuary** (Pl. D) containing the **Chapel** (Pl. C), which is open at both ends and in which was preserved the sacred boat of Khons. The reliefs on the outside of the walls of the chapel represent the king (Ramses IV. and Ramses XI.) before various gods. Blocks bearing representations and cartouches of Thutmosis III. and Amenophis III. have been built into the walls of the chapel.

On each side of this hall lie dark chambers, with reliefs by Ramses IV.; and behind it a doorway of the Ptolemaic period admits to a **Small Hall** (Pl. E), with four sixteen-sided columns. The reliefs in this hall exhibit Ramses IV. (but occasionally also the Emperor Augustus, e.g. on each side of the entrance) before the Theban gods. Adjoining are seven **Small Chambers** (Pl. F-M), with reliefs of Ramses III. and his successor. In Rooms H and I the colours are particularly well preserved: on the wide N. wall of Room I, the king, accompanied by Hathor, offers flowers to the falcon-headed Mont of Thebes and the goddess 'Sun of both lands, eye of Rē', who sit in a chapel; on the W. wall, the king offering incense and holy water to a lion-headed, ithyphallic deity and to Khons. In Room M, which was dedicated to the worship of Osiris, is a representation of the dead Osiris upon his bier, with Isis and Nephthys mourning over him.

The exit into the open air from Room L is now walled up, and the staircase ascending from Room D to the roof of the temple (view) is inaccessible.

A **Temple of Epet**, the hippopotamus-goddess (p. clvi), erected by Euergetes II. (p. cxii), adjoins the temple of Khons on the S.W.; it stands upon a basis about 10 ft. in height, crowned with a concave cornice. The keeper of the temple of Khons will open it on request. The main entrance is on the W. side; on the jambs appears the king before Osiris and other deities. We enter first a *Rectangular Hall*, with a well-preserved ceiling resting upon two columns, with flower-capitals and heads of Hathor above them. The grated windows at the top of the S. wall should be noted. To the right lie three side-rooms with crypts; the door on the left is built up. — We proceed through the central door into a *Second Hall*, with mural reliefs showing the king and various deities. This is flanked by two side-rooms.

The room on the left contains a representation of the dead Osiris on the bier, with Isis and Nephthys at his side. — The room on the right was dedicated to the birth of Horus: opposite the door, Isis suckling Horus, surrounded by gods; the king brings (left) milk and (right) a piece of cloth. On the lintel of the door, Har-sem-tewe (p. 261) as a falcon with a double crown is protected in the marsh by the hippopotamus-goddess Epet and a lion-goddess.

We then pass through a door, on the right jamb of which appears the goddess Epet, and enter the *Sanctuary*, where a figure of the goddess stood in a niche. The niche-reliefs show the king before Epet, who is represented (left) as a post with the head of Hathor and (right) as a hippopotamus. — In the E. wall of the temple is a small *Chapel of Osiris* (separate entrance on the E. side, opposite the door in the S.W. corner of the court of the Temple of Khons), constructed by Ptolemy XIII. (p. cxiii). To this belongs the shaft issuing from the sanctuary of the Temple of Epet, in which perhaps a relic of Osiris was buried.

b. The Great Temple of Amun.

The Temple of Amun, like those on the left bank (comp. p. 298 seqq.), is placed with its longer axis at right angles to the Nile. According to the practice of Lepsius and other Egyptologists, we consider the Nile as flowing from S. to N., and so use the simple expressions W., N., E., S., whereas geographical accuracy would require N.W., N.E., S.E., and S.W. On some of our plans these imaginary points of the compass are indicated as well as the true N. — Plan, see p. 279.

From the Temple of Khons we proceed in the direction of the Nile and soon reach the first pylon of the great temple of Amun. To the W. of this is the *House of the Director of the Excavations* (Director of Works, Antiquities Department). Direct route from Luxor, see p. 277. Donkeys and carriages must be left at the door to the W. of the seventh pylon (p. 295). — The rectangular terrace in front of the first pylon was even in antiquity covered by the waters of the inundation, as is indicated by marks on its front, recording the height of the inundations under the 21st-26th dynasties. On the terrace rises a small *Obelisk of Sethos II.*, beside which is the base of its companion. An avenue of recumbent rams, erected by Ramses II., extended from this point to the portal of the temple of Amun. The fragments of building to the S.W. of the right pylon-tower belong to a *Chapel* erected about 390 B.C. by King Achoris and his successor Psamuthis (p. cx). In the interior Psamuthis appears on the right and left walls, offering incense to the boat of Amun.

The great **Temple of Amun was not built on any single uniform plan. Its foundation must be dated not later than the first monarchs of the 12th Dynasty (2000-1788 B.C.), most of the Pharaohs taking some share in its enlargement or adornment. Amenophis I. (p. cv) built a second sanctuary alongside the main temple of the Middle Empire, but this was again removed at an early period (p. 294). When Thutmosis I. made Thebes the capital of the New Empire the original modest shrine seemed no longer worthy

of the dignity of the god, and the king therefore built round the temple of the Middle Empire a large court which was bounded on the W. by a pylon (No. V), and was surrounded inside by colonnades with statues of Osiris. At a later date he erected in front of this another pylon (No. IV) with an enclosing wall, placed two obelisks in front of this, and constructed a colonnade between the two pylons. In the reign of Hatshepsut (p. cv) alterations and additions were made in the interior. In front of the temple of the Middle Empire, in the court of Thutmosis I., she constructed a special sanctuary, and in the colonnade between pylons IV and V she erected two obelisks, besides practically rebuilding the colonnade itself. Her brother Thutmosis III. continued these alterations when he became sole monarch. He tore down most of the colonnades in the court of Thutmosis I. and replaced them with a series of small chapels. A new pylon (No. VI) was erected, and the court between this and the building of Hatshepsut, which had been embellished with a vestibule, was adorned with colonnades. The colonnade of Thutmosis I., between pylons IV and V, was subjected to a thoroughgoing alteration, the main object of which was to withdraw the obelisks of Hatshepsut from the gaze of visitors to the temple. Two new obelisks were raised in front of those of Thutmosis I. About twenty years later the king continued his alterations of the temple by erecting the two Halls of Annals and the antechambers between pylons V and VI. To the reign of Thutmosis III. is due also the Great Festal Temple which lies to the E., i.e. behind the main temple. Amenophis III. erected a new pylon (No. III) on the main front of the temple. All these buildings of the 18th Dynasty were thrown into the shade by the erections under the 19th Dynasty. Ramses I. raised a fifth pylon (No. II), and he and his successors, Sethos I. and Ramses II., created between this and the third pylon of Amenophis III. that gigantic hypostyle hall, probably left unfinished by Amenophis III., which has remained ever since as one of the chief wonders of Egyptian architecture. Ramses II. caused also a second girdle-wall to be built, and the temple now seemed to have received its final form. The temples of Sethos II. and Ramses III. were separate buildings, erected in front of the great sanctuary. But the Libyan kings of Bubastis (22nd Dyn.) revived the traditions of the ancient Pharaohs. A huge court, incorporating half of the temple of Ramses III., was built by Sheshonk in front of the pylon of Ramses I.; it had colonnades on two sides and ended in a great pylon (No. I). Taharka, the Ethiopian (25th Dyn.), afterwards constructed a processional way with colossal columns in this court. The temple was left unaltered under the Ptolemies, who contented themselves with a few alterations (including the erection of the granite chapel of Philip Arrhidæus). Its decay began in the time of the Roman emperors (pp. 271, 272). — Extensive excavations and restorations have been very successfully accomplished since 1895 by the Egyptian Department of Antiquities.

The *First Pylon is still 370 ft. wide, with walls 49 ft. thick and 142½ ft. high. This gigantic portal, which dates from the Ethiopian period, was never completed; and portions of the scaffolding, constructed of crude bricks, remain to this day. — The inscriptions on the door of the pylon merit notice. The one on the right, high up, placed there by the savants who accompanied the army of Napoleon to Egypt in 1799, records the latitude and longitude of the chief temples of the Pharaohs, as calculated by them; opposite, on the left, is one erected by an Italian learned society (Feb. 9th, 1841), showing the variation of the compass as 10′56″.

A magnificent *View is enjoyed from the top, which is reached by a staircase on the N. tower (comp. below). It is interesting to seek to identify, with the aid of the accompanying plan, the various columns, obelisks, and pillars, though at first we seem to see nothing but a confused system of ruins.

The *Great Court, built by the rulers of the 22nd Dynasty, is 276 ft. deep and 338 ft. wide. On each side is a row of columns, that on the right (S.) being interrupted by the temple of Ramses III. (see below).

To the left stands the small Temple of Sethos II., built of grey sandstone, with the exception of the door-frames and the lower part of the walls, for which a reddish quartzose sandstone has been used. The temple has three chapels, adorned with good reliefs, of which that in the centre was dedicated to Amun, that on the left to Mut, and that on the right to Khons. The niches contained images of the gods. A staircase inside the wall of the Khons chapel leads to the roof of the temple.

Beside the Temple of Sethos II., on the N.W. side of the court, are a number of recumbent rams, which were stored here in antiquity. They belonged to the avenue of recumbent rams, erected by Ramses II. (p. 280), which led to the second pylon, and were removed on the erection of the various buildings in the great court.

In the centre of the great court are two large *Pedestals* for statues (that on the right retains its base only). Behind was the *Colonnade of Taharka;* of the original ten columns there still stand five broken shafts on the left side and one complete column (with calyx-capital and abacus) on the right. This structure had a door on each of its four sides; in front of the W. door is a recumbent sphinx.

Upon the complete column, on the right, which was restored in 1927, Psammetichos II. (26th Dyn.) has placed his name over that of the Ethiopian Taharka (25th Dyn.); beside it is the name of Ptolemy IV. Philopator (p. cxii), which appears also on the abacus. The shaft is composed of twenty-five courses of carefully hewn stone, the capital of five courses. The height is 69 ft.; the greatest breadth of the capital 16 ft., the circumference at the top 49 ft. The columns were united by means of stone screens, dating from the reign of Philopator.

A door in the N. walk of the colonnade surrounding the great court leads out of the temple, and from this point we may skirt the outer wall to the left to the steps leading to the top of the First Pylon (see above).

The *Temple of Ramses III., to the right, facing the great court, was dedicated to Amun. It is perhaps the best extant specimen of

a simple Egyptian temple, built throughout on a single homogeneous plan. Its total length is 170 ft.

The *Pylon* with the entrance-door, which has two statues of the king, is much injured at the top. On the exterior of the left tower (E.) Ramses III., with the double crown, smites a band of prisoners with his club. Amun, in front of him, hands him the sword of victory and delivers to him chained together the representatives of the vanquished peoples, who appear in three rows. In the two upper rows are the conquered nations of the south, in the third row those of the north. On the right tower are similar representations, the king here wearing the crown of Lower Egypt. In the doorway Ramses III. receives from Amun the symbol of life, etc.

Beyond the pylon is an open *Court*, flanked by covered passages. The roofs of these passages are each supported by eight pillars, against which lean colossal figures of Ramses III. as Osiris.

On the rear walls of the pylon-towers, facing the court, are representations of Ramses III. receiving from Amun the hieroglyph for 'jubilee', as a sign that the king would yet celebrate many jubilees. — The walls of the colonnades are embellished with reliefs: in the E. arcade, the procession of the sacred boat of Amun; in the W. arcade, a procession with the statue of the ithyphallic Amun, borne by priests and accompanied by standard-bearers. — The architraves bear florid dedicatory inscriptions, recording that Ramses III. erected this monument in honour of his father Amun. — A door in the left colonnade opens into the Portico of the Bubastides (see below); and one in the right colonnade (now built up) admitted to the S. colonnade of the great court.

The court is adjoined by the *Vestibule* or *Pronaos* of the temple, which latter is on a higher level. It is supported in front by four Osiris-pillars, and in the rear by four columns with bud-capitals. The pillars are united by stone screens adorned with reliefs.

From the vestibule a door leads into a *Hypostyle Hall*, with eight columns with bud-capitals. Adjoining are three *Chapels*, dedicated respectively to Amun (in the middle; with two lattice-windows), Mut (left), and Khons (right), and each containing representations of the king sacrificing to the boat of the respective god. Beside the chapel of Khons is another chamber, and beside the chapel of Mut is a staircase, while beyond the chapel of Amun, on each side, is a chamber.

From the court of the Temple of Ramses we pass through the E. door to the so-called *Portico of the Bubastides*, situated at the S.E. corner of the great court. This portico was embellished with reliefs and inscriptions by the kings of the 22nd Dynasty.

The following reliefs may be particularized. To the left (E.; on the projecting wall), above: Amun hands King Osorkon I. the curved sword and the palm-branch (symbol of long life); below: Khnum holds the hieroglyph for 'life' to the king's nose; Hathor gives milk to the king. — Right (W.) wall: Takelothis II. and his son Osorkon, the high-priest of Amun, before Amun. Below is a long inscription.

We then return to the great court and proceed to the dilapidated **Second Pylon of Ramses I.** The two towers, with four long grooves for the flagstaffs (p. clxxii), have been freed from the ruins of later

buildings which were erected in front of it out of the materials of a temple of the heretical period (comp. p. cv). In the centre is the huge portal. In front of the portal was a kind of small *Vestibule* the entrance to which was flanked by two statues of Ramses II. The figure on the right side still stands; only the legs of the other figure remain. On the S. side of this vestibule appears Ramses II. defeating the foes of Amun. In the doorway, where the cartouches of Ramses I., Sethos I., and Ramses II. are found, an intervening door was erected by Philometor and Euergetes II. (p. cxii), during their joint reign. The lintel of this doorway is wanting, but the jambs are in good preservation, with reliefs showing the king sacrificing to the gods of the temple. On the inner sides of the earlier doorway are Ptolemaic reliefs showing the same scenes on the right and left. At the foot are the sacred boat of Amun and Ramses III. entering the temple. In the second row from the foot appears Ramses III. kneeling before Amun and holding the symbol of jubilee, indicative of long reign. Behind stands the goddess Mut, while Khons, with the moon's disk on his head, conducts Philometor to Amun. The third row from the bottom shows the king beneath the sacred tree of Heliopolis, with the goddes Seshet inscribing his name among the leaves. Probably the representations are a restoration by Philometor of older works. The other rows exhibit the king in presence of various deities.

We next enter the ****Great Hypostyle Hall,** which was justly considered one of the wonders of the world. It has been restored and had its foundations strengthened by the Department of Antiquities. Though a certain picturesque effect due to the former ruinous condition has necessarily been lost, the huge hall is still extraordinarily impressive as we look southwards from the N. side through the rows of columns. This is especially the case in the morning or evening, or by moonlight, when the columns cast intense black shadows.

The breadth of this great hall is 338 ft., its depth 170 ft., and its area 6000 sq. yds., an area spacious enough to accommodate the entire cathedral of Notre Dame at Paris. The roof was supported by one hundred and thirty-four columns arranged in sixteen rows, of which the two central rows are higher than the others and consist of papyrus-columns with open capitals, while the other rows have clustered columns with closed capitals. The hall is divided into nave and aisles. The nave, itself divided into three aisles, is c. 79 ft. in height. The roof is supported by the two central rows of columns and one of the lower rows on each side, the deficiency in the height of the latter being met by placing square pillars above them. The spaces between these pillars were occupied by windows with stone lattice-work (one on the S. side is still almost perfect). The side-aisles are 33 ft. lower than the nave.

The columns are not monolithic but are built up of semi-drums, $3^1/_2$ ft. in height and $6^1/_2$ ft. in diameter. The material is a reddish-brown sandstone. Each of the twelve columns in the two central rows is $11^3/_4$ ft. in diameter and upwards of 33 ft. in circumference, i.e. as thick as Trajan's

Column in Rome or the Vendôme Column in Paris. It requires six men with outstretched arms to span one of these huge columns. Their height is 69 ft., that of the capitals 11 ft. The remaining hundred and twenty-two columns are each $42^1/_2$ ft. in height and $27^1/_2$ ft. in circumference.

Side-doors (several now closed) lead from the hypostyle hall into the open air (comp. the plan). — A door in the N.W. corner leads to a corridor and thence to a staircase ascending to the roof of the N. tower of the 2nd pylon. — The door in the N.E. corner gives on a staircase to the roof of the hypostyle hall. A corresponding staircase on the left of the S. side-door commands a striking view of the hall; another staircase (closed) by the S.E. side-door (Pl. *k*) leads to the roof of the 3rd pylon.

Hypostyle Hall of Karnak (reconstruction, after Maspero).

On the right as we enter is a door-like frame of a vanished memorial of Ramses II., probably a kind of folding altar, in front of which lies an alabaster slab with a representation of enemies (negroes and Asiatics) 'under the soles of the king'; to the left of the door is a colossal double statue of Amun and Ramses II.

The walls of the hall, the columns, the abaci, and the architrave are covered with inscriptions and reliefs, many of which still retain their ancient colouring. These date from the reigns of Sethos I. and Ramses II., the former of whom decorated the N. half of the hall (as far as the tenth row of columns), the latter the S. half. Only a single column (the first in the sixth row) bears the names of Ramses I.

Ramses III., Ramses IV., Ramses VI., and Ramses XII. have likewise recorded their names.

Among the beautiful *Mural Reliefs of Sethos I.* those on the N. wall are of special merit. To the left of the N. side-door (Pl. *a*), below: Sethos in front of the sanctuary containing the sacred boat of Amun; Sethos conducted to the temple by Mont, with a falcon's head, and Atum; procession of sacred boats; above, Sethos and the gods of Thebes. Right of the door (Pl. *b*), below: Sethos offering incense to the sacred boats; Sethos conducted to the temple (comp. p. 285); Sethos kneeling in the chapel before Amun and Khons and receiving the symbols of a long reign; above, Sethos sacrificing to the various metamorphoses of Amun; the king kneeling to the god Harakhte, who is seated under a canopy, while behind the king stands the lion-headed goddess Wert-hekew with a palm-branch from which various symbols are suspended; to the left, the king on his knees beneath the sacred tree of Heliopolis, while Thoth inscribes the name of Sethos among the leaves. — Among the *Mural Reliefs of Ramses II.*, which seem to refer to his visit to Thebes in the first year of his reign, we note especially those on either side of the S. door. Right, the king sacrificing to the sacred boat, which is carried by priests wearing falcon or jackal masks; Ramses walks by the boat wearing priestly dress with a panther's skin; behind, the boats of Khons and Mut, likewise borne by priests. Left, below, the king in front of the chapels of the sacred boats of Amun, Mut, and Khons; farther left, the king kneels to Amun, Mut, and Khons beneath the sacred tree of Memphis and receives the symbols of a long reign, while Thoth writes the king's name among the leaves. — In the S. aisle are two fine sandstone statues of Sethos II. (headless).

On the outside walls of this hall are ***Historical Reliefs** of great importance, commemorating the victories of Sethos I. (N.) and Ramses II. (S.) over the inhabitants of Palestine and Libya (best seen by afternoon light).

We pass through the N.E. door, beside Pl. *d*, and begin with the reliefs at the E. end of the NORTH WALL (Pl. *d*). *Upper Row.* Here we see King Sethos in Lebanon. The inhabitants, whose physiognomies are distinctly characterized, are forced to fell trees for him. *Lower Row.* Battle with the Beduin of S. Palestine. Sethos is driving in his chariot and launching his arrows against the foes, who lie in confused heaps of dead and wounded. Above, to the left, is the fortress of Canaan, whose inhabitants are beseeching mercy or assisting the fugitives to ascend into it.

We now turn the corner and reach Plan *e*. *Upper Row* (partly destroyed; described from left to right). 1. Battle of Yenuam in Syria. The king, advancing to the attack in his chariot, shoots arrows against the enemy, whose charioteers, cavalry, and infantry flee in wild confusion. To the left is the fortress of Yenuam, surrounded with water. The inhabitants of the country, many of whom are represented full face (contrary to the usual Egyptian method), conceal themselves among trees. 2. The king binding captive Syrians with his own hand. 3. The king, marching behind his chariot, appears dragging four captives with him and drawing others in two rows behind him. 4. Sethos leads two rows of captured Syrians before the Theban triad, Amun, Mut, and Khons, to whom he also presents costly vessels captured amongst the booty. — *Lower Row* (from left to right). 1. Triumphal progress of the king through

Palestine. Sethos, standing in his chariot, which advances at a walk, turns towards the princes of Palestine, who do him homage with uplifted hands. Behind the king are a fortress and the costly vessels taken from the foe. Above and below the horses are seen small castles, built by the king to protect the water-stations. 2. Battle against the Beduin of S. Palestine. The king, in his chariot, shoots arrows against the enemy, the survivors of whom flee to the mountains. Beneath are several castles and wells, with the wounded lying beside them. 3. Victorious return of the king from Syria. The king stands in his chariot, preceded and followed by fettered captives. The boundary between Asia and Africa is marked by a canal bordered by reeds, in which crocodiles swim; the canal is spanned by a bridge, at each end of which is a fortified guard-house. On the Egyptian side (to the right) two groups of priests, with nosegays, and grandees welcome the returning monarch. 4. The king dedicates the captured Syrians and the booty to Amun.

To the right and left of the door are two colossal reliefs, in which the king raises his club against a band of foes whom he holds by the hair. Opposite is Amun, with several rows of captured nations and cities, presenting the curved sword of victory to Sethos.

The representations on the W. part of the N. wall (Pl. *f*) begin at the other end and run from right to left. *Top Row.* Storming of Kadesh in the land of Amor (N. Palestine). The king (figure wanting) shoots against the foe from his chariot, which has overthrown a hostile chariot. To the right, on a tree-clad height, appears the fortress of Kadesh, the defenders of which are pierced with arrows. A herd of cattle, accompanied by the herdsmen, takes to flight. — *Middle Row.* 1. Battle against the Libyans. The king in his chariot holds with his bow a Libyan, whom he is about to smite with the sword. To the right are heaps of dead and wounded enemies. The Libyans are distinguished by large pigtails worn on one side and by feathers on their heads. 2. The king transfixes a Libyan with his lance. 3. The king in his chariot, preceded by two rows of captured foes. 4. The king presents the captives and the booty to the Theban triad. — *Bottom Row.* 1. Battle against the Hittites in N. Syria. The king in his chariot shoots against his foes, who betake themselves to headlong flight in chariots, on horseback, or on foot. 2. The king in his chariot grasps cords to which are fastened several captives and two hostile chariots. In front of him are two rows of captured Hittites. 3. The king consecrates the captives and the booty to the Theban triad, who are in this instance accompanied by the goddess of truth. — We re-enter the great hypostyle hall by the N. side-door and pass through the S. door (the S.E. door being closed) to inspect the reliefs on the outside of the South Wall (Pl. *g*, *h*), which commemorate the campaigns of Ramses II. against the Hittites. They may also be visited after seeing the rest of the temple buildings, from the door beside the seventh pylon (comp. p. 295).

At the W. end of the S. wall, on the outside of the S. tower of the second pylon, is the Triumphal Inscription of Sheshonk I. (the *Shishak* of the Bible, p. cvii). This commemorates the victory won by Shishak in Palestine in the fifth year of Rehoboam, son of Solomon, King of Judah. The large form of Amun appears to the left, grasping in his right hand the sword of victory and in his left cords binding five rows of captured towns in Palestine, each of which is represented by a circular wall enclosing its name, beneath the upper part of a fettered prisoner. The curved noses, prominent cheek-bones, and pointed beards of the captives clearly identify them as Semitic. Beneath Amun appears the goddess of the Theban Nome, with the name of the nome upon her head: 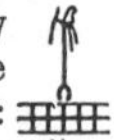 She holds a club, bow, and quiver, and leads five rows of captives with cords. To the right Shishak is seen grasping a group of cowering Semites by the hair and smiting them with his club. The figure of Shishak was left unfinished.

The Biblical passages referring to the campaign are I. Kings xiv. 25, 26 and II. Chron. xii. 2-9. Of the name-labels only a few can be identified with certainty with otherwise known names of places in Palestine, such as Rabbah (last ring of the first row), Taanach, Shunem, Rehob, Haphraim, Mahanaim, Gibeon, Beth-horon, Kedemoth, Ajalon (second row). The rest of the inscriptions, which are couched in the usual bombastic style, give no further information as to the campaign.

On the projecting wall of the court to the E. of the S. side-door is an inscription containing the *Treaty of Peace* concluded with the king of the Hittites by Ramses II. in the 21st year of his reign (comp. p. cvi). — At Pl. *i*, beyond the wall, we see Ramses II. leading two rows of captives before Amun. Beneath is the poetical account of the Hittite campaign. At Pl. *k*, on the end of the wall (beside the closed S.E. door of the hypostyle hall), we find a relief of Ramses II. presenting to Amun the captives and costly vessels taken in the Syrian campaigns.

The **Third Pylon**, built by Amenophis III. and now completely ruined, forms the rear wall of the great hypostyle hall, into which its *Vestibule* still projects. Large alabaster slabs with superb reliefs of Amenophis I., from a temple of that king, were built into it. On the rear of the S. tower (Pl. *l*) is a long inscription (imperfect at the top), recording the gifts of Amenophis III. to the god Amun; and on the rear of the N. tower (Pl. *m*) are seen the last remnants of a larger representation of a festal voyage, in the shape of a sacred bark of Amun with the king on board and another fully manned ship.

In the **Central Court** we come first upon an *Obelisk*, the last survivor of four erected in pairs by Thutmosis I. and Thutmosis III. It is 71 ft. high and stands upon a base 6 ft. square; its weight is estimated at 143 tons. On each face of the obelisk are three vertical inscriptions, the central one being the dedicatory inscription of Thutmosis I. and the other two additions by Ramses IV. and Ramses VI. The bases of the three other obelisks are adjacent. The obelisks of Thutmosis I. marked the entrance to the temple in his reign.

Next follows the **Fourth Pylon**, in a most ruinous condition. (According to the inscriptions in relief the door was restored by Alexander the Great.)

Beyond it are the scanty remains of a **Colonnade**, originally embellished with columns and with niches containing colossal statues of Osiris (with arms crossed and the symbol for 'life' in each hand). Within this colonnade rose the two great *Obelisks of Queen Hatshepsut*, made of fine pink granite from Aswân and originally covered at the apex with electrum (a natural alloy of gold and silver). The right (S.) obelisk has been overthrown and broken, and its upper portion lies on top of the rubbish heap a little farther to the right; long inscriptions on the base celebrate the power of the queen. The left *Obelisk, still standing, is 97 ft. high and its diameter at the base is $8^1/_2$ ft.; it weighs c. 320 tons and is the tallest ancient obelisk known, with the exception of the Lateran Obelisk (in Rome), which is 101 ft. high. On each of the four sides is a single vertical inscription recording the dedication of the obelisks and the fact that they were made in seven months. On the upper parts are reliefs, showing Hatshepsut, Thutmosis I., and Thutmosis III. sacrificing to Amun. The names and figures of Amun were obliterated by Amenophis IV., but restored by Sethos I. By the wall to the left is a granite statue of Thutmosis III., kneeling and holding an altar in front of him.

This colonnade underwent various transformations under the 18th Dynasty. When Thutmosis I. built it originally it had a wooden roof borne by wooden columns, afterwards replaced by stone ones, of which three bases are still in situ. The two obelisks were erected by Hatshepsut to celebrate a jubilee in the sixteenth year of her reign. Thutmosis III. afterwards surrounded the obelisks with a sandstone structure which concealed them to a height of about 82 ft., portions of which still remain. The colonnade was transformed by receiving a stone roof supported by two rows of papyrus-columns (six on the N. side, eight on the S.). The five old columns were, however, retained. Niches were formed in the walls and filled with statues of Thutmosis I., removed from the great court (p. 282). The decoration of the S. part was not concluded until the reign of Amenophis II.

Through the **Fifth Pylon**, also erected by Thutmosis I., we reach two small **Antechambers**, inserted by Thutmosis III. in front of the sixth pylon, and now in a state of ruin. To the right and left of these are two larger courts adorned with colonnades of sixteen-sided columns (comp. p. clxii) and statues of Osiris. These form the last remnant of the great court of Thutmosis I., which once surrounded the temple of the Middle Empire. In the passage leading to the N. court is a colossal seated figure of Amenophis II., in red granite. — The **Sixth Pylon**, the last and smallest of all, an erection of Thutmosis III., is now in ruins. On the walls to the right and left of the granite gateway are representations in the usual style of the cities and tribes subdued by Thutmosis III. (comp. pp. 286, 287); to the right are the tribes of the S., to the left 'the tribes of the Upper Retenu [i.e. Syria], which His Majesty took in the wretched town of Megiddo'.

Beyond the sixth pylon lies the **First Hall of Records**, erected by Thutmosis III. in a court which he had constructed some time previously. Here stand two large *Granite Pillars*, which once supported the roof. The S. (right) pillar bears the heraldic plant of Upper Egypt, the N. pillar the papyrus of Lower Egypt. Here are also the remains of wonderful *Colossal Statues of Amun* (much restored) *and the Goddess Amunet*, in reddish sandstone, dedicated by King Tutankhamûn, whose name was later replaced by that of Haremhab.

To the left and right of this Hall of Records are the court and colonnades of Thutmosis III., the ceiling of which was borne by clustered papyrus-columns with sixteen shafts. On the back of the entrance-door to the S. part are representations of Sethos II. On the E. wall, in the façade of the building of Hatshepsut, is a false door which was once lavishly adorned 'with gold and lapis lazuli'. On the S. side are five chapels for the worship of Amenophis I.

The **Granite Chapel**, in which the sacred boat stood on a pedestal (still in situ), was built in the time of Philip Arrhidæus (323-317 B.C.), probably on the site of an earlier chapel of Thutmosis III., fragments of which have been placed outside. This chapel is built of pink granite and is divided into two chambers. The front chamber, opening to the W., is 20 ft. long, the hinder one is over 25 ft. long and has in the E. wall a double window reached by four granite steps. The walls both outside and inside were covered with reliefs, the colouring of which is still in good preservation at some points. The ceiling too is well preserved.

Interior Walls. In the first chamber Philip appears offering sacrifices to various forms of Amun and performing other religious rites. The figures and inscriptions are picked out with bluish-green pigment. The reliefs in the second chamber are larger, but in poorer preservation. Here, to the left, Philip is seated at a banquet. — *Exterior Walls.* On the S. side of the first chamber are four rows of reliefs, the lowest of which is destroyed: 1. Rites attending the entrance of the chapel by the king; the goddess Amunet gives milk to the king. 2, 3. The sacred boats of Amun, borne by priests, going and returning on a festal occasion. On the S. wall of the second chamber are four sadly damaged reliefs, side by side, representing the king sacrificing to various forms of Amun or performing religious ceremonies. On the N. wall of the first chamber the king offers two small trees to Amun-Kamephis. On the N. wall of the second chamber are representations of foundation ceremonies and of sacrificial scenes.

On the N. wall of the **Second Hall of Records** of Thutmosis III. (enclosing the chapel) are long inscriptions detailing the military achievements of that monarch. The relief above the inscription to the right of the black granite door depicts Thutmosis III. conferring gifts on the temple (two obelisks, vases, necklaces, chests). — Opening off the Hall of Records to the N. and S. are a number of rooms, all more or less in ruins, which were built and embellished with reliefs by Queen Hatshepsut. As in all other places, the names and figures of the queen have been scratched out or replaced by those of Thutmosis II. or Thutmosis III. In the S. half are a room containing a staircase leading to the roof, and a chamber with a granite altar dedicated by Thutmosis III. Here is also a fine statue of Amenophis II. (sitting beside a damaged figure of Amun).

The **Reliefs of Queen Hatshepsut*, in a room to the N. shut off by a black granite door (opened by the keeper), are very fine and have retained their colour well. The left wall, which originally adjoined the N. wall of the second record hall, was removed thence and re-erected here. The portraits of Hatshepsut have been deleted and here and there replaced by poor reliefs of Thutmosis II. and III. Note the difference between the red-skinned Amun of Karnak and the black-skinned Amun-Kamephis.

We now descend to the E. to an open space, strewn with the scanty relics of the earliest *Temple of the Middle Empire*. In front of the chambers of Thutmosis III., which may be recognized on the N. side, ran a path, on which the Pharaohs erected statues to the grandees judged worthy of that honour.

We next reach the ***Great Festal Temple of Thutmosis III.** We enter by the main portal on the S.W. (Pl. *a*), in front of which stand two statues of the king as Osiris (the left one only complete) and the stumps of two sixteen-sided columns (comp. p. clxiv). We turn to the left, traverse the antechambers, and find ourselves in the *Great Festal Hall*, which has five aisles and is 144 ft. wide and 52 ft. deep. The roof of the three central aisles, which were higher than the others, was supported by twenty columns in two rows and thirty-two square pillars. The tent-pole shaped columns (p. clxviii) are unique, and indicate that the architect conceived the central aisles as forming a huge festal tent. The pillars, not so tall as the columns, were of the same height as the outer walls and with the latter supported the pentagonal roofing slabs of the lower side-aisles. At the same time they were prolonged to the same height as the columns by means of imposts and architrave, in order to assist the columns in supporting the roof of the central aisles. The reliefs on the pillars show Thutmosis III. in presence of the gods. The hall contains several torsos of statues found there.

In the Christian era the hall was converted into a *Church* (comp. p. clxxxviii), and the columns still show paintings of the 6-7th cent. portraying personages of the Coptic church.

At the S.W. corner of the hall is the chamber (Pl. *c*) in which was found the so-called *Karnak Table of the Kings*, a list of the Egyptian monarchs from the earliest times down to the 18th Dyn. (removed in 1843 to the Bibliothèque Nationale in Paris). The statues of the ancient kings which were carried in procession by the priests were probably kept in this room. — On the N. side of the three central aisles lie three *Chapels;* the one on the W. (Pl. *x*) contains a colossal group of Thutmosis III. between Amun and Mut. — From the N.W. corner of the hall we next pass through an antechamber (Pl. *z*) into a narrow corridor, the N. side of which is adorned with fine reliefs: Thutmosis III. offering incense to the ithyphallic Amun; the king pouring water over Amun, while on the right priests and singing men and women approach; the king pouring water on an altar in presence of Amun and burning incense. From the N.E. angle of the Festal Hall a flight of steps ascends within a tower-like structure to a chamber of unknown purpose, which still contains an alabaster altar. — The rooms on the E. side of the Festal Hall are in a very ruinous condition. On the N.E. is a chamber with two pillars, and adjoining it lies a dilapidated chapel with a large granite altar. — The central door in the E. aisle leads into three chambers, of which only the lower part of the walls is now left. Adjoining, on the N., and reached by steps, is a Small Room (known as the 'Botanical Garden'), with its roof supported by four clustered papyrus-columns with bud-capitals (still in good preservation);

on the lower part of the wall are representations of the plants and animals brought from Syria to Egypt by Thutmosis III. in the 25th year of his reign. To the S. steps lead to the chambers of the sanctuary, adjoining which is the ALEXANDER ROOM, built by Thutmosis III. and embellished with reliefs and inscriptions in the time of Alexander the Great. The reliefs show Alexander (or occasionally Thutmosis) sacrificing. Farther on is a beautiful HALL with eight sixteen-sided columns (seven still erect), and to the E. of it are rooms with pillars in two stories; beyond that, forming the end of the temple on the S. side, runs a CORRIDOR, opening off which are two small rooms with pillars and seven other chambers with reliefs of Thutmosis III.

The central and E. portions of the Temple of Amun (from Pylon III onwards) were surrounded by a GIRDLE WALL, the extant remains of which are covered with reliefs of Ramses II. sacrificing to the gods. On the E. side of this girdle-wall and to the E. of the Festal Temple of Thutmosis III. lies a second *Sanctuary of Thutmosis III.*, which was probably dedicated to the cult of that king and his sister Hatshepsut after their death. In the central chapel (Pl. *a*) are colossal seated figures of the royal pair; in front of it, to the E., is a pillared hall, containing six gigantic statues of the king as Osiris, which were 'usurped' by Ramses II. — Farther E., in the same main axis (beyond a still unexcavated rubbish-mound), lie the scanty ruins of a *Temple of Ramses II.*, which interrupts an old brick girdle-wall. Beyond the entrance gateway, which is situated on the E. side, we enter a room with eight columns and with two pillars embellished with Osiris-statues; beyond that is a narrow hypostyle hall. To the E., in front of the portal, lay a hall with twenty columns connected by screens, of the time of Taharka (p. cviii). To the N. of this are the remains of another *Temple of Ramses II.*, which was restored in the time of the Ptolemies and was perhaps dedicated to the cult of King Mentuhotep III. (11th Dyn.). To the S., to the E. of the Sacred Lake, are the remains of a brick building dating from a period anterior to the Middle Empire.

Farther on is the well-preserved *East Gateway* (closed) of the great brick girdle-wall which enclosed the whole area of the temple. The gate was built by Nektanebis I. (378-361 B.C.) and is 62 ft. in height. It lies 510 yds. distant from the first pylon (p. 282).

Against the girdle-wall stands a small *Temple of Osiris*, erected by Osorkon III. (22nd Dyn.; p. cviii), his son and co-regent Takelothis III., and his daughter Shepenupet. The first chamber was added later by Princess Amenerdaïs (p. 348), sister of Shabako (25th Dyn.) and mother-in-law of Psammetichos I. Near it are several small chapels of the same period (26th Dyn.). — The destroyed *Temple of Amenophis IV.*, outside the gateway, has a pillared hall once adorned with colossal statues of the king (p. 93); its mural reliefs were broken up and built into the ninth and tenth pylons (p. 296). — If we turn to the right (S.) outside the gateway, we soon reach a small building bearing the cartouches of Ramses III. and Ramses IV.

c. The Northern Buildings at Karnak.

Of the buildings to the N. of the Temple of Amun the Temple of Ptah alone is worth a visit; the others are in such bad preservation that hurried travellers may omit a visit to them altogether.

From the N. side-door of the Great Hypostyle Hall an ancient paved road leads N.E. to the Temple of Ptah, within the precincts of the Temple of Amun, passing (left) a small brick fortress and three small *Chapels of the Late Period.*

The largest or SOUTHERNMOST CHAPEL was built towards the close of the 26th Dyn. by the major-domo Pedeneit. In the doorway we see Psammetichos III. (p. cix) and Queen Enkh-nes-nefer-ib-rē in presence of Amun and other gods. Beyond is a hall built of brick, with four stone columns To the right of the entrance to the sanctuary is Nitocris, wife of Psammetichos II., to the left is Amasis. — The CENTRAL CHAPEL was erected by a court official named Sheshonk in the reign of Amasis, who is represented on the left jamb of the entrance-door. On the right jamb is Queen Enkh-nes-nefer-ib-rē, to whose household Sheshonk belonged. The walls of this chapel are of unburnt brick, with the exception of the gates, the columns of the court, and the sanctuary, which are of stone. — The NORTHERN CHAPEL, the oldest, was built in the reign of Taharka (25th Dyn.), who, along with the princess Shepenupet, appears on the walls.

The ***Temple of Ptah,** patron-god of Memphis, was built by Thutmosis III. and enlarged and restored by Shabako the Ethiopian (p. cviii) and by several of the Ptolemies.

As we approach from the W., we reach five successive *Gateways*, of which the second and fourth (Pl. *a* and *b*) were built by Shabako, whose names have been scratched out, the others by a Ptolemy. Farther on is a *Colonnade*, enclosed by four columns (rich foliage capitals) connected by screens. The small *Pylon* beyond the colonnade has a portal bearing the name of Thutmosis III., restored in the Ptolemaic period. This admits to a *Court* (Pl. *c*), embellished at the back with a porticus supported by two sixteen-sided columns. Two pedestals of red granite stand here, dedicated by Amenemmēs I. (12th Dyn.) and Thutmosis III. In the walls are six ancient recesses. A staircase ascends to the upper story. A doorway (with restored reliefs of Thutmosis III.) in the main axis of the temple leads into the *Sanctuary*, which retains the original reliefs of Thutmosis III. Here stands the image (now headless) of Ptah, which is illuminated with weird effect through an aperture in the ceiling (the modern wooden door should be closed). To the right is a room with a statue of the lion-headed goddess Sakhmet; to the left, another with ancient reliefs of Thutmosis III. — It is instructive to observe the difference in style between the ancient and the restored reliefs.

To the S.E. of the Temple of Ptah, on the way to the Temple of Osiris (p. 292), is a *Storehouse*, built by the Ethiopian Shabako, consisting of a single hall borne by twelve columns. Round the brick walls run stone tables on which the sacrificial gifts were laid.

From the Temple of Ptah a gate in the N. girdle-wall of the Temple of Amun leads to the **North Temple Precincts,** which are surrounded by a brick wall. Here stands the TEMPLE OF MONT, which is now so ruined and covered with rubbish that its ground-plan can scarcely be made out. The temple was built for the war-god Mont (the oldest local deity at Thebes, p. 270) by Amenophis III. (18th Dyn.), though it was subsequently several times enlarged (last in the time of the Ptolemies). The earlier sculptures and architectural fragments are of great beauty. Two obelisks of red granite once stood in front of the N. entrance, of which the bases and some fragments are still extant. The N. gateway of the N. temple precincts, built of sandstone, dates from Ptolemy Euergetes. — In the girdle-wall to the S.

of the Temple of Mont is a gate (comp. p. 271) adorned with the name of Nektanebis II. (Nekht-Har-ehbēt, p. cix) and remains of a list of conquered peoples.

From the sandstone gateway we proceed S.W., passing the remains of a *Ptolemaic Temple* (not yet freed from rubbish), of which the staircase is still to be seen, to *Six Small Chapels*, each of which is entered by a sandstone gateway in the girdle-wall (no inscriptions). Only the two chapels farthest W. have left any considerable remains. The second from the W. contains the name of Amenerdaïs, with that of her brother Shabako. The fine alabaster statue of the princess now in the Cairo Museum (p. 96) was found here. — Farther on towards the river are numerous brick houses of a later date, which have been largely demolished. Among them are the remains of a small temple dedicated by Philopator (p. cxii) to Thoth. — To the extreme N., amidst the houses of the village of Karnak, stands a *Small Temple*, erected by Shepenupet, daughter of the Ethiopian king Piankhi (p. 348), and adorned with palm-columns.

d. The Southern Buildings at Karnak.

Situated to the S. of Ramses II.'s girdle-wall (p. 292) is the **Sacred Lake**, named by the Arabs *Birket el-Mallâḥa* or 'Lake of the Salt Pit', as the water has become saline through infiltration. The banks were anciently faced with hewn stones, and traces of these are still to be seen on the W. and S. sides, and even better on the N., where steps descend into the lake. On the N. bank of the lake stands a structure of Thutmosis III. Near the N.W. corner are the ruins of a building of Taharka (25th Dyn.), and on the bank of the lake is a colossal **Granite Scarabaeus*, which was dedicated by Amenophis III. (18th Dyn.) to the sun-god Atum-Khepre, who was pictured in the form of a scarabæus.

We now proceed to visit the **Connecting Buildings** between the Temple of Amun and the Temple of Mut.

Quitting the central court of the Temple of Amun, we enter a court enclosed on two sides by walls and on the rear by Pylon VII, all of which are in ruins. Here stood two temples taken down under Thutmosis III., one dating from the Middle Empire, the other erected by Amenophis I. The limestone blocks of the latter, which are adorned with fine reliefs, have been rediscovered in the third pylon of Amenophis III. (p. 288). Adjacent is the so-called 'Karnak Cachette' (now closed up again), a large pit in which a profusion of statues of all periods was discovered in 1902-9 (779 of stone, 17,000 of bronze; now mostly in the Cairo Museum); they came from the Temple of Amun and were probably buried here when no longer used. — On the exterior of the W. wall was inscribed the famous treaty made by Ramses II. with the Hittites (p. 288). On the E. wall is a long inscription (Pl. *a*), describing the contests of King Menephthes (Merneptah, p. cvii) with the Libyans and the peoples of the Medi-

terranean (Etruscans, Achæans, etc.), and a triumphal relief (Pl. *b*) of Menephthes, in the presence of Amun, smiting his enemies.

Pylon VII, built by Thutmosis III., whose victories are celebrated on it, originally served, like the following Pylon VIII, as the S. entrance to the Temple of Amenophis I. (see p. 294). In front of the N. façade are seven colossal red granite statues of kings of the Middle and New Empires; in front of the S. façade are the lower parts of two colossal statues of Thutmosis III.; in front of the easternmost of these stands the lower part of a large obelisk of Thutmosis III.

In front of the E. façade of the *East Tower* stand a figure of Osiris (on which is an inscription of Ramses II. added at a later date) and a colossal statue of Thutmosis III. In front of the *West Tower* are (left to right) a colossal statue of Thutmosis III. with the double crown, an Osiris figure of the same (its head on the ground before it), a seated figure of a king of the Middle Empire, a seated figure of Sebek-hotep, a fine statue of Amenophis II., and the left half of a memorial inscription of Haremhab (p. cvi).

Beside Pylon VII is a modern door, by which visitors usually quit the temple precincts (comp. p. 280) in order to inspect the S. exterior walls of the great hypostyle hall (p. 287).

Beside the E. wall of the court between Pylon VII and Pylon VIII lies (immediately to the left) a small much-ruined *Chapel* dating from the reign of Thutmosis III. (in peripteral form, p. clxxi). Farther on, on the same wall, is a representation (Pl. *c*) of Ramses II. sacrificing.

Pylon VIII is in comparatively good preservation. It was built by Queen Hatshepsut and is thus the most ancient part of the entire building. Hatshepsut's names were removed from the reliefs by Thutmosis II. Sethos I. restored the reliefs which Amenophis IV. (p. 271) had destroyed; but in many cases he inserted his own name instead of replacing those of the former kings.

North Side. *Left Tower (E.).* Above, 1. Sethos I. sacrificing to various gods; farther to the right, 2. Thutmosis II. (originally Hatshepsut) led into the temple by the lion-headed goddess Wert-hekew, followed by Hathor; behind the king are priests carrying the sacred boat of Amun; beneath appears Thutmosis I. before the Theban triad. The inscription in front of this king refers to the accession of Hatshepsut. — *Right Tower (W.)*, from left to right: 1. Sethos I. (originally Hatshepsut) led into the temple by the falcon-headed Mont, who holds to his nose the symbol for 'life'; behind are priests carrying the boat of Amun. 2 (upper row, to the right). Thutmosis II. (originally Hatshepsut) before Amun and Khons; behind the king are the goddess Wert-hekew and Thoth, the latter writing upon a palm-branch; beneath (in two rows), Ramses III. before various gods. — On the *Door Jambs* are inscriptions of Thutmosis II. (originally Hatshepsut) and Thutmosis III.

On each side in the Gateway is Ramses II. before various deities.

South Side. Amenophis II. seizing fettered enemies by the hair and smiting them with his club; before him is Amun (inserted later by Sethos I.). — On the *Door Jambs* are inscriptions of Thutmosis II. (left; originally Hatshepsut) and Thutmosis III. (right). — Leaning against the right doorpost is a red granite stele, much damaged, recording the Asiatic campaigns of Amenophis II. — By a side-entrance leading on the E. side into the E. tower are reliefs and inscriptions of high-priests of Amun in the reign of Sethos II. — The outer side of the E. wall of the court (in the direction of the Sacred Lake) is decorated with reliefs of the high-priest Amenhotep in the presence of Ramses IX.

Four colossal seated figures of kings were placed before the S. side of this pylon, the best-preserved of which is that of Amenophis I. (to the W.; of limestone). The two figures of Thutmosis II. retain their lower part only; the one to the W. is of reddish-brown silicious sandstone and bears an inscription on the back recording that Thutmosis III. restored it in the 42nd year of his reign.

The following **Pylon IX**, built by King Haremhab, partly with the remains of a temple of Amenophis IV. (p. 292), has collapsed.

Between Pylons IX and X lies a square court, surrounded by a wall, which is interrupted on the left (E.) side by the ruins of a small **Temple of Amenophis II.** (18th Dyn.).

This temple, probably erected to celebrate the king's jubilee, stands on a basement surmounted by a cavetto cornice and reached by an inclined plane on the W. side. In front of the temple is a *Porticus*, borne by twelve square pillars embellished with reliefs. Thence a granite portal admits us to a large five-aisled *Hall*, the roof of which rested on twenty square pillars with cavetto cornices at the top. A smaller *Pillared Hall* on the right contains the lower portion of a colossal alabaster statue; the corresponding *Hall* on the left is separated from the main hall by a narrow corridor. Most of the sculptures on the walls and pillars are executed in fine low-relief, only a few being in sunk relief; much of the colouring is in good preservation. They all depict the king before various deities.

On the E. wall of the court are several important reliefs of Haremhab (19th Dyn.). At Pl. *d* the king conducts to the Theban triad captives with costly gifts from the land of Punt (p. 233), while at Pl. *e* he appears with fettered Syrian captives.

On the outside of the wall, behind Pl. *e*, is a procession of priests carrying the sacred boats. Beside it is an inscription of the time of the high-priest Pinutem II. (see p. cvii), recording the appointment of a priest in deference to an oracle of Amun.

The reliefs on the W. wall of the court, which also date from Haremhab, are in poor preservation.

Pylon X, which formed the S. entrance to the precincts of the great temple of Amun from the end of the 18th Dynasty onwards, was likewise built by Haremhab, who used the stones of a temple raised by Amenophis IV. (p. 292) in Karnak to his new deity (p. 245). The reliefs on the central granite doorway exhibit Haremhab sacrificing and performing other religious rites. — In front of the N. side of the pylon stand two headless statues of Ramses II., of fine-grained limestone (adjoined by a smaller figure of his wife). Here also are the remains of a stele with a manifesto of Haremheb, intended to restore order to the distracted state. In front of the S. side of the pylon are the remains of colossal statues of Amenophis III. (E.) and Haremhab (W.) and the lower part of a colossus of Osiris.

From Pylon X the *East Avenue of Sphinxes*, erected by Haremhab (stones of Amenophis IV. from Pylon X are now deposited here), leads to a *Gate* in the girdle-wall of the **South Temple Precincts**, built by Ptolemy II. Philadelphus (p. cxi) and embellished with reliefs and long inscriptions. On the E. side of this road is a *Chapel of Osiris-Ptah* (closed), with well-preserved painted reliefs;

the chapel was built by the Ethiopian kings Tanutamun and Taharka (25th Dyn.). From the gate we proceed to an open space (not yet excavated) containing large figures of rams, sphinxes, and a large alabaster stele of Amenophis III., usurped by Ramses II.

To the E. is a ruined *Temple of Amenophis III.*, orientated W. and E. and dedicated to Amon-Rē. It consists of a colonnaded court, a pillared hall, two antechambers, the sanctuary, and side-rooms.

Farther S., in a remarkably picturesque site, is the **Temple of Mut**, built by Amenophis III.

Outside the *Gateway* (Pl. *A*) are pillars with figures of the god Bes. On the gateway are lengthy inscriptions of the Ptolemaic period (hymns to the goddess Mut) and an inscription of Ramses III., who restored the temple. The gateway admits us to a large *Court*, the centre of which was occupied by a processional way flanked with columns and laid out in the main axis of the temple. The court contains numerous seated figures of the lion-headed goddess Sakhmet (placed on a par with Mut), dedicated by Amenophis III. On several of these Sheshonk I. (p. cvii) has placed his own name in place of that of Amenophis. The overthrown colossal statues of Amenophis III. (usurped by Ramses II.) stood in front of the entrance to the temple. — Farther on is a *Second Court*, with the continuation of the colonnade of the processional way and with colonnades also along the walls. Fragments of the Hathor capitals of the columns and of statues of Sakhmet strew the ground; on the left, a black granite statue of Amenophis III. The court is adjoined by a hall borne by papyrus-columns, the sanctuary, and other rooms, all of which are very ruinous.

Behind the Temple of Mut lies a *Sacred Lake*, shaped like a horseshoe, and at its W. end are the remains of a small **Temple of Ramses III.** (19th Dyn.; p. cvii).

The entrance, on the N. side, is formed by a much damaged pylon with two statues of the king. On the W. exterior wall are interesting representations of scenes from the king's campaigns: 1. Battle in Syria; 2. Syrian captives brought before the king; adjoining, heaps of hands cut off from the enemy are being counted; 3. Battle with the Libyans; 4. Triumphal procession of the king, and train of Libyan captives; 5. The king inspecting the captives; 6. Train of captives; 7. Dedication of the spoil to the Theban triad. On the S. wall: the king in the presence of Sakhmet, who is leading Amun by the hand.

Excursion to Medamût (3-4 hrs. there and back), strongly recommended if time permit. The site is reached after $1^1/_4$ hr.'s riding on donkey-back. We take the road to Karnak (p. 277), diverge from it to the E. at the Temple of Mut, and then follow the railway embankment to the right or N. [Or we may traverse the village of Karnak and Nagʿ el-Fôqâni, and then go to the E. towards the railway.] Beyond kilometre-stone 667 we turn E. and soon reach the village of *Medamût (El-Madamûd)*. A somewhat longer route is by the motor-road to Qena (p. 277).

The **Temple of Medamût** was situated in *Medu*, the N. sister-town of Thebes, and now lies in a cultivated district, surrounded by peasants' huts and palm-groves. The excavations of the Institut Français d'Archéologie Orientale (p. 44), begun in 1925 by Ferdinand Bisson de la Roque under the direction of Georges Foucart, have laid bare a large part of the temple. The finds are in the Cairo Museum and the Louvre. The temple was erected in the Ptolemaic period (3rd cent. B.C.) on the site of temples of the Middle and New Empires, and was extended in the Roman imperial age; it was dedicated to the war-god Mont (p. 293) and his sacred bull. The lay-out, orientated W. and E., differs in many respects from other Ptolemaic temples. The entrance in the brick enclosure-wall was a *Gateway* built by Tiberius

now collapsed. The *Main Façade* of the temple resembles a pylon and in front of it were three curious kiosks. Thence doors led to the great *Colonnaded Court*, which was adorned with reliefs of Antoninus Pius. The rear of this was formed by a *Vestibule* (pronaos, p. clxxii), of which five columns are still standing: the two central ones with rich foliage-capitals (with a half-door between them) and three papyrus-columns with bud-capitals. Then come a small *Hypostyle Hall*, two *Antechambers*, and the *Sanctuary*, the last adjoined by several chapels. Behind the temple buildings proper, which were bounded by corridors on the N. and S., lay a separate temple, probably intended for the worship and stable of the sacred bull. At the base of the N., E., and S. exterior walls is represented a procession of the Nile deities, coming from the S. and the N. with their offerings. A memorial inscription on the S. exterior wall represents a Roman emperor sacrificing to the sacred bull and refers to an oracle which formerly existed in this temple. — About 150 yds. to the W. of the entrance gateway (see above) is a *Quay* resembling that at Karnak and formerly adorned with two obelisks. The pavement bears drawings of visitors' footprints and demotic inscriptions.

Near Medamût, to the N.E. of Luxor, is the Coptic convent of **Deir Amba Pakhôm** (about 1 hr.'s donkey-ride), reached by the motor-road branching off from the Karnak road (p. 277), whence we subsequently diverge N.E. across the fields. The convent is occupied by a few Coptic families. The Sun. service in the church, which is unimportant, is attended by the Copts of the neighbourhood, and the large cemetery on the edge of the desert is the burial-place of the Copts of Luxor.

B. THE WEST BANK AT THEBES.

Comp. the adjoining plan of the Necropolis of Thebes.

Donkeys and *Carriages* (p. 268) had better be ordered the night before to be in readiness on the W. bank. — An early start should be made. Luncheon baskets, etc., comp. p. 268. Near the temple of Deir el-Bahari lies Cook's rest-house (p. 317), and near the Ramesseum (p. 324) that of the Anglo-American Nile & Tourist Co. Ferry-boats ply from the chief hotels at Luxor to the W. bank (p. 268).

On the W. bank lay the *Necropolis*, or City of the Dead, and also a large number of temples.† These latter, dating mostly from the New Empire, were dedicated to Amun, the principal deity of Thebes, and were used also as mortuary temples (p. 301) in the worship of deceased kings. They were adjoined by priests' dwellings, libraries, and sometimes schools. In the vicinity were groves and lakes, besides granaries, stables for the sacrificial animals, barracks for the guards, prisons, etc. Close by lay the villages of the numerous workmen who found employment in connection with the cemeteries: masons, painters, builders, and above all embalmers (p. clv), to whose care the bodies were committed. Gradually a whole city arose here, like the quarters beside the tombs of the Mamelukes at Cairo. Under the New Empire its management was placed in the hands of a special official, known as 'prince of the West and general of the soldiers of the Necropolis'.

---

† All the temples on the left bank have their entrances on one of the short sides, facing the Nile. The longer axes of these temples lie from S.E. to N.W., but in conformity with the system mentioned on p. 280 the text speaks of them as if they lay from N. to S.

III. The Temple of Sethos I. at Qurna.

From the landing-place of the ferry-boat and the adjoining stand for carriages and donkeys the road leads past several farms to a narrow branch of the Nile. Beyond this we cross a bridge over the Fâḍilîya Canal and follow the canal bank to the right (on the left, near the estate of Bûlus Bey Ḥanna, is the road to the Colossi of Memnon, p. 345) to the farm of ʿEzbet el-Gineina, where we take the cart-track to the left.

The **Mortuary Temple of Sethos I.** (Pl. F 2) was founded in honour of Amun by Sethos I., and at the same time was devoted to the worship of the king's father, Ramses I. Sethos left it unfinished and Ramses II. 'renewed' it, i.e. embellished it with reliefs and inscriptions. The beautiful execution of these recalls the contemporary sculptures at Abydos (p. 253). The original building was 518 ft. in length, but of this only the actual sanctuary with its halls and chambers, 154 ft. in depth, remains, while there are but scanty relics of the former courts and pylons.

The COLONNADE on the front of the temple originally displayed ten clustered papyrus-columns with bud-capitals, but only nine are now left. On the architrave is the dedicatory inscription of Ramses II. In its inner wall are three doors (Pl. *a*, *b*, *c*), which lead into the three divisions of the temple. On this wall, to the left of Pl. *b*, are representations of the provinces of Upper Egypt (a man and woman alternately), bearing dedicatory gifts; to the right, similar reliefs of the nomes of Lower Egypt. The former have sedges on their heads, the latter papyri — the floral emblems of the two regions. Above the former the king offers incense to the bark of Amun carried by priests; above the latter the king appears before various deities.

Passing through the middle door (Pl. *b*) we enter a HYPOSTYLE HALL with six papyrus-bud columns, flanked on each side by three chambers. On the slabs of the roof of the middle aisle appear the winged sun-disk, flying vultures, and the names of Sethos I., in a frame of serpents, between two vertical rows of hieroglyphics. The low reliefs on the walls show Sethos I. and Ramses II. sacrificing to various deities. Those at Pl. α and at Pl. β represent respectively Mut and Hathor of Dendera suckling Sethos. — SIDE CHAMBERS (Pl. *d*-*i*). *Chamber g* is ruined; the ceilings in *d*, *f*, *h*, and *i* are in good condition. The finely executed reliefs in *e*, *f*, *h*, and *i* depict Sethos I. offering sacrifices or performing sacred ceremonies in presence of various deities. In *i*: on the left wall, Thoth before the sacred bark of the king; on the right wall, (left) the king seated at the banquet with the goddess of the temple behind him, and (right) the king in priestly vestments performing ceremonies before himself; on the rear wall, the king as the god Osiris, seated in a chapel, surrounded by the gods of Thebes (Amun and Mut; left) and of Memphis (Ptah and Sakhmet; right). In *d* are sunk reliefs of Ramses II., showing (right) the king pacing off the temple (comp. p. 325) before Amun

and Amunet, and (left) the king burning incense before Amun, Khons, and Mut. — The hypostyle hall is adjoined in the longer axis of the temple by a higher TRANSVERSE CHAMBER, off which open five other chambers. The middle one of these is the SANCTUARY, which still contains the base for the sacred boat of Amun. The mural reliefs show Sethos I. burning incense to the boat. Then follows a ROOM (with bas-reliefs of Sethos I.) borne by four pillars, with ruined side-chambers.

We now turn (through Chamber *d*, see p. 299) to the right-hand division of the temple, which is in a very ruinous condition. It consisted of the large COURT OF THE ALTAR (Hall of Ramses II.) and of several rooms adjoining it. The sunk reliefs of Ramses II. sacrificing to various gods are inferior to those of the central building and left-hand portion of the sanctuary. The court was used as a church in the Christian period, whence date the seven wall-niches.

We return to the hypostyle hall and pass through Chamber *g* to visit the left-hand division of the temple. In the small CHAPEL OF RAMSES I. (borne by two papyrus-bud columns) are low-reliefs, which were probably 'usurped' by Ramses II.: to the right the king kneeling before Amun, Khons, and the deified Sethos, while behind him is the goddess Mut. — Adjoining are three CHAMBERS (Pl. *A*, *B*, *C*). On the side-walls of the central chamber (Pl. *A*) Sethos I. offers incense to the boat of Amun and anoints the statue of his father Ramses I. with his finger. On the rear wall is a double door-shaped stele to Ramses I., with a representation of the Osiris-coffin of the king, on which Isis is seated in the form of a falcon. The two other rooms (Pl. *B* and *C*) were built by Ramses II. and contain rather crude reliefs (the king before the gods). — A side-door (Pl. *l*) leads from the chapel of Ramses I. to a narrow corridor, the left wall of which is now represented only by the lowest courses of masonry (the steps descend to two underground chambers). Thence we enter (to the right) ROOM *D*, with sunk reliefs dating from Ramses II., showing that king and his father Sethos sacrificing before various deities and performing other sacred rites.

A road leads W. from the Temple of Sethos to the village and necropolis of **Dirâ' Abu'n Naga** (Pl. E 2), situated on the slope of the foot-hills of the Libyan mountains. The rock-tombs date from the New Empire. The following (opened by the keeper) are the most interesting: No. 17, the tomb of *Neb-Amun*, physician to the king (18th Dyn.), a short distance above the prominent reddish house of the Department of Antiquities and the adjacent inconspicuous village mosque. On the right half of the rear wall of the vestibule are representations of Asiatics; the ceiling has beautiful ornamentation. — Farther N., beyond scree-slopes, is No. 20 (near the keeper's hut), the tomb of the fan-bearer *Mentu-her-khopshef*, with funeral scenes. — Adjoining this and reached through a breach in the wall is No. 24, the tomb of another *Neb-Amun*, steward to a queen of Thutmosis III., with pretty stucco reliefs (funeral scenes, fields of the blessed, banquet) and ceiling decorations; on the short wall, a stele with a long inscription. — To the N., higher up, No. 13, the tomb of *Shuroy*, of the 20th Dyn. (Ramesid period), with beautiful funeral scenes. — Farther N., a little lower down, No. 19, the tomb of *Amenmose*, high-priest of a temple of Amenophis I.

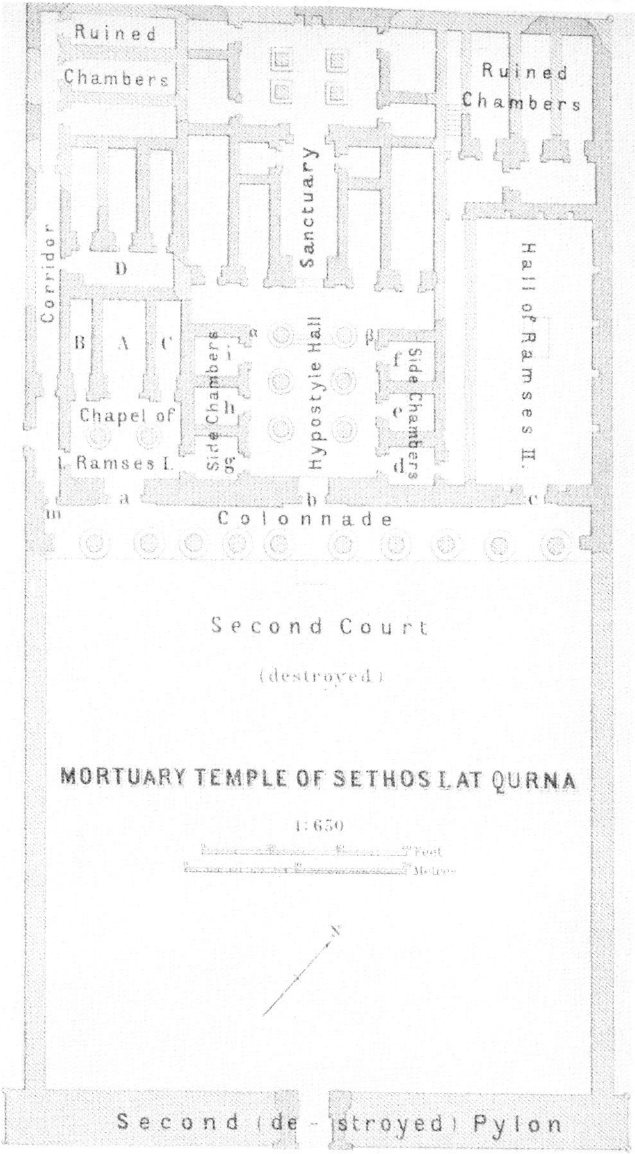

Ruined Chambers
Ruined Chambers
Sanctuary
Corridor
D
B A C
Chapel of Ramses I.
Side Chambers
i
h
gg
a
β
Hypostyle Hall
Side Chambers
f
e
d
Hall of Ramses II.
l
m
a
b
c
Colonnade
Second Court
(destroyed)
MORTUARY TEMPLE OF SETHOS I. AT QURNA
1:650
Feet
Metres
N
Second (destroyed) Pylon

at the beginning of the 19th Dynasty. About one-half of the mural reliefs in the tomb-chamber have survived: they represent the funeral procession and the ceremonies at the tomb. On the right half of the rear wall, the sacred boat with the image of Amenophis I. is drawn out of the temple of which the deceased was high-priest. — A little farther N., No. 155, the tomb of *Entef* (18th Dyn.). We first enter the vestibule, which is covered by a shelter-hut; it was once an open chamber borne by seven pillars. On the rear wall are remains of coloured stucco reliefs: 1. The deceased, accompanied by his wife, receives offerings of every kind; on the right, the grape-harvest, a wine-press, delivery of the jars filled with wine; above, on the extreme right, a fragmentary hunting scene (with hippopotamus). The remains of the stele are on the right short wall. The inner chambers are very ruinous. — Somewhat higher up is *No. 255, the tomb of *Roy* (18th Dyn.), a royal scribe and estate manager of King Haremhab, excavated by Howard Carter (p. 315). On the left entrance-wall, field work. The long wall on the left (S.) shows (above) the deceased and one of his relatives, each accompanied by his wife, praying to various deities; the deceased and his sister are conducted by the hawk-headed Horus to the scales on which their hearts are weighed; Harsiēsis conducts them to Osiris; below, the funeral. On the right (N.) long wall: the deceased, his sister, and various relatives receive offerings from the priest, who is clothed with a panther-skin.

IV. Bîbân el-Mulûk. Tombs of the Kings.

The Tombs of the Kings at Bîbân el-Mulûk (see Pl. B C 1 and the inset) belong to the 18-20th Dyn. and consist of a series of passages and chambers hewn in the rock. Like the corridors within the pyramids that mark the graves of kings up to the beginning of the New Empire, they were intended only for the reception of the sarcophagus; the temples dedicated to the cult of the deceased, in which the offerings to the dead were made and which lay on the E. side of the pyramids, were built in the plain, at some distance from the rock-tombs.

The STRUCTURE of the tombs is practically the same in nearly all. *Three Corridors*, placed one beyond the other, led into the innermost recesses. Small side-chambers sometimes opened off the first corridor, and recesses for the reception of the tomb-furniture were provided in the second and third. The third corridor led into an *Anteroom*, beyond which lay the *Main Hall*, where, in a hollow in the floor, the heavy granite sarcophagus was deposited. The main hall, the roof of which was frequently supported by pillars, was often adjoined by other chambers.

The WALLS of the tombs, from the entrance to the final chamber, were covered with sacred pictures and texts, a knowledge of which was essential for the deceased in the future life. The prevailing conception at Bîbân el-Mulûk was that the deceased king, as companion of the sun-god (or rather absorbed in the sun-god), sailed through the underworld at night in a boat; thus those scenes and texts were preferred which described this voyage and instructed the deceased as to the exact route. These texts were chiefly taken from two books closely related to each other. One was called '*The Book of that which is in the Underworld*' (*Amduat*). According to this, the underworld (*Dēt;* p. cxlix) is divided into twelve regions ('caverns'), corresponding to the twelve hours of night; and the descriptions in the book were therefore likewise in twelve chapters. In each of these the river bearing the boat of the sun is represented in the middle; in the boat stands the ram-headed sun-god, surrounded by his retinue, and bringing for a short time light and life to the regions he traverses. Above and below are shown the two banks of the river, thronged by all manner of spirits, dæmons, and monsters, which greet the sun and ward off his enemies.

The second book, known as the '*Book of Portals*, reproduces the same conceptions. The nocturnal journey of the sun through the twelve regions of the underworld is again represented. Massive gates or pylons, guarded by gigantic serpents, separate one region from another; each

serpent bears a name known to the sun-god, and the deceased must know it also. Two gods and two fire-spitting snakes guard the approach and greet the sun-god.

A third work, which may be called '*The Sun's Journey through the Underworld*', contains still more gloomy and unattractive representations. The sun-god has arrived in the underworld and addresses a speech to the spirits and monsters, which are carefully depicted in long rows.

Recourse was had to other works also for the decoration of the kings' tombs. The chief of these were the '*Sun Litany*' and '*The Book of the Opening of the Mouth*'. The former, which was used in the first corridors, contains a long-winded hymn to the sun-god, to be recited in the evening as the sun entered the underworld. In the course of the hymn the god is invoked under seventy-five different names and is depicted in as many forms. — The text and illustrations in the second of these works teach the multifarious ceremonies which had to be performed before the statue of the deceased king in order to ensure it the use of its organs, so as to enable it to eat and drink in the tomb.

Strabo tells of forty tombs 'worthy of a visit', *Richard Pococke* (1737; p. 135), the first modern traveller to write an account of the valley, describes fourteen, while at present sixty-one are known, but only seventeen of these are accessible. Pausanias (2nd cent. of our era), Ælian (under Septimius Severus, 193-211), Heliodorus (3rd cent.), Ammianus Marcellinus (4th cent.), and other ancient authors refer to them as the *Syringes* of Thebes, from the resemblance of the long corridors to the reeds of a shepherd's pipe. The name occurs also in the Greek inscriptions within the tombs.

There are two routes to Bîbân el-Mulûk (a donkey-ride of 3/4 hr.). The lower of these, described below (see Pl. F 1), leads past the Temple of Sethos at Qurna (p. 299). The mountain-track viâ Deir el-Baḥari (Pl. C 1) is better followed on the return (comp. p. 316).

The well-kept lower road leaves the necropolis of Dirâ' Abu'n-Naga (p. 300) to the left, and winds, first N.W., then W., up the southernmost of two desert valleys known as the *Wâdiyein* ('the two valleys'). The gorge gradually contracts, between walls of naked yellowish rock on which the midday sun pours its perpendicular rays, and a gloomy solitude broods over the scene, which is of a sublimity unmatched elsewhere in the Nile valley.

After riding for about 3/4 hr. through the valley we reach a place where the road divides. The right branch leads to the seldomer visited West Tombs of the Kings (p. 316). The left branch leads to the **Bîbân el-Mulûk** proper ('Doors of the Kings'; Pl. B 1). We dismount at a wooden barrier near Tombs 6 and 7 (comp. the inset plan on p. 298).

The most important tombs (Nos. 6, 8, 9, 11, 16, 17, 35, and the tomb of Tutankhamûn) are lighted up by electricity thrice weekly (Tues., Thurs., and Sat.; mornings only). Special arrangements are in force for the tomb of Tutankhamûn (inquire at the hotels). After the visit to Tomb 11 we should proceed to Tomb 35. Hurried or fatigued travellers may content themselves with the tombs of Ramses VI. (9), Menephthes (8), Amenophis II. (35), Sethos I. (17), and Tutankhamûn. The other accessible tombs (unlighted) are Nos. 1-4, 14, 15, 19, 34, 47, but they are of interest only to specialists. Any other tombs than these may be visited only by express permission from the chief inspector at Luxor. We describe the tombs in numerical order.

The tombs occur both in the main valley and in its branches and are made accessible by easy paths, which, unfortunately, somewhat impair the imposing impression of solitude made by the valley.

On the right (W.) side of the path: *No. 1. Tomb of Ramses X., Yet-Amun.* A Greek inscription proves that it was known and accessible in Greek times.

No. 2. **Tomb of Ramses IV.** An ancient staircase, with an inclined plane in the centre, leads to the entrance. Above the door are Isis and Nephthys worshipping the solar disk, in which stand the ram-headed sun-god and a scarabæus. On the right wall, behind the door, are two Copts raising their hands in prayer; an inscription indicates one of these as 'Apa Ammonios, the martyr'. The designs and inscriptions were painted upon stucco, which has fallen off in nearly every case. In the main chamber is the king's sarcophagus, measuring $10^1/_4$ ft. long, 7 ft. wide, and 8 ft. high, with inscriptions and representations. The tomb was used in the Christian period as a hermit's chapel, and later as a place of pilgrimage (whence the Christian graffiti, about fifty in number, and the above-mentioned saints' picture).

No. 3, to the left of the path, is filled with rubbish; it was originally intended for Ramses III. — *No. 4. Tomb of Ramses XII.*, last of the Ramessids. This tomb has no reliefs and is unfinished. — *No. 5*, farther on, to the left, is the entrance to a corridor.

No. 6. ***Tomb of Ramses IX.**, *Nefer-ke-rē* (lighted), approached by a flight of steps with an inclined plane in the centre. On the staircase to the right is an unfinished inscription of the king. On the door-lintel is the disk, with the king on both sides worshipping it. Behind the latter are (l.) Isis and (r.) Nephthys.

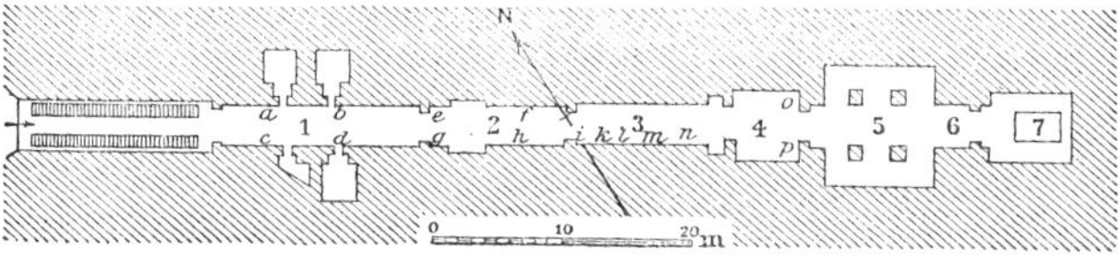

CORRIDOR 1 (comp. the plan). At the beginning of the *Left Wall* is a chapel, beside which (Pl. *a*) the king stands before Harakhte and Osiris. Two doors farther on admit to small chambers without decoration; over the doors is a text from the 'Sun Litany'. At Pl. *b* is a text from the 125th chapter of the 'Book of the Dead' (p. 111), containing the deceased's profession of his sinlessness, beneath which a priest, clad like the god Hor-Enmetf, pours the symbols for 'life', 'stability', and 'welfare' upon the king, who is clad like Osiris. On the *Right Wall*, at Pl. *c*, we see the king in a chapel before Amun and Meret-seger, a goddess of the dead. Two doors here also admit to side-chambers. Over the doors and at Pl. *d* are representations of serpents and of spirits with the heads of dogs and bulls. The text contains the beginning of 'The Sun's Journey through the Underworld' (p. 302).

CORRIDOR 2. On the *Left Wall*, at Pl. *e*, is a serpent rearing itself, to the right of which and in the recess are figures of the sun-god (from the 'Sun Litany'). Below the recess is the king followed by Hathor. At Pl. *f* is a text from the 'Book of the Dead'; farther right the king, over whom hovers a falcon, appears before the falcon-headed Khons-Neferhotep. On the *Right Wall*, at Pl. *g*, is a serpent; and at Pl. *h*, dæmons and spirits (some enclosed in oval rings). The *Ceiling* is adorned with stars.

Corridor 3. On the *Left Wall* is the course of the sun during the second hour of night and the beginning of the course during the third hour. On the *Right Wall*, at Pl. *i*, the king presents an image of Maat to Ptah, beside whom stands the goddess Maat. Adjacent at Pl. *k* is a representation of the resurrection: the mummy of the king lies across a mountain, with the arms raised above the head; above are a scarabæus and the sun-disk. At Pl. *l*, *m*, and *n* three rows of dæmons are shown, one above the other. In the top row are eight suns, in each of which is a black man standing upon his head; in the central row are serpents pierced by arrows, praying women standing upon mounds, and a scarabæus in a boat, ending at stem and stern in serpents' heads; in the lowest row are dæmons upon serpents, also four men bent backwards, spitting out scarabæi, etc.

Room 4. At Pl. *o* and *p* appear two priests, each with a panther-skin and side-lock, sacrificing before a standard.

Room 5. This room, the ceiling of which is supported by four pillars, and then a passage (6) lead downwards to Room 7, which contained the sarcophagus. On the walls are gods and spirits. On the vaulted ceiling are two figures of the goddess of the sky (representing the morning and evening sky), beneath whom are constellations, boats of the stars, etc.

Opposite, on the right side of the path, is *No. 7*, the *Tomb of Ramses II.*, which was plundered in antiquity. The king's mummy was afterwards buried at Deir el-Baḥari (comp. pp. 101, 102).

On either side of the entrance-passage are raised hieroglyphics with texts from the 'Sun Litany'; on the left are the king before the sun-god Rē-Harakhte and a representation of the sun with the ram-headed sun-god and the scarabæus. Some of the inner rooms are still filled with rubbish, and their designs and inscriptions in flat relief are much damaged.

No. 8, the ***Tomb of Menephthes**, *Merneptah* (lighted), lies in a side-gorge, a little to the right of the path. Over the entrance are Isis and Nephthys worshipping the sun-disk, in which are a scarabæus and the ram-headed sun-god.

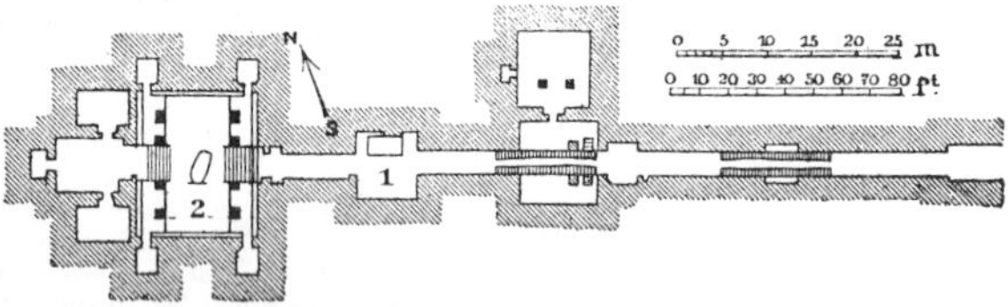

Entrance Corridors, adorned with texts from the 'Sun Litany', with figures of gods (on the left, a beautiful coloured bas-relief of the king before Rē-Harakhte), and with scenes from the realm of the dead (from the 'Book of Portals'), lead down somewhat steeply to an Anteroom (Pl. 1), in which lies the granite lid of the outer coffin. Farther on steps descend into a Pillared Chamber (Pl. 2). The central space is barrel-vaulted, the aisles have flat roofs. This contains the **Lid of the Royal Coffin*, on which the figure of the ruler rests as on a mattress. The lid, which, as usual, is in the form of a cartouche (p. cxxxvii), is beautifully executed in pink granite. The face is very impressive when lighted up by electricity. The chambers adjoining and behind the Pillared Chamber are unimportant and inaccessible.

No. 9. ***Tomb of Ramses VI.**, *Neb-ma-rē* (lighted). This tomb was named by the French Expedition *La Tombe de la Métempsycose*, and by British scholars, following the traditions of the Romans, the

Tomb of Memnon, as Ramses VI. bore the same prænomen as Amenophis III. (p. cv), who was called Memnon by the Greeks. The tomb, which was originally intended for Ramses V., is distinguished by the excellent preservation of its coloured sunk reliefs, which, however, are inferior in style to those of the 19th Dynasty.

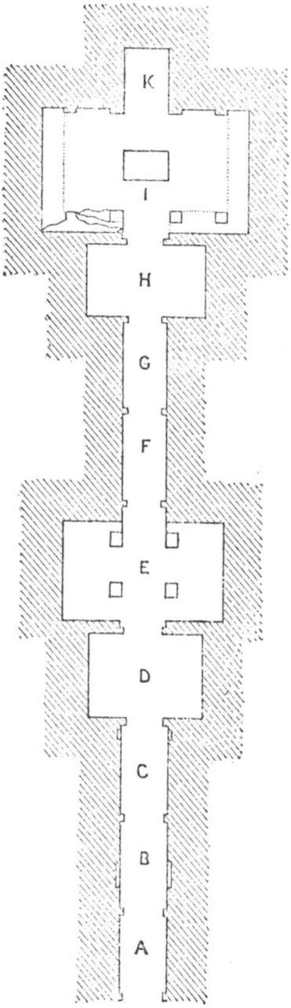

Three Corridors (Pl. *A*, *B*, *C*) lead to an Antechamber (Pl. *D*) and then on to the First Pillared Hall (Pl. *E*), with which the original construction of Ramses V. ended. On the left walls of these chambers appears the journey of the sun through the realms of the dead as related in the 'Book of Portals' (p. 301). On the walls to the right are other texts and pictures relating to the world beyond the tomb. On three pillars in the Pillared Room the king is seen sacrificing to the gods of the dead; the ceiling is adorned with astronomical tables. Two Corridors (Pl. *F*, *G*), the walls of which depict the subterranean journey of the god of the sun, according to the 'Book of that which is in the Underworld', lead to a Second Antechamber (Pl. *H*), the walls of which are covered with inscriptions and scenes from the 'Book of the Dead'. The wall to the left is occupied by chapter 125 (see p. 303). Next comes the Second Pillared Hall (Pl. *I*), still containing remnants of the great granite sarcophagus. On the walls are texts relating to the underworld. In the rear wall is a niche (Pl. *K*). On the vaulted ceiling the goddess of the sky appears twice, representing the sky by day and by night, with the hours. — This tomb contains numerous Greek and Coptic inscriptions.

Immediately below No. 9 lies the tomb of Tutankhamûn (p. 315).

No. 10 is the *Tomb of Amen-meses*, one of the claimants of the throne at the end of the 19th Dyn. (p. cvii). His mother Takhat and his wife Beketwerer also were buried here. The representations in this tomb have been deliberately destroyed.

No. 11. **Tomb of Ramses III. (lighted). This imposing tomb, usually called '*Bruce's Tomb*' after its discoverer (p. 136; 1769) or '*The Harper's Tomb*' (comp. p. 307), is inferior in size to Nos. 17 and 14 only. The execution of the sunk reliefs is not of the best, but their variety is exceptional and the colouring is well preserved.

This tomb possesses a unique peculiarity in the ten side-chambers, opening off the first two corridors. It was begun and finished as far as Room III by Seth-nakht, father of Ramses III.; his cartouches are still to be seen at various places where the later stucco has fallen off.

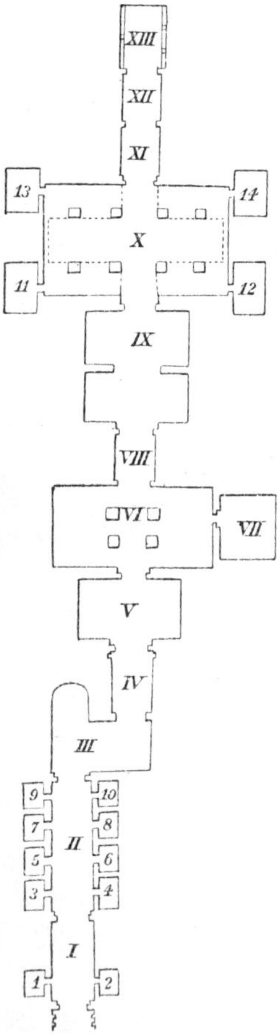

The entrance is approached by the usual flight of steps with an inclined plane in the middle; on each side of it are two pilasters adorned with bulls' heads. On the lintel of the door is the customary representation of Isis and Nephthys worshipping the sun-disk, in which are a scarabæus and the ram-headed sun-god.

CORRIDOR I. To the right and left of the entrance are kneeling figures of the goddess of truth, sheltering those who enter with her wings. On the *Left Wall* is the king before Harakhte, followed by the title of the 'Sun Litany', the sun between a serpent, a crocodile, and two gazelles' heads. Then follows the text of the 'Sun Litany', which is continued on the *Right Wall.* — SIDE CHAMBER 1 (to the left): Scenes from the royal kitchen. — SIDE CHAMBER 2 (to the right): Two rows of ships, in the upper row with sails set, in the lower row with sails furled.

CORRIDOR II, with chambers on both sides. On both sides the 'Sun Litany' is continued, with the appropriate figures of the sun-god (p. 302), who approach Isis on the left wall and Nephthys on the right. — SIDE CHAMBER 3 (to the left). In the *Upper Row* (beginning on the entrance-wall, to the left) we see a kneeling Nile-god bestowing his gifts upon seven gods of fertility (with ears of corn on their heads); and (beginning on the entrance-wall, to the right) a Nile-god before the serpent-headed goddess Napret ('corn'), five Uræus-snakes, clad with aprons, and two gods of fertility. In the dilapidated *Lower Row*, to the left, the Nile-god of Upper Egypt presents gifts to ten clothed Uræi; to the right, the Nile-god

of Lower Egypt before Napret and three Uræi. — SIDE CHAMBER 4 (to the right) may be called the king's armoury, for its walls are covered with representations of weapons, standards, armour, etc. On the *Entrance Wall* the sacred black bull Meri stands on the 'southern lake' (to the left) and the black cow Hesi upon the 'northern lake' (to the right). On the *Left Wall*, at the top: standards with pictures of sacred animals, heads of the goddess Hathor, etc. On the *Rear Wall*, at the top, are arrows, bows, and quivers. On the *Right Wall*, at the top, are standards with gods' heads. The lower representations have been destroyed. — SIDE CHAMBER 5 (to the left). In the upper row are various local deities (alternately hermaphroditic and female) with offerings; in the lower row are kneeling Nile-gods. — SIDE CHAMBER 6 (to the right) is the king's 'treasury'. On its walls are depicted utensils and furniture of various kinds: vases, jars, bottles (including so-called false-necked vases, such as were imported from the isles of Greece), elephants' tusks, necklaces, chairs, and couches with head-rests and ascended by steps. — SIDE CHAMBER 7 (to the left). On each side of the entrance the guardian spirit of the king is shown, bearing a staff ending in a king's head. On the other walls are two rows of representations of oars with serpents and sacred cattle. The lower row is much damaged. — In SIDE CHAMBER 8 (to the right) we see the sacred fields, with ploughing, sowing, reaping, etc., in progress; the king sails by on a canal. — SIDE CHAMBER 9 (to the left). To the left we see a harper singing to Onuris and the falcon-headed Harakhte. To the right is a similar representation, badly mutilated. The text of the songs is inscribed on the entrance-wall. — SIDE CHAMBER 10 (to the right). Twelve different forms of Osiris.

ROOM III represents the usual third corridor, the tomb here having had to be deflected to the right in order to avoid the adjoining tomb No. 10. On the *Rear Wall* is a goddess, representing the South, raising a water-jar. The king appears on the other walls sacrificing to various gods. — CORRIDOR IV. The journey of the sun during the 4th hour *(Left Wall)* and 5th hour of night *(Right Wall)* is here illustrated from the 'Book of that which is in the Underworld' (p. 301). — ROOM V. Figures of gods.

ROOM VI is a sloping passage with side-galleries supported by four pillars on which the king is depicted before various gods. On the *Left Walls* (beginning at the entrance-wall) is the sun's journey through the 4th division of the underworld (4th chapter of the 'Book of Portals'; p. 301). In the bottom row the representatives of the four chief races of men known to the ancient Egyptians (pp. 309, 310) should be noticed. On the *Right Walls* is the journey through the 5th region of the underworld ('Book of Portals'). On the rear wall, left and right, the king in the presence of Osiris. — ROOM VII. *Entrance Wall:* to the right, the king led by the god Thoth and the falcon-headed Har-khentekhtaï; to the left, the

king presenting Osiris with an image of truth. On the remaining spaces are scenes from the 'Book of that which is in the Underworld' (deities felling trees, etc.).

The other rooms, which are not lighted by electricity, are much damaged and need detain the traveller but a short time. — ROOM X, with pillars and, on the walls, mythological and astronomical scenes, contained the sarcophagus of the king (now in the Louvre, the lid in the Fitzwilliam Museum at Cambridge). The mummy of the king, now at Cairo, was found hidden at Deir el-Baḥari (comp. (pp. 101, 102).

No. 12. Cave without inscriptions.

No. 13, very low, and largely filled up, was not a king's tomb, but seems to have belonged to *Bay*, chancellor to King Siptah (19th Dyn.).

No. 14, originally the *Tomb of Queen Tewosret*, wife of Siptah (comp. p. 104), was afterwards appropriated and enlarged by *Sethnakht* (p. cvii), who caused the names and figures of the queen to be covered with stucco.

No. 15. Tomb of Sethos II. The first corridor of this tomb contains good reliefs. The tomb is at present used as a laboratory for the restoration of the objects found in Tutankhamûn's tomb (p. 315).

No. 16. ***Tomb of Ramses I.** (lighted). A wide flight of steps leads to the entrance. Beyond this are a sloping corridor and a second flight of steps (steep), which lead to the SARCOPHAGUS CHAMBER. In the middle stands the open coffin of the king, in red granite, with pictures and texts in yellow paint. The walls of the room are covered with coloured scenes and inscriptions on a grey ground.

Entrance Wall. To the left, Maat and Ramses I. before Ptah, behind whom stands the symbol of Osiris (p. clviii). To the right, the goddess of truth and the king offering wine to Nefertēm; behind the god is the symbolic knot of Isis (p. clxxxvi). — *Left Wall.* To the left of the door leading to a small side-room: Ramses I. led by the dog-headed Anubis and the falcon-headed Harsiēsis. To the right of the door and above it: the 3rd chapter of the 'Book of Portals'. Beyond the gate guarded by the serpent Djetbi we see the journey through the third region of the underworld. In the middle the boat is being drawn by four men towards a long chapel, in which lie the mummies of nine gods. Then follow twelve goddesses, representing the hours of the night; these, divided into two groups of six, separated by a serpent, ascend a mountain, beneath which is a pond, indicated by zigzag lines. — In the *Rear Wall* opens a small chamber, on the back-wall of which is represented Osiris between a ram-headed deity and a sacred snake. Above the door are dæmons with the heads of dogs and falcons (the souls of Pe and Nekhen). On the rear wall, farther to the right: Ramses I. dedicates four packages to the beetle-headed sun-god Atum-Rē-Khepre; Harsiēsis, Atum, and Neith conduct the king to the throne of Osiris. — The *Right Wall*, pierced by the entrance to a small unadorned chamber, is decorated with representations and texts from the second chapter of the 'Book of Portals' (p. 301).

No. 17. ****Tomb of Sethos I.** (lighted), usually known as *Belzoni's Tomb* from its discoverer (p. 136; Oct. 1817). The reliefs here, which are extraordinarily well preserved, far surpass all others at Bîbân el-Mulûk in beauty of execution and even rival those at Abydos

(p. 253). In size the tomb resembles Nos. 11 and 14; its length is 328 ft. A flight of wooden steps descends to the entrance.

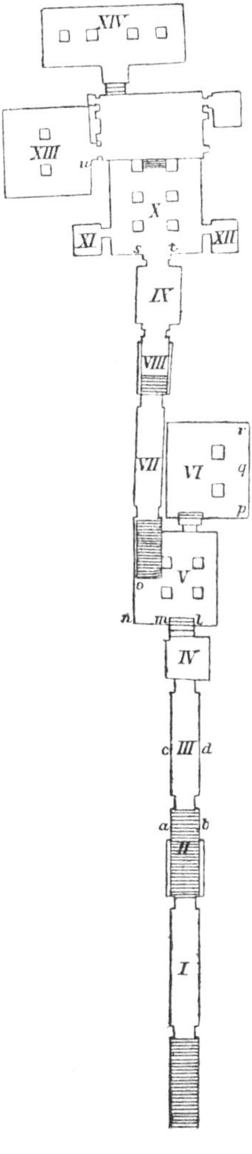

Corridor I. On the *Left Wall* is the king before the falcon-headed sun-god Harakhte. Then follows the title of the 'Sun Litany' (p. 302), with the sun-disk bearing a scarabæus and the ram-headed sun-god, between a serpent, a crocodile, and two cows' heads. The adjoining text is taken from the 'Sun Litany', which is continued on the *Right Wall.* The *Ceiling* is decorated with hovering vultures.

Corridor II (with staircase). On the upper part of the recess in the *Left Wall* are represented thirty-seven forms of the sun-god, from the 'Sun Litany'; below the recess is a text from the 'Book of that which is in the Underworld'. This is repeated on the *Right Wall.* At Pl. *a* is Isis, at Pl. *b* Nephthys.

Corridor III. On the *Left Wall* (Pl. *c*) is the journey of the sun during the 5th hour of night, from the 5th chapter of the 'Book of that which is in the Underworld'. On the *Right Wall.* at Pl. *d*, appears the journey of the sun during the 4th hour of night, from the 4th chapter of the 'Book of that which is in the Underworld'.

Antechamber IV. Representations of the king in the presence of various deities.

Room V, with pillars. On the *Left Walls* is the journey of the sun through the 4th region of the underworld, from the 4th chapter of the 'Book of Portals'.

At the beginning is the 4th gateway, guarded by the serpent Teke-hor. In the *Middle Row* appears the boat of the sun towed by four men, preceded by spirits with a coiled snake, three ibis-headed gods, and nine other gods ('the spirits of men who are in the underworld'). To the right is a god with a sceptre. In the *Top Row* various men greet the god,. while others hold a twisted cord. In the *Bottom Row*, to the left, Horus and the representatives of the four chief races of men known to the Egyptians, viz. four 'human beings' (i.e. Egyptians),

four Asiatics, with pointed beards and coloured aprons, four negroes, and four Libyans identified by the feathers on their heads and their tattooed bodies. Farther on are genii, with a snake, on which stand the hieroglyphs for 'time', etc.

On the *Right Walls* is the sun's journey through the 5th region of the underworld, from the 5th chapter of the 'Book of Portals'.

Middle Row: The boat of the sun towed by four men, preceded by dæmons. *Top Row:* Twelve gods with forked sticks, twelve gods with a serpent from which human heads project, and twelve gods with a twisted cord attached to a mummy. *Bottom Row:* A god leaning upon a staff; twelve mummies upon a couch formed by a serpent, etc.

In the centre of the *Rear Wall* is Osiris enthroned, with Hathor behind him, while the falcon-headed Horus leads the king into his presence. On the *Pillars* the king is shown before various divinities.

A few steps lead hence to Room VI, the decorations of which bave been sketched on the stucco in red chalk and finished in black. On the *Pillars* the king stands in front of various deities. On the *Entrance Wall* (to the left) and the *Left Wall* is the journey of the sun during the 9th hour of night, from the 9th chapter of the 'Book of that which is in the Underworld'.

Middle Row: The boat of the sun, preceded by twelve star-gods with oars; three sacred animals (cow, ram, bird with a human head); a mummy standing upright, the guardian deity of the sacrifices. *Top Row:* Twelve genii crouching upon curious stands, and twelve women. *Bottom Row* (partly destroyed): Serpents spitting fire; men with sticks; a mummy.

On the *Rear Wall* is the journey of the sun during the 10th hour of night (from the 10th chapter of the 'Book of that which is in the Underworld'), continued on part of the right wall.

Middle Row: The boat of the sun, preceded by various deities, including a falcon upon a two-headed serpent with four legs; four spirits, having sun-disks in place of heads, carrying arrows; four spirits with lances, and four with bows. *Top Row:* A god with a sceptre; scarabæus holding in its fore-legs the hieroglyph for 'land'; the patron goddesses of Upper and Lower Egypt seated beside two erect serpents, bearing the sun-disk; two goddesses beside the hieroglyph for 'god', upon which rests the sun-disk; goddesses with lions' heads and human heads, etc. *Bottom Row* (partly destroyed): Horus leaning upon his staff watches twelve condemned souls swimming in the waters of the underworld; four goddesses with serpents; head of the god Seth upon a sceptre.

On the *Right Walls* is the journey of the sun during the 11th hour of night (from the 11th chapter of the same book).

Middle Row: Boat of the sun, preceded by twelve men carrying a serpent; two serpents bearing on their backs the two Egyptian crowns, from which heads project; four goddesses. *Top Row:* Two-headed god; serpent (the god Atum), with four legs and two wings, held by a god (the soul of Atum) standing behind; the constellation of the 'tortoise', in the shape of a serpent on which a god sits; two-headed god; four goddesses, each seated upon two serpents, etc. *Lower Row.* The condemned. The enemies of the sun-god are being burned in curious furnaces, under the inspection of the falcon-headed Horus (on the right); adjacent stand goddesses with swords, breathing flames; in the last furnace, four corpses standing on their heads; various deities.

We return to Room V, whence a flight of eighteen steps, to the left, descends through Corridors VII and VIII (with representations of the 'Opening of the Mouth' ceremony) to *Antechamber IX,

where admirable reliefs show the king before Osiris, Isis, Harsiēsis, Hathor, Anubis, and other gods of the dead.

Hall X, whence an incline with steps at the side leads to the mummy-shaft, consists of two portions — a front portion with pillars and a rear portion on a lower level with a vaulted ceiling. The scenes in the former are taken from the 'Book of Portals' (p. 301). — The alabaster sarcophagus of the king, now in the Soane Museum in London, stood in the rear portion of the hall; the mummy, which was hidden at Deir el-Baḥari, is now in the Cairo Museum (comp. pp. 101, 102). On the *Left Wall* here (over the door leading to Room XIII) the king is shown offering a libation of wine to Harakhte. Farther on the journey of the sun during the 1st hour of night (1st chapter of the 'Book of that which is in the Underworld') is represented in four rows.

In the two *Middle Rows* we see (above) the boat of the sun, adorned in front with a rug and bearing the ram-headed sun-god, seven other gods, and the 'mistress of the boat'. It is preceded by two goddesses of truth, Osiris, the lion-headed Sakhmet, and other deities. Below in his boat is the sun-god, in the form of a scarabæus, worshipped by two figures of Osiris; in front are three serpents and several deities. In the *Top* and *Bottom Rows* (representing the banks of the river) are small square panels, containing reliefs of spirits in human and animal shapes (i.e. cynocephali, fiery serpents), which greet the god on his entrance into the lower world or drive away his foes.

In a *Niche* at the end of the left wall is the dog-headed Anubis, performing the ceremony of the 'Opening of the Mouth' before Osiris. — On the *Rear Wall* is the journey of the sun in the 2nd hour of night (2nd chapter of the 'Book of that which is in the Underworld').

Middle Row. In the boat of the sun the sun-god is accompanied by other deities, including Isis and Nephthys in the form of uræus serpents. In front of it are four smaller boats, in one of which are three deities without arms, in the second a crocodile with a human head upon its back, in the third (which is decorated with two gods' heads) a sistrum (p. clxiv), two goddesses, and a scarabæus, and in the fourth (similarly adorned) a god holding a large ostrich feather, the symbol of justice, and the moon upon a head-rest. *Top* and *Bottom Rows.* Various spirits and dæmons to protect the sun-god.

On the *Right Wall* is the sun's journey during the 3rd hour of night (3rd chapter of the 'Book of that which is in the Underworld').

In the *Middle Row* is the boat of the sun, preceded by three smaller boats. Four gods, with arms interlaced, approach to meet them. In the *Top* and *Bottom Rows* spirits of various forms (a ram with a sword, five dæmons with birds' heads, four figures of Osiris enthroned, etc.) greet the procession.

On the vaulted *Ceiling* are some interesting astronomical figures, lists of the so-called decani-stars, constellations, etc.

Side Room XI. Here is represented the gate of the underworld and the sun's journey through the 3rd region (from the 'Book of Portals', p. 301). — Side Room XII (Room of the Cow). The interesting texts in this room contain a very ancient myth of a rebellion of mankind against the sun-god, their punishment, and the final

rescue of the survivors. The scene on the rear wall is an illustration from this myth: the heavenly cow, supported by the god Show and other spirits, with two boats of the sun floating on its body.

Side Room XIII (the sacrificial chamber) contains two pillars. On the left-hand pillar appears the king before Ptah and Osiris. Round the three main walls runs a bench, decorated with a cavetto cornice; the small pillars which originally supported it have been destroyed. The representations upon it are almost entirely obliterated. On the *Entrance Wall* (to the left) and the *Left Wall* appears the sun's journey during the 7th hour of night (from the 'Book of that which is in the Underworld').

Middle Row. The sun-god once more is shown in his boat, on the prow of which stands Isis, to drive away evil spirits with her spells. In front of the boat a large serpent has been overcome by the goddess Selket and a god. Farther on are four goddesses with swords, and the graves, adorned with human heads, of the gods Atum, Khepre, Rē, and Osiris. *Top Row.* Spirits and dæmons; human-headed serpent; a god ('Flesh of Osiris') seated upon a throne beneath a serpent; three foes of Osiris, beheaded by a lion-headed god; a god holding a cord binding three foes lying on the ground; three human-headed birds wearing crowns; a god borne on a serpent; etc. *Bottom Row.* Horus, before whom are the twelve star-gods who conduct the sun at night; twelve star-goddesses approaching the grave of Osiris, upon which a crocodile rests. The god's head projects from the grave-mound.

On the *Rear Wall* is the sun's journey during the 8th hour of night (from the 'Book of that which is in the Underworld').

Middle Row. The boat of the sun towed by eight men, preceded by nine followers of Rē, who are represented by the hieroglyph for 'follow', with a head attached to it in front. Four rams (forms of the god Tatenen) head the procession. *Top* and *Bottom Rows.* Dwellings of deceased gods and spirits, the doors of which open as the sun-god approaches, showing the occupants restored to life. In each house in the top row are three gods (first the nine gods of Heliopolis, p. cxlviii), in the bottom row snakes and other spirits.

On the *Entrance Wall* (to the right) and *Right Wall* is the sun's journey during the 6th hour of night (from the 'Book of that which is in the Underworld').

Middle Row. The boat of the sun is here preceded by Thoth with the head of a cynocephalus (his sacred animal), holding in his hand an ibis (also sacred to him), and by a goddess carrying the pupils of the eyes of Horus. The remainder of the row is taken up by sixteen spirits together with the god Khepre, who are surrounded by a serpent with five heads. Four of the sixteen spirits represent the kings of Upper Egypt, four the kings of Lower Egypt, while the rest are in the guise of mummies. In the *Top* and *Bottom Rows* are other spirits. In the latter is a serpent, with the heads of the four genii of the dead upon its back, also nine fiery serpents with swords, all intended to annihilate the foes of the sun-god.

The second side-chamber on the right is unnumbered and has no decorations. — Room XIV has no decorations and is inaccessible.

No. 18. Tomb of Ramses XI., Kheper-ma-rē.

No. 19. Tomb of Mentu-her-khopshef, a prince of the close of the 20th Dynasty. The inner part is unfinished.

No. 20. Tomb of Queen Hatshepsut (p. 317), consisting of a series of corridors, 700 ft. long and descending to a depth of 318 ft.,

has neither inscriptions nor reliefs. In the tomb-chamber were found the sarcophagi of Queen Hatshepsut (now in the Cairo Museum, p. 94) and her father Thutmosis I. (now in the Boston Museum).

No. 21 has no inscriptions.

Nos. 22-25 lie in the West Valley of the Tombs of the Kings (p. 316).

Nos. 26-33 are insignificant.

No. 34. **Tomb of Thutmosis III.** This tomb is situated in an abrupt and narrow rocky ravine, about 275 yds. S. of the tomb of Ramses III. (No. 11). The entrance is high up and difficult of access.

A sloping corridor descends to a staircase (Pl. 1), with broad niches to the right and left, beyond which another corridor leads to a rectangular shaft (Pl. 2), 16-20 ft. deep, probably intended as a protection against grave-robbers but now crossed by a foot-bridge. The ceiling is adorned with white stars on a blue ground.

Farther on we enter a Room (Pl. 3) borne by two unadorned pillars. The ceiling is decorated with stars and the walls bear the names of 741 different divinities. — In the left corner of the rear wall is a staircase leading to the Tomb Chamber (Pl. 4), which has the oval form of a royal cartouche. Two square pillars bear the ceiling, with its yellow stars on a blue ground. The walls are covered with excellently preserved scenes and citations from the 'Book of that which is in the Underworld'. The representations on the pillars are of special interest. On one face of the first pillar stands a long religious inscription; on the second face are Thutmosis III. and the Queen-Mother Êset in a boat (at the top), the king suckled by his mother Êset in the form of a tree (below), and the king followed by his wives and a princess; on the third face are dæmons. The second pillar has dæmons and another long inscription. The Sarcophagus is of red sandstone, and its scenes and inscriptions are in red paint; it was empty when the tomb was opened, and the mummy of the king was found at Deir el-Baḥari (p. 323). The objects found in the four small adjoining rooms (Pl. 5-8) are now in the Cairo Museum (p. 101).

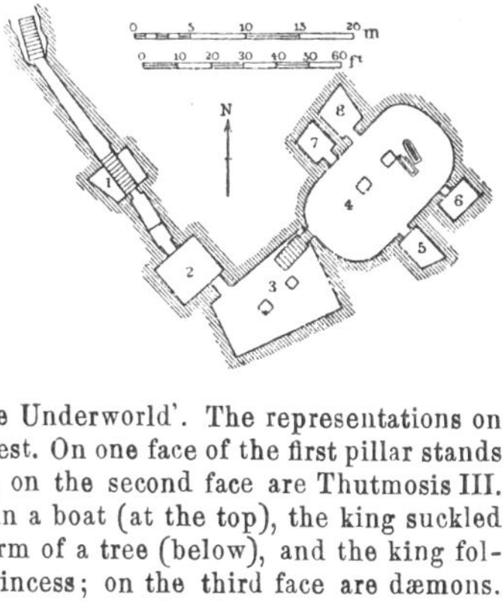

No. 35. ***Tomb of Amenophis II.** (lighted). This tomb lies about 200 yds. W. of the tomb of Ramses III. Part of its contents has been left on the spot (comp. p. 101). From the entrance steep flights of steps and sloping corridors descend to a shaft (now bridged; Pl. 1), in the depth of which is the opening to a small chamber

(Pl. 2), and then to a Room (Pl. 3) whose walls and two pillars are quite unadorned. From the left rear corner of this apartment a staircase descends to a sloping corridor and to a Room (Pl. 4) borne by six pillars. At the back of this is a kind of crypt. On the pillars Amenophis II. is represented before the gods of the dead. The blue ceiling is dotted with yellow stars. The walls, painted yellow (in imitation of a papyrus), bear beautifully executed citations and scenes from the 'Book of that which is in the Underworld'. In the crypt stands the sandstone *Sarcophagus of the king (effectively shown by electric light), containing a mummy-shaped coffin with the body of Amenophis II., wrapped in its shroud and still adorned with garlands. On each side of the main room are two small chambers (Pl. 5-8). In the first to the right (Pl. 5) lie three mummies. The second to the right (Pl. 6; inaccessible) contained nine royal mummies, placed here to conceal them from grave-robbers. Among them were the mummies of Thutmosis IV., Amenophis III. (18th Dyn.), Siptah, and Sethos II. (19th Dyn.), now in the Cairo Museum (comp. pp. 101, 102).

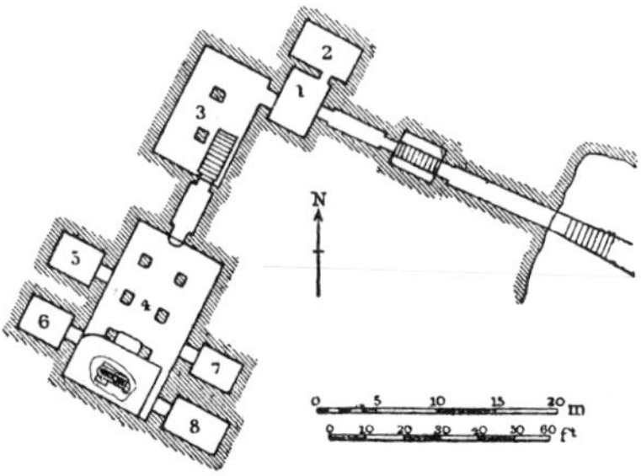

No. 36. Tomb of Mey-her-peri, a standard-bearer (comp. p. 100), without inscriptions. *No. 37* also has no inscriptions.

No. 38. **Tomb of Thutmosis I.** This is the earliest royal tomb in the Valley of the Kings; it lies in the abrupt slope at the end of the valley, between Tombs 14 and 15.

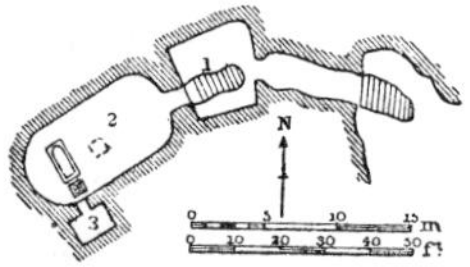

A steep flight of steps descends to Room 1, whence another flight leads to the roughly hewn Tomb Chamber (Pl. 2), the ceiling of which was originally supported by a column. The walls were once covered with painted stucco. The sarcophagus found here is now in the Cairo Museum (p. 94). — To the left is another small room (Pl. 3).

Nos. 39-41, unimportant.

No. 42, which may be the *Tomb of Thutmosis II.*, is unimportant.

No. 43. Tomb of Thutmosis IV. This tomb is unfinished; two of its chambers contain representations of the king in the presence of different gods. For the battle chariot and other objects found in the tomb, see pp. 98, 100, 102.

No. 44. Tomb of Tent-Karu, and *No. 45. Tomb of Userhēt*, are devoid of interest.

No. 46. Tomb of Yu'e and Tu'e, the parents-in-law of Amenophis III. (p. cv). This tomb, which lies between Tombs 3 and 4 and contains no inscriptions, was discovered by Theodore M. Davis, the American, in 1905; its rich contents were transferred to the Cairo Museum (see p. 102).

No. 47. Tomb of King Siptah (19th Dyn.). This tomb contains the king's coffin and a few good scenes: the king before Rē-Harakhte; the sun-disk between two mountains; Isis, Nephthys, and Anubis waiting upon the body of Osiris. Part of the tomb equipment is in the Metropolitan Museum of New York.

No. 48, Tomb of the Vizier Amenemopet (18th Dyn.), and *Nos. 49-54* are without inscriptions.

No. 55. Tomb of Queen Teye (p. 104), wife of Amenophis III. and mother of Amenophis IV. This tomb, which is without inscriptions, lies close to No. 6; Amenophis IV. also was buried here.

No. 56, the so-called 'Gold Tomb', without inscriptions.

No. 57. Tomb of King Haremhab (comp. p. 100). Some of the scenes on the walls are excellently executed. The tomb-chamber still contains the sarcophagus.

No. 58. ***Tomb of Tutankhamûn** (adm., see p. 302). This famous tomb lies immediately below that of Ramses VI. (No. 9, p. 304). Tutankhamûn (p. cvi), son-in-law of Amenophis IV., died at the age of about eighteen. The tomb was discovered by Howard Carter on Nov. 4th, 1922, and opened by him and the 5th Earl of Carnarvon (d. 1923) on Nov. 26th. Though it had been broken into and plundered soon after the king's burial, its marvellously rich contents (now in the Cairo Museum, pp. 105 seqq.) were found practically undamaged. They form the most complete and most valuable collection of the kind ever discovered in Egypt and afford an excellent idea of the magnificence with which a Pharaoh was interred.

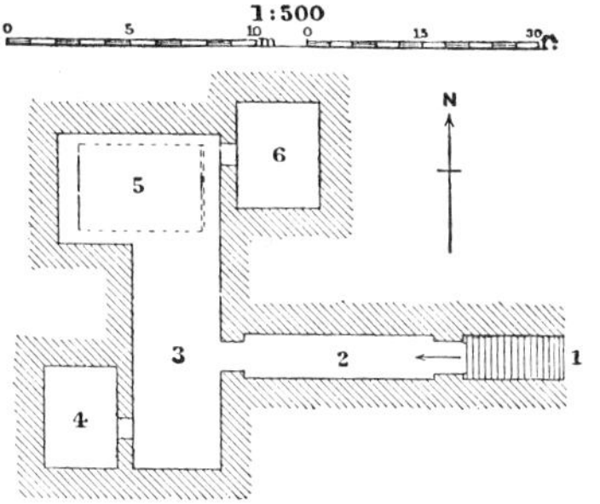

From the floor of the valley a flight of sixteen steps (Pl. 1), 5 ft. wide and 13 ft. long, descends in a W. direction. After passing a door which was sealed up on a subsequent occasion but is now open, we reach a passage (Pl. 2), 25 ft. long and $5^1/_2$ ft. wide, at the end of which another door gives on the ANTECHAMBER (Pl. 3), which is 26 ft. long and $8^1/_2$ ft. wide, the largest chamber in the tomb. At the

time of its discovery it was crowded with funeral furniture and offerings of every description. To the W. is a Side Chamber (Pl. 4). The N. wall, by the door of which stood two lifesize wooden statues of the king (p. 106), has been removed, and its place taken by scaffolding, through which the visitor surveys the electrically lighted Tomb Chamber (Pl. 5). In the centre of this stands the rectangular *Sarcophagus* of yellowish crystalline sandstone. Its sides are covered with religious representations and texts, and at the corners are four goddesses, executed in relief, who protect the dead king with their wings. The sarcophagus contains a mummy-shaped *Wooden Coffin*, covered with stucco and lavishly gilded. The face is a portrait of the king, the eyes being inserted. On the brows, decorated with a withered wreath of flowers, are the vulture and serpent, symbols of royalty. The arms are crossed over the breast, and the hands hold a flail and a crook, each made of gold and faience. This coffin now contains the king's mummy, which is greatly decayed. The inner wooden coffin and the gold coffin, in which the mummy was found, are now at Cairo (pp. 107, 108). The four shrines of gilded wood, in which the stone sarcophagus was enclosed, have been taken to pieces. The walls of the tomb-chamber are decorated with hastily executed paintings: E. wall, the king's funeral; N. and W. walls, King Eye, Tutankhamûn's successor, performing the ceremony of the 'Opening of the Mouth' on the mummy, and Tutankhamûn sacrificing to various gods of the dead. On the right (E.) is the Treasury (Pl. 6).

The Western Valley of *Bîbân el-Mulûk* (Pl. A 1; comp. p. 302), usually named by the Arabs *Gabbânet el-Qurûd* or 'Cemetery of the Apes', after Tomb 23 (see below), is seldom visited, in spite of its scenic attractiveness. The keys are usually kept by the guards in the E. valley. Visitors should inquire whether the guard with the keys is on the spot.

The first tomb here (No. 22) is that of *Amenophis III.*, found by the savants of the French Expedition. We enter from the W.; the tomb soon bends N., but finally resumes its original direction.

The second tomb (No. 23), called *Turbet el-Qurûd* (Tomb of the Apes), is in a very retired spot. It belonged to *King Eye* (p. 250), whose coffin is in the Cairo Museum (p. 94).

Tombs No. 24 and No. 25 are without inscriptions.

V. From Bîbân el-Mulûk to Deir el-Baḥari and El-ʿAsâsîf.

To return from Bîbân el-Mulûk to the plain we should take the mountain-path (Pl. B C 1) viâ Deir el-Baḥari. It is possible to ride to the top of the hill, but walking all the way is preferable (strong shoes necessary). — Another very pleasant route leads from Bîbân el-Mulûk up the steep hill and then, above Sheikh ʿAbd el-Qurna (Pl. C 2), descends to Deir el-Medîna (p. 338; the donkey-boy should be given definite instructions). — The morning or late afternoon is the best time to visit the temple of Deir el-Baḥari, for during the hotter hours of the day the oppressive rays of the sun are reflected from the rocks here with peculiar intensity.

The path begins at Tomb 16, ascends the hill separating Bîbân el-Mulûk from Deir el-Baḥari and El-ʿAsâsîf, and descends in zigzags. It is fatiguing but safe, and is easily accomplished in $^3/_4$ hr. The **View* is most remarkable: first we look into the desolate Valley of the Kings; then, from the summit and as we descend, we see the peculiarly shaped ravine of Deir el-Baḥari, the steep projecting mountain-side with its tombs and buildings old and new, and the rich green of the fertile plain below, spread out on both sides of the Nile, with its groups of palms and gigantic temples, as far as Karnak and Luxor on the E. bank. The situation of the temples of Deir el-Baḥari is remarkably fine; on the W. and N. they are framed by precipitous rocks of a light-brown and golden colour, against which the dazzling white walls once stood out in magnificent relief. — Near the great temple, to the S.E., lies the rest-house of Thos. Cook & Son (open only to the company's tourists and to patrons of the hotels of the Upper Egypt Hotel Co., p. 267).

The **Great Temple of Deir el-Baḥari** (*Deir el-Baḥri;* Pl. C 1) lies in a semicircular basin originally reserved exclusively for the monument of the Mentuhotep kings. Its slopes were occupied by the tombs of grandees of the 11th Dyn., including the rock-tomb of Queen Nofru (p. 321). The temple dates from the beginning of the New Empire and was built and adorned with statues, reliefs, and inscriptions by *Queen Hatshepsut*, the sister, wife, and co-regent of Thutmosis III. (p. cv). Like the 11th Dyn. mortuary temple (p. 322) lying to the S. of it, it is constructed in terraces; it occupies a portion of the court of the 11th Dyn. temple. The construction of the temple shared the chequered fortunes of its foundress. When Hatshepsut was expelled from the throne by her brother and husband, after a brief reign, the building operations came to a halt, and Thutmosis caused the statues to be removed and the names and figure of his sister to be obliterated in all the finished sculptures and inscriptions at Deir el-Baḥari as well as elsewhere throughout the country. Thutmosis II., who succeeded his brother, continued the work of destruction by inserting his own name in place of that of Hatshepsut. When Thutmosis II. died, however, Hatshepsut regained the throne and the building was resumed. Operations were not carried on with any remarkable activity, for when the queen's long reign came to an end the temple was still unfinished. Thutmosis III., once more on the throne, so far from supplying what was still wanting, resumed his former tactics, destroying all allusions to his sister and sometimes inserting his own name and figure in place of hers. Amenophis IV. (p. 245) carefully destroyed all reference to Amun, and the inscriptions and reliefs were left thus mutilated until the reign of Ramses II., who restored them, though with inferior workmanship. For centuries afterwards the temple remained unaltered; but under Euergetes II. (p. cxii) a few slight restorations were undertaken and some unimportant

additions were made, without, however, affecting the original plan. On the introduction of Christianity a community of monks established themselves in the temple and founded a monastery, known to the Arabs as *Deir el-Bahari* (the 'Northern Monastery'). The chambers of the temple were converted into chapels and the 'heathen' representations on the walls were barbarously defaced. — Mariette (p. 157) made a few excavations here, but finally in 1894-96 the entire temple was exhumed at the cost of the Egypt Exploration Fund under the direction of Edouard Naville (d. 1926), the Geneva archæologist; more recently it has been carefully examined and set to rights by the expedition of the Metropolitan Museum of New York under Herbert E. Winlock.

It should be noted that Hatshepsut in her capacity as ruler of Egypt is uniformly represented with the traditional attributes of kingship, viz. the short apron and the beard, though these, of course, are properly appropriate to men only.

The temple was dedicated to Amun; but the goddess Hathor and Anubis, god of the dead, also had chapels here, and several chambers were devoted to the worship of the queen, who was buried at Bîbân el-Mulûk (p. 312), and to that of her parents. The building occupies a part of the courtyard of the 11th Dyn.; three terraces, rising one above the other from the level ground, are connected with each other by inclined planes, which divide the whole into a N. half, to the right, and a S. half, to the left. At the W. side of each terrace is a raised colonnade. The stages were cut out of the E. slope of the mountain, and support was given to the outer and inner walls by means of blocks of the finest limestone. The chapels devoted to the cult of the various deities were likewise cut out of the rock.

An *Avenue of Sphinxes* led from the plain to the temple, ending at the gateway (now almost totally destroyed) forming the entrance to the temple precincts. In front of the gate, in square enclosures of masonry, stood two persea trees (Mimusops Schimperi), the stumps of which are still extant.

We first enter the **Lower Court**, on the W. side of which is an inclined plane leading to a terrace adorned with colonnades. The slope is enclosed by balustrades. On the left is a remarkable recumbent figure of a lion. The terrace is in a very dilapidated condition, but is being restored. Each colonnade consisted of twenty-two columns arranged in a double row. The columns in the back row were sixteen-sided, while those in the first row were square pillars in front, ornamented at the top with hawks, uræi, and vultures. Little now remains of the reliefs and inscriptions that once decorated the walls.

On the rear wall of the *North Colonnade*, at Pl. *a*, are traces of the representation of a pond, on which water-fowl are being caught with nets. — On the rear wall of the *South Colonnade* (right to left): Pl. *b*. The queen (figure chiselled out) sacrificing to the ithyphallic Amun; Pl. *c*. Erection and dedication of the temple obelisks; ships and soldiers hastening to a festival; Pl. *d*. Ships bringing two obelisks from the quarries of Aswân to Thebes.

TEMPLE OF DEIR EL-BAHRI

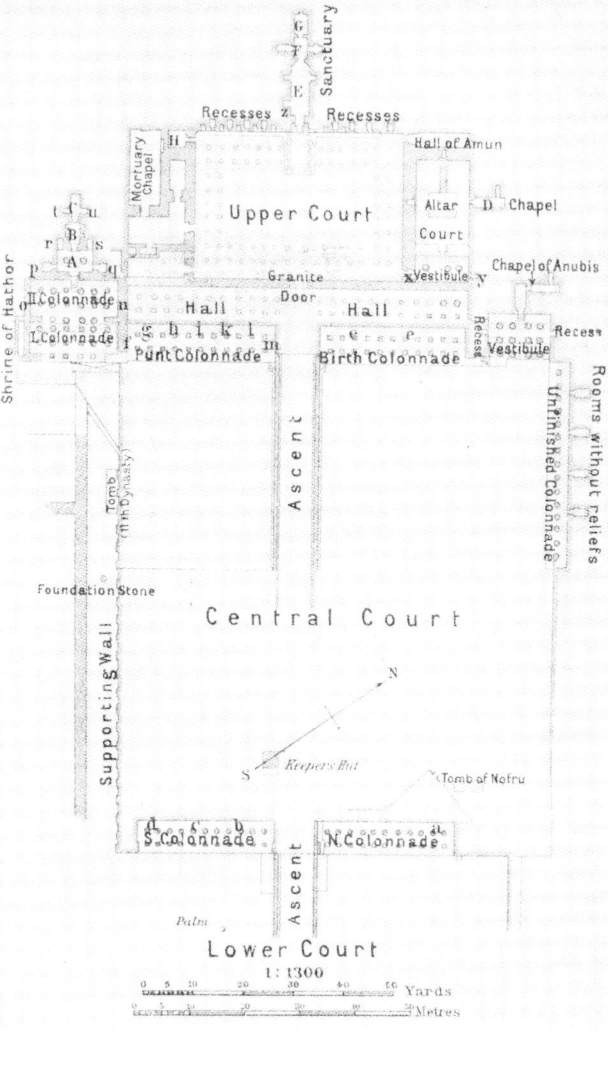

Sanctuary
G
F
E
Recesses
z
Recesses
H
Mortuary Chapel
Hall of Amun
Upper Court
Altar Court
D
Chapel
t
C
u
B
r
s
p
A
q
Granite Door
x
Vestibule
y
Chapel of Anubis
Shrine of Hathor
o
II. Colonnade
u
Hall
Hall
I. Colonnade
g
h
i
k
l
e
f
Recess
Vestibule
Recess
m
Punt Colonnade
Birth Colonnade
Rooms without reliefs
Unfinished Colonnade
Ascent
Tomb (11th Dynasty)
Foundation Stone
Central Court
Supporting Wall
N
S
Keeper's Hut
Tomb of Nofru
a
c
b
d
S. Colonnade
N. Colonnade
Ascent
Palm
Lower Court
1:1300
0 5 10 20 30 40 50
Yards
0 5 10 20 30 40 50
Metres

In front of the inclined plane may be seen two excavations, in which papyrus was planted. There were also circular holes (now filled up) for flowers.

The lower court commands the best view of the carefully constructed S. retaining wall, which consists of finely polished blocks of limestone with simple but effective ornament, reproducing the original decoration of the columns in the lower colonnade (p. 318).

We now ascend the approach to the **Central Court**, which is likewise bounded on the W. by a terrace with colonnades. On the right is the Birth Colonnade; on the left, the Colonnade of Punt.

The Birth Colonnade contains eleven pairs of square pillars supporting the roof. On all four sides of the pillars is the same scene: Amun laying his hand in blessing upon the shoulder of Hatshepsut (figure defaced throughout) or Thutmosis III. The inscriptions and representations on the walls of the colonnade refer to the procreation and birth of the queen (Pl. *e*). Among these are two fine figures of the queen-mother Ahmes, once in presence of the ram-headed Khnum and the frog-headed Heket, and once in presence of the ibis-headed Thoth. — Two steps at the N. end of this colonnade descend to a Vestibule with twelve sixteen-sided columns. On the walls are fine reliefs.

In the *South Wall* is a small *Recess* with representations of the queen (effaced) before various deities; at the top appears the queen (again scratched out) before Osiris. To the left of the recess is Anubis, behind whom stood the queen; to the right are Nekhbeyet and Harakhte, between whom were the names of the queen. — In the *North Wall* is a similar *Recess*. Above it is Thutmosis III. making a libation of wine to the falcon-headed Soker, god of the dead; to the right, Anubis and the queen (scratched out); to the left, the queen (scratched out) standing in a chapel before the symbol of Eme-wet (p. clvi). — On the *West* (rear) *Wall*, the queen (scratched out) sacrificing to Amun (left) and to Anubis (right), with sacrificial gifts heaped up before each god.

Three steps at the back of the vestibule lead to a Chapel of Anubis, consisting of three chambers with vaulted ceilings. The colouring of the bas-reliefs is admirably preserved, though the figure of the queen is invariably scratched out. They represent Hatshepsut before various deities, especially Anubis. Thutmosis III. occurs once on the E. wall of the second chamber, pouring water before Soker.

On the N. side of the central court is an unfinished Colonnade, the roof of which is supported by fifteen sixteen-sided columns. Behind it are four chambers (now walled up).

We now turn to the Colonnade of Punt, on the S. side of the W. terrace, exactly corresponding with the Birth Colonnade. The *Scenes on the walls, some of which are unfortunately much damaged, commemorate a trading expedition to Punt (p. 233), undertaken during the queen's reign. On the *South Wall* we see a village in Punt (Pl. *f*). The beehive huts are built over the water amongst palms and incense-trees; ladders lead up to the entrances. In the lower row, to the right, is the reception of the Egyptian envoy and his suite by the prince of Punt; above, the envoy in front of his tent, looking at the gifts that have been heaped upon him. — On the *West Wall* we see, to the left (Pl. *g*), the arrival of the

Egyptian fleet at Punt, where it is laden with precious merchandise; to the right is the return of the fleet. Above are the inhabitants of Punt and the Egyptians with their gifts; while prostrate grandees do homage to the queen. Farther on (Pl. *h*) the queen (effaced), followed by her guardian spirit, dedicates to Amun the spoils of the expedition; the cattle feeding beneath the trees are especially worthy of notice. At Pl. *i* gold and other precious metals are being weighed in presence of the goddess Seshet, who records the results; Horus presides at the scales, and behind him is the Nubian god Dedun. Below we see the incense being measured, while Thoth notes down the results; close by are seven incense-trees in tubs, imported from Punt. At Pl. *k* Thutmosis III. offers incense to the boat of Amun, which is borne by priests. At Pl. *l* is Hatshepsut before Amun (a long inscription between them has been erased). — On the *North Wall*, at Pl. *m*, the queen (chiselled out) is seated beneath a canopy, with her guardian spirit behind her. In front are her grandees, to whom she is speaking, and a long inscription.

At the left (S.) end of the Punt Colonnade is a Shrine of Hathor, goddess of the necropolis at Thebes (p. clvi), which was originally reached also from below by a flight of steps. The innermost chambers are preceded by two covered *Colonnades* (now in ruins). The first of these had sixteen-sided columns and square pillars with Hathor capitals; the second, which lies at a slightly higher level, had round Hathor columns (three of them in partial preservation) and also sixteen-sided columns (six partly remaining).

There are still a few *Wall Decorations* in the second colonnade. On the N. wall (Pl. *n*): Thutmosis III. with an oar, in presence of a goddess; to the right is a procession, consisting of three rows with two ships in each and (below) soldiers with standards and axes (to the right two soldiers dancing to castanets). — On the S. wall (Pl. *o*; much dilapidated): Sacrificial scene, and a boat containing a Hathor cow, with Queen Hatshepsut drinking from the udder. — On the W. wall (right): Thutmosis II. (replacing Hatshepsut), with an oar and a builder's square, before Hathor (whose figure was defaced by Amenophis IV.); the king, whose hand is licked by the Hathor cow. These are repeated to the left.

We ascend two steps to the *Shrine* proper, which comprised three rock-hewn chambers (Pl. *A*, *B*, *C*), each one step higher than its predecessor and containing several niches. The ceiling of *Room A*, which is decorated with stars on a blue ground, is supported by two sixteen-sided columns. The reliefs, which those who have leisure may examine, show Hatshepsut (everywhere defaced) or Thutmosis III. before various deities. — *Room B* contains *Wall Reliefs of unusual beauty. They represent Hatshepsut (chiselled out) presenting offerings of all kinds to the Hathor cow, which stands in a boat beneath a canopy. The traces of a second and smaller figure of the queen, represented as imbibing milk from the udder of the cow, are still visible. The little nude boy, holding a sistrum, in front of the queen, is Ehi, son of Hathor (p. 261). — *Room C* has a roof of parabolic vaulting. On each of the side-walls is an admirable relief of Hat-

shepsut drinking from the udder of the Hathor cow, before which stands Amun (on a smaller scale). Rear Wall: Hatshepsut between Hathor and Amun, who holds the hieroglyph for 'life' to her nose. Above the niches (Pl. *t*, *u*) Hatshepsut and Thutmosis III. offer milk and wine to Hathor.

We return to the central court, at the N.E corner of which is the entrance to the *Tomb of Queen Nofru* (11th Dyn.). Candles or an electric torch are essential to inspect the sarcophagus-chamber.

From the court we ascend the inclined approach which brings us first to a much ruined HALL, the roof of which was borne by pillars (originally colossal statues of Hatshepsut, converted into pillars by Thutmosis III.) and sixteen-sided columns. A granite doorway here gives access to the upper court.

The central part of the **Upper Court** was occupied by a large HYPOSTYLE HALL, now in a state of complete ruin. Its walls were adorned with reliefs of a festal procession, which have suffered severely at the hands of the Coptic monks. — Turning sharp to the right (N.), we reach a door (Pl. *x*) admitting to a VESTIBULE, which had three sixteen-sided columns. Opposite the door is a small *Niche* (Pl. *y*), with well-preserved representations of Hatshepsut.

Rear Wall of the recess: Hatshepsut (erased) before Amun. Side Walls: Hatshepsut seated at table, with a priest clad like the god Enmetf in front of her. The figure of the queen is uninjured, contrary to the usual practice, but the priest's figure was defaced by Amenophis IV.

To the left of the vestibule we enter an OPEN COURT, in which is an **Altar*, approached by ten steps and dedicated by Hatshepsut to the sun-god Rē-Harakhte. This is one of the very few altars that have come down to us from Egyptian antiquity on their original sites. In the W. wall of this court is a small niche with sacrificial scenes on the walls (the figure of Hatshepsut erased). — A door in the N. wall of this court admits to a *Chapel*, comprising two chambers. With a few unimportant exceptions the reliefs on the walls have been chiselled away by Thutmosis III. and Amenophis IV.

On the side-walls of the *1st Chamber* (Pl. *D*) Hatshepsut offers sacrifices to various deities, mainly deities of the dead, such as Anubis, Soker, Osiris, and Eme-wet, and also to Amun. Above a bench against the end wall is a representation of Hatshepsut and Thutmosis I. before the symbol of Eme-wet (p. clvi). *2nd Chamber*. On the right wall: Thutmosis I. (originally Hatshepsut) and his mother Seniseneb, sacrificing to Anubis. On the left wall: Hatshepsut and her mother Ahmes sacrificing to Amun. On the end-wall: Hatshepsut and Anubis. On the ceiling are representations of stars during the hours of the night.

On the S. side of the upper court are several chambers now in ruins and a well-preserved MORTUARY CHAPEL, with a vaulted roof, which was used for the cult of the manes of Hatshepsut and is adorned with reliefs.

To the right and left of the entrance, the slaughter and cutting up of the sacrificial beasts. On the side-walls are shown three rows of priests and officials bringing sacrificial gifts to Hatshepsut, and above are sacrificial objects of various kinds. Hatshepsut herself (effaced) is seated with a list of the offerings before her, while priests offer incense or perform

other rites. On the end-wall is represented the door that led into the realm of the dead.

In the W. wall of the court is a series of recesses, containing representations of Thutmosis III. and Hatshepsut in presence of the gods. The larger recesses were occupied by statues of the queen. In the middle is the entrance to the sanctuary. — In the left corner opens the small *Room H*, in the right corner the so-called *Hall of Amun*, both of which may be omitted by hurried visitors.

Room H. The ceiling is well preserved. On the right wall appears Amon-Rē in front of a table of offerings, which replaces the effaced figure of Hatshepsut. Behind the table is the queen's guardian spirit. On the rear wall are Thutmosis III. and Thutmosis I. (substituted for the queen) making an offering of clothes to Amun. On the left wall Thutmosis II. (substituted for the queen), with his guardian spirit, offers sacred oil to the ithyphallic Amun.

Hall of Amun. Part of the ceiling, decorated with stars on a blue ground, still remains. On the left side-wall we observe Hatshepsut pacing out the temple precincts, before Amun, before the ithyphallic Amon-Min, and before the enthroned Amun. On the right wall is Thutmosis III. before these same gods. On the rear wall is Thutmosis II. (originally Hatshepsut) before Amun. The figures of the gods here were defaced by Amenophis IV. and were not replaced at the restoration under Ramses II.

A granite portal, reached by a porch dating from the 18th Dyn., with balustrades, forms the entrance to the Sanctuary. The three chambers (Pl. *E*, *F*, *G*) are unfortunately much damaged. The first two have vaulted ceilings and wall-niches. The scenes in the *1st Chamber* (Pl. *E*) show Hatshepsut (sometimes Thutmosis III.) sacrificing to various deities, among whom figures the deceased Thutmosis II. The *3rd Room* was added under Euergetes II. and was dedicated to the saints Imhotep and Amenhotep, who were revered in the Ptolemaic period (comp. p. 339). The reliefs and inscriptions of this late period compare very unfavourably with the masterly sculptures of Hatshepsut.

On the upper part of the right wall of the 1st Chamber is a noteworthy scene: Hatshepsut, Thutmosis III., and the princess Ra-nofru sacrifice to the sacred boat of Amun, behind which stood Thutmosis I. with his consort Ahmes, and their little daughter Bit-nofru. A similar scene was represented above the niche (Pl. *z*) on the left wall; the kneeling Thutmosis III. and Princess Ra-nofru may still be distinguished.

Immediately to the S., adjoining the temple of Hatshepsut, lies a temple which dates from the beginning of the Middle Empire and is the best surviving monument of its period. This is the ***Mortuary Temple of Kings Mentuhotep II. and III.** (*Neb-hepet-rē* and *Neb-khru-rē*; Pl. C 1, 2), begun by Mentuhotep II., who erected over his tomb (p. 323) a terrace with colonnades and a pyramid, as well as tombs and chapels for the women of his harem. The structure was extended and completed by his successor Mentuhotep III., who also chose to have his tomb here. This is the earliest Theban temple known to us and it is of great interest from the simplicity of its architecture. It was excavated by the Egypt Exploration Fund in 1905-7 and more carefully explored by the expedition of the Metropolitan Museum (p. 324) in 1922-25. — From the

cultivated fields, where we see the ruins of a temple of the Ramessid era and a brick structure belonging to the tomb of a Sheshonk, a wide avenue led to the great court in front of the temple. The holes in which trees were planted are still recognizable here. The temple itself was constructed in terraces. From the COURT, bounded on the W. side by two COLONNADES with rectangular pillars (with the cartouche of Neb-khru-rē), an inclined plane leads to a higher TERRACE, on which stood the actual mortuary temple with the pyramid. Beyond a vestibule which has almost completely disappeared, but which formerly extended to the N. and S., lies the *Ambulatory*, a sort of corridor with 140 octagonal pillars encircling the base (cased with fine limestone slabs) of the *King's Pyramid*. In the W. wall of the gallery were the *Sepulchral Chapels of the Favourites of the Royal Harem*. On the W. we next reach a *Court* surrounded by colonnades. In the pavement of this court was the entrance to a sloping passage 164 yds. long, leading to the subterranean tomb-chamber of Mentuhotep III. On the E. side of the court are openings admitting to the shaft-tombs of the favourites. A large *Pillared Hall* (only the bases of its eighty octagonal pillars remain) and a *Chapel* with a recess (hewn in the rock) terminated the temple. — To the N.W. of this building stood a *Sanctuary of Hathor*, built by Thutmosis III. and now destroyed. The shrine, constructed in the rock and containing the image of the deity as a cow, is now in the Cairo Museum (p. 92).

Numerous very important discoveries have been made in the VALLEY-BASIN OF DEIR EL-BAḤARI. Thus, in 1881, the *Royal Mummies* mentioned on pp. 101, 102 were found in a shaft in a little valley to the S. of the great temple, while in 1891 a *Common Tomb for Theban Priests* was discovered immediately to the N. of the lower courtyard (contents now in the museums of Cairo and Alexandria, pp. 97, 23). In the courtyard in front of the temple of Mentuhotep is situated the subterranean *Tomb of Mentuhotep II.* (see p. 322), known to the Arabs as *Bâb el-Ḥuṣân* and discovered by Howard Carter (p. 315) in 1900.

By proceeding E. from Deir el-Baḥari we soon reach the small depression known as **El-ʿAsâsîf** (Pl. C D 2). This contains a large NECROPOLIS, the tombs in which date mostly from the beginning of the Saïte period (25th and 26th Dyn.). Various brick buildings are noticed also. The arched gateway belonged to the tomb of Ment-em-hēt, 'prophet of Amun' (p. 324). The tombs consist of a superstructure enclosed by brick walls, with an entrance pylon on the E., and of subterranean tomb-chambers, to which we descend by a gate on the N. side.

An interesting example of a burial-place of the Saïte period is the **Tomb of Pbes* (*Pabasa*, No. 279), who was chief steward to Nitocris, daughter of Psammetichos I. and 'divine' princess of Thebes (c. 610 B.C.). The superstructure is in a very ruinous state. The subterranean chambers are reached on the N. side by an inclined plane enclosed by brick walls. A steep staircase descends at first to the ANTECHAMBER, which is decorated with reliefs and inscriptions. On the short wall to the left (W.) and the rear wall (S.): the de-

ceased (note the gazelle under the chair) at table with his son, or a priest, in front of him; below, scenes from the funeral procession. Next follows an open Court of Sacrifice. This lies at the foot of a shaft 46 ft. deep, the walls of which are lined with brickwork above, while below they are hewn out of the solid rock. On the W. and E. sides of the court are narrow Colonnades, each of four pillars. The inscriptions on the architraves enumerate the titles of Pbes. The walls are adorned with sunk reliefs of sacrificial scenes or of the deceased at table. Some of the pillars have (besides the usual pictures of offerings to the deceased) vintage, fishing, and bee-keeping scenes. The ceiling pattern is pleasing and in good preservation. On the S. wall, to the right of the door leading to the next room: Nitocris, escorted by Pbes, offers wine to Osiris, Isis, and Horus; on the left, Psammetichos, followed by Nitocris (with rattles) and Pbes, offers milk to Rē-Harakhte. The reliefs and inscriptions of the Hall, which is borne by eight pillars, are badly damaged. Adjacent are several chambers with tomb-shafts.

Of especial interest also is the **Tomb of Ibi** (No. 36), an official of Nitocris (see p. 323), which contains reliefs copied from originals of the time of the Ancient Empire. It lies close to the American House (see below) and resembles the tomb of Pbes in its lay-out. A flight of steps leads into the antechamber, where the deceased is represented sitting at the table of offerings and receiving sacrificial gifts. In the room adjoining this on the right are tasteful reliefs of artisans and dances. Farther on we come to what was originally an open court with arcades at the sides; the reliefs on the walls represent sacrificial scenes, among which one of a hunt should be noticed. The adjacent colonnade leads to several chambers farther on. — Among the other tombs of the same epoch may be mentioned the *Tomb of Ment-em-hēt* (p. 323; No. 34; inaccessible), a 'prophet of Amun' of the time of Taharka (25th Dyn.); and the **Tomb of Pedamenōpet** (No. 33; inaccessible), a high official under the 26th Dyn. (comp. p. 354). This last tomb is larger than any of the kings' tombs at Bîbân el-Mulûk, being 287 yds. in length and 2710 sq. yds. in area. The carefully executed inscriptions and reliefs, now much injured and blackened, refer almost without exception to life after death.

On the N. slope of the hill of *El-Khôkha* (p. 337), near El-ʿAsâsîf, is the *American House* (Pl. C 2), belonging to the expedition of the Metropolitan Museum of New York.

VI. The Ramesseum.

This temple may be reached on donkey-back from the landing-place on the W. bank in 3/4 hr.; from the Colossi of Memnon in 1/4 hr.; and from Medînet Habu or Deir el-Bahari in 20 minutes. — On the S.W. side of the temple is the rest-house of the Anglo-American Nile & Tourist Co., open only to the company's tourists and to patrons of the hotels of the Upper Egypt Hotels Co. (p. 267).

The ****Ramesseum** (Pl. C 3), the large mortuary temple built by Ramses II. (p. cvi) on the W. bank and dedicated to Amun, is unfortunately only half preserved. We may in all probability identify it with the '*Tomb of Osymandyas*' described by the historian Diodorus (1st cent. B.C.), Osymandyas being regarded as a corrupt form of *User-ma-rē*, the prænomen of Ramses II.

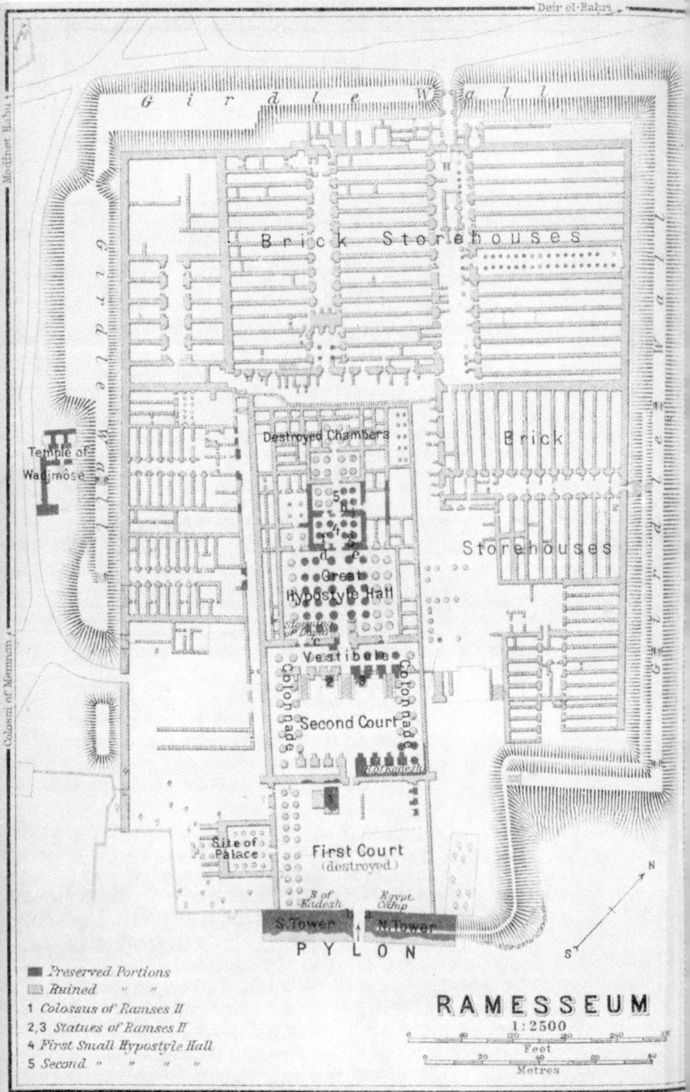
Deir el-Bahri
Medinet Habu
Colossi of Memnon
Girdle Wall
Girdle Wall
Girdle Wall
Brick Storehouses
Brick Storehouses
Destroyed Chambers
Temple of Wadjmose
Great Hypostyle Hall
Vestibule
Colonnade
Colonnade
Second Court
First Court (destroyed)
Site of Palace
B. of Kadesh
Egypt. Camp
S. Tower
N. Tower
PYLON
N
S
Preserved Portions
Ruined " "
1 Colossus of Ramses II
2,3 Statues of Ramses II
4 First Small Hypostyle Hall
5 Second " " "
RAMESSEUM
1:2500
Feet
Metres

Wagner & Debes, Leip

We begin our inspection at the great **Pylon**, or E. entrance to the temple. This was originally 220 ft. broad, but its ruined exterior now resembles a quarry. Many reliefs on its inner (W.) side, next the court, are in fair preservation and are recognizable with a field-glass (best by afternoon light). They refer to the Syrian campaigns of Ramses II., notably to the war with the Hittites which began in the fifth year of his reign (comp. p. 274).

On the North Tower, to the extreme *Left*, we observe the Asiatic fortresses taken by Ramses in the eighth year of his reign. Thirteen of the original eighteen are still recognizable, each with an inscription containing its name. The captives are being led away. In the *Middle* are scenes from the war with the Hittites, which are continued on the S. tower. Below is the Egyptian army on the march; above appears the Egyptian camp, within a rampart of shields, presenting an animated scene. The chariots are drawn up in long lines, with the unharnessed horses beside them; close by are the heavy baggage-cars with their teams, unperturbed by the great lion of the king, which reclines before him. The asses employed in the commissariat service of the army are conspicuous in the camp; now released from their burdens, they show satisfaction by means of movements and attitudes which the artist seems never tired of drawing. The soldiers are conversing with each other, and one drinks from a water-skin. Disputes and quarrels are not wanting. Above, to the right, the tranquillity of the camp is rudely disturbed by an attack of the Hittites. To the *Right* the king holds a council of war with his princes. Beneath captured spies are being beaten.

The *Left Half* of the South Tower of the pylon is occupied by the picture of the battle of Kadesh, which we have already seen on the pylon at Luxor (p. 274). Ramses in his chariot dashes against his foes, who are either slain by his arrows or flee in wild confusion and fall into the Orontes. Behind the king are other war-chariots. To the right, at a distance from the scene of action, is the Hittite prince. Above is a second, now scarcely distinguishable, representation of the Hittites fleeing to their fortress. The reliefs on the *Right Half* show the usual presentment of the king, grasping enemies by the hair and smiting them; farther to the right is the king holding a long staff and accompanied by fan-bearers.

On the interior walls of the *Portal* of this pylon are the usual reliefs of Ramses sacrificing to various gods. At the top of the *Jambs* (Pl. *a*, *b*) Ramses appears pacing out the precincts of the temple (a rite performed at the foundation of a temple; comp. pp. 257, 299); at the bottom, various deities.

The **First Court** is utterly ruined. In front of the fragments of the wall on the W. side lie the remains of a **Colossus of Ramses II.* (Pl. 1), the largest statue in the country, celebrated in Shelley's sonnet 'Ozymandias of Egypt'. The name of Ramses II. appears in well-preserved hieroglyphics on the upper arms and on the seat of the statue. The face is completely destroyed. The remains (breast, upper part of the arms, one foot, etc.) testify to the care with which the monument was chiselled and polished.

The length of the ear is 3½ ft., surface of face from ear to ear 6⅘ ft., surface of breast from shoulder to shoulder 23⅓ ft., from one shoulder to the other in a straight line 22½ ft., circumference of the arm at the elbow 17½ ft., diameter of the arm between the elbow and shoulder 4⅘ ft., length of the index finger 3¼ ft., length of the nail on the middle finger 7½ inches, breadth of the foot across the toes 4½ ft. The total height seems to have been 57⅖ ft., and its total weight c. 1000 tons.

The head of another colossal *Statue of Ramses II.*, found in 1816, has been since 1817 in the British Museum.

On the S. side of the court lay a colonnade (now completely destroyed), forming the front of a royal palace of which only scanty traces survive.

The **Second Court** is entered through a gap in the wall to the right of the colossus. It is in better preservation than the first court, and is mentioned with its caryatids in Diodorus's description. On the right and left were double colonnades (almost wholly destroyed); those on the front had square pillars with statues of Osiris, while at the back was a raised terrace with Osiris-pillars and papyrus-bud columns. Four of the Osiris-pillars in front are still extant, and also four at the back. On the shafts of the columns and the sides of the pillars are representations of Ramses II. sacrificing to the gods. The figures of Osiris, most of which are headless, likewise represent Ramses II.

The part of the front wall which is still standing is now supported on the side next the court by modern brick buttresses. Upon it are two rows of interesting reliefs, bearing traces of colouring and easily distinguishable with the aid of a field-glass. Those in the *Lower Row* once more refer to the Hittite war and commemorate Ramses II.'s great exploits at the *Battle of Kadesh*. The king (to the left), much larger than the other warriors, dashes along in his chariot. The Hittites, pierced by his arrows or trodden down by the horses, fall in confused heaps; crowds of them are hurled into the Orontes. Farther to the right appears the battlemented fortress of Kadesh, round which the river flows. Beside it, on the other side of the river, are Hittite troops that have had no share in the battle; some of them hold out helping hands to their drowning comrades. The *Upper Row* contains scenes from the *Festival of Min* (the harvest-god), which was celebrated when the king ascended the throne (p. 350). To the left stands the king, awaiting the procession, which is headed by priests carrying the images of the royal ancestors. Two tall poles erected in front of the king bear the god's head-dress. Adjacent are priests letting four birds fly, for the purpose of carrying tidings to the four quarters of the globe that the Pharaoh has attained the crown; to the right the king appears cutting a sheaf with a sickle for presentation to the god.

This second court also contained colossal statues of the king. Fragments of one of these (in black granite) lie upon the ground, notably the head, which is well preserved except for the nose. On the throne are the names of Ramses II., beside which Belzoni the explorer (p. 136) has immortalized his own.

The **Vestibule**, situated on a terrace, was reached by three flights of steps, of which that to the N. is in excellent preservation. Only the S. part of the *Rear Wall* (Pl. *c*) is still standing; on it are three rows of bas-reliefs. In the bottom row are eleven sons of the king; in the middle row, to the left, is the king conducted by Atum and the falcon-headed Mont, who holds the hieroglyph for 'life' to the king's nose; to the right is the king kneeling before the Theban

triad, while Thoth, behind him, writes the king's name on a palm-branch; in the top row the king is shown sacrificing to Ptah, to the left, and offering incense to the ithyphallic Min and a goddess, to the right.

Beyond this vestibule is the **Great Hypostyle Hall**, which had three entrances and, like the great hall at Karnak (p. 284), a nave of three aisles, which were higher than the six side-aisles. The nave, part of the roof of which still remains, has six couples of columns with calyx-capitals and six couples with bud-capitals. The latter were lower than the former, but upon them rose a wall, with pillars and window-openings, to the height of the others. Eleven columns of each kind still stand. Each of the side-aisles had columns with bud-capitals; to the left six columns and a part of the roof still remain. On the smooth shafts of the columns appears Ramses II. sacrificing to the gods.

On the *South Half of the East Wall* (Pl. *a*) the storming of the Hittite fortress of Dapur is shown in the lower row. To the left is the Pharaoh dashing in his chariot against the enemy, some of whom are slain, while the rest, horse, foot, and chariots, betake themselves to flight. To the right is the fortress, defended by the Hittites, while the Egyptians are attacking it on ladders or push up to the walls under the protection of sheds and shields. The sons of the Pharaoh, the names of whom are given, distinguish themselves in the battle. — In the upper row are several representations of the king sacrificing to the gods.

On the *West Wall*, in the lower row (Pl. *d, e*), appear the sons of the Pharaoh; in the upper row, above Pl. *e*, is the king before Amun and Khons, with the lion-headed Sakhmet behind him, and above Pl. *d*, the king followed by a goddess, in presence of Amun and Mut.

The **First Small Hypostyle Hall** (Pl. 4), with four couples of papyrus-bud columns, has a well-preserved roof decorated with astronomical representations and pictures of the king before the gods.

The Reliefs on the walls are not uninteresting. On the *East Wall* (Pl. *g, f*) are priests bearing the sacred boats of Amun, Mut, and Khons, each decorated with the head of its god. On the N. part of the *West Wall* (Pl. *i*) the king is seated beneath the sacred tree of Heliopolis, on the leaves of which his names are being written by Atum (seated on a throne to the left), the goddess Seshet, and Thoth (to the right).

Of the following **Second Small Hypostyle Hall** (Pl. 5) only the N. (r.) half, with four columns, survives. The sacrificial representations here are of little interest; at Pl. *h* the king is shown burning incense to Ptah and the lion-headed Sakhmet.

Behind the main temple, towards the N.W., are the remains of a number of extensive *Brick Buildings*, some of which were erected in the time of Ramses II., as we learn from the stamps on the bricks. Among the rest are some well-constructed vaults, originally covered by a platform. From the fragments of wine-jars and the stoppers found here we may reasonably conclude that these were store-rooms in connection with the temple. Adjacent is an altar, resembling that of Deir el-Bahari (p. 321). — To the W., adjoining the brick vaults, are the ruins of a large rectangular *Hall*, the ceiling of which was borne by thirty-two columns (the stumps of twelve of them still remain).

About 500 yds. N.E. of the Ramesseum we reach the *Mortuary Temple of Thutmosis III.* (Pl. D 2, 3), protected by a modern enclosing wall. Its ancient girdle-walls are partly hewn out of the rock and partly built of crude bricks. The inner chambers are in a very dilapidated condition, but we

can still recognize traces of hypostyle halls, brick chambers, etc. Many of the bricks bear the name of the royal builder. — Between the Ramesseum and this temple of Thutmosis lay the *Mortuary Temples of Amenophis II.* (18th Dyn.) and *Siptah* (19th Dyn.), the scanty remains of which were discovered by Sir Flinders Petrie in 1896. — Farther N.E., not far from Qurna, are the remains of the *Mortuary Temple of Amenophis I.* (Pl. E 2).

To the S. of the Ramesseum (see Pl. C 3) were similar temples of *Thutmosis IV.*, *Prince Wedjmose* (18th Dyn.), *Queen Tewosret* (wife of Siptah, p. 308), and *King Menephthes* (*Merneptah;* p. 304), all of which were explored by Sir Flinders Petrie in 1896; but the remains of these are very scanty.

Near the temple of Menephthes is the **Chicago House** (Pl. C 3, 4) of the University of Chicago Expedition, a large building provided by Mr. Julius Rosenwald, of Chicago, with an Egyptological library. — To the W. of the Ramesseum, on the way to Deir el-Medîna, lies the **German House** (Pl. C 3), erected as a lodging for the German savants at Thebes.

VII. The Tombs of Sheikh ʿAbd el-Qurna.

The Rock Tombs of ʿIlwet Sheikh ʿAbd el-Qurna (Pl. C 2), situated in the hill behind the Ramesseum to the N., form in conjunction with the Tombs of El-Khôkha (Pl. D 2), to the E., the largest and most important group among the private burial-grounds of Thebes. These were laid out among the foot-hills at the W. edge of the mountains by the grandees, the higher and the minor officials, and the priests of the New Empire. The S. group includes the vaults in the hill of *Qurnet Murʿai* (Pl. B 3; p. 341) and the valley of Deir el-Medîna (Pl. B 3; p. 338), while to the N. are the tombs in the long hill-slope of *Dirâʿ Abu'n-Naga* (Pl. E 2; p. 300). The total number of tombs in these cemeteries is over 330; they are numbered and usually have locked doors, which are opened by the keeper. The majority consist of three parts: a *Forecourt*, a wide *Hall*, with a roof frequently borne by pillars or columns, and a *Passage* or *Corridor*, ending in a recess in which the statues of the deceased and his favourite relatives were erected. Not infrequently there is a small chamber on each side of the passage. In front of the tomb was an open court where offerings were made to the dead. As the limestone of the hill of Sheikh ʿAbd el-Qurna is of poor quality, ill adapted for sculpture, the walls of most of the tombs were covered with clay, then whitewashed, and adorned with paintings. The representations on the side-walls of the hall, many of which are among the most valuable examples of Egyptian painting that we possess, depict the deceased in his earthly circumstances and duties, and thus shed a flood of light upon Egyptian life of the New Empire in its heyday. The end-walls of the hall are shaped like huge grave-stones; one usually bears prayers for the dead, while on the other is recorded the biography of the deceased. The representations on the walls of the passages illustrate the various funeral rites. — Some of the tombs that contain no inscriptions are inhabited by the poorer fellahin, while the forecourts serve for their livestock. In front of most of these cave-dwellings stand covered cylinders like gigantic mushrooms, of Nile mud and straw kneaded together. These are primitive granaries, while their flat roofs serve as sleeping places.

The tombs of Sheikh ʿAbd el-Qurna (see Pl. C D 2 and the inset) fall into four topographical groups. 1. The *Upper Enclosure*, surrounded by a low stone wall, on the E. and N. slopes of the hill, to the W. of the road from the Ramesseum to Deir el-Bahari. It has two entrances, one on the S. near Tomb 100 and another on the N. near Tomb 68. — 2. The tombs in the *Plain* between the Ramesseum and the Upper Enclosure. — 3. The *Lower Enclosure*, between the N.E. side of the hill of Sheikh ʿAbd el-Qurna and the hill of El-Khôkha, to the E. of the above-mentioned road. The entrance is opposite the N. entrance of the Upper Enclosure. — 4. The tombs of *El-Khôkha*, situated some near the American House, others between the Lower Enclosure and El-Khôkha.

If time be limited, it will be sufficient to visit the tombs of *Sennufer* (96 B) in the Upper Enclosure; *Ramose* (55), *Kha-em-hēt* (57), *Userhēt* (51), and *Nakht* (52), all in the plain; and *Menna* (69), near the N. gate of the Upper Enclosure.

a. Upper Enclosure.

From the Ramesseum we proceed N. towards the E. side of the hill and enter the Upper Enclosure (see Pl. C 2 and the inset) by the S. gate, whence paths lead to the various tombs.

Opposite the entrance lies the **Tomb of Rekhmerē** (No. 100), a vizier under Thutmosis III. and Amenophis II. It consists of a forecourt and a large hall, from the centre of which a long passage of considerable and gradually increasing height runs into the rock. At its end, about 18 ft. above the floor, is a small niche (serdâb, p. clxxvi; originally closed by a false door of granite) that probably held a statue of the deceased.

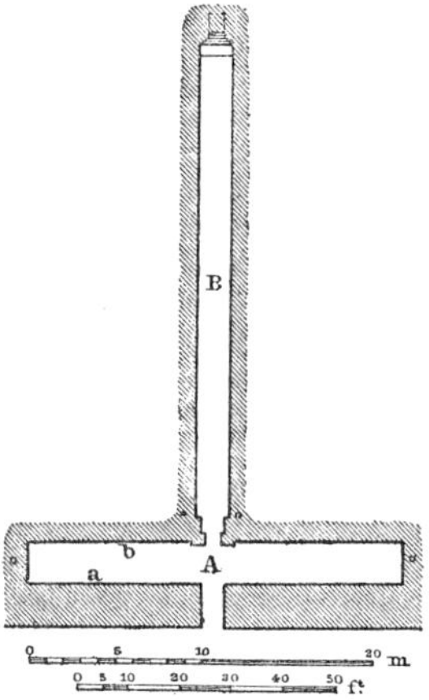

Hall (Pl. A). On the entrance-wall, to the left (Pl. a), Rekhmerē (r.) receiving petitioners; people (l.) with tribute. On the rear wall (Pl. b) Rekhmerē receives tribute and gifts from foreign peoples, who are arranged in five rows: 1. People of Punt (p. 233); 2. Princes of Keftiu (Crete) and the islands of the Ægean, bringing costly vases; 3. Nubians, with a panther, a giraffe, apes, gold, skins, etc.; 4. Syrians, with chariots, horses, an elephant and a bear, and costly vases; 5. People of the South, men, women, and children. — Passage (Pl. B). On the left wall (left to right): 1. Rekhmerē superintends the delivery of temple dues (corn, wine, cloth, etc.). 2. Rekhmerē inspects the workmen placed under him (carpenters, leather-workers, goldsmiths, makers of vases); below, the inspection of temple works, the building of a pylon and the polishing of statues. 3. Funeral scenes. On the right wall (left to right): 1. Rekhmerē at table. 2 (above). Offerings before the statues of the deceased; below is the statue of Rekhmerē in a boat, towed by men on the bank of the pond. 3. Banquet, musicians, and singers. 4. Boats.

From this tomb we ascend the hill to the subterranean ***Sepulchral Chambers of Sennufer** (No. 96 B), mayor of the southern city (i.e. Thebes) and overseer of the gardens of Amun under Amenophis II. (p. cv). These chambers are distinguished by the freshness of their paintings. The upper chambers are uninteresting and are now used as a magazine. A steep flight of steps descends to an antechamber and to a hall with four pillars. The mural decorations all represent religious subjects.

Antechamber (Pl. A). The ceiling is adorned with grapes and vine branches. On the left wall *(a)* sits Sennufer (l.), to whom his daughter

(partly destroyed) and ten priests bring offerings. On the right wall *(b)* servants bring the funeral equipment, while his daughter stands behind; to the right is the deceased entering and quitting the tomb. On the rear wall, to the right and left of the door *(d* and *c)*, the deceased and his daughter worshipping Osiris, who was represented above the door. — HALL (with pillars; Pl. B). The ceiling is adorned with network pattern and vine branches; the latter occur also in the wall-frieze. Above the door lie two dogs (Anubis); below and on the door-posts are the usual prayers for the dead. On the entrance-wall, to the left *(e)*, the deceased and his sister Merit appear emerging from the tomb and seated on a bench. On the left side-wall *(f)* are depicted the funeral ceremonies, with the deceased himself (left) looking on. On the rear wall *(g)* the deceased and his sister (destroyed) sit at table, while priests offer the sacrifice for the dead; farther to the right are the ships that take the mummy to Abydos (p. 253) and bring it back to the grave. On the right side-wall *(h)* the deceased and Merit are seen in an arbour, praying to Osiris and Anubis; in the middle, Anubis by the bier of Osiris; other religious scenes and texts; priest pouring the water of purification over Sennufer and Merit. On the entrance-wall, to the right *(i)*, the same couple are seen at table, with a priest sacrificing. Most of the pillars also bear the same two figures.

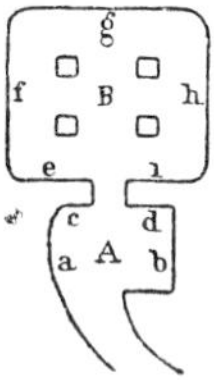

We ascend a flight of steps to the **Tomb of Kenamun** (No. 93), chief steward to Amenophis II. This was once one of the largest and finest tombs in the cemetery, but is now very ruinous, and little is left of the excellent paintings on yellow stucco.

From the wide forecourt we enter a HALL supported by ten columns. On the right entrance-wall the deceased was represented (his portraits and names have been everywhere obliterated) receiving the cattle tax; on the left entrance-wall, funeral rites (men hauling the statues to the tomb, women, ships; slaughter of sacrificial animals). On the rear wall, right, musicians performing before the infant Amenophis II., who is being nursed; left, Amenophis II., enthroned beneath a canopy, receiving New Year's gifts (statues of the king and the Queen Mother Hatshepsut, jewellery, furniture, weapons, chariots) displayed before him by the deceased. In the barrel-vaulted PASSAGE: right wall (right to left), remains of a hunting scene in the desert (ostriches, ibex and hound, jackals, etc.); hunting in the marshes; funeral banquet. In the SHRINE: right and left, the deceased and his wife at table; on the rear wall, the deceased praying to Osiris (l.) and Anubis (r.).

We return to No. 96 and ascend on the right to the **Tomb of Emunedjeh** (No. 84), a government official under Thutmosis III. In the hall appear representatives of the South and the North Lands (Nubians and Asiatics) bringing tribute to the king; in the passage is the deceased hunting. The tomb was used as a church in the Christian period (comp. p. clxxxviii).

We next reach, farther to the right, the **Tomb of Amenemhab** (No. 85), an officer of the time of Thutmosis III., consisting of a hall with pillars, a passage, and side-chambers.

PILLARED HALL (Pl. A). On the left of the entrance *(a)*: Amenemhab superintends the distribution of bread and meat to his troops. On the pillars, portraits of Amenemhab and his wife Bek. Above, between the two central pillars (but on the farther side), an hyæna hunt. The tasteful designs on the ceiling should be observed. On the rear wall, to the right *(b)*, the king was represented seated under a canopy, while in front of him stood Amenemhab, who described the part which he took in the Asiatic campaigns of Thutmosis III., in a long inscription written in blue characters, on

a white ground. Below this inscription, to the right, are seen Syrians, in their peculiar white garments with coloured borders, bringing tribute.

PASSAGE (Pl. B). On the left wall *(c)* is Amenemhab receiving vases, caskets, sandals, shields, and other objects presented to him by the king for the equipment of his tomb. — LEFT SIDE CHAMBER (Pl. C). Funeral rites. — RIGHT SIDE CHAMBER (Pl. D). On the wall *(d)*, to the left, are the deceased and his wife (effaced) at table; on the right is an Egyptian dinner-party. The servants in attendance carry flowers on their arms. The guests, two of them on easy chairs and three on stools, are offered refreshments. Below, in the second row, the ladies are seated. An attendant carries staves wreathed and crowned with flowers, and all the lady guests have blossoms in their hair and round their necks and hold lotus-flowers in their hands. In the lowest row is a band of musicians in full activity. It consists of two harpers (a man sitting and a woman standing), a flute-player (a woman standing), and a lute-player (a woman standing). On the rear wall *(e)* are fowling and fishing scenes. — On the left wall *(f)* in the continuation of the PASSAGE (Pl. B 1) are representations of funeral rites and sacrificial scenes. On the right wall *(g)* is Amenemhab's garden, with a fish-pond in the centre. To the left flowers are being presented to the deceased and his wife.

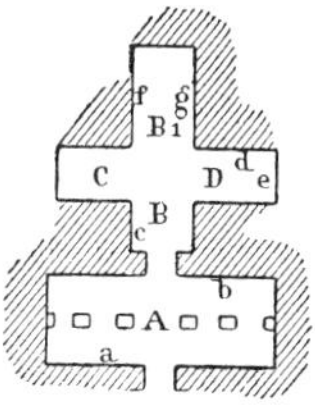

The **Tomb of Men-kheper-rē-seneb** (No. 86), high-priest of Amun in the time of Thutmosis III., is a little farther up the hill. The only paintings are in the hall. On the entrance-wall, to the right, are chariot-makers, leather workers, and herds of cattle; on the entrance-wall to the left, harvest scenes; on the right end-wall, the deceased takes the tribute of the Southlanders into his custody; on the wall to the right of the door leading to the corridor, Asiatics bringing tribute, including a curious goblet brought by a Keftiu or Cretan.

We ascend again to the **Tomb of Amenemhēt** (No. 82), who was scribe, steward, and granary superintendent to the vizier User in the time of Thutmosis III.

Note the remains of a picture of a banquet at the New Year feast with musical accompaniment, on the left rear wall; below is a bull fight. In the passage: left wall, funeral ceremonies and the voyage to Abydos; right wall, funeral banquet with musicians and persons bringing offerings.

We next reach the **Tomb of Enene** (No. 81), overseer of the granaries of Amun, who flourished at the beginning of the New Empire and had charge of the building of the tomb of Thutmosis I. (p. 314). The arrangement of this tomb is somewhat unusual. The entrance is formed by a pillared portico. The reliefs depict the life of the deceased.

On the 1st Pillar (to the left) are fishing scenes. 2nd Pillar: Harvest scenes (a woman gleaning; three men mowing). 3rd Pillar: Tillage. 5th Pillar: Enene at table. 6th Pillar: Enene's garden, with his house and storehouse below, surrounded by a wall. 7th Pillar: Hunting scene: an hyæna, struck by an arrow in the mouth, rears on its hind-legs while a dog dashes at it; hare, mountain-goats, gazelles. Back Wall: to the right of the door, peasants bringing tribute; adjoining, Enene hunting in the marshes and spearing fish. To the left of the door, Enene receiving tribute (in the upper row are dark-brown Nubians, including two women carrying their children in baskets on their backs); Enene inspecting the contributions of the peasants (observe the lines to guide the artist's hand); Enene

receiving tribute (only two rows remain, in one of which are necklaces, in the other incense is being weighed). — PASSAGE. On the left wall is the funeral, with female mourners; next, the deceased in the Temple of Abydos (p. 253), which is seen to the left; to the right, Enene and his wife seated at a table. On the right wall offerings are being brought to Enene and his wife. — In the SHRINE are four statues: one of the deceased, two of women, and one of a man. The shaft in front of it has been filled up.

From the tomb of Enene we ascend the hill to the highest row of tombs. There is a fine *VIEW from the top, including the Ramesseum and the Colossi of Memnon and extending across the Nile to the buildings of Luxor and Karnak; to the left are the hills, with the temple of Deir el-Baḥari at their feet. — In the highest row is the **Tomb of Haremhab** (No. 78), an army-officer under Thutmosis IV.

HALL. To the right and left of the entrance is a banquet scene with lute-players. On the rear wall, to the left, Haremhab presents to the king the contributions of the peasants; above, soldiers being recruited. On the right part of the rear wall the tribute from the Syrians and negroes is brought to the king. On the left wall of the PASSAGE are shown the funeral procession, with a collection of costly gifts comparable in its variety with the treasure of Tutankhamûn (p. 106), and the voyage to Abydos. Farther right are the remains of a picture of the Judgment of the Dead. On the right wall, to the right, funeral rites (purification of two mummies); left, hunting in the marshes (beautifully drawn birds) and bird-snaring with the clap-net (note the pelicans). Both the hall and the passage have fine ceilings. The latter leads to a wide pillared hall, left unfinished.

Close by to the N. is the much mutilated **Tomb of Tjenena** (No. 76), a fan-bearer on the king's right hand, of the time of Thutmosis IV.; on the rear wall to the right the deceased is seen bringing the representatives of the Asiatic peoples, who have come with tribute, into the presence of Thutmosis IV. This tomb is connected by a breach in the wall with the **Tomb of Amenhotepsise** (No. 75), second prophet of Amun in the time of Thutmosis IV. On the wall to the left of the entrance, the deceased inspects artisans working for the temple, and surveyors. On the opposite wall, statues, harps, vessels, a pillared arcade, and other gifts made to the temple of Amun; on the wall to the right of the entrance, the banquet of the dead; on the opposite wall, the deceased is escorted to the temple of Amun at Karnak, the façade of which (pylon with flagstaffs and statues) is represented to the right, and is here greeted by his relatives, the priestesses of Amun.

We ascend to the ridge of the hill and then descend N. to the **Tomb of Tjeneni** (No. 74), chief scribe and commander of the soldiers under Thutmosis IV. HALL. On the rear wall, to the right, the deceased inspecting tribute brought to the king (in the lower row are horses). To the left is Tjeneni inspecting a parade of the troops under his command (note the drummer with the drum on his back).

A little to the N. of No. 74 lies the **Tomb of Senmut** (No. 71), chief architect and favourite of Queen Hatshepsut and creator of the great temple of Deir el-Baḥari (p. 317). This tomb is of great historical importance but is badly damaged. At the back of the chamber, which was once supported by pillars, in the right-hand corner (now protected from damage), is a representation of three Keftiu (Cretans) bringing curiously shaped vessels. Above is a frieze of Hathor heads.

Lower down, on the N. side of the conspicuous *Wilkinson's House*, is the **Tomb of Entef-oker** (No. 60), vizier to Sesostris I. (12th Dyn.), the oldest in the cemetery. A long passage leads to a chamber with

a recess, in front of which stands a mutilated lifesize statue of *Senet*, wife of Entef-oker. The painted walls of the corridor illustrate the old-fashioned style of the Middle Empire. Right wall: bird-snaring with the clap-net; hunt in the desert; kitchen, bakehouse, and brewery; the deceased and his wife inspecting their New Year's presents. Left wall: the voyage to Abydos; funeral ceremonies; dancing girls and musicians.

Thence we descend to the **Tomb of Imisib** (No. 65), an official of the temple of Amun at the end of the 20th Dynasty. This tomb was originally constructed under the 18th Dyn., but Imisib coated the old reliefs with a layer of stucco, on which he placed his own paintings.

From the forecourt we enter a HALL borne by six sixteen-sided pillars, whence a long vaulted passage leads to a statue-niche. The faded wall-paintings in the hall show festal barges with the name of Ramses IX., golden utensils, and (left wall) the king sacrificing to the sacred boat of Amun and to the statues of his ancestors. The ceiling decoration is admirable.

We now descend to the N. gate of the enclosure, by which is the ***Tomb of Menne** (No. 69), scribe of the fields and estate inspector under the 18th Dynasty. On the entrance-wall to the right in the hall the deceased and his wife are represented receiving sacrificial gifts; their relatives bring flowers and eatables. On the entrance-wall to the left we see the deceased superintending the labours of the field in his official capacity; at the top a field is being measured with a rope (the details are very fine). On the rear wall to the right, the deceased and his relatives at table. On the end-wall to the left, the deceased and his wife praying to Osiris. On the left wall in the passage are burial-scenes and Osiris judging the dead; on the right wall the representations of the deceased hunting in the marshes, the voyage to Abydos (comp. p. 253), and the ceremonies in the mummy's presence are notable. Fine ceiling decoration.

b. THE TOMBS IN THE PLAIN.

The tombs among the rubbish-mounds in the desert, between the Ramesseum and the Upper Enclosure, to the W. of the road to Deir el-Baḥari, are among the most interesting in the whole cemetery.

The largest and most important, both historically and artistically, is the ***Tomb of Ramose** (No. 55; comp the inset), governor of the metropolis and vizier to Amenophis IV. (p. cv). It dates from the beginning of the reign of the heretical king and is one of the few monuments belonging to the period at which the transition from the ancient religion to pure sun-worship was accomplished; owing to the removal of the court from Thebes to Tell el-ʿAmârna (p. 245) it was left unfinished. Some of the scenes are executed in delicate bas-relief and some are painted in bright colours or just sketched in in black pigment. Most of them are still in the old style of the time of Amenophis III., but several already display the new forms of ʿAmârna art. The tomb has been completely excavated and restored in recent years by Robert Mond.

From the open court we enter the large PILLARED HALL, the roof of which is borne by four rows of eight columns each. The left or N. half of the *East Wall* has fine reliefs in the style of Amenophis III.: right to left, Ramose and his wife, followed by several officials, bring offerings; above, the deceased, followed by his wife Merit-Ptah and preceded by his three daughters; below, holy water is poured over the statue of the deceased; Ramose and his wife, and another married couple, receive all sorts of gifts from the hands of servants; below, Ramose and his wife, and Amenhotep ("chief steward of the king's house in the nome of Memphis") and his wife, seated at table, while a priest in a panther's skin officiates in their presence. On the *South Wall* are brightly painted burial-scenes; the groups of mourning women in the animated ʿAmârna style are excellent; below, on the right, is Ramose entering the palace. A shaft in the corner descends obliquely to the sarcophagus-chamber. On the left half of the *West Wall* is Amenophis IV., still represented in the old conventional manner, seated below a canopy with Maat, the goddess of truth, while Ramose is represented twice; on the right half (ʿAmârna style) the king and his consort are shown on a balcony of the palace, watching Ramose being adorned with the golden chains they have thrown down to him. The unattractive figure of the king is here reproduced with great fidelity to nature; the figure of Ramose is merely sketched in. Above are the sun and its rays; behind, the royal bodyguard. Farther to the right is Ramose leaving the palace with his decorations and receiving the congratulations of the populace. In the doorway to the lower chamber: left, Ramose and his wife (partly obliterated) praying; right, Ramose and his wife entering the tomb. — The PASSAGE, supported by eight papyrus-columns, is unfinished and undecorated. Adjacent is a small room with unfinished niches.

Adjoining this tomb on the S. is the **Tomb of Userhēt** (No. 56), a royal scribe of the period of Amenophis II. (p. cv), with tasteful ceiling-patterns and excellent mural paintings.

On the right half of the rear wall is the deceased offering gifts to the king; to the left, store-chambers with all sorts of loaves; below, on the left, barbers at work. The left-hand wall of the passage depicts the deceased hunting gazelles in his chariot and hunting in the marshes; below, fishing and the vintage; on the right wall, burial-scenes.

Beside No. 56 lies the **Tomb of Kha-em-hēt** (No. 57), superintendent of the royal granaries under Amenophis III. It is adorned with admirable bas-reliefs.

The court contains remains of the tomb-stele. To the left in the doorway is Kha-em-hēt with uplifted hands offering a prayer to the sun-god. In the niche to the left in the first wide HALL are two mutilated statues of Kha-em-hēt and his relative Imhotep, a royal scribe, who was interred in an adjoining but now inaccessible tomb. On the wall to the right of the entrance is the deceased offering two vessels with two geese in each; to the left of this relief two upper rows depict the surveying of the fields; below are cheerful agricultural scenes. On the rear wall to the left Kha-em-hēt presents a report on the harvest to Amenophis III., who is sitting

beneath a canopy (figures much mutilated). The nine captive tribes at the foot of the canopy should be noticed. On the right is a similar scene with the king seated upon a magnificent throne, on which he is represented in the guise of a sphinx. Behind Kha-em-hēt are two rows of his officials in humble attitudes. The top row shows Kha-em-hēt being attired and anointed. — The mutilated texts and scenes in the long PASSAGE relate to the life beyond the tomb. The INNER HALL at the end of the passage contains large seated statues, very highly polished. Adjoining it opens a small unadorned chamber.

A little to the W. of the tomb of Ramose (No. 55) is the **Tomb of Pere** (No. 139), a priest of Amun, perhaps dating from the time of Amenophis III., with a few well-preserved paintings.

On the right entrance-wall and the opposite rear wall, the deceased and his wife receiving offerings. On the short wall, the deceased and his wife, followed by their family, praying to Osiris; below, pictures of the obsequies in three rows (funeral procession, voyage to Abydos, ceremony of the 'Opening of the Mouth').

A little E. of the tomb of Kha-em-hēt (No. 57), close to the road, is a COURT adjoined by four tombs. To the S. is the ***Tomb of Neferhotep** (No. 50), a priest who lived under King Haremhab (p. cvi). This tomb dates from the beginning of the 19th Dyn. and its sunk reliefs already show a lack of the animation characteristic of the art of the 18th Dyn. and approach the dull style of the Ramessid period. The HALL contains some beautiful and well-preserved ceiling-paintings. On the left end-wall we see the deceased being decorated with chains of honour in the presence of the king. On the rear wall, to the left of the door to the passage, are the deceased and his family at a banquet, with a son bringing food to them. Below this, to the left, is a harper, with the text of the song he is singing in front of him. On the right wall of the PASSAGE, where the deceased and his wife are seen sitting at the table of offerings, is a second copy of this song, which encourages us to leave all cares behind and think of the joys of life. In the recess are statues of the deceased and his family. — To the N. of the court is the **Tomb of Userhēt** (No. 51), the first prophet of Thutmosis I. (p. cv). This tomb was constructed in the time of Sethos I. (p. cvi). A charming scene on the right end-wall represents the deceased and two women under a fig-tree, with their souls shown in the form of birds (comp. p. cliv). Other birds sit in the branches, while to the right stands a tree-goddess giving water to the deceased. Some of the other details also are very attractive. On the rear wall, to the right of the door to the passage (blocked up), the deceased and his sisters are shown sacrificing to Osiris at the top, while below they stand in the presence of Thutmosis (represented with a black skin). — To the E. is the **Tomb of Amen-wehsu** (No. 111), a painter who with his own hands has decorated the walls with scenes on stucco and texts of religious import (period of Ramses II.). — The *Tomb of Khensumose* (No. 30), on the W., of the Ramessid period, is much dilapidated and not accessible.

The northernmost of all, not far from the N. gate of the Upper

Enclosure, is the ****Tomb of Nakht** (No. 52), an official and priest of Amun under the 18th Dyn. (c. 1425 B.C.). From the entrance (Pl. 1) we enter the first chamber (Pl. 2) which is alone decorated. The paintings on the walls are in an excellent state of preservation. Under Amenophis IV. (p. cv) the name of Amun has been obliterated wherever it occurred. — *Wall a.* In the lower row is the deceased superintending his labourers, who are ploughing, hoeing, and sowing; two men are breaking the clods with hammers; to the left a labourer drinks from a water-skin hanging from a tree; a tree is being felled. In the upper row, to the right, the deceased inspects harvest operations represented in three rows: below, three men reaping with sickles, behind them a woman gleaning, two men packing the ears of corn in a basket, two women plucking flax; in the middle, the threshed corn being measured; above, winnowing the grain. To the left, the deceased and his wife sacrificing. — *Wall b.* False door painted to imitate granite. In the upper compartment are the deceased and his wife at table, and beside it are attendants with offerings; below the door, a heap of offerings, by which stand two tree-goddesses and two servants (note the painting of the grapes). — *Wall c* (in poor preservation). In the lower row, to the right, the deceased and his wife (much damaged) are seated at table, upon a bench, below which is a cat eating fish; their son brings flowers and geese to them, while three women make music; other relatives sit in two rows to the left. Only the left half of the upper row remains: a blind harper and women seated on the ground conversing. —

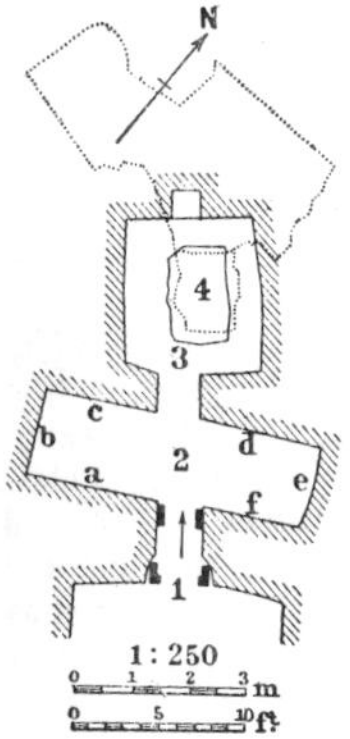

Wall d. In the lower row, the deceased and his wife seated in an arbour, while servants bring them flowers, grapes, poultry, fish, etc.; to the right birds are being caught in nets and plucked; above, vintage and wine-pressing. In the upper row, to the left, are the deceased and his wife, to the right, the deceased spearing fish and fowling. — *Wall e* (unfinished). Nakht and his wife seated at table, while their relatives bring offerings. — *Wall f.* The deceased and his wife, followed by three rows of servants, offer a sacrifice (as on Wall e). — From the second chamber (Pl. 3) a shaft (Pl. 4) descends to another underground chamber (shown by a dotted line on our plan), which is now inaccessible.

c. Lower Enclosure.

This group, which is best visited from the tomb of Nakht (No. 52) or that of Menne (No. 69), includes several interesting tombs. No. 106 is the **Tomb of Pesiur,** governor of the metropolis and

vizier of Sethos I. (p. cvi). The forecourt contains a fine stele and statues of the deceased; in the entrance and on the pillars, Pesiur in his official uniform with his wife. — No. 41 is the **Tomb of Amenemopet**, chief steward of Amun at the beginning of the 19th Dynasty. By the pillars of the courtyard are statues of the deceased; on the walls, memorial inscriptions and religious paintings. — No. 42 is the **Tomb of Amenmose,** governor of the foreign lands in the N. (18th Dyn.). On the left rear wall and the left short wall of the first hall is the deceased displaying before the king the tribute of the Asiatics.

No. 23 is the **Tomb of Tjay,** archivist in the reign of Menephthes (19th Dyn.).

A flight of steps, in front of which there was formerly another hall, leads to the open Court, which is surrounded by colonnades (rebuilt). In the E. corner of the S. colonnade was a representation of the royal chancery. Then comes a Hall, with wall-paintings mostly of sacrificial scenes; on the right entrance-wall, Tjay is decorated with golden chains of honour by the king on his throne. — On the left wall of the Passage, the funeral procession and Judgment of the Dead (partly destroyed); right wall, sacrificial scenes and the deceased, in many cases accompanied by his wife, praying to the gods of the dead. — The following Chamber contains the granite sarcophagus; in a recess in the rear wall are half-statues of Osiris, Isis, and Horus.

No. 38 is the **Tomb of Djeserkerē-seneb,** inspector of the granaries of Amun under Thutmosis IV. (p. cv). The right-hand rear wall of the hall is adorned with an excellent painting of a banquet, with the deceased and his sister being entertained by musicians and dancers.

d. The Tombs of El-Khôkha.

Among the tombs situated to the S. of the hill of *El-Khôkha* (Pl. D 2), and in the hill itself, the following merit inspection.

The **Tomb of Neferronpet** (No. 178), also known as *Kenro*, a scribe of the treasury of Amon-Rē in the reign of Ramses II. (p. cvi), lies a little to the N.W. of the house of the ʿomda or village headman. The well-preserved mural paintings and ceiling-decorations of its two chambers are typical specimens of Ramessid art. The first chamber contains burial-scenes; on the rear wall of the second are four statues.

The **Tomb of Surer** (No. 48), whose full name was *Amenemhēt*, lies a little E. of No. 178, not far from the N.W. corner of the temple walls of Thutmosis III. (p. 327). It is an imposing structure of the time of Amenophis III. (p. cv), resembling the tomb of Ramose (p. 333) and possessing remarkable reliefs in the best style of the period. The open court is adjoined by a transverse hall with fluted columns; on the right rear wall, the king enthroned; farther to the right are statues being hauled. The stele is large but badly mutilated. The second axial hall, constructed deep in the rock, is supported by papyrus-columns and has a vaulted ceiling, but it is unfinished and in a very ruinous state.

The **Tomb of Nebamun and Ipuki** (No. 181), two sculptors of the end of the 18th Dyn., lies on the S. slope of El-Khôkha and has excellent paintings of fresh colouring.

On the left entrance-wall (W. half of S. wall) of the HALL: Nebamun and his mother sacrificing; a banquet; below, Ipuki and his wife receiving gifts from their relatives. Right entrance-wall (E. half): the deceased praying to the deified Amenophis I. and Queen Ahmes-Nofreteroy (p. cv); below, he is seated supervising the work of his craftsmen (carpenters, goldsmiths, jewellers). Right short wall: the deceased praying to Osiris and the four sons of Osiris (see p. clvi, Emset); below, two married couples seated. On the left half of the rear wall and on the left short wall, burial scenes, the voyage to Abydos, and funeral ceremonies.

The **Tomb of Puimrē** (No. 39), priest of Amun in the time of Thutmosis III. (p. cv), is at the N.E. end of El-Khôkha. This tomb, though remarkable for its fine reliefs (some with well-preserved colouring), is badly mutilated and has of recent times been reconstructed out of the numerous fragments by Norman de Garis Davies.

From the large FORECOURT, the rear of which was adorned with a colonnade and six memorial inscriptions, a central door leads to the HALL, in the back-wall of which are three doors leading to three chapels. On the right entrance-wall of the hall (N. half of E. wall): above, hunting in the swamps; below, tribute from the marsh districts (poultry, cattle); wine-pressing, bird-snaring, fishing, men binding and carrying bundles of papyrus. Left entrance-wall, the workshops of the temple of Amun (chariot-builders, goldsmiths, jewellers, carpenters, makers of stone vessels). On the right (N.) short wall, driving game in the desert. Rear wall: receipt of tribute from the N. lands and the lands by the Red Sea; the best-preserved reliefs are those on the right of the central door. — On the walls of the right-hand or NORTH CHAPEL: funeral rites, voyage to Abydos, the deceased at table. In the CENTRAL CHAPEL: sacrifice of animals; the deceased receiving offerings. On the S. wall of the adjoining niche, the ceiling of which is decorated with door-ornamentation, the deceased and his wife at table; by the rear wall stood a stele (now in the Cairo Museum). The reliefs in the SOUTH CHAPEL show the deceased and his wife receiving offerings and seated at table.

The **Tomb of Prennufer** (No. 188), a royal steward of the beginning of the reign of Amenophis IV. (p. cv), lies to the W. of No. 39, close to the house of the Metropolitan Museum expedition (p. 324). The reliefs (in the ʿAmârna style) of the hall are badly damaged, and their subjects are barely distinguishable.

VIII. Deir el-Medîna.

Qurnet Murʿai. Tombs of the Queens.

No one should miss seeing the beautiful little Ptolemaic temple of *Deir el-Medîna.* The tomb of Huye at *Qurnet Murʿai* (p. 342) and the *Cemetery of Deir el-Medîna* (p. 340) need be visited only by those who have plenty of time. The *Tombs of the Queens* (p. 342), for which at least $1^1/_4$ hr. must be allowed, lie somewhat out of the way but should be inspected even by the hurried traveller. We may, however, visit them from Medînet Habu (p. 347) and take Deir el-Medîna in returning.

About $^1/_2$ M. to the W. of the Ramesseum, on the way to the Tombs of the Queens (p. 342), is the graceful little ***Temple of Deir el-Medîna** (or *el-Madîna;* Pl. B 3), begun by Ptolemy IV Philopator, completed by Philometor and Euergetes II. (p. cxii),

and principally dedicated to Hathor, goddess of the dead, and to Maat, goddess of truth. It lies in a barren hollow and is surrounded by a lofty wall of dried bricks which are fitted together in wavy lines. Through this a doorway of stone (on the S.E.) leads into the temple precincts, at the back of which (N.) are steep rocks. The temple is of freestone, on the smooth façade of which, crowned with a cavetto cornice, many Greeks and Copts have written their names. In Christian times it was used by the monks as a dwelling-place, and to this is due the mutilation of many of the inscriptions and reliefs. Adjoining the temple on the left is an archway of bricks.

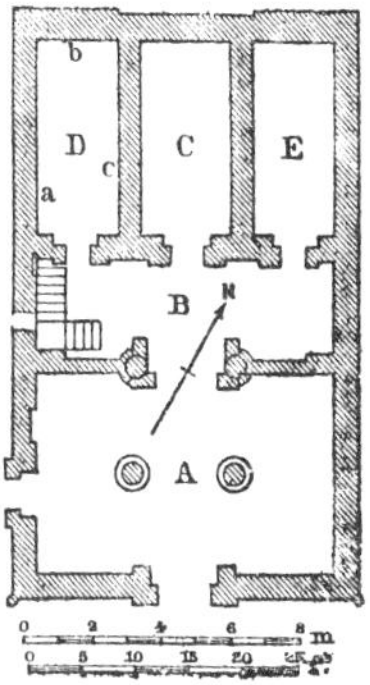

We first enter a large Vestibule (Pl. A), the roof of which (now mostly fallen in) was supported by two flower-columns. Separated from it by two columns with rich foliage-capitals and two pillars adorned with heads of Hathor is the Pronaos (Pl. B; p. clxxii). Stone screens rose between the pillars and columns, and between the columns, which bear figures of the deified sage Amenhotep (p. 89; No. 3) and the god Imhotep (p. clvii), was a doorway, open at the top. Only the left screen now remains. The walls of this hall are embellished with incised reliefs, representing the king sacrificing to various deities. Towards the top of the left wall is a tasteful window, which originally lighted a staircase. — From the pronaos three doors open into as many Chapels. Above the cavetto cornice over the doorway to the *Central Chapel* (Pl. C) are seven heads of Hathor. On the interior walls appears Philopator, sometimes accompanied by his sister Arsinoë, sacrificing to various gods; and on the jambs of the entrance-door are four gods with bulls' heads. — On the left wall of the *Left Chapel* (Pl. D) is a well-executed representation of the Judgment of the Dead (Pl. a; p. cliv). To the right is enthroned Osiris, god of the underworld, and in front of him are the symbol of Eme-wet (p. clvi), the four genii of the dead upon a lotus-flower, the 'Devourer of the Underworld' in the form of a hippopotamus, and Harpocrates (p. clvi), resting upon a crooked staff. The ibis-headed Thoth inscribes the verdict. To the left Anubis and Horus weigh the heart of the deceased; two goddesses of truth, with feathers on their heads, conduct the deceased into the judgment hall. Above is the deceased praying to the forty-two judges of the dead. On the rear wall (Pl. b) of this chapel Philopator offers incense before Osiris and Isis. On the right wall (Pl. c) appears, to the left, the sacred boat of Soker-Osiris (comp. p. clix) on a pedestal, with standards, etc., beside it. To the right the king offers incense to Anubis, who holds a disk,

and to the ithyphallic Min (p. clvii). On the lintel of the door is a four-headed ram (the god of the four winds), above which is a flying vulture, worshipped by four goddesses. On the door-jambs, the king with three falcon-headed and three dog-headed genii. — The good reliefs in the *Right Chapel* (Pl. E) show the king before different gods.

To the S. of the temple, in the valley between the escarpment of the W. hills and the W. side of the hill of Qurnet Murʿai (Pl. B 3), are the ruins of a settlement of the New Empire, inhabited by the artists and workmen employed in the construction of the royal and private tombs. On the slope of the W. hills is the **Cemetery of Deir el-Medîna,** with numerous rock-tombs, mostly of necropolis officials of the 19-20th Dyn., though some date back to the 18th. Excavations by the Institut Français d'Archéologie Orientale (p. 44), under the direction of B. Bruyère, are in progress.

Hurried visitors may restrict their attention to Nos. 3, 340, and 217, though several others with paintings in good condition merit inspection. In the tombs of the 19-20th Dyn. (Ramessid period) the scenes of daily life which constitute the charm of the 18th Dyn. tombs practically disappear and are replaced by conventional scenes of sacrifice and burial and by subjects from the Book of the Dead (p. 111). — The tombs are locked, the keys being kept by the custodian and at the offices of the French excavations.

From the floor of the valley we climb the hillside to the **Tomb of Sennutem** (No. 1), of the Ramessid period, with a vaulted tomb-chamber and religious reliefs and paintings, including a very pretty picture of the funeral banquet. The valuable contents of this tomb, which was discovered in 1886, are now in the Cairo Museum (p. 100). — Adjacent are the **Family Tombs of Amennakht, Nebenmaat, and Kha-em-tōre** (Nos. 218-220; Ramessid period). A staircase leads to a *Chamber* with a vaulted roof and religious scenes (above the entrance, the Hathor cow). Next comes an *Antechamber* (undecorated), whence steps on the left lead to the *Chamber of Nebenmaat:* right wall, Anubis at the bier; rear wall, obsequies by the tomb (behind the pyramid is a goddess welcoming the setting sun in the W. mountain); left wall, the deceased and his sister praying to Osiris, the deified Amenophis I., and Queen Ahmes-Nofreteroy (p. cv). We return to the antechamber, on the right of which lies the *Chamber of Kha-em-tōre* (paintings damaged). Another staircase leads to the *Chamber of Amennakht*, which has scenes and texts from the Book of the Dead (the deceased and his sister in the fields of the blessed, etc.); on the left short wall, Anubis at the bier.

Higher up are the **Tombs of Khonsu and Khabekhnet** (Nos. 2 and 2 B), sons of Sennutem (No. 1). No. 2 is uninteresting. In No. 2 B steep steps lead to the tomb-chamber, on the left wall of which is a remarkable painting of Anubis at the bier of Osiris, who is represented as a fish.

Thence we proceed N. to the **Tomb of Ramose,** a scribe in the necropolis (No. 250; Ramessid period), which has well-preserved paintings (yellow on a white ground). Right wall: the deceased with his wife and family praying to the Hathor cow issuing from the rock. Rear wall, above: (right) the deceased in presence of Osiris, (left) his wife praying to Amenophis I.; below, procession of mourners and sacrifice to the mummies at the tomb. — **Tomb of Erenufer** (No. 290; Ramessid period). A staircase leads to an anteroom with the opening of the tomb-shaft and thence to a vaulted chamber with excellently preserved texts and scenes from the Book of the Dead (in colours on a yellow ground). On the left entrance-wall, Erenufer and his parents (with grey hair) praying to Ptah. — Adjacent is the **Tomb of Nu and Nakht-Min** (No. 291). From the small forecourt we enter a vaulted chamber with admirable ceiling-painting. Left wall, the funeral procession and ceremonies, fluently drawn in white on a grey ground. The other wall-

paintings represent sacrifices to various members of the family and to Osiris and Hathor.

To the N. of No. 291, just behind the temple of Deir el-Medîna, is the **Tomb of Nefrabet** (No. 5; Ramessid period). A staircase leads to a vaulted chamber, the walls of which represent the deceased and his relatives praying to the Hathor cow issuing from the mountain (right) and to the Horus falcon (left). Steps lead thence to a second chamber with religious paintings (yellow on a white ground): Horus and Thoth pouring holy water over the deceased; Amenophis I. praying to Meret-seger, the serpent-headed goddess of the dead, and to Hathor; the sun supported by two lions. On the short rear wall, above the opening of the shaft, are represented the mummies of the deceased and his wife. — We now ascend the hill again to the S. to the **Tomb of Kha** (No. 8), dating from the time of Amenophis III. The vaulted chapel has a pretty ceiling-pattern. This tomb is noteworthy for the lavish tomb-equipment discovered here (now at Turin).

Farther S. is the ***Tomb of Peshedu** (No. 3; Ramessid period). A steep staircase descends to several chambers and finally through a low vaulted *Passage*, in which the chapel with the recumbent Anubis jackal is depicted on either side, to the *Sepulchral Chamber*. Right entrance-wall, the deceased prostrate in prayer beneath a palm. Right long wall: above, the deceased (small figure) praying to Osiris and other gods of the dead; below, Peshedu and his small daugther in presence of Re-Harakhte, Atum, Khepre, Ptah, and the sacred Osiris post (p. clviii). By the rear wall stood the sarcophagus, which was composed of limestone blocks; above is Osiris and the mountain of the dead. On the left long wall (continued on the left entrance-wall): above, Osiris and his circle; below, texts from the Book of the Dead; the deceased and his family, headed by his white-haired father, adoring the Horus falcon.

Adjoining No. 3 is the **Tomb of Amenemhēt** (No. 340), a necropolis official of the end of the 18th Dynasty. Steps lead to the vaulted entrance, through which we reach the small tomb-chamber. The paintings, in colours on a yellow ground, are excellently preserved. Left short wall: above, the deceased praying to Anubis (l.) and Osiris (r.); below, the deceased and his wife at the table of offerings, with his sons and daughters on the left and attended by servants. Rear wall, on either side of a small recess, the deceased and his wife at table. Right short wall (unfinished): above, the same scene as on the left short wall; below, the funeral cortège in two rows. The ceiling is adorned with grapes and vine leaves, in squares. — Not far off is the **Tomb of Nekht-Amun** (No. 335), a sculptor of the 20th Dynasty. A steep staircase leads to an upper room adjoined by a small chamber with pretty paintings (the deceased praying to his patron saint Thoth, etc.). Another staircase leads to a lower sepulchral chamber with fluently painted family pictures (on the right short wall, Anubis at the bier). — On the same level, but a little further S., are the tombs of the sculptor *Ken* (No. 4) and the necropolis official *Amenmose* (No. 9), both of the Ramessid period, with fairly well preserved reliefs. — Finally we proceed N. again to the highest row of tombs to visit the **Tomb of Ipuy** (No. 217), a sculptor of the 19th Dynasty. On the right short wall, very pretty representations of the manufacture of the tomb equipment (carpenters making two chapels). On the right entrance-wall, scenes of daily life: wine-pressing, craftsmen at work, fishing.

From the valley of Deir el-Medîna to the Tombs of the Kings, see p. 316.

The hill of **Qurnet Murʿai** (Pl. B 3), which separates the valley of Deir el-Medîna from the arable district, is occupied by a number of fellah huts and by the ruins of a brick convent. Scattered among these are rock-tombs of the 18th Dyn., most of which are of no interest.

The most important is the **Tomb of Huye** (*Amenhotep;* No. 40), who was governor of Ethiopia (Nubia) under Tutankhamûn. The key is kept by the custodian.

Entrance Wall. To the left appears the ceremonial investiture of Huye as governor, in presence of the king; his relatives and officials congratulate him. To the right stands Huye, with his relatives, and in front of him are two gaily decorated Nile boats; farther on is Huye as governor of Ethiopia, with five rows of people bringing tribute, etc. — On the Left End Wall appears the deceased, sacrificing to the dog-headed Anubis on the left and to Osiris on the right. — On the Rear Wall (left) is Huye bearing the flail and the crook, symbols of his dignity (comp. p. clxxxvi), with three rows of Nubian chiefs. Behind him is the tribute from Nubia, including a Nubian landscape standing upon a table covered with panther-skins and cloths: in the centre is a conical hut, with dûm-palms, giraffes, and negroes at the sides. Higher up are bowls of jewels, rings of gold, sacks of gold-dust, shields covered with golden plates and dappled skins, footstools, chairs, benches of ebony, a chariot, etc. The Nubian chiefs, dressed (with a few exceptions) in the Egyptian style, are received by Huye and his brother Amenhotep. In the top row, behind the chiefs, their princess, shaded by an umbrella, approaches in a chariot drawn by oxen, and is followed by chiefs wearing ostrich-feathers in their hair, which is plaited into a kind of hood (as is the custom to this day among these tribes). The procession is closed by two negresses with pendent breasts. One of them carries a child on her back, and each woman leads a boy behind her. In the second and third rows are Nubians bringing gold, panther-skins, a giraffe, and oxen. Between the horns of the last, which are represented as arms, are heads of supplicating negroes. More to the left, the arrival of Huye from Nubia with transport vessels. Five Ethiopian princes crouch in the second boat. Cattle and other goods are being brought to Egypt in the smaller vessels below. — On the right side appears the king, seated under a canopy; before him stands Huye presenting the Syrian tribute, which includes artistic gold vases. The other representations are almost entirely obliterated. — The sepulchral inscription, which should have occupied the Right End Wall, was never executed. On each side of the vacant space are offerings to Huye. The rest is destroyed.

Below No. 40 are two tombs of the Ramessid period. No. 277 is the **Tomb of Amen-em-ōnet,** a priest, with funeral scenes (ships with the shrine of the dead; mourning women; statues of Amenophis III. and Queen Teye being conveyed to the tomb on sledges; the mountain-side with the tomb surmounted by a pyramid and preceded by the great tomb-stele). No. 278 is the **Tomb of Amenemhab,** containing religious scenes (the Hathor cow issuing from the mountain, etc.).

The **Tombs of the Queens,** called by the Arabs *Bîbân el-Ḥarîm* (Pl. A 3), should not be missed if time permit.

On the way from Deir el-Medîna to the (1 M.) Tombs of the Queens we pass a number of inscribed steles, formerly in niches. The first of these shows Ramses III. before Amun and Ptah. On the next Meret-seger, goddess of the West, offers the same monarch her breast; behind is the sun-god Rē-Harakhte; to the right is Amun, investing the king with the sickle-shaped sword. The inscription refers to the campaigns of the king. We then ascend through a mountain valley with bare and lofty sides of limestone, picturesquely formed and carved with inscriptions to the gods of the regions of the dead. — The road from Medînet Habu (p. 347) to the (about $1^1/_4$ M.) Tombs of the Queens unites with that described above.

Both routes end in an enclosed *Valley*, which is of great beauty, though not so imposing as that of Bîbân el-Mulûk (p. 302). At its entrance are the remains of a Coptic monastery (7th cent.). From the farther end of the valley an especially fine view is enjoyed of the Theban plain and the Colossi of Memnon.

The tombs belong mainly to the 19th and 20th Dynasties. Altogether upwards of seventy have been discovered, most of which were explored in 1903-5 by the Italian archæological mission under E. Schiaparelli († 1928). Many of them are unfinished and entirely without decoration, and in their rough and blackened condition resemble mere caves in the rocks. It is rare to find either inscriptions or representations carved in the stone; even in the finest tombs the limestone walls were more often covered with plaster, which could be adorned with paintings without much difficulty. The more important tombs are designated by tablets with Italian inscriptions, and the best-preserved ones, which alone are worth visiting, must be opened by the keeper, who provides candles.

We ride or drive to the end of the valley and begin with Tomb 66, after which hurried visitors content themselves with Nos. 44 and 43. Or we may choose the reverse direction and proceed along the E. wall of the valley, passing a tablet commemorating the Italian excavations. The graves we first reach are *No. 36* (of an unknown princess), *No. 39* (of *Sitrē*, mother of Sethos I.), *No. 40* (of an unknown princess), and *No. 42* (of *Prē-her-wnamf*, a son of Ramses III.).

Beyond these is *No. 43*, the **Tomb of Prince Seth-her-khopshef,** son of Ramses III. (p. cvii). Two narrow corridors lead to a somewhat wider chamber, which is adjoined by a small room. The reliefs, which were formerly coloured but are now smoke-blackened, show the prince and the king praying to various deities and performing other religious rites. On the rear wall of the innermost chamber Osiris is seen to the right and left, while on the side-walls are various other deities arranged in two rows.

No. 44. **Tomb of Prince Kha-em-wēset,** son of Ramses III., with coloured reliefs in good preservation. In the *First Passage* are seen the deceased and his royal father in the presence of various deities. Adjoining are two lateral chambers with reliefs of the prince in the presence of the gods; on the rear wall are Isis and Nephthys with Osiris. The mural representations in the *Second Passage* show the king and prince in front of the gates and guards of the Fields of the Blessed; adjoining are citations from the 'Book of the Dead' (p. 111). In the last room the king is seen before various deities.

Beyond the tomb of Prince Kha-em-wēset we pass *No. 51*, the *Tomb of Queen Eset*, mother of Ramses VI.

No. 52, the *Tomb of Queen Titi*, consists of the usual antechamber, a long passage, and a large chapel with a small chamber on each of its three sides. The reliefs have been badly damaged.

Close by is *No. 55*, the ***Tomb of Prince Amen-her-khopshef,** son of Ramses III. The scenes in this tomb are remarkably fresh in colour.

In the *First Room* (Pl. 1) we see, to the left, Ramses III. embraced by Isis; farther on, Ramses III., accompanied by Prince Amen-her-khopshef, offers incense to Ptah; representations of the king before various divinities (Ptah-Tenen, Dwe-metf with the dog's head, and Emset, the guardian spirits of the dead, and Isis), who take him by the hand. To the right are similar pictures: the king embraced by Isis; the king and the prince burning incense before the god Show; Kebeh-senuf, Hapi, and Isis holding the king by the hand. — The *Side Rooms* (2 & 4) contain no pictorial decorations and are locked. — The following *Passage* (3) is adorned with pictures from the 'Book of Portals' (p. 301). — *Room 5* contains the granite sarcophagus.

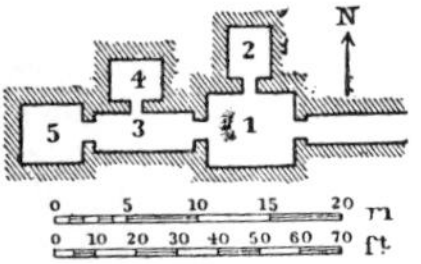

Adjacent is *No. 66*, the ****Tomb of Mer-en-Mut Nofret-ere,** wife of Ramses II., the arrangement of which differs from that of the other tombs of the queens. Its beautiful pictures take the form of the finest painted stucco reliefs, which have, however, suffered in places from the infiltration of water; the portraits of the queen deserve particular attention. The ceilings represent the starry firmament.

A staircase leads down to the *Hall* (Pl. 1), along the left *Walls* (Pl. *a*) of which runs a bench for the reception of sacrificial gifts, crowned with a cavetto cornice. The inscriptions consist of religious texts from the 17th chapter of the Book of the Dead. The accompanying pictures represent the queen, seated under a canopy, playing draughts; the soul of the queen, represented as a bird with a human head (comp. p. cliv); the queen, kneeling, worships the sun borne by two lions; the god Thoth as an ibis; the mummy on the funeral couch; various divinities. On the walls to the right, the queen before Osiris, praying to the sun-god Harakhte and to the goddess of the West (Pl. *b-d*); similar picture of the queen, followed by Isis, before the sun-god Khepre, his head in the form of a scarabæus (Pl. *e*); the goddess Selket (Pl. *g*). — In the *Side Room* (Pl. 2) we see (beginning on the right) the god Khnum, accompanied by Isis and Nephthys; the queen worshipping the sacred bull and seven sacred cows; the queen before Atum and (farther on) before Osiris; the queen offering writing materials to Thoth and sacrificing to Ptah. — On the side-walls of the *Staircase* (Pl. 3) leading from the hall (Pl. 1) we see above, to the right and left, the queen in presence of various divinities; below are Isis and Nephthys kneeling and mourning. On the architrave of the door, the goddess of truth with outstretched wings. — We now enter the *Pillared Hall* (Pl. 4), containing the coffin of the queen. The reliefs here and in the smaller Rooms 5-7 are much damaged.

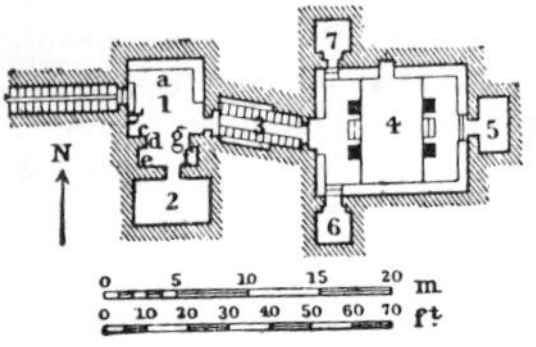

IX. The Colossi of Memnon.

The route diverges at the estate of Bûlus Bey Ḥanna (comp. the map, p. 270) from the road along the Fâḍilîya Canal and runs straight across the fields to the Colossi and to the ($1^1/_2$ M.) edge of the desert. Here it divides: to the right, past Chicago House (p. 328), for the Ramesseum, to the left for Medînet Habu (each $^3/_4$ M. from the Colossi).

The ***Colossi of Memnon** (Pl. C 4; called by the Arabs *Eṣ-Ṣanamât*, and also, of late, *El-Qolossât*) form the most prominent landmark on the W. bank at Thebes and are visible from a great distance on all sides. These two colossal statues have suffered severely from the hand of time and have lost their artistic value, but they still exert all their old attraction in virtue of the innumerable associations that cling to them. The two immense figures and the cubical thrones on which they are seated are carved out of a pebbly and quartzose sandstone-conglomerate found in the sandstone mountains beyond Edfu (p. 359), of a yellowish-brown colour and very difficult to work. Both represent Amenophis III. (p. cv) and they originally stood in front of the mortuary temple erected by that monarch, of which only the scantiest relics are now left. In the Roman imperial epoch they were taken for statues of Memnon, son of Eos and Tithonus, who slew Antilochus the brave son of Nestor, during the Trojan war, for which he was himself slain by Achilles.

The *Southern Colossus* is in better preservation than the N. one, but there is little difference between them in point of size. The dimensions of the former, in which the original form is more easily seen, are as follows: height of the figure 52 ft., height of the pedestal (partly hidden) on which the feet rest 13 ft., height of the entire monument 64 ft. But when the figure was adorned with the long-since vanished crown, the original height may have reached 69 ft. The legs from the sole of the foot to the knee measure $19^1/_2$ ft., and each foot is $10^1/_2$ ft. long. The breadth of the shoulders is 20 ft.; the middle finger on one hand is $4^1/_2$ ft. long; and the arm from the tip of the finger to the elbow measures $15^1/_2$ ft.

The *Northern Colossus* is the famous vocal statue of Memnon. To the left of the king stands his mother Mut-em-weye, to the right his wife Teye; a third figure, between the legs, has been destroyed. On each side of the seat two Nile-gods were represented in sunk relief, twining the representative plants of Egypt (sedge and papyrus) round the hieroglyph for 'to unite', a symbol of the union of Upper and Lower Egypt.

Attention began to be directed to the *Musical Phenomenon* connected with the colossus about the beginning of the Roman empire, after it had been broken. When it became known that the N. colossus emitted a musical note at sunrise, a new myth was invented to explain the fact. Memnon, who had fallen at Troy, appeared as a stone image at Thebes and greeted his mother Eos with a sweet and plaintive note when she appeared at dawn. The goddess heard the sound and the morning dews are the tears she

shed upon her beloved child. If the sound was not heard, it was taken as a sign that the god was angry. Strabo (p.cxiv), who is the first author to mention the phenomenon, expresses doubt as to its genuineness; but Pausanias (2nd cent. of our era) and Juvenal (p. 380) accept it as a fact. The phenomenon ceased altogether after the time of Septimius Severus (p. cxv), who caused the restoration of the upper portions, perhaps with a view to propitiate the angry god. The restoration was rather clumsily carried out with five courses of sandstone blocks. None of the various attempts made to explain the resonance of the stone are scientifically satisfactory.

The numerous Greek and Latin *Inscriptions*, in prose and verse, inscribed upon the legs of the figure by travellers under the Roman Empire, are peculiarly interesting. These are more numerous on the left than on the right leg, and none are beyond the reach of a man standing at the foot of the statue. The earliest was carved in the 11th year of the reign of Nero, the latest in those of Septimius Severus and Caracalla (p. cxv), and the most numerous (27) in that of Hadrian. Only one Egyptian (who is responsible for a short demotic inscription) is found among these scribblers. The inscriptions were for the most part the work of men of some eminence, including eight governors of Egypt, three epistrategi of the Thebaïd, two procurators, etc. A large number, though not all, are dated. Many of the great officials who visited the marvels of Thebes were accompanied by their wives. The colossus was frequently dumb, in which case the visitor usually waited until a more favourable occasion. Some were so struck with the phenomenon that they were not content till they had heard it three or four times. Hadrian (A.D. 130) spent several days here along with his wife Sabina and a large retinue. In his reign a perfect flood of Greek verses spread over the legs of the colossus, most of them by the court-poetess *Balbilla*. One of her effusions (on the left leg) relates in twelve hexameters that Memnon greeted Hadrian "as well as he could" when he perceived the emperor before sunrise, but that a clearer note, like that caused by a blow on an instrument of copper, was emitted at the second hour, and that even a third sound was heard, so that all the world could see how dear the emperor was to the gods.

By far the best verses are those on the front of the pedestal by *Asclepiodotus*, who calls himself imperial procurator and poet. They may be translated as follows: —

"Sea-born Thetis, learn that Memnon never suffered pangs of dying.
Still, where Libyan mountains rise, sounds the voice of his loud crying
(Mountains which the Nile-stream, laving, parts from Thebes, the hundred-gated)
When he glows, through rays maternal with warm light illuminated.
But thy son who, never-sated, dreadful battle still was seeking,
Dumb in Troy and Thessaly, rests now, never speaking."

Among the ruins in the neighbourhood of the colossi are the remains of another *Statue* of great size, lying 3 min. W., amidst arable land. Close by is a large *Sandstone Stele*, now broken in two, which is almost the only relic of the temple in front of which the colossi stood. The hieroglyphics and the representations refer to the dedication of the temple. In the rounded pediment the Pharaoh appears receiving the symbol of life from Amun on the right and from Soker-Osiris on the left; above are the winged sun-disk and the name of Amenophis III. Behind the Pharaoh in each case is his consort Teye. — Still farther N.W., at the edge of the desert, are two fragments of an ancient brick building, known as *Kôm el-Ḥeiṭân.*

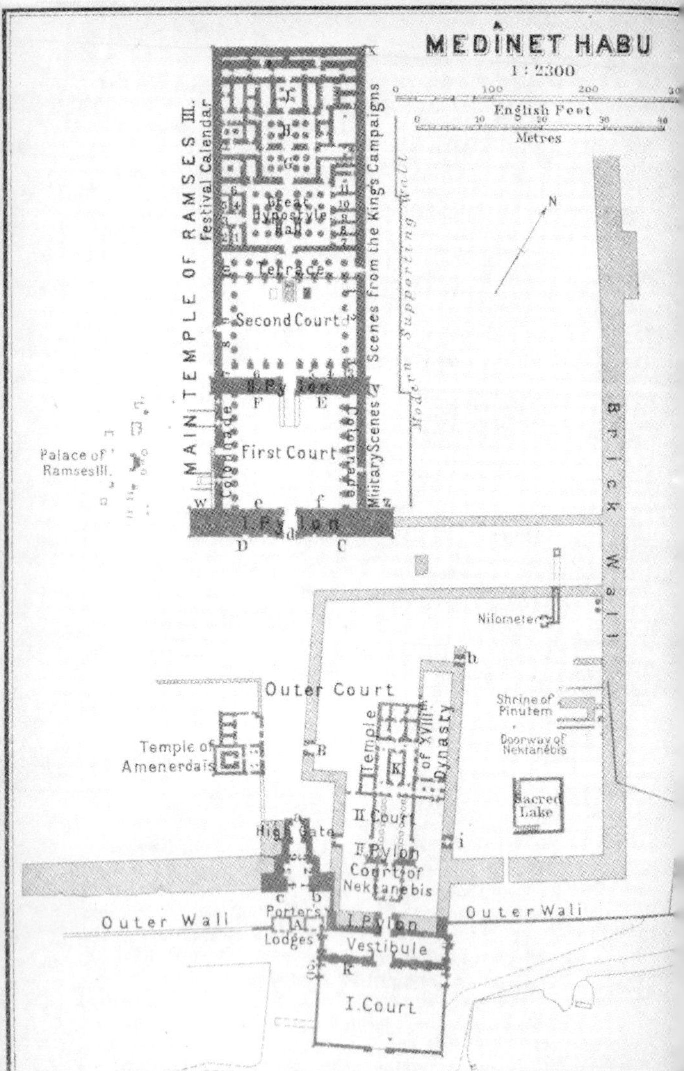
MEDINET HABU
1 : 2300
English Feet
Metres
MAIN TEMPLE OF RAMSES III.
Festival Calendar
Scenes from the King's Campaigns
Great Hypostyle Hall
Terrace
Second Court
II. Pylon
First Court
Colonnade
Military Scenes
I. Pylon
Modern Supporting Wall
Brick Wall
Palace of Ramses III.
Nilometer
Outer Court
Temple of XVIII. Dynasty
Shrine of Pinutem
Doorway of Nektanebis
Sacred Lake
Temple of Amenerdaïs
High Gate
II Court
II Pylon
Court of Nektanebis
Outer Wall
Porter's Lodges
I. Pylon
Vestibule
I. Court
Qaṣr el-'Agûz

Engraved & printed by Wagner & Debes, Leip

X. **Medînet Habu.**

About 1 M. from Deir el-Medîna and 3/4 M. from the Memnon colossi (p. 345), in a conspicuous situation, lies the southernmost temple-group on the W. bank at Thebes. Before we reach it we leave on the left the scanty ruins of the *Mortuary Temple of Thutmosis II.*, excavated in 1926 by the expedition of the Institut Français d'Archéologie Orientale at Cairo (p. 44). — The temples bear the name of **Medînet Habu** (*Madînet Habu*, 'town of Habu'; Pl. B 4), a Christian village which arose around and even within the ancient sanctuary as early as the 5th cent., and of which considerable traces still remain.

The entire edifice may be divided into two easily distinguished portions. One of these is a smaller and older temple of the 18th Dynasty (p. 354), afterwards enlarged. The other is the main temple of Ramses III. (p. 349), which was connected with the royal palaces (p. 352). Its precincts were enclosed by a brick wall, 59 ft. high, and by a crenellated outer wall, 13 ft. high. We pass the pylon and other buildings in front of the small temple and visit first the structure of Ramses.

We pass through the outer wall by means of a *Gate* (Pl. *A*), about 13 ft. wide, flanked by two small *Porter's Lodges.* Beyond these we are confronted by the remarkable edifice resembling the gateway of a fortress and called the **High Gate.** Formerly known also as the *Pavilion of Ramses III.*, it forms the entrance to the temple precincts instead of the usual massive pylon and portals of stone. This structure interrupts the great inner wall of brick which enclosed all the temples within a rectangle and was connected with the royal palaces (p. 352). The pavilion thus formed a part of the palaces, which stood at some distance from it. Its apartments were occasionally used as a residence by the Pharaoh and his harem and were decorated accordingly (comp. p. 348). Two tall towers (Pl. *b*, *c*), with almost imperceptibly sloping walls and with their E. sides resting upon a battering foundation-wall, enclose a narrow court, gradually contracting towards the back, where there is a gateway (Pl. *a*) in the central erection joining the towers. The reliefs on the *Façade of the Right Tower* (Pl. *b*) show the king smiting his foes in presence of Rē-Harakhte; below are seven fettered princes, representing the vanquished peoples (Kheta or Hittites, Emor or Amorites, Tjakari, Shardana or Sardinians, Shakalasha or Sicilians, Tuirsha or Tyrrhenians, and Peleste or Philistines; comp. p. 349). On the *Façade of the Left Tower* (Pl. *c*) is a corresponding picture of Ramses smiting his Nubian and Libyan foes before Amon-Rē.

In the *Court* between the towers are two seated figures of the lion-headed goddess Sakhmet, in black granite (found in front of the gate). On the walls, between the first and second stories, are some curious consoles or brackets, which are adorned with the busts of four captive enemies, and formerly bore statues of the king. The reliefs on the walls are mostly sacrificial in character.

Right (N.) Wall of the Court. The representations from right to left are: 1. Ramses sacrificing to Seth (defaced) and to Nut; below is the king presenting two rows of captives to Amun. 2. The king offering wine to Atum and a goddess; below, the same offering flowers to Onuris and to a goddess. 3. Mont (defaced) and Atum conduct the king before Amun. — *Left (S.) Wall of the Court.* 4. The king presents an image of Amun to Harakhte and Maat; below, he leads two rows of captives before Amun (the Libyan in the lower row, drawn full-face, should be noticed). 5. The king offers incense to the moon-god and to Seshet; below, he presents an image of Maat to Ptah and Sakhmet. In the second story is a window with attractive ceiling-decorations. 6. The king before Amun, with Mut and Thoth behind him.

In the *Gateway* (Pl. *a*) leading to the forecourt the king appears conducting two rows of fettered captives before Amun (on the left) and smiting a band of enemies (on the right).

A modern staircase in the S. tower ascends to two **Apartments* in the upper part of the middle structure, the floor between which has disappeared. The wall-reliefs of the lower room have vanished, but those of the upper room (harem scenes) are still quite distinct. The windows command a fine view of the temples and ruined village on the W. and of the plain to the E. Similar reliefs adorn the walls of the other (inaccessible) rooms. Note the curious head-dress of the women.

Some of these Reliefs may be seen from below. One, on the W. wall of a room in the upper story of the *North Wing*, is visible from the entrance; it represents the king seated with five maidens standing round him. — From the N.E. corner of the outer court (see below) we observe in the upper story of the N. wing two windows. To the right and left of these is the king, again surrounded by maidens. More to the right, near a hole in the wall, the king, with a maiden standing in front of him; of the kneeling and standing women to the left only the lower portions remain. Below is a narrow window, with vases of flowers above and to the right the king listening to girl-musicians. — In this part of the N. wing we may observe the holes in which the ends of the rafters supporting the floors of the upper stories were inserted.

The inner (W.) side of the central edifice, through which we pass by the gateway *a*, bears reliefs showing the king in various positions as the conqueror of his enemies. — We have now entered the extensive *Outer Court*, between the pavilion and the main temple. In the middle stands a small *Gateway* (Pl. *B*), erected by Nektanebis I. (p. cx). To the right lies the Temple of the 18th Dyn. (p. 354). To the left is a small Mortuary Temple of Amenerdaïs, a princess who was the ecclesiastical ruler of Thebes under the last Ethiopian monarchs and Psammetichos I. (p. cix). Comp. p. 292.

Through a *Portal* we enter a *Forecourt*, formerly with an arcade on either side, each borne by two columns, and thence pass to the vaulted *Sanctuary*, which is completely surrounded by a corridor. On the *Left Wing* of the portal we see Amenerdaïs sacrificing to Amun (above) and standing holding two sistra before Amun and Mut (below). On the *Right Wing* Amenerdaïs sacrifices to Amun (above) and to a goddess (below). The temple is adjoined on the right by three chapels, dedicated to *Nitocris* (daughter of Psammetichos I.), *Shepenupet* (daughter of the Ethiopian king Piankhi, p. 294), and *Meht-wesekhet* (wife of Psammetichos I.). The last chapel had a kind of crypt, with inscriptions, visible beneath the broken flooring.

The ***Main Temple of Ramses III.** was built on nearly the same plan as the Ramesseum (p. 324) and was dedicated like it to Amun.

The façades of both towers of the large **First Pylon** are covered with representations and inscriptions commemorating the king's warlike exploits. On the *Right Tower* (Pl. *C*), to the right, the king is shown before Amon-Rē-Harakhte, grasping a band of enemies by the hair and smiting them with his club. The falcon-headed god hands him the curved sword and leads to him by a cord the captured lands, which are represented in the accustomed manner (p. 287) by circular walls enclosing their names and surmounted by bound enemies. Beneath are two other rows of names of conquered lands. Farther to the left, between two grooves for the flagstaffs, is a similar but much smaller scene, and beneath is a long inscription, describing in exceedingly exaggerated language the victory won by Ramses III. over the Libyans in the 11th year of his reign. At the foot Amun is seated to the left, with Ptah standing behind, inscribing the years of the king's reign on a palm-branch. The king kneels before Amun, under the sacred tree, and receives from the god the symbols of a long reign, suspended on a palm-branch. Thoth writes the king's name among the leaves of the tree, and beside him stands the goddess Seshet. To the right of the portal, below, is a stele of the 12th year of the king (imitated from a stele of the 35th year of Ramses II. at Abu Simbel, p. 434), commemorating the gifts made to the god Ptah. The *Left Tower* (Pl. *D*) bears similar scenes.

Through the *Central Portal* (Pl. *d*), embellished within and without by representations of the king worshipping the gods, we enter the **First Court**, forming an approximate square of 115 ft. The inner side of the first pylon is adorned with scenes from the Libyan campaign of Ramses (see above). To the S. (Pl. *e*) is a battle, in which the Egyptians are aided by mercenaries from among the Shardana (p. 347), who are distinguished by their round helmets ornamented with horns. To the N. (Pl. *f*) are the captured Libyans marshalled before the king, and an inscription. — The court is flanked on the right and left by covered *Colonnades*. The ceiling of that to the right is borne by seven square pillars, against which stand colossal statues of the king as Osiris. The left (S.) colonnade has eight papyrus-columns with calyx-capitals. These last belonged to the façade of the royal palaces (p. 352), which stood to the S. of the temple and communicated with the first court by three doors and a large balcony-window. To the right and left of this window the king is seen standing on a bracket formed of hostile heads and slaying his foes. Under the window are dancers, wrestlers and merrymakers, represented as greeting the king on his appearance at the window with unrestrained joy (for the back of the window, see pp. 352, 353). The scenes on the colonnade walls represent the wars, victories, and captives of the king. At the ends the king is seen on his way to the feast of Amun, attended by his fan-bearers.

The inscriptions and sculptures on the **Second Pylon** are still more interesting. On the *Right Tower* (Pl. *E*) is a long inscription recording the triumph won by the king in the eighth year of his reign over a league of peoples from the lands of the Mediterranean, who menaced Egypt by sea and by land from Syria. On the *Left Tower* (Pl. *F*) the king leads before Amun and Mut three rows of prisoners, representing the conquered in this campaign. These have beardless faces and wear curious caps adorned with feathers; their pointed aprons, decorated with tassels, differ from those of the Egyptians. The inscription describes them as belonging to the tribes of the Danauna and Peleste (Philistines).

The granite gateway of the second pylon, which is approached by an inclined plane, admits us to the **Second Court**, which is 125 ft. deep and 138 ft. broad. In the Christian period it was converted into a church, the remains of which have been cleared away (comp. p. clxxxviii). This court is almost an exact reproduction of the second court of the Ramesseum (p. 326), even to part of the relief-embellishments; but it is in much better preservation. On all four sides are colonnades. On the N. and S. these are supported by columns with bud-capitals; on the E. are square pillars with Osiris-statues, and on the W. is a terrace (pronaos) with eight Osiris-pillars in front and eight columns behind. On the columns and pillars the king is shown sacrificing to the gods.

The reliefs on the back-walls of the colonnades illustrate events in the life of Ramses, some showing great festivals in which he took part, others the warlike deeds of himself or his army. — NORTH AND NORTH-EAST COLONNADES. In the upper row are *Scenes from the Great Festival of the God Min* (p. clvii), which was celebrated also as a coronation festival, as we have seen in the Ramesseum (p. 326). First (Pl. 1) appears the Pharaoh, borne from his palace by his sons (names wanting) on a richly decorated litter with a canopy. He is followed by numerous courtiers, while he is preceded by priests carrying censers, a priest who recites, and a troop of soldiers, each of whom wears two feathers on his head. The trumpeter and drummer in the upper row, and the castanet-players in the lower row, should be noticed. In the next scene (Pl. 2) the king is shown sacrificing and offering incense before the image of Min. The following scene (Pl. 3), continued on the E. wall, exhibits the sacred procession. The image of Min is borne on a litter by priests, while fan-bearers walk by the side and priests carrying the sacred shrines follow. In front marches the king, who in turn is preceded by a white bull (the sacred animal of Min), the queen, and a long procession of priests carrying standards, temple utensils, and images of the king and his ancestors. To the right is the king awaiting the procession, with two emblems in front of him. Priests let four birds escape (comp. p. 326). Farther to the right (Pl. 4) the Pharaoh cuts with his sickle the sheaf of corn handed to him by a priest (as in the Ramesseum,

p. 326). Behind him stands the reciting priest, who intones a hymn to Min, while another priest presents the sheaf to the god. The queen (above) also is present at this ceremony. The white bull again appears in front of the king, and beneath is a series of images of the royal ancestors. Finally (Pl. 5) the king is shown offering incense to the god Min, who stands under a canopy.

The lower series of representations on the N. and N.E. walls are less interesting. To the left (Pl. 1) are the sacred boats of Khons, Mut, and Amun, to which the king sacrifices; to the right (Pl. 2) priests bear the boats out of the temple, while the king, behind a fourth boat, approaches to meet them.

South and South-East Colonnades. In the upper rows in these a *Festival of Ptah-Soker* is displayed. It begins to the left of the door (Pl. 6) with a train of priests, bearing sacred boats, images of the gods, standards, and temple utensils. Behind stand the king and his dignitaries. We next observe (Pl. 7; S. wall) a colossal symbol of the god Nefertēm, son of Ptah, borne by eighteen priests. The king (Pl. 8) holds a cord, which is being pulled by sixteen courtiers. Two priests offer incense before the king. Then follow sixteen priests (Pl. 9) bearing the boat of Soker (p. clix), followed by the king. The king (Pl. 10) sacrifices before the sacred boat; and finally the king before the ram-headed Khnum and two other gods, and before the falcon-headed Soker-Osiris, to whom he offers a platter with bread. — Below are *Warlike Reliefs*. The *1st Scene* (Pl. 6, on the S.E. wall) depicts the king attacking the Libyans with his charioteers and shooting with his bow. The infantry fight in wild confusion. The Egyptians are assisted by the Shardana mercenaries (in the lower row; p. 347). The *2nd Scene* shows the return of the king from the battle. He drives in his chariot, with three rows of fettered Libyans in front of him and two fan-bearers behind him. *3rd Scene.* The king leads the Libyan captives before Amun and Mut. On the S. wall is a relief (Pl. 7) showing the king seated in his chariot (with his back to the horses) and receiving the Libyan captives (light-red in hue), who are conducted to him in four rows by his sons and other notabilities. The hands, etc., cut off from the slain are being counted. The greater part of this wall is occupied by a 75-line inscription, recording incidents of the war.

The rear wall of the West Corridor, on the terrace, has three rows of representations. In the two upper rows Ramses III. is shown worshipping various deities. In the lowest row (as in the Ramesseum, p. 327) are royal princes and princesses. The names beside these were added under Ramses VI.

Of the following chambers only the lower parts of the walls and columns remain.

We first enter the **Great Hypostyle Hall.** The roof was formerly supported by twenty-four columns in four rows of six, of which the eight central ones were considerably thicker than the others. On the walls are representations of the king in the presence of various

deities. An interesting relief on the S. wall shows the magnificent gold vases presented by Ramses III. to Amun, Mut, and Khons.

Three *Smaller Halls* (Pl. *G*, *H*, *J*) follow, two with four couples of columns, and one with four pillars. In Room *H* are two groups of red granite, one (left) representing Amun and Maat, the other (right) the king and the ibis-headed Thoth. — The other rooms at the back were dedicated to different deities. Those to the left of Room *J* were devoted to Osiris. One has a vaulted ceiling, with astronomical representations. From Room *G* a staircase ascended to other chambers on the upper floor.

The great hypostyle hall is adjoined also at the sides (N. and S.) by two series of rooms (Pl. 1-11), of which those to the S. formed the *Treasury* of the temple.

The *Representations* on the walls of these treasure-chambers refer to the costly objects stored within them. *Room 1:* The king presents Amun with papyrus-holders held by lions with the king's head or by kneeling figures of the king. *Room 2:* The king presents to Amun costly vessels and boxes with lids in the shape of rams or sphinxes or of the heads of rams, falcons, or kings. *Room 3:* The king presents Amun with sacks of precious stones. *Room 4:* The king offers costly table-services, ornaments, golden harps, silver, and lead. *Room 5:* The king offers heaps of gold and other precious metals. — In *Rooms 6-11* we see the king sacrificing to various deities. In Room 7 the princes and princesses present gifts to the king and queen. In Room 10 stands a colossal alabaster statue of Ptah (headless), dating from the time of Amenophis III. (found in the first court).

To the S. of the temple are the ruins of two **Royal Palaces** (comp. p. 319), a small portion of which was laid bare by Henry Burton in 1913. They are now being fully excavated by an expedition from the University of Chicago (comp. p. 328), under the direction of Prof. Uvo Hoelscher. One of the palaces was superimposed upon the other, and both were built by Ramses III. The throne-room of the more recent still contains the alabaster dais for the throne, approached by three short flights of steps. On the left is the king's bedchamber with a raised platform for the bed in a recess. On the right are the bath-room and a room for the king's wardrobe. Adjacent on the W. are rooms for the harem, with a place for the throne of the king, and a bath. Beyond this, on the S., are three sets of apartments belonging to the harem, each with two living rooms, a bath, and a dressing room. — On the W. side of the palace is a *Well*, approached by a staircase; the string-board represents Nile-gods drawing water, Ramses III. sprinkled with water by Thoth and Horus, and the king in presence of Khons-Neferhotep.

We now quit the temple and proceed to examine the interesting **Historical Reliefs** on the *Outside of the Temple Walls*, which chiefly commemorate the wars of Ramses III.

We begin with the *South Wall, the first pylon of which (Pl. *w*) is adorned with admirable hunting scenes. Above is the king hunting mountain-goats and wild asses; below he appears with his retinue, pursuing wild bulls in a marshy district abounding with fish and waterfowl.

On the W. part of the S. wall is a long *Festival Calendar*, which contains a list of the appointed sacrifices for the period between the 26th Pakhons (the day of Ramses III.'s accession) and the 19th Tybi. Beneath is a procession of priests, carrying food. — To the right and left of the balcony-window of the palace (see above), to which a flight of steps ascends,

the king appears in the act of slaying his prisoners (comp. p. 349). In the embrasure of the window the king and his retinue are seen going to the balcony-window.

On the West Wall are scenes from a war with the negroes of the Sûdân and the first of a series illustrating the Libyan war.

S. half of the wall: 1. The king in battle; 2. Triumphal procession with captive negroes; 3. Captives brought before Amun. — N. half (Libyan war): 4. The king, behind whom stands Thoth, in front of Amun and Khons; 5. The king, the falcon-headed Mont, and four priests carrying idols on the ends of poles; 6. The king in his war-chariot, accompanied by his guards.

On the W. part of the North Wall (Pl. *x*, *y*) are ten scenes from the wars against the Libyans and a naval victory over Northern maritime peoples; in the E. part are the Syrian wars.

W. half: *1st Scene.* The Egyptian army on the march. A lion walks beside the chariot of Ramses. In another chariot before that of the king is the standard of Amon-Rē with the ram's head. — *2nd Scene.* Battle with the Libyans. — *3rd Scene.* The king harangues five rows of soldiers, who bring captive Libyans. The severed hands, etc., are counted, amounting to 12,535. — *4th Scene.* The king in the balcony of his palace inspects the levying of troops. Standards are brought out and weapons distributed to the soldiers. — *5th Scene.* The king starts for Syria; before him march soldiers with lances and bows. Below are the Shardana mercenaries (p. 347). — *6th Scene.* Battle with the seafaring tribes of the Mediterranean in Palestine (see below). The king in his chariot shoots arrows against the enemies, identified as Tjakari by their curious caps. The children of the foe await the result in ox-carts. — *7th Scene.* The king at a lion-hunt. One of the lions, hidden in a thicket, has been pierced by the king's spear and arrows; another lies dying beneath the horse's feet. Underneath is a procession of the Egyptian army and mercenaries. — *8th Scene* (not very distinct except when the light falls on it obliquely). *Naval battle with the maritime peoples of the Mediterranean, who were met and conquered by the Egyptian fleet at the mouth of the Nile. The king shoots from the shore against the hostile fleet. One of the hostile ships (below) has capsized. The Egyptian vessels are denoted by the lion's head on the prow. One of these (below, on the right) has a large number of oarsmen and contains Tjakari who have been captured and pinioned; in the lower row other prisoners are being conveyed away. The king himself is treading upon captive foes. In front of him are some archers, and above him, in the form of a vulture, hovers the goddess of Lower Egypt. — *9th Scene.* The king, having alighted from his chariot, receives in a balcony the grandees who conduct the prisoners. In the lower row the severed hands are being counted. To the left is the royal chariot. Above is the 'Ramses Castle', perhaps the palaces of Medînet Habu. — *10th Scene.* The king presents two rows of captives, Tjakari (above) and Libyans (below), to Amun, Mut, and Khons, the Theban triad.

E. half of N. wall (Pl. *y*, *z*). First Court. *Upper Row* (from left to right): 1. Ramses storms a Syrian fortress; 2. The king alights from his chariot after the victory and stabs a Syrian with his lance; 3. The king receives the prisoners and (4.) presents them, along with magnificent vases, to Amun and Khons. — *Lower Row* (left to right): 1. Ramses in his chariot attacking a Libyan castle; 2. Libyan prisoners; 3. Three rows of captives brought to the king by his officers; 4. Return with the captives, greeting by Egyptian grandees; 5. Captive Libyans presented to Amun and Mut.

On the first pylon (Pl. *z*) are three scenes: in the top row, the king storming a fortress defended by the Hittites; below, battle with the Libyans; the king alighting from his chariot and binding two Libyans.

On the N. side of the outer court between the High Gate and the main temple (p. 348) stands the small but elegant peripteral

Temple of the 18th Dynasty (comp. p. clxxi), the oldest building at Medînet Habu, erected in the reign of Queen Hatshepsut and Thutmosis III. (p. cv). The figures and inscriptions of the queen, in the first completed (inner) chambers, have been chiselled out here also or replaced by those of others. The figures and names of the gods defaced by Amenophis IV. were restored under Haremhab and Sethos I. The entrance was originally on the E. side, but the restorations carried out under the later Pharaohs (particularly Ramses III.) and in the Ptolemaic and Roman periods were so extensive that little of the ancient ground-plan is distinguishable. The reliefs on the outside date from the reign of Ramses III.

To the N. of the High Gate is a gate leading into the second court, whence we enter the temple on the left. The temple comprises a *Cella* (Pl. *K*), surrounded by a *Colonnade* (decorated by Thutmosis III.), and six *Chambers* behind. The colonnade is enclosed on the outside by a parapet upon which rise square pillars, which, together with the sixteen-sided columns (comp. p. clxiv), support the roof. The representations show Thutmosis III. sacrificing or performing other sacred rites in presence of the gods. In the inner chambers Thutmosis I. and Thutmosis II. also appear in place of the original figures of Hatshepsut. The inscriptions on the pillars on each side of the entrance refer to the restorations by Haremhab, Sethos I., and Pinutem (p. cvii). The cella, the reliefs in which were restored at a later period, had a door at each end (restored by Euergetes II., p. cxii). The last room on the right still contains a naos of red granite (unfinished). — The structures to the N. and S. of the anterior colonnade were added at a later period. That to the N. was erected with blocks taken from earlier edifices, bearing the names of Ramses II., Pinutem, and Achoris (p. cx). The small grated windows and the rings on the upper part of the column-shafts should be noticed. In the Christian period the temple was converted (comp. p. clxxxviii) into a church dedicated to St. Menas (p. 30); the inscriptions and remains of frescoes date from the 7th century.

We now return to the *Second Court*, which dates from the reign of Achoris and was originally a covered hypostyle hall. The granite gateway to the N. is a relic of a building of the beginning of the 26th Dyn. (erected by Pedamenōpet, p. 324). On the E. the court is bounded by the *Second Pylon*, which was erected by Shabako (p. cviii), the Ethiopian, and restored under Ptolemy X. Soter II. (p. cxiii). On the back of the pylon appears Taharka (p. cviii), grasping a band of enemies by the hair and smiting them. — The adjoining *Vestibule of Nektanebis I.* (p. cx), 31½ ft. long and 26 ft. wide, was supported on each side by four clustered columns with bud-capitals (two restored), connected with each other by stone screens. On the E. side was a portal. — About 13 ft. to the E. of the last rises the large *First Pylon*, which was built in the later Ptolemaic epoch, largely with blocks taken from earlier edifices (especially from the

Ramesseum). Ptolemy X. Soter II. and Ptolemy XIII. Neos Dionysos (p. cxiii) appear on the central portal, worshipping the gods.

In front of the pylon and dating from Ptolemaic times stood an airy, two-columned *Vestibule* with beautiful flower-capitals (note the traces of colour) and wooden beams. In the Roman period it was enlarged to form a wide eight-columned *Hall* with lofty unfinished screens. In front of this was constructed a *Forecourt* 130 ft. wide and $83^1/_2$ ft. deep. In front of one of the screens is placed a door-shaped stele of Thutmosis III. in red granite, discovered in the flooring of the first pylon. The *Gateways* in the wall surrounding the court are now built up; that on the S. (Pl. *g*) is adorned with inscriptions by the Emperor Antoninus Pius (p. cxv).

In the N.E. angle of the great girdle-wall, near the small temple, lies the *Sacred Lake*, a basin about 60 ft. square, with two flights of steps. — About 45 yds. N.W. of it is a *Nilometer*. A doorway, bearing the name of Nektanebis I., admits to a chamber beyond which is a corridor, whence the staircase of the nilometer descends to a depth of 65 ft. — Between the temple of the 18th Dynasty and the nilometer stands a small *Gateway*, with inscriptions of the Emperor Domitian (p. cxiv). Its original position is unknown, but it was re-erected on this spot with blocks found immured in a Coptic building.

About 200 paces S. of the High Gate (p. 347) is a small unfinished **Temple of Thoth,** now known as *Qaṣr el-ʿAgûz*, erected in the Ptolemaic period by Euergetes II. to *Teephibis*, a god of similar character to Thoth. It consists of a wide vestibule and three rooms, one behind another. On the entrance-wall of the second room, to the left, we see the king sacrificing to Thoth, Imhotep, and the deified sage Amenhotep (comp. p. 89); the lower row of reliefs alone is finished, the others are merely sketched out.

About $^2/_3$ M. to the S.E. of Medînet Habu are the ruins of a *Royal Town of Amenophis III.*, which included a large *Palace* (Pl. A 4) known as the 'House of Joy'. The site, known as *Malqata*, was excavated in 1910-18 by the Metropolitan Museum of New York. The palace contains living and state apartments for the king, quarters for the courtiers and the harem, a residence for Queen Teye, a large festal hall erected for the celebration of the king's second jubilee, workshops, etc.

Still farther S., about $2^1/_2$ M. from Medînet Habu, on the road to Armant (see below), stands a well-preserved **Roman Temple,** dedicated to Isis, and now known as *Deir esh-Shelwît*. It was erected by Hadrian and Antoninus Pius, while the ruined pylon bears the names of Vespasian, Domitian, and Otho. The temple consists of a cella surrounded by apartments. A staircase leads to the roof from a room to the extreme left of the entrance.

22. From Luxor to Aswân by Railway.

Comp. the Map, p. 232.

129 M. One express (the 'night express', p. 216) daily in $4^1/_2$ hrs., and one ordinary train in $5^1/_2$ hrs. During the season the sleeping and dining cars of the train de luxe from Cairo run through to Aswân (Shellâl); when required, the train de luxe itself runs through (comp. p. 216).

Luxor, see p. 267. — The line sometimes skirts the right bank of the Nile, sometimes the edge of the desert.

$12^1/_2$ M. **Armant** *(Arment)*, with an important sugar-factory and post and telegraph offices, lies on the left bank of the river, whence a secondary line runs to Esna (p. 357; $25^1/_2$ M., two trains daily

in either direction). Armant was called in antiquity *On*, or, to distinguish it from On in Lower Egypt (Heliopolis, p. 129), the *Upper Egyptian On* or *Per-Mont* (i.e. 'House of Mont'), whence the Greek name *Hermonthis* was formed. Its deity was the falcon-headed Mont, god of war (p. clvii). In the Roman imperial period it was the capital of a province.

The bank is shaded by stately lebbakh-trees (p. lxxvii). From the point where the bazaar reaches the bank of the river a flight of steps, incorporating several ancient sculptured fragments, descends to the stream. The large temple-buildings, dating from the Ptolemaic and imperial periods, which lay about $1/2$ hr. N.E., have been almost entirely destroyed, the stones being used to build the sugar-factory. The burial-place of the Buchis bulls, sacred to Mont (comp. the Serapeum at Ṣaqqâra, p. 158), was discovered by Robert Mond and Walter B. Emery in 1927.

At *Er-Rizeiqât (Rezikat)*, 4 M. to the S.W. of Armant, on the W. bank (a station on the secondary line to Esna, see p. 355), is a necropolis of the Middle Empire. — The village of Ṭôd *(Toud)*, the ancient *Tuphium*, $1^3/_4$ M. to the E. of Armant station, on the E. bank, contains the picturesque remains of a large temple of the Ptolemaic and imperial periods, dedicated to Mont. One chamber of the Ptolemaic period, in perfect preservation, is inhabited by a sheikh. The building in front, probably the ancient vestibule, is represented by a wall and by the lower halves of columns.

The railway quits the cultivated lands and skirts the edge of the stony desert. The E. mountains display beautiful forms and colours.

$17^1/_2$ M. *Esh-Shaghab (Ech-Chaghb, Shagab)* is the station for **Gebelein** (i.e. 'the two mountains'; W. bank), two parallel hills divided from each other by a depression 164 ft. wide. To the N.W. is *El-Gabalîn (Gabalein)*, a station on the secondary line to Esna (see p. 355). The summit of the *Gebel Mûsa*, the smaller hill, to the E., is crowned with the conspicuous tomb of a sheikh *(Sîdi Mûsa)* and with the remains of a walled temple of Hathor, which dates back to the 3rd Dynasty. Rebuilt in the 11th, it was enlarged by Thutmosis III. and after its subsequent destruction was rebuilt in the Ptolemaic period. Near the village of Gebelein, at the W. base of the hill, lie the ruins of the ancient town of *Crocodilopolis*. The larger hill, to the W., is $2/3$ M. long, and on its E. and N. slopes are old burial-grounds, mostly of the prehistoric period and of the end of the Middle Empire, which were examined by the Italian Archæological Mission in 1910-11. In the neighbourhood once stood the ancient *Aphroditespolis*, also called *Pathyris* (House of Hathor, p. clvi), which for some time was the capital of a separate nome.

On the E. bank, to the S.E. of Shaghab, lie the villages of *Ed-Dibâbîya (Ed-Dabaïbah)*, near which are quarries with inscriptions, and *El-Mi'alla (Mu'alla, Ma'alla)*, near which are tombs of the New Empire. — $28^1/_2$ M. *El-Maṭâ'na (Matana, Meta'anah)* is the station for *Aṣfûn el-Maṭâ'na* (the ancient *Asphynis*, Egyptian *Hesfun*), on the W. bank (station on the secondary line) and on the Aṣfûn Canal,

with a large sugar-factory (conspicuous chimney-stacks). — The railway now skirts a canal, traversing a cultivated district, until just before Esna, when it returns to the river-bank.

33 M. **Esna** or **Isna** (motor-cars and cabs at the station, fare to the town and back P.T. 20; New Grand Hotel, modest, R. 12 P.T., by the river) lies on the W. bank of the Nile, which is crossed here by a dam (p. 363; trolley P.T. 2 per person). Near the station are pretty gardens and the trim houses of the officials employed at the dam. — The village of *El-Ḥilla*, 2 M. to the S.E. of the station, occupies the site of the ancient *Contra-Latopolis*, of whose late-Ptolemaic temple no trace survives.

Esna, which in antiquity adjoined the town of *Enit*, was one of the most important places in Upper Egypt. Its Egyptian name was *Te-snēt*, whence came the Coptic *Sne* and the Arabic *Isna*. The Greeks called it *Latopolis*, after the latos, a kind of Nile fish venerated here. Esna is now a district capital (20,000 inhab. in 1927), with a post office (near the temple), a druggist's shop, and numerous cafés. The station on the secondary line to Armant (p. 355), school, markaz (district offices), tribunal (with telegraph office), and other public buildings stand in the pleasant street skirting the Nile. On the old quay, near the markaz, are some fragmentary inscriptions and the remains of a nilometer of the Roman imperial epoch. A road leading to the right from the New Grand Hotel on the river-bank brings us in a few minutes to the temple, which is situated near the bazaars, several feet below the street-level.

The ***Temple of Khnum,** the ram-headed local deity, associated with whom were the goddesses Satet and Neith (the latter identified by the Greeks with Athena), is the chief object of interest in the town. The lion-goddess Menheyet and Nebt-uu, who corresponds to Isis, appear here as companions to Khnum. The extant edifice was built in the Ptolemaic period and was extended and embellished with inscriptions and reliefs by the Roman emperors. The façade, 120 ft. wide and 50 ft. high, is turned towards the E. and is crowned by a cavetto cornice, in which stand the names of Claudius and Vespasian (p. cxiv) on either side of the winged sun-disk. On the architrave below are the votive inscriptions of these emperors. Vespasian is referred to as lord of 'Rome the capital'. The screens connecting the front columns bear representations of the Pharaoh being conducted by the gods into the temple. On the last screen to the left, Harsiēsis and Thoth pour holy water over the king, with the lion-headed goddess Menheyet on the right. The seven-aisled vestibule, which belongs almost entirely to the Roman era, is the only completed portion of the temple. It corresponds in arrangement to the vestibule of the temple of Hathor at Dendera (p. 261) and is 108 ft. broad and 54 ft. deep. The roof, embellished with astronomical representations over the side-aisles and two rows of vultures in flight over the central aisle, is borne by twenty-four columns (in

four rows), which have elaborate floral capitals and are covered with reliefs and inscriptions. Each column is 37 ft. high and $17^3/_4$ ft. in circumference. — The walls are lined with four rows of reliefs, showing emperors in the costume of the Pharaohs sacrificing to the gods of Esna or carrying out ceremonies connected with the building of the temple. In the middle of the *Rear Wall* (W.) projects a portal, resembling a pylon and crowned with a cavetto cornice; its door (now walled up) gave access to the inner parts of the temple. The reliefs and inscriptions upon it date from the reign of Ptolemy VI. Philometor (p. cxii). On each side is a smaller door (walled up); to the right of the left-hand door appears the Emperor Decius (p. cxv) sacrificing to Khnum. — Towards the foot of the *North Wall* is a relief of the falcon-headed Horus, the Emperor Commodus (p. cxv), and Khnum drawing a net full of waterfowl and fishes; to the left stands the ibis-headed Thoth, to the right the goddess Seshet. — Adjoining the *East Wall*, at the screen immediately to the left of the entrance, a small chapel has been added. — Inscriptions and representations were placed also on the *Outer Walls* by the Roman emperors: on the S. wall, Domitian (p. cxiv) slaying a heap of enemies, with Khnum and Menheyet looking on; N. wall, Khnum, behind whom is the goddess Nebt-uu, hands the curved sword to Trajan (p. cxv) as he slays his enemies.

From the open space in front of the temple a long and very picturesque bazaar-street, still roofed-over in parts, runs parallel with the Nile.

In the neighbourhood of Esna are the remains of several Coptic Monasteries and Churches. About $3^1/_4$ M. to the S. is the ***Monastery of SS. Manaos and Sanutios***, also called *Deir esh-Shúhadâ* ('Monastery of the Martyrs', p. cxc), which is said to have been founded by the Empress Helena (p. cxvi) but belongs to the 10-11th centuries. It possesses a new and an old church, the latter containing some ancient frescoes, now covered with whitewash. — About $5^1/_2$ M. to the N. is the ***Deir Amba Matteos***, or monastery of St. Matthew, with interesting frescoes; and $^1/_2$ M. to the W. is an ancient *Church* hewn out of the rock, also with frescoes.

Near the village of *Zarnîkh*, $2^1/_2$ M. to the S.W. of Esna station, are two rock-steles of historical importance, dating from the beginning of the reign of Amenophis IV. — $45^1/_2$ M. *Es-Sibâ'îya (Sabaia, Es-Siba'ieh)*. There are phosphate deposits in the vicinity. The village lies on the left bank of the Nile.

$51^1/_2$ M. **El-Maḥâmîd** is the station for visitors to the ruined town of **Elkâb** (p. 365), lying $1^1/_2$ M. to the S.E., between the railway and the Nile. A short visit to the ruins and tombs may be made on foot, but those who wish to do more should communicate in advance with the postmaster or station-master of El-Maḥâmîd, either by post or telegraph, so that donkeys may be in waiting at the station and the guardians of Elkâb at their post. — Behind the station are stone-quarries and, on the hill, the conspicuous white tomb of a sheikh. Farther on, to the left, is the isolated hill of tombs, and to the right is the old town wall of Nekhab.

The railway traverses the desert. In the distance to the right the pylon-towers of Edfu come into sight.

65 M. **Edfu** (*Idfu*, p. 369). The town and temple lie on the W. bank. Visitors ferry across the river in small boats in 1/4 hr. from beside the station and are met by donkeys on the opposite bank; the temple is within 1/2 hr.'s walk. — Behind the station are the pumping works for the estates of Count Blücher.

The strip of arable land widens, and the railway approaches the Nile. — 69 M. *Taftîsh ʿAṭîya (Taftiche Attia)*, station for Owen Pasha's estates.

Beyond (75 M.) *Es-Sîrâg (Sirag)* the line hugs the river for some time, passing below rocks crowned by the ruins of a late-Byzantine fortress (p. 364). — 82 M. *Silwa.*

Near the village of **El-Ḥôsh** *(El-Hoch)*, beside the *Gebel Abu Shega*, on the W. bank, are a number of quarries. From masons' marks and Greek inscriptions in these we learn that sandstone blocks were quarried here in the 11th year of Antoninus Pius (A.D. 149) for a temple of Apollo (i.e. Horus, probably at Edfu.)

A short distance above El-Ḥôsh is the valley of *Khôr Tangûra*, in which, on a cliff to the right, about 1/2 hr. inland, are good prehistoric carvings (elephants, antelopes, giraffes, a ship, etc.). Similar sculptures are to be seen on the rocky bank of the Nile, to the S. of the mouth of the valley. — Farther S., about 3/4 hr. below Silsila (see below), is a cliff known as *Shaṭb er-Rigâl*, on the left side of which, a few paces from the river-bank, is a most interesting *Relief* representing the homage of an inferior king Entef before King Neb-hepet-rē Mentuhotep II. (11th Dyn.) and the king's mother Yoh. Behind Entef is an official named Kheti. On the same cliff-face, farther up in the valley, occur representations and inscriptions from the Middle Empire and the beginning of the New Empire.

88 M. *El-Kâgûg*. On the E. bank, about 2 M. to the S.W. of the station, lie the extensive **Quarries of Silsila**, which are best visited in conjunction with the temple of Kôm Ombo (p. 374); we spend the night at the Hotel Kôm Ombo and take the early train to Kâgûg. It is thus possible to return to Kôm Ombo by the midday train and go on to Luxor by the afternoon train. It is advisable to notify the custodian at Silsila through the inspector of antiquities at Luxor, so that he may have a boat in readiness.

The quarries of Silsila were worked especially under the New Empire. In the reign of Ramses II. no fewer than 3000 workmen were employed here for the Ramesseum (p. 324) alone. An inscription of Amenophis III. (p. cv) records the transport of stones by the Nile for a temple of Ptah. At the N. end of the hill are found the scanty ruins of the ancient town of *Khenit* and its temple (fragmentary inscriptions of Ramses II.). The abandoned workmen's dwellings near the river are of modern construction. To the E., towards the top of the rock on the N. face of the hill, is a stele of

Amenophis IV. (marked No. 37), recording that Amenophis caused an obelisk for the temple of the sun at Karnak to be quarried here. Below, to the right, are prehistoric rock-carvings, and lower down at the foot of the hill are the numerous mouths of small rock-tombs. — By following the hill S., we first reach a large cave-quarry supported by pillars and open to the W. Next come a small empty quarry and, on the hill above, a large unfinished sphinx (No. 40). Then a larger quarry, in which pylons scratched on the cliff facing N. indicate that the stones for the pylon of a temple were quarried here in ancient times. A modern inscription commemorates the cutting of stone for the Esna barrage (p. 363) in 1906-9. At the entrance of two of the quarries are two memorial inscriptions of Sethos I. The largest quarry, which lies to the S. of this, is closed by a gate, which the custodian will open. On the N. wall of the narrow passage leading to it is the drawing of an obelisk.

To visit the more important monuments, situated on the W. bank, we ferry to the steamer landing-place, whence we turn N. The well-trodden track skirts the river, passing a number of small tomb-like recesses (cenotaphs) and memorial tablets. Beyond some quarries we reach the **Rock Chapel** (unlocked by the keeper), which was hewn in the rock under Haremhab (19th Dyn.) and in the following centuries was embellished with inscriptions and reliefs, of great artistic and historical value, in honour of kings and high officials. In front are five doorways, separated from each other by pillars (Pl. *a-d*) at varying distances, and crowned with the torus and cavetto cornice. We enter by the middle door (now the sole entrance), on the lintel of which are chiselled the sun-disk and the names of Haremhab. The interior consists of a wide but shallow vaulted hall (Pl. *A*), at the back of which is an oblong room (Pl. *B*). All the walls are covered with carving and inscriptions.

On the *South Wall* (Pl. *f*) is a fine relief of a goddess offering the breast to King Haremhab, while Khnum stands behind her and Amon-Rē behind the king.

On the *Rear Wall*, at Pl. 1, to our left as we enter, is a *Relief of King Haremhab returning in triumph from his campaign in Nubia. The Pharaoh is seated on his throne, which is borne by twelve soldiers adorned with feathers. Behind and before him are soldiers with the long-handled flabellum. A priest precedes the litter, offering incense, with a train of captured Nubians and three rows of soldiers (among whom is a trumpeter). To the left the king and Amun stand upon prostrate negroes. Beneath the main scene is a recess, to the left of which are negro prisoners, and to the right Egyptian soldiers marching off captives. Note the free style of the attitudes of the barbarians. Poetic inscriptions above both reliefs extol the king as the conqueror of the inhabitants of Kush (provinces of the Upper Nile, p. 411): "Hail to thee, King of Egypt, thy name is extolled in the land of the Nubians", etc. — To the right in this wall is a recess (Pl. 2) with the figure in high-relief (full-face) of Khay, an official under Ramses II. — Pl. 3. Above, inscription with a representation of King Siptah (p. cvii) bringing flowers to Amun, while his official Bay holds the flabellum behind; below, King Haremhab shooting arrows against an enemy. — Pl. 4. Memorial tablet of the 2nd year of Menephthes: the king offering an image of Maat, goddess of truth, to Amon-Rē and Mut; behind the king are Queen Eset-nofret, with a sistrum, and the vizier Pinehas, with

a flabellum. — Pl. 5 (recess). Figure in high-relief of a man holding his left hand before his breast. — Pl. 6. Tablet placed by Kha-em-wēset, son of Ramses II., in memory of the fourth jubilee of Ramses II. — Pl. 7 (to the right of the door). Similar inscription of Kha-em-wēset. — Pl. 8. Small relief of a man named Moy, in prayer. — Pl. 9 (in a recess). Large figure, in high-relief, of Prince Kha-em-wēset. — Pl. 10. Defaced relief of Kha-em-wēset receiving offerings. — Pl. 11. Tablet, erected by the fan-bearer Moy, in memory of the jubilees of Ramses II.; to the left is the kneeling figure of Moy; above is Ramses II. presenting an image of Maat to Amun, Harakhte, Maat, Ptah, and Suchos (p. clix), the local deity of Silsila. — Pl. 12. Relief of a vizier, beneath which is a dainty little representation of a column with a palm-capital. — Pl. 13. Memorial tablet of the 45th year of Ramses II., dedicated by a high official, who appears kneeling below, with a flabellum; above, the king presents an image of Maat to Amun, the great Mut, Khons, Harakhte, and Suchos (head injured). — Pl. 14. Three men praying.

On the *North Wall* (Pl. *h*) is a recess with six figures in high-relief. On the *East Wall*, at Pl. *i*, and on the *Entrance Pillars* are numerous memorial inscriptions.

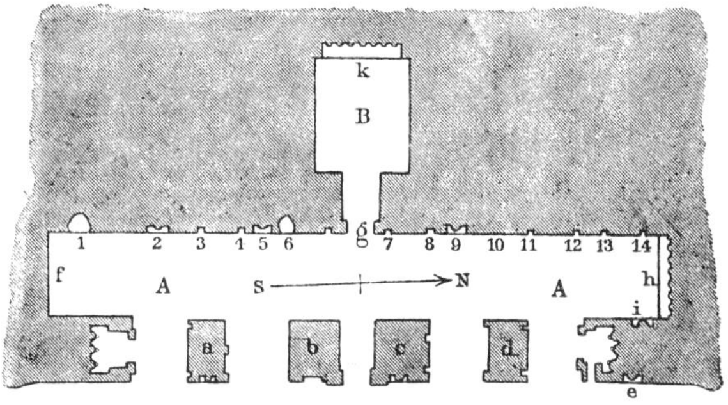

In the *Doorway* (Pl. *g*) from the first chamber to the second (*B*) are representations of King Haremhab sacrificing to Harakhte and the goddess Ews-os of Heliopolis (on the left) and to Amun and Mut (on the right). — On the side-walls of *Room B* are representations of the gods; in the rear wall is a recess (Pl. *k*) with the much damaged figure of Amun seated in the midst of six other gods.

The route goes on S. from the Rock Chapel, sometimes skirting the river-bank, sometimes leading through the ancient quarries, which were probably exhausted during the Roman period. It passes a number of rock-inscriptions and chapel-like recesses (cenotaphs).

We first reach a rock facing the river, with three *Memorial Inscriptions* upon it: to the left, Ramses III. before Amun, Mut, and Khons; in the middle, Sheshonk I. (who erected the tablet; p. cvii) conducted by the goddess Mut before Amun, Harakhte, and Ptah, while behind the king is his son, Yewpet, high-priest of Amon-Rē and general-in-chief; to the right, Ramses IX. (p. cvii), worshipping Amun, Mut, Khons, and Suchos.

Farther on is a *Cenotaph Recess* with a painted ceiling, on the left door-jamb of which is the praying figure of Thutmosis, scribe of the treasure-house. Another *Recess*, with a ceiling finely painted with spiral patterns, etc., has the cartouches of Thutmosis III. and of Hatshepsut (destroyed) on the lintel.

Farther S., close to the river, are three *Cenotaph Recesses* side by side. The northernmost of these belonged to Nekht-Min, royal scribe and overseer of the granaries of Upper and Lower Egypt; on the left wall is a fine relief showing the deceased and a companion at table; on the rear wall are three seated figures. — Another *Tomb Recess*, belonging to Amenemhēt, priest of Amun, has fine reliefs and well-preserved colouring; in the rear wall appears the deceased, to whom attendants bring food and drink, and on the side-walls are the deceased and his wife Mimi, etc.

After skirting the bushy river-bank for 1/4 hr. we reach the Southern Monuments, offering a picturesque appearance. The chief of these are two *Recesses* (cenotaphs) about 6 ft. deep, which lie close beside each other. The architraves over the entrances are adorned with cavetto cornices and uræus serpents and are borne by clustered columns. That to the N. (right) was constructed in the first year of Menephthes (p. cvii); it represents the king sacrificing to Harakhte, Ptah, and the Nile-god (right), and to Amun, Mut, and Khons (left). Beneath is a long hymn to the Nile and lists of offerings to be made to the river-god. — The scenes in the S. recess are repetitions of these, except that Menephthes is replaced by Ramses II., in the first year of whose reign the recess was constructed. — On the rock between these recesses is a door-shaped *Stele*, on which King Menephthes is shown presenting a figure of the goddess of truth to Amun; the king is followed by a prince and by the vizier Pinehas, who erected this stele to his master. — Farther to the S. is another *Stele*, on which Menephthes sacrifices to Amun, while behind him is Roy, high-priest of Amun, who dedicated this monument.

On a curious isolated sandstone rock, to the right, is a *Stele* of the 6th year of Ramses III. (p. cvii), showing the king sacrificing to Amun, Harakhte, and the god of the Nile. On the same rock, to the left, appears a priest adoring the names of Sethos I. — Farther to the S., and at a lower level than those steles, is another and much ruined recess, dating from the reign of Sethos I. (p. cvi). On the river-bank are traces of an ancient flight of steps descending to the stream.

The Railway traverses, past the river-defile of Gebel es-Silsila (94 M. *Gebel es-Silsila* station, p. 364), a district which has lately been brought under cultivation (see below).

102 M. **Kôm Ombo** (Hotel Kom Ombo, at the station, the property of the under-mentioned company, 17 R., pens. P.T. 70-80, good) is the headquarters of the Egyptian Société de Wadi Kom Ombo. On the bank of the Nile are the large pumping works of the company (with three powerful pumps, each of 1500 h.p.), conspicuous for miles around by their tall chimney, by which the waters of the Nile are raised to a height of about 80 ft. and used for the irrigation of an area, formerly quite unproductive, of 22,000 feddân (22,836 acres; to be increased to 30,000 feddân or 31,000 acres). The pumping works are connected by a trolley-line with the railway station, where a factory deals with the sugar-cane raised in the reclaimed area. —

The *Temple of Kôm Ombo* (p. 374), on the bank of the Nile, may be reached in 1/2 hr. by trolley from the station (P.T. 20 there and back). — The train next traverses a reclaimed district, intersected by embankments and canals.

106 M. **Darâw** *(Darau)*, a large village with several mosques, marks the boundary between the Arabic and Nubian languages. It has a station of the Sûdân Pioneer Mission (German). Fans, baskets, and other Nubian articles may be purchased here very cheaply. A large and interesting market is held on Tues., to which the Bishârîn and the ʿAbâbda (p. 398) bring hundreds of camels to be sold. These tribes may be studied here much better than at their now much diminished camping ground at Aswân (p. 381). Both speak a peculiar language, allied to Egyptian and other E. African (Hamitic) idioms. They support themselves by cattle-raising and by trading in charcoal, sheep, and camels, which they fetch from the Eastern Desert (comp. p. lx). The Bishârîn have a curious head-dress of plaited hair. — 113 M. *El-Khannâq (Khannak).*

The line approaches the river and passes fine groves of palms as it traverses the granite district of Aswân. — 122 M. *El-Khaṭṭâra.* In the Nile here is the large island of *Bahrîf* (p. 365). On the left bank appears the hill of tombs (p. 384), with the picturesque grave of a sheikh.

129 M. **Aswân** (p. 378).

23. From Luxor to Aswân by the Nile.

Comp. the Map, p. 232.

65 M. Tourist Steamer, up in 1 1/2-2 days, down in 1-1 1/2 day. — Motor-boats, see p. 268.

Luxor, see p. 267. — The picturesque forms of the E. bank of the Nile remain long in view, the colossi of Memnon being the last of the ruins to disappear. On the W. bank is *El-Marîs*, with a steam-pump. Sugar-cane fields occupy the W. bank. A large island is passed.

In about 2 hrs. the steamer reaches (9 1/2 M.; W. bank) *Armant* (railway stations, p. 355).

The Nile describes a wide curve. — On the W. bank, opposite a large island, rises (18 1/2 M.) the long ridge of *Gebelein* (p. 356). — Farther on, on the same bank, is *El-Maṭâʿna* (railway station, p. 356).

The river-banks are picturesquely clad with extensive groves of palms, but the smoking chimneys of the sugar-factories impair the beauty of the scenery. The steamer passes the **Esna Barrage** by means of a lock (262 ft. long) next the W. bank. The dam was constructed in 1906-9 by John Aird & Co. (p. 396) at a cost of £E 1,000,000. It is 955 yds. long, 20 ft. broad at the top, and rises 30 ft. above the Nile at its lowest. Its 120 sluices are intended mainly to regulate the irrigation of the province of Qena (comp. p. lxxiii). On both banks of the river are large canals with sluices.

36 M. (W. bank) **Esna** (*Isna;* railway station; see p. 357).

In the Nile is the cultivated island of *Er-Rîqîya;* on the W. bank of the river lies the village of *Es-Sibâ'îya* (railway station, on the E. bank, p. 358).

At *El-Qannân*, on the W. bank, there are ancient river-embankments. On the W. bank stretches a broad and fertile plain, on the E. is the finely shaped *Gebel esh-Sharâwna (Gebel Sharôna).* In the river is another large island. — At *El-Khiwi (El-Khewa)*, on the E. bank, appears the first sandstone.

On the W. bank, about 3/4 hr. farther S., near the village of *El-Biṣalîya (Baṣalîya)*, is the pyramid of *El-Kûla*, which now presents the aspect of a step-pyramid, owing to the decay of the filling-in material. This pyramid is still about 30 ft. high, while its base occupies an area of about 350 square yards.

On the E. bank lie *El-Maḥâmîd* (railway station, p. 358) and (44 M.) **Elkâb**, with its ruined town and rock-tombs (p. 365).

65 M. **Edfu** (*Idfu ;* railway station; see p. 359).

On the E. bank, 5 M. above Edfu, is the village of **Er-Ridîsiya** *(Redesîya, Rodsieh)*, after which a temple of Sethos I., lying 37 M. to the E., has been named (see p. 401). — Farther along the E. bank (12 M. from Edfu), on the mountain-slopes approaching close to the river near the hill of *Es-Sîrâg*, are the picturesque remains of a late-Byzantine fortified town (perhaps the ancient *Thmuis*), with a church or convent. In the neighbourhood are ancient quarries with inscriptions (one of Thutmosis III.). The nummulite limestone of the hills here gives place to sandstone (comp. p. lxix), which has furnished the material for most of the gigantic buildings of Upper Egypt.

18 1/2 M. (E. bank) *Silwa* (railway station, p. 359).

26 M. **Gebel es-Silsila** ('Mountain of the Chain'; so called from a chain that is said once to have blocked the passage of the river). The hills on the two banks of the river approach close together, and in very ancient times there were probably rapids at this point (like those at Aswân, p. 389). These were regarded as the beginning of the Nile, and even in later periods the Nile-god *Hapi* enjoyed special reverence at Silsila (p. 362), where great festivals were held in his honour.

Above the defile of Gebel es-Silsila the landscape changes its character. The mountains recede from the river, giving space to the desert, which appears grey on the E. side and yellow on the W. The narrow cultivable strip is tilled by peasants of a distinctly darker complexion than the fellahin of N. Egypt. Both land and people approach gradually nearer to the Nubian type.

On the E. bank lies *Iqlît (Aklit)*. — At the village of *Muneiḥa* (*Miniha;* E. bank) we enter the E. branch of the stream, which here encircles the island of *El-Manṣûrîya*, with a village of the same name.

On the E. bank are the large pumping works of the Kôm Ombo Co. (p. 362). On a hill appear the conspicuous ruins of the beautiful temple of Kôm Ombo (p. 374), especially picturesque by the light of the full moon. The islands opposite the E. bank were, perhaps, in former times united with the mainland, or separated from it only by a narrow channel; but in the course of centuries the Nile has gradually extended its channel farther E.; and during the 19th cent. alone about 20 ft. were washed away from the E. bank, along with a large portion of the building. An embankment has been constructed to prevent further mischief.

$41^1/_2$ M. **Kôm Ombo** (railway station; see p. 362).

The channel of the river narrows. — *Darâw*, a railway station (p. 363), lies on the E. bank. — On the W. bank, near *Er-Raqaba*, are the ruins of the ancient *Contra-Ombos*.

The scenery becomes tamer beyond the village of *El-Kûbânîya*, on the W. bank, near which are early-Egyptian cemeteries excavated by the Vienna Academy of Sciences in 1910-11.

Opposite rises the *Gebel el-Ḥammâm*, with quarries which yielded stone for the temple at Ombos (now vanished, comp. p. 374) as early as the reign of Hatshepsut (18th Dyn.). To the W. the yellow sand of the desert often extends right down to the river. At *El-Khaṭṭâra* (railway station, p. 363) granite appears for the first time.

We now pass the large and well-tilled island of *Bahrîf* (p. 388), with its palm-groves and fields. Opposite, near *El-Wâreṣâb*, on the W. bank, are some quarries (with graffiti).

As we approach Aswân (E. bank) the scene presented to us is one of great and peculiar beauty. On the hill to the right is the *Qubbet el-Hawa* (p. 386); straight in front of us lies the N. extremity of the island of *Elephantine* (p. 382), with the Savoy Hotel. Sandstone now gives place to masses of granite on the banks and in the channel of the stream. On the left are the harbour, the Roman Catholic church, and the hotels.

65 M. **Aswân** (p. 378).

24. Elkâb.

The monuments of Elkâb are visited from the station of *El-Maḥâmîd* (p. 358). Those unwilling to spend the night there should take the early train from Luxor to Esna (p. 357), drive thence by motor-car (to be ordered in advance) to ($18^1/_2$ M.) El-Maḥâmîd, and return from Esna to Luxor by the afternoon train. This allows time for the inspection of the chief monuments at least.

Elkâb or *El-Kâb*, the ancient *Nekhab*, once ranked among the chief cities of Egypt and was in prehistoric times the capital of Upper Egypt (p. ci). Even under the Ptolemies it was the capital of the third nome of Upper Egypt, which was afterwards named Latopolites. Nekhbeyet, the goddess of the town, was represented either as a vulture or as a woman with the crown of Upper Egypt;

she was regarded as a protecting deity of Upper Egypt. She also assisted women in childbirth, and was therefore identified with Eileithyia by the Greeks, who named the town *Eileithyiaspolis*. Half-a-day suffices for a visit to the chief antiquities.

The ***Ruins of Nekhab**, which are surrounded by a massive girdle-wall of sun-dried bricks, lie near the river. The wall, which probably dates from the Middle Empire, has been damaged on the S.W. side by the Nile, but is otherwise intact. It is of immense thickness (37 ft.) and encloses a rectangle, 620 yds. by 590 yds., with gates on the E., N., and S. sides, beside which broad ascents lead to the top of the wall. The N. wall intersects a necropolis of the Ancient Empire, excavated by J. E. Quibell in 1897. The city itself, enclosed by another double wall, of which distinct traces are still to be seen, occupied only about one-fourth of the space within the girdle-wall. Very scanty ruins now remain of the temple, built during the 18th Dyn. on the site of an earlier sanctuary and enlarged by Nektanebis I. (p. cx) and others.

Visitors should not omit to ascend to the top of the N. wall, for the sake of the admirable view: to the E., at the head of a desert valley, appear the isolated rock with inscriptions, the temple of Amenophis III., and, a little nearer, the chapel of Thoth (comp. below); to the N. is the hill with the rock-tombs, and a little farther away is a mushroom-shaped rock, with the quarries that yielded the stone for the city temple.

We follow the route leading due E. from the E. gateway in the girdle-wall and cross the dazzlingly white sand, past a small ruined *Sandstone Chapel* (no inscriptions) close to the wall. In rather more than $^1/_2$ hr. we reach a ruined *Chapel of Thoth*, known to the Arabs as *El-Ḥammâm*, i.e. 'the bath', and built by Setaw (p. 420), governor of Nubia in the time of Ramses II.

We keep straight on, leaving the larger temple of the Ptolemies on the left, and soon reach two *Rocks* projecting from the plain, at the point where the road turns N. towards the desert, halfway between El-Ḥammâm and the E. temple of Amenophis III. Both rocks bear numerous inscriptions and figures of animals. Most of these date from the 6th Dyn. and were probably placed here by priests of Elkâb.

The charming small temple or ***Chapel of Amenophis III.** lies fully $^1/_4$ hr. E. It may be reached direct in about an hour from the Nile. The little temple, which is about 50 ft. deep, was dedicated to Nekhbeyet, 'mistress of Re-yant' (i.e. of the entrance to the desert valley). It consists of a ruined *Vestibule* of the Ptolemaic period, with papyrus-columns (the capitals of which strew the ground), and of a *Hall*, the roof of which was borne by four sixteen-sided columns embellished with heads of Hathor. The names of the king, Amun, and Nekhbeyet, and several representations of the gods were defaced under Amenophis IV. and restored under Sethos I. Many of them were again renewed in the Ptolemaic period.

On the *Entrance Door* of the hall are a votive inscription and a representation of Amenophis III. The exterior walls bear only a few in-

scriptions and representations (ships) that were added at a later date; to the right of the door is Kha-em-wēset, in presence of Ramses II., his father, in commemoration of the king's fifth jubilee, in the 41st year of his reign. Another hieroglyphic inscription here ('In the 13th year of his majesty, lord of the world, Napoleon III.') is certainly the latest in Egypt, with the exception of that added to celebrate 'King Henri V.' (i.e. Count Chambord, d. 1883). On the pavement outside the chapel representations of footprints have been scratched by pilgrims.

The representations within the hall have retained their colouring in good condition. On each side of the entrance, Amenophis III. and his father Thutmosis IV. seated at banquet-tables. *Left Wall.* Amenophis III. sacrificing to the sacred boat, which is decorated with falcons' heads; Amenophis III. presenting incense and water to Nekhbeyet; Amun (blue) embracing the king and holding the hieroglyph for 'life' to the king's nose. *Rear Wall.* On each side of the recess, Amenophis III. sacrificing to Nekhbeyet. *Right Wall.* The falcon-headed Horus handing the hieroglyph for 'life' to the king, who stands before him; the king presenting two wine-jars to Nekhbeyet; the king sacrificing to the sacred boat. Adjacent are demotic inscriptions in red, written by visitors to the chapel. The names of Amenophis alternating with heads of Hathor are arranged as a frieze in this hall and as an embellishment on the architrave; at the base of the walls are bulls in a marsh.

Turning here, we direct our steps towards the Nile and in $^1/_4$ hr. reach the **Rock Temple**, on the right side of the valley, recognizable from a distance by the *Staircase* leading up to it. The latter consists of forty-one steps hewn in the rock, with a massive balustrade on each side. The temple, dedicated to Nekhbeyet, was constructed under Ptolemy IX. Euergetes II. (Physcon, p. cxii), and provided with reliefs and inscriptions by him and by Ptolemy X. Soter II.

On reaching the platform at the top of the stairs we pass through a doorway to a *Vestibule*, not quite 33 ft. wide, which was supported by columns with elaborate floral capitals, while the façade was formed of stone screens built between columns. Thence another door, the right half of which is still standing, leads into a smaller *Hall* (only 20 ft. wide), which also was bounded by screens between columns. The floor is covered with ruins. Behind this is the Rock Chamber. This chamber, which was originally a tomb-chamber dating from the New Empire, has a vaulted ceiling, with vultures hovering in the centre. At the top of the walls is a frieze made of the name of Ptolemy X. Soter II. between heads of Hathor. Below are inscriptions and much injured representations of the king and queen before various deities.

On an isolated hill, about 1 M. from the steamer landing-place, are a number of ***Rock Tombs,** placed side by side on the S. slope. Most of these date from the end of the Middle Empire or from the beginning of the New Empire. There are thirty-one tombs in all, but only six repay a visit. These tombs, like all the monuments at Elkâb, are of small dimensions, but their distinct pictures of ancient Egyptian domestic life are not without interest.

We first enter the tomb of **Peheri** *(Pehray)*, nomarch of Elkâb, which is conspicuous by its wide opening. It dates from the reign of Thutmosis III., and is distinguished by a series of representations from the life of the deceased, with well-preserved colouring. The faces have all been obliterated.

In front of the entrance is a platform in which is the opening of a deep mummy-shaft. We enter the vaulted Tomb by a much damaged door. *Entrance Wall*, to the left: the deceased with a long staff; above is a sailing

ship. — *Left Wall (W.).* In the upper row is the deceased inspecting agricultural operations (ploughing, sowing, reaping with sickles, collecting and binding the sheaves, oxen treading out the corn, winnowing the grain, bringing home the grain in sacks). In the lower row the deceased inspects his herds (cattle, asses, etc.); he superintends the weighing of gold made into rings and the shipping of his grain. In the upper row farther on Peheri holds on his lap the young Prince Wedjmose, whose tutor he was; Peheri and his wife in a bower receiving flowers, fruit, etc.; above, vintage scenes. In the lower row Peheri superintends his fowlers and fishers; the captured birds and fish are being prepared and the nets mended. Farther on to the right the burial of Peheri and the accompanying rites are shown in five rows one above the other. — *Right Wall (E.).* Peheri and his wife at a banquet, with their son officiating as a priest before them. Below their chair is a tame baboon. Opposite them are their relatives at table, and in the lower row are a female harpist and flute-player. Farther on to the right are Peheri and his wife, praying and sacrificing. A door was afterwards made through this wall to two other chambers. — *Rear Wall.* In the recess here sit Peheri, his wife, and his mother. On the side-walls of the recess are various persons at a banquet.

Of the tombs to the right of the tomb of Peheri that of **Ahmose Pen-Nekhbeyet** is noteworthy. It consists of a single vaulted chamber, the fine reliefs in which have, however, left no traces. Ahmose was prominent, especially in war, under the first kings of the New Empire, from Amosis to Thutmosis III. (p. cv). His biography is recorded in the doorway.

To the left of the tomb of Peheri is that of **Setaw**, high-priest of Nekhbeyet. This tomb, dating from the time of Ramses IX. (20th Dyn.), is the latest grave with inscriptions at Elkâb. Though four hundred years later than the others, it is decorated on the same plan and in the same style.

On the *Left Wall* nothing can now be distinguished but four sacred boats, apparently bound for a festival of the king. *Right Wall.* To the left are Setaw and his wife at table; below their chair is a baboon. Before them their son-in-law officiates as priest, in a panther-skin; and opposite are their relatives at table, seated in rows. The artist has included his own portrait, identified by the palette. Part of this scene is destroyed by a door made at a later period to a side-chamber. Farther to the right are Setaw and his wife sacrificing. — The stele on the *Rear Wall* is much injured.

To the left of this tomb lies that of **Ahmose**, an admiral, which is noted for its long inscription recording the life and deeds of the deceased, more especially his share in the war of liberation against the Hyksos (p. civ).

The tomb comprises a rectangular chamber, with vaulted ceiling, and another room (right), with the mummy-shaft. Main Room. On the *Right Wall* appears the deceased with staff and sceptre, accompanied by the painter Peheri, his grandson, who constructed the tomb. In front is the above-mentioned inscription, continued on the entrance-wall. The designs on the *Left Wall* are unfinished; the red lines to assist the draughtsmen may still be noticed. The *Rear Wall* is much damaged; to the right we see the deceased and his wife at table, to the left, the relatives in rows.

The tomb of **Reni**, nomarch of Elkâb and high-priest at the beginning of the 18th Dyn., still farther to the left (W.), contains representations resembling those in the tomb of Peheri (p. 367), but not so skilfully executed.

On the *Left Wall* are harvest scenes; the deceased superintends the counting of the stock in his district; close by are a herd of swine, animals which were much appreciated in Elkâb, in contradistinction to the rest of Egypt (comp. p. 417); the deceased and his wife at table, with their relatives seated opposite. On the *Right Wall*, the funeral and accompanying ceremonies. In the *Rear Wall* is a niche with a seated statue of the deceased, now quite destroyed.

The last three tombs farther to the left (W.) appear to date from a period before the New Empire.

One of these, badly mutilated, belongs to Ah-nofru, a lady attached to the royal harem, and her husband. Another (with a vaulted ceiling) belonged to Bebi and his wife Sebk-nakht, who also was a lady of the harem. The third (now inaccessible) consists of a vaulted chamber with a tastefully adorned ceiling and a room with the shaft. It dates from the reign of Sebek-hotep II. (13th Dyn.).

A little W. of the hill of tombs stood a small *Temple of Thutmosis III.*, now destroyed.

On the W. bank opposite Elkâb, about 10 min. from the river, lies the village of *Muissât (Mo'isât)*, and farther on, about 1 hr. from the river, on the edge of the desert, rises the *Kôm el-Aḥmar* ('Red Hill'), with the extensive ruins and tombs of Hierakonpolis.

Hierakonpolis (Egyptian *Nekhen*) was one of the most ancient cities in the country and in prehistoric times was probably the capital, along with Elkâb, of Upper Egypt (p. ci). Its god was a Horus, to whom the falcon was sacred, whence arose the Greek name Hierakōnpolis ('city of falcons'). A little to the N., beyond a broad desert route, is a second mass of ruins, amongst which is a large *Fort* (Hint Amm Sefian) or royal castle, dating from the earliest period of the kings, with a low outer wall and a higher inner wall of unburnt bricks. On the E. side is the gate. In the adjoining cultivated land lay the *Temple* of Nekhen, in which J. E. Quibell discovered in 1897-98 some important sculptures of the period of the earliest kings, besides others of later date, including the copper statue of Phiops I. mentioned on p. 91. — To the W. is a hill with tombs of the Ancient and Middle Empires, two with designs and inscriptions upon stucco. — About 1/4 hr. farther W., also on the hill of Kôm el-Aḥmar, are eight rock-tombs, dating from the beginning of the New Empire, of which only the first to the right or N. (*Dhuti*, of the time of Thutmosis I.) and the first to the left or S. (*Harmose*, high-priest of Nekhen) repay a visit. The structure of these tombs resembles that of the tombs at Elkâb. At the inner end of each is a recess with a statue of the deceased and his wife. In the tomb of Harmose dancing girls are painted upon stucco.

25. Edfu.

Tourist Steamers, see p. 364. — The Railway Station (p. 359) is on the E. bank.

Hotels. *Ptolémée* (proprietor André Lagoudakis), near the station, 15 R. at P.T. 25, pens. 80, new; *National* (same proprietor), 10 R. from P.T. 12, pens. 45, modest but clean. — Donkeys are to be had at the landing-place.

Edfu (Idfu), a district capital (15,000 inhab. in 1927), was called in antiquity *Dbôt*, Coptic *Atbô*, whence is derived the modern Arabic name Idfu. In Græco-Roman times it was called *Apollonopolis Magna*, after its chief god Horus-Apollo, and was the capital of the second nome of Upper Egypt, the Apollonopolites. *Horus*, who, according to the myth, here waged one of his great combats with Seth (comp.

pp. cxlviii, 238), was surnamed 'He of Beḥdet', Beḥdet being probably a district of ancient Edfu; he was represented as a flying falcon, as a man with a falcon's head, or as the sun with outspread wings.

The way from the landing-place to the (20 min.) temple of Horus leads almost due W., passes through the main street of the village (with the Ophthalmic Hospital and Government Offices), crosses the *Ramâdi Canal*, and ends at the N. gate of the later girdle-wall. Route from Edfu railway station, see p. 359.

The ****Temple of Horus,** built of sandstone, stands in wonderful, almost perfect preservation, exceeding that of any other Egyptian temple or even of any antique building in the world, in spite of the two thousand years that have passed over it. Unfortunately the reliefs all over the temple were mutilated in the Christian period (comp. p. clxxxviii). The present temple occupies the site of an earlier sanctuary and was dedicated to the sun-god *Horus*, *Hathor* of Dendera, and the youthful *Horus*, 'Uniter of the Two Lands' (*Har-semtewe*, *Harsomtus;* comp. p. 261). The history of its construction and an account of the entire structure are detailed in lengthy inscriptions on the exterior of the girdle-wall (at Pl. *i* and *k*). The temple proper was begun in 237 B.C. by Ptolemy III. Euergetes I. and completed, so far as the masonry was concerned, by his successor Philopator in 212 B.C. The decoration of the walls with reliefs and inscriptions, postponed by the death of Philopator and the disturbed reign of Epiphanes his successor, was resumed in 176 B.C. under Philometor and completed in 147 B.C. (under Euergetes II.), i.e. ninety years after the laying of the foundation-stone. Euergetes II. built the great vestibule (completed 122 B.C.) and embellished it with reliefs, and under Ptolemy X. Soter II. and Ptolemy XI. Alexander I. (p. cxiii) the colonnaded court, the girdle-wall, and the pylon were added, though the reliefs on the latter date from Neos Dionysos (p. cxiii). The final touch was given in 57 B.C.

The temple was originally surrounded by a lofty *Brick Wall*, still partly preserved, pierced by a large gateway on the S., in the axis of the temple, and by a smaller gateway to the W.

The great **Pylon** stood in an inner girdle-wall of brick, and its entrance was closed by a double door. It is covered on all sides with reliefs and inscriptions. On the front of each of the towers the colossal figure of King Neos Dionysos is conspicuous, smiting his foes, whom he holds by the hair, in presence of the falcon-headed Horus of Edfu and Hathor of Dendera. In two rows, above, the king appears praying and offering sacrifices before Horus, before Hathor and Horus, 'Uniter of the Two Lands', and before other gods of Edfu. The four wide incisions, two on each side of the central portal, were intended to support large flagstaffs, which were further secured by means of clamps fastened in the holes still to be seen in the masonry directly above. The small rectangular apertures in

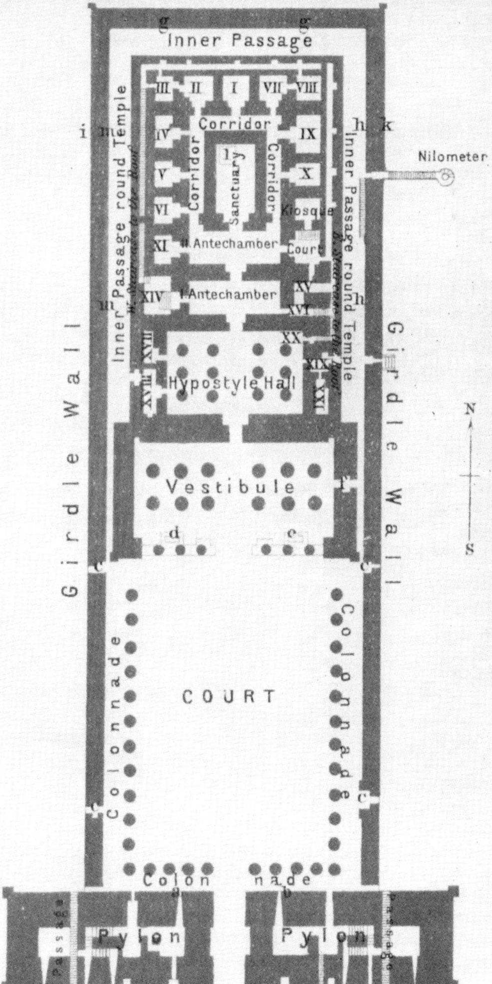

TEMPLE OF HORUS AT EDFU

1:1000 — Feet 0 20 40 60 80 100; Metres 0 10 20 30

Wagner & Debes' Geog! Estab! Leipzig

the towers served to admit light and air to the chambers and staircases within (see p. 373).

A passage leads through each pylon-tower to the outside of the girdle-wall, which is embellished with religious reliefs (Ptolemy XI. Alexander I. before the gods of Edfu) and inscriptions giving the history of the structure mentioned on p. 370. In front of the pylon stand two colossal falcons in dark granite. One has the figure of a priest in Roman costume before it.

The **Court**, between the pylon and the vestibule, is a spacious enclosure, paved with broad flags and surrounded on three sides by a covered colonnade of thirty-two columns. In this court rose the great altar upon which offerings were made to the gods of Edfu in presence of the assembled people. The columns supporting the roof of the colonnade are embellished with rich floral and palm capitals. The incised reliefs on the shafts show the king before Horus and the other gods of Edfu; the name of the king has not been inserted in the inscriptions. On the rear walls of the colonnades are three rows of large reliefs, showing the Pharaoh (Ptolemy X. Soter II. or Ptolemy XI. Alexander I.) in communion with the gods or triumphing over his foes, as the earthly representative of Horus. The same representations occur over and over again in wearisome repetition throughout the temple.

On the S. wall (Pl. *a*), to the left of the entrance: the king, wearing the crown of Lower Egypt, quits his palace in order to visit the temple; Horus and Thoth pour the water of consecration upon him. — These scenes are repeated to the right of the entrance (Pl. *b*), where, however, the king wears the crown of Upper Egypt.

The doors to the right of *a* and left of *b* lead to the staircases in the interior of the pylon (ascent, see p. 373). The E. and W. exits (Pl. *c*) are built up. — Outside the E. exit are the remains of a building of Ramses III.'s time.

The back of this court is formed by the front of the vestibule, which is crowned by a cavetto cornice. On each side of the large portal are three stone screens between the columns. The reliefs upon these, facing the court, represent Euergetes II. in a reverential attitude with pendent arms or offering sacrifice to Hathor of Dendera (on the two central screens) or to the falcon-headed Horus of Edfu (on the others). To the left of the entrance stands a colossal falcon with the double crown; the falcon on the right lies on the ground.

The **Vestibule**, or *Pronaos*, has twelve columns with elaborate floral capitals. The ceiling is covered with astronomical representations, now blackened beyond recognition. On the walls are four rows of incised reliefs, showing Euergetes sacrificing to the gods and performing other religious rites, such as the ceremonies at the foundation of the temple (in the lower row on the left wall), etc. Above are a row of astronomical representations and a frieze consisting of the names of the king guarded by two falcons. Close to the pavement we see Euergetes and his wife Cleopatra and a long procession of local deities bringing sacrificial gifts to the three chief

gods of Edfu. — To the right and left of the entrance are two small *Chapels*. One (Pl. *d*) is the 'Consecration Chamber', as is indicated by the relief on the rear wall, representing Horus (r.) and Thoth (l.) pouring consecrated water upon the king. The chapel to the right (Pl. *e*) was the library; upon its walls is a catalogue of the books preserved here. On the left wall Seshet, goddess of literature, appears writing upon a palm-branch. — A side-door (Pl. f) in the E. wall admits to the inner passage (p. 373) round the temple. — On the architrave of the door leading to the hypostyle hall is a curious representation. Ptolemy IV. Philopator offers an image of the goddess of truth to the boat of the sun, which appears guided by two figures of the falcon-headed Horus as pilot and helmsman. In the boat the sun is adored by Thoth (l.) and Neith (r.). In an attitude of worship, at the sides, are Four Senses: to the right, sight and hearing; to the left, taste and reason.

Next follows the **Hypostyle Hall**, the roof of which is borne by twelve columns with rich floral capitals. Apertures near the top of the walls and in the ceiling admit light to this hall. The representations on the walls resemble those of the preceding great vestibule. Of the adjoining side-chambers, two (Pl. XVIII and XIX) served as accesses to the inner passage round the temple, one (Pl. XVII) was a laboratory, while from another (Pl. XX) the great E. staircase led up to the roof of the temple.

On each side of the adjoining FIRST ANTECHAMBER is an approach to one of the *Staircases* leading to the temple-roof. The mural reliefs on the staircases resemble the corresponding reliefs at Dendera (p. 265). On that on the E. (Pl. XVI) is a procession of priests ascending, headed by the king; on that on the W. (Pl. XIV) is the same descending. The corridors and chambers on the roof contain nothing of interest, those to the E. being probably intended for the cult of Osiris. — On the E. of the SECOND ANTECHAMBER is a small *Sacrificial Court*, in which (to the N.) is an elegant little *Kiosk*, with two columns with floral capitals supporting the roof. Upon the ceiling is Nut, goddess of the sky, beneath whom appear various forms of the sun in boats. — To the left of the Second Antechamber is a small *Room* (Pl. XI) dedicated to the god Min (p. clvii).

In the **Sanctuary**, which forms a separate building shut off from the rest of the temple and lighted by three small rectangular apertures in the ceiling, the most interesting *Reliefs* are those in the lower row on the right (E.) wall. 1. The king (Philopator) removes the lock from the shrine of Horus. 2. He opens the door of the shrine. 3. He stands in a reverential attitude, with pendent arms before the god. 4. He offers incense to his deified parents, Euergetes I. and Berenice. 5. He offers incense before the sacred boat of Hathor. By the rear wall is a granite shrine (Pl. *l*), with a pointed roof, dedicated to Horus by King Nektanebis II. (p. cx). This is a relic of the original pre-Ptolemaic temple (p. 370). In front of the shrine

is a pedestal of dark granite (found in another part of the temple), intended to support the sacred boat and indicated by an inscription as the votive gift of a private citizen.

The sanctuary is surrounded by a Corridor, resembling the ambulatory of a Christian church, from which ten small Side Chambers (Pl. i-x) open. These, used for various religious rites and for store-rooms, are adorned with reliefs (well-preserved colouring in Rooms IX and VI) and are faintly lighted by holes in the roof. In the flooring of each of the corner-rooms (Pl. iii and viii) is the entrance to a crypt, formerly closed by a stone slab.

We return to the hypostyle hall and pass through Room xix to the **Inner Passage** between the exterior of the temple proper and the interior of the girdle-wall. On the outside of the temple walls are lions' heads as water-spouts and four rows of religious reliefs. At the foot of the wall appear the king, the queen, and a procession of local deities approaching the three chief gods of Edfu. On the inner side of the E. girdle-wall (Pl. *hh*) the king appears before the various gods of Edfu; on the N. wall (Pl. *gg*) are similar scenes and long hymns to the god of Edfu. On the W. wall (Pl. *mm*) are more important reliefs representing the contests of the god Horus with his enemies, who are depicted as crocodiles and hippopotami.

The chief are the following: *1st Scene* (below, to the right). The king, standing on shore, attempts to transfix a hippopotamus, which bends its head aside. Horus does the same; in his left hand he holds a chain, and in his right a javelin; beside him is his mother Isis, and behind, at the helm, is a small Horus. — *2nd Scene.* The king appears on land (to the left), before two ships, in each of which are a Horus and an assistant. Horus holds the hippopotamus with a chain and pierces its head with a javelin. — *5th Scene.* The hippopotamus lies on its back, with a chain fastened to its hind-feet. — *7th Scene.* Horus, in a ship with expanded sail, aims a blow at the head of a hippopotamus, the hind-foot of which is caught in a line held in the god's left hand. Isis kneeling in the bow of the boat holds the head of the animal by a cord. The king, standing on the bank with two attendants, seeks to pierce the skull of the hippopotamus. — Farther to the left (opposite the pylon): The king, the ram-headed Khnum, the falcon-headed Horus, and the ibis-headed Thoth are dragging a net, in which are not only waterfowl, fishes, and a stag, but also two Asiatics and some negroes, the ancestral foes of Egypt.

A subterranean staircase leads from the E. part of the passage round the temple to an ancient *Nilometer*, a round well situated outside the temple, and encircled by a spiral staircase which was formerly also reached from without. On the walls of the latter is the scale, with demotic numbers. The subterranean communication with the river has been interrupted.

Finally, an *Ascent to the Top of the Pylon is recommended. The doors on the S. side of the court (to the right and left of Pl. *a* and *b*) lead into dark chambers, from each of which an easy staircase of 242 steps in fourteen flights ascends to the platforms of the towers. Doors on the landings of the staircase admit to small chambers, constructed in the solid masonry and lighted, like the staircases, by means of small window-openings (see pp. 370, 371). The staircases in the two towers are connected with each other by a pass-

age running above the central portal; and in each tower there is a door affording access to the roof of the colonnade in the court. On the roof of the W. colonnade are the workmen's drawings for the cavetto cornice of the pylon. The view from the top is unusually attractive, commanding not only the most imposing survey of the temple buildings, but also ranging over the plain through which the Nile flows, with its verdant crops and its villages fringed with palms and mimosas, framed by the desert mountains in the distance.

The **Birth House** lies to the W. of the entrance to the great temple of Horus. It was built by Ptolemy IX. Euergetes II., while the interior decorations date from Ptolemy X. Soter II. It is surrounded by a colonnade, supported by columns with clustered foliage-capitals and cubes adorned with figures of Bes (comp. p. 266). Besides the main chamber there is a vestibule adjoined by two small rooms.

MAIN CHAMBER. On the right wall (left to right): Hathor of Dendera nurses Horus, while seven other Hathors play musical instruments. Behind the goddess is her youthful son Ehi-wēr, with a sistrum (p. clxiv). To the right is the confinement of Hathor, to the left the king holding two sistra, with seven figures of Hathor giving suck. The king before various deities and (left) before the sacred boat of Hathor. On the left wall are scenes referring to the birth of Harsomtus (Khnum shaping the child on the potter's wheel, etc.).

The *Court* in front of the Birth House was enclosed with columns connected by stone screens. On the shafts of the columns are goddesses with musical instruments and a representation of Hathor suckling Horus.

To the W. of the temple of Horus are the **Rubbish Mounds** of the old town, partly excavated in 1921-24 by the Institut Français d'Archéologie Orientale (p. 44). Beneath the houses of the Arabo-Coptic period lie Græco-Roman ruins. Papyri and all kinds of household utensils have been recovered.

26. The Temple of Kôm Ombo.

The STEAMER stops here on the way upstream (p. 365), allowing about 1 hr. for a visit to the temple. From the landing-place a path leads along the bank to a modern flight of steps, which ascend to the S. entrance of the temple. — RAILWAY STATION, see p. 362. We take the field-railway (trolley) to the temple and from its terminus follow a path to the N. entrance. — Tickets of admission (p. 212) must be shown. — Kôm Ombo may be conveniently visited as a one-day excursion from Aswân.

The ancient Egyptian city of *Ombos*, whose name survives in *Kôm Ombo* ('Hill of Ombos'), probably owes its foundation to the strategic importance of its site, upon a hill commanding both the Nile and the routes from Nubia to the Nile valley. Yet the town attained no great prosperity until the Ptolemaic era, when it was converted from an ordinary provincial town into the capital of the separate nome of *Ombites*. It was at this era that the mighty temples were built, which excite our admiration to-day; the earlier sanctuaries have left scarcely a trace. Ombos possessed two chief gods, the crocodile-headed *Suchos (Sobk)* and the falcon-headed *Haroēris.*

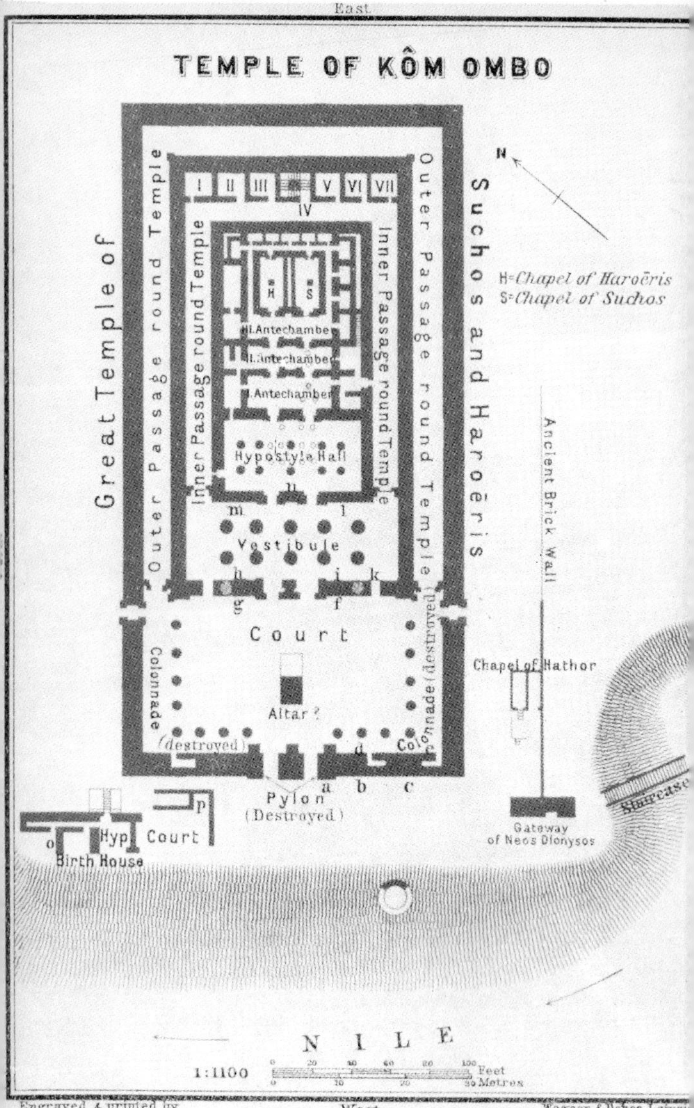
East
TEMPLE OF KÔM OMBO
Great Temple of
Suchos and Haroëris
Outer Passage round Temple
Inner Passage round Temple
I
II
III
IV
V
VI
VII
H
S
H=Chapel of Haroëris
S=Chapel of Suchos
III. Antechamber
II. Antechamber
I. Antechamber
Hypostyle Hall
n
m
l
Vestibule
h
i
k
g
f
Court
Colonnade
Colonnade (destroyed)
(destroyed)
Colonnade
Altar ?
d
a
b
c
Pylon
(Destroyed)
p
Hyp.
Court
o
Birth House
Ancient Brick Wall
Chapel of Hathor
Gateway of Neos Dionysos
Staircase
N
NILE
1:1100
Feet
Metres
Engraved & printed by
West
Wagner & Debes, Leipzig

With the former were specially associated *Hathor* and the youthful moon-god *Khons-Hor;* with the latter, the 'Good Sister' (*T-sent-nofret*, a special form of Hathor) and the 'Lord of Both Lands' (*P-neb-tewe).* The ruins of the town, now buried in sand, lie in the N.E. corner of the plateau. In 1893 all the temple buildings in the S. part of the plateau were cleared of rubbish and restored under the directions of J. de Morgan (d. 1924). A marble tablet on the right door of the vestibule (p. 376) commemorates the fact.

The temple precincts, which lie about $49^1/_4$ ft. above the average level of the Nile, were enclosed by a brick girdle-wall. The S. entrance is formed by a massive *Gateway*, erected by Ptolemy Neos Dionysos (p. cxiii). Only the right (E.) half is now standing; the other has sunk into the river. The reliefs show Neos Dionysos presenting various offerings to the gods of Ombos.

The *Great Temple of Suchos and Haroëris was built on a uniform plan, combining two temples side by side in the same building, and was embellished with reliefs by Philometor (p. cxii), Euergetes II. (p. cxii), and Neos Dionysos. The reliefs in the court and on the outer walls, however, were added under the Roman emperors, more especially under Tiberius (p. cxiv). In its general arrangements the temple of Ombos resembles other temples of the same period (at Dendera, Edfu, and Philæ), but it differs from them in being dedicated to two deities instead of to one only. Each of these two deities had his own special worship and festivals, so the entire building is bisected longitudinally by an imaginary line, each half having its own gateways, doorways, and chapels. The S. or right half was dedicated to Suchos, the N. or left half to Haroëris.

The Pylon, at the entrance to the temple court, had two doors. The left wing has completely vanished; while only the lower part of the central pillar (between the doors) and of the right wing remain.

On the outer side (facing the river) of the right wing are the following representations, from left to right: Pl. *a*. Suchos, Hathor, and Khons-Hor, the gods worshipped in the right half of the temple. Pl. *b*. Hieroglyphic text of fifty-two lines. Pl. *c*. Emperor Domitian (p. cxiv), with the crown of Upper Egypt, accompanied by fourteen gods and goddesses, offering gifts to the above-mentioned deities.

At the corner to the right (above Pl. *c*) the upper row of representations also has been preserved: six spirits (the last three, the 'Souls of Hierakonpolis', with dogs' heads) carry the newly crowned king (defaced) to his palace, on a portable throne; they are followed by the symbols  ('life') and  ('happiness'), bearing images of the gods on long poles; finally a large figure of the king leaving the palace on his way to the temple; he is preceded by a priest offering incense and followed by his guardian spirit (with a king's head upon a sceptre).

The Court, as at Edfu, was surrounded on three sides by colonnades. Only the lower portions of the sixteen columns are now left. The reliefs on these, the colouring of which is in places well preserved, represent Tiberius sacrificing to the gods. On the inner

side of the right wing of the pylon are two doors, one of which (Pl. *d*) admits to a small apartment, while the other (Pl. *e*) leads to a staircase by which the roof of the pylon was gained. The square base in the centre of the court was probably an altar; let into the ground beside it are two small granite troughs. In this, as in all the other rooms of the temple, the ancient pavement is in excellent preservation. The rear of the court is separated from the adjoining pronaos by stone screens, which are pierced by two large portals and two smaller doorways. On the screen to the right (Pl. *f*) is a relief of the falcon-headed Horus and the ibis-headed Thoth pouring the water of consecration upon King Neos Dionysos, to the left of whom is the crocodile-headed Suchos, the lord of the right half of the temple. On the left screen (Pl. *g*) the same scene takes place before the falcon-headed Haroëris (upper half restored), to whom the left half of the temple is dedicated. The screens are crowned by a row of serpents, with sun-disks on their heads.

The Vestibule, or *Pronaos*, contains ten columns with rich floral and palm capitals and was decorated by Neos Dionysos (sunk reliefs on the columns, bas-reliefs on the walls). On the shafts appears the king sacrificing to the gods. The ceiling of the two main aisles is embellished with flying vultures; while the under side of the architraves supporting this ceiling bears astronomical designs (star-gods in their boats, etc.). We may observe the lines dividing the surface into squares to guide the artist in drawing the figures, and also some older sketches that were not carried to completion. The mural reliefs here are especially beautiful, the finest being that to the right of the N. portal (on screen *h*). We here see the king (Neos Dionysos), in presence of Haroëris (to the right), being blessed by a lion-headed Isis and the falcon-headed Harsiësis, on the right, and by the goddess Nut and the ibis-headed Thoth, on the left.

The remaining mural reliefs may be inspected by those who are not pressed for time. On *Screen i:* the guardian goddesses of Upper and Lower Egypt blessing the king; to the left stand the crocodile-headed Suchos and his companion Hathor. — To the left, above the small *Door k:* Neos Dionysos sacrificing to four fabulous monsters (including a winged lion with four heads); the animals have been scratched out. — Opposite, on *Wall l* (the exterior wall of the hypostyle hall), are three rows. Bottom Row: to the right are Euergetes II. and Cleopatra (comp. p. 377; upper parts wanting) in presence of Suchos and his fellow-gods Hathor and P-neb-tewe; in the middle, the king before the falcon-headed Haroëris and the 'good sister'; to the left Euergetes presents the temple of Ombos to Suchos and Hathor. Middle Row: to the right the king (wanting) sacrifices to Osiris enthroned, Isis (before whom is her youthful son), and Nephthys; in the middle Euergetes presents flowers to the earth-god Geb and the sky-goddess Nut; to the left Euergetes offers two jars of wine to Show and the lion-headed Tefnut. Top Row: to the right, the king (wanting) before Haroëris, the 'good sister', and P-neb-tewe; in the middle he offers an ornament to Suchos and Khons-Hor; to the left Euergetes offers milk to Suchos and Hathor (badly damaged). — On *Wall m*, to the left of the left entrance to the next room, are three rows of similar scenes.

The Hypostyle Hall is entered by two doors. Its ceiling, which was lower than that of the pronaos, was supported by ten papyrus-

columns with umbellate (open) capitals. On each shaft Euergetes II. is seen sacrificing to a god; the mural reliefs show him in communion with the gods. The relief on the left (N.) wall should be noticed: the falcon-headed Haroëris presents the curved sword and the symbol for eternal life to Euergetes II., behind whom are his sister Cleopatra and his wife of the same name. The sacred crocodile of Ombos is represented at Pl. *n*, between the doors leading from the pronaos.

Between the doors leading hence to the inner rooms of the temple are reliefs showing Philometor, elder brother of Euergetes II., sacrificing to the falcon-headed Haroëris.

The following three smaller ANTECHAMBERS, each of which lies a little higher than the preceding, also are embellished with fine reliefs. Adjoining are a number of side-chambers, which may have been used as store-rooms; those to the left (N.) have almost completely disappeared. On the rear wall of Antechamber III, between the doors, is a fine relief: Philometor, clad in a white mantle and accompanied by Cleopatra, stands before the falcon-headed moon-god Khons, who writes the name of the king upon a palm-branch, from which hangs the symbol for length of reign; behind are Haroëris and Suchos, the chief gods of Ombos.

Two doors lead from Antechamber III to the two SANCTUARIES, the basements only of which are preserved, that to the left (Pl. *H*) being dedicated to *Haroëris*, that to the right (Pl. *S*) to *Suchos*. In each is a pedestal of black granite on which the sacred boat with the image of the god was placed. Beside and behind these sanctuaries were smaller apartments with crypts. Other crypts were constructed within the wall dividing the two sanctuaries.

Two small side-doors lead from the pronaos to an INNER PASSAGE round the temple proper, at the innermost part of which are seven doors opening into as many CHAMBERS (Pl. I-VII). These contain unfinished reliefs, which are interesting on account of their various stages of completion, and inscriptions that were sketched out but never finished. In the central room (Pl. IV) is a staircase to the upper story.

The E. walls of the OUTER PASSAGE round the temple are decorated with reliefs showing the Emperor Trajan sacrificing to Egyptian gods. At the N.E. corner, the emperor kneeling before two deities; close by is the representation of a set of medical instruments.

On the terrace in front of the temple lies a small **Birth House**, facing S.E. and now in a most ruinous condition. It was built or restored by Euergetes II. Among the extant reliefs one (at Pl. *o*) deserves notice. It represents Euergetes II. with two gods sailing in a boat through the marshes, which are bordered with papyrus-plants thronged with birds; to the left is the ithyphallic god Min-Amon-Rē. — On the S. side is a subterranean staircase (Pl. *p*) leading to the river, on the bank of which is a nilometer (much damaged), like that at Edfu.

In the open space to the E. of the Birth House and to the N. of the great temple are two fine architrave blocks (one with the name of Neos Dionysos) and the remains of several small buildings. The latter include a *Roman Gate* and a ruined chapel on a raised base; a large and a small *Well* lined with masonry and communicating with each other (the larger approached by steps inside and a covered staircase outside; the smaller connected by pipes with a small basin, in which perhaps young sacred crocodiles were kept); a small *Chapel* erected to Suchos by Caracalla (p. cxv); a *Coptic Church*, of which only a single column survives; and a large *Coptic House*.

Finally we visit the small unfinished CHAPEL OF HATHOR, to the S. of the temple court, built of red sandstone under the Emperor Domitian. In one of its rooms are mummies of sacred crocodiles found in the vicinity.

The terrace in front of the temple commands a beautiful *View of the Nile and the districts on the W. bank, while from the rubbish-mounds beside the temple we may survey the newly irrigated region beside Kôm Ombo, the villages of Shaṭb and Darâw, the island of Manṣûrîya, and the desert to the W.

27. Aswân and its Environs.

The TOURIST STEAMERS usually remain here two days. — RAILWAY, see p. 363; the station lies to the N. of the town.

Hotels (prices highest in Jan. and Feb.). **Cataract* (Pl. b), opposite the island of Elephantine, with a pretty garden and a large terrace on the Nile (sand, light, and sun baths), 280 R. at 90-210 (before the season 70-160), B. 15, L. 45, D. 55, pens. 180-300 (140-240), omnibus 20 P.T., open in winter only; **Grand* (Pl. c), on the quay, 80 R. at 60-150 (before the season 40-90), B. 12, L. 35, D. 45, pens. 130-200 (90-150), omnibus 16 P. T.; *Savoy* (Pl. a; closed at present), on Elephantine, with a large garden. These three, all with lifts, belong to the Upper Egypt Hotels Co.; pension rates are granted only for a stay of five days or more. — *St. James* (Pl. e), on the quay, 38 R., pens. P.T. 70-80. — *Ghezireh Palace*, on the Nile to the N. of the town, with a large garden, 45 R. at P.T. 25-40, pens. 60-80 (Viennese cuisine; free motor-car for the use of guests going into the town). — *Khedivial*, unpretending. — *Assuân Camp* (M. G. Hedra), in the desert, near the station, $1/2$ M. to the N.E. of the town, a sanatorium for sufferers from kidney disease and rheumatism, 40 R., pens. 70-100, omnibus P.T. 6; closed from the middle of April to the end of October.

Motor Cars, Carriages, Camels, Donkeys (P.T. 5 per hour), and **Boats**, all at fixed tariffs, which may be seen at the stands and in the railway time-table mentioned on p. xvii (a little dearer if hired through an hotel). — MOTOR BOATS. The Cataract Hotel has two motor-boats on hire, well fitted up, with sleeping berths; fare to Luxor £E 25-30, according to the size of the party. By the motor-boat 'Dixie' (belonging to S. Papayannis): fare to the Dam P.T. 120, to Kôm Ombo £E 5, to Edfu £E 11, to Luxor £E 22, to Abu Simbel £E 35.

Post Office, Shâriʿ el-Manshîya; also at the Cataract Hotel during the season. — **Telegraph Office** at the old station building, near the landing-place. — **Bank.** *National Bank of Egypt*, Shâriʿ el-Manshîya. — **Shipping Offices and Tourist Agents.** *Thos. Cook & Son*, *Anglo-American Nile & Tourist Co.*, both at the Grand Hotel; *Sûdân Government Steamers*, at the station and the Grand Hotel.

Physicians. *Dr. Moore*, *Dr. Neylon*, both English; *Dr. Schacht*, *Dr. Lahmeyer*, both German. — CHEMIST. *Savoy Pharmacy*, at the Grand Hotel.

Churches (hours of service are posted up in the hotels). Anglican: *St. Mark's* (p. 380), near the Cataract Hotel; *Roman Catholic Church*, Shâriʿ el-Manshîya (p. 380).

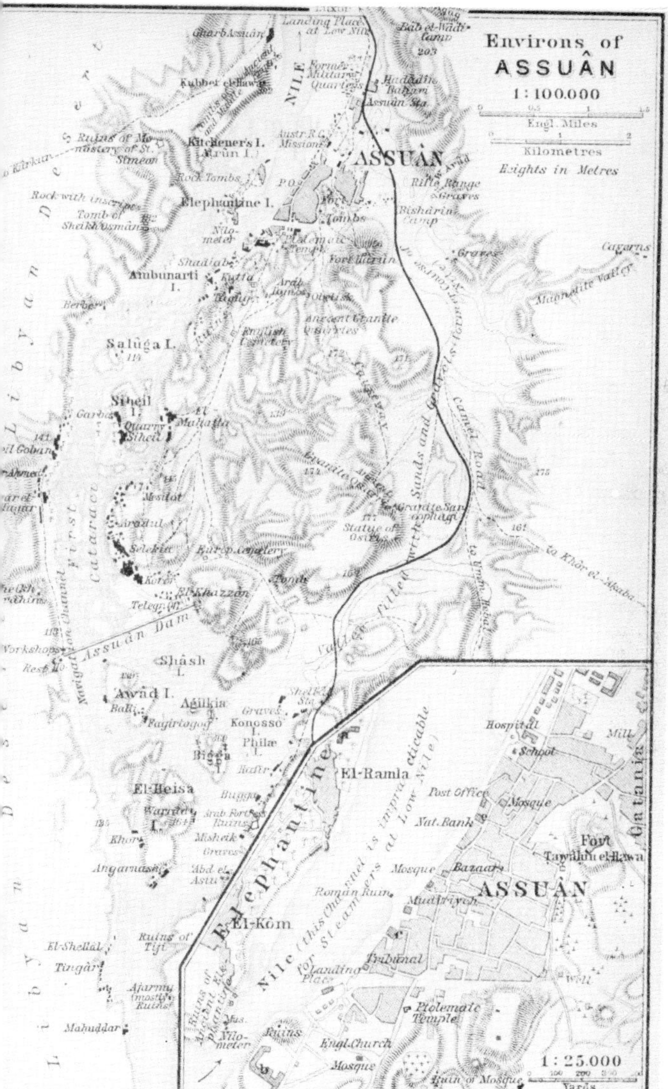

Geograph. Establ. Wagner & Debes Leipzig

Photographs (films developed; also photographic materials, books, etc.): *Bishareen Bazaar* (Aram Sempad); *MacGillivray*, next to the Grand Hotel; *Nile Photo Store* (Ibrahim Bros.), at the German Mission (p. 380); *Royal Photo-Book Stores* (P. Gondopoulo), at the Grand Hotel.

Golf Course (9 holes), near the Assuân Camp Hotel (comp. p. 378). — *Racecourse*, see p. 381.

Nubian and Sudanese Articles are everywhere offered for sale: silver rings and armlets, dervishes' weapons (mostly, however, manufactured in Aswân or in Europe), amulets, horns, panther-skins (generally poor and dear), basket-work, etc. — Persian and Indian Embroideries are sold by *Dhanamall Chellaram* and *Pohoomull*, both on the quay. — Oriental Wares: *Leon Gani*, at the Old Tribunal, on the quay; *Bishareen Bazaar* (see above); *Assuan Art Gallery* (G. Léon), Shâri el-Manshîya, at the entrance to the bazaars.

Guides. *Muhammed Sherqâwi* and *Ahmad 'Abd el-Maula* are good and reliable dragomans (for Nubia and the Sûdân also).

Plan of Visit. 1st Day. *Rock Tombs* on the W. bank (p. 384) and the island of *Elephantine* and *Aswân Museum* (p. 383; steamer passengers may use the afternoon of the day of arrival for the visit to these); in the afternoon, the *Granite Quarries*, with the great *Obelisk* (p. 381), and Aswân and its *Bazaars*. — 2nd Day. Island of *Philae* (p. 390) and the *Nile Dam* (p. 396). — 3rd Day. Excursion to the *Monastery of St. Simeon* (p. 386; 1/2 day), or a ride in the desert. — The excursion to the *Temple of Kôm Ombo* (p. 374), including a visit to the market of *Darâw* (p. 363), takes a day; by motor-boat, see p. 378.

Aswân, *Assuân*, or *Assouan* (Greek *Syene*, Coptic *Suan*), a clean town of 16,366 inhab., is the capital of the province of Aswân, the southernmost of Upper Egypt, which has an area of 363 sq. M. and extends S. from Isna to the frontier of the Anglo-Egyptian Sûdân (p. 441). The once considerable trade in the products of the Sûdân and Abyssinia has almost entirely ceased since the Mahdist revolt and the construction of the railway to Port Sudan. Aswân lies on the E. bank, partly on the plain and partly on a hill, in N. Lat. 24° 5′. The fertile strip here is narrow, but supports numerous date-palms, the fruit of which enjoys a high reputation. The Nile divides into several arms, separated by granite rocks and islands, the largest of which is Elephantine (p. 382). The horizon on the W. is bounded by the Libyan hills, on the E. by the Arabian mountains. On account of its charming situation and its equable and dry climate Aswân is in great favour as a health resort, especially from Nov. to Feb. or even later (comp. p. lxxx). The constellation of the Southern Cross is visible here in Jan. about 3 a.m. and in April about 10 p.m.

History. The district around the modern Aswân, including the island of Elephantine, bore in antiquity the name of *Yēbu*, or 'Elephant Land', probably because the Egyptians here first saw the African elephant. At a later date that name was restricted to the island and town of Elephantine. From the erection of the Pyramids to the Roman period the ancient Egyptians found material for their great temples and statues in the quarries of Yēbu (Syene), which yielded fine coloured granite, containing a large proportion of translucent quartz, yellow or brick-red feldspar, and black mica. Curiously enough, however, the term 'syenite', which was used by Pliny, is now applied by geologists to a different variety of stone, containing a much larger proportion of hornblende. Strategically, Yēbu commanded the Nile cataracts and the waterways between Egypt and Nubia. It was also the starting-point of the great caravan routes leading to Nubia and the Sûdân, along which passed the earliest commercial and military

expeditions of the Egyptians. The ancient capital of the province was likewise named Yēbu and lay on the S. side of the island (p. 383). The existence here of a Jewish military colony, with a temple of Jehovah, in the 6th and 5th cent. B.C. has been proved by the discovery in 1906-8 of a large number of Aramaic papyri (now mostly in Berlin).

Another town, named *Swĕnet*, the *Syene* of the Greeks, was situated on the E. bank of the Nile, but appears not to have attained any great importance until a late period. *Juvenal*, the Latin satiric poet, who lived at the beginning of the 2nd cent. of our era, was appointed prefect of the garrison at Syene, or, in other words, was banished to the most remote frontier of the empire, as a punishment for his biting attacks on the court. A famous curiosity of ancient Syene was a well, into which, at midday during the summer solstice, the sun's rays descended perpendicularly, casting no shadow, thus proving that Syene was situated under the tropic (which, however, has now shifted somewhat to the S.). The report of its existence led the learned Athenian *Eratosthenes* (276-196 B.C.), attached to the Museum at Alexandria (p. 14), to the discovery of the method of measuring the size of the earth that is still employed. — The place suffered greatly at the hands of the Blemmyes (p. 413), but became the seat of a Christian bishop, and appears to have rapidly regained its prosperity under the Caliphs. Arab authors record that no fewer than 20,000 inhabitants died of the plague at one time, a fact that points to a very large total population. After the close of the 12th cent. Aswân suffered severely from the incursions of plundering Arab tribes, finally put a stop to by a Turkish garrison stationed here by the sultan Selîm, after the conquest of Egypt in 1517.

The railway station lies to the N. of the town. From the landing-place of the steamers the attractive riverside street, Shâriʿ el-Manshîya, leads N. along the Nile to ($2^1/_4$ M.) the Ghezireh Palace Hotel, passing the principal public buildings, the Summary Tribunal, the German Sûdân Pioneer Mission, the Grand Hotel (beside a rock with inscriptions), and the mudîrîya or government buildings. Opposite the last a ruined building, for which stones of earlier structures were used, projects into the river. This, known to the Arabs as *El-Ḥammâm* (bath) and as the Bath of Cleopatra, probably dates from the Roman period and was perhaps a lock or a bridge-head. Farther on rises the lofty minaret of the chief mosque, beside which the Shâriʿ el-Maḥkama diverges on the right for the bazaars; then, as we descend the river, we pass the police station (markaz), the National Bank, the St. James Hotel, the post office, the government hospital, the flourishing trade school, and the Roman Catholic church, with the school of the Catholic Sûdân Mission. Across the river appears the hill with the rock-tombs and the Qubbet el-Hawa (p. 386). In the highly picturesque inner town are the large Coptic church and the Coptic school. A hill at the S. end of the Shâriʿ el-Manshîya (see above) is laid out with beautiful gardens, and on it are ruins (Qaṣr Mulla), perhaps of a convent. Opposite, on the E. side of the road, stands the *English Church*, built in 1899-1900 from a design by Somers Clarke in the style of a Coptic church, with a dome. The font was a gift of Queen Victoria. Farther on is the Cataract Hotel (p. 378). The Shâriʿ esh-Shellâl, which diverges E. (l.) near the ruins, forks after about 300 yds.: the broad road on the right (S.) leads to the Nile Dam (comp. p. 389), while the left (N.) branch leads in a few minutes to a small

Ptolemaic Temple (open to holders of the general admission ticket, p. 212). Built by Euergetes I. (p. cxi) and Philopator (p. cxii) but never completed, the temple was dedicated to Isis of Syene.

The Main Portal is crowned with a cavetto cornice. *Left Jamb:* above, Euergetes presenting an image of Maat to Amun; below, Euergetes making a libation of milk to a goddess. *Right Jamb:* above, Euergetes before Min-Amun, and before Mut and Isis. *Lintel:* Euergetes, in one case accompanied by his wife Berenice, before various deities. In the *Doorway* to the right, the king before Thoth; to the left, the king before Harsiēsis; above is an inscription. — The Interior consists of a hall with two pillars, in which stand the bases of several statues and sacred boats, and of three chapels, the middle one of which has on its rear wall reliefs showing Euergetes (once accompanied by Berenice) before the deities of Syene.

To the E. of the Cataract Hotel, on a granite rock below a Roman stone wall on which stands a modern house, is an inscription of the reign of Amenophis IV.: to the right is Men, 'superintendent of works', before Amenophis III.; to the left is Men's son Bek, chief architect at ʿAmârna (p. 245), before Amenophis IV. (defaced), upon whom the sun's rays descend.

On the hill above the Cataract Hotel to the S. is *Fort Tâgûg (Tâqûq)* or *Gamalîya*, used as the barracks of the Camel Corps. A beautiful view is enjoyed thence, especially towards evening. Visitors should prolong their walk along the hill, to the S., for the sake of the views of the Nile valley, the islands, and the dam, and descend, to the right, to the village of *El-Maḥaṭṭa* (p. 389).

A ride (donkey, carriage, or motor-car) may be taken to the *Market* (market-day Thurs.) and the *Camp of the Bishârîn*, situated within an Arab cemetery, 3/4 M. to the E. of the town. These Beduin live with their families in wretched tents covered with mats (comp. p. 363). — Between the camp and the Assuan Camp Hotel is the *Racecourse* of the Assuan Sporting Club (race-meetings weekly during the season, including interesting donkey and camel races). — A fine *View is commanded by the *Tomb of Sheikh Hârûn*, above the camp, to the right. Close by is an ancient fort.

We may return viâ the old *Arab Cemeteries*, which are situated in the desert to the S. of the town and may be reached viâ the Shâriʿ esh-Shellâl (p. 380). Each grave is marked by a rectangle of unhewn stones. The tombs of the richer dead are small domed erections. At the top is a sheikh's tomb.

On the hills to the right of the road are some large mosque-like *Cenotaphs* of famous saints, such as the Sheikh Maḥmûd, the Sheikh ʿAli, the Lady (Es-Saiyida) Zeinab, etc., whose memory is celebrated by festivals on their birthdays (mûlid), etc. The domed 12th cent. tomb of *El-Arbaʿîn*, i.e. 'the forty' (martyrs), is noteworthy.

The **Granite Quarries** (Arabic *Maḥâgir*), from which the ancient Egyptian builders and sculptors drew their supplies (comp. p. 379), are situated in the hills to the S., and may be reached in 1/4 hr. from the town by a route viâ the Arab cemeteries (see above) and then E., past a grove of tamarisks. In the N. quarry is an unfinished **Obelisk*, 137 ft. long and 13 3/4 ft. thick at its broader end, which, had it been completed, would have weighed 1168 tons. Around the obelisk is a trench 2 1/2 ft. wide, dividing it from the surrounding rocks. The

moderately lofty cliffs show manifold traces of the industry of the ancient stone-cutters. The blocks were detached from the cliffs by boring numerous holes along a prescribed line, driving wooden wedges into these, and then wetting the wedges. Statues, sarcophagi, obelisks, etc., were roughly dressed by the stone-cutters in the quarries in order to lessen the weight for transport. The hill above the obelisk commands a wide prospect, including the monastery of St. Simeon (p. 386) in a desert valley, to the W., beyond the Nile. A massive *Causeway*, by which the huge blocks were conveyed to the Nile, runs from the N. quarry to Aswân and is used to this day.

From the N. quarry we follow the causeway, which first crosses the mountain (fine view), then descends into a picturesque valley, and finally runs along on a level to (3/4 hr.) the S. quarry, which opens to the E., facing the desert. This also contains rough-hewn blocks ready for removal. On a rock here may be seen an inscription with the name of Amenophis III., though the name and figure of the stone-cutter who carved it have been obliterated. Beside it two trough-shaped sarcophagi have been begun (in the Ptolemaic or Roman period); and in the vicinity are the unfinished colossus of a king (covered, except the feet, with sand) and a large quadrangular block, perhaps intended for the shrine of a god. About 5 min. farther on, on the hill above the wide valley traversed by the railway to Shellâl, is a figure of Osiris (called Ramses by the natives), about 20 ft. in height, with crown and beard and with folded arms. This point commands a fine view of the desert and in the direction of Philæ.

If we follow the railway-line we reach in 1/4 hr. the cattle-yards where cattle imported from the Sûdân are inspected before being despatched to Egypt. Farther on is the railway station of Shellâl (p. 389). — If we diverge to the right at the cattle-yards, we pass through the village of Shellâl, skirting the ancient brick wall (p. 389), and in 1/4 hr. reach the village of Khazzân and the dam (p. 396).

The verdant island of **Elephantine**, with its luxuriant palm trees, attracts all travellers. The Arabs call it merely *El-Gezîra*, 'the island', or *Gezîret Aswân*. It is reached by rowing boat (return fare P.T. 5). The entire visit takes barely an hour (2 hrs. including the museum). There are two villages on the island, whose inhabitants speak Nubian (p. lxii).

Close to the landing-stage, on the E. side of the island, facing Aswân, is a stone staircase leading to the ***Nilometer** (*Miqyâs;* comp. p. 112). After more than a thousand years of neglect it was restored to use in 1870 in the reign of Khedive Ismâ'îl, as is recorded by French and Arabic inscriptions. On the walls of the staircase are damaged Greek inscriptions of the Roman epoch, giving the water-levels. The scales date from the later Roman period, and the ells

are marked in Greek (and also in demotic) characters. The new scale is inscribed on marble tablets.

Strabo's description is not yet antiquated: "The Nilometer is a well built of regular hewn stones, on the bank of the Nile, in which is recorded the rise of the stream, not only the maximum but also the minimum and average rise, for the water in the well rises and falls with the stream. On the side of the well are marks, measuring the height sufficient for the irrigation and the other water levels. These are observed and published for general information. . . . This is of importance to the peasants for the management of the water, the embankments, the canals, etc., and to the officials on account of the taxes. For the higher the rise of water, the higher are the taxes."

Near the staircase leading to the nilometer, in a pretty garden, is the **Aswân Museum** (open 9-4, closed on Fri. and holidays; adm. P.T. 5). It contains an interesting collection of antiquities, mostly found in Lower Nubia and affording a good idea of the stage of civilization attained in the district.

ENTRANCE HALL. Mummy of a sacred ram (p. 384); Egyptian, Greek, and Coptic tombstones and tables of offerings, one with a Meroïtic inscription (p. cxxxviii). — We turn to the left and pass through Room 2 to reach ROOM 1. Prehistoric antiquities (4000-3200 B.C.). *Case A:* Red polished black-topped pots; pale jugs with dark-red paintings (ships, men, animals); hand-wrought stone vessels. *Frame B:* Slate palettes for cosmetics. *Show Case C:* Combs, bodkins, and needles of bone; club-heads; flint knives and arrow-heads; two palettes for cosmetics. *Case D:* Chains, amulets, and cylindrical seals. — ROOM 2. Ancient Empire (c. 3200-2270 B.C.). *Case E:* Pottery. *Case F:* Copper weapons and tools; pear-shaped club-heads; skull with a healed fracture; clay doll; ostriches' eggs inscribed with figures of animals. *Case G* (by the window): Porphyry dish; bead chains and bracelets. — We pass through the entrance hall to enter ROOM 3. Middle and New Empires (2100-1500 B.C.). *Case H:* Earthenware vases, including red and black polished ware with incised patterns filled in in white; quartz bracelets; crude figures of women and cattle. *Case I:* Finds from tombs of the New Empire, quite similar to those from Egypt; alabaster vessels; boxes for cosmetics; small mummy-masks of painted plaster, which were fastened to the wrappings; earthenware; Mycenæan false-necked amphora; set of draughts in blue faience. *Case J:* Mirrors, daggers, knife of copper and bronze. *Case K* (by the window): Chains, rings, amulets; small steatite stele with a representation of Amun as a ram. *Case L:* Scarabæi. — ROOM 4. Late Period. *Cases O* and *P:* Mummies of the Ptolemaic era with coloured cartonnages. *Cases Q* and *R:* Mummies of a priest and priestess of Isis of Philæ. *Case M:* Bronze vessels and lance-heads; heavy bronze armlets; Meroïtic glass vessels with incised patterns. *Case N:* Nubian pottery of the late-Roman period (c. A.D. 400); bead chains; earthenware censer and small bronze incense-burner from a Christian church at El-Maḍîq (p. 424).

Farther S., opposite the Cataract Hotel, lies a massive ancient *Embankment*, many of the blocks in which were taken from earlier edifices and bear inscriptions. The rock-inscriptions close to the stream should be noticed also (the large ones bear the name of Psammetichos).

The entire S. part of the island is covered with great mounds of rubbish formed by the ruins of the ancient **Town of Elephantine.** Among some brick walls a few paces W. of the quay we may distinguish the foundations of a small temple, constructed with stones brought from earlier edifices, including drums of columns and blocks with the cartouches of Thutmosis III., Ramses III., and

other monarchs. From an inscription on the solitary stump of a column now standing we learn that Trajan (p. cxv) was the builder. About 50 paces W. a granite portal, once the entrance to a large temple, dominates all this part of the island. The reliefs upon it show Alexander II. (p. cxiii) sacrificing to the ram-headed Khnum and other deities of Elephantine. Inscribed blocks and sculptured fragments lie scattered about. On a wall still standing is represented the emperor, followed by Nile-gods, sacrificing to Khnum; the faces of the emperor and the god have been mutilated. Close by is the necropolis of the sacred rams, whose sarcophagi are still to be seen (mummies, see p. 383). Various other buildings, seen and described by the French Expedition (p. 136), were pulled down about the beginning of the 19th century. Among these were temples built by Amenophis III. and Thutmosis III.

The higher parts of the island, especially a granite promontory on the W. bank, command a *View of the black and brown, rough and smooth rocks of the cataract, among which the Nile flows.

The trip round the island by small boat, which takes about 1 hr. (fare P.T. 10 per person), is full of interest. On an islet, about 550 yds. S., not far from the right bank of the Nile, are several smoothly polished and cylindrical 'pot-holes', caused by the action of high water. — The island between Elephantine and the W. bank, named *El-Aṭrûn* or *Kitchener's Island*, formerly belonged to Lord Kitchener and is now the property of the government. It is covered with palms, bananas, oleanders, pomegranates, and roses.

On the W. bank, to the N. of Elephantine, rises a hill, crowned with the sheikh's tomb (p. 386), in which are the ***Rock Tombs** of the princes and grandees of Elephantine (by boat P.T. 10 per person there and back; general admission tickets should not be forgotten). These, which were opened in 1885-86 by Lord Grenfell, date from the close of the Ancient Empire and from the Middle Empire and are therefore contemporary with the tombs at Beniḥasan (p. 241), which they resemble both in construction and decoration. The view from the tombs is fine.

From the landing-place we ascend a sandy path, which reaches the top at Tomb 31. The ancient staircases, hewn in the rock and consisting of two parallel flights of steps with an inclined plane between them up which the sarcophagi were drawn, are more fatiguing; they reach the top at Tombs 25 and 26.

We begin with Tomb 25, belonging to **Mekhu**. This dates from the 6th Dyn. (p. ciii), and both its construction and its decoration are somewhat crude. It contains eighteen roughly worked columns in three rows. Between two columns opposite the entrance is a stone table with three legs, which was perhaps used as an altar. On the rear wall, opposite the entrance, is a false door within a recess

approached by steps and closed by a stone screen. The representations on the walls and columns show the deceased receiving various offerings. To the right of the entrance sacrifices are being made to the deceased; to the left of this are agricultural scenes (ploughing; harvest; asses bringing home the harvest). — Adjoining is Tomb 26, belonging to **Sabni**, son of Mekhu. The remarkable entrance (now walled up) is divided by a cross-beam into two parts. In front are two small obelisks and sacrificial basins. The tomb-chamber contains fourteen square pillars. The *Rear Wall* represents the deceased in a boat, accompanied by his daughters, hunting in the marshes: to the left he appears holding the throw-stick in one hand and the slain birds in the other; to the right he harpoons two fish at a blow; in the middle is a papyrus thicket with birds fluttering about it.

Climbing up to the right (N.) from this double tomb we pass several others (Nos. 27, 29, 30), which are sanded up. — No. 28 (locked) is that of **Heke-yeb**. In the small chamber is a representation of the deceased as a Nubian with a curious curled wig and a dark-brown skin.

*No. 31, the tomb of **Si-renpowet**, son of Satet-hotep, and a prince under Amenemmēs II., is one of the largest and best-preserved. Beyond a narrow *Passage* follow an undecorated pillared *Hall*, in which, on the right, is the fine granite table of offerings, and then a *Corridor* with three recesses on each side. Each of these recesses contains a statue (chiselled out of the rock) of the deceased in the guise of the Osiris mummy. To the left of the first recess is a painted figure of the deceased (colours excellently preserved), followed by his son. At the end of the corridor is a small *Hall*, with four pillars, on each of which appears the deceased. The lines dividing the scene into squares for the guidance of the artist's hand may still be seen in several of these designs. At the back of this hall opens a *Recess* with good paintings on stucco and delicately executed hieroglyphics. On the back wall of the recess the deceased is shown at table, with his son before him carrying flowers; on the right wall the mother of the deceased sits at table, the deceased standing to the right; on the left wall is the deceased with his wife and his son.

Farther on are the tombs of *Aku* (No. 32), *Khuy* (sanded up), and *Khunes*. The first contains a recess with a representation of the deceased and his wife seated at a meal in an arbour, with their son before them. On the left wall of the eight-pillared hall of the tomb of Khunes are representations of Egyptian craftsmen: bakers, potters, metal-workers beside a furnace, brewers, leather-workers, etc. The two last-named tombs were used as dwellings by Coptic monks (comp. p. clxxxviii), who have added various inscriptions. — Then follow the tombs of *Khenusew* and of **Harkhuf**. The latter has inscriptions of historical importance outside the tomb, on each side of the entrance, above and beside figures of the deceased (to the left, Harkhuf leaning on a staff with his son holding a censer in front of him).

The inscriptions form an extract from the biography of Harkhuf, recording especially four successful trading expeditions to Nubia, three of which were made in the reign of Methusuphis (Merenrē, 6th Dyn., p. ciii) and one in that of Phiops II. (Nefer-ke-rē). Among the goods brought back on the fourth journey was a dwarf.

Adjoining is the small tomb of **Pyopi-nakht** (No. 35; sanded up), with inscriptions on each side of the doorway. These extol the exploits of the deceased in the campaigns led by King Nefer-ke-rē (Phiops II.) against Nubia and the Beduin dwelling to the E. of Egypt. Farther on are the grave of *Senmose* and finally the interesting tomb (*No. 36) of **Si-renpowet**, son of Sat-tjeni, who flourished in the reign of Sesostris I. (12th Dyn.). A doorway of fine limestone, with portraits of the deceased, admits to the *Court.* The shafts of the six pillars, which here supported the roof of a colonnade, bear inscriptions and figures of the deceased. On the *Back Wall*, to the left of the door, is a large figure of the deceased followed by his sandal-bearer and two dogs; cattle are being brought to him (notice the enraged bulls); he appears in a boat spearing fish. To the right of the door is a large figure of the deceased followed by his bow-bearer, a dog, and his three sons. Above, the deceased is shown seated in a colonnade, with four women with flowers in front of him; below are a woman and two men gambling. The mural paintings on stucco in the first pillared hall are badly injured. A vaulted corridor, now shut off by a modern wall, leads hence to a second *Hall* with pillars and a recess.

Farther N. is the tomb of *Ka-kem-kaw*, discovered by Lady William Cecil in 1902 and dating from the time of Amenophis III. It has superb ceiling-paintings (birds on the wing; spirals with bulls' heads) and on the pillars is represented the deceased before the gods of the dead (Osiris, etc.). — On the way down to the river-bank we pass several more small tombs. Above the tombs are the remains of a Coptic convent.

The summit of the hill, which, however, is not reached without some difficulty, is crowned by the *Qubbet el-Hawa*, the small tomb of a sheikh. It commands a *View (especially fine by full moon) of the Nile valley, the district of the cataracts, and the desert. — From this point we may reach the monastery of St. Simeon (see below) in 40 min., by a route leading S.S.W.

The ruined ***Monastery of St. Simeon** *(Deir Amba Samaʿân,* usually called *Deir Amba Hadra)* is situated on a hill in the desert on the W. bank of the Nile. Landing opposite the S. end of Elephantine, we follow a valley, and in 20 min. reach our goal. This is one of the largest and best-preserved Coptic buildings in existence (p. cxc). It was founded in the 7th cent. and has been deserted since the 13th. The buildings, erected on a doubly terraced rock-platform, are surrounded by a ring-wall 20-23 ft. high, the lower part of which is built

of rough stone, the upper part of crude bricks; the lower W. portion is hewn out of the rock.

We enter the buildings of the lower stage (excavated and restored in 1925-26 by Professor U. Monneret de Villard, head of the Italian Archæological Mission) by a tower on the E. and reach the *Forecourt*. On the left is a gate-keeper's room; on the right, a large stone bench (maṣṭaba) which served as sleeping quarters for pilgrims. Adjoining the court on the S. is the **Church**, an aisled basilica. The wide nave was formerly roofed with two domes, and the large *Apse* at its E. end has three rectangular niches covered with half-domes. In the central niche is a damaged fresco of Christ enthroned among the angels. The rooms on either side of the apse contain Coptic inscriptions. Behind is the baptistery. The smaller apse at the W. end of the nave likewise contains remains of frescoes. A small door at the W. end of the N. aisle leads to a small *Rock Chapel*, with fine ceiling-designs (8th cent.) and a niche with six medallions of saints. To the N. and W. of the church are outbuildings and small caves, and there is a tomb built up against its S. side. The court to the S.E. is adjoined by bedrooms (each with three beds) and other rooms with barrel-vaulting.

A flight of stone steps to the N.W. of the church leads to the upper stage, which is $16^1/_2$ ft. higher. Here we find the *Living Quarters (Qaṣr)*, a large three-storied building. The two lower floors are well preserved. On each floor is a large vaulted central corridor, adjoined on either side by the monks' cells with their brick couches. On the walls are Coptic and Arabic inscriptions. Near the living quarters are numerous *Outbuildings* (mill, bake-house, oil and wine presses, store-rooms, bath), some in a very ruinous state, and a small domed chapel. — The house of the Archæological Mission, to the S. of the monastery, commands a splendid view of Aswân and the desert.

From the monastery we may, if time permit, go S. along the ridge to ($^1/_2$ hr.) two high *Cliffs*, one of which, looking from the Cataract Hotel like a gigantic pig, is covered with inscriptions. In 10 min. more we reach a hill of dark stone, which affords a superb *View of the cataract district, extending S. to Philæ and N. to the island of Bahrîf (p. 388). A similar view is obtained from the tomb of *Sheikh ʿOsmân*. — The direct route from the monastery to the Nile passes an extensive cemetery, on a plateau strewn with dark stones. On the river-bank are numerous rock-tombs.

Another very interesting excursion may be made through the Western Desert to the **Quarries** to the N. of the Monastery of St. Simeon (there and back 2 hrs.). From the rock-tombs (p. 384) we follow a route, indicated by heaps of stones, which runs N. to a *Sandstone Quarry*, still containing the upper part of an obelisk with a representation and inscription of Sethos I. We return viâ the village

of *Gharb Aswân* (West Aswân) to the landing-stage at the rock-tombs (p. 384).

A favourite afternoon excursion is N. from the Ghezireh Palace Hotel to the so-called *Alabaster Hill*, marking the site of an ancient quartz-quarry, whence the Egyptians obtained the necessary material for polishing hard stone. Near the hill to the N. of this point (with rock-inscriptions of various dates) opens the Wâdi Abu Agag (see below), running thence to the E.

In addition to the trip mentioned on p. 384, pleasant afternoon trips may be made by Boat from Aswân to the Nile islands of the cataract district (Siheil, etc.; p. 389), and downstream past the palm and orange groves of (2½ M.) *Nag' esh-Shîma* to the (5 M.) island of *Bahrîf* (p. 365). On the N. end of the latter (1¼ M. farther) is a pavilion where visitors are accustomed to make the tea they have brought with them.

In the case of a longer stay visits may be paid to the highly picturesque valleys of the Arabian and Libyan deserts, which debouch in the neighbourhood of Aswân. These excursions are made by camel.

Short Excursions. 1. To the *Khôr el-'Aqaba*, S.E. of the ancient quarries, 3 hrs. there and back. — 2. To the E. by the *Wâdi Arûd* as far as the top of the plateau (views; the Gebel Garra, see below, is visible to the W. beyond the Nile), and back to the N.W. through the *Wâdi Abu Agag* (see above; ½ day). — 3. From the Qubbet el-Hawa (p. 386) S.W. along the picturesque hills on the W. bank to the dam (p. 396), 4 hrs. The camels should be sent on the night before to the Qubbet el-Hawa.

Longer Excursions. 1. Through the E. desert to the well of *Umm Hebal*, about 25 M. to the S.S.E.; 4-5 days there and back. As the way lies through the territory of the Bishârîn (pp. 363, 381), a member of that tribe should be selected as guide. From Shellâl (p. 389) we proceed to the S.E. through the *Wâdi Duëra*, then follow the *Wâdi Barâmram* past the conspicuous sharp ridge of *Gebel Kurtunos* (1200 ft.; on the left), and in 11-12 hrs. (from Shellâl) reach the well of *El-Muelha*, in the wide and pleasant *Wâdi Dimhîd (Dihmît)*. Thence we lay a S.E. course through the *Wâdi Umm Hebal* to the (7 hrs.) well of *Umm Hebal*. A longer (3 days) but more picturesque route leads S.E. from the Wâdi Abu Agag (see above) or the Wâdi Arûd (see above) through the *Wâdi el-Hûdi*, which merges into the broad *Wâdi el-'Arab* at an abandoned gold-mine; and thence by the winding *Wâdi Umm Hebal* to the (18 hrs. from Aswân) well of Umm Hebal. — 2. Through the Libyan desert to the (38½ M.) uninhabited *Oasis of Kurkur* (1050 ft.; numerous fossils), 4-5 days there and back. The route leads W.S.W. from the Qubbet el-Hawa (comp. above). After about 21 M. it passes 2¾ M. to the left of the conspicuous *Gebel Garra* (1770 ft.; wide views), and after 16 M. more it surmounts the hill of *Gebel Kurkur* (1225 ft.), behind which lies the oasis. Comp. *John Ball's* 'Jebel Garra and the Oasis of Kurkur' (with maps; Cairo, Survey Department, 1902; P.T. 15).

Excursion to Philæ and the Nile Dam.

Many travellers to Philæ avail themselves (for the outward journey at least) of the Railway to Shellâl (6¼ M. in ¼-½ hr.; fares P.T. 7, 4, 2). But the Desert Route is preferable (1 hr.; motor-cars and carriages, see p. 378; donkey there and back P.T. 8, including a 2 hrs.' wait), whether we follow it throughout or diverge from it to follow the river for part of the way. The best way to return is to arrange to take a boat from Philæ to the Nile Dam (fare from Shellâl station to the island and thence to the dam, P.T. 10 each person) and have a motor-car to meet us there for the return to El-Khazzân (p. 389). Or we may go on from the dam in another boat

through the cataracts to Aswân (fare P.T. 20 each pers.). — Provisions and tickets of admission must be taken.

The Railway (station, see p. 378) runs through the desert in a wide curve round the ancient granite quarries (p. 381) and ends at the station of *Shellâl* (see below).

The Desert Route diverges from the Shâriʿ esh-Shellâl (p. 380) and follows the broad road described by Strabo, who assigns it a length of fifty stadia. Beside the road lie large blocks of granite, with ancient inscriptions carved by Egyptian officials, now numbered in white. On the right are the British and Arab cemeteries. About 1/2 M. beyond the former is a ravine (telegraph-line) diverging towards the village of *El-Maḥaṭṭa* (see below). Farther on we reach the golf-course (where the direct route to Shellâl diverges) and after 1/2 hr. the outskirts of the village of *El-Khazzân*. Here our route forks: left for Shellâl (see below); straight on an avenue of lebbakh-trees (p. lxxvii) leads in a few minutes through the village, with its pretty bungalows and gardens, to the dam. Thence to Shellâl, see below.

A Shorter Route diverges at the golf-course and follows the railway (disused) constructed for the transport of building material for the dam. We skirt the remains of an ancient *Brick Wall*, which was erected, perhaps as early as the Middle Empire, to protect the Nile traffic against the predatory attacks of the tribes of the E. desert. The wall is 6 1/2 ft. thick and, at places, 13-20 ft. high, and consists of two faces of bricks filled up with pieces of granite. It leads as far as *Shellâl* (see below).

The Riverside Route leads from the Cataract Hotel viâ Fort Tâgûg (on the hill; p. 381) to the village of *El-Maḥaṭṭa*, opposite the island of Siheil.

The island of **Siheil** (*Seheil*), reached from Aswân by boat (p. 388), was dedicated to Anuket, and contains over two hundred rock-inscriptions, besides the ruins of two temples. One of the temples, near the village of Siheil on the W. side of the island, dates from the 18th Dyn., the other (to the S.) from the reign of Ptolemy Philopator (p. cxii). High up on the S.E. rocks of the island is an important inscription of the Ptolemaic period, recording that in the reign of the primæval King Djoser (p. 156) the Nile failed to rise during a period of seven years and that a famine arose in the land in consequence.

The view of the stream with its numerous dark-coloured granite rocks, covered with a smooth glaze, like enamel, is very fine, although the foaming rapids of the *Great Cataract* are now things of the past. — From El-Maḥaṭṭa the route leads through the dirty village of *Korôr (El-Kurûr)*, wedged in among the granite rocks. It then passes the hamlet of *El-Khazzân* and then again turns E., passing a cemetery for Christian workmen, and joins the desert route (see above) at the tomb of a sheikh, near the ancient brick wall.

The village of *Shellâl* (*Esh-Shallâl*, 'the cataract'), where both the railway and the desert route end, lies on the E. bank of the Nile, opposite Philæ. Good ferry-boats are in waiting (P. T. 5 there and back).

The Island of Philæ.

Philae, once the 'pearl of Egypt', is 500 yds. in length and 160 yds. in breadth, and consists of a crystalline granite mixed with hornblende, beneath the alluvial deposits of the Nile. The modern name is borrowed from the Greeks, and is derived from the ancient Egyptian *Pi-lak*. The Copts called it *Pilakh*, i.e. 'the corner', and the Arabs used to call it *Bilâq*.

Nowadays the island is called *El-Qaṣr* or *Gezîret Anas el-Wogûd*, after the hero of one of the tales in the Thousand and One Nights, which has its scene transferred to Philæ in the Egyptian version. The name *Philae* is known to the natives only through its use by tourists.

Herodotus, who visited Elephantine c. 450 B.C., makes no mention of Philæ. The first reference to it dates from the reign of Nektanebis I. (c. 370 B.C.), to which the oldest temple buildings on the island belong. But there is little doubt that it was inhabited and adorned with temples at an earlier period than that.

The chief deity of Philæ was the goddess *Isis;* but *Osiris* and *Nephthys*, *Hathor* (p. 395), *Khnum* and *Satet*, the gods of the cataracts, and other deities were likewise worshipped here. The imposing buildings which still survive were erected by the Ptolemies during the last two centuries B.C. and by the Roman emperors during the first three Christian centuries. Numerous inscriptions inform us that Greek and Roman pilgrims flocked in crowds to the shrine of the mysterious, benign, and healing goddess Isis. We know also that the goddess of Philæ was worshipped by the predatory Nubians and by the Blemmyes (p. 413), and that, even after their battles with the Emperor Marcian (A.D. 451), the priests of these tribes were permitted to offer sacrifices to Isis along with the Egyptian priests, and also obtained the right of removing the miraculous image of the mighty goddess from the island at certain solemn festivals and of retaining it for some time. Even after all Egypt had long been Christianized the ancient Isis worship still held sway in Nubia. In spite of the edicts of Theodosius the temples of Philæ were not closed until the reign of Justinian (527-565), when some of their chambers were used for Christian services. After the conquest of Egypt by the Arabs Philæ embraced Islâm, but in the meantime a Coptic town had been established on the island.

The island, which formerly ranked as one of the most beautiful points in Egypt, has lost much of its charm since the construction of the Nile Dam, whereby its rich vegetation has been destroyed. It is only between August and December, when the water is allowed to flow freely through the gates of the dam and the surface regains about the same level it had before the construction of the barrier, that all the temples become accessible. The water, however, has covered the walls and columns several feet high with a layer of slime, blurring the outlines of all the reliefs and inscriptions. The further heightening of the dam (comp. p. 396) will increase the extent and period of submersion of the island.

The traveller should visit the various points in the following order, without lingering too long over any of them, if his time be limited. It is better to obtain a good general impression of the whole than to examine the details minutely.

The extensive **Outer Temple Court**, at the S.W. end of the island, is bounded on the N. by the first pylon of the Temple of Isis, on the S. by the porch of Nektanebis, and on the E. and W. by colonnades.

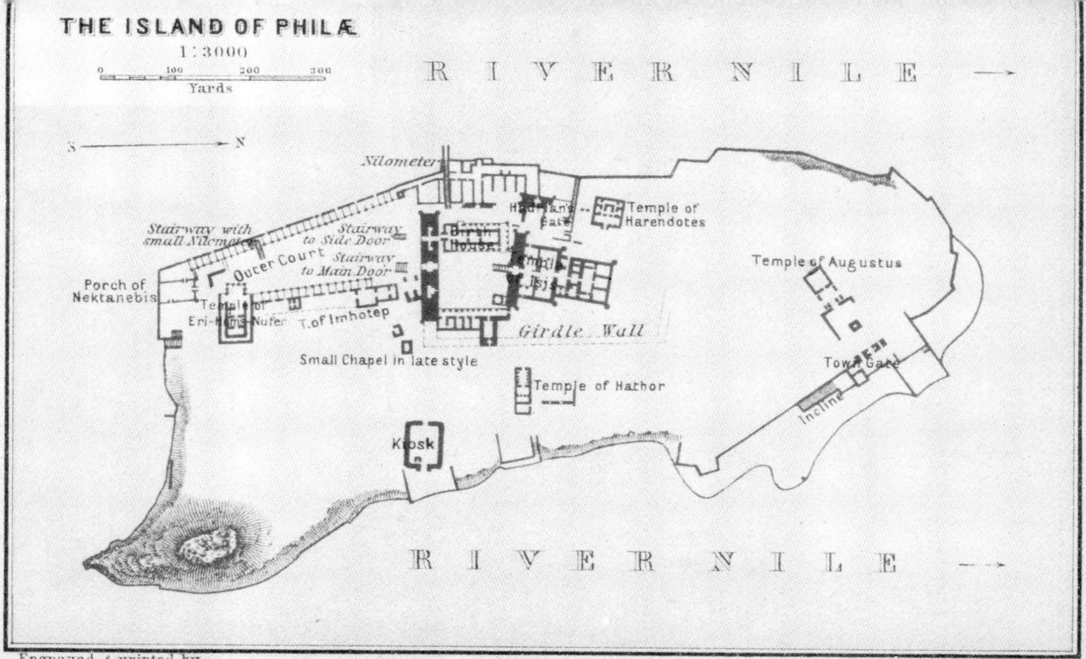

Engraved & printed by Wagner & Debes, Leipzig

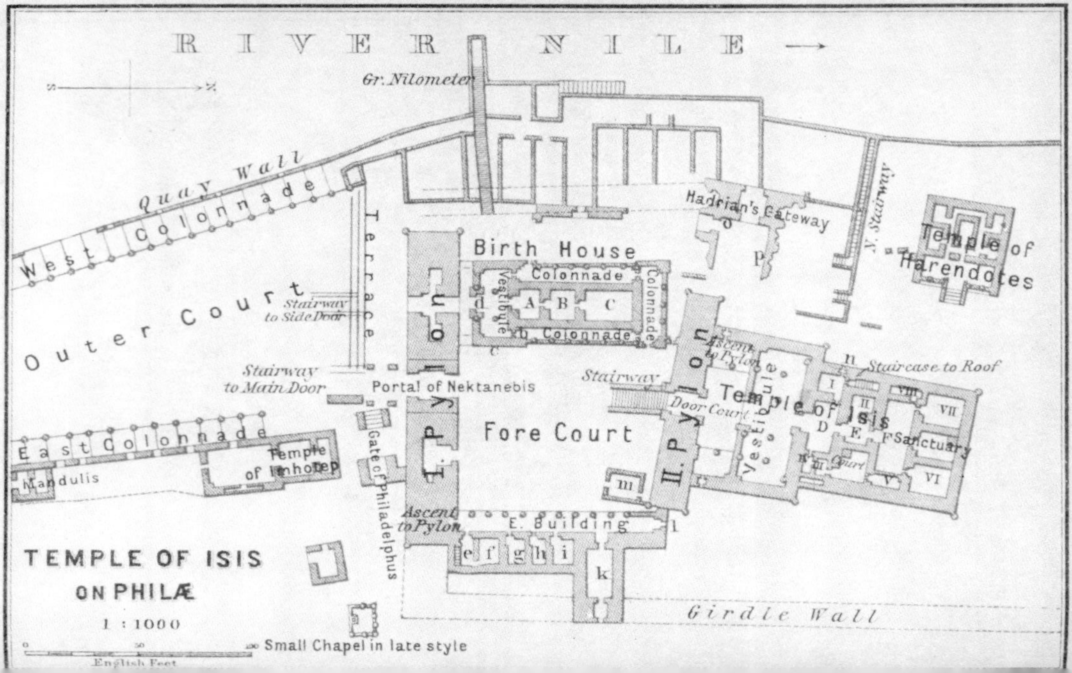

RIVER NILE
S
N
Gr. Nilometer
Quay Wall
West Colonnade
Outer Court
Terrace
Stairway to Side Door
Stairway to Main Door
Portal of Nektanebis
Birth House
Colonnade
Vestibule
A B C
I. Pylon
II. Pylon
Hadrian's Gateway
N. Stairway
Temple of Harendotes
Ascent to Pylon
Staircase to Roof
Stairway
Door Court
Temple of Isis
Vestibule
Sanctuary
Court
Fore Court
E. Building
East Colonnade
Temple of Imhotep
Mandulis
Gate of Philadelphus
Girdle Wall
TEMPLE OF ISIS
ON PHILÆ
1 : 1000
English Feet
Small Chapel in late style

This court dates from the late-Ptolemaic period or from the reign of Augustus. Fragments survive of the strong *Quay Wall* that perhaps was carried round the greater part of the island, with flights of stone steps at various points.

The PORCH OF NEKTANEBIS I. was built by Nektanebis as the entrance-hall for a temple dedicated to 'his mother Isis, revered at Abaton, mistress of Philæ, and to the Hathor of Senmet' (p. 395). The temple was swept away by the Nile shortly after its completion; but Ptolemy II. Philadelphus (p. cxi) restored the porch. The elegant little structure was supported by fourteen columns with varying floral capitals, above each of which was a second sistrum-capital. Only six of the columns are standing, and the roof has disappeared. Between the columns were stone screens, over 6 ft. in height, crowned with cavetto cornices and rows of uræus serpents, and interrupted on the E., W., and N. sides by exit-doors. These screens bore reliefs showing Nektanebis sacrificing to the gods.

Before the river front of the temple two *Obelisks* upon chest-shaped bases were erected in the Ptolemaic period. These were made of sandstone instead of the usual granite. The W. obelisk, bearing a Greek and several Arabic inscriptions, is still standing, though it has lost its apex; the E. obelisk is represented by its base only.

The WEST COLONNADE, which follows the line of the shore of the island, is 100 yds. in length and has a row of thirty-one (formerly thirty-two) plant columns, each 16 ft. high, no two capitals of which are alike. Most of the columns have reliefs showing Tiberius offering gifts to the gods. The ceiling, which is partly destroyed, is decorated with stars and flying vultures. The rear wall is embellished with two rows of bas-reliefs, representing the Pharaoh (usually Augustus or Tiberius) offering gifts to the gods. — A subterranean stairway leads outside this colonnade to a small *Nilometer*.

The EAST COLONNADE is unfinished; only six of its sixteen columns are completed, the remainder were left merely rough-hewn. The unfinished capitals should be noticed. In the back-wall are five doors, which led to various chapels.

This colonnade is adjoined at its S. end by the now very ruinous TEMPLE OF ERI-HEMS-NUFER (*Harensnuphis*, p. clvi), erected by Ptolemy IV. Philopator (p. cxii) and Ergamenes, his Nubian contemporary, and extended by Ptolemy V. Epiphanes. — Behind the central part of the colonnade lay the small CHAPEL OF MANDULIS (a Nubian deity), now in a very fragmentary condition; and at the N. end is a well-preserved little TEMPLE OF IMHOTEP (*Æsculapius;* p. clvii), built by Ptolemy II. Philadelphus.

The ***Temple of Isis**, dedicated to Isis and her son Harpocrates, was the principal sanctuary on the island and probably occupies the site of an earlier shrine. Its erection, begun by Ptolemy II. Philadelphus (p. cxi), was completed in its essential details by Euergetes I., but its embellishment with inscriptions and reliefs was a very gradual process, and at not a few points was never finished.

The **First Pylon**, 150 ft. broad and 60 ft. high, consists of two towers and a central portal, decorated by Nektanebis I. with the cus-

tomary reliefs. On the front of the right (E.) tower appears a huge figure of the Pharaoh (Ptolemy XIII. Neos Dionysos, p. cxiii) in the usual attitude, grasping a band of enemies by the hair and raising his club for the fatal stroke. To the left stand Isis, the falcon-headed Horus of Edfu, and Hathor. Above are two reliefs: to the right, the king (Neos Dionysos) presents the crown of Upper and Lower Egypt to Horus and Nephthys; to the left, he offers incense to Isis and Harpocrates. On the left (W.) tower are similar representations, and at the foot are numerous demotic and Greek inscriptions. A doorway, embellished with reliefs by Ptolemy VI. Philometor, leads through the left tower direct to the entrance of the Birth House (see below). In front of the pylon formerly stood two obelisks, erected by Euergetes II. (p. cxii), and two lions, all of granite. One of the obelisks was removed by W. J. Bankes in 1819 to Kingston Lacy, Wimborne, Dorset.

Adjoining the E. pylon-tower, to the right, is an elegant *Gateway*, which was built by Ptolemy II. Philadelphus and originally stood in a brick wall. It is embellished with reliefs of Ptolemy (on the lintel) and Tiberius (on the jambs).

The *Ascent of the Pylon is recommended. The winding staircase begins in the S.E. angle of the forecourt (see the plan, p. 391). Several unadorned and feebly lighted chambers are found within the towers. The view from the top commands the whole island and its surroundings.

We now pass through the central gateway, within which, to the right, is a French inscription ('an 7 de la république') commemorating Napoleon's Egyptian campaign and the pursuit of the Mamelukes by General Desaix in 1799.

The **Forecourt**, which we next enter, is bounded on the S. by Pylon I and on the N. by Pylon II. On the E. and W. are edifices, each with a colonnade on the side next the court.

On the W. (left) is the Birth House, dedicated to Hathor-Isis and to the memory of the birth of her son Horus (comp. pp. 266, 374). It is reached also by a doorway in the W. tower of Pylon I (see above); on the back of the pylon is a relief of four priests carrying the boat of Isis, preceded by the king burning incense. The birth house is surrounded on all four sides by colonnades, the columns of which have floral capitals surmounted by sistrum-capitals. The walls, the columns, and the stone screens between the columns are adorned with the conventional reliefs and inscriptions, mostly dating from Euergetes II., Neos Dionysos, Augustus, and Tiberius. The reliefs in the last chamber are especially interesting: Horus as a falcon in the marshes, Isis suckling Horus in the marshes of the Delta, and other scenes from the childhood of the god.

The East Building, opposite the birth house, was occupied by the priests, partly for scientific purposes. The colonnade of plant columns is very elegant. The reliefs and inscriptions date from Neos Dionysos, the votive inscription on the architrave from Euergetes II. At the N. end of the colonnade is a *Door* (Pl. *l*), approached by

several steps, opening upon the inner passage round the temple. The reliefs upon this show Neos Dionysos before the gods.

The **Second Pylon** is 105 ft. broad and 40 ft. high. The *Portal* between the towers was embellished by Euergetes II. with reliefs of the usual type. The large relief on the right (E.) tower represents the Pharaoh Neos Dionysos dedicating the slaughtered sacrificial animals to Horus and Hathor. Above are two small reliefs: on the right, Neos Dionysos presenting a wreath to Horus and Nephthys; on the left, Neos Dionysos offering incense and pouring water upon an altar, in presence of Osiris, Isis, and Horus. The granite of the site at the foot of the tower has been smoothed to form a stele, with a six-lined inscription and reliefs relating to a grant of lands made to the temple of Isis by Philometor in the 24th year of his reign (157 B.C.). In front of it are the foundations of a small *Chapel* (Pl. *m*). — On the left (W.) tower are similar scenes (figures defaced).

An inner staircase ascends to the W. tower (comp. the plan), whence we proceed across the central portal to the E. tower. The ascent, however, is not worth making except when the first pylon is inaccessible.

Within the doorway, at the top, to the right, are some much faded early-Christian pictures.

The **Temple of Isis** proper, entered by this portal, consisted of an open court (here very small), a vestibule or pronaos, several antechambers, and a sanctuary, with smaller chambers adjoining. The walls are covered both outside and inside with reliefs of Ptolemies (Philadelphus, Euergetes II., etc.) and Roman emperors (Augustus, Tiberius, Antoninus) performing the customary ceremonies in the guise of Pharaohs; but the traveller will find detailed descriptions of similar scenes in our accounts of the temples of Dendera (p. 261) and Edfu (p. 370).

The **Court** had a small colonnade on each side, the roof of which rested on a single column. The uncovered portion could be shaded from the sun by means of a velarium; the holes for the cords are still visible in the upper part of the cavetto cornice turned towards the second pylon.

The **Vestibule**, with eight columns, was originally separated from the preceding court by stone screens between the first row of columns. Christian services were celebrated in the court and vestibule, of which the numerous Coptic crosses chiselled in the walls are memorials. A Greek inscription in the doorway to Room *D*, on the right, records that "this good work" took place under Bishop Theodorus (in the reign of Justinian, p. 390). An inscription over the door commemorates the archæological expedition sent hither by Pope Gregory XVI. in 1841.

The small **Antechambers** (Pl. *D*, *E*, *F*) preceding the sanctuary are adjoined by chambers lying in darkness. The **Sanctuary**, which has two tiny windows, still contains a pedestal placed here by Euergetes I. and his wife Berenice, on which stood the sacred boat with

the image of Isis. The other rooms in the inner part of the temple do not repay a visit.

To the W. of Antechamber *D* is a small room (Pl. I) embellished with representations of the king before Isis. A door (Pl. *n*; see p. 391) here affords an exit from the temple. Here also is the approach to the Staircase, ascending first to a chamber situated above Room VII, and thence to the Roof of the sanctuary. — A few steps descend here to the ***Osiris Chambers,** with some interesting reliefs referring to the death of Osiris (p. cxlix). On the left wall of the anteroom (above Room *F*): 1. The (N.) Nile-god offers a libation of milk to the soul of Osiris, sitting before him in the form of a bird; 2. The falcon-headed Harendotes pours the sacred water over the falcon-headed mummy of Osiris, behind which stand the sisters of the god. 3. Four dæmons, the god Show, and the Emperor Antoninus (builder of this room) before Osiris and his two sisters Isis and Nephthys. In the small Main Chamber (above Room II), on the wall opposite the entrance: *Central Row*, beginning to the left: 1. Isis and Nephthys by the bier of Osiris Onnophris, who is nude; 2. Two goddesses beside the tomb of Osiris, whose head is wanting; on the door to the tomb strides a lion; 3. Four dæmons carrying the falcon-headed mummy of Osiris. *Lower Row:* 1. The frog-headed Heket and the falcon-headed Harsiēsis by the bier of Osiris, beneath which stand the jars for the entrails; 2. The corpse of Osiris amongst marsh-plants; a priest pouring the consecrated water; 3. The dog-headed Anubis by the bier of Osiris, beside which kneel Isis and Nephthys, the sisters of Osiris.

We quit the temple of Isis by Door *n* (see above), turn to the W., and proceed to visit **Hadrian's Gateway,** a small portal in the ancient girdle-wall of the temple, adjoined by a much-ruined vestibule. This structure was built by Hadrian (p. cxv) and embellished by Hadrian, Marcus Aurelius, and Lucius Verus. Probably because this door led to Abaton (p. 395) the reliefs upon it refer to the cult of Osiris. On the lintel: Hadrian before Osiris, Isis, and Harsiēsis, and before Osiris, Nephthys, and Harendotes. On the left jamb is the sacred relic of Abydos; on the right jamb, the fetish of Osiris. Within the gateway, at the top of the right wall: Marcus Aurelius before Osiris and Isis (note the lines to guide the artist); below, Marcus Aurelius bringing offerings, grapes and flowers, to Isis.

The Vestibule, which was never completed and is now much ruined, contains some interesting reliefs. Above the door in the S. wall (Pl. o) of the chamber are two rows of reliefs. Above: Nephthys presenting the crown of Lower Egypt, and Isis that of Upper Egypt to Horus, who is seated on a bench; the king's name is being inscribed on a palm branch by Thoth, to the left, and by Seshet (goddess of writing), to the right; behind Thoth sits the god Show, holding a sail, and still farther back are another god and a goddess playing the lyre. Below: The Osiris tomb at Abaton, with the body of Osiris borne by a crocodile; to the left stands Isis, higher up is the sun among mountains, and above the whole are the sun, a half-moon, and stars. The whole design is shown within a small temple, with a door to the left, and two large pylons and one small one in

front; to the right are rocks. — To the left of the door is an unfinished relief of the king presenting a field. Above are three lines in Meroïtic cursive characters (p. cxxxviii). — In the second row from the top, on the *Right Wall* (Pl. *p*), is the celebrated *Representation of the Source of the Nile:* at the foot of a rock, on which perch a vulture and a falcon, the Nile-god, surrounded by a serpent, pours water from two vases. — To the right of this is the soul of Osiris (in the form of a bird) in the sacred grove, worshipped by Hathor (l.) and Isis, Nephthys, Horus, and Amun (r.).

To the S. of Hadrian's Gateway is a *Nilometer* (now inaccessible), which has hieratic and demotic scales as well as the customary Coptic one.

From Hadrian's Gateway we proceed N. to the scanty ruins of a *Temple of Harendotes* (p. clvi), built by the Emperor Claudius.

In the N. part of the island (comp. the map, p. 390) are two *Coptic Churches*, the remains of a *Coptic Convent*, and a ruined *Temple of Augustus*, built in the 18th year of that emperor's reign.

At the extreme N.E. of the island, and in the axis of the temple of Augustus, is a large *Roman Town Gate*, probably erected by Diocletian, with three arches, the side-arches being lower than that in the centre. The N. side-arch has a domical stone vault.

About 50 paces to the E. of the Temple of Isis lies the small ***Temple of Hathor,** dedicated to Hathor-Aphrodite by Philometor and Euergetes II. (p. cxii). The colonnade in front of it (restored) and the sanctuary (now vanished) were both added by Augustus.

The columns in the former were united by stone screens, on which Augustus appeared sacrificing to various forms of Hathor. On the columns themselves are charming representations of flute-players, harpers, figures of Bes playing the tambourine and the harp and dancing, apes playing the lyre, priests carrying an antelope, etc. The temple proper is in better preservation; in front of it are two plant columns, which were joined to the walls by means of screens.

To the S.E. of this temple, on the bank, rises the so-called ***Kiosk,** the chief decoration and the characteristic symbol of the island, which, however, is generally so submerged that only the upper part of its columns are visible. It dates from the Roman imperial period and was never completed. Above the floral capitals of the columns it was intended to add sistrum-capitals.

The rocky island of **Bigga** *(Bîga*, Egyptian *Senmet)*, the chief deities of which were Ups, goddess of fire, and Hathor, deserves a visit chiefly for the sake of the charming view of Philæ. It is reached by boat in a few minutes. We land at the ancient quay and ascend by a staircase. In front of us lie the remains of a Ptolemaic temple (Ptolemy XIII. Neos Dionysos, p. cxiii), of which part of the hypostyle court is still standing, with its plant-columns united by stone screens. On the E. side is a door, into which an apse has been built. Bigga was the site also of the famous sanctuary of *Abaton*, with a tomb of Osiris (p. cxlix). Active travellers are recommended to climb one of the rocks of Bigga, for the sake of the remarkable view over the whole cataract district.

The rocky islets off the N. end of Philæ, now called *Konosso* ('great rock'), were formerly considered the S. limit of Egypt (see

p. 412). The islets, now generally submerged, contain numerous rock-inscriptions, among which the cartouches of Psammetichos II. (p. cix) are conspicuous on a massive double rock.

The Nile Dam at Aswân.

Those who wish to visit the dam only may go by the shorter route described on p. 389, and return by the rather longer route along the bank.

The **Aswân Dam* or *Barrage* (Arabic *Es-Sadd*, i.e. 'the dam', or *El-Khazzân*, i.e. 'the reservoir'), built in 1898-1912 below Philæ, is one of the largest structures of the kind in the world and ranks among the sights of Egypt. It was constructed in order to dam up the water of the Nile so that a regular supply could be furnished during time of low water. By this means the country can be regularly irrigated all the year round, and many irrigation canals that used formerly to run dry periodically now receive a constant supply of water. The dam is built of granite blocks brought from the old quarries at Aswân (p. 387) and runs straight across the river-channel for a distance of 2150 yds. ($1^1/_4$ M.). The original height of the dam was 130 ft. above the foundation, while its thickness varied from 23 ft. at the top to 98 ft. at the bottom. In 1907-12, however, it was raised another $16^1/_2$ ft. and its thickness increased by about as much; so that the storage-lake formed above the dam has now a capacity of 594,000 million gallons, a depth of 88 ft., and an extent upstream, when full, of 185 M. On the recommendation of three expert engineers (British, American, and Dutch), the Egyptian government has decided to raise the dam (in 1929-33) by another 18 ft. The masonry is penetrated by 180 sluice gates for regulating the flow of the water. These include 140 lower sluices (each measuring $23 \times 6^1/_2$ ft.) for the distribution of the water and 40 upper sluices (each $6^1/_2 \times 11$ ft.) to permit the escape of surplus water. The iron gates of the sluices ('Stoney patent') are regulated by hand-winches on the dam. When the Nile begins to rise in the first half of July all the sluices are opened. At the end of November the gates are gradually closed, and the lake above the dam is filled. When the want of water in Egypt begins to be noticeable (about the end of March) the quantity required for cultivation is drawn off gradually from the accumulated stores in the reservoir, which last until the river once more begins to rise at the middle or end of July.

To the W. of the dam is a *Navigation Canal*, by which the boats are locked up and down stream. It is $1^1/_4$ M. long and the difference in level (75 ft.) is surmounted by four locks, each 230 ft. long and 31 ft. wide. The two upper gates of the locks are 63 ft. high, the five others 49 ft., 39 ft., and 36 ft. high.

The original plan for the two dams of Aswân and Asyûṭ (p. 237) was worked out by *Sir William Willcocks* at the Egyptian Ministry of Public Works. The execution was entrusted to the British contractors *John Aird & Co.* The work was begun in the summer of 1898; the foundation-stone

was laid on Feb. 12th, 1899, by the Duke of Connaught; and on Dec. 10th, 1902, the dam was formally declared complete in the presence of the Khedive ʿAbbâs II., the Duke and Duchess of Connaught, and Lord Cromer. The cost of the two dams amounted to £E 3,237,000. — The plan for the raising of the dam at Aswân was prepared by *Sir Benjamin Baker* and *Sir William Garstin* (p. 237). The new works cost £E 1,500,000, besides £E 300,000 spent on the expropriation of the Nubian villages. — Comp. 'The Assuân Reservoir and Lake Mœris', by *Sir William Willcocks* (1906).

Those who come from Philæ by boat (p. 388) land to the S.E. of the dam, which is crossed by small trolleys pushed by Arabs (fare P.T. 5, there and back). Visitors alight at the various view-points. On the W. bank is a small *Restaurant* (rfmts. only), affording a view of the whole structure.

The Return to Aswân by boat (p. 388, 389) through the cataracts is well worth making and is free from danger. We embark at the lowest of the four locks. The course follows the W. bank of the river, through another lock and past Siheil (p. 389), Salûga, and other picturesque rocky islands. Aswân is reached in 1½ hr.

28. Routes through the Eastern Desert.

Comp. the Map in front of the Title Page.

The necessary *Camels* (P.T. 20-30 per day) are obtained with the aid of a resident friend or one of the consular agents. Tents and other requisites must be brought from Cairo (comp. p. xxvi). The *Khabîr*, or guide in charge of the caravan, is held responsible for the safe conduct of the entire party, and obedience to his marching orders is advised. For the character of the scenery, comp. p. lxxi. The shooting of gazelles is forbidden.

Comp. *T. Barron & W. F. Hume*, Topography and Geology of the Eastern Desert of Egypt (Central Portion; Cairo, Survey Department, 1902); *Arthur E. P. Weigall*, Travels in the Upper Egyptian Deserts (Edinburgh & London, 1909); *Eberhard Fraas*, Geognostisches Profil vom Nil zum Roten Meer (Zeitschrift der Deutschen Geologischen Gesellschaft, Band 52, Heft 4, 1900); *Georg Schweinfurth*, Aufnahmen in der Östlichen Wüste von Ægypten (in 10 sheets, 1:200,000, with the exception of Sheet 1 mentioned on p. 178; 1897-1910).

The desert routes between the Nile and the Red Sea were important in antiquity both for the trade with the seaports and the land of *Punt* (p. 233) and for the gold-mines and valuable quarries of green breccia and several varieties of granite in the mountains of the Arabian Desert. *Qena* (p. 232) is now the usual starting-place of the caravans, but in antiquity it was *Koptos* (*Qifṭ*; p. 232). The most important harbours on the Red Sea, named from N. to S., were *Myós Hórmos* (now *Abu Shaʿr el-Qibli*), *Leukós Limēn* (now *Qoṣeir*), and *Berenike*. — A railway from Qena to Qoṣeir is projected.

From Qena to Abu Shaʿr el-Qibli, 5-6 days. The route leads N.E. from the *Wâdi Qena* to the (3 days' march) *Wâdi Faṭîra*, on the N. side of which lies the *Gebel Faṭîra* (4920 ft.; *Mons Claudianus*). About ½ M. to the S. of the latter wâdi are the granite quarries, known as *Umm Diqâl* ('mother of columns'), which were worked by captives and convicts, chiefly in the reigns of Trajan and Hadrian. Traces have been found also of old gold-mines, the exploitation of

which is again being attempted, without much success, by the Fatirah Exploring Co. Here are situated also the ruins of the Roman settlement of *Hydreuma Trajani* ('watering station of Trajan'). These consist mainly of a fort about 82 yds. square surrounded by walls and towers. Outside the walls lie a temple and other buildings, and some large columns and Greek inscriptions have been found in the quarries. About two days' journey farther N. is the *Mons Porphyrites*, now called *Gebel ed-Dukhkhân* ('smoke mountain'; 4460 ft.), the ancient porphyry quarries of which were worked by the Romans. Here are the ruins of an Ionic temple of the time of Hadrian (never completed), remains of an irregularly built settlement, and two large reservoirs. We follow the ancient route hence to the plateau of *Abu Sha'r el-Qibli*, on the E. slope of which lie the ruins of *Myós Hórmos* (p. 397). On the coast, 3 M. to the E., are the remains of a Roman fort. — A second route (the ancient 'Porphyry Road'), running farther S., ascends the large *Wâdi Qena*, then proceeds to the *Wâdi Qattar*, and finally skirts the S. base of the Mons Porphyrites to the sea.

The Journey from Qena to Qoṣeir (4-5 days, or 10 hrs. by motor-car) is much more interesting. [It can also be made from Qifṭ or Luxor by a good road (about 93½ M.; comp. below).] The route from Qena follows the valley of the Nile for the first day and leads near the edge of the desert, past the villages of *El-Gabalâw*, with the tomb of *Sîdi Rukâb* (a Moslem saint), *El-Ashrâf esh-Sharqîya*, *Nag' el-Ḥai*, and *Nag' Karam 'Imrân*. The first night is generally spent at the large caravanserai of **Bîr 'Ambar,** about 3½ hrs. from Qena. This was erected at the expense of an Ibrâhîm Pasha and comprises several separate buildings, covered with dome-shaped roofs and surrounded by courts and colonnades.

On the second day we advance E. through a monotonous plain intersected in all directions by small undulating heights. All around us extend the interminable yellowish-grey, sun-bleached rocks of the desert. To the E. of the **Gebel el-Qarn** ('mountain of the horn'), about midway between Bîr 'Ambar and Laqeiṭa, the road from Qena is joined by that from Luxor. The only variety is afforded by an occasional *mabwala* (a place where the camels halt from time to time to make water) or a *maḥaṭṭa* (ancient halting-places 6-9 M. apart, which serve as guide-posts showing the road). Here and there we observe some of the semaphore-towers of an optical telegraph dating from the time of Muḥammed 'Ali. The Qoṣeir caravans usually pass the second night in the village of **Laqeiṭa** (*Bîr el-Laqîṭa*, *El-Gheiṭa*; 9 hrs. from Bîr 'Ambar, 12½ hrs. from Qena), at a small oasis with two wells, some palms, a few mud-huts, and a half-ruined caravanserai. A detachment of the camel corps is stationed here. Near the chief well are some fragments of a Greek inscription containing the name of Tiberius Claudius. The manners and customs of the 'Abâbda (p. 363) who live here repay observation; the way in which the children wear their hair is especially notable.

About $2^1/_2$ hrs. E. of Laqeiṭa we quit the plain and enter a wâdi, flanked by abrupt terraces belonging to the upper cretaceous formation and containing petrified oyster-shells. In $^3/_4$ hr. more we reach the *Qaṣr el-Banât*, or 'Castle of the Maidens', a picturesque rock of sandstone formed by atmospheric erosion and covered with numerous graffiti in Greek, Coptic, Arabic, Himyaritic, and Sinaitic characters, engraved here by caravans. Adjacent lies a Roman watering station *(hydreuma)*, forming an oblong 125 ft. in length and 102 ft. in breadth. The enclosing wall, formed of courses of sandstone without cement, was $6^1/_2$ ft. high. Within the wall lie twenty small chambers opening on a rectangular inner court, the only exit from which is on the N. side. No water is now procurable here.

At about 2 hrs. from the Roman watering station begins the winding pass named *Muṭraq es-Selâm.* On the *Gebel Abu Kûʿ* ('father of the elbow'), at the entrance to the pass, are more graffiti, older than those at Qaṣr el-Banât; in one of them Amenophis IV. (p. cv) is mentioned. Beyond the pass we approach the fine mountain scenery through which the second part of the Qoṣeir route leads. In the distance (r.) rise the S. foot-hills of the *Ḥammâmât Mts.*, while nearer and in front are the S.W. spurs. These mountains rise in terraces to a height of 4200 ft. and outvie in impressive scenery the rocks of Aswân. The outliers of the range consist of a yellow sandstone, belonging to the cretaceous formation, followed by the red 'Nubian' sandstone, also of the cretaceous system (comp. p. lxxi).

Among these hills, to the N. of the caravan route, lies a second Roman station, with a well (water unfit for drinking). About 2 hrs. farther on we reach the older (palæozoic) formations of the Ḥammâmât Mts. proper. The character of the scenery suddenly changes; the hard, dark rocks rise perpendicularly and the mountains assume an abrupt, Alpine appearance. Here begins the **Wâdi el-Ḥammâmât,** the *Rehenu* valley of the Egyptians, who quarried its hard dark stone for statues and sarcophagi in the most ancient times. [This was the *Niger* or *Thebaicus Lapis* of the ancients, according to Fraas a greywacke rock with outcroppings of later granite.] In 1 hr. more we reach the *Bîr el-Ḥammâmât*, a well 16 ft. in diameter (excellent water); an aged ʿAbâbda sheikh, who occupies a position of authority and is ready to give help to travellers, lives here. Near the well are the remains of a Roman wall and five unfinished and now shattered sarcophagi. The quarries contain numerous Egyptian inscriptions. The earliest expedition to Ḥammâmât of which we have any knowledge took place in the reign of King Isesi (5th Dyn.). At a later period, especially under the Middle Empire, the quarries were diligently worked, and even under the New Empire they were in operation. We hear of a great undertaking under Ramses IV. (p. cvii) for the purpose of procuring blocks for the temple of Amun at Thebes, in which no fewer than 8368 workmen and soldiers were employed. The quarries were worked under Darius, Xerxes, and Artaxerxes also.

Just beyond the quarries the route turns from the N.E. to the S. and passes the ruins of *El-Fawâkhir* ('the potsherds'). Traces of the ancient open workings and deep subterranean adits (very difficult of access), the foundations of hundreds of workmen's cottages, and numerous inscriptions bear witness to the former importance of the place.

About 1 hr. beyond El-Fawâkhir we reach *Bîr es-Sidd*, a small and picturesquely situated spring, adjoined by settlements of the ʿAbâbda. In 4 hrs. more we reach the top of the pass, on the other side of which we descend through the *Wâdi Abu Siran* to (3 hrs.) the *Wâdi Rôṣafa*, containing a large well, the water of which, however, is considered unwholesome. The route now makes a wide curve to the N. and at the plain of 'Liteima' reaches the dividing line between the central mountain range and the outlying chains consisting of cretaceous sandstone and tertiary rocks (white limestone). After $2^1/_2$ hrs. we pass through the *Wâdi Beiḍa* and proceed to (3 hrs.) the *Bîr el-Inglîz* (dug by British troops in 1800), the cisterns of which are generally dry. Thence we go on through the *Wâdi ʿAmbagi*, with a spring of brackish water, to (4 hrs.) Qoṣeir.

El-Qoṣeir (*Qosseir*, *Kosseir;* accommodation at the Italian canteen, pens. P.T. 16-18), on the Arabian Gulf, with 2000 inhab. in 1927, is an unimportant harbour with a stone jetty, an old fort, two mosques, several bazaars, and a wireless station. In the Ptolemaic period the desert route ended here at the *Leukós Limēn* or 'White Harbour', and in earlier times in the vicinity of the *Wâdi el-Gâsûs*, about 35 M. farther N.W. A light railway runs from El-Qoṣeir to some phosphate mines worked by an Italian company, which sends a motor-car to Luxor every fortnight. — About 50 M. to the N. of El-Qoṣeir, on the Red Sea, is the village of *Safâga*, with the mines of the Egyptian Phosphate Co. — Still farther N. (87 M. from El-Qoṣeir; 220 M. to the S. of Suez) is *El-Hurghâda*, capital of the Red Sea District (2123 inhab.; comp. p. xlix). The office of the ma'mûr is $1^1/_2$ M. to the N.W., at the workmen's colony (with mosque and school) of the Anglo-Egyptian Oil Fields Co., which has oil-fields here. Another $1^1/_2$ M. farther is the settlement of the company's European officials, with a club-house. In the vicinity rises the *Gebel esh-Shâyib* (7156 ft.).

On the return journey from El-Qoṣeir towards the Nile the Beduin sometimes prefer another and more southerly route ('Moʿila Route'), diverging from the route described above at the *Bîr el-Inglîz*. This alternative route, which may be strongly recommended, leads at first through the winding *Wâdi Qabr el-Khâdim*, afterwards passing the *Gebel Nuḥâs* and through the pass of *Rîʿat el-Ghazâl* into the *Wâdi Ghazâl*. To the right rise the imposing phonolithic cones of the *Gebel Daghanîya* and the *Gebel Moshâghir* (6 hrs. from Bîr el-Inglîz), the ascent of which from the E. is easy and well worth while, as it commands an excellent survey of the abrupt peaks of the Ḥammâmât. We next follow the *Wâdi Homûda*, which farther on takes the name of *Wâdi el-Ḥomr*, with the fine *Gebel Ḥomr* flanking it on the right. On the way are numerous traces of ancient gold-mines, especially noticeable in the thick beds of quartz to which the Gebel Ḥomr owes its formation. The night is spent at (4 hrs.) *Bîr el-Moʿila*, a well beside a few huts of the ʿAbâbda. At the *Gebel Wâqif* we cross the *Ṭarîq eḍ-Ḍahrâwi*,

a road running from N. to S., and farther on we reach *ʿAmâra*, with another well and ʿAbâbda huts. Thence our route lies through the *Wâdi Nûr* and the *Wâdi el-Qash* to the ($3^1/_2$ hrs.) *Bîr el-Qash*, a dried-up well. The route now leads through palæozoic greywacke rocks, which, beyond Bîr el-Moʿila, assume the same breccia formation as in the Ḥammâmât. The Wâdi el-Qash bends S., but we quit the mountains ($2^1/_2$ hrs. from Bîr el-Qash) by the pass of *Rîʿat el-Kheil*, and re-enter the desert of sand and gravel, the heights of which are formed of cretaceous sandstone. We proceed across the pass of *Rîʿat el-Hamra* to *Mabwalat Râs Aṣfar*, whence we go on through the *Wâdi Mághlaṭ* to *Mabwalat Khôr el-Ghîr*. Lastly we proceed viâ *Gáhrat ed-Dabʿa* to (10 hrs. from Rîʿat el-Kheil) *Laqeiṭa* (p. 398), where our route unites with the more northerly one already described.

The Journey to Berenike through the territory of the ʿAbâbda Beduin is seldom undertaken. We may start from Qena or Qifṭ, diverging at Laqeiṭa (p. 398), or from Edfu (see below). On both routes traces of old watering stations are discernible. The Antonine Itinerary (3rd cent. of the Christian era) gives a list of the ancient stations (starting from Koptos) with their distance from each other in Roman miles, as follows: Phœnicon 24, Didyme 24, Afrodito 20, Kompasi 22, Jovis 23, Aristonis 25, Phalacro 25, Apollonos 23, Kabalsi 27, Kænon Hydreuma 27, Berenike 18, in all 258 Roman miles = about 236 English miles. A third route, established by Hadrian, led from Antinoupolis (p. 221) to the Red Sea, and then S. along the coast to Berenike. *Golenishev*, the Russian Egyptologist, who described his journey in the 'Recueil de travaux relatifs à la philologie et à l'archéologie égyptiennes et assyriennes' (xiii, 1890, p. 75 seqq.), took eleven days from Ridîsîya (p. 364) to Berenike. One day may be saved on the outward journey by starting from Edfu (p. 359). The temple of Sethos I. is then reached late in the afternoon of the first day.

1st Day. From Ridîsîya to *Bîr ʿAbbâd* (3 hrs.), in the *Wâdi Miâḥ*. In the wâdi, which is entered opposite the mouth of the *Wâdi Ammerikba*, is an ancient station with masons' marks like those at El-Ḥôsh (p. 359). Lepsius mentions a ruin here, named *Herhush* (i.e. sandstone), dating from some ancient settlement.

2nd Day. The **Temple of Sethos I.** is reached in the afternoon. This temple, about 37 M. from Ridîsîya (p. 364), after which town it is sometimes called, was discovered in 1816 by Frédéric Cailliaud. It was built by Sethos I. (p. cvi) beside an ancient watering station, and was dedicated to Amon-Rē. The vestibule is built of blocks of sandstone and has four papyrus-columns with bud-capitals. The reliefs represent the king as victor over negroes and Asiatics. The following hall, hewn out of the rock, contains four square pillars, reliefs of the king sacrificing, and long inscriptions recording the sinking of the wells and the building of the temple. In the rear wall are three niches, with statues of the king and various gods. — A *Small Building* beside the temple perhaps marks the site of the well. On an adjoining rock, to the E., are three steles. On one of these is an Asiatic goddess on horseback, with shield and spear; the second is dedicated by the official entrusted with the sinking of the well; and on the third is Eni, viceroy of Ethiopia, kneeling before the king. Higher up on the rock are rude figures of gazelles, Greek graffiti, and an inscription of a Prince Mermes, dating from the reign of Amenophis III.

3rd Day. More masons' marks discovered on small rocks. Ancient station of *Abu Greïa*, with two cisterns and chambers (not to be confounded with the place of the same name near Berenike, see p. 402).

4th Day. Descent into the *Wâdi Beizaḥ*, with its acacias. Rude designs and graffiti on the rocks. We cross the *Wâdi Higelîg*. On the rocks to the right are rude representations of giraffes, camels, and ibexes. Remains of an ancient station named *Sammut*, with a cistern and chambers, occur in the wâdi of the same name. We next proceed through the broad green *Wâdi Moëlha (Bîr Muëliḥ)* towards the *Gebel Mûgef* (3935 ft.), near which is a well of good water.

5th Day. We pass several groups of rude stone huts, probably built by miners. View of Gebel Zúbara (p. 402). On a rock to the right is a

representation of an Egyptian bark, with sails and oars. Farther on is another ruined station.

6th Day. Ancient station of *Ed-Dueïg.* Adjacent is another smaller building. About 3 hrs. farther on we cross the watershed between the Nile and the Red Sea. Two more cisterns, within a semicircular enclosure. We pass the granite hill of *Abu Hâd* (2075 ft.).

7th Day. Descent into the *Wâdi Gemâl.* Station in the form of a right-angled triangle, with two cisterns. Lateral valley diverging towards the emerald-mines (see below). To the right rises the *Gebel Abyad.*

8th Day. We proceed through the *Wâdi Abyaḍ* and the *Wâdi Ḥigelîg*, leaving the *Gebel Hamâta* (6490 ft.) to the right; then along the *Wâdi Rûmît.* On a height in the *Wâdi Huṣûn* are some sheikhs' graves, in a circular form.

9th Day. Seven other circular tombs; the well of *El-Haratra* lies to the right; old structure of a large cistern in the *Wâdi el-Hasîr.* Through the *Wâdi Amrugûm* to the *Wâdi Lâhemi*, which descends from the mountain of that name, crosses our route, and proceeds in windings to the Red Sea. The last station is *Abu Greïa* (see remark on p. 401), comprising several buildings, the largest of which contains the remains of rooms. Another rectangular building seems to have been a reservoir.

10th Day. Arrival at *Sikket Bender*, near the temple of Berenike.

The town of **Berenike** *(Berenice)*, situated in the same latitude as Aswân, was founded in 275 B.C. by Ptolemy II. Philadelphus, who revived the commerce of the Red Sea by the establishment of several new ports. The town, which was named by Ptolemy after his mother, was the terminus of the main desert routes from Egypt, and for four or five hundred years was the entrepôt of a maritime commerce carried on mainly with Arabia and India. The ruins, still extant, surround the *Temple*, which faces E.N.E. In front is a forecourt 28½ ft. in width and 12 ft. in depth, which was adjoined by the temple proper (inner length 31 ft.), comprising two rows of apartments. The representation on the left outside wall shows a Roman emperor appearing before a goddess, who seems to be, according to the inscription, the tutelary deity of the green (i.e. emerald) mine.

The Emerald **Mines,** ½° to the N. of Berenike, were worked by the Arabs down to the year 760 of the Hegira (A.D. 1370), after which they were abandoned. Muhammed ʿAli made an unavailing attempt to reopen them. They lie partly in the *Wâdi Sakeit* and partly on the *Gebel Zúbara* (*Gebel ez-Zabâra;* 4465 ft.), 14 M. to the N.E. They are best visited from Edfu (p. 359), but may, like Berenike, be approached by following the coast of the Arabian Gulf from Qoṣeir. The first route diverges from the road to Berenike in the *Wâdi Gemâl* (see above). To the S. of the Gebel Zúbara lies the village of *Sakeit (Bîr Sikait)*, with numerous miners' huts and a small rock-hewn temple, with a few Greek inscriptions.

Farther N. (25° 30′ N. Lat.), in the *Wâdi Umbârek*, lie the ancient gold-mines of **Umm Rus,** reopened by the Um Rus Gold Mines of Egypt, a British company. Hundreds of labourers' huts are still visible here besides the ruins of about three hundred houses dating from a Græco-Roman settlement (called by Ptolemy *Nechesia*). A light railway leads from Umm Rus to (4½ M.) the small port of *Mirsa Umbârek* or *Mersa Imbarak*, on the Red Sea.

Travellers going on from Abu Shaʿr el-Qibli, Qoṣeir, or Berenike to Sinai (comp. Baedeker's 'Palestine & Syria') or Arabia cross the Red Sea to one of the ports on the E. coast, where *Tûr*, *Mînet el-Wejh* (p. 451), *Yanboʿ el-Bahr*, and *Jidda* (p. 452) are called at every ten or twenty days by steamers of the Khedivial Mail Line (comp. R. 36).

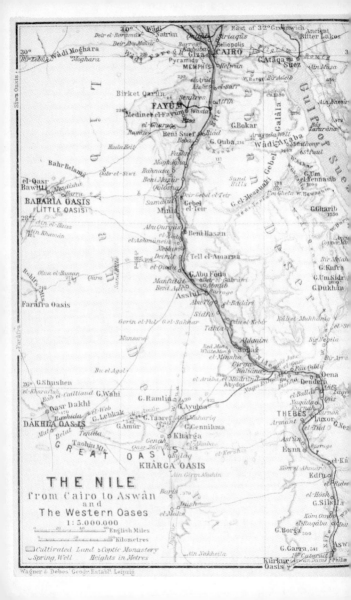

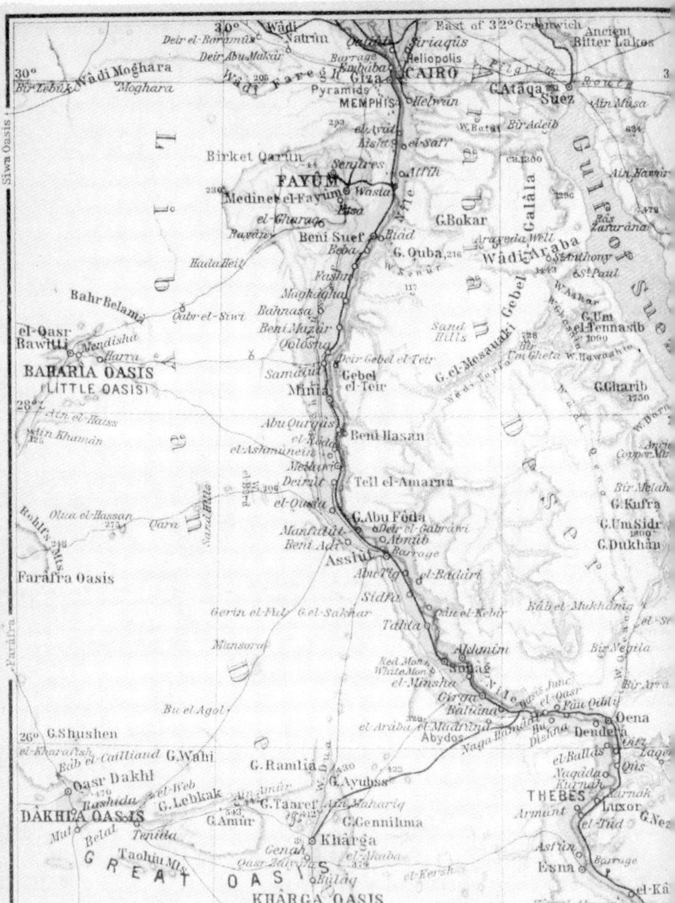

Wagner & Debes' Geogr. Establ. Leipzig

29. The Western Oases.

By the term Oasis (Egyptian *waḥet;* Arabic *wâḥ*, plural *wâḥât*) is generally understood a fertile and inhabited spot in the midst of the desert. More correctly, however, the oases are large depressions in the desert plateau, of which a comparatively very small area is really fertile, by far the larger portion being desert. The fertility of the oases depends upon the existence of a water supply lying in a stratum of sandstone, from 300 to 550 ft. below the surface, and rendered available either by natural springs or by deep artesian wells. Fertile land, therefore, is usually found in the lowest parts of an oasis (comp. p. lxxii).

Comp. 'Problems of the Lybian Desert' by *John Ball* (Geographical Journal, 1927).

The five Egyptian oases, situated in the Libyan desert, had in 1927 an aggregate population of 75,644. They form the Western and Southern Desert Provinces (p. xlix) and are under the control of the Frontiers Administration (a branch of the War Office, Cairo, 5 Shâriʻ el-Falaki; Pl. D 4-6). All persons proceeding to the W. desert, whatever route they choose, should report to the Director General at Cairo or at the office of the Administration at Burg el-ʻArab (p. 31). Motorists proceeding viâ Burg el-ʻArab must report to the authorities there; those approaching by other routes must notify their intended route and their day of departure to the Director General of the Frontiers Administration at Cairo (see above). *Khârga* is connected with the Nile valley by railway, and is therefore easily visited; the others *(Sîwa, Baharîya, Farâfra,* and *Dâkhla)* are reached by motor-car. Camel-caravans (comp. p. xxvi) are too slow to be of much use. — The shooting of gazelles is forbidden.

Sîwa.

The *Oasis of Sîwa,* the *Ammonium* or seat of the oracle of Jupiter Ammon (p. clv; visited by Alexander the Great in 331 B.C.), is the westernmost of the oases and lies 2-3 days' journey (c. 400 M.) by motor-car from Alexandria. Full information is supplied by the 'Libyan Oases Association' at Alexandria (26 Rue de l'Eglise Copte, p. 10), which arranges a nine days' circular tour (going viâ Burg el-ʻArab and Mirsa Maṭrûḥ; returning viâ El-Qâra, p. 404) for £E 3 per day per person, including board and lodging. 1st Day: along the railway-line from Alexandria to Mirsa Maṭrûḥ (c. 205 M.; p. 31; rest-house). 2nd or 3rd Day: by the Sikket es-Sulṭân ('sultan road'), also called Sikket el-Isṭabl ('stable road'), the ancient caravan route used by Alexander the Great (see p. 31), through the *Wâdi er-Raml* to *Bîr Goaiferi (Bîr Guʻeifiri),* then through the *Pass of Kanâyis* past several wells (at a half-way point, known as El-Buweib, the *Bîr Fu'âd el-Auwal,* dug in 1928 in memory of King Fu'âd I.'s tour of the Western Desert) to the *Râs el-Ḥamrâya* and Sîwa (c. 195 M.). —

The caravan route from Cairo leads viâ *Abu Roâsh* (p. 149) to the *Deir Abu Maqâr* (Convent of St. Macarius, p. 35) in the Wâdi en-Naṭrûn, and thence W. to the uninhabited depression of *Moghara* (*Ḥaṭîyet el-Maghara*; 7-8 days from Cairo; comp. p. lxx), in the N.E. part of the Qaṭṭâra Depression (see below). In seven days more, proceeding viâ *Bîr Gharâdiq* (*Bîr Abu 'l-Gharâdiq*, i.e. 'the well of the ghardaq shrubs', Nitraria retusa) and *Wâdi Letheila* (*Wâdi el-Etheila*), we reach the small oasis of *El-Qâra* (*Qârat Umm eṣ-Ṣughaiyar*, *Gara*; about 130 inhab.). Thence three days' march brings us to Sîwa. — From Alexandria the caravan route leads S.W. viâ the *City of St. Menas* (p. 29) to join the Cairo route at *Moghara* (see above).

The *Qaṭṭâra Depression*, named after one of the principal springs within it (55 M. to the N.E. of El-Qâra, see above), begins 130 M. to the W. of Cairo and extends, about 185 M. in length, S.W. in the direction of Sîwa; N. of Moghara (see above) it approaches to within 35 M. of the Mediterranean coast. The perimeter of the depression at its sea-level contour is over 684 M. long; quite one-half of its total area of c. 6950 sq. M. lies over 164 ft. below the level of the Mediterranean, while the lowest point yet found (c. 20 M. to the S.E. of El-Qâra) is 440 ft. below it.

The *Oasis of Sîwa*, with beautiful gardens (over 160,000 date-palms; pomegranates, limes, grapes, olives, vegetables), lies about 56 ft. below the level of the sea, in N. Lat. 29°12′ and E. Long. 25°30′ (comp. p. lxxii). After the visit of Pausanias in A.D. 160, the first European to penetrate to this oasis was W. G. Browne (p. 135; 1792), who may thus rank as the rediscoverer of the Ammonium. The inhabitants (3900 in number) are chiefly Berbers and, like the Berbers of North Africa, have a language of their own, though the men speak and understand Arabic also. Besides a number of smaller settlements there are two large villages, built upon isolated rocks, viz. *Sîwa* (Prince Fârûq Hotel, at the foot of the Qâret el-Muṣabbirîn, 12 R., good) and *Aghurmi*. Sîwa is the seat of a ma'mûr (district officer, p. xlix), and has a mosque (begun in 1907, work resumed in 1928) and a government hospital (foundation-stone laid in 1928). The most important relics of antiquity are the rock-tombs of the *Qâret el-Muṣabbarîn* (*Gebel el-Môta*), near Sîwa; the temple of Aghurmi (now almost entirely taken up by modern dwellings), in which we may recognize the seat of the oracle of Jupiter Ammon (see below); and the almost wholly destroyed temple at *Ummebeida*, $^1/_2$ M. from Aghurmi.

Sal-ammoniac (ammonium chloride or hydrochlorate of ammonium) is said to have been first obtained by distillation of camels' dung near the temple of Jupiter Ammon (see above). The ammonites, a fossil genus of cephalopods, are so-called because their coiled shell resembles the ram's horns on the statue of this god.

The oasis of *Jarabûb* (p. 31) is about 75 M. to the N.W. of Sîwa, in Italian territory.

Comp. *C. Dalrymple Belgrave's* 'Siwa, the Oasis of Jupiter Ammon' (London, 1923; 15*s*.), *G. E. Simpson's* 'The Heart of Libya: the Siwa Oasis, its People, Customs, and Sport' (London, 1928; 7 *s*. 6 *d*.), and ***Steindorff's*** 'Durch die Libysche Wüste zur Amonsoase' (Leipzig, 1904).

Baharîya.

The *Oasis of El-Baharîya* (*Baharia*, *Bahrîya*; 'the northern'), called also *Oasis of Bahnasa* (*Wâh el-Bahnasa*), the 'Little Oasis' of the ancients, is reached by motor-car viâ tolerable desert tracks from Sandafa (p. 219; 125 M.), and from Gîza viâ Madînet el-Faiyûm (p. 203; 196 M.), or from Burg el-'Arab (p. 31; 217$^1/_2$ M.). The oasis is 11 M. long and 5$^1/_2$ M. broad and is situated in N. Lat. 28°23′ and E. Long. 28°19′. The population numbers 6800. The chief villages are *El-Qasr* (635 ft.) and *Bâwîti* (*Bawitti*; 370 ft.), a district capital, to the E. of which are the hamlets of *Mandîsha* (*Mendîsha*) and *Ez-Zabw* (*Zabu*, *Zubbo*). The remains of antiquity in this oasis are scanty. Bâwiti has an interesting church of the 6-7th centuries.

Comp. *Ball & Beadnell's* 'Baharia Oasis, its Topography and Geology' (Cairo, 1903) and *Steindorff's* volume mentioned at p. 404.

Farâfra.

The *Oasis of El-Farâfra* (230 ft.), with 630 inhab., is of little importance except as a station on the route between Baharîya and Dâkhla. The village of *Qasr el-Farâfra* lies 295 ft. above the level of the sea, in N. Lat. 27°3′ and E. Long. 27°57′, about 72 M. to the N.N.W. of Dâkhla. Asyût (p. 226) is the best starting-point for a visit from Egypt (8-10 days). Desert route to Mîr and Manfalût, see p. 225.

Comp. *H. J. L. Beadnell's* 'Farafra Oasis' (Cairo, 1901).

Khârga.

The *Oasis of Khârga* is connected by a railway, 122 M. in length. with *Oasis Junction*, on the line from Cairo to Luxor (p. 231). A visit to it is recommended to travellers who are attracted by the prospect of a railway journey through the desert and an opportunity of becoming acquainted with the scenery and life of an oasis. An introduction to the governor at Khârga is desirable.

There is one train weekly in either direction in 8-9$^1/_4$ hrs.: from Oasis Junction on Tues., returning from Khârga on Friday. The night express from Cairo (p. 216) connects at (337$^1/_2$ M.) Oasis Junction with the oasis train. — Those who reach the junction at other times (e.g. coming from Luxor) proceed by motor-car or motor-trolley (for 10 pers.; to be ordered 48 hrs. in advance through the Chef du Service de l'Exploitation, Cairo Station, or the Chef Divisionnaire de l'Exploitation, Luxor Station), by which *Khârga* is reached in 4 hrs. Fare for the outward journey P.T. 400 for one person, for each extra person P.T. 118; for the return journey P.T. 118 per person. Fares for those travelling only as far as *Kâra* (p. 406): by motor-car or motor-trolley, P.T. 50 for one person, for each extra person P.T. 5 (return journey P.T. 5 per person); by hand-trolley P.T. 12 for two persons, for each extra person P.T. 6.

Comp. *John Ball's* 'Kharga Oasis, its Topography and Geology' (Cairo, 1900) and *H. J. L. Beadnell's* 'An Egyptian Oasis' (London, 1909).

The oasis of Khârga, Arabic *El-Wâhât el-Khârga* ('the outer oases'), the 'Southern Oasis' of the ancient Egyptians, the 'Great Oasis' of the Greeks and Romans, is 185 M. long and 20-50 M. broad,

and is situated in N. Lat. 25°26′ and E. Long. 30°33′. Like other oases Khârga is surrounded by a fairly steep chain of cretaceous limestone hills, which rise in terraces to the height of 1410 ft. on the side next the desert. Thanks to numerous springs issuing from clefts in the cretaceous marl, the oasis was extremely fertile in antiquity and contained many towns and settlements, whose ruins exist to this day. In the middle ages, however, its prosperity waned. In modern times an effort was made by the Corporation of Western Egypt, the company which built the railway, to extend the area of cultivation by boring artesian wells; the enterprise, however, was unsuccessful, and the railway was sold to the government. The main wealth of the oasis consists in its date-palms, about 50,000 in number, but fruit-trees, rice, and other crops are grown. Khârga and Dâkhla (p. 408) form the province of the Southern Desert, the governor of which has his headquarters at Khârga. The aggregate population of the two oases is about 29,000.

Diverging from the Cairo and Luxor line at *Oasis Junction* (p. 231), the Oases Railway runs W., at first through cultivated land but afterwards ascending towards the desert, to (3½ M.) *Kâra* (resthouse, 4 beds, P. 70 P.T., good). A halt for breakfast is made here. The line follows the edge of the cultivated land a little farther, then strikes off into the desert, gradually ascending through the wide *Wâdi Samhûd*, which narrows as we ascend and is flanked by picturesque sand-eroded rocks. At 25 M. the plateau is reached, and a boundless sea of gravelly desert extends on every hand, giving place farther on to a rocky waste. After 90 M. the railway begins to descend through the *Wâdi Refûf* (12½ M. long), a rocky valley of peculiar beauty. It then crosses a wide plain and at (106 M.) *Meherîq (Maḥârîq)* reaches the level of the oasis.

122 M. **El-Khârga** (190 ft.; Rest House, 6 beds, P. 100 P.T., good, previous notice to be given at the Kâra rest-house, see above; tents and provisions for excursions supplied), with about 8000 inhab., fine palms, two mosques, a school, and a large hospital, is the chief town in the oasis. The post office is situated in the principal square. Part of the town is a labyrinth of narrow dark lanes, which resemble tunnels, being roofed over with palm-trunks or palm-branches daubed with mud. In the N. part of the town are the new government buildings (markaz) and a government rest-house.

The chief Ruins in the N. part of the oasis may be visited from Khârga in a day (donkeys available).

The large ***Temple of Hibis**, 2½ M. to the N. of Khârga, is picturesquely situated in a grove of palms. This temple, built by Darius I. (521-486 B.C.) in honour of Amun (comp. p. clxxiv), was excavated by the archæological expedition of the Metropolitan Museum of New York in 1909-11 and has been restored by the Egyptian Department of Antiquities. The axis of the temple runs E. and W., and the building is approached through four gateways. On the right wing of

the second gateway is a Greek inscription of sixty-six lines, dating from the 2nd year of the Roman Emperor Galba (A.D. 69). We enter the temple through a *Colonnade*, built by Nektanebis II. (358-341 B.C.), which is adjoined by a *Colonnaded Court*. Beyond these are a *Vestibule* (pronaos) and the small *Hypostyle Hall*, borne by four columns. A staircase to the left leads to a chamber dedicated to the cult of Osiris. In the *Sanctuary* are some interesting representations of gods (Astarte on horseback, Astarte with bow and arrows, etc.). To the left is a staircase ascending to the roof, to the right is a small chamber with a representation of the god Khnum shaping the king on the potter's wheel.

On a sandstone hill, 20 min. S.E., is the **Temple of Nadûra**, dating from the time of Antoninus Pius (A.D. 138-161) and surrounded by a lofty brick wall. The pronaos (p. clxxii), which was separated from the forecourt on the E. by columns connected by stone screens, is in good preservation. — The trigonometrical survey mark beside the temple commands a view of the N. portion of the oasis.

On a ridge about 1/2 M. to the N. of the temple of Hibis is the ***Christian Cemetery**, with several hundred brick tombs dating from the period of the banishment of Bishops Athanasius (p. cxvi) and Nestorius (p. 230). Most of these are arranged on either side of a broad avenue. The typical tomb consists of a domed chamber, frequently with an E. apse and side-recesses, and a vestibule; the larger tombs are practically miniature basilicas (comp. p. clxxxvii). The façades are not unfrequently adorned with pilasters or semi-columns and contain triangular recesses for the reception of lamps. Few of the internal decorations are preserved; in one tomb is a representation of Daniel in the den of lions, another has scenes from Biblical history. Close by is the rest-house of the Department of Antiquities (key kept by the custodian of the cemetery). — Between the temple and the cemetery lie the **Ruins of the Roman Town of Hibis** (Egyptian *Hibet*), some of the houses of which are in good preservation. — About 1/2 M. to the N. of the cemetery stands the **Christian Monastery** *(Qaṣr 'Ain Muṣṭafa Kâshif)*, a brick structure in admirable preservation. The entrance, on the N. side, is protected by a lofty square tower. In the W. half are the monks' cells, with vaulted roofs, arranged one above the other in several stories, in the E. half are the refectory, common room, chapel, etc.

An expedition should be made to the large *Roman Fort of Ed-Deir*, 15 1/2 M. to the N.E. of Khârga, on the caravan route to Girga (p. 231). The fort is provided with round towers; on the N. side is a temple. There are other ruins in the vicinity, and 1 3/4 M. to the S. is the flat-topped *Gebel Umm el-Ghenneim* (1270 ft.; view).

Excursions to the Southern Portions of the Oasis are very interesting, but are practicable only for those who know Arabic or who bring a dragoman with them from Cairo or Luxor. Camels and other necessaries may be obtained at Khârga, preferably through a government official (introduction desirable). — About 1/2 day's march brings us to the villages

and ruins of *Qaṣr el-Ghueida*, situated about the middle of the oasis, to the S. of the *Qurn el-Gennah (Ganâh, Ginâh)*. A lofty brick wall surrounds an enclosure covered with small brick houses and containing a temple of the Ptolemaic period, built of red sandstone and adorned with reliefs and inscriptions. About 2½ M. farther on is *Qaṣr ʿAin ez-Zaiyân*, with a Roman temple. A journey of 1½-2 days to the S. from this point, viâ the large village of *Berîs (Bârîs)* or *Berys* (170 ft.; rest-house to the E. of the village) and *El-Maks*, brings us to the *Qaṣr Dûsh*, the *Kysis* of the ancients, with a large temple of the Roman imperial epoch. There is another brick temple in the vicinity.

Dâkhla.

The *Oasis of Dâkhla* (*Dakhel*, Arabic *El-Wâḥât ed-Dâkhla*, i.e. 'the inner oasis'), the most populous of the oases, is situated in N. Lat. 25°28′ and E. Long. 28°58′, 43 M. to the W. of Khârga, and is reached from the town of Khârga by motor-car in 9 hrs. (to Gedîda; P.T. 150 per person), or by camels in 3-4 days. From Asyûṭ (p. 226) it is reached in 7 days. The chief places in the oasis are *El-Qaṣr* (394 ft), *Gedîda* (accommodation at the ʿomda's), *Balâṭ (Balat)*, *Mûṭ* (390 ft.; rest-house), and *Qalamûn*. About 2 hrs. S.W. of El-Qaṣr is a large ruined temple of the Roman imperial time.

Comp. *H. J. L. Beadnell's* Dakhla Oasis (Cairo, 1901).

III. LOWER NUBIA.

Tickets of Admission to the antiquities, see p. 212. — As *Shellâl (Philae)* is not yet united by railway with *Wâdi Halfa*, visitors to Lower Nubia are practically dependent upon the steamers. The journey by land, on camels or donkeys, is fatiguing and by no means recommended; and the costly dahabîya (p. 216) will be employed only by travellers with special aims. By small parties or single travellers the trip may well be made by motor-boat (to be hired at Aswân: comp. p. 378). — All the ruined sites of Nubia are free from floods in summer and autumn.

Nile Steamers. Regular communication between Shellâl and Wâdi Halfa (214 M.; railway connection for Kharṭûm) is maintained by the Sûdân Government Express Steamers *(Sudan, Britain, Lotus*, and *Meroë)*, which run in connection with the express trains, leaving Shellâl on Mon. and Thurs. afternoons and returning from Wâdi Halfa on Mon. and Thurs. evenings. The boats are stern-wheelers and are well fitted up. The voyage upstream takes 41-42 hrs., downstream 37½ hrs., a stay of 1 or 2 hrs. usually being made at Es-Sebûʿa (p. 424), and Abu Simbel (p. 431). The Mon. steamer remains at Wâdi Halfa from Wed. to Mon., and the Thurs. steamer from Sat. to Thurs., so that ample time is available for the excursion to the Second Cataract (p. 439). Fare from Shellâl to Wâdi Halfa 1st class P.T. 560, 2nd class P.T. 350; meals 1st class P.T. 80 per day, 2nd class P.T. 50. During the season tickets for 'independent tours' also are issued (1st class, including meals): from Shellâl to Wâdi Halfa and back, with a motor-boat excursion to the Second Cataract, in 4-6 days, £E 12½-17 according to the month; from Shellâl to

Kharṭûm (comp. p. 445) and back (including 1st class railway fare and hotel charges) in 9 days, £E 42 (early season, £ 31). Although these steamers make no halt of any duration except at Wâdi Ḥalfa, travellers who are not specially interested in archæology will obtain a sufficiently adequate idea of the scenery of Nubia on this voyage. — There is also a weekly mail-steamer ('intermediate service'), starting from Shellâl on Tues. (from Wâdi Ḥalfa on Sat.), which calls at almost all stations and completes the voyage in 60 hrs.; fares as for the express-steamers (no meals provided). Information and time-tables may be obtained on application to the tourist agents at Cairo (p. 40) or from the agency of the Sûdân Government Steamers at Aswân railway station, and the Grand Hotel (p. 378).

Tourist Steamers. Travellers who desire to inspect the ruined sites of Nubia more closely will avail themselves of Messrs. Thos. Cook & Son's tourist steamer *Thebes* (comp. p. 214), which plies during the season (in 1928-29 every Mon. from the beginning of Dec. to the beginning of March) and takes seven days for the trip from Shellâl to Wâdi Ḥalfa and back; return-fare, including meals, 30*l.* (single-berth cabin with private bath 40*l.*, double cabin for one passenger 35*l.*), from Cairo 100-160*l.*

The Itinerary of Cook's steamer was as follows in 1928-29.

1st Day. Start from Shellâl (Philæ) on Mon. at 3.30 p.m. and proceed S. past Debôd and Qertassi.

2nd Day. To Dendûr (visit to the temple, p. 419) and Garf Ḥusein (visit to the temple, p. 420), and thence viâ Ed-Dakka to Eṣ-Sebûʿa (visit to the temple, p. 424) and Korosko (p. 426).

3rd Day. To El-ʿÁmada (visit to the temple, p. 426) and thence past Ed-Derr and Qaṣr Ibrîm to Abu Simbel, which is reached about 6 p.m.

4th Day. Visit to the temples of Abu Simbel (p. 431). Start again at 11 a.m. and reach Wâdi Ḥalfa (p. 438) about 5 p.m.

5th Day. Excursion to the Second Cataract (p. 439).

6th Day. Start at 8.30 a.m. for Abu Simbel (p. 431).

7th Day. To Ed-Derr (p. 427), Korosko (p. 426), and Kalâbsha (visit to the temples, pp. 416, 418), arriving at Shellâl on Sun. evening.

Land and People. *Nubia* (Arabic *Bilâd el-Barâbra*, 'land of the Berbers', p. lxii) extends from the First Cataract to Merowe (p. 446), i.e. to 18° N. Latitude. It is divided into *Lower Nubia* (from Philæ to Wâdi Ḥalfa) and *Upper Nubia* (from Wâdi Ḥalfa southwards). Politically, the portion to the N. of Faras (p. 437) belongs to the Egyptian mudîrîya of Aswân, in which it forms the district of Ed-Derr (p. 427). The rest of Lower Nubia and the whole of Upper Nubia has, since its reconquest in 1898 (p. cxxx), been placed under the administration of the Anglo-Egyptian Sûdân. In Lower Nubia the arable area is seldom more than a few hundred yards in width; and at not a few points, especially on the W. bank, the desert advances right up to the river-brink. Moreover in the neighbourhood of

the Aswân Dam (comp. p. 396) the possibility of cultivation is greatly restricted. The population (c. 120,000) is in consequence very scanty. Comp. p. lxiii. — Lower Nubia was known to the ancient Egyptians as the land of *Wewet*, while the countries on the Upper Nile, from Wâdi Ḥalfa southwards, were included under the single name of *Kush*, the *Cush* of the Bible. The Greeks and Romans called them *Æthiopia*. The present inhabitants of Nubia are more faithful to their ancient manners and customs than the Egyptians. When the huge storage-lake, extending far into Northern Nubia, was formed by the dam at Aswân, the villages within its basin were removed to the heights (comp. p. 397). This fact accounts for the numerous ruined villages seen under water or on the edge of the lake.

History. In prehistoric times, a light upon which has been thrown of recent years by the systematic excavation of Nubian cemeteries, Lower Nubia was inhabited by the same race (a branch of the brown Mediterranean stock) as Egypt proper. A uniform culture thus prevailed from the Nile delta southwards to the Second Cataract. At the beginning, however, of the historical period (3200 B.C.), which coincides with the foundation of the united kingdom of Egypt, the latter's civilization made great strides, reaching its material and artistic zenith in the Pyramid age. Meanwhile Nubia remained in its original condition. The burials of those times bear witness to the dire poverty of the inhabitants. The cultural connection with Egypt was practically destroyed. In the earliest Egyptian texts Lower Nubia is the country through which the products of the Sûdân (ebony, ivory, leopard-skins, gums and resins, etc.) were imported. Under the 6th Dyn. (p. ciii) Nubian mercenaries were enlisted by the Pharaohs, and the princes of Elephantine (p. 383) undertook trading expeditions to the lands of the upper Nile. A great change took place in the population of Lower Nubia in the period between the Ancient and Middle Empires, towards the end of the 3rd millennium B.C. Nubian tribes, pressing forwards from the S., took possession of the districts between the First and Second Cataracts. They brought with them to their new territory their own African culture, which, however, embodied many local traditions and did not altogether escape the influence of Egypt. Thus arose a characteristic Nubian civilization, which reached its apogee under the Middle Empire (p. ciii). At the same time political differences with Egypt sprang up. Even in the time of the 11th Dyn. the Pharaohs attempted to subdue Nubia and gain control of the important trade route to the Sûdân. But it was not until the 12th Dyn. that the conquest of Nubia was successful and the frontier of Egypt advanced to *Semna* (p. 440). In order to guard the newly acquired possessions a chain of forts was erected in the rocky valley of Baṭn el-Ḥagar (p. 439), with its numerous cataracts, between Ḥalfa and Semna. Nubia regained its independence during the decline of Egypt under the Hyksos kings (p. civ), but became an Egyptian

possession again at the beginning of the New Empire. The Pharaohs of the 18th Dyn. penetrated still farther S. and made themselves masters of the land of Kush as far as *Napata* (p. 445), which then became the southernmost city of the empire. The conquered regions were incorporated with the southernmost province of Egypt proper, which began at Elkâb (p. 365), and the whole of the great province thus formed was placed under an official who bore the title of 'Prince of Kush and Governor of the Southern Lands'. Under the established rule of Egypt Nubia rapidly prospered. Egyptian civilization, which had already penetrated Nubia before the time of the 18th Dyn., now spread throughout the land, gradually obliterating the Nubian culture of the Middle Empire. Under the 18th Dyn. Nubia was completely Egypticized. Beautiful temples, little inferior in size and embellishment to those of the motherland, arose in profusion, especially on the W. bank of the Nile, which was safer from the attacks of the E. Beduin. Most of them were dedicated to the great Egyptian gods, Amun, Rē-Harakhte, and Ptah; but in some of them other deities also were worshipped, such as Isis and others of the Egyptian gods, the local Nubian god Dedun, the deceased King Sesostris III. (p. civ), who united the rôles of first conqueror and patron-saint of Nubia, and occasionally also the reigning king and queen (pp. 421, 424, 431, 435). The temple inscriptions were composed in the Egyptian language and written in the Egyptian character, and Egyptian became the official language, although the great mass of the people adhered to the Nubian tongue.

Nubia continued to be a political and cultural dependency of Egypt until about 1100 B.C. But when the power of the Pharaohs waned under the 21st Dyn. (p. cvii) Nubia shook off her allegiance again and a native Ethiopian Monarchy was established, with *Napata* as its capital (p. 445). But the civilization of this kingdom continued to be Egyptian; and its monarchs, who were dependent on the priests, regarded themselves as the true protectors of the Egyptian religion and as the legitimate rulers of Egypt. About 730 B.C. the Ethiopian *Piankhi* (p. cviii) temporarily overran all Egypt, and shortly afterwards an Ethiopian dynasty (the 25th; p. cviii) established itself firmly on the Egyptian throne. But in little more than a century (about 654 B.C.) the kingdom of these Ethiopian Pharaohs was restricted to Nubia, of which the N. border then lay near Philæ (Konosso, p. 395).

Comparatively full information is available regarding the kings of the next period, who resided at Napata, and we hear of the fruitless expedition into Lower Nubia of the army of *Psammetichos II.* (c. 590 B.C.) and of *Cambyses'* attempts at conquest (525 B.C.). After that time the history of the country is obscure. The capital was transferred from Napata to *Meroë* (p. 448) about 300 B.C., but a branch of the royal family continued to rule over N. Ethiopia from Napata.

Egyptian civilization gradually declined in Nubia. The Egyptian hieroglyphic writing became corrupted and a native Meroïtic hieroglyphic and cursive character was developed (p. cxxxviii), which, about the beginning of the Christian era, began to be used for writing the native (so-called Meroïtic) language even in official documents.

During the PTOLEMAIC AND ROMAN IMPERIAL EPOCHS the S. frontier of Egypt was near *Hierasykaminos* (p. 423), and it was occasionally pushed farther S. as far as *Primis* (p. 429). On the other hand the Ethiopians sometimes succeeded in extending their power as far N. as Philæ, and perhaps even occupied part of Upper Egypt. When the Romans first came to Egypt *Candace*, queen of N. Ethiopia, attacked the Roman province, but was repulsed by the Roman governor Petronius in 23 B.C. (p. 421). About this time also the *Blemmyes*, a nomadic race of the E. desert (comp. p. lx), who had previously acknowledged the suzerainty of Ethiopia, assumed an aggressive attitude. Not content with harassing the N. parts of Lower Nubia, they carried their depredations also into the Roman territory in S. Egypt (comp. p. cxv), until finally the Romans gave way before them. *Diocletian* (c. A.D. 300) withdrew from Nubia altogether, retiring within the bounds of Egypt proper, to the N. of Philæ. The Blemmyes, however, in alliance with the Nubians, continued their attacks on Upper Egypt; but in A.D. 451 they were defeated by *Marcian*, who concluded a peace with them (comp. p. 390). Previously (c. A.D. 350) the Abyssinian kings of Aksum had conquered the upper valley of the Nile and put an end to the Meroïtic kingdom.

Christianity established itself at Philæ in the 4th cent., and thence extended throughout Nubia, where the temples were converted into churches. In A.D. 640 Egypt and the Upper Nile Valley fell into the hands of the Arabs. *ʿAmr* (p. cxvii) penetrated as far as Dongola and imposed tribute upon Nubia, but no enduring subjugation of the country was effected. Shams ed-Dôla, brother of Saladin, took possession of the fortress of Ibrîm (p. 429) in 1173 and plundered the church treasury; but Christianity yielded to Islâm very gradually, and a Christian kingdom lingered at Sôba on the Blue Nile (p. 460) until the middle ages. We know little of the Mohammedan principalities established at Ed-Derr (p. 427), Dongola (p. 447), Sennâr (p. 461), and other points in Nubia. In 1821 Ismâʿîl Pasha conquered the whole of Nubia for his father, Muḥammed ʿAli (pp. cxxv, cxxvi). For the later history of the country, the Mahdist rebellion, and the reconquest by Kitchener, see pp. cxxvii seqq.

30. From Shellâl to Kalâbsha.

31 M. BY STEAMER (comp. pp. 409, 410). — During the winter season the quarries and fort at *Qertassi* and the temples at *Tâfa* and *Kalâbsha* are flooded and therefore inaccessible except by small boat.

As we leave *Shellâl* (p. 389) we have a fine view of the ruined temples of *Philæ* (p. 390) and of the rocks of *Bigga* (p. 395). To the S.W. of Bigga lies *El-Heisa (El-Hesseh)*, the largest of the cataract islands, where the cemetery of the priests of Philæ was discovered. On the E. bank is the village of *El-Mashhad*, with picturesque old mosques. On the rocks above is a sheikh's tomb. — On the E. bank, opposite the S. end of El-Heisa, is a rock-inscription of Phiops I. (p. ciii), relating to his victory over the Nubians.

At *Gûdhi* the river bends S.W., afterwards returning to its S. direction. The scenery becomes less wild, and a narrow strip of verdure appears on each bank. — To the W. is the *Gebel Sheimet el-Wâḥ*. From time to time we observe on both banks, at low water, ancient dykes of huge stones, and on the summits of the higher hills are ruined guard-houses, dating from the Mahdist insurrection.

$9^1/_2$ M. **Debôd** *(Dâbûd)*, a village community on both banks. On the W. bank are traces of an ancient quay and the **Temple of Debôd**, situated near the river. This temple was built by the Nubian king Ezekher-Amun, a contemporary of the earlier Ptolemies, and it was enlarged by Ptolemy VI. Philometor (p. cxii). From a modern flight of steps we pass through two *Doorways*, on the second of which appear the winged sun-disk and a Greek inscription in favour of Philometor and his consort Cleopatra. About 42 ft. beyond a third doorway (now ruined) is the temple proper.

Of the *Vestibule*, the façade of which was borne by four columns with rich floral capitals, connected by stone screens, little now remains. The reliefs on the façade show Augustus or Tiberius in the presence of various deities. The side-walls of the *First Hall* are decorated with reliefs in two rows, exhibiting Ezekher-Amun sacrificing to various deities. Over the door is a votive inscription of the same monarch. Thence we proceed through an *Antechamber* (without decoration) to the *Sanctuary*, which contains a granite *Naos*, dating from Euergetes II. and Cleopatra (p. cxii). The adjoining chambers contain nothing of interest.

At *Dimri* (W. bank) is an ancient wall; and on the E. bank farther on is the fragment of a quay-wall, with a staircase. The island of *Morgos (Murquṣ, Markos)*, next passed, has some picturesque ruins of houses, apparently of mediæval origin.

$17^1/_2$ M. *Dihmît (Dehmîṭ)*, on both banks, is a steamer station. — 25 M. *El-Umbarakâb (Amberkâb)*, with considerable hamlets on both banks.

To the right (W. bank) next appears the small temple of Qertassi *(Girtâs)*, an attractive building on a rocky plateau, recalling the 'kiosk' at Philæ (p. 395). It is only 25 ft. square. Columns,

connected by stone screens, once supported the roof, of which only a single cross-beam now remains. Two Hathor-columns (at the entrance, which faces N.) and four other columns with elaborate flower-capitals (two on each side) are now standing.

To the S. is an embankment constructed to protect the valley from inundation, and farther on are extensive **Sandstone Quarries*, which yielded the stone for the temples at Philæ. They contain numerous Greek votive inscriptions (and one demotic) dating from the Roman imperial epoch (Antoninus, Marcus Aurelius, Septimius Severus, Caracalla, Gordian). These are addressed to Isis and to the Nubian deities Sruptichis and Pursepmunis. Two busts in high relief and an empty niche, with an Egyptian doorway, also deserve notice. — At the end of the quarries ($^3/_4$ M. from the temple) is a *Roman Fort* (perhaps the ancient *Tzitzi*), with a girdle-wall of large hewn stones, the inner core of which has disappeared, leaving only the outer shell. The gateway on the N. side shows the Egyptian cavetto cornice. On the W. side we may trace the ancient ditch.

Farther on the river-valley narrows and lofty cliffs approach close to the stream.

Tâfa (*Teifa;* W. bank), the ancient *Taphis*. On the river bank are the remains of a narrow quay, on the S. side of which is a small nilometer. The little *Temple*, of the Roman period, was left unfinished and has no mural reliefs. The entrance faces S. The façade is supported by two columns with elaborate floral capitals. In the interior of the temple are four standing columns, with floral capitals. — To the N. are the remains of some large structures, perhaps the relics of a fortified camp. — To the S. of the village lay a second temple, which, however, was entirely destroyed in the latter half of the 19th century. To the W. is a Mohammedan cemetery of an early period. On the hill above is a castellated building.

Beyond Tâfa the dark shining rocks advance close to both river banks, forming a kind of rocky gateway, known as the *Bâb el-Kalâbsha*. At a few isolated points a narrow strip of cultivated land borders the river, and on the E. bank lies a small village. The navigation of this reach is somewhat intricate, owing to the numerous rocky islands. At the point where the valley expands again lies a small island, with some ruined buildings.

31 M. *Kalâbsha* forms a large commune on both banks of the Nile. — From *Kharṭûm*, a small village on the W. bank, a desert route leads round the Bâb el-Kalâbsha to Tâfa (see above). On this route, about 10 min. from the village, is a rock-inscription, dating from the 19th year of King Taharka (p. cviii). About $1^1/_4$ M. farther on, on a small plateau, is the ruined church of *Sitta Gasma*, built of rough stones.

Hard by the river, as we proceed S., lie the ruins of the ancient town of *Talmis*. Closely hemmed in by modern houses appears the

large and picturesque ***Temple of Kalâbsha,** built in the reign of Augustus on the site of an earlier sanctuary founded by Amenophis II. (p. cv) and refounded by one of the Ptolemies. This is the finest building in Nubia after the great temple of Abu Simbel (p. 431). It was never completely adorned with reliefs and inscriptions; and the reliefs that are finished are very crude, while the subjects of the representations are frequently misunderstood. The temple was probably dedicated in the first place to the Nubian god Mandulis (p. 391), to whom are addressed most of the dedicatory inscriptions found on the pylons, the walls of the vestibule, and elsewhere. It was converted into a church on the introduction of Christianity. The building is in comparatively good preservation and has recently been restored.

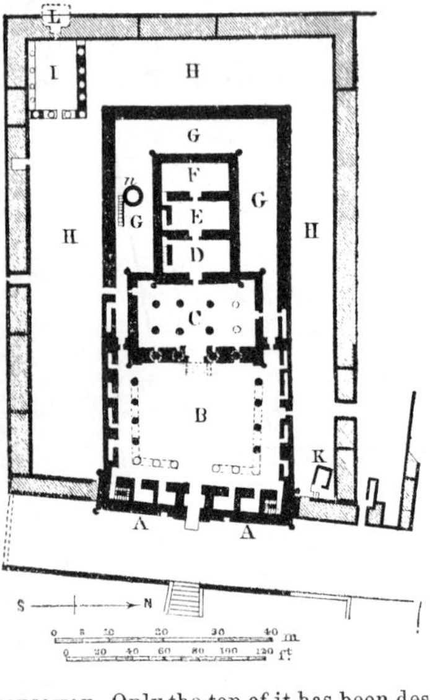

The approach to the temple is formed by a *Causeway*, about 100 ft. long and 25 ft. broad, constructed of hewn stones and still in excellent preservation. At the end next the river is a rectangular projection, below which passes a road; at the landward end a flight of low steps ascends to a long and narrow platform immediately in front of the pylon.

The Pylon (Pl. AA), the principal entrance to the temple precincts, stands at a slight angle with the axis of the temple and causeway. Only the top of it has been destroyed, but it has no reliefs whatever, with the exception of two representations of gods in the doorway. Each tower of the pylon has a groove for a flagstaff (comp. p. 370).

The Court (Pl. B), between the pylon and the vestibule, was surrounded on three sides by colonnades, of which four columns (with rich foliage-capitals) on each side (N. and S.) are now erect. In the court side of the S. pylon-tower are three doors, the two N. ones leading to two chambers, the third (S.) to a staircase ascending in three flights to the roof (fine view). The N. tower also contains a staircase. On each side of the court four narrow chambers have

been constructed in the wall; and a door in the N. colonnade communicates with the passage round the temple and with a crypt. The rear wall of the court forms the imposing façade of the vestibule, which is entered by the large portal in the middle. Between the columns are four stone screens.

On the first screen to the left Thoth and Horus are shown pouring the consecrated water (typified by the hieroglyphs for 'life' and 'purity') upon the king. Adjacent sits the god Harsiēsis of Talmis.

On the first screen to the right is a Greek inscription. This is a decree of Aurelius Besarion, also named Amonius, governor of Ombos and Elephantine, ordering the owners of swine to remove their animals from the holy Talmis. It probably dates from A.D. 248-9. — On the second column to the right are two Greek inscriptions, between which is a long inscription in the Meroïtic cursive character (p. cxxxviii). — The most interesting inscription, however, is on the right corner of the façade. This is the *Memorial Inscription of Silko*, sub-king of the Nubians and all the Ethiopians (c. 5th cent. of the Christian era), in which he celebrates, in bad Greek, his victory over the Blemmyes, whom he defeated "from Primis to Talmis, advancing as far as Taphis [Tâfa] and Talmis".

The Vestibule, or *Pronaos* (Pl. C), the roof of which has fallen in, has twelve columns, with elaborate floral capitals. Most of the reliefs represent the emperor in presence of the gods; two, on the rear (W.) wall, to the left of the door, deserve notice. One shows one of the Ptolemies presenting a field to Isis, Mandulis, and a third deity; the other (right) represents Amenophis II., founder of the original temple (p. 416), offering a libation of wine to Min and Mandulis. On the stone screen to the left of the entrance is a later Christian painting of the three men in the fiery furnace.

The following *Three Rooms (Pl. D, E, F) have well-preserved reliefs, with vivid colouring, depicting the emperor in presence of the gods of Talmis and other deities. At the foot of the walls of Room D are depicted local deities with their offerings. Many of the inscriptions are merely sketched in in red. Small chambers have been constructed in the S. walls of Rooms D and E. From Room D we reach the *Staircase*, which ascends in the thickness of the wall to the roof of Room F. Thence the higher roofs of the front portions of the temple are reached by steps. Another staircase leads from the roof of Room E to the top of the external wall. Descending a few steps to the left, we reach a *Chapel* formed in the thickness of the wall. This comprises two rooms (with a crypt in the second) and was probably intended for the cult of Osiris.

The Inner Passage (Pl. G) round the temple is entered by doors in the court and vestibule. The unfinished lions' heads on the exterior of the temple proper are water-spouts. On the rear wall is a large relief of the emperor before the gods; below are smaller reliefs. The two representations of Mandulis, on the girdle-wall opposite these reliefs, were probably originally protected by a small wooden chapel. On the S. side is a well-preserved *Nilometer* (Pl. *n*).

The W. part of the girdle-wall of the Outer Passage (Pl. H) round the temple was built against the rock. The small *Chapel*

(Pl. I) in the S.W. angle was perhaps a birth house (p. 266). It includes an unfinished open court enclosed by columns and stone screens, and a *Rock Chamber* (Pl. L), of which only the door has reliefs (the emperor before the gods). — Another well-preserved *Chapel* (Pl. K), in the N.E. angle, probably dates from the Ptolemaic temple.

Outside the temple are *Gateways* and ruins of a massive wall of hewn stones. On the W. hill-slope are *Quarries*, while the *Remains of the Ancient Town*, the houses and girdle-wall of which are easily traceable, stretch down into the plain. In the latter are towers of rough stone.

We now proceed N. from the temple of Kalâbsha, turn to the left, and reach the (1/4 hr.) ***Rock Temple of Beit el-Wâli** ('House of the Wâli'), situated halfway up a hill, at the mouth of a side-valley. The temple, founded under Ramses II. (p. cvi), consists of a vestibule, a hypostyle hall hewn in the rock, and a small sanctuary. The Vestibule, of which only the side-walls so far as they were formed by the rock are now standing, was used as a church in Christian times, being divided into nave and aisles and provided with a vaulted brick roof. Our interest is excited by the animated **Historical Reliefs* on the side-walls, of which coloured casts have been placed in the British Museum.

Two scenes on the left wall represent the king's triumph over the Ethiopians. In the first relief we see the king, to the right, under a canopy, while (in the row below) Egyptian grandees present him with tribute of various kinds, the principal object being a tablet adorned with plants, from which hang rings and skins. Behind these are two fettered negroes, after whom come negroes with offerings (monkeys, greyhounds, a leopard, a giraffe, an ostrich, cattle) and women with their children (one carrying her children in a basket held on her back by a strap round her forehead). One of the oxen has horns represented as arms, between which is the head of a negro suing for mercy. In the upper row we see the above-mentioned tablet placed before the king, while the governor of Ethiopia is being adorned with gold chains of honour; farther on are rings of gold, chairs, elephants' tusks, bows, shields, leopard-skins, ebony, fans, and other articles brought as tribute; negroes approach with their offerings (cattle, antelopes, a lion, etc.). — In the second relief the king and his sons appear in chariots dashing against the negro foe. The negroes flee to their village, which lies among dûm-palms. A wounded negro is led by two comrades to his wife and children, while another woman crouches over a fire and cooks a meal.

The reliefs on the right wall refer to the wars against the Syrians and Libyans. In the first scene (beginning to the right) the Pharaoh stands upon two prostrate enemies, grasping three others (Syrians) by the hair, while a prince leads fettered prisoners before him. — In the second relief the king appears before a Syrian fortress; on

the battlements are men and women suing for mercy (notice the woman holding her child by the arm); the king seizes one of the enemy (who holds a broken bow) by the hair to kill him; below, one of the royal princes is beating in the doors with an axe. — The third relief shows the king in his chariot, charging the fleeing Syrians; he kills two of the foes, while two others are bound to his chariot. — In the next scene the king smites a Libyan, while his dog seizes the foe. — In the fifth relief we see King Ramses II. enthroned beneath a canopy, with his lion at his feet. His son Amen-her-wnamf leads Syrian prisoners to him.

Three doors lead from the vestibule into the Hypostyle Hall, which was hewn in the rock. The ceiling of the hall is borne by two 'proto-Doric' columns (p. clxiv), each with four plain sides on which are inscriptions. The mural reliefs are well executed, but their subjects are of no special interest. They represent the king before the gods and (on each side of the side-doors) smiting his enemies (a Syrian and an Ethiopian). — The Sanctuary has similar reliefs. By the rear wall are three statues of the gods, now defaced beyond recognition. These two rock-chambers also were used as a Christian church.

31. From Kalâbsha to Korosko.

Comp. the Map, p. 414.

87 M. by Steamer (comp. pp. 409, 410). — During the winter season the temple at *Dendûr*, the fortress at *Kushtamna*, the temple of *Dakka*, part of the fortress at *Kûbân*, and the temples at *Qûrta* and at *El-Maḥarraqa* are flooded and inaccessible.

Kalâbsha, see p. 415. — $4^1/_2$ M. *Abu Hôr*, on both banks, is situated under the tropic of Cancer. On the E. bank lie *Sheqîq* (*Shigeig*) and, farther on, the chief village *Abu Hôr*, with post and telegraph offices. It is also a steamer station. On the rocks on the barren W. bank are numerous graffiti of ships and animals (some of them of hoary antiquity) and a few inscriptions of the Middle Empire.

Abu Ṭarfa (W. bank). About 1 M. to the S. is a rock-cave with the tomb of a sheikh. The low rapids here, caused by granite rocks in the Nile, are known as the *Bâb Abu Hôr*.

$12^1/_2$ M. *Murwâw* (on both banks) is a steamer station. At *Kubôshâb (Kobosh)*, on the W. bank, are ancient quay-walls with a nilometer and an unfinished little rock-chapel. A little to the N. is a curious irrigation arrangement hewn in the rock.

On the W. bank, opposite the village of *Dendûr*, appears the small **Temple of Dendûr**, built by Augustus on the site of the ancient *Tutzis* and dedicated to various gods, including *Pede-ēse* and *Pe-Hôr*, the sons of Kuper, two local deified heroes. The temple stands upon a platform, immediately at the foot of the mountains, and is preceded by a broad terrace. Of the Pylon, which formed

the entrance to the temple, only the stone doorway remains; the towers, probably built of brick, have disappeared. At the top of the portal is the winged sun-disk, and within and on the front (E.) and back (W.) is the emperor sacrificing to various gods. Beyond the portal we enter an open COURT, which was originally enclosed by brick walls. The façade of the TEMPLE is adorned with two fine columns with floral capitals, once connected with the side-walls by stone screens. The walls of the *Vestibule* are embellished with reliefs of the emperor in presence of the gods. The other two *Small Rooms* have no decoration. In the rear wall of the innermost is a *False Door*, surmounted by serpents, with representations of Pede-ēse and Pe-Hôr praying to Isis and Osiris. The *N.* and *S. Exterior Walls* of the temple are adorned with interesting reliefs. On the N. wall, to the left of the door from the vestibule, appears the emperor offering a piece of cloth to Pe-Hôr, on the S. wall, below, to the left of the door, he sacrifices to Pede-ēse, who is accompanied by a woman, probably his wife.

Among the various *Inscriptions* placed on the walls by visitors to the temple is one in Coptic, in which a certain presbyter Abraham records that he erected a cross here in the church at the command of the Nubian king Eispanome. This appears within the S. side-door of the vestibule.

Above the temple is a small *Rock Chapel*, with a door showing the Egyptian cornice. In the cliffs to the N. of the temple are *Quarries*. The stones lying in front of these are, perhaps, remains of ancient houses.

Beyond the steamer station at ($18\frac{1}{2}$ M.) *Mârîya (Marîa)*, a commune on both banks, the banks of the Nile become flatter and are partly cultivated.

23 M. *Qirsha* (*Qersha*, *Girsha*; E. bank), situated in a wide belt of cultivated land, lies beside the ruins of the ancient Byzantine fortress of *Sabagûra*, which stretches up the hill from the river and is enclosed by strong stone walls.

Opposite, on the W. bank, lie the village (steamer station) and **Rock Temple of Garf Ḥusein** *(Gerf Hussein)*. The Egyptian name of this temple was *Per-Ptah*, the 'House of Ptah'. It was founded in the reign of Ramses II. by *Setaw*, governor of Nubia (p. 427), and it was dedicated to Ptah of Memphis and his fellow-gods. In front of the rock-temple proper lay a quadrangular COURT (Pl. A), which was surrounded by covered colonnades. The E. colonnade had plant-columns, while the others were supported by pillars, against which stood figures of Ramses II. Two of the columns and five of the pillars, with the remains of the architrave, are still extant. The W. side of the court is bounded by the rock-façade of the temple, hewn to imitate a pylon and decorated in a corresponding style. On the left side of the portal is a relief of Ramses offering fresh vegetables to Ptah. Passing through this portal, we enter a large HALL (Pl. B), 45 ft. square, hewn out of the rock. The ceiling is supported by six pillars, 28 ft. high, against which are statues of the king like those in the court. On each side of the

hall are four recesses, each with the king, in the guise of a god under various titles, standing between two deities.

In the recesses on the *Left (S.) Side* (from left to right): 1. The king between Amon-Rē and Mut; 2. between Horus, lord of Beki (Kûbân), and Horus, lord of Buhen (Ḥalfa); 3. between Ptah-Tenen and the cow-headed Hathor; 4. between Ptah and Sakhmet. — In the recesses on the *Right (N.) Side* (from left to right): 1. The king between Khnum and Anuket; 2. between Nefertēm and Satet; 3. between Horus, lord of Mem (ʿAnîba), and Isis; 4. between Harakhte and Ews-os. — The reliefs on the walls of the hall, showing the king before various deities, are unimportant.

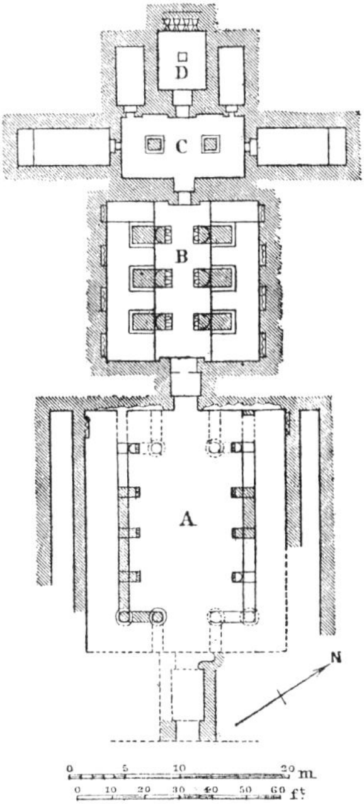

The following Anteroom (Pl. C), about 36 ft. wide though only 17 ft. deep, is entered by a small door, on the left side of which is the king before Ptah. The ceiling is supported by two square pillars. The walls and pillars are embellished with representations of the king in presence of various gods (including the deified Ramses). To the right and left lie two chambers. At the back are three chapels, the central and largest of which is the Sanctuary (Pl. D). On the walls of this chamber are reliefs. On the left wall Ramses before the boat of Ptah; on the right wall, the king before the boat of Harakhte. In the centre of the sanctuary is a pedestal, wrought out of the rock, for the sacred boat. At the back is a recess with four seated figures, representing (from left to right) Ptah, the deified Ramses, Ptah-Tenen, and Hathor with the cow's head.

Above Qirsha and Garf Ḥusein the scenery relapses into monotony. — 29 M. *Kushtamna (Koshtamna)*, a commune on both banks (steamer station on the E. bank). On the E. bank rises the *Gebel Ḥayâti*. On the W. bank is a brick-built fortress of the Middle Empire, known to the natives as *Kuri*. Extensive sandbanks and granite rocks interrupt the course of the river.

35 M. **Ed-Dakka,** on the W. bank, is a steamer station. Dakka is the Greek *Pselchis*, near which the Roman general Petronius defeated the Ethiopians in 23 B.C. (comp. p. 413).

A little to the S. of the landing-place and not far from the river bank is the **Temple of Dakka**, which occupies the site of an earlier shrine, probably of the New Empire, and was dedicated to Thoth of Pnubs, an Ethiopian town. By the Greeks this god was called Paotnuphis. The most ancient part of the building dates from the time of the Ethiopian king Ergamenes and his contemporary Ptolemy IV. Philopator (p. cxii). Euergetes II. (p. cxii) added a vestibule, and the temple received its final form under the Roman emperors by the addition of the sanctuary and pylon. The temple lies with its main axis parallel to the river (i.e. running N. and S.), contrary to the usual rule in Nubian temples.

The entrance is by a well-preserved Pylon, which stood in the outer girdle-wall. Each pylon-tower has a groove for a flagstaff; and both have a few isolated reliefs on the outside and numerous inscriptions, chiefly Greek, though some, added by visitors to the temple, are demotic and Meroïtic (p. cxxxviii). Within the central gateway, on the left side, is a representation of the king making offerings to Thoth, Tefnut, and Hathor, and (below) to Isis.

The Ascent of the Pylon is attractive. In each tower there is a staircase, beginning in a guard-room at the foot and passing three other rooms in the successive stories. On the platform at the top of the W. tower are numerous inscriptions written by visitors and also carved representations of footprints, indicating the spots where the worshippers stood. The roof of the central portal may be reached from the W. tower.

No trace now remains of the court between the pylon and the vestibule. The façade of the Vestibule has two columns with floral capitals, connected with the side-walls by means of screens. On the walls are representations of the king before the gods of Dakka. On the E. wall the Pharaoh proffers to the god Thoth, patron of the scribes, a palette, which is borne by Isis and Nephthys and is, perhaps, symbolical of Osiris. Reliefs of an Ethiopian king occur on the rear wall (at the top, to the left). The vestibule was at a later date used as a church and was painted over with sacred subjects, traces of which are still visible. — The doorway in the rear wall was originally the main entrance to the earlier temple. On the jambs are a number of reliefs: left, Philopator before Rē, Khnum, and Isis; right, Philopator before Amon-Rē, Harendotes, and Isis. Within the portal an emperor dedicates the figure of Maat to the god Thoth of Pnubs and to the lion-headed Tefnut.

We next enter the Transverse Chamber. A staircase, on the right, led hence to the roof of the temple in the Roman period; at the top is a crypt in the thickness of the wall. — The following Chamber was built by Ergamenes. Of its reliefs only one is interesting (right wall): Ergamenes making a libation of wine to a god described as 'Pharaoh of Senmet' (Bigga) and to the goddess Anuket. — A small door (of later construction) in the E. wall admits to Two Chambers. On the back-wall of the second are two lions sitting face to face; above them is a baboon (Thoth)

worshipping the goddess Tefnut (in the form of a lioness); higher up are two ibises.

The SANCTUARY, containing the granite shrine, is embellished with clumsy reliefs by an unidentified emperor, who appears in them before various deities. An interesting relief represents the Nile gods approaching the sacred fig-tree, beneath which sits Thoth in the form of a baboon. In the rear wall are a door (of later construction) and two windows (surmounted by the winged sun-disk). On the outside of this wall was a large door-shaped recess, containing a relief of Thoth of Pnubs.

On the E. bank, nearly opposite Dakka, lies the commune of *El-ʿAllâqi*. A little to the N. of the steamer station is **Kûbân** (or *Kubbân*), the ancient *Beki*, with the ruins of a *Fortress* of the Middle Empire (p. ciii), commanding the road to the under-mentioned gold mines. The fortress was enclosed by a lofty wall of sun-dried bricks, mats, and wooden logs, and was defended by a ditch. Within the wall, on the S. side, lay a small temple. — Adjacent are two almost completely demolished *Temples*, one to the S., the other to the N. of the village. Near the former is a rock-hewn *Cistern*, to the E. of which, in the desert, are several tombs of the Middle Empire.

From Kûbân a route leads through the extensive WÂDI ʿALLÂQI to (40 M.; a camel-ride of 1½ day) the *Gold Mines of Umm Garayât* (*Wâdi Khawanib*), situated in 22°40′ N. Lat. and 33° 18′ E. Long. These were worked until the middle ages, and granite mortars and mills and other apparatus used in the search for gold are still to be seen. The mines are now (since 1902) being worked again by an English company. In the same neighbourhood are traces of various other ancient mines.

At (38 M.) *Qûrta*, on the W. bank, are the ruins of a small temple, dedicated to Isis, on the site of an earlier shrine of the New Empire. — In the river lies the large and usually flooded island of *Zerâr*, known also as *Gezîret Qûrta*. On the W. bank, 1¼ M. farther on, and to the S. of the villages of *Ofeduîna* (*Ofedunîa*) and *Birba*, lies the small **Temple of El-Maḥarraqa**, better known as the *Temple of Ofeduîna*. This marks the site of the ancient town of *Hierasykaminos* ('the sacred sycamore'; p. 413), which lay on the extreme boundary of the Egyptian kingdom under the Ptolemies and the Romans. The unfinished temple (restored) dates from the Roman period and was dedicated to Sarapis. It includes a rectangular court, surrounded on three sides by covered colonnades. The entrance is on the E. side. The columns on the S. side are connected by stone screens, and through the central one of these a door leads to the rest of the temple. The spiral staircase of masonry, which leads to the roof of the colonnade from the N.E. corner of the court, is an unusual feature.

44 M. *El-Maḥarraqa* (*Miḥarraqa*), on both banks. On a flat-topped hill on the W. bank, 1¼ M. to the S. of the temple, stands the Byzantine *Fortress of Mehendi*. This is surrounded by a thick wall strengthened with towers, except on the side next the river,

where the steepness of the hill was considered protection enough. From the main entrance, on the S. side, a street leads to a church and thence to an open space. The houses, built of brick and stone, have vaulted roofs and are in good preservation.

50 M. *Saiyâla (Seyala)*, on both banks, with a post and telegraph office; the steamer station is on the E. bank. — 56 M. *El-Madîq* is a steamer station on the W. bank. The mountains on the E. become higher. The river makes a wide bend to the W.

68 M. *Wâdi el-'Arab*, on both banks, is inhabited by an Arabic-speaking population.

The village of **Es-Sebû'a** *(Es-Sibû')* consists of two parts, one on each bank of the Nile. On the W. bank (station of the government steamer), amid the tawny desert-sand, lies the well-preserved **Temple of Sebû'a**, called by the Egyptians *Per-Amun* ('House of Amun'). This temple was dedicated to Amun and the sun-god Rē-Harakhte by Ramses II., and is constructed on the same plan as the temple at Garf Ḥusein (p. 420). Ramses himself also was worshipped here as a god. The temple precincts are enclosed by a partly demolished brick wall, in which is a Stone Gateway (Pl. 1), flanked by a statue of Ramses II. and a royal sphinx and leading to the First Forecourt (Pl. 2). The central path is lined with six lion-sphinxes wearing the double crown, whence the modern name of Es-Sebû'a ('the lions') is derived. Behind we note the stone basins for ablutions. We pass through a demolished Brick Pylon (Pl. 3) to reach the Second Forecourt (Pl. 4), adorned on either side with two very fine hawk-headed sphinxes, images of the sun-god Rē-Harakhte. On the left of this court lies another small Brick Temple, with a main chamber (Pl. 5) containing an altar dedicated to Amon-Rē and Rē-Harakhte; in an adjoining room (Pl. 6) are two round storage-places.

A staircase (Pl. 7; restored) ascends to the terrace on which stands the temple proper. Its entrance is a well-preserved Stone Pylon (Pl. 9; 65 ft. high, 80 ft. wide), in front of which stood four colossal statues of the king. One of these, on the left, holding a staff with a ram's head, the symbol of Amon-Rē, is still upright; the prostrate statue on the right holds the symbol of Rē-Harakhte, a staff with a hawk's head. The weathered reliefs on the towers show the king slaying a heap of enemies in the presence of Amon-Rē or Rē-Harakhte. Passing through the central doorway (with reliefs of Ramses II. sacrificing to the gods), we enter the Court (Pl. 10), which is 65 ft. square and is adorned on either side with colonnades of five pillars with colossal statues of the king in front of them. The crude mural reliefs, with the usual scenes of sacrifice, are devoid of interest. To the left of the court lies a Slaughter Court (Pl. 11), with perforated stones to which the animals were tethered.

A staircase ascends from the court to a narrow terrace (Pl. 12) and to the double door (built into the ancient doorway in Christian times)

of the great HYPOSTYLE HALL (Pl. 13; 41 ft. long, 52 ft. wide, and 19 ft. high), constructed partly in the rock, with a roof borne by six pillars with statues of the king (now destroyed) and by six plain pillars. As in the case of many other Egyptian temples it was converted into a Christian church, orientated W. and E. The apse, which opens towards the W., and the altar in front of it are still in existence. Many of the reliefs were painted over by the Christians. Beyond the hall is a rock-hewn TRANSVERSE CHAMBER (Pl. 14), adjoined on either side by rooms. Its wall-reliefs show Ramses II. and various deities, also the king sacrificing to his own image. Of the three chapels opening off the rear wall, the central one, as at Garf Ḥusein, forms the SANCTUARY (Pl. 15). Here, on the right wall, we see the king offering flowers to the sacred bark of Harakhte, which is adorned with hawks' heads; on the left he offers them to the bark of Amun, with its decoration of rams' heads. On the rear wall is the ship of the sun, with the ram-headed sun-god Rē-Harakhte seated beneath a canopy and worshipped by the king (l.) and by three apes (r.). Below is a niche with the mutilated statues of the three deities

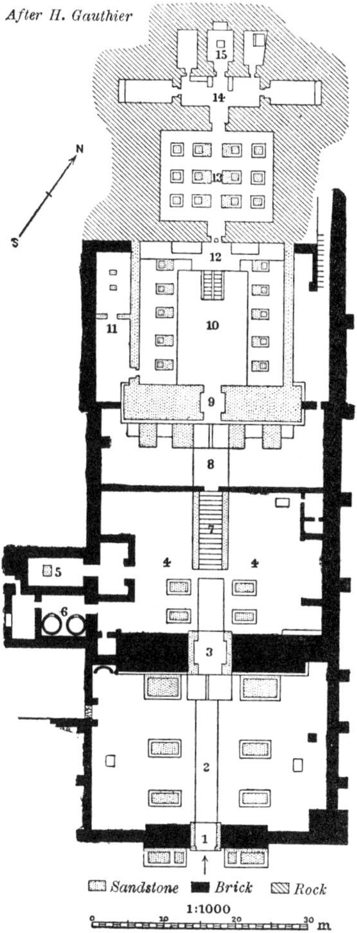

worshipped in this temple, Amun, Ramses, and Rē-Harakhte; on either side is represented the king offering flowers. Over the middle statue is a painting of St. Peter with the key of heaven.

76 M. *Shâturma*, a village situated among palms on the E. bank. The Nile now bends to the S., and the mountains approach close to the E. bank, their steep slopes lending a peculiar charm to the scenery.

$81\frac{1}{2}$ M. *Es-Singâri-Dakhlanîyeh* (E. bank) and *El-Mâlki* (W. bank), a steamer station.

87 M. **Korosko** (*Kurusku;* E. bank), a steamer station with a post and telegraph office and a small mosque, is situated in a plain, bounded by a semicircle of mountains. It is the starting-point of the great caravan route to Abu Ḥamed (p. 445; 8-10 days' journey). This road strikes direct across the desert, the chief haunt of the ʿAbâbda and Bishârîn Beduin (p. lx), avoiding the three upper cataracts and cutting off the windings of the Nile. During the Mahdist insurrection Korosko was of considerable strategical importance and was held by a strong garrison; now, however, the forts and barracks are deserted and many houses are in ruins. In the valley behind the town is a British military cemetery. — The traveller may ascend ($\frac{3}{4}$-1 hr.) the steep and stony hill of *Aweis el-Gurani*, close to Korosko. The view extends over the caravan route, the loop of the Nile, the W. mountains, and far over the Libyan desert.

32. From Korosko to Abu Simbel.

56 M. BY STEAMER (comp. pp. 409, 410). — *Comp. the Map, p. 414.*

The E. bank of the Nile between Korosko (see above) and Arminna (p. 431) is the most fertile portion of Nubia. The belt of cultivable land along the river is comparatively broad and is irrigated by means of water-wheels (sâqiyas) of curious construction, worked by oxen. — Beyond Korosko the Nile valley trends to the N., so that the N. wind which prevails in winter frequently retards the sailing boats. On the right bank is (3 M.) *Abu Ḥandal* (steamer station). On the left bank lies the district of *Er-Rîqa (Areiqa)*, in which, near *El-Gezîra*, are the ruins (explored in 1907 by the expedition of the University of Philadelphia) of a Nubian castle still occupied in the time of Thutmosis III.

About 3 M. farther lies ($9\frac{1}{2}$ M.) the **Temple of El-ʿAmada**, which dates from the 18th Dyn. (p. cv) and was dedicated to Amon-Rē and to Rē-Harakhte, the sun-god. It was erected under Thutmosis III. and Amenophis II. and was extended under Thutmosis IV. The figures of Amun were defaced by Amenophis IV. and restored by Sethos I. In Christian times the temple was used as a church and the reliefs were covered with whitewash, which has had the effect of preserving the original colouring (comp. p. clxxxviii).

We enter the temple, which is orientated practically S. and N., by a stone Portal, which was originally flanked by pylon towers of brick. On the right side of the doorway appears Thutmosis III., to the left Amenophis II., in the presence of Rē-Harakhte. On the inside of the doorway, to the left, is an inscription referring to a campaign of Menephthes (p. cvii) against the Ethiopians; farther on appears the praying figure of Setaw, who was governor of Nubia under Ramses II. (p. 430). — A court enclosed by brick walls extended originally beyond the pylon, while at the back stood a colonnade with four proto-Doric (p. clxiv) columns. This court was afterwards converted by Thutmosis IV. into a covered Hypostyle Hall (still in good preservation; $32^1/_2$ ft. long, 26-$28^1/_2$ ft. wide, and $14^1/_2$ ft. high) by the addition of twelve pillars and stone side-walls. The reliefs on the pillars and walls show Thutmosis IV. in intercourse with the gods, and the inscriptions on the architraves also date from that king. The columns are embellished with perpendicular bands of inscriptions, containing dedications by Thutmosis III. or Amenophis II., who are represented also on the rear wall before the gods. — The following Transverse Chamber is $24^1/_2$ ft. broad, $24^1/_2$ ft. long, and 12 ft. high. On the right half of the entrance-wall is Thutmosis III. embraced by Isis, and then Amenophis II. sacrificing to Amon-Rē. On the left half Thoth and Horus of Edfu pour the consecrated water, symbolized by the hieroglyphs for 'life', over Amenophis II. Of the three doors in the back-wall of this room the side-doors lead into two Chambers; in the right-hand or E. chamber the reliefs on the right wall represent the ceremonies at the foundation of a temple. — The central door gives access to the Sanctuary, on the back-wall of which is a stele of the third year of the reign of Amenophis II. At the top is a relief of the sacred boat of the sun with the gods Rē-Harakhte and Amun, to whom Amenophis II. is making a libation of wine; beneath is an inscription recording the completion of the temple and the king's campaign in Syria. Among other details Amenophis records that he captured seven Syrian princes and hanged six of them on the walls of Thebes and the seventh at Napata (p. 445). — To the right and left of the sanctuary are two small rooms, connected with the side-chambers of the transverse chambers by doors constructed at a later date but now walled up.

Between the temple and the river are the foundations of a small building, either a chapel or a quay.

The Nile here describes a curve from E. to W. On the right bank are (10 M.) *Ed-Dîwân* and **Ed-Derr** (*Ed-Dirr;* steamer station), a district capital, the chief town in Nubia, prettily situated beneath sycamores and date-palms. On the river-bank are the government building and the school. A little down-stream is the large brick residence of the Kâshif, who was formerly independent ruler of Nubia. A cemetery close by contains the tasteful tomb of a sheikh.

Most of the tombs here are surrounded by low mud-walls and strewn with pebbles; at the head of each is placed a large dish for water and frequently a censer also.

Close by, at the foot of the hills, lies the small **Rock Temple of Derr** ('Temple of Ramses in the House of Rē'), built by Ramses II. and dedicated to the sun-god Rē-Harakhte. The temple lies N. and S. The pylon and court having disappeared, we first enter the much-ruined Hall, the sides of which were partly formed by the smoothed rocks of the hill. The roof was supported by twelve square pillars in three rows. The pillars in the back rows, against which rose colossal statues of Ramses II., still stand to a considerable height. Only the lower portion of the walls, the reliefs on which were of historical importance, is now standing. On the left (E.) half of the *Entrance Wall* are traces of warlike scenes with chariots and warriors. On the *Right (W.) Wall* are scenes from the Nubian campaign of the king. In the upper row (much damaged) we see Ramses II. in his chariot, accompanied by his lion, conducting a group of captives before the god; adjacent the king sacrifices to Amon-Rē. The lowest row shows the king in his chariot launching arrows against his fleeing foes. We see the fugitives conveying their wounded to the mountains, where a herdsman's family, surrounded by their cattle, wait in grief and anxiety. To the left are Egyptian soldiers with negro captives. On the *Left (E.) Wall* also are remains of several reliefs: (left to right) 1. Captives led before the king; 2. The king in battle; 3. The king smiting his enemies; 4. The king leads two rows of captives before Rē-Harakhte, in whose temple they are to be slaves. Above, the king appears before Atum. *Rear (S.) Wall:* To the left of the door appears the king grasping a group of enemies by the hair and smiting them with his club, while the king's lion seizes a foe by the leg, and the falcon-headed Rē-Harakhte hands the king the sickle-shaped sword; to the right the king presents an image of Maat to the ram-headed Khnum. At the foot of the wall are princes with their fans. To the right of the door is the king smiting his enemies in presence of Amon-Rē; to the left, above, the king makes a libation of wine to Ptah and another god, below, he burns incense before Thoth.

The following Hypostyle Hall, which is almost square, is hewn entirely out of the rock. The roof rests upon six pillars, on which are reliefs of the king before various deities. One scene on the *West Wall* shows Ramses burning incense before the sacred boat of Rē-Harakhte, which is adorned with falcons' heads and carried by priests. On the *East Wall* is a similar scene, in which the king offers flowers to the sacred boat. — Adjoining this hall are three chapels, the central one being the Sanctuary, in which the sacred boats were kept, as is depicted on the side-walls. On the rear wall are four seated figures (in poor preservation) of the gods worshipped in the temple, viz. (left to right) Ptah, Amon-Rē, the king, and Rē-Harakhte.

On the hill-slope to the E. of the temple are a ruined Egyptian rock-tomb, a rocky memorial niche dedicated to Amenemhab in the reign of Ramses II., inscriptions of the Middle and New Empires, and very old carefully chiselled graffiti of ships, giraffes, etc. At the entrance of the valley traversed by the road to the Bîr Murat (p. 445) is a small and ancient recess, in which a fire is made on feast-days in honour of Sheikh Yûsuf, who is buried beneath. — To the W. of the temple are nine shallow rock-recesses, some Coptic graves, and an ancient cistern.

Beyond Derr the Nile valley again turns S.W. The W. bank becomes more fertile, and numerous water-wheels enliven the water's edge. The landscape takes on quite a new character. On the W. bank lies *Tumâs*, with a large, partly flooded island. Behind the village are rock-inscriptions of the Ancient Empire. — 15 M. *Tunqâla* (E. bank) and *'Áfya* (*Afia;* W. bank), the latter situated beyond palm-groves and fields. The hills on the E. bank approach closer to the stream. — 20 M. *Qatta* (E. bank). On the W. bank lies the ruined castle of *Karanóg*, a lofty brick edifice on a substructure of sandstone; it is of late Nubian origin and may date from the 3rd or 4th cent. of our era. To the S. of it are the ruins of an ancient town.

On the E. bank, near ($23^1/_2$ M.) the large island of *Gezîret Ibrîm* or *Gezîret Abu Râs*, is the prosperous village of **Ibrîm** (steamer station), with fine groves of palms and two mosques. In the N. part of the village, near a cemetery with the picturesque tomb of a sheikh, are the rock-grottoes of Elleisîya (*El-Leisîa).* The largest of these dates from the reign of Thutmosis III. On each side of the entrance of the largest grotto are inscriptions of Thutmosis III., and on the rocks farther on are numerous memorial inscriptions.

Opposite Ibrîm, on the green W. bank, lies the pretty village of **'Anîba** (*'Ineiba)*, shaded by palms. It occupies the site of the ancient *Mem*, capital of Nubia and residence of the Egyptian viceroy under the New Empire. About $^1/_2$ hr. from the river, in a solitary rock, is the dilapidated *Tomb of Pennet*, an official under Ramses VI. (20th Dyn.). The entrance is on the S.E. side and was originally approached by a still traceable rough causeway.

Midway between Pennet's tomb and the river lies an extensive cemetery of the New Empire, with the remains of pyramidal and other *Brick Tombs* and a large Nubian cemetery of the Middle Empire. Both were explored in 1912-14 by the German Ernst von Sieglin Expedition, directed by Georg Steindorff.

The E. bank of the river is now approached by lofty and precipitous rocks. Upon one of these stands the extremely picturesque ruined fort of ***Qaṣr Ibrîm**, dating from Roman times. A visit to it is interesting.

Qaṣr Ibrîm is identified with the Roman *Primis*, which was one of the most important strategic points in Nubia (comp. p. 413). At the beginning of the 16th cent. the sultan Selîm I. (p. cxxiv) placed a garrison of Bosnians here. The fortress was occupied in 1812 by the fleeing Mamelukes (p. cxxvi), but in the same year Ibrâhîm Pasha recaptured and destroyed it.

An easy path ascends on the N. to the only *Gate* of the fortress, which lies on the N. side. This is embellished with the Egyptian cavetto cornice and the sun-disk. The *Girdle Wall* of rough stones is supported on the S. side by an older substructure of carefully hewn blocks. The interior of the fortress is occupied by a confused group of houses of the Turkish period, built of rough stones, but incorporating fragments of older buildings, such as portions of columns used for thresholds. Two of the larger buildings are still in good preservation, viz. a Byzantine *Church* in the middle and a *Temple* in the Egyptian style in the N.W. corner. The church stands on the site of an older Coptic church; it was afterwards used as a mosque, but a consecration cross is still to be seen on one of the columns. The temple has no inscriptions. Steep flights of steps, cut in the rock, descended on the W. side to the river. The view from the castle hill is very fine; to the E. rise the hills of the Arabian desert (one eminence crowned by the tomb of a sheikh), while the Nile flows far below; to the W. lies the tawny desert with its pyramidal hills, contrasting with the verdant cultivated land and the grey houses of ʿAnîba.

Close to the S. slope of the castle hill lie the ruins of a small *Town*, surrounded by a wall. Farther up the valley is a large *Cemetery*, with simple Christian graves and some brick tombs on a more ambitious scale. There is a similar cemetery in the valley to the N. of the castle.

In the steep W. slope of the castle hill are several large *Memorial Recesses*, dating from the New Empire. These now lie at some height above the river-bank and some are very difficult of access, but originally they were reached by means of steps from a path skirting the river at a higher level than the present path. The first recess (on the S.) was constructed in the reign of Thutmosis III. by Nehi, governor of Ethiopia. The second was constructed in the reign of Ramses II. by Setaw (p. 437), governor of Ethiopia, who is represented in it with his officials. The third recess dates from the joint reign of Thutmosis III. and Hatshepsut, but the name of the latter is everywhere defaced. Both rulers, each beside a deity, are represented on the rear wall. The fourth recess, the most important, belongs to the reign of Amenophis II. On the right side-wall the king receives tribute of all kinds (including leopards) from two officials. On the left wall the king appears conducted by Horus, lord of Buhen (Wâdi Ḥalfa), before a row of gods. In a niche in the back-wall is the statue of the king, embraced by Horus of Mem (ʿAnîba), on the right, and by the goddess Satet, on the left. The walls are further adorned with Meroïtic paintings. The fifth recess has no sculptures.

On a steep cliff facing the river, to the S. of Qaṣr Ibrîm, are a *Relief and Inscription of Sethos I.*, commemorating a victory. Beside it are very early graffiti of elephants, giraffes, etc.

The mountains on the E. bank presently retire, leaving room for a strip of cultivated land. Numerous sâqiyas or water-wheels

are seen. — 30 M. *El-Gineina* (E. bank); $33^1/_2$ M. *Esh-Shibbâk* (*Esh-Shabbâk;* E. bank), opposite which is *Maṣmaṣ*. — 36 M. *Tûshka* (*Toshka, Toski;* steamer station), on both banks. On the W. bank here, 7 M. from the river, a large force of dervishes was defeated, with the loss of their cannon, by the British on Aug. 3rd, 1889; several thousand slain were left on the battlefield. Near the village is a large Nubian cemetery of the Middle Empire, excavated by Hermann Junker in 1911-12 at the expense of the Vienna Academy of Sciences. — $45^1/_2$ M. *Arminna* (*Ermenne;* E. bank). The ancient cemeteries near the village were examined in 1911-12 by the expedition of the Vienna Academy (see above). The desert approaches close to the river, and the banks often rise steeply from the water. The large ruined building on the W. bank was, perhaps, a storehouse dating from the time of Muḥammed ʿAli. — 54 M. *Farrîq* (E. bank), a commune including the villages of *Furqundi* and *Demîd*. The hills on both banks become higher. At the point where they touch the river on the W. bank lie the great rock-temples and colossi of (56 M.) *Abu Simbel* (steamer station).

33. The Rock Temples of Abu Simbel.

The two rock-temples of *Abu Simbel*, known also as *Ibsambul*, built by Ramses II., are among the most stupendous monuments of ancient Egyptian architecture and challenge comparison with the gigantic edifices situated in Egypt proper. Tickets of admission (p. 212) should not be forgotten. The temples produce a very grand effect by moonlight or at sunrise. The interior of the great temple is illuminated at night by electricity provided from the steamer.

The ****Great Temple of Abu Simbel** is entirely excavated out of the solid rock. It was dedicated in the first place to Amon-Rē of Thebes and Rē-Harakhte of Heliopolis, the leading deities of Egypt, but Ptah of Memphis and the deified Ramses himself were likewise worshipped here. Its longer axis runs almost due E. and W., so that at sunrise the sun's rays penetrate to the innermost sanctuary. *Burckhardt*, in 1812, was the first modern traveller to examine this temple, which was excavated by Belzoni (p. 136) in 1817. It was cleared from fresh sand-drifts by Lepsius (p. 136) and again by Mariette (p. 157) in 1869. In 1909 *Alessandro Barsanti* discovered the small court to the N. of the terrace, freed the N. colossus from the rubbish concealing it, and built walls on the plateau to protect the temple from sand.

From the landing-place the temple is 5 min. walk across the fields. We ascend a modern staircase to the **Forecourt** in front of the temple, which is hewn out of the rock and enclosed on the N. and S. by ancient brick walls that have been repaired in places. Adjoining this on the W. is a *Terrace* reached by a flight of steps

with an inclined plane in the middle. To the right and left, in front of the inclined plane, are steps leading to two recesses (Pl. *a*, *b*), which perhaps contained basins for the ablutions of those entering the temple. In these recesses are inscriptions in honour of Ramses II.; that to the right (N.) represents the king burning incense before Amun, Rē-Harakhte, and Ptah and presenting them with flowers; in that to the left (S.) the king burns incense before Amun, Ptah, and the lion-headed Sakhmet. The terrace is embellished in front with rows of captives and a cavetto cornice, and is bounded by a balustrade, bearing the dedicatory inscription (comp. above). Behind the balustrade stand figures of falcons and small statues of the king. Here our attention is attracted by the four *Colossi of Ramses II. (Pl. A-D), hewn out of the cliff against which their backs are placed, and arranged in pairs on either side of the entrance to the temple. Each of these figures is over 65 ft. in height, i. e. larger than the Colossi of Memnon (p. 345), but the workmanship is good and the proportions just, while their size is in admirable keeping with the scale of the façade of the temple and the surrounding cliffs. The mild countenance and characteristic nose of Ramses II. are best preserved in the first colossus. The second has unfortunately lost its head and shoulders, which lie on the ground before it. The upper part of the third colossus was patched up under Sethos II., who added the support under the right arm.

Upon his head the king wears the double crown; his hands rest upon his knees; and from his neck hangs a ring bearing the prænomen of Ramses II., which is carved also upon the upper arms and between the legs. To the right and left of each colossus and between their legs are smaller figures of other members of the royal family. To the left of the first colossus is Princess Nebt-tewe, to the right Bent-Anat, between the legs an unidentified princess. To the left of the second colossus is Tuʿe, mother of Ramses II., to the right is his wife Nofret-ere (comp. p. 435), and between his legs is Prince Amen-her-khopshef (comp. p. 436). On each of the thrones of colossi B and C, on the sides next the entrance, are two Nile-gods, wreathing the floral emblems (papyrus and sedge) of Lower and Upper Egypt round the hieroglyphic symbol for 'to unite' (comp. p. cii), while below is a row of fettered prisoners, those on the left being negroes, those on the right Syrians.

Upon the two S. colossi are a number of Greek, Carian, and Phœnician *Inscriptions*, of considerable interest. These were carved by mercenaries, who had penetrated thus far in the course of military expeditions. The most remarkable is a Greek inscription on the left leg of the second colossus, written by mercenaries sent by Psammetichos II. from Elephantine to Nubia (comp. p. 412). They had advanced to the second cataract and wrote this inscription on their way back. The English translation runs as follows: "When King Psammetichos came to Elephantine, they wrote this, who came with Psammetichos, son of Theocles, and proceeded viâ Kerkis as far as the river allowed of it. Potasimto led the foreigners, Amasis the Egyptians. Archon, son of Amoibichos, and Pelekos, son of Udamos, wrote this." Kerkis is probably the modern Qirsha (p. 420).

The Façade, which here represents the pylon of the ordinary temples, is crowned by a cavetto cornice, above which is a row of cynocephali worshipping the rising sun. Within the cornice are the cartouches of Ramses II., surrounded by uræus serpents, and inter-

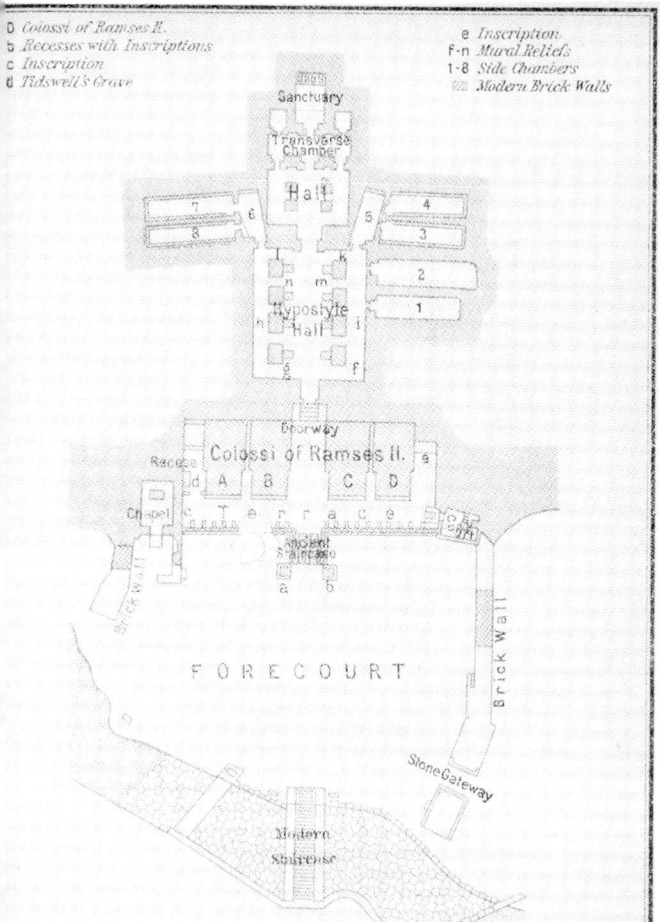
a Colossi of Ramses II.
b Recesses with Inscriptions
c Inscription
d Tidswell's Grave
e Inscription
f-n Mural Reliefs
1-8 Side Chambers
Modern Brick Walls
Sanctuary
Transverse Chamber
Hall
Hypostyle Hall
Doorway
Colossi of Ramses II.
Recess
Chapel
Terrace
Court
Ancient Staircase
Brick Wall
FORECOURT
Brick Wall
Stone Gateway
Modern Staircase
N
GREAT TEMPLE of ABU SIMBEL
1:950
Feet
Metres
Wagner & Debes, Leipzig

rupted by figures of Amun (left) and Rē-Harakhte (right). Then follows the dedication-inscription of the king to Amon-Rē and Rē-Harakhte. In a niche above the ENTRANCE DOOR the prænomen of the king is represented by large figures in relief, amongst which that of the falcon-headed sun-god is conspicuous. To the right and left the king presents an image of Maat to this god and to his own deified name. On the lintel of the door Ramses is shown laying the foundation-stone of the temple before Amun and Mut, on the left, and before Rē-Harakhte and the lion-headed Wert-hekew, on the right. Within the portal a smaller doorway was built by Ramses II.

We now enter the rock-temple, the interior of which measures about 180 ft. from the threshold to the back of the innermost chamber. The first room, the **Great Hypostyle Hall**, corresponding to the open court with covered colonnades in temples built in the open air, is 54 ft. broad and 58 ft. deep. The ceiling is supported by eight square pillars, against which stand Osiris-figures of the king (30 ft. high), holding the flail and the crook. The figures in the N. row wear the double crown, those in the S. row the crown of Upper Egypt. The artistic effect of these admirably executed statues is very fine; the best is the fourth figure in the N. row, with its intelligent expression and well-preserved characteristic nose. The ceiling of the central aisle is adorned with flying vultures, those of the side-aisles with stars. Some of the reliefs on the wall, still vividly coloured, are of great historical value. On the right half of the ENTRANCE WALL (Pl. *f*) the king is shown smiting a band of enemies in presence of Rē-Harakhte, who hands the curved sword to Ramses. Above the king hovers a vulture and behind him is his guardian spirit or Ka. Beneath are the king's daughters, with sistra. The left half of this wall (Pl. *g*) is occupied by a corresponding scene, in presence of Amon-Rē. Beneath are the king's sons.

SOUTH WALL (Pl. *h*). At the top are five reliefs: 1. The king before a ram-headed god and a lion-headed goddess; 2. The king dedicates four packages; 3. The king offers incense to Ptah; 4. The king kneeling under the sacred tree of Heliopolis, before Rē-Harakhte, while Thoth and Seshet stand close by; 5. The king before Amun. Beneath are three large warlike scenes (left to right). 1. The king in his chariot storms a Syrian fortress. The defenders on the battlements sue for mercy, but are pierced with his arrows. The king is followed by three of his sons. Beneath, a herdsman flees with his herd towards the town. 2. The king pierces a prostrate Libyan with a lance. 3. The triumphal return of the king from battle with the captured negroes.

The NORTH WALL (Pl. *i*) represents scenes from the king's campaign against the Hittites, with which we have already become acquainted in the Ramesseum (p. 325) and at Luxor (p. 274) and Abydos (p. 260). In the *Lower Half* of the representation we see

first (left) the march of the Egyptian army, which consists of infantry and charioteers; then (between the doors to Rooms 1 and 2), the Egyptian camp, with the shields of the soldiers arranged round it in a kind of stockade. The bustle of the camp is represented with great vivacity: the unharnessed horses receiving their fodder, the resting soldiers, the camp-followers, etc. To the right is the royal tent. The third picture shows the king on his throne, holding a council of war with his officers. Below information is extorted from two spies by means of blows. In the last scene (to the right) the chariots of the Egyptians and Hittites are already engaged in battle. The scenes in the *Upper Half* transport us to the midst of the fight. To the left the king dashes in his chariot against his enemies, who have surrounded him in their chariots. In the centre is the fortress of Kadesh, surrounded by the Orontes. Its defenders watch the fight from the battlements. To the extreme right is the king in his chariot, inspecting his officers, who count the severed hands of the enemy and bring fettered prisoners.

Rear Wall. To the right (Pl. *k*) of the central door is Ramses II. leading two rows of captured Hittites before Harakhte, his own deified figure, and the lion-headed Wert-hekew; to the left (Pl. *l*) he leads two rows of negroes before Amun, the deified Ramses, and Mut. — Between the two last pillars on the left stands a *Stele* (Pl. *n*), dating from the thirty-fifth year of the reign of Ramses II., on which is a long inscription recording that Ramses erected edifices for Ptah of Memphis and presented rich gifts to him.

Adjoining this large hall are eight Chambers (Pl. 1-8) with religious scenes. Several of them were probably used to store the temple utensils and treasure. Round the walls of these run stone tables.

We now enter a **Hall**, 36 ft. broad and 25 ft. deep, supported by four pillars. On the S. wall the king, followed by his wife Nofretere holding two sistra, appears offering incense before the sacred boat with the shrine of Amun, which is carried by priests; and on the N. wall is a similar scene before the boat of Rē-Harakhte. Three doors lead from this hall into a **Transverse Chamber**, and thence three other doors admit to three apartments. The central apartment is the **Sanctuary**, containing a rock-hewn support for the sacred boat, behind which are mutilated figures of the four deities worshipped in the temple: Ptah, Amun, the deified Ramses, and Rē-Harakhte.

We now proceed to visit the smaller monuments outside the rock-temple. On the smoothed S. wall of the forecourt is a *Stele* (Pl. *c*) of the thirty-fifth year of the reign of Ramses II., commemorating the marriage of the Pharaoh with the daughter of the King of the Hittites, who was brought to Egypt by her father. At the top the king appears seated between two gods beneath a canopy, while the king of the Hittites and his daughter worship him. — The space between the

southernmost colossus and the face of the cliff has been converted into a small open recess by the erection of a doorway. On its W. wall is a long poetic inscription placed here by Ramses II. On the left is the grave of Major Tidswell (Pl. *d*), who died in 1884, during the Nile Exedition. — In the space between the northernmost colossus (Pl. D) and the face of the cliff, on the W. wall, is a large memorial inscription (Pl. *e*), also erected by Ramses II., and representing him in the presence of Rē-Harakhte. — On the N. wall, to the left of the entrance of the court, is a memorial inscription of Siptah (p. cvii), in which he is represented burning incense to Amon-Rē, Mut, Rē-Harakhte, etc.

The terrace is adjoined on the N. by an OPEN COURT dedicated by Ramses II. to the worship of the sun. The walls surrounding it rise on the E. side to form a sort of pylon. In the court are two pedestals with cavetto cornices. On the S. one, to which steps ascend, stood four praying baboons; the one on the N. bore a chapel containing the images of a scarabæus (the sun-god Khepre) and of a baboon (the moon-god Thoth; now in the Cairo Museum, see p. 95). On the N. wall of the court we see the boat of the sun, drawn by jackals, in which Ramses is sacrificing to Rē-Harakhte.

Immediately to the S. of the great temple is a small **Chapel** discovered in 1874 by a party of travellers including Amelia Edwards, the novelist (1831-92), who has described it in her interesting 'Thousand Miles up the Nile'. This is possibly a birth-house (comp. p. 266). It consists of a *Vestibule* and a rock-hewn *Sanctuary*, which is embellished with well-preserved reliefs.

Entrance Wall. On each side appears the king entering the temple. — *Left Wall.* The king, followed by his guardian spirit, offers incense to the sacred boat of Thoth. — *Rear Wall.* To the left, the king presents his own cartouche to Amon-Rē of Napata; to the right, he makes a libation of wine to Rē-Harakhte. — *Right Wall.* The king, accompanied by his guardian spirit, sacrifices to the boat of Amun-Harakhte. The king's prænomen is represented behind by the goddess Maat, who is equipped with special symbols.

A *Marble Tablet* on the rock in front of the chapel commemorates the battle of Tûshka (p. 431) in English and Arabic.

From the forecourt of the temple we pass through a stone gateway made by Ramses II. in the brick enclosure and proceed to the small ***Temple of Hathor.** This temple is hewn in a rock separated by a valley from the great temple. It also was founded by Ramses II. and was dedicated to Hathor and to the deified Nofret-ere, consort of Ramses. The façade is turned more to the S. than that of the great temple. The quay on the river and the approach thence to the entrance have been washed away.

The FAÇADE, 92 ft. long and 39 ft. high, is hewn in imitation of a pylon with receding front, crowned by a cavetto cornice. The cornice, however, has fallen. On each side of the narrow entrance, with their backs against the façade, are three *Colossal Statues*, 33 ft. in height, representing Ramses II. and Nofret-ere. Beside these

are smaller figures of the royal children: beside the colossi of the queen are the princesses Merit-Amun (right) and Hent-tewe (left); beside the outer colossi of the king are the princes Meri-Atum (right) and Meri-Rē (left); and beside the colossi of the king on the right and left of the door are the princes Amen-her-khopshef (right) and Ra-her-wnamf (left). On the receding façade are projecting parts resembling buttresses, separating the colossi, so that each of the latter appears to be in a kind of niche. On these buttresses are votive inscriptions.

We now enter the Hypostyle Hall (Pl. A), the roof of which is borne by six pillars, decorated in front with sistra with the head of Hathor, while the other sides bear representations of the king, the queen, and various deities.

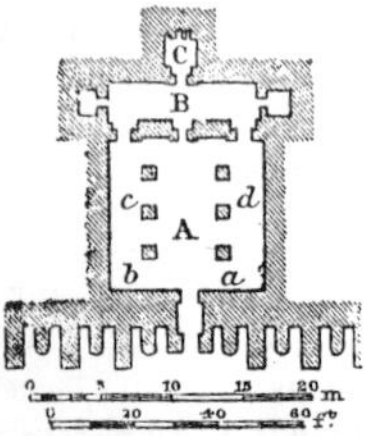

Mural Reliefs. On the *Entrance Wall* (Pl. *a*, *b*) Ramses, accompanied by his wife, smites (left) a negro in presence of Amon-Rē and (right) a Libyan before Rē-Harakhte. — *Left Wall* (Pl. *c*; from left to right): 1. Ramses before Hathor; 2. Ramses crowned by Seth and Horus; 3. The queen before Anuket; 4. Ramses presenting an image of Maat to Amun. — *Right Wall* (Pl. *d*; from right to left): 1. Ramses offering food to Ptah; 2. Ramses before the ram-headed god Herishef of Heracleopolis; 3. The queen before Hathor; 4. Ramses making a libation of wine to Rē-Harakhte. — *Rear Wall.* To the left, the queen before Hathor; to the right, the queen before Mut.

Three doors lead into a Transverse Chamber (Pl. B), with unimportant mural reliefs. Adjoining are two rooms, barely begun, over the doors of which are tasteful reliefs of the Hathor cow in a papyrus marsh, worshipped in one case by the king, in the other by the queen. From the transverse chamber we enter the Sanctuary (Pl. C). In the rear wall is a chapel-shaped recess, with its roof supported by sistra. Within this is a high relief, representing (full face) a figure of Hathor in the form of a cow, below the head of which appears the king under her protection. On the *Left Wall* the queen offers incense to Mut and Hathor; on the *Right Wall* the king offers incense and pours a libation before his own image and that of his wife. Two rooms adjoining the sanctuary were originally planned, and spaces for doors to these have been left free in the rear wall of the transverse chamber.

On the smoothed face of the rocks, both to the N. of the small temple and to the S. of the 'birth-house' near the great temple, are numerous **Memorial Inscriptions* and *Niches*, most of which date from the reign of Ramses II.

34. From Abu Simbel to Wâdi Ḥalfa.

40 M. by Steamer (comp. pp. 409, 410). — *Comp. the Map, p. 414.*

As we proceed S. from Abu Simbel we notice the village of *Ballâna* on the W. bank. On the E. bank, below *Abahûda (Abu Oda)*, a village belonging to Farrîq (p. 431), the hills approach close to the stream. On one of these, the **Gebel Adda,** lies a small Rock Temple, founded in the reign of King Haremhab (19th Dyn.) and dedicated to Amon-Rē and Thoth of Shmun (p. 221). This temple was afterwards used as a Christian church. The *First Hall* contains four papyrus-columns with bud-capitals. The architectural details have been painted over with Byzantine ornamentation, and the ancient mural reliefs project from beneath figures of Christian saints. On the left half of the entrance-wall, Haremhab suckled by Anuket, beside whom stands the ram-headed Khnum; on the right half Haremhab before Thoth. On the left wall, the king before Thoth and Horus; right of the door, Haremhab accompanied by Horus and Seth. On the right wall, Christian paintings of Epimachus and other saints on horseback and Coptic inscriptions. On the ceiling, figures of Christ (with raised right hand) and an Apostle. The hall is adjoined by two side-chambers, and behind it is the sanctuary.

The ruins of a *Mediaeval Fortress* rise on an isolated rock to the S. of the Gebel Adda. In the valley are numerous domed brick tombs, probably Christian. — Farther S., in the face of an isolated cliff opposite the large island of *Shatawi*, are several *Memorial Niches*. One of these dates from the reign of King Eye (18th Dyn.), who here prays to six gods. Another was constructed by Pesiûr, governor of Nubia in the reign of Haremhab.

On the E. bank rise numerous isolated rocks, while the mountains recede far from the river. — 11 M. *Qusṭul* (*Qostol;* E. bank). The Nile expands; the large sand-banks in the river-bed are a great hindrance to navigation. — $17^1/_2$ M. *Adindân* (E. bank; steamer station) is the last commune belonging to Egypt. In the village are the remains of a church, and there is another ruined church farther inland. The frontier of the Anglo-Egyptian Sûdân (comp. p. 441) is indicated on the bank of the river.

On the W. bank, near the river, lie the remains of a fortress of a late period and some ruined houses.

Faras (W. bank). On the bank of the Nile is a rectangular wall of the Meroïtic period (328 yds. by 197 yds.), with towers of defence, enclosing the remains of a castle, blocks of masonry belonging to an Egyptian temple (ascribed to the time of Thutmosis III.), and the ruins of two churches. To the S.W. is an isolated rock with the remains of a temple of Hathor and with a memorial niche of Setaw, governor of Nubia under Ramses II. (p. 366). To the N.W. of the walled enclosure, near a modern Mohammedan cemetery, is the débris of a temple erected by Tutankhamûn and a Meroïtic necro-

polis, which, together with the rest of the antiquities of Faras, were explored in 1910-12 by the Oxford University Expedition under Prof. F. L. Griffith. — On the W. bank curious dunes consisting of sand and the feathery leaves of tamarisks extend between the villages and the desert expanse. In the river lies *Gezîret Faras*, a large island, known as *Artikargu* ('rich island') by the Nubians, with the village of *Artinōg* ('breast of the island').

Opposite the island, on the W. bank, lies the village of *Aksha*, with the remains of a small temple built by Ramses II.

We next reach the scattered village of *Serra (Sara)*, on both banks of the Nile. Here, on the E. bank, are the remains of Coptic conventual buildings and a church, all within a fortress dating perhaps from the Middle Empire. To the N. and S. of the fortress are two more churches, and about 1 M. farther S. lies a fourth church, to the E. of which is a hill with graffiti of the Middle Empire.

Farther on, on the W. bank, are remains of Coptic buildings and a ruined Coptic church. — 29 M. *Dibeira*, on both banks, with fine palm-groves. In the river lies the *Island of Dibeira*. We pass (33½ M.) *Ashkît* (*Ishket;* E. bank) and *Arqîn* (*Argîn;* W. bank), beyond which the river-banks again become flat and barren.

40 M. **Wâdi Ḥalfa,** a clean little town on the E. bank, founded by the British on the site of several Nubian villages, is the capital of the province of Ḥalfa in the Anglo-Egyptian Sûdân. It contains a small bazaar, a pretty mosque, a Coptic church (to the N. of the village), a Greek church (near the station), and an English church, and, including the Nubian village of *Dabarôsa* on the N., has 2700 inhabitants. Wâdi Ḥalfa is the starting-point of the government railway to Kharṭûm (p. 445). — To the S. of the village are the *British Lines*, with the government hospital, the mudîrîya (government buildings), and the pretty houses and gardens of the officials. The railway goods yard and workshops are farther upstream.

On the W. bank of the Nile are the ruins of the ancient walled town of **Buhen,** which is reached by motor-boat or sailing vessel from the town of Wâdi Ḥalfa in 1-2 hrs. Buhen was an Egyptian colony established under the Middle Empire and still contains two temples of the New Empire. The North Temple, founded by Amosis (p. civ) at the end of the 17th Dyn., dates from the beginning of the 18th Dyn., when Amenophis II. (p. cv) constructed a new building. It is a plain structure, built of brick, with the exception of the pillars in the first hall and the jambs of the entrance-door, which were of sandstone. It is much damaged and sanded up. The South Temple, 40 yds. distant, was exhumed in 1887 by Gen. Sir Charles Smith and is now protected by a wooden structure (adm. P.T. 5). It is in better preservation than the other, its sandstone walls and pillars still rising to the height of 5-6 ft. This S. temple was built by Thutmosis III. and Hatshepsut and dedicated to Horus of Buhen. The cartouches and figures of Hatshepsut have been defaced or converted

into those of Thutmosis II. (p. cv). The temple stands E. and W. Close to the river-bank is a brick *Pylon* (a relic of the fortifications of the Middle Empire), whose S. tower rises like a massive pillar. Behind is a large *Hall*, the present form of which is due to a reconstruction, probably at the beginning of the 20th Dynasty. The pillars and columns on which the roof rested bear not only the original reliefs and inscriptions of Thutmosis III. but also numerous hieroglyphic inscriptions added by officials of the New Empire. There are also Greek, Carian, and Meroïtic inscriptions. On one pillar is a long inscription celebrating the deeds of Thutmosis III. Behind this hall lies the *Temple Proper*, the back of which adjoined the cliff, while on the other three sides were colonnades with 'proto-Doric' columns (p. clxiv). Within are a transverse hall, communicating with the sanctuary, and several other chambers. The mural reliefs, many of which retain their colouring, represent the Pharaoh in presence of the gods.

In the desert to the W. and N. of the site of the town are large cemeteries of the Middle and New Empires, excavated in 1909-10 by D. Randall-MacIver and C. Leonard Woolley (Eckley B. Coxe jun. Expedition of the University of Philadelphia).

*Excursion to the Second Cataract (5-9 hrs.). We proceed by boat from Wâdi Ḥalfa to the ruined temples on the W. bank (p. 438) and thence through the rocks of the cataract (by motor-boat in 1 hr.). Beyond the temples the land route skirts the stream, then turns towards the desert, and finally, gradually ascending, returns to the stream shortly before the cataract is reached. On a hill between Buhen and the rocks of Abuṣîr is the tomb of *Sheikh ʿAbd el-Qâdir*. At the foot of the hill is a small *Coptic Church* (after c. 1000), built entirely of crude bricks, with well-preserved frescoes. — The drive by motor-car along the E. bank to the cataract is also recommended; if time permit it may be extended to Gumai (there and back £E 2; comp. p. 440).

The **Second Cataract** is superior in scenic beauty to the First Cataract at Aswân. It lies at the N. end of the gorge of the *Baṭn el-Ḥagar* ('belly of stones'; see p. 440), which begins at the island of Dâl, about 90 M. to the S., and through which the river descends in a series of rapids, over rocks of greywacke, greenstone, and granite, forming numerous rocky islands in its course. The best point of view is the abrupt rocky hill of *Abuṣîr*, on the W. bank. At the foot of the hill, contrasting strongly with the green of the tamarisks, lies a chaos of glistening black boulders, through which the river forces its way in foaming cataracts, especially fine at the time of the inundation. In the distance to the N. are the white houses and slender minaret of Wâdi Ḥalfa on the E. bank, and the ruined temples of Buhen (p. 438) on the W. bank; to the E., beyond the broad river, rise the mountains of the desert; to the S. lie the rocky islets among the rapids.

From Wâdi Ḥalfa to Semna.

About 40 M. — A visit to the naturally beautiful and historically interesting N. part of the *Baṭn el-Ḥagar* (p. 439), which formerly required four or five days, can now be accomplished by motor-car in a single day. — Motor trip to the Second Cataract and Gumai, see p. 439.

The road follows the abandoned Kerma railway on the E. bank of the Nile (comp. the map, p. 414). We first reach the village of *Matûga* (*Maʿtûqa;* W. bank). Farther on, also on the W. bank, is *Mirgissa*, a fortress of the Middle Empire, on a steep rock close to the Nile. Within the girdle-wall are the scanty ruins of a small temple erected by Sesostris III. On the island of *Daba*, nearly opposite, are ancient Egyptian fortifications. — We then pass *ʿAbka* (E. bank; c. 10 M. from Wâdi Ḥalfa), the straggling commune of *Gumai* (*Gamai, Gemmei;* 15 M.; government rest-house), with some ruined Christian domed tombs, and *Murshid East* (24 M.; on the opposite bank is *Murshid West*). — About 32 M. from Wâdi Ḥalfa is *Sarras*, where numerous rocky islets interrupt the stream; on one of these, to the S., are the ruins of an Arab castle, perched upon a rock. We next reach *Shalfak* (W. bank), with a well-preserved fortress of the Middle Empire, and the rocky island of *Uronarti* (Arabic *Gezîret el-Malik*, i.e. 'king's island'), on the N. end of which are the ruins of a fortress of the Middle Empire and of a chapel built by Thutmosis III. On the W. side of the island are considerable rapids. — Soon afterwards the road diverges W. (r.) from the railway embankment and reaches (c. 40 M. from Wâdi Ḥalfa) the village of *Kumma (Semna East)*, with a ruined fortress of the Middle Empire and a temple of the time of Thutmosis III. and Hatshepsut. On the opposite (W.) bank is *Semna (Semna West)*, to which the traveller is ferried on a raft. Under the Middle Empire it marked the S. limit of Egypt. On the top of the hill are massive fortifications, with well-preserved girdle-walls. Within the latter is a temple, built by Thutmosis III. and Hatshepsut and dedicated to the Nubian deity Dedun. The river, here flowing between granite cliffs, forms numerous rapids. The numerous inscriptions on both banks of the stream are interesting, especially those of the end of the 12th and of the 13th Dyn. with flood-marks, from which it would appear that the Nile used to rise about 26 ft. higher than it does at present. The explanation probably is that the river undermined the W. bank and washed out a considerable passage, so that the high water escaped round the W. end of the granite barrier and never again rose to its former level.

To the W. of the Wâdi Ḥalfa-Dongola reach of the Nile (pp. 445-447) extends the *Southern Libyan Desert*, 180,000 sq. M. of which are between the boundaries of the Anglo-Egyptian Sûdân. Much of this desert tract is still unexplored, but some oases, e. g. *Selîma*, *Bîr en-Naṭrûn*, lie on the famous *Darb el-Arbaʿîn* ('forty days' road') running from Asyûṭ (p. 226) to El-Fâsher (p. 463; province of Dârfûr).

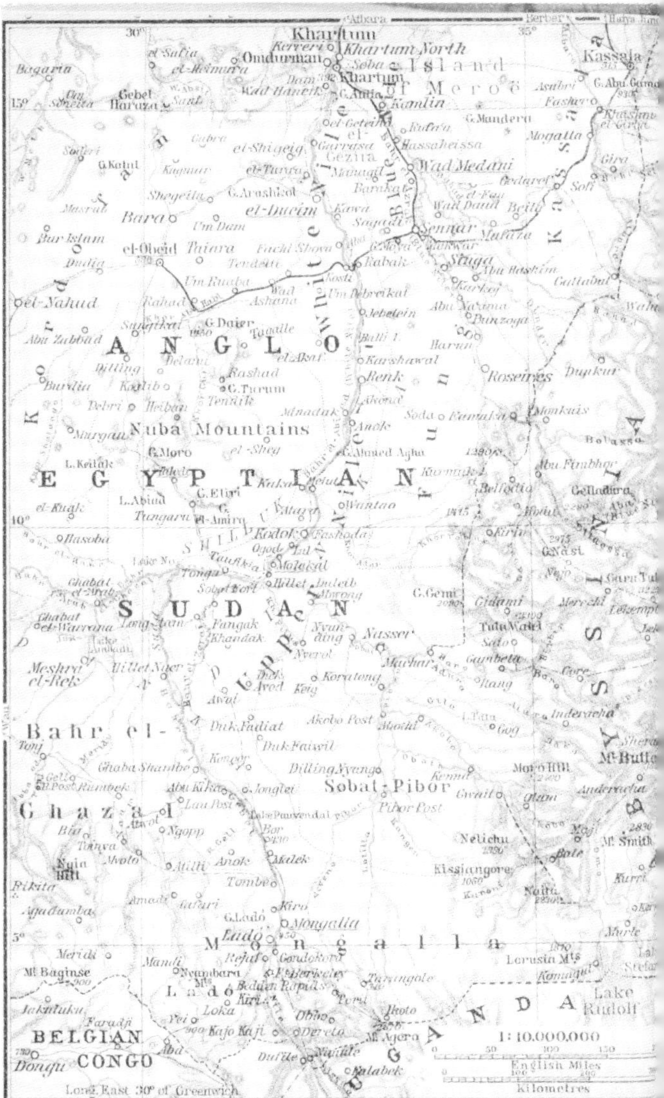

Capitals of Provinces   Heights in Metres   Telegraphs or Telephones

IV. UPPER NUBIA AND THE SÛDÂN.

The Anglo-Egyptian **Sûdân** or *Soudan* (pp. xlviii, cxxix), occupying an area (1,008,100 sq. M.) approximately equal to that of Central Europe, extends from almost exactly the 22nd parallel of latitude on the N. to the 4th parallel of latitude on the S. It includes the fourteen provinces (mudîrîya) of *Baḥr el-Ghazâl* (capital, Wau), *Berber* (capital, Ed-Dâmer), *Blue Nile* (capital, Wad Medani), *Dârfûr* (capital, El-Fâsher), *Dongola* (capital, Merowé), *Fûng* (capital, Singa), *Ḥalfa* (Wâdi Ḥalfa), *Kassala*, *Kharṭûm*, *Kordofân* (capital, El-Obeid), *Mongalla*, *Red Sea* (capital, Port Sudan; for the Beja or Nomads Administration, Sinkât), *Upper Nile* (capital, Malakal), and *White Nile* (capital, Ed-Dueim). The population was estimated at 7,005,966 in 1926. The British and Egyptian flags fly side by side in the Sûdân, and the rights of the joint possessors are defined by a convention signed on Jan. 19th, 1899. The interest on the Sûdân loan is guaranteed by the British government. The cost of the civil administration is borne by the Sûdân. Since the withdrawal of the Egyptian troops in 1924 (comp. p. cxxxii) the army, to the support of which Egypt still contributes £E 750,000 annually, consists of the Sudan Defence Force, which is recruited from the Sudanese, and of a detachment of British troops, quartered at Kharṭûm. The total revenue of the Sûdân government in its first year (1899) amounted to £E 126,596, its expenditure to £E 230,238; in 1927 the revenue and expenditure were respectively £E 5,929,944 and £E 5,550,489. The Governor-General (Arabic *Ḥâkim ʿAmm*) is a British official, appointed by the

King of Egypt on the recommendation of the British government. The mudîrs (p. xlix) of the provinces and the district commissioners are British, but the ma'mûrs (district officers) are Arabs. The development of the railway system, which received an important extension in 1924-28 through the opening up of the Eastern Sûdân by the Kassala Railway, and irrigation, now being actively carried out, by which cotton-growing especially is furthered, ensure a great economic future for the Sûdân. The total value of exports in 1923 was £E 2,562,091, in 1924 £E 3,541,866, in 1925 £E 3,801,348, in 1926 £E 4,876,236, in 1927 £E 5,229,419, and in 1928 £E 5,879,421; the value of imports in each of these years was £E 4,669,004, £E 5,474,910, £E 5,437,727, £E 5,574,401, £E 6,155,314, and 6,672,425. The most important articles of export (comp. p. 452) are gum arabic, a large part of the world's supply being derived through the Sûdân, and cotton. The amount of gum exported in 1924 was 20,363 tons, with a value of £E 846,879; in 1926, 22,744 tons, with a value of £E 844,198. The cultivation and export of cotton, which rivals that of Egypt in quality, is rapidly increasing. In 1927 the total area planted with cotton amounted to 208,539 acres, producing an average annual harvest of 29,200 tons. The completion of the Sennâr dam in 1925 and the consequent irrigation of the Gezîra (p. 461) increased the area available for cotton-planting by about 100,000 acres, the possibilities of future extensions being considerable. — Other products and exports of the Sûdân are sesame, senna leaves and pods, ground-nuts, skins and hides, salt, and gold. Among cereals wheat, barley, and maize are grown and especially durra (sorghum millet), the natives' chief foodstuff, and dukhn (pennisetum, another kind of millet). The average annual production from 1915 to 1925 of durra, which is grown in the provinces of Blue Nile, Fûng, White Nile, and Kassala, was 197,000 tons. Large numbers of cattle and sheep are exported, mainly to Egypt. Gold is mined chiefly at Gabeit, in the Red Sea Province. Salt is derived from the extensive salt-pans on the Red Sea near Port Sudan, and in such amounts as to supply the whole of the Sûdân, while considerable quantities are exported to Abyssinia. An ad valorem export duty of 1%, and an import duty of 8% is levied on most articles. Tobacco, spirits, coal, petroleum, cattle, etc., are subject to special import duties. The considerable import trade in cotton goods, hardware, machinery, timber, flour, coffee, tea, spirits, and sugar is in the hands of Greek and Arab merchants (gallâba). The great bulk of these goods comes viâ Port Sudan (p. 452). Beside the Egyptian coins the silver 'Maria Theresa' dollar, a reproduction of the Austrian issue of 1780 (Arabic *riyâl abu nuqṭa*), equivalent to P.T. 8½ or 9, is current in the districts adjoining the Abyssinian frontier and in Eritrea. British shillings (P.T. 5), florins (P.T. 10), and sovereigns (P.T. 97½) also are current in the Sûdân and are accepted by the government.

The CLIMATE resembles that of Upper Egypt (p. lxxx), though the maximum temperature is higher and the occasional variations have a greater range. From December to March cold winds often prevail, and warm clothing is necessary. At Kharṭûm the maximum heat is reached twice a year, in May or June (in 1928, 113° Fahr.) and in September (in 1927, 105° Fahr.; October, 107° Fahr.). Violent sand-storms (Arabic *habûb*) are frequent from May to September, followed by deluges of rain, which are apt to breed fever.

The best SEASON for a visit to the Sûdân is between Nov. and Feb. inclusive, though March also is frequently suitable. Visitors are recommended to make the outward journey viâ Aswân and Wâdi Ḥalfa and to return by the Red Sea (R. 36) viâ Port Sudan to Suez, or to reverse this route. The direct railway journey from Cairo to Kharṭûm (steamer between Shellâl and Wâdi Ḥalfa) takes 87$^1/_2$ hrs. and costs £E 18 P.T. 43$^1/_2$, including sleeping car supplements. Circular tour tickets are issued for the section from Shellâl to Kharṭûm and back; these are available for nine days and include four days' hotel charges at Kharṭûm and visits to Kharṭûm and Omdurmân (price £E 42; comp. pp. 409, 410). Details are given in the official time-tables of the Sûdân Government Railways, which may be obtained from the Sûdân Agencies in London (Wellington House, Buckingham Gate, S.W. 1), Cairo (p. 39), and Alexandria (p. 10), from the tourist agents, and from the railway authorities. — Travellers entering the Sûdân require to have their passports visé at the Sûdân Agency at Cairo (fee P.T. 5).

OUTFIT. Light clothing, of flannel or tussore silk, with a sun-helmet to protect the temples and neck, should be worn by day; but a warm rug and overcoat for night-travelling and during cold winds should be taken. Stout boots for visiting ruins and riding breeches and leggings for camel excursions are convenient. Summer-weight underclothing is recommended. Evening dress need not be cooler than that worn at home. — Ladies should take plenty of summer dresses, especially light washing frocks; for travelling a tweed costume is desirable. Photographic materials are best brought from home, although they are obtainable in Kharṭûm. Those who do not travel by the tourist trains and steamers should provide themselves with camp-beds and bedding, mosquito-nets, filters, cooking apparatus, provisions, and a small medicine chest. All these are to be obtained at Kharṭûm at fair prices. Fuller information is obtainable from the offices of Messrs. Thos. Cook & Son or D. E. Munari at Cairo and Kharṭûm, or from the Sûdân Agency at Cairo (p. 39).

Travel in the Sûdân outside the ordinary tourist-tracks was formerly dependent on camels, sailing boats, or privately chartered steamers, but has been revolutionized by the introduction of *Motor Cars*, which can be hired at the following stations: Wad Medani (for Geḍâref, Gallâbât, and Kassala), Makwâr (for the Blue Nile and the Dinder), Port Sudan (for Tokar), Kassala (for Eritrea), El-Obeid (for Nuba Mountains and Dârfûr), Mongalla and Juba (for the Belgian Congo and Uganda). Cars are also used in the Baḥr el-Ghazâl. Tariffs may be ascertained on application to the district

commissioners. Permission to use the *Rest Houses* maintained by the government (sleeping accommodation only) must be obtained from the authorities at Kharṭûm. *Steamers* fully equipped for shooting parties may be hired from the General Manager of the Sûdân Government Railways & Steamers at Atbara (p. 448). Travellers hiring *Camels* have to provide their own equipment (saddles, saddle-bags, and water-skins; average load per camel 360 lb.).

Sport. Excellent big-game and other shooting may be enjoyed in the Sûdân, the best months being Jan., Feb., and March, when the long grass has disappeared. The fee for a *Game Licence* varies according to the kind of game and the period. *Licence A* (£E 60) entitles the holder to shoot any unprotected animal or bird, including elephants and large or small antelopes. *Licence B* (£E 6) is valid only for the smaller antelopes. *Special Licence D* (£E 10), available only in the Red Sea Province, is valid for bustard, dikdik, gazelles, ibex, klipspringer, kudu, oryx beisa, wart-hog, and wild sheep. *Special Licence C* (£E 15) is restricted to addra gazelle or ril, kudu, wild sheep, addax, etc., in N. Kordofân, N. Dârfûr, and N. Dongola. All licences are subject to a limitation of bag with regard to both animals and birds. The shooting of the wild ass, egret, flamingo, ground hornbill, giraffe, heron, ibis, jaribu stork, otter, hoopoe, marabou, ostrich, pelican, rhinoceros bicornis, secretary bird, shoe-bill, and spoon-bill is strictly forbidden. — Further information will be found in the *Preservation of Wild Animals Ordinance 1927*, the *Notes on Big Game Shooting in the Sudan*, and *A. L. Butler's* Brief Notes for Identifying Game Animals of the Sudan (P. T. 5), which are obtainable from the Sûdân Agencies in London and Cairo and from the Game Warden at Kharṭûm. — For the importation of guns and ammunition a permit from the Sûdân Agency at Cairo is necessary, which will supply information concerning the quantity of ammunition permissible. The importation of rifles of ·303 calibre (that of the standard British military rifle) and of revolvers and pistols of ·450 and ·455 calibre is forbidden. — Everything necessary for a shooting expedition is obtainable at reasonable prices from D. E. Munari at Cairo (p. 40). Dragomans, gun-bearers, servants, etc., may be hired at Kharṭûm through the Sûdân government.

Literature (on sale at Cairo). *Sir Ernest A. Wallis Budge's* The Egyptian Sudan, its History and Monuments (illus.; London, 1907; 2 vols.), and A History of Ethiopia (Nubia and Abyssinia; illus., 2 vols., London, 1928); *H. A. MacMichael's* History of the Arabs in the Sudan (2 vols.; Cambridge, 1922); *Winston Churchill's* The River War (London, 1899, 3rd ed. 1915), the best book on the Mahdist War; *Sir Rudolf Slatin's* Fire and Sword in the Sudan (London, 1896); *G. W. Steevens's* With Kitchener to Khartum (London, 1898); *Wingate's* Mahdism and the Egyptian Sudan (London, 1900); *Henry Cecil Jackson's* Osman Digna (London, 1926; comp. p. cxxix). — *Abel Chapman's* Savage Sudan, its Wild Tribes, Big Game, and Bird Life (London, 1921); "*Ben Assher's*" A Nomad in the South Sudan (London, 1928). — *S. Hillelson's* Sudan Arabic, English-Arabic Vocabulary (Sûdân Government; London, 1925). — *Percy Falcke Martin's* The Sudan in Evolution, a study of the economic, financial, and administrative conditions of the Anglo-Egyptian Sudan, etc. (London, 1921); *Artin Pasha's* England in the Sudan (London, 1911); *Henry Darley's* Slaves and Ivory (London, 1926). The *Sudan Almanac* is a useful annual publication of the Intelligence Department of the Sûdân Government (London; 1*s*. 3*d*.).

Maps, see p. ccviii.

35. From Wâdi Ḥalfa to Kharṭûm.

Comp. the Map before the Title Page.

581 M. Sûdân Government Railways. A *Train de Luxe*, with sleeping and dining cars, runs twice a week (Wed. and Sat.) in 24 hrs., in connection with the government express steamers (p. 409; fare 1st cl. £E 8 P.T. 19, 2nd cl. £E 5 P.T. 73½, meals c. 15s. per day; sleeping car supplement £E 1). — Detailed information may be obtained from the Sûdân Agencies and tourist agents at Alexandria (p. 10) and Cairo (pp. 39, 40) and from the Sûdân Government Steamer Agency at Aswân (p. 378).

Wâdi Ḥalfa and excursions thence to the Second Cataract and to Semna, see pp. 438-440.

The construction of the railway to Kharṭûm was undertaken in 1896-97 in order to support the advance of the Anglo-Egyptian army; and the work of laying a railway line across the sandy and stony surface of the desert was so energetically carried on that it advanced as much as a mile-and-a-half daily. For want of local names the passing-stations are numbered from 1 to 10. The provision of an adequate water supply being essential, wells were sunk at Nos. 4 and 6 on Kitchener's initiative and water was found in both cases at a depth of about 80 ft. — On the E. rises a bare, violet-coloured chain of hills, beyond which lies (124 M.) *Bîr Murrât* and behind which runs the caravan route from Korosko to Abu Ḥamed (comp. p. 426). At No. 10 station the railway to Kareima diverges on the right (S.W.; see below). As the train approaches Abu Ḥamed the dark-coloured ranges of hills, which border the left bank of the Nile, become visible in the distance. Isolated dûm palms (p. lxxviii), fields of barley, conical sayal-acacias (ṭalḥ), and finally a grove of palms announce the proximity of the river.

232 M. **Abu Ḥamed** (1132 ft.). From the station we have a glimpse of the poor village, which takes its name from a sheikh buried in the neighbourhood. The important position at the bend of the river, which here turns abruptly to the S.W., was captured from the dervishes in Aug. 1897 by General Hunter, who had advanced from Dongola.

From Abu Ḥamed to Kareima, 145 M., railway in 10½ hrs. (1st cl. fare £E 1 P.T. 68½); trains twice weekly in either direction, in connection with the trains to and from Kharṭûm. This line evades the difficult navigation of the *Fourth Cataract* and provides connection with the rich province of Dongola. There is a rest-house near *Kareima* station; boats for Nûri and Kurru (p. 446) may be hired at Kareima. — On the right bank, above the cataract, lies *Kirbekan*, where Major-General William Earle fell in 1885.

About 1½ M. below Kareima rises the **Gebel Barkal**, the 'sacred mountain' of ancient inscriptions. This isolated rocky hill rises abruptly from the plain to a height of 302 ft. At its base extend the ruins of the ancient Ethiopian city of *Napata*. Under the New Empire Napata was the southernmost town under Egyptian rule and the chief depot of the trade with the Sûdân. It attained the zenith of its prosperity in the 8th cent. B.C., when it became the capital of an independent Ethiopian kingdom (p. 412). Piankhi, Sabakon, Taharka, and their successors (p. cviii) resided here and built sumptuous temples for Amon-Rē and other deities. When the royal residence was transferred about 300 B.C. to Meroë (p. 448), farther S., Napata began to decline; and although it subsequently, after the division

of the kingdom, became the seat of a branch of the royal family (300-225 and 200-20 B.C.) and remained the religious centre of the kingdom, it never regained its former prosperity. The extant ruins include many pyramids, differing from those of Egypt by their slender form, and several temples and other structures. Cailliaud explored the site in 1822 and Lepsius in 1844, but more thorough excavations were carried out in 1916 and 1919 by the Harvard-Boston Expedition, directed by George A. Reisner.

At the S.E. base of the Gebel Barkal lies the great *Temple of Amon-Rē*, built at the end of the 18th Dyn. by Tutankhamûn or his viceroy Huye (p. 342), enlarged by Sethos I. and Ramses II., and renewed by Piankhi and Taharka. The sanctuary still contains the granite base for the sacred boat of the gods, dedicated by Taharka to Amon-Rē. The pylon and the columns of the forecourt behind it belong to a restoration of the temple in the Meroïtic period. — Of the other temples that situated by the S.E. angle of the hill merits attention; it was built by Taharka for Amon-Rē and Mut. The front portions (pylon and two hypostyle halls) are very ruinous; the two columns with Hathor capitals in the second room, the only ones that are still upright, form the chief feature of the ruined site. The further rooms are entirely hewn out of the rock: the small transverse chamber was supported by two pillars adorned with figures of the god Bes, of which only one has survived; in the sanctuary beyond, the smoke-blackened mural reliefs show King Taharka praying and sacrificing to the Theban deities. — The *Pyramids* situated to the W. of the hill date from the Meroïtic age; the oldest and largest, in the central group, has a wide staircase descending to underground tomb-chambers.

On the left bank of the Nile, 4 M. above Kareima, is the village of *Nûri*, 2 M. from which, in the desert, lies a large *Pyramid Field*, comprising fifty-eight tombs. Twenty of these mark the resting-places of Ethiopian kings, while the others are tombs of queens and princesses and are of later date than those at Kurru (see below). The pyramids are built of soft sandstone and have weathered badly. The oldest and largest is the tomb of Taharka (p. cviii). — The third large group of the Napata pyramids is at *Kurru*, 8 M. downstream from Kareima and a few minutes' walk from the Nile. The earlier kings of Ethiopia were buried here. The tomb-chapels of the pyramids of Tanutamun (663-653 B.C.) and Queen Kalhata, with their excellently preserved reliefs, deserve a visit (shown by the guardian).

From Kareima to Kerma viâ Debba and Dongola, 209 M., steamer weekly in winter in either direction in 2½ days. Passengers must cater for themselves. There is also a frequented caravan route from Kareima to Dongola. The first station is (6 M.) *Merowé* (rest-house), 'capital' of the province of Dongola, on the left bank of the Nile, beside which lies the large village of *Sanam Abu Dôm*, with a temple of Taharka excavated by the Oxford University Expedition in 1913. A small museum at Merowe contains statues from the temples near the Gebel Barkal, a lifesize black granite statue of Taharka, and the granite sarcophagus of King Antaman (623-593 B.C.) from his pyramid at Nûri. To the E., in the desert, is the *Wâdi Ghazâl*, with the ruins of a large Christian convent. On the right bank, opposite Merowe, is the abandoned village of Merowe, with the ruins of the government building, erected on the remains of a mediæval fortress, which was built in its turn with the stones of an ancient edifice. Among the ruins is an altar dedicated by Piankhi, the Ethiopian king. — Both banks of the river are covered with cotton-fields. — 12½ M. *Tangassi Sûq*, on the left bank, the next steamer station, is the scene on Tues. of one of the largest markets in the Sûdân. In the neighbourhood are some ancient pyramids; and on the opposite bank lies the pyramid-field of *Kurru* (see above). About ¾ hr. farther on, near the village of *Zûma*, on the right bank, is another group of more than thirty pyramids. — Still farther S.W. in the Nile valley, on the left bank, lies (46½ M.) *Kôrti* (steamer station; rest-house), which was General Wolseley's headquarters in Dec. 1884, during his unavailing dash to relieve Gordon (comp. p. 449). On the same bank, 14 hrs. by steamer from Kôrti, lies (82 M.) *Ed-Debba* (rest-house), an important trading point with the Kabâbîsh Beduin, who bring salt from the desert, and the starting-point of a caravan route to El-Obeid (p. 463; 14-20 days' journey). On the right

bank, 5 M. farther down, lies *Dongola el-ʿAgûza* ('Old Dongola'), the former capital of the province, now deserted. It still contains a very interesting early Christian church. Beyond the steamer stations of ($135^1/_2$ M.) *Khandak* (rest-house) and *Urbi* we reach (175 M.) New Dóngola or *El-ʿOrdi* (784 ft.; rest-house), a thriving town of 15,000 inhab., on the left bank of the Nile. Finally, passing the island of *Argo* (rest-house), the steamer arrives at Kerma (781 ft.; rest-house), on the right bank of the Nile.

Close to the river at Kerma is the ruin of a largish brick building, the so-called *Lower* (W.) *Defûfa* (i. e. fortress), a fortified Egyptian trading factory dating from the Middle Empire. The *Upper* (E.) *Defûfa*, a second and externally similar brick ruin, lies about 2 M. farther E.; this contained a chapel of the same period. Close by is a large *Burial Ground*, containing both single tombs and large circular tumuli in which the Nubian grandees of Kerma under the Middle Empire were interred together with their families and servants; the latter, according to the barbarous native custom, seem to have been buried alive with the corpse of their lord and master. The various sites were explored by G. A. Reisner in 1913-16 (comp. p. 446).

The so-called *Third Cataract*, with the rapids of Abu Fâtma and Ḥannak, is situated below Kerma. At its S. end is the island of *Tombos*, and opposite, on the granite rocks of the E. bank, are five memorial inscriptions of Thutmosis I., conqueror of Upper Nubia (p. cv). The most important of the Egyptian ruins in the province of Ḥalfa, between the second and third cataracts, can only be visited by caravan or in a native boat (gyassa): 1. The *Temple of Sesebi*, situated on the left bank of the Nile at the N. end of the Kaibâr rapids, opposite the district capital Delgo. This was a temple of the sun built by Amenophis IV. in the N. W. corner of the fortress of Gematon and is the only Aton temple (p. cv) that has survived. It measures 130 ft. by 65 ft. Of the columns in the first hall only three are still standing. The reliefs of Amenophis IV. have been mutilated and replaced by those of Sethos I. 2. The *Temple of Sôleb* (W. bank; about 55 M. to the N. of the third cataract), built by Amenophis III. for Amun and for the worship of the king himself. On the front of the pylon are reliefs of Amenophis IV. The reliefs on the back of the pylon and on the N. side of the gateway between the two colonnaded courts refer to the jubilee of Amenophis III. 3. The very ruinous *Temple of Sedeïnga*, about 13 M. below Sôleb, built by Amenophis III. for his wife Teye, who was venerated as the patron goddess of Nubia.

Beyond Abu Ḥamed the railway ascends the valley of the Nile on the border line between the *ʿAtmûr* (steppe) on the E. and the arable belt on the river-bank on the W. The latter is marked by palm-trees and, lower down, by a bushy undergrowth. Between Nov. and Jan. the verdant strip reminds one of the bank of the Nile in Egypt. In the settlements on the banks we now for the first time see the typical round straw huts (tukul) of Central Africa, with their pointed roofs and airy 'rekubas' or porches.

$248^1/_2$ M. *Dagash.* The *Robâtâb* and *Shaiqîya* tribes here, together with a few sub-tribes, constitute the great Arab group of the *Monâṣîr.* The Monâṣîr preserve a number of ancient legends concerning the wanderings, feuds, and intermarriages of their ancestors, and are exceedingly proud of these 'histories of God's people'. — 267 M. *Abu Dîs;* 291 M. *Shereik*, prettily situated among palms near the river.

347 M. *El-ʿAbîdîya* is situated above the *Fifth Cataract.*

362 M. **Berber** (1048 ft.; rest-house), or *El-Mekheirif*, capital of the N. district of the province of Berber, was destroyed during the Mahdist rebellion, but it was afterwards rebuilt a little to the N. and is gradually recovering its importance (pop. 10,000 in 1928).

The town stretches along the E. bank of the Nile for a distance of $5^1/_2$ M. The river-banks here are exceedingly fertile but very scantily populated, though the government actively encourages the settlement of peasant proprietors. Berber is noted for riding camels, woven fabrics, leather goods (e.g. red shoes), camel-saddles, water-skins, saddle-bags, and saddle-rugs. The Sûdân salt prepared here formerly circulated throughout all Central Africa as an article of barter, in the form of small brown cones.

388 M. **Atbăra** (*'Aṭbara*, 1162 ft.; plain hotel near the railway station), situated to the N. of the junction of the Atbara River and the Nile, is a flourishing place, the headquarters of the Sûdân Government Railways and Steamers, with large railway-workshops. This is the point of divergence of the Nile & Red Sea Railway, which runs to Port Sudan and Suâkin (see p. 453). To the left of the railway is a cemetery containing graves of the British soldiers who died in hospital after the battle of Atbara. The railway is here carried by an iron bridge over the river *Atbara* (p. lxvi), the channel of which is dry from April to June. — The battle of Atbara took place on April 8th, 1898. Kitchener marched from Berber to Hûdi on the Atbara, whence he attacked the Emîr Maḥmûd, who was strongly posted at a place called *Nakhfîla*. The victory of the British opened the way for a further advance to the Sûdân.

395 M. *Ed-Dâmer* (post office and Government rest-house near the station) is the capital of the province of Berber.

From Ed-Dâmer a caravan route leads S.E. to *Kassala* (p. 453; 242 M. in 6 days; by motor-car in $14^1/_2$ hrs.).

The railway runs for a long distance close to the bank of the Nile. — 408 M. *Ez-Zeidâb*, a cotton-growing centre. The scenery now assumes a savanna-like character, with a bushy undergrowth, intersected by the usually dry beds of 'khôrs' or mountain-torrents. — $433^1/_2$ M. *Mutmîr*. Good examples of baskets made by the villagers are offered for sale alongside the train. — 437 M. *Umm 'Ali.* — The pyramids of Meroë become visible to the E. — 449 M. *El-Kabûshîya*, with a rest-house close to the railway station.

About 4 M. to the N. of the station of El-Kabûshîya the railway intersects the extensive **Ruins of Meroë**, capital of the Ethiopian empire (p. 445) from 300 B.C. to about A.D. 350, which were excavated in 1909-14 by Prof. J. Garstang of Liverpool (comp. his 'Meroë, the City of the Ethiopians', Oxford, 1911). About $^1/_4$ hr. E. of the railway-line is the large *Temple of the Sun*, mentioned by Herodotus, which seems to have been built by King Aspalta (593-568 B.C.). It rises in several terraces, the lowest of which is surrounded by an arcade. On the highest terrace is the sanctuary, with the remains of an obelisk, the symbol of the sun-god. The pavement was of blue and yellow tiles. On the exterior of the walls are interesting reliefs, commemorating the victories of the king. Also to the E. of the railway, among ancient cemeteries, stand two small *Chapels*, one dedicated to the Ethiopian lion-god Apezemak, the other probably to a sacred cow. — To the W. of the railway, beyond the village of Begrawîya, are the ruins of a royal city, enclosed by a stone wall, and the large *Temple of Amun* (443 ft. long), built c. 300 B.C. The entrance to the latter, which is formed by a pylon, gives access to several halls, of the columns of which only

the stumps survive. Among the objects of interest are a stone throne, whence the god Amun pronounced his oracles, and an altar embellished with reliefs. We cross the town wall to the W. of the temple to the ruins of two *Royal Palaces*, dating from the 2nd or 3rd cent. of our area. Near these are the *Royal Baths*, protected by a wooden structure (opened by the custodian). The façade of the large swimming bath, into which steps descend, is adorned with statues, brilliant frescoes, and glazed tiles. Adjacent is a semicircular chamber with three seats, probably the tepidarium. The remains of a quay wall in the vicinity show that in antiquity the bed of the Nile ran several hundred yards to the W. A large cemetery in the plain to the E. of the ruined town contains about eight hundred tombs, mostly pyramidal, in which the nobles of Meroë and members of the royal family were buried. The pyramids are small and in ruins.

About 1 hr. N.E. of Kabûshîya and visible from the railway rise the *Pyramids of Meroë*, in two main groups on two chains of hills separated by a valley, the Wâdi et-Tarabil. Like the earlier pyramids of Napata (p. 445) these Meroïtic pyramids are distinguished by their slender form. Many of them are still adjoined on the E. by mortuary chapels decorated inside with religious reliefs in the peculiar Egypto-Ethiopian style and with hieroglyphic inscriptions. The pylon-shaped portals are usually embellished, after the Egyptian fashion, with figures of kings grasping their foes by the hair and smiting them with the sword. The *South Group* is the older, roughly contemporary with the pyramids of Kurru and Nûri (p. 446). Here were buried the viceroys ruling the S. half of the Ethiopian empire as vassals of the kings of Napata; the earlier independent kings and some of the queens of Meroë (down to c. 250 B.C.) were also interred here. — The *North Group* of forty-one pyramids (thirty-four kings, five queens, and two crown princes) date from the period of the Meroïtic empire (from 250 B.C. down to the Roman Empire).

474 M. *Shendi*, one of the principal towns in the ancient Fûng kingdom, is an industrial centre of some importance, with cotton-weaving factories, dye-works, and foundries. Products of the local industries (including excellent cotton homespun or 'damûr', natural and dyed) are offered for sale in the market. — On the left bank, opposite Shendi, lies *Metemma*, captured by Wolseley on Jan. 21st, 1885, after the battle of *Abu Klea* (*Abu Ṭileiḥ;* 31 M. to the N.). This was the final act in the campaign (comp. p. 446).

The Fûng tribes distinguished themselves by their warlike ability in the 18th and beginning of the 19th centuries. Their emîrs wore shirts of chain-mail and helmets with nose-pieces; specimens of both were captured as late as 1897. Ismâ'îl, son of Muḥammed 'Ali, was treacherously captured and burned at Shendi in 1822, though his army was rescued by the hasty advance of the Daftardâr Muḥammed from Kordofân.

At (497 M.) *Wad Benâga (Wad Ben Naga)* are the scanty remains of several late-Ethiopian temples.

In the fertile *Wâdi Awateib*, 22 M. to the S.E. of Benâga, are the ruins of *Nâga*, reached in $1^1/_2$ hr. by motor-car, or in 7-8 hrs. on camels, which must be ordered five days in advance from the ma'mûr of Shendi. Among the ruins are several ancient houses, three well-preserved late-Ethiopian temples, a graceful Roman chapel (2nd or 3rd cent. B.C.), and also the remains of several smaller sanctuaries. The largest temple, consisting of a pylon and a chamber behind it, was dedicated to the lion-god Apezemak by king Netekaman and Queen Amantere (15 B.C. to A.D. 15). The S. tower of the pylon shows the king (on the N. tower, the queen), accompanied by a lion, slaying his enemies. The inner and outer walls of the chamber are covered with reliefs; on the exterior of the rear wall is the three-headed lion-god. In the vicinity are two ancient reservoirs. The Arabs water their herds at the well here. — A journey of 4 hrs. N.E. from this point viâ the ($11^1/_2$ M.) well of Bîr Benâga brings us to the (2 M. farther)

well-preserved ruins of *Muṣauwarât*, in the *Wâdi eṣ-Ṣofra*, probably at one time the residence of an Ethiopian king. Among the extensive remains are those of a large palace, several sanctuaries, and stables for cattle, etc. Thence we return viâ Bîr Benâga to Shendi (28 M.; p. 449).

This district was brutally laid to waste in 1895 by the dervishes, whose animosity was directed against the Ethiopic-Semitic *Ja'alîn*, whom, in the true spirit of Arab vendetta, they endeavoured to exterminate, root and branch, in revenge for alleged treachery. To-day, however, the traces of the dervishes' raid have disappeared. The tribes have multiplied, and the villages have been repopulated and rebuilt. Members of the Ja'alîn tribe are now frequently met in Kharṭûm as servants, scribes, or watchmen.

526 M. *Gebel Gerri* lies $8^1/_2$ M. to the E. of the *Sixth* or *Shablûka Cataract*. On each side rise numerous conical summits. — To the right, beyond the Nile, the hills of Kerreri (p. 459) come into sight. During the war the German Zeppelin L 59, starting from Jamboli in Bulgaria in an attempt to convey munitions to the troops in German East Africa, succeeded in reaching this district before being recalled by wireless; between Nov. 21st and Nov. 26th, 1917, it covered 4198 M. in 95 hrs. without a landing.

579 M. *Kharṭûm North* (*Ḥalfâya*; p. 455), with 14,319 inhab., magazines, barracks, etc. The railway crosses the Blue Nile by a bridge, 710 yds. in length, with seven main spans of 217 ft. each and a swing-section for the passage of boats. The bridge was designed by the French engineer G. C. Imbault and was built in 1908-10 by the Cleveland Bridge & Engineering Co. of Darlington, England. It is used also for ordinary traffic.

581 M. **Kharṭûm** (*Central Station*, Pl. D 4), see p. 454.

36. From Suez to Kharṭûm viâ Port Sudan.

Comp. the Map before the Title Page.

From Port Taufîq at Suez (p. 200) to *Port Sudan*, steamers of the Khedivial Mail Line on the 1st, 11th, and 21st of the month (1st class £E 13, 2nd class £E 10). The S.S. 'Taif' calls at Ṭûr, Yanbo' el-Baḥr, Jidda, and Suâkin, and arrives at Port Sudan on the 6th, 16th, and 26th, while the S.S. 'Talodi', calling also at Mînet el-Wejh (every twenty days only), arrives on the 7th, 17th, and 27th. Many of the large British liners (P. & O., Bibby, Henderson, etc.) call at Port Sudan on the way from Port Said or Suez (inquire at a tourist agency). — From Port Sudan to *Kharṭûm*, 487 M., express twice weekly (Tues. and Sat., with dining and sleeping cars) in 32 hrs. (1st class £E 7 P.T. 3, 2nd class £E 4 P.T. 92; sleeping car supplement £E 1). Special trains are run to meet the steamers when sufficient passengers are embarking or landing.

Suez, see p. 199. — On the left, soon after our departure, appear the palms at the Springs of Moses (p. 201), 1 M. from the coast; on the right is the lightship 'Zenobia', marking the *Newport Reefs*. The gulf expands, but the reddish cliffs on both sides remain in sight. About 47 nautical miles from the Newport reefs, on the right, rises the white lighthouse (80 ft. high) on the *Râs Za'farâna*, whose

light is visible for 14 sea-miles. Farther on, on the same side, rises the picturesque *Gebel Gharîb* (5742 ft.), at the foot of which, on the cape of the same name, is another lighthouse with an iron framework and a round base serving as the keeper's dwelling. — To the left are the imposing mountains of Sinai, the most conspicuous summits of which are the serrated pyramid of the *Gebel Serbâl* (6736 ft.) and, to the S., the sugar-loaf of the *Gebel Umm Shômar* (8448 ft.). At their base stretches the barren desert of *El-Qâʿa*, following the undulations of the coast-line and rising to the height of 984 ft. In front of us lies the solitary little port of *Ṭûr* or *Ṭôr* (2nd day), which is a quarantine station during the period of the Mecca pilgrimage (p. 452). To the N.W. of it lies a small grove of palms. Among the central mountains of Sinai we obtain a brief glimpse of the *Gebel Mûsa* (7520 ft.; 'Mountain of Moses'), the traditional Mount of the Covenant, and of the *Gebel Kâterîn* (8530 ft.) to the right of it (comp. Baedeker's 'Palestine'). The peninsula of Sinai ends on the S. in the steep *Râs Muḥammed* (98 ft.). — The coast on the right is fringed by a series of rocks and islets; on the *Ashrafi Reef* is an iron lighthouse (140 ft. high) with a revolving light, and on the rugged islet of *Shadwân* (1214 ft.) is a flash-light.

Passing through the *Straits of Jubal*, 4 M. wide, the steamer enters the **Red Sea**. On the left we have a view up the *Gulf of ʿAqaba*, through which the Erythræan depression is continued N. towards the Syrian depression (Dead Sea, Valley of the Jordan). We now lose sight of the coast on both sides. Excluding the gulfs at its N. end the Red Sea is 1080 nautical miles in length, 120 to 190 nautical miles in breadth, and has a maximum depth of 7740 ft. The name dates from antiquity and is supposed to have some connection with the tribes of the Homerites ('the red'). The colour of the water is bluish-green. The sultry climate, which is rendered more oppressive by the extreme moisture of the atmosphere due to evaporation, is notorious. In August the temperature frequently rises to above 104° Fahr. in the shade, when sunstroke is to be guarded against; but during the travelling season (Oct.-May) the heat is often so modified in the N. part of the sea by the prevailing N. winds that travellers returning from the tropics run the risk of taking cold. During this season a strong S. wind usually blows in the S. part of the sea, rendering the outward journey at least endurable. In any case, in winter the steamer is seldom more than one or two days within the zone of extreme heat.

There are several islands and islets in the N. part of the Red Sea. About 80 nautical miles from Shadwân (see above) lie the *Brothers*, two low coral islands, with a lighthouse (69 ft. high) whose light is visible for 12 nautical miles. On the third day we call at *Mînet el-Wejh* (*El-Wejh, Wedj;* comp. p. 450) on the coast of Arabia. About 100 nautical miles to the S. of the Brothers is the *Daedalus Shoal*, a submarine coral reef, marked by a lighthouse (59 ft. high), with a

light visible for 14 nautical miles. Beyond that point the steamer's course is free of islands for more than 650 nautical miles. On the fourth day we reach *Yanboʿ el-Baḥr (Yamboʿ, Yenboʿ).* At about lat. 22 we descry on the Egyptian coast the *Gebel Soterba* or *Gebel Ten* (7287 ft.). On the fifth day we touch at *Jidda* or *Jeddah* (20,000 inhab.; British consul), a trading town on the Arabian coast, which has been in the hands of the Wahhabis (comp. p. xciv) since 1925. Jidda is the harbour for *Mecca*, which lies 59 M. inland, and about 100,000 pilgrims land here annually, on their way (now mostly by motor-car) to the birthplace of the Prophet (comp. pp. xc, xci).

From Jidda the ship crosses the Red Sea in a S.W. course to *Suâkin* (p. 453), which we reach on the 6th or 7th day.

As we enter the harbour of Port Sudan several lighthouses and coral reefs are passed. To the right, at the mouth of the harbour, is the whitewashed tomb of *Sheikh Barghût* ('Sheikh Flea'), which was the only building at this place before the founding of Port Sudan. Farther on are the harbour stores, custom house, railway station, hotel (r.), and Government House (straight on).

Port Sudan. — Porterage of luggage from the steamer to the custom house (where luggage is examined) and thence to the train, P.T. 1 per package.

HOTEL. *Port Sudan*, to the S. of the town, belonging to the Sûdân Government Railways, pens. 110 P.T. per day, good.

POST, TELEGRAPH, and WIRELESS TELEGRAPH OFFICES. — BANKS. *National Bank of Egypt; Barclay's* (Anglo-Egyptian Bank).

STEAMSHIP AGENTS. *A. Frank & Co.* (Khedivial Mail Line); *Gellatly, Hankey & Co.* (Ellerman's Wilson, Union Castle, Messageries Maritimes); *Contamichalos, Darke & Co.* (Ellerman's City & Hall, Ellerman's Bucknall, Henderson, Hamburg-America, etc.).

HOSPITAL (well-equipped). — CHURCHES. *Anglican; Coptic; Greek.* — CLUBS. *Red Sea; Sport.*

FISHING. Excellent fishing from boats may be enjoyed in the harbour, the waters of which abound with the bayardo or bayad, sirroe, barracouta (up to 40 lb.), and other fish. Tackle should be brought from home, including a tarpon-rod (9-10 ft. long) or a strong salmon-rod (c. 14 ft.) and a metal reel with not less than 200 yds. of tarpon line.

Port Sudan, with 29,000 inhab. in 1928, the flourishing port of the Anglo-Egyptian Sûdân and the chief town of the Red Sea province, is situated in N. lat. 19°38′ and E. long. 37°8′, on a deep bay running inland in a N. direction, which affords an anchorage for ships of considerable size. It was founded as the terminus of the railway from the Nile to the Red Sea, opened in 1906, as the dangerous harbour of Suâkin (p. 453) could not be adapted to the requirements of modern shipping. The imports (sugar, cotton goods, flour, timber, cement, machinery, coffee, tea, clothing, etc.) amounted in 1928 to £6,672,425, and the exports (chiefly gum, cotton, cotton-seed, sesame, cattle, and hides) to £5,879,421. The town proper (West Town), with its clean streets and neat houses, lies on the W. bank of the harbour, opposite the quays. Outside the town to the S.W. are settlements of Arabs and negroes and of the Beja-Hadendoa, a nomad tribe frequenting the mountains between the Nile and the Red Sea (comp. p. lx).

From Port Sudan to Suâkin, 38 M., branch-line in $2^1/_2$ hrs., five trains weekly in either direction. When the large liners stay long enough, special trains are run from the quay at Port Sudan to Suâkin (fare £E $1^1/_2$, including luncheon and tea). By motor-car Suâkin is reached from Port Sudan in $2^1/_2$ hrs. (there and back P. T. 300 for 4 passengers). — To ($18^1/_2$ M.) *Sallôm Junction*, see below. — 38 M. **Suâkin** (*Suakin Shata* station) or *Suâkim*, more correctly *Sawâkin* (no hotel; post office), a picturesque town of 2000 inhab., situated at the W. end of an inlet (3 M. long), was the chief trading place on the African coast of the Red Sea before the foundation of Port Sudan, but is now rapidly decaying. It consists of an inner town, built on an island, and of an outer town on the mainland; a causeway connects the two. From the railway station on the mainland it is about 20 min. walk to the inner town, which has a large number of tall, clean houses with pretty bow windows. By the water's edge is the picturesque Government House, once the headquarters of both Gordon and Kitchener. In the outer town are several large bazaars. A lofty wall built by Kitchener, with the battlemented 'Kitchener Gate', defends the town on the landward side, and farther inland is a ring of small forts constructed during the Mahdist war. All these buildings are now falling into ruin, but the government has voted funds for the preservation of those of special value.

The Railway from Port Sudan to Atbara (Kharṭûm) crosses the harbour by a bridge to the station of *Port Sudan Town* and thence runs S. through the desert-plain bordering the Red Sea. — 6 M. *Asôteriba.* — $18^1/_2$ M. *Sallôm Junction*, for the line to Suâkin (see above). — The line gradually ascends among the picturesque mountains that stretch parallel with the Red Sea from the Abyssinian highlands to the Gulf of Suez. — $66^1/_2$ M. *Gebeit.* — 75 M. *Sinkât* (2933ft.), a hill-station for the officers and officials of the Sûdân government, is the capital of the Hadendoa district. The clean village, mainly inhabited by the Hadendoa (comp. p. 452), lies on the right of the railway. — The line reaches the crest of the ridge at (81 M.) *Summit* (3008 ft.), the station for *Erkowît* (c. 3600 ft.), a summer resort with a golf-course, among the mountains, about 4 hrs.' camel ride to the E. (1 hr. by motor-car, P.T. 50 per pers.). In spring Erkowît is the headquarters of the Governor-General. For accommodation, motor-car, and camels application must be made not less than two days in advance to the general manager of the Sûdân Government Railways at Atbara (p. 448). — The line now descends rapidly across the wide steppe that stretches W. towards the Nile. — 118 M. *Tehamiyam (Thamiam).* — $127^1/_4$ M. *Haiya Junction*, for the line to Kassala (see below). — 181 M. *Musmâr.* — At (297 M.) *Atbara* we join the main line from Wâdi Ḥalfa to Kharṭûm, see p. 448.

From Haiya Junction viâ Kassala and Gedâref to Makwâr, 491 M., one train weekly in either direction; through-carriages (1st and 2nd class) from Port Sudan. — This line, constructed in 1923-29, intersects the province of Kassala from N. to S. and is intended to open up the Eastern Sûdân, the trade of which hitherto depended on caravans, and to encourage the development of the great cotton plantations in the delta of the river Gâsh. — $215^1/_2$ M. **Kássala** (1591 ft.) is a picturesque town of 50,000 inhab., situated in 15° 25′ N. lat. and 36° 26′ E. long., on the E. bank of the Gâsh. It lies about 3 M. from the *Gebel Kassala* (4560 ft.), not far from the Eritrean frontier. Kassala was founded as a military camp in 1834, during the eastward advance of the Egyptian army, and is now the seat of the provincial government. In 1885 it fell into the hands of the Mahdists, from whom it was captured by the Italians in Jan. 1894; in 1897 it was handed over to

the Anglo-Egyptian Sûdân. Kassala is the junction of a caravan route E. to Agordat in Eritrea, whence a railway runs S.E. viâ Keren and Asmara to Massaua (Massawa) on the Red Sea. — Beyond Kassala the railway turns S.W. and after about 4 hrs., just short of *Khashm el-Girba*, crosses the Atbara. In another 6 hrs. we arrive at (351 M.) *Gedâref*. The line goes on viâ the Sennâr Dam to (491 M.) *Makwâr;* thence to Sennâr (for Kharṭûm and El-Obeid), see p. 461.

37. Kharṭûm and Omdurmân.

Arrival. The *Central Railway Station* (Pl. D 4) is on the S. side of Kharṭûm; it is the starting-point for the line to El-Obeid (p. 460). — *Kharṭûm North Station* (Pl. E 3; p. 450) is of no importance to tourists.

Hotels. **Grand Hotel Khartum* (Pl. a, D 3; belonging to the Sûdân Government Railways), on the Blue Nile (p. 456), with garden and fine view, 50 R. at 40-90, B. 20, L. 35, D. 50, pens. (5 days minimum stay) 140-190 P.T. — *Gordon* (Pl. b; D 4), 29 R., B. 15, L. 20, D. 30, pens. 80-120 P.T., good; *Royal* (Pl. c; E 4), with a pretty garden, 14 R. from 30, B. 16, L. 20, D. 25, pens. 75-80 P.T.; *New Khedivial* (Pl. d; D 4). — *Victoria* (Pl. e; D 4), quite unpretending.

Post and Telegraph Offices. In the Khedive Avenue at Kharṭûm, S. of the Government Offices (Pl. 6, D 3; p. 457); near the Large Market at Omdurmân (Pl. 20, B 1; p. 459).

Tramways. Cars start every 10 min. from Sirdâr Avenue at Kharṭûm (Pl. D 4; *Khartum Central*) and run W. past the Gordon Hotel and behind the Grand Hotel (stopping-place) to *Mogren* (Pl. B 3), then over the new bridge to *Omdurman Central* (Sûq; Pl. A 1) and *Abu Rûf* (Pl. C 1; p. 459). Here the tramway connects with a ferry-boat to the *Government Farm* (Pl. D 1), on the right bank of the Nile, whence a tramway runs to *Kharṭûm North* and across the Blue Nile Bridge to the *Central Station* (Pl. D 4).

Motor Cars and Cabs, with fixed tariff.

Banks. Branch-offices of the *National Bank of Egypt* (Pl. 12; D 4) and *Barclay's Bank* (formerly *Anglo-Egyptian*). — **Travelling Requisites** from *Vanian*. — **Forwarding Agents.** *Gellatly, Hankey & Co.; Contomichalos, Darke & Co.; Albert Frank & Co.*

Tourist Agents. *Thos. Cook & Son*, at the Grand Hotel (during the season); *E. D. Munari*, Sirdâr Avenue (Pl. D E 4).

Newspapers. *Sudan Herald* (daily and weekly editions). The official *Sudan Gazette* (P.T. 2), containing the government notices and ordinances as to shooting, travelling, and the export of curiosities (weapons, ostrich-feathers), may be obtained from the Civil Secretary, Kharṭûm.

Golf Courses both at Kharṭûm (see Pl. D 4) and at Omdurmân (Pl. A 1).

English Church. *All Saints' Cathedral* (Pl. 8, E 3; p. 456). — Missions. *Church Missionary Society; American Mission; Italian Roman Catholic Mission* (with church; p. 456). — *Greek Girls' School.*

Distribution of Time. A stay of four or five days allows sufficient time for the principal sights and for excursions to the battlefield of Kerreri and the Sennâr Dam (comp. pp. 459, 460). — *First Day.* Visit the sights of Kharṭûm and ride to the native village (p. 457). — *Second Day.* Omdurmân (guide convenient). — *Third Day.* Excursion to the battlefield of Kerreri (p. 459) and second visit to Omdurmân. — *Fourth and Fifth Days.* Excursion to the Sennâr Dam (p. 461). — Those who make a longer stay should undertake trips up the White Nile and the Blue Nile, a visit by steamer to Kosti on the White Nile (p. 462), or the very attractive excursion to Meroë, Nâga, and Muṣauwarât (pp. 449, 450), which requires special arrangements with the tourist agents.

Kharṭûm or *Khartoum* (1252 ft.), the capital of the Sûdân and the residence of the Governor-General, is situated in N. lat. 15°36′

and E. long. 32° 32′, on the left bank of the *Blue Nile*, immediately above its confluence with the *White Nile* (comp. p. lxvi). The name, meaning 'elephant's trunk', refers to the shape of the long peninsula that ends on the N.W. in *Mugran* or *Mogren Point* (Pl. B 3; formerly called *Râs Kharṭûm*). The town was built in 1822-30 by Muḥammed 'Ali and quickly rose to prosperity as the southernmost depot of the trade of Egypt, so that it is said to have had 70,000 inhab. in 1882. During the rebellion of the Mahdi (p. cxxix) General Gordon, who was despatched hither by the British government to withdraw the garrisons in the Sûdân, entered the town on Feb. 18th, 1884, and defended it until Jan. 26th, 1885 (comp. p. 456). The town was reduced to ruins by the Mahdists, but has been rebuilt since the capture of Omdurmân in 1898 (p. cxxx). Its ground-plan was designed by Lord Kitchener as a series of 'Union Jacks', with broad streets and large squares. The town, including Omdurmân, now contains 123,740 inhab. (Kharṭûm 30,797; Omdurmân 78,624; Kharṭûm North 14,319), to which may be added a peasant population of 61,975 living without the confines of the town. Most of the houses have but one story and are built of sun-dried bricks, though in the better ones free use is made also of white Kerreri sandstone; and of red sandstone from Gebel Auliya (p. 463); they are frequently surrounded by fine gardens.

The TREES and PLANTS that occur in the private and public gardens at Kharṭûm nearly all belong to the Sudanese flora, with the exception of the date-palm and some of the shade trees along the avenues (*Albizzia lebbakh*, p. lxxvii; *Ficus indica*, or banyan; *Ficus religiosa*, peepul or botree; *Ficus nitida; Dalbergia sissoo*), which have been imported. The SÛDÂN FLORA is represented in avenues and gardens by *Kigela aethiopica* (Umm shuṭûr), the sausage-tree, named from its curious fruit; *Tamarindus indica*, the tamarind ('ardēb); *Balanites aegyptiaca* or soap-tree (hejlij, heglig), the date-shaped fruit of which is eaten in times of famine; *Ficus sycomorus*, the sycamore (comp. p. lxxviii); *Khaya senegalensis* (African mahogany). Mimosas are represented by *Acacia arabica* (ṣunṭ; p. lxxviii) and *Acacia albida* (ḥarâz). There are specimens of *Calotropis procera* ('ushar), a species of the Indian mudar plant, poisonous, but used for flavouring the native beer (merîsa); *Dodonea viscosa*, Erkowit privet, is used for hedges. Specimens of the gigantic *Adansonia digitata*, or baobab (tebeldi), are to be seen in the town; in Kordofân its thick trunk is often hollowed out by the natives and used as it stands as a cistern. There are also a number of gum-acacias, parkinsonias (comp. p. lxxviii), sesbanias, and a few coffee-plants. — AGRICULTURE is carried on by the Nubian fellahin in the primitive manner of the Dongolese, without plough or harrow, but none the less industriously (comp. p. lxxv). Their sâqiyas, or water-wheels (p. lxxiv), are sometimes 25 ft. and more in height, and are worked by zebus. Wooden posts are occasionally placed beside these wheels in such a way as to form a kind of sun-dial, by which the hours of labour are regulated. The chief crop is durra (*Sorghum vulgare*, Arabic *dura;* comp. p. lxxvi), the staple food of the country, but sweet potatoes (*Ipomœa batatas;* Arabic bombai), maize, and the Sudanese sugar-cane (*Sorghum saccharatum;* el-'ankûlîb) are cultivated also. The last-named ripens between February and May.

Along the bank of the Blue Nile runs the EMBANKMENT, a promenade 3 M. in length, planted with lebbakh and other trees. The view hence is very fine. Opposite is *Kharṭûm North* (p. 450), with the dockyard, at the W. end of which is preserved the 'Bordein', one

of Gordon's paddle-steamers. On *Tûti Island* are a village and a fort that offered a desperate resistance to the dervishes in 1885. Downstream we see the Omdurmân bridge (p. 457) and the junction with the White Nile. To the W., beyond Tûti Island, is the desert-town of Omdurmân, marked by the minaret of the new mosque. Farther N. are the hills of Kerreri and Sûrqab (p. 459).

Following the Embankment to the E. from the Grand Hotel (p. 454) we pass the *Coptic Church* (Pl. 2), with its two towers, and a number of attractive villas and bungalows, including those of the Mudîr, the Financial Secretary, and the Commandant (Pl. 4; D 3). We next reach the *War Office* (Pl. 5; D 3) and the *Government Offices* (Pl. 6; D 3), containing the Civil Secretary's and Financial Secretary's Departments; in the garden is an equestrian statue of Lord Kitchener. Adjacent is the picturesque Gothic *Palace of the Governor-General* (Pl. 11; D 3), occupying the site of the building on the steps of which Gordon fell under the lances of the dervishes (memorial tablet in the corridor). Visitors are admitted to the palace and grounds (inquire at the office just inside the N. entrance). — Farther on are the *Public Works Department* (Pl. 7; E 3) and the gardens and villas of the British officials. At the corner of Muḥammed ʿAli Street is the attractive building of the *Sudan Club* (Pl. E 3), with gardens. Farther on are the *Italian Mission* (Pl. 9, E 3; formerly the Austrian Mission, the oldest in the Sûdân) and the *Military Hospital.*

We then reach the **Gordon Memorial College** (Pl. E F 3; director, N. R. Udal), opened in 1902, for which Lord Kitchener obtained the necessary funds by public subscription throughout the British Empire. This is a large and substantial building in which native youths (about 370 in number) are trained by British and native teachers "to earn their own livelihoods in their own country and to provide the Sudan government and business houses with staffs." The college contains a higher elementary school, a higher school for technical education (surveying and engineering), and a training college for schoolmasters and cadis. Associated with it are instructional workshops, a *Museum* (with interesting ethnographical and natural history collections and a fine collection of antiquities from the ruined sites of the Sûdân; guide P.T. 5), and the *Wellcome Tropical Research Laboratories* (open 9-1), founded in 1901 by Henry S. Wellcome of Messrs. Burroughs, Wellcome & Co., London. Beyond the railway are the barracks and the suburb of *Burri* (Pl. G 3), with the waterworks.

We return from Gordon College by *Khedive Avenue*, which runs parallel with the Embankment. Here are the *Maronite Church* (Pl. 13; E 3) and *All Saints' Cathedral* (Pl. 8; E 3), consecrated in 1912, the N. transept of which forms the Gordon Memorial Chapel. In the open space behind the Governor-General's Palace is a *Statue of Gordon* (represented as riding on a camel), a bronze copy of that executed

by E. Onslow Ford in 1890 for the Royal Engineers' Institute at Chatham. — Farther on, to the right, are the *Anglo-Egyptian Bank*, the *General Post Office* (1927), the *Law Courts*, the offices of the *Irrigation Department*, and the *Mudîrîya* (Pl. 3; D 3), or office of the mudîr; to the left is the *National Bank of Egypt* (Pl. 12; D 4).

To the W. of the Grand Hotel, on the Embankment, lies the *Zoological Garden* (Pl. 1; C 3), which contains a representative collection of Sudanese animals. A very attractive walk is afforded by the promenade extending to *Mogren Quays* (Pl. C 3), which are used for the river traffic to the White Nile districts, and to the picturesquely sited Nubian village of *Mandara*. On the left are all sorts of warehouses. Along the bank are numerous sâqiyas, for watering the fields and palm-groves. We return from the Omdurmân bridge (see below) either by tram or on foot viâ Khedive Avenue.

The business part of Kharṭûm, which is chiefly inhabited by Greeks, is restricted to the portion of the town lying to the S. of Khedive Avenue, and is intersected by the tramway. Its central point is the large *'Abbâs Square* (Pl. D 4), with a handsome *Mosque;* to the N.W. are the interesting *Markets*. The *Bazaars* are especially animated in the afternoon.

Victoria Avenue, leading S. from the Gordon statue (p. 456), passes (l.) the domed tombs of two governors of the Sûdân, Aḥmed Pasha el-Minikli (1844-46) and Mûsa Pasha Ḥamdi (1863-65); farther on are the synagogue and the Civil Hospital. The avenue ends at the *Central Station* (Pl. D 4), which may be reached also by the streets parallel with Victoria Avenue. Opposite the station, to the right, is the *Lord Kitchener Memorial School of Medicine*, opened in 1924, which trains native doctors; the similar building on the left accommodates the Wellcome Medical Laboratories (1928; comp. p. 456). At the S. end of the Mosque Avenue (parallel with Victoria Avenue) is the *Christian Cemetery*, with a war memorial cross (1928). — Beyond the station are the *Fortifications* constructed by Gordon. To the right and left are barracks. To the S.E. lie the *Racecourse* and the *Sudanese Village* (Pl. E 4), known to the natives as *Ed-Deim* and largely inhabited by pilgrims on their way to Mecca. It shelters various tribes of the Sûdân (Shilluks, Dinkas, Bornawis, Gebelawis, etc.), partly in mud hovels, partly in the characteristic round straw huts.

Communication between Kharṭûm and Omdurmân is maintained by a new bridge over the White Nile at Mogren Point (Pl. B 3; p. 455). Constructed of steel in 1925-28 by Messrs. Dorman, Long & Co., it consists of seven spans each 244 ft. long, with a swing span of 304 ft. for navigation (total length 2012 ft.). From the bridge we obtain a wonderful view of the 'meeting of the waters', the different colours of the two rivers being clearly discernible for some distance beyond their confluence (comp. p. lxvi); Omdurmân and the island of Tûti (p. 456) also are well seen from here.

The native town of **Omdurmân**, where the Mahdi Muḥammed Aḥmed (p. 455) established his military camp in 1884, was after his death in 1885 the residence of the Khalîfa ʿAbdullâhi et-Taʿâïshi for fourteen years, during which it became the scene of the most atrocious cruelties and extravagant orgies. It extends for about 5 M. along the left bank of the united Nile, and has room for upwards of 100,000 inhabitants. The name is said to be derived from an old woman who once spent a solitary existence here. The S. part is the *Umm* or *Omm Durmân* proper. The central part, formerly including the holy buildings and the walled inner town inhabited by the Baggâra (Baqqâra) tribe, to which ʿAbdullâhi belonged, is called by the natives *El-Buqʿa*, i. e. 'the (holy) place', a name always given to the wandering headquarters of the Mahdists. To the N. is the *Ḥâret en-Nuṣâra* or *el-Mesîḥîyîn*, the Christian quarter, inhabited by Abyssinians, Copts, and Greeks.

The warlike oppression of the Mahdist period, the fanatical enthusiasm for pilgrimages, the desire for plunder, and the devastation of whole provinces have assembled here a confused medley of the most diverse races and stocks: Bantus and grotesque negroes from the W. Sûdân; Semitic and Hamitic tribes from the desert, such as the Nûba, Baggâra, Kabâbîsh, Gawâmʿa, and Kawâhla; Nubians, fellahin, Jaʿalîn (p. 450). To these must now be added Egyptians, Syrians, and Greeks. The shopkeepers are mostly Dongolese. The fashions prevalent among the natives are very curious, such as their methods of shaving, tattooing, perfuming, and greasing themselves, and otherwise altering their personal appearance.

Omdurmân is reached from Kharṭûm either by the electric tram or by motor-car. On the bank of the White Nile, beyond the bridge, are (l.) the barracks of the Sudanese troops and a neglected cemetery; on the right are various military buildings. Following the tram-lines we cross the *Khôr Angar* and pass the small market (sûq; Pl. B 2) of the village of *Ḥillet el-Mûrada*, near which, on the river bank, is the large and picturesque *Boat Harbour (Mûrada)*. Farther on (r.) is the *Beit el-Amâna* (Pl. 19; B 2) or former arsenal of the dervishes, burnt down in 1922. The large *Mosque Square* (Pl. B 2), surrounded by a brick wall and now used as a sports-ground, was a place of prayer and assembly under the Khalîfa ʿAbdullâhi. To the left of it lies the *Zabṭîya* or office of the ma'mûr (Pl. 22). On the E. are the remains of the *Tomb of the Mahdi* (Pl. 15), which was erected, at the order of the Khalîfa, by an Arab architect, and consisted of a square building 85 ft. high, surmounted by a lofty dome, and furnished with three arched windows on each side. After the capture of Omdurmân the tomb was destroyed by the British and its contents scattered. Fragments of the Mahdi's dwelling are still to be seen by the tomb. — Opposite the tomb, adjoining the great mosque, is the *House of the Khalîfa ʿAbdullâhi* (Pl. 16; see above), still in good preservation, a large enclosure including several courts and colonnades, numerous thambers, and a bath-house. Numerous mementos of the dervishes' rising and the battle of Omdurmân are exhibited here (adm. P.T. 10, including the Mahdi's Tomb). The upper story commands a fine view

of Omdurmân and its environs. Adjacent are the house of the British District Commissioner (Pl. 17) and the memorial stone of the Hon. H. G. L. Howard, an English war correspondent who fell here in 1898. A little to the S. are the ruins of the Sudanese *Guard House* (Kommândânîya), formerly the house of the Emîr Ya'qûb. To the S.E., by the Nile, is the old *Prison* (Pl. 25; B 2), where many Europeans languished. It is sometimes known as the 'Saier Prison', from the name of the jailor under the Mahdi and Khalîfa. Slatin Pasha (Sir Rudolf Slatin, baron of the Austrian Empire; b. in Austria 1857), who was appointed governor of Dârfûr by Gen. Gordon and was obliged to surrender after the battle of Kashgil near El-Obeid (p. 463), was imprisoned here for eleven years but eventually succeeded in escaping. From 1900 to 1914 he was the British Inspector-General of the Sûdân. — To the E. of the Mahdi's tomb, facing an open space, stands the modern *Prison* (Pl. 18), formerly the house of *Sheikh ed-Dîn*, son of the Khalîfa. To the N. of this are the barracks of Sudanese machine-gun batteries.

We now skirt the N. wall of the Great Mosque to regain the broad street traversed by the tramway, which we follow to the N. To the right is the *Government School* (Pl. 24; B 1); behind it, to the E., on the site of the walled inner town of *El-Buq'a* (p. 458), with the quarters of the Khalîfa's bodyguard, stands the *Civil Hospital* (Pl. 22; B 1). To the left, in an open space, is the *Post & Telegraph Office* (Pl. 20). The street ends at the *New Mosque* (Pl. A B 1). Near by is the *LARGE MARKET or *Sûq* (Pl. A 1), on which the various bazaars converge and which presents a busy and variegated scene of African life. All the articles of consumption of Central Africa are to be seen here in profusion: curious spices of a hundred different varieties, drugs, and perfumes; soda, saltpetre, salt; betel, bead-nuts, seeds, and wood of every kind; ostrich-feathers, glass beads, toilet-butter, 'angarîbs (bedsteads), the dried flesh of wild animals, etc. The silver and ivory bazaar is especially interesting. Skilful smiths, and saddlers dealing with hippopotamus hide, may be seen at work. Many articles here, however, are manufactured specially for tourists. The place of execution (Pl. 23) under the Khalîfa was in the date market. The *Sûq el-Ḥarîm* (formerly limited to women-dealers) is devoted to fruit, milk, ornaments, ointments, and basket-work.

At the Large Market the main street turns to the right (E.) and intersects the poverty-stricken quarter of *Abu Rûf*, with its grey mud-hovels and picturesque market (sûq; Pl. C 1). It ends at the Nile, near the Abu Rûf quays (p. 454).

Excursions. To the N. to (6 M.) the BATTLEFIELD OF KERRERI, on the left bank of the Nile. This excursion is made by motor-car from Kharṭûm or Omdurmân; large parties may hire a steamer. We first proceed to the *Khôr Shambat*, and thence to the *Gebel Sûrqab* (commonly called *Gebel Surgham*), which affords the best general view of the battlefield. On the way we pass a large marble *Obelisk*, erected to the memory of the officers and men of the 21st Lancers who fell in the engagement. The monument, which has been damaged by natives, is surrounded by an iron railing. —

Near the village of *Kerreri* and the Gebel Sûrqab, on the left bank of the Nile, Kitchener, with 22,000 men, defeated, on Sept. 2nd, 1898, a dervish army of 45,000 men, whose fanatical onslaughts were shattered by the steady fire of the Anglo-Egyptian troops. The dervishes are estimated to have lost 10,000 killed, 16,000 wounded, and 4000 prisoners, while of the British 25 were killed and 99 wounded, of the Egyptians 21 killed and 230 wounded. On the afternoon of the same day Kitchener entered Omdurmân. ʿAbdullâhi (p. 458) fled S., but was slain in 1899 at the battle of Umm Debreikat (p. 462).

The Ruins of Sôba, on the right bank of the Blue Nile, to the S.E. of Kharṭûm, are most easily reached by motor-car (9 M.), following a well-marked road along the right bank of the river. *Sôba* was the capital of the Christian kingdom of *Aloa*, which existed until the middle ages. The extensive field of the ruins is covered with fragments of baked bricks. The large tumuli rising here and there probably mark the sites of churches and public buildings. One church, with granite columns, has been partly brought to light.

The excursion to *Sennâr* and the *Sennâr Dam* (p. 461) is made in one day by motor-car. By the special train of the Sudan Government Railways (Mon. and Fri. from Jan. to March; return fare, including meals and sleeping car, £E 10), a day and a half is necessary.

38. The Southern Sûdân.

Longer excursions to the Southern Sûdân are mostly undertaken only by sportsmen. The expense of such excursions is necessarily great, and the equipment must be very carefully selected. The *Motor Car*, *Railway*, and *Steamer Routes*, however, mentioned below, afford an excellent opportunity for those who wish to become acquainted with the wonderful scenery of the tropics. — For *Caravan Journeys* the best plan is to hire camels, with the help of competent advice, in Kharṭûm. The rest of the equipment, such as beds, cooking utensils, provisions, mosquito-nets, etc. (but not rifles and ammunition), is also procurable at Kharṭûm.

A. From Kharṭûm viâ Wad Medani and Sennâr to Kosti and El-Obeid.

427 M. Railway to *Sennâr* daily in 8½ hrs., thence to *El-Obeid* viâ Kosti (Sun. and Thurs.) in another 15 hrs. Fares to El-Obeid 1st class £E 6 P.T. 7, 2nd class £E 4 P.T. 25.

Kharṭûm, see p. 454. — The line skirts the left (W.) bank of the Blue Nile. Shortly after (35 M.) *El-Masîd* cotton-fields are reached. From this point to Wad en-Nau (p. 461) irrigation is by free flow from the canals. — 56½ M. *El-Miʿeiliq* is the station for *Kâmlîn*, a district capital.—80 M. *El-Hasîheisa*, a district capital with a market; ferry to *Rufâʿa*, on the E. bank, whence there is a motor route to Geḍâref (p. 454). — 101 M. *Ṭaiyiba*. — 108 M. **Wad Médani** (1358 ft.), with 33,000 inhab. in 1928, the capital of the Blue Nile province, lies near the confluence of the *Rahad* and the Blue Nile; it has broad streets lined by brick houses. On the river-bank stands the palace of the mudîr, a brick building with beautiful tropical gardens. Adjoining the town is a large native village with conical thatched huts. — 114¼ M. *Barakât* is the headquarters of the Sudan Plantations Syndicate (p. 461), with four large cotton factories in the neighbourhood. Beyond Barakât the Blue Nile is joined by the *Dinder*. — From

(122 M.) *Wad en-Nau* to Sennâr the irrigation water is to be raised from the main canal by pumps.

167 M. **Sennâr,** on the left bank of the main irrigation canal (see below), with numerous round huts. Old Sennâr, see p. 462.

A branch-line runs from Sennâr in 1/4 hr. to (6 1/4 M.) *Makwâr,* a negro village converted into a town of several thousand inhabitants by the construction of the dam, since the completion of which, however, it has dwindled considerably. It has clean streets, pleasant houses, and a nice tropical garden. The native town is rapidly growing. Close to the station is a rest-house with restaurant (6 R.; lodging 20, board P.T. 55); notice should be given at least twenty-four hours in advance to the Irrigation Department at Makwâr.

The ***Sennâr** or **Makwâr Dam,** constructed in 1922-25, is one of the greatest valley barrages in the world and the chief means by which the British government has fostered the economic prosperity of the Sûdân. Its purpose was to irrigate and fertilize the so-called *Gezîra* or 'island', the triangular steppe between the White and the Blue Nile, to the N. of the Sennâr-Kosti railway, and thus to provide fresh arable areas for cotton and corn. The waters of the Blue Nile are dammed to a height sufficient to fill the canals necessary for the irrigation of the Gezîra. A storage reservoir is also provided, so that the canals can be fed during the dry season; this forms a lake extending upstream as far as Singa (p. 462), about 50 M. distant, and estimated to contain as much as 140,000 million gallons.

The length of the dam is 1 3/4 M., of which the dam proper comprises 1970 yds., the bridge-heads and approaches 1312 yds. Its height is 85 ft. above the river-bottom, and the foundations had to be taken down in places to a depth of 33-39 ft. before reaching firm rock (hard gabbro). The masonry (450,000 cubic yds.) consists of granite blocks brought from a quarry on the Gebel Ságadi (Saqadi; 492 ft.), 35 M. to the W. The dam has eight main sluices, each 27 1/2 ft. high and 6 1/2 ft. wide, besides forty large and seventy-two smaller spillways. The railway to Geḍâref and Kassala (p. 453) runs over the dam.

At the W. end of the dam diverges the main canal, which is regulated by fourteen separate sluices, measuring 16 ft. by 10 ft. It is 85 ft. wide and can take 18,480 gallons of water per second. Some 35 M. in length, it follows the river from S. to N. and feeds a whole system of canals, the total length of which, including field channels, amounts to 9286 M. The allotment of the water and the agricultural development of the irrigated territory are in the hands of the Sudan Plantations Syndicate (p. 460). According to the complete scheme three million feddân will be irrigated; at present it is only intended to cultivate 300,000 acres. In 1925-26 80,000 acres were sown with cotton, and the durra fields yielded a harvest of 80,000 ardebb (435,947 bushels). In 1926-27 100,000 acres were under cotton (130,000 in 1927-28), 50,000 under durra, and 50,000 under lûbiya (p. lxxvi).

The first idea of irrigating the Gezîra by means of a dam came from a German, and was taken up by Sir William Garstin (d. 1925), the engineer,

with the support of Kitchener. The enterprise was begun in 1921 from the plans of Sir Murdoch Macdonald. The work of construction, in which as many as 19,000 workmen were employed, was at first in the hands of the Sudan Construction Co., who were succeeded in 1922 by S. Pearson & Son Ltd. The work was completed in July 1925 and was officially opened in Jan. 1926, the total cost amounting to 13,000,000*l*.

Cotton-growing in the Gezîra was first tested by experimental plantations at Ṭaiyiba (p. 460; established in 1911) and Barakât (p. 460; 1914). Owing to the heat of the summer climate of the S. Sûdân it was decided to sow in July-September. Picking begins about the end of December, the last watering takes place in April, and the harvest is completed in May. The practice of the N. Sûdân and Egypt is thus reversed (comp. p. lxxv). The Gezîra already supplies Lancashire mills with 100,000 bales a year of the highest grade long-staple cotton.

From Makwâr to Singa, a very interesting excursion (about 5 hrs. there and back by motor-car, including 1 hr.'s stay at Singa). The road leads through durra fields and then through bush. We pass several native villages, which are more African in character than the new villages in the district irrigated by the Sennâr Dam. The scenery is extremely attractive. *Singa* is the capital of the Fûng province. The government building is situated by the river, and close by is a beautiful tropical garden. Steamer to Suki or Roṣeireṣ, see below.

Another pleasant excursion (about $^3/_4$ hr. by motor-car) may be made from Makwâr to the ruined site of *Old Sennâr*, which lies between the main irrigation canal and the Blue Nile. This town, which had some 20,000 inhab., was completely destroyed by the Khalîfa in 1885. In the immediate vicinity is the forest of *Deim el-Mesheikha*, rich in monkeys and bird-life.

From *Suki*, to the S. of the dam, a steamer plies fortnightly on the Blue Nile when the Nile is high (Oct. to the beginning of Jan.) to (54 M.) *Singa* (see above), (97$^1/_2$ M.) *Abu Na'âma*, and (174 M., in three days) *Roṣeireṣ* (1539 ft.), situated on the right bank of the Blue Nile. Higher up the river forms rapids, rendering further navigation impossible. — The storage reservoir (p. 461) is navigable from Jan. to June as far as Singa.

Beyond Sennâr the railway turns W. and crosses the *Gezîra* (p. 461). — Near (120 M.) *Gebel Môya* is an ancient negro cemetery, excavated by H. S. Wellcome (p. 456). — 230$^1/_2$ M. *Ḥillet 'Abbâs*. The railway now crosses the White Nile by a remarkable iron bridge, completed by the Cleveland Bridge & Engineering Co. in 1910; it is 1510 ft. long and has eight fixed spans and a central swing-span, 246 ft. wide, open during the day for the passage of boats.

236 M. **Kosti** (rest-house, 6 beds at P.T. 20; steamer station, see p. 464), on the left bank of the White Nile, near the S. end of the island of Abba (p. 464), was named after a Greek settler. It is a rising place, being the headquarters of the S. district of the White Nile province and one of the chief markets for the produce of the province of Kordofân. It lies on the borders of the negro lands, and representatives of the nearest tribes (Habbânîyas, Danâglas, Dinkas, and occasionally Shilluks) are seen in the market-place.

The battlefield of *Umm Debreikat*, where the Khalîfa 'Abdullâhi (comp. p. 460), with the last of the chiefs, was defeated and slain by the Anglo-Egyptian troops under Sir Reginald Wingate (Nov. 24th, 1899), lies about 30 M. to the S.W. of Kosti. The Khalîfa was buried on the battlefield.

The railway runs W. through the White Nile province. — 294$^1/_2$ M.

Tendelti, a district capital and the seat of a ma'mûr (p. 442), carries on a busy trade in gum arabic, sesame, ground-nuts, and dura. The market, close to the station, is worth seeing. — Near (309 M.) *Wad 'Ashâna* the railway enters Kordofân, a fertile province, rich in cattle. — 339 M. *Umm Ruwâba*; 385 M. *Er-Rahad.*

427 M. **El-Obeid** (*El-Ubaiyaḍ*; 1903 ft.), the railway terminus, capital of the province of Kordofân, has taken on a new lease of life as the centre of the gum trade. It is situated in N. lat. 13° 11′ and E. long. 30° 14′, and extends over a flat hollow, at the lowest parts of which are numerous springs of good water. The population, at one time numbering about 35,000, consists of Arabs and Nûba negroes, and in the dry season, when the neighbouring villages are out of water, it now amounts to about 17,000. With the exception of the mosques and a few large buildings the houses are mostly round straw huts with conical roofs. To the S. lie the barracks of the Sûdân Camel Corps and the government building. An Egyptian force under Hicks Pasha (Col. William Hicks), which attempted to take El-Obeid from the Mahdi, was annihilated on Nov. 5th, 1883 in the 'Battle of Kashgil' (comp. p. cxxix).

A road passable for motors leads S.W. from El-Obeid to the native town of *En-Nahûd* (130 M.; pop. 12,000), whence another road leads W. to *El-Fâsher* (270 M.; pop. 12,000 in 1928), capital of the Dârfûr province, which was conquered in 1916 after the revolt of the tributary sultan 'Ali Dînâr. It marches on the W. with French Equatorial Africa and on the N. with the Libyan Desert. *Gebel Marra* (9875 ft.) rises in the centre of the province.

B. From Kharṭum viâ Ed-Dueim, Kosti, and Renk to Juba.

1089 M. The Mail Steamers of the Sûdân Government (flat-bottomed, stern-wheel steamers burning wood and oil) ascend the White Nile every Sat. from the middle of Dec. to the middle of April and fortnightly at other seasons (starting on Fri.), the return journey being completed in 23-26 days (1st class fare £E 58 P.T. 80 plus P.T. 75 daily for meals; 2nd class £E 24 P.T. 50 plus P.T. 50 daily for meals). — There is also a fortnightly passenger service (starting on Thurs. morning) throughout the year from Kharṭûm to Renk (there and back in 10 days; fare £E 16 P.T. 11).

Kharṭûm, see p. 454. — We steer W. and in 1/2 hr., at Mogren Point (p. 455), reach the White Nile, which forms the verdant island of *Dakin* at its confluence with the Blue Nile. The steamer enters the W. arm of the White Nile. 'Gordon's Tree' or 'Maho Bey' forms a conspicuous landmark. When the river is high it is 2-3 M. wide and resembles a great lake. Herds of camels, goats, and sheep are seen grazing on the low flat banks. — On the E. bank of the river, 29 M. from Kharṭûm, rises the volcanic hill of *Gebel Auliya (Aulia)*, near which a barrage resembling the Sennâr Dam (p. 461) is projected by the Egyptian government. The quarries on the S. slope of the hill yielded the material for many of the buildings at Kharṭûm.

58 M. *El-Geteina*, on the E. bank, near the *Gebel Mandara*, is a district capital in the White Nile province and is inhabited mainly by Danâgla Arabs. On the W. bank are great fields of safra dura, a

kind of large-grained millet forming the staple food of the N. Sûdân. The banks are covered farther on with thick groves of mimosa and acacia. In the distance to the S.W. we see the *Gebel Arashkol*, a group of bare rocky hills about 330 ft. in height. — 100½ M. *Tur'a el-Khaḍra* was formerly the harbour for Kordofân and the W.

128 M. **Ed-Dueim** (W. bank; 1266 ft.), the capital of the province of the White Nile, with regularly laid out streets, is inhabited by Danâgla and Ḥassânîya Arabs. It has a small mosque, designed by a Greek architect, and an unpretending Greek café. Barley, wheat, onions, and hibiscus plants (p. lxxvi) are cultivated here. Ed-Dueim was once the chief trading centre for gum arabic, which was brought hither from Kordofân and unloaded for Port Sudan. Hicks Pasha organized here his ill-fated expedition to Kordofân in 1883 (p. 463). — 151½ M. *Kawa* (E. bank), the chief town of a district. The straw roofs (tukuls) of the houses are curious. — The steamer now reaches the N. end of the densely wooded island of *Abba* or *Aba* (28½ M. long), the base of the Mahdi in his religious war of 1883 (p. cxxix). — 182 M. *Fashâshôya*, on the W. bank, was the home of the Mahdi and the starting-point of Sir Reginald Wingate's expedition against the Khalîfa 'Abdullâhi in 1899 (comp. p. 462). — 198 M. *Kosti* (W. bank), see p. 462. On the opposite bank lies the village of *Gôz Abu Gum'a*.

About 4 M. beyond Kosti the steamer passes through the large railway bridge mentioned on p. 462. We now enter the region of the negro tribes. The scenery alters. Cultivated fields cease. Narrow belts of forest near high water level separate the river from the open plains. Hippopotami, crocodiles, gazelles, and innumerable waterfowl may be seen. On the E. bank is the territory of the Dinka negroes (see below). — About 245 M. from Kharṭûm we see on the E. bank the ridge of *Gebelein* (*El-Jebelein*, 'the two mountains') with its five quaint peaks and the district capital of the same name, with a busy market in gum arabic and ground-nuts. — Some 45 M. farther S. we reach the N. boundary of the Upper Nile province. — 306 M. *Er-Renk* (E. bank), a district capital. — At 340 M. we pass the *Gebel Aḥmed Agha*, a cliff 345 ft. in height. — 405 M. *Kâka* (W. bank) consists of a group of settlements of Shilluk negroes, who live by agriculture and fishing and who build ingenious boats. Short of Kâka we pass a gum plantation. — The river sweeps round towards the E., separating the Dinka negroes on the E. bank from the Shilluk negroes on the W. bank. The Dinkas do not wear clothes. Both tribes adorn themselves with all kinds of ornaments and carry long spears. The Shilluks, who often have a curious tall coiffure, are tall and slender of stature (some as much as 7 ft.) and are of a much higher culture than the Dinkas. — 421 M. *Melût* (E. bank), a district capital. The river again bends towards the S.

466 M. **Kodok** (*Fâshôda*; 1035 ft.), a district capital on the W. bank, was occupied by the French under Major Marchand from July 10th to Dec. 11th, 1898, when a serious dispute was avoided by its cession

to the British (p. cxxx). In the vicinity is the capital of the Shilluks and the residence of their 'Mek' (from melek, i. e. king), or hereditary headman. — 497 M. *Lul*, a station of the Italian Roman Catholic Mission (p. 454).

509 M. **Malakal**, on the E. bank, is the capital of the Upper Nile province and the headquarters of the irrigation authorities for the upper White Nile.

From Malakal to Meshra' er-Req, 225½ M., monthly steamer in four days, in connection with the mail steamer from Kharṭûm (fare about £E 7). — 10 M. *Taufîqîya* (see below). — The steamer ascends the *Sobat* to (20½ M.) *Doleib Hill (Hillet Duleib)*, an American mission station, and then returns to the White Nile. Thence to *Tonga* and *Lake No*, see below. We follow the *Bahr el-Ghazâl* ('Gazelle River') S.W. to *Ghâbat el-'Arab*, at the mouth of the *Baḥr el-'Arab*, which debouches from the W. We then steam S. At the mouth of the *Jur (Agur)* the Baḥr el-Ghazâl widens into *Lake Ambadi*. — 225½ M. **Meshra' er-Req** is a district capital in the province of Baḥr el-Ghazâl.

519 M. *Taufîqîya (Taufikia)*, a district capital, founded by Sir Samuel Baker (p. 467) in 1870, was formerly the chief garrison in the Upper Sûdân.

From Taufîqîya to Gambeila on the Sobat, 342 M. (from Kharṭûm 869 M.), steamer monthly from June to Nov., while the Sobat is navigable, in 13 days from Kharṭûm (1st class £E 23 P.T. 88, 2nd class £E 11 P.T. 94). — To (10½ M.) *Doleib Hill*, see above. — Thence we ascend the *Sobat* S.E. to (79½ M.) *Abwong*, capital of the Lau district in the Upper Nile province. — 188 M. *Fort Nâṣir (Old Nasser*; 1525 ft.). — A little farther up, on the right bank, is *Nâṣir (New Nasser)*, a district capital and American mission station. — On the 5th day after leaving Taufîqîya we reach (218 M.) the mouth of the *Bâro* (at the confluence of the *Pibor*). Following the Bâro, we pass (233 M.) the mouth of the *Adura* and, beyond (312 M.) *Itang*, arrive at (342 M.) *Gambeila* (1700 ft.), a district capital and trading place leased from Abyssinia.

About 4 M. beyond Taufîqîya, on the E., the *Sobat* joins the White Nile, which now expands and flows from W. to E. The low river-banks are covered with mimosa shrub. On either side are Shilluk villages and vast expanses of grass with isolated trees and, here and there, large termite ant-hills. We pass the mouth of the *Bahr ez-Zerâf* ('Giraffe River'), which flows into the White Nile from the S. — 575 M. *Tonga*, a station of the Italian Roman Catholic Mission. Fully 60 M. to the N. we may distinguish the *Gebel el-Amira* (2280 ft.) and *Gebel Eliri*, near which lies *Talôdi*, the capital of the former province of Nuba Mountains. Elephants, buffaloes, and some rare species of antelope are seen from time to time.

At 615 M. we reach *Lake No*, where the *Albert Nile (Baḥr el-Gebel)*, coming from the S., and the *Baḥr el-Ghazâl* (see above) unite to form the *White Nile*. The steamer turns S. up the Albert Nile, through the *Sudd* district, a great stretch of swamp one-third the size of the British Isles. This name, which means hindrance or barrier, has been given on account of the blockading masses of water-plants which used to form floating islands considerable enough to obstruct the course of the river at frequent intervals. Since 1900, however, the channel has been cleared of these barriers of vegetation at several points, and

the strong current has prevented fresh accumulations from forming. On either side are lakes and lagoons; papyrus seems to be the only vegetation. At (749 M.) *Hillet en-Nuer (Ḥillet en-Nuweir)* definite banks appear again; these are occupied by villages of the *Nuer*, a warlike tribe that appears to have been driven by its neighbours to its present habitat around the two great feeders of the White Nile. — The marsh district then begins again.

854 M. *Shambé*, the chief town of a district in the province of Baḥr el-Ghazâl. Thence a caravan route leads W. viâ *Rûmbek* (1509 ft.) to *Wau* (*Wâw;* 1395 ft.), capital of the province. Large quantities of hippopotami inhabit the lagoons here. — At *Kenîsa* is a deserted station of the Austrian Mission (comp. p. 456). The region becomes more wooded; dûm and fan or doleib palms (Borassus flabelliformis) abound.

985 M. *Bôr* (1410 ft.) is the chief place in the Dinka-Nuer district of the province of Baḥr el-Ghazâl, with a government gum plantation. The village of Bôr lies 9 M. to the E. and is the largest settlement of the Dinka negroes. To the S. begins the territory of the *Bâri* negroes. The scenery changes: numerous villages with the clean huts of the Bâri and their herds of cattle are seen; the banks are cultivated at many points. — We next reach the English Mission station of (980 M.) *Malek.* The river divides into two arms, then reunites to form the E. frontier of the former 'Ladó Enclave', which was leased to the Congo Free State in 1894-1910 but now belongs to the province of Mongalla. The scenery assumes a park-like character.

"Luxuriant tropical vegetation abounds. Giant Euphorbia are a marked feature of the forest. The whole of the banks and most of the trees are covered with a velvety-looking mass of creepers. A bluff, 10-13 ft. high, projects into the stream . . . . . The face of this cliff is perforated by myriads of holes made by a very beautiful and tiny species of bee-eater. These birds have rose-coloured wings, with bronze coloured bodies. They add much to the beauty of a lovely scene" *(Garstin).*

1034 M. *Terakeka*, on the W. bank, is a district capital of the Mongalla province. To the S. lies the military station of *Kiro*, prettily situated in the midst of trees. The *Gebel Ladó* comes in sight.

1067½ M. **Mongalla,** on the E. bank, is the centre of the local rain-grown cotton industry and the capital of the province of Mongalla, which is remarkable for the large number of elephants and giraffes it contains. Coffee has recently been planted with success in the district. From Mongalla a broad fair-weather motor road (North Equatorial Road) runs viâ Juba to Uganda and Kenya Colony (comp. p. 467). The *Nyambara Mts.* on the W. and the mountain ranges of Uganda on the S. now become visible. Navigation is impeded here by shoals and sandbanks. — 1068 M. *Ladó* (1475 ft.), founded by Gordon in 1874, was in 1878-85 the headquarters of Emin Pasha (Eduard Schnitzer, 1840-92), the German explorer, at that time governor of the Equatorial Province of Egypt; later it became a Belgian military station (comp. above). It has now been abandoned.

1071 M. **Gondókoro** is wonderfully situated on the lofty and thickly wooded bank of the river, with the mountains of Ladó (N.W.) and Rejâf (S.W.) in the background. On the lofty bank close by are the remains of the headquarters of Sir Samuel Baker, the explorer (1821-93). — 1089 M. **Juba** (rest-house), a mission station on the W. bank, has been since Dec. 1928 the terminus of the Nile steamers, which previously went on to *Rejâf (Rejjâf)*, a district capital 7 M. farther S. Rejâf lies on the W. bank, at the foot of the conspicuous *Gebel Rejâf* (328 ft.). Quarters at the house of the Société du Haut Uële et du Nil (P. 120 P.T.).

From Juba a motor road leads S.W. viâ *Loka* (3314 ft.) and the neat settlement of *Yei* (a district capital) to (124 M.) *Aba* (2790 ft.) in the Belgian Congo. Thence viâ *Faraje* and through the alluvial gold-mine district (Moto Mines) to *Aru*, and then through beautiful mountain scenery, reminiscent of Switzerland, to *Arua* (Uganda) and (379 M.) *Rhino Camp* (see below; four days' motoring from Juba).

From Rejâf a motor road runs to *Stanleyville*, connecting the Nile with the Congo. A regular service for passengers and mails is maintained on it, the journey being made in 5 days.

From Juba viâ Uganda and Kenya Colony to Mombasa. From Juba to (104 M.) *Nímule* (1010 ft.), on the Uganda frontier, by motor-car (accommodating three passengers) during the dry season (Dec.-March), to be ordered three weeks in advance from the General Manager of the Sûdân Government Railways & Steamers at Atbara (p. 448, fare £E 6 per person, minimum £E 10); provisions and cooking utensils must be taken; there are several rest-houses en route. From Nimule we proceed by steamer to *Rhino Camp* on *Lake Albert* or *Albert Nyanza* (p. lxvi), and thence across the lake to (200 M. from Juba) *Butiaba* in two days.

From Butiaba we go E. by motor-car to *Masindi Town* (Masindi Hotel, pens. 15*s.*) and (75 M.) *Masindi Port* (3610 ft.), at the efflux of the Victoria Nile from *Lake Kioga*. Thence a steamer plies fortnightly on Lake Kioga S.E. to *Namasagalli* on the Victoria Nile.

From Namasagalli we go on by the Busuga Railway to (18 M.) *Mbulamuti* (to Mombasa, see below) and (61 M.) *Jinja* (Ibis Hotel, pens. 18*s.*), near the *Ripon Falls* (492 ft. wide, 13 ft. high) on the Victoria Nile, which here issues from *Lake Victoria* or *Victoria Nyanza* (3725 ft.; comp. p. lxvi).

From Jinja we may proceed by steamer to (24 hrs.) *Kisumu (Port Florence)*, on the Kawirondo Bay of Lake Victoria. This is the starting-point of the narrow-gauge Uganda Railway, which attains an altitude of 7825 ft. before reaching Nakuru (p. 468).

A railway, begun in Dec. 1928, will connect Jinja with *Kampala*, situated on Lake Victoria, 60 M. to the W., the commercial capital of the Uganda Protectorate. To connect the new railway with the main line the Victoria Nile will be bridged near Jinja.

At Mbulamuti (see above) the new section (opened in Jan. 1928) of the Kenya and Uganda Railway diverges to the E. It runs viâ

Tororo (railway projected to Mbale and Nimule, p. 467) and *Turbo* to *Nakuru* (near the lake of that name), and has its highest point (9040 ft.) between the last two stations. From Nakuru the old section of the railway runs on to *Nairobi* (5560 ft.), capital of Kenya Colony, a pleasant, typically English garden city, and thence to *Mombasa* on the Indian Ocean. By this new route Mombasa is reached from Mbulamuti in two days, the distance being 778 M.

Steamers ply regulary from Mombasa to Egypt (Suez) and Europe.

INDEX.

Besides place-names this index contains a number of personal names (printed in italics) and other words occurring in the text. — The following is a short list of Arabic words of frequent occurrence (comp. the vocabulary, p. xxxiii): —

ʿAin, spring.
Bâb, gate.
Bahr, sea, river (Nile).
Balad, *Beled*, village.
Beit, house.
Bilâd, land, district.
Bîr, well, cistern.
Birba, temple-ruin.
Birka, pool.
Darb, *Derb*, road.
Deir, monastery.
ʿEzba, *ʿIzba*, hamlet, farm.
Gâmiʿ, mosque.
Gebel, mountain.
Gezîra, island.
Kafr, village.
Kôm, mound of rubbish.
Madîna, *Medîna*, town.
Meidân, *Mîdân*, square, place.
Nagʿ, hamlet.
Qalʿa, fortress.
Qanṭara, bridge.
Qaṣr, castle.
Râs, promontory.
Shâriʿ, street.
Tell, hill.
Wâdi, valley.
